HISTORY

OF THE VARIATIONS OF THE

PROTESTANT CHURCHES

Real View Books

J. H. Newman, *Anglican Difficulties*

A. Carrel, *Voyage to Lourdes*

J. H. De Groot, *The Shakespeares and the "Old Faith"**

K. A. Kneller, *Christianity and the Leaders of Modern Science*

A. Barruel, *Memoirs Illustrating the History of Jacobinism*

H. E. Manning, *The True Story of the Vatican Council*

Saint John Fisher, *The Defense of the Priesthood*

All titles with an Introduction (*Postscript)
by Stanley L. Jaki

J.-B. BOSSUET

HISTORY

OF THE VARIATIONS OF THE

PROTESTANT CHURCHES

with an Introduction by

Stanley L. Jaki

Real-**V**iew-**B**ooks

Published by
AMERICAN COUNCIL ON ECONOMICS AND SOCIETY
34152 Doreka Drive
Fraser, Michigan, 48026

1997

J.-B. Bossuet (1627-1704)
1. Doctrinal variations of the Protestant Churches (1517-1687)
2. Controversial theology

ISBN 0-9641150-8-5

Printed in the United States of America

Contents

Introduction

"L'Histoire des variations des Eglises protestantes is certainly one of Bossuet's most beautiful works and possibly the most accomplished and yet the least read work of his." So wrote a hundred years ago Ferdinand Brunetière, the foremost French literary critic of his time.[1] By beauty Brunetière meant stylistic quality, a praise all the more to the point as according to him Bossuet was one of the few great masters of French prose who did not write for the sake of writing. Among the few minor faults Brunetière found with the *Variations* was its author's occasional sermonizing. Such a fault derived from an enormous virtue. Bossuet was known to his contemporaries as the Eagle of Meaux. He earned this renown as a preacher whose words soared to levels much higher than mere rhetoric, however skillful, can ever reach. A rhetorician he certainly was and in the best sense of that word. With Pascal, Bossuet is the creator of that French style that rightly prides itself on saying the most with the fewest words and with a finesse in which precision matches beauty and power. Not a few pages of Bossuet's sermons stand for the finest specimens of French prose. His sermons are still being reprinted; selections from them reappear at regular intervals. Evidently he still attracts many readers.

Bossuet's sermons were read even during the first century following his death, or the period when the popularity of a first-rate author may suffer a temporary eclipse. One of Bossuet's late-18th-century admirers was none other than Boswell, who wondered why Samuel Johnson found praise for the French language only as a means of circulating knowledge more effectively than any other tongue. Boswell countered by referring to the excellence of French literature. He mentioned Fénelon and then Voltaire, only to be brushed off by Johnson. "What do you say to the Bishop of Meaux?"—insisted Boswell. "Sir, nobody reads him," went Johnson's reply. In reporting this, Boswell added in a note: "I take leave to enter my strongest protest against this judgment. Bossuet I hold to be one of the first luminaries of religion and literature. If there are such who do not read him, it is full time they should begin."[2]

Anyone who reads Johnson's posthumously published sermons can but suspect that his indirect slighting of Bossuet indicated his uneasiness in the presence of a preacher incomparably superior to him.[3] As to Boswell, he is no longer regarded as a mere reporter, however assiduous, but rather as one whose day-to-day portrayal of Johnson shows time and again the touch of a genius.[4] Moreover, for all his moral lapses, Boswell had a far deeper religious sense than his idol, whose undeniably strong common sense hardly ever went much beneath the surface. Boswell's reference to Bossuet as a first-rate luminary of religion is an uncanny proof of the penetration of Bossuet's sermons into Protestant countries, which by then had increasingly lost touch with genuine Christianity. Boswell's remark also reveals his accurate grasp of the chief characteristic of Bossuet's sermons—keen interest in what is universally human in the religious quest, even while never leaving out what is unmistakably Christian and Catholic.

This was, of course, natural for one in whom brilliant mental qualities and personal probity united with a profound commitment to the ideal of the priesthood. Prior to his ordination as a priest on March 18, 1652, in his twenty-fifth year, Bossuet had spent two years preparing for that event. He did so in semi-retirement under the direction of a future saint, then simply spoken of as Monsieur Vincent. Five years later, it was the same Monsieur Vincent who prevailed on Bossuet to go to Paris from Meaux, where he had been a canon of the cathedral.

Had Bossuet not seen preaching as a pivotal part of his being a priest and therefore a fisher of men, Monsieur Vincent would hardly have cast out his net for him. He certainly knew the effectiveness of the young priest's manuscript booklet, "Exposition de la doctrine de l'Eglise catholique sur les matières de controverse." Once it became public knowledge that Turenne, the famed marshal of the French army, had abandoned Calvinism for the Catholic faith after reading that booklet, Calvinists in France realized the formidable adversary they had in its author. Scores of lesser, though still eminent names found the road to truth in that booklet, which, following its publication in 1671, went through five editions within ten years, without counting various reimpressions. In 1686 alone it came out in ten new editions.[5]

To Paris Bossuet went in 1657 to preach, and for the next twelve years preaching was his chief work. Over a hundred and thirty sermons of his are extant from that period, with about a hundred lost. Among the surviving sermons are two Lenten series preached before the Court in 1662 and 1666. The voice of the public soon demanded that Bossuet be made a bishop. He was forty-two when in 1669 the King appointed him to the See of Condom, a small town near the Pyrenees. It was as a bishop that he delivered his famed funeral sermons for Henrietta of France, and a year later for her daughter, the Duchess of Orléans. Beset with anxiety that his duties in Paris prevented his residence in his diocese, Bossuet resigned his bishopric in 1670. Appointed in the same year to be the preceptor of the Dauphin, that is, Louis, the nine-year-old son of Louis XIV and heir to the French throne, Bossuet became tied to the Court. He nevertheless achieved some independence from royal power and flattery by choosing to live in a religious house in Paris.

For Bossuet the new assignment was a unique means to further the implementation of Providence, taken in that concrete sense in which the Old and the New Covenants represented God's specifically providential plan for mankind. It was that sense which Bossuet felt called upon to instill in the Dauphin. One of Bossuet's means of achieving this aim consisted in writing books of instruction. They covered grammar, sacred and profane history, geography, the classics, devotion, such as preparation for first communion, and philosophy, including special treatises on logic, theodicy, and free will.[6] Bossuet even composed a Latin dictionary for the benefit of his young Royal charge. His high hopes were shared by none other than the Pope, Innocent XI, who would have regaled Bossuet with the red hat but for the opposition of Louis XIV, who knew that Bossuet's ultimate loyalty lay with the Church and not with the Throne.

That loyalty was part of Bossuet's dedication to the highest Christian moral standards. It was no secret to Louis XIV that Louise de la Vallière, his mistress and mother of four of his children, had no firmer support in her growing spiritual distress than in Bossuet, who invariably stood by her in her efforts to break out of a sinful liaison and find peace by joining the Carmelites. This she did in 1674, and a year later Bossuet preached the sermon when she took her vows. Again, at variance with Archbishop Harlay of Paris and the King's Jesuit confessor, Père La Chaize, Bossuet firmly upheld the decision of the parish priest in Versailles who refused to give absolution to Mme Montespan, the next mistress of the King. In fact, on seeing that the King was ready to re-establish his liaison with Mme Montespan upon his return from the campaign in Flanders, Bossuet wrote to him: "You will never be at peace with God as long as this violent passion, which has for so long separated you from him, possesses you. Everyone praises your troops, and what they achieve under such a leader. But, all this time, Sire, I think within myself of a more important war and a more difficult victory. Meditate upon our Lord's words for they seem destined for great kings and conquerors: 'For what shall it profit a man, if he shall gain the whole world, and lose his own soul?' What will it profit you, Sire, to be victorious and feared in this world, if in your soul you are defeated? Pray God that he will free you, as I pray the same with my whole heart."[7]

Such utterly sincere words could only come from one steeped in spiritual life. Bossuet became a close friend of Armand Bouthillier de Rancé only after the latter had reformed his life in a spectacular way. In religious history the name of de Rancé and La Trappe will forever remain united. Time and again Bossuet visited the founder of the Trappists of La Trappe, Normandy. Again, Bossuet's posthumously published *Meditations sur l'Evangile* would not still be a bestseller had its contents not come from genuinely spiritual depths.

Of Bossuet's works written for the Dauphin's benefit two appeared in print. One, *Introduction à la philosophie ou Connaissance de Dieu et de soi-même*, was published posthumously in 1722 and thereafter reprinted countless times. The other appeared in 1681, or just when Bossuet had completed his preceptorship of the Dauphin. It was the famed *Discours sur l'histoire universelle*, a book still being reprinted and translated.[8] At first glance, the *Discours* may appear a mere rearticulation of Augustine's *City of God*. Yet the dozen or so centuries that separated the two works meant much more than distance in time. Augustine wrote to show that the Church was not responsible for the collapse of Rome or civilization. Bossuet's concern was to instill in the Dauphin's mind a deep appreciation for Christian civilization as the embodiment of God's plan, which he, as the future King of France, had a special calling to defend and promote. Given the fact that God has entered human history with a very specific plan, any other consideration of history has to be, so Bossuet thought, merely a distraction from that all-important perspective.[9]

This is why Bossuet presented universal history in terms of sacred history. There was no room there for the histories of China or India, not even for Babylon, Persia or Egypt, taken for their own sakes. Greece and Rome fared differently, but only because they witnessed the New Covenant become a historical reality. This is not to suggest that one cannot find traces of modernity in Bossuet's portrayal of history. Thus, for instance, he stressed the importance of climate, a point subsequently taken up by Montesquieu on a grand scale in his *L'esprit des lois* (1748), in which no attention was paid to sacred history. Although Bossuet had not only the

Dauphin in mind as he wrote his *Discours* but also the "libertins" of his times, he did not seem to suspect that they would ever dominate the scene, and indeed in the rather short run at that. Bossuet could hardly imagine that Montesquieu's purely secularist analysis of history and society was but half a century away, or that only a little farther away in the future lay Voltaire's *Siècle de Louis XIV* (1751), which, though still fairly free of vitriolic attacks on Church and Throne, represented the very opposite of Bossuet's own satisfaction with that century.

Today, Bossuet's approach has in the eyes of many only one usefulness: to provide a dark, or at best a naive background to an "enlightened" or "mature" view of history. Such a view was in fact already in the making when Bossuet died in 1704 at the age of seventy-six. A few years earlier Pierre Bayle came out with his *Dictionnaire historique et critique* (1697), in which the champions of the Enlightenment, such as Voltaire, Diderot and others, were to find inspiration and guidance. Bossuet to the end considered intramural problems of theology to be the central issues. He would not have understood that most learned pope, Benedict XIV, who voiced his dismay when presented with a tome which the Faculty of Theology of Nantes had composed "on certain propositions having to do with probabilism." The work, which dealt with a dispute among Catholic moral theologians, visibly upset the pope: "It is high time," he wrote to a confidant, "that all these quarrels were settled; Catholic theologians should not have to write except against materialists, atheists and Deists who are trying to destroy the very foundation of religion."[10] Bossuet in his old days still found Molinism a worthy cause to combat and denounce in Rome.

But Bossuet was not altogether blind about the future course of history. The proof of this is in the work *L'Histoire des variations des églises protestantes*. To the composition of this work, which is reprinted here in its English translation, he devoted much of the decade of his life that followed the completion of his preceptorship of the Dauphin and found him fully immersed in his episcopal duties in Meaux. In this work he predicted that Protestants in large numbers would fall prey to a Socinianism[11] in which there was no room for genuine supernatural tenets and certainly not for the doctrines of Trinity and Incarnation. Bossuet therefore would not have been surprised by a telling outcome: in those late 18th-century defenses of God's plan that were so highly acclaimed outside Catholic circles, such as Herder's *Ideen zur Geschichte der Philosophie der Menschheit* (1784-91), one would look in vain for an endorsement of these very tenets. In such works,

Christ and his Church are espoused only as facets of a cultural progress generated by the human genius, certainly not as supernatural gifts to man that are the crowning acts of divine Providence in history. Bossuet would have been the last to be surprised by the wide reception given to Higher Criticism and rationalist Lives of Jesus within Protestant circles from the early nineteenth century onward.

Of course, Benedict XIV would have been the last to suggest that anti-Christian trends, so subversive of the Christian perspective on history, could be effectively opposed by a Christianity fractured into a growing number of camps. Being an Italian and never having been exposed to Protestant activities, Benedict XIV could not feel so keenly as Bossuet did the threat which Protestantism posed to God's providential plan. The threat was to the unity of that plan and all the more so as Protestantism proved itself to be the logical breeding place of disunity. Herein lies the perennial timeliness of Bossuet's overriding concern for the Church and its Unity. It was a genuinely supernatural concern, in spite of the all too close tie which Bossuet supported between Rome and the French Throne in the interest of the Church's unity.

He never truly perceived the extent to which the Throne promoted its unity with the Church by trying to subjugate it. The Abbé Le Dieu, who served as Bossuet's secretary from 1684, noticed no grave emotion in Bossuet's tone as he replied to his question about who had really planned the famed convention of the French bishops and clergy that sat from the Fall of 1681 till the late Spring of 1682. Bossuet's apparent equanimity should seem all the stranger since he knew that Colbert planned it and that he himself would never condone the crude domination of the Church by the State which Colbert sought to achieve thereby.

Bossuet may not have been the actual drafter of the Four Gallican Articles. He may have merely put them into a Latin that did not smack of scholasticism. However, he fully agreed with their thrust. The first article stressed the restriction of the pope's authority to strictly spiritual matters. Bossuet disagreed with Bellarmine who held that the pope can depose sovereigns. The second declared the superiority of the Ecumenical Council over the pope. The third laid it down that hallowed customs, traditions, and privileges cannot be changed or annulled by the pope. Finally, the pope was held infallible, but only through the consent given by the Church to his utterances.

That Bossuet spent much of the decade after 1682 writing, in Latin, a massive defense of those articles[12] makes doubly intriguing the fact that simultaneously he wrote another massive work, the one whose English translation is reprinted here. He did not suspect that, as will be seen later, those two works were in a sense at cross purposes. At first Bossuet planned to write something much smaller than the *Variations* and rather different from it. In 1682 a Protestant pastor took issue with the "variations" he had found in the various editions of Bossuet's *Exposition de la foi catholique,* which he took for so many evidences of inconsistencies in Catholic doctrine. At that time Bossuet was reading the *Corpus syntagma confessionum fidei,* or a collection of Protestant credal statements, from the Augsburg Confession down to the mid-17th century.[13] Bossuet at first thought that he would turn the tables on Protestants by exposing their chronic inconsistencies in a new introduction to his *Exposition.* But soon he saw that the subject was vast and deserved a commensurate treatment. Such is the immediate origin of the *Variations.*[14]

Bossuet's plan soon began to leak out. As the publication fell more and more behind, Protestants began to suggest that Bossuet found it increasingly difficult to gloss over the inconsistencies of Catholic doctrine by a portrayal of Protestant variations. Actually, his energies were also spent in writing his defense of the Gallican articles. Dividing his energies between two massive projects did not prevent Bossuet from turning the *Variations* into a most original book, and easily the greatest book he would write. The originality of the book lies in Bossuet's carrying the interconfessional disputes to their basics. Bossuet was the one who perceived that it was largely futile to continue such disputes as long as they dealt with particular points of disagreememt, such as this or that dogma or scriptural phrase. Bossuet saw that it was much more effective to focus attention on a facet of Protestantism that had plagued it from its very inception: it necessarily produced rank inconsistencies both in the thinking of its chief protagonists and in its official pronouncements, a process further aggravated by the growing number of Churches to which it kept giving rise.

The *Variations* first appeared in two quarto volumes in May 1688. Between that publication and the second revised edition (1702), to which Bossuet himself added some corrections, the book appeared four times. The second edition was reprinted eleven times during the eighteenth century, and six times between 1817 and 1845. After that the *Variations* appeared anew only in various complete editions of Bossuet's works, of which the nineteenth century saw several. A Latin translation, produced between 1688-1710, was never published except for the Preface. Another Latin translation of the entire work was, however, published in Tyrnavia

(Nagyszombat, Hungary) in 1718. There one still vividly remembered the great Hungarian counter-reformer, Cardinal Pázmány, and his exceedingly effective work, "Guide leading to the Divine Truth."[15]

Broad and enduring interest in the *Variations* was witnessed by its translation into Italian (1733), German (1823-25), and Spanish (1852). The English translation, made from the sixth French edition by someone in all appearance connected with the English seminary in Douay, first appeared in Antwerp in 1742 in two volumes.[16] It resembled the French original also in that it carried as marginal notes all the section headings as well as the references to works quoted. This translation was reprinted with slight stylistic corrections in Dublin in 1829, with the section headings printed in the text itself and the references given as footnotes. This edition came out twice in New York (Sadler, 1845 and 1885). It is the text of the 1885 printing which is presented here, entirely reset, of course.[17]

A mere look at the numerous references throughout the whole book will show the thoroughness with which Bossuet did his research. While one can regret his ignorance of the German tongue, the fact is that the vast majority of relevant Protestant writings and statements were quickly translated into Latin, and in fact often appeared originally in that tongue. Bossuet, who worked without research assistants, did his best, however, to secure information from time to time about material not yet in print. At any rate, since A. Rébelliau, librarian of the Institut de France, published in 1891 his vast study on Bossuet's *Variations,* under the title *Bossuet, historien du Protestantisme,*[18] attacks on Bossuet's historical scholarship have failed to be persuasive.

By modern standards of historical scholarship, so intent on using unpublished material, Bossuet's almost exclusive use of printed material may seem gravely defective. Yet it would be a great defect to think that the published material available to Bossuet could not give him a reliable picture of his subject matter. Also, Bossuet's critics reveal great bias when they deplore his method, which consists in judging Protestants by words taken from their own mouths. Thus, in dealing with the Reformation in England, Bossuet avoided using the work of the Catholic recusant, Nicolas Sander, although it was full of facts unavailable elsewhere.[19] Bossuet satisfied himself with the material in *The History of the English Reformation* (1679) written by Gilbert Burnet, subsequently bishop of Salisbury, of which two volumes were available in French early enough for Bossuet's purposes.[20] Burnet, a noted latitudinarian, was, as it turned out, incensed not only by Bossuet's finding his book an arsenal against English Protestantism, but also by Bossuet's most benevolent view of the Catholic elements in the Established Church as it stood before the 1688 revolution.

Also, Bossuet did not portray Luther, for instance, as an unmitigated misfit. He recognized good qualities in him. Perhaps he should have seen more of such qualities in Luther, but his picture was far more balanced than those apotheoses of Luther that were published by Lutherans and even secular historians in large quantities, with rank disregard of historical scholarship. There was indeed a great need for works on Luther such as the ones by Heinrich Denifle[21] and Hartmann Grisar.[22] The violent Protestant reaction to these works merely showed the fragility of the halo which a so-called scholarship placed around the head of Luther, the blameless knight of pure Christianity. Strangely, the very same scholars who applauded the champions of Higher Criticism as they lowered Christ to the level of a mere religious enthusiast, felt stung to the quick by the critical evidence presented by Denifle about Luther's enjoying some moral lowlands.[23]

It hardly bespeaks respect for scholarship among latter-day Catholic specialists on Luther and Protestantism that they dismiss Denifle, a first-rate historian, as a caricaturist of Luther. They do the same with Grisar's vast tomes on Luther, in spite of their overwhelming and devastating documentation. They never consider the possibility that the new ecumenical atmosphere is no different from other atmospheres. It also has its index of refraction, which at times makes a scholar's vision refractory to plain written evidence. Again, scholars too attentive to minute details can easily blind themselves to the massive reality of great contours. One need not explore each and every crevasse of the Alps to be impressed by their monumentality. Doctrinal history can speak clearly, even though some details may be missing. Or as Newman put it: "Bold outlines and broad masses of color rise out of the records of the past. They may be dim, they may be incomplete; but they are definite." Such was Newman's chief assurance about the fact that "whatever history teaches, whatever it omits, whatever it exaggerates, whatever it says and unsays, at least the Christianity of history is not Protestantism. If ever there were a safe truth, it is this."[24]

One can indeed safely say that Bossuet's portrayal of the first one and a half centuries of Protestantism proved that it could not help but generate further protests among the protesters, who finally found that they agreed only in one thing: their protestations against Rome. Apart from this, they would at first settle their burgeoning differences rather reluctantly, and later take them for a normal state of affairs. In fact they were to take them, in the long run, for their very glory. This is not to suggest that Protestants did not want to notice something which remained essentially the same in Protestant teaching and was indeed the same with what the Church had always held unchanged. But, as Brunetière aptly noted, in trying to articulate it, they heaped confusion on confusion. Bossuet saw this all too clearly, and he saw no less sharply, Brunetière rightly argued, the clarity of the logic of Catholicism: "Even if Luther and Calvin had, for instance, been a hundred times more in the right on the question of the Eucharist and justification by faith than the Catholic theologians, they would have been still wrong, according to Bossuet, in their being separated from the Church, because there is no Church without an absolute power to define its dogmas, and, on the other hand, without the Church, there is no Christianity, and perhaps not even religion."[25]

This principle of continuity did not seize Bossuet's mind only when he sat down to write the *Variations*. Brunetière called attention to the fact that as a young priest Bossuet, in a sermon delivered at the entry of a new convert from Protestantism into religious life, extolled the unbroken chain of tradition, as a chain anchored in God himself: "*Ecclesia ab apostolis, apostoli a Christo, Christus a Deo tradidit*. There one finds the entire *Variations*."[26]

Whatever one's eagerness to find fault here and there with Bossuet's marshalling of facts in the *Variations*, their vastness rises massively. Furthermore, he makes that vastness rise before his readers' eyes with a disarmingly simple method, that of plain chronology, which is broken only late in the book where he shows in a long section that Cathars, Albigenses, Waldenses and Wickliffites were not the forerunners of Luther for at least one crucial reason: they did not anticipate Luther's idea of justification by faith alone.

Justification by faith alone, which in turn is but an imputed justice that does not wipe away man's sins but merely covers them, was a radical novelty, undreamed of either in the Patristic or in the Scholastic period of doctrinal and exegetical history. For this reason alone Luther could not be a reformer, that is, one who restores a former image that had been deformed. Rather, Luther effectively shaped that modernity on the religious level where subjective experience is preferred to objective reality. Living in an age and a country where classical standards still prevailed, Bossuet could not be expected to emphasize what Newman eventually did in a book he authored while still an Anglican: "Luther found Christians in bondage to their works and observances; he released them by his doctrine of faith and he left them in bondage to their feelings."[27] The sickeningly modern preoccupation with personal sentiments is crowned in that subjectivist deformation of religion which Luther launched while trying to bring about a radical reformation of the Church.

Out of that syndrome, that cannot be cured with further emphasis on feelings, a most effective rescue offers itself in a return to facts, including the facts and march of history. The chapters of *Variations* have years for their title. Books I-IV cover the period 1517-1537, or the span from Luther's first challenge to Rome to the formulation of the Articles of Smalkald. Book V deals with Melancthon, by far the most balanced theologian in Luther's camp, who was particularly in the center of the storm in the 1530s. The subject of Book VI centers on the year 1540 when the bigamy of Philip of Hesse was perpetrated with full Lutheran assistance. The English Reformation, taken up in Book VII, is followed by the narrative of the Protestants' disagreements during the first sixteen years of the Council of Trent. Book IX deals largely with Calvin's person and work. In Book X Bossuet returns to the English Reformation under Elizabeth. The digression on the Cathars and similar medieval sects constitutes the subject of the longest section, Book XI, of the *Variations*. Book XII is taken up with the activities of Calvinists in France during two periods full of civil disturbances, the 1570s and the years 1603-1615. In Book XIII Bossuet lays bare the contradictory efforts of various Protestant pastors in France to present Rome as the Antichrist. Book XIV takes the reader to Holland where Calvinism asserted strongly its radical tenets during the first half of the 17th century and provoked heated disagreements among its adherents. Book XV, another very long section, is an analytical discussion of the differences between Protestants and Catholics in their respective understanding of the Creed's article: I believe in the Holy Catholic Church.

Along this long narrative, at times burdensome by its minute marshalling of facts and dicta, the reader comes across sparkling observations, time and again. Such are Bossuet's dicta on the two sides of Luther's presentation—one for friends, one for the public—of his doctrine of imputed justice (Bk VI, sec. 30); on the inability of the Protestants to find in the clarity of the Bible a clear means of putting an end to all disputes among themselves (Bk VIII, sec. 34); on the Reformers' effort to mimic the Church (Bk IX, sec. 72); on the Protestants' civic disobedience as contrasted with the early Christians' submission to the State (Bk X, sec. 53); on the failure of typical Protestants to realize the extent to which their ministers have a sway over them (Bk XII, sec. 36); on Calvin's evasiveness about the failure of Luther's prophecy to come true, regarding the quick demise of the papacy (Bk XIII, sec. 2); on the harshness of the Calvinist denial of free will (Bk XIV, sec. 14); on error as of necessity generating further errors (Bk XIV, sec. 53); and finally on the four points that are implied in the Catholic belief in the Church (Bk XV, sec. 3).

In bringing his work to a head with a dicussion of the differences among Protestants concerning belief in the Church, as contrasted with the uniformity among Catholics, Bossuet certainly showed his perspicacity. Leaving aside the idea of justification by faith alone as essentially being a proposition about sentiments, the crux of the difference between Catholics and Protestants resides in their respective understanding of the reality of the Church as a tie to Jesus Christ. On that score, one could either agree or disagree with Bossuet and take the consequences. It is not possible to disagree with Bossuet to any substantial extent concerning his presentation of facts, data, and statements. He was and still is a respectable historian of Protestantism.[28] No critic of his, old or new, could catch him in a serious misrepresentation of facts. No critic of his, except those intentionally blind, could deny that his book contained, even apart from his main theme, strikingly original sections. One of them was his account of Melancthon, whom he portrayed as a profoundly torn mind, who would have fared far better had he not come, as a youthful professor of Greek, under the sway of Luther, the powerful speaker and personality. The most balanced and clear-sighted among the first generation of Protestant theologians, Melancthon in the end hoped, as Bossuet pointedly recalled, to find spiritual freedom among the Turks! A principal reason for this was that he could never stomach Luther's, let alone Calvin's denunciations of free will. Common sense prompted Melancthon also to recognize that without a pope somehow involved in convoking an ecumenical council, the disintegration of European Christendom could not be reversed. With an almost fatherly compassion did Bossuet report Melancthon's sundry agonies, such as his perplexities in the face of adverse astrological forecasting. Thus on one occasion Melancthon canceled a trip to England because the stars predicted storms in the Baltic. Recent scholarship on Melancthon still has to emulate some sterling qualities of Bossuet's account of him.[29]

Bossuet's portrayal of Melancthon occupied much of Book V, and by then he pressed relentlessly the main theme of his great work as set forth in its Preface. That theme, Bossuet said, had been articulated by the Church Fathers. He quoted Saint Hilary's graphic comment on the Arians'

ready compliance with Emperor Constantius' orders to hold one Council
after another. The policy merely imitated "unskillful architects, who are
never pleased with their own work [and] do nothing but to build up and
pull down." On the contrary, in its first assembly at Nicæa, the Catholic
Church "raised an immortal edifice," so that "to condemn Arianism for
ever, nothing more is necessary than to repeat that first creed." In fact the
pattern was noted, as Bossuet was eager to point out, by the pagan
historian Ammianus Marcellinus, an adversary of Saint Ambrose. In
addition to a famed passage of Tertullian on the proverbial fickleness of
heretics, Bossuet quoted "two holy authors of the eighth century," as if to
underline that the same view did not disappear from the Catholic
perspective as time went on. Those "two holy authors" stated that "heresy,
old and new, is always itself a novelty; . . . it innovates daily, and daily
changes its doctrine."[30] Twelve centuries later none other than Rudolf
Bultmann had to register the same pattern in a letter to Karl Rahner:
"How fortunate you must be to be able to appeal to the Pope; appeal to
the Lutheran synods merely leads to greater disunity."[31] The tack taken
by Bossuet was indeed the correct one.

In almost the same breath Bossuet referred to a book, published in
Geneva in 1654, that contained all the credal statements and conciliar
definitions issued by Protestant bodies since the Augsburg Confession in
1530. That work, *Corpus syntagma confessionum fidei* turns up again and
again in the Notes as a storehouse of information.[32] In the preface
Bossuet also pointed out that he had in view mainly the Lutherans and the
Calvinists, and especially the nature and consequences of their differing on
whether Christ was present in the Eucharist in a literal or in a purely
figurative sense. There were, of course, other points too, such as the nature
of imputed justice and its co-existence with sin in man, and, last but not
least, the question of free will, good works, and predestination. No less
important, Bossuet noted, was the fact that already the first generation of
Protestants had to acknowledge that somehow salvation was also to be
found in the Roman Church. Yet while a Catholic could say, without
undermining his notion of the Church, that those who for no fault of their
own were outside the Church could still be saved, a similar admission by
Protestants would have struck at the very roots of their ecclesiology, if
there ever was a coherent one.[33]

Bossuet made it clear, right in the preface, that his portrayal of
Protestant variations, inconsistencies, and contradictions was meant chiefly
to help Catholics appreciate the consistency and clarity of their faith.

Catholics "will learn to despise that knowledge which puffs up, and that eloquence, which dazzles. . . . They will deplore the errors of the human mind, and be convinced that the only remedy for these great evils, is to break off all attachment to private judgment, for it is this which distinguishes the Catholic from the Protestant. The property of the heretic, that is, of one who has a particular opinion, is, to be wedded to his own conceits: the property of the Catholic, that is, universal, is, to prefer the general sense of the church to his own sentiments; this is the grace for which we shall petition in behalf of those that err." The Catholic therefore "will everywhere praise the Almighty for the continual protection He affords His church, in order to maintain its simplicity, and inflexible uprightness, amidst the subtleties with which men strive to bewilder the truths of the Gospel." For a dark contrast there is, for the modern Catholic, the admission of Harnack, whose Protestantism largely consisted in an anti-Catholic rationalism, that "the Reformation ended in contradiction."[34]

The greatest surprise which Bossuet offered to the readers of the *Variations* was his narrative and documentation of what is undoubtedly the darkest blot on the far from shiny moral armor of Luther and his chief allies. The blot had its remote origin in the resolve of a maiden not to yield to Philip, Landgrave of Hesse, unless he, already married for years, was ready to take her for wife. It would have already been inexcusable on the part of Luther, Melanchton and Bucer, if they had merely yielded to the threats of the Landgrave, a noted lecher, and allowed him the marriage ceremony, which took place on March 4, 1540. But the Landgrave insisted on theological justification of the bigamous marriage after he had vainly tried to obtain a "dispensation" from the pope in return for 4000 golden ducats! Luther and his allies had therefore to engage for over a year in perpetrating the worst of all possible sins, the sin against the Holy Spirit, by calling sin virtue. They indeed bent over backward to make it appear to the Landgrave and to themselves that polygamy could somehow have a place, however restricted, in the New Dispensation if it served a good and important cause. The end, they argued for all practical purposes, justified the means because the very cause of the Reformation depended on the Landgrave's armed support. But that cause would have also been lost if somebody had learned of the bigamous marriage ceremony, unheard of in the annals of the Church. To be sure, the Landgrave kept his part of the bargain by keeping everything secret, and for a good reason: in the Holy Roman Empire bigamy was a crime that called for beheading as its punishment. Those who aided and abetted such a crime had also much to fear.

But here too, as in countless other instances, the Gospel proved true: nothing is concealed that will not ultimately come to light. The documentary disclosure could not have a more ironic background. The Palatine Elector, Carl-Ludwig, a descendant of the Landgrave, became furious at the Lutheran ministers in his Court, who looked askance at his having a concubine. He decided to take revenge on them by divulging his ancestor's crime and their predecessors' part in it. In this he was assisted by his relative, Ernest, Landgrave of Hesse-Rheinfels-Rothenburg, a Catholic since 1652, who provided copies of relevant documents from his Archives. These were used by the numismatic writer, Lorenz Beger, who at the command of Carl-Ludwig presented the story in 1679.[35] The Elector then distributed copies of the story among his officials, one of whom was a certain Obrecht. The latter, in a letter of June 20, 1687, to Bossuet, reported also the fact that the Elector forbade all recipients to disclose that it was he who provided them with copies. To crown the comedy and perhaps to cover himself, the Elector forced Beger to write a refutation of the work, which, however, was never published.[36]

At any rate, it was no longer possible for Lutherans to dismiss what had been public knowledge by June 1540, when the bride's mother told the story to the Prince of Saxony. It was no longer possible to denounce Catholics, such as Bellarmine, for having reported the rumors circulating about that bigamous wedding. It was no longer possible not to see the stark contrast between the "corrupt" pope Clement VII, who in 1531 refused the feelers of Henry VIII about permission to have a second wife, and the cowardly moral compromise of the self-styled restorer of pristine Christianity.[37] Now, largely through Bossuet's alertness, the story loomed large as a dark blot on Luther's reputation. Bossuet was the first to add the Landgrave's instructions (and threats) to Luther and his allies, and, as Bossuet remarked, "the history is now complete."[38]

Likewise, Bossuet's history of the doctrinal variations of Protestant churches up to his time was, in substance, complete. No less important, Bossuet's prediction that Protestant churches would in ever greater numbers adopt some form of Socinianism, has indeed come true. The naturalism of Socinianism, present everywhere in main-line Protestant churches, proved no barrier against the purely pragmatist ethics of the new secularist consensus. Hence the exodus from those churches of so many, some of whom simply abandon Christianity, others look towards the

Catholic Church, but most of them swell the ranks of the Evangelicals. The latter represent another variation of Protestantism, insofar as they try to safeguard belief in the supernatural with practically no insistence on ordained ministry as conceived either in Lutheranism or Calvinism. Many evangelicals also obey the logic emphasized by Bossuet as they find that only the Catholic Church assures a supernatural dispensation that satisfies legitimate questions about it.[39]

While Bossuet was right on a great many points, he was clearly wrong on some and very wrong on a most fundamental one. After finding so many inconsistencies in Burnet's account of the English Reformation, Bossuet should have been more cautious in attributing so much catholicity to the Church of England and in taking so seriously its interest in the Church Fathers. Even in his wildest dreams Bossuet would not have considered the possibility of an Oxford Movement, which was propelled, at least in Newman's case, by the realization that the Church of England deteriorated into an ecclesial version of a purely naturalistic form of religion, totally subservient to the Establishment.[40] It would have been utterly inconceivable for Bossuet to entertain the possibility that the Church of England would eventually ordain women and have bishops who condone the homosexuality of some of their clergy. Yet in doing so the Church of England merely obeys the logic of naturalism which Bossuet forcefully intimated to be at work within the Reformation.

In failing to see the Church of England in its true reality, Bossuet may have been influenced by his admiration for the close unity of Church and State. Sainte-Beuve's caption of Bossuet's sphere of vision—"Un Dieu, un Christ, un évêque, un roi"[41]—may be too confining, but there can be no doubt about Bossuet's profound loyalty to the Throne. He, wrongly though understandably enough, saw in the close union of Church and Throne an indispensable bulwark of securing the providential plan of God through social tranquillity. Born into a family of magistrates, he naturally became a staunch supporter of "law and order." Any threat to this was in his eyes a crime crying to high heaven, a breach of the loyalty imposed by Saint Paul toward temporal power, a loyalty fully obeyed by the first Christians, though violently persecuted. Therefore he could see no saving grace whatever in the subversive scheming and insurrections of the Calvinists in France. Historians will never agree about the true extent to which such insurrections were or were not justified prior to the Saint Bartholomew's Day massacre. Nor will they ever agree on the true measure in which Calvin hatched those insurrections and became therefore responsible for the horrible ravages that sapped France's vitality by the end of the sixteenth century. Bossuet's portrayal of the coolness with which the aged Calvin viewed the beginning of those ravages is one of the most chilling details in the *Variations*.

The debate that arose in the wake of the publication of the *Variations* engaged a good deal of Bossuet's time and energy until 1691. He countered with six *Avertissements aux Protestants* the eight Pastoral Letters which the Calvinist minister, Pierre Jurieu, wrote against the *Variations*. In the first *Avertissement* Bossuet took Jurieu to task for dismissing the great conciliar definitions of the fourth and fifth centuries as so many useless errors. In the second Bossuet took for his target Jurieu's efforts to show that according to Luther and Calvin, God is not the author of sin. In the third he dealt with the idolatry which Jurieu attributed to the great Church Fathers and with the inconsistencies of Protestant ecclesiology. The fourth had for its subject the Landgrave's bigamous marriage. The fifth was devoted to the differences between the ancient Church and the Churches issued from the Reformation. Then came the *Défense de l'histoire des variations*, or Bossuet's reply to a history of the Calvinist Church, which another Calvinist minister, Jacques Basnage, brought out in Holland in 1690. There Bossuet also replied to Burnet's *Censure of M. de Meaux's History*. But with the publication of the sixth and the longest *Avertissement*, a reply to Jurieu's last three Letters, Bossuet considered the dispute closed as far as he was concerned: "Let Mr Jurieu dogmatize from early morning on, let him issue prophecies as many as he wants, I leave it to history to refute his prophecies, and I leave him alone with his teaching. All that remains for me is to pray that God may open the eyes of Protestants, so that they may perceive the sign of error Mr Jurieu raises in their midst in the instability of their teaching."[42]

None of those critics saw, or wanted to see the point where Bossuet entangled himself in a grave inconsistency and exposed the *Variations* to serious objections. The point related to his unabashed endorsement of conciliarism, despite of his being adamant on the point that there can be no unity of the Church without union with the See of Rome. Yet while he asserted the indefectibility of that See, he attributed no infallibility to its occupant. Bossuet made much of the fact that in his time it was not heretical to deny infallibility. Yet, a defense of conciliarism had to include this lame escape hatch, which even in Bossuet's time amounted to a desperate rear-guard defense of a position more and more at variance with the thrust of true development.[43] Bossuet expected the college of bishops and the sense of the faithful to bring an errant pope quickly back to the right track. The fact that bishops spoke with one voice only to the extent that individual bishops cherished union with the Pope, should have given Bossuet second thoughts on his ideas on unity. His position received its sharpest rebuke in the spontaneous loyalty which the faithful manifested, then as later, towards the occupant of the See of Rome. For all his faithfulness in discharging his pastoral duties as bishop of Meaux, and for all his readiness to help the poor, Bossuet remained loftily detached from the ordinary faithful and their sense of reality, spiritual and physical.

Bossuet was too much attached to the highest intellectual circles, taking its atmosphere for true and decisive reality. Hence his support of Arnauld and his cohorts at Port-Royal, who were most careful not to alienate him by probing into the inconsistencies of his conciliarism. This was done by his fellow bishop, Choiseul-Praslin, a radical defender of the Gallican position, who in a conversation with Bossuet insisted that anyone who attributed indefectibility to the See of Rome could not logically deny infallibility to its occupant.[44] Although, as the years went by, Bossuet kept correcting his *Defensio* so that it approached Rome's position, even so he did not want it ever to be published. But Bossuet's Jansenist nephew, the Abbé Bossuet, brought out the work in 1740, though without corrections.[45]

One can only guess the kind of corrections Bossuet had formulated. Perhaps they contained his recognition of why the Catholic "variations," which he carefully distinguished in the *Variations* from their Protestant kind, never contradicted one another. For any argument, however sound, that the Catholic variations did not become divergences from truth, remains hanging in mid-air without a reference to a certain factor at play. That factor is not so much the councils and the bishops, as the bishop of Rome who, time and again, proved to be the sole factor that set effective limits to variations that might have grown into sheer errors.

Bossuet did not live to see the unfolding of the weak points of his conciliarism. They lay in his all too high esteem of the Church in France ever from its inception in the still Roman province of Gaul. Bossuet's stature remained a chief asset for all supporters of the Gallican position, including Napoleon, who used to refer to Bossuet as "his bishop." Dupanloup and other French bishops made much of that "asset" as they tried to remove the discussion of papal infallibility from the agenda of Vatican I, only to find Manning carrying the day.[46]

Yet to Bossuet's undying credit, he held nothing so dear as the unity of the Church. He did not lend his support to the Gallican position insofar as he perceived it to be a direct threat to this unity. This is why Louis XIV and his counsellors, who believed in the supremacy of the Throne over the Church, were of two minds about inviting Bossuet to that famed gathering of the representatives of bishops and clergy that approved the Four Articles of the freedom of the Gallican church. But however incomplete the support they could expect from Bossuet, his absence from that gathering would have been considered a fatal blow to the Gallican cause.

The sermon, still to be translated into English, which Bossuet preached at the opening of that council on November 9, 1681, has, tellingly, "L'Unité de l'Eglise," for its title and theme. It masterfully creates the impression that he had successfully avoided both Scylla and Charybdis. Bossuet owed it more to his unbending attachment to the See of Rome as the pledge of unity than to the logic of his sermon that years later he successfully prevented a number of French bishops from opting for an open break with Rome. But his inability to see and to point out that no local Church's traditional privileges, however ancient, enjoy immutability contributed greatly to the unpreparedness of many French bishops and priests for the crucible of the Revolution.

It did not follow from Bossuet's ecclesiology that of all factors in the Church, the papacy should come out victorious from a cruel contest in which the greatest losers were the French bishops. They lost because of their being tied to the Ancien Régime as a chief tool of God's providential plan which Bossuet portrayed so effectively. For the Concordat of 1801, which forced Pius VII to declare all episcopal sees in France to be vacant and to fill them with new appointments, turned out to be the initial phase of modern Church history wherein the papacy is less and less the object of serious challenges from within the fold. From then on the appointment of new bishops by Rome became less and less interfered with either by tradition or by particular State-Church relations. Contrary to the expectations of Napoleon, who thought that the Concordat assured him of domination over the pope, it actually opened the road to Vatican I.

But long before anyone could perceive this course of events, Bossuet's staunch loyalty to the See of Rome spoiled Napoleon's final scheme to turn the Pope into a lackey of his political megalomania. In June 1811 Napoleon made the bishops of the Empire assemble in Notre Dame so that a National Council would teach the Pope obedience to the Emperor in matters "temporal" which would have included the Emperor's right to appoint bishops. But the bishops refused to be intimidated. They thought not only of the Pope, deprived of all means of communication with the outside world, but also of Bossuet. In fact they were forcefully reminded of Bossuet by Mgr Boulogne, bishop of Troyes, who opened the Council with a sermon in which he declared, in a direct reference to Bossuet's sermon on the unity of the Church, that he and his fellow bishops would "never detach themselves from that first link in the chain, without which all the others would fall away and would leave nothing to be seen save confusion, anarchy, and ruin."[47] The Emperor denounced the bishops as traitors, threw three of them into prison, but was unable to force a break in that chain. Within a year and a half he was fleeing from Moscow across endless snowfields towards what ultimately became his own enchainment on the Island of Saint Helena. More than one contemporary saw in that outcome God's answer to Napoleon's scornful question: "Does he [the Pope] suppose that the arms will fall from my soldiers' hands?"[48]

So much for the broader context and for a balanced view of the real chink in the fearsome armor which the *Variations* proved itself to be. There was no point in adhering to that first link, if it was not a very special link, indeed the only link in the chain that would never fail. This is not to suggest that Bossuet's contemporary critics in France, especially the Calvinist pastors Jurieu and Claude, had thought it useful to press Bossuet on a point which might have acted as a boomerang against them. For by pressing that point, Bossuet's Protestant antagonists would have bared the far more grievous inconsistencies of their own ecclesiology. That Gibbon never pressed that point, it had to be for a reason worth exploring. Gibbon, as is well known from his posthumously published Autobiography, became a Catholic as a young Oxford undergraduate in 1752. The motive is best reported in his own words: "The English translations of two famous works of Bossuet, Bishop of Meaux, *The Exposition of the Catholic Doctrine* and *The History of the Protestant Variations,* achieved my conversion, and I surely fell by a noble hand. I have since examined the originals with a more discerning eye, and shall not hesitate to pronounce that Bossuet is indeed a master of all the weapons of controversy. In the *Exposition,* a specious apology, the orator assumes with consummate art, the tone of candor and simplicity; and the ten horned monster is transformed at his magic touch, into the milk-white hind, who must be loved as soon as she is seen. In the *History,* a bold and well-aimed attack, he displays, with a happy mixture of narrative and argument, the faults and follies, the changes and contradictions of our first reformers, whose variations (as he dexterously contends) are the mark of historical error, while the perpetual unity of the Catholic Church is the sign and test of infallible truth."[49]

Actually, Gibbon owed his conversion to the consideration that if there were a divinely revealed truth, it had to be protected infallibly, which the Protestant reliance on the private interpretation of the Bible could not provide. Forced by his father, most indignant at the news of his son's becoming a Catholic, to repair to Lausanne and lodge there with Mr Pavilliard, a Calvinist minister, young Gibbon made quick progress in his studies as well as in his enlightenment. Two years later the pastor reported young Gibbon's pious return to Protestantism. But by 1764 and after some trips to Paris and elsewhere, Gibbon, aged thirty-one, was fully convinced of the falsity of all Christianity. The memorable proof of this is his response to hearing the friars chant the vespers in the church of Ara Coeli on the Capitoline. Gibbon no longer had any doubt about his slowly maturing perception that the Rome of Christian superstitions was the cause of the decline and fall of ancient Rome, that epitome of noble human virtues unfettered by supernatural vagaries. Gibbon apparently did not meditate on Suetonius' *Lives of the Twelve Caesars.*

While Bossuet still saw Protestantism as a road to Socinianism, the logical continuation of that road clearly pointed to plain agnosticism. Gibbon's spiritual journey served as an early proof of this, and a celebrated one. A century later, leaders of the Oxford Movement, disillusioned by the practical paganism of an England still under the external sway of one of the Churches issued from the Reformation, were ready to articulate that logic bluntly. Thus Manning, a year before his conversion, wrote to the still Anglican James Hope: "It is Rome or licence of thought and will."[50]

Undoubtedly, the growth of licentiousness in a formerly Christian Western culture did much to spark Christians to seek their unity. Rome's response in Vatican II gave further powerful impetus to ecumenism. Yet, three decades after Vatican II, after so many much publicized meetings of three popes with various leaders of Protestant Churches, and after so many sessions of sundry interconfessional committees, the unity of Christians does not seem to be any closer, and certainly not as far as the eventual unity of Catholics and Protestants is concerned.

One may list a number of reasons for this painful impasse. Undoubtedly too high hopes were raised too soon, as if four centuries of at times very hostile separation could be undone in four decades or even less. But the slow pace of history should not be taken for an explanation for the slowness of humans to make amends, for it is man who makes history and not the other way around. Man, however, is a fallen being and nothing shows this more, apart from an examination of one's own conscience, than a look at human history. There one also sees the long-range effects of initial missteps. It is here that a re-reading of Bossuet's *History of the Variations of the Protestant Churches* may be a much needed help.

For even if one is willing to take, at variance with Bossuet, a most benevolent look at the thinking and actions of Luther and Calvin and of their erstwhile chief associates, it remains a fact that Protestant Churches proliferate as distinct denominations.[51] And so does their doctrinal message, the ecumenical movement known as Faith and Order notwith-standing.[52] Here it is not possible to disagree with Bossuet. Worse, the diversities of the Protestant message are less easy to specify and distinguish today than was the case with the message of those whom Bossuet had in view. Faced with this additional difficulty, one cannot help looking for its source. In taking Bossuet for a guide here too, one will not go away empty-handed. For Bossuet already noted that the sudden proliferation of diversities among various early Protestant groups gave way, before long, to a trend which shows Protestants escaping into the art of generalities.

This is precisely the stumbling block of ecumenism today on at least the level of conceptualization. Cultivation of generalities, such as the emphasis put on having faith, though not on its object, is not a means toward unity, but a pull away from it. While Rome is under constant pressure to give up this or that of its "Tridentine doctrines," hardly ever anyone asks Protestants what are they willing to give up from their Reformation inheritance. They are not asked partly because they cannot answer clearly and with one voice. Further, they are not asked partly because Rome has been portrayed for long as the chief source of all troubles besetting Christians in an increasingly un-Christian world. The Protestant side appears by comparison the embodiment of truthfulness and therefore not in obligation to answer. But there is a problem with a truthfulness which increasingly resists clear definitions. In that predicament it becomes doubly resented that Rome cannot but insist on truth. Indeed the same pope, John Paul II, who more than any other pope in history held out the prospect of great concessions, noted in his Encyclical *Ut unum sint,* of all places, that "The unity willed by God can be attained only by the adherence of all to the content of revealed faith in its entirety. In matters of faith compromise is in contradiction with God who is Truth."[53]

In this age of utter relativism and subjectivism it is hardly popular to speak of truth, let alone Truth writ large. Yet while truth, especially its moral kind (which counts most), is at a discount, facts are not so easy to dispose of. The fact is clearer than daylight that the Reformers kept breeding contradictory variations as they aimed at rescuing the Christian ecclesial reality from its allegedly total deformation by restoring its erstwhile pristine form. The effort has now largely become a tendency to submerge all variations thus bred into a studied cultivation of vagueness, as if one could know only opinions (called various traditions) but no truth, and as if this were not a proposition of truth. In a more theological vein, the same intrinsic vaguenes and the dialectic contradiction it leads to is voiced by that Lutheran theologian, according to whom "Ever again and always for Lutherans the greatest obstacle in the path of ecumenism is the Gospel. . . . The unity of the Church is not an end itself, the unity of the Church is important for the sake of the Gospel."[54] According to Christ, however, the unity of his disciples was the *par excellence* means to reveal the fact that he had come to us from the Father.

It has also become all too clear that Rome alone shows courage and firmness in voicing age-old truths. It is hardly an enviable role. Bossuet put this all too well as he summed up the connection of the "forerunners" of the Reformers with the work of the latter: "A reformation was necessary—who denies it? but it was still more necessary to refrain from schism. Were those who promoted this schism by their preaching any better than their neighbors? They acted as if they were; this was enough to delude and 'spread like a canker' (2 Tim 2:17), according to St. Paul's expression. The world was desirous of condemning and rejecting their leaders; this is called Reformation. A specious name dazzles the people, and, to stir up hatred, calumny is not spared; thus is our doctrine blackened; men hate it before they know it."[55]

Nothing would be more self-defeating than to get lost in vain debates about words like formation, reformation and deformation. The fact of schism, of separation, which Paul called heresy, and about which he knew that in man's fallen state it had to come so that truth might become manifest—such facts, however saddening, cannot be talked away. Nor should one forget that the age of the great Church Fathers, to which Vatican II wanted to redirect late-20th-century Catholics, heard Saint Augustine state, and in reference to the testimony of the Scriptures, that "there can be no just cause for severing the unity of the Church." In the same breath he called schism "the most sacrilegious of all sins."[56]

In uttering these strong words, Augustine served merely as a faint echo to some words of Saint Dionysius, most of whose extant writings are part of Eusebius' *Church History*. There we read that in his letter to Novatian, Dionysius addressed him the strongest conceivable reproach: "You ought to have been ready to suffer anything whatever rather than split the Church of God, and martyrdom to avoid schism would have brought you as much honor as martyrdom to escape idolatry.—I should say, more. For in the latter case a man is martyred to save his own single soul, in the former to save the whole Church."[57]

These two passages, capital as they are, have not been quoted here as a hint about respective responsibilities for the disunity of Christendom. Today's Protestants are not guilty of what Luther and others wrought four hundred years ago. Nor are the Catholics of today responsible for whatever grounds their forebears provided for the Reformation. The responsibility of present-day Catholics and Protestants lies on a higher level than that of mutual recrimination. But regardless of the importance of the irenic atmosphere that should rule on that level, its high grounds must not lack serious attention to truth, which, in the case of the Church, is never ahistorical.

The unity of Christians, which is not a commodity but a sacred duty, can only be a unity in a Church which is a visible, living, historical continuity. Here the lessons of facts, statements, and events, now almost five centuries old, are of paramount instructiveness. Those who ignore or slight the lessons of history are bound to repeat its missteps. Here a careful study of Bossuet's *History of the Variations of the Protestant Churches* may profit all those who, in their ecumenical commitment, search for factual information about the past so that they may all the more securely orient themselves toward that future which will come in God' good time.

Notes

[1] F. Brunetière, *Bossuet* (2d rev. ed.; Paris: Hachette, 1914), p. 68.

[2] J. Boswell, *The Life of Samuel Johnson, together with the Journal of a Tour to the Hebrides,* new ed., with notes and introduction by A. Napier (London: George Bell and Sons, 1889), vol. V, p. 268.

[3] The twenty-eight sermons preached by Johnson and published posthumously could have been composed by any deist, and perhaps even by a Buddhist, devoted to pedestrian moralizing. Christianity is mentioned occasionally, but Christ never. See

Samuel Johnson. Sermons, ed. J. Hagstrom and J. Gray (New Haven, CT: Yale University Press, 1978).

[4] In the plethora of recent studies on Boswell, one may note the collection of essays, *Boswell: Citizen of the World, Man of Letters,* ed. I. S. Lustig (Lexington, KY: University Press of Kentucky, 1995).

[5] *Dictionnaire raisonnée des Oeuvres de Bossuet,* par l'Abbé V. Verlaque (Paris: Alphonse Picard et Fils, 1903), reprinted (Nendeln, Lichtenstein: Kraus, 1975); see pp. 9-10, for the list of the 7th to 12th editions.

[6] For a brief list, see H.-M. Bourseaud, *Histoire et description des manuscrits et des éditions originales des ouvrages de Bossuet* (Paris: A. Picard & Fils, 1898), p. 227.

[7] Quoted from E. E. Reynolds, *Bossuet* (Garden City, N.Y.: Doubleday, 1963), p. 85.

[8] A new translation by E. Forster, with introduction by O. Ranum, was published by the University of Chicago Press in 1976 in its series, Classic European Historians.

[9] This aspect of Bossuet's thought is best set forth in Brunetière's *Bossuet.* An excellent summary of it was provided by Brunetière himself in his article, "Bossuet," in *The Catholic Encyclopedia* (New York, 1907), vol. 2, pp. 699-702.

[10] See R. Haynes, *Philosopher King: The Humanist Pope Benedict XIV* (London: Weidenfeld and Nicholson, 1970), p. 199.

[11] The system evolved from the ideas of the Italian reformer, Lelio Sozzini, or Lelius Socinus (1525-62), through the efforts of his nephew, Fausto Sozzini, or Faustus Socinus (1539-1604), who was active in Poland.

[12] *Defensio declarationis ecclesiae gallicanae.* See note 39 below. Incidentally, those Four Articles received a swift and massive rebuttal from the Spanish Benedictine, Joseph Saenz de Aguirre, whose *Auctoritas infallibilis et summa Cathedra Sancti Petri* (Salamanca, 1683) won him a cardinal's hat.

[13] *Corpus syntagma Confessionum fidei quae in diversis regnis et nationibus, ecclesiarum nomine fuerunt authentice editae,* ed. nova (Geneva: Petri Chouer, 1654). Incidentally, it was heavily used by P. Schaff in his *The Creeds of Christendom* (1877; 6th ed., 1985) where the more recent material further illustrates the same lack of consistency.

[14] For details, see Louis François de Bausset's *Histoire de Bossuet, Evêque de Meaux* (5th ed.; Paris: Beauce-Rusand, 1828), vol. 3, pp. 90-91. The four volumes of this work, first published in 1814, are still an indispensable source of information. Bausset, consecrated bishop of Alais in 1784 and imprisoned briefly during 1792, was a good friend of Abbé Emery, director of Saint Sulpice, from whom he obtained the manuscripts of Fénélon. This served as the basis of Bausset's three-volume *L'Histoire de Fénélon* (1809). He took a prominent part in public life after 1815, and was created a cardinal in 1817, seven years before his death, at the age of seventy-six.

[15] Petri Card. Pázmány, *Hodoegus* (1613).

[16] It was translated from the sixth French edition. The name of the publisher was not given.

[17] The work of resetting was done by Anne Sinclair Williams, the proofreading and reindexing by Thomas Mauro, to both of which the editor wishes to express here his profound appreciation.

[18] Paris: Hachette, 1891. I have used the third revised edition from 1909.

[19] Sander's work was originally published in Latin in Cologne in 1585 as *De origine ac progressu schismatis Anglicani*. Its English translation, *The Rise and Growth of the Anglican Schism*, first published in 1877, has since been many times reprinted.

[20] *Histoire de la Réformation de l'Eglise d'Angleterre* (Londres: chez Richard Chisnel, 1683-85).

[21] The first Part of Volume 1 of Denifle's *Luther und Luthertum* (1904) appeared in English translation as *Luther and Lutherdom* (Somerset, Oh.: Torch Press, 1917).

[22] H. Grisar, *Luther*, translated from the German in five volumes (London: K. Paul, Trench, Trubner, 1913-1917).

[23] A point emphatically made and carefully documented by Denifle in his *Luther and Lutherdom*, pp. 13-26.

[24] Newman, *An Essay on the Development of Christian Doctrine* (Garden City, N.Y.: Doubleday Image Books, 1960), p. 34.

[25] Brunetière, *Bossuet*, p. 74.

[26] Ibid., p. 76.

[27] Newman, *Lectures on the Doctrine of Justification* (5th ed.; London: Rivington, 1890), p. 340.

[28] In addition to Rébelliau's work, there is also L. Crousle's shorter monograph, *Bossuet et le protestantisme: étude historique* (Paris: H. Champion, 1901), where much attention is paid to many other evidences of Bossuet's concern for Protestantism.

[29] Bossuet's engaging, though still critical portrayal of Melancthon shows up to good advantage against modern monographs on him, such as *Melancthon, Alien or Ally* by F. Hildebrandt (Cambridge, Eng.: University Press, 1946) and *Melancthon, the Quiet Reformer* by C. L. Manschreck (New York: Abingdon Press, 1958).

[30] They were Beatus, abbot of Libana, and Etherus, bishop of Osma, authors of a long letter of Elipandus, archbishop of Toledo, who preached a form of adoptionism. Their letter also contains a passage which, in fact, may have even better suited Bossuet's purpose. Beatus and Etherus noted that heretics, being so numerous, "come up with many lies, and since they think diversely about the Catholic faith, they cannot agree among themselves." The letter also deplores the confusion among the bishops. See *Heterii et sancti Beati ad Elipandum epistola*, Migne, PL vol. 96, cols. 902 and 946.

[31] Rahner repeatedly quoted this and other passages from that letter during his lecture trip in England in 1971, which later was recalled in *The Tablet*, March 10, 1979, p. 238.

[32] This book, already referred to in note 12 above, is invariably referred to by Bossuet as *Synt. conf. fid.* His omission of the first word in the title is no help in tracking it down, something true of many of his references. They were never made more explicit in subsequent editions of the *Variations*, whether printed separately or as part of the various editions of his *Oeuvres complètes*. It is not likely that a critical edition of the *Variations* that would satisfy the meticulous reader, will soon be forthcoming.

[33] See my *Les tendances nouvelles de l'ecclésiologie* (Rome: Herder & Herder, 1957; reprinted, 1962), pp. 83-98.

[34] A. Harnack, *Lehrbuch der Dogmengeschichte,* (3d ed.; Freiburg: Mohr, 1897), vol. 3, p. 788.

[35] Bossuet gives in French translation only one half of the book's title. The full title of the book, of which no copies are in the United States, reads as follows: *Kurtze, doch unpartheyisch- und gewissenhaffte Betrachtung des in dem Natur- und Göttlichen Recht gegründeten Heiligen Ehstandes, in welcher die bisher strittigen Fragen vom Ehbruch, der Ehscheidung, und sonderlich von dem vielen Weibers nehmen mit allem beiderseits gegebenem Beweisthumb dem christlichen Leser vorgestellt werden.* The book, which ran to 249 quarto pages, contains no indication of the place of publication. No detail given by Bossuet differs from the wealth of material offered by Grisar in chapter xxi, "Princely Marriages," in volume 4 of his *Luther,* that deals with Luther's and his associates' involvement in the affairs of Henry VIII and mostly those of the Landgrave, as well as with modern reactions to it.

[36] See *Deutsche Gelehrten Lexicon* (1750); reprinted, Hildesheim: Georg Olms, 1960, vol. A-C, col. 912.

[37] For details, see L. Pastor, *The History of the Popes,* vol. X, tr. F. R. Kerr (London: Kegan Paul, Trench and Trübner, 1930), pp. 276-77.

[38] Book VI, 9.

[39] See Elizabeth Altham's report, "Protestant Pastors on the Road to Rome," in *Sursum Corda* (Ft. Collins, Co., Special Promotional edition, 1995), pp. 2-13.

[40] A main theme in Newman's Twelve Lectures delivered in the London Oratory in 1850, known as *Anglican Difficulties.* See reprint by Real View Books (Fraser, MI, 1994), with introduction and notes by S. L. Jaki.

[41] Sainte-Beuve, *Les grands écrivains français. XVIIe siècle. Ecrivains et orateurs religieux* (Paris: Garnier Frères, 1928), p. 25.

[42] *Oeuvres de Bossuet* (Paris: Firmin Didot Frères, 1860), vol. IV, p. 538.

[43] See especially the conclusion in A.-G. Martimort's standard monograph, *Le gallicanisme de Bossuet* (Paris: Le Cerf, 1953).

[44] The conversation, first reported by Fénelon, was made much by J. de Maistre in his spiritedly anti-gallican *Du Pape* (1821; Lyon: H. Pélagaud Fils & Roblot, 1873), p. 88.

[45] Such is at least the view of none other than Döllinger. For details, see Hergenröther's *Anti-Janus,* tr. J. B. Robertson (Dublin: W. B. Kelly, 1870), p. x.

[46] As is all too clear from his *The True Story of the Vatican Council* (1875; reprinted, with an introduction by S. L. Jaki; Fraser, MI: Real View Books, 1996).

[47] Quoted from E. E. Y. Hales, *Revolution and Papacy 1769 - 1846* (London: Eyre & Spottiswoode, 1960), p. 210.

[48] One of them was the Protestant historian A. Alison in his *History of Europe from the Commencement of the French Revolution in 1789 to the Restoration of the Bourbons in 1815* (New York: Harper and Brothers, 1842), vol. III, p. 286.

[49] *Autobiography of Edward Gibbon as originally edited by Lord Sheffield,* with an introduction by J. B. Bury (London: Oxford University Press, 1907), p. 47. As Reynolds pointed out in his *Bossuet* (p. 163), Gibbon refers to John Dryden's *The Hind and the Panther* (1687), in which the first line reads, "A milk-white Hind, immortal and unchanged." While Gibbon saw clearly that the Catholic Dryden seriously took the image of that Hind as a symbol of the Catholic Church, subsequent literary criticism tried to make it appear as something which Dryden himself did not take seriously. This

obfuscation in literary criticism has just been exploded by Anne Barbeau Gardiner in her *Ancient Faith and Modern Freedom: John Dryden's The Hind and Panther* (Washington DC: Catholic University of America Press, 1997).

[50] Letter of December 11, 1850, to James Hope.

[51] The unabated proliferation of Protestant denominations is well attested in the *Oxford Dictionary of World Religions*. Protestant groups, basically independent of one another, make up the largest part of the approximately 28,000 distinct associations within Christendom. For the situation in America four decades ago, one can profitably consult J. A. Hardon's *The Protestant Churches in America* (Westminster, MD: The Newman Press, 1957).

[52] For the origin and early history of that movement, see my book, *Les Tendances nouvelles de l'ecclésiologie* (quoted in note 28 above), pp. 129-138. The movement was a reaction to the earlier and purely pragmatic trend, known as Life and Work, that survived in the heavily politicized World Council of Churches.

[53] *Ut unum sint* (1995) #18.

[54] J. A. Burgess, "Lutherans and the Papacy: Review of Some Basic Issues," in P. J. Mc Cord (ed.), *A Pope for all Christians? An Inquiry into the Role of Peter in the Modern World*: Paulist Press, 1976), p. 21.

[55] Book XI, 206.

[56] "Haec de Scripturis sanctis documenta proferimus, ut appareat facile non esse quidquam gravius sacrilegio schismatis: quia praecidendae unitatis nulla est justa necessitas," *Contra epistolam Parmeniani*, Lib. 2, c. 25 (PL 42:176).

[57] *Eusebius. The History of the Church*, tr. G. A. Williamson (Penguin Book, 1965), p. 285.

THE

HISTORY

OF THE

VARIATIONS

OF THE

PROTESTANT CHURCHES.

By *JAMES BENIGN BOSSUET*,
Bifhop of MEAUX, one of His moft Chriftian
Majefty's Honourable Privy-Council, heretofore
Preceptor to the DAUPHIN, and Chief Almoner
to the DAUPHINESS.

IN TWO PARTS.

Tranflated from the *Sixth Edition* of the *FRENCH*
Original printed at *PARIS*, M DCC XVIII.

PART I. VOL. I.

ANTWERP:
Printed in the YEAR M DCC XLII.

Preface

The Design of This Work

1.—A general idea of the Protestant Religion, and the variations of it. The discovery of them useful to true doctrine and the peace of the human mind.—The Authors to whom reference is made in this History

IF Protestants knew thoroughly how their religion was formed; with how many variations and with what inconstancy their confessions of faith were drawn up; how they first separated themselves from us, and afterwards from one another; by how many subtleties, evasions, and equivocations they labored to repair their divisions and to re-unite the scattered members of their disjointed reformation; this reformation of which they boast would afford them but little satisfaction, or rather, to speak my mind more freely, it would excite in them only feelings of contempt. It is the history of these variations, these subtleties, these equivocations, and these artifices, which I design to write; but in order to render this detail more useful to them, some principles must be laid down which they cannot contravene, and which the current of a narration would not permit me to deduce, when once engaged in it.

2.—Variations in faith a certain proof of falsehood.—Those of the Arians.— Steadiness of the Catholic Church.

When in expositions of faith, variations were seen among Christians, they were ever considered as a mark of falsehood and inconsistency, if I may so speak, in the doctrine propounded. Faith speaks with simplicity; the Holy Ghost sheds pure light; and the truth which he teaches has a language always uniform. Whoever is but the least conversant in the history of the Church, must know she opposed to each heresy appropriate and precise expositions which she never altered; and if we attend to the expressions by which she condemned heretics, it will appear that they always proceed by the shortest and most direct route to attack the error in its source. She acts thus, because all that varies, all that is overlaid with doubtful or studiously ambiguous terms, has always appeared suspicious, and not only fraudulent, but even absolutely false, because it betrays an embarrassment with which truth is unacquainted.

This was one of the grounds on which the ancient doctors condemned the Arians, who were constantly making new confessions of faith, without ever being able to settle themselves. Since their first confession of faith, which was made by Arius, and presented by this arch-heretic to his bishop, Alexander,

1

they never ceased to vary. With this did St. Hilary reproach Constantius, the protector of those heretics; and whilst this emperor called new councils to reform their creeds and frame new confessions of faith, this holy bishop addressed him in these forcible words: "Your case is similar to that of unskilful architects, who are never pleased with their own work. You do nothing but build up and pull down; whereas the Catholic Church, the first time it assembled, raised an immortal edifice, and gave in the symbol of Nice so full a declaration of truth, that to condemn Arianism for ever, nothing more is necessary than to repeat that creed."[1]

3.—The character of heresies is to be changeable—a celebrated passage of Tertullian.

But they are not the Arians alone who have varied in this manner. From the origin of Christianity, all heresies have had the same character, and long before the time of Arius, Tertullian had said: "Heretics vary in their rules; namely, in their confessions of faith; every one of them thinks he has a right to change and model what he has received according to his own fancy, as the author of the sect composed it according to his own fancy. Heresy never changes its proper nature in never ceasing to innovate; and the progress of the thing is like to its origin. What is permitted to Valentine is allowed to Valentinians; the Marcionites have equal power with Marcion, nor have the authors of a heresy more right to innovate than their disciples. All changes in heresy, and when examined to the bottom, it is found, in course of time, entirely different in many points from what it had been at its birth."[2]

4.—This character of heresy recognised in all ages of the Church.

This character of heresy has been always observed by Catholics, and two holy authors of the eighth century have written "that heresy, however old, is always in itself a novelty; but that, the better to retain the title of being new, it innovates daily, and daily changes its doctrine."[3]

5.—The charter of immutability in Faith of the Catholic Church.

But whilst heresies, always varying, agree not with themselves, and are continually introducing new rules, that is to say, new symbols, Tertullian says, "That in the Church the rule of faith is unalterable, and never to be reformed."[4] It is so, because the church which professes to speak, and teach nothing but what she hath received, does not vary; and on the contrary, heresy, which began by innovating, daily innovates, and changes not its nature.

6.—The principle of instability in all new doctrines.—St. Paul.—St. Chrysostom.

Hence, St. Chrysostom, speaking of this precept of the Apostle, "Shun profane babblings which will increase into more ungodliness," "avoid novelties in your discourses, for things do not stop there; one novelty begets another, and there is no end to error when once you have begun to err."[5]

7.—Two causes of instability in heresies.

In heresies, two things cause this disorder: one drawn from the nature of the human mind, which having once tasted the bait of novelty, ceases not to seek with disordered appetite this deceitful allurement; the other is drawn from the difference that exists between the works of God and those of man. The Catholic truth proceeding from God, has its perfection at once; heresy, the feeble offspring of the human mind, can be formed only by ill-fitting patches. When, contrary to the precept of the wise man, we venture to remove "the ancient landmarks set by our fathers,"[6] and to reform the doctrine once received among the faithful, we launch forth, without a thorough insight into the consequences of our attempt. That, which at the commencement, a false light, made us hazard, is found attended with such inconsistencies, as to oblige these reformers every day to reform themselves, so that they cannot tell when their own minds are at rest, or their innovations terminated.

8.—What those variations are, which we undertake to show in Protestant Churches.

These are the solid and steady principles by which I undertake to demonstrate to Protestants the falsehood of their doctrine, from their continual variations, and the unstable manner in which they have explained their dogmas. I do not speak of the unsteadiness of individuals, but of the body of the church, in the books which they call symbolical; namely, those that have been made to express the consent of the churches; in a word, from their own confessions of faith, decreed, signed and published: the doctrine of which has been given out as the doctrine containing nothing but the pure word of God, and which, notwithstanding, has been changed in so many different ways in its chief articles.

9.—The Protestant party divided into two main bodies.

But when treating of those who, in these latter ages, have called themselves Reformed, it is not my design to speak of the Socinians, nor the different societies of Anabaptists, nor of the other different sects which have sprung up in England and elsewhere, in the bosom of the new reformation; but of those two bodies only, one of which is composed of Lutherans, namely, those who have for their rule the Confession of Augsburg; the other, who follow the sentiments of Zwinglius and Calvin. The former, in the institution of the Eucharist, defend the literal sense; the latter, the figurative. By this character shall I distinguish one from the other; though many other very weighty and very important differences exist between them, as will appear by what follows.

10.—The variations of one party are a proof against the other, chiefly those of
Luther and the Lutherans.

The Lutherans will tell us here, that they are very little concerned in the variations and conduct of Zwinglians and Calvinists; and some of those may imagine in their turn, that the inconstancy of Lutherans affects them as little: but both one and the other are mistaken, since the Lutherans can see in the

Calvinists the consequences of those commotions which they excited; and, on the contrary, the Calvinists ought to remark in the Lutherans the disorder and uncertainty of that original which they have followed. But the Calvinists in particular, cannot deny, that they have always looked upon Luther and the Lutherans, as the authors of their reformation, and not to speak of Calvin, who often mentioned Luther with respect, as the head of the reformation, we shall see, in the sequel of this history, that all the Calvinists, (by this name I call the second party of Protestants,) the Germans, English, Hungarians, Poles, Dutch, and all others in general, who assembled at Frankfort, through the influence of Queen Elizabeth, all these having acknowledged "those of the Confession of Augsburg," namely, the Lutherans, "as the first that gave a new birth to the church," acknowledge also the Confession of Augsburg as common to the whole party, "which they did not pretend to contradict, but 'to understand correctly';"[7] and this in one article only, that of the Supper; for this reason also naming amongst their fathers, not only Zwinglius, Bucer, and Calvin but Luther and Melancthon and placing Luther at the head of all the reformers.

After that, let them say that the variations of Luther and the Lutherans affect them not; we will tell them, on the contrary, that, according to their own principles, and their own declarations, to show the variations and inconsistencies of Luther and the Lutherans, is to point out the spirit of giddiness in the source of the reformation, and the head where it had been first conceived.

11.—*The collection of the Confessions of Faith, printed at Geneva.*

A long time since, a collection of Confessions of Faith has been printed at Geneva,[8] in which with that of the defenders of the figurative sense, namely, that of France and the Swiss, are also those of the defenders of the literal sense, namely that of Augsburg and some others. What is still more remarkable is this, that though the confessions there collected be so different, and in many articles of faith condemn one another, in the preface to this collection, they are, notwithstanding, proposed "as one entire body of sacred divinity, and as authentic records, which men ought to have recourse to in order to know the ancient and primitive faith." They are dedicated to the kings of England, Scotland, Denmark, and Sweden, and those princes and republics by whom they are followed. That those kings and states should be separated from each other in communion, as well as in faith, is a matter of no consequence. Those of Geneva address them, notwithstanding, as true believers, "enlightened in these latter times by the special grace of God, with the true light of the Gospel," and then present them with all these confessions of faith, as "an external monument of the extraordinary piety of their ancestors."

12.—*The Calvinists approve of the Lutheran Confessions of Faith, at least, as containing nothing contrary to fundamental points.*

It is because these doctrines are equally adopted by the Calvinists, either as absolutely true, or at least as having nothing in them contrary to the foundation of faith; hence it follows, that when we shall see in this history the doctrine of the confessions of faith not only of France and Switzerland, and the other defenders of the figurative sense, but of Augsburg and others set forth by the Lutherans, this doctrine must not be considered as foreign to Calvinism, but as a doctrine which the Calvinists have approved expressly as true, or left uncensured in the most authentic acts that have passed among them.

13.—*The Lutheran Confessions of Faith.*

I shall say less of the Lutherans, who instead of being moved by the authority of those who defend the figurative sense, have nothing but a contempt and aversion for their sentiments. Their own inconstancy ought to confound them. When we should but read the titles of their Confessions of Faith, in this Geneva collection, and in the other books of the same kind, where they are collected together into a body, we would be astonished at their multitude. The first that appears is that of Augsburg, whence the Lutherans derive their name. It will be seen as presented to Charles V, in 1530, and after that to have been touched and retouched several times. Melanchton, who had penned it, entirely altered the sense of it in the apology which he wrote afterwards. This apology was subscribed to by the whole party. Thus it was changed in coming forth from the hands of its very author. From that time they never ceased reforming and explaining it in different ways; so difficult these reformers found it to satisfy themselves, and so little accustomed to teach precisely what was to be believed. But, as if one confession of faith alone were not sufficient on the same subject, Luther judged it necessary for him to deliver his sentiments after another manner; and in 1537, he drew up the articles of Smalcald, in order to have them presented to the council which Paul III had called at Mantua. These articles were signed by the whole party, and are inserted in what the Lutherans call the Book of Concord.[9]

This explication did not fully satisfy. It was necessary to draw up the confession called Saxonic, presented to the Council of Trent in 1551, and that of Wirtemberg, which in 1552 was also presented to the same council.

To these are to be added the explications of the church of Wirtemberg, the birthplace of the Reformation, and the rest of them, which shall in order take their place in this history; particularly those of the Book of Concord, in the "Abridgment of Articles," and also in the same book, the "Explications Repeated." All these are so many several confessions of faith, authentically published by the party, embraced by some churches, impugned by others in points the most important; and yet these churches would wish to appear as forming one body, because, through policy, they dissemble their dissensions on ubiquity and other matters.

14.—*The Confessions of Faith of the Figurative-Sense Defenders, and the second party of Protestants.*

Nor was the other party of Protestants less fruitful in confessions of faith. At the same time that the Confession of Augsburg was presented to Charles VI, those who dissented from it presented to him their own, published in the name of four cities of the empire, the first of which was Strasburg.

This so little pleased the defenders of the figurative sense, that every one would make his own; we shall see four or five after the fancy of the Swiss. But if the Zwinglian ministers had their way of thinking, others were no less singular in theirs: this diversity gave rise to the confession of France and Geneva. About the same time were published two confessions of faith in the name of the Church of England; as many in the name of the Kirk of Scotland. Frederick III, Elector Palatine, would make his own separately and apart; this, with the others, took its place in the collection of Geneva. The Dutch would adhere to none of those already made: we have, therefore, a Dutch confession of faith approved by the Synod of Dort. But why should not the Calvinists of Poland have theirs? Indeed, though they had subscribed the last confession of the Zuinglians, yet we still find they published another at the synod of Czenger. Not satisfied with this, assembled at Sendomir, with the Lutherans and Vaudois, they agree to a new way of expounding the article on the Eucharist,—yet so that none of them departed from their former sentiments.

15.—*Other authentic Acts.—How these variations prove the weakness of the Protestant Religion.*

To omit the confession of faith framed by the Bohemians who wished to please both parties of the new reformation—I speak not of the treaties of concord which were made between the churches with so many variations and so many equivocations, they will appear in their proper place, with the decisions of national synods, and the other confessions of faith made in different circumstances. Great God! Is it possible, that upon the same matters and the same questions, so many multiplied acts, so many decisions, and different confessions of faith are necessary? And yet I cannot boast that I know all, and I know that I cannot find all. The Catholic Church never had occasion to oppose the same heresy a second time; but the churches of the new reformation, which has produced such a number, strange to say, and yet true, are not yet content! And we shall see in this history that the Calvinists have new confessions, which have suppressed or reformed all the others.

These variations fill us with astonishment. They will appear worse when we learn the detail and the manner in which these acts, so authentic, were drawn up. We are amused—I speak it without exaggeration—with the name of a confession of faith—and nothing has been less serious in the new reformation than that which is most serious in all religion.

16.—*The Protestants are ashamed of so many Confessions of Faith.—The vain pretexts by which they endeavor to excuse them.*

This prodigious multitude of confessions of faith has alarmed those who made them: we shall see the weak reasons by which they endeavor to excuse them: but I cannot avoid mentioning those which have been set forth in the preface of the collection of Geneva,[10] because they are general, and bear equally upon all the churches which call themselves reformed.

The first reason assigned to establish the necessity of multiplying these confessions is, that as many articles of faith were attacked, it became necessary to oppose many confessions to this great number of errors. I agree to the justice of this reasoning and at the same time, by a contrary reason, I demonstrate the absurdity of all these confessions of faith of the Protestants, since all, as it appears by reading the titles, only regard articles precisely the same; so that we can address them with St. Athanasius, "Why a new council—new confessions—a new creed? What new question has been raised?"[11]

Another excuse alleged is, that the whole world ought (as the apostle says) to render an account of their faith, so that the churches spread in different places, have a right to declare their belief by a public testimony; as if all the churches in the world, however separated they may be, cannot agree in the same testimony, when they have the same belief; as, in fact, from the origin of Christianity we have witnessed a like consent in the churches. Who will show me that the churches of the east have had in primitive times a confession different from that of the west? Has not the symbol of Nicea served equally as a testimony against all the Arians—the definition of Chalcedon against all the Eutychians—the eight chapters of Carthage against all the Pelagians? and so of the rest.

But, say the Protestants, was there one of the reformed churches which could make a law for the rest? No, certainly; all these new churches, under the pretext of shaking off domination have deprived themselves of order, and are unable to preserve the principle of unity. But, in fine, if the truth governs all, as they boast, to unite them in one confession of faith, nothing more is necessary than that all should enter into the sentiment of him to whom God had given the grace first to explain the truth.

In fine, we read in the preface of Geneva, that if the reformation had produced but one confession of faith, this consent might have been taken for a studied combination; whereas, a concordance between so many churches, and confessions of faith, without agreement, is the work of the Holy Ghost. This agreement would indeed be surprising; but, unfortunately it is not found in these confessions of faith; and from this history it will appear, that in a matter so serious there never was such inconstancy.

17.—*The Protestants of the two parties in vain endeavor to reunite under one sole and uniform Confession of Faith.*

This great evil was deeply felt in the reformation, and the attempt to remedy it proved fruitless. All the second party of Protestants held a general assembly to draw up a common confession of faith; but we see by the acts, that having no principle of unity, an agreement was impossible.[12]

The Lutherans, who appeared more united in the confession of Augsburg, were not less embarrassed with different editions, and could find therein no better remedy.[13]

18.—*How much these varieties degenerate from the ancient simplicity of Christianity.*

We shall be tired, no doubt, of witnessing these variations, and so many false subtleties of the new reformation; so many cavils on words; so many different agreements; so many equivocations and forced explanations, on which these have been founded. Is this, it will be often said, the Christian religion, perfect and simple? No, certainly it is not. Ammian Marcellin was right when he said, that Constantius, by all his councils and all his symbols, had strayed from this admirable simplicity, and that he had weakened the whole vigor of the faith, by the perpetual fear which he entertained lest he should be deceived in his sentiments.[14]

19.—*Why it will be very necessary in this history to speak of those whom the Protestants call the Reformers*

While it is my intention to represent in this work the confessions of faith and the other public acts, where the variations appeared not only of individuals, but of entire churches of the new reformation, at the same time I cannot avoid speaking of the chiefs of the party who have drawn up these confessions, or have made those changes. Thus Luther, Melancthon, Carlostad, Zuinglius, Bucer, Ecolampadius, Calvin, and the others, will appear often in their places; but I shall not say anything which is not taken from their own writing, or authors above suspicion, so that there will not be in all this narrative any fact that is not certain and useful in elucidating the variations whose history I write.

20.—*Parts of this history, whence they are drawn.—Why no history more certain and more authentic than this.*

With regard to the public acts of Protestants, besides their confessions of faith and their catechisms, which are in the hands of the whole world, I have found some others in the collection of Geneva; others in the book called the "Concord," printed by the Lutherans in 1654; others in the result of the national synod of the pretended reformers, which I have seen in an authentic form in the king's library; others in the Sacramentarian History, printed at Zurich in 1602, by Hospinian, a Zuinglian author; or, in fine, in other Protestant authors; in a word, I shall say nothing which is not authentic, and incontestable. As to the rest, to speak plainly, it is well known of what persuasion I am; for certainly I am a Catholic, as submissive as any other to the decisions of the church, and so disposed, that no one fears more to prefer his own private opinion to the universal judgment. After that, to pretend to be neutral or indifferent to the cause whose history I write, or to dissemble what I am, would be to offer a gross illusion to the reader; but with this sincere avowal, I maintain that Protestants cannot deny that I am entitled to belief, and that they will never read a history more indubitable than this; since in all that I have to say against their churches and their authors, I will mention nothing which is not clearly proved by their own witnesses.

21.—Some objections that may be made against this work.

I have not spared pains to transcribe them. The reader will perhaps complain that I have not spared his. Others will probably condemn my dwelling upon things which may appear trivial to them; but besides that those, who are accustomed to treat on matters of religion, well know, in a subject of such delicacy and importance, every thing, even to the least word, is essential; we ought to consider not what things are in themselves, but what they have been, and what they are in the minds of those with whom we have to deal; and, after all, it will be easily seen that this history is entirely of a description quite peculiar; that it ought to come forth to the world with all its proofs, and armed as it were on all sides; and in order to render it more convincing and useful, it was necessary to make it less amusing.

22.—Some things which it was necessary to trace farther back; as the history of the Vaudois, of the Albigenses, of John Wickliff, and of John Huss.

Though my plan may appear to confine me to the history of Protestants, in certain places I judged it necessary to ascend to matters of a more distant date; at that period especially, when the Vaudois and Hussites were seen to re-unite themselves with the Calvinists and Lutherans. In this place it was necessary to know the origin and sentiments of these sects, to point out their extraction, and to distinguish them from those with whom some have wished to confound them; to detect the Manicheism of Peter of Bruis, and the Albigenses, and show how the Vaudois emanated from them; to give an account of the blasphemies of Wickliff, from whom Huss and his disciples took their birth; in a word, to reveal the shame of all these sectaries to those who glory in such predecessors.

23.—Why the order of time is followed without distinction of the subject matter.

As to the arrangement of this work, the disputes and decisions will, without the distinction of matter, be seen to proceed in it in the same order in which they happened. By this means, it is certain that the variations of Protestants, and the state of their churches, will be more clearly marked. By thus taking in at one view the circumstances of time and place, we shall obtain a clearer view of what may serve for the conviction or defence of the parties concerned.

24.—The whole dispute regarding the Church put together.—The present state of this famous question, and to what terms it is reduced by the ministers Claude and Jurieu.

There is but one controversy, the history of which I give separately; it is that which regards the church. This is a matter of such importance, that by its decision alone all disputes might be terminated, were it not as much obscured in the writings of Protestants, as it is clear and intelligible in itself. To restore it to its native plainness and simplicity, I have collected, in the last book, all I had to mention on this subject; that the reader, having once seen the difficulty to the bottom, may perceive what obliged these new churches to change into so many shapes in succession,—what in the end is but one and the same. For, in a word, the whole matter at issue is to show where the church was before the reformation. Naturally and accordingly to the commonly received opinions of all Christians, it ought to be acknowledged as visible; and in their first confessions of faith, namely those of Augsburg and Strasburg, the first of each party, they went thus far. By this they obliged themselves to show, as agreeing with them in one and the same belief, not private individuals scattered up and down, some on one point and some on another, but bodies of a church, namely, bodies composed of pastors and people. For a long time they amused men in saying, that the church indeed was not always in a state of splendor, but in all times there was at least, some little assembly where truth made itself heard; at last they having well perceived they could not point out any one, either little or great, obscure or illustrious which was of the Protestant belief, the subterfuge of an invisible church very opportunely occurred to them, and the dispute long turned upon this question. In our days they have more clearly perceived, that a church reduced to an invisible state was a chimera, irreconcilable with the plan of scripture, and common notions of Christians, and this bad position is now abandoned. The Protestants have been obliged to seek for their succession in the church of Rome. Two celebrated ministers of France vied with each other which should best cover the inconsistencies of this system, to use an expression then in fashion. It is well known, that those two ministers are M. Claude and Jurieu. These men were gifted with wit and learning, subtlety and address, and every qualification necessary to make a good defence. None put on a better countenance than they, nor classed their adversaries, with a more haughty and disdainful air, with weak people and missionaries for whom they entertained so great contempt; the difficulty, however, which they would make appear so light, proved at last so great, that it raised a division in the party. At length they were obliged to acknowledge publicly, that in the Church of Rome, as in other churches, eternal salvation with the essential succession of true Christianity were found—a secret which the policy of the party had so long kept concealed. They have given us great advantages besides; they were driven into such visible excesses; they have so far forgotten both the ancient maxims of the reformation, and their own confessions of faith, that I could not but relate this change in full. Having applied myself with great care to trace out exactly the plan of these two ministers, and show plainly the state in which they have placed the question, I must acknowledge sincerely, that I have found in their writings, with the most dexterous shifts, as much erudition and as much subtlety as ever I have observed in all the Lutheran or Calvinistic authors with whom I am acquainted. If among Protestants it should be judged advisable, under the pretext of the absurdities into which they have been forced to contradict and recall what they have granted, and again take shelter in the invisible church, or other retreats equally abandoned, this would be like the disorder of a defeated army, who, dismayed at their overthrow, should seek to re-enter those forts which they had been unable to maintain, at the peril of being soon forced out a second time: or like the restlessness of a sick person, who, after much turning to-and-fro in bed in search of a more easy place, comes back to that he had just left, where he soon finds himself as uncomfortable as before.

      25.—*What complaints Protestants may make, and how frivolous.*

I have but one thing to fear: it is, if I may be allowed to speak it, lest I should lay too open to our brethren the weakness of their reformation. Some there are, who, seeing their religion so manifestly in the wrong, rather than be pacified, will be exasperated against us, though alas! I am far from imputing to them the misfortunes of their birth, and I pity, much more than I blame them. But they will not fail to rise up against us. What recriminations will be prepared against the church, and what reproaches against myself, probably, on the nature of this work? How many of our adversaries, though without reason, will tell me, that departing from my own character and maxims, and converting disputes of religion into personal and particular accusations, I have abandoned that moderation, which they themselves have praised? But certainly they will merit the blame,—if this history renders the reformation odious, honest minds will clearly see, that it is not I, but the thing itself that speaks. In a discourse in which with regard to matters of faith, I propose to show the most authentic acts of the Protestant religion, nothing less than personal facts can be the question in hand; and if these be found in their authors, whom they represent as men sent in an extraordinary manner to revive Christianity in the sixteenth century, a conduct directly opposed to such a design; if through the whole party they have formed, characters quite contrary to a reviving of Christianity be seen; in this part of the history, Protestants will learn not to dishonor God and his providence, by attributing to him a special choice which would be evidently bad.

      26.—*What recriminations may be allowed them.*

We must bear with recriminations, together with all those inventions and calumnies with which our adversaries are accustomed to load us. I require of them but two conditions, which they must allow to be just. The first is, not to think of accusing us of variations in matters of faith, until after they have cleared themselves; for they cannot deny, that this course would not be an answer to this history, but would tend to bewilder and delude the reader; secondly, not to oppose reasonings or conjectures to certain facts; but certain facts to certain facts, and authentic decisions of faith to authentic decisions of faith.

      And if by such proofs they show us the least inconsistency, or the least variation, in the dogmas of the Catholic Church, from her first origin down to us, that is from the foundation of Christianity, I will readily own to them that they are right, and I myself will suppress my whole history.

27.—This History very conducive to the knowledge of Truth.

It is not, however, my design to make a jejune and insipid recital of Protestant variations. I shall disclose their causes; I shall show that no change happened among them, which does not argue an inconsistency in their doctrine, and is not the necessary result of it. Their variations, like those of the Arians, will discover what they would have excused, what supplied, what disguised in their belief. Their disputes, their contradictions, and their equivocations, will bear witness to Catholic truth, which, from time to time, must also be represented such as it is in itself, in order to make it appear by how many ways its enemies have been forced at length to draw near to it again. Thus, in the very midst of so many disputes, the dark and inevitable confusions of the new reformation, Catholic truth, like a beautiful sun piercing through opaque clouds, will everywhere display its lustre; and this treatise, should the execution equal the desire with which God has inspired me, will be the more convincing demonstration of the justice of our cause, as it will proceed from principles and facts allowed for certain by all.

28.—And to facilitate a re-union.

In short, the contests and agreements of Protestants will point out to us in what, on one side or the other, they have placed the fundamentals of religion, and the point at issue: what they must aver, what, at least, they must support in conformity with their own principles. The Confession of Augsburg alone, with its apology, will decide more in our favor than one thinks, and, I presume, what is most essential, we shall convince the Calvinists, complaisant to some, inexorable to others, that what appears odious in the Catholic, and not so in the Lutheran, at bottom is not essentially different; when it will appear, that what is aggravated against one, is extenuated and tolerated in the other; this will prove sufficiently, that such conduct proceeds not from principle, but aversion, which has ever been the true spirit of schism. This trial to which the Calvinist subjects himself, will reach much further than he is aware. The Lutheran will also find disputes greatly lessened by the truths he already acknowledges, and this work which at first might seem contentious, will tend more to promote peace than strife.

29.—How Catholics ought to be affected by this History.

As to the Catholic, he will everywhere praise the Almighty, for the continual protection he affords his church, in order to maintain her simplicity, and inflexible uprightness, amidst the subtleties with which men strive to bewilder the truths of the Gospel.

The perverseness of heretics will be a great and instructive spectacle to the humble of heart. They will learn to despise that knowledge which puffs up, and that eloquence which dazzles; and the talents which the world admires will appear to them of little value, when they see such vain curiosities, such caprices in learned men, such dissimulation, such artifices in the most polite writers; so much vanity and ostentation, such dangerous illusions amongst those called men of wit; and finally, so much arrogance and passion, and consequently so many and so manifest errors in men that appear great, because they are followed by the crowd. They will deplore the errors of the human mind, and be convinced that the only remedy for these great evils is to break off all attachment to private judgment, for it is this which distinguishes the Catholic from the Heretic. The property of the heretic, that is, of one who has a particular opinion, is, to be wedded to his own conceits: the property of the Catholic, that is, universal, is to prefer the general sense of the whole church to his own sentiments; this is the grace for which we shall petition in behalf of those that err. We shall, however, be filled with a salutary and holy awe, when we contemplate the dangerous and slippery temptations with which God tries his church, and the judgments which he exercises on her; nor shall we cease to pour forth prayers to obtain for her, pastors equally enlightened and exemplary, since it is through want of them that the flock, which has been redeemed at so great a price, has been so miserably ravaged.

Notes

[1] Lib. contra Const. N. 23 Col. 1254
[2] De Praeter, c. 42.
[3] Eth. et Beat. lib. 1 contra Eliss.
[4] De Berg. vel. N, 1.
[5] Thom. 5 in 2, ad Tim.
[6] Proverbs xxii, 28.
[7] Act. Auth. Blond. p. 65.

[8] Syntagma Conf. Fidei. Gen. 1654.
[9] Concord. pp. 298, 730, 570, 778.
[10] Syn. Conf. Præf.
[11] Athan. de Syn. et Ep. ad Afr.
[12] Book 2.
[13] Ibid. 3, 8.
[14] Ammian Marcel, lib. 21.

Book I

[From the year 1517 to the year 1520]

Brief summary: The beginning of Luther's disputes.—His agitations.—His submissions to the Church and Pope.—The foundations of his Reformation laid in imputed justice; his unheard of propositions; his condemnation.—His passion, furious threats, vain prophecies, and the miracles of which he boasts.—The Papacy to be overthrown all of a sudden, without violence.—He promises he will not permit men to rise in arms for the maintenance of his gospel.

1.— Reformation the Church desired many ages ago.

A REFORMATION of ecclesiastical discipline had been desired several ages since. "Who will grant me," says St. Bernard, "before I die, to see the church of God such as she had been in the primitive times?"[1] If this holy man had any thing to regret at his death, it was, that he had not witnessed so happy a change. During his whole life he bewailed the evils of the church: he never ceased to admonish the people, the clergy, the bishops, and the Popes themselves of them. Nor did he conceal his sentiments on this subject from his own religious, who partook of his affliction in their solitude, and extolled the Divine goodness in having drawn them to it so much the more gratefully, as the world was more universally corrupted. Disorders had still increased since that time. The Roman church, the mother of churches, which for nine whole ages had, by setting the example of an exact observance of ecclesiastical discipline, maintained it throughout the universe to her utmost power, was not exempt from evil; and from the time of the council of Vienne, a great prelate, commissioned by the Pope to prepare matters there to be discussed, laid it down as a groundwork to this holy assembly, "to reform the church in the head and members."[2] The great schism which happened soon after made this saying common, not only with particulars doctors, Gerson, or Peter D'Aily, and other great men of the time, but also with the councils; and nothing was more frequently repeated in those of Pisa and Constance. What happened in the council of Basil, where a reformation was unfortunately eluded, and the church reinvolved in new divisions, is well known. The disorders of the clergy, chiefly those of Germany, were represented in this manner to Eugenius IV, by Cardinal Julian. "These disorders," he said, "excite the hatred of the people against the whole ecclesiastical order, and should they not be corrected, it is to be feared lest the laity, like the Hussites, should rise against the clergy, as they loudly threaten us."[3] If the clergy of Germany were not quickly reformed, he predicted, that after the heresy of Bohemia, and when it would be extinct, another still more dangerous would soon succeed; for it will be said, proceeded he, "that the clergy are incorrigible, and will apply no remedy to their disorders. When they shall no longer have any hopes of our amendment," continued this great Cardinal, "then will they fall upon us. The minds of men are pregnant with expectation of what measures will be adopted, and are ready for the birth of something tragic. The rancor they have imbibed against us becomes manifest; they will soon think it an agreeable sacrifice to God to abuse and rob ecclesiastics, as abandoned to extreme disorders, and hateful to God and man. The little respect now remaining for the ecclesiastical orders will soon be extinguished. Men will cast the blame of these abuses on the court of Rome, which will be considered the cause of them, because it had neglected to apply the necessary remedy."[4] He afterwards spoke more emphatically: "I see," said he, "the axe is at the root: the tree begins to bend, and instead of propping it whilst in our power, we accelerate its fall." He foresees a speedy desolation in the German clergy. The desire of depriving them of their temporal goods would form the first spring of motion. "Bodies and souls," says he, "will perish together. God hides from us the prospect of our dangers, as he is accustomed to do with those whom he destines for punishment: we run into the fire which we see lighted before us."[5]

2.—*The desired reformation regarded not faith, but only discipline.*

Thus in the fifteenth century, did this Cardinal, the greatest man of his time, lament the abuses of those days, and foresee their alarming consequences. He seems to have foretold those evils in which Luther was about to involve all Christendom, beginning with Germany. Nor was he mistaken, when he supposed that a reformation which was despised, and a hatred redoubled against the clergy, would speedily bring forth a sect more terrible to the church than that of the Bohemians. Under the banner of Luther appeared this sect, and in assuming to themselves the title of Reformed, they boasted they had realized the wishes of Christendom, because a reformation had been long desired by the Catholic world, people, doctors, and prelates. In order to justify this pretended reformation, whatever had been said by the writers of the church against the disorders of the clergy and people, was collected with great industry.

But here is a manifest deceit in the passages cited; not one of those doctors even for once thought of changing the faith of the church, or of correcting her worship, which chiefly consisted in the sacrifice of the altar, or of subverting the authority of her prelates, and chiefly that of the Pope, which was the great end of this new reformation as founded by Luther.

3.—*The testimony of St. Bernard.*

Our reformers cite to us St. Bernard, who enumerating the grievances of the church, all those she sustained at the beginning during the persecutions, and those she suffered from heresies in their progress, and those she was exposed to in latter days, through the corruption of morals, allows the latter to be far more frightful, because they corrupt the very vitals, and spread infection through all the members of the church: whence, concludes this great man, the church may truly say with Isaiah, "her bitterest and most painful bitterness is in peace,;"[6] "when left in peace by infidels, and unmolested by heretics, she is most dangerously assaulted by the depraved morals of her own children."[7] Even this were sufficient to show that he did not deplore, as the reformers did, the errors into which the church had fallen, since, on the contrary, he represented it as safe on that side; but such evils only as proceeded from relaxed discipline: accordingly, when, instead of discipline, the dogmas of the church were attacked by turbulent and restless men,—such as Peter of Bruis, as Henry, as Arnauld of Bresse,—this great man would not suffer one of them to be weakened, but fought invincibly for the faith of the church, and the authority of the prelates.[8]

4.—*The testimony of Gerson, and Cardinal Peter D'Aily, Bishop of Cambray.*

It was so with the other Catholic doctors, who in the succeeding ages lamented abuses, and demanded a reformation of them. Gerson was the most celebrated of these, and none proposed with more energy a reformation of the church in her head and members. In a sermon, which he made after the council of Pisa, before Alexander the Fifth, he introduces the church demanding of the Pope a reformation and re-establishment of the kingdom of Israel: but to show he complained of no error that could be observed in the doctrine of the church, he addresses the Pope in these words: "Why," says he, "do you not send the Indians, whose faith may have been easily corrupted, as they are not united to the church of Rome, whence certainty of faith must be derived?"[9] His master, Cardinal Peter D'Aily, sighed also for a reformation, but he fixed its foundation on a principle entirely different from that on which Luther would establish it, since the latter wrote to Melancthon, "that sound doctrine could not subsist, whilst the authority of the Pope existed;" and, on the contrary, the Cardinal thought "that the members of the church being separated from their head, during the schism, and there being no administrator, and apostolic director, namely no Pope, that all the church acknowledged no hope could be entertained of effecting a reformation."[10] Thus one made the reformation to consist in the subversion of the papacy, and the other in the perfect re-establishment of that sacred authority, which was instituted by Jesus Christ to preserve unity amongst its members, and retain all in their respective duties.

5.—*Two ways of desiring the reformation of the Church.*

There were then two different sorts of persons, who called for the reformation; one, the truly peaceable and true children of the church, without bitterness bewailed her grievances, and, with respect, proposed a reformation of them, and in humility bore with a delay. Far from desiring to effect this object by schism, they, on the contrary, looked on schism as the greatest of all evils. In the midst of these abuses, they admired the providence of God, who, according to his promises, knew how to preserve the faith of the church. And, though they could not accomplish a reformation of morals, free from all bitterness and passion, they deemed themselves happy that nothing prevented them from accomplishing it in themselves. These were the strong ones of the church, whose faith no temptation could shake, nor induce to deviate from unity. Besides these, there were proud spirits, who, struck with the disorders they saw prevailing in the church, especially in her ministers, did not believe the promises of her eternal duration could subsist in the midst of such abuses; whereas, the Son of God had taught to respect the chair of Moses, notwithstanding the evil actions of the Scribes and Pharisees who sat therein.[11] These became proud, and thereby weak, yielding to the temptation which inclines to hate the chair itself, in hatred to those who sat upon it; and, as if the wickedness of man could make void the work of God, the aversion they had conceived against the teachers, made them both hate the doctrines they taught, and the authority they had received from God to teach.

Such were the Vaudois and Albigenses; such were John Wickliffe and John Huss. The ordinary bait by which they induced weak souls into their nets, was the hatred with which they inspired them against the pastors of the church. Influenced by this spirit of bitterness, they sighed for a rupture. It is not therefore surprising that, in the time of Luther, when invectives and animosities were carried to the highest pitch, the most violent schism and apostacy of course ensued, that, perhaps, till then had ever been seen in Christendom.

6.—*Luther's commencements and qualities.*

Martin Luther, an Augustinian Friar, by profession Doctor and Professor of Divinity in the University of Wittenberg, first excited these commotions. The two parties which called themselves reformed, have equally acknowledged him to be the author of this new reformation. Not only his followers, the Lutherans, vied with each other in extolling him, but even Calvin, often admires his virtues, his magnanimity, his constancy, and the incomparable industry with which he opposed the Pope. He is the trumpet, or rather he is the thunder, he is the lightning that awaked the world from their lethargy: it was not Luther that spoke, but God that thundered from his mouth.[12]

True it is, he had a strength of genius, a vehemence in his discourses, a lively and impetuous eloquence, which captivated the people and bore all before him, an extraordinary boldness when supported and applauded, with an air of authority which made his disciples tremble, insomuch that neither in little things, nor in great, dared they venture to contradict him.

Here I should relate the beginnings of the quarrel in 1517, were they not known by all mankind. For who is ignorant of the publication of the Indulgences of Leo X, and the jealousy of the Augustinian Friars against the Dominicans, who, on this occasion, were preferred to them? Who does not know that Luther, an Augustinian Doctor, being selected to maintain the credit of his order, first attacked the abuses many made of indulgences, and the extravagances that were uttered from the pulpit on that subject? But he had too much fire to keep himself within these limits: from the abuses of the thing, he came to the thing itself. He went on step by step, and though always diminishing indulgences and reducing them almost to nothing by his mode of explaining them, however, he seemed to agree with his adversaries in the essential part; for when he began to write his propositions, one of them was couched in the following terms: "Whoever denies the truth of the indulgences of the Pope, let him be accursed."[13]

7.—*The groundwork of Luther's Reformation.*—*What imputed Justice, and Justification by Faith means.*

Meanwhile, one subject led him on to another. As that of justification, and of the efficacy of the sacraments bordered nearly upon indulgences, Luther fell on these two articles; and this dispute soon became the most important.

Justification is that grace which, remitting to us our sins, at the same time renders us agreeable to God. Till then, it had been believed that what wrought this effect proceeded indeed from God, but yet necessarily existed in man; and that to be justified,—namely, for a sinner to be made just,—it was necessary he should have this justice in him; as to be learned and virtuous, one must have in him learning and virtue. But Luther had not followed so simple an idea. He would have it, that what justifies us and renders us agreeable to God was nothing in us: but we were justified because God imputed to us the justice of Jesus Christ, as if it were our own, and because by faith we could indeed appropriate it to ourselves.

8.—*Luther's special Faith, and the certainty of Justification.*

But the mystery of this justifying faith had something in it that was very singular. It did not consist in believing in general in a Saviour, his mysteries and his promises; but in believing most assuredly, each one in his heart, that all our sins are forgiven us. "We are justified," said Luther without ceasing, "from the time we with certainty believe ourselves so." The certainty which he required was not that moral certainty alone, which, grounded on reasonable motives, excludes trouble and perturbation; but an absolute and infallible certainty, by which the sinner is to believe himself justified with the same faith as he believes Christ came into the world.

Without this certainty there was no justification for the faithful; for they were told that they could neither call on God nor trust in him alone, whilst they had the least doubt, not merely of the Divine Goodness in general, but of that particular goodness by which God imputes to each of us the justice of Jesus Christ; and this is what he called special faith.

9.—*According to Luther, man is assured of his Justification, without being assured of his Repentance.*

Here a new difficulty arose, whether, in order to be assured of his justification, it was necessary, at the same time, that man should be satisfied with the sincerity of his repentance. This immediately occurred to every one; and, since God promised to justify the penitent only, if we are assured of our justification, it seems necessary that we should be certain of the sincerity of our repentance. But Luther abhorred this last certainty; and so far from being assured of the sincerity of repentance, "one was not even assured," said he, "by reason of the most hidden vice of vain-glory or self-love, that he did not commit many mortal sins in his very best actions."[14]

Luther went still much further; for he had invented this distinction between the works of God and those of men, "that the works of men, however beautiful in appearance, might seemingly be good, yet were they grievous sins; on the other hand, the works of God, however deformed in appearance, might seemingly be bad, yet were they of an eternal merit."[15] Deceived by his antithesis and by this play of words, Luther imagined that he had discovered the true difference between the works of man and those of God; not reflecting that the good works of men are also the works of God, who, by his grace, produces them in us, which, according to Luther himself, should give them an eternal merit; but this is what he was resolved to avoid,—on the contrary concluding, "That all the works of the just would be mortal sins were they not fearful of their being so; nor could there be any avoiding presumption, or having a true hope, if, in every action they performed, they did not fear damnation."[16]

Repentance, doubtless, is not compatible with mortal sins actually committed; for to be truly repentant of some grievous sins, and not of all, or to be sorry for them, whilst one commits them, is impossible. If, therefore, we are never certain, that in every good work we fall not into divers grievous sins—, if, on the contrary, we ought to fear our constantly falling into such, we can never be assured of being truly penitent; and could we be assured of this, we need not, as Luther prescribes, fear damnation, unless we at the same time believe that God, contrary to his promise, would condemn to hell the contrite of heart. And if, on account of his own want of disposition, of which he was not assured, a sinner should happen to call in doubt his justification, Luther told him he was not assured of his good disposition, nor did he know, for example, whether he were truly penitent, truly contrite, truly afflicted for his sins; yet he was not the less assured of his entire justification, because it depended not on any good disposition on his part. On this account this new Doctor declared to the sinner, "Believe firmly that thou art absolved, and thou art so, whatever be thy contrition."[17] This is the equivalent to saying, whether you be penitent or not, you need not concern yourself. All consists, said he continually, "in believing, without hesitation, that you are absolved;" whence he concluded, whether the priest baptized or gave you absolution in earnest or in jest, is a matter of no consequence;[18] because in the sacraments there was only one thing to fear, namely, the not believing strongly enough that all your crimes were forgiven you, when you had once wrought on yourself to believe so.

10.—The Inconsistency of this Doctrine.

The Catholics perceived that this doctrine labored under a most grievous difficulty, because the believer, being obliged to hold himself assured of his justification, and not of his repentance, consequently ought to believe he might be justified in the sight of God, though he were not truly penitent, which opened the way to impenitence.

True it is, however, (for nothing ought to be concealed,) that Luther did not exclude from justification a sincere repentance, namely, the horror of sin, and the will to do good, and, in short, the conversion of the heart, and judged it as absurd, as we do, to be justified without contrition or repentance. Between him and Catholics, on this head, there appeared no difference, unless that the Catholics called these acts the dispositions of the sinner to justification, and Luther judged he styled them more justly, the necessary conditions. But this subtle distinction, at bottom, did not extricate him from the difficulty: for these acts are essential for the remission of sin, name them as you will, either condition, or disposition, or necessary preparation; so that the question still returned: How Luther could say the sinner ought to believe most assuredly that he was absolved, be his contrition what it may, that is, be his repentance what it may; as if the being penitent, or not, were a thing quite indifferent to the remission of sins.

11.—Whether we may be assured of our Faith without being assured of our Repentance.

Here, then, was the great difficulty in the new dogma, or, in modern phrase, the new system of Luther. How was it possible to have assurance of the entire remission of sin, when not assured, nay, it was impossible one should be certain of true repentance, and true conversion? But it was enough, said Luther, one was assured of faith. A new difficulty, to be assured of faith, and not of repentance; which faith, according to Luther, always produces. "But," answers he, "the faithful can say, 'I believe' and thereby his faith becomes sensible to him;" as if the same person might not in like manner say, "I repent," and so become alike assured of his repentance. "If, lastly, it be replied that the doubt will still remain, whether he repent or not as he ought to do, I say the same of faith; and the sum of the whole is this,—that the sinner must rest assured of his justification, without the possibility of an assurance that he hath fulfilled as he ought that necessary condition of obtaining it, which God required at his hands."[19]

Here there was a new labyrinth. Although faith did not, in the opinion of Luther, dispose to justification, (for he ever had an aversion to these dispositions,) it was, however, the necessary condition, and the only means of appropriating to us Jesus Christ and his justice. If, therefore, after all the efforts that a sinner makes, in order to persuade himself fully that his sins are forgiven him through his faith, this question should arise within, Who will tell me, weak and imperfect as I am, whether or not I have that true faith which changes the heart? This is a temptation, according to Luther. We must believe, that by faith all our sins are forgiven us, without troubling ourselves whether this faith be such as God requires; nay, without so much as thinking of it. For this thought alone would be making the grace of justification depend on a thing which may be in us; which the gratuitousness, as I may say, of justification, according to him, would not suffer.

12.—The Security which Luther blames.

With this certainty of the remission of sin, advanced by Luther, he however declared there was a certain state dangerous to the soul, which he called security. "Let the faithful take care," says he, "that they come not to a security;" and immediately after, "There is a detestable arrogance and security in those who flatter themselves, and are not truly afflicted for their sins, which are still deeply rooted in their minds."[20] If to these two theses of Luther, we join that in which he said, as has been seen already, that, on account of self-love, one could never be assured he did not commit many mortal sins in his very best actions, insomuch that he ought always to fear damnation,[21] it might seem that this Doctor, at bottom, agreed with Catholics, and that this certainty, which he lays down, was not to be taken, as it has been by me, in the most rigorous sense. But in that we should be deceived; Luther literally maintains these two propositions, which appear so contrary—"Man is never assured that he grieves for his sins as he ought to do; and he must rest assured that he has gained the forgiveness of them." Whence follow those two propositions, which seem not less opposite: certainty is to be admitted, security is to be feared. But what is, then, this certainty, if it be not security? This was the inexplicable knot of the doctrine of Luther, which never could be unravelled.

13.—The Answer of Luther, by the distinction of two kinds of Sin.

For my part, all I could ever find in his works tending to unfold this mystery, is the distinction he makes between sins committed with knowledge, and those committed "without knowledge and against conscience—lapsus contra conscientiam."[22] It seems, therefore, that Luther would have said, a Christian cannot be assured of his being exempt from sins of the first kind, but may be so with regard to the second; and if in the committing these he held himself assured of the remission of his sins, he fell into that pernicious security condemned by Luther; whereas, avoiding them, he may have a full assurance that all the rest, even the most hidden, are forgiven him; which is sufficient for that certainty which Luther would establish.

14.—The difficulty still remains.

But still the difficulty returned; for, according to Luther, it remained indubitable that it is never known by man whether this vice of self-love, so hidden, does not infect the best of all his actions: on the contrary, in order to avoid presumption, he must look upon it as unquestionable that they are mortally infected with it: "that he flatters himself;" and that when he believes himself "truly grieved for his offences," it does not follow that he really is as much so as is necessary for the remission of them. If this be so, whatever he may think he feels within himself, he never knows whether sin reigns not in his heart, the more dangerously the more hidden it is. We must, therefore, be brought to believe we may be reconciled to God, whilst sin predominates in us, or there never will be any such thing as certainty.

15.—*The Contradiction of the Doctrine of Luther.*

Thus all we are told of the certainty man may have with respect to sin committed against conscience, is nothing to the purpose. Luther should have gone farther and acknowledged that this sin which hides itself, this secret pride, this self-love, which lurks in so many shapes, and even assumes the form of virtue, may be, perhaps, the grand obstacle to our conversion, and the inevitable subject of that continual fear which, after St. Paul, is taught by Catholics. The same Catholics observed, that the answers on this subject were manifestly contradictory. Luther had advanced this proposition: "No man should answer the priest that he is contrite, that is, penitent."[23] And as the proposition seems very strange, he cites these passages to support it: "I am not conscious to myself of any thing, and yet I am not on that account justified."[24] David says, "Who knoweth his sins?"[25] St. Paul says, "He that commendeth himself is not approved, but he whom God commendeth."[26] From these texts Luther concluded that no sinner is so qualified as to answer the priest, "I am truly penitent;" and understanding it rigorously, and for an entire certainty, he was right. According to him, therefore, man was not absolutely assured he was penitent. According to him, however, he was absolutely certain his sins were forgiven him; he was absolutely certain, therefore, that forgiveness is independent of repentance. Catholics labored in vain to understand these novelties: here is a prodigy, said they, in doctrine and morals, nor can the church bear this scandal.[27]

16.—*The Sequel of the Contradictions of Luther.*

"But," said Luther, "we are assured of our faith, and faith is inseparable from contrition." To which was replied, "Allow, therefore, the faithful to answer for their contrition equally with their faith, or prohibiting one, prohibit the other." "But," proceeded he, "St. Paul has said, 'Examine yourselves whether you be in the faith; prove yourselves.'[28] Therefore we feel faith," concluded Luther: "Therefore we feel it not," concluded his adversaries. If it be a matter of proof, if a subject of examination, it is not a thing we know from feeling, nor, as they say, from conscience. That which is called faith, continued they, may be, perhaps, nothing more than an illusory image of it, and a weak repetition of what has been read in books, or heard from the mouths of others. In order to be certain we have that lively faith which works the true conversion of the heart, we ought to be sure that sin no longer reigns in us; which Luther neither can nor will guarantee to us, whilst he guarantees what depends thereon, namely, the forgiveness of sins. Here is the contradiction, and the inevitable weakness of his doctrine.

17.—*The Continuation of them.*

Nor let this text of St. Paul be alleged: "What man knoweth the things of a man, save the spirit of man, which is in him?"[29] True it is, no other creature, neither man nor angel, sees any thing in us but what we see: otherwise, how could David have said what Luther objected—"Who knoweth his sins?" These sins, are they not in us? And since it is certain we do not always know them, man will be always a mystery to himself, and his own mind an eternal and impenetrable subject of doubt. It is, therefore, manifest folly to seek for a certainty of the forgiveness of our sin, if we be not certain that we have entirely withdrawn our hearts from it.

18.—*Luther forgot all that he had said well at the beginning of the Dispute.*

At the beginning of the dispute Luther spoke much better; for here are his first theses on Indulgences, in 1517, and at the first rise of the discussion: "None is assured of the truth of his confession, much less of the fulness of his pardon."[30] At that time, on account of the inseparable union of repentance and forgiveness, he acknowledged that the uncertainty of the one implied that of the other. He afterwards changed, but from good to bad; still retaining the uncertainty of contrition, he took away the uncertainty of forgiveness, and no longer allowed forgiveness to be dependant on repentance. Thus Luther reformed himself; such was his progress, as his anger against the church increased, and as he sunk deeper into schism. In every thing he made it his study to take the reverse of the sentiments of the church. Far from endeavoring, as we do, to inspire sinners with a fear of the judgments of God, to excite repentance in them, Luther went to such excess as to say, "That contrition, which looked back, in the bitterness of heart, on years past, weighing the grievousness of sins, their deformity, their multitude, beatitude lost, and damnation incurred, served only to make men greater hypocrites;"[31] as if it were hypocrisy in the sinner to rouse himself from insensibility. But, perhaps, he meant no more than that these sentiments of fear were not sufficient, unless they are united with faith and the love of God. I acknowledge he afterwards explained himself thus,[32] but in contradiction to his own principles; for on the contrary, he required, (and this, as we shall hereafter see, is one of the fundamentals of his doctrine) that forgiveness of sin should precede love; and to establish this, abused the parable of the two debtors in the Gospel of whom our Saviour said, "He to whom is forgiven the greatest debt loveth most."[33] From this Luther and his disciples concluded, one did not love till after the debt, namely, the sin, was remitted to him. Such was the great indulgence preached by Luther, and opposed by him to those that were published by the Dominicans, and granted by Leo X. No occasion for exciting fear, no necessity for love; to be completely justified from all kinds of sins, man required no more than to believe without hesitation that they were all forgiven him, and in a moment the affair was settled.

19.—*Luther's strange doctrine concerning the war against the Turks.*

Among the extraordinary things which he every day advanced, there was one that astonished the whole Christian world. Whilst Germany, threatened with the formidable arms of the Turk, was all in motion to oppose him, Luther established this principle—"That it was necessary, not only to will what God requires us to will, but all absolutely that God himself wills." Whence he concluded, "that to fight against the Turk, was to resist the will of God, who designed to visit us."[34]

20.—*Luther's outward humility, and his submission to the Pope.*

In the midst of so many bold propositions, nothing in the exterior was more humble than he—a man timid and retired. He said, "By force he had been drawn into the world, and rather by chance than design, thrown into those troubles."[35] His style had nothing uniform, was even unpolished in some places, and this on purpose. So far from promising immortality to his name and writings, he had never so much as sought it. Nay, he waited the decision of the Church respectfully, so far as to declare expressly, "should he not abide by her judgment, he consented to be treated as a heretic." In a word, all he said breathed his submission, not only to the council, but to the holy see, and the Pope himself, who, moved by the clamor which the novelty of the doctrine had excited over all the church, had taken cognizance of the cause; and thus it was, that Luther appeared most respectful. "I am not so rash" said he,[36] "as to prefer my private opinion to that of all other men." As to the Pope, this is what he wrote to him in 1518, on Trinity Sunday: "Whether you give life or death, call me this or that way, approve or reprove as best seems fitting, I will hearken to your voice, as to that of Christ himself."[37] For three entire years, all his discourses were filled with similar protestations: nay, more, he referred himself to the decision of the universities of Basil, Fribourg, and Louvain. A while after, he joined to them that of Paris; nor was there a tribunal in the church which he would not acknowledge.

21.—*The reasons on which he grounded his submission.*

What he uttered concerning the authority of the holy see had the appearance of sincerity; for the reasons which he assigned for his attachment to this great see were, indeed, the most capable of affecting a Christian heart. In a book which he wrote against Sylvester Prierius, a Dominican, he begins with citing these words of Jesus Christ, "Thou art Peter," and these, "Feed my sheep." The whole world, says he, confesses, that from these texts proceeds the authority of the Pope. In the same place, after saying that the faith of the whole world ought to be regulated by that which the church of Rome professes, he thus proceeds: "I give thanks to Jesus Christ, for preserving on earth this only church by a great miracle, and which alone may demonstrate that our faith is true, insomuch as never, by any one decree, hath she departed from the true faith." Even after the ardor of dispute had shaken a little these good principles, "the consent of all the faithful retained him in a reverence for the authority of the Pope." "Is it possible," said he, "for Jesus Christ not to be with this great number of Christians?"[38] Thus he condemned the Bohemians, who separated from our communion, and protested it should never be his fate to fall into a like schism.

22.—His sallies of passion, for which he begs pardon.

However, there was something haughty and violent perceptible in all his writings. But though he attributed his passion to the violence of his adversaries, whose excesses, in that way, were not inconsiderable, yet he asked pardon for it. "I acknowledge," (thus he wrote to Cardinal Cajetan, legate then in Germany) "I have been transported indiscreetly, and have been wanting in due respect to the Pope. I am sorry for it. Though urged to it, I should not have answered the fool that wrote against me, according to his folly. Be so good," continued he, "as to represent the matter to the holy father; I desire no more than to hear the voice of the church, and to obey it."

23.—A new protestation of submission to the Pope.—He offers Leo X, and Charles V, to be silent for the future.

After his citation to Rome, and whilst appealing from the Pope ill-informed to the Pope well-informed, he did not cease to say, "that the appeal, inasmuch as it regarded him, did not seem necessary to him," he always abiding submissive to the judgment of the Pope, yet excused his going to Rome on account of the expense.[39] And moreover, said he, this citation before the pope was needless to a man who waited for nothing but the decree of the Pope, in order to comply with it.[40]

In the course of this proceeding, on Sunday, the 28th of November, he appealed from the Pope to the council; but in his act, he persisted in always saying, "that he neither presumed to doubt the supremacy, or authority of the holy see, nor yet to say any thing contrary to the power of the Pope well-advised and well-informed." And, indeed, on the third of March, 1519, he wrote again to Leo X, that "he did not design in anywise to interfere with his authority, or that of the church of Rome."[41] And, provided a similar injunction were laid on his adversaries, he bound himself, as he had all along done, to an eternal silence; for he could not bear a partial judgment; and, if we may believe him, he would have remained satisfied with the Pope, had he but imposed on both parties an equal silence. So little was this reformation, so much boasted of since, deemed by him necessary to the welfare of the church. As for retractation, he would never hear it mentioned, however sufficient matter there was for it, as observed above. And yet, so far from exaggerating, I do not tell the whole. But, said he, "being once engaged, his Christian reputation would not suffer him to abscond in a corner," or to retreat. This was his excuse after the rupture commenced; but, during the contest, he assigned one, the more probable as it was more submissive. "For, after all," said he, "I do not see what use would be my retractation, since it is not what I have said, but what the church will say to me, whom I shall not pretend to answer as an adversary, but to hear as a disciple."[42]

In the beginning of the year 1520, he spoke somewhat higher; the contest, too, grew warmer, and the party was increased. He wrote, therefore, to the Pope,—"I abhor disputes; I will attack no man, nor be myself attacked; if I be, having Jesus Christ for my lord and master, they shall not go unanswered: as for recanting what I have said, let no man look for it. Your holiness, with one word, may terminate all these contests, by bringing the cause to your own tribunal, and imposing silence on both parties."[43] This is what he wrote to Leo X, dedicating to him, at the same time, the Book of Christian Liberty, full of new paradoxes, the dreadful effects of which we shall soon witness. The same year, after the university of Louvain and Cologne had censured this, and the other books of Luther, he complained thus: "Wherein hath Leo, our holy father, offended these universities, that they should snatch out of his hands a book dedicated to his name, and laid at his feet, there to await his sentence?" In short, he wrote to Charles V, "that he would be an humble and obedient son of the Catholic Church, even unto death; and promised to hold his peace, if his enemies would but let him."[44] He called the whole universe, and the two greatest powers thereof to witness, that these disputes might be terminated; and to this he bound himself in the most solemn manner.

24.—*He is condemned by Leo X, and flies into horrible excesses.*

But this affair had made too great a noise to be dissembled. The sentence issued from Rome; Leo X published his Bull of condemnation, dated June 18, 1520; and, at the same time, Luther forgot all his submissions, as if they had been empty compliments. From that time he became furious; clouds of libels were scattered against the Bull: first, appeared his notes and comments on it, filled with contempt; a second pamphlet bore this title, "Against the execrable Bull of Antichrist," which he concluded with these words, "In the same manner that they excommunicate me, I excommunicate them again."[45] Thus did this new Pope pass sentence. He put out a third in "defence of the articles condemned by the Bull."[46] Far from retracting any of his errors, or in the least moderating his excesses, he went beyond them, and confirmed every thing, even to this proposition, namely, "Every Christian woman or child, in the absence of the priest, may absolve, in virtue of these words of Jesus Christ,—All that ye shall unbind, shall be unbound;" even to that wherein he said, that to fight against the Turk was to resist God. Instead of correcting so scandalous a proposition, he maintained it anew, and assuming the tone of a prophet, spoke thus: "If the Pope be not brought to an account, Christendom is ruined; he that can, let him flee to the mountains; or let this Roman homicide be slain. Jesus Christ shall destroy him by his glorious coming; it shall be he and no other."[47] Thus, borrowing the words of the prophet

Isaiah, "Oh Lord," cried out this new prophet, "who believeth in thy word?" And concluded, in delivering to men this commandment, as an oracle sent from heaven: "Forbear ye to make war against the Turk, until the name of the Pope be taken from beneath the heavens; I have said it."

25.—His fury against the Pope and those Princes who supported him.

This was plainly declaring to them, that henceforward the pope was to be held as their common enemy, against whom all were to unite. But Luther spoke much plainer afterwards; when disappointed that these prophesies did not proceed fast enough, he endeavored to accelerate their accomplishment by these words; "The Pope is a wolf, possessed by an evil spirit; from every village and every borough men must assemble against him; neither the sentence of the judge, nor the authority of a council must be waited for; no matter if Kings and Caesars make war in his behalf; he that rises in arms under a thief, does it to his own cost. Kings and Caesars bear not themselves guiltless, by saying they are the defenders of the church, because they ought to know what is the church."[48] In short, whoever had believed him, must have set all on fire, and reduced to one heap of ashes, both Pope and princes that supported him; and what is still more strange, as many propositions as we have seen were as many theses of divinity, which Luther undertook to maintain. Nor was this an orator whom the warmth of the harangue might have betrayed into indeliberate conclusions; but a doctor, that dogmatized in cold blood, and erected all his phrenzies into theses.

Although he did not, as yet, exclaim quite so high in that libel which he published against the Bull, yet the commencement of that intemperance might have been discovered in it; and it was the same passion which made him say, on the subject of the citation on which he did not appear, "I defer my appearing there, till I am followed by five thousand horse, and twenty thousand foot; then will I make myself be believed."[49] All was of this character: and through his whole discourse appeared mockery and violence; the two marks of exasperated pride.

He was reproved in the Bull for maintaining some of the propositions of John Huss; instead of excusing himself, as he would have done heretofore, "It is true," said he to the Pope, "all that you condemn in John Huss I approve; all that you approve I condemn. Here is the recantation you enjoin me: do you require more?"[50]

The most burning fevers cause not more frantic ravings. This was called by the party the height of courage; and Luther, in the notes he made on the Bull, told the Pope under the name of another, "We know full well that Luther will not bate you an inch, because so great a courage cannot relinquish the defence of the truth he has once undertaken."[51] When, through hatred that the Pope had caused his works to be burned at Rome, Luther, in his turn, caused the Decretals to be burnt at Wittenberg; the acts recording this exploit, ordered by hims to be registered, said, "That he had held forth with a surprising beautifulness of diction, and a happy elegance, in his mother tongue."[52] With this charm he ravished and led away mankind. But, above all, he forgot not to mention it was not enough to have burnt those Decretals, and it had been much more to the purpose, if the like had been done to the Pope himself; "that is to say," added he, moderating a little his expression, "the Papal chair."

26.—How Luther came at last to reject the authority of the Church.

When I consider so much passion after so much humility, I am at a loss whence this apparent humility could proceed in a man of such temper. Was it from artifice and dissimulation? Rather, was it not that pride, unacquainted with itself in its beginnings, and fearful at first, hides behind its contrary, till an occasion presents of appearing to advantage?

After the rupture was opened, Luther himself confesses, "that in the beginning he was like one in despair, nor could man comprehend from what weakness God had raised him to such courage; nor how, from such trembling, he came to so great strength."[53]

Whether God or the occasion made this change, I shall leave to the judgment of the reader, and, for my part, am content with the fact which Luther owns during this alarm: in one sense, it is very true that his humility was not feigned. What might cause one, however, to suspect artifice in his discourses, is, that occasionally he forgot himself so far as to say, "that he never would change his doctrine; and though he had referred his whole dispute to the determination of the supreme bishop, it was because respect ought to be observed towards him who bore so great a charge."[54] But whoever shall reflect on the interior conflicts of a man, whom pride on one side, and the remains of faith on the other, never ceased to distract interiorly, will not consider it at all impossible that such different sentiments should appear alternately in his writings. Be that as it may, it is certain the authority of the Church restrained him for a long time, nor can we read without indignation, as well as pity, what he writes regarding it. "After," says he, "I had gotten the better of all the arguments which were opposed to me, one remained still which, with extreme difficulty and great anguish, I could scarce conquer even with the assistance of Jesus Christ; namely, that we ought to hear the church."[55] Grace, I may say, with reluctance abandoned this unhappy man. He prevailed at length; and to complete his blindness, mistook Jesus Christ's abandonment of him, for the immediate assistance of his hand. Who would have thought, that refusing presumptuously to hear the church, contrary to the express command of Christ, should be attributed to the grace of Christ? After this fatal victory, which cost Luther so dear, he cries out like one set free from irksome bondage, "Let us break their bands asunder, and cast their yoke from us;"[56] for he made use of these words in answering the Bull; and in his last struggle to shake off church authority, not reflecting that this inauspicious canticle is what David put into the mouth of rebels, whose conspiracies were against the Lord, and against his anointed, Luther, in his blindness, applies to himself, exulting that, exempt from all constraint, he may henceforward speak and decide, as he wishes, in all things. His despised submissions rankle in his breast;—he keeps no temper;—his sallies, that should scandalize his disciples, encourage them; they catch, by hearing, the contagious phrenzy; so rapid a motion reaches soon to a great distance; and numbers look on Luther as sent by God for the reformation of mankind.

27.—Luther's Letter to the Bishops.—His pretended extraordinary mission.

Then he applies himself to maintain his mission as extraordinary and divine. In a letter he wrote to the bishops, "falsely so styled," said he, he assumed the title of Ecclesiastes or Preacher of Wittenberg, which none had ever given him; nor does he pretend any thing else, but that he gave it to himself; "that so many Bulls, and so many excommunications, so many condemnations from the pope and emperor, had stript him of all his former titles, and defaced the character of the beast in him; yet he could not remain without a title, and had therefore given himself this, as a token of the ministry to which God had called him, and which he had received not from man, nor by man, but by the gift of God, and by the revelation of Jesus Christ."[57] Here we have his vocation as immediate, and as extraordinary, as that of St. Paul. On this foundation, at the beginning, and throughout the entire body of the letter, he qualifies himself "Martin Luther, by the grace of God, Ecclesiastes of Wittenberg;" and declares to his bishops, "lest they should pretend ignorance, that this is his own title which he bestows on himself, with an egregious contempt of them and Satan; and that he might, with as good a claim, have called himself evangelist by the grace of God: for Jesus Christ most certainly named him so, and considered him as Ecclesiastes."[58]

By virtue of this celestial mission he did every thing in the church; he preached, he visited, abrogated some ceremonies, left others remaining, instituted and deposed. He that never was more than a priest, dared to make, I do not say other priests, which itself would be an attempt unheard of in the entire Church since the origin of Christianity; but what is much more unheard of, even a bishop. It was deemed expedient by the party to invade the bishopric of Nuremberg. Luther went to this city, and by a new consecration ordained Nicholas Amsdorf bishop of it, whom he had already made minister and pastor of Magdeburg. He did not, therefore, make him bishop, in the sense he sometimes calls by that name all pastors, but he made him bishop, with all the prerogatives annexed to this sacred name, and gave him that superior character which himself had not; but all was comprised in his extraordinary vocation; and an evangelist, sent immediately from God like another Paul, could do all he pleased in the church.

28.—Luther's arguments against the Anabaptists, who preached without ordinary mission and miracles.

Such attempts as these, I know very well, are esteemed nothing in the new reformation. These vocations and missions, so much respected in all ages, are nothing more, after all, than formalities to these new doctors, who require only what they call essentials; but these formalities established by God, preserved what is essential. They are formalities, if they please, but in the same sense the sacraments are so—divine formalities which are the seals of the promise, and the instruments of grace. Vocation, mission, succession, lawful ordination, are alike with them to be called formalities. By these sacred formalities God seals the promise he made to his church of preserving her for ever. "Go, teach and baptize; and lo, I am with you always, even to the end of the world:"[59] with you, teaching and baptizing; not with you here present only, and whom I have immediately chosen, but with you in the persons of those who shall be for ever substituted in your place by my appointment. Whoever despises these formalities of legitimate and ordinary missions, may, with the same reason, despise the sacraments, and confound the whole order of the church. And without entering further into this subject, Luther, who said he was sent with an extraordinary title immediately from God as an evangelist and apostle, was not ignorant himself that that extraordinary vocation ought to be confirmed by miracles. Therefore, when Muncer, with his Anabaptists, assumed the title and function of a pastor, Luther would not suffer the question to turn on what he might call essential, or admit he should prove his doctrine from the Scriptures; but ordered he should be asked, "Who had given him commission to teach?" "Should he answer—God; let him prove it," says Luther, "by a manifest miracle; for when God intends to alter any thing in the ordinary form of mission, it is by such signs that he declares himself."[60]

Luther had been educated in good principles, and could not avoid sometimes returning to them. Witness the treatise which he wrote of the authority of magistrates, in 1534. This date is remarkable, forasmuch as four years after the Augsburg Confession, and fifteen after the rupture, it cannot be said that the Lutheran doctrine had not at that time taken its form; and yet Luther there declared again, "that he had much rather a Lutheran should leave the parish, than preach there against his pastor's consent; that the magistrate ought not to suffer either private assemblies, or any to preach without lawful vocation; if they had suppressed the Anabaptists when they began to spread their doctrine without vocation, the many evils which desolated Germany would have been prevented; that no man truly pious should undertake any thing without vocation, which ought to be observed so religiously, that even a gospeller (for so he calls his own disciples) might not preach in the parish of a papist or a heretic, without the consent of him who was pastor of it"; "which he spoke, " proceeds he, "in warning to the magistrates, that they might shun those prattlers, who brought not good and sure testimonials of their vocation, either from God or men; without this, though they preached the pure gospel, or were angels dropt from heaven, yet they ought not to be admitted." This is to say, sound doctrine is not sufficient; but, besides this, one of two things is requisite, either miracles to testify God's extraordinary vocation, or the authority of those pastors who were already qualified to confer the ordinary vocation in due form.

When Luther wrote this, he was well aware it might be asked, whence he himself had received his authority? and therefore answered, "He was a doctor and a preacher who had not intruded himself, nor ought he to cease to preach, after it had been forced upon him, neither could he dispense with himself in teaching his own church; but for other churches, he did no more than communicate his writings to them, which was but what charity required."

29.—*What were the miracles by which Luther pretended to authorize his mission.*

But when he spoke with this assurance of his church, the question was, who had given him a charge of it; and how that vocation which he had received with dependance, on a sudden became independent of the whole ecclesiastical hierarchy? However that be, Luther, for this time, was willing his vocation should be ordinary; at other times, when he was more sensible of the impossibility of maintaining it, he styled himself, as above, God's immediate envoy, and boasted he was deprived of all these titles which had been conferred on him by the church of Rome, that he might enjoy so celestial a vocation. Then, as for miracles, he was at no loss: he would have the great success of his preaching considered miraculous; and, at his renouncing the monastic life, he wrote to his father, who seemed a little shocked at this change, that God had withdrawn him from that state by visible miracles. "Satan," says he, "seems to have foreseen from my infancy all that one day he was to suffer from me. Is it possible, that I, of all mortals, should be the only one he attacks at this time? Formerly, you were desirous of taking me from the monastery; God hath taken me thence without you. I send you a book wherein you will see, by how many miracles and extraordinary instances of his power he hath absolved me from monastic vows."[61] These wonders and prodigies were not only the boldness, but also the unlooked for success of his undertaking. It was this he gave for miraculous, and his disciples were persuaded of it.

30.—*Sequel of Luther's boasted Miracles.*

They even accounted it supernatural that a *petty monk* had conceived the courage to attack the Pope, and stood intrepid amidst so many enemies. The people took him for a hero, a man from heaven, when they heard him defy threats and dangers, and say, "though he absconded for awhile, the devil knew full well" (a fine witness) "it proceeded not from fear;—that when he appeared at Worms before the emperor, nothing was capable of terrifying him; and though he had been assured of meeting there as many devils ready to seize him as were tiles on the house-tops, he would have dared them all with the like resolution."[62] These were his ordinary expressions. He had always in his mouth the devil and the pope, as enemies he was about to crush; and his disciples discovered in these words a divine ardor, a celestial instinct, and the enthusiasm of a heart influenced with the glory of the gospel.

When some of his party undertook, as we shall see, during his absence, and without consulting him, to destroy images at Wittenberg,—"I am quite unlike these new prophets," said he, "who think they do something marvellous and worthy of the Holy Ghost, when they pull down statues and pictures. For my part, I have not lent my hand to the overthrowing of the least single stone; I have set fire to no monastery, yet, by my mouth and my pen, almost all monasteries have been laid waste; and the report is public that I alone, without violence, have done more injury to the Pope, than any King could have done with all the power of his kingdom."[63] These were the miracles of Luther. His disciples admired the force of this plunderer of monasteries, never reflecting that this formidable strength might be the same with that of the angel whom St. John calls "the destroyer."[64]

31.—*Luther acts the Prophet: promises to destroy the Pope immediately without suffering the taking of arms.*

Luther assumed the tone of a prophet against those who opposed his doctrine. After admonishing them to submit to it, he threatened at last to pray against them. "My prayers," said he, "will not be Salmoneus's thunder, no empty rumbling in the air. Luther's voice is not to be stopt so, and I wish your highness find it not to your cost." Thus he wrote to the Prince of the House of Saxony. "My prayer," continued he, "is an impregnable bulwark, more powerful than the devil himself. Had it not been for that, long ago, Luther would not be so much as spoken of; and men will not stand astonished at so great a miracle!"[65] When he threatened any with the divine judgments, he would have it believed he did it upon general views. You would have said that he read it in the book of fate. Nay, he spoke with such certainty of the approaching downfall of the Papacy, that his followers no longer doubted it. Upon his assertion, it was deemed certain that two antichrists, the Pope and the Turk, were clearly pointed out in Scripture. The Turk was just falling, and the attempts he was then making in Hungary were to be the last act of this tragedy. As for the Papacy, it was just expiring, and the most he could allow was two years' reprieve: but above all, let them beware of employing arms in this work. Thus he spoke, whilst yet but weak; and prohibited all other weapons than the word, in the cause of his gospel. The Papal reign was to expire on a sudden by the breath of Jesus Christ;—namely, by the preaching of Luther. Daniel was express on the point; St. Paul left no doubt; and Luther, their interpreter, would have it so. Such prophesies are still in fashion. The failure of Luther prevents not our ministers from venturing at the like event now; they know the infatuation of the vulgar, ever destined to be charmed with some spell. These prophecies of Luther stand in his works upon record to this day, an eternal evidence against those who so lightly gave them credit.[66] Sleidan, his historian, relates them with a serious air. He lavishes all the elegance of his fine style, all the purity of his polished language, to represent to us a picture which Luther had dispersed throughout Germany,[67] the most foul, the most base, the most disgraceful that ever was. Yet, if we believe Sleidan, it was a prophetic piece; nay, the accomplishment of many of

Luther's prophecies had been seen already, and the remainder of them was still in the hands of God.

Luther was not looked on as a prophet by the people alone. The learned of the party would have him esteemed such. Philip Melancthon, who, from the beginning of the disputes, had entered himself on the list of his disciples, and was the most able as well as the most zealous of them all, conceived at first a firm persuasion that there was something in this man extraordinary and prophetic; and, notwithstanding all the weaknesses he discovered in his master, he was a long time before he could relinquish the conviction; and, speaking of Luther, he wrote to Erasmus, "you know we ought to prove and not to despise prophecies."[68]

32.—*The boastings of Luther and the contempt he entertained for all the Fathers.*

This their new prophet, however, fell into unheard-of extravagances. He was always in extremes. Because the prophet made terrible invectives by God's commandment, he becomes the most profuse of abusive language, and the most violent of men. Because St. Paul, for man's good, had extolled the gifts of God in his own ministry with that confidence which proceeded from manifest truth, confirmed by divine miracles from above, Luther spoke of himself in such a manner, as made all his friends blush for him. They, however, grew accustomed to it, and called it magnanimity, admired the holy ostentation, the holy vauntings, the holy boasts of Luther; and Calvin himself, though prejudiced against him, styled them so.[69] Elated with his learning, superficial in reality, but great for the time, and too great for his salvation and the peace of the church, he set himself above all mankind, not his contemporaries only, but the most illustrious of past ages.

In the question of free-will, Erasmus objected to him the consent of the Fathers, and all antiquity. "You do very well," said Luther; "boast to us of ancient Fathers, and rely on what they say, when you have seen that all of them together have neglected St. Paul; and buried in a carnal sense, have kept themselves, as on set purpose, at a distance from this morning star, or rather from this sun." And again, "What wonder that God hath left all the nations of the earth, and all the churches, to go after their own ways?" What a consequence! If God abandoned the gentile world to the blindness of their hearts, does it follow that churches, delivered from it with such care, must be abandoned like them? Yet this is what Luther says in his book of "Man's Will Enslaved." And what deserves still more to be observed here, is, that in what he there maintains, not only against all the Fathers, and all the churches, but against all mankind, and their unanimous consent,—namely, that there is no such thing as free-will, he is abandoned, as will be seen, by all his disciples, and that even in the Confession of Augsburg; which shows to what excess his rashness was carried, since he treated with such outrageous contempt all churches and Fathers, in a point where he was so manifestly in error. The praises, which these holy doctors have, with one voice, bestowed on chastity, rather disgust than move him. St. Jerome is not to be endured for recommending it. He pronounces that all the holy Fathers, together with him, would have done much better, if they had married. In other matters he is not less extravagant. In a word, Fathers, Popes, councils, general and particular, in every thing, and every where, are esteemed nothing by him, unless they concur in his sentiments. He disposes of them in a moment, by quoting Scripture, interpreted in his own way, as if, before his time, men had been ignorant of Scripture; or the Fathers, who so religiously kept and studied it, sought not, but neglected, its true sense.

33.—*His buffoonery and extravagances.*

To such a degree of extravagance did Luther now arrive from that excessive modesty he professed at first, he passed to this extreme What shall I say of his buffooneries, no less scandalous than degrading, with which he stuffed his writings? Let but one of his most partial disciples take the trouble to read that one discourse he composed against the Papacy, in the time of Paul III, certain I am he would blush for Luther. He will there find throughout the whole, I do not say so much fury and transport, but such wretched puns, such low jests, and such filthiness, and that of the lowest kind, as is not heard but from the mouths of the most despicable of mankind. "The Pope," says he, "is so full of devils, that he spits and blows them from his nose." Let us not finish what Luther was not ashamed to repeat thirty times. Is this the language of a reformer? But the Pope was in question; at that name alone he fell into all his fury and he was no longer master of himself. But may I venture to relate what follows in this foolish invective? It must be done, though abhorrent to my feelings, that it may appear, for once, into what paroxysms of fury the chief of this new reformation fell. I will, then, force myself to transcribe these words, addressed by him to the Pope:—My little Paul, my little Pope, my little ass walk gently; 'tis freezing: thou wilt break a leg; thou wilt befoul thyself; and they will cry out, Oh the devil! how the little ass of a Pope has befouled himself!"[70] Pardon me, Catholic readers, for repeating these irreverences. Pardon me, too, ye Lutherans, and reap at least the advantage of your own confusion. But after these foul ideas, it is time to see the beautiful parts. They consist in thus playing on words; cœlestissimus, scelestissimus, sanctissimus, satantissimus; and it is what you find in every line. But what will you say of this fine figure? "An ass knows that he is an ass, a stone knows that it is a stone: but these little asses of Popes do not know that they are asses."[71] And lest the same should be returned upon him he obviates the objection: "And," says he, "the Pope cannot take me for an ass; for he knows very well that, through God's goodness, and by his particular grace, I am more learned in Scripture than he and all his asses put together."[72] To proceed; here the style begins to rise: "Were I a sovereign of the empire, [where will this fine beginning lead him?] I would make but one bundle of both pope and cardinals, and place them altogether in the little ditch of the Tuscan sea; this bath would cure them, I pass my word for it, and give Jesus Christ for security."[73] Is not the sacred name of Jesus Christ brought in here much to the purpose? Enough is said; let us be silent, and tremble under the dreadful judgments of God, who, in punishment of our pride, has permitted that such gross intemperance of passion should have so powerfully swayed to seduction and error.

34.—*Sedition and violence.*

I say nothing of seditions and plunderings, the first fruits of the preachings of this new evangelist. These served but to foment his vanity. The gospel, said he, and his disciples after him, has always caused disturbances, and blood is necessary for its establishment.[74] Calvin defends himself the same way. Jesus Christ, all of them cried out, came to send a sword into the midst of the world.[75] Blind! not to perceive, or unwilling to learn, what sword was sent by Jesus Christ, and what blood was shed on his account. True it is, the wolves, in the midst of whom Christ sent his disciples, were to spill the blood of his innocent sheep; but did he say the sheep should cease to be sheep—should form seditious confederacies, and, in their turn, spill the blood of the wolves? The sword of persecutors was drawn against his faithful; but did they draw the sword,—I do not say to assault their persecutors,—but to defend themselves against their onsets? In a word, seditions were raised against the disciples of Jesus Christ; but the disciples of Jesus Christ, during three hundred years of an unmerciful persecution, never so much as raised one. The gospel rendered them modest, peaceable, submissive to the lawful powers, even though these powers were hostile to the faith; and filled them with true zeal—not that bitter zeal which opposes sourness to sourness, arms to arms, violence to violence. Supposing, then, if they please, Catholics to be unjust in persecuting; those who gave themselves out for reformers, on the model of the church apostolic, ought to have begun their reformation with an invincible patience: but, on the contrary, said Erasmus, who witnessed the birth of their beginning, "I behold them coming out from their sermons, with fierce looks and threatening countenances, like men that just came from hearing bloody invectives and seditious speeches." Accordingly, we find "these evangelical people always ready to rise in arms, and equally as good at fighting as disputing."[76] Perhaps the ministers may grant us, that the Jewish and the idol priests gave room for as bitter satires as those of the church of Rome, however hideous they may represent them to have been. When did it ever happen that St. Paul's new converts, on their return from hearing his sermons, fell to pillaging the houses of these sacrilegious priests, as the auditors of Luther and his disciples have been known to do so frequently at their separation, promiscuously flying to the plunder of all ecclesiastics, without distinction of good or bad? What do I say of idol priests? The very idols themselves were spared, in some measure, by the Christians. When did it happen at Ephesus or Corinth, when they absconded, after St. Paul's or the apostles' preaching, that they overthrew so much as one of them? On the contrary, the town-secretary of Ephesus bears witness to his fellow-citizens, that St. Paul and his companions "did not blaspheme against their goddess;"[77] namely, that they spoke against false deities, without raising disturbances, or breaking the public peace.

Yet I cannot but believe the idols of Jupiter and Venus were full as odious as the images of Jesus Christ, of his blessed mother, and his saints, which our reformers trampled under foot.

Notes

1 Bern. Epist. 257, ad Eugen. Papam. nunc 238. N. 6.
2 Guil. Durand. Episc. Mimat. Speculator dictus, Tract. de Modo Gen. Conc. celeb. tit. 1. part. 3 ejusd. part. Tit. 33, &c.
3 Epist. 1. Julian Card. ad Eug. iv. inter Op. Æn. Silv. p. 66.
4 Ibid.
5 Ibid.
6 Isaiæ xxxviii. 17.
7 Bern. Serm. 33. lin Cant. N. 10.
8 Bern. Serm. 65, 66 in Cant.
9 Gers. Serm. de Ascens. Dom. ad Alex. V, vol. ii, p. 131.
10 Ibid. 137.
11 Matth. xxiii, 2, 3.
12 Calv. II, Def. Cont. Vestph. opusc. F. 785-787, et seq. Resp. Cont. Pigh. Ibid. fol. 137-141, &c.
13 Prop. 1517, 71, vol. i, Vited.
14 Luther, T. i. Prop. 1518. Prop 48.
15 Prop. Heidls. 1518. Prop. 3, 4, 7, 11.
16 Ibid.
17 Serm. de Indulg. vi. p. 52.
18 Prop. 1518. Ibid. Serm. de Indulg.
19 Ass. artic. damnat. v. ii. ad Prop. 14.
20 5 Disp. 1538. Prop. 44, 45. 1. T.
21 Prop. 1518, 48, v.i.
22 Luth. Themat. v. i. p. 490. Conf. Aug. cap. de bon. op. Synt. Gen. 2. part. p. 21.
23 Assert. art. Damnat. ad art. 14. T. ii.
24 1 Cor. iv. 4.
25 Ps. xviii. 13.
26 2 Cor. x. 18.
27 Ibid. ad Prop. 12. 14.
28 2 Cor xiii. 5.
29 1 Cor. ii. 2.
30 Prop. 1517. Prop. 20. T. i.f. 50.
31 Serm. de Indul.
32 Adver. execr. Anticrist. Bull. t.ii. fol. 93.
33 Luc. vii. 42, 43.
34 Prop. 1517, 98, f. 56.
35 Resol. de Pot. Papæ. Praef. T. 1. f. 310. Præf. oper. ibid. 2.
36 Cont. Prieri. t. i. f. 177.
37 Protest. Luth. t. i. f. 195.
38 Disput. Lips. t. i. f. 251.
39 Ad Card. Cajetan.
40 Ibid.
41 Luth. ad Leon. X. 1519.
42 Ad Card. Caj. t. i. p. 216.
43 Ad Leon. X. t. ii. f. 2-6.
44 Luth. ad Car. V. ib. 44.
45 T. i. 88, 91.
46 Assert. art. per Bull. Damnat.
47 Ibid. t. ii. Prop. 33.
48 Disp. 1540, Prop. 59, et seq. t.i. f. 407.
49 Adv. execr. Antchr. Bull. t.ii. f. 91.
50 Ibid. Prop. 30. f. 109.
51 Not. in Bull. t. ii. f. 56.
52 Exust. acta. t. ii. f. 123.
53 Præf. Op. t. i. f. 49, 50, et seq.
54 Pio. Lect. t. i. f. 212.
55 Præf. Oper. Luth. t. i. f. 49.
56 Not. in Bull, t. i. f. 63. Ps. ii. 3.
57 Ep. ad falso nominat. ordin. Episcoporum, t. ii. f. 305.
58 Ibid. 14. 220.
59 Mat. xxviii. 20.
60 Sleid. lib. v. Edit. 1555-69. in Ps. lxxxii. de Magis. t.iii.
61 De Vot. Monas. ad Johannem Lut. Parent. suum. t. ii. 263.
62 Ep. ad Frid. Sax. Ducem, apud Chyt. l. x. p. 247.
63 Frider. Duc. Elect. &c., t. vii. p. 507-509.
64 Apoc. ix. 11.
65 Ep. ad George Duc. Sax. t. ii. f. 491.
66 Assert. art. Damnat. t.v. f. 3. ad Prop. 3. ad Prop. 33. Ad. lib. Amb.

Cathar. ib. f. 161. Cont. Reg. Aug.
ib. 331, 332, et seq.
[67] Sleid. 1. iv. 70. xiv. 225. xvi.261, &c.
[68] Mel. lib. iii. Epist. 65.
[69] Defen. Cont. Vestph. opusc. f. 788.
[70] Papapismus.
[71] Papapismus.

[72] Adv. Papism. p. 474.
[73] Ibid.
[74] De Serv. Arb. f. 431, &c.
[75] Matt. x. 34-47.
[76] Lib. xix. 113, 24, 31, 47. p. 2053 &tc.
[77] Acts xix. 37.

Book II

A brief summary.—Luther's variations on Transubstantiation.—Carlostadius begins the Sacramentarian contest.—The circumstances of this rupture.—The Boors revolt; the part Luther acts.—His Marriage, of which himself and his friends are ashamed.—The extremes into which he runs on Free-Will, and against Henry VIII, King of England.—Zuinglius and Œcolampadius appear.—The Sacramentarians prefer the Catholic to the Lutheran doctrine.—The Lutherans take up arms, contrary to all their promises.—Melancthon is afflicted at it.—They unite themselves under the name of Protestants.—Fruitless projects of agreement between Luther and the Zuinglians.—Conference of Marpurg.

1.—*The Book of the Captivity of Babylon.*—*Luther's Sentiments concerning the Eucharist, and his great desire of destroying the reality.*

THE first treatise, in which Luther fully discovered himself, was that which he composed in 1520, of the captivity of Babylon. In it he loudly exclaimed against the church of Rome, which had just condemned him; and amongst the dogmas, whose foundations he aimed to destroy, one of the first was transubstantiation. He would most willingly have undermined the real presence, had he been able; and every one knows what he himself declares in his letter to those of Strasburg, where he writes, that "it would have been a great pleasure to him, had some good means been afforded him of denying it, because nothing could have been more agreeable to the design he had in hand of prejudicing the Papacy."[1] But God sets hidden boundaries to the most violent minds, and permits not innovators to afflict his church equally with their desires. Luther was irrecoverably struck with the force and simplicity of these words—"This is my body, this is my blood; this body given for you, this blood of the New Testament, this blood shed for you, and for the remission of your sins;"[2] for thus ought these words of our Lord to be translated, in order to give them their full force. The church had believed without difficulty, that Jesus Christ, to consummate his sacrifice and the figures of the old law, had given us his proper flesh sacrificed for us. She judged the same of the blood shed for our sins. Accustomed from her infancy to mysteries incomprehensible, and to ineffable tokens of the divine love, the impenetrable miracles included in the literal sense had not shocked the faith; nor could Luther ever persuade himself, either that Jesus Christ would have obscured, on set purpose, the institution of his sacrament, or that simple words were susceptible of such violent figures, or could possibly have any other sense than that which naturally entered into the minds of all Christians in the east and the west; insomuch, that they never could be diverted from it, either by the sublimity of the mystery, or the subtleties of Berengarius and Wickliffe.

2.—*The change of substance attacked by Luther, and his gross way of explaining it.*

He was determined, however, to mix with it something of his own. All those who, to his time, had well or ill explained the words of Jesus Christ, had acknowledged they wrought some sort of change in the sacred gifts. Those that would have the body there in a figure only, said that our Saviour's words wrought a change which was purely mystical, so that the consecrated bread became the sign of the body. Those that maintained the literal sense, with a real presence, by an opposite reason, admitted accordingly an effectual change. For which reason, the reality together with the change of substance, had naturally insinuated itself into the minds of men; and all Christian churches, in spite of whatever sense could oppose, had come into a belief so just and so simple. Luther, however, would not be directed by such a rule. "I believe," says he, "with Wickliffe, that the bread remains; and with the Sophists, (so he called our divines,) I believe the body is there."[3] He explained his doctrine in several ways, which, for the most part, were very gross. One time he said the body was with the bread, as fire is with red-hot iron. At other times he added these expressions,"that the body was in the bread, and under the bread, as wine is in and under the vessel;"—from this the celebrated propositions *in*, *sub*, *cum*; importing that the body is in the bread, under the bread, and with the bread. But Luther was very sensible that these words, "This is my body," required something more than placing the body in this, or with this, or under this; and to explain, "This is," he thought himself obliged to say that these words—"This is my body," imported,—this bread is substantially and properly my body; a thing unheard of, and embarrassed with insuperable difficulties.

3.—*Impanation asserted by some Lutherans—rejected by others.*

However, in order to surmount them, some of Luther's disciples maintained that the bread was made the body of our Lord, and the wine his precious blood, as the Divine Word was made man: so that, in the Eucharist, a true impanation was made, as in the Virgin's womb a true incarnation. This opinion, which had appeared at the time of Berengarius, was renewed by Osiander, one of the principal Lutherans;—a thing unintelligible to man. Every person saw, that for bread to be the body of our Lord, and wine his blood, as the Divine Word is man, by that kind of union which divines call personal or hypostatic, how necessary it was that, as man is the person, the body should also be the person, and the blood likewise; which destroys the very principles of reasoning and of language. The human body is part of the person, but not itself the person, nor the whole, nor, as they speak in schools, the suppositum. The blood is still less so; and this is in no respect the case when personal union can find admittance. Every one is not learned enough rightly to employ the term hypostatic union: but when it is once explained, every person must perceive to what it can be applied. So Osiander was left to defend alone his impanation and invination, and to say as much as he pleased. This bread is God; for he went to that excess.[4] But so strange an opinion required not refutation: it fell of itself by its own absurdity; nor was it approved by Luther.

4.—*Luther's variations on Transubstantiation—a new way of deciding in matters of faith.*

Yet what he himself said led the direct way to it. No one could conceive how bread, remaining bread, could be at the same time the true body of our Lord, as he asserted, without admitting, between both, this hypostatic union rejected by him. But he was resolute in rejecting it; and yet united both substances, even so far as to say one was the other.

At first, however, he spoke but doubtfully of the change of substance; and though he preferred the opinion which retains the bread, to that which changes it into the body, the matter seemed but trivial to him. "I permit," says he, "both one and the other opinion; the scruple is the only thing I take away."[5] Such was the decision of this new pope; transubstantiation and consubstantiation were alike indifferent to him. In another place, having been upbraided with making the bread remain in the Eucharist, he owns as much: "but," adds he, "I do not condemn the contrary opinion; I only say it is not an article of faith."[6] But in the answer he made to Henry VIII, King of England, who refuted his Captivity, he soon advanced much further. "I had taught," says he, "it was a matter of no importance whether, in the sacrament, bread remained or not; but now I transubstantiate my opinion; I say it is an impiety and a blasphemy to hold that the bread is transubstantiated;" and he carries his condemnation to an anathema.[7] The motive which he alleges for this change is remarkable. This is what he writes in his book to the Vaudois: "True it is, I believe it an error to say the bread does not remain, although this error hath hitherto appeared to me of light importance; but now that we are too much pressed to admit this error without the authority of Scripture, to spite the Papists, I am determined to believe that the bread and wine remain." This is what drew on Catholics the anathema of Luther. Such were his sentiments in 1523. We shall see whether he will persist hereafter in them; but it may not be amiss to observe, even in this place, that a letter is produced by Hospinian, in which Melancthon accuses his master of allowing transubstantiation to certain churches in Italy, to whom he had written on that subject. The date of this letter is in 1534, twelve years after he had answered the King of England.

5.—*Strange flights of passion in the books against Henry VIII, King of England.*

Now his transports of passion against this prince were so violent, that the Lutherans themselves were ashamed of them. There was nothing but atrocious contumelies, and outrageously giving him the lie in every page—"He was a fool, an idiot, the most brutal of all swine and asses."[8] Sometimes he addresses him in this terrible manner: "Beginnest thou to blush, Henry?--no longer king, but sacrilegious wretch!" His beloved disciple, Melancthon, durst not reprove, and knew not how to excuse him. Some even of his own disciples were scandalized at the outrageous contempt with which he treated all that the universe had esteemed most grand, and at his capricious manner of deciding in controversies in faith. To define one way, and then, all of a sudden, the very opposite, merely in despite of the Papists, was too visibly abusing the authority which was given him, and insulting, as we may say, the credulity of mankind. But he was complete master in his own party, and they dared not disapprove whatever he said.

6.—*A Letter of Erasmus to Melancthon concerning Luther's transports.*

Erasmus, astonished at the extravagance of passion which he had endeavored in vain to moderate by his advice, in a letter to his friend Melancthon explains the causes of it: "What shocks me most in Luther is," says he, "that whatever he takes in hand to maintain, he carries to extremity and excess. Warned of his excesses, so far from moderating them, he runs on more headstrong; and seems to have no other design than to proceed to still greater intemperance. By his writings," adds he, "I know the man's temper as much as if I had lived with him—a fiery and impetuous spirit. You see an Achilles, whose warmth is invincible, through the whole tenor of them. You are no stranger to the artifices of the Enemy of mankind. Add to this, so great success, so declared an approbation, so universal applause of his audience,—against such allure-ments a modest mind would scarce stand uncorrupt."[9] Although Erasmus never left the communion of the church, yet he maintained amid these disputes of religion a particular character, which makes Protestants give him credit for those facts of which he was witness. But it is on other grounds most certain, that Luther, elated with the victory which he thought he had already gained over the power of Rome, no longer kept himself within bounds.

7.—*Division amongst the pretended Gospellers.*—*Carlostadius attacks Luther and the reality.*

Strange! that he and his party should have looked upon the prodigious number of their followers, as they all did, for a mark of divine favor, without reflecting that St. Paul had foretold of heretics and seducers, that their speech spreadeth like a cancer,"[10] that "they grow worse and worse, erring and driving into error."[11] But the same St. Paul says also, that their progress is limited, "they shall proceed no farther."[12] The unhappy conquests of Luther were checked by the division which broke out among these new reformers. It has been long since said, that the disciples of innovators believe they have a right to innovate after the example of their masters;[13] the leaders of rebels meet with rebels as rash as themselves. But without more reflections, to speak the simple fact, Carlostadius, whom Luther had so much commended,[14] however unworthy he may have been, and whom he called his venerable preceptor in Jesus Christ, found himself able to oppose him. Luther had attacked the change of substance in the Eucharist.—Carlostadius attacked the reality, which Luther had not dared to undertake.

Carlostadius, if we believe the Lutherans, was a brutal, ignorant person, yet artful and turbulent; void of piety, without humanity, and rather a Jew than a Christian. This is what Melancthon, a man moderate and naturally sincere, says of him. But without citing the Lutherans in particular, his friends as well as enemies are agreed he was the most restless and impertinent of men. No more proof of his ignorance is necessary than the exposition he gave of the Eucharistic institution , where he maintained that, by these words, "This is my body," Jesus Christ, without any regard to what he gave, meant no more than to show himself seated at table, as he then was with his disciples;—so ridiculous a conceit, that one has a difficulty to believe it ever entered into the mind of man.[15]

8.—Origin of the contests between Luther and Carlostadius.—Luther's pride.

Before he had given this monstrous interpretation, two great contests had already happened between him and Luther. For in 1521, whilst Luther lay concealed for fear of Charles V, who had put him under the ban of the empire, Carlostadius had thrown down images, taken away the elevation of the blessed sacrament, and even low masses, and set up communion under both kinds in the church of Wittenberg, where Lutheranism began. Luther did not so much disapprove of those changes, but rather judged them as done in an improper time, and in themselves unnecessary. But what provoked him the most, as he shows plainly in the letter he wrote on the subject, was that Carlostadius had despised his authority,[16] and would have set himself up for a new doctor. Remarkable are the sermons he made on this occasion; for, without naming Carlostadius, he reproached the authors of these enterprises, that they had acted without mission, as if his own had been more valid. "Easily," said he, "could I defend them before the Pope, but I know not how to justify them before the devil, when this evil spirit shall, at the hour of death, oppose against them these words of Scripture, 'Every plant that my father hath not planted shall be rooted up;' and again, 'They did run, and it was not I that sent them.' What will they answer then? They shall be cast down into hell."

9.—Luther's sermon, wherein to spite Carlostadius and those who followed him, he threatens to retreat and re-establish the mass.—His extravagances in boasting of his power.

Thus spoke Luther whilst he yet lay concealed. But coming forth from his Patmos (for he so called the place of his retreat) he made a quite different sermon in the church of Wittenberg. He there undertook to prove that hands ought not to be employed in the forming of abuses, but the word alone. "It was the word," said he, "whilst I slept quietly, and drank my beer with my dear Melancthon and Amsdorf, that gave the Papacy such a shock as never was given by prince or emperor. Had I been inclined," he proceeds, "to have done things in a tumultuary way, all Germany should have swam in blood; and when at Worms, I could have put things into such a state that the emperor himself had not been safe in it."[17] This is what history had not informed us of. But people once prejudiced believed every thing; and so sensible was Luther of his being master, that he had courage to tell them in full audience, "moreover, if you pretend to continue doing things by these common deliberations, I will unsay, without hesitation, all that I have written or taught. I will make my recantation, and leave you. Remember, I have said it; and, after all, what hurt will the popish mass do you?" One thinks himself in a dream when he reads these things in the writings of Luther printed at Wittenberg; you return to the beginning of the volume to see if there be no mistake, and say in astonishment,—What is this new gospel? Could such a one as this pass for a reformer? Will men never open their eyes? Is it, therefore, so difficult a thing for man to confess his error?

10.—*Luther decides in the most important matters from spite.—The elevation; two kinds.*

Carlostadius, on his side, did not remain quiet, but, provoked at being so warmly treated, labored to combat the real presence, as much to attack Luther as from any other motive. Luther also, though he had thoughts of laying aside the elevation of the host, yet retained it out of spite to Carlostadius, as he himself declares, "and lest," proceeds he, "it might seem we had learned something from the devil."[18]

He spoke not more moderately of communion under both kinds, which the same Carlostadius had introduced by his private authority. Luther, at that time, held it for a thing quite indifferent. In the letter he wrote on the reformation of Carlostadius, he reproaches him "with having placed Christianity in things of no account,—communicating under both kinds, taking the sacrament into the hand, abolishing confession, and burning images."[19] And again, in 1523, he says in the formulary of the mass, "if a council did ordain or permit both kinds, in spite of the council we would take but one, or take neither one nor the other, and would curse those who should take both in virtue of this ordinance."[20] Behold what was called Christian liberty in the new reformation! Such was the modesty and humility of these new Christians!

11.—*How the war was declared between Luther and Carlostadius.*

Carlostadius being driven from Wittenberg, was obliged to retire to Orlemond, a town of Thuringia, subject to the Elector of Saxony. At this time all Germany was in a flame. The boors, revolting against their lords, had taken up arms, and implored the aid of Luther. Besides their following his doctrine, it was supposed that his book of Christian liberty had not a little contributed to inspire them with rebellion, by that bold manner with which he spoke against laws and legislators.[21] For, though he defended himself by saying, that he meant not to speak of magistrates, or of civil laws, it was, however, true that he made no distinction between secular and spiritual powers; and to pronounce in general, as he did, that a Christian was not subject to any man, was, till the interpretation came, nourishing the spirit of insubordination in the people, and giving dangerous views to their leaders. Add to this, that to despise the powers supported by the majesty of religion, is to leave others destitute of support. The Anabaptists, another shoot of the doctrine of Luther, who were formed by pushing his maxims to their greatest extent, mixed in the tumult of the boors, and began to turn their sacrilegious inspirations to manifest rebellion. Carlostadius was infected with these novelties, at least Luther accuses him of it; and true it is, he held a great intimacy with the Anabaptists, murmuring continually with them, as well against the Elector as against Luther, whom he called a flatterer of the Pope, chiefly on account of what little he had preserved of the mass and real presence;[22] for the contest was, who should the most condemn the church of Rome, and depart farthest from its doctrine. These disputes having raised great commotions at Orlemond, Luther was sent there by the prince to appease the tumult. In his way he preached at Jena, in the presence of Carlostadius, whom he failed not to charge with sedition. From this began the rupture; the memorable account of which I shall relate exactly as it is found in the works of Luther, as it is acknowledged by the Lutherans, and as Protestant historians have delivered it.[23] The sermon of Luther being over, Carlostadius went and visited him at the Black Bear, where he lodged, a place famous in this history for giving birth to the Sacramentarian war between the new-reformed. There, amongst other discourses, Carlostadius having excused himself in the best manner he was able as to sedition, he declares to Luther he could not bear his opinion of the real presence. Luther, with a disdainful air, defies him to write against him, promising him, at the same time, a florin of gold if he would undertake it. The money is produced. Carlostadius puts it into his pocket. They shake hands mutually, promising each other fair play. Luther drinks to the health of Carlostadius, and to the success of the fine work he was about to publish. Carlostadius pledges him in a bumper; and thus was the war declared, German-like, the twenty-second of August, 1524. The parting of the champions was as remarkable. "May I see thee broken on a wheel!" says one; "Mayest thou break thy neck before thou leaves town!" says the other.[24] The entry of Luther had not been less extraordinary; for upon his arrival at Orlemond, Carlostadius had ordered it so, "that he was received with great vollies of stones, and almost smothered with dirt." Such is the new gospel. Such the acts of the new apostles!

12.—*The wars of the Anabaptists, and that of the revolted peasants.—The share that Luther had in these revolts.*

Soon after occurred more bloody battles, but, perhaps, not more dangerous. The revolted peasants had met together to the number of forty thousand. The anabaptists rose in arms with unheard-of fury. Luther, called upon by the peasants to pronounce upon the claims they had against their lords, acted a very strange part. On one hand, he wrote to the peasants, that God had forbid sedition. On the other hand, he wrote to the lords, that they exercised such a tyranny "as the people could not, would not, ought not to endure."[25] By these last words, he rendered back to sedition those arms which he seemed to have taken from it. A third letter, written in common to both sides, laid the fault on both, and denounced the dreadful judgments of God against them, should they not dispose matters amicably. Here his weakness was blamed. Soon after, occasion was given of reproaching him with intolerable cruelty. He published a fourth letter, exciting the princes, powerfully armed,"to exterminate, without pity, those miserable wretches who had not followed his advice, and to spare those only who should voluntarily lay down their arms;" as if a seduced and vanquished populace were not a fit object of compassion, but ought to be treated with as much rigor as the heads that misled them. But Luther would have it so; and when he saw so cruel a sentiment was condemned, incapable of owning himself ever in the wrong, he made a book expressly to prove that truly, "no mercy at all ought to be showed rebels, nor were even those to be forgiven, whom the multitude had drawn by force into any seditious action."[26] Then were seen those famous battles which cost Germany so much blood. Such was its state when the Sacramentarian dispute added new fuel to the flames.

13.—*The Marriage of Luther, which had been preceded by that of Carlostadius.*

Carlostadius, who began it, had already introduced a novelty singularly scandalous; for he was the first priest of any reputation that took a wife; and this example was attended with surprising effects in the sacerdotal order, and in the monasteries. Carlostadius was not as yet at variance with Luther. The marriage of this old priest was laughed at, even among the party; but Luther, who earnestly desired to do the same, uttered not a word. He was fallen in love with a nun of quality, and singular beauty, whom he had taken out of her convent. It was a maxim of the new reformation, that vows were a Jewish practice, and none of them less obligatory than that of chastity. The Elector Frederick suffered Luther to speak after this manner, but could not bear that he should reduce these opinions to practice. He had nothing but contempt for those priests and religious who married, contrary to the canons, and that discipline which had been revered for so many ages. Therefore, not to lose his credit with that prince, Luther was obliged to have patience during the prince's life; but he was no sooner dead that Luther married his nun. This marriage happened in 1525, that is, in the height of the civil wars of Germany; at which time the Sacramentarian disputes were inflamed to the utmost violence. Luther was then forty-five years old; and this man, who, under the shelter of religious discipline, had passed his whole youth blameless in continency, in so advanced an age, and whilst he was hailed throughout the universe as the restorer of the Gospel, blushed not to abandon so perfect a state of life, and look behind him. Sleidan passes lightly over this fact. "Luther," says he, "married a nun, and thereby gave room for fresh accusations from his adversaries, who called him madman and slave of Satan;"[27] but he does not disclose the whole secret; nor were they only Luther's adversaries who blamed his marriage; he himself was ashamed of it; his disciples, the most devoted to him, were surprised at it; and all this we learn from a curious letter of Melancthon to his intimate friend, the learned Camerarius.

14.—*A remarkable Letter of Melancthon to Camerarius on Luther's marriage.*

It is written all in Greek, for so they corresponded on secret matters. He informs him, that "Luther, when least expected, had taken Boren to wife, (this was the nun's name,) without the least intimation of it to his friends: but that, one evening, having invited Pomeranus the minister to supper, together with a painter and a lawyer, he had the usual ceremonies performed; that it was astonishing to see that at so miserable a time, when good men had so much to suffer, he could not command himself so as to compassionate, at least, their misfortunes; but on the contrary, seemed so regardless of the miseries that threatened them, as to suffer his reputation to be weakened, even at a time when Germany stood most in need of his prudence and authority." Then he relates to his friend the causes of this marriage: "that he very well knows Luther was no enemy to human nature, and that natural necessity, he really believes, was what engaged him in this marriage; therefore, he ought not to wonder that Luther's magnanimity should thus be mollified; that this manner of life is low and common, but holy: and after all, the scripture allows marriage as honorable; in the main, there is no crime in it; and if more than this be laid to Luther's charge, it is a manifest calumny." This he says on account of a rumor which had spread of the nun's being with child, and ready to lie in when Luther married her, which proved false. Melancthon was therefore in the right to justify his master on this head. He adds, "that all that can be blamed in this action of his, is the unseasonable time in which he did so unexpected a thing, and the pleasure he thereby gave his enemies, who only seek to accuse him. In conclusion, he beholds him full of trouble and vexation for this change, and does what he can to comfort him."

It is plain enough how much Luther was ashamed of and concerned at his marriage, and how greatly Melancthon was struck, notwithstanding all the respect he had for him. What he adds in the conclusion, intimates likewise, how much he believed Camerarius would be affected since he says he was desirous of preventing him, "lest through his zeal for the continuation of Luther's glory, always untarnished and reproachless, he should give himself over to too much trouble and dejection at this surprising news."

They had at first regarded Luther as a man superior to all ordinary weakness. That which he evinced by this scandalous marriage dejected them. But Melancthon comforts his friend and himself as well as he is able, by reason that "there may, perhaps, be something in it that is hidden and divine; that he has certain marks of Luther's piety; and some humiliations befalling them may turn to good, there being so much danger in elevated stations, not only for the ministers of holy things, but for all mankind in general; and after all, the greatest saints of antiquity had their failings; and lastly, that we ought to embrace the word of God for its own sake, not for the merits of those who preach it, there being nothing more unjust than to blame the doctrine for the faults into which its teachers fall."

Doubtless, the maxim is good; but they ought not to have laid much stress on personal defects—not built so much on Luther, whom, however presumptuous, they experienced to be so weak; nor, lastly, have boasted to us so much of their reformation, as the marvellous work of God's hand, seeing the chief instrument of this wondrous work was a man, not only so vulgar, but swayed by such violent passions.

15.—*A notable diminution of Luther's authority.*

It may easily be judged from the conjuncture of affairs, that the unseasonable-ness of time at which Melancthon is so much disturbed, and that unfortunate diminution of Luther's glory, which he is troubled should happen then when most required, regarded it is true, those horrible disasters, by which Luther foreboded the ruin of Germany; but more especially bore a relation to the Sacramentarian dispute, which Melancthon well knew would weaken the authority of his master. And, indeed, Luther was not believed innocent of the disturbances of Germany, as they originated with those who followed his gospel, and appeared animated by his writings; besides, we have seen that, at the commencement, he had as much encouraged as restrained these rebel peasants. The Sacramentarian contest also was esteemed the effect of his doctrine. Catholics reproached him that, by exciting so great a contempt for church authority, and shaking this foundation, he brought every thing into question. "See," said they, "what it is to place the authority of deciding in the hands of every private person; to have given the scripture for so plain and easy, that, to understand it, no more is necessary than to read it, without consulting church or antiquity." All these things grievously troubled Melancthon; he that was naturally a man of discernment, saw a division rising in the midst of the reformation, which not only rendered it odious; but enkindled in it an endless war.

16.—*A dispute on Free-Will between Erasmus and Luther.—Melancthon bewails the transports of Luther.*

Other things happened at the same time, which gave him great anxiety. The dispute about free-will had grown warm between Erasmus and Luther. Erasmus was held in great esteem throughout all Europe, though he had many enemies on all sides. At the beginning of these troubles, Luther used all his efforts to gain him and wrote to him in such respectful terms as approximated even to meanness.[28] At first Erasmus favored him, yet not to such an extent as to leave the church. When he saw the schism manifestly declared, he abandoned him entirely, and wrote against him with great temper. But Luther, instead of imitating him, published so acrimonious a reply, as induced Melancthon to say, "I wish to God Luther had been silent. I had hopes that old age would have rendered him more mild; and I see that, pushed on by his adversaries, and the disputes into which he is obliged to enter,[29] he daily grows more violent." As if a man, who called himself the reformer of the world, ought so soon to forget his character as not to remain master of himself, whatever might be the provocation! "That torments me strangely (said Melancthon;) and if God lend not his helping hand, these disputes will be attended with an unfortunate event."[30] Erasmus, finding himself treated so rudely by one to whom he had been so mild, said, pleasantly enough, "I thought marriage would have tamed him;" and deplored his fate in seeing himself, notwithstanding his meek temper, "condemned, old as he was, to fight against a savage beast, a furious wild boar."

17.—The blasphemies and audaciousness of Luther in his treatise on Man's Will Enslaved.

The outrageous language of Luther did not constitute his greatest excess in those books he wrote against Erasmus. The doctrine itself was horrible; for he not only concluded that free-will was totally extinguished in mankind since their fall—a common error in the new reformation—"but, moreover, that it is impossible any other should be free but God; that his presence and divine providence are the cause of all things falling out by the unchangeable, eternal, and inevitable will of God, who thunder-strikes and breaks to pieces all free-will: that the name of free-will is a name which appertains to God alone, incompatible either with man, with angel, or any other creature."[31]

From these principles he was obliged to make God the author of crimes; nor did he conceal the thing, saying in express terms, that "free-will is a vain title; that God works the evil in us, as well as the good; that the great perfection of faith consists in believing God to be just, although, necessarily, by his will, he renders us worthy of damnation, so as to seem to take pleasure in the torments of the wretched."[32] And again: "God pleases you when he crowns the unworthy; he ought not to displease you when he condemns the innocent:"[33] he adds for conclusion, "that he said these things not by way of examination, but by way of deciding; that he meant not to subject them to the decision of any person; but advises the whole world to submit to them."

It is not surprising that such excesses troubled the modest mind of Melancthon; not that he himself, at the commencement, had not approved these prodigies of doctrine, having himself said with Luther, "that God's foreknowledge renders free-will absolutely impossible; and that God was not less the cause of the treason of Judas, than of the conversion of St. Paul." But besides that he had been drawn into these opinions, rather by the authority of Luther than his own choice, nothing was more opposed to his character than such opinions, established in so violent a manner, and he knew not where he was, when he witnessed the transports of his master.

18.—New transports against the King of England.—Luther boasts of his own meekness.

He saw them redoubled at the same time against the King of England. Luther, who had conceived a somewhat good opinion of this prince, because of his mistress Anne Boleyn, who was favorable enough to Lutheranism, had so far relented as to make excuses to him for his violence at first.[34] The king's answer was not such as he expected. Henry VIII reproached him with the levity of his temper, the errors of his doctrine, his scandalous and shameful marriage. Then Luther, who never humbled himself except to induce others to crouch to him, and never failed to attack those who did not do so immediately, answered the king, "That he was sorry for having treated him mildly; that he did it at the request of his friends, in hopes such sweetness might be serviceable for this prince; with the same view he had formerly written to the Legate Cajetan, to George Duke of Saxony, and to Erasmus, but he found it succeeded badly; for which reason he should not be guilty of the like fault for the future."[35]

Amidst all these excesses, he even boasted of his extreme meekness. "For, relying on the ever firm support of his learning, he yielded not in pride either to emperor, or king, or prince, or Satan, or the whole universe; but if the king would lay aside his majesty, to treat more freely with him, he should find that he would conduct himself humbly and meekly to the most inferior persons; a true sheep in simplicity, that could believe no evil of any one."[36]

19.—*Zuinglius and Œcolampadius undertake the defence of Carlostadius.—* *Where Zuinglius was: his doctrine on the salvation of heathens.*

What could Melancthon think, in his own temper the most peaceable of men, when he saw the outrageous pen of Luther raise up so many enemies abroad, whilst the Sacramentarian contest created him so many formidable ones at home?

And indeed, at this time, the best pens of the party were directed against him. Carlostadius had found such defenders as placed him above the reach of contempt. Eagerly attacked by Luther, and driven from Saxony, he had retired to Switzerland, where Zuinglius and Œcolampadius took up his defense. Zuinglius, minister of Zurich, had begun to disturb the church, on account of indulgences, as well as Luther, but some years after him. He was a daring man, whose fire surpassed his learning;—in language, clear and intelligible; nor excelled by any of the pretended reformers, in a precise, uniform, and coherent way of expressing his thoughts; nor, indeed, did any carry them to a greater length, or with more presumption.

As the character of his genius will be better known by his own sentiments than my words, I shall produce a part of the most finished piece of his whole works: it is the "Confession of Faith," which, a little before his death, he sent to Francis I. There, explaining the article of life everlasting, he says to this prince, "that he must hope to see the assembly of all men that ever have been holy, valiant, faithful, and virtuous, from the beginning of the world. "There you will see," he proceeds, "both Adams—the redeemed and the Redeemer. You will there see an Abel, an Enoch, a Noah, an Abraham, an Isaac, a Jacob, a Juda, a Moses, a Joshua, a Gideon, a Samuel, a Phineas, an Elias, an Eliseus, an Isaiah, with the Virgin Mother of God, whom he announced; a David, an Ezekiahs, a Josiah, a John Baptist, a St. Peter, a St. Paul. You will there see Hercules, Theseus, Socrates, Aristides, Antigonus, Numa, Camillus, the Catos and Scipios. There you will see your predecessors and all your ancestors who have departed this world in faith. In a word, not one good man, one holy spirit, one faithful soul, whom you will not there behold with God. What more beautiful, what more glorious, more agreeable, can be imagined, than such a sight?"[37] What man had ever dreamed of thus placing Jesus Christ confusedly with the saints? And in the train of patriarchs, prophets, apostles, and our Saviour himself, even Numa, the father of Roman idolatry, even Cato, who killed himself like a maniac, and not only so many worshippers of false divinities, but even the gods, the heroes whom they worshipped? I cannot conceive why he did not rank amongst them Apollo, or Bacchus, and Jupiter himself; and if such crimes prevented him as poets lay to their charge, were those of Hercules less infamous? This is what heaven is composed of, according to the head of the second party of the Reformation: this is what he wrote in a confession of faith, dedicated by him to the greatest King in Christendom; and what Bullinger, his successor, has given us as "the masterpiece and last song of this melodious swan."[38] And is it not astonishing that such as these could pass for men sent in an extraordinary manner by God for the reformation of his church.

20.—The frivolous Answer of those of Zurich in defence of Zuinglius.

Luther did not spare him on this head, but declared openly "that he despaired of his salvation; because, not satisfied with continuing to impugn the sacrament, he had become a heathen by placing impious heathens, even Scipio the Epicurean, even Numa, the devil's instrument in founding idolatry among the Romans, in the number of blessed souls. For what does baptism avail us—what the other sacraments, the Scriptures, and Jesus Christ himself, if the impious, the idolaters, and the Epicureans, are saints and in bliss? And what is this else than teaching, that every man may be saved in his own faith and religion?"[39]

To answer him was no easy task. Nor did they answer him at Zurich in any other way than by a wretched recrimination, accusing him also of placing amongst the faithful, Nebuchadnezzar, Naaman the Syrian, Abimelech, and many others, who, born out of the Covenant and race of Abraham, were however saved, as Luther says, "by a fortuitous mercy of God,"[40] But not to defend this "fortuitous mercy of God," which in reality is something strange, it is one thing to have said with Luther, that there may have been men out of the number of Israelites, who knew God; another thing, to place with Zuinglius in the number of blessed souls, such as worshipped false divinities; and if the Zuinglians were right in condemning the excesses and violence of Luther, there was much more reason to condemn this prodigious extravagance of Zuinglius. For, in short, this was not one of those mistakes into which a man may be betrayed in the heat of discourse: he was writing a confession of faith, and intended to make a simple and brief exposition of the Apostles' Creed; a work that, above all others, required a mature consideration, exact doctrine, and a settled head. It was in the same strain he had before spoken of Seneca "as of a most holy man, in whose heart God had written the faith with his own hand,"[40] because he had said in his letter to Lucilius "that nothing was hidden from God."[41] Thus we have all the platonic, peripatetic, stoic philosophers enrolled amongst the saints, and full of faith, because St. Paul acknowledges they had understood the invisible things of God by the visible works of his power;[42] and what furnishes this Apostle with reasons to condemn them in his Epistle to the Romans, has justified and sanctified them, in the opinion of Zuinglius.

21.—*The Error of Zuinglius upon original Sin.*

To teach such extravagances as these, a man must have no notion of Christian justice, or of the corruption of our nature. And, indeed, Zuinglius was quite a stranger to original sin. In that confession of faith, which he sent to Francis I, and in four or five treatises which he made expressly to prove the baptism of the little children against anabaptists, and explain the effect of baptism in this infant age, he does not so much as speak of its cancelling original sin, which, however, is allowed by all Christians to be the chief fruit of their baptism. He had done the same in all his other works; and when this omission of an effect so considerable was objected to him, he shows that he did so designedly, because, in his opinion, *no sin is taken away by baptism.* He carries still farther this rashness, when he says, "It is no sin, but a misfortune, a vice, a distemper; that nothing is weaker or more distant from the Scripture sense, than to say, original sin is not only a distemper, but also a crime."[43] In conformity to these principles, he decides that men indeed are born "prone to sin from their self-love," but not sinners, except improperly, by taking the penalty of sin for sin itself: and this "proneness to sin," which cannot be sin, makes, according to him, the whole evil of our origin. In the sequel of his discourse, it is true, he acknowledges that all men would perish, were it not for the grace of the Mediator, because this proneness to sin would not fail in time to produce it, were it not stopped; and it is in this sense he acknowledges that all men are damned by the "force of original sin;" a force which consists not, as we have just now seen, in making men truly sinners, as all Christian churches have decided against Pelagius, but in making them only "prone to sin," through the weakness of their senses and self-love, which the Pelagians and heathens themselves would not have denied.

The decision of Zuinglius, on the remedy of this evil, is not less strange; for he maintains that it is taken away from all men whatever, by the grace of Jesus Christ, independently of baptism: insomuch that original sin damns no man, not even the children of the heathens. As to those, though he dares not fix their salvation in the same degree of certainty with that of Christians and their children, he says, however, that, like the rest, as long as they are incapable of the law, they are in the state of innocence, alleging this text of St. Paul—"where no law is there is no transgression."[44] "Now," proceeds this new doctor, "it is certain that children are weak, without experience, and ignorant of the law, and are not less without law than St. Paul, when he said, 'I lived without the law heretofore.'[45] Therefore, as there is no law for them, neither is there any transgression of the law, and, by consequence, no damnation. St. Paul says, that he lived without the law once, but there is no age in which man is more in this state than his infancy; consequently, it must be said, with the same St. Paul, that without the law sin was dead in them."[46] Just so disputed the Pelagians against the church. And although, as above stated, Zuinglius here speaks with greater assurance of the children of Christians than of others, he, however, in reality speaks of all children whatever, without exception. It is plain to what point his proof is directed; and certainly, since the time of Julian there never was a more complete Pelagian than Zuinglius.

22.—The error of Zuinglius on Baptism.

Nay, the Pelagians acknowledged, that baptism could at least give grace, and remit the sins of the adult. Zuinglius more rash than they, ceases not to repeat what has been already told of him, "that baptism takes away no sin, and gives no grace." "It is the blood of Jesus Christ," says he, "that remits sins, therefore, it is not baptism." Here an instance may be seen of that perverted zeal the reformation had for the glory of Jesus Christ. It is more clear than day, that to attribute the remission of sins to baptism, which is the means of taking them away established by Jesus Christ, does no more injury to Jesus Christ, than you offer a painter, by attributing the fine coloring and the beautiful touches of his picture to the pencil he makes use of. But the reformation carries its vain reasoning to such excess, as to imagine it gives glory to Jesus Christ, to destroy the efficacy of these instruments which he employs. And to continue so gross an illusion to the utmost extremity, when a hundred passages from the Scriptures were objected to Zuinglius, where it is said, that Baptism saves us, that it remits our sins; he thinks he has fully satisfied by answering, that baptism is here taken for the blood of Jesus Christ, of which it is the sign.

23.—Zuinglius accustomed to wrest the Scripture in every thing.—His contempt
for antiquity, the source of his error.

Such licentious explications make every thing one wishes to be found in Scripture. It is not surprising that Zuinglius there finds that the Eucharist is not the body, but the sign of the body, though Christ has said, "This is my body;" since he is able to find that baptism does not indeed give the remission of sins, but figures it to us as already given; though the Scripture has said a hundred times, not that it figures, but gives it to us. It is no matter of surprise that the same author, to destroy the reality which incommoded him, eludes the force of these words, "This is my body;" since to destroy original sin, which shocked him, he was able to evade these words; "all have sinned in one man," and again, "by the disobedience of one man many were made sinners."[47] But still more strange is the confidence of this author in supporting his new interpretations against original sin, with a manifest contempt of all antiquity. "We have seen," says he, "The ancients teach another doctrine concerning original sin: but in reading them it is easily perceived how obscure and embarrassed, not to say entirely human, rather than divine, is all they say on that head. For my part, this long time I have not leisure to consult them." In 1526 he composed this treatise; and for many years before, he had no leisure to consult the ancients, nor go back to the fountain-head. Meanwhile he reformed the church. Why not, will our Reformers say? And what had he to do with the ancients, since he possessed the Scriptures? but on the contrary, here is an instance how little safety there is in searching the Scriptures, when one pretends to understand them, without having recourse to antiquity. By understanding the Scriptures in such a manner, Zuinglius discovered there was no original sin, that is to say, there was no redemption; and the scandal of the cross was made void; and pushed his notions to such a length, as to place among the saints those, who, indeed, whatever he might say, had no part with Jesus Christ. Thus is the church reformed, when men undertake its reforma-tion without concerning themselves about what was the sense of past ages; and, according to this new method, it is easy to arrive at a reformation like that of the Socinians.

24.—*The character of Œcolampadius.*

Such were the heads of the new reformation. Men of talent, it is true, and not deficient in literature, but bold, rash in their decisions, and puffed up with their vain learning: men who delighted in extraordinary and particular opinions, and therefore aimed, not only to raise themselves above those of their own age, but also above the most holy of ages past. Œcolampadius the other defender of the figurative sense amongst the Swiss was both more moderate, and more learned; and if Zuinglius appeared by his vehemence another Luther, Œcolampadius more resembled Melancthon, whose particular friend he was also. In a letter, which, when a youth, he wrote to Erasmus, you observe the marks of a piety equally affectionate and enlightened, together with much wit and politeness.[48] From the feet of the crucifix, before which he had been accustomed to pray, he wrote such tender things to Erasmus on the ineffable sweetness of Jesus Christ, whom this pious image represented so lively to his imagination, that there is no reading it without being affected. The reformation which came to trouble these devotions, and account them idolatry, began at that time; for it was in 1517 that he wrote this letter. He entered into religion in the first heat of these disturbances, with much courage and reflection; at an age, as Erasmus observes, too advanced for any imputation of youthful precipitancy.[49] We also learn from the letters of Erasmus, that he was greatly enamoured with the course of life he had undertaken, and relished God in peace of mind, and therein lived quite remote from the novelties that were then spreading. However, (such is human weakness, so great the contagion of novelty,) he left his monastery, preached the new reformation at Basil, where he was pastor, and tired of celibacy, like the rest of the reformers, married a young girl, with whose beauty he was enamoured. "This is the way," said Erasmus, "they choose to mortify themselves;"[50] he could not but admire these new apostles, who were sure to abandon the solemn profession of celibacy to take wives; whereas, the true apostles of our Saviour, according to the tradition of all the fathers, in order to attend to God and the Gospel only, left their wives to embrace celibacy. "It seems," said he, "as if the reformation aimed at nothing more than to strip a few monks of their habits, and to marry a parcel of priests; and this great tragedy terminates at last in a conclusion that is entirely comical, since, just like comedies, all ends in marriage."[51] The same Erasmus complains, in other places,[52] that after his friend Œcolampadius had abandoned his tender devotion, together with the church and monastery, in order to embrace this impious and contemptible reformation, he was no longer the same man; instead of candor, which this minister professed whilst he acted of himself, nothing but artifice and dissimulation could be found in him, after he had once entered into the spirit of the party.

25.—*The progress of the Sacramentarian doctrine.*

After the Sacramentarian dispute had been raised in the manner we have seen, Carlostadius scattered abroad little tracts against the real presence; and, although on all hands they were allowed to be replete with ignorance,[53] yet they were relished by the people already charmed with novelty. Zuinglius and Œcolampadius wrote in defence of this new doctrine: the first with much wit and vehemence; the other with much learning, and so sweet an eloquence, that "were it possible," says Erasmus, "and would God have permitted it, it were capable of seducing even the elect."[54] God put them to this trial; but his promises and truth upheld the simplicity of the faith of the church against human reasoning. A little after Carlostadius was reconciled with Luther, and appeased him by saying that what he had taught upon the Eucharist, was rather by the way of proposing and examining, than deciding.[55] This man's life was one uninterrupted scene of feuds; and the Swiss, who received him a second time, were never able to calm his turbulent temper.

His doctrine spread more and more, but on more plausible interpretations of our Saviour's words than what he had formerly given. Zuinglius said, "the good man said well enough, there was some hidden sense in these divine words, but could never find out what it was." He and Œcolampadius, with somewhat different expressions, agreed on the whole, that these words, "This is my body," were figurative: "Is," said Zuinglius, "is as much as to say, signifies;" "body," said Œcolampadius, "is the sign of the body." Their leaders, Bucer and Capito, became zealous defenders of the figurative sense. The reformation divided itself; and those who embraced this new party were called Sacramentarians. They were also named Zuinglians, either because Zuinglius had first supported Carlostadius, or because his authority prevailed in the minds of the people, who were led away by his vehemence.

26.—*Zuinglius careful to take from the Eucharist whatever was raised above the senses.*

We must not be surprised that an opinion so favorable to human sense became so fashionable. Zuinglius said positively there was no miracle in the Eucharist, or any thing incomprehensible; that the bread broken represented to us the body immolated; and the wine, the blood shed: that Jesus Christ, at the institution of these sacred signs, had given them the name of the thing itself: that it was not, however, a simple spectacle, nor signs wholly naked, for as much as the remembrance of, and faith in, the body immolated and the blood shed, supported our souls; that the Holy Ghost meanwhile sealed in our hearts the remission of sins; and therein consisted the whole mystery. Human reason and sense had nothing to suffer from this explication.[56] The Scripture was all the difficulty: but when one side opposed "This is my body," the other answered, "I am the vine; I am the door; the rock was Christ." True it is these examples came not to the point. It was not in proposing a parable, or explaining an allegory, that Jesus Christ said, "This is my body; this is my blood." These words, entirely detached from the context, carried their full meaning in themselves,—a new institution was in hand,—which ought to be made in simple terms, and yet no place in Scripture had been found, where the sign of the institution received the name of the thing itself the moment it was instituted, and without any previous preparation.

27.—*Of the Spirit which appeared to Zuinglius, to furnish him with a passage, where the sign of the institution, received immediately the name of the thing instituted.*

This argument tormented Zuinglius; he sought day and night for a solution. In the meantime, however, mass was abolished, in opposition to all the exertions of the town-secretary, who disputed powerfully for the Catholic doctrine and the real presence. Twelve days after, Zuinglius had this dream, with which he and his disciples have been so much upbraided. In it he tells us, that imagining he was disputing against the town-secretary, who pressed him closely, on a sudden, he saw a phantom, white or black, appear before him,[57] who spoke these words: "Coward, why answerest thou not what is written in Exodus,—'The Lamb is the passover,'[58]—intimating it was the sign?" This is the celebrated passage so often repeated in the writings of the Sacramentarians, in which they thought to have found the name of the thing given to the sign, and in the very institution of the sign; and thus it was conceived by Zuinglius, who availed himself of it. His disciples will contend, when he said he knew not who suggested this thought, whether he was white or black, he meant only, that it was an unknown person, and true it is, the Latin terms will bear this explication. But, besides that concealing himself, so as not to discover what he was, is the natural character of an evil spirit, Zuinglius was also manifestly in error:—these words, "The Lamb is the passover," by no means signify it was the figure of the passover. It is a common Hebraism, where the word sacrifice is understood; so sin merely is the sacrifice for sin; and barely passover is the sacrifice of the passover; which the Scripture itself explains a little farther on, where it says at full length, not that the Lamb is the passover, but the sacrifice of the passover. This most certainly was the sense of that place in Exodus. Other examples were afterwards produced, as we shall see in due time; but this was the first. There was nothing in it, as we see, that should much comfort the mind of Zuinglius, or that showed him the sign at the very institution received the name of the thing. He awoke, however, at this next explication of his unknown friend, read the place of Exodus, and went to preach what he had discovered in his dream. Men were too well prepared not to believe him; the mists which still remained on their minds were dissipated.

28.—*Luther writes against the Sacramentarians, and why he treated Zuinglius more severely than the rest.*

It provoked Luther to see, not only individuals, but whole churches of the new reformation, now rise up against him. But he abated nothing of his accustomed pride. We may judge from these words,—"I have the Pope in front; I have the Sacramentarians and Anabaptists in my rear; but I will march out alone against them all; I will defy them to battle; I will trample them under my feet." And a little after,—"I will say it without vanity, that for these thousand years the Scripture has never been so thoroughly purged, nor so well explained, nor better understood, than at this time it is by me."[59] He wrote these words in 1525, a little after the contest had commenced. In the same year he composed his book "against the heavenly prophets;" thereby ridiculing Carlostadius, whom he accused of favoring the visions of the Anabaptists. This book consisted of two parts. In the first he maintained the impropriety of breaking down images; that in the law of Moses nothing was prohibited as the object of adoration, but the images of God; that the images of crosses and of saints were not comprehended in this prohibition; that none under the gospel were obliged to destroy images by force, because that was contrary to gospel-liberty; and those who destroyed them were doctors of the law, and not of the gospel. By this reasoning he justified us from all those accusations of idolatry, with which we were unreasonably charged on this head. In the second part he attacked the Sacramentarians. But Œcolampadius he treated with moderation at the commencement; yet he attacked Zuinglius with violence. This doctor had written, that before the name of Luther was known, he had preached the gospel,—that is, the reformation in Switzerland—ever since the year 1516; and the Swiss gave him the glory of this beginning, which Luther arrogated to himself.[60] Offended at these words he wrote to those of Strasburg, "that he durst assume to himself the glory of first preaching Jesus Christ, but that Zuinglius wished to deprive him of that glory. How is it possible," proceeds he, "to be silent whilst these men disturb our churches and impugn our authority? If they are unwilling to suffer their own to be weakened; for the same reason, they ought not to weaken ours." In conclusion, he declares, "there is no medium, either he or they must be the ministers of Satan."[61]

29.—*The words of a celebrated Lutheran on the jealousy of Luther against Zuinglius.*

An ingenious Lutheran, and the most celebrated of those that have written in our days, here makes this reflection:—"Those who despise all things, and expose not only their fortunes, but their lives, often are not able to raise themselves above glory, so flattering are its charms, so great is human weakness. On the contrary, the higher a man's courage is elevated the more does he covet praises—the more concerned to see those bestowed on others, which he believes due to himself."[62] It should not be, therefore, a matter of surprise, if a man of Luther's magnanimity wrote these things to those of Strasburg.

30.—*Luther's strong arguments for the real presence; and how he boasts of them.*

In the midst of these strange transports, Luther, by powerful arguments, confirmed the faith of the real presence. Both the Scripture, and ancient tradition, supported him in this cause. He demonstrated, that to convert so simple, so precise words of our Saviour to a figurative sense, under pretext that there were figurative expressions in other places of the Scripture, was to open a way by which the whole Scripture, and all the mysteries of our religion, would be turned to figures; that the same submission was, therefore, required here, with which we receive the other mysteries, without attending to human reasoning, or the laws of nature, but to Jesus Christ and his words only; that our Saviour spoke not, in the institution, either of faith or the Holy Spirit, but said, "This is my body," and not that faith would make you partake of it; wherefore, the eating, of which Jesus Christ there spoke, was not a mystical eating, but an eating by the mouth; that the union of faith was consummated out of the sacrament,[63] nor could it be believed that Jesus Christ gave us nothing that was particular by such emphatic words;[64] that it is evident his intention was to render certain his gift, by giving us his person; that the remembrance he recommended to us of his death, excluded not his presence, but obliged us to receive this body and this blood as a victim immolated for us; that the victim became ours, indeed, by manducation; that, in reality, faith ought then to intervene, in order to make it profitable to us; but to show that, even without faith, the word of Jesus Christ had its effect, there needed but to consider the communion of the unworthy. He urged here forcibly the words of St. Paul, when, after relating these words, "This is my body," he condemned so severely those "who discerned not the body of the Lord, and who rendered themselves guilty of his body and blood."[65] He added, that St. Paul meant to speak throughout of the "true body," and not of the body in figure; and that it was evident from his expressions, that he condemned those impious persons of insulting Jesus Christ, not in his gifts, but immediately in his person.

But where he manifested his greatest strength, was in demolishing the objections which were raised against these heavenly truths. He asked of those who objected to him, "flesh profiteth nothing,"[66] with what assurance they durst say, that the flesh of Jesus Christ profiteth nothing, and apply to this life-giving flesh what Jesus Christ said of the carnal sense, or, at most, of the flesh taken after the manner in which the Capharnaites understood it, or evil Christians received it, not uniting themselves thereto by faith, nor receiving at that same time that spirit and life with which it abounds? When they presumed to ask him, What, therefore, did this flesh avail taken by the mouth of the body, he again asked of these proud opponents, What did it avail that the Word was made flesh? Could not truth have been announced, nor mankind redeemed, but by this means? Are they acquainted with all God's secrets, to say unto him, he had no other way by which to save man? And who are they, thus to set laws to their Creator, and prescribe to him the means by which he would apply his grace to them? If, at last, they opposed against him human reasons, how a body could be in so many places at once—a human body, whole and entire, in so small a space? He destroyed all these engines levelled against God, by asking, how God preserved his unity in the trinity of persons? how of nothing, he had created heaven and earth? how he had clothed his Son in a human body? how he made him be born of a virgin? how he delivered him up to death? and how he was to raise up all the faithful on the last day? What did human reason pretend by opposing these vain difficulties against God, which he blasted with a breath? They say that all the miracles of Jesus Christ are sensible.[67] "But who has told them that Jesus Christ did resolve never to work any other? When he was conceived by the Holy Ghost in the womb of a virgin, to whom was this, the greatest miracle of all, become sensible? Could Mary have known what it was she bore in her womb, had not the angel announced the divine secret to her? But when the divinity dwelt corporeally in Christ Jesus, who saw it, or who comprehended it? Now who sees him at the right hand of his Father from whence he exerts his omnipotence over the whole universe? Is this what obliges them to wrest, to break to pieces, to crucify the words of their Master? I do not comprehend, say they, how he can execute them literally. They prove to me very well, by this reason, that human sense agrees not with God's wisdom; I allow it; I agree with them; but I never knew before that nothing was to be believed but what we discovered by opening our eyes, or what human reason can comprehend."

Lastly, when it was said to him, that this matter was not of consequence, or of sufficient importance for breaking peace:—"who then obliged Carlostadius to begin this quarrel? What forced Zuinglius and Œcolampadius to write? May that peace for ever be accursed, that is made to the prejudice of truth!" By such arguments he often silence the Zuinglians. It must be acknowledged, he had a great strength of genius; he wanted nothing but the rule, which can be had no where but in the Church, and under the yoke of a legitimate authority. Had Luther continued obedient to that yoke, so necessary for the regulation of all minds, but especially for fiery and impetuous minds like his, he might have kept his writing free from those transports, those buffooneries, that brutal arrogance, those excesses, or rather extravagances; and the force with which he treated some truths, would not have contributed to seduction. It is for this reason we see him still invincible, when he sets forth the ancient doctrines he had learned in the bosom of the Church; but pride closely pursued his victories. So much was this man captivated with himself for having fought so strenuously for the proper and literal sense of our Saviour's words, that he could not refrain from boasting of it. "The Papists themselves," said he, "are obliged to allow me the praise of having defended the doctrine of the literal sense much better than they. And, in reality, I am assured, were they all melted down into one mass, they never would be able to maintain it with the strength that I do."[68]

31.—*The Zuinglians prove against Luther that Catholics understand the literal sense better than he.*

He was mistaken; for although he fully proved that the literal sense was to be maintained, he knew not how to understand it in all its simplicity; and the supporters of the figurative sense demonstrated to him, that if the literal sense were to be followed, transubstantiation would carry it. This is what Zuinglius, and all the defenders of the figurative sense, in general, proved most clearly. They observe, that Jesus Christ has not said, "My body is here, or my body is under this, and with this, or this contains my body, but only, 'This is my body.'" Thus, what he is to give the faithful is not a substance which contains his body, or which accompanies it, but his body, "without any other foreign substance."[69] Neither has he said, "This bread is my body," which is another of Luther's explications; but he has said, "This is my body," by an indefinite term, to show that the substance he gives is no longer bread, but his body.

And when Luther explained, "This is my body;" that is, this bread is my body, really and without figure, contrary to his intentions, he destroyed his own doctrine. For we may very well say with the Church, that bread becomes body, in the same sense that St. John has said, "the water was made wine,"[70] at the marriage-feast in Cana of Galilee, namely, by the change of one into the other. In the same manner may it be said, that what is bread in appearance, is, in effect, the body of our Lord; but that true bread, remaining such, should be at the same time the true body of our Lord, as Luther maintained, the defenders of the figurative sense proved to him, as did the Catholics, that it was a reasoning void of sense, and concluded that he ought either to admit a moral change only, together with them, or a change of substance, together with the Papists.

32.—*Beza proves the same truth.*

It is for this reason that Beza, at the Conference of Montbeliart, maintains against the Lutherans, that of the two explications which adhere to the literal sense—namely, that of the Catholics, and that of the Lutherans, "It is that of the Catholics which departs least from the words of the institution of the Lord's Supper, were they to be expounded word for word." He proves it by this reason: because "the Transubstantiators say, that by virtue of these divine words, that which before was bread, having changed its substance, becomes immediately the body itself of Jesus Christ, to the end that, by this means, this proposition may be true, 'This is my body.' Whereas the exposition of the consubstantiators, saying, that these words, 'This is my body,' do signify my body is essentially in, with, or under this bread, declares not what is become of the bread, and what that is, which is the body, but only where it is."[71] This reason is plain and intelligible. For it is clear, that Jesus Christ, having taken bread in order to make it something, must have declared to us what kind of something he did intend to make it; it is not less evident, that the bread became that which the Almighty did intend to make it. Now these words show he intended to make it his body, whatever that is understood, since he said, "This is my body." If, therefore, this bread is not become his body in figure, t is become so in effect; and there is no way to avoid admitting either the change in figure, or the change in substance.

Thus if we only understand simply the words of Jesus Christ, the doctrine of the Church must be embraced, and Beza is correct in stating, that it is attended with less difficulties, as to the manner of speaking, than that of the Lutherans, that is to say it is more agreeable to the literal sense.[72] Calvin frequently confirms the same truth; and, not to dwell on the sense of individuals, a whole Synod of Zuinglians have acknowledged it.

33.—A whole Synod of Zuinglians in Poland establishes the same truth.

It is the Synod of Czenger, a town in Poland, published in the Collection of Geneva. This synod, after having rejected Papistical Transubstantiation, shows "that Lutheran Consubstantiation is untenable," because, "as the wand of Moses was not a serpent but by transubstantiation, and the water in Egypt was not blood, nor, at the marriage of Cana, wine, without a change; so the bread of the supper cannot be the body of Christ substantially, if it be not changed into his flesh, by losing the form and substance of bread."[73]

It was good sense that dictated this decision. In fact, the bread remaining bread, can be no more the body of our Lord, than the wand remaining the wand, could be a serpent, or than the water remaining water, could be blood in Egypt, or wine at the marriage of Cana. If, therefore, what was bread becomes of body of our Lord, either it becomes so in figure by a mystical change, according to Zuinglius's doctrine, or it becomes so, in effect, by a real change, as is maintained by Catholics.

34.—Luther understood not the force of these words, "This is my body."

Thus, Luther, who boasted that he alone had defended the literal sense better than all the Catholic divines, was greatly mistaken; since he did not even comprehend the true ground which holds us to this sense, nor understand the nature of those propositions which operate what they express. Jesus Christ says to that man, "Thy son liveth."[74] Jesus Christ says to that woman, "Thou art loosed from thine infirmity."[75] In speaking, he does what he says: nature obeys; things are changed, and the sick person becomes sound. But words, which regard only accidental things, as health and sickness, operate only accidental changes. Here, where a substance is concerned, for Jesus Christ said, "This is my body, This is my blood," the change is substantial; and by an effect as real as it is surprising, the substance of the bread and of the wine is changed into the substance of the body and the blood. Consequently, when we follow the literal sense, we must not only believe that the body of Jesus Christ is in the mystery, but also that it makes the whole substance of it; and this is what the words themselves lead us to, in Jesus Christ, not having said, my body is here, or this contains my body, but this is my body; and he would not even say this bread is my body, but this, indefinitely. And in the same manner as if he had said, when he changed the water into wine; that which you are going to drink is wine, it ought not to be understood that he had preserved together both water and wine, but that he had changed the water into wine; so when he declares, that what he presents as his body, it ought not in any way to be understood that he mixes his body with the bread, but that he effectually changes the bread into his body. To this the literal sense leads us, as the Zuinglians themselves acknowledge, and this it is which Luther could never understand.

35.—*The Sacramentarians proved to Luther that he admitted a kind of figurative sense.*

On account of not understanding it, this great defender of the literal sense fell necessarily into a kind of figurative sense. According to him, "This is my body," imported, this bread contains my body, or this bread is joined with my body; and by this means, the Zuinglians forced him to acknowledge, in this expression, that grammatical figure which substitutes that which containeth for that which is contained, or the part for the whole.[76] Then they pressed him in this way: if it be lawful for you to admit in the words of the institution, that figure which puts the part for the whole, why will you prevent us from admitting in them that figure which substitutes the thing for the sign? Figure for figure, the metonomy which we acknowledge is worth full as much as the synecdoche which you receive. These gentlemen were humanists and grammarians. All their books were soon filled with the synecdoche of Luther, and the metonomy of Zuinglius; it was necessary for Protestants to engage on one side or other of these two figures of rhetoric; and it appeared manifest, that none but the Catholics, equally distant from one and the other, and admitting in the Eucharist neither the bread nor a bare sign, justly established the literal sense.

36.—*The difference between doctrine invented, and doctrine received by tradition.*

Here was perceived the difference between the doctrines introduced anew by particular authors, and those which come in their natural channel. The change of substance had of itself spread over both the east and the west, entering into all minds together with the words of our Lord, without ever causing any disturbance; neither were those who believed it, ever marked by the Church as innovators. When it was contested, and men labored to wrest the literal sense with which it had spread over the whole earth, not only the Church remained firm, but also her very adversaries were seen to combat for her, whilst they combated against each other. Luther and his followers proved invincibly that the literal sense ought to be retained. Zuinglius, with his party, established with no less force, that it could not be retained without the change of substance: thus they agreed in this only, to prove against each other, that the Church, which they had abandoned, had more reason on her side than any of them: by I know not what force of truth, all those who abandoned her, retained something of it, and the Church which kept the whole, gained the victory.

37.—The Catholic sense is visibly the most natural sense.

Hence, it clearly follows, that the interpretation of Catholics, who admit the change of substance, is the most natural and the most simple; both because it is followed by the greatest number of Christians, and because of these two, who impugn it by different ways, one of them, that is Luther, undertook to oppose it purely out of a spirit of contradiction, and in spite of the Church; and the other, that is Zuinglius, agrees, that if with Luther the literal sense is to be received, the change of substance must be received also with the Catholics.

38.—Question: whether the Sacrament be destroyed in Transubstantiation?

Afterwards, the Lutherans, once engaged in error, confirmed themselves therein with this argument, that it is destroying the sacrament, to take from it, as we do the substance of bread and wine. I am obliged to acknowledge I have not found this reason in any of the writings of Luther; and, indeed, it is too weak and too far-fetched to occur immediately to the mind; for it is known that a sacrament, that is, a sign, consists in that which it appears, not in the interior or substance of the thing. It was not necessary to show Pharaoh seven real kine, and seven ears of real corn to notify to him the fertility and the famine of seven years. The image that was formed in his mind was quite sufficient for that purpose; and if we must come to things with which the eyes have been affected, in order that the dove should represent the Holy Ghost, and that chaste love with all its sweetness, which he inspires into holy souls, it was not at all necessary that it should be a real dove which descended visibly upon Jesus Christ; it was sufficient it had the whole exterior; in the same manner, in order that the Eucharist might specify to us that Jesus Christ was our bread and our drink, it was sufficient that the characters and ordinary effects of these aliments were preserved: in a word, it was enough, there was nothing changed with regard to the senses. In the signs of the institution, that which denotes their force is the intention declared by the words of the institutor; now, by saying over the bread, "This is my body," and over the wine, "This is my blood," and seeming, by virtue of these divine words, actually invested with all the appearances of bread and wine, he shows clearly enough, that he is truly a nourishment, who has taken on him the resemblance of it, and under that form appears to us. If, to the reality of the sacrament, true bread and true wine be necessary, it is likewise true bread and true wine that are consecrated; and which, by consecration, are made the true body and true blood of our Redeemer. The change that is made in the interior, without any alteration of the exterior, makes also one part of the sacrament—namely, of the sacred sign; inasmuch as this change, become sensible by the words, makes us see that by the words of Jesus Christ operating in a Christian, he ought to be most really, though in a different manner, changed inwardly, retaining only the exterior of other men.

39.—*How the names of bread and wine may remain in the Eucharist.*
—Two rules drawn from Scripture.

Thereby those passages are explained, in which the Eucharist is called bread, even after consecration; and this difficulty is manifestly solved, by the rule of changes, and the rule of appearances. By the rule of changes, the bread become the body, is called bread, as in Exodus, the wand become a serpent, is called a wand, and the water become blood, is called water. These expressions are made use of to show at once, both the thing which was made, and the material employed to make it of. By the rule of appearances, in the same manner that, in the Old and New Testament, the angels who appeared under human shape, are called, at he same time, angels[77] because they are so, and men, because they appear so; so the Eucharist will be both called the body, because it is so, and bread, because it so appears. If, then, one of these two reasons is sufficient to preserve to it the name of bread without prejudicing the change, the concurrence of both will be much stronger. And no difficulty should be imagined of discerning truth amidst these different expressions; for, when the Holy Scripture explains the same thing by different expressions, to prevent all ambiguity, there is always a principal place, to which the rest are to be reduced, and where things are expressed, such as they are, in precise terms. What if these angels be called men in some places? there will be a place where it will be clearly seen that they are angels. What if this blood and this serpent be called water and wand? you will find the principal place, where the change will be specified; and it is by that the thing should be defined. What will be the principal place, by which we are to judge of the Eucharist, if it be not that of the institution, where Jesus Christ made it to be what it is? So, when we would name it with relation to what it was, and what it appears, we may call it bread and wine; but when we would name it with respect to what it is in itself, it will have no other name than that of body and blood. And it is by this it ought to be defined, since it can never be anything else than what it is made by the all-powerful words which gave it being. Both of you, as well Lutherans as Zuinglians, do, contrary to nature, explain the principal text by other places, and both of you, departing from the rule, do separate still to a greater distance from one another, than you do from the Church which you chiefly aimed to oppose. The Church, which follows the natural order, and reduces all the passages where the Eucharist is mentioned, to that which, beyond dispute, is the principal and foundation of all the others, holds the true key of the mystery; and triumphs not only over both one and the other, but also over the one by the other.

40.—*Luther dismayed at these disputes; his dejection deplored by Melancthon.*

In effect, during these Sacramentarian disputes, those who called themselves Reformed, notwithstanding their common interest, which at times united them in appearance, waged a more cruel war against each other than against the Church itself, mutually calling each other "furies, maniacs, slaves of Satan, greater enemies to the truth and the members of Jesus Christ, than the Pope himself;" which to them was saying every thing.

In the meantime, the authority which Luther was desirous of maintaining in the new Reformation, that had arisen under his standard, was becoming contemptible. He was overwhelmed with grief; and that haughtiness, which he showed exteriorly, could not support him under that dejection of mind which he felt interiorly; on the contrary, the more haughty he was, the more insupportable it was to him to be despised by a party, of whom he wished to be the sole leader. The concern he felt communicated itself to Melancthon; "Luther," says he, "causes in me great troubles, by the long complaints he makes to me of his afflictions; writings, judged not contemptible, have quite dejected and disfigured him; through the compassion I have for him, I find myself afflicted to the utmost extremity, for the calamities of the Church. The doubtful vulgar divide themselves into contrary sentiments; and had not Jesus Christ promised to be with us even to the consummation of ages, I should apprehend the utter destruction of religion from these dissensions; for nothing is more true than the sentence which says, through much disputing, truth escapes from us."[78]

41.—Luther teaches Ubiquity. [1527, 1528]

Strange agitations of a man, who hoped to see the Church repaired, and now sees her ready to fall by the very means taken for her re-establishment! What comfort could he find in the promises made to us by Jesus Christ, of being always with us? It is for Catholics to nourish themselves with this faith; for them, who believe the Church can never be overcome by error, however violent the assault, and who, in fact, have ever found her to be invincible. But how can they advance claims to this promise in the new Reformation, whose first foundation, when they separated from the Church, was that Jesus Christ had so forsaken her, as to let her fall into idolatry! Moreover, though it is true that truth remains always in the Church, and becomes the more purified in proportion as it is attacked, Melancthon was right in thinking, that by much disputation individuals fell into error. There was no error so monstrous, into which the heat of dispute had not impelled the passionate mind of Luther. It made him embrace that monstrous opinion of ubiquity. These are the arguments on which he grounded this strange notion. The humanity of our Lord is united to his divinity; therefore, the humanity, as well as the other, is every where: Jesus Christ, as man, is seated at the right hand of God; the right hand of God is every where; therefore, Jesus Christ, as man, is every where. As man, he was in heaven before he had ascended into it. He was in the monument when the angels said he was not there. The Zuinglians fell into a worse extreme, by saying that God had it not even in his power to put the body of Jesus Christ in several places. Luther runs into another excess, and maintains that this body was necessarily in every place; that is what he taught in a book already mentioned, which he wrote in 1527, in order to defend the literal sense, and what he ventured to insert in a "Confession of Faith," which he published in 1528, under the title of "The Great Confession of Faith."[79]

42.—*Luther declares anew that it imports little whether the substance of bread be admitted or taken away; the gross divinity of this Doctor, at which Melancthon is scandalized.*

He says, in this last book, that it is of little importance, whether the bread be admitted in the Eucharist or not; but that it was more reasonable to acknowledge therein. "A carnal bread and a bloody wine—*panis carneus et vinum sanguineum.*" This was the new language, by which he expressed that new union he placed between the bread and the body. These words seemed to aim at impanation, and often such fell from him, which had a further tendency than he meant. But, at least, they proposed a certain mixture of bread and flesh, of wine and blood, which appeared very gross, and was insupportable to Melancthon—"I have spoken," says he, "to Luther, concerning this mixture of the bread and the body, which appears a strange paradox to many people. He answered me peremptorily, that he would alter nothing in it; and, for my part, I do not think it proper to meddle any more in this affair."[80] Which is as much as to say, he was not of Luther's mind, yet dared not to contradict him.

43.—*The Sacramentarian contest upset the foundations of the Reformation.—Calvin's words.*

Meanwhile, the excesses into which they fell on both sides of the new reformation, discredited it with men of good sense. This dispute alone destroyed the common foundation of each party. They believed they could terminate all disputes by the Scripture alone, and would have no other judge than that; and the whole world was witness, there was no end to their disputes on Scripture, even on one passage of it, than which none ought to be more clear, since it regarded a last will and testament. They exclaimed one to the other, "All is clear and nothing more is necessary than to open your eyes." By this evidence of Scripture, Luther discovered that nothing was more impious and daring than to deny the literal sense; and Zuinglius found nothing more gross and absurd than to follow it. Erasmus, whom both were desirous of gaining, said the same to them that all Catholics did:—"You all appeal to the pure word of God, and believe yourselves its true interpreters. Agree, then, amongst yourselves, before you set laws to all mankind."[81] Whatever excuse they invented, they were quite ashamed that they could not agree, and in the bottom of their hearts, all thought the same that Calvin wrote to his friend Melancthon,—"It is of great importance, that the least suspicion of the divisions, which are amongst us, pass not to future ages; for it is ridiculous beyond any thing that can be imagined, after we have broken off from the whole world, we should so little agree amongst ourselves ever since the beginning of our reformation."[82]

44.—*The Lutherans take up arms under the Landgrave's command,
who owns that he is in the wrong.*

Philip, Landgrave of Hesse, very zealous for the new gospel, had foreseen this disorder, and from the beginning of the rupture endeavored to effect a reconciliation. As soon as he saw the party sufficiently strong, and, moreover, threatened by the emperor and the Catholics, he began to form designs of a confederacy. The maxims laid down by Luther for the foundation of his reformation, to seek no support from arms, were soon forgotten. They rose in arms under pretext of an imaginary treaty, said to have been made between George, Duke of Saxony, and the other Catholic princes, to exterminate the Lutherans.[83] The matter indeed was adjusted: the Landgrave was satisfied with the great sums of money, which some ecclesiastical princes were obliged to pay down, to indemnify him for raising forces, which he himself acknowledged he had done on false reports.

Melancthon, who did not approve of this conduct, found no other excuse for the Landgrave, but the reluctance he felt to let it appear that he had been deceived, and had nothing more to say in his defence, than that an "evil shame"[84] had influenced him. But other thoughts gave him much more uneasiness. They had boasted among themselves that the Papacy should be destroyed, without making war and shedding blood. Previous to the time of the Landgrave's tumult, and a little after the revolt of the peasants, Melancthon had written to the Landgrave himself, "That it was better to suffer every thing than to take up arms in the gospel cause;"[85] and now it happened, that those who had labored so much to convince the world of their pacific principles were the first to run to arms, and that on a false report, as Melancthon himself acknowledges.[86] Accordingly he adds, "When I see what a scandal the good cause is liable to, I am almost overwhelmed with this concern."[87] Luther was far from these sentiments: though in Germany it was known as certain, and Protestant authors have acknowledged it,[88] that this pretended treaty of George of Saxony was a mere illusion. Luther wished to believe it true; and wrote several letters and libels, in which he is so transported against that prince, even as to call him, "of all fools, the greatest fool; a proud Moab, who always undertook what was above his strength," adding that he would pray to God against him: then that he would give notice to the princes to exterminate such people, who wished to see all Germany in blood:[89] that is to say, lest the Lutherans themselves should be placed in that condition, and begin by exterminating such princes as were opposed to their designs.

This George, Duke of Saxony, so insulted by Luther, was as much opposed to the Lutherans, as his kinsman the Elector was favorable to them. Luther prophesied against him with all his strength, regardless that he was of the same family with his Lord and master; and it is plain that it was not his fault that his prophesies were not fulfilled with the edge of the sword.

45.—The name of Protestants.—The conference of Marpurg, where the Landgrave labors in vain to reconcile both parties of Protestants.—1529.

This armament of the Lutherans, which in 1528 made all Germany tremble, had raised their pride to such a height, that they judged themselves in a condition to protest openly against the decree, published against them the year following in the Diet of Spires, and to appeal from it to the emperor, to the future general council, or to that which should be held in Germany. It was on this occasion they re-united themselves under the name of Protestants; but the Landgrave, who had more sagacity, more capacity and more valor than any of them, perceived that the diversity of sentiments would be an everlasting obstacle to that perfect union, which he desired to form amongst them; therefore, the same year that the decree passed at Spires, he procured the conference of Marpurg, where he caused all the leaders of the new reformations to meet, namely, Luther, Osiander, and Melancthon, on one side; Zuinglius, Œcolampadius, and Bucer, on the other, to pass over those less distinguished. Luther and Zuinglius were the only speakers; for the Lutherans, long before this, were silent when Luther was present; and Melancthon frankly acknowledges that he and his companions were but "mute figures."[90] They thought not then of amusing each other with equivocal explications, as they did afterwards. The true presence of the body and blood was plainly maintained on one side, and denied on the other. On both sides it was understood, that a presence in figure, and a presence by faith, was not a true presence of Jesus Christ, but a moral presence—a presence improperly so called, and in metaphor. They agreed, in appearance, on all articles, except the Eucharist. I say in appearance, for it is clear from two letters, which, during this conference, Melancthon wrote to his princes to give them an account of it, that, in reality, they very little understood each other's meaning.—"We discovered," says he, "that our adversaries understood very little of Luther's doctrine, although they endeavored to imitate his language;"[91] that is, they agreed through complaisance, and in words, though in reality they understood not each other; and the truth is, Zuinglius had never comprehended any thing of Luther's doctrine on the sacraments, nor of his imputed justice."[92] Those of Strasburg, with Bucer their minister, were also accused of not having good sentiments, that is, as they meant it, not Lutheran enough on this head, and so it afterwards appeared, as we shall soon perceive. The truth of the thing is, Zuinglius and his companions were somewhat troubled about these matters, and spoke whatever might please Luther, having nothing in their thoughts but the real presence. As to the manner of treating things, Luther, as usual, spoke with haughtiness. Zuinglius showed much ignorance, so far as to ask several times,"How a wicked priest could perform a sacred thing?"[93] Luther pressed him closely, and made him see from the example of baptism that he knew not what he said. When Zuinglius and his companions saw they could not prevail on Luther to admit their figurative sense, they entreated him at least to hold them for brethren, but were sharply repulsed. "What fraternity do you ask of me," replied Luther, "if you persist in your belief? It is a sign you doubt of it, since you desire to be their brethren who reject it."[94] Thus ended the conference. However, they promised mutual charity. Luther interpreted this charity such as we owe to enemies, and not such as is allowed to those of the same communion. "They were indignant," said he, "to see themselves treated like heretics." They agreed, however, to write no more against each other. "But it was only to give time," continued Luther, "to come to themselves."

This agreement, such as it was, continued but a short time; on the contrary, by the different accounts that were given of this conference, their minds were more exasperated than before. The proposal of fraternity made by the Zuinglians was considered by Luther a stratagem, and he said, "that Satan so reigned in them that they had it no longer in their power to advance any thing but lies."[95]

Notes

[1] Ep. ad. Argentin. t. vii. f. 501.
[2] Matt. xxvi. 28. Luike xxii. 19,20. 1 Cor. xi. 24.
[3] De Capt. Bab. t. ii.
[4] Mel. lib. ii. Ep. 447.
[5] De Cap. Babyl. t. ii. f. 66.
[6] Resp. ad art. extract. ibid. 172.
[7] Contra Reg. Aug. T 11.
[8] Cont. Reg. Aug. 333.
[9] Erasm. lib. vi. Epist. 3, ad Luther, lib. xiv. Ep. 1, &c.—Id. lib. xix. Ep. 3 ad Melanct.
[10] 2 Tim. ii. 17.
[11] Ibid. iii. 13.
[12] Ibid. iii. 9.
[13] Tert. de Præser. c. 42.
[14] Ep. Dedic. Comm. in Gal. ad Carlo-stad.
[15] Zuin. Ep. ad. Matt.
[16] Ep. Luth. ad Gasp. Gustol. 1522.
[17] Serm. Quid. Christiano præstandum, t. vii. f. 273.
[18] Luth. par Confess. Hospin. part. ii. f. 188.
[19] Epist. ad Gasp. Gustol.
[20] Form. Miss. t. ii. 384, 386.
[21] De Libert. Christ. t. ii. f. 10. 11.
[22] Sleidan, lib. v. xvii.
[23] Luth. T. 11. Jen. 447, Calixt. Jud. N. 49. Hosp. 2. Part. ad an. 1524 f. 38.
[24] Epist. Luth. ad Argent. t. vii. f. 602.
[25] Sleid. lib. v. Ibid. 75.
[26] Sleid. lib. x. p. 77.
[27] Sleid. lib. v. p. 77.
[28] Ep. Luth. ad. Erasm. inter. Erasm. Ep. lib. vi. 3.
[29] Ep. Mel. lib. iv. Ep. 28.
[30] Lib. xviii. Ep. 11, 22.
[31] De Serv. arb. t. ii. 426, 429, 431, 435.
[32] Ibid. f. 444.
[33] Ibid. f. 46 .
[34] Epist. ad. Reg. Ang. t. ii. 92.
[35] Ad maled. Reg. Angliæ. Resp. t. ii. 493. Sleid. lib. v. p. 80.
[36] Ibid. 494. 495.
[37] Christ. Fidei clara expos. 1536. p. 27.
[38] Præf. Balling.
[39] Parv. Conf. Luth. Hosp. p. 2. 187.
[40] Luth. Hom. in Gen. c. iv. 20.
[41] Oper. ii. 6, Declar. de Pec. Orig.
[42] Rom. i. 19.
[43] Declar. de Pec. Orig.
[44] Rom. iv. 15.
[45] Rom. vii. 9.
[46] Rom. vii. 8.
[47] Rom. v. 12, 19.
[48] Ep. Erasm. Lib. vii. Ep. 42, 45.
[49] Erasm. Lib. xiii. Ep. 12, 14. Lib. x.
[50] Lib. xix. Ep. 41.
[51] Ep. Erasm. Lib. xix.
[52] Lib. xviii. Ep. 23, 19, 113, 31, 47, Col. 2057, &c.
[53] Ibid. Lib. xix. Ep. 113, 31, 59. p. 2106.
[54] Lib. 18. Ep. 9.
[55] Hosp. 2 part. ad an. 1225—f. 40

[56] Zuing. Conf. Fid ad Franc. et Epist. ad car. 5.
[57] Hosp. ii. p. 25, 26. Exod. xii. 11
[58] Exod. xii. 11.
[59] Ad Maled. Reg. Ang. t. ii. 498.
[60] Zuing. in explan. artic. 18. Ges. in Bibl. etc. Calix. Judic. 53.
[61] T. ii. J.. epist. p. 2 2.
[62] Calix. Judic. n. 53.
[63] Serm. de Corp. et Sang. Christ. defen. Verbi Cœnæ. t. vii. 277, 381.
[64] Cat. Mag. de Sac. alt. Concord. p. 551.
[65] 1 Cor. xi. 24, 28, 29.
[66] John vi. 63.
[67] Serm. quod verba stent. ibid.
[68] Epist. Luth. ad Hosp. 2 Part, ad An. 1534, f. 132.
[69] Hosp. ad an. 1527, f. 49.
[70] John ii. 9.
[71] Conf. de Mont. Imp. à Gen. 1587, p. 52.
[72] Conf. de Mont. Imp. à Gen. 1587, p. 52.
[73] Syn. Czeng. tit. de Cœna. in Synt. Gen. part 1.
[74] John iv, 50, 51.
[75] Luke xiii, 12.
[76] Vid. Hosp. 2 Part. 12, 35, 47, 61, 76, 161, &c.

[77] Exod. vii. 12, 18.
[78] Luth. ad Jac. Præp. Brem. Hosp. 82. Luth. Maj. Conf. ibidem. Zuing. Resp. ad Luth. Hosp. 44. Lib. iv. Ep. 76, ad Camer.
[79] Serm. quod verba stant. t. iii. Jen. Conf. Maj. t. iv. Jen. Calix. Jud. N. 40. et. seg.
[80] Lib. iv. Ep. 76. 1528
[81] Lib. xviii. 3, xix. 3, 113, xxxi, 59, p. 2108.
[82] Calvin epist. ad Mel. p. 145.
[83] Sleid. Lib. vi. 92. Mel. Lib. iv. Epist. 70.
[84] Ibid.
[85] Mel. Lib. iii. Epist. 16.
[86] Lib. iv. Ep. 70, 72. Ibid. 72
[87] Ibid.
[88] Mel. ibid. Sleid. ibid. Dav. Chyt. in Saxon. ad an 1528, p. 312.
[89] Luth. Ep. ad Vences. Lync. t. vii. et ap. Chyt. in Sax. p. 312 et 982.
[90] Mel. Lib. iv. Ep. 88.
[91] Ibid. Ep. ad Elect. Sax. et ad Hen. Duc. et ap Luth. T. iv. Jen.
[92] Mel.
[93] Hosp. Ibid.
[94] Luth Ep. ad Jen. Præp. Bremens. Ibid.
[95] Luth. Ep. ad Jen.

Book III

A Brief summary.—The Confessions of Faith of both parties of Protestants.—That of Augsburg composed by Melancthon.—That of Strasburg, or of the Four Towns, by Bucer.—That of Zuinglius.—Variations in that of Augsburg concerning the Eucharist.—The ambiguity of that of Strasburg.—Zuinglius alone plainly asserts the figurative sense.—The term substance, why applied to explain the reality.—The Apology of the Augsburg Confession penned by Melancthon.—The Church calumniated in almost every point, chiefly in that of Justification, Operation of the Sacraments, and Mass.—The merit of good works acknowledged on both sides; also Sacramental Absolution, Confession, Monastic Vows, with many other Articles.—The Church of Rome many ways acknowledged in the Confession of Augsburg.—A demonstration, from the Augsburg Confession and Apology, that the Lutherans would return to us, did they but lay aside their calumnies, and well comprehend their own doctrine.

1.—The famous Diet of Augsburg, where the Confessions of Faith are presented to Charles V.

IN the midst of all these differences, preparations were making for the famous Diet of Augsburg, which Charles V had called in order to pacify the troubles which this new gospel had raised in Germany. He came to Augsburg, the 15th of June, 1530. This period is remarkable; for then it was, for the first time, that the Confessions of Faith, published under the name of each party, appeared in form. The Lutherans, defenders of the literal sense, presented to Charles V the Confession of Faith, called the Confession of Augsburg. The four towns of the empire, Strasburg, Meiningen, Lindau, and Constance, which defended the figurative sense, gave in their Confessions of Faith separately to the same prince. This was called the Confession of Strasburg, or of the four towns; and Zuinglius, who was not inclined to be silent on so solemn an occasion, although he was not of the body of the empire, also sent to the emperor his Confession of Faith.

2.—The Confession of Augsburg digested by Melancthon, and presented to the emperor.

Melancthon, the most eloquent, the most polite, and at the same time the most moderate of all the disciples of Luther, drew up the Augsburg Confession in concert with his master, on whom they had prevailed to approach near the place of the diet. This Confession was presented to the emperor in Latin and in German, the 25th of June, 1530, subscribed by John, Elector of Saxony, by six other princes, of whom one of the chief was Philip, Landgrave of Hesse, and by the towns of Nuremberg and Reutlingen, to which four other towns associated themselves. It was read publicly in the diet, in presence of the emperor; and agreed that no copy of it should be spread abroad, either printed or written, but by his orders.[1] Many editions of it have been since made, as well in the German as in the Latin language, all materially differing; and yet it has been received by the whole party.

3.—*Of the Confession of Strasburg, or of the Four Towns, and of Bucer who formed it.*

Those of Strasburg, with their associate defenders of the figurative sense, offered to subscribe it, excepting only the article of the Lord's Supper. They were not admitted on those terms, so they compiled their own confession, which was drawn into form by Bucer.

He was a man of sufficient learning, of a pliant mind, and more fruitful in distinctions than the most refined scholastics; an agreeable preacher; his style something heavy; but the advantage of his figure and sound of voice gained upon his hearers. He had been a Dominican, and was married like the rest, and even, as I may say, more so than the others, for on the death of his first wife he proceeded to a second, and so to a third marriage. The holy fathers received not to priesthood any person who, whilst a layman, had been twice married, Bucer, both a priest and a religious, during his new ministry married three times with scruple. This circumstance recommended him to the party; they wished by these daring examples to confound the superstitious observances of the ancient church.

It does not appear that Bucer had concerted any thing with Zuinglius; the latter with the Swiss spoke plainly and openly; Bucer's thoughts were wholly intent on compounding matters, and never was man so fertile in equivocations. Yet neither he nor his party could at that time unite themselves with the Lutherans, and the new reformation made two bodies visibly separated by two different confessions of faith.

After they had been drawn up, these Churches seemed to have assumed their last form, and it was time, at least at that juncture, to hold themselves steady; but, on the contrary, here it was they betrayed most of their variations.

4.—*Of the Confession of Augsburg, and its Apology; the authority of these two pieces throughout the whole party.*

The Augsburg Confession is the most considerable of all in every respect. Besides that it was first presented and subscribed by a greater body, and received with more ceremony, it has also this advantage, that it was considered afterwards, not only by Bucer, and by Calvin himself in particular, as a work common to the Reformation, but also by the whole party of the figurative sense assembled in a body, as will appear from what follows. The Emperor had caused some Catholic divines to refute it; Merlancthon made its Apology, which he enlarged a short time after. This Apology, however, must not be regarded as a particular work, since it was presented to the Emperor in the name of the whole party who laid before him the Confession of Augsburg, and the Lutherans have held no assembly since that time to declare their belief, in which the Confession of Augsburg and Apology were not placed by them upon equal authority, as appears from the acts of the assembly of Smalkald, in 1537, and from others.[2]

5.—*The tenth article of the Confession of Augsburg, which relates to the Lord's Supper, expressed four different ways.—The Variations of the two first.*

It is certain, the intention of the Confession of Augsburg was to establish the real presence of the body and blood; and, as the Lutherans say in the Book of Concord, "It was then expressly designed to reject the error of the Sacramentarians, who, at the same time, presented their own particular Confession of Augsburg."[3] But the Lutherans were so far from speaking in a uniform manner on this subject, that, on the contrary, we see at first sight the tenth article of their confession, which is that in which they design to establish the reality; we behold, I say, this tenth article couched in four different forms, being scarcely able to discern which is the most authentic, since they all appeared in editions which had the marks of public authority.

Of these four ways we see two in the Geneva Collection, where the Confession of Augsburg is delivered to us as it was printed in 1540, at Wittenberg, the birthplace of Lutheranism, in the presence of Luther and Melancthon. We there read the article of the last supper two different ways. In the first, which is that of the Wittenberg edition, it is said, that "with the bread and wine, the body and blood of Jesus Christ are truly given to those who partake of the supper."[4] The second speaks not of bread and wine, and is expressed in these terms; "They (the Protestant churches) believe that the body and blood are truly distributed to those who eat, and disapprove of those who teach the contrary."[5]

Here is a variation of the first step of sufficient importance, since the last of these expressions agrees with the doctrine of the change of substance, and the other seems calculated to oppose it. The Lutherans, however, stopped not there; and although, of the two ways of expressing the tenth article, which appear in the Geneva Collection, they have followed the last in their Book of Concord, at the place where the Augsburg Confession is there inserted; however, this same tenth article is seen two other ways expressed in the same book.[6]

6.—*Two other ways in which the same Article is couched, and their differences.*

And truly, the Apology of the Augsburg Confession will be found in this book, where the same Melancthon who had drawn it up, and defends it, transcribes the article in these terms: "In the Lord's Supper the body and blood of Jesus Christ are truly and substantially present, and are truly given together with the things that are seen, that is, with the bread and wine, to those who receive the sacrament."

In fine, we also find these words in the same Book of Concord: "The article of the supper is thus taught from the word of God in the Augsburg

Confession: that the true body and the true blood of Jesus Christ are truly present, distributed and received in the holy supper, under the species of bread and wine; and those are disapproved of who teach the contrary."[7] And it is in this manner also that the tenth article is delivered in the French version of the Confession of Augsburg, printed at Frankfort in 1673.[8]

If these two ways of expressing the reality be compared, there is no person who does not see that this of the Apology expresses it in stronger words than did the two preceding ones from the collection of Geneva, but at the same time departs farther from transubstantiation; and that the last, on the contrary, accommodates itself to the expressions which the Church makes use of, that Catholics might subscribe it.

7.—Which of these ways is the original one.

If it be asked, which of these four ways is the original one presented to Charles V, the thing admits of no small doubt.

Hospinian maintains the last to be the original because it is that which appears in the impression which was made in the year 1530, at Wittenberg, that is in the seat of Lutheranism, the abode of Luther and Melancthon.[9]

He adds the cause why this article was changed, because it too openly favored transubstantiation, signifying the body and blood to be truly received, not with the substance, but under the species of bread and wine, which is the very expression made use of by Catholics.

And this is the very thing which enforces the belief that the article was thus expressed at first, since it is certain from Sleidan and Melancthon, as well as from Celestin and Chytræus, in their histories of the Confession of Augsburg, that the Catholics contradicted not this article in the refutation of the Augsburg Confession, which they there made by the order of the Emperor.[10]

Of these four ways, the second was that which was inserted in the Book of Concord; and it might seem that this was the most authentic, because the princes and states who subscribed this book, seem to affirm in the preface that they transcribed the Augsburg confession, as it is still to be found in the archives of their predecessors, and in those of the empire.[11] But, upon more exact inquiry, this will be found inconclusive, since the authors of this preface only say, that having compared their copies with the archives, "they found that theirs was wholly and throughout of the same sense with the Latin or German originals;" which shows the pretension of agreeing in substance with the other editions, but not the positive fact, that is, that the words are throughout the same; otherwise, such different ones would not be found in another part of the same book, as we observed before.

Be that as it may, as the Confession of Augsburg could be presented to the emperor but in one way, it is strange there should appear three others so different from that, and altogether as authentic, as we have just seen, and that so solemn an act should be so many times altered by its authors in an article so essential.

8.—*The Fifth way in which this same Tenth Article is expressed in the Apology of the Confession of Augsburg.*

But they stopped not in so fine a way, but immediately after the Confession of Augsburg, they gave the emperor a fifth explication of the article of the supper, in the Apology for their Confession of Faith, drawn up at their order by Melancthon.

In this Apology, Melancthon being careful to express in formal terms the literal sense, approved, as has been seen, by the whole party, was not content to have already acknowledged a true and substantial presence, adding, that Christ was "corporeally given to us," and that this was the "ancient and common" sentiment, not only of the "Church of Rome," but also of the "Greek Church."[12]

9.—*The manner in which the Reality is explained in the Apology, tends at the same time to establish the Change of Substance.*

And although this author but little favors the change of substance even in this book, yet his dislike to it is not so great, but that he makes honorable mention of the authorities which establish it; for in order to prove his doctrine of the "corporeal presence," from the sentiment of the eastern church, he cites the canon of the Greek mass, when the priest prays expressly, says he, that the proper body of Jesus Christ be made in the change of bread, or by the change of bread. Far from condemning anything in this prayer, he makes use of it as a record whose authority he owns; and with the same judgment produces the words of Theophylas, archbishop of Bulgaria, who affirms that the bread is not the figure only, but is truly changed into flesh.[13] It also happens, that of the three authorities which he adduces to confirm the doctrine of the real presence, two there are which assert the change of substance; so necessarily do these two truths follow each other, so natural a connexion is there between them. When these passages, which appeared at the first publication, were afterwards mutilated in some editions by the enemies of transubstantiation, it was because they were displeased that they could not establish the reality, which they approved, without admitting transubstantiation at the same time, which they had been determined to deny.

10.—*The evasion of the Lutherans, with regard to these Variations.*

Such were the uncertainties into which the Lutherans fell at their commencement; no sooner did they undertake to give a settled form to their church, by a confession of faith, than they were so irresolute, that they immediately published an article of such importance as that of the Eucharist, in five or six different forms. They were not more unchangeable, as shall be seen, in the other articles: and what they commonly answer, that the council of Constantinople added something to that of Nice, avails them nothing; for the truth is, a new heresy rising up, after the council of Nice, which denied the divinity of the Holy Ghost, it was necessary to add some words for its condemnation; but in our present case, where nothing new occurred, it was nothing but want of steadiness which introduced among the Lutherans the variations we have seen.

11.—The Sacramentarians are not more steady in explaining their Faith.

If the defenders of the figurative sense reply that their party fell not into similar inconsistencies, let then not flatter themselves with this persuasion. In the "Diet of Augsburg," where the confessions of faith commence, it has been demonstrated that the Sacramentarians at first produced two different ones; and we shall soon see the diversity of them. In course of time they were not less fruitful in different confessions of faith than the Lutherans, and have appeared no less embarrassed, no less uncertain, in the defence of the figurative, than the others in that of the literal sense.

This is what may justly surprise us; for it would seem that a doctrine so easy to be understood, according to human reason, as is that of the Sacramentarians, should afford no embarrassment to those who undertook to explain it. But it is because the words of Jesus Christ naturally made an impression of reality on the mind, which all the refined subtleties of the figurative sense are not able to destroy. As, therefore, the greatest part of those who opposed it, could not divest themselves of this entirely; and, on the other hand, were desirous to please the Lutherans, who retained it, we must not be surprised that, with their figurative interpretations, they mingle so many expressions which savor of the reality; nor that, having left the true idea of the real presence taught them by the Church, they were so pressed to please themselves with the terms they had chosen, in order to retain some image of it.

12.—The indefinite and ambiguous expressions of the Confession of Strasburg,
on the article of the Lord's Supper.

This was the cause which introduced these equivocations, we shall see, into their Catechisms and Confessions of Faith. Bucer, the great architect of all these subtleties, gave a slight specimen of them in the Strasburg Confession; for, though unwilling to make use of the same terms as the Lutherans to explain the real presence, he affects to say nothing that might be contrary to it, and expresses himself in words ambiguous enough to bear that sense. Thus he speaks, or rather makes those of Strasburg and the others to speak: "When Christians repeat the supper, which Jesus Christ made before his death, in the manner that he instituted it, he gives to them, by the Sacraments, his true body and blood to eat and drink truly, to be the food and drink of souls."[14]

In reality, they say not with the Lutherans, "That this body, and this blood, are truly given with the bread and wine;" and yet less, "that they are truly and substantially given;" Bucer, as yet, had not proceeded so far; but he says nothing contrary to it, and nothing, in fact, which a Lutheran, and even a Catholic might not approve. We all consenting to this, "that the true body and true blood of our Lord are given to us to eat and drink truly" not for the food of bodies, but, as Bucer said, for the food of souls. So this confession kept itself within general expressions; and even when it says, "We truly eat and drink the true body and true blood of our Lord," it seems to exclude eating and drinking by faith; which, indeed, is no more than a metaphorical eating and drinking: so much were they afraid of acknowledging that the body and blood are only spiritually given, and of inserting into a confession of faith, what to Christians was so great a novelty. For although the Eucharist, as well as the other mysteries of our salvation, had a spiritual effect for its end, it had, like the other mysteries, that which was accomplished in the body for its foundation.—Jesus Christ was to be born, to die, to be spiritually risen again in the faithful; yet he was also to be born, to die, and to rise again really, and according to the flesh. In the same manner, we were to partake spiritually of his sacrifice; yet also we were corporally to receive the flesh of this victim, and to eat of it indeed. We were to be united spiritually to the heavenly spouse; yet his body which he gave to us in the Eucharist, in order to a mutual possession of ours, was to the pledge and seal, as well as the foundation of this spiritual union; and this divine marriage, as well as the ordinary ones, though in a far different way, was to unite minds by uniting bodies. To speak therefore of the spiritual union was, in reality, to explain the last end of this mystery; but to that intent, the corporal union, on which the other was grounded, ought not to have been forgotten. At least, since it was that which separated the Churches, they ought, in a confession of faith, to have spoken distinctly for or against it,—a course which Bucer had not sufficient resolution to pursue.

13.—*The progress of these same ambiguities, and the remarkable effect they had on those towns that subscribed to them.*

He was fully sensible he should be reproved for his silence; and to obviate the objection, after having said in general, "That we truly eat and drink the true body and true blood of our Lord, for the food of our souls," he makes those of Strasburg say, "that keeping themselves at a distance from all dispute, and all curious and superfluous inquiry, they call back the mind to that only which profits, and which by our Saviour was alone regarded, namely, that, feeding on him, we may live in him, and by him:"[15] as if explaining the principle end proposed by our Saviour were sufficient, without speaking one way or the other of the Real Presence, which the Lutherans, as well as Catholics, granted to be the means.

Having declared these things, they conclude, by protesting "that they are calumniated when they are accused of changing the words of Jesus Christ, and mutilating them by human interpretations, or of administering nothing in their supper but mere bread and wine, or of despising the Lord's Supper; for, on the contrary," they say, "we exhort the faithful to give ear to the words of the Lord with a simple faith, by rejecting all false comments, and all human inventions, and by adhering closely to the sense of the words, without hesitating in any way; finally, by receiving the sacraments for the food of their souls."

Who condemns not, with them, superfluous refinements, human inventions, false comments on the words of our Lord? What Christian does not profess to adhere closely to the sense of these divine words? But since this sense had been the subject of disputation for six whole years, and so many conferences had been held to settle it, they ought to have determined what it was, and what were those false glosses which were to be rejected. What advantage is it to condemn that in general, and by indefinite terms, which is rejected by all parties? and who sees not, that a confession of faith requires decisions more clear and more precise? Certainly, were we to judge of Bucer's sentiments, and those of his brethren, by this Confession of Faith only, and knew not from other sources that they were not favorable to the Real and Substantial Presence, we might believe they were not, at least, far from it. They have terms to flatter those who believe it, others by which to escape if pressed; in a word, we may say, without doing them an injustice, that whilst confessions of faith are generally made to explain our thoughts on disputes which disturb the peace of the Church, these, on the contrary, by lengthened discourses and tedious circumlocution, discovered the secret of saying nothing distinctly on the subject of discussion.

From thence an odd effect followed: namely, that of the four towns which had united themselves by this common confession of faith, and had all embraced, at that time, sentiments contrary to the Lutherans, three, namely, Strasburg, Meningen, and Lindau, without scruple, a short time afterwards, went over to the doctrine of the Real Presence: so well had Bucer succeeded by his ambiguous discourses in rendering their minds pliant, so that they could easily turn to any side.

14.—*The Confession of Faith of Zuinglius very clear and free from all equivocation.*

Zuinglius dealt more frankly. In the Confessions of Faith which he sent to Augsburg, and which received the approbation of all the Swiss, he declared plainly, "That the body of Jesus Christ, after his ascension, was no where else but in Heaven; nay, could be no where else; that truly, in the supper, it was, as it were, present by the contemplation of faith, and not really, or by its essence."[16]

To defend this doctrine, he wrote a letter to the Emperor and the Protestant Princes, where he establishes this difference between him and his adversaries; that these would have "a natural and substantial body, and he a sacramental body."[17] He is uniform in the use of the same language; and in another Confession of Faith, which, at the same time, he directs to Francis the First, he explains, "This is my body," "of a symbolical, mystical, and sacramental body; of a body by denomination and signification;" in the same manner," says he, "as a queen, showing amongst her jewels her nuptial ring, says readily, 'This is my king, that is, this is the ring of the king my husband, wherewith he hath espoused me.'"[18] I know not of any queen that ever used such an odd phrase; but it was not easy for Zuinglius to find, in ordinary language, such a mode of speaking as he would ascribe to our Saviour. Nay, he acknowledges no more in the Eucharist than a moral presence, which he calls "Sacramental and Spiritual." He always places the force of the sacraments in this,"that they assist the contemplation of faith; that they serve for a bridle to the senses, and make them concur better with the thoughts." As to the manducation, "which the Jews understood in the same sense with the Papists," according to him, "it ought to cause the like horror a father would feel who has his son given him to eat." In general, "faith has a horror of a visible and corporal presence, which makes St. Peter say, 'depart from me, O Lord;' Jesus Christ must not be eaten in this carnal and gross way: a faithful and religious soul eats his true body sacramentally and spiritually." Sacramentally, that is to say, in sign; spiritually, that is, by the contemplation of faith, which represents to us Jesus Christ suffering, and shows us he is wholly ours.

15.—*The state of the question appears clearly in the Confession of Zuinglius.*

It is not our business here to complain, that he calls our manducation gross and carnal, though so much elevated above the senses; nor that he would raise a horror of it, as a cruel and bloody object. These are the usual reproaches which those of his party have ever made to us and the Lutherans. We shall see, by what follow, how those who now reproach will justify us; it is enough that we here observe, that Zuinglius speaks plainly. From these two Confessions of Faith we learn in what the difficulty precisely consists; on one side, a presence in sign, and by faith; on the other, a real and substantial presence; and this it is which separated the Sacramentarians from Catholics and Lutherans.

16.—*What reason there was for making use of the word Substance in the Eucharist; that it is the same which made it necessary in the Trinity.*

It will now be easy to comprehend what was the reason why the defenders of the literal sense, both Catholics and Lutherans, used so much the words "true body, real body, substance, proper substance," and others of a similar nature. They made use of the words "real and true," to signify that the Eucharist was not a mere sign of the body and blood, but the very thing itself.

For this reason, also, they employed the word substance; and if we trace it up to its origin, we shall find, that what introduced this word into the mystery of the Trinity, rendered it likewise necessary in the mystery of the Eucharist. Before the subtleties of heretics had confounded the true sense of these words of our Saviour, "I and my father are one,"[19] the perfect unity of the Father and Son was believed to be sufficiently expressed by this text of Scripture, without the necessity of always saying they were one in substance; but ever since the time that heretics would persuade the faithful the unity of the Father and Son was only a unity of concord, of thought, of affection, it was deemed expedient to banish these pernicious equivocal terms, by establishing consubstantiality—namely, the unity of substance. This term, which was not in Scripture, was judged necessary to the right understanding of it, and keeping at a distance the dangerous interpretations of those who adulterated the simplicity of God's word.

By adding these expressions to Scripture, it was not pretended it explained itself, in respect of that mystery, obscurely or ambiguously; but it grew out of the necessity which existed of opposing by these express words the evil interpretations of heretics, and of preserving that nature and primitive

Scripture sense, which would immediately have made impression on the mind, were not the ideas confused by prejudice or false subtleties.

It is easy to apply this to the subject of the Eucharist. Had the natural and just sense, without refinement, been preserved of these words "This is my body, this is my blood," we should have thought we had sufficiently explained a real presence of Jesus Christ in the Eucharist, by saying, that what he there gives is his body and blood; but since it has been said that Jesus Christ was then present in figure only, or by his spirit, or by his virtue, or by faith, then, to remove all ambiguity, it was believed necessary to say, that the body of our Lord was given to us in its proper and true substance, or what comes to the same, that he was really and substantially present. It is this which gave rise to the term Transubstantiation, just as natural to express a change in substance, as that of consubstantial was to express a unity of substance.

17.—*The Lutherans had the same reason as we to make use of the word Substance; Zuinglius never used it, nor Bucer at the commencement.*

For the same reason, the Lutherans, who acknowledge the reality without the change of substance, when they rejected the term Transubstantiation, retained that of "the true and substantial presence," as we have seen in the Apology of the Augsburg Confession; and these terms were chosen to fix the natural sense of these words, "This is my body," as the word consubstantial was chosen by the fathers of Nicæa to fit the literal sense on these words, "I and my Father are one," and these other, the "Word was God."

Accordingly, we do not find that Zuinglius, who first reduced to form the opinion of the figurative sense, and explained it in the frankest manner, ever employed the word substance. On the contrary, he perpetually excluded "the manducation" as well as the substantial "presence," in order that he might leave nothing but a figurative manducation, that is, "in spirit and by faith."[20]

Bucer, although more inclined to ambiguous expressions, did not, in the beginning, make use of the word substance, or communion and substantial presence, but was content not to condemn these terms, and confined himself only to the general expression which we have seen. Such was the first state of the Sacramentarian controversy, into which Bucer's subtleties introduced afterwards such a number of unseasonable variations as we shall be obliged to relate in the sequel. For the present it is sufficient to have pointed out the cause.

18.—*Of the doctrine of Justification; that there is no difficulty in it after what has been said on it in the Confession of Augsburg and in the Apology.*

The question of justification, in which that of free-will was contained, seemed to Protestants of a far different importance, for which reason they twice demand of the emperor, in the Apology, a particular attention to this subject, as being the most important of the whole gospel, and that also on which they have labored most.[21] But I hope it will soon be discovered they have labored in vain, to say nothing more, and that in this dispute there is much more of misunderstanding than real difficulty.

19.—*That the doctrine of Luther on Free-Will is retracted in the Confession of Augsburg.*

And first, we must remove from this dispute the question of free-will. Luther had returned from that excess, which induced him to say, that God's prescience wholly destroyed free-will in all creatures; and had consented to have this article placed in the Augsburg Confession:—"That free-will is to be acknowledged in all men that have the use of reason, not for the things of God, which men cannot commence or at least finish without him, but only with regard to the works of this present life and the duties of civil society."[22] Melancthon added to it in the Apology, "with respect to the exterior works of God's law."[23] These are two truths already which admit of no discussion; one, that there is a free-will; and the other, that of itself it can do nothing in works that are truly Christian.

20.—*A word in the Augsburg Confession which tended to Semi-Pelagianism.*

There was, moreover, a word, in that passage we have just seen of the Augsburg Confession, which, from men who would attribute all to grace, was not near so correct as we speak in the Catholic Church. It is in that place where it is said, that of itself "free-will cannot commence, or at least finish the things of God," a restriction which seems to insinuate it can at "least commence" them by its proper strength—a Semi-Pelagian error, from which we shall hereafter see the Lutherans at present are not far removed. The following article[24] explained how "the will of the wicked was the cause of sin;" where, although it be not distinctly enough said that God is not the author of it, as much at least was insinuated, in opposition to the first maxims of Luther.

21.—*All the reproaches made to Catholics founded on calumnies; the first calumny on gratuitous Justification.*

But what is most remarkable, with respect to the other points of Christian grace in the Confession of Augsburg is this, that it every where supposes errors in the Catholic Church, which errors were always detested by her; so that they seemed rather to have sought a subject for quarrelling than reforming, and the thing will appear manifest upon expounding historically the belief of the one and the other.

In the Confession of Augsburg and in the Apology, they grounded themselves much on the remission of sins being purely the result of generosity which ought not to be attributed to the merit and worth of precedent actions. Strange! the Lutherans every where ascribed to themselves the honor of this doctrine, as if they had brought it back again into the Church, and reproached Catholics, "that they believed they obtained forgiveness of their sins by their own works; that they believed they could merit it by doing, on their side, what they were able, and even by their own strength; that all they attributed to Jesus Christ was the having merited for us a certain habitual grace, whereby we may more easily love God; and although the will had it in its power to love him, it did it more willingly from this habit; that they taught no other justice than that of reason; that we could draw near to God by our proper works, independently of the propitiation of Jesus Christ, and that we had dreamt of a justification without speaking one word of him;"[25] which they repeat incessantly, to conclude as often, "That we had buried Jesus Christ."

22.—*They attributed to Catholics two propositions that were contradictory: 'ex opere operato,' what it means.*

But whilst they reproached Catholics with so gross an error, they, on the other hand, imputed to them the opposite sentiment, accusing them of "believing themselves justified by the sole use of the sacrament, 'ex opere operato,' as they speak in schools, without any good disposition."[26] How could the Lutherans imagine, that amongst us so much was given to man, and at the same time so little? But both one and the other are very distant from our doctrine, inasmuch as the Council of Trent is quite full, on the one side, of the good sentiments by which we ought to dispose ourselves for baptism, for penance, and for communion, declaring even in express terms, "that the reception of grace is voluntary;" and on the other side, it teaches, that the forgiveness of sins is purely gratuitous; and that all which prepares us for it, either proximately or remotely, from the beginning of the vocation and the first horrors of a conscience shaken by fear, even to the most perfect act of charity, is the gift of God."[27]

23.—*According to the Lutheran doctrine, the Sacraments operate 'ex opere operato.'*

True it is, we say with regard to infants, that by his infinite mercy baptism sanctifies them, though they co-operate not by any good motives to this great work; but besides, that in this the merit of Jesus Christ, together with the efficacy of his blood, displays itself, the Lutherans themselves say as much; they themselves confessing that "little children ought to be baptized; that baptism is necessary for their salvation; and that by this sacrament they are made the children of God."[28] Is not this an acknowledgment of the force of the sacrament, of itself and by its own action effectual, "ex opere operato," in children? For I do not find that the Lutherans consider themselves bound to maintain with Luther, that children brought to baptism, produce therein an act of faith. They must then necessarily say with us, that the sacrament, by which they become regenerated, operates by its own proper virtue.

If it be objected, that amongst us the sacrament has the same efficacy in the adult, and operates in them 'ex opere operato,' it is easy to comprehend that this is not admitted to exclude the necessary good dispositions in them, but only to show that what God works in us, when he sanctifies us by the sacrament, is above all our merits, all our works, all our foregoing dispositions; in a word, the pure effect of his grace, and of the infinite merits of Jesus Christ.

24.—*That according to the Council of Trent, the remission of sins is purely gratuitous.*

There is no merit therefore of ours that obtains the remission of sins; and the Confession of Augsburg ought not to have assumed the glory of this doctrine, as if it were peculiar to itself; since the Council of Trent equally acknowledged, "that we are said to be justified gratuitously, because all that precedes justification, whether faith or works, cannot merit this grace;" conformably to what the Apostle says, "if it be grace, it is not therefore works, otherwise grace is no longer grace."[29]

Here then is the remission of sins, and justification gratuitously and without merit, established in as express terms in the Catholic Church as it could possibly have been done in the Confession of Augsburg.

25.—*The second calumny on the Merit of Works; that is is acknowledged in the Augsburg Confession, and by Luther, in the same sense as it is in the Church.*

If after the remission of sins, when the Holy Ghost dwells, and charity reigns in us, and the soul is rendered agreeable by a gratuitous bounty, we acknowledge merit in our good works,—the Confession of Augsburg agrees with us in this, seeing that in the Geneva edition, printed after that of Wittenberg, which was made under the inspection of Luther and Melancthon, we read that "the new obedience is reputed a justice, AND MERITS reward." And yet more expressly, that "although far distant from the perfection of the law, it is a justice, AND MERITS reward." And a little after, that "good works are worthy of great praises, that they are necessary, and that THEY MERIT recompenses."[30]

Afterwards, explaining these words of the Gospel, "Whosoever hath, to him shall be given," it says, "that our action must be joined to God's gifts, which it preserves in us; and that IT MERITS their increase;" and praises this saying of St. Austin,[31] "that charity, when it is exercised, MERITS the increase of charity." Here then is our co-operation necessary in express terms, and its merit confirmed by the Confession of Augsburg. Therefore they thus conclude this article: "thereby good men may understand what true good works are, and how they please God, and how THEY ARE MERITORIOUS."[32] Merit cannot be better established, nor more inculcated; nor does the Council of Trent insist further on this matter.

All this was taken from Luther, and from the grounds of his sentiments; for in his commentary on the Epistle to the Galatians, he writes, that "where he speaks of justifying faith, he means that which works by charity; for," says he, "faith MERITS that the Holy Ghost be given us."[33] He had just said, that with this Holy Ghost all virtues are given us, and it was thus he explained justification in that famous commentary: it was printed at Wittenberg, in 1553, so that twenty years after Luther had commenced the Reformation, nothing as yet was found in merit that deserved correction.

26.—*The Apology asserts the Merit of Works.*

It must not then be a matter of surprise, if in the Apology of the Augsburg Confession, this opinion be found so strongly grounded. There Melancthon makes new efforts to explain the subject of justification, as his letters testify, where he thus teaches, "that there are rewards proposed and promised to the good works of the faithful, and that they are MERITORIOUS, not of forgiveness of sins or of justification, (which we have not otherwise than by faith,) but of other corporal and spiritual rewards in this life, and that to come;" according to what St. Paul saith, "that each one shall receive his reward according to his works."[34] And Melancthon is so full of this truth that he confirms it anew in the answer to the objections by these words: "We confess, as we have often done already, that although justification and life eternal appertain to faith, good works, however, MERIT other corporal and spiritual rewards, and different degrees of rewards, according to what St. Paul says, 'that each one shall be rewarded according to his labor:' for gospel justice being occupied about the promise of grace, gratuitously receives justification and life; but the fulfilling of the law, which proceeds as the result of faith, is occupied about the law itself; and then the recompense, continues he, IS OFFERED NOT GRATUITOUSLY, but according to works, AND IT IS DUE; and according those WHO MERIT this reward are justified before they fulfil the law."[35]

Thus the merit of works is constantly recognized by those of the Augsburg Confession as a thing comprised in the notion of a reward, there being nothing indeed more naturally united than merit on one side, when reward is promised and proposed on the other.

And verily, what they reprehend in Catholics is not their admission of merit, which is also asserted by them, but is, says the Apology, "that as often as merit is spoken of, they transfer it from other rewards to justification."[36] If, then, we acknowledge no merit but what follows and not precedes justification, the difficulty will be removed; and it is the very thing that was done at Trent by this decision,"that we are said to be gratuitously justified, because not any of those things, whether faith, or works, which precede justification, can merit it."[37] And again, "that our sins are gratuitously forgiven us, by the divine mercy, for the sake of Jesus Christ."[38] Whence it follows, also, that the Council admits no merit, "but in regard to the augmentation of grace, and life eternal."[39]

27.—Melancthon is inconsistent with himself in the Apology, when he there denies that good works merit eternal life.

As to the augmentation of grace, it was agreed to at Augsburg, as already seen; and for life eternal, true it is, Melancthon would not acknowledge it was merited by good works, since, according to him, they merited other recompenses only, which are promised to them in this life and the next. But when Melancthon spoke this, he did not reflect what he had said in this same place, that it is "eternal glory which is due to those who are justified," according to this saying of St. Paul, "Those whom he hath justified, he hath glorified also."[40] Again, he reflected not that eternal life is the true recompense promised by Jesus Christ to good works, conformably to that text of the Gospel cited by him in another place in support of merit, that those who shall obey the Gospel "shall receive a hundred fold, in this world, and life everlasting in the next;"[41] where is seen, besides the hundred fold which shall be our recompense in this life, that life eternal is promised as our reward in the life to come: so that if merit is grounded on the promise of a recompense, as Melancthon asserts, and with truth, nothing is more merited than eternal life, though, in other respects, nothing more gratuitous, according to that excellent doctrine of St. Augustin, "Life eternal is due to the merits of good works; but the merits unto which it is due are gratuitously given us by our Lord Jesus Christ."[42]

28.—*That there is something in eternal life which falls not under merit.*

It is also true, that what prevents Melancthon from absolutely holding eternal life as a recompense promised to good works, is, that eternal life being always, in a certain manner, annexed to grace, it is without works given to little children, and would be given to the adult in case they were even surprised by death the very moment they were justified, without their having had time to act afterwards; which prevents not, in another respect, the eternal kingdom, eternal glory, eternal life, from being promised as a reward to good works, and also from being merited, in the sense expressed by the Augsburg Confession.

29.—*Variations of the Lutherans in that which they curtailed in the Confession of Augsburg.*

What does it avail the Lutherans to have altered this Confession, and to have erased in their Book of Concord, and other editions, those passages which sanction merit? Can they, by this act, prevent this confession of faith from having been printed at Wittenberg, under the eyes of Luther and Melancthon, with no contradiction from any of the party, and with all the passages we have cited? What other effect does the erasure of them produce, but to make us remark the force and importance of them? But to what purpose is it to erase the merit of good works in the Confession of Augsburg, whilst they themselves leave it as entire in the Apology, as they have caused it to be printed in their Book of Concord? Is it not certain the Apology was presented to Charles V by the same princes and in the same diet as the Confession of Augsburg?[43] But what is still more remarkable, it was presented, as the Lutherans confess, "in order to preserve its true and proper sense;"[44] for so it is worded in an authentic writing, in which the Protestant princes and states declare their faith. Therefore, it is not to be doubted but the merit of works is agreeable to the spirit of Lutheranism, and of the Confession of Augsburg, and it is unjustly that the Lutherans disturb the Church of Rome on this head.

30.—*Three other calumnies against the Church.*—*The fulfilling of the law acknowledged in the Apology in the same sense as in the Church.*

I foresee, however, it may be said they have not approved the merit of works in the same sense as we do, for three reasons;—first because they do not acknowledge with us, that the just man can and ought to fulfil the law; secondly, because for this very reason they do not admit that merit which is called of condignity, whereof all our books are full; thirdly, because they teach that the good works of man justified stand in need of the gratuitous acceptation of God in order to obtain for us eternal life, which they will not allow that we admit. Here, it will be said, are three characters by which the doctrine of the Confession of Augsburg and of the Apology will stand separated externally from ours. But these three characters subsist not, except by as many misrepresentations of our belief: for, in the first place, if we say we ought to satisfy the law, the whole world agrees in it, since all agree we ought to love, and the Scripture pronounces that "love or charity is the fulfilling of the law."[45] There is even an express chapter in the Apology which bears this title: "Of love and the fulfilling of the Law."[46] And we have just seen in it, that "the fulfilling of the law proceeds as the result of justification;" and this is there repeated in a hundred places, and cannot be called in question. But further, it is not true that we pretend, after one is justified, he satisfies the law of God in full rigor, since, on the contrary, we are taught by the Council of Trent that we are daily under the necessity of saying, "Forgive us our trespasses."[47] So that, however perfect our justice may be, there is always something God amends in it by his grace, renews by his holy spirit, supplies by his bounty.

31.—*The merit of Condignity.*

As to the merit of condignity, besides that the Council of Trent has not made use of this term, the thing bears no difficulty, since, at the bottom, it is agreed upon, that after justification, that is, after the person has become agreeable, and the Holy Ghost dwells, and charity reigns in him, the Scripture attributes to him a kind of dignity: "They shall walk with me in white because they are worthy."[48] But the Council of Trent has clearly explained that all this worthiness proceeds from grace; and the Catholics have declared it to the Lutherans ever since the time of the Augsburg Confession, as appears from the history of David Chytræus, and from that of George Cælestin, both Lutheran authors.[49] Both these historians give an account of the confutation of the Augsburg Confession made by the Catholics at the Emperor's command, when they declare,"that man cannot merit eternal life by his own proper strength, and without the grace of God, and that all Catholics confess our works of themselves are not of any merit; but that the grace of God render them worthy of eternal life."

32.—*The merit of Congruity.*

With regard to the good works we perform before we are justified—because the person then is neither agreeable nor just, on the contrary, is accounted still as in sin, and an enemy—in this state he is incapable of any true merit; and the merit of congruity or seemliness which divines allow in him, is not, in their opinion, any true merit, but a merit improperly so called, which has no further signification, than that it is suitable to the Divine Goodness to have a regard to the sighs and tears which he himself has inspired into the sinner who begins to be converted.

This same must be answered with regard to alms which a sinner bestows to "redeem his sins," according to the advice of Daniel;[50] and to that "charity which covereth the multitude of sins,"[51] and forgiveness promised by Jesus Christ himself to "those who forgive their brethren."[52] The Apology answers here, that Jesus Christ does not add "By doing alms, or by forgiving, one merits forgiveness, *ex opere operato*, in virtue of this action, but in virtue of faith."[53] Who has ever said that good works, which please God, must not be done according to the spirit of faith, without which, as St. Paul says "it is impossible to please God?"[54] Or who ever thought that these good works, and the faith which produces them, merited forgiveness of sins *ex opere operato*, and were capable of operating it of themselves? None so much as ever thought of employing this expression, *ex opere operato,* in the good works of the faithful; it was applied only to the Sacraments, which are nothing but instruments of God. It was employed to show that their action was divine, all-powerful, and effectual of itself; and nothing but a calumny, or gross ignorance, could suppose that in Catholic doctrine, good works wrought, after this manner, the forgiveness of sins, and justifying grace. God, who inspires them, has regard thereunto, of his bounty for the sake of Jesus Christ; not because we are worthy he should have a regard to them in order to justify us, but because it is worthy of him to look down with pity on humble hearts, and therein complete his own work. Such is the merit of congruity, which may be attributed to man even before he is justified. The thing, at bottom, is indisputable; and truly, if the term displeases, it is not used in the Council of Trent, even by the Church herself.

33.—The Mediation of Jesus Christ always necessary.

But although God looks with another eye on sinners already justified, and the works which he then produces by his spirit dwelling in them tend more immediately to eternal life, it is not true, according to us, that a voluntary acceptation of them is not requisite on God's part, because all is here grounded, as says the Council of Trent, on the promise which "God has made to us mercifully," that is gratuitously, "for the sake of Jesus Christ,"[55] of giving eternal life to our good works, without which we could not promise ourselves so high a recompense. Thus, when in the Confession of Augsburg, and the Apology,[56] it is every where objected against us, that after justification we believe we have no further need of Jesus Christ's mediation, we cannot be more visibly calumniated; since, beside that it is through Jesus Christ alone we preserve the grace received, we stand in need of God's incessantly having regard to that promise which he of his sole mercy, and by the blood of the Mediator, has made unto us in the new covenant.

34.—How the merits of Jesus Christ appertain to us; and how they are imputed to us.

In a word, whatever the Lutheran doctrine has that is good, had not only been entire in the Church, but also had been much better explained, inasmuch as all false ideas were clearly removed from it. The truth of this assertion appears principally in the doctrine of imputed justice. The Lutherans imagined they had discovered something wonderful and peculiar to themselves, when they said, "God imputed to us the justice of Jesus Christ, who had perfectly satisfied for us, and rendered his merits ours." Yet the Scholastics, so much censured by them, were full of this doctrine. Who amongst us has not ever believed and taught that Jesus Christ superabundantly satisfied for men, and that the Eternal

Father, contented with this satisfaction of his Son, dealt with us as favorably as if we ourselves had satisfied his justice? If this be all that is understood, when the justice of Jesus Christ is said to be imputed to us, it is what no one doubted, nor should they have disturbed the whole world, nor taken on themselves the title of reformers, for so known and so avowed a doctrine. The Council of Trent did acknowledge, with sufficient fulness, that "the merits of Jesus Christ, and of his passion," were rendered ours by justification, since it repeats so often, "that by it they are communicated to us," and without it none can be justified.[57]

35.—Justification, regeneration, sanctification, renovation, how in substance they are all the same grace.

What Catholics, together with this council, understand, when, not satisfied with the simple imputation of the merits of Jesus Christ, they permit not that alone to be relied on, is, that God himself is not satisfied with that only; but in order to apply those merits to us, he at the same time regenerates us, vivifies us, renovates us, diffuses his holy spirit into us, which is the spirit of holiness, and by that means does sanctify us: and all this together in our doctrine makes up the justification of a sinner. This also was the doctrine of Luther and Melancthon.[58] Those subtle distinctions between justification and regeneration or sanctification, in which at present the whole nicety of the Protestant doctrine is placed, were born after them, and since the Confession of Augsburg. The Lutherans now acknowledge that these things were confounded by Luther and Melancthon, even in the Apology, so authentic a work of the whole party. Luther, indeed, thus defines justifying faith: "True faith is the work of God in us, by which we are renovated, and born again of God and the Holy Ghost. And this faith is that true justice which St. Paul calls the justice of God, and which God approves."[59] By this, therefore, we are both justified and regenerated at the same time; and since the Holy Ghost, that is, God himself, acting in us, interposes in this work, it is no imputation out of us, as Protestants will now have it, but a work within us.

And as to the Apology, Melancthon repeats there in every page, "that faith justifies and regenerates us, and brings to us the Holy Spirit." And a little after, that "it regenerate hearts, and brings forth a new life."[60] And again, more clearly: "To be justified, is of unjust to be made just; and to be regenerated is to be declared and reputed just:" which shows that these two things concur together. Not the least appearance of the contrary is to be found in the Confession of Augsburg; and there is nobody but perceives how well those two ideas which the Lutherans then had coincide with ours.

36.—Satisfactory works acknowledged in the Apology, and Monks reckoned among the Saints.

It seems as if they had separated farther on satisfactory works, and the austerities of a religious life; for they reject them frequently, as contrary to the doctrine of gratuitous justification. But, in reality, they do not condemn them so severely as one might at first be induced to think; for not only St. Anthony and the monks of the first ages, men of frightful austerity, but also those of these latter days, St. Bernard, St. Dominic, and St. Francis are numbered amongst the holy fathers in the Apology. Their mode of life, far from being censured, is judged worthy of the saints, "because," say they, "it prevented them not from believing themselves justified by faith for the love of Jesus Christ."[61] A sentiment far removed from the excesses which we at this day witness in the new reformation, where they blush not to condemn St. Bernard, and rank St. Francis in the list of fools. True it is, after having placed these great men in the number of holy fathers, the Apology condemns the monks who followed them, upon the pretence that "they believed they merited the forgiveness of sins, grace, and justice, by these works, and did not receive it gratuitously."[62] But the calumny is manifest, since the religious now-a-days still believe, as did those of old, together with the Catholic Church and the Council of Trent, that the forgiveness of sins is purely gratuitous, and given thorough the merits of Jesus Christ alone.

And that it may not be supposed the merit which we attribute to these works of penance was then disapproved of by the defenders of the Augsburg Confession, they teach, in general, "of works and afflictions, that they do not MERIT many benefits from God; THAT THEY MITIGATE PAINS; that they MERIT that we should be assisted against the perils of sin and death."[63] What prevents their saying as much of fasting and other mortifications? And all this, well understood, is nothing in substance, but what is taught by all Catholics.

37.—*The necessity of baptism, and the admissibility of justice taught in the Confession of Augsburg.*

Calvinists have departed from the true ideas of justification, by saying, as we shall see, that baptism is not necessary for little children; that justice once received is never lost, and, what is a consequence of this, that it is preserved even in crime. But the Lutherans, when they saw these errors spring up among the Anabaptist sects, condemned them by these three articles of the Confession of Augsburg:

"That baptism is necessary to salvation, and that they condemn the Anabaptists who assert children may be saved without baptism, and out of the Church of Jesus Christ."[64]

"That they condemn the same Anabaptists, who deny the Holy Ghost may be lost after a man is once justified."[65]

"That those who fall into mortal sin are not just; that we ought to resist evil inclinations; that those who, contrary to God's commandment, obey them, and act contrary to their conscience, are unjust, and have neither the Holy Ghost, nor faith, nor confidence in the divine mercy."[66]

38.—*The inconsistencies of certainty, and of special faith, are not removed by the Augsburg Confession.*

One will be astonished to see so many articles of importance decided in the Augsburg Confession conformably to our sentiments; and truly, when I consider what it is which they have discovered, that is particular, I see nothing but that special faith of which we spoke at the commencement of this work, and the infallible certainty of the forgiveness of sins which they will have it to produce in consciences. And, indeed, it must be acknowledged that this is what they give us as the capital point of Luther's doctrine, the masterpiece of his reformation, and the strongest foundation of piety and comfort to the faithful. However, no remedy was discovered against that terrible difficulty we at first observed,—in being assured of the forgiveness of sin, without ever being able to be certain of the sincerity of repentance. For after all, let imputation be what it may, it is certain that Jesus Christ imputes his justice to none but those who are penitent, and sincerely penitent, that is, sincerely contrite, sincerely afflicted for their sins, sincerely converted. Let this sincere repentance have in itself whatever of worth, perfection, merit, there may be, or let it not, I have sufficiently explained myself before on the subject, and shall add no more upon this occasion. Let it be either condition, or disposition and preparation, or in a word what you please, it concerns me not, since, whatever it may be, it must be had, or there is no forgiveness. But, according to the principles of Luther, I can never be assured whether I have or have it not; since, according to him, I can never know whether my repentance be not an illusion, the vain conceit of my own self-love; nor whether the sin I believe rooted out of my heart, reign not there more securely than ever, as it escapes my sight.

It is to no purpose to say with the Apology, "that faith is incompatible with mortal sin;"[67] now I have faith; therefore, I have not mortal sin. For it is from this springs all the difficulty, since it ought to be said on the contrary, "Faith is incompatible with mortal sin." It is what the Lutherans have now just taught. Now I am not assured that I have not mortal sin; it is what we have proved by the doctrine of Luther:[68] I am not, therefore, certain that I have faith. In effect, they exclaim in the Apology, "Who loves God sufficiently? Who fears him sufficiently? Who suffers with sufficient patience?" Now, it may be said in the same manner, Who believes as he ought? Who believes sufficiently to be justified before God? And what follows in the Apology confirms this doubt; for it proceeds, "Who doubts not frequently whether it be God or chance that governs the world? Who doubts not frequently whether he shall be heard of God?"[69] Therefore, you doubt frequently of your own proper faith. How, then, are you assured of the forgiveness of sins? You have not, therefore, this forgiveness; or else, contrary to the dogma of Luther, you have it without being assured you have it: or, which is the height of blindness, you are assured of it without being assured of the sincerity of your faith, or of that of your repentance; and so the forgiveness of sins becomes independent of both one and the other. See to what this certainty conducts us–this groundwork, on which is wholly built the confession of Augsburg, this fundamental dogma of Lutheranism.

39.—*That, conformably to the principles of Lutherans themselves, the uncertainty acknowledged by the Catholics should give no trouble, nor disturb the repose of conscience.*

Now what they oppose to us, namely, that by the uncertainty, wherein we leave afflicted consciences, we cast them into trouble, or even into despair, is not true; and to this the Lutherans must agree, for this reason—because, however they may boast of the assurance they have of their justification, they dare not absolutely assure themselves of their perseverance, nor consequently of their eternal happiness. On the contrary, they condemn those who say, justice once received can never be lost.[70] But by this loss, one forfeits all right he had, as a justified person, to eternal inheritance. Therefore, one is never certain of not losing this right, since he is not certain that he shall never lose that justice to which it is annexed. Yet he hopes, however, for this blessed inheritance. In this sweet hope he lives happy, according to St. Paul, "rejoicing in hope."[71] Therefore, exclusive of this last assurance which prohibits all kind of doubt, one may enjoy as much repose as the state of this life permits.

40.—*What is the true repose of Conscience in Justification, and what certainly is received therein.*

Hence is seen what must be done in order to the acceptance of the promise, and the application of it; it is to believe, readily, that the grace of Christian justice, and, consequently, life eternal, belong to us in Jesus Christ; and not only to us in general, but also to us in particular. On the part of God, I acknowledge, there is no impediment to this ready and firm belief: heaven and earth shall pass away sooner than his promises fail us. But that we have no impediment, nothing to fear on our side, the terrible example of those who persevere not to the end; and who, according to the Lutherans, were not less justified than the elect themselves, evidently establishes the contrary. Here, then, in a few words, is the whole doctrine of justification. Although to nourish humility in our hearts, we are always in fear as regards ourselves, with respect to God all things are made sure to us; so that our repose in this life consists in a firm confidence in his paternal goodness, and in a perfect resignation to his high and incomprehensible will, together with a profound adoration of this his impenetrable secret.

41.—*The Confession of Strasburg explains Justification like the Church of Rome.*

As to the Confession of Strasburg, if we consider its doctrine, we shall see how much reason there was, at the Conference of Marpurg, to accuse those of Strasburg, and the Sacramentarians in general, of understanding nothing of the justification as expounded by Luther and the Lutherans: for this confession of faith says not a word either of justice by imputation, or of the required certainty thereof. On the contrary, it defines justification to be that by which "of unjust we become just, and of wicked good and upright,"[72] without giving us any other idea of it. It adds, that it is gratuitous, and attributes it to faith; but to faith joined with charity, and fruitful in good works. Thus it says, with the Confession of Augsburg, "that charity is the fulfilling of the whole law, conformably to the doctrine of St. Paul;"[73] yet explains more strongly than Melancthon had done, how necessarily the law ought to be fulfilled, asserting "that no one can be completely saved, if he be not so guided by the spirit of Jesus Christ as not to fail in any of those good works, for the practising of which God has created us; and that it is so necessary the law should be fulfilled, that heaven and earth shall sooner pass away than an abatement be made in the least tittle of the law, or in one single iota." No Catholic ever spoke more strongly of the accomplishment of the law than this Confession. But, although this be the foundation of merit, Bucer spoke not a word of it there; though elsewhere, he makes no difficulty of acknowledging it in the sense of St. Augustin, which is that of the Church.

42.—*Of Merit, according to Bucer.*

Whilst we are on this subject, it may not be unnecessary to consider what were the opinions of this Doctor, one of the chief leaders of the second party of the new Reformation, in a solemn conference, where he expressed his sentiments in these terms:—"Whereas, God will judge each one according to his works, we must not deny that good works performed by the grace of Jesus Christ, and which he himself operates in his servants, do *merit* eternal life; not, indeed, from their intrinsic worth, but from the acceptation and promise of God, and the covenant made with him; for it is to such works the Scripture promises the reward of eternal life, which, in another respect, however, is a favor, because these good works, to which a recompense is given, are the gifts of God."[74] This is what Bucer wrote in 1539, in the dispute of Leipsic, that it may not be supposed these things were written at the beginning of the Reformation, before they had time for reflection. Conformably to this same principle, the same Bucer decides, in another place, that it must not be denied but "one may be justified by works, as St. James teaches, since God will render to each man according to his works." And he proceeds,—"The question is not of MERITS: we reject them not in any way, and even acknowledge that eternal life is MERITED according to this saying of our Savior, 'He that shall leave off all for the love of me, shall have a hundred fold in this life, and hereafter, life everlasting.'"[75]

43.—*Bucer undertakes to defend the Prayers of the Church, and shows in what sense the merits of the Saints profit us.*

The merits which every one may acquire for himself, and even with respect to eternal life, cannot be more clearly acknowledged. But Bucer advanced still farther; and, whereas the Church was accused of attributing merits to Saints, not only for themselves, but for others also, he justified it by these words:—"With regard to the public prayers of the Church, called Collects, where mention is made of the prayers and merits of the Saints; whereas, in these same prayers, whatever is entreated in that way, is entreated of God and not of the Saints, and, moreover, is entreated through Jesus Christ, by this all those who make this prayer, acknowledge that all the merits of the Saints are gifts of God gratuitously granted." And, a little after, "For we, moreover, do confess and preach with joy, that God rewards the good works of his servants, not in themselves alone, but in those also for whom they pray, since he has promised he will do good to those who love him, to a thousand generations."[76] Thus Bucer disputed for the Catholic Church, in 1546, at the Conference of Ratisbon; and, indeed, these prayers were made by the greatest men of the Church, and in the most enlightened ages; and St. Augustin himself, however great an enemy he was to presumptuous merit, acknowledged, however, that the merits of the Saints were useful to us, when he said, "one of the reasons for celebrating in the Church the memory of martyrs, was in order that we might be associated to their merits, and assisted by their prayers."[77] Thus, let what may be said, the doctrine of Christian justice, of its works, and its merits, was acknowledged by both parties of the new Reformation; and what has since raised so much difficulty, at that time made none at all, or at most, if it did, it was from this cause alone,—that frequently, in the Reformation, men were swayed by the spirit of contradiction.

44.—Strange doctrine of the Confession of Augsburg on the Love of God.

I cannot here omit an odd doctrine of the Augsburg Confession on justification; namely, that not only the love of God was not necessary for it, but necessarily supposes it already accomplished. Luther had told as much before; but Melancthon explains it at length in the Apology. "It is impossible to love God," says he, "if previously, one has not, by faith, the forgiveness of sins; for a heart that has a true feeling of an incensed Deity cannot love him—it must see him appeased; whilst he threatens, whilst he condemns, human nature cannot so far elevate itself as to love him in his wrath. It is an easy matter for idle contemplatives to imagine these dreams of the love of God, that a man guilty of mortal sin may love him above all things; because they are not sensible what the wrath and judgment of God are; but a troubled conscience perceives the vanity of these philosophical speculations." From this he concludes every where—"That it is impossible to love God, if, previously, one be not assured of forgiveness obtained."[78]

That we are justified, therefore, before we have the least spark of divine love, is one of the niceties of Luther's justification: for the whole tenor of the Apology is not only to establish that one is justified before he loves, but, also, that it is impossible to love unless he be justified previously; insomuch that pardon offered with so great bounty can gain nothing on our hearts—we must have received it already to be capable of loving God. Not so speaks the Church in the Council of Trent:—"Man excited and assisted by grace," says this Council, believes all that God has revealed, and all he has promised; and this he believes before all things, that the impious man is justified by the grace, by the redemption which is in Christ Jesus. Conscious, then, to himself, that he is a sinner, from that justice by which he is alarmed, he turns towards the Divine mercy, which raises up his hope IN THE CONFIDENCE HE HAS THAT GOD WILL BE PROPITIOUS TO HIM THROUGH JESUS CHRIST, and he begins to love him as the author of all justice,"[79] namely, as the gracious being who gratuitously justifies the impious. This love, so happily commenced, moves him to detest his crimes; he receives the sacrament—he is justified. Charity is gratuitously diffused into his heart by the Holy Ghost; and having commenced to love God when he offered to him his grace, he loves him still more when he has received it.

45.—*Another error in the Lutheran Justification.*

But here is a new *finesse* of the Lutheran justification. St. Augustin, after St. Paul, establishes, that one of the differences of Christian justice from that of the law, is, that the justice of the law is built on the spirit of fear and terror; whereas, Christian justice is inspired by the spirit of affection and love. But the Apology expounds it in a different way; and that justice, to which the love of God is judged necessary, into which it enters, in which consists its purity and truth, is there throughout represented as the justice of works, the justice of reason, justice through its own proper merits; in a word, as the justice of the law, a Pharisaical justice. These were new ideas, with which Christianity was as yet unacquainted: a justice which the Holy Ghost infuses into our hearts, by infusing charity, is a Pharisaical justice, which cleanses but the exterior; a justice infused gratuitously into our hearts for the sake of Jesus Christ, is a justice of reason, a legal justice, a justice through works; and, finally, they accuse us of maintaining a justice by its own proper powers, whereas it appears clearly from the Council of Trent, that we maintain a justice which has faith for its foundation, grace for its principal cause, the Holy Ghost for its author from its very beginning, even to the last perfection to which it can arrive in this life.

I believe it now appears how necessary it was to give a clear idea of the Lutheran justification from the Confession of Augsburg and Apology, because, as this exposition has fully discovered that in an article which is considered by the Lutherans as the masterpiece of their Reformation, after all nothing has been done except to calumniate us in some points, to justify us in others, and even in those, when some dispute may still remain, evidently to leave us the advantage.

46.—*The Lutherans acknowledge the Sacrament of Penance, and Sacramental Absolution.*

Besides this principal article, there are others in the Augsburg Confession or Apology, of the highest importance: for example, that "particular absolution ought to be retained in confession; that to reject it is an error of the Novatians, and a condemned error: that this absolution is a true sacrament, and properly so called; that the power of the keys remits sins, not only in the sight of the Church, but also in the sight of God."[80] As to their reproaching us with maintaining that "this sacrament conferred grace without any good motive on the part of him who receives it," I believe the reader is already tired with hearing a calumny already refuted so frequently.

47.—*Confession, with the necessity of Enumerating Sins.*

As to what is taught in the same place, that confession being retained, "the enumeration of sins ought not to be exacted in it, because the thing is impossible, according to these words, 'who is there that knoweth his sins?'"[81] For sins that are not known, this was indeed a good excuse, but no sufficient reason for not subjecting to the keys of the Church those that are known. And, truly, it must be candidly acknowledged, neither Luther nor the Lutherans differ in sentiments from us on this subject; since, in Luther's little Catechism, which is unanimously received by the whole party, we find these words:—"In the sight of God we must hold ourselves guilty of our hidden sins; but, with respect to the Minister, we must confess those only which are known to us, and which we feel within our hearts."[82] And, the better to discover the Lutheran conformity with us in the administration of this sacrament, it will not be irrelevant to consider the absolution, which, as the same Luther, in the same place, sets its down, the confessor gives the penitent, after confession, in these terms:—"Do you not believe that my forgiveness is that of God? "Yes!" answers the penitent. "And I," replies the confessor, "by the order of our Lord Jesus Christ, forgive you yours sins, in the name of the Father, and of the Son, and of the Holy Ghost."[83]

48.—*The Seven Sacraments.*

For the number of sacraments, the Apology teaches us that Baptism, the Supper, and Absolution are three true sacraments. Here is a fourth, since "No difficulty ought to be made of admitting Orders into this rank, by taking it for the ministry of the word, because it is commanded of God, and has great promises."[84] Confirmation and Extreme Unction are specified as "ceremonies received by the fathers," which, however, have not an express promise of grace. I know not, then, what can be the meaning of these words of St. James's epistle concerning the unction of the sick: "If he be in sin, it shall be forgiven him;"[85] but the thing was, perhaps, that Luther had no opinion of this epistle, though the Church had never called it in question. This daring Reformer cut off from the canon of Scriptures whatever did not accord with his opinions; and it is on account of this Unction that he writes, in his Captivity of Babylon, without the least testimony of antiquity, that this epistle seems not to be St. James's, nor worthy of the apostolic spirit."[86]

As for Marriage, those of the Augsburg Confession acknowledge its divine institution, its promises too, yet temporal; as if it were a temporal concern to bring up in the Church the children of God, and to save one's own soul in thus taking care of them;[87] or that one of the fruits of Christian matrimony were not to provide that the children born in it be named saints, as destined to sanctity."[88]

But the Apology, at bottom, seems not much to oppose our doctrine concerning the number of sacraments, "provided," it says, "this sentiment, which predominates throughout the whole Pontifical kingdom, be rejected, that the sacraments operate grace without any good motion of him that receives them."[89] For they are never tired with making us this unjust reproach. It is there they place the whole stress of the question; that is, were it not for the false ideas of our adversaries, scarcely any difficulty would remain about it.

49.—Monastic Vows, and that of Continency.

Luther had expressed himself in a revolting manner against monastic vows, even to say on that of Continency, (stop your ears, chaste souls!) that "it was impossible for one to keep it as to divest himself of his sex."[90] Modesty would be offended should I repeat the words he, in many places, makes use of on this subject; and to see how he delivers himself on the impossibility of continence. For my own part, I know not what will become of that life he says he led without reproach, during the whole time of his celibacy, and to the forty-fifth year of his age. Be this as it may, all is softened in the Apology, since not only St. Anthony and St. Bernard, but also St. Dominic and St. Francis, are there numbered among the saints; and all that is required from their disciples is, that, after their example, they seek the forgiveness of their sins from the gratuitous bounty of God, which the Church has too well provided for to fear any reproach on that head.[91]

50.—St. Bernard, St. Francis, St. Bonaventure, placed by Luther amongst the Saints; his strange doubt regarding the Salvation of St. Thomas of Aquin.

This place of the Apology merits attention, those of the latter ages being there placed on the list of saints, so that the Church which brought them forth and nourished them at her breast, is acknowledged for the True Church. Luther could not refuse this glorious title to these great men. He enumerates every where among the saints, not St. Bernard only, but also St. Francis, St. Bonaventure, and others of the thirteenth century. St. Francis, above all, seemed to him an admirable man, and animated with a wonderful fervor of spirit. He carries down his praises as far as Gerson, the same that, in the Council of Constance, had condemned Wickliffe and John Huss, and calls him "a great man in every respect."[92] Thus the Church of Rome was still the mother of saints in the fifteenth century. There is but St. Thomas of Aquin of whom Luther would doubt; for what reason I know not, unless it were that this saint was a Dominican, and Luther could not forget the sharp disputes he had held with that order. Whatever it might be, "he knows not," so he says, "if Thomas be damned or saved;"[93] though, doubtless, he made no other kind of vows than the other religious, had said no other mass, and had taught no other faith.

51.—The Lutheran Mass.

To return to the Augsburg Confession and the Apology, even the article of the Mass is passed over there so lightly, that it can scarcely be perceived that Protestants designed any change in it. They commence by complaining of the "unjust reproach against them of abolishing the mass."—"It is celebrated," say they, "amongst us with extreme reverence, and in it are preserved almost all the ordinary ceremonies."[94] In reality, when, in 1523, Luther reformed the mass, and drew up his formula,[95] scarcely any thing was altered by him that struck the eyes of the people. The Introit was there retained, the Kyrie, the Collect, the Epistle, the Gospel, with the wax candles and incense, if they pleased; the Credo, the Preaching, the Prayers, the Preface, the Sanctus, the Words of Consecration, the Elevation, the Lord's Prayer, the Agnus Dei, the Communion, the Thanksgiving. Such is the order of the Lutheran mass, which exteriorly appeared little different from ours; moreover, the singing was retained, and even in Latin: and this is what was said of it in the Confession of Augsburg,—"Together with the chanting in Latin, are mingled prayers in the German tongue, for the instruction of the people. In this mass we see the altar ornaments and sacerdotal garments, and great care was taken to retain them, as appeared from their practice, and the conferences then held."[96] What is still more, nothing was said in the Augsburg Confession against the oblation; on the contrary, it is insinuated in this passage cited from the tripartite history:—"In the city of Alexandria they assembled together on Wednesday and Friday, and the whole service is then performed, except the solemn oblation."[97] The reason was, they were unwilling to discover to the people that they had made any alteration in the public service. To judge by the Augsburg Confession alone, it might seem that masses only, without communicants, were objected to, "which were abolished," said they,"because they were scarcely ever celebrated but for lucre;"[98] so that, on considering merely the terms of the Confession, one would have said that nothing except the abuse was the object of attack.

52.—The Oblation, how taken away.

Meanwhile, those words in which there is mention of the oblation made to God of the proposed gifts, were cut off from the canon of the mass. But the people, always struck exteriorly with the same objects, attended not to it at the commencement; and to render, however, this change supportable to them, it was insinuated that "the canon was not the same in all churches; that the canon of the Greeks differed from that of the Latins—and even among the Latins, that of Milan from that of Rome."[99] This was done to amuse the ignorant; but they did not think proper to acquaint them that these canons or liturgies had none other than accidental differences; that all the liturgies agreed unanimously as to the oblation, which was made to God of the proposed gifts before they were distributed; and this is what they changed in practice, without daring to acknowledge as much in the public Confession.

53.—What was invented in order to render the Oblation in the Mass odious.

But, in order to render this oblation odious, they would pretend to make the Church believe she attributed to it "a merit of remitting sins, without the necessity of bringing to it either faith or any good motive;" which was repeated three times in the Confession of Augsburg, and they omitted not in the Apology to inculcate the same—insinuating that Catholics admitted the mass for no other reason than to extinguish piety.

In the Confession of Augsburg they even attribute to the Catholics this strange doctrine, "That Jesus Christ had satisfied for original sin in his passion, and had instituted the mass for mortal and venial sins, which were committed every day;"[100] as if Jesus Christ had not equally satisfied for all sins; and, by way of a necessary elucidation, they added, that Jesus Christ had offered himself to bear the cross, "not for original sin only, but for all others too,"[101] a truth of which none ever doubted. It is not a matter of surprise that the Catholics, as Lutherans themselves relate, on hearing this reproach, all, as if with one common voice, cried out against it, saying: "That never had such a thing been heard among them."[102] But the people were to be made to believe that these wretched Papists were even ignorant of the first elements of Christianity.

54.—The Prayer and Oblation for the Dead.

Now, whereas the faithful, at all times, had the oblation made for the dead deeply impressed upon their minds, the Protestants would not seem to be ignorant of, or conceal a thing so well known, and in the Apology spoke of it in these terms—"With regard to what is objected against us concerning oblation for the dead having been practised by the Fathers, we acknowledge they prayed for the dead, AND WE PREVENT NONE FROM NOW DOING IT; but we do not approve of the application of the Lord's Supper for the dead, in virtue of the action, *ex opere operato*."[103] Here every thing abounds with artifice: for, in the first place, whilst they say they do not prevent this prayer, they had it cut off from the canon, and by so doing defaced a practice as ancient as the Church. Secondly, the objection spoke of the oblation, and their answer is concerning prayer, not daring to let the people see that antiquity had offered for the dead; because that was too convincing a proof that the Eucharist was profitable even to those who received not the communion.

55.—The Lutherans reject the doctrine of Arius, contrary to prayer for the Dead.

But the following words of the Apology are remarkable: "Unjustly do our adversaries reproach us with the condemnation of Arius, whom they will have condemned for denying that the mass was to be offered for the living and the dead. This is their custom—to oppose the ancient heretics against us, and to compare our doctrine with theirs. St. Epiphanius declares, that Arius taught that prayers for the dead were unprofitable. We support not Aerius, but dispute against you—who say, contrary to the doctrine of the Prophets, of the Apostles and Fathers, that the mass justifies men in virtue of the action, and merits the forgiveness for sinners, to whom it is applied, of the guilt and pain, provided they put no obstacle to it."[104] Thus is an imposition practised upon the ignorant. If it were not the intention of the Lutherans to maintain Arius, why do they maintain this particular dogma, which this Arian heretic had added to the Arian heresy—"That we ought not to pray or offer up oblations for the dead?"[105] This is what St. Augustin relates of Arius after St. Epiphanius, of whom he had given an epitome. If they reject Aerius, if they dare not support a heretic condemned by the holy Fathers, they ought to replace in the Liturgy, not only prayer, but also the oblation for the dead.

56.—How the Oblation of the Eucharist is profitable to the whole world.

But here is the great subject of complaint in the Apology: namely, say they, that St. Epiphanius, by condemning Aerius, did not assert as you do, "That the mass justifies men in virtue of the action, *ex opere operato*, and merits for the wicked to whom it is applied, the forgiveness of the guilt and the pain, provided they put no obstacle thereto." To hear them speak, one would say, that the mass of itself was to justify all kinds of sinners for whom it is said, without their so much as thinking of it. But where is the advantage of thus deceiving men? The manner, say we, by which the mass is profitable, even to those who think not of it, even the most wicked, contains no difficulty at all. It is profitable to them like prayer, which certainly we should never offer for the most obdurate sinners, did we not suppose it could obtain of God that grace which would overcome their obduracy of heart, if they did not resist it, and which often obtains it so abundantly as to prevent their resistance. It is thus the oblation of the Eucharist is profitable to the absent, the dead, and even sinners themselves; because, in reality, the consecration of the Eucharist, placing before the eyes of God so agreeable an object as the Body and Blood of his Son, cries with it a most powerful manner of intercession, which, however, sinful men too often render useless by the impediment which they oppose to its efficacy.

What could be offensive in this manner of explaining the effect of the mass? As for those who converted so pure a doctrine to sordid gain, Protestants know very well the Church did not approve of them; and for masses without communicants, the Catholics told them ever since that time, what since has been confirmed at Trent, that, if none communicate at it, it is not the fault of the Church; "since, on the contrary, she wished the assistants would communicate at the mass they hear;"[106] so that the Church resembles a rich benefactor, who always keeps an open table, and ready served, although the guests come not to it.

The whole artifice of the Augsburg Confession, concerning the mass, is now seen: it consists in scarcely touching the exterior; in changing the interior, even what was most ancient, without apprising the people of the alteration; in accusing Catholics of the grossest errors—even so as to make them say, contrary to their own principles, that "the mass justified the sinner," (a thing always reserved to the Sacraments of Baptism and Penance,) and that too without any good motive, in order to make the Church and her Liturgy more odious.

57.—A horrible calumny, grounded on Prayers made to Saints.

They were not less industrious in disfiguring the other parts of our doctrine, and particularly that of prayer to the saints. "There are those," says the Apology, "who attribute downright divinity to the saints, by saying, they see in us the hidden thoughts[107] of our hearts." Where are those divines, who attribute to saints the seeing of the hidden secrets of hearts like to God, or seeing them otherwise than by that light he imparts to them, as, when he pleased, he did to the Prophets? "They make the saints," said they, "not only intercessors, but also the MEDIATORS OF REDEMPTION. They devised that Jesus Christ was more difficult, and the saints more easy, to be appeased; they confide more in the mercy of the saints, than in that of Jesus Christ; and, FLYING FROM JESUS CHRIST, they seek the saints."[108] It is unnecessary to justify the Church from these abominable excesses. But to remove all doubt that this was literally Catholic doctrine, "We speak not now," added they,"of popular abuses; we speak of the opinion of doctors." And a little after, "they exhort to confide more in the mercy of the saints than in that of Jesus Christ. They enjoin to trust in the merits of the saints, as if we were reputed just by reason of their merits, as we are reputed just by reason of the merits of Jesus Christ." After imputing such excesses to us, they say gravely, "We invent nothing; they state in the indulgences that the merits of the saints are applied to us."[109] A little equity would have enabled them to see in what manner the merits of the saints are useful to us; and Bucer himself, an unsuspected author, has sufficiently vindicated us from the reproach which they objected to us on that head.

58.—*Calumnies regarding Images, and a gross imposture with respect to Invocation of Saints.*

But their object was to exasperate and irritate the minds of men; and, therefore, they further add: "From the invocation of saints they proceed to images. They honored them, and believed there was a certain virtue in them, as the magicians make us believe there is in the images of the constellations when they are made at a certain time."[110] Thus they excited the public hatred. It must be acknowledged, however, that the Confession of Augsburg proceeded not to this extremity; and that these images were not so much as mentioned in it. To satisfy the party, something more severe must be said in the Apology. Particular care, however, was taken not to let the people see that these prayers, addressed to the saints, that they might pray for us, were common in the ancient Church. On the contrary, they spoke of it as "a new custom, introduced without the testimony of the Fathers, and of which nothing had been seen before St. Gregory, that is, before the seventh century."[111] The people were not yet accustomed to despise the authority of the ancient Church; and the Reformation, as yet timorous, reverenced the great names of the Fathers. But now it assumed boldness, and knew not how to blush; insomuch that they have conceded to us the fourth century, and are not ashamed to assure us that St. Basil, St. Ambrose, St. Augustin, in a word, all the Fathers of this so venerable an AGE, have, with the invocation of saints, set up, in the new idolatry, the reign of Antichrist.[112]

59.—*The Lutherans durst not reject the authority of the Church of Rome.*

Then, during the time of the Augsburg Confession, the Protestants boasted, that they had on their side the holy Fathers, chiefly in the article of justification, which they esteemed most essential; and they not only pretended the ancient Church was for them, but this concluded the exposition of their doctrine. "Such is the abridgment of our faith, where nothing will be seen contrary to Scripture, nor to the Catholic Church, nor even to THE CHURCH OF ROME, as far as she can be known from her writers.[113] The matter which is the subject of dispute regards some few abuses, which, without any certain authority, have been introduced into the Churches; and though there should be some difference, it ought to be tolerated, since it is not necessary that Church rites should be every where the same."[114]

In another edition are read these words: "WE DESPISE NOT THE CONSENT OF THE CATHOLIC CHURCH, nor will we maintain the impious and seditious opinions she has condemned, for it is not irregular passions, but the authority of God's word, and OF THE ANCIENT CHURCH, that has moved us to embrace this doctrine, in order to increase the glory of God, and provide for the advantage of pious souls in the Universal Church."[115]

Also in the Apology, after the exposition of the article of Justification, considered without comparison the most important, they said, "That it was the doctrine of the Prophets, the Apostles, and the Holy Fathers, of St. Ambrose, St. Augustin, and the greatest part of the other Fathers, and of the whole Church, who acknowledged Jesus Christ for propitiator, and author of justification; and that all which was approved by the Pope, some cardinals, bishops, divines, or monks, was not to be taken for the doctrine of the Church of Rome:[116]" whereby particular opinions were manifestly distinguished from the received and constant doctrine, which they professed not to interfere.

60.—*Memorable words of Luther, acknowledging the true Church in the Communion of Rome.*

The people, therefore, still believed they followed in every thing the sentiments of the Fathers, the authority of the Catholic Church, and even that of the Church of Rome, a veneration for which was deeply imprinted upon all minds. Even Luther himself, however arrogant and rebellious, returned at times to his good sense, and manifested plainly, that the ancient veneration, which he had formerly entertained for the Church, was not wholly extinguished. About the year 1534, so many years since his revolt, and four years after the Confession of Augsburg, was published his treatise for abolishing the Private Mass. It is the same in which he relates his famous conference with the prince of darkness.[117] There, though so much incensed against the Catholic Church, even so far as to hold it for the seat of Antichrist and abomination, so far from taking from it the title of Church, on that account, he concluded, on the contrary, "That she was the true Church, the pillar and ground of truth, and the most holy place. In this Church," he continued, "God miraculously preserves baptism, the text of the Gospel in all languages, the remission of sins, and absolution as well in Confession as in public; the Sacrament of the altar towards Easter, and three or four times a year, though one kind has been taken away from the people; the vocation and ordination of pastors, comfort in the agony of death; the image of the crucifix, and at the same time the remembrance of the death and passion of Jesus Christ: the Psalter, Lord's Prayer, the Symbol, the Decalogue, and many pious canticles in Latin and German." And a little after:—"Where the true relics of saints are to be found, there, without doubt, has been, and still is, the Holy Church of Jesus Christ; there the saints have dwelt; for the institutions and sacraments of Jesus Christ are there, excepting one kind that has been forcibly taken away. For which reason it is certain, Jesus Christ has been there present, and his Holy Spirit there does preserve his true knowledge, and the true faith in his elect." Far from looking on the cross put into the hands of dying persons as an object of idolatry, he, on the contrary, holds it for a monument of piety, and a wholesome admonition, that recalled to our minds the death and passion of Jesus Christ. As yet, the revolt had not extinguished in his heart those good remnants of the piety and doctrine of the Church; nor am I surprised that, in the frontispiece of all the volumes of his works, he is represented, with the Elector his master, kneeling before a crucifix.

61.—Both kinds.

As to what he says of taking away one kind, the Reformation found itself very much embarrassed about this article, and this is what was said of it in the Apology: "We exclude the Church, which, not being able to receive both kinds, has suffered this injury; but we excuse not the authors of this prohibition."[118]

To comprehend the mystery of this part of the Apology, but few words are necessary. Its author, Melancthon, writes to Luther, consulting him on this subject whilst Catholics and Protestants were disputing it at Augsburg. "Eckius believed," said he, "that communion under one or both kinds should be held for indifferent. Which I would not allow; and yet I excused those who hitherto, through error, had received but one; for they exclaimed, we condemned the whole Church."[119]

They durst not then condemn the whole Church: they abhorred the very thought; which led Melancthon to this pure expedient of excusing the Church in an error. What more could those who condemn her say, since the error here meant, is supposed to be an error in faith, and an error tending even to the entire subversion of so great a sacrament as that of the Eucharist? But no other method was to be found: Luther approved it; and the better to excuse the Church, which communicated under one kind only, he joined the violence she suffered from her pastors in that point, to the error into which she was led: thus she was admirably excused, and by this method the promises of Jesus Christ never to abandon her were excellently well preserved.

The words of Luther in reply to Melancthon merit observation: "They cry out, that we condemn the whole Church." The whole world was astonished at this idea. "But," answers Luther, "we say that the Church being oppressed and deprived by violence of one kind, ought to be excused; as we excuse the synagogue in not having observed all the ceremonies of the law during the captivity of Babylon, when she had it not in her power."[120]

The example was unhappily cited; for certainly those who detained the synagogue captive were not of her body, as the pastors of the Church, whom they here represented as her oppressors, were of the body of the Church. Again, the synagogue, though externally under control as to its observances, was not on that account drawn *into error*, as Melancthon maintained the Church had been, in being deprived of one kind: but, in short, the article passed. Lest they should condemn the Church, it was agreed to excuse her, as to the error she had been in, and *the injury* which had been done her; and the whole party subscribed to this answer of the Apology.

All this but little coincided with the seventh article of the Augsburg Confession, where it is declared, "That there is one Holy Church, which shall remain for ever. Now the Church is the assembly of the Saints, where the Gospel is taught, and the sacraments rightly administered."[121] To salve this idea of the Church, not only the people were to be excused, but the sacraments also were to be well administered by the pastors; and if that of the Eucharist did not subsist under one kind only, no longer could the Church herself be made to subsist.

62.—*The body of the Lutherans submit themselves in the Augsburg Confession to the judgment of the General Council.*

The difficulty in condemning the doctrine of the Church was not less pressing, and this was the reason that the Protestants durst not acknowledge that their confession of faith was opposite to the Church of Rome, or that they had withdrawn themselves from her. They endeavored to have it believed, as we have just seen, that they were not distinguished but by certain rites and some slight observances. And, moreover, to show they always pretended to make one body with her, they openly submitted to her council.

This appears in the preface of the Confession of Augsburg, addressed to Charles V. "Your imperial majesty has declared, that you could determine nothing in this affair, wherein religion was concerned, but would have recourse to the Pope, to procure the convention of an universal council. You repeated the same declaration in the last year in the last diet held at Spire, and manifested that you persisted in the resolution of procuring this assembly of a general council: adding that the affairs between you and the Pope being concluded, you believed he might easily be induced to call a general council." By this it is seen what council it was, of which there was question. It was a general council, to be assembled by the Pope, and the Protestants submitted themselves to it in these terms: "If matters of religion cannot be amicably arranged with our parties, we offer in all obedience to your imperial majesty, to appear and plead our own cause before such a general, free, and Christian council." And, finally, "It is to this general council, and to your imperial majesty conjointly, that we have and do appeal, and we adhere to this appeal."[122] When they spoke in this manner, it was not their intention to give the emperor authority to pronounce on the articles of faith: but upon appealing to the council, they also named the emperor in their appeal as the person who was to procure the convocation of this holy assembly, and whom they solicited to retain in the meantime all things in suspense. So solemn a declaration will remain for ever upon record in the most authentic act the Lutherans have ever made, and in the very front of the Augsburg Confession, in testimony against them, and in acknowledgment of the inviolable authority of the Church. All then submitted to it, and whatever might be done before her decision arrived, was all provisional. With this specious appearance they retained the people, and perhaps even deceived themselves. They involved themselves still further, however, and the horror they had for schism diminished daily. After they had been accustomed to it, and the party had gained strength by treaties and leagues, the Church was forgotten; all they had said of her holy authority vanished like a dream, and the title "of a free and Christian Council," used by them, became a pretext to render their calling for a council illusory, as will be seen hereafter.

63.—*The Conclusion of this matter; how useful it ought to be in reclaiming the Lutherans.*

This is the history of the Augsburg Confession and of its Apology. We see the Lutherans would relinquish many things, and almost all, I dare say, should they only take the trouble to lay aside the calumnies with which they there charge us, and comprehend fully the dogmas in which they are so visibly conformable to our doctrine. If they had been advised by Melancthon, they would have drawn still nearer to Catholics, for he spoke not all he wished; and whilst he was laboring at the Confession of Augsburg, he, himself, writing to Luther, concerning the Articles of Faith, which he entreated him to revise, "They must," says he, "be often changed, and fitted to the occasion."[123] Thus did they patch up this famous Confession of Faith, which is the foundation of the Protestant religion; and thus were the dogmas therein treated. Melancthon was not permitted to soften matters as he wished:—"I changed something," says he, "every day, and changed again, and should have changed much more if our companions would have suffered me."[124] "But," proceeded he, "they are concerned at nothing;" the meaning was, as he explained it every where, that, without foreseeing what might happen, they thought of nothing but carrying all to extremities; for which reason Melancthon, as he acknowledges himself, "was always oppressed with cruel anxieties, endless cares, and insupportable regrets."[125] Luther held him under greater restraints than all the rest together. We see, in the letters which he wrote to him, that he knew not how to assuage this proud spirit; sometimes he was carried against Melancthon "into such a passion, that he even refused to read his letter."[126] Express messengers were sent to him in vain; they returned without an answer; and under these restraints the unfortunate Melancthon, who did all he could to check the impetuosity of his master, and of the party, always weeping and sighing, wrote the Confession of Augsburg.

Notes

1 Chyt. Hist. Confess. Aug.
2 Præf Apol. in Lib. Concord, p. 48.
 Act. Smal. ibid. 356. Epitome
 Act. ib. 571. Solid. Répét. ibid.
 633. 726.
3 Concord, p. 728.
4 Conf. Aug. art. 10.
5 Conf. Aug. art. 10. Syntagm. Gen.
 2 part, p. 13.
6 Conf. Aug. art. 10, in Lib. Concord,
 p.13.
7 Apol. Conf. Aug. Conc. p. 157.
8 Solid. Répét.
9 Hospin. part 2, p. 94, 132, 173.
10 Sleid. Apol. Conf. Aug. ad. Art. 10.
 Chytr. Hist. Conf. Aug. Cœlest
 Hist. Conf. Aug. t. iii.
11 Præf. Con.
12 Apol. Confess. Aug. in Art. 10, p.
 157.
13 Apol. Aug. Conf.
14 Conf. Arc. Gent. c. xviii. de Cœna.
 Synt. Gen. part. i. p. 195.
15 Conf. Argent. c. 18. de Cœna. Synt.
 Gen. part. 1. p. 195.
16 Conf. Zuing. int. Oper. Zuing. et
 ap. Hosp. ad an. 1530; 101, et seq.
17 Epist. ad Cæs. et Princ. Prot. ibid.
18 Conf. ad Franc. I.
19 John x. 30.
20 Ep. ad Cæs. et Princ. Prot.
21 Ad Art iv. de Justif. p. 60. de
 pœn. p. 161.
22 Conf. Aug. Art. xviii. Apol. ad eund.
 Art.
23 Apol. ad eund. Art.
24 Art. xix. ibid.
25 Conf. Art. xx. Apol. Cap. de Justif.
 Conc. p. 61. Ibid. pp. 62, 74, 102,
 103.
26 Conf. Augu. Art. xiii. etc.
27 Sess. 6. cap. v. vi. 14. Sess. xiii. 7.
 Sess. xiv. 4. Sess. vi. 7. Ibid. cap. viii.
 ibid. cap. v. vi. Can. 1, 2, 3. Sess.
 xiv. 4.
28 Art. ix.
29 Conc. Trid. Sess. vi. cap. 8.
30 Art. vi. Synt. Gen. p. 12. Ibid. p. 20.
 cap. de Bon. Oper.

31 Ibid. p. 21.
32 Page 22.
33 Comment. in Ep. ad Gal. t. v. 243.
34 Apol. Conf. Aug. ad Art. iv. v. vi.
 Resp. ad Object. Concord. p. 96.
35 Resp. ad Object. Com. p. 137.
36 Apol. Conf. Aug. p. 137.
37 Sess. vi. cap. 8.
38 Ibid. cap. 9.
39 Ibid. cap. 16. et Can. 32.
40 Apol. Conf. Aug. 137.
41 In Locis Comm. cap. de Justif. Mat.
 xix. 29.
42 Aug. ep. 105, num. 194. N. 19. De
 Comp. et Grat. cap. 13. N. 41.
43 Præf. Apol. Conc. p. 48.
44 Solid. repet. Conc. 633.
45 Rom. xiii. 10.
46 Apol. 83. Ib. p. 137.
47 Sess. vi. c. 11.
48 Apoc. iii.
49 Chyt. Hist. Conf. Aug. post Conf.
 George Cæl. Hist. Conf. Aug.
 t. iii.
50 Dan. iv.
51 1 Peter, iv. 8.
52 Luke vi. 37.
53 Resp. ad Arg.
54 Heb. xi. 6.
55 Conc. Trid. Sess. vi. c. 16.
56 Apol. Resp. ad Arg. p. 127.
57 Sess. vi. c. 3-7.
58 Solid. Répét. Conc. p. 686. Epit.
 artic. Ibid. 185.
59 Præf. in Epist. ad Rom. t. v. f. 97, 98.
60 Cap. de Justif. Conc. pp. 68, 71, 72,
 73, 74, 82. Cap. de Dilect. 83.
61 Apol. Resp. ad Arg. vi. 99. De Vot.
 Monast. 281.
62 Apol. Resp. ad Aug. vi. 99. De Vot.
 Monast. 281.
63 Ibid. p. 136.
64 Art. ix. p. 12.
65 Art. xi. p. 13.
66 Art. vi. p. 12. Cap. de bon. Oper. p.
 21.
67 Apol. Cap. de Justif. 71-81.
68 Sup. Book I.
69 Apol. Cap. de Justif. 91.

[70] Conf. Aug. Art. vi. 11. Cap. de Bon. Operib. pp. 12,13, 21.
[71] Rom. xii. 12.
[72] See before, Book II.
[73] Conf. Argent. cap. iii. et iv.
[74] Disp. Lips. an. 1539.
[75] Resp. ad Abrinc.
[76] Disp. Ratisb.
[77] Lib. xx. contra Faust. Manich. 31.
[78] Art. v. 20. cap. de bon. Oper. Synt. Gen. ii. 2d part. Apol. cap de Justif. p. 81.
[79] Sess. vi. cap. 6.
[80] Art. xi. xii. xxii. Gen. p. 21. Apol. de Pœnit. p. 167. 200, 201.
[81] Conf. Aug. art. xi. cap. de Conf.
[82] Cat. Min. Concord. p. 378.
[83] Ibid. p. 380.
[84] Apol. cap. de Num. Sac. ad art 13. p. 200. et seq.
[85] James v. 18.
[86] De C. Babyl. t. xi. 86.
[87] 1 Tim. ii. 15.
[88] 1 Cor. vii. 14.
[89] Apol. p. 203.
[90] Ep. ad Vol. t. vii. p. 505.
[91] Apol. resp. ad Arg. p. 99. De Vot. Mon. p. 281.
[92] Thess. 1522. t. i. p. 377, adv. Paris Theologast. t. ii. p. 193, de abrog. Miss. priv. primo. Tract. Ibid. 258, 259, de Vot. Mon. Ibid. 271, 278.
[93] Præf. adv. Latom. Ibid. 243.
[94] Cap. de Miss.
[95] Form. Miss. t. ii.
[96] Chyt. Hist. Conf. Aug.
[97] Conf. Aug. cap. de Miss. ibid.
[98] Ibid.
[99] Consult Lut. apud. Chyt. Hist. Aug. Conf. tit. de Canone.
100 Conf. Aug. edit Gen. cap. de Miss. p. 25. Apol. cap. de Sacram. et Sacrif. et de Vocab. Miss. p. 269.
[101] Conf. Aug. in tit. Conc. cap. de Miss.
[102] Chyt. Hist. Conf.
[103] Apol. c. de Voc. Miss. p. 274.
[104] Ibid.
[105] Aug. Lib. de Hær. 53. Ep. Hær. 75.
[106] Chyt. Hist. Conf. Cath. c. de Miss. Conc. Trid. Sess. 22. c. 6.
[107] Ad Art xxi c. de Invoc. SS. p. 225.
[108] Ad Art. xxi. cap de Invoc.
[109] Ibid.
[110] Ibid. 229.
[111] Ibid.
[112] Dall. de Cult. Satin. Josep. Mida in Comment. ap. Jur. Acc. de Prop.
[113] Conf. Aug. Art. xxi. edit. Gen. p. 22.
[114] Apol. Resp. ad Arg. p. 141. &c.
[115] Edit Gen. Art. xxi. p. 22.
[116] Apol. Resp. ad Arg. p. 141.
[117] Tr. de Misssa, t. vii. p. 236, et seq.
[118] Cap. de utriusque Specie, p. 235.
[119] Mel. lib. i. Ep. 15.
[120] Resp. Luth. ad Mel. t. ii. Sleid. lib. vii. p. 112.
[121] Conf. Aug. Art. vii.
[122] Præf. Conf. Aug. Concord. p. 8.
[123] Lib. i. Ep. 2.
[124] Lib. iv. Ep. 95.
[125] Ibid.
[126] Lib. i. Ep. 6.

Book IV

A Brief summary:—The Protestant Leagues, and the resolution of taking up arms warranted by Luther.—Melancthon's embarrassment upon these new projects so contrary to the first plans.—Bucer displays his Equivocations, in order to unite the whole Protestant party and the Sacramentarians with the Lutherans.—They are equally rejected by Zuinglius and Luther.—Bucer at length deceives Luther, by acknowledging that the unworthy do receive the Truth of the Body.—The Agreement of Wittenburg concluded on that foundation.—Whilst they are returning to the opinion of Luther, Melancthon begins to doubt of it, however subscribes every thing required by Luther.—The Articles of Smalkald, and Luther's new explication of the Real Presence.—Melancthon's limitation of the Article which regards the Pope.

1.—*The Leagues of the Protestants after the Decree of the Diet of Augsburg, and the resolution of taking up arms approved by Luther.*

RIGOROUS was the decree of the Diet of Augsburg against Protestants. As the Emperor then set up a kind of defensive league with all the Catholic states against the new religion, the Protestants, on their part, resolved more than ever to unite among themselves. But the division regarding the Lord's Supper, which had broken out so openly at the Diet, was a perpetual obstacle to the reunion of the whole party. The Landgrave, in no way scrupulous, made his treaty with those of Basil, Zurich, and Strasburg. But Luther would not hear it mentioned; and the Elector, John Frederick, persisted in the resolution of making no league with them: in order, therefore, to settle this matter, the Landgrave despatched Bucer, the great negotiator of those times in matters of religion, who, by his orders, had an interview with Zuinglius and Luther.[1]

At this time a little pamphlet of Luther's put all Germany in a ferment. We have seen that the great success of his doctrine had made him believe that the Church of Rome was going to fall of itself; and he then maintained strongly that arms ought not to be employed in the cause of the Gospel, not even to defend themselves against oppression.[2] The Lutherans agree, that nothing was more inculcated in his writings than this maxim. He was desirous of giving his new church this beautiful character of primitive Christianity, but he could not adhere to it long. Immediately after the Diet,[3] and while Protestants were laboring to form the league of Smalkald, Luther declared, that although he had constantly taught hitherto, "it was not allowable to resist lawful powers, at present he referred to the lawyers, to whose maxims he was a stranger when he wrote his first works: moreover, that the Gospel was not contrary to political laws; and in such bad times one might be brought to extremity, when not only the civil law, but conscience also, would oblige the Faithful to take up arms, and associate themselves against all those who should make war upon them, even against the Emperor."[4] The letter, which Luther had written against George, Duke of Saxony,[5] had already given a full evidence that the evangelical patience, so boasted of in their first writings, was considered by them as at an end; but that was a letter written to a private individual alone. Here, however, is a public writing, by which Luther authorized those who took up arms against their prince.

2.—Melancthon's concern at these new resolutions of war.

If we credit Melancthon, Luther had not been consulted particularly about the leagues; the affair was somewhat palliated to him, and this writing came forth without his knowledge. But either Melancthon spoke not all he knew, or all was not discovered to Melancthon. It is certain, from Sleidan, that Luther was expressly consulted; nor is it found that his writing was published by any but himself, and truly who would have dared to do it without his orders?[6] This writing set all Germany in a flame. Melancthon complained of it, but in vain. "To what purpose," says he, "was the circulation of this writing throughout all Germany? Ought the alarm to have thus been sounded to excite all the towns to make confederacies?"[7] It was with difficulty he was brought to renounce that beautiful idea of reformation Luther had instilled into him, and which he had so well maintained, when he wrote to the Landgrave, "That it was better to suffer every thing than to take up arms in the cause of the Gospel."[8] He had said as much about the leagues the Protestants were treating about, and which he had endeavored to prevent, as far as he was able, at the time of the Diet of Spire, to which he had been conducted by his Prince, the Elector of Saxony. "It is my opinion," said he, "that all good men ought to oppose these leagues:"[9] but in such a party these fine sentiments could not be supported. When it was seen that prophecies went on too slowly, and Luther's blast was too weak to cast down this so much detested Papacy, instead of entering into themselves, they permitted themselves to be carried away by the most violent measures. At length Melancthon hesitated, but not without extreme reluctance: nay, the agitation he showed while these confederacies were forming excites compassion; he writes to his friend Camerarius, "We are no longer consulted about the question—whether or not it be lawful to defend ourselves by making war: there may be just reasons for it. So great is the malice of some, that should they find us defenceless, they would be capable of any enterprise. Strange are the aberrations of men, and their ignorance extreme! None are touched with this saying,—'Be not solicitous, for your heavenly Father knoweth what is needful for you.' Man believes not himself secure unless he has good and secure supports. In this weakness of minds our theological maxims could never make themselves be heard."[10] Then he ought to have opened his eyes, and seen that the new Reformation, incapable of maintaining the maxims of the Gospel, was not what he imagined it to be until then. But let us attend to the following part of the letter: "I will not," says he, "condemn any person; neither do I believe the precautions of our people ought to be blamed, provided that they do nothing that is criminal, which we shall well know how to provide against." No doubt these Doctors knew perfectly well how to withold armed soldiers, how to set bounds to the ambition of princes, after they have engaged them in a civil war. Alas! if this war itself was a crime, according to the maxims he had always maintained, could he hope to prevent crimes during the course of this war? But he durst not admit his party to be in the wrong; and after he was unable to frustrate their resolutions to a war, he found himself under the obligation of supporting them by arguments. This caused him to sigh. "Oh!" says he, "how well did I foresee, at Augsburg, all these commotions!" It was then he so bitterly lamented the transports of his friends, who pushed all to extremities, and were, said he, "concerned at nothing." For this he wept incessantly; nor could Luther, with all the letters he wrote, give him relief. His grief increased when he saw so many projects of leagues warranted by Luther himself. But, "in conclusion, my dear Camerarius," finishes his letter, "this thesis is wholly singular, and may be considered several ways, for which reason we must pray to God."[11]

His friend Camerarius, in his heart, approved no more than he of these warlike preparations; and Melancthon did always what he could to support him. Above all, Luther was to be excused. A few days after the above letter, he acquaints the same Camerarius, "that Luther had written extremely moderately, and it was with great difficulty they had extorted his determination from him. I believe," says he, "you see completely we are not in error. In my opinion, we ought to give ourselves no more concern about these same leagues; and, truly, such is the present conjuncture, that, in my opinion, we ought not to condemn them. So let us again pray to God."[12]

Very right; but God holds in derision prayers made to him in deprecation of public calamities, when we do not oppose such proceedings as bring them on us. What do I say? When we approve, when we subscribe to them, though with reluctance. Melancthon was sensible of this; and troubled, as well for what he himself, as what others did, entreats his friend to comfort and support him. "Write to me often," thus he speaks; "I have no ease but from your letters."

3.—*Bucer's negotiations.*—*The death of Zuinglius in battle.*

This, then, was a point determined in the new Reformation, that it was lawful to take up arms, and necessary to join in leagues. At this period Bucer entered upon his negotiations with Luther; and whether it was that he found him inclined to peace with the Zuinglians, from a desire to form a strong league, or that by some other means he was able to meet him in good humor, he obtained from him fair words. He sets off immediately to obtain the adhesion of Zuinglius; but the negotiation was interrupted by the war that intervened between the Catholic and Protestant cantons. The latter, though stronger, were vanquished; Zuinglius was killed in battle, and manifested, that however warm a disputant, he was no less bold a combatant. The party found it difficult to defend, in a pastor of souls, this unbecoming bravery, and the excuse was, that he followed the Protestant army in the capacity of a minister, rather than that of a soldier;[13] but, after all, it was certain that he had advanced far into the hottest of the engagement, and died sword in hand. His death was followed by that of Œcolampadius. Luther says he was beaten to death by the devil, whose assault he was unable to resist;[14] and others, that he died of grief, being unable to support the anguish which so many troubles brought upon him. In Germany, the peace of Nuremberg moderated the rigors of the decree of the Diet of Augsburg; but the Zuinglians were not included in this agreement, either by Catholics or Lutherans; and the Elector, John Frederick, obstinately refused to admit them into the league until they should have agreed with Luther in the article of the Real Presence. Bucer, not desponding, pursued his object, and, by all possible ways, labored to surmount this only obstacle to the reunion of the party. To persuade either party was deemed impossible, and already fruitlessly attempted at Marpurg. A mutual toleration, each one retaining his own sentiments, had been rejected there by Luther with contempt, who persisted to say, with Melancthon, that this would be injurious to the truth, which he defended. No other method was left for Bucer, but to have recourse to equivocation, and to acknowledge the substantial presence so as to leave himself a way of escaping.

4.—*The grounds of Bucer's equivocations, in order to reconcile parties.*

The plan he adopted to effect so considerable a concession is surprising. It was an ordinary discourse with the Sacramentarians, that they ought to be cautious not to place simple signs in the sacraments. Zuinglius himself had made no difficulty of acknowledging something more in them; and, to verify his words, some promise of grace annexed to the sacraments was sufficient. The example of baptism sufficiently proved this. But, whereas the Eucharist was not only instituted as a sign of grace, but, moreover, was called the body and blood,—not to be a simple sign, it was necessary the body and blood should be received in it. It was said, therefore, they were received by faith: the true body was therefore received, for Jesus Christ had not two. When they had come so far as to say the true body of Jesus Christ was received by faith, they acknowledged the proper substance was received. To receive it, without it being present, was a thing incomprehensible. Behold, then, said Bucer, Jesus Christ substantially present. There was no further occasion for speaking of faith; it was sufficient to understand it. Thus did Bucer, absolutely and without restriction, acknowledge the real and substantial presence of our Lord's body and blood in the Eucharist, although they were only in heaven; which, however, was afterwards softened by him. In this manner, without admitting any thing new, he changed his whole language; and by habituating himself to speak like Luther, began at length to say, they never had understood each other, and that this long discussion, which had caused so much excitation, was nothing but a dispute on words.

5.—*The agreement Bucer proposes is only in words.*

He had spoken more justly, had he said their agreement was in words only; since, after all, this substance, which was said to be present, was as distant from the Eucharist as heaven is from earth, and was no more received by the faithful than the substance of the sun is received by the eye. This is what Luther and Melancthon said. The first called the Sacramentarians a double-tongued faction,[15] on account of their equivocations; and said, They made a devilish game with the words of our Lord."[16] "The presence which Bucer admits," says the latter, "is but a presence in word, and a presence of virtue. But it is the presence of the body and blood, and not that of their virtue, which we require. If this body of Jesus Christ be no where else but in heaven, and is not with the bread, nor in the bread,—if, finally, it is not to be found in the Eucharist but by the contemplation of faith, it is nothing but an imaginary presence."

6.—*Equivocation on spiritual presence and real presence.*

Brucer and his companions were displeased that what was done by faith was here called imaginary, as if faith were nothing but a simple imagination. "Is it not enough," said Bucer, "that Jesus Christ is present to the pure spirit and to the soul elevated on high?"[17] There was much equivocation in these words. The Lutherans agreed that the presence of the body and blood, in the Eucharist, was above the senses, and of a nature not to be perceived by the mind and by faith; but required, however, that Jesus Christ should be present, in the sacrament, in his proper substance. Whereas Bucer would not have him present, indeed, elsewhere than in heaven, where the mind, by faith, sought him; which had nothing in it that was real, nothing that answered to the idea given by these sacred words,—"This is my body, this is my blood."

7.—*The presence of the body, how spiritual.*

But that which is spiritual, it is not real also? and is there nothing real in baptism, because there is nothing in it that is corporeal? Another equivocation.—Spiritual things, such as Grace and the Holy Ghost, are as present as they can be, when they are spiritually present. But what is a body present in spirit only, if not a body absent in reality, and present only in thought? a presence which cannot, without fallacy, be called real and substantial. But would you, then, said Bucer, have Jesus Christ corporeally present, and do not yourselves acknowledge the presence of his body in the Eucharist to be spiritual? Neither Luther, with his companions, no more than the Catholics, denied that the presence of Jesus Christ in the Eucharist was spiritual as to the manner, provided it were granted to them, that it was corporeal as to the substance: that is, in more plain words, the body of Jesus Christ was present, but in a divine, supernatural, incomprehensible manner, which the senses could not reach; spiritual, inasmuch as the mind alone, subject to faith, could know it, and that its end was entirely celestial. St. Paul had justly called the human body, raised from the dead, "a spiritual body,"[18] on account of the qualities with which it was invested, divine, supernatural, and above the reach of the senses: with much more reason, the body of the Savior, placed after so incomprehensible a manner in the Eucharist, might be so called.

8.—*If the presence of the body be only spiritual, the words of the institution are nugatory.*

Again, all they said of the mind being elevated on high, to seek a Jesus Christ at the right hand of his Father, was no more than a metaphor, not at all capable of representing a substantial reception of the body and blood, since this body and blood remained only in heaven, as the soul, united to its body, remained only on earth; nor was there any more a true and substantial union between the faithful and the body of the Lord, than if there never had been a Eucharist, and Jesus Christ had never said, "This is my body." Let us suppose these words had never been uttered by him at all; the presence, by the mind and by faith, would still subsist in a manner entirely similar, and never mortal man have dreamt of calling it substantial. Now, if the words of Jesus Christ oblige us to more strong expressions, it is because they grant us what would not have been given without them, namely, the proper body and the proper blood, whose immolating and effusion have saved us on the cross.

9.—*Whether a local presence were to be admitted.*

Two fruitful sources of cavilling and equivocation remained for Bucer; one in the word local, and the other in the word sacrament or mystery. Luther and the defenders of the real presence never had pretended that the body of our Lord was contained in the Eucharist, as in a place to which it was commensurate, and in which it was comprehended after the ordinary manner of bodies; on the contrary, they believed nothing to be in the flesh of our Lord which was distributed to them at the holy table, but the simple and pure substance, together with the grace and life with which it abounded; nay, more than this, divested of all sensible qualities and modes of existence with which we are acquainted. Accordingly, Luther easily granted to Bucer that the presence under debate was not local, provided it were granted to him it was substantial; and Bucer strongly insisted on the exclusion of local presence, believing he had weakened as much by this as he had been forced to allow of the substantial presence. He even made use of this artifice to exclude the oral manducation of our Lord's body. He conceived it to be not only useless, but even gross, carnal, and little worthy of the spirit of Christianity; as if this sacred pledge of the flesh and blood, offered on the cross, which our Savior still gave us in the Eucharist, to certify to us that the victim and immolation of it were wholly ours, had been a thing unworthy of a Christian; or that this presence ceased to be true, under pretext that, in a mystery of faith, God had not designed to make it sensible; or, lastly, that a Christian was not touched with this inestimable token of divine love, because it was not known to him otherwise than by the word alone of Jesus Christ; things so far distant from the spirit of Christianity, that the grossness of their minds is inconceivable, who, not able to relish them, look on others, that do, as gross minded.

10.—*Equivocation on the word Sacrament and Mystery.*

The other source of equivocation was in the words Sacrament and Mystery. Sacrament, in the ordinary acceptation, means a sacred sign: but in the Latin language, from which this word is taken, sacrament often signifies a high, secret, and impenetrable thing. This also is the signification of the word mystery. The Greeks have no other word to express sacrament than that of mystery; and the Latin Fathers frequently call the mystery of the Incarnation, the sacrament of the Incarnation, and so of the rest.

Bucer and his followers thought they had gained their point, when they said the Eucharist was a mystery, or a sacrament of the body and blood: or, that the presence acknowledged in it, and the union then effected with Jesus Christ, was a sacramental presence and union; and, on the contrary, the defenders of the Real Presence, both Catholics and Lutherans, understood it to be a presence and union, real, substantial, and properly so called; but hidden, secret, mysterious, supernatural in its manner, and spiritual in its end, proper, in a word, to this sacrament; and it was for all these reasons that they called it sacramental.

Far, therefore, were they from denying that the Eucharist was a mystery in the same sense as the Trinity and Incarnation; namely, a thing high as well as secret, and altogether incomprehensible to the mind of man.

11.—*The Eucharist is a sign, and how?*

Nor did they even deny that it was a sacred sign of the body and blood of our Lord; for they knew that the sign does not always exclude the presence; on the contrary, there are signs of such a nature as denote the thing present. When it is said, a sick person has given signs of life, the meaning is, from these signs it is seen that the soul is still present in its proper and true substance. The external acts of religion are intended to manifest, that truly we have religion in our hearts; and when the angels appeared in human shape, under this appearance, which represented them to us, they were in person present. Thus, the defenders of the literal sense spoke nothing incredible, when they taught that the sacred symbols of the Eucharist, accompanied by the words, "This is my body, this is my blood," denote to us Jesus Christ present, and that the sign is most closely and inseparably united to the thing.

12.—*All the Mysteries of Jesus Christ are signs in certain respects.*

It must be acknowledged still further, that what is most true in the Christian religion, if I may so speak, is both together a mystery, and a sacred sign. The incarnation of Jesus Christ figures to us that perfect union we ought to have with the Divinity in grace and glory. His birth and death are the figure of our spiritual birth and death. If, in the mystery of the Eucharist, he condescends to approach our bodies in his own proper flesh and blood, thereby he invites us to the union of minds, and figures it unto us. In a word, until we have arrived to the full and manifest truth, which will render us for ever happy, every truth will be to us the figure of a truth more intimate: we shall not taste Jesus Christ all pure and in his proper form, and entirely disengaged from figure, until we shall see him, in the fulness of his glory, at the right hand of his Father: for which reason, if in the Eucharist he is given to us in substance and in truth, it is under a foreign species. This is a great Sacrament and great Mystery, in which, under the form of bread, is hidden from us a true body; in which, in the body of a man, the majesty and power of God are hidden from us; in which such great things are performed after a manner impenetrable to human senses.

13.—*Bucer plays with words.*

What latitude for the equivocations of Bucer, in these several significations of the word Sacrament and mystery! And how many evasions might not be prepared from terms, which each one wrested to serve his own purpose! If he granted a real and substantial presence and union, though he did not always express that he understood it by faith, he believed he saved all, by adding to expressions the word Sacramental; this done, he exclaimed, they disputed only on words, and how strange it was they should disturb the Church, and prevent the progress of the Reformation, for so frivolous a dispute.

14.—*Œcolampadius had warned Bucer of the fallacy there was in his equivocations.*

No person would credit him in this. Not only Luther and the Lutherans laughed at his pretence, that the whole Eucharistic dispute was only a dispute on words,—even those of his own party told him plainly he imposed on the world by his substantial presence, which, after all, was only a presence by faith. Œcolampadius had observed how much he had confused the subject by this his substantial presence of the body and blood, and a little before he died, had written to him, that in the Eucharist, there was only for those "Who believed, an effectual promise of the remission of sins, by the body given, and the blood shed; that our souls were nourished therewith, and our bodies associated to the resurrection by the Holy Ghost: that we thus received the true body, and not bread only, nor a simple figure," (he took good care not to say that we received it substantially;) "that in truth the wicked received but a figure; but that Jesus Christ was present to those who were his, as God, who strengthens and who governs us."[19]

This was all the presence Œcolampadius would allow, who concluded in these words: "This is all, my dear Bucer, we can grant the Lutherans.—Obscurity is dangerous to our Churches. Act after such a manner, my dear brother, as not to deceive our hopes."

15.—The sentiments of those of Zurich.

Those of Zurich declared to him with still greater freedom, that it was an illusion to say, as he did, that this dispute was only verbal, and warned him that his expressions led him to the doctrine of Luther, to which he arrived at length, but not so soon. Then they raised loud complaints of Luther, who would not treat them like brethren; yet, however, acknowledged him "for an excellent servant of God;"[20] but it was observed by the party, this suavity served only to make him "more inhuman and more insolent."[21]

16.—The Confession of Faith of those of Basil.

Those of Basil showed themselves far removed both from the sentiments of Luther and the equivocations of Bucer. In the confession of Faith, which is placed in the collection of Geneva in the year 1532, and in Hospinian's history in the year 1534, because, perhaps, is was published for the first time in the one of these two years, and renewed in the other, they say, that "as water remains in Baptism, where the forgiveness of sins is offered to us; so the bread and wine remain in the Supper, where, with the bread and wine, the true body and true blood of Jesus Christ are figured to us, and offered by the minister."[22] To explain this more plainly, they add, "Our souls are nourished with the body and blood of Jesus Christ by a true faith," and by way of elucidation put in the margin, "That Jesus Christ is present in the Supper, but sacramentally, and by the remembrance of faith, which raises man up to heaven, and does not take Jesus Christ from thence."—Finally, they conclude by saying, "That they confine not the natural, true and substantial body of Jesus Christ in the bread and wine, commonly called the Sacrament of the body and blood of Jesus Christ; but in heaven at the right hand of God his Father, whence he shall come to judge the living and the dead." This is what Bucer would neither say, nor explain clearly; that Jesus Christ, as man, was no where than in heaven, although, as far as a judgment can be formed, he was then of that opinion. But he plunged still more deeply into notions so metaphysical that neither Scotus, nor the most refined Scotists, came near to him; and all his equivocations turned on these abstracted ideas.

17.—Luther's Conference with the Devil.

At this time Luther published his book against private mass, where that famous conference is to be found, which he formerly had with the angel of darkness, and where, convinced by his reasons, he abolishes, like an impious wretch, that mass he had said for so many years with so much devotion, if we may believe him.[23] It is surprising to see how seriously and lively he describes his awakening, as in a surprise, in the dead of night; the manifest apparition of the devil to dispute against him. "The terror with which he was seized, his sweat, his trembling, and the horrible palpitation of his heart in this dispute; the strong arguments of the demon, who leaves no repose to the mind; the sound of his thundering voice; his oppressive ways of arguing, when he makes both question and answer perceptible at once. I then was sensible," says he, "how it so often happens that men die suddenly towards the dawn of day: it is by means of the devil, who can kill and strangle them, and without all that, by his disputes reduce them to such difficulties, that it is enough to cause death, as I have many times experienced." He informs us in passing, that the devil frequently attacked him in this manner, and to judge of the other attacks by this, it is to be believed he had learned many things from him besides the condemnation of the mass. It is here he attributes to the evil spirit the sudden death of Œcolampadius, as well as that of Emzer, formerly so great an enemy to Lutheranism in its birth. I mean not to enlarge on so trite a subject: I am satisfied with having observed, that God, for the confusion, or rather for the conversion of the enemies of the Church, has permitted Luther to fall into so great a blindness, as to acknowledge, I do not say, that he was frequently tormented by the devil, which might be common to him with many saints; but what is peculiar to him, that he was converted by his industry, and that the spirit of falsehood had been his tutor in one of the principal points of his reformation.

In vain do they pretend here, that the devil disputed against Luther, only to overwhelm him with despair, by convincing him of his crime; for the dispute had not that tendency. When Luther appears convinced, and unable to answer any thing more, the devil presses no farther, and Luther rests satisfied he had learned a truth of which he was before ignorant. If this be true, how horrible to be tutored by such a master! If Luther fancied it, what illusions, what dismal thoughts occupied his mind! If he invented it, how sad a story had he to boast of!

18.—*The Swiss are incensed against Luther.*

The Swiss were scandalized at the conference of Luther, not so much because the devil appeared there in the capacity of a doctor: they were embarrassed enough to defend themselves against a similar vision, of which Zuinglius boasted,[24] as we have already seen; but they could not endure the manner in which he there treated Œcolampadius. Most severe libels came out on this subject: but Bucer went on negotiating; and through his mediation a conference was held in Constance, for the reunion of both parties. There, those of Zurich declared they would compromise with Luther, provided, on his side, he would grant them three points: one, that the flesh of Jesus Christ was not eaten but by faith; another, that Jesus Christ, as man, was only in a particular place in heaven; the third, that he was present in the Eucharist, by faith, in a manner proper to the sacraments. These words were plain and void of equivocation. The other Swiss, and in particular those of Basil, gave their joint approbation to so clear a proposal. And, indeed, it was wholly conformable to the Basil Confession of Faith: but, although this confession gave a perfect idea of the doctrine of the figurative sense, those of Basil, who had drawn it up, failed not to draw up another, two years after, on the occasion we are going to relate.

19.—Another Basil Confession of Faith, and the former modified.

In 1536, Bucer and Capito came from Strasburg. These two celebrated architects of the most refined equivocations, taking occasion from the Confessions of Faith, which the churches separated from Rome prepared to send to the council which the Pope had just convened, solicited the Swiss to make one, "which might be so framed as to assist the agreement they had considerable hope of effecting;"[25] that is, it was proper to select such terms as the Lutherans, ardent defenders of the Real Presence, might take in good part. With this view, a new Confession of Faith was drawn up, which is the second of Basil; the expressions we have related in the first, which specified, too precisely, that Jesus Christ was not present, except in heaven, and that nothing but a Sacramental Presence, and by remembrance only, was to be acknowledged in the Sacrament, are here retrenched. In reality, the Swiss appeared strongly intent on asserting, as they had done in the first Basil Confession, "that the body of Jesus Christ is not contained in the bread." Had they used these terms without some modification, the Lutherans would easily have perceived their object was directly to oppose the Real Presence; but Bucer had expedients for every thing. By his insinuations, those of Basil were determined to say, "That the Body and Blood are not naturally united to the Bread and Wine; but that the Bread and Wine are symbols, by which Jesus Christ himself gave us a true communication of his Body and Blood, not to serve as a perishable nourishment to the stomach, but to be a food of life eternal."[26] The remainder is nothing but a somewhat long application of the fruits of the Eucharist, which all the world receives.

20.—Equivocation on this Confession of Faith.

There was not here so much as one word to which the Lutherans might not agree; for they do not pretend the body of Jesus Christ is a food for our stomachs, but teach that Jesus Christ is united to the bread and wine, in an incomprehensible, celestial, and supernatural manner; so as, it may well be said, without offending them, that he is not "naturally united" to them. The Swiss proceeded no farther; so that by means of this expression, the article passed in terms a Lutheran might admit, and wherein nothing else, at most, could be desired but more precise and less general expressions. Of the substantial Presence, a thing discussed at that time, they would say neither good nor evil; this was all Bucer could gain of them. Afterwards, they neither adhered to the first nor the second Confession of Faith, which they had published by mutual agreement; and in due time we shall see a third make its appearance, with quite new expressions.

21.—Each one followed the Impressions of his Guide.

Those of Zurich, taught by Zuinglius, and full of his spirit, made no compromise with Bucer; and instead of drawing up, like those of Basil, a new Confession of Faith, to manifest how they persevered in the doctrine of their master, they published that which he had sent to Francis I, which has been mentioned already; and in which he will admit of no other presence in the Eucharist, than that which is made "by the contemplation" of Faith, clearly excluding the substantial presence. Thus they continued to speak naturally. They alone did so among all the defenders of the figurative sense; and it may be seen at this time, how, in the new Reformation, every Church acted according to the impression received from their respective masters. Luther and Zuinglius, ardent, and in extremes, inspired the Lutherans and those of Zurich with similar dispositions, and rejected all temperate measures: if Œcolampadius were more gentle, those of Basil were on that account more pliant; and the people of Strasburg entered into all the mitigations, or rather all the equivocations and fallacies of Bucer.

22.—Bucer acknowledges that the unworthy really receive the Body.

He carried the thing so far, that, after granting all that could be desired, on the real, essential, and substantial, even natural presence, that is, the presence of Jesus Christ according to his nature, he found out expedients to make the faithful, unworthily communicating, receive him really. He required only that the impious and infidels, for whom this holy mystery was not instituted, should be excepted: yet, however, said he was resolved, even in that point, to have no difference with any person.[27]

1536. With all these explications, it is not surprising he appeased Luther, until then implacable. Luther believed the Sacramentarians truly came over to the doctrine of the Augsburg Confession and Apology. Melancthon, with whom Bucer was negotiating, acquainted him that he found Luther more tractable, and that he began to speak more amicably of him and his companions. At last the Assembly of Wittenberg, in Saxony, was held, at which the deputies of the German churches, on both sides, were present.[28] Luther at first spoke in a lofty tone. He would have Bucer and his companions declare that they retracted, and entirely rejected all they said to him of the thing itself, as being not so much the subject of discussion as the manner. But at length, after much discussion, in which Bucer displayed all his pliancy, Luther took those articles, which this minister and his companions granted him, for a retractation.

23.—The Agreement of Wittenberg, and its Six Articles.

1. "That, according to the words of St. Irenæus, the Eucharist consists of two things—the one terrestrial, and the other celestial; and, by consequence, the body and blood of Jesus Christ are truly and substantially present, given, and received with the bread and wine."

2. "That, although they had rejected Transubstantiation, and did not believe that the body of Jesus Christ was contained locally in the bread, or had with the bread any union of long continuance out of the use of the sacrament, it ought, however, to be acknowledged that the bread was the body of Jesus Christ, by a sacramental union; that is, that the bread being present, the body of Jesus Christ was at the same time present, and truly given."

3. They add, however, "That out of the use of the sacrament, whilst it is kept in the ciborium, or shown in processions, they believe it is not the body of Jesus Christ."

4. They concluded by saying, "That this institution of the sacrament has its force in the Church, and depends not on the worthiness or unworthiness of the minister, nor of him who receives."

5. "That as for the unworthy, who, according to St. Paul, truly eat the sacrament, the body and blood of Jesus Christ are truly presented to them, and THEY TRULY RECEIVE THEM, when the words of Christ's institution are observed."[29]

6. "That, however, they take it to their judgment" as says the same St. Paul, "because they abuse the sacrament, by taking it without repentance, and WITHOUT FAITH."[30]

24.—*Bucer deceives Luther, and evades the terms of agreement.*

Luther, it seems, had nothing more to desire. When they grant him that the Eucharist consists of two things—the one heavenly and the other terrestrial, and from this conclude, that the body of Jesus Christ is substantially present with the bread, they manifest sufficiently that he is not present only to the mind, and by faith. But Luther, who was not unacquainted with the subtleties of the Sacramentarians, urges them on still further, and induces them to say, that those even "who have not faith, do, however, truly receive the body of our Lord."[31]

One would not have suspected they believed the body of Jesus Christ was not present to us but by faith, since they acknowledged that it was present and truly received by those who were without repentance, and without faith. After this avowal of the Sacramentarians, Luther easily believed that he had nothing more to demand, and judged they said all that was necessary to confess the reality: but he had not as yet sufficiently understood that these Doctors had particular secrets to explain every thing. However lucid the words of agreement appeared to him, Bucer had reserved a way of escaping. He has published several writings, where he acquaints his friends in what sense he understood each word of the agreement: he there declares, that "Those who, according to St. Paul, are guilty of the body and blood, receive not only the sacrament, but the thing itself indeed, and are not without faith; although," says he, "they have not that lively faith which saves us, nor a true devotion of heart."

Who would ever have believed that the defenders of the figurative sense could have acknowledged a true reception of the body and blood of our Lord in the Supper, without having the faith which saves us? What! is a faith, which is unable to justify us, sufficient, according to their principles, to communicate Jesus Christ truly to us? Their whole doctrine contradicts this sentiment of Bucer. Nor can this minister, however subtle, possibly reconcile what he says here with his other maxims. But it is not my object, in this place, to examine the subtleties by which Bucer extricates himself from the agreement of

Wittenberg: I am content with remarking this undoubted fact—that all the churches of Germany which defended the figurative sense, assembled in a body, by their deputies agreed, in an authentic act, "That the body and blood of Jesus Christ are truly and substantially present, given and received in the Supper, with the bread and wine; and that the unworthy, who are WITHOUT FAITH, do, however, receive this body and this blood, provided they adhere to the words of the institution."

If these expressions can accord with the figurative presence, henceforth it is no longer known what is the meaning of words, and all things may be discovered in any thing. Men, who have accustomed themselves to wrest in this manner human language, will make the Scripture and Fathers speak what they please; nor must we be surprised at so many violent interpretations they give to the most plain passages.

25.—Calvin's Sentiments on Equivocations in matters of Faith.

Whether Bucer had a settled design of amusing the world with these affected equivocations, or whether some confused idea of the reality induced him to believe he might safely subscribe these expressions, so evidently contrary to the figurative sense, I leave the Protestants to determine. Certain it is, Calvin, his friend, and, in some manner, his disciple also, when he wished to express a reprehensible obscurity in a profession of faith, said, "There was nothing so embarrassed, so ambiguous, so intricate in Bucer himself."[32]

These artificial ambiguities were so congenial to the spirit of the new reformation, that Melancthon himself, naturally the most sincere of men, who had most condemned equivocations in matters of faith, permitted himself to be drawn into them contrary to his inclinations. We find a letter of his in 1541, where he writes that nothing is more unworthy of the Church, "than to use equivocations in Confessions of Faith, and to draw up articles which required other articles to explain them; that it was establishing peace in appearance, and in fact exciting war;" and, in short, that it was "similar to the false council of Sirmium and the Arians, mingling truth and error."[33] His judgment was certainly correct; and, at the same time, however, when the first assembly of Ratisbon was held, to reconcile the Catholic religion with the Protestant, "Melancthon and Bucer (it is not Catholics that write it, but Calvin, who was present, and the intimate friend of both) composed, on transubstantiation, equivocal and deceitful forms of faith, on order to satisfy, if possible, their adversaries in conceding nothing to them."[34] Calvin was the first to condemn these affected obscurities and shameful dissimulations: "With reason," says he, "you blame the obscurities of Bucer."[35] "It must be spoken freely," says he in another place, "It is not lawful to embarrass that with obscure and equivocal words which requires light; those who would hold a medium, forsake the defense of truth."[36] And with regard to those snares just mentioned, which Bucer and Melancthon, by their ambiguous discourses, laid for the Catholics nominated to confer with them at Ratisbon, this is what the same Calvin says of them: "As to myself, I do not approve of their design, although they have their reasons; for they hope the points of discussion will emit light, and be elucidated of themselves. For this reason they pass over many things, and fear not these ambiguities; they do it with a good design, but yield too much to the times."[37] Thus did the authors of the new Reformation, with very bad reasons, either practise or excuse the most criminal of all dissimulations—that is, affected equivocations in points of faith. We shall learn from what follows, if Calvin, who seems as much opposed to the practice himself, as he is indulgent to it in others, will always continue of the same opinion; and we must return to the artifices of Bucer.

26.—Whether the presence be permanent in the Eucharist.

In the midst of the advantages he conceded to the Lutherans in the Agreement of Wittenberg, he gained at least one thing which Luther let pass,—that the body and blood of Jesus Christ had no permanent union, out of the sacramental use, with the bread and wine; and that the body was not present, when shown, or carried in procession.[38] This was not the sentiment of Luther; till then he had always taught that the body of Jesus Christ was present from the time the words were said, and remained present till the species was altered;[39] so that, according to him, "he was present even when carried in procession," although he would not approve that custom. And truly, if the body was present in virtue of the words of institution, and these words be understood according to the letter, as Luther maintained it, it is clear the body of Jesus Christ ought to be present at the instant he says, "This is my body," since he does not say, "this will be," but "This is." It was suitable to the power and majesty of Jesus Christ, that his words should have a present effect, and the effect subsist as long as things should remain in the same state. Nor was it ever doubted, from the earliest times of Christianity, that the portion of the Eucharist reserved for the communion of the sick, and for that which the faithful practised daily in their houses, was as much the true body of our Savior as that distributed to them at Church. Luther had always understood it thus; and yet he was induced, I know not how, to tolerate the contrary opinions which Bucer proposed at the time of the agreement.

27.—Sequel.—Conclusion of the Agreement.

He would not, however, permit him to say that the body was not in the Eucharist, except precisely at the time of using it, that is, in the reception; but only "that, out of the sacramental use, there was no permanent union between the bread and the body."[40] This union subsisted, therefore, out of the use, that is, out of communion; and Luther, who made the holy sacrament be elevated, and adored, even at the time the Agreement was framing, would not permit it should be denied him, that Jesus Christ was there present during these ceremonies; but in order to take away the presence of the body of our Lord in the tabernacles and procession of Catholics, which was the object of Bucer, it was sufficient to permit him to say, that the presence of the body and blood in the bread and wine was not of long duration.

Now, had it been asked of these doctors how long, therefore, this presence was to remain, and to what time they limited the effect of the words of our Lord, they would have been strangely embarrassed. It will appear from what follows, and we shall see, when they abandoned the natural sense of the words of our Savior, as they had no longer any certain rule, so they no longer had precise terms, nor certain faith.

Such was the issue of the Concord of Wittenberg. The articles are reported in the same manner by both parties of the new Reformation, and were signed at the end of May in 1536.[41] It was agreed that it should not have force until it had received the approbation of the Churches. Bucer and his companions so little doubted of the approbation of their party, that immediately after the Agreement was signed, they celebrated the Supper with Luther in token of perpetual concord. The Lutherans have always praised this agreement. The Sacramentarians refer to it as an authentic treaty, which had reunited all Protestants. Hospinian pretends that the Swiss—a part, at least, of that body—and Calvin himself, gave it their approbation."[42] An express approval of it, in fact, is found among the letters of Calvin:[43] so that this Agreement ought to have place among the public acts of the new reformation, since it contains the sentiments of all Protestant Germany, and of almost all the reformation.

28.—*Those of Zurich laugh at the equivocations of Bucer.*

Bucer was solicitous to have it approved by those of Zurich. He went to their assembly, and harangued them in words lofty and indefinite; then presented them a long writing.[44] In such verbosity equivocations lie concealed, and a few word are sufficient to speak the faith plainly. In vain did he display his subtleties; he could not make the Swiss digest his substantial presence, nor his communion of the unworthy; they wished always to express their thoughts just as they were, in plain terms, and to say, as Zuinglius did, that there was no physical or natural presence here, nor a substantial one, but a presence *by faith,* a presence *by the Holy Ghost,* reserving to themselves the liberty of speaking of this mystery as they should find suitable, and always in the most plain and intelligible manner that is possible. That is what they wrote to Luther; and Luther, scarcely recovered from a dangerous illness, and fatigued, perhaps, with so many disputes, sought repose, and referred the affair to Bucer, with whom he imagined that he perfectly agreed.[45]

29.—*The Zwinglians will not hear miracles mentioned, nor Omnipotence in the Eucharist.*

But having mentioned in his letter, that, agreeing about the Presence, they were to leave the manner to the Divine Omnipotence; those of Zurich, astonished that he should speak to them of Omnipotence in an action, where they conceived nothing that was miraculous, no more than their master Zuinglius, complained of it to Bucer, who took great pins to satisfy them; but the more he insisted with them that there was something incomprehensible in the manner Jesus Christ gave himself to us in the Supper, the more the Swiss, on their part, repeated to him, that there was nothing more easy. A figure in these words, "This is my body;" the meditation on the death of our Lord, and the operation of the Holy Ghost in the hearts of the faithful, were attended with no difficulty, and they were determined to admit no other miracles in it. So, indeed, should the Sacramentarians speak, would they speak naturally. The Fathers, it is true, did not speak so; they found no example too elevated to raise up the minds of men to the belief of this mystery; but employed for the purpose the creation, the incarnation of our Lord, his miraculous birth, all the miracles of the Old and New Testament, the wonderful change of water into blood, and of water into wine; persuaded as they were, that the miracle, which they acknowledged in the Eucharist, was not less the work of Omnipotence, and yielded in nothing to the most incomprehensible miracles of the hand of God. Thus it was proper to speak in the doctrine of the Real Presence, and Luther had, with this faith, retained the same expressions. From a contrary reason, the Swiss found all easy, and chose rather to turn the words of our Lord into a figure, than to call upon his Omnipotence to verify them; as if the most simple manner of explaining the Holy Scriptures were always that in which reason encounters the least difficulty; or miracles cost the Son of God any thing, where he wished to give us a pledge of his love.

30.—*Doctrine of Bucer, and return of the Towns from his belief to that of the Real Presence.*

Although Bucer could not prevail on those of Zurich, during two years continually treating with them, after the Agreement of Wittenberg, and foresaw very well that Luther would not always be so peaceable as at that time, he used every expedient in order to retain him in this quiet disposition. As for his part, he adhered so closely to the Agreement, that, even after, he was considered by those of the Augsburg Confession as a member of their churches, and in every thing acted conjointly with them.

Whilst he treated with the Swiss, and endeavored to make them comprehend something in the Supper more high and impenetrable than they imagined, among other things he told them, that although there was no doubt of Jesus Christ being in heaven, they did not well understand where this heaven was, nor what it was, and that "heaven was even in the Supper;"[46] which carried with it so clear an idea of the Real Presence, that the Swiss could not bear to hear him.

The comparisons he employed tended rather to enforce than weaken the reality. He often instanced that ordinary action of shaking one another by the hand;[47] a very plain example to show that the same hand used to execute treaties may be a pledge of the will to fulfil them; and that a transitory contract, yet real and substantial, may become, by the institution and usage of men, the most effectual sign they can give to each other of perpetual union.

Since he had commenced to treat about the Agreement, he was not fond of saying with Zuinglius, that the Eucharist was the Body, as the Rock was Christ, and as the Lamb was the Passover. He chose rather to say it was so, as the Dove is called the Holy Ghost, which shows a Real Presence; there being none that doubt that the Holy Ghost was present, in a particular manner, under the form of the dove. He adduced also the example of Jesus Christ breathing on the Apostles, and at the same time giving them the Holy Ghost:[48] which still proved that the body of Jesus Christ is not less communicated, nor less present, than the Holy Ghost was to the Apostles.

With all this, however, he approved of the doctrine of Calvin, replete with sacramentarian notions;[49] and was not afraid to subscribe a confession of faith, where the same Calvin said, that the manner in which the body and blood of Jesus Christ were received in the Supper consisted in the Holy Ghost uniting therein what was separated in place. This, it seems, was clearly acknowledging Jesus Christ to be absent. But Bucer explained every thing, and had surprising solutions for all kinds of difficulties. But what is here most remarkable, the disciples of Bucer, and as we have before observed, whole towns, that under his guidance had so far removed from the Real Presence, came now again insensibly into this belief. The words of Jesus Christ were so well deliberated on, and so often repeated, that at last they produced their effect, and men naturally returned to the literal sense.

31.—*Melancthon begins to doubt the doctrine of Luther.—The Weakness of his Theology.*

While Bucer and his disciples, the declared opponents of the doctrine of Luther on the real presence, drew near to him, Melancthon, the dear disciple of the same Luther, the author of the Augsburg Confession, and of the Apology, in which he had maintained the reality, to such a length as to appear inclined to transubstantiation, began to waver.

In 1535, or about that time, this doubt came into his mind;[50] before that time, it may be seen how very steady he had been. He had even composed a book of the sentiments of the holy Fathers on the Supper, in which he had collected many passages most expressly for the real presence.

As the criticism of those days was not very accurate, he perceived, at length, that some of them were spurious,[51] and that the transcribers, through ignorance or carelessness, had attributed to the ancients some works of which they were not the authors. This troubled him, although he had cited a sufficient number of passages which were incontestable. But he was more embarrassed to find many places in the ancients where they called the Eucharist a figure.[52] He collected these passages, and was astonished, said he, "to see in them so great a diversity." Weak divine! not to understand that neither the condition of faith, nor of this present life, could permit us to enjoy Jesus Christ face to face, for which reason he gave himself unto us under a borrowed form, necessarily joining truth with figure, and the Real Presence with an exterior sign that concealed it from us. From this proceeds that apparent diversity of the Fathers which surprised Melancthon. The same difficulty would have appeared to him, had he closely investigated the mystery of the Incarnation, and the divinity of the Son of God, before the disputes of heretics had induced the Fathers to speak of these matters with more precision. In general, where two truths that appear contrary are to be reconciled, as in the mystery of the Trinity, and that of the Incarnation, to be equal and to be inferior; and in the Eucharist, to be present and to be in figure; naturally, a sort of language is used that appears confused, unless we have the key of the Church, as we may say, and the full comprehension of the entire mystery: besides the other reasons which obliged the Fathers to conceal the mysteries in some places, affording in others the certain means by which to understand them. Melancthon did not know so much. Dazzled with the name of reformation, and the exterior of Luther then somewhat specious, he immediately enlisted in the party. As yet but young and a great humanist, and only a humanist, newly called by the Elector Frederick to teach the Greek language in the University of Wittenberg, he could have made but little progress in the investigation of ecclesiastical antiquity with his master Luther, and was strangely shocked at the contrarieties he supposed he found in the Fathers.

32.—*A dispute in the time of Ratramnus, that confounds Melancthon.*

To embarrass himself completely, he must also read the book of Bertram or Ratramnus, which then began to appear; an ambiguous book, where certainly the author did not always understand himself:[53] the Zuinglians support their cause much by it. The Lutherans cite it for themselves, and find nothing in it to condemn, but that it sowed the seeds of Transubstantiation. There is, indeed, sufficient to content, or rather to embarrass both sides. Jesus Christ, in the Eucharist, is so much a human body by his substance, and so unlike a human body by his qualities, that it may be said he is one, and is not one, in different respects; that in one sense, considering his substance only, it is the same body of Jesus Christ, which was born of Mary; but that in another sense, considering the manner alone, it is a different one, which he has made himself by his own word, which he conceals under shadows and figures, whose truth reaches not the senses, but discovers itself to faith alone.

This is what raised a dispute amongst the faithful in the time of Ratramnus. Some, with respect to the substance, said, the body of Jesus Christ was the same in the womb of the Virgin and the Eucharist: others, with respect to the qualities, or rather manner of existence, would have it another. Thus we see St. Paul, speaking of a body risen again, makes, as it were, another body of it, far different from what we have in this mortal life, though in reality it be the same:[54] but, on account of the different qualities with which this body is vested, St. Paul makes of it as it were two bodies, one of which he calls "the animal body," and the other "the spiritual body."[55] In this same sense, and with much more reason, one might say, that the body received in the Eucharist, was not that which came from the blessed womb of the Virgin. But though this might be said in a certain sense, others feared, by saying it, they should destroy the truth of the body. Thus did Catholic Doctors, agreeing in substance, dispute about the manner; some following the expressions of Paschasius Rathbert, who would have the Eucharist to contain the same body which came from the Virgin; others adhering to those of Ratramnus, who maintained it was not the same. With this another difficulty was connected, inasmuch as a strong persuasion of the real presence, which obtained over the whole Church, both in the East and West, had induced many Doctors no longer to permit in the Eucharist the term "figure," which they believed was contrary to the truth of the body; and others, who considered that Jesus Christ does not give himself in the Eucharist in his proper form, but under a foreign one, and in a manner so full of mysterious significations, acknowledged, indeed, that the body of our Savior was really in the Eucharist but under figures, under veils, and in mysteries: which to them appeared the more necessary, as, in other respects, it was most certain that, to possess Jesus Christ in his manifest truth, under the cover of no figure, was a privilege reserved for the next life. All this was true in the main; but, before it could be well explained, there was room for long disputes. Ratramnus, who followed the last party, had not sufficiently investigated this matter, and, without differing in substance from other Catholics, sometimes fell into obscure expressions, which it was difficult to reconcile: the very cause that all his readers, Protestants as well as Catholics, have understood him in so many different senses. Melancthon found that this author left his reader to guess at his meaning, instead of explaining it with clearness, and, with him, lost himself in a subject which neither he nor his master Luther had ever well comprehended.

33.—*Melancthon wishes for a new decision.—Luther's tyranny.*

By this reading, and these reflections, he fell into a deplorable uncertainty; but whatever might be his opinion, of which we shall hereafter speak, he began to dissent from his master, and wished most ardently that an assembly might be held to treat anew on this subject, "without passion, without sophistry, and without tyranny."[56] This last word visibly regarded Luther, for in all the assemblies, till then, held in the party, as soon as Luther appeared, and declared his opinion, Melancthon himself assures us the others had no alternative but silence, and all was terminated. But whilst, disgusted with such proceedings, he demanded new deliberations, and receded from Luther, yet he rejoiced that Bucer, with his companions, drew near to him. We have but just seen him approve the agreement in which the real presence was fixed more than ever to the external symbols;[57] because it was there established that it subsists in the communion of the unworthy, "although there be neither faith nor repentance." It is necessary to cast our eyes only for a moment on the Agreement of Wittenberg, not only subscribed but also obtained by Melancthon, to be convinced how positively he there assents to a thing of which he had conceived so great a doubt.

34.—*Luther makes a new declaration of his Faith, in the Articles of Smalkald.*

The reason was, Luther always pushed forward, and was so resolute upon this point, that he knew not how to contradict him. The year after the agreement, that is, in 1537, while Bucer continued negotiating with the Swiss, the Lutherans met at Smalkald, the ordinary place of their assemblies, and where all their leagues were formed. The Council summoned by Paul the Third gave occasion to this assembly. Luther could not be well satisfied with the Confession of Augsburg, nor the Apology, nor the manner in which his doctrine was there explained, since he himself draws up new articles, "in order," says he, "that it may be known what are the points from which he is resolved never to depart;"[58] and for this reason he procured this assembly. There Bucer declared himself so explicitly on the Real Presence, "that he satisfied," says Melancthon, who mentions it with joy, "even those of our people who were the most difficult to be pleased."[59] Consequently, he satisfied Luther; and here, again, Melancthon is delighted that the sentiments of Luther are followed, whilst he himself abandons them; that is, he was delighted to see all the Protestants of Germany reunited. Bucer had given his assent; the town of Strasburg, with their Doctor, declared for the Confession of Augsburg; human policy, their most important object, had attained its end; and, as for doctrine, they were afterwards to provide for that.

35.—A new way of explaining the Words of the Institution.

It must be acknowledged, however, that Luther proceeded in this with more sincerity. He was determined to speak plainly on the subject of the Eucharist, and thus explained the sixth article of the Sacrament of the Altar:—"As to the Sacrament of the Altar," says he, "we believe that the bread and wine are the true body and true blood of our Lord; and are not only given and received by pious Christians, but also by the impious."[60] These last words are the same we have seen in the Concord of Wittenberg, except that, instead of the word "unworthy," he uses the word "impious," which is stronger, and removes the idea of faith to a still greater distance. It is also to be observed that, in this article, Luther says nothing against the presence out of the use of the Sacrament, nor against the permanent union; but only, "that the bread was the true body;" not determining when it was, nor for how long a time.

36.—Whether Bread can be the Body.

Yet this expression, "that the bread was the true body," before that time had never been inserted by Luther in any public act. The terms which he generally used were, that the body and blood were given "under the bread" and "under the wine;"[61] thus he explains himself in his little Catechism. He adds a word in the large one, and says, "that the body is given to us in the bread and under the bread."[62] I cannot discover exactly at what time these two Catechisms were written, but it is certain the Lutherans acknowledge them both for authentic acts of their religion. To the two particles, "in," and "under," the Confession of Augsburg adds "with;" and it is the ordinary phrase of the true Lutherans, "that the body and blood are received in, under, and with the bread and wine;" but, hitherto, it had never been said in any public act of the whole party, that the bread and wine were the true body and true blood of our Lord. Luther here decides the point, and necessary it was for Melancthon, how great soever his repugnance might be, to unite the bread with the body,—to subscribe even that the bread was the true body.

37.—Luther cannot evade the equivocations of the Sacramentarians who elude all.

The Lutherans in their Book of Concord assure us, that Luther was forced to this expression by the subtleties of the Sacramentarians,[63] who invented evasions to accommodate to their moral presence Luther's strongest and most precise expressions, for the real and substantial presence: from this we may again, as we go on, observe, that it is not a matter of surprise, if the defenders of the figurative sense invent expedients to call in the support of the fathers; since Luther himself living and speaking, who knew their subtleties, and who undertook to oppose them, found it difficult to prevent them from wresting his words to their own sense by their interpretations: fatigued with their subtleties, he directed his mind to the discovery of such expressions as they might no longer wrest, and drew out the article of Smalkald in the above form.

And, indeed, as we have before observed,[64] if the true body of Jesus Christ, according to the opinion of the Sacramentarians, be not received except by means of a lively faith, it cannot be said with Luther, that "the impious receive it;" and as long as they shall maintain, that the bread is not the body of Jesus Christ, except in figure, without doubt they will never say with the Article of Smalkald, "That the bread is the true body of Jesus Christ;" thus Luther, by this expression, excluded the figurative sense, and all the Sacramentarian interpretations. But he was not aware he no less excluded his own doctrine, since we have shown that the bread cannot be the true body, unless it become so by a true and substantial change, which Luther would not admit.

Thus when Luther, and the Lutherans, after turning the Article of the Real Presence so many different ways, endeavor at last to explain it so precisely, as that the Sacramentarian equivocations might remain entirely excluded, we see them fall insensibly into expressions, which, according to their principles, have no sense, and cannot be maintained except in the Catholic doctrine.

38.—The violence of Luther against the Pope in the Articles of Smalkald.

At Smalkald, Luther expresses himself with great asperity against the Pope, who, as we have seen, was not even named in the Articles of the Augsburg Confession, nor in the Apology; and lays down, among the articles from which he resolved never to depart, "That the Pope is not of divine right; that the power he has usurped is full of arrogance and blasphemy; that all he has done or now does, in virtue of this power, is diabolical; that the Church can and ought to subsist, without a head; that although the Pope should acknowledge he is not of divine right, but was made purely to maintain, more conveniently, the unity of Christians among sectaries, yet no good could ever come from such authority; and that the best way to govern and preserve the Church, is for all the bishops, though unequal in their gifts, to remain equal in their ministry, under the one only head Christ Jesus: lastly, that the Pope is antichrist."[65]

39.—Melancthon wishes that the authority of the Pope should be acknowledged.

I expressly mention, at length, these decisions of Luther, because Melancthon gave them a limitation which cannot be sufficiently considered.

At the conclusion of the Articles are seen two lists of subscriptions, in which appear the names of all the Ministers and Doctors of the Confession of Augsburg.[66] Melancthon signed with all the others; but because he refused to agree to what Luther had said of the Pope, he made his subscription in these terms, "I, Philip Melancthon, approve the foregoing articles as pious and Christian. As for the Pope, my opinion is, if he would receive the Gospel, that for the peace and tranquillity of those who are already under him, or shall be hereafter, we may grant to him that superiority over the bishops, which he enjoys already by human right."[67]

This superiority of the Pope, however established, was the object of Luther's aversion. Ever since the time the Popes condemned him, he became irreconcilable to this power, and induced even Melancthon to sign an act, by which the whole new reformation declared in a body, "We never will approve of the Pope's having power over the rest of the bishops."[68] At Smalkald, Melancthon retracts it. It was the first and only time he ever, by a public act, opposed his master; and because his complaisance, or submission, or some similar motive, whatever it might be, induced him to pass over, in spite of all his doubts, the much more difficult point of the Eucharist, we must believe that powerful reasons influenced him to resist in this. These reasons merit investigation the more, as by this examination we shall discover the true state of the new reformation; the particular dispositions of Melancthon; the cause of all the troubles which constantly agitated him, even to his death; how a man engages on the side of error with general good intentions; and how he there remains in the midst of the most violent anxieties that can be felt in this life. The thing merits to be deeply understood, and Melancthon himself, by his own writings, will discover it to us.

Notes

[1] Recess. Arg. Sleid. Lib. vii. 3.
[2] Lib. i. n. 3. ii. 9.
[3] Sleid. Lib. vii. viii.
[4] Sleid. Lib. vii. 117.
[5] Sleid. Lib. ii. n. 42.
[6] Lib. iv. Ep. 3. Lib. vii. 117.
[7] Lib. iv. Ep. 3.
[8] Lib. iii. Ep. 16.
[9] Lib. iv. Ep. 85. 3. Ib. Ep. 85.
[10] Lib. iv. Ep. 110.
[11] Lib. iv. Ep. iii.
[12] Ibid.
[13] Hosp. ad an. 1521.
[14] Tr. de abrog. Miss. t. vii. p. 230.
[15] Luth. Ep. ad Sen. Francof. Hosp. ad an. 1533, 128.
[16] Ep. Mel. apud Hosp. 1530. 110.
[17] Ep. Mel. p. 3.
[18] 1 Cor. xv. 44. 46.
[19] Epist. œcol. ap. Hosp. an 1520. 112
[20] Ep. ad March. Brand. ib.
[21] Hosp. 127.
[22] Conf. Bas. 1532. Art. ii. Synt. i. Part. 72.
[23] De abrog. Miss. priv. t. vii. p. 226.
[24] Hosp. ad an. 1533. 131.

[25] Synt. Conf. Gen. de Helv. Conf. Hosp. Part ii. 141.
[26] Conf. bas. 1536. Art. xxii. Synt. p. 1, 70.
[27] Hosp. Part. ii. fol. 135.
[28] Hosp. an. 1535, 1536
[29] Hosp. p. ii. an. 1535. f. 145. in Lib. Conc. 729.
[30] Art. i. Art. v. et vi.
[31] Buc. Declar. Conc. Vit., Id. ap. Hosp. an. 1536. 148, et seq.
[32] Ep. Cal. p. 50.
[33] Lib. i. Ep. 25. 1541. Ib. Ep. 76.
[34] Ep. Cal. p. 38.
[35] Ep. p. 50.
[36] Ep. p. 50.
[37] Ep. p. 38.
[38] Art. ii. 3.
[39] Luth. Ser. cont. Lucr. et. Ep. ad quend. Hosp. ii. p. 14, 44, 132.
[40] Form. Miss. b. ii. Hosp. an. 1536. p. 148.
[41] Conc. p. 729. Hosp. part ii. fol. 145. Chytr. Hist. Confess. Aug.
[42] Ann. 1536, 1537, 1538.
[43] Calv. ep. p. 324.
[44] Hosp. p. ii. f. 150. et seq.
[45] Hosp. p. ii. f. 157.
[46] Hosp. 162.
[47] Ep. ad Ital. int. Calv. Ep. p. 44.
[48] Ep. ad Ital. int. Calv. Ep. p. 44.
[49] Int. Ep. Calv. p. 378.
[50] Hosp. an 1535. 137, et seq.
[51] Lib. iii. Epist. 114, ad Joan. Brent.
[52] Ibid.
[53] Lib. iii. Ep. 188, ad Vit. Theod.
[54] 1 Cor. xv. 37, et seq.
[55] Ibid. 42, 43, 44, 46.
[56] Lib. ii. Ep. 40. iii. Ep. 188, 189.
[57] Lib. iii. Ep. 114. ad Brent.
[58] Art. Smal. Præf. in lib. Conc.
[59] Ap. Hosp. an. 1537, p. 155. Mel. iv. Ep. 196.
[60] Conc. p. 330.
[61] Conc. p. 330.
[62] Ibid. p. 553.
[63] Ibid. p. 720.
[64] Lib. ii. N. 3. p. 3.
[65] Art. iv. p. 312.
[66] Conc. p. 336.
[67] Conc. p. 338
[68] Mel. Lib. x. Ep. 76.

Book V

[General Reflections on the Agitations of Melanchthon, and the state of the Reformation]

A brief summary.—Melanchton's agitations, regrets, vacillating condition.—The cause of all his errors, and of his disappointed hopes.—The unhappy success of the Reformation, and the wretched motives that attract men to it, acknowledged by the Authors of the party.—Melancthon in vain acknowledges the perpetuity of the Church, the authority of her judgments, and that of her Prelates.—Imputed Justice leads him away, though, by his Confession, he does not find it in the Fathers, not even in St. Augustin, on whom he had formerly rested.

1.—*How Melanchthon was attracted to Luther.*

THE first proceedings of Luther, at which time Melancthon devoted himself entirely to him, were attended with a specious appearance. Exclaiming against abuses, which were but too true, with much force and liberty; mingling with his discourses pious sentiments, the remnants of a good education; and at the same time leading a life, if not perfect, at least blameless in the eyes of men, are things which have no small attractive influence. We are not to suppose that heresies always have for their authors libertines and wicked men, who designedly make religion subservient to their passions. St. Gregory Nazianzen does not represent to us Heresiarchs as men destitute of religion, but as men who mistake it. "They are," says he, "men of great minds, for weak minds are equally useless for good or evil. But these great wits," proceeds he, "are withal ardent and impetuous, who pursue the affair of religion with a boundless warmth:"[1] that is, who have a false zeal, and mingling proud disgust, and invincible assurance, and their own conceits with religion, urge all to extremes: to this also must be united an air of regularity, or where would be that seduction so often predicted in the Scripture? Luther had formerly a zest for devotion. In his early life, alarmed by a clap of thunder, which he thought would have struck him dead, he entered into religion with dispositions sufficiently sincere. What occurred with regard to indulgences has already been explained. If he advanced extraordinary tenets of doctrine, he submitted himself to the Pope. Condemned by the Pope, he appealed to the Council, which the whole Christian world, many ages before, had deemed necessary to redress the grievances of the Church. To reform corrupt morals was an object desired by the universe: and although sound doctrine always subsisted equally well in the Church, yet it was not explained equally well by all preachers. Many preached nothing but indulgences, pilgrimages, almsgiving to the religious, and made those practices, which were only the accessaries of piety, the foundation of religion. They spoke little of the grace of Jesus Christ; and Luther, who, by the dogma of imputed justice, took a new view of it, appeared to Melancthon, as yet but young, and more acquainted with polite literature than theology, to be the only preacher of the Gospel.

2.—*Melancthon captivated with novelty, and the deceitful appearance of imputed justice.*

It is but just to give all to Jesus Christ. The Church attributed all to him in the justification of the sinner, as well and better than Luther, but in a different manner. We have seen how Luther attributed all to him, by absolutely taking all from man; and, on the other hand, the Church attributed all to him, by maintaining, for an effect of his grace, all the good man has, and even the right use of his free-will in all that regards a Christian life. The novelty of Luther's doctrine and opinions captivated men of wit. Melancthon was the chief of them in Germany. To erudition, to politeness, and to elegance of style, he united a singular moderation. He was considered to be the only person capable of succeeding in learning, to the reputation of Erasmus; and Erasmus himself, by his own choice, would have elevated him to the first honors among the learned world, had he not seen him engaged in a party against the Church; but the tide of novelty bore him down with the crowd. From the beginning of his attachment to Luther, he wrote to one of his friends, "I have not yet treated the matter of justification as it should be treated, and I am aware that none of the ancients treated it in this manner."[2] These words demonstrate a man captivated with the charms of the new doctrine; and yet he has but touched so great a subject, and already knows more than all the ancients. We see him charmed at a sermon, which Luther made on the subject of the Sabbath-day.[3] He there taught that repose, in which God did all, and man nothing. A young professor of the Greek language heard such novel ideas, promulgated by the most lively and vehement orator of his age, with all the ornaments of his native language, and immense applause: it is not a matter of surprise that he was captivated. To him Luther appears the greatest of all men—a man sent by God—a Prophet. The unexpected success of the new reformation confirmed this opinion. Melancthon was sincere and credulous; men of talent are often so: there he was taken. All the votaries of polite literature follow his example—Luther becomes their idol. He is attacked, and perhaps with too much acrimony. The ardor of Melancthon is enkindled; the confidence of Luther engages him still more; and with his master, he permits himself to be captivated with the temptation of reforming Bishops, Popes, Princes, Kings, and Emperors, even at the expense of unity and peace.

3.—*How Melancthon excused the violence of Luther.*

Luther, it was true, was the slave of unheard-of excesses: this was a subject of sorrow to his moderate disciple. He trembled whenever he thought of the implacable wrath of this Achilles; and feared "nothing less from the old age of a man, whose passions were so violent, than the transports of a Hercules, a Philoctetes, and a Marius;"[4] that is, he anticipated what, indeed, happened, something furious. This he writes confidentially, and in Greek, according to his custom to his friend Camerarius: but, as with men of wit, a witty saying often has great influence, a bonmot of Erasmus supported him. Erasmus said that the world, stubborn and obdurate as it was, required a master as rude as Luther:[5] that is, as he explained it to him, Luther seemed necessary to the world, as tyrants are, whom God sends for its correction; as a Nebuchadnezzar, a Holofernes; in a word, as a scourge of God. In this there was no subject in which to glory; but Melancthon, who had understood it on the fair side, persuaded himself, at the commencement, that, in order to awaken the world, nothing less was necessary than the violence and thunder of Luther.

4.—The commencement of the agitations of Melancthon.

But at length the arrogance of this imperious master declared itself. The whole world rose up against him, even those who were equally intent upon the reformation of the Church. A thousand impious sects enrolled themselves under his banner, and, under the name of Reformation, arms, seditions, and civil wars, devastated Christianity. To increase these sorrows, the Sacramentarian contest divided the new-born reformation into two almost equal parts. However, Luther urged every thing to extremes; and his discourses, instead of calming, imbittered the minds of men. His conduct appeared so weak, and his excesses so singular, that Melancthon neither could excuse nor support them. From that time his agitations were exceedingly great. Every moment he wished for death. For thirty hears his tears ceased not to flow.[6] "And the Elbe," said he, "with all it streams, would not have furnished him with water sufficient to weep for the sorrows of the divided reformation."[7]

5.—Melancthon acknowledges at length that Luther's great success proceeded from a bad principle.

The unexpected success of Luther, with which he had been at first dazzled, and which with all others he considered as a mark of the finger of God, was but a weak relief to him, when time had discovered to him the true causes of this great progress and its deplorable effects. He soon perceived that licentiousness and independence had been the great supporters of the reformation. If the cities of the empire were seen to run in crowds to this new gospel, it was not to adopt its doctrine. Our reformed will feel pain at these words, but it is Melancthon who writes them and writes them to Luther:—"Our people blame me because I restore the jurisdiction to Bishops. The people accustomed to liberty, having once cast off the yoke, will not receive it again: and the imperial towns are most averse to this authority. They seek not doctrine and religion, but power and liberty."[8] He repeats this complaint again to the same Luther:—"Our associates," says he, "dispute not for the Gospel, but who shall govern."[9] These towns, therefore, sought not for doctrine but independence;

and if they were averse to their Bishops, it was not because they were pastors, but because they were sovereigns.

6.—He anticipates the disorders which were to arise from the contempt of Episcopal authority.

To speak all, Melancthon was not anxious to re-establish the temporal power of the Bishops; but what he wished to have restored, was the ecclesiastical government, the spiritual jurisdiction, and, in a word, "the Episcopal administration;" because he saw that without that every thing would fall into confusion. "Would to God I could confirm, not the sovereignty of Bishops, but restore their administration; for I see what kind of Church we are likely to have if we subvert the ecclesiastical government. I see that TYRANNY WILL BE MORE INSUPPORTABLE THAN EVER."[10] It is what always happens when the yoke of lawful authority is thrown off. Those who excite the people to insurrection under the pretext of liberty, become tyrants themselves; and if it be not yet sufficiently seen that Luther was of that number, what follows will establish it beyond all doubt. Melancthon proceeds; and after blaming those who loved Luther, only because, through his means they removed the Bishops, he concludes, "They had gained a liberty which would do posterity no good. For what will be," proceeds he, "the state of the Church, if we change all the ancient customs, and there be no more prelates nor certain guides?"

7.—Ecclesiastical authority and discipline entirely despised in the New Churches.
—The testimony of Capito and others.

In this disorder he anticipates each one will become his own master. If the ecclesiastical powers, to whom the authority of the Apostles came by succession, be not acknowledged, how will the new ministers subsist who have taken their places? It is only necessary to hear Capito speak, the colleague of Bucer in the administration of the Church of Strasburg:—"The authority of the ministers," says he, "is wholly abolished; all is lost—all falls to ruin. There is not any Church amongst us, not so much as one, where there is any discipline. The people say boldly to us—you wish to tyrannize over the Church which is free—you wish to establish a new Papacy." And a little after: "God has given me to understand what it is to be a pastor, and the injury we have done the Church by our precipitate judgment, and the inconsiderate vehemence which induced us to reject the Pope. For the people, accustomed to, and nourished, as it were, in licentiousness, have rejected the curb altogether, as if, by destroying the power of the Papists, we, at the same time, destroyed the force of the Sacraments and the Ministry. They loudly tell us, I know enough of the gospel; what need have I of your aid to find out Jesus Christ; go and preach to those that are disposed to hear you."[11] What Babylon more confused than this Church, which boasted she had come forth from the Church of Rome as from a Babylon? Such was the Church of Strasburg; that Church which the new reformed incessantly proposed to Erasmus, when he complained of their disorders, as the most orderly and modest of all the churches. Such was this Church in 1537, that is, in her vigor and in her bloom.

Bucer, the colleague of Capito, entertained no better opinion of it in 1549; and acknowledges that nothing had been there more sought after, "than the pleasure of living after their own fancy."[12]

Another minister complains to Calvin, that there was no order in their churches, and gives this reason, "That a great number of their people believed they had withdrawn themselves from the power of Antichrist, by revelling with the wealthy of the Church, as pleased them best, and by despising all discipline."[13] These are not discourses which censure disorders with exaggeration; they are what the new Pastors write to each other in confidence; and by them are seen the sad effects of the new reformation.

8.—*Another fruit of the Reformation.—The servitude of the Church, in which the Magistrates make themselves Popes.*

One of the fruits it produced was the slavery into which the Church fell. It is not surprising if the new reformation pleased princes and magistrates, who then became masters of all, even of doctrine itself. The first effect of the new gospel, in a town adjoining Geneva, Montbeliart, was an assembly there held, by the principal inhabitants, in order to know "what the Prince could ordain concerning the Supper."[14] In vain Calvin resists this abuse: he has little hope of a remedy; and all he can do is to complain of it, as the greatest disorder that can be brought into the Church. Mycon, the successor of Œcolampadius in the ministry of Basil, makes a similar complaint to as little purpose: "The laymen," says he, "assumes all to themselves, and the magistrate has made himself Pope."[15]

This was an evil unavoidable in the new Reformation; it established itself by rising up against the Bishops, by warrant from the magistrates. The magistrate suspended the mass at Strasburg, abolished it in other places, and modelled the divine service; the new pastors were instituted by his authority; after that it was but just that he should have all power in the Church. Thus all that was gained in the new reformation, by rejecting the Pope, the ecclesiastical successor of St. Peter, was to give themselves a lay-pope, and place the authority of the Apostles in the hands of the magistrates.

9.—*Luther receives the Mission of the Prince to make the Ecclesiastical Visitation.*

Luther, proud as he was of his new Apostleship, could not defend himself against so great an abuse. Sixteen years had elapsed since the establishment of his Reformation in Saxony, without ever thinking of visiting the Churches, even to see if the pastors whom they had appointed discharged their duty, or if the people knew, at least, their Catechism. "They were taught very well," says Luther, "to eat flesh on Fridays and Saturdays, to lay aside confession, to believe they were justified by faith alone, and that good works merited nothing;"[16] but seriously to preach repentance, Luther well assures us, was a thing they never thought of.—The Reformers were otherwise employed. At

last, to restrain this disorder, in 1538, they thought of the remedy of a
Visitation, so recommended in the Canons. "But not a man amongst us," says
Luther, "was as yet called to this ministry; and St. Peter prohibits any thing
being done in the Church without being assured by a certain deputation, that
what one does is the work of God;" that is, in a word, "a mission, a vocation,
a lawful authority is necessary for that end."[17] Observe, these new evangelists
were assured of their extraordinary mission from above, to cause the people
to rise up against their bishops, to preach in opposition to them, to take upon
themselves the administration of sacraments, contrary to their prohibition: but
for the true episcopal function, which is to visit and correct, not one of them
had received the vocation or appointment from God, so imperfect was this
heavenly mission; so much those, who boasted of it, did distrust it in reality.
The remedy discovered for this defect was to have recourse to "the Prince, as
to a power undoubtedly ordained by God in this country."[18] Thus Luther
speaks. But was this power of God's appointment established for this function?
Luther acknowledges it was not, and rests upon this foundation, that a
visitation is an apostolic function. Why, then, have recourse to the prince?
"Because," says Luther," although the secular power be not charged with this
office, they will not fail, in charity, to name visitors;" and Luther exhorts the
other princes to follow this example; that is, he would have the function of
Bishops be exercised by the authority of princes; and this attempt, in the
language of the Reformation, was called charity.

10.—*The Lutheran Churches have no better discipline, and Melancthon
acknowledges it.*

This statement demonstrates that the Sacramentarians were not the only people
who, destitute of lawful authority, had filled their Churches with confusion:
Capito, it is true, after complaining, as we have seen, that discipline was
unknown in the Churches of his sect, adds, "there was no discipline except in
the Lutheran Churches."[19] But Melancthon, who was acquainted with them,
speaking of these Churches, in 1532, and much about the time that Capito
wrote his letter, relates, "that discipline was destroyed among them, and they
doubted of the most important matters: however, that, like the others, they
would take no care to explain their tenets, and these evils were incurable:"[20]
so that no advantage remains on the part of the Lutherans, unless that their
discipline, such as it was, so much excelled that of the Sacramentarians as to
excite their envy.

11.— *Melancthon laments the Licentiousness of the party, in which people at table decided points
of Religion.*

It is expedient we should also learn, from Melancthon, in what manner the
great men of the party treated theology and ecclesiastical discipline. Confession
of sins was but feebly spoken of among the Lutherans; and though little was
said of it, and though the remains of Christian discipline which they wished
to retain were small, yet they had such an influence on a man of importance,

as Melancthon relates, that he openly declared at a "great banquet (for there only, says he, they treat theology) that they ought to oppose it; that they ought to be on their guard, lest that liberty they had recovered should be taken from them, otherwise they would be enchained by a new slavery, and that already, by little and little, the ancient traditions were renewing."[21] This is the consequence of exciting the spirit of rebellion among people, and indiscreetly inspiring them with a hatred of traditions. We have in one single banquet a representation of what was done in the others. This spirit prevailed among all the people; and Melancthon himself says to his friend Camerarius, speaking of these new churches, "You see the excesses of the multitude, and their blind desires:"[22] no order could be established among them.

12.—*Imputed justice diminished the necessity of good works.*

Thus the true reformation, namely, of morals, retrograded instead of advancing, and this for two reasons—one, because authority was destroyed, and because the new doctrine inclined to favor human passions. I undertake not to prove that the new Justification had this bad effect. It is a subject often treated of before, and foreign to my purpose. I shall speak only of those notorious facts that, after the establishment of imputed justice, the doctrine of good works fell into such disrepute, that some of the chief disciples of Luther said it was a blasphemy to teach they were necessary. Others went so far as to say they were contrary to salvation; all concurred in deciding they were not necessary. It is permitted, in the new Reformation, to say, that good works are necessary, as things, which God requires from man, but it cannot be said that they are necessary to salvation. And why, then, does God require them? Is it not in order to save us? Has not Jesus Christ himself said, "If thou wilt enter into life, keep the commandments?"[23] It is, therefore, precisely for obtaining life and eternal salvation that good works are necessary according to the Gospel, and it is what the whole Scripture preaches to us. But the new Reformation has discovered this subtlety, that one may without difficulty allow them to be necessary, provided it be not for salvation. The question regarded the adult, for as to little children, all were agreed. Who would have believed the Reformation was to bring forth such a prodigy? and that this proposition, good works are necessary to salvation," should ever have been condemned? It was done by Melancthon and all the Lutherans in many of their conventions[24] and particularly that of Worms, in 1557, the acts of which we shall see in their proper place.

13.—*No Reformation of Morals in the Protestant Churches; the testimony of Erasmus.*

I intend not here to impeach Protestants with their bad morals; our own, with relation to most men, did not appear better. I wish only to disabuse them of the idea that their Reformation was attended with the fruits that might be anticipated from so beautiful a name, or that their new justification had produced one good effect. Erasmus frequently said, that of the many whom he had seen embrace the new Reformation, (and he maintained a familiarity with most of their chiefs,) he had not seen so much as one whom it had not made worse instead of making better. "What an evangelical generation this is!" said he.[25] "Nothing was ever seen more licentious, and, withal, more seditious; nothing, in a word, less evangelical than these pretended evangelists: they abrogate vigils, and the divine service of the night and day. They were, said they, Pharisaical superstitions; but then they should have substituted something better in their place, and not become Epicureans to escape Judaism. All is carried to extremes in this new Reformation. They root up only what ought to be pruned; they set fire to the house in order to cleanse it. Morals are neglected; luxury, debauchery, adulteries, increase more than ever; there is no order, no discipline among them. The people indocile, after having shaken off the yoke of their superiors, will believe no person; and in so disordered a licentiousness Luther will soon have reason to regret what he calls the tyranny of bishops." When he wrote in this way to his Protestant friends regarding the unhappy fruits of their reformation,[26] they candidly agreed with him. "I had much rather," said he to them, "have to do with those Papists you decry so much."[27] He reproaches them with the malice of Capito, the malignant falsehoods of Farel, whom Œcolampadius, at whose table he lived, could neither suffer nor restrain; the arrogance and violence of Zuinglius, and in a word, with those of Luther, who sometimes seemed to speak like the Apostles, and at other times abandoned himself to such strange excesses, and such vile scurrility, that it was plainly seen the apostolic air he affected at times proceeded not from his heart. The others with whom he was acquainted were no better. "I find," said he, "more piety in one good Catholic bishop than in all these new evangelists."[28] What he said was not to flatter the Catholics, whose disorders he impeached with sufficient freedom. But, besides that he disapproved their boasting of the reformation, without any superior merit of their own, he judged there was an essential difference between those who neglected good works through weakness, and those who lessened their dignity and necessity by maxim.

14.—*The testimony of Bucer.*

But here is a testimony which will press the Protestants more closely: it is that of Bucer. For in 1542, and more than twenty years after the reformation, this minister writes to Calvin, "that among them the most evangelical did not so much as know what true repentance was"[29]—so much had they abused the name of reformation and gospel. We have just heard as much from the lips of Luther.[30] Five years after this letter of Bucer, and in the midst of the victories of Charles V, Bucer writes again to the same Calvin: "God has punished the injury we have done to his name by our long and pernicious hypocrisy."[31] This was confining a sufficiently proper name to licentiousness covered with the title of reformation. In 1549, he describes in stronger terms the little fruit of the pretended reformation, when he writes again to Calvin. Our people have passed from the hypocrisy so deeply rooted in the Papacy, to a profession, such as it is, of Jesus Christ; and there is but a small number who have departed from his hypocrisy."[32] Now he certainly seeks for a subject of dispute, and endeavors to render the Church of Rome guilty of that hypocrisy, according to the style of the reformation, he understands the watchings, the abstinence, and devotions performed in honor of the saints, and similar practices, it was impossible for the new Reformed to be more detached from these things than they were, having all of them passed to the opposite extreme; but as the foundation of piety consisted not in these external things, it consisted still less in abolishing them. If it were the opinion of merits that Bucer here calls our hypocrisy, this was an evil, which the reformation had too well corrected, which had taken away even that merit which is the gift of grace, though the truth sometimes forced its acknowledgment. However that may be, the reformation had prevailed so little against hypocrisy, that very few, according to Bucer, had abandoned so great an evil. "For which reason," proceeds he, "our people labored more to appear disciples of Jesus Christ than to be so in reality; and when this appearance injured their interests, they relinquished it. What pleased them was the separation from the tyranny and superstitions of the Pope, and LIVING AFTER THEIR OWN FANCY." And a little after, "Our people would never receive sincerely the laws of Jesus Christ: neither have they courage to enforce the laws against others, with a Christian constancy. As long as they believed they had the arm of flesh to support them, they generally returned answers of some vigor; but when this arm of flesh was broken, and they no longer had any human aid, they forgot them."

Doubtless, the true reformation hitherto—I mean that of morals—had but weak foundations in the pretended reformation; and the work of God, so much boasted of, and so much desired, was neglected by them.

15.—*The insupportable tyranny of Luther; what Calvin writes to Melancthon.*

What Melancthon most expected in Luther's reformation, was Christian liberty, and freedom from human authority; but he found himself much disappointed in his hopes. For almost fifty years together, he beheld the Lutheran Church always under tyranny or in confusion. She long had to sustain the punishment of despising lawful authority. Never was there a master more severe than Luther, nor a tyranny more insupportable than what he exercised in points of doctrine. This arrogance was so well known, as to induce Muncer to say there were two popes—that of Rome and Luther; and this latter was the more rigorous. Had it been only Muncer, a fanatic, and the leader of fanatics, Melancthon might have consoled himself; but Zwinglius, Calvin, and all the Swiss and all the Sacramentarians—men not at all despised by Melancthon—said, loudly, without his being able to contradict them, that Luther was another pope. None are unacquainted with what Calvin wrote to his friend Bullinger, "that the excesses of Luther could be no longer borne, whose self-love would not permit him to see his own defects, nor bear contradiction."[33] Here doctrine was in question, and it was principally in doctrine that Luther would make himself absolute. The thing was carried to such excess, that Calvin complained of it to Melancthon himself. With what excess does your Pericles deal out his thunder!"[34] It was thus Luther was called, when they wished to give a fine name to his intemperate eloquence. "We owe much to him, I acknowledge, and I will readily allow him a very great authority, provided he knows how to govern himself; though it is time for him now to reflect how much deference ought, in the Church, to be given to men. All is lost where one alone has more power than all the others, particularly if he fears not to use the extent of his power. And certainly, we leave a singular example to posterity, whilst we rather relinquish our liberty than by the least offence provoke one single man. His temper, you may say, is violent, and all his motives impetuous; as if his violence were not augmented by the obsequiousness of the whole world. Let us once have courage to sigh freely." How great must be the captivity of man when he may not sigh with freedom! A man, I acknowledge, may be chagrined; though one of the first and least effects of virtue is to overcome himself in this inequality of temper; but what is to be hoped of a man who has no more authority, nor perhaps more learning than the others, who will hear nothing, and must rule all things by his word?

16.—Melancthon, tyrannized over by Luther, thinks of retiring.

Melancthon could make no reply to those just complaints, nor was he of a different opinion from the others. Those who lived with Luther, never knew how this rigorous master would take their sentiments in point of doctrine. He menaced them with new formularies of faith, chiefly with regard to the Sacramentarians, whose pride Melancthon was accused of fomenting by "his meekness." This pretext was made use of to incense Luther against him, as his friend Camerarius writes in his life.[35] Melancthon knew no remedy for those evils, except that of flight; and his son-in-law, Bucer, acquaints us, that he was resolved upon it."[36] He writes himself, that Luther was so incensed against him, n account of a letter received from Bucer, that he thought of nothing but of withdrawing for ever from his presence.[37] He was under such restraint with Luther, and the heads of the party, and they had so overwhelmed him with labor and uneasiness, that, quite exhausted, he wrote to his friend Camerarius, "I am," says he, "in slavery, as one in the den of the Cyclops; for I cannot conceal my thoughts from you, and I often think of flight."[38] Luther was not the only one that so enchained him; amongst those who have withdrawn themselves from lawful authority, every one is master at certain times, and the most moderate man is always the greatest slave.

17.—He passes his whole life, without ever daring to explain his doctrine entirely.

When a man has entered into a party to speak his sentiments with freedom, and this illusion has induced him to renounce the established government, if he subsequently find the yoke to enslave him, and not only the master he has chosen, but even his companions, retain him in more subjection than before, what he has not to suffer, and how can we feel surprise at the continual lamentations of Melancthon? No, Melancthon never spoke his full sentiments, with regard to doctrine, not even at Augsburg, when he wrote his Confession of Faith, and that of all the party. We have seen how "he accommodated his dogmas to the occasion:"[39] he was ready to say many milder things, that is, approximating more closely to the tenets received by Catholics, "if his companions would have permitted him." Constrained on all sides, but more by Luther than any other, he never dares to speak, and reserves himself for "better times, if such should happen," says he, "for the designs I entertain."[40] This is what he writes in 1537, in the assembly of Smalkald, where the articles above-mentioned are drawn up. Five years after that time, and in 1542, we find him again sighing for a free convention of the whole party, "where doctrine may be explained in a firm and precise manner."[41] Again, after this, and towards the latter end of his life, he writes to Calvin and Bullinger, that some were about to write against him, on the subject of the Eucharist, and the adoration of the bread. The Lutherans were to be the authors of this book. "If they publish it," said he, "I will speak freely."[42] But these better times, these times of speaking freely, and declaring without fear what he called truth, never came for him; nor was he deceived when he said, that, "Let matters turn out as they may, never should they have the liberty of speaking freely on points of doctrine."[43] When Calvin and the others encourage him to speak his sentiments, he always speaks like one under the obligation of great caution, and awaits an opportunity of explaining himself on certain matters[44] which, however, he never performed.—Thus one of the chief teachers of the new reformation, and he who may be said to have given Lutheranism its form, died without fully explaining himself on the most important controversies of his time.

18.—*New Tyranny in the Lutheran Churches after that of Luther.*

The reason was, while Luther lived, he was forced to silence; after his death, they were not more free. Other tyrants took his place. They were Illyricus, and the other leaders of the people. The unhappy Melancthon considers himself, among the Lutherans his colleagues, as in the midst of enemies, or, to use his own words, in the midst of furious wasps, "and has no hopes of finding sincerity, except in heaven."[45] I wish it were allowed me to employ the word "Demagogue," which he uses. Those were certain orators in Athens, and the popular states of Greece, who became all-powerful with the people, by flattering them. The Lutheran churches were led by similar speakers: "Ignorant men," so speaks Melancthon, "who are strangers to both piety and discipline. Such are they who domineer; and I am like Daniel among the Lions."[46] This is the picture which he draws of the Lutheran Churches. They had already fallen into anarchy, that is, as he says himself, "into a state that at once involves all evils:"[47] he wishes for death, and sees no hopes but in Him who has promised to support his Church, "even in her old age, and to the end of the world." Happy, could he have perceived that consequently he never ceases to support her!

19.—*Melancthon knows not where he is, and all his life searches after Religion.*

Here it is that men should have stopped; and since it was necessary ultimately to return to the promises made to the Church, Melancthon had only to reflect, that they ought to have been as immutable in ages past, as he wished to believe they were to be in ages subsequent to the Reformation. The Lutheran Church had no particular assurance of her eternal duration, nor ought the reformation made by Luther to remain more immoveable than the first institution established by Jesus Christ and his Apostles. How was it possible for Melancthon not to see that the reformation, whose faith he would change daily, was not the work of man? We have seen how he changed, and changed again, many important articles of the Augsburg Confession, even after it had been presented to the Emperor.[48] At different times, he even took many important things from the Apology, although it had been subscribed by the whole party with as much submission as the Confession of Augsburg. In 1532, after the Confession of Augsburg and Apology, he writes again, "That most important points remain undecided, and that they ought, without noise, to seek means to explain their dogmas."[49] "How much," says he, "do I wish this to be done, and done well!" like a man that knew in his conscience nothing hitherto had been done as it ought. In 1533, "Who is there," says he, "that so much as thinks of healing the conscience agitated with doubts, and of discovering truth!"[50] In 1535, "How much," says he, "do we deserve to be blamed, we that take no care to heal the conscience agitated with doubts, nor to explain the dogmas, purely and simply without sophistry! These things torment me terribly."[51] He wishes in the same year, "that a pious assembly would determine the Eucharistic contest, without sophistry, and without tyranny."[52] He judges then the thing as undecided; and five or six ways of explaining this article, which we find in the Augsburg Confession, and Apology, have not satisfied him. In 1536, accused of still raising many doubts of the doctrine he professed, he replies at once, that it was immoveable, for so it was necessary he should speak, or abandon the cause.[53] But immediately after, he gives to understand that, indeed, many defects remained in it; and it must not be forgotten that he speaks of doctrine. Melancthon imputes these defects to the vices and obstinacy of ecclesiastics, "by whose means it happened," says he, "that amongst us things have been left to take their own course, to say nothing worse; that we have fallen into many faults, and, at the commencement, have done many things without reason." He acknowledges the disorder; and the vain excuse he seeks, by imputing the defects of his own religion to the Catholic Church, will not conceal it. He had advanced no further in 1537; and whilst all the Doctors of the party assembled with Luther at Smalkald, there explained anew the points of doctrine, or, rather, there subscribed to the decisions of Luther, "I was of opinion," says he, "that, rejecting some paradoxes, they should explain doctrine more simply;"[54] and although he subscribed, as we have seen, these decisions, he was so little satisfied with them that, in 1542, we have heard him still wish for another assembly, "where the dogmas might be explained in a firm and precise manner."[55] Three years after, and in 1545, he acknowledges that truth had been but very imperfectly discovered to the preachers of the new gospel. "I beseech God," says he, "to prosper this glimmering of doctrine, such as he has discovered to us."[56] He declares that, as to himself, he has done all in his power: "The will," says he, "was not wanting to me, but time, guides, and doctors." How! was his master, Luther, then wanting him—the man he had believed to be raised by God to dispel the darkness with which the world was covered? Without doubt he confided but little in the doctrine of such a master, when he so bitterly laments the want of a doctor. And, indeed, after the death of Luther, Melancthon, who in so many places so highly extols him, writing in confidence to his friend Camerarius, contents himself with saying, coldly enough, that "he had at least well explained some part of the heavenly doctrine."[57] A little after, he confesses "that he and the others fell into many errors, which they could not avoid, upon coming forth from so much darkness:"[58] and is satisfied with saying that "many things have been well explained;" which agreed perfectly with the desire he had, that the rest should be better explained. We see, in all the above passages, that the dogmas of faith were the things in question; since decisions, and new decrees on doctrine, are there spoken of in every place. Men, if they please, may now be surprised at those they call Seekers in England. Here is Melancthon himself, who still seeks for many articles of his religion forty years after the preaching of Luther and the establishment of the Reformation.

20.—*What were the dogmas which Melancthon found badly explained.*

If it be asked what were the dogmas Melancthon pretended were badly explained, it is certain that they were most important ones—that of the Eucharist was in the number. In 1553, after all the changes of the Augsburg Confession, after the explanations of the Apology, after the Articles of Smalkald, which he had signed, he still demands "a new formulary for the Supper."[59] It is not well known what he wished to insert in this new formulary; it appears only, that neither those of his own nor those of the opposite party pleased him, since he says, that both one and the other did nothing but obscure the subject. Another article which he wished might be decided was that of free-will, the consequences of which so very much affected the subjects of justification and grace. In 1548 he writes to Thomas Cranmer, that Archbishop of Canterbury who completely destroyed the King, his master, by his obsequiousness: "Ever since the commencement," says he, "the doctrines which have been advanced amongst us on free-will, according to the opinions of the stoics, were too harsh, and we must think of making some new formulary on this head."[60] That of the Augsburg Confession, though he himself had drawn it up, no longer pleased him; he began to think that free-will did not only act in the duties of civil life, but moreover in the operations of grace, and by its assistance. These were not the notions he had received from Luther, nor what Melancthon himself had explained at Augsburg. This doctrine raised him opponents among the Protestants. He prepared himself for a vigorous defence, when he wrote to a fried, "If they shall publish their stoical disputes, (regarding fatal necessity and free-will,) I shall answer very gravely and very learnedly."[61] Thus in the midst of his misfortunes, he is pleased with the thoughts of writing a fine work, and persists in his belief, as the following will more fully discover to us.

21.—*Melancthon declares that he adheres to the Confession of Augsburg, at the time he thinks of reforming it.*

We might point out other things which Melancthon wished to see decided, long after the Confession of Augsburg. But what appears more singular is, that whilst he, who had made it, found in his conscience, and acknowledged to his friends, the necessity of reforming it in so many important articles, he himself, in the public assemblies then held, never ceased to declare, with all the others, that he adhered precisely to this Confession, such as it was presented at the Diet of Augsburg, and to the Apology, as the pure exposition of the word of God. Policy required this; and it would have too much dishonored the Reformation to admit that it had erred in its foundation.

What repose could Melancthon have during these uncertainties? The evil was, they arose from the very grounds, and, as I may say, from the constitution of his church in which there was no regular power, no legitimate authority. Usurped authority has no uniformity; it bends or relaxes without moderation. Thus tyranny and anarchy are felt in it alternately; nor is it known to whom application should be made to arrange matters in a steady frame.

22.—*These uncertainties proceeded from the constitution of the Protestant Churches.*

So essential, and, at the same time, so inevitable a defect in the constitution of the new Reformation, gave extreme trouble to the miserable Melancthon. If any questions arose, there were no means of terminating them; the most certain traditions were despised; the Scripture was rested and forced by the caprice of every man; all parties believed they understood it—they all proclaimed it was clear; not a man would yield to his companion. Melancthon called out in vain for an assembly, to terminate the Eucharistic dispute, which tore in pieces the new-born Reformation. Conferences which they called amicable had nothing but the name, and served only to exasperate the minds of men and embarrass the cause: a juridical assembly was necessary, a council which should have the power of deciding, and to which the people should submit. But where was this to be had in the new Reformation? The remembrance of the despised bishops was still too recent; the individuals, who had possessed themselves of their places, could not assume to themselves a more inviolable character; and, indeed, both sides, Lutherans and Zuinglians, wished to have their mission judged of by the merits of the cause. He who spoke the truth had, according to them, the true mission. The difficulty was to know who spoke the truth, which every person claimed; and all those who rested their mission on this examination made it doubtful. The Catholic bishops had a certain title, and their vocation alone was indisputable. It was said they abused it, nor was it denied that they had. Thus Melancthon always wished to acknowledge them, and always maintained that it was wrong "to yield nothing to the sacred order."[62] If their authority was not re-established, he anticipated, with a lively and inconsolable sorrow, that "discord would have no end, and would be attended with ignorance, barbarity, and all kinds of evil."

23.—*The authority of the Church absolutely necessary in matters of Faith.*

It is very easy to say, as our reformed do, that they have an extraordinary vocation; that the Church, like kingdoms, is not attached to an established succession; and matters of religion ought not to be judged in the same form that causes are at tribunals. Conscience, say they, is the true tribunal, where each one is to judge matters as they are in themselves, and hear truth from himself: these things, I repeat, are very easily said. Melancthon said them, like the others; but, in his conscience, was very sensible some other foundation was necessary on which to build the Church. For, in reality, why should she have less order than empires? Why should she not have a legitimate succession in her magistrates? Ought a way to be left open to every man who would say he was sent from God, or the faithful to be obliged to investigate the cause to the bottom, though the greatest part of men are incapable of such inquiry? Such language may serve for disputation; but when a matter is to be terminated,—the peace of the Church to be established,—and true repose, without impediment, given to the consciences of men, we must have recourse to other means. Do what we may, we must return to authority, which is neither certain nor lawful, when, proceeding from nothing higher, it rests on itself for a foundation. It is for this reason Melancthon wished to acknowledge the bishops, whom succession had established, and saw no other remedy for the evils of the Church.

24.—*The sentiments of Melancthon on the necessity of acknowledging the Pope and Bishops.*

The manner in which he explains himself, in one of his letters on this subject, is admirable. "Our people are agreed that ecclesiastical polity, by which Bishops are acknowledged the superiors of many churches, and the Bishop of Rome superior to all Bishops, is allowable. It was also lawful for kings to endow churches with revenues: so there is no dispute about the superiority of the Pope, and the authority of Bishops; and the Bishops, as well as the Pope, may easily retain this authority: for guides are necessary to retain the Church in order, to watch over those who are called to the Ecclesiastical ministry and the doctrine of priests, and to exercise Ecclesiastical judgments. If there were not such Bishops, IT WOULD BE NECESSARY TO CREATE THEM. THE POPE'S MONARCHY would also be of great use to the agreement of doctrine between different nations. Thus the SUPERIORITY OF THE POPE might easily be admitted, were we but agreed in all the rest; and Kings themselves might easily moderate the attempts of Popes on the temporalities of their kingdoms."[63] This was what Melancthon thought of the authority of the Pope and Bishops. The whole party entertained the same sentiments when he wrote this letter.

"Our people," says he, "are agreed:" far from looking upon the authority of Bishops with the superiority and *monarchy* of the Pope, as a mark of the anti-Christian empire, he held it for a thing desirable, and which ought to be created, if not established. It is true that he added this condition, that ecclesiastical powers "should not oppress sound doctrine:" but, if it may be permitted to say they do oppress it! and, under this pretext, refuse the obedience due to them, they fall again into the difficulty they seek to avoid, and the ecclesiastical authority becomes a mock authority for all that wish to contradict.

25.—*Melancthon, in the Assembly of Smalkald, is of opinion that they should acknowledge the Council convened by the Pope—and why?*

It was for this reason also that Melancthon always sought for a remedy to so great an evil. It was not certainly his design that the disunion should remain for ever. Luther submitted to the Council at the time Melancthon embraced his doctrine. The whole party pressed its convocation, and Melancthon hoped from it the termination of the schism, without which, I presume, he never would have engaged in it. But, after the first step, men venture farther than they had intended. To the demand of the Council, the Protestants added, that they demanded it "free, pious, and Christian." The demand is just—Melancthon agrees to it; but such fair words concealed a profound artifice. By the name of a free Council, they explained their meaning to be such a Council as the Pope, and all those who professed submission to him, should be excluded from. These, they said, were interested persons—the Pope was the guilty party, the Bishops were his slaves—they could not be judges. Who, then, should hold the Council? The Lutherans, mere private individuals? or priests in rebellion against their bishops? What an example to posterity! And, again, were they not also interested? Were they not considered guilty by Catholics, who, without doubt, formed the greatest, not to say the best part of the Christian world? What! to have indifferent judges, should then the appeal be made to Turks or Heathens, or ought God to send us angels? And was anything more necessary than to accuse all the magistrates of the Church, in order to deprive them of their power, and render judgment impossible? Melancthon had too much sense not to see this was but an illusion. What can he do? He informs us himself. In 1537, when the Lutherans were assembled at Smalkald, in order to discover what was best to be done with regard to the council Paul the Third had summoned at Mantua, it was said the Pope ought not to be allowed the authority of forming a convention in which himself was to be accused, nor should a council so convoked be acknowledged by them. But Melancthon could not agree with this. "My opinion was," says he, "not to refuse the Council absolutely, because, although the Pope cannot be judge therein, however HE HAS THE RIGHT OF CALLING IT TOGETHER, and the Council must order the proceeding on to judgment."[64] Here he immediately acknowledges the Council; and what is still more remarkable, the whole world allowed he had, on the whole, reason on his side. "Men more acute than myself," proceeds he, "said that my reasons were subtle and TRUE, but useless; that the tyranny of the Pope was such, that if we once consented to be present at the Council, it would be understood that we thereby granted to the Pope the power of judging. I saw very well there was some difficulty in my opinion; but, after all, it was the most honest. The other carried it, after great disputes, and I believe there is in this somewhat of fatality."

26.—*When certain principles are overturned, all we do is unwarrantable and contradictory.*

This is generally said when one knows not what to say. Melancthon seeks for an end to the schism, and, for want of comprehending truth whole and entire, what he says is not consistent. On one side he was sensible what service an acknowledged authority does the Church. He saw clearly, among so many dissensions then arising, that a principal authority was then necessary to maintain unity, nor could he recognise this authority any where but in the Pope. On the other hand, he would not have him to be judge in the impeachment the Lutherans brought against him. Thus he grants him the authority of calling the Assembly, and, after that, will have him excluded from it—an odd opinion, I acknowledge. But for all this, Melancthon ought not to be deemed a person unskilled in these matters: he was not so reputed by his own party,—the only person, I may say, in whom they could boast, and excelled by none among them in sense or erudition. If he proposes things contradictory, it was because the new Reformation allowed nothing that was right or consistent. He was correct in saying that it belonged to the Pope to call the Council, for who else should call it, particularly in the present state of Christianity? Was there any other power, except that of the Pope, which the whole world would acknowledge? and to deprive him of it at once, before the Assembly, in which they said they had intended to accuse him, was not this too unjust a prejudice? Above all, when the matter in debate was no personal crime of the Pope, but the doctrine which he had received from his predecessors so many ages ago, and which was common to him with all the Bishops of the Church? These reasons were so solid, that the rest of the Lutherans, opposed to Melancthon, acknowledged them, as he himself has just told us, "to be true." But those who acknowledged this truth, however, maintained at the same time, and with good reason, that if they granted the Pope the power of forming the Assembly, they could no longer exclude him from it. The bishops, who ever acknowledged him the Chief of their order, and saw themselves in a synodical body convened by his authority, would they suffer their assembly to commence with dispossessing a natural President for a cause common to them all? Would they given an example unheard of in all past ages? These things were inconsistent; and in this conflict of the Lutherans it appeared manifestly that, after certain principles are overthrown, every thing that follows is untenable and contradictory.

27.—Reasons for the restriction which Melancthon placed to his Subscription
in the articles of Smalkald.

If they persisted in refusing the Council which the Pope had convened, Melancthon had no further hopes of a remedy for the schism; and it was on this occasion he spoke the words above cited, "that discord would be everlasting,"[65] in consequence of not recognising the authority of the sacred order. Afflicted at so great an evil, he pursues his point; and although the opinion he had proposed for the Pope, or, rather, for the unity of the Church, in the Assembly of Smalkald, was there rejected, he made his own subscription to the above form, as we have seen, reserving the authority of the Pope. The important causes and reasons which obliged him to concede the superiority of the Pope over the Bishops are now seen. Peace,—which reason and experience of the dispositions of his own sect made him consider impossible without these means,—forced him, in opposition to Luther, upon so necessary an expedient. His conscience, at this time, triumphed over his complaisance; and he added only, that he gave the Pope a superiority of "human right:" unhappy in not seeing that a Primacy which experience showed him to be so necessary for the Church, well deserved to have been instituted by Jesus Christ; nay more, what is found established in all ages, could proceed from none but him!

28.—The words of Melancthon on the authority of the Church.

Surprising were the sentiments he had with regard to the authority of the Church. For, although, like other Protestants, he would not allow the infallibility of the Church in disputes, lest, said he, too great a prerogative should be given to men, the dictates of his mind carried him still farther. He frequently repeated, that Jesus Christ had promised his Church to support her for ever; that he had promised his "work," that is, his Church, "should never be dissipated nor abolished;" and therefore to ground himself upon the faith of the Church, was to ground himself not on man, but on the promise of Jesus Christ himself.[66] This induced him to say even, "Sooner may the earth open under my feet, than it happen to me to depart from the sentiment of the Church in which Jesus Christ does reign." And in other numberless places, "Let the Church judge—I submit myself to the judgment of the Church."[67] The truth is, that faith, which he had in the promise, vacillated frequently; and once, after having said, according to the sentiments of his heart, "I submit myself to the Catholic Church," he adds, "that is to say, to good men, and learned men."[68] This, his limitation, I acknowledge, destroyed the whole; and it is easily seen what that submission was, which, under the name of good and learned men, acknowledges none, at the bottom, but such as he pleases: for this reason he wished always to come to a fixed character, an avowed authority, which was that of the Bishops.

29.—*Melancthon cannot depart from the opinion of imputed justice, whatever grace God bestows on him for his return.—Two truths acknowledged by him.*

If it be now asked, How it happened that a man so desirous of peace did not seek it in the Church, but remained separated from that sacred order he was so intent on establishing? it is easily answered—it was chiefly because he could never abandon his imputed justice. God, however, had given him great graces, since he had the knowledge of two truths capable of reclaiming him: one, that a doctrine not found in antiquity ought not to be followed. "Consult," said he, to Brentius, "with the ancient Church:"[69] and, again, "Opinions unknown to the ancient Church are not to be received."[70] The other truth, that is, his doctrine of imputed justice, was not to be met with in the Fathers. As soon as he began to set about explaining it, we have heard him say, "He found nothing like it in their writings."[71] Nevertheless, they thought fit to say, in the Augsburg Confession and Apology, that nothing was advanced therein but was conformable to their doctrine. Above all, St. Augustin was cited; and it had been too shameful to the Reformers to own that so great a Doctor, the defender of Christian grace, had been ignorant of the foundation of it. But what Melancthon writes to a friend in confidence, shows us plainly that it was only for form sake, and to save appearances, they named St. Augustin in the party. For he repeats three or four times, with a kind of concern, that what hinders his friend from well understanding the matter is, because, "he is still too much wedded to St. Augustin's imagination," and that "he must turn away his eyes entirely from the imagination of this Father."[72] But, then, what is this imagination he must turn his eyes from? Why it is, says he, the imagination of being held for just by the fulfilling of the law, which the Holy Ghost works within us. This fulfilling, according to Melancthon, avails nothing towards rendering man agreeable to God, and it was a false imagination in St. Augustin to have thought the contrary: thus does he treat so great a man. And nevertheless, he cites him, on account, says he, of the public opinion men have of him. But, in the main, continues he, "he does not sufficiently explain the justice of faith." As if he said, on such a subject, we ought at least to cite a Father the whole world considers the best interpreter of this article, although, to speak the truth, he makes not for us. He found nothing more favorable in the rest of the Fathers. "What dense darkness," said he, "do we find on this subject in the common doctrine of the Fathers and our adversaries."[73] What became of those fine words, Consult with the ancient Church? Why did he not practise what he advised others? And seeing he knew no piety, (as, indeed, none there is but what is grounded on the true doctrine of justification,) how could he believe so many saints were ignorant of it? How could he imagine he saw so clearly in Scripture what he did not see in the Fathers, not even in St. Augustin, the doctor and defender of justifying grace against the Pelagians, whose doctrine also, in this point, the whole Church had constantly followed?

30.—*Melancthon can neither satisfy himself in imputed justice, nor resolve to abandon it.*

But what most deserves our observation in this place is, that he himself, smitten as he was with the specious idea of his imputed justice, never could succeed in explaining it to his own liking. Not content with laying down the dogma regarding it in the most ample manner in the Confession of Augsburg, he applies himself wholly to the expounding of it in the Apology; and whilst he composed it, he wrote to his friend Camerarius, "I truly suffer a very great and painful labor in the Apology, in the points of justification, which I desire to explain profitably."[74] But, however, after all this pains-taking, has he fully explained it? Let us hear what he writes to another friend; it is the same we have seen him reprove as too much wedded to St. Augustin's imagination. "I have endeavored," says he, "to explain this doctrine in the Apology but, in such discourses as these, the calumnies of our adversaries permit not the explaining of myself so as I do to you at present, though, in reality, I say the same thing."[75] And, a little after, "I hope you will find some kind of help from my Apology, although I there speak with caution of so great matters." This whole letter scarcely contains one single page, the Apology has more than a hundred on the subject; and, notwithstanding, this letter, according to him, explains it better than the Apology. The thing was, he durst not say in the Apology as clearly as he did in this letter, "that we must entirely take off our eyes from the accomplishment of the law, even from that which the Holy Ghost works in us." This is what he called rejecting St. Augustin's imagination. He saw himself always pressed with this question of the Catholics: If we are agreeable to God independently of all good works, and all fulfilling of the law, even of that which the Holy Ghost works in us, how and whereto are good works necessary? Melancthon perplexed himself in vain to ward off this blow, and to elude this dreadful consequence: "Therefore good works, according to you, are not necessary." This is what he called calumnies of adversaries, which hindered him from owning frankly, in the Apology, all he had a mind to say—this was the cause of that great labor he had to undergo, and of those precautions of which he spoke.

To a friend the whole mystery of the doctrine was disclosed, but in public he was to be on his guard; he yet further added to his friend, that, after all, this doctrine is not well understood, except in "the conflicts of conscience:" which was as much as to say, that when a man could do no more, and knew not how to assure himself of having a will sufficient for fulfilling the law, the remedy for preserving all this, notwithstanding the undoubted assurance of pleasing God preached up in the new Gospel, was to take off their eyes from the law and the fulfilling of it, in order to believe that, independently of all this, God reputed us for just. This was the repose Melancthon flattered himself with, and which he never would relinquish. This difficulty, indeed, always occurred, that of holding oneself assured of the forgiveness of sins without like assurance of conversion; as if these two things were separable, and independent one of the other. This occasioned, in Melancthon, that great labor; and therein he could never satisfy himself; so that after the Confession of Augsburg, and so many painful inquiries of the Apology, he comes besides, in the Confession called Saxonic, to another exposition of justifying grace, where he advances other novelties, which we shall see in time.

Thus is man agitated when smitten with an idea that has but a delusive appearance—fain would he explain his thoughts, but knows not how—fain would he find in the Fathers what he searches after; no such principle is to be found in them, yet he cannot renounce the flattering idea that so agreeably prepossesses him. Let us tremble and humble ourselves—let us acknowledge that, in man, there is a profound source of pride and error; and that the weakness of the human mind, like to the judgments of God, are unfathomable.

31.—*Melancthon's grievous agonies—he foresees the dreadful consequences of the overthrow of Church authority.*

Melancthon was persuaded he saw truth on one side, and lawful authority on the other. His heart was divided, and the struggle to reunite these two gave him continual torment. He was not able to renounce the charms of imputed justice, nor to make the body of the bishops receive a doctrine unknown to those who had governed the Church till then. Hereupon, the authority which he loved for being lawful, became odious to him, because it opposed that which he mistook for truth. At the same time that you hear him say "he never called the authority of bishops in question," he arraigns their "tyranny," chiefly because they opposed his doctrine, and believes "he weakens his own cause by laboring to re-establish them."[76]

Mistrusting his own conduct, he racks himself, nor foresees any thing but disasters. "What will this Council be," says he, "if held, but a tyranny either of Papists or of others: a battle of divines more cruel and stubborn than that of centaurs?"[77] Well was he acquainted with his master, Luther, and feared no less the tyranny of his own than that he attributed to the adverse party! The fury of divines makes him tremble. He sees, authority once shaken, that all the dogmas, even the most important, will be called in question, one after another, without knowing where to stop. The disputes and differences about the Lord's Supper discovered to him what was to happen on other articles. "Good God!" says he, "what tragedies will posterity behold, if these questions ever come to be moved, whether or no the Word, whether the Holy Ghost be a person!"[78] These matters began to be moved in his time, but he judged this beginning to be but weak as yet; for he perceived the minds of men to become insensibly bolder and bolder against the established doctrines, and the authority of ecclesiastical decisions. What would have been the case had he seen the other pernicious consequences of the doubts which the Reformation started? the whole order of discipline publicly overthrown by some, and independence set up, that is, anarchy, with its whole train of evils, under the specious and flattering name of liberty; the spiritual power placed by others in the hands of princes; Christian doctrine impugned in every point; Christians denying the work of creation, and that of man's redemption; destroying hell;

abolishing the soul's immortality; stripping Christianity of all its mysteries, and changing it into a sect of philosophy wholly adapted to the senses: thence indifference of religions arising, and, what naturally ensues, the very foundation of religion sapped; the Scripture directly combatted; the way opened to Deism, that is, to Atheism in disguise; and the books that broach these prodigious doctrines issuing from the bosom of the Reformation, and from whose quarters where she predominates. What would Melancthon have said had he foreseen all these evils? and what would have been his lamentations? He had seen enough to trouble him his whole life long. The contests of his own times and party were sufficient to make him say that without a visible miracle, all religion would be soon extinct.

32.—*The causes of Melancthon's errors—He alleges the promises he made to the Church, but trusts not enough in them.*

What benefit did he then find in those divine promises, whereby, as he himself attests, Jesus Christ had bound himself to maintain his Church, even in her extreme old age, and never to suffer her to perish?[79] Had he thoroughly considered this blessed promise, he would not have been satisfied with owning, as he has done, that the Gospel doctrine would subsist eternally, in spite of errors and disputes: but would have owned, moreover, that it ought to subsist by the means established in the Gospel, that is, by an inviolable succession of the ecclesiastical ministry. He would have seen that it was to the Apostles and to the successors of the Apostles this promised was ad-dressed—"Go, teach, baptize; and lo, I am with you always, even unto the end of the world."[80] Had he comprehended well these words, he would never have imagined that truth could be separated from that body, wherein succession and lawful authority were found; and God himself would have taught him, that as the profession of truth can never be overruled by error, the force of the apostolic ministry can receive no interruption by any relaxation of discipline. This is the faith of Christians: thus, with Abraham, they must believe in the promise, "In hope against hope;"[81] and further believe that the Church will preserve her succession, and bring forth children even then when she shall appear the most barren, and her strength, through length of days, the most exhausted. Melancthon's faith could not stand this trial. He believed, indeed, in the promise in general, whereby the profession of truth was to subsist, but had not sufficient faith in the means God had appointed for its maintenance. What did the retaining so many good sentiments avail him? The enemy of our salvation, says St. Gregory, the Pope,[82] does not always wholly extinguish them; and as God leaves in his children some remains of concupis-cence, which keeps them in humility, Satan, his imitator, in a contrary sense, leaves also in his slaves, however strange it may seem, some remains of piety, (false, to be sure, and deceitful,) but yet apparent, whereby he accomplishes their seduction. To complete the mischief, they believe themselves saints, without reflecting that piety unattended with all its requisites, is nothing but hypocrisy.

Melancthon, from some interior impulse, was moved to think that peace and unity, without which there is neither faith nor Church, had no other support on earth but the authority of the ancient pastors. He did not follow this divine light to its whole extent; his foundations were all subverted; every thing fell out contrary to his hopes. He aspired to unity; he lost it for ever, without being able to meet with so much as the shadow of it in the party wherein he had sought it. The Reformation, brought about or supported by arms, filled him with horror; he saw himself under the necessity of finding out excuses for an extravagance which he detested. Let us reflect on what he wrote to the Landgrave of Hesse, whom he saw ready to take up arms:—"May your Highness be persuaded that it is better to endure all extremities than to take up arms for the Gospel cause."[83] But he was forced to retract this fine maxim, when the party had entered into a confederacy to make war, and Luther himself had declared for them.

The unfortunate Melancthon could not even retain his natural sincerity; but was obliged to join with Bucer in laying snares for the Catholics, in affected equivocations; to load them with calumnies in the Confession of Augsburg;[84] to approve publicly this Confession, which he wished from the bottom of his heart to see reformed in so many points; to speak always as best pleased others; to pass his whole life in perpetual dissimulation; and that even with respect to religion, the first act whereof is to believe, as the second is to confess. What constraint! what corruption! But party zeal carries all before it; one hardens and animates another; they must not only defend themselves, but multiply; the fine name of Reformation makes all lawful, and the first engagement makes all necessary.

33.—*The Princes and Doctors of the party are alike insupportable to him.*

Meanwhile the heart is stung with secret reproaches, and such a state becomes irksome. Melancthon often declares that strange things pass in his mind, and knows not how to express his internal anguish. In the account he gives his intimate friend Camerarius, concerning the decrees of the Assembly of Spire, and the resolutions taken by the Protestants, all the terms he employs to represent his grief are extreme. "They are incredible agitations and the torments of hell; he is almost brought to death's door. What he feels is horrible: his consternation is astonishing. During his oppressions he is sensibly convinced how much certain people are to blame."[85] When he dares not to speak out, it is some head of the party that is to be understood, and principally Luther: it was not certainly out of any fear of Rome that he wrote with so much precaution, and kept within such bounds; and, on the other hand, it is most certain nothing troubled him so much as what passed in the party itself, where all things were carried on by political interests, underhand contrivances, and violent counsels; in a word, nothing was there treated on but leagues, "which all good men," said he, "ought to prevent."[86] All the affairs of the Reformation turned on these leagues of princes with the confederate towns, which the emperor had a mind to break, and the Protestant princes were resolved to maintain; and this is what Melancthon wrote to Camerarius on the subject:—"You see, my dear friend, that in all these conventions nothing is less thought on than religion; fear makes them propose agreements, such as they are, for a time and with dissimulation; and no wonder if such treaties succeed ill; for is it possible that God should bless such counsels?"[87] Far from exaggerating when he speaks thus, it is perceived, even from his letters, that he saw something in the party still worse than what he wrote. "I see," says he, "that there is something secretly contriving, and I wish I were able to stifle all my thoughts."[88] He had such a disgust against the princes of his own party and their assemblies into which they always brought him, in order to draw from his eloquence and facility excuses for counsels he approved not of, that at length he cried out—"Happy are they who meddle not with public affairs."[89] Nor did he ever find the least repose, till, after a too clear conviction of the evil intentions of those princes, "he had quite left off giving himself any concern about their projects."[90] But they entangled him again in their intrigues in spite of him; and we shall soon see how he was obliged to authorize, by writing, their most scandalous proceedings. The opinion he had of the Doctors of the party, and how little he was satisfied with them, has been already shown: but here is something still stronger. "Their manners are such," says he, "that, to speak very moderately, many people, moved at the confusion they behold amongst them, think any other state a golden age comparatively to that they put us in."[91] He judged "these wounds incurable;"[92] and the Reformation, from the very beginning, stood in need of another reformation.

34.—*The prodigies, the prophecies, the horoscopes, wherewith Melancthon was disturbed.*

Besides these agitations, in his correspondence with Camerarius, Osiander, and the rest of the heads of the party, and with Luther himself, he was continually upon the subject of the prodigies that happened, and the dreadful threats of the angry heavens. Sometimes you know not what he would be at: but it is always something terrible—something, I know not what, which he promises to disclose in private to his friend Camerarius, raises a kind of horror when you read him.[93] Other prodigies, almost coincident with the sitting of the Diet of Augsburg, appeared to him favorable to the new Gospel. At Rome, "the extraordinary overflowing of the Tiber, and a mule's bringing forth whose foal had a crane's foot;" in the territory of Augsburg, the birth of a "calf with two heads," were to him a sign of an unquestionable change in the state of the universe, and in particular of "Rome's approaching ruin by schism:"[94] it is what he writes most seriously to Luther himself, informing him withal, that this happened on that same day the Confession of Augsburg was presented to the emperor. Here we see with what notions the authors of this Confession, and the heads of the Reformation, fed themselves at so great a conjuncture: Melancthon's letters are quite full of dreams and visions, and one is apt to think he is reading Titus Livius, upon viewing all the prodigies there related. Is this all? Oh the extreme weakness of a mind in others respects admirable, and, but for his prepossession, so penetrating! The threats of astrologers terrify him. He is continually under frights from the ominous conjunctions of the stars—"a dreadful aspect of Mars" makes him tremble for his daughter, whose horoscope he himself had cast. He is not less "dismayed at the horrible flame of a comet extremely northern."[95]

While the conferences were held at Augsburg upon matters of religion, he comforts himself for their proceeding so slowly on, because "the astrologers foretell that the stars will be more propitious to ecclesiastical disputes towards autumn."[96] God was above all these presages, it is true; and Melancthon repeats it frequently, as well as the almanac-makers; but, after all, the stars rule even Church affairs. We find his friends, that is, the heads of the party, entered with him into these reflections: as for himself, his unlucky nativity promised him nothing but endless contests on doctrine, great labors, and little fruit. He is astonished, born as he was on the hills adjacent to the Rhine, that it should have been foretold him he was to suffer shipwreck on the Baltic Sea;[97] and being sent for into England and Denmark, he is determined not to venture himself on that sea. To so many prodigies and so many threats of unfriendly constellations, to complete the illusion, he joined also prophecies. It was one of the party's weaknesses to believe that their whole success had been foretold; and here is one of the most remarkable predictions they boast of. In 1516, as they say, a year before the commotions of Luther, some cordelier or other, commenting on Daniel, had taken it into his head to say, that the "Pope's power was going to decline, and would never rise again."[98] This prediction was equally true with that other which this new prophet tacked to it, namely, that in 1600, "the Turk would be master of all Italy and Germany." Notwithstanding, Melancthon seriously relates the vision of this fanatic, and boasts of having the original by him, just as it was written by the brother cordelier. Who would not have trembled at this news? The Pope, it seems, already staggered at Luther's blow, and now they will have it that he is quite laid flat. Melancthon takes all this for prophecy; so weak is man when prepossessed. After the Pope's downfall he believes he sees the victorious Turk pressing forward; nay, the earthquakes that happened then confirm him in this thought.

Who would believe him capable of all these impressions, if all his letters were not full of them? We must do him this honor—they were not his own dangers which caused him so much trouble and anxiety. In the midst of his most violent agitations we hear him say confidently, "our dangers disturb me less than our faults."[99] He assigns a fine motive for his grief—the public grievances, and particularly the grievances of the Church: but the truth is, he was sensible in his conscience, as he frequently acknowledges, how great a share those persons had in these grievances who boasted of being the reformers of them. But enough of the troubles which afflicted Melancthon in particular: the reasons of his behavior at the Assembly of Smalkald, and the motives for the restriction he put to that furious article which Luther proposed against the Pope, have been sufficiently explained.

Notes

[1] Orat. p. 26.
[2] Lib. iv. Ep. 126. Col. 574.
[3] Ibid. Col. 575.
[4] Lib. iv. Ep. 240, 315.
[5] Lib. xviii. Ep. 25, 19, 3.
[6] Lib. iv. Ep. 100-119, 842.
[7] Lib. ii. Ep. 202.
[8] Lib. i. Ep. 17.
[9] Lib. i. Ep. 20.
[10] Lib. iv. Ep. 104.
[11] Ep. ad Far. Int. Ep. Calv. p. 5.
[12] Int. Ep. Calv. p. 509, 510.
[13] Int. Ep. Calv. p. 43.
[14] Calv. Ep. p. 50, 51, 52.
[15] Int. Ep. Calv. p. 52.
[16] Visit. Sax. c. de Doct. c. de Libert. Christ.
[17] Ibid.
[18] Visit. Sax. cap. de Doct. cap. de Libert. Christ.
[19] Int. Epist. Calv. p. n. 7.
[20] Lib. iv. Ep. 135.
[21] Ibid. 71.
[22] Ibid. p. 769.
[23] Matt. xix. 17.
[24] Mel. Ep. Lib. i. p. 70. col. 84.
[25] Ep. p. 818, 822. Lib. xix. Ep. 3, 31, 47. p. 2063.
[26] Lib. xix. 2, 30, 62.
[27] Lib. xix. 3.
[28] Lib. xxxi. Epist. 59. col. 2118.
[29] Int. Ep. Calv. p. 54.
[30] Visit. Sax. Cap. de Doct. c. de lib. chr.
[31] Int. Ep. Calv. p. 100.
[32] Ibid. p. 509, 510.
[33] Ep. p. 526.
[34] Calv. Ep. ad Mel. p. 72.
[35] Cam. in. Vit. Phil. Mel.
[36] Peuc. ep. ad Vit. Heod. Hosp. p. 2.
[37] Mel. lib. iv. ep. 315.
[38] Ibid. p. 255.
[39] Lib. iii. N. 59.
[40] Lib. iv. ep. 204.
[41] Lib. i. ep. 110. col. 147.
[42] Ep. Mel. int. Calv. ep. p. 218, 236.
[43] Lib. iv. ep. 136.
[44] Ep. Mel. int. Calv. ep. p. 199. Calv. Resp. p. 211.

[45] Mel. epist. ad Calv. int. Calv. epist. p. 144.
[46] Lib. iv. ep. 836, 842, 845.
[47] Lib. iv. et lib. i. ep. 107, 4, 76, 876.
[48] V.S. lib. iii. N. 5. et seq. 23, 24, 27.
[49] Lib. iv. ep. 135.
[50] Ibid. ep. 140.
[51] Lib. iv. ep. 170.
[52] Lib. iii. ep. 114.
[53] Lib. iv. ep. 194.
[54] Ibid. ep. 98.
[55] Lib. i. ep. 110.
[56] Lib. iv. ep. 662.
[57] Lib. iv. ep. 662.
[58] Ibid. ep. 699.
[59] Lib. ii. Ep. 447.
[60] Lib. iii. Ep. 42.
[61] Lib. ii. Ep. 200.
[62] Lib. iv. Ep. 196.
[63] Resp. ad Bell.
[64] Lib. iv. Ep. 196.
[65] Lib. iv. Ep. 196.
[66] Lib. i. Ep. 107. iv. 76, 733, 845, 876, etc.
[66] Lib. iii. Ep. 44. Lib. i. Ep. 67, 105. Lib. ii. Ep. 159, etc.
[67] Lib. iii. Ep. 44. Lib. i. 67. 105. Lib. ii. Ep. 159 etc.
[68] Lib. i. Ep. 109.
[69] Lib. iii. Ep. 114.
[70] Mel. de Eccles. Cath. ap. Lut. t. i. p. 444.
[71] Lib. iii. Ep. 126, col. 574. S. n. 2.
[72] Lib. i. Ep. 94.
[73] Lib. iv. Ep. 228.
[74] Lib. iv. Ep. 110. Omnino valde multum laboris sustineo, &c.
[75] Lib. i. Ep. 94.
[76] Lib. iv. Ep. 228.
[77] Ibid. Ep. 140.
[78] Ibid.
[79] Lib. i. Ep. 107, 476, etc. v. n. 28.
[80] Matt. xxviii. 20.
[81] Rom. iv. 18.
[82] Pastor, part iii. Adm. 31.
[83] Lib. iii. Ep. 16. Lib. iv. Ep. 110, 111.
[84] V.S. lib. iv. n. 2 et seq. Ib. n. 24.
[85] Lib. iv. Ep. 85.
[86] Sleid. lib. viii.

[87] Lib. iv. Ep. 137.
[88] Ibid. Ep. 70.
[89] Ibid. Ep. 85.
[90] Lib. iv. Ep. 228.
[91] Ibid. Ep. 742.
[92] Ibid. Ep. 759.
[93] Lib. ii. Ep. 89, 269.
[94] Lib. i. Ep. 120. iii. 69.

[95] Lib. ii. Ep. 37. 445. Lib. iv. Ep. 119, 135, 137, 195, 198, 759, 844, etc. 119, 146.
[96] Ib. Ep. 93.
[97] Lib. ii. Ep. 448. 37.
[98] Mel. Lib. i. Ep. 65
[99] Lib. iv. Ep. 70.

Book VI

A brief Summary.—The Landgrave endeavors to maintain union between the Lutherans and Zuinglians.—A new remedy discovered for the incontinence of this Prince, by allowing him to marry a second wife, the first being alive.—The remarkable instruction he gives to Bucer, in order to induce Luther and Melancthon to adopt this sentiment.—The dogmatical judgment of Luther, Bucer, and Melancthon, in favor of Polygamy.—The new marriage ensues in consequence of this consultation.—The Party is ashamed, and has not courage to deny or acknowledge it.—The Landgrave prevails on Luther to suppress the elevation of the Holy Sacrament in favor of the Swiss, whom this ceremony had alienated from the League of Smalkald. On this occasion Luther is provoked anew against the Sacramentarians.—Melancthon's design to destroy the foundation of the Altar Sacrifice.—It is acknowledged in the Party that this Sacrifice is inseparable from the Real Presence and Luther's doctrine.—As much confessed concerning Adoration.—A Momentaneous Presence, and in the sole reception, how allowed.—Luther's sentiment despised by Melancthon and the Divines of Leipsic and Wittenberg.—Luther's furious Theses against the Divines of Louvain.—He acknowledges the Sacrament to be adorable, detests the Zuinglians, and dies.

1.—*The scandalous Incontinency of the Landgrave, and what remedy was found for it in the Reformation.*

THE agreement of Wittenberg continued not long; it was foolish to imagine that a peace so patched up could be of long duration, and that so great an opposition in doctrine, with so great an emotion in the minds of men,could be surmounted by equivocations. Luther could not forbear uttering angry words and venting his spleen against Bucer. Those of Zurich were not backward in defending their Doctor; but Philip, Landgrave of Hesse, who had always warlike projects in contemplation, kept the whole Protestant party united, as far as he was able, and for some years withheld them from coming to an open rupture. This Prince was the support of the League of Smalkald, and, considering the great need they had of him in the party, they allowed to him what no example before had warranted among Christians—it was to have two wives at once; nor could the Reformation find out any other remedy for his incontinence.

The historians who have written that this Prince was, in other respects, very temperate,[1] were not let into the whole secret of the party; they did all they could to conceal the intemperance of a Prince whom the Reformation cried up above all others. We find from Melancthon's letters, in 1539,[2] at the time when the League of Smalkald became so formidable, that this Prince had a distemper which was carefully concealed; it was one of those that are not to be named. He recovered; and, for his intemperance, the heads of the Reformation prescribed the new remedy above-mentioned. They concealed, as much as they were able, this shame of the new doctrine. M. de Thou, with all his penetration into foreign affairs, could, it seems, discover no more than that this Prince, "by the advice of his pastors," had a concubine together with his wife. This is enough to cover these false pastors with confusion who thus authorized concubinage: but it was not then known that these pastors were Luther himself and all the heads of the party, and that they permitted the Landgrave to have a concubine under the title of a lawful wife, although he had then another whose marriage subsisted in full force. At present this whole mystery of iniquity is discovered by the authentic papers which the late Elector Palatine, Charles Lewis, caused to be printed, and part of which, Ernest, Prince of Hesse, descended from Philip, has made public since his becoming Catholic.

2.—*Important acts relating to this matter, taken from a book printed by order of the Elector Charles Lewis, Count Palatine.*

The book which the Prince Palatine caused to be printed bears this title, "Conscientious Considerations on Marriage, with a Dilucidation of the Questions till the present time debated, touching Adultery, Divorce, and Polygamy." The book came out in German, in 1679, under the borrowed name of Daphneus Arcuarius, under which was concealed that of Laurentius Bœger, that is, Laurence Archer, one of this Prince's counsellors. The design of the book is, apparently, to justify Luther against Bellarmine, who accused him of authorizing polygamy, but, in reality, he shows that Luther favored it; and lest it might be said he, perchance, advanced this doctrine at the beginning only of the Reformation, he produces what was done long after, in this new marriage of the Landgrave. He instances in three pieces, the first of which is an instruction of the Landgrave himself delivered to Bucer, for he was the person commissioned to negotiate with Luther the whole business, whence it is plain that the Landgrave at times employed him in adjusting matters of a quite different nature than were the Sacramentarian contests. You have here a faithful copy of this instruction; and as the piece is remarkable, it may be here seen entire, translated word for word, from German into Latin, and by a good hand.[3]

3.—*Bucer sent to Luther and other heads of the Party to obtain leave for marrying a second wife—this Prince's instructions to his Envoy.*

The Landgrave begins by setting forth how that, "since his last illness, he had reflected much on his state, and chiefly upon this, that a few weeks after his marriage he had begun to wallow in adultery: that his pastors had frequently exhorted him to approach the holy table, but he did believe he should there meet with his judgment, because he will not abandon such a course of life."[4] He imputes to his wife the cause of all his disorders, and gives the reasons for his never loving her; but, having a difficulty in explaining himself on these matters, he refers them to Bucer, whom he had made privy to the whole affair. Next he speaks of his complexion, and the effects of high living at the assemblies of the empire, at which he was obliged to be present. To carry thither a wife of such a quality as his own, would be too great an encumbrance. When his preachers remonstrated to him that he ought to punish adulteries and such like crimes, "How," said he, "can I punish crimes of which I myself am guilty? When I expose myself in war for the Gospel cause, I think I should go to the Devil should I be killed there by the sword or musket-ball.[5] I am sensible that, with the wife I have, NEITHER CAN I, NEITHER WILL I, change my life, whereof I take God to witness; so that I find no means of amendment but by the remedies God afforded to people of old, that is to say, polygamy."[6]

4.—*Sequel to Instruction—the Landgrave promises the revenues of Monasteries to Luther if he will favor his design.*

He there states the reasons which persuade him that it is not forbidden under the Gospel; and what deserves most notice, is his saying, "that to his knowledge, Luther and Melancthon advised the King of England not to break off his marriage with the Queen, his wife; but, besides her, also to wed another."[7] This, again, is a secret we were ignorant of: but a Prince, so well informed, says he knows it; and adds, that they ought to allow him this remedy so much the readier, because he demands it only "for the salvation of his soul." "I am resolved," proceeds he, "to remain no longer in the snare of the Devil; NEITHER CAN I, NEITHER WILL I, withdraw myself but by this way; wherefore I beg of Luther, of Melancthon, of Bucer himself, to give me a certificate, that I may embrace it. But if they apprehend that such a certificate may turn to scandal at this time, and prejudice the Gospel cause, should it be printed, I desire at least they will give me a declaration in writing, that God would not be offended should I marry in private; and that they will seek for means to make this marriage public in due time, to the end that the woman I shall wed may not pass for a dishonest person, otherwise, in process of time, the Church would be scandalized."[8] Then he assures them that " they need not fear lest this second marriage should make him injure his first wife, or even separate himself from her; since, on the contrary, he is determined on this occasion to carry his cross, and leave his dominions to their common children. Let them, therefore, grant me," continues this Prince, "in the name of God, what I request of them, to the end that I may both live and die more cheerfully for the Gospel cause, and more willingly undertake the defence of it; and, on my part, I will do whatsoever they shall in reason ask of me, whether they demand the revenues of monasteries, or other things of a similar nature."[9]

5.—Continuation of it—The Landgrave proposes to have recourse to the Emperor,
and even to the Pope, in case of refusal.

We see how artfully he insinuates the reasons which he, who knew them so thoroughly, was sensible would have most influence on them; and, as he foresaw that scandal was the thing they would most dread, he adds, "That already the ecclesiastics hated the Protestants to such a degree, that they would not hate them more or less for this new article allowing polygamy: but if, contrary to his expectation, Melancthon and Luther should prove inexorable, many designs ran in his head—amongst others, that of applying to the Emperor for this dispensation, whatever money it might cost him."[10] This was a ticklish point—"For," continues he, "there is no likelihood of the Emperor's granting this permission without a dispensation from the Pope, for which I care but little,"[11] says he; "but for that of the Emperor I ought not to despise it, though I should make but little account of that too, did I not otherwise believe that God had rather allowed than forbidden what I wish for; and if the attempt I make on this side (that is upon Luther) succeed not, a human fear urges me to demand the Emperor's consent, certain as I am to obtain all I please, upon giving a round sum of money to some one of his ministers. But although I would not for any thing in the world withdraw myself from the Gospel, or be engaged in any affair that might be contrary to its interest, I am, nevertheless, afraid lest the Imperialists should draw me into something not conducive to the interests of this cause and party. I, therefore, call on them," concludes he, "to afford me the redress I expect, lest I should go seek it in some other place less agreeable; desirous a thousand times rather to owe my repose to their permission than to all other human permissions. Finally, I desire to have, in writing, the opinion of Luther, Melancthon, and Bucer, in order that I may amend myself, and with a good conscience approach the Sacrament."—Given at Melsinguen, the Sunday after St. Catherine's Day, 1539.

"PHILIP, LANDGRAVE OF HESSE."

6.—The dogmatical advice of Luther.—Polygamy allowed by him and the other
heads of the Protestants.

The instruction was equally pressing and ticklish. We see the secret springs which the Landgrave sets in motion: he forgets nothing, and whatever contempt he showed for the pope, the very naming him on this occasion was too much for these new Doctors. So dexterous a Prince let not a word slip without design; and, besides, the very hint of entering into conjunction with the Emperor, was enough to make the whole party tremble. These reasons carried with them much more weight than those the Landgrave had striven to draw from Scripture. To cogent reasons there was joined an artful agent. Accordingly, Bucer obtained of Luther a consultation in form, the original of which in German, in Melancthon's hand and style.[12] It is permitted to the Landgrave, according to the Gospel,[13] (for every thing is done in the Reformation under that name,) to marry another wife besides the one he has already. They deplore, indeed, the condition he is in, "that he cannot refrain from his adulteries as long as he shall have but one wife;"[14] and represent to him this state as very bad in the sight of God, and contrary "to the security of his conscience."[15] But at the same time, and in the next period, they grant him their leave, and declare to him that "he may marry a second wife, if he be fully bent upon it, provided only he keep it secret." Thus the same mouth pronounces good and evil;[16] thus the crime becomes lawful by concealing it. I blush to write these things, and the Doctors who wrote them were themselves ashamed of them. This may be seen through the whole tenor of their perplexed and winding sentences: but they, in the end, were obliged to speak the word, and allow the Landgrave, in express terms, this bigamy he so much coveted. This was the first time it was ever said, since the birth of Christianity, by men styling themselves Doctors in the Church, that Jesus Christ had not forbidden such marriages: that text of Genesis, "They shall be two in one flesh,"[17] was eluded, although Jesus Christ had reduced it to its first sense and primitive institution, which suffers but two persons in the nuptial band.[18] The resolution, in the German language, was signed by Luther, Bucer, and Melancthon. Two other Doctors, one of them Melander, the Landgrave's minister, signed it also, in Latin, at Wittenberg, in the month of December, 1539.[19] This permission was granted in form of dispensation, and reduced to a case of necessity,[20] for they were ashamed of passing this practice into a general law. They found out necessities against the Gospel, and, after having so much blamed the dispensations of Rome, they ventured to give one of that high importance. All the most renowned persons of the Reformation in Germany consented to this iniquity: God visibly gave them over to a reprobate sense; and those who exclaimed against abuses in order to render the Church odious, themselves commit much stranger and more numerous ones at the very beginning of their Reformation, than they could either rake up or invent during the course of so many ages that they upbraid the Church with her corruption.

7.—What was answered in this Consultation with relation to the Emperor.

The Landgrave had very well foreseen he should make his Doctors tremble with the bare mentioning his thoughts of treating with the Emperor on this affair. They answer him, that this Prince has neither faith nor religion—"that he is a cheat, who has nothing of German manners in him, with whom it is dangerous to enter into any engagements."[21] Writing thus to a Prince of the empire, what is it else but putting all Germany in a flame? Then what can be more abject than what appears at the beginning of this advice? "Our poor, little, miserable, and abandoned Church," say they, "stands in need of virtuous governing princes."[22] Here is the reason, if taken right, these new Doctors go upon. But these virtuous princes the Reformation stood in need of, were princes who would make the Gospel subservient to their passions. The Church, indeed, may want the support of princes for her temporal repose; but to broach pernicious and unheard-of points of doctrine purely to please them, and, by this means, to sacrifice to them the Gospel they boast of re-establishing, is the true mystery of iniquity, and the abomination of desolation in the sanctuary.

> 8.—*The secret of the second Marriage, which was to pass for Concubinage—this scandal despised by those who were of the Consultation.*

So infamous a Consultation was enough to discredit the whole party; nor could the Doctors who subscribed to it have silenced the clamors, nor shunned the odium of he people, who, as themselves do own, would have "ranked them with Mahometans, or Anabaptists, that make a jest of marriage."[23] Accordingly, they took their measures, and, in their advice, forbade the Landgrave, above all things, ever to discover this new marriage. There were but a very small number of witnesses to be present, who were also to be bound to secrecy "under the seal of confession,"[24]—thus spoke the Consultation. The new bride was to pass for a concubine. They preferred this scandal in the house of this Prince to that which would be caused throughout all Christendom by the sanctioning of a marriage so contrary to the Gospel, and to the common doctrine of all Christians.[25]

> 9.—*The second Marriage is made in private—the contract agreed upon.—1540.*

The consultation was followed by a marriage, in form, betwixt Philip, Landgrave of Hesse, and Margaret of Saal, by the consent of Christina of Saxony, his wife. The Prince had no more to do but declare, at his marriage, that he did not take this second wife "through any levity or curiosity, but from inevitable necessities of body and conscience, which his Highness had laid before many learned, prudent, Christian, and devout preachers, who had advised him to put his conscience in repose by this means."[26] The instrument of this marriage, dated the 4th of March, 1540, may be found, together with the consultation, in the book which was published by order of the Elector Palatine. Prince Ernest has also furnished the same pieces, so that they are become public in two ways. It is ten or twelve years since copies of them have been produced in a book dispersed through all France,[27] and never contradicted; and now we have them in such an authentic form that there is no room left for doubt. That nothing further might be required, I have added thereto the Landgrave's instruction, and the history is now complete.

> 10.—*The Landgrave's and Luther's Answer to those who reproach them with this Marriage.*

Evil deeds generally come out one way or other. Whatever caution was used to conceal this scandalous marriage, it began, nevertheless, to be suspected; and certain it is, both the Landgrave and Luther were upbraided with it in public writings, but they shifted off the matter by equivocating. A German author has published a letter of the Landgrave's to Henry, the young Duke of Brunswick, where he speaks to him in these words:—"You reproach me with a report that prevails of my having taken a second wife, whilst the first is still living:

but I declare to you, that if you or any other person say that I have contracted an unchristian marriage, or that I have done any thing unworthy of a Christian Prince, it is all downright calumny: for although, towards God, I look upon myself as a miserable sinner, I live, however, before him, in my faith and in my conscience, after such a manner that my confessors do not hold me for an unchristian person. I give scandal to no one, and live with the Princess, my wife, in a perfect good understanding."[28] All this was true, in his way of thinking, for he did not allow that the marriage he was reproached with was unchristian. His first lady was satisfied with it, and the Consultation had stopped the mouths of the Confessors of this Prince. Luther answers with no less artifice. "They reproach the Landgrave," says he, "with being a polyga-mist. I have not much to say on that subject. The Landgrave is able, and has men learned enough to defend him. As for myself, I know one only Princess and Landgrave of Hesse, who is and ought to be named wife and mother in Hesse; and there is no other that can give young Landgraves to this Prince, but the Princess who is the daughter of George, Duke of Saxony."[29] And, indeed, they had ordered matters so that neither the new bride nor her children could bear the title of Landgraves. To defend themselves thus, is aiding their own conviction, and acknowledging the shameful corruption introduced in doctrine by those who, in all their works, spoke of nothing but re-establishing the pure Gospel.

11.—*Luther's scandalous Sermon on Marriage.*

After all, Luther did but follow those principles he had laid down in other places. I have always dreaded speaking of these "inevitable necessities" which he recognised in the union of the two sexes, and of that scandalous sermon he delivered at Wittenberg on marriage; but, since the series of this history has made me at once break through that barrier which modesty has laid in my way, I can no longer dissemble what is found printed in Luther's works.[30] It is true, then, that in a sermon which he delivered at Wittenberg, for the reformation of marriage, he blushed not to pronounce these infamous and scandalous words—"If they are stubborn (he speaks of wives) it is fitting their husbands should tell them, if you will not another will: if the mistress refuse to come, let the maid be called." A man would blush to hear such words in a farce, and on the stage. The chief of the reformers preaches this seriously in the Church; and, as he turned all his excesses into dogmas, he adds:—"However, it is necessary for the husband to bring his wife first before the Church, and to admonish her two or three times; after that put her away, and to take Esther instead of Vashti." This was a new cause for divorce superadded to that of adultery. Thus did Luther handle the subject of the reformation of marriage. We must not ask him in what Gospel he found this article; it is sufficient that it is included "in those necessities," which he fain would believe were above all laws and precautions. After this, will any one wonder at what he allowed the Landgrave? In this sermon, it is true, he orders to repudiate the first wife before the other be taken; and, in the consultation, he permits the Landgrave to have two at once. But, then, the sermon was pronounced in 1522, and the Consultation was penned in 1539. It was but fair that Luther should have learned something after seventeen or eighteen years spent in reforming.

12.—*The Landgrave obliges Luther to suppress the elevation of the blessed Sacrament in the Mass.—How this occasion was made use of to inflame him anew against the Sacramentarians.—1542, 1543.*

From that time forward the Landgrave had almost an absolute sway over this patriarch of the Reformation; and after having found out his weak side in so essential a point, he no longer thought him capable of resisting him. This Prince was little versed in controversies; but, to make amends, like an expert politician he knew how to conciliate the minds of men, to manage different interests, and keep up confederacies. His chief aim was to prevail upon the Swiss to enter into that of Smalkald; but he perceived they were offended at many things in practice among the Lutherans, and particularly at the elevation of the Holy Sacrament, which was still in use, with the ringing of the bell, and the people striking their breasts, with sighs and groans. Five-and-twenty years had Luther preserved these motions of a piety which he knew had Jesus Christ for its object: but nothing was permanent in the Reformation. The Landgrave never ceased attacking Luther on this head, and importuned him in such a manner, that after suffering this custom to be abolished in some Churches of his party, he at length set it aside in the Church of Wittenberg, which was under his immediate direction. These changes happened in 1542 and 1543.[31] The Sacramentarians triumphed at it; they believed that Luther was now relenting: and even, among the Lutherans, it was said he was at length falling off from that admirable resolution, wherewith he had, up to that period, maintained the ancient doctrine of the Real Presence, and that he was about coming to an understanding with the Sacramentarians. He was nettled at these reports; for he was impatient of the most trifling circumstance that infringed on his authority.[32] Peucer, Melancthon's son-in-law, from whom we have taken this account, observes, he took no notice of it for awhile; for, says he, "his great heart was not easily wrought upon."[33] We shall now, however, see by what means they roused him. A physician named Wildus, of great repute in his profession, and much esteemed by the nobility of Misnia, where these reports were most spread against Luther, came to visit him at Wittenberg, and met with a kind reception at his house. "It fell out," proceeds Peucer, "that, at a feast, where Melancthon was also present, this physician being heated with wine, (for at the Reformers' tables men drank as in other places, and such abuses as these were not what they had undertaken to correct;) this physician, I say, began to talk unguardedly of the elevation lately suppressed, and told Luther very frankly, that the common opinion was, he had made this alteration only to please the Swiss, and that he had at length adopted their opinions. This great heart was not proof against these words uttered in liquor; his emotion was perceptible, and Melancthon foresaw what ensued.

13.—*Luther's old jealousy awakened against Zuinglius and his disciples.*—*1545.*

In this matter was Luther animated against the Swiss, and his wrath became implacable on account of two books, which those of Zurich caused to be printed the same year. One was a translation of the Bible made by Leo of Juda, that famous Jew who embraced the Zuinglian doctrine; the other was the works of Zuinglius, carefully collected, with great eulogiums of this author. Although there was nothing in these books against Luther's person, immediately upon their publication he flew out into the greatest extravagance, nor had his transports ever appeared so violent. The Zuinglians published, and the Lutherans have almost owned the same, that Luther could not endure that any one, besides himself, should meddle with translating the Bible.[34] He had made a very elegant version of it in his own language, and thought it was not consistent with his honor that the Reformation should have any other, at least where German was understood. The works of Zuinglius awakened his jealousy,[35] and he believed they were always resolved to set up this man against him, to dispute with him the glory of being the first reformer.[36] Be that as it will, Melancthon and the Lutherans all owned that, after a truce of five or six years' standing, Luther first renewed the war with greater fury than ever. Whatever power the Landgrave had upon Luther, he could never restrain his transports for any considerable time. The Swiss produce letters in Luther's own hand, where he forbids the bookseller, who had made him a present of Leo's translation, ever to send him any thing from those of Zurich, "for they were damned men, who dragged away others into hell; and the churches no longer could communicated with them, nor consent to their blasphemies, and he had resolved to oppose them by his writings and his prayers, to his very last breath."[37]

14.—*Luther will not suffer the Sacramentarians to be any longer prayed for, and believes them inevitably damned.*—*1544.*

He kept his word. The year following he published a comment upon Genesis, where he placed Zuinglius and Œcolampadius with Arius, with Muncer, and the Anabaptists, among the Idolaters, who made for themselves "an idol of their own thoughts, and adored them in contempt of God's word." But what he afterwards published was much more terrible—it was his little "Confession of Faith," madmen, blasphemers, miserable wretches, damned souls, for whom it was no longer lawful to pray:"[38] for he carried matters to this extremity, and protested he never would have any further communication with them, "neither by letters, nor by words, nor by works," if they did not confess, "that the bread of the Eucharist was the true natural body of our Lord, which the impious, and even the traitor Judas, received not less by the mouth than St. Peter and the rest of the faithful."

15.-*Luther's Anathemas.*

By that means he believe he had put an end to the scandalous interpretations of the Sacramentarians, who turned all to their own sense; and declared he held all for fanatics, who should refuse subscribing this last "confession of faith."[39] For he now assumed so high a tone, and so threatened the world with his anathemas, that the Zuinglians no longer called him any thing but the "new Pope, and new Anti-Christ."

16.—*The Zuinglians reprove Luther for always having the Devil in his mouth, and call him a madman.*

Thus not less vigorous was the defence than the attack. Those of Zurich, scandalized at this strange expression, "the bread is the true natural body of our Lord," were much more so at Luther's outrageous contumelies; insomuch that they wrote a book, entitled, "Against the vain and scandalous Calumnies of Luther," in which they maintain "that a man must be as mad as himself to bear with his furious sallies; that he dishonored his old age; and, by his violence, rendered himself contemptible; and he ought to be ashamed of filling his books with so much abusive language, and so many devils." The truth is, Luther had taken care to place the devils within and without, at top and at bottom, at the right hand and the left, before and behind the Zuinglians; inventing, withal, new phrases to pierce them through and through with devils, and repeating this odious name even so as to excite horror.

17.—*Luther's scandalous Prayer, who says he never offended the Devil.*

Such was his custom: in 1542 the Turk threatened Germany more than ever; he had published a prayer against him, where he brought in the Devil after a strange manner. "Thou knowest," said he, "O Lord, that the Devil, the Pope, and the Turk have neither right nor reason to torment us, for we have never offended them: but because we confess that thou, O Father, and the Son, Jesus Christ, and the Holy Ghost, are but one only God eternal—there is our sin, there is our whole crime; for that it is they hate and persecute us; and we should no longer have to fear any thing from them, did we but renounce this faith."[40] What a blindness, to jumble together the Devil, the Pope, and the Turk, as the three enemies of the faith in the Trinity! what a calumny to aver that the Pope persecutes them for this faith! and what folly to exculpate himself to the enemy of mankind as one that never had given him any displeasure!

18.—*Bucer's own Confession of Faith—He confirms that the unworthy do really receive the body of our Lord.—Invention of solid Faith.*

Sometime after Luther had renewed his indignation against the Sacramentarians, in the manner already mentioned, Bucer framed a new confession of faith. These men were never tired of that; it seemed as if he had a mind to oppose it to the little confession which Luther had but just published. That of Bucer came up pretty near to the expressions of the Wittenberg agreement, whereof he was the mediator; but he would not have made a new confession of faith, had he not intended to change something. The thing was (he would no longer say as distinctly and generally as he had done) that the body of our

Saviour might be taken without faith, and taken very really in virtue of our Lord's institution, which our evil disposition could not deprive of its efficacy.[41] Bucer here corrects that doctrine, and seems to lay it down as a condition for the presence of Jesus Christ in the Supper, not only that it be celebrated according to Christ's institution, but also "that men have a solid faith in those words by which he gives himself."[42] This Doctor, who durst not give a lively faith to those who communicated unworthily, in favor of them invented "this solid faith," which I leave to the examination of Protestants; and he would have it, that, by such a faith, the unworthy one received "not only the sacrament, but the Lord himself."[43]

19.—*The same Author's perplexities with relation to the Communion of the Impious.*

He seems puzzled what to say of the communion of the impious; for Luther, whom he would not openly contradict, decided, in his little confession, that they as truly received Jesus Christ as the saints. But Bucer, who feared nothing so much as speaking plainly, says, that those amongst the impious, "who have faith for awhile, receive Jesus Christ in an enigma, as they receive the Gospel." What prodigies of expression! and for those who have no faith at all, it seems he ought to say, they do not at all receive Jesus Christ. But that would have been too clear; he is content with saying, "they do not see, nor touch in the Sacrament, any thing but what is sensible." But what else would he have men see and touch therein, besides what is capable of striking the senses? The rest, that is, the body of our Saviour, may be believed, but no one boasts of either seeing him, or touching him in himself; nor have the faithful any advantage in that respect above the impious. Thus Bucer, according to his custom, does nothing but perplex; and by his subtleties, prepares the way, as we shall see, to those of Calvin and the Calvinists.

20.—*Melancthon labors to make the Real Presence momentaneous, and places it only in the act of using it.*

Meanwhile, Melancthon made it his particular endeavor to diminish, as I may say, the Real Presence, by striving to reduce it to the precise time of its reception. This is a principal dogma of Lutheranism, and it is of great moment clearly to understand how it was established in the sect.

21.—*The aversion for the Mass is the true foundation of this dogma.*—*Two things the Protestants cannot bear therein.*

The Mass was the great aversion of the new Reformation, though, in point of fact, it was nothing else but the public prayers of the Church, consecrated by the celebration of the Eucharist, wherein, Jesus Christ present, honors his Father, and sanctifies the faithful. But two things offended the new Doctors, because they never thoroughly had understood them: one was the oblation, the other the adoration given to Jesus Christ present in these mysteries.

22.—*Luther's bind hatred to the Oblation and the Canon of the Mass.*

The oblation was nothing but the consecration of the bread and wine, in order to make them the body and blood of Jesus Christ, and render him, by this means, truly present. It was impossible this action should not, of itself, be agreeable to God; nor that the sole presence of Jesus Christ, showed to his Father, by honoring his supreme majesty, should not be capable of drawing down his graces on us. The new Doctors were bent to believe that a virtue of saving men, independently of faith, was attributed to this presence, and to the action of the Mass: we have seen their error, and on so false a pre-supposition, did the Mass become the object of their aversion. The most holy words of the canon were decried. Luther discovered poison in every part thereof, even in that prayer we there make a little before Communion—"O Lord Jesus Christ, Son of the living God, who by thy death has given life to the world, by thy body and blood free me from all my sins." Luther, who could believe it! condemned these last words, and would imagine that we attributed our deliverance to the body and blood, independently of faith, without reflecting that this prayer, addressed to Jesus Christ, Son of the living God, who by his death has given life to the world, was itself, in every part, an act of the most lively faith. No matter: "Luther said, that the monks attributed "their salvation to the body and blood of Jesus Christ, without mentioning one word of faith."[44] If the priest, at communion, said with the Psalmist, "I will take the heavenly bread, and call upon the name of the Lord,"[45] Luther found fault with it, and said, "that we improperly, and unseasonably, turned of the mind from faith to works." How blind is hatred! How envenomed must that heart be which poisons such holy things!

23.—*In what sense we offer in the Mass for the redemption of mankind.*—*The Ministers forced to approve this sense.*

No wonder if, after this, they showed the same virulence against the words of the canon, where it is said that "the faithful offer this sacrifice of praise for the redemption of their souls." The most passionate of their ministers are now obliged to own, that the intention of the Church here is to offer for the redemption, not to merit it anew, as if the cross had not merited it, but "in thanksgiving for so great a benefit," and with the design of applying it to us.[46] But never would Luther or the Lutherans enter into so natural a sense; nothing would they see in the Mass but horror and abomination: thus, all that was most holy in it was wrested to an evil sense; and thence concluded Luther "that the Canon ought to be as much abominated as the Devil himself."

24.—*The whole Mass is comprehended in the Real Presence alone.*—*This Presence cannot be admitted without owning it permanent, and existing out of the Reception.*

In the hatred which the reformation had conceived against the Mass, nothing was so much desired as to sap the foundation of it, which, after all, was nothing else but the Real Presence. For upon this presence did the Catholics ground the whole worth and virtue of the Mass: this was the only basis of the oblation, and all the other worship; and Jesus Christ there present constituted its very essence. Calixtus,[47] a Lutheran, has owned, that one of the reasons, not to say the principal one, which made so great a part of the Reformation to deny the Real Presence, was, because they knew no better way to destroy the Mass and the entire worship of Popery. Luther, could he have done it, would himself have come into this sentiment; and we have seen what he said of the inclination he had to shake off Popery in this particular as well as others. And yet, whilst he retained, as he saw himself forced to do, the literal sense, and the Real Presence, it was evident that the Mass subsisted entire; for, upon his retaining this literal sense, the Catholics concluded, not only that the Eucharist was the true body, since Jesus Christ had said "this is my body," but also that it was the body from the time Christ had pronounced it so; consequently, before the manducation, and from the very instant of consecration, since it was not then said, "this shall be," but "this is;" a doctrine wherein we shall now perceive the whole Mass to be contained.

25.—*The Real Presence permanent and independent of the Reception retained by Luther, even after he had suppressed the Elevation.*

This consequence which the Catholics drew from the Real Presence to the Permanent Presence, and subsisting independent of its use, was so clear that Luther had acknowledged it;[48] it was on this foundation that he had always retained the Elevation of the Host, even to the year 1543, and, even after he had abolished it, he writes, in his "Little Confession," in 1544, that "it might be retained with piety, as a testimonial of the real and corporeal presence in the bread, since, by this action, the priest did say, 'Behold, Christians, this is the body of Jesus Christ, which was given for you'." Whence, it appears, that, although he had changed the ceremony of Elevation, he did not change the foundation of his sentiment on the Real Presence, but continued to own it immediately after the Consecration.

26.—*Melacthon finds no other means of destroying the Mass, but by denying the Permanent Presence.*

With this faith it is impossible to deny the sacrifice of the altar; for what will they have Jesus Christ do before his body and blood are eaten, but to render himself present for us before his Father? It was, then, in order to hinder so natural a consequence, that Melancthon sought always to reduce this presence to the sole manducation; and it was chiefly at the conference of Ratisbon that he displayed this part of his doctrine. Charles the Fifth had ordered this conference in 1541, betwixt the Catholics and Protestants, that means might be found for reconciling both religions. It was there that Melancthon, acknowledging, according to his custom, the real and substantial presence together with the Catholics, took great pains to show that the Eucharist, like other sacraments, was not a sacrament, except in the lawful use thereof, that is, as he understood it, except in the actual reception.[49]

27.—Melancthon's frivolous reasons.

The comparison he drew from the other Sacraments was very weak; for, in signs of this nature, where all depends on the will of the institutor, it appertains not to us to prescribe him general laws, nor to tell him he can make but one kind of sacraments; in the institution of his sacraments he might have proposed to himself divers designs, which must be understood from the words he employed at each particular institution. Now, Jesus Christ having said, precisely, "this is," the effect ought to be as speedy as the words are powerful and true; nor was there room for further reasoning.

28.—Other, as frivolous, reasons.

But Melancthon replied; and this was his main argument, which he ceased not to repeat, that God's promise not being made to the bread, but to man, the body of our Lord ought not to be in the bread but when man received it.[50] By a similar method of reasoning it might as well be concluded, that the bitterness of the waters of Mara was not corrected,[51] nor the waters of Cana made wine,[52] but at the time they were drunk, since these miracles were wrought only for the men who drank of it. As, then, these changes were made in the water, but not for the water, there is no reason we should not likewise acknowledge a change in the bread which is not for the bread; there is no reason why this heavenly bread, as well as the terrestrial, should not be made and prepared before it be eaten, nor can I conceive how Melancthon should lay such stress on so pitiful an argument.

29.—These reasons of Melancthon destroyed all Luther's doctrine.

But the most considerable thing here is, that by this reasoning he attacked his master Luther, no less than he did the Catholics; for, by proving that nothing at all was done in the bread, he proved that nothing was done in it in any instant, and that the body of our Lord is not there, either in the reception, or out of the reception; but that man, to whom this promise is addressed, receives it at the presence of the bread, as at the presence of water he receives in baptism, the Holy Ghost and sanctifying grace. Melancthon saw well this consequence, as it will appear hereafter; but whether he had the cunning to conceal it then, or Luther looked not so narrowly into it, the hatred he had conceived against the Mass, made him pass over all that was advanced in order to destroy it.

30.—Melancthon's last reason more weak than all the rest.

Melancthon made use of another argument still weaker than the foregoing ones. He said that Jesus Christ would not be tied; and that to bind him to the bread, further than the time of using it, was to take away his free-will.[53] How can one think such a thing, and say, that the free-will of Jesus Christ is destroyed by a tie that proceeds from his own choice? His word binds him, without doubt, because he is faithful and true; but this bond is not less voluntary than inviolable.

31.—*Melancthon's true reason was, because he could not separate the Mass from the Real Presence, were that owned permanent.—Luther's saying.*

This was what human reason opposed to the mystery of Jesus Christ; vain subtleties, mere quirks: but a weightier motive lay at the bottom of all this. Melancthon's true reason was, because he could not deny but that Jesus Christ, placed on the holy table before the manducation and by the sole consecration of the bread and wine, was an object of itself agreeable to God, which attested his supreme excellence interceded for men, and had all the conditions of a true oblation. In this manner the Mass subsisted, neither could it be overthrown, but by overthrowing the Real Presence out of the manducation. Accordingly, when Luther was told that Melancthon had strenuously denied this presence at the Conference of Ratisbon, Hospinian reports, he cried out, "Cheer up, my dear Melancthon, the Mass is now fallen to the ground—thou hast destroyed the mystery which, hitherto, I had struck at, but in vain."[54] Thus, by the Protestants' own confession, the sacrifice of the Eucharist will ever remain immoveable, as long as in these words, "This is my body," an effectual presence shall be admitted; and in order to destroy the Mass, the effect of our Saviour's words must be suspended, their natural sense be taken away, and "this is" be changed into "this shall be."

32.—*Melancthon's dissimulation.—Luther's notable Letters in favor of the Permanent Presence.*

Although Luther permitted Melancthon to say whatever he pleased against the Mass, yet he in nowise departed from his former notions, nor did he reduce the presence of Jesus Christ in the Eucharist to the bare reception of it. It is even plain that Melancthon shifted with him on this subject; and there are two of Luther's letters, in 1543, wherein he commends a saying of Melancthon's, "that the presence was in the action of the Supper, but not in a precise and mathematical point."[55] As for Luther, he determined the time to be from the Pater Noster which was said in the Lutheran Mass immediately after the Consecration, until all the people had communicated, and all the remaining particles were consumed. But why stops he there? If, at that instant, the communion had been carried to the absent, as St. Justin tells us was done in his time,[56] what reason would there have been to say, that Jesus Christ had immediately withdrawn his sacred presence? But why should he not continue it for some days after, when the Holy Sacrament should be reserved for the communion of the sick? It is nothing but mere caprice to take away the presence of Jesus Christ in this case; and Luther and the Lutherans had no longer any rule, when, out of the actual reception, they admitted the use of it but for ever so short a time. But what made still more against them is, that the Mass and Oblation always remained; and, had there been but one moment of presence before the communion, this presence of Jesus Christ could not be deprived of any of the advantages which attended it. For which reason Melancthon always aimed, whatever he might say to Luther, at placing the presence in the precise time of the reception alone, and this only way could he find of destroying the Oblation and Mass.

33.—The Elevation irreprehensible, according to Luther's sentiments.

Nor was there any other way for destroying the Elevation and Adoration. It has been shown that, at taking away the Elevation, Luther, so far from condemning it, approved the principle of it. I repeat once more his words:—"The Elevation," he says, "may be preserved, as a testimonial of the real and corporal presence; since the doing that is saying to the people, Behold, Christians, this is the body of Jesus Christ, which was given for you."[57] This was what Luther wrote after abolishing the Elevation; but why, then, one may say, did he abolish it? The reason is worthy of the man; and we learn from himself, "that if he attacked the Elevation, it was only out of spite to the Papacy; and, if he retained it so long, it was out of spite to Carlostadius. In a word," concludes he, "it should be retained when it was rejected as impious, and it should be rejected when commanded as necessary."[58] But, upon the whole, he acknowledged what, indeed, is not to be doubted—that there could be no difficulty in showing to the people this divine body from the very time it began to be present.

34.—The Adoration necessary.—Formal avowal of Luther after many variations.

As to the Adoration, after having one while held it as indifferent, and another laid it down as necessary, he at length adhered to his last conclusion;[59] and in the positions which he published against the Doctors of Louvain, in 1545, that is, a year before his death, he called the Eucharist "the adorable sacrament."[60] The Sacramentarian party, who had so much triumphed when he set aside the Elevation, was in a consternation; and Calvin wrote, "that, by this decision, he had raised up the idol in God's temple."[61]

35.—The divines of Wittenberg and Leipsic own, with Melancthon, that there is no avoiding the sacrifice, the Transubstantiation and the Adoration, but by changing Luther's doctrine.

Melancthon was then more than ever convinced that it was impossible to destroy the Adoration, or the Mass, without reducing the whole Real Presence to the precise moment of the manducation. He saw, even, that it was necessary to go further, and that all the points of Catholic doctrine relating to the Eucharist returned upon them one after another, if they did not find out a way to separate the body and blood from the bread and wine. He then pushed the principle already spoken of so far as that nothing was done for the bread and wine, but all for man: insomuch, that in man only was the body and blood to be really found. Melancthon has never explained in what manner he would have this to be done: but as to the foundation of this doctrine, he never left off insinuating it with great secrecy, and in the most artful manner he was able: for there were no hopes, as long as Luther lived, of making him relent on this point, nor of being able to speak freely what men thought: but Melancthon so deeply rooted the doctrine in the minds of the Wittenberg and Leipsic divines, that, after Luther and he were dead, they plainly explained themselves in favor of it in an Assembly, which, by the Elector's orders, they held at Dresden, in 1561. There they feared not to reject Luther's proper doctrine, and the Real Presence which he admitted in the bread; and finding no other means of defending themselves against Transubstantiation, the Adoration, and Sacrifice, they went over to the Real Presence taught them by Melancthon; not in the bread and wine, but in the faithful who received them.[62] They declared, therefore, "That the true substantial body was truly and substantially given in the Supper, although there was no necessity of saying that the bread was the essential body or the proper body of Jesus Christ, or that it was corporally and carnally taken by the corporeal mouth; that ubiquity raised a horror in them; that it was a subject of astonishment that men should be so positive in affirming that the body was present in the bread, since it was of much more importance to consider what is done in man, for whom, and not for the bread, Jesus Christ rendered himself present." After that they explained their sentiments concerning the Adoration, and maintained that it could not be denied, admitting the Real Presence in the bread, although it should even be explained that the body is not present in it except in the actual use: "That the Monks would always have the same reason for beseeching the Eternal Father to hear them through his Son, whom they rendered present in this action; that the Supper having been instituted for the remembrance of Jesus Christ, as he could not be taken nor remembered without believing in, and calling on him, the addressing one's self to him in the Supper as present, and as placing himself in the hands of sacrificing priests after the words of Consecration, could by no means be hindered." By the same reason they maintained that, admitting this Real Presence of the body in the bread, the sacrifice could not be rejected, and they proved it by this example: "It was," said they, "the ancient custom of all suppliants, to take in their arms the children of those whose assistance they implored, and present them to their fathers, in order to prevail with them by their interposition." They said, in the same manner, that having Jesus Christ present in the bread and wine of the Supper, nothing could hinder us from presenting him to his Father, in order to render him propitious to us; and, lastly, they concluded "that it would be much more easy for the monks to establish their Transubstantiation, than for those to impugn it, who, rejecting it in word, affirmed, nevertheless, that the bread was the essential body, that is, the proper body of Jesus Christ."

36.—*Luther's doctrine, immediately after his death, changed by the Divines of Wittenberg.*

Luther had said at Smalkald, and made the whole party subscribe to it, that the bread was the true body of our Lord equally received by saints and sinners: he himself had said, in his last "Confession of Faith," approved by the whole party, "that the bread of the Eucharist is the true natural body of our Lord."[63] Melancthon and all Saxony had received this doctrine with all the rest, for Luther would be obeyed: but, after his death, they fell off from it, and owned with us, that these words, "the bread is the true body," import necessarily the change of bread into the body; since, it being impossible for the bread to be the body by nature, it could not become so but by a change; thus they openly rejected their master's doctrine.[64] But they went much further in the above declaration, and confess that, admitting, as Lutherans had hitherto done, the Real Presence in the bread, there could be no objection to the sacrifice, which Catholics offer to God, nor to the adoration they pay to Jesus Christ in the Eucharist.

37.—No answering the arguments of these Divines.

Their proofs are convincing. If Jesus Christ is believed to be in the bread, if faith lays hold of him in this state, can this faith subsist without adoration? Does not this faith itself necessarily imply the highest adoration, since it draws after it the invocation of Jesus Christ, as Son of God, and as there present? The proof of the sacrifice is not less conclusive: for, as these divines say, if, by the sacramental words, Jesus Christ is rendered present in the bread, is not this presence of Jesus Christ itself agreeable to the Father, and can our prayers be sanctified by a more holy oblation than that of Jesus Christ present? What do Catholics say more, and what is their sacrifice else but Jesus Christ present in the sacrament of the Eucharist, and representing himself to his Father the victim by which he had been appeased? There is no way, then, of avoiding the sacrifice, no more than the adoration and transubstantiation, without denying this real presence of Jesus Christ in the bread.

38.—The Wittenberg Divines return to Luther's sentiment, and why? The Catholics alone have a consistent doctrine.

Thus the Church of Wittenberg, the Mother of the Reformation, and whence, according to Calvin, the light of the Gospel proceeded in our days as it proceeded formerly from Jerusalem, no longer can maintain the sentiments of Luther, her first founder.[65] The whole doctrine of this head of the Reformation contradicts itself: he invincibly establishes the literal sense and Real Presence: he rejects the necessary consequences therefrom, as maintained by Catholics. If, with him, the Real Presence is admitted in the bread, the whole Mass, with the Catholic doctrine, must of course be admitted without reserve. This seems too grating to these new Reformers; for what good have they been doing, if they must be forced to approve these things, with the whole worship of the Church of Rome? but, on the other side, what more chimerical than a Real Presence separated from the bread and wine? Was it not, in showing the bread and wine, that Jesus Christ said,"This is my body"? Has he said, we should receive his body and blood divided from those things wherein it was his pleasure they should be contained; and if we are to receive the proper substance of them, must it not be after such a manner as he declared at the institution of this mystery? In these inextricable difficulties, the desire of abolishing the Mass prevailed; but the method which Melancthon and the Saxons had taken to destroy it was so bad, that it could not subsist. Those of Wittenberg and Leipsic themselves soon after came back, and Luther's opinion, which placed the body in the bread, kept its ground.

39.—*Luther more furious than ever towards the end of his days: his transports against the doctors of Louvain.*

Whilst this head of the Reformers drew near his end, he daily became more and more furious. His theses against the doctors of Louvain are a proof of it. I never can believe that his disciples will behold, without shame, the prodigious aberrations of his mind even to the last period of his life. Sometimes he plays the buffoon, but in the lowest way imaginable, and fills his theses with these wretched equivoques; *vaccultas*, instead of *facultas*; *cacolyca ecclesia*, instead of *catholica*; because he finds in these two words, *vaccultas* and *cacolyca*, a frigid allusion to kine, wicked men, and wolves. To scoff at the custom of calling doctors our masters, he always styles those of Louvain, *nostrolli magistrolli, bruta magistrollia*: persuaded he makes them very odious or contemptible by these ridiculous diminutives of his own coining. When he has a mind to speak more seriously, he calls these doctors "Downright beasts, hogs, Epicureans, pagans, and atheists, who are unacquainted with any other repentance but that of Judas and Saul, who do not take from Scripture, but from the doctrine of men, all they vomit out; and adds, what I dare not translate, *quicquid ructant, vomunt, et cacant*."[66] Thus did he forget all kind of shame, and valued not the making himself a public laughing-stock, provided he drove all to extremes against his adversaries.

40.—*His last sentiments concerning the Zuinglians.*

He treated the Zuinglians no better; and, besides what he said of the adorable sacrament, which utterly destroyed their doctrine, he declared seriously that he held them for heretics, and shut out of the pale of God's Church.[67] He wrote, at the same time, a letter, wherein, upon the Zuinglians having called him an unhappy wretch, "They have afforded me a great pleasure," says he: "I, therefore, the most unhappy of all men, esteem myself happy for one thing only, and covet no other beatitude than that of the Psalmist: happy is the man that hath not been in the council of the Sacramentarians, and hath never walked in the ways of the Zuinglians, nor sat in the chair of those of Zurich." Melancthon and his friends were ashamed of these extravagances of their master. There were secret murmurings in the party, but none durst speak out. If the Sacramentarians complained of Luther's transports to Melancthon, and those who were better affected towards them, they answered, "That he softened the expressions in his books by his familiar discourses, and comforted them, for that their master, when he was heated, spoke more than he meant to speak; which," said they, "was a great inconvenience,"[68] but what they could not help.

41.—*Luther's Death.*

The above letter was of the twenty-fifth of January, 1546. The eighteenth of February following, Luther died. The Zuinglians, who could not refuse him praises without ruining the Reformation, of which he had been the founder, to comfort themselves for the implacable enmity he had evinced towards them, even to his death, spread abroad some conversations he had held with his friends, wherein they pretended he was much mitigated. These accounts carried no appearance of truth; but truly, whether they did or not, it is of little importance to the design of this work. I write not on private conversations, but acts only and public works; and if Luther had given these new instances of his inconstancy, it would, however, be the business of the Lutherans to furnish us wherewith to defend him.

42.—*A new piece produced by Mr. Burnet on Luther's sentiment.*

To omit nothing of what I know concerning this fact, I shall observe, moreover, that I find in Mr. Burnet's "History of the English Reformation," a letter of Luther's to Bucer, which is given us under this title: "A paper concerning a reconciliation with the Zuinglians."[69] This piece of Mr. Burnet, if considered, not in the extract which this artful historian makes of it in his history, but as it is in his "Collection of Records,"[70] will set forth the extravagances that pass in the minds of innovators. Luther begins with this remark, "That it must not be said, they understood not one another." This is what Bucer always pretended, that their disputes were only on words, and that they understood not one another; but Luther could not suffer such an illusion. In the second place, he proposes a new thought to reconcile the two opinions: "The defenders of the figurative sense must allow," says he, "that Jesus Christ is truly present: and we," proceeds he, "will grant that the bread alone is eaten: *panem solum manducari.*" He does not say, we will grant, "that in the sacrament there is truly bread and wine," as Mr. Burnet has translated it; for that had not been a new opinion, such as Luther here promises. It is sufficiently known that consubstantiation, which admits both the bread and wine in the Sacrament, had been received in Lutheranism from its first beginning.

But the new thing he proposes is, that although the body and blood be truly present, nevertheless there is nothing eaten but bread alone: so absurd a refinement, that Mr. Burnet could not hide the absurdity of it in any other way than by suppressing it. But there is no need of troubling oneself to find out sense in this new project of agreement. After having proposed it as useful, Luther turns short; and considering what an inlet would thereby be opened to new questions tending to introduce Epicurism: "No," says he, "it is better leaving these two opinions just as they are, than proceed to these new explications of them, which, far from making them pass on mankind, would indeed only serve to exasperate them the more." Finally, to allay this dissension, which, he says, he would have redeemed with his body and blood, he declares on his side, that he is willing to believe his adversaries are sincere.

He demands they would believe as much of him, and concludes for mutually bearing with one another, without specifying in what manner that was to be done: so that he seems to mean nothing else by it, than abstaining from writing and giving one another abusive language, as had already been agreed upon, but with very little success, at the conference of Marpurg. This is all that Bucer could obtain for the Zuinglians, even when Luther was in his best humor, and, probably, during those years when there was a kind of suspension of arms. However that may be, he soon returns to his old temper; and, for fear the Sacramentarians should endeavor, after his death, to wrest him by their equivocations to their own sentiments, toward the end of his life, he made those declarations against them we have already seen, leaving his disciples as much animated against them as he himself had been.

RECORDS CONCERNING THE SECOND MARRIAGE OF THE LANDGRAVE SPOKEN OF IN THIS BOOK VI.

INSTRUCTIO.

Quid doctor Martinus Bucer *apud Doctorem* Martinum Lutherum, *et* Philippum Melancthonem *solicitare debeat, et, si id ipsis rectum videbitur, postmodum apud Electorem* Saxionæ.

I. Primo, ipsis gratiam et fausta meo nomine denunciet, et si corpore animoque adhuc bene valerent, quod id libentor intelligerem. Deinde incipiendo quod ab eo tempore quo me noster Dominus Deus infirmitate visitavit, varia apud me considerassem, et præsertim quod in me repererim quod ego ab aliquo tempore, quo uxorem duxi, in adulterio et fornicatione jacuerim. Quia vero ipsi et mei prædicantes sæpe me adhortati sunt ut ad Sacramentum accederem: Ego autem apud me talem præfatam vitam deprehendi, nulla bona conscientia aliquot annis ad Sacramentum accedere potui. Nam quia talem vitam DESERERE NOLO, qua bona conscientia possem ad mensam Domini accedere? Et sciebam per hoc non aliter quam ad judicium Domini, et non ad Christianam confessionem me perventurum. Ulterius legi in Paulo pluribus quam uno locis, quomodo nullus fornicator, nec adulter regnum Dei possidebit. Quia vero apud me deprehendi quod apud meam uxorem præsentem a fornicatione ac luxuria, atque adulterio abstinere non possim: nisi ab hac vita desistam, et ad emendationem me convertam, nihil certius habeo expectandum quam exhæredationem a regno Dei et æternam damnationem. Causæ autem, quare a fornicatione, adulterio, et his similibus abstinere non possim apud hanc meam præsentem uxorem sunt istæ.

II. Primo quod initio, quo eam duxi, nec animo nec desiderio eam complexus fuerim. Quali ipsa quoque complexione, amabilitate, et odore sit, et quomodo interdum se superfluo potu gerat, hoc sciunt ipsius aulæ præfecti, et virgines, aliique plures: cumque ad ea describenda difficultatem habeam, Bucero tamen omnia declaravi.

III. Secundo, quia valida complexione, ut medici sciunt, sum, et sæpe contingit ut in fœderum et Imperii comitiis diu verser, ubi lautà vivitur et corpus curatur; quomodo me ibi gerere queam absque uxore, cum non semper magnum gynæceum mecum ducere possim, facile est conjicere et considerare.

IV. Si porro diceretur quare meam uxorem duxerim, vere imprudens homo tunc temporis fui, et ab aliquibus meorum consiliariorum, quorum potior pars defuncta est, ad id persuasis sum. Matrimonium meum ultra tres septimanas non servavi, et sic constanter perrexi.

V. Ulterius me concionatores constanter urgent, ut scelera puniam, fornicationem, et alia; quod etiam libenter facerem: quomodo autem scelera, quibus ipsemet immersus sum, puniam, ubi omnes dicerent, "Magister, prius teipsum puni?" Jam si deberem in rebus evangelicæ confœderationis bellare, tunc id semper mala conscientia facerem et cogitarem: Si tu in hac vita gladio, vel sclopeto, vel alio modo occubueris, ad Demonem perges. Sæpe Deum interea invocavi, et rogavi: sed semper idem remansi.

VI. Nunc vero diligenter consideravi scripturas antiqui et novi Testamenti, et quantum mihi gratiæ Deus dedit, studiose perlegi, et ibi nullum aliud consilium nec medium invenire potui; cum videam quod ab hoc agendi modo penes modernam uxorem meam NEC POSSIM, NEC VELIM abstinere (quod coram Deo testor) quam talia media adhibendo, quæ a Deo permissa nec prohibita sunt. Quod pii Patres ut Abraham, Jacob, David, Lamech, Solomon, et alii, plures quam unam uxorem habuerint, et in eundum Christum crediderent, in quem nos credimus, quemadmodum S. Paulus ad Cor. x. ait; et præterea Deus in veteri Testamento tales Sanctos valde laudarit: Christus quoque eosdem in novo Testamento valde laudat, insuper lex Moisis permittit, si quis duas uxores habeat, quomodo se in hoc gerere debeat.

VII. Et si objiceretur, Abrahamo et antiquis concessum fuisse propter Christum promissum, invenitur tamen clare quod Lex Moisis permittat, et in eo neminem specificet ac dicat, utrum duæ uxores habendæ, et sic neminem excludit. Et si Christus solum promissus sit stemmati Judæ, et nihilominus Samuelis pater, Rex Achab et alli, plures uxores habuerunt, qui tamen non sunt de stemmate Judæ. Idcirco hoc, quod istis id solum permissum fuerit propter Messiam, stare non potest.

VIII. Cum igitur nec Deus in antiquo, nec Christus in novo Testamento, nec Propheta, nec Apostoli prohibeant, ne vir duas uxores habere possit; nullus quoque Propheta, vel Apostolus propterea Reges, Principes, vel alias personas punierit aut vituperarit, quod duas uxores in matrimonio simul habuerint, neque pro crimine aut peccato, vel quod Dei regnum non consequentur, judicarit; cum tamen Paulus multos indicet qui regnum Dei non consequentur, et de his qui duas uxores habent, nullam omnino mentionem faciat. Apostoli quoque cum gentibus indicarent quomodo se gerere, et a quibus abstinere deberent, ubi illos primo ad fidem receperant, uti in Actis Apostolorum est: de hoc etiam nihil prohibuerunt, quod non duas uxores in matrimonio habere possent; cum tamen multi Gentiles fuerint qui plures quam unam uxorem habuerunt: Judæis quoque prohibitum non fuit, qui lex illud permittebat, et est omnino apud aliquos in usu. Quando igitur Paulus clare nobis dicit oportere Episcopum esse unius uxoris virum, similiter et Ministrum: absque necessitate fecisset, si quivis tantum unam uxorem deberet habere, quod id ita præcepisset et plures uxores habere prohibuisset.

IX. Et post hæc ad hunc diem usque in orientalibus regionibus aliqui Christiani sunt, qui duas uxores in matrimonio habent. Item Valentinianus Imperator, quem tamen Historici, Ambrosius, et alii Docti laudant, ipsemet duas uxores habuit, legem quoque edi curavit; quod alii duas uxores habere possent.

X. Item, licet quod sequitur non multum curem, Papa ipsemet Comiti cuidam, qui sanctum sepulchrum invisit, et intellexerat uxorem suam mortuam esse, et ideo aliam vel adhuc unam acceperat, concessit ut is utramque retinere posset. Item scio Lutherum et Philippum Regi Angliæ suasisse, ut primam uxorem non dimitteret, sed aliam præter ipsam duceret quemadmodum *præter propter* consilium sonat. Quando vero in contrarium opponeretur, quod ille nullum masculum hæredem ex prima habuerit, judicamus nos plus hic concedi oportere causæ quam Paulus dat, unumquemque debere uxorem habere propter fornicationem. Nam utique plus situm est in bona conscientia, salute animæ, christiana vita, abstractione ab ignominia et inordinata luxuria, quam in eo ut quis hæredes vel nullos habeat. Nam omnino plus animæ quam res temporales curandæ sunt.

XI. Itaque hæc omni a me permoverunt, ut mihi proposuerim, quia id cum Deo fieri potest, sicut non dubito, abstinere a fornicatione, et omni impudicitia, et via, quam Deus permittit, uti. Nam diutius in vinculis diaboli constrictus perseverare non intendo, et alias absque hac via me præservare NEC POSSUM, NEC VOLO. Quare hæc sit mea ad Lutherum, Philippum et ipsum Bucerum petitio, ut mihi testimonium dare velint, si hoc facerem, illud illicitum non esse.

XII. Casu quo autem id ipsi hoc tempore propter scandalum, et quod Evangelicæ rei fortassis præjudicare aut nocere posset, publice typis mandare non vellent; petitionem tamen meam esse, ut mihi scripto testimonium dent: si id occulto facerem me per id non contra Deum egisse, et quod ipsi etiam id promatrimonio habere, et cum tempore viam inquirere velint, quomodo res hæc publicanda in mundum, et qua ratione persona quam ducturus sum, non pro inhonesta, sed etiam pro honesta habenda sit. Considerare enim possent, quod alias personæ quam ducturus sum graviter accideret, si illa pro tali habenda esset quæ non Christiane vel inhoneste ageret. Post quam etiam nihil occultum remanet, si constanter ita permanerem, et communis Ecclesia nesciret quomodo huic personæ cohabitarem, utique hæc quoque tractu temporis scandalum causaret.

XIII. Item non metuant quod propterea, etsi aliam uxorem acciperem, meam modernam uxorem malo tractare, nec cum ea dormire; vel minorem amicitiam ei exhibare velim, quam antea feci: sed me velle in hoc casu crucem portare, et eidem omne bonum præstare, neque ab eadem abstinere. Volo etiam filios, quos ex prima uxore suscepi, Principes regionis relinquere, et reliquisd aliis honestis rebus prospicere: esse proinde adhuc semel petitionem meam, ut per Deum in hoc mihi consultant, et me juvent in iis rebus, quæ non sunt contra Deum, ut hilari animo vivere et mori, atque Evangelicas causas omnes eo liberius, et magis Christiane suscipere possim. Nam quidquid me jusserint quod Christianum et rectum sit, SIVE MONASTERIORUM BONA, seu alia concernat, ibi me promptum reperient.

XIV. Vellem quoque et desidero non plures quam tantum unam uxorem ad istam modernam uxorem meam. Item ad mundum vel mundanum fructum hac in re non nimis attendendum est; sed magis Deus respiciendus, et quod hic præcipit, prohibet, et liberum relinquit. Nam imperator et mundus me et quemcunque permittent, ut publice meretries retineamus; sed plures quam unam uxorem non facile concesserint. Quod Deus permittit hoc ipsi prohibent: quod Deus prohibet, hoc dissimulant, et videtur mihi sicut matrimonium Sacerdotum. Nam Sacerdotibus nullas uxores concedunt, et meretrices retinere ipsis permittunt. Item Ecclesiastici nobis adeo infensi sunt, ut propter hunc articulum quo plures Christianis uxores permitteremus, nec plus nec minus nobis facturi sint.

XV. Item Philippo et Luthero post modem indicabit, si apud illos, præter omnem tamen opinionem meam de illis nullam opem inveniam; tum me varias cogitationes habere in animo: quod velim apud Cæsarem pro hac re instare per mediatores, etsi multis mihi pecuniis constaret, quod Cæsar absque Pontificis dispensatione non faceret; quamvis etiam Pontificum dispensationem omnino nihili faciam: verum Cæsaris permissio mihi omnino non esset contemnenda; quam Cæsaris permissionem omnino non curarem, nisi scirem quod propositi mei rationem coram Deo haberem, et certius esset Deum id permisisse quam prohibuisse.

XVI. Verum nihilominus ex humano metu, si apud hanc partem nullum solatium invenire possem, Cæsareum consensum obtinere, uti insinuatum est, non esset contemnendum. Nam apud me judicabam si aliquibus Cæsaris Consiliariis egregias pecuniæ summas donarem, me omnia ab ipsis impetraturum: sed præterea timebam, quamvis propter nullam rem in terra ab Evangelio deficere, vel cum divina ope me permittere velim induci ad aliquid quod Evangelicæ causæ contrarium esse posset: ne Cæsareani tamen me in aliis sæcularibus negotiis ita uterentur et obligarent ut isti causæ et parti non foret utile: esse idcirco adhuc petitionem meam, ut me alias juvent, ne cogar rem in iis locis quærere, ubi id non libenter facio, et quod millies libentius ipsorum permissioni, quam cum Deo et bona conscientia facere possunt, confidere velim, quam, Cæsarea, vel ALIIS HUMANIS permissionibus: quibus tamen non ulterius confiderem nisi antecedenter in divina Scriptura fundatæ essent, uti superius est declaratum.

XVII. Denique iterato est mea petitio ut Lutherus, Philippus, et Bucerus mihi hac in re scripto opinionem suam velint aperire, ut postea vitam meam emendare, bona conscientia ad Sacramentum accedere, et omnia negotia nostræ religionis eo liberius et confidentius agere possim.

Datum Melsingæ Dominica post Catharinæ Anno 1539.

PHILIPPUS LANDGRAFFIUS HASSIAE

THE CONSULTATION OF LUTHER AND THE OTHER PROTESTANT DOCTORS CONCERNING POLYGAMY.

To the most serene Prince and Lord Philip Landgrave of Hesse, *Count of Catzenlembogen, of Diets, of Ziegenhain, and Nidda, our gracious Lord, we wish above all things the Grace of God through Jesus Christ.*

Most Serene Prince and Lord,

I. Postquam vestra Celsitudo per Dominum Bucerum diuturnas conscientiæ suæ molestias, nonnullas simulque considerationes indicari curavit, addito scripto seu instructione quam illi vestra Celsitudo tradidit; licet ita properanter expedier responsum difficile sit, noluimus tamen Dominum Bucerum, reditum, utique maturantem, sine scripto dimittere.

II. Imprimis sumus ex animo recreati, et Deo gratias agimus, quod vestram Celsitudinem difficili morbo liberaverit, petimusque, ut Deus Celsitudinem vestram in corpore et animo confortare et conservare dignetur.

III. Nam prout Celsitudo vestra videt, paupercula et misera Ecclesia est exigua et derelicta, indigens probis Dominis Regentibus, sicut non dubitamus Deum aliquos conservaturum, quantumvis tentationes diversæ occurrant.

IV. Circa quæstionem quam nobis Bucerus proposuit, hæc nobis occurrunt consideratione digna: Celsitudo vestra per se ipsam satis perspicit quantum differant universalem legem condere, vel in certo casu gravibus de causis ex concessione divina, dis-

I. We have been informed by Bucer, and in the instruction which your Highness gave him, have read, the trouble of mind, and the uneasiness of conscience your Highness is under at this present; and although it seemed to us very difficult so speedily to answer the doubts proposed; nevertheless, we would not permit the said Bucer, who was urgent for his return to your Highness, to go away without an answer in writing.

II. It has been a subject of the greatest joy to us, and we have praised God, for that he has recovered your Highness from a dangerous fit of sickness, and we pray that he will long continue this blessing of perfect health both in body and mind.

III. Your Highness is not ignorant how great need our poor, miserable, little, and abandoned Church stands in of virtuous Princes and Rulers to protect her; and we doubt not but God will always supply her with some such, although from time to time he threatens to deprive her of them, and proves her by sundry temptations.

IV. These things seem to us of greatest importance in the question which Bucer has proposed to us: your Highness sufficiently of yourself comprehends the difference there is betwixt settling an universal law, and using (for urgent reasons and with God's permission) a dispensation in a particular case:

pensatione uti; nam contra Deum locum non habet dispensatio.

V. Nunc suadere non possumus, ut introducatur publice, et velut lege sanciatur permisso plures quam unam, uxores ducendi. Si aliquid hac de re prælo committeretur, facile intelligit vestra Celsitudo, id præcepti instar intellectum et acceptatum iri, unde multa scandala et difficultates orirentur. Consideret, quæsumus, Celsitudo vestra quam sinistre acciperetur, si quis convinceretur hanc legem in Germaniam introduxisse, quæ æternarum litium et inquietudinum (quod limendum) futurum esset seminarium.

VI. Quod opponi potest, quod coram Deo æquum est id omnino permittendum, hoc certa ratione et conditione est accipiendum. Si res est mandata et necessaria, verum est quod objicitur; si nec mandata, nec necessaria sit, alias circumstantias oportet expendere ut ad propositam questionem propius accedamus: Deus matrimonium instituit ut tantum duarum et non plurium personarum esset societas, si natura non esset corrupta; hoc intendit illa sententia: *Erunt duo in carne una*, idque primatus fuit observatum.

VII. Sed Lamech pluralitatem uxorum in matrimonium invexit, quod de illo Scriptura memorat tanquam introductum contra primam regulam.

VIII. Apud infideles tamen fuit consuetudine receptum; postea Abraham quoque et posteri ejus plures duxerunt uxores. Certum

for it is otherwise evident that no dispensation can take place against the first of all laws, the divine law.

V. We cannot at present advise to introduce publicly, and establish as a law in the New Testament, that of the Old, which permitted to have more wives than one. Your Highness is sensible, should any such thing be printed, that it would be taken for a precept, whence infinite troubles and scandals would arise. We beg your Highness to consider the dangers a man would be exposed unto, who should be convicted of having brought into Germany such a law, which would divide families, and involve them in endless strifes and disturbances.

VI. As to the objection that may be made, that what is just in God's sight ought absolutely to be permitted, it must be answered in this manner. If that which is just before God, be besides commanded and necessary, the objection is true: if it be neither necesssary nor commanded, other circumstances, before it be permitted, must be attended to; and to come to the question in hand: God hath instituted marriage to be a society of two persons and no more, supposing nature were not corrupted; and this is the sense of that text of Genesis, "There shall be two in one flesh," and this was observed at the beginning.

VII. Lamech was the first that married many wives, and the Scripture witnesses that this custom was introduced contrary to the first Institution.

VIII. It nevertheless passed into custom among infidel nations; and we even find afterwards, that Abraham and his posterity had many wives. It is also

est hoc postmodum lege Mosis permissum fuisse, teste Scriptura, Deuter. 2. 1. 1. ut homo haberet duas uxores: nam Deus fragili naturæ aliquid indulsit. Cum vero principio et creationi consentaneum sit unica uxore contentum vivere, hujusmodi lex est laudabilis, et ab Ecclesia acceptanda, non lex huic contraria statuenda; nam Christus repetit hanc sententiam: *Erunt duo in carne una*, Matt. xix. et in memoriam revocat quale matrimonium ante humanam fragilitatem esse debuisset.

IX. Certis tamen casibus locus est dispensationi. Si quis apud exteras nationes captivus ad curam corporis et sanitatem, inibi alteram uxorem superinduceret; vel si quis haberet leprosam; his casibus alteram ducere cum consilio sui Pastoris, non intentione novam legem inducendi, sed suæ necessitati consulendi, hunc nescimus, qua ratione damnare licerit.

X. Cum igitur aliud sit inducere legem, aliud uti dispensatione, obsecramus vestram Celsitudinem sequentia velit considerare.

Primo ante omina cavendum, ne hæc res inducatur in orbem ad modum legis, quam sequendi libera omnium sit potestas. Deinde considerare dignetur vestra Celsitudo scandalum nimium, quod Evangelii hostes exclamaturi sint, nos similes esse Anabaptistis, qui

certain from Deuteronomy, that the law of Moses permitted it afterwards, and that God made an allowance for frail nature. Since it is then suitable to the creation of men, and to the first establishment of their society, that each one be content with one wife, it thence follows that the law enjoining it is praiseworthy; that it ought to be received in the Church; and no law contrary thereto be introduced into it, because Jesus Christ has repeated in the nineteenth chapter of St. Matthew that text of Genesis, "There shall be two in one flesh:" and brings to man's remembrance what marriage ought to have been before it degenerated from its purity.

IX. In certain cases, however, there is room for dispensation. For example, if a married man, detained captive in a distant country, should there taken a second wife, in order to preserve or recover his health, or that his own became leprous, we see not how we could condemn, in these cases, such a man as, by the advice of his Pastor, should take another wife, provided it were not with a design of introducing a new law, but with an eye only to his own particular necessities.

X. Since then the introducing a new law, and the using a dispensation with respect to the same law, are two very different things, we entreat your Highness to take what follows into consideration.

In the first place, above all things, care must be taken, that plurality of wives be not introduced into the world by way of law, for every man to follow as he thinks fit. In the second place, may it please your Highness to reflect on the dismal scandal which would not fail to happen, if occasion be given to

simul plures duxerunt uxores. Item Evangelicos eam sectari libertatem plures simul ducendi, quæ in Turcia in usu est.

XI. Item principum facta latius spargi quam privatorum consideret.

XII. Item consideret privatas personas, hujusmodi principum facta audientes, facile eadem sibi permissa persuadere, prout apparet talia facile irrepere.

XIII. Item considerandum Celsitudinem vestram abundare nobilitate efferi spiritus, in qua multi, uti in aliis quoque terris sint, qui propter amplos proventus, quibus ratione cathedralium beneficiorum perfruuntur, valde evangelio adversantur. Non ignoramus ipsi magnorum nobilium valde insula dicta; et qualem se nobilitas et subdita ditio erga Celsitudinem vestram sit præbitura, si publica introductio fiat, haud difficile est arbitrari.

XIV. Item Celsitudo vestra, quæ Dei singularis est gratia, apud reges et potentes etiam exteros magno est in honore et respectu; apud quos merito est, quod timeat ne hæc res pariat nominis diminutionem. Cum igitur hic multa scandala confluant, rogamus Celsitudinem vestram, ut hanc rem maturo judicio expendere velit.

XV. Illud quoque est verum quod Celsitudinem vestram omni modo rogamus et hortamur, ut fornicationem et adulterium fugiat. Habuimus quoque, ut, quod res est, loquamur, longo tempore non parvum mærorem, quod intellexe-

the enemies of the Gospel to exclaim, that we are like the Anabaptists, who have several wives at once, and the Turks, who take as many wives as they are able to maintain.

XI. In the third place, that the actions of Princes are more widely spread than those of private men.

XII. Fourthly, that inferiors are no sooner informed what their superiors do, but they imagine they may do the same, and by that means licentiousness becomes universal.

XIII. Fifthly, that your Highness's estates are filled with an untractable nobility, for the most part very averse to the Gospel, on account of the hopes they are in, as in other countries, of obtaining the benefices of cathedral churches, the revenues whereof are very great. We know the impertinent discourses vented by the most illustrious of your nobility, and it is easily seen how they and the rest of your subjects would be disposed, in case your Highness should authorize such a novelty.

XIV. Sixthly, that your Highness, by the singular grace of God, hath a great reputation in the empire and foreign countries; and it is to be feared lest the execution of this project of a double marriage should greatly diminish this esteem and respect. The concurrence of so many scandalds obliges us to beseech your Highness to examine the thing with all the maturity of judgment God has endowed you with.

XV. With no less earnestness do we entreat your Highness, by all means, to avoid fornication and adultelry; and, to own the truth sincerely, we have a long time been sensibly grieved to see your Highness abandoned to such impurities, which might be followed by

rimus vestram Celsitudinem ejus-
modi impuritate oneratam, quam
divina ultio, morbi, alique pericula
sequi possent.

XVI. Etiam rogamus Celsitudinem vestram ne talia extra matrimonium, levia peccata velit æsti-
mare, sicut mundus hæc ventis
tradere et parvi pendere solet:
Verum Deus impudicitiam sæpe
severissime punivit: nam pœna
diluvii tribuitur regentum adulte-
riis. Item adulterium Davidis est
severum vindictæ divinæ exem-
plum, et Paulus sæpius ait; Deus
non irridetur. Adulteri non introi-
bunt in regnum Dei: nam fidei
obedientia comes esse debet, ut
non contra conscientiam agamus, 1
Tim. iii. Si cor nostrum non re-
prehenderit nos, possumus læti
Deum invocare; et Rom. viii. Si
carnalia desideria spiritu mortifica-
verimus, vivemus; si autem secun-
dum carnem ambulemus: hoc est,
si contra conscientiam, agamus,
moriemur.

XVII. Hæc referrimus, ut
consideret Deum ob talia vitia non
ridere, prout aliqui audaces faciunt,
et ethnicas cogitationes animo
fovent. Libenter quoque intellexi-
mus vestram Celsitudinem ob ejus-
modi vitia angi et conqueri. In-
cumbunt Celsitudini vestræ negotia totum mundum concernentia.
Accedit Celsitudinis vestræ com-
plexio subtilis, et minime robusta,
ac pauci somni, unde merito corpori parcendum esset, quemadmodum multi alii facere coguntur.

the effects of the divine vengeance,
distempers, and many other dangerous
consequences.

XVI. We also beg of your Highness not to entertain a notion, that the
use of women out of marriage is but a
light and trifling fault, as the world is
used to imagine; since God hath often
chastised impurity with the most severe
punishment: and that of the deluge is
attributed to the adulteries of the great
ones; and the adultery of David has
afforded a terrible instance of the divine
vengance; and St. Paul repeats frequently, that God is not mocked with impunity, and that adulterers shall not enter
into the Kingdom of God. For it is said,
in the second chapter of the first Epistle
to Timothy, that obedience must be the
companion of faith, in order to avoid
acting against conscience; and in the
third chapter of the first of St. John, if
our heart condemn us not, we may call
upon the name of God with joy: and in
the eighth chapter of the Epistle to the
Romans, if by the spirit we mortify the
desires of the flesh, we shall live: but,
on the contrary, we shall die, if we
walk according to the flesh, that is, if
we act against our own consciences.

XVII. We have related these passages, to the end that your Highness
may consider seriously that God looks
not on the vice of impurity as a laughing matter, as is supposed by those
audacious libertines, who entertain
heathenish notions on this subject. We
are pleased to find that your Highness is
troubled with remorse of conscience for
these disorders. The management of the
most important affairs in the world is
now incumbent on your Highness, who
is of a very delicate and tender complexion; sleeps but little; and these

XVIII. Legitur de laudatissimo Principe Scanderbego, qui multa præclara facinora patravit contra duos Turcarum Imperatores, Amurathem et Mahumetem, et Græciam dum viveret, feliciter tuitus est, ac conservavit. Hic suos milites sæpius ad castimoniam hortari auditus est, et dicere, nullam rem fortibus viris æque animos demere ac Venerem. Item quod si vestra Celsitudo insuper alteram uxorem haberet, et nollet pravis affectibus et consuetudinibus repugnare, adhuc non esset vestræ Celsitudini consultum ac prospectum. Oportet unumquemque in externis istis suorum membrorum esse dominum, uti Paulus scribit: Curate ut membra vestra sint arma justitiæ. Quare vestra Celsitudo in consideratione aliarum causarum, nempe scandali, curarum, laborum ac solicitudinum, et corporis infirmitatis velit hanc rem æqua lance perpendere, et simul in memoriam revocare, quod Deus ei ex moderna conjuge puchram sobolem utriusque sexus dederit, ita ut contentus hac esse possit. Quot alii in suo matrimonio debent patientiam exercere ad vitandum scandalum? Nobis non sedet animo Celsitudinem vestram ad tam difficilem novitatem impellere, aut inducere; nam ditio vestræ Celsitudinis, aliique nos impeterent, quod nobid eo minus ferendum esset, quod ex præcepto divino nobis incumbat matrimonium, ominaque

reasons, which have obliged so many prudent persons to mange their constitutions, are more than sufficient to prevail with your Highness to imitate them.

XVIII. We read of the incomparable Scanderberg, who so frequently defeated the two most powerful Emperors of the Turks, Amurat II and Mahomet II, and whilst alive, preserved Greece from their tyranny, that he often exhorted his soldiers to chastity, and said to them, that there was nothing so hurtful to men of their profession, as venereal pleasures. And if your Highness, after marrying a second wife, were not to forsake those licentious disorders, the remedy proposed would be to no purpose. Every one ought to be master of his own body in external actions, and see, according to the expression of St. Paul, that his members be the arms of justice. May it please your Highness, therefore, impartially to examine the considerations of scandal, of labors, of care, of trouble, and of distempers, which have been represented. And at the same time remember that God has given you a numerous issue of such beautiful children of both sexes by the Princess your wife, that you have reason to be satisfied therewith. How many others, in marriage, are obliged to the exercise and practice of patience, from the motive only of avoiding scandal? We are far from urging on your Highness to introduce so difficult a novelty into your family. By so doing, we should draw upon ourselves not only the reproaches and persecution of those of Hesse, but of all other people. The which would be so much the less supportable to us, as God commands us in the ministry which we exercise, as

humana ad divinam institutionem dirigere, atque in ea quoad possibile conservare, neque scandalum removere.

XIX. Is jam est mos sæculi, ut culpa omnis in Predicatores conferatur, si quid difficultatis incidat; et humanum cor in summæ et inferioris conditionis hominibus instabile, unde diversa pertimescenda.

XX. Si autem vestra Celsitudo ab impudica vita non abstineat, quod dicit sibi impossibile, optaremus Celsitudinem vestram in meliori statu esse coram Deo, et secura conscientia vivere ad propriæ animæ salutem, et ditionum ac subditorum emolumentum.

XXI. Quod si denique vestra Celsitudo omnino concluserit, adhuc unam conjugem ducere, judicamus id secreto faciendum, ut superius de dispensatione dictum, nempe ut tantum vestræ Celsitudini, illi personæ, ac paucis personis fidelibus constet Celsitudinis vestræ animus, et conscientia sub sigillo confessionis. Hinc non sequuntur alicujus momenti contradictiones aut scandala. Nihil enim est inusitati Principes concubinas alere; et quamvis non omnibus e plebe constaret rei ratio, tamen prudentiores intelligerent, et magis placeret hæc moderata vivendi ratio, quam adulterium et alii belluini et impudici actus; nec curandi aliorum sermones, si recte cum conscientia agatur. Sic et in tantum hoc approbamus: nam quod circa matrimonium in lege Mosis fuit permissum, Evangelium non revocat, aut vetat, quod exter-

much as we are able, to regulate marriage, and all the other duties of human life, according to the divine Institution, and maintain them in that state, and remove all kind of scandal.

XIX. It is now customary among worldlings, to lay the blame of every thing upon the Preachers of the Gospel. The heart of man is equally fickle in the more elevated and lower stations of life; and much have we to fear on that score.

XX. As to what your Highness says, that it is not possible for you to abstain from this impure life, we wish you were in a better state before God, that you lived with a secure conscience, and labored for the salvation of your own soul, and the welfare of your subjects.

XXI. But after all, if your Highness is fully resolved to marry a second wife, we judge it ought to be done secretly, as we have said with respect to the dispensation demanded on the same account, that is, that none but the person you shall wed, and a few trusty persons, know of the matter, and they, too, obliged to secrecy under the seal of confession. Hence no contradiction nor scandal of moment is to be apprehended; for it is no extraordinary thing for Princes to keep concubines; and though the vulgar should be scandalized thereat, the more intelligent would doubt of the truth, and prudent persons would approve of this moderate kind of life, preferably to adultery, and other brutal actions. There is no need of being much concerned for what men will say, provided all goes right with conscience. So far do we approve it, and in those circumstances only by us specified; for the Gospel hath neither recalled nor forbid what was permitted in the law of

num regimen non immutat, sed adfert æternam justitiam et æternam vitam, et orditur veram obedientiam erga Deum, et conatur corruptam naturam reparare.

XXII. Habet itaque Celsitudo vestra non tantum omnium nostrum testimonium in casu necessitatis, sed etiam antecedentes nostras considerationes quas rogamus, ut vestra Celsitudo tanquam laudatus, sapiens, et Christianus Princeps velit ponderare. Oramus quoque Deum, ut velit Celstitudinem vestram ducere ac regere ad suam laudem et vestræ Celsitudinis animæ salutem.

XXIII. Quod attinet ad consilium hanc rem apud Cæsarem tractandi; existimamus illum, adulterium inter minora peccata numerare; nam magnopere verendum, illum Papistica, Cardinalitia, Italica, Hispanica, Saracenica imbutum fide, non curaturum vestræ Celsitudinis postulatum, et in proprium emolumentum vanis verbis sustentaturum, sicut intelligimus perfidum ac fallacem virum esse, morisque Germanici oblitum.

XXIV. Videt Celsitudo vestra ipsa, quod nullis necessitatibus Christianis sincere consulit. Turcam sinit imperturbatum, excitat tantum rebelliones in Germania, ut Burgundicam potentiam efferat. Quare optandum ut nulli Christiani Principes illius infidus machinationibus se misceant. Deus conservet vestram Celsitudinem.

Moses with respect to marriage. Jesus Christ has not changed the external economy, but added justice only, and life everlasting, for reward. He teaches the true way of obeying God, and endeavors to repair the corruption of nature.

XXII. Your highness hath therefore, in this writing, not only the approbation of us all, in case of necessity, concerning what you desire, but also the reflections we have made thereupon; we beseech you to weigh them, as becoming a virtuous, wise, and Christian Prince. We also beg of God to direct all for his glory and your Highness's salvation.

XXIII. As to your Highness's thought of communicating this affair to the emperor before it be concluded, it seems to us that this Prince counts adultery among the lesser sort of sins; and it is very much to be feared lest his faith being of the same stamp with that of the Pope, the Cardinals, the Italians, the Spaniards, and the Saracens, he make light of your Highness's proposal, and turn it to his own advantage by amusing your Highness with vain words. We know he is deceitful and perfidious, and has nothing of the German in him.

XXIV. Your Highness sees, that he uses no sincere endeavor to redress the grievances of Christendom; that he leaves the Turk unmolested, and labors for nothing but to divide the empire, that he may raise up the house of Austria on its ruins. It is therefore very much to be wished that no Christian Prince would give into his pernicious schemes. May God preserve your High-

Nos ad serviendum vestræ Celsitudini sumus promptissimi.

Datum Vittenbergæ die Mercurii post festum Sancti Nicolai, 1939.

Vestræ Celsitudinis parati ac subjecti servi,

MARTINUS LUTHER.
PHILIPPUS MELANCTHON.
MARTINUS BUCERUS.
ANTONIUS CORVINUS.
ADAM.
JOANNES LENINGUS.
JUSTUS WINTFERTE.
DIONYSIUS MELANTHER.

Ego Georgius Nuspicher, accepta a Cæsare potestate, Notarius publicus et Scriba, testor hoc meo chirographo publice, quod hanc copiam ex vero et inviolato originali propria manu a Philippo Melancthone exarato, ad instantiam et petitionem mei clementissimi Domini et Principis Hassiæ ipse scripserim, et quinque foliis numero excepta inscriptione complexus sim, etiam omnia proprie et diligenter auscultarim et contulerim, et in omnibus cum originali et subscriptione nominum concordet. De quare rerum testor propria manu.

GEORGIUS NUSPICHER,
Notarius.

ness. We are most ready to serve your Highness.

Given at Wittenberg the Wednesday after the feast of Saint Nicholas, 1539.

Your Highness's most humble, and most obedient subjects and servants,

MARTIN LUTHER.
PHILIP MELANCTHON.
MARTIN BUCER.
ANTONY CORVIN.
ADAM.
JOHN LENINGUE.
JUSTUS WINTFERTE.
DENIS MELANTHER.

I George Nuspicher, Notary Imperial, bear testimony by this present act, written and signed with my own hand, that I have transcribed this present copy from the true original which is in Melancthon's own handwriting, and hath been faithfully preserved to this present time, at the request of the most serene Prince of Hesse; and have examined with the greatest exactness every line and every word, and collated them with the same original; and have found them conformable thereunto, not only in the things themselves, but also in the signs manual, and have delivered the present copy in five leaves of good paper, whereof I bear witness.

GEORGE NUSPICHER,
Notary.

Instrumentum Copulationis
Philippi Landgravii,
et Margaretæ de Saal.

In nomine Domini Amen.

Notum sit omnibus et singulis, qui hoc publicum instrumentum vident, audiunt, legunt, quod Anno post Christum natum 1540, die Mercurii mensis Martii, post meridiem circa secundam circiter, Indictionis Anno 13, potentissimi et invictissimi Romanorum Imperatoris Caroli-quinti, clementissimi nostri Domini Anno regiminis 21, coram me infrascripto Notario et teste, Rotemburgi in arce comparuerint serenissimus Princeps et Dominus Philippus Landgravius Comes in Catznelenbogen, Dietz, Ziegenhain, et Nidda, cum aliquibus suæ Celsitudinis consiliariis ex una parte; et honesta, ac virtuosa Virgo Margareta de Saal, cum aliquibus ex sua consanguinitate ex altera parte; illa intentione et voluntate coram me publico Notario ac teste, publice confessi sunt, ut matrimonio copulentur; et postea ante memoratus meus clementissimus Dominus et Princeps Landgravius Philippus per Reverendum Dominum Dionysium Melandrum suæ Celsitudinis Concionatorem, curavit proponi ferme hunc sensum: —Cum omnia aperta sint oculis Dei, et homines pauca lateant, et sua Celsitudo velit cum nominata virgine Margareta matrimonio copulari, etsi prior suæ Celsitudinis conjux adhuc sit in vivis, ut hoc non tribuatur levitati et curiositati, ut evitetur scandalum, et nominatæ virginis et illius honestæ consanguinitatis honor et fama non patia-

The Marriage Contract of Philip,
Landgrave of Hesse,
with Margaret de Saal.

In the name of God, Amen.

Be it known to all those, as well in general as in particular, who shall see, hear, or read this public instrument, that in the year 1540, on Wednesday, the fourth day of the month of March, at two o'clock or thereabouts, in the afternoon, the thirteenth year of the Indiction, and the twenty-first of the reign of the most puisssant and most victorious Emperor Charles V, our most gracious lord; the most serene Prince and Lord Philip Landgrave of Hesse, Count of Catznelenbogen, of Dietz, of Ziegenhain, and Nidda, with some of his Highness's Counsellors, on one side, and the good and virtuous Lady Margaret de Saal with some of her relations, on the other side, have appeared before me, Notary, and witness underwritten, in the City of Rotenburg, in the castle of the same city, with the design and will publicly declared before me, Notary public and witness, to unite themselves by marriage; and accordingly my most gracious Lord and Prince Philip the Landgrave hath ordered this to be proposed by the Reverend Denis Melander, preacher to is Highness, much to the sense as follows:—"Whereas the eye of God searches all things, and but little escapes the knowledge of men, his Highness declares that his will is to wed the said Lady Margaret de Saal, although the Princess his wife be still living, and that this action may not be imputed to inconstancy or curiosity; to avoid scandal and maintain the honor of the said Lady, and the reputation of her kindred, his Highness makes oath

tur; edicit sua Celsitudo hic coram
Deo, et in suam conscientiam et
animan hoc non fieri ex levitate,
aut curiositate, nec ex aliqua vili-
pensione juris et superiorum, sed
urgeri aliquibus gravibus et inevitabilibus necessitatibus conscientiæ et
corporis, adeo ut impossibile sit sine
alia superinducta legitima conjuge
corpus suum et animan salvare.
Quam multiplicem causam etiam
sua Celsitudo multis prædoctis, piis,
prudentibus, et Christianis Prædi-
catoribus antehac indicavit, qui
etiam consideratis inevitabilibus
causis id ipsum suaserunt ad suæ
Celsitudinis animæ et conscientiæ
consulendum. Quæ causa et necessitas etiam Serenissimam Principem
Christianam Ducissam Saxoniæ, suæ
Celsitudinis primam legitimam
conjugem, utpote alta principali
prudentia et pia mente præditam
movit, ut suæ Celsitudinis tanquam
dilectissimi mariti animæ et corpori
et serviret, et honor Dei promove-
retur ad gratiose consentiendum.
Quemadmodum suæ Celsitudinis
hæc super relata syngrapha testatur;
et ne cui scandalum detur eo quod
duas conjuges habere moderno
tempore sit insolitum; etsi in hoc
casu Christianum et licitum sit, non
vult sua Celsitudo publice coram
pluribus consuetas ceremonias usur-
pare, et palam nuptias celebrare
cum memorata virgine Margareta
de Saal; sed hic in privato et silen-
tio in præsentia subscriptorum
testium volunt invicem jungi matrimonio.—Finito hoc sermone nomi-
nati Philippus et Margareta sunt
matrimonio juncti, et unaquæque
persona alteram sibi desponsam
agnovit et acceptavit, adjuncta

here before God, and upon his soul
and conscience, that he takes her to
wife through no levity, nor curiosity,
nor from any contempt of law, or
superiors; but that he is obliged to it
by such important, such inevitable
necessities of body and conscience, that
it is impossible for him to save either
body or soul, without adding another
wife to his first. All of which his Highness hath laid before many learned, devout, prudent, and Christian preachers,
and consulted them upon it. And these
great men, after examining the motives
represented to them, have advised his
Highness to put his soul and conscience at ease by this double marriage.
And the same cause and the same
necessity have obliged the most serene
Princess, Christina Duchess of Saxony,
his Highness's first lawful wife, out of
her great prudence and sincere devotion, for which she is so much to be
commended, freely to consent and
admit of a partner, to the end that the
soul and body of her most dear spouse
may run no further risk, and the glory
of God may be increased, as the deed
written with this Princess's own hand
sufficiently testifies. And lest occasion
of scandal be taken from its not being
the custom to have two wives, although this be Christian and lawful in
the present case, his Highness will not
solemnize these nuptials in the ordinary
way, that is, publicly before many people, and with the wonted ceremonies,
with the said Margaret de Saal; but
both the one and the other will join
themselves in wedlock, privately and
without noise, in presence only of the
witnesses underwitten."—After Melander had finished his discourse, the said
Philip and the said Margaret accepted
of each other for husband and wife,

metua fidelitatis promissione in nomine Domini. Et antememoratus princeps ac Dominus ante hunc actum me infrascriptum Notarium requisivit, ut desuper unum aut plura instrumenta conficerem, et mihi etiam tanquam personæ publicæ, verbo ac fide Principis addixit ac promisit, se omnia hæc inviolabiter semper ac firmiter servaturum, in præsentia reverendorum prædoctorum Dominorum M. Philippi Melancthonis, M. Martini Buceri, Dionysii Melandri, etiam in præsentia strenuorum ac præstantium Eberhardi de Than Electoralis Consiliarii, Hermanni de Malsberg, Hermanni de Hundelshausen, Domini Joannis Fegg Cancellariæ, Lodolphi Schenck, ac honestæ ac virtuosæ Dominæ Annæ natæ de Miltitz viduæ defuncti Joannis de Saal memoratæ sponsæ matris, tanquam ad hunc actum requisitorum testium.

Et ego Balthassar Rand de Fulda, potestate Cæsaris Notarius publicus, qui huic sermoni, instructioni, et matrimoniali sponsioni, et copulationi cum supra memoratis testibus interfui, et hæc omnia et singua audivi, et vidi, et tanquam Notarius publicus requisitus fui, hoc instrumentum publicum mea manu scripsi, et subscripsi, et consueto sigillo munivi in fidem et testimonium.

BALTHASAR RAND.

and promised mutual fidelity in the name of God. The said Prince hath required of me, Notary underwritten, to draw him one or more collated copies of this contract, and hath also promised, on the word and faith of a prince, to me a public person, to observe it inviolably, always and without alteration, in presence of the Reverend and most learned masters Philip Melancthon, Martin Bucer, Denis Melander; and likewise in the presence of the illustrious and valiant Eberhard de Than, counsellor of his electoral Highness of Saxony, Herman de Malsberg, Herman de Hundelshausen, the Lord John Fegg of the Chancery, Rudolph Schenck; and also in the presence of the most honorable and most virtuous Lady Anne of the family of Miltitz, widow of the late John de Saal, and mother of the spouse, all in quality of requisite witnesses for the validity of the present act.

And I Balthasar Rand, of Fuld, Notary public imperial, who was present at the discourse, instruction, marriage, espousals, and union aforesaid, with the said witnesses, and have heard and seen all that passed, have written and subscribed the present contract, being requested so to do; and set to it to the usual seal, for a testimony of the truth thereof.

BALTHASAR RAND.

Notes

[1] Thuan. Lib. iv. ad an. 1557.

[2] Mel. Lib. iv. Ep. 214.

[3] See the end of this (6th) book.

[4] Inst. N. 1, 2. Ib. n. 3.

[5] Inst. N. 5.

[6] Ibid. N. 6.

[7] Ibid. N. 6. et seq. Ibid. N. 10. Ibid. N. 11, 12.

[8] Inst. N. 12.

[9] Ibid. N. 13.

[10] Ibid. N. 14.

[11] Ibid. N. 15. et seq.

[12] See the end of this (6th) Book.

[13] Consul. de Luther, N. 21, 22.

[14] Ibid. N. 20.

[15] Ibid. N. 21.

[16] Jam. iii. 10.

[17] Gen. ii. 24.

[18] Matt. xix. 4, 5, 6.

[19] Book of Conscien. Confid. S. N. 2.

[20] Consult. N. 4, 10, 21.

[21] Ibid. N. 23, 24.

[22] Ibid. N. 2.

[23] Consult. N 10, 18.

[24] Consult N. 21.

[25] Ibid.

[26] Inst. Copalat.—See the end of this (6th) Book.

[27] Lettres de Gastineau.—Varill. Hist. de l'Heres. liv. xii.

[28] Hortlederus de Caus. Bell. Germ. An. 1540.

[29] Jen. T. vii. fol. 425.

[30] Serm. de Matrim. t. v. fol. 123.

[31] Gas. Peuc. Nar. Hist. de Phil. Mel. soceri. sui. sent. de Cœn. Dom. Ambergæ, 1596, p. 24.

[32] Peuc. ibid. Sultzeri. id. Ep. ad Cal. inter. Calv. Ep. p. 52.

[33] Peuc. ibid.

[34] Hosp. part ii. p. 183. Calix. Judicium, N. 72. p. 121, 122.

[35] Hosp. ibid. f. 184.

[36] Ibid.

[37] Ibid. f. 183.

[38] Hosp. Ibid. p. 186, 187. Calix. Jud. N. 73. p. 123. et seq. Lut. parv. Cons.

[39] Conc. p. 734. Luth. t. ii. f. 325. Hosp. 193.

[40] Sleid. lib. xiv.

[41] Ibid. lib. iv. N. xxiii.

[42] Conf. Bucer, ibid. art. 22.

[43] Ibid. 23.

[44] De abomin. Mis. priv. seu Canonis, t. ii. pp. 393, 394.

[45] Ps. cxv.

[46] Blond. Præf. in lib. Albert de Euchar.

[47] Judic. Calix. N. 47, p. 70, N. 51, p. 78. S. lib. ii. N. 1.

[48] Luth. parv. Conf. 1544. Hosp. p. 13.

[49] Hosp. pp. 154, 179, 180.

[50] Hosp. pp. 154, 179, 180. Mel. Lib. ii. ep. 25, 40. Lib. iii. 188, 189, &c.

[51] Exod. xv. 23.

[52] Joan. ii.

[53] Mel. ep. Sup. cit. Hosp. Part. ii. p. 184, etc. Joan. Sturm. Antip. iv. Part 4.

[54] Hosp. p. 180.

[55] Jen. t. iv. pp. 585, 586, et ap. Cælest.

[56] Just. Apol. ii.

[57] S. u. 24. Parv. Conf.

[58] Ibid.

[59] Hosp. 14, 1545.

[60] Ad Art. Lov. Thesi. 16. t. ii. 501.

[61] Ep. ad Buc. p. 108.

[62] Wit. et Lips. Theol. Orthod. Conf. Heidelb. an. 1575. Hosp. an. 1561, p. 291.

[63] Art. vi. Conc. p. 330.

[64] S. lib. iv. Parva. Conf. S. n. 14.

[65] Ep. Calv. p. 590.

[66] Cont. Art. Lov. Thes. 28.

[67] Hosp. 199.

[68] Ep. Crucig. ad Vit. Theod. Hosp. 194, 199, &c.

[69] The author was not apprised that Bishop Burnet had falsified this record by changing *nihil minus* into *nihilominus*. This he was first charged with, and the fact proved against him, by Dr. Hicks. In the latter editions of his history the fault is corrected in the "Collection of Records," though his inferences from it still remain in the body of his work. T. xi. l. i. Au. 1549. p. 105.

[70] Collect. of Records, part ii. lib. i. n. 34.

Book VII

[An Account of the Variations and Reformation of England under Henry VIII, from the year 1529 to 1547; and under Edward VI, from 1547 to 1553; with the subsequent history of Cranmer, until his death, in 1556.]

A brief summary.-The English Reformation condemned even from Mr. Burnet's own history.—The divorce of Henry VIII.—His furious transports against the Holy See.—His Ecclesiastical Supremacy.—The grounds of, and consequences from, this doctrine.—This point excepted, the Catholic Faith remains whole and entire.—Henry's decisions in matters of Faith.—His Six Articles.—The History of Thomas Cranmer, Archbishop of Canterbury, author of the English Reformation.—His base compliances, corruption, and hypocrisy.—His shameful sentiments concerning the Hierarchy.—The conduct of the pretended Reformers, and in particular of Thomas Cromwell, the King's Vicar-General and Vicegerent in Spirituals.—That of Anne Boleyn, against whom the divine vengeance declares itself.—The prodigious blindness of Henry through the whole course of his life.—His death.—The minority of Edward VI, his son.—Henry's decrees reversed.—The King's Ecclesiastical Supremacy alone remains in force.—It is carried to such a pitch, that even Protestants are ashamed of it.—Cranmer's Reformation built on this principle.—The King looked upon as judge in matters of Faith.—Antiquity despised.—Continual variations.—The death of Edward VI.—Cranmer's treason, in conjunction with others, against Queen Mary, the late King's sister.—The Catholic Religion re-established.—Cranmer's ignominious end.—Some particular remarks on Mr. Burnet's History and the English Reformation.

1.—The death of Henry VIII, King of England.—On this occasion the account of the beginning and progress of the English Reformation is entered upon.—1547.

THE death of Luther was soon followed by another death, which caused great changes in religion. It was that of Henry VIII, who, after giving such great hopes in the first years of his reign, made so bad use of the rare qualifications of body and mind, with which the divine bounty had so liberally endowed him. Nobody is ignorant of the irregularities of this Prince, nor of the blindness he fell into by his unhappy amours, nor how much blood he shed after he had given himself up to them, nor of the dreadful consequences of his marriages, fatal, almost every one of them, to those he took to his bed. Nor is it less known on what occasion he, once a very Catholic Prince, made himself the author of a new sect, equally detested by Catholics, Lutherans, and Sacramentarians. The Holy See having condemned the divorce, which, after a marriage of five-and-twenty years, he had made from Catherine of Arragon, relict of his brother Arthur, and the marriage he had contracted with Anne Boleyn, he not only rose up against the authority of that See which condemned him, but also, by an attempt till then unheard of among Christians, declared himself head of the Church of England, as well in spirituals as temporals; and from thence begins the English Reformation, whereof so ingenious a history has been given us of late years, and, at the same time, so full of rancor against the Catholic Church.

2.—The foundation here built upon is Mr. Burnet's own history.—The Doctor's pompous words concerning the English Reformation.

The author of it, Dr. Gilbert Burnet, upbraids us in his very Preface, and through the entire progress of his History, with having derived great advantage from the conduct of Henry VIII, and that of England's first Reformers. Above all, he complains of Sanders, a Catholic historian, whom he accuses of having invented heinous facts to make the English Reformation odious. These complaints are then turned against us and the Catholic doctrine. "A religion," says he, "whose foundation was laid in falsehood, and superstructure raised on imposition, may be supported by the same means which gave it birth."[1] He even carries out this outrageous invective to a higher pitch: "Sanders's book might well serve the ends of that Church, which has, all along, raised its greatness by public cheats and forgeries." The colors he paints us in are not more black than the ornaments he decks his own Church with are pompous and glittering. "The Reformation," proceeds he, "was a work of light, and needs not the aid of darkness to give it a lustre. A full and distinct narrative of what was then done will be its apology as well as its history." These are fine words, nor could more magnificent ones be used, if, in the changes that happened in England, he had been to show us even the same sanctity which shone forth at the first birth of Christianity. Since he desires it, let us then consider this history, which, by its naked simplicity alone, justifies the Reformation. We stand not in need of a Sanders; Mr. Burnet will suffice to let us clearly see what was this work of light, and the bare series of facts related by this artful defender of the English Reformation is enough to give us a just idea of it. And if England there finds the sensible marks of that blindness, which God sometimes diffuses over kings and nations, let her not blame me, who do but follow a history which the whole body of the Parliament has honored with so authentic an approbation;[2] but let her adore the hidden judgments of God, who has permitted the errors of this learned and illustrious nation to rise to so visible a height, only to the end she might, by this means, the more easily know herself.

3.—The first fact avowed that the Reformation began by a man equally rejected by all parties.

The first important fact I observe in Mr. Burnet, is what he advances even in his preface, and continues to give proofs of through the whole body of his book: that "when Henry VIII began the Reformation, the King's design seemed to have been in the whole progress of these changes to terrify the Court of Rome, and force the Pope into a compliance with what he desired: for, in his heart, he continued addicted to the most extravagant opinions of that Church, such as Transubstantiation and the other corruptions in the Sacrifice of the Mass, so that he rather died in this communion than in that of the Protestants." Whatsoever Mr. Burnet may please to say of this matter, we shall not admit this Prince, whom he seems to offer us, a member of our communion; and since he casts him off from his own, the immediate result of this fact is, that the author of the English Reformation, and who, in reality, laid the true foundation of it, in the hatred he excited against the Pope and Church of Rome, is one equally rejected and excommunicated by all sides.

4.—What was the Faith of Henry VIII, author of the Reformation.

What in this place mostly deserves our observation is, that this Prince was not content with believing in his heart, and outwardly professing all those points of faith, which Mr. Burnet calls the greatest and most extravagant of our corruptions, but even by law, in his new capacity of supreme head, under Jesus Christ, of the Church of England, made them that church's articles of faith. He caused them to be approved by all the Bishops and all his Parliaments, that is, by all the tribunals in which the highest degree of ecclesiastical authority in the Church of England resides at this day, he made them be subscribed, and put in practice throughout all England, and in particular by the Cromwells, the Cranmers, and all the rest of Mr. Burnet's heroes, who, whether Lutherans or Zuinglians in their hearts, and zealous for setting up the new Gospel, went nevertheless, as usual, to Mass, as to the public worship which was paid to God, or said it themselves; in a word, practised all the rest of the doctrine and service received in the Church in spite of their religion and consciences.

5.—What were the instruments made use of by Henry VIII in the Reformation.— Cromwell, his Vicegerent in spirituals.

Thomas Cromwell was the person the King appointed his Vicar-General in spirituals, in 1533, immediately after his condemnation; and whom, in 1536, as Supreme Head of the Church, he made his Vicegerent, whereby he placed him at the head of all ecclesiastical affairs, and of the whole sacred order, though he were no more than a layman, and always remained such.[3] Till then that title had not been met with on the lists of the Crown-officers of England, nor among the employments recorded in the review of the empire,[4] nor in any Christian kingdom whatsoever; and it was Henry VIII that first showed

England, and the Christian World, a Lord Vicegerent and a King's Vicar-General in spirituals.

6.—*Thomas Cranmer is Mr. Burnet's hero.*

Cromwell's intimate friend and chief manager of the English Reformation was Thomas Cranmer, Archbishop of Canterbury. This is Mr. Burnet's great hero. He abandons Henry VIII, whose scandals and cruelties are too flagrant. But he was well aware, should he do the same by Cranmer, whom he looks upon to be the author of the Reformation, this would be giving us at once too bad an idea of this whole work. Therefore he enlarges much in praise of this prelate; and not content with admiring every where his moderation, his piety, and prudence, he stops not at making him as irreprehensible, or even more so, than St. Athanasius and St. Cyril; and of such extraordinary worth, that "we shall find as eminent virtues, and as few faults in him, as in any prelate that has been in the Christian Church for many ages."[5]

7.—*Mr. Burnet's heroes are not always, even in his judgment, the best of men.—What he relates of Montluc, Bishop of Valence.*

The truth is, we must not rely much on the praises Mr. Burnet gives the heroes of the Reformation: witness those he bestowed on Montluc, Bishop of Valence. "He was," says he, "one of the wisest minsters of his time, and always for moderate councils in matter of religion, which made him be sometimes suspected of heresy. And, indeed, the whole sequel of his life declared him to be one of the greatest men of that age: only being so long, and so firmly, united to the interest of Queen Catharine Medicis, takes off a great deal of the high character which the rest of his life has given him."[6] The crime certainly was not very great, since he owed all to this Princess, who besides was his Queen, the wife and mother of his Kings, and always in union with them; so that this Prelate, against whom this only exception could be made of being faithful to his benefactress, in Mr. Burnet's judgment, must have been the most irreproachable of all his contemporaries. But the eulogiums the Reformers bestow on the great men of their sect are not to be taken literally. The same Mr. Burnet, in the very book wherein he so highly extols Montluc, speaks thus of him—"This Bishop was eminent; but he had his faults." After what he has said of him, these faults, we ought to think, will be but trifling; but read to the end, and you will find they consisted in this, that "he had endeavored to corrupt the daughter of an Irish gentleman who had received him into his house; and had with him an English mistress whom he kept,"[7] who having drunk, without reflection, the precious balm which Solyman the Magnificent had made this Prelate a present of, "he fell into such a rage, that all the house was disturbed with it, whereby he discovered both his lewdness and passion at once." Here are the trifling faults of a Prelate, "the whole course of whose life declared him to be one of the greatest men of that age. The Reformation, either not over nice in virtue, or indulgent to her heroes, easily forgives them such abominations; and if Montluc, for having only a little spice of Reformation, was a man, notwithstanding such crimes, almost irreproachable, no wonder so great a reformed as Cranmer should have merited such high encomiums.

Thus warned against any imposition for the future from the great commendations, wherewith Mr. Burnet extols his Reformers and Cranmer most particularly; let us now form the history of this Prelate on the facts related by this historian, his perpetual admirer, and observe, at the same time, in what spirit the Reformation was conceived.

8.—*Cranmer, a Lutheran according to Mr. Burnet.—How he came into the King's favor and that of Anne Boleyn.*

Ever since the year 1529, Thomas Cranmer had put himself at the head of that party, which favored the Queen's divorce, and the marriage the King was resolved upon with Anne Boleyn. In 1530, he wrote a book against the validity of Catharine's marriage, and we may judge how successfully, by thus flattering the predominant passion of his Prince, he made his court. From that time, he began to be considered at Court as a kind of favorite, and looked on as the person likeliest to succeed in credit to Cardinal Woolsey. Cranmer was then devoted to Luther's doctrine, and as Mr. Burnet says, was looked on as the most learned of those who had embraced it.[8] Anne Boleyn, proceeds this author, had also received some impressions of this doctrine.[9] Afterwards he makes her appear wholly devoted to the sentiments of those whom he calls the Reformers. By this word we must always understand the hidden or avowed enemies of the Mass and Catholic doctrines. Crome, Shaxton, Latimer, and others, adds he, of that society, favored the King's cause.[10] Here we have the secret which linked Cranmer and his adherents with Henry's mistress: here lies the foundation of this new favorite's interest, and the beginnings of the English Reformation. The unhappy Prince, who knew nothing of these associations and designs, did himself insensibly combine with the enemies of that faith, which he till then had so well defended, and through their secret machinations, became unwittingly subservient to the designs of destroying it.

9.—*Cranmer, sent to Rome on account of the divorce, is there made the Pope's Penitentiary.—He marries, though a Priest, but in private.*

Cranmer was sent into Italy and Rome in behalf of the divorce, and there carried the dissimulation of his errors so far, that the Pope made him his Penitentiary; which shows he was a priest. He accepted of this employment, Lutheran as he was. From Rome he went into Germany, there to manage his good friends the Protestants; and then it was he married Ossiander's sister. Some say, he had debauched her, and was forced to marry her; but I shall not vouch for these scandalous facts till I find them well attested by those of the party or at least by unsuspected authors.[11] As for the marriage, the fact is certain. These men are accustomed, in spite of the canons, in spite of the profession of continency, to look on such marriages as good. But Henry was of another mind, and held married priests in abhorrence.[12] Cranmer had been already expelled from Jesus College, in Cambridge, for a former marriage. The second he contracted, whilst a priest, would have brought him into much more dreadful circumstances, since, by the canon law, he would have been excluded from this holy order by a second marriage, though contracted even before priesthood. The Reformers, in their hearts, made but a jest both of the sacred canons and their own vows; but for fear of Henry, it was necessary to keep this marriage private, and this great Reformer set out by deceiving his master in a concern of this importance.

10.—*Cranmer, nominated Archbishop of Canterbury, receives the Pope's Bulls, though a married man and a Lutheran.*

Whilst he was in Germany, in the year 1533, the Archbishopric of Canterbury became vacant by Warham's death. The King of England nominated Cranmer, and he accepted of it.[13] The Pope, who knew no error in him, but that of maintaining the nullity of Henry's marriage, (a thing at that time undecided), gave him his bulls; Cranmer received them, and dread not, by so doing, to contaminate himself by receiving, as the party used to speak, with the character of the beast.

11.—*Cranmer's consecration; profession of submission to the Pope; his hypocrisy.*

At his consecration, and before they proceeded to ordain him, he took the usual oath of fidelity to the Pope, introduced some ages before. This was not without scruple, as Mr. Burnet tells us; but Cranmer had ways and means of coming off, and salved all by protesting that he intended not to restrain himself by this oath from what he owed his conscience, his king, and his country: a protestation in itself quite needless; for who of us imagines he engages himself by this oath to any thing that is contrary to his conscience, or the service of his king and country? Far from thinking we prejudice any of these, it is even expressed in the oath, that we take it without prejudice to the rights of our order, *Salvo ordine meo*. The submission which is sworn to the Pope in spirituals,[14] is of a different order from what we naturally owe our Prince in temporals, and without protesting, we have always well understood, that one does not interfere with the other. But in a word, either this oath is a mere empty form, or it obliges to acknowledge the Pope's spiritual jurisdiction. The new Archbishop, therefore, acknowledged it in word, though he believed no such thing. Mr. Burnet[15] grants that this expedient did but little agree with Cranmer's sincerity; and in order to extenuate as far as he was able so criminal a dissimulation, adds a little after, "by which, if he did not wholly save his integrity, yet it was plain he intended no cheat." What is it, then, we call a cheat, or can there be a greater than to swear what you do not believe, and come prepared with shifts to elude your oath, by a protestation conceived in words so indeterminate? But Mr. Burnet thinks not fit to tell us that Cranmer, who was consecrated with all the ceremonies of the Pontifical, besides this oath he pretended to evade the force of, made other declarations against which he did not protest: viz. "to receive with submission the traditions of the

Fathers and the constitutions of the Holy See-Apostolic, to render obedience to St. Peter in the person of his vicar the Pope and his successors, according to canonical authority; to keep chastity," which in the intention of the Church, as expressly declared from the time one is admitted to subdeaconship, imported celibacy and continency. This is what Mr. Burnet makes no mention of. He does not tell us that Cranmer said Mass according to custom together with his consecrator. Cranmer ought also to have protested against this act, and against all the Masses he said when officiating in his Church; or, at least, during the whole reign of Henry VIII, that is for thirteen years successively. Mr. Burnet speaks not a word of all these fine actions of his hero. He tells us not, that when he made priests, as doubtless he did in the space of so many years as he was Archbishop, he made them according to the terms of the Pontifical wherein Henry changed nothing, no more than in the Mass. He, therefore, gave them power "of changing the bread and wine into the body and blood of Jesus Christ by their holy benediction, of offering the sacrifice, and saying Mass as well for the living as the dead."[16] It would have been much more important to protest against so many acts so contrary to Lutheranism, than against the oath of obedience to the Pope. But the thing was, Henry VIII, whom a protestation against the Pope's supremacy did not offend, would not have endured the rest. This was the cause of Cranmer's dissimulation. Here then we have him, all at once, a Lutheran, a married man, a concealer of his marriage, an Archbishop according to the Roman Pontifical, subject to the Pope, whose power he detested in his heart, saying Mass which he did not believe in, and giving power to say it; yet, nevertheless, if we believe Mr. Burnet, a second Athanasius, a second Cyril, one of the most perfect prelates the Church ever had. What a notion would he give us, not only of St. Athanasius and St. Cyril, but also of St. Augustin, St. Ambrose, St. Basil, and all the Saints in general, had they nothing in them more excellent, nor less defective, than a man who practises, for so long a time, what he believes the very height of sacrilege and abomination? Thus are men blind in the new Reformation; and thus the darkness which overcast the minds of the first Reformers, is diffused around their defenders to this very day.

12.—*Reflection on Cranmer's pretended moderation.*

Mr. Burnet pretends that his Archbishop did all he could to waive this eminent dignity, and admires his moderation. For my part, I am far from disputing with the greatest enemies of the Church, certain moral virtues, to be met with in heathens and philosophers; which, in heretics, were nothing else but a snare of Satan to entrap the weak, and a party of that hypocrisy which seduces them. But Mr. Burnet has too much wit not to see that Cranmer, who had on his side Anne Boleyn, with whom the King was so smitten; who did all which could be required to favor the amorous passion of that prince; and who, after declaring against Catharine's marriage, had made himself so necessary to the breaking of it, was very sensible Henry could never choose an Archbishop more favorable to his designs: so that nothing was more easy for him than to obtain the Archbishopric by refusing it, and thus add the reputation of moderation to the honor of so great a prelacy.

13.—*Cranmer proceeds to a sentence of Divorce.—He takes the title of Legate of the Apostolic See in giving the sentence.*

Accordingly, no sooner was Cranmer raised to this dignity, but he bestirred himself to make an interest in the parliament in favor of the divorce. Before this time, in the year 1532, the King had already privately married Anne Boleyn: she was with child, and the secret was ready to break out. The Archbishop, who was privy to it, signalized himself in this juncture, and evinced much vigor in flattering the King. By his archiepiscopal authority, he wrote him a very serious letter on his incestuous marriage with Catharine: "a marriage," said he, "the world had long been scandalized with;"[17] and declared to him that, for his part, he was determined to suffer no longer so great a scandal. Here is a man of wonderful resolution, a second John the Baptist. Thereupon he cites the King and Queen to appear before him: he proceeds: the Queen does not appear: the Archbishop declared her contumacious, and the marriage null from the beginning; nor did he forget, in his sentence, to take upon him, as was customary with the Archbishops of Canterbury,[18] the quality of Legate to the See Apostolic. Mr. Burnet insinuates,[19] this might be done in order to make the sentence firmer: that is to say, the Archbishop, who in his heart neither owned Pope nor Holy See, was willing, for the King's sake, to take that title which would best authorize his pleasures. Five days after, he confirmed the private marriage of Anne Boleyn, though contracted before that of Catharine was declared void, and the Archbishop hesitated not to ratify so irregular a proceeding.

14.—*The sentence of Clement VI, and Henry's rage against the Holy See.*

The definitive sentence of Clement VII against the King of England is known sufficiently. It followed soon after that which Cranmer had given in his behalf; Henry, entertaining still some hopes from the Court of Rome, had again submitted himself to the decision of the Holy See, even after the Archbishop's judgment. There is no need of relating to what excess of wrath the King was transported, and Mr. Burnet himself owns "he kept no measure in his resentments."[20] Accordingly, from that period he began to carry his title, of Supreme Head of the Church of England, to its utmost extent.

15.—*More and Fisher condemned to Death for refusing to own the King Head of the Church.—1534.*

Then it was the world lamented the death of two, the greatest men of England for piety and learning: of Thomas More, Lord High Chancellor; and Fisher, Bishop of Rochester.[21] Mr. Burnet himself grieves at the occurrence, and looks upon the "tragical end of these two great men to have left one of the greatest blots on this King's proceedings."[22]

These were the two most illustrious victims of the ecclesiastical supremacy. More, being very much urged to own it, made this fine answer: "That he should distrust his own understanding, were he alone against the whole Parliament: but, although the great council of England was against him, the whole Church, the great Council of Christendom, was on his side." Fisher's end was not less glorious, nor less Christian.

16.—*The memorable date of Henry's Cruelties and other excesses.*

Then began executions indifferently against Catholics as well as Protestants, and Henry became the most sanguinary of all princes. But remarkable is the date: "It does not appear," says Burnet, "that cruelty was natural to him. For, in twenty-five years' reign, none had suffered for any crime against the State"[23] but two men, whose punishment could not be imputed to him. "Yet, in the ten last years of his life," says the same author, "many instances of severity occurred."[24] Mr. Burnet will not have him imitated, nor condemned with too much severity; but none condemns him more sharply than Burnet himself, who thus speaks of this Prince: "The vastness and irregularity of his expense procured many heavy exactions, and twice extorted a public discharge of his debts, debased the coin, with other irregularities. His proud and impatient spirit occasioned many cruel proceedings; the taking so many lives only for denying his supremacy, particularly Fisher's and More's, the one being extremely old, and the other one of the glories of his nation, for probity and learning." The rest may be seen in his Preface; but I cannot omit the last touch: "that which was the first of all, and deserved most to be blamed, was the laying a precedent for the subversion of justice, and oppressing the clearest innocence, by attainting men without hearing them." All this notwithstanding, Mr. Burnet would have us believe, that although "upon slight grounds he was too ready to bring his subjects to the bar, yet they were indicted and judged always according to law,"[25]—as if the making unjust laws, such as condemning the accused without allowing them a hearing, and laying snares for the innocent in the formalities of justice, were not the height of cruelty and tyranny. But what can be more horrible than what is added by the same historian? "That this Prince, whether impatient of contradiction, or perhaps blown up, either with the vanity of this new title of Head of the Church, or with the praises which flattery bestowed on him; he thought all persons were bound to regulate their belief by his dictates."[26] These are, indeed, "such odious blemishes in the life of a Prince," as Mr. Burnet speaks, "that no honest man can excuse;" and we are obliged to this author for having saved us the trouble of looking out for proofs of all these excesses in histories that might be more suspected. But what cannot be dissembled is, that Henry, so averse before to these horrible disorders, did not fall into them, according to Mr. Burnet's own confession, till the ten last years of his life; that is, he fell into them immediately after his divorce, after his open rupture with the Church, after he had usurped, "by an example unprecedented" in all ages, the ecclesiastical supremacy: and forced he is to own, that one of the causes of his prodigious blindness was, "this glorious title of Head of the Church," which his people had bestowed on him. I now leave the Christian reader to judge, whether these be the characters of as Reformer; or rather, of a Prince, whose excesses the divine justice revenges by other excesses; whom it delivers over to the desires of his own heart, and abandons visibly to a reprobate sense.

17.—*Cromwell made Vicegerent.*—*Every thing concurs to excite the King against the Faith of the Church.*—*1535.*

The death of Fisher and More, and so many other bloody executions, cast terror into all minds; every body swore to Henry's Supremacy, and none durst stand up against it. This Supremacy was established by divers Acts of Parliament, and "the first act of the king's supremacy was the nominating Cromwell vicar-general in spirituals, and visitor of all the monasteries and other privileged places throughout England."[27] This was properly declaring himself Pope; and what is more remarkable, this was placing the whole ecclesiastical power in the hands of a Zuinglian, for I am persuaded Cromwell was one, or, if Mr. Burnet likes better, at least a Lutheran. It has appeared, that Cranmer, Cromwell's intimate friend, was of the same party, and that both of them acted unanimously, in order to excite the incensed King against the ancient faith.[28] The new Queen favored them with all her power, and took Shaxton and Latimer, hidden Protestants, to be her chaplains, and promoted them to the bishoprics of Salisbury and Worcester. But although every thing went contrary to the old religion, and the chief ecclesiastic and secular powers conspired its utter subversion, it is not always in the hands of men to carry on their evil purposes as far as they desire. Henry was provoked only against the Pope and Holy See. Accordingly, he attacked only this authority; and God willed it so, that the Reformation, from her infancy, should bear marked on her forehead the impression of this Prince's hatred and revenge. Whatever, therefore, might be the vicar-general's aversion to the Mass, power was not then given him, like another Antiochus, against the perpetual sacrifice;[29] one of his visitorial injunctions was, that every priest should say Mass daily, and the religious observe their rule carefully, and particularly their three vows.[30]

18.—*Cranmer's Metropolitical Visitation by the King's authority.*

Cranmer also made his metropolitical visitation, but it was after he had obtained the King's license for it: they began to perform all acts of ecclesiastical jurisdiction in virtue of the royal authority. The whole drift of this visitation, as of all the actions of those days, was firmly to establish the King's ecclesiastical supremacy.[31] At that time, the complying archbishop had nothing so much at heart as this, and the first act of jurisdiction, which the bishop of the first See in England did, was to enslave the Church, and subject to the earthly Kings that power which she had received from heaven.

19.—*The Plundering of Monasteries.*

The visitations were followed by the suppression of Monasteries, whose revenues the King appropriated to himself. Protestant and Catholic countries indifferently cried out shame against the sacrilegious rapine of goods consecrated to God; but to the character of revenge, which the English Reformation bore from the beginning, was to be joined that also of an infamous avarice; and this was one of the first fruits of Henry's supremacy, who made himself head of the Church, to have a title to plunder it.

20.—*The death of Queen Catharine.—A comparison betwixt this Princess and Anne Boleyn.—1536.*

Soon after this, died Queen Catharine: "She was a devout and pious Princess," says Mr. Burnet, "and led a severe and mortified life. In her greatness, she wrought much with her own hands, and kept her women well employed about her;"[32] and to join common with great virtues, the same historian adds that, by the writers of those times, "she is represented as a most wonderful good woman."[33] These characters are widely different from those of her rival Anne Boleyn. Allowing she might be vindicated from those infamous actions, which her favorites, at their death, charged her with, Mr. Burnet[34] does not deny that her gaiety was immodest, her liberties indiscreet, her behaviour irregular and licentious. A virtuous woman, not to say a queen, never bears with the failure of due respect, so far as to suffer such declarations as men of all degrees, even the lowest, made to this Princess. Why do I say suffer?—be pleased with them,—and not only take part therein, but also draw them on herself, and not blush to say to one of her gallants, "that he looked for dead men's shoes, and if aught came to the King but good, he would look to have her."[35] All these things are owned by Anne, and far from showing a greater discountenance to those bold lovers, it is certain, without entering farther into the matter, she did but treat them the better for it. In the midst of this strange conduct, "we are assured that she grew more full of good works, and almsdeeds,"[36] and with the exception of her advancing the pretended Reformation, which nobody disputes, this is all that is told us of her virtues.

21.—*Sequel of the comparison, and visible mark of God's Judgment.—Cranmer annuls the King's Marriage with Anne.*

But if we carry our reflections still higher, we cannot but acknowledge the hand of God on this Princess. She enjoyed but three years that glory to which so many troubles had elevated her: a new fit of love raised her up, and a new amour pulled her down; and Henry, who had sacrificed Catharine to her, soon sacrificed Anne to the youth and charms of Jane Seymour. But Catharine, when she lost the King's affections, preserved, at least, his esteem to the very end; whereas, he had Anne executed infamously on a scaffold.[37] This death happened a few months after that of Catharine. But Catharine preserved to the very last the character of gravity and constancy, which she had kept up during the entire course of her life. As for Anne, at the moment she was taken, whilst she prayed to God in tears, she was observed to break out into a fit of laughing, like a distracted person:[38] the words she vented in passion against her lovers, who had betrayed her, showed the disorder she was in, and the troubled state of her conscience. But here is a visible mark of the hand of God. The King, always hurried on by his new amours, caused his marriage to Anne to be annulled in favor of Jane Seymour, as he had annulled Catharine's in favor of Anne. Elizabeth, Anne's daughter, was declared illegitimate, as Mary, Catharine's daughter, had been before. By a just retaliation, Anne fell into the same pit she had dug for her innocent rival. But Catharine, even to death, maintained the dignity of a Queen, the truth of her marriage, and the honor of Mary's birth. Anne on the contrary, through a shameful compliance, owned what was false,—that she had married Henry whilst Lord Piercy was living, with whom she had before contracted; and by confessing, contrary to her conscience, the nullity of her marriage with the King, involved her daughter Elizabeth in her own shame. To the end that God's justice might appear more manifest in this memorable event, Cranmer, that same Cranmer who had annulled Catharine's marriage,[39] annulled, likewise, that of Anne, to whom, of all persons living, he was most obliged. God struck with blindness all who had contributed to the breach of so solemn a marriage as was that of Catharine: Henry, Anne, the archbishop himself, not one escaped. Cranmer's base pusillanimity, and his extreme ingratitude to Anne, excited the abhorrence of all good men; and his shameful compliance, in breaking all marriages just as it pleased Henry, took from his first sentence all the appearance of authority which the name of an Archbishop could have given to it.

22.—Cranmer's base compliance ill excused by Mr. Burnet.

Mr. Burnet[40] sees with great concern so odious a blot in the life of his great Reformer, and to excuse him says, that Anne declared, in his presence, her marriage with Lord Piercy; by which it was evident, that which she had made with the King was not valid; upon which confession he could not but separate her from this Prince, and give sentence for the nullity of the marriage. But here is a too manifest imposition; it was notorious in England that Anne's engagement with Piercy, far from being a concluded marriage, was not even a promise of marriage to be concluded, but a bare proposal of a marriage desired by this lord: which, so far from invalidating a subsequent marriage, would not even have been an impediment to the contracting of it. Mr. Burnet agrees herein and lays down all these facts as certain.[41] Cranmer, who knew the whole secret of what had passed between the King and Anne, could not be ignorant of them; and Piercy, the Queen's pretended husband, had "taken his oath before the two Archbishops, that there was no contract, nor promise of marriage even between them, and received the Sacrament upon it before the principal of the King's privy-council; wishing it might be to his damnation, if there were any such thing."[42] So solemn an oath received by Cranmer discovered to him plainly that Anne's confession was not free. When she made it, she was adjudged to die, and, as Mr. Burnet says, "even thunderstruck with the terrible sentence of being burnt."[43] This the laws had condemned her to; and the mitigating so cruel a part of her judgment depended on the King alone. Cranmer might easily judge that, in such a condition, she might be wrought upon to confess what they pleased, "either by some hopes of life, or by mitigating her sentence."[44] Then was the time for an Archbishop to lend his helping hand to an oppressed person, whom trouble, or hopes of softening her punishment, makes to speak against her conscience. If Anne, his benefactress, did not move him, he ought, at least, to have compassionated the innocence of Elizabeth just going to be declared born in adultery, and, as such, incapable of inheriting the crown, and this on no other grounds but a declaration extorted from the Queen her mother. Nor does God bestow so great an authority on bishops, but with the obligation of lending the assistance of their eloquence to the infirm, and their strength to the oppressed. But virtues, to which Cranmer was a stranger, were not to be expected from him: not even the courage to represent to the King, the manifest contrariety of the two sentences, which he caused to be pronounced against Anne; one of which condemned her to death for defiling the King's bed by her adulteries; the other, by reason of a pre-contract, declared she never had been married to the King.[45] Cranmer dissembled so flagrant an iniquity; and all he did in behalf of the unhappy Princess was to write a letter to the King, wherein he wishes she may declare herself innocent;[46] which he concludes with a postscript, protesting he is exceedingly sorry that such faults can be proved, as he heard by relation:[47] so much did he fear giving Henry the least suspicion that he disapproved of any thing he did.

23.—*The Execution of Anne Boleyn.*

It had been thought his credit was shaken by Anne's downfall. And, indeed, immediately upon it, he was forbidden to approach the King; but he soon found means of ingratiating himself at the expense of his benefactress, and by cancelling her marriage.[48] The unfortunate Princess was in hopes of moving the King, by owning all he desired. This confession only saved her from the stake, and Henry condemned her to the block. She comforted herself on the day of her death, because she had heard say, the executioner was very dexterous; and besides, said she, I have a slender neck. At the same time, adds the witness of her death, she put her hands about it, laughing heartily; either from ostentation of an uncommon intrepidity, or because her head was turned at death's approach; and it seems to have been God's judgment on that unhappy Princess, that her end, dismal as it was, should yet have something in it no less ridiculous than tragical.

24.—*Henry's decisions of Faith.—He confirms that of the Church concerning the Sacrament of Penance.*

It is time to relate the definitions of faith which Henry made in quality of Supreme Head of the Church of England. In these articles, drawn up by the king himself, we have a confirmation of the Catholic doctrine. Here we find "the absolution of the priest taught, as instituted by Jesus Christ, and to be looked upon as valid as if given by God himself, with the necessity of confession to a priest, if it may be had."[49] On this foundation are built the three acts of penance divinely instituted, contrition and confession in express terms, and satisfaction under the name of worthy fruits of penance, which we must bring forth, although it be true that God pardons sins only for the satisfaction of Jesus Christ, and not on account of our merits. Here is the whole substance of the Catholic doctrine. Nor must it be imagined by Protestants, that what is said of satisfaction is peculiar to themselves, since the Council of Trent has ever believed that the forgiveness of sins is a pure grace, granted on account of the sole merits of Jesus Christ.

25.—Concerning the Eucharist.

In the Sacrament of the Altar is owned, "The very same body of Christ, that was born of the Virgin Mary, truly and substantially given under the forms of bread and wine;" or, as the English original speaks, "Under the form and figures of bread:" which marks most distinctly the Real presence of the body, and gives to understand, according to the usual expression, that nothing but the species of bread remains.

26.—Concerning Images and Saints.

Images were retained, with full liberty of incensing them, kneeling before them, bringing offerings, and showing respect to them, in consideration that these homages were a relative honor, directed to God, and not to the Image.[50] This was not only approving the honor of Images in general, but those things, in particular, wherein it is carried to its greatest height.

The people were taught that it was good to pray to the saints, that they would pray for, and with us, yet so as not to think to obtain these things at their hands which were only to be obtained of God.[51]

When Mr. Burnet looks upon this as a kind of "Reformation, that the immediate worship of Images was removed, and the direct invocation of saints changed into a simple prayer of praying for the faithful,"[52] He does but trifle; since there is not a Catholic but will own to him that he hopes for nothing from the saints but their prayers, nor renders any honor to images but what is here expressed with relation to God.

27.—Of Ceremonies.—Of the Cross.

Touching ceremonies, these are expressly approved of, viz. "holy water, blessed bread, hallowing the font, the exorcisms in baptism, giving ashes on Ash-Wednesday, bearing palms on Palm-Sunday; creeping to the cross on Good-Friday, and kissing it in memory of Christ's death:"[53] all these ceremonies were looked upon as a kind of mysterious language, which brought to mind God's benefits, and excited the soul to raise itself up to heaven, which, in reality, is the very notion all Catholics have of them.

28.—*On Purgatory and Masses for the dead.*

The custom of praying for the dead is warranted as having a certain foundation in the book of Maccabees, and a continuation in the Church from the beginning: all is approved of, and it is held "consistent with the due order of charity to pray for them, and to make others pray for them, in Masses and Exequies, and to give alms to them for that end:"[54] whereby that was acknowledged in the Mass, which was the great aversion of the new Reformation, viz. that virtue by which, independently of communion, it profited those for whom it was said, inasmuch as those souls, doubtless, did not communicate.

29.—*The King decides concerning Faith, by his own authority.*

With relation to each of these articles the King said, that he enjoined all bishops to announce them to the people, "By him committed to their spiritual charge;" a language till then quite unheard of in the Church. The truth is, when he decided these points of Faith, he had before heard the bishops, as judges hear lawyers; but it was he that prescribed and decided. All the bishops signed, after Cromwell, the Vicar-general, and Cranmer, Archbishop of Canterbury.

30.—*Cranmer and the rest subscribed Henry's articles*
against their consciences.—Mr. Burnet strives in vain to excuse them.

Mr. Burnet is ashamed to see his reformers approve the chief articles of the Catholic doctrine, and even the Mass itself, which alone contained them all. But he excuses them, saying, "That some of the bishops and divines were not then so fully convinced about some matters, which afterwards they arrived to a clearer understanding of, and so it was their ignorance and not their cowardice or policy, that made them compliant in some things."[55] But is not this bantering the world in too gross a manner, to make the Reformers ignorant of what was most essential in the Reformation?[56] If Cranmer and his adherents sincerely approved all these articles, even the Mass, wherein could they be called Lutherans? and if, from that time, they rejected in their hearts all these pretended abuses, as doubtless they did, what was their signing them else but a shameful prostitution of their consciences? Nevertheless, Mr. Burnet will have it, at all events, that the Reformation took a great step at that very time, because in the first of Henry's articles the "Scriptures and the ancient Creeds were made the standards of the people's faith,"[57] with a prohibition of saying any thing that was not conformable to them; a thing which nobody denied, and which, consequently, stood in no need of being reformed.

Such are the articles of faith which were established by Henry in 1356. But although he had omitted some, and in particular no mention was there made of four Sacraments, Confirmation, Extreme Unction, Order, and Matrimony, it is certain, however, that he altered nothing therein no more than in the other points of our faith; but his design was to express particularly, in those articles, what was most controverted at that time, to the end that he might leave no doubt of his perseverance in the ancient faith.

31.—To draw in the Gentry, Church lands are sold at low rates.

At the same time, by Cromwell's advice, and in order to draw in the gentry to his sentiments, he sold them in their several counties the lands of those monasteries that had been suppressed, and at very low prices.[58] Such was the cunning of the Reformers, and such the ties that linked men to the Reformation.

32.—Cromwell and Cranmer confirm anew the Faith of the Church,
which they detested in their hearts.

The Vicegerent published also a new ecclesiastical regulation, which had the doctrine of the above articles, so conformable to Catholic doctrine, for its foundation. Mr. Burnet finds a great likelihood that these injunctions were opened by Cranmer,[59] and gives us a new instance, that, in point of religion, this Archbishop was capable of the most criminal dissimulations.

33.—Henry's Six Articles.—1439.

Henry explained himself more distinctly as to the ancient faith, in the famous declaration of those six articles which he published in 1539. In the first, he established Transubstantiation; in the second, Communion in one kind; in the third, the Celibacy of Priests, with the penalty of death for those who should trespass against it; in the fourth, the obligation of keeping Vows; in the fifth, the use of private Masses; in the sixth, the necessity of auricular Confession.[60] These articles were published by authority of the King and parliament; and it was enacted that those who obstinately opposed them should suffer death, and the rest be prisoners during the King's pleasure.

34.—The King's marriage with Anne of Cleves, Cromwell's design, who pro-
posed it.—The King's new amours.—Cromwell condemned to death.—1540.

Whilst Henry declared himself in so terrible a manner against the pretended Reformation, Cromwell, the Vicegerent, and the Archbishop, saw no other way of advancing it, than by giving the King a wife, who might protect them and their designs. The Queen, Jane Seymour, died in the year 1537, in childbed, of Edward. If she experienced not Henry's fickleness, Mr. Burnet is of opinion, it was owing, in all likelihood, to the shortness of her life. Cromwell, who remembered how much power Henry's wives had over him as long as they continued in his affection, believed that Anne of Cleves'[61] beauty would be a great prop to his measures, and prevailed with the King to marry her; but unluckily this Prince fell in love with Catharine Howard,[62] and scarce had he accomplished his marriage with Anne, but he bent all his thoughts to break it off. The Vicegerent underwent the punishment of having advised him to it, and found his ruin where he thought to meet with his support. It was perceived that he gave private encouragement to the new preachers, enemies of the Six Articles and Real Presence,[63] which the King defended vehemently. Some words spoken by him on this occasion against the King, were brought to his ears.[64] Whereupon the Parliament, by the King's orders, condemned him for a heretic and traitor to his country.[65] It was observed, he was condemned without being heard, and so bore the punishment of that detestable advice he had been the first author of, to attaint people without hearing them. And after this, will any one say that the arm of God was not visible on these miserable Reformers, the most wicked, as we see, no less than the greatest hypocrites of all mankind?

35.—Cromwell's hypocrisy—Mr. Burnet's vain artifices.

Cromwell, above all the rest, prostituted his conscience to flattery; he, in his quality of Vicegerent, authorizing in public all Henry's articles of faith, which he strove secretly to destroy. Mr. Burnet's conjectures that if he was refused a hearing, it was because "It was very probable that in all he had done that way," viz. for the pretended Reformation, "he had the King's warrant for it, and acted only by his order, whose proceedings towards a Reformation are well known."[66] But this time the artifice is too gross, and to be deluded by it a man must wilfully blind himself. Will Mr. Burnet have the face to say, that the proceedings towards a Reformation, which he attributes to Henry, were in prejudice to his Six Articles, or the Real Presence, or the Mass? This would be giving himself the lie, since he owns throughout his whole work, that this Prince was always very zealous for, or, to use his own words, addicted to, all these articles. Nevertheless he would here have us believe, that Cromwell had secret orders to undermine them, when at the same time he is put to death for having favored those who impugned them.

36.—Cranmer's prostitution of conscience—he annuls the King's marriage with Anne of Cleves—the magnificent terms of this unjust sentence—the King marries Catharine Howard, who is favorable to the Reformation, and soon beheaded for her infamous behaviour—the judgment of the Convocation.

But let us leave Mr. Burnet's conjectures, and his vain shifts to color the Reformation, and confine ourselves to facts which truth will not suffer him to deny. After Cromwell's attainder, it was still requisite, for the King's satisfaction, to rid him of his odious wife, by making void the marriage with Anne of Cleves. The pretext was very gross. The betrothing of this Princess to the Marquis of Lorrain whilst both parties were minors, and which they never ratified when of age, was alleged as the cause of nullity. It was plain nothing could be more weak in order to dissolve a perfectly complete marriage. But, though reasons were wanting, the King had a Cranmer ready for all jobs. By means of this Archbishop this marriage was cancelled similarly to the two others. "The sentence was pronounced on the 9th of July, 1540, and the whole convocation, without one dissenting vote, judged the marriage null. The sentence was signed by all the ecclesiastics of both chambers, and sealed with the seals of both Archbishops." Mr. Burnet is ashamed, and owns[67] "this was the greatest piece of compliance that ever the king had from his clergy; for they all knew there was nothing of weight in that pre-contract," which was made the foundation of the divorce.[68] Therefore they acted openly against their consciences; but lest we should, at another time, be imposed upon by the specious terms of the new Reformation, it is proper to take notice that they pass this sentence, as representing the great Council, after having said that the King required nothing of them but what was true, was just, was honorable, and holy: in this manner spoke those corrupted Bishops.[69] Cranmer, who presided over this assembly, and carried the result of it to the Parliament, was the greatest coward of them all; and Mr. Burnet, after having strained hard to palliate the matter, is forced to own that, overcome with fear, (for he knew it was contrived to send him quickly after Cromwell,) he consented with the rest.[70] Such was the courage of the second Athanasius, the virtue of this second Cyril. Upon this unjust sentence the King married Catharine Howard, no less zealous for the new Reformation than Anne Boleyn. But strange was the destiny that attended these female Reformers. Her scandalous life soon brought her to the scaffold, nor was Henry's house ever clear from the stains of blood and infamy.

37.—A new declaration of Faith conformable to the Church's doctrine.

The prelates made a new confession of faith, which this Prince confirmed by his authority; wherein the belief of the seven sacraments was declared in express terms, that of penance, in the absolution given by the priest; the necessity of confession, transubstantiation, concomitancy. "So that," says Mr. Burnet, "communion in both kinds was not necessary; the veneration of images and praying to saints, in the same sense we have seen in the King's first declaration, which is the sense of the Church; the necessity and merit of good works in order to obtain life everlasting; prayers for the dead; and, in short, all the rest of the Catholic doctrine, except the article of Supremacy, whereof we shall speak apart."[71]

38.—Cranmer's hypocrisy, who signs all of them.

Cranmer, with the rest, subscribed to every one; for, although Mr. Burnet asserts that some articles passed which were contrary to his sentiments, yet he yielded to the plurality, and we observe no opposition on his part to the common judgment. The same exposition had been published by the King's authority ever since the year 1538, signed by nineteen Bishops, eight Archdeacons, and seventeen Doctors, without any opposition. Such, at that time, was the faith of the Church of England and of Henry, whom she had owned for her head. The Archbishop approved of all against his conscience. His master's will was his sovereign rule; and, instead of the Holy See with the Catholic Church, the King alone was to him infallible.

39.—Nothing considerable was changed in the Missals and the other books of the Church.—Continuation of Cranmer's hypocrisy.

Meanwhile, he continued saying Mass, which he rejected in his heart, although nothing was changed in the Mass-books. Mr. Burnet agrees, "The alterations they made were inconsiderable, and so slight, that there was no need of reprinting either the Missals, Breviaries, or other Offices: for," proceeds this historian,"a few erasures of these Collects, in which the Pope was prayed for, of Thomas Becket's Office (St. Thomas of Canterbury,) and the Offices of other Saints, whose days were, by the King's injunctions, no more to be observed, with some other deletions, made that the old books did still serve."[72] After all, then, the same worship was still practised, Cranmer complied with it; and if you would know all that troubled him, it was, as we learn from Mr. Burnet, because, excepting Fox, Bishop of Hereford,[73] as great a dissembler as himself, the other Bishops that adhered to him[74] were rather clogs than helps to him, because they would not be managed and governed by politic and prudent measures, but were flying at many things that were not yet abolished. Cranmer, who betrayed his conscience, and attacked in secret what he approved and practised in public, was more cunning, since he knew how to introduce his skill, in managing his politic measures, into the very heart and vitals of religion.

40.—*Cranmer's behaviour in relation to the Six Articles.*

One may wonder, perchance, how a man of this temper ventured to speak against the Six Articles; for this is the only place where Mr. Burnet makes him courageous; but he himself discovers the cause to us. It was because he had a *particular interest* in the article which condemned married priests to death, for he was then married himself.[75] It had been too much to suffer his own condemnation to pass in Parliament for a standing law, and his fear even made him then show some kind of courage: accordingly, though he spoke but faintly against the other articles, yet he delivered himself fully against this. But, after all, it does not appear that he did any more on this occasion than, after a vain struggle to dissuade the passage of the law, to fall in at last, as his custom was, with the general opinion.

41.—*Mr. Burnet's account of Cranmer's resistance.*

But here is the greatest act of his resolution. Mr. Burnet would have us believe, upon the credit of an author of Cromwell's life, that the King, being concerned for Cranmer on account of the act on behalf of the Six Articles, was desirous of knowing why he opposed them, and ordered him to put all his arguments in writing, which he did.[76] The paper, written out fair by his secretary, fell into the hands of one of Cranmer's enemies. It was immediately carried to Cromwell, then living, with the design of having the author taken up; but Cromwell stifled the thing, and so Cranmer escaped this hazard.[77]

This account naturally leads us to believe that the King knew nothing at all of Cranmer's writing against the Six Articles; and that, had he known it, this prelate would have been utterly ruined; and, lastly, that he escaped purely by his cunning and perpetual dissimulation: however, if Mr. Burnet had rather have it so, I am willing to believe the King found so great a propensity in Cranmer to approve, in public, all his master could desire, that this prince had no reason to be under any concern what a person of such compliance might think in private, nor could he find it in his heart to part with so commodious a counsellor.

42.—Cranmer's shameful sentiments on the Ecclesiastical authority, which he sacrifices to the Crown.

It was not only with regard to his new mistresses that the King experienced him to be so great a flatterer: Cranmer had forged for him, in his own brain, that new idea of supremacy annexed to the Crown: and what he says concerning it, in a paper produced by Mr. Burnet among his Records, is unexampled.[78] He teaches then, "That all Christian Princes have committed unto them immediately of God the whole cure of all their subjects, as well concerning the administration of God's word, for the cure of souls, as concerning the ministration of things political and civil governance; and, in both these ministrations, they must have sundry ministers under them to supply that which is appointed to their several offices; as for example, the Lord Chancellor, Lord Treasurer, Lord Great Master, and the Sheriffs for Civil Ministers; and the Bishops, Parsons, Vicars, and such other Priests *as be appointed by his Highness* in the ministration of the word; as for example, the Bishop of Winchester, the Parson of Winwick, &c. All the said officers and ministers, as well of that sort as the other, must be appointed, assigned, and elected and in every place, by the laws and orders of Kings and Princes, with divers solemnities, *which be not of necessity*, but only for good order and seemly fashion: for is such offices and ministrations were committed without such solemnity, they were, nevertheless, truly committed; and there is no more promise of God, that grace is given in the committing of the ecclesiastical office, than it is in the committing of the civil office."

43.—Cranmer's Answer to an Objection.—Shameful Doctrine concerning the authority of the Church during persecutions.

After thus making all ecclesiastical ministry to rest on a simple delegation of princes, without so much as ordination or ecclesiastical consecration being necessary on the occasion, he obviates an objection which immediately occurs; to wit, how pastors exercised their authority under princes that were not Christians; and answers conformably to his principles, that there was no remedy then for the correction of vice, or appointing of ministers in the Church of God; but the people accepted of such as were presented to them by the apostles, or others whom they looked upon as filled with the spirit of God, and this of their own voluntary will; and afterwards gave ear to them, as a good people ready to obey the advice of good counsellors. This is what Cranmer spoke in an assembly of bishops; and this was the notion he had of that divine power which Jesus Christ gave to his ministers.

44.—Cranmer always persisted in these sentiments.

I am under no necessity of rejecting this prodigy of doctrine so strongly refuted by Calvin and all other Protestants, since Mr. Burnet himself blushes for Cranmer, and is willing to take for a retractation of this opinion, what he elsewhere signed concerning the divine institution of bishops. But, besides what has already appeared, that his subscriptions are not always a proof of his real sentiments, I must tell Mr. Burnet, that he conceals from us, with too much artifice, Cranmer's true notions. It made not against him, though the institution of bishops and priests was divine, and he acknowledges this truth in that very piece of which we have just produced the extract. For at the close of this ninth question, it is expressly mentioned, that "all of them were agreed," and consequently Cranmer, "that the apostles had received from God the power of creating bishops or pastors."[79] Neither could it be denied, without too manifestly contradicting the Gospel. But what Cranmer and his adherents pretended was, that Jesus Christ had instituted pastors to exercise-their power dependantly of the prince in every function; which certainly is the most monstrous and the most scandalous flattery that ever entered into the heart of man.

45.—*The dogma which makes all ecclesiastical power flow from the Crown, reduced to practice.*

Accordingly, it thence came to pass, that Henry VIII gave the bishops power to visit their diocese with this preface;—"That all jurisdiction, as well ecclesiastical as secular, proceeded from the regal power, as from the first foundation of all magistracy in all kingdoms; that those who, till then, had exercised this power *precariously*, were to acknowledge it as coming from the liberality of the prince, *and give it up to him when he should think fit*; and upon these grounds he gives power to such a bishop, *as to the King's vicar*, to visit his diocese by the regal authority; and to promote whom he shall judge proper to holy orders, and even priesthood;" and, in short, to exercise all the episcopal functions, "with power to subdelegate," if he thought it necessary.[80]

46.—*Cranmer acts conformably to this dogma,—the only one wherein the Reformation has not varied.*

Let us say nothing against a doctrine which destroys itself by its own enormity, and only take notice of that horrid proposition which makes the power of bishops so to flow from that of the King, that it is even revocable at his will. Cranmer was so persuaded of this royal power, that he was not ashamed, himself archbishop of Canterbury, and primate of the whole Church of England, to take out a new commission of the same from under Edward VI, though but a child, when he reformed the Church according to his own model; and of all the articles published by Henry, this was the only one he retained.[81]

47.—*Queen Elizabeth's scruple concerning the power given her in the Church.*

This power was carried to such a pitch in the English Reformation, that Elizabeth had some scruples about it; and the horror men had of seeing a woman the Church's supreme head, and the fountain of all pastoral power, whereof, by her sex, she was incapable, opened their eyes at length to see, in some measure, the excesses to which they had been carried.[82] But we shall see, without diminishing the force, or removing the grounds of it, they did no more than just palliate the matter; nor can Mr. Burnet, at this day, but lament to see excommunication, belonging only to the spiritual cognisance, and which ought to have been reserved for the bishop with the assistance of the clergy, by a fatal neglect given over to secular tribunals; that is, not only to Kings, but likewise to their officers:—"an error," proceeds this author, "grown since into so formed a strength, that it is easier to see what is amiss, than to know how to rectify it."

48.—*A manifest contradiction in the English doctrine.*

And, certainly, I do not conceive any thing can be imagined more contradictory, than to deny their Kings, on one side, the administration of the word and sacraments; and grant them, on the other hand, excommunication, which, in reality, is nothing else but God's word armed with the censure which comes from Heaven, and one of the most essential parts of the administration of the sacraments: since, undoubtedly, the right of depriving the faithful of them can appertain to none else but those who are appointed by God to give them to the people. But the Church of England went much further, inasmuch as she has attributed to her Kings and to the secular authority, the right of making rituals and liturgies, and even of giving final judgment without further appeal, in points of faith; that is, of that which is most essential in the administration of the sacraments; and the most inseparably annexed to the preaching of God's word. And as well under Henry VIII as in the succeeding reigns, we find no ritual, no confession of faith, no liturgy, which derives not its ultimate sanction and force from the authority of the King and parliament, as the sequel will make plain. They went even to that excess, that whereas the orthodox emperors, if formerly they made any constitutions concerning faith, either they made them in order to put in execution Church decrees, or at least waited for the confirmation of their ordinances. In England they taught, on the contrary, "that the decrees of councils, in points of faith, were not laws, nor of any force, till they were ratified by princes;"[83] and this was the fine idea which Cranmer gave of Church decisions in a discourse of his reported by Mr. Burnet.

49.—*Cranmer's flattery, and Henry's disorders, the cause of the English Reformation.*

This Reformation, therefore, took its rise from Henry's vices, and the flatteries of this archbishop. Mr. Burnet takes great pains to heap up examples of very vicious princes, whom God has made subservient to great ends.[84] Who questions it? But without examining the histories he quotes, where he blends truth with falsehood, and what is certain with what is doubtful; can he show one only example, where God, intending to reveal to men some important, and, during so many ages, unknown truth—not to say utterly unheard of—ever did choose so scandalous a King as Henry VIII, and so base, so corrupt a bishop as Cranmer? If the schism of England, in the English Reformation, be a divine work, nothing in it is more divine than the King's ecclesiastical supremacy, since, by that, not only did commence the breach with Rome, the necessary foundation, according to Protestants, of every good reformation, but that also is the only point wherein they have never varied since the schism. God made choice of Henry VIII to introduce this new article of faith among Christians, and, withal, made choice of this very prince to be a remarkable instance of his most profound and most terrible judgments; not of that sort by which he subverts monarchies, and gives to impious Kings a manifestly disastrous end; but of that other, whereby, delivering them over to their flatteries and passions, he suffers them to run headlong into the utmost excess of wilful blindness. Meantime, while he thinks fit, he witholds them on this brink in order to make manifest in them those mysteries of his counsels he is willing men should know. Henry VIII attempts nothing against the other Catholic verities. All his attacks are levelled only at St. Peter's chair; by that, it became apparent to the whole universe, that this prince's design was only to revenge himself on that pontifical power which had condemned him, and that his hatred was his sole rule of faith.

50.—*It concerns not Faith to examine the conduct of Clement VII, and his methods of proceeding.*

After that, I am under no necessity of examining all Mr. Burnet relates, whether as to the intrigues of Conclaves, or the behaviour of Popes, or the artifices of Clement VII. What advantage can he draw from thence? Neither Clement, nor the other Popes are, amongst us, the authors of any new article of faith. Nor have they separated us from the holy Society in which we were baptized; nor have they taught us to condemn our ancient pastors. In a word, they make no sect among us, and their vocation has nothing in it that is extraordinary. If they enter not by the door, which is always open in the Church, that is, by canonical ways, or, if they make ill use of the ordinary and lawful ministry intrusted to them from above, this is the very case specified in the Gospel,[85] of honoring the chair without approving, or imitating the persons. Nor ought I at all concern myself whether Julius II's dispensation were well given, nor whether Clement VII could, or ought to revoke it, and annul the marriage. For, although I look upon it as certain, that this last Pope acted well in the main, and, in my opinion, nothing can be blamed on this occasion but, at the most, his policy, which was at one time too timorous, and at another too hasty: this is not a question for me to decide in this place, nor a pretext for impeaching the Church of Rome for error. These matters of dispensation are often regulated by simple probabilities; nor is one obliged to look therein for the certainty of faith, whereof they are not always even capable. But since Mr. Burnet makes from this a capital accusation against the Church of Rome, I cannot, methinks, but dwell a little upon it.

*51.—The account of the Marriage Dispute entered upon.—The fact is laid down.
—The vain pretexts with which Henry covered his passion.*

It is a fact, notoriously known, that Henry VII had obtained a dispensation from Julius II to marry the widow of Arthur, his eldest son, to Henry, his second son and successor. This Prince, after he had seen all the reasons for doubting, consummated, when a King, and at age, this marriage, with the unanimous consent of all the estates of his realm, the 3d of June 1509, that is, six weeks after his coming to the crown.[86] Twenty years elapsed without calling in question a marriage so sincerely and honestly contracted. Henry, falling in love with Anne Boleyn, called conscience in to assist his passion; and his marriage becoming odious to him, at the same time became doubtful and suspected. Meanwhile, a Princess had sprung from this marriage, who from her infancy had been acknowledged heiress of the kingdom;[87] so that the pretext which Henry took for breaking off the marriage, lest, said he, the succession of the realm should be doubtful, was a mere trick, since non dreamed of disputing it with his daughter, Mary, who, in fact, was unanimously owned for Queen, when the order of birth called her to the crown. On the contrary, if any thing could obstruct the succession of this great kingdom, it was Henry's doubt; and it appears, that all he published relating to the doubtfulness of his succession, was nothing but a cloak, as well for his new amour, as for the disgust he had taken to the Queen his wife, on account of some infirmities she had contracted, as Mr. Burnet himself owns.[88]

52.—Julius's dispensation attacked by Arguments from fact and right.

A Prince, whom passion rules, would have it believed he has reason on his side: so to please Henry, the dispensation, on which his marriage was grounded, was attacked several ways, some taken from fact, others from right. As to fact, the dispensation was maintained to be null, because granted on false allegations. But as these arguments of fact, reduced to these minute niceties, were over-ruled by the favorable condition of a marriage that had subsisted so many years; those from right were chiefly insisted on, and the dispensation maintained null, as granted in prejudice to the law of God, which the Pope could not dispense with.

53.—Arguments of right grounded on Leviticus.—The state of the question.

The question was, whether or no the prohibition in Leviticus, not to contract within certain degrees of consanguinity or affinity, and, among others, that of marrying the brother's widow, did so appertain to the law of nature, as to be obligatory in the Gospel law.[89] The reason for doubting was, because we do not read that God ever dispensed with what was purely of the law of nature: for example, since the multiplication of mankind there has been no instance of God's permitting the marriage of brother and sister, nor others of this nature in the first degree, whether ascending, or descending, or collateral. Now, there was an express law in Deuteronomy,[90] which, in certain cases, enjoined a brother to take his sister-in-law and the widow of his brother to wife. God, therefore, not destroying nature, which he is the author of, gave thereby to understand that this marriage was not of that sort which nature rejects; and this was the foundation which Julius II's dispensation was grounded upon.

54.—*The Protestants of Germany favorable to Julius' dispensation, and Henry's first marriage.*

We must do the Protestants of Germany this justice: Henry could never obtain from them the approbation of his new marriage, nor the condemnation of Julius II's dispensation. When this affair was spoken of in a solemn embassy, which this Prince sent to Germany, in order to join himself to the Protestant confederacy, Melancthon decided thus: "We have not been of the English Ambassador's opinion; for, we believe, the law of not wedding a brother's wife, is susceptible of dispensation, although we do not believe it to be abolished."[91] And again, more concisely in another place: "The Ambassadors pretend, that the prohibition against marrying a brother's wife is indispensable; and we, on the contrary, maintain it may be dispensed with."[92] This was exactly what they stood for at Rome, and Clement VII's definitive sentence against the divorce rested on this foundation.

55.—*Bucer of the same opinion.*

Bucer was of the same opinion upon the same motives; and we learn from Mr. Burnet, that, according to this author, one of England's Reformers, "The law of Leviticus did not bind, and could not be moral, because God hath dispensed with it."[93]

56.—*Zuinglius and Calvin of the contrary opinion.*

Zuinglius and Calvin, with their disciples, were favorable to the King of England; and it is not unlikely but that a design of settling their doctrine in that kingdom, contributed not a little to their complaisance: but the Lutherans sided not with them, although Mr. Burnet makes them to vary a little in the matter: At first, "they thought," says he, "the laws in Leviticus were not moral, and did not oblige Christians; yet, after much disputing, they were induced to change their minds, but could not be brought to think that a marriage once made might be annulled."[94]

57.—*The odd decision of the Lutherans.*

And truly their decision, as reported by Mr. Burnet, is a very odd one; since, after their owning that "The law of Leviticus is divine, natural, and moral, and to be observed as such in all churches, insomuch that a marriage, contracted contrary to this law with a brother's widow, is incestuous;"[95] they conclude, nevertheless, that this marriage ought not to be broken; with some doubt at first, but, at length, by a final and definitive determination, as Mr. Burnet owns; so that an incestuous marriage, a marriage made contrary to divine, moral and natural laws, which still remain in their full force throughout the whole Christian Church, ought to subsist, in their judgment; nor is a divorce, in this case, allowable.

58.—*Remarks on the conformity of the Protestants' opinions with the sentence of Clement VII.*

This decision of the Lutherans is, by Mr. Burnet, referred to the year 1530: that of Melancthon, just mentioned, is posterior, and in 1536. However, it is a favorable precedent for Julius II's dispensation, and the sentence of Clement VII, that these Popes have met with defenders among those who sought nothing more than to censure their proceedings at any rate. The Protestants of Germany were so resolute in this sentiment that, for all the ties and interests Cranmer had then with them, he could engage none on his master's side, but only his brother-in-law, Osiander, whose authority will hereafter appear of no great weight.

59.—*Henry bribes some Catholic Doctors.*

As for Catholics, Mr. Burnet acquaints us that Henry VIII had bribed two or three Cardinals. Without informing myself of the truth of these facts, I shall observe only, that a cause must be bad indeed that stands in need of such infamous supports. And as for the Doctors, whose subscriptions Mr. Burnet boasts to us, where is the wonder that, in so corrupted an age, so great a King was able to find those who were not proof against his presents and solicitations? Our historian will not allow us to call in question the authority of Fra-Paolo, nor of De Thou.[96] Let him give ear to these two historians. One says, "that Henry having consulted in Italy, in Germany, and in France, he found one part of the divines favorable, and the other contrary. That the greatest number of those of Paris were for him, and many believed they had done it more from the persuasion of the King's money than that of his arguments."[97] The other says, "that Henry made diligent inquiry into the opinions of divines, and in particular of those of Paris, and the report ran, that these being gained by money, had subscribed in favor of the divorce."[98]

60.—*Concerning the pretended Consultation of the Paris Faculty of Divinity.*

I will not decide whether the conclusion of the Faculty of Divinity, at Paris, produced by Mr. Burnet[99] in favor of Henry's pretensions, be true or not; others will take this question in hand: this only shall I say, that it is very much to be suspected, as well on account of the style, far different from that which the faculty is accustomed to make use of, as because Mr. Burnet's conclusion is dated the 2nd of July, 1530, at the Mathurins; whereas, at that time, and for some years before, the assemblies of the faculty were held commonly in the Sorbonne.

61.—*The testimony of the Lawyer, Charles du Moulin.*

In the notes which Charles du Moulin, that renowned civilian, has made on Decius's Consultations, he speaks of the debate of the Doctors of Divinity at Paris, in favor of the King of England, the 1st of June, 1530, but this author places it in the Sorbonne.[100] He makes but little account of this declaration, wherein the party that favored the King of England carried it by fifty-three votes against forty-two; "which majority of eight voices," says he, "deserved no great weight, on account of the English *angels* of gold which were distributed for the purchase of it: this," he affirms, "he knew from the attestations which the President du Fresne and Poliot had given in by order of Francis I." Whence he concludes, the true judgment of the Sorbonne, that is, their genuine and unbought judgment, was that which favored the King's marriage with Catharine. It is, moreover, very certain that, during the deliberation, Francis, who then favored the King of England, had charged M. Lisset, the first President, to solicit the Doctors in his behalf, as appears by the original letters still kept in the King's library, wherein the President gives an account of his diligent compliance. Whether, then, this deliberation was made by the faculty in body assembled, or whether it was only the judgment of several Doctors, published in England under the name of the faculty, as happens in like cases, is a matter which I am not interested in examining into at present. It is apparent enough that the King of England's conscience was rather burdened than eased by such consultations, carried on by intrigue, by money, and by the authority of two so great monarchs. The rest of them, alleged by our author, were not transacted with more integrity. Mr. Burnet himself assures us, "that the King of England's agent in Italy, in many of his letters, said that, if he had money enough, he did not doubt but he should get the hands of all the divines in Italy."[101] Money, therefore, not the good-will, was wanting.[102] But not to dwell any longer on the minute stories Mr. Burnet is so triflingly circumstantial in, there is nobody but will own that Clement VII had been too unworthy of his place, if in an affair of this importance, he had shown the least regard to these mercenary consultations.

62.—*Reasons for the decision of Clement VII.*

And, indeed, the question was determined on more solid principles. It appeared, clearly, that the prohibition of Leviticus bore not the character of a natural and indispensable law, since God derogated from it in other places. The dispensation of Julius II, grounded on this reason, had so probable a foundation, that it appeared such even to the Protestants of Germany. No matter what diversity of sentiments there might have been on this subject, it was sufficient that the dispensation was not evidently contrary to the divine laws, which obliged Christians. This matter, then, was of the nature of such things, wherein all depends on the prudence of superiors, where sincerity and uprightness of heart must give all the repose conscience can have. It was also but too manifest that, had it not been for Henry VIII's new fit of love, the Church never would have been troubled with the shameful proposal of a divorce, after a marriage contracted and continued with a good conscience so many years. Here is the knot of the affair; and without speaking of the process, wherein, perchance, policy, good or bad, might intervene, Clement VII's decision, when all is said, will be a testimony to future ages, that the Church knows not how to flatter the passions of Princes, nor approve their scandalous proceedings.

63.—Two Points of Reformation under Henry VIII, according to Mr. Burnet.

We might here conclude what concerns the reign of Henry VIII, did not Mr. Burnet oblige us to consider two commencements of Reformation, which he remarks at this time: one is, his putting the Scriptures into the hands of the people; the other, his showing that every nation might reform itself independently of all others.

64.—First Point—The reading of the Scriptures, how granted to the people under Henry VIII.

As for what regards the Bible; this is what Henry VIII said in 1540, in his Preface to the Exposition of the Christian Faith above spoken of: "That, whereas there were some teachers whose office it was to instruct the people; so the rest ought to be taught, and to those it was not necessary to read the Scriptures; and that, therefore, he had restrained it from a great many, esteeming it sufficient for such to hear the doctrine of the Scriptures taught by their preachers." Afterwards he allowed the reading of them that same year, upon condition "that his subjects should not presume to expound, or take arguments from Scripture;"[103] which was obliging them anew to refer themselves to the pastors of the Church for Scripture interpretations;[104] in which case it is agreed the reading of this divine book must undoubtedly be very wholesome. Moreover, if at that time the Bible was translated into the vulgar language, there was nothing new in that practice. We have the like versions for the use of Catholics in ages preceding the pretended Reformation; nor is that a point of our controversies.

65.—Whether the progress of the Reformation be owing to the reading of the Scriptures, and in what manner.

Mr. Burnet, pretending to show that the progress of the new Reformation was owing to the reading of Scripture allowed to the people, ought to have stated that this reading was preceded by artful and cunning preachers, who had filled their heads with new interpretations. In this manner was it that an ignorant and headstrong people found, indeed, nothing in Scripture but those errors they had ben prepossessed with: and what hastened and completed their ruin was the rashness inspired into them, of every man's deciding for himself which was the true sense of Scripture, of every man's making for himself his own creed. Thus it was that ignorant and prejudiced people found in Scripture, the pretended Reformation: but what man is there of the least sincerity that will deny me, that, by the same means, they would as clearly have found Arianism in it, as they conceived they did Lutheranism or Calvinism?

66.—How men are deceived by Scripture ill-interpreted.

When this notion is once put into the heads of the ignorant, that all is clear in Scripture, that they understand it in all that is necessary for them, and, therefore, that the judgment of all pastors and of all ages is quite needless to them, they take for certain truth the first sense that offers, and what they are accustomed to always appears the most genuine. But, they ought to be made sensible that, in this case, it is the letter often which kills, and in those very passages, which appear the most plain, God has often hid the greatest and most awful mysteries.

67.—Proof from Mr. Burnet of the snares laid for the unlearned in the pretended perspicuity of Scripture.

For example, Mr. Burnet proposes to us this text, "Drink ye all of this," as one of the most clear that can be imagined, and which leads us the most directly to the necessity of both kinds. But it will now appear to him, from what he owns himself, that what he thinks so plain becomes a snare to the ignorant; for these words, "Drink ye all of this," in the institution of the Eucharist, are not, after all, more plain than these in the institution of the Passover: "Thus shall ye eat the paschal lamb, with your loins girded, and your staff in your hand:"[105] consequently, standing; and in the posture of people ready to depart, for that, indeed was the spirit of this Sacrament. Nevertheless, we are assured by Mr. Burnet,[106] this was not practised by the Jews, who, afterwards, changed this custom into the common table posture, and lay down, according to the custom of the country, at the eating of the lamb, as at other meals; and that this change, which they made in the Divine institution, we are sure was not criminal, since our Saviour made no scruple in complying with it.[107] I ask him in this case, whether a man who should have taken this divine commandment literally, without consulting the tradition and interpretation of the Church, would not have found in it his certain death, since he would have found in it the condemnation of Jesus Christ;[108] and whereas this author adds afterwards, it seemed reasonable to allow the Christian Church the like power in such things with the Jewish, why then should a Christian, in the new Passover, believe he has seen every thing relating to the Supper, upon reading the words only of the institution? and will not he be obliged to examine, besides these words, the tradition of the Church, in order to know what she always looked upon as necessary and indispensable in the Communion? Without pushing this examination any further, this is enough to show Mr. Burnet they must of necessity come into it; nor can the pretended perspicuity, which the illiterate think they find in these words, "Drink ye all of this," be any thing but an illusion.

68.—Henry VIII's second point of Reformation according to Mr. Burnet; that the Church of England acted by a schismatical principle, when she believe she could regulate her Faith independently of all the rest of the Church.

The second ground of Reformation, pretended to be laid by Henry VIII, Mr. Burnet makes to consist in the establishment of this principle, that every national Church was a complete body within itself, so that the Church of England, with the authority and concurrence of their head and King, might examine and reform all errors and corruptions, whether in doctrine or worship. These are fine words. Discover but their meaning, and you will find that such a reformation is nothing but a schism. A nation, which looks on itself as a complete body, which regulates its faith, in particular, without regard to what the rest of the Church believes, is a nation which separates itself from the universal Church, and renounces unity of faith and sentiments, so much recommended to the Church by Jesus Christ and his Apostles. When a Church thus cantoned makes the King her head, she gives herself, in matters of religion, a principle of unity, which Jesus Christ and the Gospel have not established;[109] changes the Church into a body politic, and gives room to erect as many separate Churches, as states may be formed. This idea of Reformation and Church was first conceived in the brain of Henry VIII and his flatterers, nor had Christians ever before been acquainted with it.

69.—Whether the Church of England in this followed the ancient Church, as Mr. Burnet pretends it did.

We are told, that all the provincial councils in the ancient Church were so many precedents for this, who condemned heresies, and reformed abuses."[110] But this is visibly imposing on mankind. True it is, provincial councils were obliged immediately to condemn heresies which arose in their respective countries: for in order to suppress them, ought they to have waited till the contagion had spread and alarmed the whole Church? Nor is that our question. What he should have made appear to us is, that these Churches looked on themselves as a complete body, in the same manner they do in England; and reformed their doctrine, without taking for their rule what the whole body of the Church unanimously did believe. Of this, I say no example will ever be produced. When the African Fathers condemned the infant heresy of Celestius and Pelagius, they laid for a foundation the prohibition of interpreting the Holy Scripture otherwise than the Catholic Church, spread over the whole earth, had always interpreted and understood it. Alexander of Alexandria laid down the same foundation against Arius, when, condemning him, he said, "We know but one Catholic and Apostolic Church, which, incapable of being subverted by the world's whole power, overthrows every impiety and every heresy." And again, "In every one of these articles we believe what hath pleased the Apostolic Church."[111] Thus did the Bishops and particular Councils condemn heresies by a prior judgment, by conforming themselves to the common faith of the whole body. These decrees were sent to all churches, and from this unity they drew their utmost force.

*70.—Whether the Church of England had reason to believe, that now-a-days it
is too difficult a thing to consult the Faith of the whole Church.*

But, say they, the remedy of a universal council, easy as it was under the
Roman empire, when the Churches had one common sovereign, is become
too difficult, now that Christendom is divided into so many states: another
fallacy. For, in the first place, the consent of Churches may be declared
otherwise than by general councils: witness, in St. Cyprian, the condemnation
of Novatian; witness that of Paul of Samosata, of whom it was written, that
he had been condemned by the council and judgment of all the bishops of the
world, because all had consented to the council held against him at Antioch;[112] lastly, witness the Pelagians, and so many other heresies, which,
without a general council, have been sufficiently condemned by the united
authority of the Pope and all the Bishops. When the necessities of the Church
required a general council to be assembled, the Holy Ghost always provided
means; and so many councils, as have been held since the fall of the Roman
empire, have made it plainly appear, that to assemble the pastors when
requisite, there needed not its assistance. The reason is because, in the Catholic
Church there is a principle of unity independent of the kings of the earth. To
deny this, is making the Church their captive, and rendering the heavenly
government, instituted by Jesus Christ, defective. But the English Protestants
would not acknowledge this unity, because the Holy See is the external and
common bond thereof; and it was more agreeable to them to have, in matters
of religion, their king for their head, than to own, in St. Peter's chair, a
principle by God established for the unity of all Christians.

*71.—All sorts of novelties crept into England in spite of the severities of Henry
VIII.—The reason why.*

The Six Articles published by the authority of King and Parliament had the
force of law during the whole reign of Henry VIII. But what sway over
consciences can decrees concerning religion have, which, drawing all their
strength from regal authority, to which God has intrusted no such commission,
have nothing in them but what is political? Though Henry VIII enforced them
with innumerable executions, and cruelly put to death, not only Catholics,
who detested his supremacy, but also the Lutherans and Zuinglians who
impugned the other articles of his faith, all manner of errors crept insensibly
into England, nor did the people any longer know what to stand to, when
they saw St. Peter's chair despised, from whence it was notorious faith first
came to this great isle, whether the conversion of its inhabitants under pope
Eleutherius be considered, or that of the English, which was procured by St.
Gregory the Great.

    The whole establishment of the Church of England, the whole order of
her discipline,—the whole disposition of the hierarchy in this kingdom; in a
word, the mission, as well as the consecration of bishops, was so certainly
derived from this great Pope and the chair of St. Peter, or from bishops
holding him for the head of their communion, that the English could not

renounce this power without weakening among them even the origin of Christianity, and all the authority of ancient traditions.

72.—They argued in England from false principles, when they rejected the Pope's Supremacy.

When they set about rejecting the authority of the Holy See in England, it was observed by them "that Gregory the Great had exclaimed against the ambition of that title of Universal Bishop, and refused it much about the time that England received the faith from those he sent over;" whence, concluded Cranmer and his associates, "When our ancestors received the faith, the authority of the See of Rome was within the limits of a laudable moderation."[113]

73.—Whether St. Gregory, Pope, under whom the English were converted, had different notions of the authority of his See from what we have.

Not to dispute, in vain, on this title of Universal which the Popes never do assume, and may be more or less supportable according to the different senses it is taken in; let us consider for a moment what St. Gregory, who rejected it, believed nevertheless relating to the authority of his See. Two passages known to the whole world will decide this question. "As for what concerns," says he, "the Church of Constantinople, who questions its being subjected to the See Apostolic, which neither the Emperor nor our brother Eusebius, bishop of that city, do cease to acknowledge?"[114] And in the following letter, speaking of the primate of Africa, as to what he says, "that he is subject to the See Apostolic, I know no bishop that is not subject to it when delinquent. Furthermore, when delinquency requires not otherwise, we are all brethren according to the law of humility."[115] Here, then, have we all bishops manifestly subject to the authority and correction of the Holy See, and this authority acknowledged even by the Church of Constantinople, at that time the second Church of the whole world in dignity and power. Here is the foundation of the pontifical power; the rest, which custom or toleration, or, if you please, even abuse might have introduced or increased, might be preserved, or suffered, or extended more or less, as order, peace, and public tranquillity should require. Christianity was born in England with the confession of this authority. Henry VIII could not endure it, even with this laudable moderation owned by Cranmer in St. Gregory: his passion and policy made him annex it to his crown, and by this so strange an innovation, he opened the way for all that followed.

74.—Death of Henry VIII.

Some say this unhappy Prince, towards the end of his days, felt some remorse for the excesses he had run into; and, in order to calm his conscience, sent for some bishops to him. I vouch it not; those who, in scandalous sinners, but particularly in Kings, are for discovering such biting stings of conscience as appeared in an Antiochus, are not acquainted with all God's ways, nor reflect sufficiently on that deadly insensibility and false peace he sometimes suffers his greatest enemies to fall into. Be that as it will, should Henry have consulted his bishops, what could be expected from a body which had enslaved the Church? Whatever indications Henry might give of desiring to be sincerely advised in this juncture, he could not restore to the bishops that liberty which his cruelties had deprived them of; dreadful to them were the vicissitudes of temper this prince was subject to; and he could not brook truth from the mouth of Thomas More, his Chancellor, nor from the holy Bishop of Rochester, both of whom he put to death for speaking it freely to him, never more deserved to hear it.

75.—*Every thing is changed after his death.*—*The young King's Guardian is a Zuinglian.*—*1547, 1548.*

In this state he died; and no wonder if, after his death, things grew worse. The foundations once shaken, by little and little, all goes to ruin. Edward VI, his only son, succeeded him according to the law of the land. As he was scarce ten years old, the kingdom was governed by a Council, appointed by the deceased king: but Edward Seymour, brother to Queen Jane, and the King's uncle by the mother's side, had the chief authority, with the title of Protector of the Kingdom of England. He was a Zuinglian in his heart, and Cranmer was his bosom friend. This Archbishop then threw off the mask, nor did he longer conceal any of that venom which lay lurking in his heart against the Church.

76.—*The Reformation founded on the ruin of ecclesiastical Authority.*

In order to prepare the way for their intended reformation under the King's name, they set out by declaring him, as Henry had been before, the supreme head of the Church of England in spirituals and temporals.[116] In Henry's time it was a settled maxim, that the King was Pope in England. But far different prerogatives were conferred on this new papacy than the Pope had ever pretended to. The bishops took out new commissions from Edward, revocable at the King's pleasure, as heretofore had been enjoined in King Henry's time; and, in order to advance the reformation, it was judged necessary to keep them under the subjection of an arbitrary power. The Archbishop of Canterbury, and primate of all England, was the first to bend his neck under this shameful yoke. This is not to be wondered at, since he was the person who inspired all these sentiments: the rest did but follow the pernicious example he set to them.[117] This was somewhat moderated afterwards, and the bishops were obliged to look upon it as a favor to hold their bishopricks of the King during life.[118] In the tenor of their commissions, it was plainly expressed, as under Henry, pursuant to Cranmer's doctrine, that the episcopal power, as well as that of the secular magistracy, flowed from the crown as from its source, that the bishops exercised it only precariously as delegates in the King's name, and which they were to deliver up again when it should please him to call for it, from whom they had received it.[119] The King gave them faculties to ordain and deprive ministers, inflict censures and punish scandalous persons, and to do all the other parts of the episcopal function, all which they were to execute and do in the King's name and under his authority.[120] At the same time, it was owned, that this pastoral charge was committed to bishops by the word of God. It was necessary to make use of this word to give themselves credit. But although nothing was found therein for the regal power, except what related to the concerns of this world, it was nevertheless extended to what is most sacred in the pastoral charge. Commissions for consecrating bishops were issued out by the King, and directed to whom he pleased: so that according to this new hierarchy, as the bishops were not consecrated but by the royal authority, so by the same only could they proceed to ordination.[121] Even the form and prayers of ordination, as well of bishops as of priests, were regulated by Parliament. The same was done in respect to the liturgy and public service, and the whole administration of the sacraments. In a word, all was subject to the King, and, upon abolishing the ancient law, the Parliament, it seems ,was to make an new body of canons. All these attempts were grounded on a maxim which the Parliament of England had laid down for a new article of their faith, viz., that all jurisdiction, both spiritual and temporal, was derived from the King, as from its source.[122]

77.—*Sequel of the ruin of Ecclesiastical Authority.*

It is not here to our purpose to deplore the calamities of the Church thus enslaved, and shamefully degraded by her own ministers. Our business is to relate facts, and a bare relation of them will suffice to show their enormity. "Not long after, the king declared he intended to visit his kingdom, therefore, neither the archbishops nor any other should exercise any jurisdiction while that visitation lasted.[123] There was proclamation from the King, commanding all to remember him in the public prayers as the supreme head of the Church of England, which was to be observed under the pains of excommunication, sequestration, or deprivation."[124] Thus, together with ecclesiastical censures, the whole pastoral authority is openly invaded by the King, and the most sacred depositum of the sanctuary wrested from the priestly order, without sparing even that of faith, which the Apostles had left to their successors.

78.—*Reflection on the miserable beginnings of the Reformation, wherein the sacred order had no share in the affairs of Religion and Faith.*

I cannot but stop here a moment to consider the groundwork of the English Reformation, "that work of light, a full and distinct narrative whereof makes its apology as well as history." The Church of England glories above all the other Churches of the Reformation, for having proceeded all orderly and by lawful assemblies. To afford some color for this boasting, it was, in the first place, and above all, necessary that ecclesiastics should have had the chief share in the management of this great alteration in religion. But quite the reverse was done, and ever since the time of Henry VIII, "they were cut off from meddling with it, except as they were authorized by the King."[125] All the complaint they made amounted to no more than that an encroachment was made on their privileges; as if for them to meddle with religion were only a privilege, and not essential to the very being of the ecclesiastical order.

But perchance one may imagine they met with better treatment under Edward, when, as Mr. Burnet pretends, the Reformation was set on a more solid basis. Quite the contrary; they begged it as a favor of the Parliament, "at least, that matters of religion should not be determined till they had been consulted, and had reported their opinions and reasons."[126] What a wretched state had they brought themselves to, not to intermeddle otherwise than by barely offering their opinions; they who were the proper judges in such cases, and of whom Christ had said, "He that hears you, hears me!" but this, says our historian, could not be obtained.[127] But, at least it may be allowed them to decide on articles of faith of which they were the preachers. By no means. The King's counsellors resolved to follow the method begun by the late King, of sending visiters over England with ecclesiastical injunctions and articles of faith; and it was the business of the King's council to regulate the articles of religion that were to be proposed to the people by his authority.[128] Meanwhile, the Six Articles of Henry VIII were to be adhered to, until they should think better of the matter; nor were they ashamed to require of the bishops an express declaration, "to make profession of such doctrine as afterwards, at any time, should be certified by the archbishop to the other bishops in the King's name."[129]

79.—The King is made absolute master of the Pulpit, and forbids Preaching all over his Kingdom till further orders.

It seems we need say no more, after the relation of such great excesses. But lamentable as it is, let us continue it. It is in some manner laboring to heal the Church's wounds to bewail them in the sight of God. The King took to himself so absolute an authority over the word and preaching, that a proclamation was issued, by which none were to preach without license from the King or his visiters—the Archbishop of Canterbury or the bishop of the diocese; so that the chief right was in the King, nor had the bishops, but by his permission only, any share therein. Sometime after, the Council allows those to peach who were likely to set forth the pure word of God after such sort as the Holy Ghost should for the time put in the preacher's mind.[130] The Council, it seems, had changed their minds; after they had made preaching depend on the regal power, they here leave it to the discretion of those who should imagine themselves filled with the Holy Ghost, and by this means all fanatics are admitted to it. The year following they changed again. "To restrain the clashing and contention of pulpits, the power of granting licenses to preach was taken from the bishops of each diocese, so that none might give them but the King and the archbishop."[131] By this means it is an easy matter to authorize the preaching up of any heresy. But the effects of this restraint are not what we are now upon. What ought to be considered is, that the whole authority of the word was delivered up to the prince alone. Things were carried so far, that after declaring to the people that the King had employed learned men to take away all subjects of controversies, "till the order now preparing should be set forth, he did inhibit all manner of persons to preach in any public audience."[132] Here then was preaching suspended throughout the whole kingdom, the bishops silenced by the King's proclamation, and all waiting in suspense, ignorant what religion the King would think fit to coin for them. "To this was tacked an admonition, exhorting all persons to receive with submission the orders that should, in a short time, be sent down to them." Thus was the English Reformation brought about; that work of light, a distinct narrative whereof makes, according to Mr. Burnet, its history as well as its apology.

80.—The Six Articles abolished.

These preparations being thus made, the English Reformation was set on foot, in the King's name, by the Duke of Somerset and Cranmer; and here the regal power pulled down that faith which the regal power had before set up. The Six Articles, which Henry VIII had caused to be published with his whole spiritual and temporal authority, were repealed;[133] and, notwithstanding all the precautions he had taken in his will to preserve those precious remains of the Catholic religion, and perhaps, in time, to restore it wholly, the Zuinglian doctrine, so much detested by this prince, gained the ascendant.

81.—Peter Martyr called over, and Zuinglianism established.—1549, 1550, 1551.

Peter Martyr, a Florentine, and Bernardin Ochin, afterwards the declared enemy of Jesus Christ's divinity, were called over to begin this Reformation. Both of them, like the rest of the reformers, had exchanged the monastic state for that of wedlock. Peter Martyr was a downright Zuinglian. The doctrine which he proposed in England concerning the Eucharist in 1549 was reduced to these three positions:—

I. There is no transubstantiation.

II. The body and blood of Jesus Christ are not corporeally in the Eucharist, nor under the species of bread and wine.

III. The body and blood of Christ are united to the bread and wine sacramentally, that is, figuratively, or at most, virtually.[134]

82.—Bucer not hearkened to.

Bucer did not approve the second proposition; for, as hath been seen, he was for excluding a local presence, but not a corporeal and substantial one. He maintained that Jesus Christ could not be separated from the Supper, and that he was after such a manner in heaven, as not to be substantially removed out of the Eucharist. Peter Martyr believed it was an illusion to admit a corporeal and substantial presence in the Supper, and not admit in it the reality which Catholics maintained, together with Lutherans; and what respect soever he might have for Bucer, the only Protestant he had any consideration for, yet he did come into his sentiments. A set of articles[135] was drawn up in England, comformable to Peter Martyr's opinion: it was there specified, "That the body of Jesus Christ was no where but in heaven: that he could not be really present in different places; so that no corporeal or Real Presence of the body and blood of Jesus Christ in the Eucharist was to be believed." This is what was defined. But, as yet, their faith was not in its utmost perfection, and, in due time, we shall see this article pretty much reformed.

83.—*Mr. Burnet's Confession concerning the Belief of the Greek Church.*

We are here obliged to Mr. Burnet for owning a thing of no small weight: for he grants us that the Real Presence is acknowledged by the Greek Church. These are his words: "The Lutherans seemed to agree with that which had been the doctrine of the Greek Church, that in the Sacrament, there was both the substance of bread and wine, and Christ's body likewise."[136] Herein he is more sincere than the greatest part of those of his religion; but, at the same time, opposes a greater authority against the novelties of Peter Martyr.

84.—*The Reformers repent themselves of having said that in the Reformation of the Liturgy they had acted by the assistance of the Holy Ghost.*

Then did the spirit of change entirely possess England. In the Reformation of the Liturgy and common prayers, which was made by the authority of Parliament, (for God gave ear to none but such,) it had been set forth in the preamble to the Act, that the commissioners named by the King to draw them up "had finished the work with one uniform agreement, and by the aid of the Holy Ghost."[137] Men were astonished at this expression. But the Reformers had their answer ready, viz., "That this was not so to be understood, as if they had been inspired by extraordinary assistance; for then there had been no room for any correction of what was now done."[138] Now these Reformers were still for correcting and changing on; and never did pretend to frame their religion all at once. And, indeed, very considerable alterations were soon made in this Liturgy, and their chief aim was to deface all the tracks of antiquity that hitherto had been preserved.

85.—*All the remains of Antiquity at first retained in the Liturgy are now destroyed.*

In the consecration of the Eucharist this prayer had been retained, "With thy Holy Spirit vouchsafe to bless and sanctify these thy gifts and creatures of bread and wine, that they may be unto us the body and blood of thy most dearly beloved son,[139] &c. They were willing to preserve, in this prayer, somewhat of the Church of Rome's Liturgy, which St. Augustin, the Monk sent to the English by St. Gregory, had brought in with Christianity. But although they maimed it by lopping off some words, yet still it was found "too much to favor transubstantiation,"[140] or even the corporeal presence, and was afterwards entirely erased.

86.—*England abrogates the Mass, which she had heard from her first conversion to Christianity.*

The words of that prayer were yet much stronger, as the Church of England used it at the time she embraced Christianity: for, whereas they had put in the reformed Liturgy, that these gifts may be unto us the body and blood of Jesus Christ; in the original it stands thus, that "This oblation be made unto us the body and blood of Jesus Christ." This word *made*, imports a true action of the Holy Ghost, who changes the gifts, conformably to what is said in the other liturgies of antiquity: "Make, O Lord, of this bread, thy own body; and of this wine, the own blood of thy Son; changing them by the Holy Spirit."[141] And these words, "be made unto us the body and blood," were said in the same spirit with those of Isaiah, "Unto us a child is born, unto us a son is given:"[142] not implying, that the sacred gifts are then only made the body and blood when we receive them, as the Reformers will have it; but signifying that it is for us they were formed in the Eucharist, as for us they were formed in the Virgin's womb. The English Reformation has corrected every thing that too much favored transubstantiation. The word oblation would likewise have too much favored a sacrifice: to give the sense of it in some manner, they substituted gifts. At length, it was wholly taken away, and the Church of England would no longer hear that sacred prayer she heard, when, coming forth from the baptismal font, she first received the bread of life.

87.—*The Gallican Mass and the rest, in the main, are the same with that of Rome.*

If it be insisted on that the holy priest Augustin brought them the Gallican Liturgy or Mass, rather than the Roman, the free choice of either having been left to him by St. Gregory, that alters not the case: the Gallican Mass, said by the Hilaries and the Martins, in the main, differed not from the Roman, nor the rest.[143] The Kyrie Eleison, the Pater, the Pax, or the blessing, may be given in one place of the Mass rather than another, and such things, as little essential, made the whole difference; and for this reason was it that St. Gregory left the choice thereof to the holy priest he sent into England.[144] As well in France, as at Rome, and in all the rest of the Church, a prayer was made to beg the transformation and change of bread and wine into the body and blood; the merit and mediation of saints with God was every where employed, but a merit grounded on the divine mercy, and a mediation supported by that of Jesus Christ. In all of these Liturgies the dead were frequently prayed for; and, with respect to all these things, there was but one language in the East and West, in the South and North.

88.—*The Reformation corrects itself with respect to Prayers for the Dead.*

The English Reformation had retained, in Edward's time, something of prayer for the dead; for, at funerals, they recommended the soul departed to God's mercy, and, as we now do, they prayed that his sins might be pardoned.[145] But all these remains of the primitive spirit are abolished: this prayer savored too much of purgatory. It is certain it was said from the first ages, both in the East and the West: no matter, it was the Pope's Mass, and that of the Church of Rome: it must be banished England, and every word of it turned to the most odious sense.

89.—Sequel of Alterations.

The Church of England, I may venture to say it, altered every thing she derived from antiquity.[146] Confirmation must be nothing but a catechism to renew the baptismal vows. But, said Catholics, the fathers, from whom we receive it by a tradition founded on the Acts of the Apostles, and as ancient as the Church, say not so much as a word of this notion of catechism. This is true, and they are forced to own it. Confirmation, nevertheless, is turned to this form, otherwise it would be too papistical. The holy chrism is taken away, which the most ancient fathers had called the instrument of the Holy Ghost;[147] the use of oil, even in extreme unction, will at last be laid aside, whatever St. James may say; and though St. Innocent Pope spoke of this unction in the fourth age, it will be decided that extreme unction was not heard of till the tenth century.

90.—Ceremonies and the sign of the Cross retained.

Among these alterations three things remained; holy ceremonies, the festivals of saints, abstinence and Lent. They thought it but meet that priests, in the public service, should put on a mysterious dress, symbols of purity and the other dispositions which the divine worship does require. Ceremonies were looked upon as a mystical language, and Calvin appeared too extravagant in rejecting them.[148] The use of the cross was retained, "as a public declaration that they were not ashamed of the cross of Christ."[149] At first, it was ordered to be kept up "in the sacrament of baptism, and in the office of confirmation, and in the consecration of the sacramental elements, as an outward expression of the veneration" they had for this holy ceremony.[150] Nevertheless, it was at last suppressed, in confirmation and the consecration, in which St. Augustin, with all antiquity, bears testimony, that it was ever practised; nor can I devise why it was retained only in baptism.

91.—England justifies us in the observance of Festivals, even those of Saints.

Mr. Burnet justifies us with relation to fasts and holydays; which days he will not have accounted holy of their own nature, nor from any magical virtue in that time.[151] This we consent to, and certainly, such a natural or magical virtue, which he thinks himself obliged to reject, never entered into any man's head. He says, "that none of these days were properly dedicated to any saint; but only to God in remembrance of such saints."[152] This is our very doctrine. In a word, he every where, and in every thing, vindicates us on this subject, since he agrees to a conscientious observing of such times.[153] Wherefore, those who object to us, that we follow the commandments of men,[154] need but object this to the Church of England, and she will vindicate us.

92.—*The same in abstinence from Flesh.*

They do no less evidently justify us from the reproach of teaching the doctrine of devils, when we abstain from certain meats for penance sake. Mr. Burnet answers for us, when he blames carnal men, who will not conceive, "that the frequent use of fasting, with prayer and true devotion joined to it, is perhaps one of the greatest helps that can be devised to advance one to a spiritual temper of mind, and to promote a holy course of life."[155] Since it is from this spirit, not a kind of temporal policy, as many do imagine, that the Church of England had forbidden flesh on Fridays and Saturdays, on Vigils, the four Ember-weeks, and throughout Lent, we have nothing on this subject to upbraid one another with. There is only reason to wonder that the King and Parliament should command these holydays and abstinences;[156] that the King should declare what were fish-days, and grant licenses and dispensations from these observances;[157] and lastly, that in matters of religion they should prefer the King's commandments to those of the Church.

93.—*Cranmer in his Reformation inverts all order.*

But something still more surprising in the English Reformation, was a maxim of Cranmer's. Whereas, in reality, the worship depends on faith, and should by that be regulated, Cranmer confounded this order; and, before he had examined the doctrine, suppressed, in the worship, what most displeased him. According to Mr. Burnet, the belief of Christ's presence in every crumb of bread gave occasion to laying aside the cup.[158] And indeed, argues he, in this hypothesis, "communion in both kinds was not necessary."[159] So that the question about the necessity of both kinds depended on that of the Real Presence. Now, in 1548, England still believed in the Real Presence, and the Parliament declared, that "the whole body of Christ was contained in every piece of consecrated bread, whether it were small or great."[160] The necessity, nevertheless, of communicating under both kinds had been already established; that is, they had drawn the consequence before they were well assured of the principle.

94.—*Sequel.*

The year following, Christ's presence in the sacrament was greatly called in question, and the thing left undecided. Yet the adoration of Jesus Christ in the sacrament had already been suppressed provisionally; as if one, seeing the people stand in great awe as in the King's presence, should say,—Good people, let us, in the first place, lay aside these exterior tokens of respect; there will afterwards be time to examine whether the King be present or no, and whether this honor be agreeable to him. The oblation of the body and blood was in like manner taken away; although this oblation, after all, be nothing else but the consecration made before God of this body and blood so really present before the manducation; and without examining the principle, that which inevitably ensued from it, was already destroyed.

The cause of so irregular proceeding was the leading the people by motives of hatred, and not of reason. It was an easy matter to excite hatred against certain practices, whereof they concealed from the people the beginning and right use, especially when some abuses were interwoven with them:[161] thus it was easy to render priests odious who abused the Mass for sordid gain; and hatred once inflamed against them, was by a thousand artifices insensibly turned against the mystery they celebrated, and even, as hath appeared, against the Real Presence, the foundation of it.

95.—*How the public hatred was raised against the Catholic doctrine.—Example in the Instruction of young Edward, and concerning Images.*

The same was done with respect to Images, and a French letter, which Mr. Burnet gives us of Edward VI to his uncle, the protector, makes it palpable. To exercise this young prince's style, his master sent him about collecting all the passages wherein God speaks against idols. "In reading the Holy Scripture, I was desirous," said he, "to note several places which forbid both *to adore and to make* any images, not only of strange Gods, but also to form any thing; thinking *to make it like to the Majesty of God* the Creator." In this credulous age, he had simply believed what was told him, that Catholics made images, thinking they made them like to the Majesty of God. "I am quite astonished," proceeds he, "God himself and his Holy Spirit having so often forbidden it, that so many people have dared to commit idolatry *by making and adoring images.*"[162] He fixes the same hatred, as we see, on the making, as on the adoring them; and, according to the notions that were given him, is in the right, since, undoubtedly, it is not lawful to make images with the though of making something *"like to Majesty of the Creator."* For, as this prince adds, God cannot be seen in things that are material, but will be seen in his own works. Thus was a young child deluded by them. His hatred was stirred up against Pagan images, in which man pretends to represent the Deity: it was shown him that God forbids to make such images, but they not having as yet taken it into their heads to say that it is unlawful to make such as ours, or unlawful to represent Jesus Christ and his saints, they took care to conceal from him, that those of Catholics were not of this nature. A youth of ten or twelve years old could not discover it of himself: to make images odious to him in general, and confusedly, was enough for their purpose. Those of the church, though of a different order and design, passed in the same light as the others: dazzled with the plausible reasoning and authority of his masters, every thing was an idol to him; and the hatred he had conceived against idolatry was easily turned against the Church.

96.—*Whether any advantage can be drawn from the sudden progress of the pretended Reformation.*

The people were not more cunning, and it was but too easy to animate them by the like artifices. After this, can the sudden progress of the Reformation be taken for a visible miracle, the work of God's own hand? With what assurance could Mr Burnet say it;—he! who has so thoroughly discovered to us the deep causes of this lamentable success? A prince blinded with inordinate passion, and condemned by the Pope, sets men at work to exaggerate particular facts, some odious proceedings and abuses which the Church herself condemned. All pulpits ring with satires against ignorant and scandalous priests; they are brought on the stage, and made the subject of farce and comedy, insomuch that Mr. Burnet himself expresses his indignation at it.[163] Under the authority of an infant King, and a protector violently addicted to Zuinglianism, invective and satire are still carried to a higher pitch. "The laity, that had long looked on their pastors with an evil eye,"[164] greedily swallowed down the poisonous novelty. The difficulties in the mystery of the Eucharist are removed, and the senses, instead of being kept under subjection, are flattered. Priests are set free from the obligation of continency; monks from all their vows; the whole world from the yoke of confession, wholesome, indeed, for the correction of vice, but burdensome to nature. A doctrine of great liberty was preached up, and which, as Mr. Burnet says, "showed a plain and simple way to the kingdom of heaven."[165] Laws so convenient met with but too ready a compliance. Of sixteen thousand Ecclesiastics, who made up the body of the English clergy, we are assured by Mr. Burnet, three parts renounced their celibacy in Edward's time;[166] that is, in the space of five or six years; and good Protestants were made of these bad Ecclesiastics, who thus renounced their vows. Thus was the clergy gained. As for the Laity, the Church revenues, exposed to rapine, became their prey. The vestry-plate enriched the prince's exchequer: the shrine alone of St. Thomas of Canterbury, with the inestimable presents that had been sent to it from all parts, produced a royal treasure of immense sums of money.[167] This was enough to degrade that holy martyr. He was attainted, that he might be pillaged; nor were the riches of his tomb the least of his crimes. In short, it was judged more expedient to plunder the Churches, than, conformably to the intention of the founders, to apply their patrimony to its right use. Where is the wonder, if the nobility, the clergy, and the people were so easily gained upon? is it not rather a visible miracle that there remained a spark in Israel, and that all other kingdoms did not follow the example of England, Denmark, Sweden and Germany, which were reformed by the same means?

97.—*Whether the Duke of Somerset had the show of a Reformer.*

Amidst all these Reformations, the only one that visibly made no progress was that of manners. The success of Luther's Reformation in Germany, as to this point, I have already observed upon, and we need but read Mr. Burnet's history to be convinced that things went on no better in England. We have seen Henry VIII, her first Reformer; the ambitious Duke of Somerset was the second. He equalled himself to crowned heads, though but a subject; and assumed the title of "Duke of Somerset, by the grace of God."[168] In the midst of the calamities which afflicted the whole nation, when London was much disordered by the plague, his thoughts were only bent on designing such a palace as had not been seen in England; and to aggravate his guilt by sacrilege, he built it upon the ruins, and with the materials, of three Episcopal palaces and a parish church: and the revenues extorted from several Bishops and Chapters, who "had resigned many manors to him for obtaining his favor, none daring to oppose his will."[169] He did this, it is true, with leave obtained from the King; but his abusing thus the authority of a minor, and the inuring his pupil to such sacrilegious donations, inflamed the guilt. I pass over the rest of his misdeeds, for which the Parliament condemned him, first to resign the authority he had usurped over the council, and afterwards to lose his head. But not to examine the reasons he had to condemn the Admiral, his brother, to the block; how shameful a thing to have subjected a man of that dignity, and his own brother, to that iniquitous law, of "attainting a man" on the bare allegation of witnesses, "without bringing him to make his own defence!" By virtue of this law, the Admiral, besides many others, was judged without a hearing.[170] The Protector prevailed upon the King to order the Commons to proceed in it without hearing the party accused, and in this manner it was that he tutored up his pupil to do justice.

98.—*Vain forwardness of Mr. Burnet to excuse Cranmer in little things, without speaking a word of great ones.*

Mr. Burnet takes a great deal of pains to justify his Cranmer for signing, Bishop as he was, the death of this unhappy person, and meddling in a cause of blood contrary to the canons. In order to this, he lays down, according to his custom, one of those specious plans, whereby he always strives, indirectly, to make odious the Church's faith, and elude the canons, but keeps at a distance from the main point.[171] If Cranmer was to be excused, it ought not to have been merely for violating the canons which, as an Archbishop he was obliged, above all others, to have a great regard for; but for breaking through the law of nature, sacred even among heathens, of "not delivering any man to die, before that he, who is accused, have the accusers face to face, and have license to answer for himself."[172] Cranmer, notwithstanding this law, condemned the Admiral and signed the warrant for his execution. Should not so great a Reformer have stood up against so barbarous a procedure? no truly: he deemed it a business of more importance to demolish altars, beat down images, not sparing even those of Jesus Christ, and abolish the Mass, which had been said and heard by so many Saints ever since the first establishment of Christianity among the English.

99.—*Cranmer and the rest of the Reformers spirit up rebellion against Queen Mary.—1553.*

To conclude the life of Cranmer: at the death of Edward VI, he set his hand to the entail of the Crown, in which this young Prince, out of hatred to the Princess his sister, who was a Catholic, changed the order of succession. Mr. Burnet would have us believe that the archbishop signed it with great reluctance, and is satisfied if this great Reformer shows but some scruple in committing crimes.[173] Yet the Council, which Cranmer was at the head of, gave all necessary orders to arm the people against Queen Mary, and maintain the usurper Jane Grey; preachers were set to work in the cause, and Ridley, Bishop of London, had orders to "set out Queen Jane's title in a sermon at St. Paul's."[174] When her affairs proved desperate, Cranmer, with the rest of them, owned his crime, and had recourse to the Queen's clemency. This Princess resettled the Catholic religion, and England reunited herself to the Holy See. As Cranmer had always suited his religion to that of the King, it was easily believed he would also follow that of the Queen, and manifest no more difficulty with regard to saying Mass than he had done under Henry, thirteen years together, without believing in it. But his engagement was too strong, and had he thus turned with every wind, he had too openly declared himself void of all religion.[175] He was sent to the Tower both for the crime of Treason and that of heresy, and deposed by the Queen's authority.[176] This authority was lawful with respect to him who had owned and even established it. It was by this authority he himself had deposed Bonner, Bishop of London, and was therefore punished by laws of his own making. For the like reason the bishops who, by patents, had received their bishoprics for a certain time, were deprived; and till the ecclesiastical order should be entirely re-established, the Protestants were proceeded against according to their own maxims.

100.—*Cranmer declared a heretic, and for what article.* 1555.

Cranmer, after his deposition, was left some time in prison. Afterwards, declared a heretic, he himself owned that it "was because he had denied the presence of Jesus Christ on the altar."[177] By that is seen wherein the principal part of the Reformation under Edward VI was made to consist, and I am willing to take notice of it here, because all that will take a new turn under Elizabeth.

101.—*Cranmer's false answers before his judges.*—*1556.*

When Cranmer's punishment was to be determined according to form, Commissioners from the Pope and those of Philip and Mary (for the Queen had then married Philip II, King of Spain) sat in judgment against him. The accusation turned on his marriages and heresies.[178] Mr. Burnet assures us that the Queen forgave him the treason for which he had been already condemned by Parliament. He confessed the facts which were imputed to him concerning his doctrine and marriages, "only said he had never forced any to subscribe."[179]

102.—*Cranmer condemned by his own principles.*

From these words, so full of meekness, one might be induced to think Cranmer had never condemned any person on account of doctrine. Not to mention here the imprisonment of Gardiner, Bishop of Winchester, that of Bonner, Bishop of London,[180] and other things of the like nature, the archbishop had signed and consented, in Henry time, to Lambert's and Anne

Askew's death, for denying the Real Presence;[181] and under Edward, to that of Joan of Kent and of George Van Pere, both burnt for heresy. What is still more, Edward, thinking it a piece of cruelty, refused to sign the warrant for burning her, and could not be persuaded to it but by Cranmer's authority.[182] If, then, he was condemned for heresy, he himself had often enough set the example.

103.—*Cranmer twice abjures the Reformation a little before his execution.*

With the design of putting off the time of his execution, he declared "he was willing to go to Rome and defend his doctrine before the Pope, yet denied any authority the Pope had over him:"[183] from the Pope, in whose name he was condemned, he appealed to a General Council, but seeing nothing availed, he renounced all the errors of Luther and Zuinglius, and, together with the Real Presence, distinctly owned all the other points of the Catholic faith. The abjuration which he signed, was conceived in such terms as expressed the truest sorrow for his former errors. The Protestants were extremely shocked at it. However, their Reformer made a second abjuration; that is, when he saw, notwithstanding his preceding abjuration, the Queen was determined not to pardon him, he returned to his first errors; but he soon recanted them, "all this time," says Mr. Burnet, "being under some small hopes of life." So that, continues this author, having been "dealt with to renew his subscription, and then to write the whole over again, he also did it." But here was the secret he found out to secure his conscience. Mr. Burnet goes on: "But conceiving likewise some jealousies that they might burn him, he wrote secretly a paper, containing a sincere confession of his faith; and, being brought out, he carried that along with him." This confession, thus secretly written, shows us clearly enough that he was determined not to appear a Protestant as long as any hopes remained. At last, finding himself utterly disappointed, he resolved to declare what his heart had concealed, and so give himself the appearance of a martyr.

104.—*Mr. Burnet compares Cranmer's fault to that of St. Peter.*

Mr. Burnet uses all his address to hide the shame of so miserable a death; and after alleging, in behalf of his hero, the faults of St. Athanasius and St. Cyril, which we find no mention of in ecclesiastical history, he now produces St. Peter's denial, so memorable in the Gospel. But what comparison is there betwixt a momentary weakness of this great Apostle, and the wretchedness of a man who betrayed his conscience during almost the whole course of his life and for thirteen years together, to begin from the very time he was made a bishop? who never dared to avow his sentiments but when he had a King to back him? And, lastly, on the very brink of death, confessed all that was required of him, as long as he had but a glimpse of hope; so that his counterfeit abjuration was manifestly nothing else but a continuation of the base dissimulation of his whole life.

105.—*Whether it be true, that Cranmer complied no more with Henry VIII than his conscience permitted.*

Nevertheless our author will still boast to us the steady firmness (good God) of this perpetual flatterer of kings, who sacrificed every thing to the will of his masters, annulling as many marriages, setting his hand to as many condemnations, and consenting to as many laws as they pleased, even to those which were, either in fact or in his opinion, the most unjust; who, finally, was not ashamed to bring the heavenly authority of bishops under subjection to that of the Kings of the earth, and enslave the Church, in discipline, in preaching the word, in the administration of Sacraments, and in Faith. Nevertheless, but one only blemish of his life does Mr. Burnet find, that of his abjuration;[184] and, as for the rest, allows only, that he was somewhat too much subjected to the will of Henry VIII,[185] yet, to justify him completely in all his compliances, he affirms, "he thought none of them a sin,"[186] consequently was no further obsequious to Henry than his conscience allowed him. His conscience then allowed him to annul two marriages on pretexts notoriously false, founded on no other principle than Henry's new amours. His conscience allowed him, though a Lutheran, to set his hand to articles of faith, wherein Lutheranism was condemned, and the Mass, the unjust object of the horror of the new Reformation, was established. His conscience allowed him to say Mass as long as Henry lived, without believing in it; to offer to God, even for the dead, a sacrifice which he held for an abomination; to ordain priests, giving them also the power of offering; and according to the form of the Pontifical, which he durst not alter, to exact chastity of those whom he made sub-deacons, although he did not think himself obliged to it, being a married man; to swear obedience to the Pope, whom he looked upon as Antichrist; to accept his Bulls, and receive Archiepiscopal institution by his authority; to pray to Saints, and incense their images, notwithstanding that, in the Lutheran principles, all this was nothing less than idolatry; in a word, to profess and practise all that he believed ought to be banished from the house of God, as an execration and a scandal.

106.—*Mr. Burnet but ill excuses his Reformers.*

But the thing was, "the Reformers," it is what Mr. Burnet tells us, "did not know, as yet, that it was absolutely a sin to retain all these abuses till a proper occasion offered for abolishing them."[187] Doubtless, they did not know it was a sin to change, according to their notion, the Lord's Supper into sacrilege, and to defile themselves with idolatry. To make them abstain from such things, God's commandment was not sufficient: they were to wait till the King and Parliament should think it fitting.

107.—*Illusion in Mr. Burnet's examples.*

Naaman is brought forward as an instance, who, obliged by his office, to give the King his hand, would not remain standing whilst his master knelt down in the temple of Remmon; and acts of religion are compared with the duty and decorum of a secular employment.[188] The Apostles are brought forward to us, who, "After the law was dead, continued to worship at the temple, to circumcise, and to offer sacrifices;"[189] and the ceremonies, which God had instituted, and which all the Fathers allow ought to be buried honorably, are compared with actions believed to be manifestly impious.[190] The same Apostles are adduced to us, who made themselves all things to all men, and also the primitive Christians, who adopted some ceremonies of paganism. But if the primitive Christians adopted ceremonies that were indifferent, does it follow from thence, that men ought to practise such as they believe are full of sacrilege? How blind, how contradictory to itself is the Reformation, which, in order to raise a horror of the Church's practices, must call them idolatrous! Obliged to excuse the same things in her first authors, she holds them for indifferent, and makes it more conspicuous than the sun, that she banters the whole universe by calling that idolatry which is not so, or that those she admires for her heroes were, of all men, the most corrupt. But God hath revealed their hypocrisy by their own historian, and Mr. Burnet is the man that hath exposed their shame in full view.

108.—Mr. Burnet not always to be credited in his facts.

However, if to convict the pretended Reformation by their own witnesses, I have only, as it were, abridged Mr. Burnet's history, and received as true the facts I have related: I do not mean thereby to grant the rest, and allow all he relates as fact for the sake of those truths he was not able to deny, though prejudicial to his own religion. I shall not, for example, allow him what he asserts without witnesses or proof, that there was a resolution taken between Francis I and Henry VIII to withdraw themselves by agreement from the Pope's obedience,[191] and change the Mass into a bare Communion;[192] that is, to suppress the Oblation and Sacrifice. This fact, averred by Mr. Burnet, was never even heard of in France. We are as much at a loss to know what this historian means by affirming, that the reason which made Francis I alter his resolution of abolishing the Pope's power was, because Clement VII "had granted him so great power over his own clergy, that he could scarce have expected more, if he had set up a patriarch in France;"[193] for here is nothing but mere empty words, a thing unknown to our historians. Mr. Burnet is no better versed in the history of the Protestant religion, when he so boldly advances, as a thing avowed among the Reformers, that good works were indispensably and absolutely necessary to salvation,[194] for he hath seen, and will see this proposition, good works are necessary to salvation, expressly condemned by the Lutherans in their most solemn assemblies. It would be departing too much from my design, were I to descend to other facts of the like nature; but I cannot but make it known to the world, how little credit this historian merits, with relation to the Council of Trent, which he ran over in so negligent a manner, that he did not so much as take notice of the very title, which this council placed at the beginning of all its decisions. For he upbraids it with "having usurped the most glorious title of the most holy Oecumenical Council, representing the Catholic Church,"[195] although this quality be not found in any one of its decrees; a thing of little importance in itself since it is not this expression that makes a council; yet it never could have escaped a man that had but just opened the book with the least attention.

109.—*Mr. Burnet's fallacy with regard to Fra-Paolo.*

It behooves one, therefore, to be very cautious how he credits our historian in what he pronounces touching this council on the testimony of Fra-Paolo, its declared enemy rather than historian. Mr. Burnet pretends that this author ought, with respect to Catholics, to be above all exception, because he is one of their own party;[196] and this is the common artifice of all Protestants. But they are very well convinced in their consciences, that this Fra-Paolo, who counterfeited our religion, was in reality nothing but a Protestant in a monk's disguise. None knows him better than Mr. Burnet, who boasts him to us. He who, in his history of the Reformation, sets him forth for an author of our party, in another book, lately translated into our language, takes off the mask and shows him a Protestant, that had concealed himself;[197] that looked upon the English common-prayer book as his pattern; that occasionally, from the falling out between Paul V and the republic of Venice, labored for nothing more than to bring this republic[198] "to an entire separation, not only from the Court, but also from the Church of Rome; who believed himself to be in a defiled and idolatrous Church, wherein he continued nevertheless; heard Confessions, said Mass, and quieted the remorse of his conscience by passing over many parts of the canon, and not joining in those parts of the offices that went against his conscience."[199] This is what Mr. Burnet writes in the life of William Bedell, the Protestant Bishop of Kilmore, in Ireland, who was present at Venice at the time of the difference, and to whom Fra-Paolo had disclosed his sentiments. There is no need of mentioning this author's letters, which are all Protestant, and were in every library, and which Geneva at length hath made public. I speak to Mr. Burnet only of what he wrote himself, at the time he counted amongst our authors Fra-Paolo, a Protestant under a monk's disguise, who said Mass not believing it, and who remained in a Church whose worship appeared to him idolatry.

110.—*The plans of Religion which Mr. Burnet makes after Fra-Paolo's example.*

But what he deserves the least to be pardoned in is, when, in imitation of Fra-Paolo, and with as little truth, he lays before us those ingenious plans of Primitive-Church doctrine. This invention, I must own, is equally commodious and agreeable. An artful historian, in the midst of his narration, slily introduces all he pleases of antiquity, and erects for us a scheme of his own contrivance. Under pretext, that a historian ought not to enter into proofs, or play the Doctor, he is content with alleging such facts as are favorable to his own religion. Is he inclined to ridicule the veneration of images or relics, or the Pope's authority, or prayer for the dead, or even, to omit nothing, the *pallium?* he gives to these practices such a form and such a date as he thinks fit. He says, for example,[200] of the *pallium*, "that this was a device set up by Pope Paschal II;" although it be found five hundred years before, in the letters of Pope Vigilius and St. Gregory. The credulous reader, finding history all over interspersed with these reflections, and seeing every where, in a work whose character ought to be sincerity, an abridgment of the antiquities of several ages, without once dreaming that the author gives him, either his prejudices or conjectures for certain truths, admires the erudition and agreeable turns of the work, believes he has reached to the very original things, and drinks at the fountain-head. But it is not just that Mr. Burnet, under the insinuating title of a historian, should thus peremptorily decide on Church-antiquity, nor that Fra-Paolo, whom he copies after, should acquire a right to make what he pleases pass for truth concerning our religion, because that, under a Monk's habit, he hid a Calvinistic heart, and labored under-hand to discredit the Mass he said daily.

111.—*Gerson cited strangely from the purpose.*

Let not Mr. Burnet, therefore, be any longer credited as to what he relates of the Church's *dogmata*,[201] since he turns all of them to a wrong sense. Whether he speaks of himself, or introduces in his history a third person that speaks of our doctrine, his inward design is ever to decry it. Can his Cranmer be borne with, when, abusing a treatise which Gerson had made *De auferibilitate papæ*, he concludes, as from this Doctor, "That the papal power is a quite needless thing?" whereas, he means only, as the sequel of this work demonstrates, so as to leave no room for doubt, that the Pope may be deposed in certain cases. When an author relates such things seriously, his design is to trifle with mankind, and he destroys his own credit with all thinking persons.

112.—*A gross Error relating to Celibacy and the Roman Pontifical.*

But the subject on which our historian has exhausted all his ingenuity, and has employed, as I may say, as his finest coloring, is that regarding the Celibacy of Ecclesiastics. I shall not discuss what he says, either in his own, or Cranmer's name. One may judge of his remarks on antiquity,[202] by those he makes on the Roman Pontifical, which will easily be granted me has nothing in it obscure with respect to celibacy: "It was considered," says he, "that the promise made by clergymen, according to the rites of the Roman Pontifical, did not necessarily oblige them to celibate. He that confers the orders asks of him that receives them, 'wilt thou promise to live in chastity and sobriety!' To which the sub-deacon answers, 'I will.'" Mr. Burnet concludes from these words, that no other chastity was here understood, but that which one is obliged "in a state of marriage, as well as out of it." But the imposition is too gross to be borne with. The words he relates are not said on the ordination of a sub-deacon, but in that of a bishop.[203] And in that of a sub-deacon, he that presents himself to this order is stopped to hear declared to him that, till then, he was free; but if he proceeds further, he must keep chastity. Will Mr. Burnet now say again, that the chastity here in question is that which is kept in a state of marriage, and which teach us "to abstain from all unlawful embraces?"—Must we then wait for the sub-deaconship to enter into this obligation? And who is it that does not acknowledge here that profession of continency, which is imposed, according to the ancient canons, on the principal clerks from the very time they are raised to the sub-deaconship?

113.—A vain shift.

Mr. Burnet still replies,[204] that, whatever might be required by the Roman Pontifical, the English priests, who were married in the time of Edward, had been ordained without any such "question or answer made, and so were not precluded from marriage by any vow." But the contrary appears from himself, he having owned that in the time of Henry VIII nothing was altered in the rituals, nor in the other books of offices, except some extravagant prayers addressed to saints, or some other matter of light importance; and it is easy to be seen, that this Prince was far enough from taking from ordination the profession of continency, as he had even prohibited the violation of it; first, under pain of death, and when he was most mitigated, "under the forfeiture of goods and chattels."[205] And this, indeed, was the reason why Cranmer never durst declare his marriage during the life of Henry VIII; but to save himself, was forced to add to a forbidden marriage the reproach of clandestinity.

114.—Conclusion of this Book.

No wonder then, that under such an Archbishop, no regard was had to the doctrine of his holy predecessors, St. Dunstan, St. Lanfranc, St. Anselm, and such others, whose admirable virtues, and particularly that of continency, were an honor to the Church. Nor do I wonder, that in his time, St. Thomas of Canterbury's name, whose life was the condemnation of Thomas Cranmer, was effaced from their Calendar of Saints—St. Thomas of Canterbury resisted the attempts of unjust Kings; Thomas Cranmer prostituted his conscience to them, and indulged their passions. The one, banished, his goods confiscated, persecuted in his own and the persons of his dearest friends, every way afflicted, purchased the glorious liberty of speaking what his conscience dictated for truth, with a generous contempt of all the conveniences of life, and of life itself: the other, to please his Prince, spent his life under a shameful dissimulation, and an outward conformity in every thing to a religion, which he inwardly condemned. The one combated even to blood for the Church's minutest rights; and by maintaining her prerogatives, as well those which Jesus Christ had acquired by his death, as those which pious Princes had endowed her with, defended the very outworks of the holy city: the other surrendered to the Kings of the earth her most sacred trust; the word, worship, sacraments, keys, censures, authority, even faith itself. In a word, every thing was inthralled, and the whole ecclesiastical authority being united to the royal throne, the Church had no more power than the State pleased to allow. Lastly, the one, intrepid and exemplary pious through the whole course of his life, was yet more so in the last period of it: the other, always dastardly and trembling at death's approach, shrunk even below himself, and at the age of three-score and two, sacrificed even, to the dregs of a despicable life, his faith and conscience. Accordingly, he has left but an odious name amongst men; nor can any thing but stress of wit and quirk, which plain facts belie, excuse him even to his own party: but the glory of St. Thomas of Canterbury will live as long as the Church; and his virtues, which France and England have venerated with a kind of emulation, will never be forgotten. Nay, the more doubtful the cause of this holy martyr appeared to the politic world, the more did the divine power declare itself in his behalf, by the signal chastisements of Henry II, this holy Prelate's persecutor, by the exemplary penance of this Prince, which alone could appease the wrath of heaven, and by miracles of so great a lustre, wrought at his tomb, that they drew to it the Kings of France as well as England. Miracles, I say, so continual, and so well attested by the unanimous consent of all the historians of those times, that to deny them is to reject at once the truth of all history whatsoever. The English Reformation, nevertheless, hath struck the name of so great a man out of the Calendar of Saints. More flagrant still have been their attempts: nothing but the degradation of all that nation's saints, since it first became Christian, can satisfy them. Bede, their venerable historian, tells them nothing but fables; at most, but legendary stories, when he relates the miracles of their conversion, the holiness of their pastors, of their Kings, and their religions. St. Augustin, the Monk, who brought them to the Gospel, and St. Gregory, Pope, who sent him, escape not the hands of the Reformation; they are attacked and defamed by her chief writers. To believe them,[206] the mission of those saints, who laid the foundation of the English Church, was the work of the ambition and policy of Popes; and St. Gregory, so humble, so holy a Pope, by converting the English, aimed rather at subjecting them to the Holy See, than to Jesus Christ. This is what is published in England, and her Reformation establishes itself by trampling under foot and polluting the whole Christianity of the nation in its very source. But so learned a nation, it is to be hoped, will not always remain under this seduction: the respect they retain for the Fathers, and their curious and continual researches into antiquity, will bring them back to the doctrine of the first ages. I cannot believe the chair of St. Peter, whence they received Christianity, will always be the object of their hatred——The time of vengeance and illusion shall pass away, and God will give ear to the prayers of his Saints.

Notes

[1] Appen. t. iii. p. 303.
[2] Ext. from the Journ. of the House of Lords and Com., 3d Jan. 1681, 23d Dec, 1680, and 5th Jan. 1681, in

the beginning of the 2d vol. of Bur. Hist.
[3] Burn. l. iii. p. 181.
[4] Notitia Imperii.

[5] Preface, towards the end.
[6] 2d Part. l. i. p. 85.
[7] 2d Part. l. i. p. 204.
[8] Burn. lib. ii. p. 87.
[9] Ibid.
[10] Ibid.
[11] Burn. t. i. lib. ii. p. 92.
[12] Ibid. p. 75.
[13] Burn. t. i. lib. ii. p. 128.
[14] Pont. Rom. in Consc. Ep.
[15] Burn. lib. ii. p. 129.
[16] Pont. Rom. in Ord. Presbyt.
[17] Burn. lib. ii. p. 131.
[18] Ibid.
[19] Ibid.
[20] Burn. lib. ii. p. 134.
[21] P. 156.
[22] P. 155, 156.
[23] Lib. iii. p. 180.
[24] Burn. lib. iii. p. 181.
[25] Burn. lib. iii. p. 180.
[26] Ibid.
[27] P. 181.
[28] Burn. lib. ii. p. 171.
[29] Dan. viii. p. 12.
[30] Burn. lib. iii. p. 186.
[31] Ibid. p. 184.
[32] Ibid. p. 183.
[33] Burn. lib. iii. p. 192.
[34] Ibid. p. 197.
[35] Ibid. p. 199.
[36] Ibid. p. 196.
[37] Ibid. p. 192.
[38] Ibid. p. 199.
[39] Cranmer's letter, Burn. lib. iii. p. 200.
[40] Ibid. l. iii. p. 203.
[41] Ibid.
[42] Ibid.
[43] Burn. lib. iii. p. 203.
[44] Ibid.
[45] Ibid.
[46] Ibid. p. 200.
[47] Ibid. p. 201.
[48] Ibid. p. 203.
[49] Burn. lib. iii. p. 216.
[50] Ibid.
[51] Ibid. p. 217.
[52] Ibid. p. 218.
[53] Burn lib. iii. p. 217.
[54] Collec. of Records, t.i. add. p. 306.
[55] Burn. l. iii. p. 219.
[56] Ibid. p. 21.
[57] Burn. l. iii. p. 218.
[58] Ibid. p. 223.
[59] Ibid. p. 225.
[60] Ibid. p. 256.
[61] Burnet, p. 271.
[62] Ibid. p. 276.
[63] Ibid. p. 277.
[64] Ibid. p. 278.
[65] Ibid. p. 277.
[66] Ibid. p. 279.
[67] Burnet, p. 281. Coll. n. 19.
[68] Ibid.
[69] Collec. Rec. lib. iii. n. 19. p.197.
[70] Burnet, p.281.
[71] Part i. lib. iii. p. 290, et seq.
[72] Burn. lib. iii. p. 294.
[73] Burn. lib. iii. p. 254.
[74] Ibid. p. 255.
[75] Ibid. p. 257.
[76] Burnet, p. 265.
[77] Ibid. p. 266.
[78] Rec. p. i. lib. iii. n. 21. p. 220.
[79] Omnes conveniunt. Rec. part. 1. lib. iii. n. xxi. p. 223.
[80] Powers Commis. Ibid. xiv. p. 184.
[81] Burn. part. 2. lib. i. p. 6.
[82] Burn. lib. iii. p. 386, 376. part ii. lib. i. p. 44.
[83] Burnet, part ii. lib. ii. p. 176.
[84] Pref.
[85] Matt. xxiii. 2.
[86] Burn. p. i. lib. ii. p. 36.
[87] Ibid.
[88] Burn. p. i. lib. ii. p. 36.
[89] Levit. xviii. 20.
[90] Deut. xxv. 5.
[91] Melanc. lib. iv. ep. 185.
[92] Ibid. ep. 183.
[93] Burn. lib. ii. p. 92.
[94] Ibid. p. 94.
[95] Collec. of Rec. part v. lib. ii. n.
[96] Burn. t. i. Pref.
[97] Hist. del. Conc. Trid. lib. i. An. 1534.
[98] Thu. Hist. lib. i. An. 1534, p. 20.
[99] Rec. part. i. lib. ii. n. 34. p. 89.
[100] Not. ad Cons. 602.
[101] Burn. lib. ii. p. 90.
[102] Ibid.
[103] Burn. lib. iii. p. 293.

[104] Ibid. p. 303.
[105] Exod. xii. 11.
[106] Part. 2. l. i. p. 171.
[107] Ibid.
[108] Ibid.
[109] Pref. and part 1. l. iii. p. 294.
[110] Ibid.
[111] Conc. Milev. cap. 2. Epis. Alex. Episc. Alexandriæ ad Alex. Constantinop.
[112] Ep. Alex. Episc. Alex. ad Alex. Constanti.
[113] Burn. part. 1. l. ii. p. 139.
[114] Lib. vii. Ind. 2. Ep. 64.
[115] Ibid. 65.
[116] Burn. part. 1. l. iii. p. 267. part 2. l. i. p . 6. Col. of Rec. part 2. l. i. p. 90.
[117] Ibid.
[118] Ibid.
[119] Ibid. and part 1. p. 276.
[120] Part 2. l. i. p. 218.
[121] Burn. part 1. l. i. pp.141, 142, 143.
[122] Ibid. p. 43.
[123] Ibid. p. 27; and Col. n. 7.
[124] Ibid. p. 29.
[125] S.n. 2. Burn. part 2. l. i. p. 49.
[126] S.n. 2. Burn. part 2. l. i. p. 49.
[127] Rec. n. pp. 16, 17.
[128] Ibid. p. 26.
[129] Ibid. p. 59.
[130] Ibid. p. 61.
[131] Rec. n. p. 80.
[132] Ibid. p. 81.
[133] Ibid. part 2. l. i. p. 40.
[134] Hosp. part 2. An. 1547. p. 207, 208, et seq. Burn. part 2. l. i. p. 106.
[135] Burn. p. 170. Col. n. 55.
[136] Ibid. p. 104.
[137] Ibid. p. 93.
[138] Burn. p. 94. Col. n. 55.
[139] Lib. i. p. 76.
[140] Ibid. p. 170.
[141] Lit. of S. Basil, &c.
[142] Is. ix. 6.
[143] Burn. part 2, l. i. p. 72.
[144] Greg. lib. vii. ind. ii. ep. 64.
[145] Burn. p. 77.
[146] Ibid.
[147] Ibid. p. 170.
[148] Burn. p. 75.
[149] Ibid. p. 79.
[150] Ibid. p. 170.
[151] Ibid. p. 191.
[152] Ibid.
[153] Ibid.
[154] Matth. xv. 9.
[155] Burn. p. 96.
[156] Burn. p. 95.
[157] Ibid. p. 191.
[158] Ibid. part 2, p. 42.
[159] Ibid. part 1, p. 290.
[160] Ibid. p. 651.
[161] S. l. vi. n. 21, et seq.
[162] Rem. part ii. l. ii. p. 68.
[163] Lib. iii. p. 318.
[164] Ibid. p. 31.
[165] Ibid.
[166] Ibid. part ii. l. ii. p. 276.
[167] Ibid. part i. l. ii. p. 244.
[168] Burnet, part ii. lib. i. p. 134.
[169] Ibid.
[170] Ibid. p. 100.
[171] Ibid.
[172] Acts xxv. 16.
[173] Burnet, part ii. p. 223.
[174] Ibid. lib. ii. p. 238.
[175] Ibid. p. 250.
[176] Ibid. p. 274.
[177] Burn. lib. ii. p. 283.
[178] Ibid. part ii. p. 257.
[179] Ibid. p. 332.
[180] Ibid. part ii. lib. i. p. 37.
[181] Ibid. p. 112.
[182] Ibid. p. 111.
[183] Ibid. 332, 333.
[184] Burner, p. 336.
[185] Ibid.
[186] Pref. tom. i.
[187] Burn. t. i. Pref.
[188] Ibid. 4 Reg. v. 18, 19.
[189] Ibid.
[190] Ibid.
[191] Burn. part i. l. ii. p. 133.
[192] Ibid. l. iii. p. 140.
[193] Ibid. p. 133.
[194] Part i. l. iii. p. 286, 287. Sup. l. v. n. 12. Inf. l. viii. n. 30, et seq.
[195] Part ii. l. i. p. 20.
[196] Part 1. Pref.
[197] The Life of Bedell, Bishop of Kilmore, p. 8.

[198] Ibid. p. 23.

[199] Ibid. p. 16.

[200] Life of Bedell, Bishop of Kilmore, p. 340.

[201] Burn. part ii. l. ii. p. 175.

[202] Burn. part. ii. l. i. pp. 91, 92.

[203] Pont. Rom. in Consec. Ep.

[204] Ibid.

[205] Part i. l. iii. p. 282.

[206] Whitak. cont. Duræ. Fulk. cont. Stapl. Jewel. Apol Ecc. Angl.

Book VIII

[From the year 1546 to the year 1561.]

A brief Summary.—The war begun between Charles V and the Confeder-
ates of Smalkald.—Luther's Theses which had excited the Lutherans to take
up arms.—A new subject of war on account of Herman, Archbishop of
Cologne.—The prodigious ignorance of this Archbishop.—The Protestants
defeated by Charles V.—The Elector of Saxony and the Landgrave of
Hesse made prisoners.—The Interim, or the Emperor's book, which
regulates matters of Religion provisionally for the Protestants alone, till the
meeting of the Council.—The disturbance caused in Prussia by Osiander,
a Lutheran: his new doctrine concerning Justification.—Disputes among the
Lutherans after the Interim.—Illyricus, Melancthon's Disciple, strives to
undo him on account of indifferent ceremonies.—He renews the doctrine
of Ubiquity.—The Emperor presses the Lutherans to appear at the Council
of Trent.—The confession called Saxonic, and that of the Duchy of
Wirtemberg, drawn up on this occasion.—The distinction between mortal
and venial Sins.—The merit of Good Works acknowledged anew.—The
Conference at Worms for reconciling Religions.—The Lutherans at
variance among themselves, however unanimously agreeing that Good
Works are not necessary to Salvation.—Melancthon's death under a
dreadful perplexity.—The Zuinglians condemned by the Lutherans in a
Synod held at Jena.—Assembly of the Lutherans at Naumburg in order to
agree about the true edition of the Confession of Augsburg.—The
uncertainty still as great as ever.—Ubiquity set up as far almost as Lutheranism extended.—New decision on the co-operation of Free-will.—The
Lutherans inconsistent with themselves, and, in order to answer Libertines
as well as weak Christians, they fall into Demipelagianism.—An account of
the Book of Concord compiled by the Lutherans, and containing all their
decisions.

1.—*Luther's Theses in order to stir up the People to take up arms.—1540, 1545.*

FORMIDABLE was the Smalkaldic league which Luther had excited in a manner
so furious, that the worst excesses were to be dreaded from it. Elated with the
power of so many confederated Princes, he had published the Theses above
mentioned. Never was any thing seen more violent.[1] He had maintained them
from the year 1540, but we learn from Sleidan that he published them anew
in 1545, that is, a year before his death. There he compared the Pope to a

251

without waiting for commands from the magistrate. And if, after he has been shut up in an enclosure, the magistrate sets him at liberty, you may continue," said he, "to pursue this savage beast, and with impunity attack those who prevented his destruction. If you fall in the engagement before the beast has received its mortal wound, you have but one thing only to repent of, that you did not bury your dagger in its breast. This is the way to deal with the Pope; all those who defend him must also be treated like a band of robbers under their captain, be they kings, be they Cæsars."[2] Sleidan, who relates a great part of these bloody Theses, durst not venture to repeat these last words, they appeared so horrible to him; but they were in Luther's Theses, and still are to be seen in the edition of his works.[3]

2.—*Herman, Archbishop of Cologne, calls the Protestants into his Diocese.—His extreme Ignorance.*

A fresh subject of feud happened at this time. Herman, Archbishop of Cologne, took it into his head to reform his diocese after the new fashion, and to that purpose had sent for Bucer and Melancthon. Of all the prelates, this was certainly the most illiterate; a man ever resigned to the will of whomsoever governed him. Whilst he gave ear to the sage counsel of the learned Gropper, he held very holy councils for the defence of the ancient faith, for the true reformation of manners. Afterwards, the Lutherans got possession of his mind, and made him fall blindly into all their sentiments. As the Landgrave was one day speaking to the Emperor about this new reformer,[4] "What will the poor man reform?" answered he, "scarcely does he understand Latin: he never said Mass but thrice in all his life. I heard him twice; he did not know so much as the beginning of it." The fact is certain; and the Landgrave, who durst not say he knew a word of Latin, replied only, "he had read good books in the German tongue, and understood religion." Understanding it, in the Landgrave's notion, was favoring the party. As the Pope and the Emperor joined together against him, the "Protestant Princes promised him their assistance, in case he were attacked on the score of religion."[5]

3.—*It is doubted among the Confederates whether Charles V should be treated as Emperor.—The victory of Charles V.—The Book of Interim.—1546.*

They soon came to open force. The more the Emperor declared that he did not take up arms on account of religion, but in order to do himself justice on certain rebels that were headed by the Elector of Saxony and the Landgrave, the more these published in their manifestoes, that this war was not entered upon but by secret instigation of the Roman Antichrist and the Council of Trent. In this manner they endeavored, conformably to Luther's Theses, to make the war they waged against the Emperor lawful:[6] yet there was a dispute amongst them how Charles V was to be treated in their public writings. The Elector, more conscientious than the rest, would not have him styled Emperor, because, "If so," said he, "they could not lawfully wage war against him." The Landgrave had none of those scruples; and, besides, who had degraded the

Emperor? Who had deprived him of the empire? Was it to become a maxim, that whosoever united himself with the Pope, resigned the title of Emperor? The thought was as ridiculous as criminal. In conclusion, to please all parties, it was resolved, without owning or denying Charles V for Emperor, that he should be treated as bearing himself for such, and by this expedient all hostilities were allowable. But the issue of the war was not favorable to the Protestants. Overthrown by the famous victory of Charles V near the Elbe (1547), the Duke of Saxony and the Landgrave taken prisoners, they knew not which way to turn themselves. The Emperor, of his own authority, proposed to them a form of doctrine called the Interim, (1548), or the Emperor's book, which he enjoined them to follow provisionally till the Council sat. In it all the errors of the Lutherans were rejected; and the marriage of such priests as had become Lutherans, with communion under both kinds where it was re-established, were tolerated only. The Emperor was blamed at Rome for undertaking to pronounce in matters of religion. Those on his side answered, he had not taken upon him to make a decision or law for the Church, but only to prescribe to the Lutherans what they might best do till the Council met. This question belongs not to my subject; it is sufficient to observe by the way, that the Interim cannot pass for an authentic act of the Church, since neither the Pope nor the bishops have ever approved of it. Some Lutherans accepted of it rather by force than otherwise; the greatest part rejected it, and the project of Charles V had but little success.

4.—The project of the Interim.—Conference of Ratisbon in 1541.

Whilst I am on the subject of this book, it will not be amiss to observe, that it had been formerly proposed at the conference of Ratisbon in 1541. Three Catholic divines, Pflugius, Bishop of Naumburg, Gropper and Eckius, by the Emperor's orders, were there to treat about the reconciliation of religions with Melancthon, Bucer, and Pistorius, three Protestants. Eckius rejected the book, and the Prelates, together with the Catholic States, did not think it fit that a body of doctrine should be proposed, without being communicated to the Pope's Legate, then at Ratisbon. Cardinal Contarenus was the man, a very learned divine, and whom even the Protestants have praised. Wherefore, the Legate having been consulted, answered, that an affair of this nature ought to be "referred to the Pope, in order to be regulated either in the general Council, that was going to be opened, or by some other proper method."[7]

5.—Articles agreed and not agreed upon in this Conference, and in what manner.

The truth is, these conferences went on nevertheless; and when the three Protestants were agreed with Pflugius and Gropper on any articles, they were called articles accorded, although Eckius all the while opposed them.[8] The Protestants desired the Emperor to authorize these articles in the meantime, while the rest were under debate. But this was opposed by the Catholics, who declared several times, they could not consent to the changing of any dogma, or rite, received in the Catholic Church. The Protestants on their side, who pressed the exception of the articles accorded, put their own explications on them, which were not agreed to, and made a list of "things omitted in the articles accorded."[9] Melancthon, who digested these remarks, wrote to the Emperor in the name of all the Protestants, that the "articles accorded" should be received, "provided they were well understood;" that is, they themselves were sensible of their being conceived in ambiguous terms, and it was nothing but an imposition to press, as they did, the reception of them. Thus all the projects of accommodation vanished into smoke; the which I am pleased with remarking occasionally, that it may not be thought strange I should speak only, as it were, by-the-by, of so famous an action as the conference of Ratisbon.

6.—Another Conference.—The finishing stroke put to the Interim.—The little Success of this Book.—1546.

Another was held in the same city, and with as little success, in 1546.[10] The Emperor, nevertheless, ordered his book to be revised, and Pflugius, Bishop of Naumburg, Michael Helding, the titular Bishop of Sidon, and Islebius, a Protestant, put the finishing stroke to it. But he did but set a new example, how bad success these imperial decisions were used to have, in matters of religion.

7.—Bucer's new Confession of Faith.

Whilst the Emperor was exerting himself to make his Interim be received in the city of Strasburg, Bucer published there a new confession of faith, in which this Church declares, that she always unchangeably retains her first confession of faith presented to Charles V at Augsburg, in 1530, and likewise receives the agreement made at Wittenberg with Luther, namely, that act which imported that even those who have not faith, and who abuse the sacrament, receive the proper substance of the body and blood of Jesus Christ.[11] In this confession of faith, Bucer excludes nothing expressly but transubstantiation, and leaves whole and entire all that can establish the real and substantial presence.

8.—Two contrary acts are received at Strasburg at the same time.

The most remarkable thing in this is, that Bucer, who in subscribing the Articles of Smalkald, at the same time, as hath appeared, had subscribed the Confession of Augsburg, still retained the Confession of Strasburg; that is, he authorized two acts which were made to destroy each other; for it may be remembered, that the Confession of Strasburg was made only to avoid the subscribing that of Augsburg, and that those of the Confession of Augsburg would never admit for brethren, those of Strasburg, nor their associates.[12] All this is now reconciled; that is, in the new Reformation it is lawful to change, but not lawful to acknowledge that you change. The Reformation, should it own this, would appear too human a work; and it is better to approve four or five contradictory acts, provided it be not acknowledged that they are so, than to own one's self wrong, especially in confessions of faith.

9.—*Bucer goes to England, where he dies, without being able to change any thing in Peter Martyr's Articles.*

This was the last action that Bucer did in Germany. During the commotions occasioned by the Interim, he found a refuge in England among the new Protestants, who gathered strength under Edward. There he died in great esteem, yet not being able to alter any thing in the Articles which Peter Martyr had established there: so that pure Zuinglianism was the religion then. But Bucer's notions will have their turn, and we shall see Peter Martyr's Articles changed under Elizabeth.

10.—*Osiander also abandons his Church of Nuremburg, and sets all Prussia in an uproar.*

The troubles, caused by the Interim, dispersed very many of the Reformers. The Protestants even were scandalized to see them thus forsake their Churches. To venture their lives for them, or for the Reformation, was what they were not accustomed to; and it has been an observation of old standing, that none of them laid down their lives for their flock; unless it were Cranmer, who yet did all he could to save his, by forswearing his religion, as long as swearing was to his purpose. The famous Osiander was one of the first that fled. On a sudden, he disappeared at Nuremburg, and left the Church which he had governed twenty-five years, and ever since the beginning of the Reformation. Prussia was the place he retreated to. Of all countries this was one of the most addicted to Lutheranism. It belonged to the Teutonic Order (1525); but the great master of it, Prince Albert of Brandenburg, conceived all at once a desire of marrying, of reforming, and making himself a hereditary sovereign. And thus did the whole country become Lutheran, and the doctor of Nuremburg soon excited there new disorders.

11.—*What sort of man Osiander was—his doctrine about Justification.*

Andrew Osiander had signalized himself among the Lutherans by a new opinion he had introduced concerning Justification.[13] He would not have it to be by the imputation of Jesus Christ's justice, as all other Protestants maintained, but by the intimate union of God's substantial justice with our souls, grounded on that saying often repeated in Isaiah and Jeremy, "The Lord is our righteousness."[14] For, as according to him, we live by God's substantial life and love, by the essential love he bears himself, so we are just by his essential justice communicated to us; to which the substance of the word incarnate dwelling in us by faith, by the word, and the sacraments, is to be added. Ever since the time of the Confession of Augsburg was in hand, he had used his utmost endeavors to prevail with the whole party to embrace this prodigy of doctrine, and, to Luther's face, defended it with great boldness. At the Assembly of Smalkald men were astonished at his rashness; yet, fearing lest new divisions might break out in the party, wherein he had distinguished himself by his great learning, they chose to bear with him. He, above all men, had the talent of diverting Luther; and Melancthon, at their return from the

Conference of Marpurg, held with the Sacramentarians, wrote to Camerarius[15] that "Osiander had made Luther and all of them exceedingly merry."

12.—*Osiander's profane spirit observed by Calvin.*

This he did by playing the droll, chiefly at table, when his wit abounded most; but in such profane jests, that I have a difficulty in repeating them. It is Calvin who informs us,[16] in a letter which he writes to Melancthon concerning this man, "That, as often as he found good wine at an entertainment, he praised it by applying it to those words which God uttered with respect to himself, 'I am that I am.' And, again: 'Here is the Son of the living God'." Calvin had been present at the banquets in which he vented these blasphemies, at which he conceived a horror. Yet they passed off without any exception being taken to them. The same Calvin[17] speaks of Osiander as of a "brutal man, a wild beast not to be tamed. As for him," said he, "the very first time I saw him, I detested his profane spirit and infamous behavior, and always looked upon him as the shame of the Protestant party." Yet he was one of the pillars of it: the Church of Nuremburg, one of the first of the sect, had placed him at the head of her pastors from the year 1522, and he is every where found at the conferences among the chiefs of the party; but Calvin is astonished "that they were able to bear with him so long, and cannot conceive, considering all his furies, how Melancthon could have lavished so much praise upon him.

13.—*Melancthon's opinion, and that of other Protestants, concerning Osiander.*

It will be thought, perchance, that Calvin used him thus harshly from a particular hatred of his own, for Osiander was the most violent enemy the Sacramentarians had, and he it was that carried the subject of the Real Presence to such extremity as to maintain that they ought to say of the Eucharist bread, "this bread is God."[18] But the Lutherans entertained no better opinion of him; and Melancthon, who often found it served his turn to praise him, as Calvin reproaches him with doing to excess, writing to his friends,[19] does nevertheless blame "his extreme arrogance, his ravings, his other excesses, and the monstrousness of his opinions." It was not Osiander's fault that he did not go to trouble England, where he hoped that the esteem in which his brother-in-law, Cranmer, was held, would give him credit; but Melancthon acquaints us[20] that persons of authority and learning had represented the danger there was of bringing into that country a man who had spread in the Church so great a chaos of new opinions. Cranmer himself gave ear to reason on this head, and listened to Calvin,[21] who spoke to him of the illusions whereby Osiander bewitched himself and others.

14.—*Osiander, puffed up with the Prince's favor, keeps within no bounds.*

He was no sooner arrived in Prussia than he set the University of Koningsberg[22] in a flame with his new doctrine of Justification. However eager always in its defence, yet he stood in fear, say my authors, "of Luther's magnanimity," and during his life, never durst write any thing on that subject.[23] The magnanimous Luther feared him no less: in general, the Reformation, void of authority, feared nothing so much as new divisions,which she knew not how to terminate; and, lest they should irritate a man whose eloquence was formidable, he was left at liberty to utter what he pleased by word of mouth. In Prussia, finding himself free from the party's yoke, and, what elated his heart, in great favor with the Prince, who had given him the first chair in his University, he gave himself free scope, and soon divided the whole country.

15.—The dispute on Ceremonies, or things indifferent.

Other disputes were enkindled at the same time in the other parts of Lutheranism. That which arose about ceremonies, or things indifferent, was carried on with a great deal of acrimony.[24] Melancthon, supported by the Academies of Leipsic and Wittenburg, where he was all-powerful, would not have them rejected (1549). It had ever been his opinion that, in the exterior worship, the less was changed the better. For which reason, during the Interim, he made himself very easy about these indifferent practices, nor did he believe, says he,[25] "that for a surplice, for some holydays, or for the order of lessons," they ought to draw a persecution on themselves. This doctrine was made criminal in him, and it was decided in the party that these indifferent things ought absolutely to be rejected, because the use made of them was contrary to the liberty of the Churches, and contained, said they, a kind of profession of Popery.

16.—Illyricus's jealousy and hidden designs against Melancthon.

But Flacius Illyricus, who started this question, had a deeper design. His aim was directed at Melancthon's ruin, whose disciple he had been, but of whom he was afterwards become so jealous as not to endure him.[26] And now particular reasons urged him on more than ever: for, whereas Melancthon endeavored then to undermine Luther's doctrine of the Real Presence, Illyricus and his friends carried it to such extremes as to maintain ubiquity. In fact, we see it decided by the greatest part of the Lutheran Churches, and the acts thereof are printed in the Book of Concord, which almost all the Lutherans in Germany have accepted. It shall be spoken of hereafter: and, to follow the order of time, I must speak at present of the Confession of Faith called Saxonic, and of that of Wirtemberg,[27] not Wittenburg in Saxony, but the capital city of the Duchy of Wirtemberg.

17.—Saxonic Confession, and that of Wirtemburg.—Why made, and by what
Authors.—1441, 1552.

They were both made much about the same time, namely, in 1551 and 1552, in order to be presented to the Council of Trent, where the victorious Charles V would have the Protestants make their appearance. The Saxonic Confession was drawn up by Melancthon, and as we learn from Sleidan,[28] by order of Maurice, the Elector, whom the Emperor had put in the place of John Frederick. All the doctors and all the pastors, solemnly convened at Leipsic, approved it with one voice; nor ought there to be any thing more authentic than a confession of faith made by so renowned a person, in order to be presented in a general council.[29] And, truly, it was received not only throughout all the territories of the House of Saxony and of many other Princes, but also by the Churches of Pomerania and that of Strasburg, as appears by the subscriptions and declarations of those Churches. Brentius was the author of the Confession of Wirtemberg, next to Melancthon the most famous man of the whole party.[30] Melancthon's Confession was called by himself the repetition of that of Augsburg. Christopher, Duke of Wirtemberg, by whose authority the Confession of Wirtemberg was published, declares likewise that he confirms, and does but repeat, the Confession of Augsburg; but, in order to repeat it, there was no necessity of making another; and this word, *repeat*, only shows they were ashamed of producing so many new confessions of faith.

18.—*Article of the Eucharist in the Saxonic Confession.*

Accordingly, to begin with the Saxonic; the article of the Eucharist was there explained in terms very different from those employed at Augsburg.[31] For, to say nothing of the long discourse of four or five pages which Melancthon substitutes in lieu of two or three lines of the tenth article of Augsburg,[32] which decided this matter; here is what was essential in it: "It is necessary," said he, "to inform mankind that the sacraments are actions instituted by God, and that things are not sacraments except in the time of their use so established; nevertheless, in the established use of this communion, Jesus Christ is truly and substantially present, truly given to those who receive the body and blood of Jesus Christ; whereby Jesus Christ testifies that he is in them, and makes them his members."

19.—*Changes which Melancthon made by the Saxonic Confession, in the Articles of that of Augsburg and Smalkald.*

Melancthon avoid saying what he had said at Augsburg, "That the body and blood are truly given with the bread and wine," and much more, what Luther had added at Smalkald, that "the bread and wine are the true body and the true blood of Jesus Christ, the which are not only given and received by pious Christians, but also by the impious." These important words, which Luther had chosen with so great care, in order to explain his doctrine, although signed by Melancthon at Smalkald, as hath appeared, were by Melancthon himself cut off from his Saxonic Confession. It seems he was no longer of opinion that the body of Jesus Christ was taken by the mouth together with the bread, nor received substantially by the impious, although he did not deny a substantial presence, in which Jesus Christ came to the faithful, not only by his virtue and spirit, but also in his own proper flesh and substance, divided, nevertheless, from bread and wine: for it seems, among the many novelties on this subject, this, too, was to show itself, and, according to the prophecy of the venerable Simeon, Jesus Christ, in the mystery, was to be "a mark set for contradictions"[33] in these latter ages, as, with respect to his divinity and incarnation, he had been in the first ages of Christianity.

20.—*Article of the Eucharist in the Wirtemberg Confession.*

In this manner was the Confession of Augsburg and Luther's doctrine repeated in the Saxonic Confession. The Confession of Wirtemberg[34] departs no less from that of Augsburg, nor from the Articles of Smalkald. It says, "that the true body and true blood are distributed in the Eucharist, and rejects those who say the bread and wine are signs of the body and blood of Jesus Christ absent." It adds, "that it is in the power of God to annihilate the substance of bread, or to change it into his body; but that God uses not this power in the Supper, and true bread remains with the true presence of the body." It manifestly establishes concomitancy, by deciding that, "although Jesus Christ be distributed whole and entire, as well in the bread as in the wine of the Eucharist, the use, nevertheless, of both parts ought to be universal." Thus it grants us two things: one, the possibility of transubstantiation, the other the certainty of concomitancy: but though it defends the reality so far as to admit concomitancy, it explains nevertheless these words, "This is my body," by those of Ezekiel, who says, "This is Jerusalem," showing the representation of that city.

21.—*The confusion man falls into when he delivers himself over to his own conceits.*

Thus there is nothing but confusion when man departs from the straight path to follow his own ideas. As the abettors of the figurative sense receive some impression from the literal one, so the abettors of the literal sense are sometimes dazzled by the deceitful subtleties of that which is figurative. But it is not our business to examine here, whether or not, by torturing the different expressions of so many confessions of faith, some violent mode may be found out to bring them to a conformity of sense. It is enough for me to point out what difficulty those had in satisfying themselves with their own confessions of faith, who had forsaken the faith of the Church.

22.—*God wills not Sin.—An article better explained in the Saxonic Confession, than it had been in that of Augsburg.*[35]

The other articles of these confessions of faith are not less remarkable than that of the Eucharist. The Saxonic Confession acknowledgers that "the will is free; that God wills not sin, nor approves, nor co-operates to it; but that the free-will of men and devils is the cause of their sin and fall." Melancthon is here to be commended for correcting Luther and correcting himself, and for speaking more clearly than he had done in the Confession of Augsburg.

23.—*The co-operation of Free-will.*

I have heretofore observed that, at Augsburg, he did not own the exercise of free-will, except in the actions of civil life, and that afterwards he extended it even to Christian actions.[36] This he begins to discover more plainly to us in the Saxonic Confession; for, after explaining the nature of free-will and the choice of the will, and that it suffices not alone for the works, which we call "supernatural," he twice repeats, that "the will after having received the Holy Ghost, remains not idle," namely, that it is not without action; which seems to give to it, as the Council of Trent likewise does, a free action under the guidance of the Holy ghost who moves it interiorly.

24.—*Melancthon's doctrine on the co-operation of Free-will.*

And what Melancthon's doctrine gives us to understand in this confession of faith, he explains in his letters more distinctly; for he proceeds even to own the human will, in supernatural works, as "a joint agent;" *agens partiale,* according to the school language;[37] as much as to say, that man acts with God, and of both there is made one total agent. Thus he explained himself at the Conference of Ratisbon in 1541, and though he well knew that this explication would be displeasing to his companions, yet he adhered to it, because, says he, the thing is true. Thus did he come back from the excesses he had learned from Luther, though Luther persisted in them to the very last. But he delivers himself more at large on this subject, in a letter written to Calvin:[38] "I had a friend," says he, "who, reasoning on predestination, equally believed these two things,—that all happens among men as Providence ordains, and that there is a contingency nevertheless:" yet he owned he was not able to reconcile these points. "For my part," proceeds he, "who hold that God is not the cause of sin, and wills not sin, I own this contingency in the infirmity of our judgment, to the end that the ignorant may confess that David fell of himself, and by his own will, into sin; and might have preserved the Holy Ghost he had within him, and that in this combat there is some action of the will to be acknowledged," which he confirms by a passage of St. Basil, who says, "Only have the will, and God will come unto you." Whereby Melancthon seemed to insinuate, not only that the will acts, but also begins; which St. Basil rejects in other places, and Melancthon does not appear to me ever to have rejected sufficiently, since we have before taken notice, how he had introduced a word into the Confession of Augsburg,[39] by which he seemed to intimate, there was not so much harm in saying that the will could begin, as that it could finish of itself the work of God.

25.—*The exercise of Free-will plainly owned by Melancthon in the operations of grace.*

Be that as it will, it is certain he owned the exercise of free-will in the operations of grace, since he so plainly owned that David could have preserved the Holy Ghost at the time he lost it, as he might have lost it at the time he preserved it: but although this was his sentiment, he durst not declare it distinctly in the Saxonic Confession;—happy for him he could insinuate it gently by these words,—"The will is not idle, nor without action." The thing was, Luther had so dreadfully thunderstruck free-will, and bequeathed to his sect such an aversion to the exercise of it, that Melancthon durst not utter, but with fear and trembling, what he believed regarding it, and even his own confessions of faith were ambiguous.

26.—*His doctrine condemned by his Brethren.*

But all his precautions could not secure him from censure. Illyricus and his followers would never forgive him this short sentence which he had placed in the Saxonic Confession,—"The will is not idle, nor without action." They condemned this expression in two synodical assemblies, together with the text of St. Basil, which, as we have seen, Melancthon made use of.

This condemnation is set down in the Book of Concord.[40] All they did to save Melancthon's honor, was not to name him, but only to condemn his expressions under the general name of new authors, or papists, or scholastics. But whoever shall consider with what care the very expressions of Melancthon were culled out for condemnation, will plainly see that he was the person aimed at, and the sincere Lutherans own as much.

27.—*Confusion of the new Sects.*

Here is, in short, the nature of these new sects. Men suffer themselves to be prejudiced against certain doctrines, of which they take up false notions. Thus did Melancthon, at first, run into extremes with Luther against free-will, and would allow it no action in works supernatural. Convinced of his error, he leans to the opposite extreme, and so far from excluding the action of free-will, he proceeds to attribute to it even the beginning of supernatural actions. When a little inclined to return to truth, and to own that free-will hath its agency in the operations of grace, he stands condemned by his own people: such is the confusion and perplexity man falls into, by casting off the salutary yoke of Church authority.

28.—*Doctrine of the Lutherans, which contradicts itself.*

But although one part of the Lutherans will not receive these terms of Melancthon, the will is not without action in works of grace, I see not how they can deny the thing, since they all confess, unanimously, that man, under grace, may reject and lose it.

This is what they have asserted in the Confession of Augsburg; what they have repeated in the Apology; what they have anew decided and inculcated in the Book of Concord,[41] so that nothing among them is more certain. Whence it is plain they acknowledge with the Council of Trent a free-will, acting under the operation of grace, so as to be able to reject it; which thing it is proper to remark, on account of some of our Calvinists, who, for want of well understanding the state of the question, make that doctrine criminal in us, which they support, nevertheless, in their brethren the Lutherans.

29.—*A considerable article of the Saxonic Confession concerning the distinction of mortal and venial sins.*[42]

There is also an article in the Saxonic Confession, so much the more deserving of notice, as it overthrows one of the foundations of the new Reformation, which will not own that the distinction between sins, mortal and venial, is grounded on the nature of sin itself. But here the divines of Saxony confess with Melancthon, that there are two sorts of sin: "one which banishes the Holy Ghost from the heart; the other, which does not banish him." In order to explain the nature of these different sins, they observe two kinds of Christians; "one who repress concupiscence; the other, who obey it. In those who combat against it," proceed they, "sin is not reigning; it is *venial*; it bereaves us not of the Holy Ghost; it subverts not the foundation, and is not against conscience." They add, "that such sort of sins are covered," that is, they are not imputed "through God's mercy." Certain it is, according to this doctrine, that the distinction of *mortal* and *venial* sins consists, not only in God's pardoning some, and not pardoning others, as is commonly said in the pretended Reformation, but that it proceeds from the nature of the thing. Now, to condemn the doctrine of imputed justice, no more than is requisite; since it is allowed for certain, notwithstanding the sins the just man falls into daily, that sin reigns not in him, but rather charity reigns in him, and consequently justice, which suffices to denominate him truly just, since a thing takes its denomination from what is prevailing therein. Whence it follows that to explain "gratuitous justification," there is no necessity of saying, we are justified by imputation, but rather, that we are truly justified by a justice which is in us, yet proceeding from the gift of God.

30.—*Merit of Works in the Confession of Wirtemberg.*

Melancthon omitted, for what reason I know not, to insert in the Saxonic Confession, what he had inserted in the Augsburg Confession and Apology concerning the merit of good works.[43] But it must not be concluded from hence, that the Lutherans had rejected this doctrine, since, at the same time, a chapter is found in the Confession of Wirtemberg, where it is said, "that good works ought necessarily to be practised, and through the gratuitous bounty of God they merit their corporal and spiritual rewards:" which, by the way, makes it appear, that the nature of merit perfectly agrees with grace.

31.—*The Conference of Worms to reconcile both Religions.—Division of the Lutherans.—1557.*

In 1557, a new assembly, by the appointment of Charles V, was held at Worms for settling religion. Pflugius, the author of the Interim, presided in it. Mr. Burnet, ever attentive to turn every thing to the advantage of the new Reformation, gives a short account of it, in which he represents the Catholics as men, "who, unable to bear down those they call heretics with open force, divide them among themselves, and engage them into heats about lesser matters." But Melancthon's own testimony, in this case, will discover the true state of the affair.[44] As soon as the Protestant doctors named for the conference were come to Worms, the ambassadors of their respective princes assembled them together to acquaint them, from the said princes, that, above all things, and before they conferred with the Catholics, they were "to agree among themselves, and, at the same time, to condemn four sorts of errors. 1. That of the Zuinglians. 2. That of Osiander about justification. 3. That proposition which affirms good works are necessary to salvation. 4. And lastly, the error of those who had received indifferent ceremonies. This last article expressly glanced at Melancthon, and it was Illyricus with his cabal that proposed it. Melancthon had been warned of his designs, and in his journey wrote to his friend Camerarius,[45] that, "at table, and over the bottle, certain preliminary articles were drawn, with the design of making him and Brentius sign them." With the last he was very much united, and represents Illyricus, or some one of that cabal, "as a fury that went from door to door to exasperate people." It was also believed in the party, that Melancthon was pretty favorable to the Zuinglians, and Brentius to Osiander. The same Melancthon appeared much inclined to the necessity of good works, and this whole enterprise visibly aimed at him and his friends. Hitherto, therefore, it was not the Catholics that labored to divide the Protestants. They were sufficiently divided of themselves; nor was it, as Mr. Burnet pretends, "about lesser matters;" since, except the question of indifferent ceremonies, all the rest, concerning the real presence, Osiander's monstrous justification, and the manner in which good works were to be judged necessary, were of the utmost consequence.

32.—*The Lutherans unanimously condemn the necessity of Good Works for Salvation.*[46]

As to the first of these points, Melancthon agreed, that the "Zuinglians deserved to be condemned as well as the Papists." To the second, that Osiander was not less worthy of censure. To the third, that from this proposition, "good works are necessary for salvation," the last word should be cut off, so that good works, in spite of the Gospel, which denounces that, without them, we have no share in the Kingdom of God, remain "necessary" it is true, but not "for salvation;" and whereas Mr. Burnet hath affirmed that the "Protestants always declared good works indispensably and absolutely necessary to salvation;" quite on the contrary, we find this equally rejected by Melancthon's enemies, and by himself,—namely, by both parties of the Protestants in Germany.

33.—*Osiander spared by the Lutherans.*

As for Osiander, Brentius did not fail to take his part, not by defending the doctrine imputed to him, but by maintaining that they had not comprehended this author's sense, though Osiander had so plainly expressed himself, that neither Melancthon nor anybody else doubted of it. It appeared, then, to the Lutherans, a very easy matter to agree all in the condemnations required by Illyricus and his friends; but Melancthon put a stop to it, who was ever apprehensive of raising new disturbances in the Reformation, which, by its great divisions, already seemed threatened with destruction.

34.—*The Division of the Lutherans break forth, which the Catholics endeavor to improve for their Salvation.*

These disputes of the Protestants soon reached the ears of the Catholics, for Illyricus and his friends raised great clamors, not only at Worms, but over all Germany. The Catholics had resolved to press, in the conference, the necessity of submitting to the Church's judgment, in order to put an end to disputes arising among Christians; and the contentions of Protestants very opportunely fell in with this design, they making it appear that they themselves, who spoke so much of the perspicuity of Scripture, and its full sufficiency to terminate all disputes, agreed so little among themselves, nor had hitherto found out the way of finishing the least debate. The weakness of the Reformation, so ready at starting difficulties, so bad at solving them, was visible to every eye. Then Illyricus and his friends, to show the Catholics they were not unprovided of means to repress others bred in the Protestant party, laid before the Catholic deputies a copy of condemnations they had drawn, but which was rejected by their companions; thus the division blazed abroad in a manner not to be concealed. The Catholics judged it no purpose to continue on these conferences, where, indeed, every thing was at a stand, and accordingly left the Illyricans to dispute with the Melancthonists, as St. Paul[47] left the Pharisees to dispute with the Sadducees, drawing all the advantage he could from their notorious dissensions.

35.—*Osiander's triumph in Prussia.—The memorable conversion of Staphylus.*

In Prussia, something vigorous, and some resolute decision, was expected against Osiander, whose insolence was no longer to be borne with. He made it openly appear how little account he made of the Augsburg Confession, of Melancthon, its author, and of the merits even of Jesus Christ, which he did not so much as mention in the justification of sinners. Some divines of Koningsberg did what they could to oppose his doctrine, and among others, Frederick Staphylus, one of the most renowned professors in divinity of that university, who, for sixteen years together at Wittenberg, had heard Luther and Melancthon;[48] but finding they gained nothing by their learned works, and Osiander's eloquence prevailed universally, they had recourse to the authority of the Church of Wittenberg, and the rest of the Protestant Churches in Germany. When, instead of distinct and vigorous condemnations, which the weak faith of the people stood in need of, they beheld nothing come from those quarters but timorous writings, from which Osiander reaped advantage, they pitied the weakness of the party thus bereft of all authority against errors. Staphylus opened his eyes, and returned to the bosom of the Catholic Church.

36.—A new form of the Lutherans in order to explain the Eucharist in the Assembly of Franfort.—1558.

The Lutherans assembled themselves at Frankfort the year after, in order to agree about a form relating to the Eucharist, as if, till then, they had done nothing. They began, according to custom, by saying, they did but repeat the Confession at Augsburg.[49] Notwithstanding, they added to it, "that Jesus Christ was given in the use of the Sacrament, truly, substantially, and in a vivifying manner; and that this Sacrament contained two things—namely, the bread and the body; and that it is an invention of the Monks unknown to all antiquity, to say, that the body is given us under the species of bread."

Strange confusion! they did nothing, said they, but repeat the Confession of Augsburg; yet this expression, condemned by them at Frankfort, namely, "this body is present under the species" is found in one of the editions of that same Confession which they pretended to repeat, and even in that edition owned at Frankfort to be so genuine, that to this day, in the rituals used by the French church of that city, we read the tenth article of the Augsburg Confession, couched in these terms—"The body and blood are received under the species of bread and wine."[50]

37.—The question of Ubiquity made Melancthon turn towards the Sacramentarians.—1559.

But the concern of most weight among the Lutherans at that time, was that of ubiquity, which Westphalus, James Andrew Smidelin, David Chythræus, and others, set up with all their might. Melancthon opposed two reasons against them, than which nothing could be more convincing: one, that this doctrine confounded the two natures of Jesus Christ, making him immense, not only according to his divinity, but his humanity likewise, and even with respect to his body; the other, that it destroyed the mystery of the Eucharist, by taking away every thing that is peculiar to it, should Jesus Christ, as man, be no other way therein present than he is in wood and stone. These two reasons made Melancthon look with horror on the doctrine of ubiquity, and the aversion he had to it made him insensibly begin to incline towards those who defended the figurative sense. He held a particular communication with them, above all, with Calvin. But certain it is, he did not find in his sentiments what he desired.

38.—The incompatibility of Melancthon's sentiments with those of Calvin.

Calvin obstinately maintained,[51] that a believer once regenerated could not lose grace; and Melancthon agreed with the Lutherans, that this doctrine was damnable and impious. Calvin could not endure the necessity of baptism, and Melancthon would never depart from it. Calvin condemned what Melancthon taught on the co-operation of free-will, and Melancthon did not believe he could recant.

It appears sufficiently they were no less at variance about predestination; and although Calvin repeated frequently that Melancthon in his heart could not help thinking as he did, yet he never could draw any thing from him to that purpose.

39.—*Whether or not Melancthon was a Calvinists with respect to the Eucharist.*

As for what concerns the Supper, Calvin boasts every where that Melancthon was of his opinion; but as he does not produce one word of Melancthon's clearly to that purpose, but, on the contrary, taxes him in all his letters and books with having never explained himself sufficiently on that subject, methinks one may reasonably doubt of what he has advanced, and what seems to me to be most probable is this, that neither of these two authors thoroughly understood the other: Melancthon being imposed upon by the expressions of a proper substance, which Calvin every where affected, as we shall see; and Calvin, drawing to his own sense the words by which Melancthon separated the bread from the body of our Lord, yet without the design of derogating thereby from the substantial presence, which he owned in the faithful communicants.

If Peucer, Melancthon's son-in-law, may be believed, his father-in-law was a downright Calvinist. Peucer became one himself, and suffered greatly afterwards for his correspondence with Beza, in order to introduce Calvinism into Saxony.[52] He took pride in following the sentiments of his father-in-law, and wrote books where he gives an account of what he had heard from him in private relating to this subject. But without impeaching Peucer's credit, it is no unlikely thing that he, in a matter they had so perplexed with equivocal expressions, might not have fully comprehended Melancthon's meaning; and for want of that, have adapted his words to his own preconceived opinions.

After all, to know what Melancthon thought one way or other, is to me of very small importance. Many Protestants in Germany, more interested in this cause than we are, have undertaken his defence; in whose behalf I shall only say, what candor and truth oblige me to, viz., that I have no where found in any of this author's writings that Jesus Christ is not received, except by faith; which, howsoever, is the true characteristic of the figurative sense. Neither do I find that he has ever said, with those that maintain it, that the unworthy do not receive the true body and true blood; but, on the contrary, it appears to me that he persisted in what was determined on this subject in the Wittenberg agreement.[53]

40.—*Melancthon dares not speak.*

What we know for certain is, that through the fear Melancthon was in of increasing the scandalous divisions of the new Reformation, which he saw was quite void of all moderation, he scarce ventured to express himself but in terms so general, that each one might find in them whatever meaning he thought fit. The Sacramentarians did not suit him; the Lutherans ran all into ubiquity. Brentius, almost the only Lutheran he had maintained a perfect union with, went over to that side; this prodigy of doctrine spread insensibly through the whole sect. He would willingly have spoken, but knew not what to say; so great was the opposition he met with to what he believed was truth.[54] "Have I the power," said he, "to unfold truth whole and entire in the country I am in, and would the court endure it?" To which he often added: "I will speak the truth when courts shall not prevent me."

It is true, it is the Sacramentarians that make him speak after this manner: but, besides that they produce his letters, which they pretend to have the originals of, one needs but read those his friends have published, to see that these discourses, which pass for his, agree perfectly with that disposition which the implacable dissensions of the new Reformation had placed him in.

His son-in-law, who relates the facts with a great deal of simplicity, affirms he was so hated by the Ubiquitarians, that one time Chythræus, one of the most zealous of them, said, "They ought to make away with Melancthon, otherwise they should find in him a perpetual obstacle to their designs." He himself, in a letter he wrote to the Elector Palatine, which Peucer makes mention of,[55] says, "That he would no longer dispute against men whose cruelties he did experience." And this was but a few months before his death. "How many times," says Peucer, "and how many sighs, hath he unfolded to me the reasons which hindered him from discovering to the world the bottom of his sentiments?" But what could constrain him in the court of Saxony, where he then was, and in the midst of Lutherans, but the court itself, and the violence of his companions?

41.—Melancthon's sad condition, and his death.

How deplorable a state never to meet with peace, or truth, as he understood it! He had left the ancient Church, which had on her side succession, and all preceding ages. The Lutheran Church, which he and Luther had founded, and which he believed the only refuge of truth, embraced ubiquity, which he abhorred. The Sacramentarian churches, which, next to the Lutheran, he believed the most pure, were full of other errors he could not endure, and which, in all his confessions of faith, he had rejected. He was respected, as appeared, by the Church of Wittenberg; but the grievous restraints he lay under, and the measures he was bound to follow, prevented his speaking all he thought; and in this state he ended his miserable life in 1560.

42.—The Zuinglians condemned by the Lutherans, and the Catholics justified by this conduct.—1560.

Illyricus and his companions triumphed upon his death; Ubiquity was established almost throughout all Lutheranism, and the Zuinglians were condemned by a Synod held at Jena, a town in Saxony:[56] till then, Melancthon had restrained them from pronouncing such a sentence. From the time it passed, nothing in all writings against the Zuinglians was spoken of, but the authority of the Church, to which all were bound to yield without further dispute. The principal party of the new Reformation, the Lutherans, began to discover that nothing but Church authority could curb men's minds and prevent divisions; and, indeed, we see Calvin[57] never ceases to reproach them for laying greater stress on the name of the Church than the very Papists did, and for going counter to the principles established by Luther. This was true, and the Lutherans, in their turn, were obliged to answer all the arguments which the Protestant party had opposed against the Catholic Church and her council. They objected against the Church, that she made herself judge in her own cause, and that the Pope, with his bishops, were at one and the same time the accused, the accusers and the judges. The Sacramentarians said as much of the Lutherans, by whom they stood condemned. The whole body of Protestants said to the Church, that their pastors ought to take their place amongst the rest, in the council going to be held, and to judge on questions of faith; otherwise, it were prejudging against them without a hearing. The Sacramentarians made the same reproach to the Lutherans, and maintained to them, that by taking on themselves the authority to condemn them without calling their pastors to the sitting, they began themselves to do that which they had called tyranny in the Church of Rome.[58] It appeared evident that they must ultimately imitate the Catholic Church, which alone knew the true method of judging questions of faith: nor did it appear less manifest, by the contradictions the Lutherans fell into upon following this method, that it did not belong to innovators, nor could subsist but in a body, which had practised it from the origin of Christianity.

43.—Assembly of the Lutherans of Naumburg to agree about the Confession of Augsburg.—1561.

It was resolved at this time to choose, among all the editions of the Augsburg Confession, that which should be deemed authentic.[59] It was a surprising thing, that a confession which regulated the faith of all the Protestants in Germany and the whole North, and had given a name to the whole party, should have been published so many ways, and with such considerable differences, at Wittenburg and elsewhere, under Luther and Melancthon's inspection, without any care taken to adjust these variations. At last, in 1561, thirty years after this confession was made, in order to silence the reproaches which were flung at Protestants, of not having as yet fixed a confession, they met at Naumburg, a city of Thuringia, and there selected an edition; but in vain, inasmuch as the other editions having been printed by public authority, they never could suppress them,[60] nor hinder one from following one, others another, as we have elsewhere mentioned.

What is still more, the assembly of Naumburg, in choosing one edition, declared expressly, it was not thence to be concluded that they disapproved of all the rest, especially that which had been made at Wittenburg in 1540, under the inspection of Luther and Melancthon, which, besides, had been publicly made use of in the Lutheran schools, and in the conferences with Catholics.

Nay, it cannot even be decided which of these editions were preferred at Naumburg. It seems most probable to have been that which is printed with the consent of almost all the princes, and stands at the beginning of the book of Concord; but even this is not certain, since we have been shown four editions of the supper-article, equally owned in the same book.[61] Again, if the merit of good works was cut off from the Confession of Augsburg, we have found it remaining in the Apology; and that even is a proof of what was originally in the Confession, since it is certain that the Apology was made on no other account than to defend and explain it.

But the dissensions of the Protestants, on the sense of the Confession of Augsburg, were so far from being terminated at the assembly of Naumburg,[62] that on the contrary, Frederic the Elector Palatine, who was one of the members of it, believed, or would seem to believe, that he found in this Confession the Zuinglian doctrine he newly had embraced; so that he adhered to the Confession of Augsburg, and, not concerning himself about Luther, still remained a Zuinglian.

44.—*Raillery of the Zuinglians.*

Thus, it seems, every thing was found in this Confession.[63] The jeering and malicious Zuinglians called it Pandora's box, whence issued forth good and evil; the apple of discord, among the goddesses; a shoe for every foot; a vast wide cloak which Satan might hide himself in, as well as Jesus Christ. These men had proverbs at their fingers' ends, and dealt them out not sparingly to ridicule the different senses that each one found in the Confession of Augsburg. Ubiquity was the only thing that could not be discovered in it; and yet this ubiquity became a dogma among the Lutherans, authentically inserted in the book of Concord.

45.—*Ubiquity established.*

Here is what we find in that part of the book which bears this title,—"An Abridgment of articles controverted among the Divines of the Confession of Augsburg."[64] In the seventh chapter, entitled—Of the Lord's Supper:—The right-hand of God is every where, and Jesus Christ is truly and effectually united to it according to his humanity." And still more expressly in the eighth chapter, entitled—Of the Person of Jesus Christ,—wherein is explained what that Majesty is, which in the Scriptures is attributed to the word "incarnate:" there we read these words,—"Jesus Christ, not only as God, but also as man, knows all things: is able to do all things; is present to all creatures." This is a strange doctrine. True it is, the Holy Soul of Jesus Christ can do all it will in the Church, since it wills nothing but what the Divinity wills who governs it. True it is, this Holy Soul knows all that regards the world present, since all therein hath a relation to mankind, whereof Jesus Christ is the redeemer and judge, and the angels themselves, who are the ministers of our salvation, are subject to his power. True it is, Jesus Christ may render himself present where he pleases, even according to his humanity, and with respect to his body and blood; but that the soul of Jesus Christ knows, or can know, all that God knows, is attributing to a creature an infinite knowledge, or wisdom, and equalling it to God himself. To make the human nature of Jesus Christ be necessarily wherever God is, is giving it an immensity not suitable to it, and manifestly abusing the personal union; for it ought to be said by the same reason, that Jesus Christ, as man, is in all times, which would be too open an extravagancy, but, nevertheless, would follow as naturally from the personal union, according to the reasoning of the Lutherans, as the presence of Jesus Christ's humanity in all places.

46.—*Another declaration about Ubiquity, under the name of a repetition of the Confession of Augsburg.*

The same doctrine of ubiquity may be seen, but with more perplexity and a wider compass of words, in a part of this same book which bears the title:[65]—"A solid, easy, and clear Repetition of some Articles of the Augsburg Confession, which have been disputed on for some time by some Divines of this Confession, and are here decided and accorded by the rule and analogy of God's word, and the brief form of our Christian doctrine." Let who will expect from such a title the clearness and brevity it promises him; for my part, I shall only observe two things on this word repetition:[66] the first, that although the doctrine of ubiquity, which is here established, be in no kind spoken of in the Augsburg Confession, this is called, nevertheless, "a repetition of some articles of the Augsburg Confession." They were afraid of making it appear that they were obliged to tack some new doctrine to it, and all the novelties they had broached were thus made to pass under the name of repetition. The second, that it hath never been the luck of Protestants to have explained themselves aright the first time. They were always forced to come to repetitions, which, when all was said, were not a whit clearer than what went before.

47.—*The design of the Lutherans in setting up Ubiquity.*

To conceal no doctrine of the Lutherans of any importance in the book of Concord, I hold myself obliged to say, that they do not place ubiquity for the foundation of Jesus Christ's Presence in the Supper: it is certain, on the contrary, that they make this Presence depend on the words of the institution only; but they set up this ubiquity to stop the mouths of the Sacramentarians, who had ventured to say, that it was impossible for God to put Jesus Christ's body in more than one place at once; which appeared to them, not only contrary to the article of God's Omnipotence, but also to the Majesty of Jesus Christ's person.

48.—*Two memorable decisions of the Lutherans, on the co-operation of Free-Will.*

We must now consider what the Lutherans say concerning the co-operation of the will with grace: so weighty a question in our controversies, that we cannot refuse it our attention.

On this the Lutherans say two things, which will afford great light towards the finishing of our contests. I am going to propose them with as much order and clearness as I am able, and shall use my utmost to ease the reader's mind, which might be wearied with the subtlety of these questions.

49.—*Doctrine of the Lutherans, that we are without action in our conversion.*

The first thing the Lutherans do[67] in order to explain the co-operation of the will with grace, is to distinguish the moment of conversion, from what ensues; and having taught, that man's co-operation hath no place in the conversion of a sinner, they add, that this co-operation ought only to be owned in the good works which we do afterwards.

I own it is hard enough to comprehend what they would be at. For the co-operation, which they exclude from the moment of conversion, is explained in certain places after such a manner, as seems to exclude nothing,[68] but "the co-operation which is made by our own natural strength and of ourselves," as St. Paul speaks. If it be so, we are agreed: but then we do not see what need there was of distinguishing between the moment of conversion, and all that followed after, since man neither operates, nor co-operates through the whole sequel, any more than in the moment of conversion, but by the grace of God. Nothing, therefore, is more ridiculous than to say with the Lutherans,[69] that in the moment of conversion man acts no more than a stone or clay, since it cannot be denied, but in the moment of conversion he begins to repent, to believe, to hope, to love by a true action, which a log or stone can nowise do. And it is plain, that a man who repents, who believes, and loves perfectly, repents, believes and loves with more force, but not in the main after another manner, than when he begins to repent, to believe, and to love: so that, in one and the other state, if the Holy Ghost operates, man co-operates with him, and subjects himself to his grace, by an act of the will.

50.—*The confusion and contradiction of the Lutheran doctrine.*

In effect, it seems that the Lutherans, in concluding for the co-operation of free-will, would exclude that only which is attributed to our own strength. "When Luther," say they, "affirms that the will is purely passive, and in nowise acts in the conversion, his intention was not to say that no new motion was excited in our souls, and no new operation therein begun; but only to give to understand, that man can do nothing of himself, or by his own natural strength."[70]

This was setting out well: but what follows is not of a piece. For after saying, what is very true, "That man's conversion is an operation and gift of the Holy Ghost, not in any of its parts only, but in the whole," they conclude very preposterously, that "the Holy Ghost acts in our understanding, our heart, and our will, as in a subject that suffers, man abiding without action, purely passive."

This bad conclusion, which they draw from a true principle, makes it plain they do not understand themselves; for, after all, what seems to be their meaning is, that man can do nothing of himself, and that grace anticipates him in all, which, I say again, is incontestable. But if it follow from this principle, that we remain without action, this consequence reaches not only the moment of conversion, as the Lutherans pretend, but extends itself also, contrary to their notions, to the whole Christian life, since we can no more preserve grace by our own strength than acquire it, and whatever state we are in, it anticipates us in every thing.

51.—*Conclusion.—If we understand one another, there remains no dispute about co-operation.*

I know not, then, what the Lutherans mean when they say, it must not be believed, that "man converted, co-operates with the Holy Ghost, as two horses concur to draw a cart;"[71] for that is a truth which no one disputes with them, since one of these horses receives not the strength he has from the other: whereas, we agree that man co-operating hath no strength which is not given him by the Holy Ghost; and that nothing is more true than what the Lutherans say in the same place,[72] viz., "When you co-operate with grace, it is not by your own natural powers, but by new powers which the Holy Ghost bestows upon you."

Thus, the least right understanding between us clears this point of all shadow of difficulty. When the Lutherans teach, that our will does not act in the beginning of conversion, they only mean to say, that God excites good motions in us, which, though in us, are not from ourselves: the thing is unquestionable, and it is what is called exciting grace. If they say, that the will, when consenting to grace, and, by this means beginning to convert itself, acts not by its own natural strength, this again is a point avowed by Catholics. If they will say, it acts not at all, but is purely passive, they do not understand themselves, and, contrary to their own principles, destroy all action and co-operation, not only in the beginning of conversion, but also through the whole course of a Christian life.

52.—*The objection of Libertines, and the difficulty of weak Christians, concerning co-operation.*

The second thing which the Lutherans teach, concerning the co-operation of the will, deserves to be observed, because it discovers to us what a labyrinth man bewilders himself in when he forsakes his guide.

The book of Concord strives to clear the following objection raised by libertines on the foundation of Lutheran doctrine.[73] "If it be true," say they, "as taught amongst you, that the will of man hath no part in the conversion of sinners, but the Holy Ghost does all therein, I have no occasion either to read or hear sermons, or frequent the Sacraments, but will wait till the Holy Ghost sends me his gifts."

This same doctrine involved the faithful in great perplexities: for, as they were taught, that as soon as ever the Holy Ghost acted in them, he alone wrought upon them in such a manner, that they had nothing at all to do; all those, who did not feel this ardent faith, within them, but rather nothing, only misery and weakness, fell into these dismal thoughts, this dangerous doubtfulness—Am I of the number of God's elect, and will God ever send me his Holy Spirit?

53.—The Lutherans' solution grounded on eight propositions, the four first containing general principles.

In answer to these doubts the libertines and weak Christians, who deferred their conversion, there was no saying to them that they resisted the Holy Ghost, whose grace interiorly solicited them to yield themselves up to him; since they were told, on the contrary, that in these first moments of a sinner's conversion, the Holy Ghost did all himself, and a man acted no more than a log of wood. Wherefore, they take another method to make sinners comprehend that it is their fault if they be not converted, and in order to that, they lay down these positions:—

"I.[74] God wills that all men be converted, and attain to eternal salvation.

II. For that end he hath commanded the Gospel to be preached in public.

III. Preaching is the means whereby God gathers together from amongst mankind a Church, the duration whereof has no end.

IV. Preaching and hearing the Gospel are the instruments of the Holy Ghost, whereby he acts effectually in us, and converts us."

Having laid down these four general positions touching the efficacy of preaching, they apply them to the conversion of a sinner, by four other more particular ones, viz.—

54.—Four other propositions in order to apply the first.

V.[75] Before ever a man is regenerated, he may read, or hear the Gospel outwardly; and in these exterior things he hath, in some manner, his free-will to assist at Church assemblies, and there to hear, or not to hear, the word of God.

VI. They add to this: that by this preaching, and by the attention given to it, God mollifies hearts; a little spark of faith is enkindled in them, whereby the promises of Jesus Christ are embraced, and the Holy Ghost, who works these good sentiments, is, by this means, sent into the hearts of men.

VII. They observe, that, although it be true that neither the preacher nor the hearer can do any thing of themselves, and that it is necessary for the Holy Ghost to act in us, to the end we may believe the word; yet neither the preacher nor the hearer ought to have any doubt of the Holy Ghost's being present by his grace, when the word is announced in its purity according to God's commandment, and men give ear to, and meditate seriously thereon.

VIII. Lastly, they conclude that, in truth, this presence and these gifts of the Holy Ghost do not always make themselves be felt, yet, nevertheless, it ought to be held for certain that the word hearkened to is the instrument of the Holy Ghost, whereby he displays his efficacy in the hearts of men."

55.—The resolution of the Lutherans grounded on the eight preceding propositions, is downright Demipelagian.

By this way, therefore, the whole difficulty, according to them, is clearly solved, as well in regard to libertines as weak Christians. In regard to libertines, because by the first, second, third, fourth, sixth, and seventh propositions, preaching, attentively given ear to, operates grace. Now, by the fifth, it is laid down that man is free to hear preaching; he is, therefore, free to give to himself that, by which grace is given him, and so libertines are content. And for weak Christians, who, although attentive to the word, know not whether they be in grace, inasmuch as they do not feel it; there is a remedy for their doubt from the eighth proposition, which teaches them that it is not lawful to doubt but the grace of the Holy Ghost, though not felt, does accompany attention to the word: so that there remains no difficulty, according to the Lutheran principles, and neither the libertine nor weak Christian have any thing to complain of; since, for their conversion, all, in short, depends on attention to the word, which itself depends on the free-will.

56.—A proof of the Lutherans' Demipelagianism.

And that it may not be doubted what attention it is they speak of, I observe they speak of attention,[76] inasmuch as it precedes the grace of the Holy Ghost: they speak of attention, applied by the free-will to hear or not to hear; they speak of attention, whereby one gives ear externally to the Gospel, whereby one assists at Church assemblies, where the virtue of the Holy Ghost displays itself, whereby an attentive ear is given to the word, which is his organ. It is this free attention to which the Lutherans annex divine grace; and they are excessive in every thing, since they will have it on one hand, when the Holy Ghost begins to move us, that we do not act at all; on the other, that this operation of the Holy Ghost, which converts us without any co-operation on our side, is attracted necessarily by an act of our will, in which the Holy Ghost has no part, and wherein our liberty acts purely by its natural strength.

57.—Semipelagianism of the Lutherans.—An example proposed by Calixtus.[77]

This is the current doctrine of the Lutherans, and the most learned of all of them, that have written in our days, has explained it by this comparison. He supposes all mankind plunged into a deep lake, on the surface of which God has provided a salutary oil to swim, which by its virtue alone will deliver all these wretches, provided they will use the natural strength that is left them to draw near to this oil, and swallow but some drops of it. This oil is the word announced by preachers. Men of themselves may apply their attention to it; but as soon as they approach by their natural strength, in order to listen thereto, of itself, without their further intermeddling, it diffuses a virtue in their hearts which heals them.

58.—The confusion of the new Sects passing from one extremity to the other.

Thus all the vain scruples, which made the Lutherans, under pretext of honoring God, at first destroy free-will, and afterwards grow fearful at least of allowing too much to it, and at last in giving to it so great power, that to its action, and the most natural exercise of it, all is annexed. This it is to walk without rule, the rule of tradition once forsaken: they think to avoid the error of Pelagians, but winding about, they return to it another way, and the compass they take brings them back to Demipelagianism.

59.—The Calvinists come into the Demipelagianism of the Lutherans.

This Demipelagianism of the Lutherans, by little and little, spreads even to Calvinism, from the inclination that party hath of uniting itself with the Lutherans; in whose favor they have begun to say already, that Demipelagianism does not damn, that is, there is no harm in attributing to free-will the beginning of salvation.[78]

60.—A difficulty in the book of Concord, concerning the certainty of Salvation.

I find, moreover, another thing in the book of Concord,[79] which, were it not well understood, might cause a great confusion in the Lutheran doctrine. It is there said, that the faithful, in the midst of their weaknesses and combats, "ought by no means to doubt either the justice which is imputed to them by faith, or of their eternal salvation." Whereby it might seem that Lutherans admit the certainty of their salvation as well as Calvinists. But this would be too visible a contradiction in their doctrine, since, to believe the certainty of salvation in every one of the faithful, as the Calvinists believe, they ought also to believe, with them, the inamissibility of justice, which, as hath been seen, the Lutheran doctrine expressly rejects.

61.—A solution from the doctrine of Doctor John Andrew Gerard.

To adjust this contrariety, the Lutheran Doctors answer two things: one, that by the doubt of salvation, which they exclude from the faithful soul, they understood nothing but the anxiety, agitation, and trouble, which we exclude as well as they;[80] the other, that the certainty they admit in all the just, is not an absolute certainty, but conditional, and supposes that the faithful soul does not depart from God by voluntary wickedness. The matter is thus explained by Doctor John Andrew Gerard, who has published lately an entire body of controversy; the meaning of which is, that, in the Lutheran doctrine, the believer may rest fully assured that God on his side will never be wanting to him, if he be not first wanting to God—a thing not to be doubted of. To give the just more certainty, is too evidently contradicting that doctrine which teaches us that, be we never so just, we may fall from justice, and lose the spirit of adoption; a point as little questioned by Lutherans as Catholics.

62.—A brief account of the book of Concord.

Since the book of Concord has been compiled, I take it the Lutherans in body have never made any new decision of faith. The parts of which this book is composed are from different authors and of different dates; and the Lutherans' design was to give us in this collection what is most authentic amongst them. The book came out in 1579, after the famous assemblies held at Torg and Berg, in 1576 and 1577. This last place, if I am not mistaken, was a monastery near Magdeburg. I shall not relate in what manner this book was subscribed in Germany, nor the tricks and force, which, as is reported, were put on those who received it, nor the oppositions of some princes and cities who refused to sign it. Hospinian[81] has written a long history of it, which appears well enough grounded as to the chief of its facts. Let the Lutherans, who are concerned therein, contradict it. The particular decisions, which relate to the Supper and Ubiquity, were made near the time of Melancthon's death, viz., about the years 1558, 1559, 1560, and 1561.

63.—The troubles in France begin.—Confession of Faith drawn by Calvin.

These years are famous amongst us for the beginnings of our disturbances in France. In the fear 1559, our pretended Reformists drew up a confession of faith, which they presented to Charles IX in 1561, at the Conference of Poissy.[82] This was one of Calvin's productions, whom I have often already spoken of; and the reflections I must make on this confession of faith, oblige me to set forth more thoroughly the conduct and doctrine of this its author.

Notes

[1] Sleid. l. i. n. 25.
[2] Sleid. lib. xvi. p. 261.
[3] T. i. Wit. p. 407.
[4] Sleid lib. xvii. p. 276.
[5] Epist. Wit. Theod. inter. Ep. Cal. p.82.
[6] Sleid. lib. xvii. p. 289, 295, &c. Ibid. p. 297.
[7] Sleid. lib. xiv. Act. Coll. Ratisb. Argent. 1542, p. 199. Ibid. 132. Mel. lib. i. Ep. 24, 25. Act. Ratisb. Ibid. 136.
[8] Ibid. 153. Sleid. Ibid. 157.
[9] Act. Ratisb. Resp. Princ. 78. Annotata. aut omisssa in artic. Concil. 82. Lib. Ep. 29. ad Car. V.
[10] Sleid. lib. xx. p. 344.
[11] Hosp. An. 1548. p. 204.
[12] Sup. lib. iv. Sup. lib. iii.
[13] Chyt. lib. xvii. Saxon. tit. Osiandrica. p. 444.
[14] Isa. xxiii. 6, 26, 33. Jer. iii. 6.
[15] Lib. iv. Ep. 88.
[16] Cal. Ep. ad Mel. 146.
[17] Ibid. 146.
[18] S. l. ii. n. 3.
[19] Lib. ii. Ep. 240, 259, 477, &c.
[20] Ibid.
[21] Calv. Ep. ad Cranm. Col. 134.
[22] Acad. Regiomontana.
[23] Chytr. lib. xvii. p. 445.
[24] Sleid. lib. xxi. p. 365. xxii. p. 378.
[25] Lib. i. Ep. 16. ad Phil. cant. An. 1525. Lib. i. Ep. 70. Lib. ii. Ep. 36. Concord. p. 514, 789.
[26] Sleid. Ante.
[27] Synt. Gen. Part ii. p. 48, 98.
[28] Lib. xxii.
[29] Synt. Gen. Part ii. p. 94. et seq.
[30] Ibid.
[31] Cap. de Cœna.
[32] Synt. Gen. Part. ii. p. 72.

[33] Luke ii. 34. Positus in signum, cui contradicetur.

[34] Conf. Wirt. C. de Euch. Ibid. p. 115.

[35] Conf. Wirt. C. de Euch. p. 53.

[36] Cap. de rem. pecc. de lib. arb. etc. Synt. Gen. part ii. p. 54, 60, 61, etc.

[37] Demipelagian, lib. iv. Ep. 240.

[38] Ep. Mel. inter. Cal. Ep. p. 384.

[39] Conf. Aug. art. xviii. S. l. iii. n. 191. p. 20.

[40] Page 5, 82, 680.

[41] Ibid. p. 675, etc.

[42] Page 75.

[43] Conf. Wirt. c. de bonis operib. Ibid. p. 106.

[44] Mel. lib. i. Ep. 70. Burn. part ii. lib. ii. p. 355. Lib. i. Ep. 70. ejusd. Ep. ad Albert. Hardenb. et ad Bulling. apud Hospin. An. 1557, 250.

[45] Lib. iv. 868, et seq.

[46] Loc. sup. cit. S. lib. vii. n. 108.

[47] Acts xxiii. 6.

[48] Chyt. in Sax. lib. xvii. Tit. Osiand. p. 444, et seq. Ibid. 448.

[49] Hosp. f. 264.

[50] Sous les espèces du pain et du vin.

[51] Lib. i. Ep. 70.

[52] Peuc. narr. hist. de sent. Mel. It. hist. carcer. &c.

[53] S. lib. iv. n. 23.

[54] Hosp. ad An. 1557. pp. 249, 250.

[55] Peuc. Hist. car. Ep. ad. Pal. ap. Hosp. 1559. 260. Peuc. Aulicus.

[56] Hosp. 1560. p. 269. 2. Def. Cont. Westph.

[57] Cal. Ep. p. 324, ad Ill. Germ. Prin. 2. Defens. cont. West. opusc. 286. Hosp. An. 1560. p. 269, et seq.

[58] Hosp. An. 1560. pp. 270, 871.

[59] Act. conv. Naum. ap. Hosp. 1561, p. 280, et seq.

[60] S. l. iii.

[61] Ibid.

[62] Hosp. An. 1561. p. 281.

[63] Ibid.

[64] Lib. Concor. p. 600.

[65] Solida. plana. &c. Conc. p. 628.

[66] C. vii. de Cœna. p. 752, et seq. viii. de pers. Ch. p. 761, et seq. p. 782, et seq.

[67] Con. pp. 582, 673, 680, 681, 682.

[68] Pp. 656, 662, 668, 674, 678, 680, et seq.

[69] Con. p. 662.

[70] Ibid. p. 680.

[71] Ibid. p. 674.

[72] Con. p. 674.

[73] Ibid. p. 669.

[74] Con. p. 669, et seq.

[75] Ibid.

[76] Con. p. 671.

[77] Calixt. judic. n. 32, 33, 34.

[78] Jur. Syst. de l'Egl. lib. ii. ch. iii. pp. 249, 253.

[79] Con. p. 585.

[80] Con Cath. 1679, Lib. ii. Part iii. Art. 22. c. 2. Thesi. iii. n. 2, 3, 4, and Art. xxiii. c. 5. Thesi. unic. n. 6. pp. 1426 et 1499.

[81] Hosp. Concord. discors. imp. 1607.

[82] Bez. Hist. Ecc. l. iv. p. 520.

Book IX

[In the Year 1561, Calvin's Doctrine and Character.]

Brief summary.—Protestants begin to appear in France.—Calvin is their head.—His notions concerning Justification, wherein he reasons more consequently than the Lutherans; but, grounding himself upon false principles, falls into more manifest difficulties.—Three absurdities by him added to the Lutheran doctrine.—The certainty of salvation, inamissibility of justice.—Infant justification independently of Baptism.—Contradictions on this third point.—In respect to the Eucharist, he equally condemns Luther and Zuinglius, and aims at a medium between both.—He proves the necessity of admitting the Real Presence, beyond what he does in fact admit.—Strong expressions for maintaining it.—Other expressions which destroy it.—The pre-eminence of Catholic doctrine.—Those who impugn it are forced to speak our language and assume our principles.—Three different confessions of the Calvinists to satisfy three different sorts of people, the Lutherans, the Zuinglians, and themselves.—Calvin's pride and passion.—His genius compared with that of Luther.—The reason why he did not appear at the Conference of Poissy.—There Beza presents the Protestants' Confession of Faith: they tack to it a new and long explication of their doctrine about the Eucharist.—The Catholics express themselves intelligibly and in few words.—What happened with relation to the Augsburg Confession.—Calvin's sentiments.

1.—Calvin's genius.—He subtilizes more than Luther.

CALVIN's genius possibly might not have been so well adapted as Luther's was to excite people and inflame their minds: but after these commotions were once set on foot, he raised himself in many countries, in France especially, above even Luther himself, and became the head of a party, which yields but little to that of Luther.

By the penetration of his wit, and the boldness of his decisions, he refined upon, and outstript all his contemporary builders of new churches, and new-reformed the but new Reformation.

2.—Two capital points of the Reformation.—Calvin's refinements on both of them.

The two points they laid the main stresses upon, were Justification and the Eucharist.

As for justification, Calvin looking upon it as the common foundation of Protestancy, adhered to it at least equally with Luther, but grafted on it three important articles.

3.—*Three things added by Calvin to imputed justice.*—*First, the certainty of salvation.*

In the first place, that certainty which Luther owned for justification only, was by Calvin extended to eternal salvation; that is to say, whereas Luther required no more of the faithful than to believe with an infallible certainty that they were justified; Calvin, besides this certainty of justification, required the like of their eternal predestination: insomuch that a perfect Calvinist can no more doubt of his being saved, than a perfect Lutheran of his being justified.[1]

4.—*A memorable Confession of Faith made by Frederick III, Elector Palatine.*

So that, were a Calvinist to make his particular confession of faith, he would put in this article," I am assured of my salvation." We have an example of it. In the Collection of Geneva stands the confession of Prince Frederic III, Count Palatine, and Elector of the Empire. This Prince explaining his creed, after setting forth how he believes in the Father, the Son, and the Holy Ghost, when he comes to explain how he believes the Catholic Church, says, "That he believes that God never ceases gathering it together, by his word and Holy Ghost out of the mass of all mankind; and that he believes he is of that number, and ever shall be a living member of it."[2] He adds, he believes "That God being appeased by the satisfaction of Jesus Christ will not remember any of his sins, nor all the wickedness with which I shall," says he, "go on combatting through the whole course of my life; but that he will gratuitously give me the justice of Jesus Christ, insomuch that *I have no reason to apprehend the judgments of God.* Lastly, I know most certainly," continues he, "that I shall be saved, and shall appear with a cheerful countenance before the tribunal of Jesus Christ." There spoke a true Calvinist, and these are the true sentiments inspired by Calvin's doctrine, which this Prince had embraced.

5.—*The second Dogma by Calvin added to imputed justice, viz., That it never can be lost.*

Thence followed a second dogma, that whereas Luther allowed that a justified believer might fall from grace, as we have observed in the Augsburg Confession, Calvin maintains, on the contrary, that grace received can never be lost: so that, whoever is justified and receives the Holy Ghost is justified, and receives the Holy Ghost forever. For which reason the aforesaid Palatine placed amongst the articles of faith, that "he was a living and perpetual member of the Church." This is the dogma called the inamissibility of justice; namely, that doctrine by which it is believed that justice once received never can be lost. This word hath such a sanction from its universal use on this subject, that to avoid multiplying words we must accustom our ears to it.

6.—The third Dogma of Calvin: viz. That Baptism is not necessary to salvation.

There was also a third dogma, which Calvin established as a corollary from imputed justice, viz., that baptism could not be necessary to salvation, as the Lutherans maintain.

7.—Calvin's reasons drawn from Luther's principles; and first with respect to the certainty of Salvation.

Calvin was of opinion that the Lutherans could not reject these tenets, without destroying their own principles. They require of the believer to be absolutely assured of his justification, as soon as he asks it, and to trust in the divine goodness, because, according to them, neither his prayer nor trust can admit of the least doubt. Now, prayer and trust regard salvation no less than justification and forgiveness of sins; for we pray for our salvation, and hope to obtain it as much, as we pray for the forgiveness of sins, and hope to obtain it: therefore we are as much assured of the one as of the other.

8.—With respect to the inamissibility of justice.

If, then, we believe, that we cannot miss of salvation, we must also believe we cannot fall from grace, and must reject the Lutherans who teach the contrary.

9.—Against the necessity of Baptism.

Again, if we are justified by faith alone, Baptism is neither necessary in fact nor desire. For which reason Calvin will not admit that it works in us forgiveness of sins, or infusion of grace, but is a seal only, and token, that we have received them.

10.—The consequence from this Doctrine, that the Children of the Faithful are born in Grace.

It is certain, that whosoever says these things ought also to say that infants enjoy grace independently of baptism. Nor did Calvin make any difficulty of owning it. This made him broach that novelty, viz., that the children of the faithful were born in the Covenant, that is, in that sanctity, which baptism did no more than seal in them; an unheard-of doctrine in the Church, but necessary for Calvin, in order to support his principles.

11.—A passage by which Calvin upholds this new Dogma.

The foundation of this doctrine, according to him, is in that promise made to Abraham, I will be "thy God, and the God of thy seed after thee." Calvin maintained[3] that the new alliance, no less efficacious than the old, ought, for this reason, to pass like that from father to son, and be transmitted the same way; whence he concluded that, the substance of baptism, that is, its grace and covenant, "appertaining to infants, the sign of it could not be refused them; to wit, the Sacrament of baptism;" a doctrine by him held so certain, that he inserted it into his Catechism in the same terms I have now worded it, and in full as strong, into the form of administering baptism.

12.—Why Calvin is looked upon as the Author of the three precedent Dogmas.

When I name Calvin as the author of these three tenets, I do not mean to say he was the first that ever taught them; for the Anabaptists, and others, too, had maintained them before, either in the whole, or in part; but I only say he gave them a new turn, and showed better than any one else the conformity they have with imputed justice.

13.—Supposing these principles, Calvin reasoned better than Luther, but went further astray.

For my part, I cannot help thinking that, in these three articles, Calvin argued more consequently than Luther; but withal, run himself into greater difficulties, as must necessarily happen to those who reason on false principles.

14.—Difficulties attending the certainty of Salvation.

If, in Luther's doctrine, a great difficulty result from man's being assured of his justification, there is a much greater one, and which exposes human weakness to a more dangerous temptation, in being assured of his Salvation.

15.—Difficulties attending Calvin's inamissibility of justice.

Nay, by saying the Holy Ghost and justice can no more be lost than faith, you oblige the faithful, once justified, and persuaded of their justification, to believe, that no crime, be it ever so great, can cause them to fall from this grace.

In fact, Calvin maintained,[4] that, "upon losing the fear of God, faith, which justifies us, is not lost." The terms he made use of were indeed extraordinary: for he said, faith "was overwhelmed, buried, smothered; that the possession of it was lost, that is to say, the feeling and knowledge of it." But after all this he added, "it was not extinct."

An uncommon subtlety is requisite, to reconcile all these words of Calvin; but the truth is, willing as he was to maintain his tenet, he could not but allow something to that horror in man, of owning justifying faith in a soul that has lost the fear of God, and fallen into the worst of crimes.

16.—Difficulty of that doctrine which teaches that Children are born in Grace.

If to these three points you join also that doctrine which teaches that the children of the faithful bring grace with them into the world at their birth, what a horror must this raise! it following necessarily from thence, that the whole posterity of every true believer is predestined! The demonstration is obvious, according to Calvin's principles. Whosoever is born of a believer, is born in the covenant, and consequently, in grace; whosoever has once had grace, can never lose it; if he has it not only for himself, but also necessarily transmits it to his whole posterity, we have then grace extended to infinite generations. If so much as one true believer be found in a whole lineage, all the descendants of this person are predestinated. If so much as one be found to die a reprobate, it must be concluded that all his ancestors were damned.

17.—*Luther not less to be condemned for establishing these principles, than Calvin for drawing these consequences.*

But the horrid consequences of Calvin's doctrine condemn no less the Lutherans than the Calvinists; and if these last are not to be excused for running themselves into such dreadful straits, the former are not less blameworthy for laying down the principles, whence such consequences so clearly follow.

18.—*Whether these three Dogmas are to be found in the Confession of Faith.*

Notwithstanding that the Calvinists have embraced these three dogmas, as a groundwork of the Reformation, the respect they have for the Lutherans, if I am not mistaken, has been the cause that, in their confessions of faith,[5] they rather insinuated than expressly established the two first tenets, namely, the certainty of salvation, and the inamissibility of justice. An authentic declaration of them was no where made, properly speaking, till in the Synod of Dort; it shall appear in its own place. As for the dogma, which owns, in the children of the faithful, grace inseparable from their birth, we find it in the Catechism which I have quoted verbatim, and in the form of administering baptism.

19.—*Two Dogmas of the Calvinists relating to Children, little conformable to their principles.*

However, I will not aver that Calvin and the Calvinists are very steadfast in this last tenet. For although they say on the one hand, that the children of the faithful are born in the covenant, and the seal of grace, which is baptism, is not due to them, but because the thing itself, namely, grace and regeneration, is acquired to them by their being happily born of faithful parents; it appears on the other hand, they will not allow that the children of the faithful are always regenerated when they receive baptism, and this for two reasons: the first, because, according to their maxims, the seal of baptism hath not its effect with regard to the predestinated; the second, because the seal of baptism works not always a present effect, even with regard to the predestinated, since such a person may have been baptized in his infancy who was not regenerated till old age.

20.—*Agreement with those of Geneva.—1554.*

These two doctrinal points are taught by Calvin in several places,[6] but particularly in the agreement he made in 1554, between the Church of Geneva and that of Zurich. This agreement contains the doctrine of both these churches; and being received by both, it has the full authority of a confession of faith, insomuch that the two aforesaid points of doctrine being there expressly taught, they may be reckoned among the articles of faith of the Calvinistic Church.

21.—Contradictions in the Calvinist doctrine.

It is then plain, this Church teaches two things that are contradictory. The first, that the children of the faithful are certainly born in the covenant and in grace, which implies a necessary obligation of giving them baptism; the second, that it is not certain they are born in the covenant or in grace, since no one knows whether he be of the number of the predestinated.

22.—Another contradiction.

There is besides a great inconsistency in saying, on the one side, that Baptism, of itself, is a certain sign of grace, and on the other, that many of those who receive it without putting any obstacle on their part to the grace it offers them, (as in the case of infants,) yet receive from it no effect. But leaving to Calvinists the trouble of reconciling their own jarring tenets, I rest satisfied with relating what I find in their confessions of faith.

23.—Calvin's refinement on the other point of the Reformation, which is that of the Eucharist.

Hitherto Calvin soared above the Lutherans, but fell withal much lower than they had done. On the subject of the Eucharist, he not only raised himself above them, but also, above the Zuinglians, and, by the same sentence, condemned both parties, which, for so long a time, had divided the Reformation.

24.—Calvin's Treatise in order to show that, after fifteen years disputing, the Lutherans and Zuinglians had not understood one another.

They had disputed for fifteen years successively on the article of the Real Presence without ever being able to agree, whatever could be done to reconcile them, when Calvin,[7] then but young, made himself umpire, and decided that they had not understood each other, and that the heads of both parties were in the wrong; Luther, for too much pressing the corporeal Presence: Zuinglius and Œcolampadius, for not having sufficiently expressed that the thing itself, that is, the Body and Blood, were joined in the sign; a certain Presence of Jesus Christ in the Supper, which they had not sufficiently comprehended, being to be acknowledged.

25.—Calvin, already know by his Institutions, makes himself more considerable by his Treatise on the Supper.

This work of Calvin was printed in French in 1540, and afterwards translated into Latin by the author himself. He had already gained a great reputation by his Institutions, which he published, for the first time, in 1534, and which after that he made frequent editions of, with considerable additions, being extremely particular in pleasing himself, as he says in his prefaces. But men's eyes were more turned upon him, when they saw one, so little advanced in age, undertake to condemn the Chiefs of both parties of the Reformation, and the whole world was big with expectation of the novelty he was going to produce.

26.—Calvin's doctrine about the Eucharist almost forgotten by his followers.

This is, indeed, one of the most memorable points of the new Reformation, and deserves the more to be considered, the more it seems forgotten by the Calvinists now-a-days, although it makes one of the most essential parts of their confession of faith.

27.—Calvin is not content with receiving a sign in the Supper.

If Calvin had only said, that the signs of the Eucharist are not empty, or that the union we there have with Jesus Christ is effective and real, and not imaginary, this would be nothing: we have seen that Zuinglius and Œcolampadius, whom Calvin was not quite satisfied with, had said altogether as much as that in their writings. The graces we receive by the Eucharist, and the merits of Jesus Christ applied to us therein, suffice to make us understand, that, in this Sacrament, the signs are not empty, and none ever hath denied but the fruit we gather from it is very real.

28.—Not even an efficacious sign.

The difficulty then lay, not in discovering to us how grace, untied to the sacrament, became an efficacious sign, and full of virtue, but in showing how the Body and Blood were effectually communicated to us in this Sacrament: for this was the thing peculiar to this Sacrament, and what all Christians were accustomed to look for in it, by virtue of the words of the institution.

29.—Nor the virtue and merit of Jesus Christ.

To say that, together with the figure, the virtue and merit of Jesus Christ were in it received by faith, was what had been so fully said by Zuinglius and Œcolampadius, that Calvin could have found nothing wanting in their doctrine, had he not required something more than this.

30.—Calvin's doctrine partakes something of that of Bucer and the articles of Wittenberg.

Bucer, whom he acknowledged, in some measure, for his master, by confessing, as he had done at the Wittenberg agreement, a Substantial Presence common to all communicants, worthy and unworthy, thereby established a Real Presence independent of faith, and had endeavored to come up to the idea of reality, with which the words of our Saviour naturally fill the mind.

But Calvin thought he said too much,[8] and although he approved of producing to the Lutherans the articles of Wittenberg, in order to show that the quarrel relating to the Eucharist was concluded by them, yet he did not, in his heart, abide by this decision. Wherefore, he borrowed something from Bucer and this agreement, and modelling it after his own fashion, endeavored to strike out a new system peculiar to himself.

31.—*The state of the question resumed.*—*The sentiments of the Catholics on these words, "This is my Body."*

To understand the principle of it, it will be necessary to trace back in a few words the state of the question, and not fear repeating something of what has been already said on this subject. The matter in question was to know the sense of these words, "This is my Body, this is my Blood." Catholics maintained, the design of our Saviour was thereby to give us his Body and Blood to eat, as, in the old law, the flesh of the victims, sacrificed for the people, was given to them.

As this manducation was to the ancients a sign that the victim was theirs, and that they partook of the sacrifice; so the Body and Blood of our Saviour, sacrificed for us, being given us to take by the mouth with the Sacrament, are to us a sign that they are ours, and that it was for us the Son of God made a sacrifice of them on the cross.

To the end that this pledge of the love of Jesus Christ might be certain and efficacious, it was requisite we should not only have the merits, the spirit, and the virtue, but also the proper substance of the sacrificed victim, and that it should be as truly given us to eat, as the flesh of the victims had been given in the Jewish dispensation.

Thus were these words understood, "This is my Body given for you, this is my Blood shed for you,"[9] viz., This is as truly my Body, as it is true this Body was given for you; and as truly my Blood, as it is true this Blood was shed for you. By the same reason, it was understood that the substance of this flesh and blood was given to us no where but in the Eucharist, since Jesus Christ said no where else, "This is my Body, this is my Blood."

Now, we receive Jesus Christ many ways through the whole course of our lives, by his grace, by his illuminations, by his Holy Spirit, by his Omnipotent virtue; but this singular manner of receiving him, in the proper and true substance of his Body and Blood, was peculiar to the Eucharist.

Thus was the Eucharist looked upon as a new miracle, which confirmed to us all the others which God hath wrought for our salvation. A human body, whole and entire, given in so many places, to so many people, under the species of bread, was enough to startle every mind, and we have already seen, that the Fathers made use of the most surprising effects of the Divine Omnipotence, to explain this by.

32.—What Faith does in this mystery.—The sentiment of Catholics concerning these words, "Do this in remembrance of me."

Little would have availed so great a miracle wrought in our behalf, had not God afforded us the means of reaping advantage from it, and this we could not hope for, but by faith.

This mystery was, nevertheless, like all the rest, independent of faith. Believe or not believe it, Jesus Christ took flesh, Jesus Christ died, and offered himself a sacrifice for us; and by the same reason, whether we believe it or not, Jesus Christ does give us the substance of his Body to be eaten in the Eucharist; for it was requisite he should, by that, confirm to us that it was for us he took it, and for us he sacrificed it: the tokens of the divine love, in themselves are independent of our faith; our faith is only requisite to receive the benefit of them.

At the same time that we receive this precious earnest, certifying us that Jesus Christ sacrificed is wholly ours, we must apply our minds to this inestimable testimony of the divine love. And as the ancients eating the sacrificed victim, were to eat it as sacrificed, and remember the oblation, which had been made to God, in sacrifice for them; those likewise who, at the holy table, receive the substance of the body and blood of the lamb immaculate, must receive it as sacrificed, and call to mind that the Son of God had made a sacrifice of it to his Father, for the salvation, not only of the whole world in general, but also of each one of the faithful in particular; for which reason, when he said, "This is my body, this is my blood!"[10] he subjoined immediately after, "This do in remembrance of me;" that is, as the sequel makes appear, in remembrance of me sacrificed for you, and of that immense charity which made me lay down my life for your redemption, comformably to the saying of St. Paul, "ye shall show the Lord's death until he come."[11]

We must therefore be very careful not to receive only the sacred body of our Saviour into our bodies; we must also unite ourselves to it in mind, and remember that he gives us his body, to the end that we may have a certain pledge that this sacred victim is wholly ours. But whilst we stir up this pious reflection in our minds, we ought to enter into the sentiments of an affectionate acknowledgment to our Saviour; and this is the only means of perfectly enjoying this inestimable pledge of our salvation.

33.—In what manner the possessing of Christ's body is spiritual and permanent.

And although the actual reception of this body and blood be not allowed us but in certain moments, namely, in communion, our thankfulness is not confined to so short a time; and the having received this sacred pledge at certain moments, is enough to perpetuate the spiritual enjoyment of so great a good through all the moments of our lives. For though the actual reception of the body and blood be but momentary, yet the right we have to receive it is perpetual; like to that sacred right one has over another by the bond of marriage. Thus the mind and body unite themselves to enjoy their Saviour, and the adorable substance of his body and blood; but as the union of bodies is the foundation, that of minds is the perfection of so great a work. Whoever, therefore, does not unite himself in mind to Jesus Christ, whose sacred body he receives, enjoys not as he ought so great a gift: like to those brutal and treacherous spouses who unite bodies without uniting hearts.

34.—*The body and mind must be united to Jesus Christ.*

Jesus Christ wishes to find in us that love with which he abounds at his approach. When he finds it not, the union of bodies is not less real; but, instead of being fruitful, it is odious and insulting to the Son of God. Those who draw near to his body without this lively faith are "the crowd that press him;" those that have this faith are the sick woman "that touches him."[12] All touch him, rigorously speaking; but those who touch him without faith, press and importune him: those who, not content with touching him, look upon this touch of his flesh as an earnest of that virtue which goes out of him unto those who love him, touch him truly, because they touch alike his heart and body.

This it is which makes the difference between those who communicate, discerning, or not discerning, the body of the Lord; receiving, with the body and blood, the grace which accompanies them naturally, or rendering themselves guilty of the sacrilegious attempt to profane them. By this means, Jesus Christ exercises on all that almightiness given to him in heaven and on earth, applying to himself, to some as a Saviour, to others as a rigorous judge.

35.—*The precise state of the question laid down from the precedent doctrine.*

This is what was necessary to be re-considered concerning the mystery of the Eucharist, in order to understand what I have now to say; and it is plain, the state of the question is, to know, on the one hand, whether the gift which Jesus Christ bestows upon us in the Eucharist of his body and blood be a mystery, like the rest, independent of faith in its substance, and only requiring faith to profit by it; or, whether the whole mystery consists in the union we have with Jesus Christ by faith alone, without any thing else intervening on his part but spiritual promises, figured by the Sacrament, and announced by the word. By the first of these sentiments the real and substantial presence is established; by the second, it is denied that Jesus Christ is no way united to us, except in figure in the Sacrament, and in spirit by faith.

36.—*Calvin seeks to reconcile Luther and Zuinglius.*

We have seen that Luther, whatever design he might have to reject the Substantial Presence, had from the words of our Saviour so strong an impression of it, that he never could give it up. We have seen that Zuinglius and Œcolampadius, disheartened at the impenetrable loftiness of a mystery so far raised above our senses, could never enter into it. Calvin, urged on the one side with the impression of reality, and on the other with the difficulties which thwart our senses, seeks a middle way, difficult enough to make agree in all its parts.

37.—*How strongly Calvin speaks of the reality.*

In the first place he admits,[13] that we really partake of the true body and blood of Jesus Christ; and this he expressed with such energy, that the Lutherans almost believed he sided with them: for he repeats a hundred and a hundred times, that "Truth must be given us, together with the signs, that *under these signs* we truly receive the body and blood of Jesus Christ; that the flesh of Jesus Christ is *distributed* in the Sacrament; that it penetrates us; that we are partakers, not only of the spirit of Jesus Christ, but also of his flesh; that we have the proper substance, and are made partakers of it: that Jesus Christ unites himself to us whole and entire, and for that end unites himself to us in body and mind; that we must not doubt but we receive his proper body; and if there be one in the world that confesses this truth sincerely, he is the man."

38.—*One must be united to the body of Jesus Christ more than by virtue and thought.*

He not only acknowledges in the Supper, "The virtue of the body and blood, but will have the substance joined to it;" and declares,[14] when he speaks of the manner of receiving Jesus Christ in the Supper, he means not to speak of the parts you there have: "In his merits, in his virtue, in his efficacy, in the fruit of his death, in his power." Calvin rejects all these ideas and complains of the Lutherans, who, says he, reproaching him that he gave nothing to the faithful but a share in the merits of Jesus Christ, "darken the communion which he requires we should have with him." He carries his thought so far, that he excludes even as insufficient all the union that may be had with Jesus Christ, not only by the imagination, but also by the thought, or by the sole apprehension of the mind. "We are," says he, "united to Jesus Christ, not by fancy and imagination, or by thought, or the sole apprehension of the mind, but really, and in effect, by a true and substantial union."

39.—*A new effect of Faith, according to Calvin.*

Yet he still says we are united to him only by faith, which but little agrees with his other expressions; but the thing is, from a notion as odd as it is novel, he will not have that which is united to us by faith, be united to us barely by thought; as if faith were any thing else than a thought or an act of our minds, divine indeed and supernatural, which the Heavenly Father alone can inspire, but still a thought.

40.—*Calvin requires the proper substance.*

There is no knowing what all these expressions of Calvin mean,[15] if they do not signify that the flesh of Jesus Christ is in us, not only by its virtue, but in itself, and by its proper substance; nor are these strong expressions only to be found in Calvin's books, but also in his Catechisms, and the confession of faith which he gave to his disciples, which shows how literally they are to be understood.

41.—*He will have us receive the body and blood of Jesus Christ otherwise than the ancient Hebrews could do it.*

Zuinglius and Œcolampadius had often objected to Catholics and Lutherans that we received the body and blood of Jesus Christ as the ancient Hebrews received them in the desert; whence it followed that we receive them not in substance, their substance not existing then, but in spirit only. But Calvin[16] cannot suffer this reasoning, and owning that our fathers received Jesus Christ in the desert, he maintains they did not receive him like us, since we now have "the substance of his flesh, and our manducation is substantial, which that of the ancients could not be."

42.—*If we understand Calvin's expressions naturally, we must believe that the reception of the body and blood is independent of faith.*

Secondly, he teaches that this body once offered for us,[17] "Is given *to us* in the Supper to ascertain to us that we have part in his sacrifice," and in the reconciliation it brings with it; which naturally speaking, is as much as to say, we must distinguish what is on God's side from what is on ours, and that it is not our faith that renders Jesus Christ present to us in the Eucharist, but that Jesus Christ, otherwise present as a sacred pledge of divine love, serves as a support to our faith. For, as when we say, the Son of God made himself man to certify to us that he loved our nature, we own his incarnation as independent of our faith, and, withal, as means given us whereby to support it; in like manner, to teach that Jesus Christ gives us his body and blood in this mystery, to ascertain to us that we have part in the sacrifice he made of them, in truth, is owning that the body and blood are given us, not because we believe, but to the end that our faith, being excited by so great a present, may rest more assured of the divine love, which by such an earnest we are made certain of. Hereby, then, it appears manifestly that the gift of the body and blood is independent of faith in the sacrament; and Calvin's doctrine leads us to this conclusion by another way.

43.—*According to Calvin's expressions, the true body must be in the Sacrament.*

For he says in the third place,[18] and repeats it frequently, that "the Holy Supper is composed of two things, or that there are two things in this Sacrament, the material bread and the wine which we behold with our eyes, and Jesus Christ, wherewith our souls are nourished interiorly." We have seen these words in the Wittenburg agreement. Luther and the Lutherans had taken them from a famous passage of St. Irenæus, wherein it is said that the "Eucharist is composed of a celestial and a terrestrial thing;" namely, as they explained it, as well of the substance of bread as that of the body. This explanation of their was disputed by the Catholics; and, without entering here into this controversy against the Lutherans, if to them this explanation seemed contrary to Catholic transubstantiation, it manifestly overthrew the Zuinglian figure, and at least established Luther's consubstantiation: for to say we have in the Sacrament, namely, in the sign itself, the thing terrestrial together with the celestial, that is, according to the Lutherans' sense, the material bread with the very body of Jesus Christ, is manifestly placing both substances together; but to say that the sacrament is composed of bread, which we see before our eyes, and of Jesus Christ who is in the highest heavens, at the right hand of his Father, would be an expression completely extravagant. They must therefore say that both substances are indeed in the sacrament and that the figure is there joined with the thing itself.

44.—*Another expression of Calvin, that the body is under the sign of the bread,*
as the Holy Ghost is under that of the dove.

It is to this that expression tends which we find in Calvin, "that under the sign of the bread we take the body, and under the sign of the wine we take the blood, distinctly one from the other, to the end we may enjoy Jesus Christ whole and entire." And the thing here most remarkable is, that Calvin says[19] the body of "Jesus Christ is under the bread, as the Holy Ghost is under the dove;" which necessarily imports a substantial presence, nobody doubting but the Holy Ghost was substantially present under the form of the dove, as, in a particular manner, God ever was when he appeared under some figure.

The words he makes use of are precise: "we do not pretend," says he, "that a symbolical body is received; as it was not a symbolical spirit which appeared in the baptism of our Lord: the Holy Ghost was then truly and substantially present; but he rendered himself present by a visible symbol, and was seen in the baptism of Jesus Christ, because he truly appeared under the symbol, and under the external form of the dove."

If the body of Jesus Christ is as present to us under the bread as the Holy Ghost was present under the form of a dove, I know not what more can be desired for a real and substantial presence. And Calvin says all these things in a work, wherein he purposes to explain more clearly than ever how Jesus Christ is received, since he says them after having long disputed with the Lutherans on this subject, in a book which bears this title, "A Clear Exposition of the manner how we partake of the body of our Lord."

45 —*Another expression of Calvin, which makes Jesus Christ present under the*
bread, as God was in the ark.

In the same book he says, "Jesus Christ is present in the sacrament, as God was present in the ark, where,"[20] says he, "he rendered himself truly present; and not only in figure, but in his proper substance." Thus, when this mystery is very clearly and very plainly to be spoken of, expressions are naturally employed, which lead to mind the Real Presence.

46.—Calvin says he only disputes the manner, but admits the thing as much as we.

And it is for this reason, in the fourth place, that Calvin says here,[21] and every where else, that he disputes not of the thing, but only of the manner. "I dispute not," says he, "about the presence, not the substantial manducation, but about the manner both of the one and the other." He repeats, a hundred times over, that he agrees to the thing, and only questions which way it is accomplished. All his disciples speak the same language, and even to this day our reformed are angry when we tell them the body of Jesus Christ, according to their faith, is not as substantially with them, as, according to ours, it is with us; which shows that it is a dictate of the spirit of Christianity to make Jesus Christ as present in the Eucharist as possible, and that his words naturally guide us to what is most substantial.

47.—Calvin admits an ineffable and miraculous presence of the body.

Thence it comes, fifthly, that Calvin admits of a presence that is wholly miraculous and divine.[22] He is not like the Swiss, who are angry when you speak to them of a miracle in the Supper: on the contrary, he is vexed when you tell him there is none. He is continually repeating that the mystery of the Eucharist surpasses the senses; that it is an incomprehensible work of the divine power; a secret impenetrable to the mind of man; that words are wanting to express his thoughts; and his thoughts, though greatly transcending his expressions, fall far beneath the summit of this unutterable mystery: "insomuch," says he, "that he rather experiences what this union is, than understands it:" which shows he feels, or thinks he feels, the effects, but the cause is above his reach. Accordingly, he inserts in the Confession of Faith,[23] "that this mystery, by its loftiness, surpasses the measure of our senses, and the whole order of nature; and forasmuch as it is celestial, cannot be apprehended, that is, comprehended, but by faith." And laboring to explain, in the Catechism,[24] how it is possible that "Jesus Christ should make us partakers of his proper substance, considering that his body is in heaven, and we on earth," he answers, "This is done by the incomprehensible virtue of his spirit, which, indeed, conjoins things separated by distance of place."

48.—A reflection on these words of Calvin.

A philosopher would easily comprehend that the divine power is not confined within the limits of place: the meanest capacities understand how they may be united in spirit and in thought, to what is most distant from them; and Calvin, leading us by his expressions to a more miraculous union, either speaks without meaning, or excludes the union by faith alone.

49.—Calvin admits a Presence which is proper and peculiar to the Supper.

Accordingly, we see, sixthly, that he admits[25] a participation in the Eucharist which is neither in baptism nor in preaching, since he says in the Catechism, "That although Jesus Christ be therein truly communicated to us, nevertheless, it is but in part, and not fully;" which shows that he is otherwise given to us in the Supper than by faith, since faith, being as lively and perfect in baptism and preaching, he would be as fully given to us then as in the Eucharist.

50.—*The sequel of Calvin's expressions.*

What he adds, in order to explain this fulness, is yet stronger, for there it is he says what has been already cited, that "Jesus Christ gives us his body and blood, to ascertain to us that we receive the fruit thereof." Here then is that fulness which we receive in the Eucharist, and not in baptism or preaching: whence it follows, that faith alone does not give us the body and blood of our Saviour; but that this body and blood being given to us after a special manner in the Eucharist, ascertain to us, to wit, give us a certain faith, that we have part in the sacrifice which was made of them.

51.—*The Communion of the unworthy, how real, according to Calvin.*

Lastly, what Calvin lets fall, speaking even of the unworthy, makes appear how far a miraculous presence, independent of faith, is to be believed in this Sacrament: for, although what he most inculcates is,[26] that the unworthy not having faith, Jesus Christ is ready to come to them, but does not come in effect, the force of truth, nevertheless, obliges him to say, that "He is truly offered and given to all those who are seated at the holy table, although he be not received with fruit, but by the faithful only," which is the very way of speaking that we employ.

In order then to understand the truth of the mystery which Jesus Christ works in the Eucharist, it must be believed that his proper body is therein truly offered and given, even to the unworthy, and is also received, although not received with fruit: which cannot be true, if it be not also true, that what is given us in this Sacrament is the proper body of the Son of God, independently of faith.

52.—*Continuation of Calvin's expressions concerning the Communion of the unworthy.*

Calvin confirms this again in another place, where he writes thus:[27] "In this consists the integrity of the Sacrament, which the whole world cannot violate, to wit, that the flesh and blood of Jesus Christ are as truly given to the unworthy as to the faithful and elect." Whence it follows, that what is given them is the flesh and blood of the Son of God independently of faith, since it is certain, according to Calvin, that they have not faith, or at least do not exercise it in this state.

Thus have Catholics reason to say, that what makes the sacred gift, which we receive in the Eucharist, be the body and blood of Jesus Christ, is not the faith we have in his word, but the word alone by its all-powerful energy: insomuch that faith adds nothing to the truth of the body and blood, but only makes them profitable to us; and nothing is more true than this saying of St.

Augustin,[28] that the Eucharist is not less "the body of our Lord to Judas, than to the rest of the Apostles."

53.—*A comparison of Calvin, which upholds the truth of the body being received by the unworthy.*

The comparison which Calvin makes use of in the same place still more strengthens the reality: for, after having said of the body and blood, what we have just seen, "That they are not less given to the unworthy than to the worthy," he adds, this happens alike as with rain, "which, falling on a rock, runs off without penetrating: in like manner," says he, "the impious repel the grace of God, and hinder its penetrating into them."[29] Observe, he here speaks of the body and blood, which, by consequence, must be given to the unworthy, as really as rain falls upon a rock. As to the substance of the rain, it falls no less on rocks and barren places, than on those where it fructifies; and so, according to this comparison, Jesus Christ must be no less substantially present to the obdurate than to the faithful who receive his Sacrament, though only in these it fructifies. The same Calvin[30] tells us again with St. Augustin, that the unworthy who partake of his Sacrament, are those troublesome people who press him in the Gospel, and the faithful, who receive him worthily, are that pious woman that touches him. If we consider the body only, all touch him alike: but there is reason to say, those who touch him with faith alone touch him truly, because they only touch him fruitfully. Can one speak in this manner, without owning Jesus Christ is most really present both to the one and the other, and that these words, "this is my body," have always infallibly the effect expressed by them?

54.—*Calvin speaks inconsistently.*

I am well aware that when Calvin speaks thus strongly of the body being given to the impious as truly as to saints,[31] he, nevertheless, distinguishes betwixt giving and receiving; and that, in the same place, where he says, the flesh of Jesus Christ "is as truly given to the unworthy as to the elect," he hath also said that it is not received, except by the elect alone; but this is an abuse of words. For, if he means that Jesus Christ is not received by the unworthy in the same sense that St. John has said in the Gospel, "He came unto his own, and his own received him not,"[32] that is, believed not in him, he is in the right. But as those who received not Jesus Christ after this manner, did not hinder, by their infidelity, his coming as truly to them as to the rest; nor did they hinder "the word made flesh to dwell among us,"[33] from being truly received, with regard to his personal presence, in the midst of the world, nay, even in the midst of the world that knew him not and crucified him: in like manner must it be said, to speak consistently, that these words, "this is my body," render him not less present to the unworthy, who are guilty of his body and blood, than to the worthy who approach them with faith; and barely with respect to the corporeal presence, he is equally received by both.

55.—Calvin explains, as we do, these words, The flesh profiteth nothing.

I shall here observe one word of Calvin's, which vindicates us from a reproach he and his followers are continually laying at our door. How often do they object to us these words, "The flesh profiteth nothing?" and yet Calvin explains them thus,[34] "The flesh profiteth nothing, of itself alone, but it profiteth together with the spirit." This is exactly what we say, and what ought to be concluded from these words: not that Jesus Christ does not give us the proper substance of his flesh independently of our faith, for he has given it, even according to Calvin, to the unworthy; but, that it profiteth nothing to receive his flesh, if it be not received together with his spirit. And if his spirit be now always received together with his flesh, this is not because it is not always there, for Jesus Christ comes to us full of spirit and grace; but because, in order to receive that spirit which he brings, ours must be opened by a lively faith.

56.—An expression of Calvin, that the unworthy, according to us, receive only the carcass of Jesus Christ.

It is not, therefore, a body without a soul, or, as Calvin speaks, a "carcass," which we make the unworthy receive, when they receive the sacred flesh of Jesus Christ without profiting: no more than it is a carcass and a body without soul and spirit, which Jesus Christ gives them, even in the sentiments of Calvin himself.[35] It is but a vain exaggeration to call that body a carcass, which is known to be animated; for Jesus Christ, risen from the dead, dies now no more; he hath life in him, and not only that life which makes the body live, but that life also which enlivens the soul. Jesus Christ, wherever he comes, carries with him life and grace. He brought with, and in him, his whole virtue with respect to the crowd, that thronged about him; but "this virtue went not forth," but in behalf of that woman who touched him with faith. So, when Jesus Christ gives himself to the unworthy, he comes to them with the same virtue and spirit which he sheds on the faithful; but this virtue and spirit act only on those who believe; and on all these points, Calvin must speak the same things we do, to speak consistently.

57.—Calvin weakens his own expressions.

But, it is very true, he does not speak them. True, that, although he says we are partakers of the proper substance of the body and blood of Jesus Christ, he will have this substance only untied to us by faith; and after all, in spite of these great words of Proper Substance, his design is, to own nothing else in the Eucharist but a presence of virtue.

It is true, likewise, that after he had said,[36] we are partakers of the "proper substance" of Jesus Christ, he refuses to say, "he is really and substantially present;" as if the participation were not of like nature with the presence, and the proper substance of a thing could ever be received when it is present only by its virtue.

58.—He eludes the miracle which he owns in the Supper.

By the same artifice he shifts off that great miracle which he himself is sensible he is obliged to own in the Eucharist; it is, said he, an incomprehensible secret, a miracle surpassing all sense and understanding of man. And what is this secret, this miracle? Calvin thinks he has expressed it in these words: "Is it reason which teaches us, that the soul, immortal and spiritual by its creation, is enlivened by the flesh of Jesus Christ, and that so powerful a virtue flows from heaven on the earth?"[37] But he deludes us and himself too. The singular miracle which the Holy Fathers, and after them, all Christians ever believed in the Eucharist, does not regard that virtue precisely which the flesh of Jesus Christ derives from the incarnation. The miracle consists in the verifying of these words, "this is my body," when nothing but mere bread appears to the eye, and in the giving the same body, at the same time, to so many different persons. It was in order to explain these incomprehensible wonders, that the Fathers alleged all the other miracles of the divine power, the changing of water into wine, and all the other changes, even that great change which of nothing made all things. But Calvin's miracle is not of this nature, not even a miracle that is peculiar to the sacrament of the Eucharist, nor a sequel from these words, "this is my body." It is a miracle which is wrought in the Eucharist and out of the Eucharist, and which, to speak the truth, is what essentially flows from the very mystery of the incarnation.

59.—Calvin is sensible of the insufficiency of his Doctrine to explain the miracle of the Eucharist.

Calvin himself was aware that some other miracle was to be sought in the Eucharist. He had expressed as much in several places of his works, but particularly in the Catechism: "How comes it to pass," says he, "that Jesus Christ makes us partakers of the proper substance of his body, considering his body is in heaven, and we on earth."[38] In this consists the miracle of the Eucharist. What does Calvin answer to this, and what do all Calvinists answer with him? "That the incomprehensible virtue of the Holy Ghost, indeed, conjoins things separated by distance of place." Does he mean to speak like a Catholic, and say, the Holy Ghost can every where render present what he has a mind to give in substance? I understand him, and acknowledge the true miracle of the Eucharist. Would he say that things separated as far as heaven is from earth, are, nevertheless, united, substance to substance? This is no miracle of the almighty, but a chimerical and contradictory proposition, which nobody can understand.

60.—The Calvinists did not so much admit a miracle in the Eucharist, as they were sensible one ought to be admitted.

But in reality, to speak the truth, neither Calvin nor Calvinists do admit of any miracle in the Eucharist. A presence by faith, and a presence by virtue, is not miraculous; the sun has as much virtue, and produces as great effects, at as great a distance. If, therefore, Jesus Christ be only present in virtue, there can be no miracle in the Eucharist; for which reason the Swiss, men naturally sincere, who have no other use for words than to speak just as they think, would never hear it mentioned. Calvin, in this more penetrating, very well saw with all Fathers and all the faithful, that, in these words, "this is my body," there was as clear a mark of omnipotence, as in these "let there be light." To answer this idea, it was necessary, at least, to sound high the name of a miracle; but in the main, nobody was less disposed than Calvin to believe one in the Eucharist; otherwise, why does he continually upbraid us that we confound the laws of nature, that a body cannot be in several places, nor be given us whole and entire under the form of a morsel of bread? Is not this reasoning derived from philosophy? Undoubtedly; and nevertheless, Calvin, who all along employs it, declares in many places,[39] "that he will not make use of natural, nor philosophical reasons, of which he makes no account," but of Scripture only. And why? because, on one hand, he cannot divest himself of them, nor so far raise himself above man as to despise them; and, on the other hand, he is very sensible that receiving them in matters of religion, is not only destroying the mystery of the Eucharist, but all the mysteries of Christianity at once.

61.—*The perplexities and contradictions of Calvin in the defence of the figurative sense.*

The same confusion appears when these words, "This is my Body," are to be explained. All his books, all his sermons, all his discourses, are full of the figurative interpretation, and the figure metonymy, which puts the sign for the thing. This is the way of speaking, which he calls "sacramental," which he will have the Apostles beforehand well accustomed to, when Jesus Christ instituted the Supper. The Rock was Christ, the Lamb is the Passover, Circumcision is the Covenant. "This is my Body," according to him, are all the same ways of speaking; and this is what you find in every page.

Whether or not he were fully satisfied with this, the following passage will make appear.[40] It is taken out of a book entitled "A clear Explanation," already by me quoted, and which was written against Heshusius, a Lutheran minister. "Behold," says Calvin, "how this hog makes us speak. In this phrase, *This is my Body*, there is a figure like to this;" Circumcision is the Covenant, the Rock was Christ, the Lamb is the Passover. "The Forger imagined he was prattling at table, and spending his wit among his guests. Never will such fooleries be found in our writings; but, in plain words, this is what we say, viz. when we talk of Sacraments, a certain and particular way of speaking, usual in Scripture, must be followed. Thus, without escaping under the covert of a figure, we think it enough to say, what would be clear to the whole world, did not these beasts obscure even the sun himself, that the figure metonymy must here be owned, whereby the name of the thing is given to the sign."

62.—What it was that puzzled him.

Had Heshusius fallen into such a contradiction, Calvin would certainly have told him in plain terms he was drunk; but Calvin was sober, I must own, and when he confounds himself, it is because he does not find in his own expositions what can please him. He disowns here what he says through every page; he rejects that figure with contempt which he is forced to betake himself to again the same moment; in a word, he can stand to nothing he says, and is ashamed of his own doctrine.

63.—He saw further into the difficulty than the rest of the Sacramentarians—
How he endeavored to clear it.

It must be owned, nevertheless, that he was more exact than the rest of the Sacramentarians, and besides the superiority of his wit, the dispute which had been so long on foot, had given him leisure more fully to digest this matter. For he does not stand so much upon allegories and parables.—I am the door, I am the vine,—nor on other expressions of the like nature, which always carry their own expositions with them so clear and manifest, that child even could not be mistaken.[41] And besides, if because Jesus Christ made use of allegories and parables, everything was to be understood in that sense; he plainly saw that would be nothing but filling the whole gospel with confusion.

To remedy this, Calvin[42] bethought himself of these forms of expression which he calls "sacramental," wherein the sign is put for the thing; and, by admitting them in the Eucharist, which, beyond doubt, is a sacrament, he believes he has found a certain means of establishing in it a figure, without bringing the same into a precedent for other matters.

64.—The examples which he drew from Scripture.—That of Circumcision,
which confutes instead of serving him.

He also brought more apposite examples from scripture than any of the Protestant writers before him. The chief difficulty lay in finding out a sign of institution, wherein, at the institution itself, the name of the thing is immediately given to the sign without preparing the mind for it, and this with the proper word by which this sign is instituted. The question was, whether any such example could be found in scripture. Catholics maintained there could not; and Calvin thought to convince them by this text of Genesis, in which Almighty God, speaking of circumcision which he instituted, named it the Covenant:—"My covenant," says he, "shall be in your flesh."[43] But he was plainly mistaken, since Almighty God, before he had said, "my Covenant shall be in your flesh," had said already, "it shall be a sign of the covenant." The sign was therefore instituted before the name of the thing was given to it, and the mind, by this exordium, prepared to the understanding of what ensued: from whence it follows, that our Saviour should have prepared the minds of the apostles, in order to take the sign for the thing, had he designed to have given this sense to these words,—"This is my Body—this is my Blood;" but having not done this, it is to be believed he intended to leave the words in their natural and obvious sense. Calvin owns as much himself, since, by saying that the apostles ought already to have been accustomed to these sacramental ways of speaking, he owns it would have been incongruous to employ such, had they not been accustomed to them. As it then manifestly appears they could not be accustomed to give the name of a thing to the sign of institution, without being forewarned, and there being no example of this nature in the Old or New Testament, from Calvin's own principles, it must be concluded against Calvin, that Jesus Christ ought not to have spoken in that sense, and had he done it, his Apostles would not have understood him.

65.—*Another example which makes nothing to the question, viz. that the Church is also called the Body of Jesus Christ.*

And, indeed, the truth is, although he placed his chief strength in these ways of speaking, by him called sacramental, and in all intricacies, ever guided himself by this clue, he is so little satisfied therewith, that he says in other places, that the scriptures naming the Church the Body of our Lord, is the chief support of his doctrine. To make this his chief defence, shows him, indeed, conscious of his weakness. Is the Church the sign of our Lord's body, as Calvin makes the bread to be?[44] By no means; she is his body, as he is her head, by that so common way of speaking, by which a whole nation, and the prince who governs them, are represented as a kind of natural body, which hath its head and members. What can then be the reason, that after Calvin had laid his main stress on these sacramental ways of speaking, he depends still more on a manner of speaking, which is absolutely of another kind: unless it be, that to support a figure of which he stands in need, he calls to his assistance all the figurative ways of speech, of what nature soever they be, what little coherence soever they may have?

66.—*Calvin makes new efforts to preserve the idea of the Reality.*

The rest of his doctrine gives him no less pain, and the violent expressions he makes use of plainly discover it. We have seen how he will have the flesh of Jesus Christ to penetrate us by its substance. I have taken notice that, notwithstanding all these great words, he means no more by them, than that it penetrates us by its virtue; but this manner of speaking appearing weak to him, in order to mix the substance therewith, he makes us receive in the Eucharist,[45] as it were, "an extract of the Flesh of Jesus Christ, upon condition, however, that it remain in heaven, and from its substance life flow down upon us;" as if we received the quintessence and the choicest part of his flesh, the rest abiding in heaven. I will not say he believed it so; but only, that the grounds of doctrine not being able to supply him wherewith to answer the idea of reality he was so full of, he supplied this defect by far-fetched, unheard-of, and extravagant expressions.

67.—He cannot answer the idea of Reality, which our Saviour's institution impresses on the mind.

That I may not here dissemble any part of Calvin's doctrine, concerning the communication which we have with Jesus Christ, I am obliged to say, he seems in some places to make Jesus Christ as present in Baptism as in the Supper; for, in general, he distinguishes three things in the sacrament besides the sign[46]—"the signification, which consists in the promises; the matter or the substance, which is Jesus Christ, with his death and resurrection; and the effect, namely, sanctification, life eternal, and all the graces which Jesus Christ brings to us." Calvin acknowledges all these things as well in the Sacrament of Baptism, as in that of the Supper; and he teaches of Baptism in particular that[47] "the Blood of Jesus Christ is not less present to wash souls, than the water to wash bodies; and, according to St. Paul, we are indeed there clothed with Jesus Christ, and our clothing does not less encompass, than our nourishment penetrates us." Hereby, then, he openly declares that Jesus Christ is present in Baptism, as in the Supper; and the consequence from his doctrine, I own, naturally leads him to it; for, after all, he neither admits of any other presence in the Supper than by faith, nor of any faith in the Supper but what is in Baptism; consequently, I am far from pretending he admits in it any other presence in effect. What I pretend to show is the perplexity he is cast into by these words, "This is my Body." For either he must confound all mysteries, or he must be able to give a reason why Jesus Christ spoke no where else but in the Supper with this energy. If his body and blood be as present, and as really received every where else, there was no reason to choose these emphatic words for the Eucharist rather than for baptism; and the eternal wisdom would have spoken in vain. This very thing will be the everlasting and inevitable confusion of those who defend the figurative sense. On one side, the necessity of allowing something particular to the Eucharist with respect to the presence of the Body; and on the other, the impossibility of doing this, according to their principles, will always involve them in perplexities from which they can never disengage themselves; and to extricate himself was what made Calvin use so many strong expressions relating to the Eucharist, which he never durst apply to baptism, though there was the same reason for doing it, according to his principles.

68.—The Calvinists in the main have abandoned Calvin.—How he is explained in the book called the Preservative.

His expressions are so violent, and the turns he here gives to his doctrine are so strained, that his disciples have been forced to abandon him in the main, nor can I but observe in this place a notorious variation in the Calvinistic doctrine; inasmuch as the Calvinists now-a-days, under pretext of interpreting Calvin's words, reduce them to nothing at all. To receive the "proper substance of Jesus Christ" is, according to them,[48] nothing else but receiving him "by his virtue, by his efficacy, by his merit," the very things which Calvin had rejected as insufficient. All that we can hope from these great words, "the proper substance" of Jesus Christ received in the Supper, is only this,[49] viz. that what we there receive, is not the substance of another: but, as for his substance, it is no more received, than the substance of the sun is received by the eye when enlightened by its rays: the meaning of which is, that they are indeed quite strangers now to that proper substance so much inculcated by Calvin. If they defend it, it is only from a point of honor, and lest they should seem too openly to recant; and if Calvin, who abetted it with so much force in his books, had not also inserted it in the Catechisms and Confession of Faith, it would have long since been quite abandoned.

69.—*A sequel of the explanations given to Calvin's words.*

The same may be said of those words of Calvin and of the Catechism, viz. that Jesus Christ is received fully in the Eucharist, but in preaching and baptism "in part only."[50] This, naturally understood, implies, that the Eucharist hath something particular in it, which baptism and preaching have not: no such thing; it means now no more, than three are more than two; that, after having received grace by baptism and instruction by the word, when to all this God adds the Eucharist, grace increases, and is strengthened, and we possess Jesus Christ more perfectly. Thus, all the perfection of the Eucharist is its coming in the last place; and although, in instituting it, Jesus Christ made use of such particular terms, it hath nothing particular notwithstanding, nothing more than baptism, unless, perhaps, a new sign; and Calvin's talking so big of the proper substance was all to no manner of purpose.

By this means, the explanations now given to Calvin's words, and to those of the Catechism and Confession of Faith, under the pretext of interpretation, are a real variation in doctrine, and a proof that the illusions, by which Calvin endeavored to blind mankind, in order to keep up a notion of reality, could no longer subsist.

70.—*Whether there be nothing in these passages of Calvin, but bare defects of expression.*

To cover this manifestly weak side of the sect, it is true, the Calvinists answer,[51] that from these expressions we reproach them with, at most nothing can be concluded but that, perchance, the terms employed by them in explaining their doctrine at the beginning might not be quite so proper. But to answer in this manner, is affecting that they did not see the difficulty. What ought to be concluded from these expressions of Calvin and the Calvinists is, that the words of our Saviour had, at first, do what they would, made such an impression of reality on their minds, as they never could come up to by words, and which, afterwards, forced them upon expressions, which, having no sense in their belief, give testimony to ours; which is not only imposing on themselves by an erroneous way of speaking, but confessing an error in the thing itself, and, even in their confession of faith, bearing the stamp of their own conviction.

71.—Calvin wished to have understood more than in reality he said.

For instance, when he is forced to say, on one side, that the proper substance of the body and blood of our Lord is received; and on the other, that they are only received by their virtue, as the sun is received by its rays, this is confounding himself and uttering contradictions.

Then again, when he is forced to say on one side, that the proper substance of the body and blood of Jesus Christ is as much received, in the Calvinistic supper as in that of the Catholics, and that there is no difference but in manner; and on the other side, that the body and blood of Jesus Christ are far distant from the faithful as heaven is from earth, and that a Real and Substantial Presence is, after all, one and the same thing with an absence, at so prodigious a distance; this is a prodigy unheard of in human language, and such expressions only serve to make us see they would fain have it in their power to say, what, according to their own principles, they cannot say in reason.

72.—Why Heretics are obliged to imitate the language of the Church.

And that I may show once for all, not to come back to it again, the consequence of these expressions of Calvin and the first Calvinists; let us reflect, that never as yet could any heretics be found, that did not affect to speak like the Church. The Arians and Socinians say, as well as we, that Jesus Christ is God, but improperly, and by representation, because he acts in the name of God, and by God's authority. The Nestorians make no difficulty of saying, that the Son of God and the Son of Mary are but the same person; but just as an ambassador is the same person with the Prince he represents. Shall we say that they hold the same principles as the Catholic Church, and only differ in the way of expressing their thoughts? On the contrary, it will be said, they speak like her without thinking like her, because falsehood is forced at least to mimic truth. With relation to proper substance and such like expressions in the works of Calvin and the Calvinists, the case is just the same.

73.—The triumph of Truth.

Here we may observe the conspicuous triumph of Catholic verity, inasmuch as the literal sense of the words of Jesus Christ, which we defend, after forcing Luther to maintain it, however contrary to his inclinations, as hath been seen, hath also forced Calvin, who denies it, to confess nevertheless so many things, which make for, and establish it in an invincible manner.

74.—A passage in Calvin for a Real Presence, independent of Faith.

Before I quit this subject, I must observe one passage in Calvin[52] which, affording great room for speculation, I question whether I shall be able to dive to the bottom of it. It concerns the Lutherans, who, without destroying the bread, enclose the body in it. "If," says he, "what they pretend, be only this, that whilst the bread is presented in the mystery, the body is also presented at the same time, because truth is inseparable from its sign, this is what I shall not much oppose."

Here is, then, a thing which he neither altogether approves nor disapproves. It is a middle opinion, betwixt his own and that of the generality of the Lutherans: an opinion establishing the body inseparable from the sign; by consequence, independently of faith, since it is certain, that, without it, the sign may be received: and what is this else, but the opinion, which I have attributed to Bucer and Melancthon, whereby they admit a Real Presence, even in the communion of the unworthy, and without the assistance of faith; requiring this Presence to accompany the sign as to time, but not to be confined to, or contained in it, as to place? This is what Calvin will not much oppose; that is, he does not much disapprove of a Real Presence inseparable from the sacrament, and independent of faith.

75.—*Ceremonies rejected by Calvin.*

I have endeavored to make known the doctrine of this second Patriarch of the new Reformation, and persuade myself I have discovered what it was that gave him so much authority in that party. It appeared he had new ideas about imputed justice, which was the groundwork of the Reformation, and about the Eucharist which had divided them for so long a time; but there was still a third point, which greatly enhanced his credit among those who valued themselves for men of wit. It was his boldness in rejecting ceremonies much beyond whatever the Lutherans had done,[53] for they had made it a law to themselves, to retain those which were not manifestly contrary to their new tenets. But on this head Calvin was inexorable. He condemned Melancthon, who, in his opinion, thought ceremonies of too little a concern; and if the worship, introduced by him, appeared to some too naked, even this had a new charm for the men of taste and spirit, who thought thereby to raise themselves above their senses, and soar beyond the vulgar. And because the Apostles had written little on ceremonies, which they were satisfied with establishing by practice, or often left to the disposal of each Church, the Calvinists boasted, above all the Reformers, that they adhered with the greatest purity to that letter of Scripture, which in England and Scotland gave them the name of Puritans.

76.—*What opinion the other Protestants had of the Calvinists.*

By this means Calvin refined upon, and outstripped the first authors of the new Reformation. The party which bore his name was hated extremely by all the other Protestants, who looked upon them as the most haughty, restless, and seditious of any that had appeared as yet. There is no need of alleging what has, in several places, been written of them by James I, King of England and Scotland. He makes, nevertheless, an exception in favor of Puritans of other countries, thinking it enough to publish, from his own experience, that he knew none more dangerous, or greater enemies to the regal power, than those he had met with in his own kingdoms. Calvin made much progress in

France; and this great kingdom, by the attempts of his followers, saw itself on the very brink of ruin: so that he was in France much like what Luther was in Germany: and Wittenberg, which gave the new Gospel its first birth, was rivalled by Geneva, where ruled this head of the second party of the new Reformation.

77.—Calvin's pride.

How much smitten he was with this glory, we shall perceive by a few words he wrote to Melancthon. "I own myself," says he, "much your inferior; yet am nowise ignorant to what a degree God has raised me on this theatre, nor can our friendship be violated without injuring the Church."[54] To see himself as it were, exposed upon a grand theatre, and the eyes of all Europe turned upon him; to see himself advanced to the foremost rank by his eloquence; to be conscious of the name he had acquired, and an authority revered by such a party made Calvin no longer able to contain himself; to him this was too alluring a charm, and it is the same charm that has made all heresiarchs.

78.—His boasting.

It was from a sense of this secret pleasure that, in his answer to Balduinus,[55] his great adversary, he thus expressed himself: "He tells me, with reproach, that I have no children, and that God has snatched away the son he had bestowed upon me. Ought I to be thus reproached? I, who have so many thousands of children, throughout all Christendom!" To which he adds, "To all France is known my irreproachable faith, my integrity, my patience, my watchfulness, my moderation, and my assiduous labors for the service of the Church; things that, from my early youth, stand proved by so many illustrious tokens. With the support of such a conscience, to be able to hold my station to the very end of life, is enough for me."

79.—The difference between Luther and Calvin.

He had so much extolled the holy ostentation and magnanimity of Luther, that he was not easy till he had followed the example; although, to void the ridicule which Luther fell into, he particularly set up for the character of modesty, as one who had a mind to have it in his power to brag, that "he was without pride, and feared nothing so much as boasting:"[56] so that the difference between Luther's and Calvin's ostentation is, that Luther, who was hurried away by the impetuosity of his temper, ever thoughtless of moderation or restraint, praised himself as it were in transport: but the self-commendations Calvin fell into, in spite of all the law of modesty which he had set to himself, burst from the centre of his heart, and violently broke through all barriers. How pleasing was he in his own eyes, when he commends so much "His own frugality, his incessant labors, his constancy in dangers, his watchfulness to comply with his charge, his indefatigable application to extend the kingdom of Christ Jesus, his integrity in defending the doctrine of piety and the serious occupation of his whole life in the meditation of heavenly things."[57] Nothing

Luther ever said came up to this, nor did the sallies of unbridled passion ever make him say so much as Calvin utters of himself in cold blood.

80.—*How Calvin boasted of his eloquence.*

Nothing delighted him more than the glory of writing well; and Westphalus, a Lutheran, having called him a declaimer, "Do what he will," says Calvin, "nobody will ever give him credit, and the whole world is fully satisfied how well I know how to press an argument, and how distinct is that conciseness with which I write."[58]

This is giving to himself, in three words, the whole gory that the art of eloquence can bestow on man. Here is, at least, a commendation which Luther never arrogated to himself; for though he was one of the sprightliest orators of his age, so far from making it appear that he valued himself for eloquence, he took a pleasure in saying he was a poor monk, bred up in schools and obscurity, unacquainted with the art of speaking. But Calvin, wounded in this tender part, flies out, and, at the expense of modesty, cannot forbear saying that nobody delivers his thoughts more distinctly, or argues more strongly than himself.

81.—*Calvin's eloquence.*

Let us then allow him this glory, since he is so fond of it, of having written as well as any of that age; nay, if he desires it, let us even set him above Luther; for, although Luther had something more original and lively, Calvin, inferior in genius, seems to carry it by dint of study. Luther triumphed in speaking; but Calvin's pen was more correct, especially in Latin; and his style, which was more serious, was also much more coherent and more chastened. They both spoke their native language in perfection: the vehemence of both was extraordinary; both gained many disciples and admirers by their talents; elated with their success, they both despised the Fathers; both were impatient of contradiction, nor did their eloquence ever flow more copiously than when fraught with contumelies.

82.—*His temper as violent, but sourer than Luther's.*

Whoever blushed at those expressions which Luther's arrogance drew from his pen, will not be less confounded at the excesses of Calvin: his adversaries are always knaves, fools, rogues, drunkards, furies, madmen, beasts, bulls, asses, dogs, swine; and Calvin's fine style is polluted with this filth through every page. Be they Catholics or Lutherans, it is all one to him, he spares none. Westphalus's school is to him a stinking hog-sty. The Lutherans' supper is almost always called a supper of Cyclopes, "at which a barbarity may be seen becoming Scythians;"[59] if he is used to say that the devil drives on Papists, he repeats a hundred times[60] he has bewitched the "Lutherans, and that he cannot comprehend why he, above all others, is assaulted by them, unless it be that Satan, whose vile slaves they are, so much the more urges them on against him, as he sees his labors more useful to the Church than theirs."

The individuals whom he treats thus were the chief and most renowned among the Lutherans. Amidst these invectives he still boasts of his sweetness;[61] and after having stuffed his book with all that can be imagined, not only most bitter, but also most atrocious, he thinks he comes well off by saying,[62] "That he was so remote from any gall, when he penned these injurious taunts, that he himself, upon reading his work over again, stood quite astonished that so much harsh language could have ever been uttered by him, and his heart still void of bitterness. It was," says he "the heinousness of the subject which alone furnished him with all these abusive words, which stood ready to bolt from him. After all, he is not displeased that these stupid creatures have, at last, smarted under the lash, and hopes this may help to mend them." Yet he does not refuse to own he has said something more than he would have done, and that the remedy applied by him was a little too violent. But, after this modest confession, he indulges his passion more than ever, and in the very same breath that he interrogates, "Dog, doest thou understand me? Madman, dost thou comprehend me? Dost thou take me right, great beast?" he adds, "that he is well pleased that the contumelies men load him with are not retaliated."[63] Luther's passion, compared with this, was meekness itself; and, should a comparison he instituted between them, there is not a man who had not rather stand the brunt of the impetuous and insolent fury of the one, than of the profound and bitter malice of the other, who brags of being cool in the disgorging of such a flow of rancor upon all that come in his way.

83.—*The contempt he has for the Fathers.*

Both of them, after their attacks on mortal men, turned their malice against heaven, by openly despising the authority of the Holy Fathers. Every body knows how often Calvin had trampled on their decisions, what a pleasure he took in taking them to task like school-boys, in giving them their lessons, and the outrageous manner whereby he thought to elude their unanimous consent, by saying, for instance, "that these good men followed, without discretion, a custom that prevailed without reason, and which was but a little while in getting into vogue."[64]

84.—*The Fathers made themselves respected by Protestants in spite of them.*

The subject he then had in hand was prayer for the dead. All his writings are full of the like discourses. But, in spite of heretical pride, the authority of the Fathers and ecclesiastical antiquity lies weighty on their minds. For all of Calvin's avowed contempt of the Fathers, he cites them, nevertheless, as witnesses, whose authority it is not lawful to reject, when, after quoting them, he writes these words: "What will they say to the ancient Church, or will they banish St. Augustin out of the Church?"[65] The very same might be retorted on him, regarding the subject of prayer for the dead, and in the rest; where it is certain, and often by his own confession, that he hath the Fathers against him. But without entering into this particular dispute, I am satisfied with having observed that our Reformists are often constrained by the force of truth, to respect the sentiments of the Fathers more than their doctrine and inclination carries them to.

85.—*Whether Calvin ever varied in his doctrine.*

Those who have seen the endless variations of Luther may inquire whether Calvin fell into the same fault. To which I shall answer, that besides a more coherent way of thinking, he had the advantage of writing a long time after the beginning of the pretended Reformation; so that matters having been already much discussed, and doctors having had leisure to digest them, Calvin's doctrine seems more uniform than that of Luther. But, however, we shall see hereafter (whether from a policy usual to the heads of new sects to mend and perfect their own work, or, by a necessity common to those who fall into error) that Calvin also varied very much, not only in his own particular writings, but also in the public acts, which he drew in the name of all his followers, or which he inspired them with. And even to go no further, upon considering only what I have already related of his doctrine, we may have seen that it abounds with contradictions, that he follows not his own principles, and, with great words, says just nothing.

86.—*Variations in the Acts of the Calvinists.—The Agreement of Geneva compared with the Catechism and the Confession of France.—1554.*

And if we make never so little reflection on those acts which he framed, or which the Calvinists, with his approbation, published in five or six years' time,[66] neither he nor they can in any way clear themselves of the guilt of having expounded their faith with a criminal dissimulation. In 1554, we have seen a solemn agreement made between those of Geneva and Zurich; it was drawn by Calvin, and the common faith of these two Churches is there set forth. "Concerning the Supper, no more is said there than these words, 'This is my body,' must not be taken precisely in a literal sense, but figuratively; so that the name of the body and blood is by metonymy given to the bread and wine which signify them; and that if Jesus Christ nourishes us by the food of his body, and the drink of his blood, this is done by faith and the virtue of the Holy Ghost, without any transfusion or other mixture of substance, but because we have life by his body once sacrificed, and his blood once shed for us." If, in this "agreement," we find nothing mentioned either of the proper "substance" of the body and blood received in the Supper, or of the incomprehensible miracles of this Sacrament, or such like things as have been remarked in the Catechism and the Confession of Faith of the French Calvinists, the reason is obvious. Namely, because the Swiss, as hath appeared, and those of Zurich, having been instructed by Zuinglius, would never come into the notion of any miracle in the Supper; and satisfied with a virtual presence, knew not the meaning of that communication of proper substance, which Calvin and the Calvinists kept such a stir about: in order, therefore, to come to an agreement, these things were necessarily to be suppressed, and such a confession of faith as the Swiss could accept was to be presented to them.

87.—*A third Confession of Faith sent into Germany.*—*1557.*

To these two confessions of faith drawn by Calvin, one for France, the other to please the Swiss, a third also during his life was added in favor of the German Protestants. Beza and Farel, deputed by the reformed churches of France and that of Geneva in 1557, carried it to Worms, where the Princes and States of the Augsburg Confession were assembled. The design was to engage them to intercede, in the Calvinists' behalf, with Henry II, who, treading in the steps of Francis I, his father, did his utmost to depress them. The expressions of "proper substance," readily laid aside when the Swiss were treated with, were not forgotten now: nay, so many other things were added, and so much said, that, how all this can be reconcileable with the doctrine of a figurative sense is past my skill to discover. For it is there said,[67] "That not only the benefits of Jesus Christ are received in the Supper, but even his proper flesh and substance; that the body of the Son of God is not there proposed to us in figure only and by signification symbolically or typically as a memorial of Jesus Christ absent, but that he is truly and certainly rendered present with the symbols, which are not mere signs. And if," said they, "we add, that the manner whereby this body is given to us is symbolical and sacramental, this is not because it is only figurative, but by reason that, under the species of things visible, God offers to us, gives to us, and, with the symbols, renders present to us, that which is there signified to us; and this we say, to the end it may appear that in the Supper we retain the proper body and the proper blood of Jesus Christ; and, if any dispute still remain, it concerns nothing but the manner."

Till now, we had never heard the Calvinists say that the Supper was not to be looked upon as a memorial of Jesus Christ absent: we had never heard them say, that in order to give us, not his benefits, but his substance and his proper flesh, he rendered it truly present to us under the species; nor that in the Supper was to be confessed a presence of the proper body and the proper blood; and were we not acquainted with the equivocations of the Sacramentarians, we could not but take them for as zealous defenders of the Real Presence as the Lutherans themselves. To hear them talk, one might reasonably doubt if any difference between theirs and the Lutheran doctrine still remained. "If," said they, "any dispute still remain, it concerns not the thing itself, but the manner of the presence only;" so that the presence they acknowledge in the Supper must, in reality, be as real and as substantial as that which the Lutherans confess.

And, in fact, when afterwards they treat on the manner of this presence, they reject nothing in this manner but what the Lutherans reject: they reject the natural or local manner of uniting himself to us; and nobody says that Jesus Christ is untied to us in the natural and ordinary way, or that he is in the sacrament, or in the faithful, as bodies are in their place—for he is there certainly in a more elevated manner. They reject the effusion of the human nature of Jesus Christ; to wit, Ubiquity, which the Lutherans rejected likewise, and which, as yet, had not so highly gained the ascendant. They reject a gross mixture of the substance of Jesus Christ together with ours, which nobody did admit, for nothing can be less gross, and further remote from vulgar mixtures, than the union of our Lord's body with ours, which is no less avowed by Lutherans than by Catholics. But what they, above all things, reject utterly, is that gross and diabolical Transubstantiation, without saying so much as a word of the Lutheran Consubstantiation, which, as we shall see, they did not think in their hearts a whit less diabolical or less carnal. But it behooved them to be silent on that head, for fear of offending the Lutherans, whose assistance they were then imploring. And, finally, they concluded quite short, by saying that the presence which they acknowledge, is brought about in a spiritual manner, and supported by the incomprehensible virtue of the Holy Ghost;—words which the Lutherans themselves employed, as well as Catholics, in order to exclude, together with a presence in figure, even a presence in virtue, which has nothing in it that is miraculous or beyond comprehension.

88.—*Another Confession of Faith made by those in Prison, in order to be sent to the Protestants.*

Such was the Confessions of Faith which the Calvinists of France sent to the Protestants of Germany. Those who were imprisoned in France on the score of religion, joined to it their particular declaration, in which they expressly receive the Confession of Augsburg in all its articles, excepting only that of the Eucharist; adding, nevertheless, what is not less strong than the Augsburg Confession, that the Supper is not a sign of Jesus Christ absent; then, turn themselves immediately against the Papists, and their change of substance and adoration, without speaking so much as a word against the particular doctrine of Lutheranism.

This was the cause that induced the Lutherans, with the joint consent of all their divines, to judge that this declaration sent from France was conformable, in every point, to the Confession of Augsburg, notwithstanding what was there said concerning the tenth article; because, in the main, it said more on the Real Presence than this article had done.

The article of Augsburg expressed "that, with the bread and wine, the body and blood were truly present and truly distributed to those who took the Supper." These say "that the proper flesh, and the proper substance of Jesus Christ, is truly present, and truly given with the symbols, and under the visible species;" and the rest nothing less precise than what has been related; insomuch, that if it be asked which more strongly express the Substantial Presence, the Lutherans who believe it, or the Calvinists who disbelieve it, the last will certainly have the preference.

89.—*All the other articles of the Augsburg Confessions are owned by the Calvinists.*

As for the other articles of the Confession of Augsburg, they stood confirmed by the sole exception of this article of the Supper; that is to say, the Calvinists, even those who were detained in prison for their religion's sake, professed, contrary to their belief, the necessity of baptism, the amissibility of justice, the uncertainty of predestination, the merit of good works, and prayer for the dead; all points which we have read in express terms in the Augsburg Confession; and in this manner did the martyrs of the new Reformation destroy, by their equivocations, or express denial, that faith for which they died.

90.—*Reflections on these three Confessions of Faith.*

Thus have we clearly seen three different languages of our Calvinists in three different Confessions of Faith. By that which they made for themselves, they appeared anxious to please themselves: to content the Zuinglians, they lopped off something from it; and, in case of need, they knew what to add to make the Lutherans their friends.

91.—*The Conference of Poissy.—How undertaken.—Calvin comes not to it, but leaves the affair to Beza.—1561.*

We shall now hear the Calvinists explain their doctrine, not among one another, or to the Zuinglians or Lutherans, but to the Catholics. This happened in 1561, in the minority of Charles IX, at the famous conference of Poissy, where, by the orders of Queen Catharine de Medicis, his mother and regent of the kingdom, the prelates were assembled, in order to confer with the ministers about reforming those abuses which gave pretext to heresy.[68]

As in France people grew weary of the long delays of a general council, so often promised by the Popes, and of the frequent interruptions of that which was at length convened by them at Trent, the Queen, deceived by some prelates of suspected doctrine, whose sentiments were backed by the Lord Chancellor de l'Hôpital, a great personage, and very zealous for his country, believed too easily, that in so universal a commotion she might of herself take care of France apart, without the authority of the Holy See and council. She was made to believe that a conference would reconcile men's minds, and that the disputes which divided them would more surely be determined by an agreement than by a decision, which could not fail of displeasing one or the other side. The cardinal Charles of Lorrain, Archbishop of Rheims, who, having governed all under Francis II, with his brother Francis, Duke of Guise, had always maintained himself in great repute, a great genius, a great statesman, of a sparkling and winning eloquence, learned even for a man of his quality and employments, hoped to signalize himself in public, and withal to please the court by entering into the Queen's design. By this means the assembly of Poissy was set on foot. The Calvinists deputed thither the ablest men they had, excepting Calvin, whom they would not show, whether from fear of exposing to the public hatred the head of so odious a party, or he himself believed it safer for his honor to send his disciples, he remaining at Geneva where he ruled, and underhand managed the assembly, than to engage in person.

It is likewise true, that the weakness of his health, and the violence of his headstrong temper, rendered him less able to maintain a conference, than Theodore Beza, who was of a more robust constitution, and had more command of himself: Beza, then, was the man that most appeared, or rather, who alone appeared in this assembly. He was looked upon as the principal disciple, and the intimate friend of Calvin, who had chosen him for a coadjutor in his ministry and labors at Geneva, which seemed the metropolis of his Reformation. Calvin despatched his instructions to him, and Beza returned him a full account of all transactions, as appears from both their letters.

92.—*Matters treated of in the Conference, and the opening of it.*

Two points of doctrine only, properly speaking, were debated in this assembly; one relating to the Church; the other to the Supper. There lay the stress of the whole affair, because the article of the Church was looked upon by Catholics as a general principle, which subverted the very foundation of all new churches; and among the particular articles disputed on, none appeared so essential as that of the Supper. The Cardinal of Lorrain urged the opening of the Conference, though the main body of the prelates, especially the Cardinal de Tournon, Archbishop of Lyons, who presided over them in quality of the oldest Cardinal, had an extreme repugnance to it. They apprehended, and with reason too, lest the subtleties of the ministers, their dangerous eloquence heightened with an air of piety, never wanting to the most perverse of heretics, and more than all this, lest the charms of novelty might impose on courtiers, before whom they were to speak, but chiefly on the King and Queen, both susceptible, he by reason of his tender age, she from natural curiosity, of any impressions, rather bad than good, considering the wretched disposition of human nature, and the temper which then prevailed at court. But the Cardinal of Lorrain, supported by Montluc, Bishop of Valence, carried the point, and so the conference began.

93.—*The harangue of the Cardinal of Lorrain.—The Calvinists' Confession of Faith presented to the King in the Assembly.—Beza speaks, and says more than makes for him concerning the absence of Jesus Christ in the Supper.*

There is no need of my giving an account, either of the admirable harangue made by the Cardinal of Lorrain, and its merited applause, or of the honor which Beza acquired by offering to answer at the moment to the Cardinal's premeditated discourse;[69] but it is of some importance to remember, that, in this august assembly, the ministers presented publicly to the King in the name of all their churches, their joint Confession of Faith, drawn under Henry II, in their first synod held at Paris, as above mentioned. Beza, who presented it, made at the same time, by a long discourse, the defence of it, when, notwithstanding all his address, he fell into a great self-contradiction. He, who a few days before, being accused by the Cardinal of Lorrain in the presence of Queen Catharine, and the whole court, of having written in one of his books, that Jesus Christ was no more in the Supper than in the mire, *Non magis in cænâ quam in Cæno*, had rejected this proposition as impious and detested by the whole party, advanced the equivalent to it, at the Conference, even in the face of all France. For, being on the subject of the Eucharist, in the heat of his discourse, he said, that with respect to place, and the presence of Jesus Christ considered according to human nature, his body was as far distant from the Supper as the highest Heavens are from earth. The whole assembly was in a commotion at these words.[70] They remembered with what a horror he had spoken of that proposition, which as much excluded Jesus Christ from the Supper, as from the mire. He now falls into it again, when nobody urges him. The murmur from all sides made it appear how much men were struck with so strange a novelty. Beza himself, under confusion for having said so much, did not cease thereafter to importune the Queen, by frequent and reiterated requests, to obtain the liberty of explaining himself, on the plea that, being pressed by time, he had not had the leisure of making his thought rightly understood before the King. But so many words are not required to utter what a man believes. And, indeed, one may venture to say, that what disturbed Beza was not any deficiency in expounding his tenets, but rather, what gave him and his friends so much anxiety, was, that by laying open in too distinct terms the bottom of the party's doctrine on the real absence of Jesus Christ, he had made it but too visibly appear, that the great words of Proper Substance and the like which they employed to keep up some notion of reality, were nothing but mere sham.

94.—Another explanation of the Supper-article full of perplexed words.

From harangues they soon proceeded to particular conferences, chiefly on the Supper, wherein the Bishop of Valence, and Duval, Bishops of Sees, to whom a smattering of erudition, not to mention other motives, gave a secret propensity towards Calvinism, were set on nothing else, together with the ministers, but to find out some ambiguous formulary which both sides, in some measure, might rest satisfied with, without diving to the bottom of the question.

The strong expressions, which we have seen in the Confession of Faith then presented, were pretty well adapted to this scheme; but the ministers must needs make further additions which ought not to be admitted. This will appear surprising; for, as they ought to have done their best fully to explain their doctrine in the confession of faith, which they but just presented to so solemn an assembly, it seems that, when questioned concerning their belief, they should have nothing else to do than refer themselves to so authentic an act: but this is what they did not do; and behold here in what manner they proposed their doctrine by common consent. "We confess the presence of the body and blood of Jesus Christ in the holy Supper, where he truly gives us the substance of his body and blood by the operation of his Holy Spirit, and that we receive and eat spiritually and by faith, this same true body, which was sacrificed for us; to the end we might be bone of his bone, and flesh of his flesh, and be enlivened, and receive all that is profitable to our salvation; and by reason that faith, supported by God's promise, makes present the things received, and takes really and in fact the true natural body of our Lord, by virtue of the Holy Ghost; in this sense, we do believe and confess the presence of the proper body and the proper blood of Jesus Christ in the Supper." Here are still those great phrases, those pompous expressions, and those long discourses for the purpose of saying nothing. But after all this verbosity, they were not yet satisfied with their exposition, but soon after subjoined, "That the distance of place could be no hindrance to our partaking of the body and blood of Jesus Christ, by reason that our Lord's Supper is a heavenly thing, and although we on earth receive with our mouths the bread and wine as the true signs of the body and blood, our souls, which are nourished therewith, being raised up to heaven by faith, and the efficacy of the Holy Ghost, enjoy present the body and blood of Jesus Christ; and in that manner the body and blood are truly united to the bread and wine, but in a sacramental way, to wit, not according to place, or the natural position of bodies, but inasmuch as they efficaciously signify, that God gives this body and blood to those who faithfully partake of the signs themselves, and that by faith they truly do receive them." How many words, only to express, that the signs of the body and blood, received with faith, do, by this faith inspired from God, unite us to the body and blood which are in heaven! No more than this had been requisite to explain themselves distinctly; and this substantial enjoyment of the body truly and really present, and the rest of that strain, are to no other purpose than to raise a mist of confused ideas, instead of dispelling, by setting things in a clear light, which, in an explanation of faith, we are obliged to do. But in this simplicity, which we demand of them, Christians would not have found what they desired, namely, the true presence of Jesus Christ in both his natures; and, deprived of this presence, would have perceived, as it were, a certain void, which, for want of the thing itself, the ministers endeavored to fill up with this multiplicity of sounding, yet insignificant expressions.

95.—*The reflections of Catholics on these indeterminate and pompous discourses.*

The Catholics, at a loss to know the meaning of all this monstrous language, could only perceive from it that Beza's great design, by all these phrases, was to supply what he was conscious was too hollow and defective in the Calvinistic Supper. The whole force of them lay in these words, "Faith makes present the things promised." But this discourse appeared very indeterminate to Catholics. By this means, said they, judgment and the general resurrection, the glory of the blessed, as well as the fire of the damned, will be equally present to us with the body of Jesus Christ in the Holy Eucharist; and if this presence, by faith, makes us receive the very substance of things, nothing hinders the happy souls that are in heaven from receiving, actually and before the general resurrection, the proper substance of their bodies as truly as we are here made to receive by faith, the proper substance of the body of Jesus Christ. For, if faith renders things so truly present, as thereby to possess the substance of them, how much more the beatific vision! But in order to unite to us the proper substance of the body and blood, what avails this lifting up our souls to heaven by faith? Can a moral elevation, and in affection only, bring about such unions? In this manner, what substance is there that cannot be embraced? What does the efficacy of the Holy Ghost work here? The Holy Ghost inspires faith, our faith thus inspired, be it never so strong, unites itself no more to the substance of things than other thoughts, than other affections of the mind. What can be the meaning of those indefinite words, "We receive from Jesus Christ what is profitable to us," without declaring what this is? if these words of our Saviour, "Flesh profiteth nothing," are, as the Ministers will have it, to be understood of the true flesh of Jesus Christ considered as to its substance, to what purpose so much noise about what they pretend affords no profit? why is there kept so great a work about the substance of the flesh and blood received so really? why not reject, concluded Catholics, these empty words, and, in proposing their faith, at least lay cant aside and speak intelligibly?

96.—*Peter Martyr's opinion concerning the equivocations of the Ministers.*

Peter Martyr, a native of Florence, and one of the most famous Ministers that were in this assembly, was of this mind, and frequently declared that, for his part, he knew no meaning this word *substance* had; yet endeavored to explain it the best way he could, not to give offence to Calvin and his companions.

97.—*What Dr. Depense added to the expressions of the Ministers, in order to make them pass the better.*

Claude Depense, a Parisian Doctor, a man of good sense, and learned for a time when matters had not so well been canvassed and cleared up, as they have since been by so much disputation, was among those who were to labor with the Ministers to reconcile the article of the Supper. Being sincere, and of a mild temper, he was judged proper for this design: but, for all his mildness, he could not bear with the doctrine of the Calvinists; but thought those insupportable who made the work of God, namely, the presence of the body of Jesus Christ, to depend not on the word and promise of him who gave it, but on their faith who were to receive it; accordingly he disapproved their article from the first proposition, and before all the additions which they since made to it. For his part, therefore, to render our communion, with the substance of the body, independent of the faith of men, and annexed only to the efficacy and operation of the word of God, letting pass the first words as far as those where the Ministers say, "That faith makes things present," he substituted these words in lieu thereof, namely, "And because the word and promise of God makes present the things promised, and by the efficacy of this word we do really and in face receive the true natural body of our Lord, in this sense we confess and acknowledge in the Supper the presence of his proper body and proper blood." Thus he owned a real and substantial presence independently of faith, and in virtue of the sole words of our Lord; whereby he thought to determine the ambiguous and unsettled sense of those terms which the Ministers made use of.

98.—*The decision of the Prelates, delivering very plainly and in few words the whole Catholic doctrine.*

The Prelates approved of nothing in all this, and pursuant to the opinions of the Doctors, whom they had brought along with them, declared the article of the Ministers heretical, captious, and insufficient: heretical because it denied the substantial, and properly so called, presence; captious, because, in denying it, it seemed to favor the thing; insufficient, because it concealed and dissembled the ministry of priests, the force of the sacramental words, and the change of substance, the natural effect thereof.[71] On their side they opposed to the Ministers a declaration of their faith, as full and as precise as that of the Calvinists was imperfect and perplexed. Beza relates in these terms:—"We believe and confess, that in the holy sacrament of the altar, the true body and blood of Jesus Christ is really and substantially under the species of bread and wine, by the virtue and power of the divine word pronounced by the priest, the sole minister ordained for this effect, according to the institution and commandment of our Lord Jesus Christ."[72] Here is nothing captious or equivocal, and Beza owns this was all that "could be drawn at that time from the clergy, in order to allay the troubles of religion, the prelates having made themselves judges, instead of conferring amicably." I desire no other testimony than this of Beza, to show that the Bishops did their duty in fairly explaining their faith, avoiding great words which impose on men by their sound, and signify nothing distinctly, and by refusing to enter into any composition in what relates to faith. Such plain dealing as this suited not the Ministers, and so this great assembly broke up without any manner of success. God baffled the policy and pride of those who thought by their eloquence, little arts, and weak contrivances, to quench, in its first fury, so great a conflagration.

99.—*The vain discourses of the Bishop of Valence, concerning the reformation of manners.*

The reformation of discipline succeeded but little better. Fine speeches were uttered, fine proposals made, but to little or no effect. The Bishop of Valence discoursed admirably, as his custom was, against abuses, and on the duties and charge of Bishops, chiefly on that of residence, which he observed the least of any. But, to make amends, he was quite silent as to celibacy, and the exact observance of it, though, by the Fathers, it was always insisted on as the brightest ornament of the ecclesiastic order. He had not feared to violate it by a clandestine marriage, in spite of the canons; nay, a Protestant historian, who, notwithstanding he sets him off for one "of the wisest and greatest men of that age through the whole sequel of his life,"[73] reveals to us his passion, his avarice, and the shameful disorders of his life, the noise of which reached as far as Ireland, in the most scandalous manner imaginable. Yet he declaimed loudly against vice, and convinced mankind that he was one of those admirable reformers who could correct and reprove every thing in their neighborhood, provided you leave them but alone to their own corrupted inclinations.

100.—*The Tenth Article of the Augsburg Confession is proposed to the Calvinists, but they refuse to sign it.*

As for the Calvinists, it was a triumph to them to have been so much as heard in such an assembly. But this imaginary triumph was but short, for the Cardinal of Lorrain had a long while conceived a design to propose to them the signing of the Tenth Article of the Augsburg Confession; should they sign it, this would be embracing the Reality, which all those of that confession so strenuously defended; should they refuse it, this would be condemning Luther and his followers in an essential point, who were unquestionably the first authors of the new Reformation, and its main support. In order to make the division of all these Reformers more manifest all over France, the Cardinal had taken his measures beforehand, and agreed with the Lutherans of Germany to send him three or four of their ablest doctors, who, appearing at Poissy under pretext of making up their whole differences at once, should there undertake the Calvinists. Thus these new doctors, all of them proclaiming the Scripture to be so very clear, would have been seen urging one another with its authority, yet never able to come to the least agreement. The Lutheran doctors arrived too late; but the Cardinal nevertheless failed not to make his proposal. Beza and his companions, resolved not to sign the Tenth Article, as proposed, thought to escape by inquiring of the Catholics, in return, whether they were willing to subscribe the rest; by which means they should all, in every thing, agree, except the Tenth Article of the Supper alone, a subtile, but frivolous evasion.[74] For after all, the Catholics had no manner of reason to concern themselves with Luther's authority, nor the Confession of Augsburg, nor the defenders of it, all which the Calvinists could not be too tender of, for fear of condemning the Reformation in its very source. However that my be, this was all the Cardinal obtained; and content with making it appear to all France, that this party of Reformers, who outwardly appeared so terrible, were yet inwardly so weak by their own divisions, he suffered the assembly to break up. But Anthony of Bourbon, King of Navarre and first Prince of the blood, very favorable, till then, to the new party, which he was only acquainted with under the appellation of Lutherans, undeceived himself; and instead of that piety, which he had before believed in them, began, from that time, to be convinced there was nothing in it but bitter zeal and prodigious infatuation.

101.—*The Confession of Augsburg received by the Calvinists in all other points, yet through policy only.*

Yet it was no small advantage to the Catholic cause, to have obliged the Calvinists, in such an assembly, to receive anew the Confession of Augsburg, with exclusion only of the article of the Supper; since, as we have seen, they renounced by this means so many important points of their own doctrine.

Beza, nevertheless, spoke out, and made a solemn declaration of it, with the consent of all his colleagues. But whatsoever policy, and the desire of supporting themselves as much as possible by the Confession of Augsburg, might have extorted from them on this occasion, as on many others, their thoughts and words did not agree; nor can this be doubted of, when the instruction, which even during the Conference, they received from Calvin,[75] is looked into. "You," says he, "that assist at the Conference, ought to be on your guard, lest in maintaining your own just right, you appear stubborn, and so cause the whole blame of the rupture to be cast on you. The Confession of Augsburg, you are sensible, is the torch which your furies employ to light up that fire which has set all France in a combustion; but you ought to look narrowly into the reason which makes them press you so much to receive it, considering that its suppleness has ever been displeasing to men of good sense, and that Melancthon, its author, often repented of having drawn it up: and lastly, that in many places it is adapted to the practice in Germany; besides that its obscure and defective brevity has this evil in it, of omitting sundry articles of the greatest moment."[76]

It then plainly appears, that it was not the sole article of the Supper, but, in general, the whole Confession of Augsburg which displeased him. This only article, nevertheless, was excepted against; though when Germany was concerned, it was often found proper to waive even this exception.

102.—How many different parts were played by Calvin and the Calvinists with respect to the Confession of Augsburg.

This is what appears by another letter of the same Calvin, written also during the Conference, whereby we may perceive how many different parts he played at the same time. It was, I say, at this very time, and in the year 1561, that he wrote a letter to the Princes of Germany in behalf of those of Strasburg; at the beginning of which he makes them say,[77] "That they are of the number of those who receive the confession of Augsburg throughout, even in the article of the Supper;" and he adds, "that the Queen of England (Elizabeth) although she approves of the Confession of Augsburg, rejects nevertheless the carnal ways of speaking of Heshusius, and others," who could not endure either Calvin, or Beza, or Peter Martyr, or Melancthon himself, whom, with respect to the Supper, they accused of relaxation.

103.—A like dissimulation in the Elector Frederick III.

The same behaviour may be seen in the Confession of Faith of the Elector Frederick III, Count Palatine, reported in the Collection of Geneva: a confession wholly Calvinistical, and as inimical to the Real Presence as any ever was; since this Prince there declares that Jesus Christ is not in the Supper "in any manner, either visible, or invisible, comprehensible, or incomprehensible, but in heaven only."[78] Nevertheless, his son and successor, John Casimir, in the preface which he places before this Confession, says expressly, "that his father never did depart from the Confession of Augsburg, nor even from the

Apology which was joined to it:" it is that of Melancthon, which we have seen to be so distinct and full for the Real Presence; and if the son should not meet with credit, the father himself, in the body of his Confession, declares the selfsame thing, in the selfsame terms.

104.—*Calvin's shifting address with regard to the Tenth Article of the Augsburg Confession.*

It was therefore a method pretty much in vogue, even amongst the Calvinists, to approve purely and simply the Confession of Augsburg when Germany was concerned, either out of a certain respect for Luther, the common father of the whole pretended Reformation; or because that confession only had been tolerated in Germany by the States of the empire; and even out of the empire itself had obtained so great an authority, that Calvin and the Calvinists[79] durst not own, without great deference and precaution, that they departed from it; seeing that, in the exception even of the sole article of the Supper, which they often made, they rather chose the subterfuge of diversity of editions, and difference of sense put upon this article, than absolutely to reject it.

And accordingly, Calvin, who makes so free with the Confession of Augsburg, when he speaks in confidence to his friends, every where else shows an outward respect for it, even in regard to the article of the Supper, owning he receives it when right explained,[80] and in the same manner Melancthon, the author thereof, did himself understand it. But there is nothing more frivolous than this evasion; for, although this Confession was penned by Melancthon, he did not expound therein his own particular doctrine, but that of Luther and the whole party, whose secretary and interpreter he was, as he himself often declares.

And allowing that in a public act the private sentiments of that person who drew it up might be referred to, it ought, however, to be considered, not what Melancthon's notions were afterwards, but what they and those of all his sect were at that time; there being no reason to doubt but he endeavored to explain naturally what they all believed: so much the more, as we have seen that he as sincerely rejected the figurative sense at that time, as Luther himself; which he never openly approved, notwithstanding the various shifts and inconstancy he afterwards was subject to. It is not, therefore, upright and just dealing to appeal to Melancthon's judgment in this matter; and for all Calvin's continual boasts of speaking his real sentiments without the least dissimulation, yet it is plainly seen that his design was to flatter the Lutherans. Nay, so palpable became this flattery, that at length they were ashamed of it even in the party; and this was the reason that, in the acts we have just considered, especially in the Conference of Poissy, they resolved to except the article of the Supper, but that only; not at all concerned that by their approbation of all the rest, they passed sentence against their own Confession of Faith, which they had but a little before presented to Charles IX.

Notes

[1] Sup. l., iii. n. 38. Instit. l. 3. 2. n. 16. &c. 24. c. Antid. Con. Trid. in Sess. vi. cap. 13, 14. opusc. p. 185.

[2] Synt. Gen. part ii. pp. 149, 156.

[3] Inst. iv. xv. n. 22. xvi. 3, &c. 9. Gen. xvii. 7. Dom. 50.

[4] Ant. Conc. Trid., in Sess. 6. c. 16. opusc. p. 288.

[5] Conf. de Fr. Art. 18-22. Cat. Dim. 18-20. Cat. Dim. 50. Forme du Bapt. 5. n. 11.

[6] Con. Tigur. et Genev. Art. 17, 20. opusc. Cal. p. 754. Hosp. An. 1554.

[7] Tract. de Cœn. Dom. opusc. p. 1.

[8] Ep. ad Illust. Princ. Germ. p. 324.

[9] Matt. xxvi. 26, 28; Luke xxii 29; 1 Cor. xi. 24.

[10] Luke xxii. 19; 1 Cor xi. 24, 25

[11] 1 Cor. xi. 26.

[12] Mark vi. 30, 31. Luke viii. 45, 46.

[13] Instit. lib. iv. c. 17. n. 17, &c. Diluc. Expos. Adm. cont. Westph. int. opusc. &c.

[14] Tr. de Cœn. Domini, 1540. Int. opusc. &c. Inst. iv. xvi. 18, &c. &c. Diluc. Exp. opusc. 846 Ibid. Brev. Admon. de Cœna. Domini int. Ep. p. 594.

[15] Dim. 51, 52, 53. Conf. xxxvi.

[16] 2. Def. cont. Westph. p. 779.

[17] Cat. Dim. 52.

[18] Inst. lib. iv. c. 17. n. 11. 14. Catech. Dim. 53. Sup. lib. n. 23. Lib. vi. c. 34.

[19] Inst. iv. c. 17. n. 16, 17. Diluc. exp. sanæ doct. opusc. p. 839. Ibid. p. 844.

[20] Ibid.

[21] Inst. et Opusc. p. 777, et seq. pp. 839, 844, etc.

[22] Inst. iv. 17, 32.

[23] Art. 36.

[24] Dim. 53.

[25] Ibid. 52.

[26] Inst. iv. 17. 10. Opusc. de Cœna Domini. 1540.

[27] Inst. ibid. n. 33.

[28] Aug. Serm. xi. de verb. Dom.

[29] Inst. lib. iv. c. 17. n. 33. 2. Def. opusc. p. 781.

[30] Diluc. Exp. opusc. p. 848.

[31] Inst. lib. iv. c. 17, n. 33.

[32] John i. 11.

[33] Ibid.

[34] Diluc. Ex. opusc. p. 859.

[35] Inst. iv. xvii. n. 33. Ep. ad Mart. Schal. p. 247.

[36] Defens. opusc. p. 775.

[37] Diluc. Exp. opusc. p. 845.

[38] Dim. 53.

[39] Diluc. Exp. opusc. p. 858.

[40] Diluc. Exp. opusc. p. 861.

[41] Admon. ult. ad Westph. opusc. p. 812.

[42] Def. opusc. p. 781, etc.; pp. 812, 813, 818, etc.

[43] Gen. xvii. 13. Ibid. 11.

[44] Inst. iv. 17.

[45] Diluc. Expos. opusc. p. 864.

[46] Inst. lib. iv. c. xvii. n. 11.

[47] Diluc. Exp. opusc. p. 864.

[48] Preserv. p. 195.

[49] Ibid. p. 196.

[50] Dim. 52. Preserv. p. 197.

[51] Preserv. Ibid. p. 194.

[52] Inst. iv. p. 17, n. 16.

[53] Ep. ad Mel. p. 120, etc.

[54] Ep. Calv. p. 195.

[55] Resp. ad Bald. int. opusc. Calv. p. 370.

[56] 2 Def. ad Westp. opusc. 788.

[57] Ibid. 842.

[58] 2 Def. 791.

[59] Opusc. p. 799. Ibid. pp. 803, 837.

[60] Diluc. Expos. Ibid. p. 839.

[61] 2 Def. in Westph.

[62] Ult. Adm. p. 795.

[63] Opusc. 838.

[64] Tr. de Ref. Eccl.

[65] 2 Def. opusc. 777. Admon. ul. 836. Ibid.

[66] Opusc. Cal. 752. Hosp. An. 1554. Art. xxii. xxiii.

[67] Hosp. ad. 1557, f. 252.

[68] Hosp. ad An. 1561. Bez. Hist. Eccl. l. iv. La Poplin. l. vii. Thuan l. xxviii.

[69] Ep. Bez. ad Calv. inter. Ep. Calv. p. 330.

[70] Thuan. xxviii. 48.

[71] Bez. Hist. Eccl. l. iv. p. 611-614. La Poplin, I. vii.

[72] Hist. Eccl. i. iv. p. 611-614.

[73] V. S. lib. vii. n. 7.

[74] Ep. Bez. ad Calv. inter Cal. Ep. pp. 346, 347.

[75] Ep. p. 342.

[76] Hosp. ad An. 1561. Bez. Hist. Eccl. 1. iv. La Poplin. 1. vii. Thuan 1. xxviii.

[77] Ep. p. 324.

[78] Syn. Gen. part ii. pp. 141, 142.

[79] Ep. p. 319. 2. Def. Ult. Adm. ad Westp.

[80] Ep. p. 319. 2 Def. Ult. Adm. ad Westp.

Book X

Brief summary:—Queen Elizabeth's Reformation.—That of Edward corrected, and the Real Presence, which had been condemned under that Prince, held for indifferent:—The Church of England still persists in this sentiment.—Other Variations of this Church in that Queen's reign.—Her ecclesiastical Supremacy moderated in appearance, in reality left in the same state as under Henry and Edward, notwithstanding the scruples of Elizabeth.—Policy bears the sway throughout this whole Reformation.—The Faith, the Sacraments, and the whole ecclesiastical authority delivered up into the hands of Kings and Parliaments.—The same done in Scotland.—The Calvinists of France disapprove this doctrine, nevertheless let it pass.—England's doctrine upon Justification.—Queen Elizabeth favors the French Protestants.—They rebel as soon as they have it in their power.—The conspiracy of Amboise, in Francis the Second's reign.—The civil wars under Charles IX.—This conspiracy and these wars appertain to Religion, and were entered into by the authority of the doctors and ministers of the party, and grounded on the new doctrine teaching the lawfulness of making war against their prince, for the sake of Religion.—This doctrine expressly warranted by their national Synods.—The fallacy of Protestant writers, and of Mr. Burnet, amongst the rest, who pretend that the tumult of Amboise and the civil wars were state affairs.—Religion was at the bottom of Francis, Duke of Guise's murder.—Beza's and the Admiral's testimony.—A new Confession of Faith in Switzerland.

1.—*Queen Elizabeth is persuaded nothing can secure to her the Crown, but the Protestant religion.—Four points she was uneasy about.*

ENGLAND having soon returned, after Queen Mary's death, to Edward the Sixth's Reformation, set about fixing her Faith and putting the finishing stroke to her religion by the new Queen's authority. Elizabeth, daughter of Henry VIII and Anne Boleyn, was advanced to the throne, and governed her kingdom with as profound a policy as the most able kings. The step she had taken with regard to Rome, immediately upon her coming to the crown, countenanced what otherwise had been published of this princess, that she would not have departed from the Catholic religion, had she found the Pope more disposed to her interests. Paul IV, who then sat in the Apostolic Chair, gave no favorable reception to the civilities she had caused to be tendered him as to another prince, without further declaration of her mind, by the resident of the late queen her sister.[1] Mr. Burnet tells us, he treated her as illegitimate; was surprised at her great boldness in assuming the crown, a fief of the Holy See, without his consent; and gave her no hopes of receiving any favor at his hands, unless she renounced her pretensions, and submitted to the See of Rome. Such usage, if true, was not at all likely to reclaim a queen. After such a repulse, Elizabeth readily withdrew from a See, by whose decrees her birth had also been condemned, and engaged in the new Reformation; yet she did not approve that of Edward in all its parts. There were four points which caused her uneasiness,[2] that of Ceremonies, that of Images, that of the Real Presence, and that of the regal Supremacy; and what was done, in her time, with reference to these four points, we are now to relate.

2.—First Point: Ceremonies.

As for ceremonies, "her first impressions," says Mr. Burnet, "were in favor of such old rites as her father had still retained, and in her own nature loving state and some magnificence in Religion, she thought her brother's ministers had stripped it too much of external ornaments, and left religion too bare and naked. Yet I do not find she did any thing considerable in that regard."[3]

3.—Second Point: Images.—Pious sentiments of the Queen

As for Images, "That matter stuck long with her; for she inclined to keep up Images in churches, and it was with great difficulty she was prevailed upon, persuaded as she was that the use of Images in church might be a means to stir up devotion, and that at least it would draw all people to frequent them the more."[4] Herein her sentiments agreed in the main with those of the Catholics. If they stir up devotion towards God, they might well excite also the external tokens of it; this is the whole of that worship which we pay them. To be inclined to, and have favorable impressions of them in this sense, like Queen Elizabeth, was not so gross a notion as is at present imputed to our belief; and I much question whether Mr. Burnet would venture to charge a queen, who, according to him, was the foundress of religion in England, with entertaining idolatrous sentiments. But the Iconoclast party had gained their point; the queen, unable to resist them, was wrought up by them to such extremes, that not content with commanding Images to be cast out of all churches, she forbade all her subjects to keep them in their houses;[5] nothing but the Crucifix escaped,[6] and that no where but in the Royal Chapel, whence the queen could not be persuaded to remove it.

4.—They persuade her with reasons evidently bad.

It may not be improper to consider what the Protestants alleged in order to induce her to this injunction against Images, in order that the excess of vanity of the thing may be discovered. The chief foundation of their reasons is, "that the second commandment forbids the making of any Images, as a resemblance of God,"[7] which evidently proves nothing either against the Images of Jesus Christ as man, or those of the saints, or, in general, against such, with respect to which we publicly declare (as does the Catholic Church) that by them we in nowise pretend to represent the Deity. The rest is too extravagant to ear repeating: for either it concludes just nothing, or it concludes for the absolute prohibition of the use of painting and sculpture,—a weakness now-a-days so universally exploded by all Christians, as only to find place in the gross superstition of Mahometans and Jews.

5.—*Manifest Variation with respect to the Real Presence.*—*Policy regulates Religion.*

The queen showed more resolution on the subject of the Eucharist. It is of main importance well to comprehend her sentiments, such as Mr. Burnet delivers them: "She thought that in her brother's reign they made their doctrine too narrow in some points; therefore she intended to have some things explained in more general terms, that so all parties might be comprehended by them."[8] These were her sentiments in general. In applying them to the Eucharist, "Her intention was to have the manner of Christ's presence in the Sacrament be left in some *general* words. She very much disliked that those who believed the corporal presence had been driven away from the Church by too nice an explanation of it." And again, "it was proposed to have the communion-book so contrived, that it might not exclude the belief of the corporal presence; for the chief design of the Queen's council was to unite the nation in one faith."[9]

One might be apt to think, perchance, that the queen judged it needless to make any express declarations against the real presence, her subjects of themselves being sufficiently inclined to reject it: but, on the contrary, "the greatest part of the nation continued to believe such a presence. Therefore, it was recommended to the divines to see that there should be no express definition made against it; that so it might lie as a speculative opinion, not determined, in which every man was left to the freedom of his own mind."[10]

6.—*The Faith of the pretended Martyrs changed.*

Here was a strange variation in one of the main fundamental points of the English Reformation. In the Confession of Faith set forth in 1551, under Edward, the doctrine of the Real Presence was excluded in so strong a manner, that it was declared impossible and contrary to our Lord's ascension. When Cranmer was condemned for a heretic in Queen Mary's time, he owned the capital subject of his condemnation was, his not confessing a corporal presence of our Saviour on the altar. Ridley, Latimer, and others, the pretended martyrs of the English Reformation, mentioned by Mr. Burnet, all suffered for the same cause. Calvin says as much of the French martyrs, whose authority he opposes against the Lutherans."[11] This article was esteemed of that high importance even in 1549, and during the whole reign of Edward, "that when the reformation was to be carried on to the establishment of a form of doctrine," says Mr. Burnet, "which should contain the chief points of religion, inquiry was chiefly made concerning the presence of Christ in the sacrament." It was, therefore, at that time, not only one of the fundamental points, but also a capital one amongst these fundamentals. As it was of such concern, and the principal cause for which these boasted martyrs shed their blood, it could not be explained in terms too distinct. After so clear an exposition of it as that which had been made under Edward, to return, as did Elizabeth, to general terms, which left the thing undetermined, that all parties might be comprehended in them, and every man left to the freedom of his own mind, was betraying truth, and putting error on the level with it. In a word, these general terms in a confession of faith, were nothing but a fallacy in the most serious of all concerns, and wherein the utmost sincerity is required. This is what the English Reformers ought to have represented to Elizabeth. But policy outbalanced religion, nor was it now to their purpose so greatly to condemn the Real Presence. Wherefore, the twenty-ninth article of Edward's confession, wherein it was condemned, was very much changed, and a great deal left out;[12] all that showed the Real Presence was impossible and contradictory to the residence of Christ's body in heaven. "All this was suppressed, says Mr. Burnet, "and that expressed definition dashed over with minimum." The historian takes care to tell us it is still legible; but that even is a testimony against the expunged doctrine. They would have it still legible, to the end a proof might be extant, that this was the very point which they had concluded to reverse. They had remonstrated to Queen Elizabeth concerning images, "that it would cast a great reflection on the first reformers, should they again set up in churches what these so zealous martyrs of the evangelical purity had so carefully removed."[13] It was of no less a criminal nature, to rescind from the Confession of Faith of these pretended martyrs, what they had placed in it, in opposition to the Real Presence, and to annul that doctrine, in testimony whereof they had given up their lives. Instead of their plain and express definitions, they were content to say, conformably to Queen Elizabeth's design, "in general terms, that the body of Christ is given and received after a spiritual manner; and the means by which it is received, is Faith."[14] The first part of the article is very true, taking spiritual manner for a manner that is above our senses and nature, as the Catholics and Lutherans understand it; nor is the second part less certain, taking the reception for a profitable reception, and in the sense St. John meant, when he said of Jesus Christ, "that his own received him not,"[15] although he were in the world in person in the midst of them; that is to say, they neither received his doctrine nor his grace. Furthermore, what was added in Edward's Confession, with reference to the communion of the wicked who receive nothing but the symbols, was cut off in like manner, and care was taken that nothing but what the Catholics and Lutherans might approve, should be retained with respect to the Real Presence.

7.—Substantial Changes in Edward's Liturgy.

For the same reason, whatever condemned the corporal presence, was now changed in Edward's liturgy: for instance, the rubrick there explained the reason for kneeling at the sacrament, "that thereby no adoration is intended to any corporal presence of Christ's natural flesh and blood, because that is only in heaven."[16] But, under Elizabeth, those words were lopped off, and the full liberty of adoring the flesh and blood of Jesus Christ was allowed as present in the Eucharist. What the pretended martyrs and founders of the English Reformation had held for gross idolatry, became an innocent action in the reign of Queen Elizabeth. In Edward's second liturgy, these words, which had been left standing in the first, were taken away: viz., "the body or the blood of Jesus Christ preserve thy body and thy soul to everlasting life;" but these words, which Edward had left out because they seemed too much to favor the belief of the corporal presence, were replaced by Queen Elizabeth.[17] The will of kings became the rule of faith, and what we now see removed by this queen, was again inserted in the common-prayer book by King Charles II.

8.—An imposition of Mr. Burnet; who has the assurance to say, that the Doctrine established by Edward was not changed.

Notwithstanding all these changes in such essential matters, Mr. Burnet would make us believe there was no variation in the doctrine of the English Reformation. "The doctrine of the Church," says he, "was at that time contrary to the belief of a real or corporal presence in the sacrament, in like manner as at present: only, it was not thought necessary or expedient to publish it in too distinct a manner;"[18] as if one could speak too distinctly in matters of faith. But this is not all. It is a manifest variation in doctrine, not only to embrace what is contrary to it, but to leave undecided what was decided formerly. If the ancient Catholics, after deciding in express terms the Son of God's equality with his Father, had suppressed what they had pronounced at Nice, contenting themselves with barely calling him God in general terms, and in the sense the Arians could not deny it, insomuch that what had been decided so expressly should have become undecided and indifferent, would they not have altered the Church's faith, and stepped backwards? Now, this is what was done under Elizabeth by the Church of England; and non can acknowledge it more clearly than Mr. Burnet has done in the words above cited, where it stands confessed in express terms, that it was neither by chance, nor forgetfulness, but from a premeditated design, that they omitted the words used in Edward's time, and that "no express definition was made against the corporal presence;"[19] on the contrary, it was let lie as a speculative opinion, not determined, in which every man was left to the freedom of his own mind to reject or embrace it: in this manner, either sincerely or politically, the faith of the reformers was forsaken, and the dogma of the corporal presence left for indifferent, against which they had combated even unto blood.

9.—England indifferent as to the Real Presence.

This, if we believe Mr. Burnet, is yet the present state of the Church of England. It was on these grounds that the Bishop William Bedell, whose life he has written, believed that a great company of Lutherans who had fled to Dublin for refuge, might without difficulty communicate with the Church of England,[20] "which in reality," says Mr. Burnet, "hath so great a moderation in that matter (the Real Presence) that no positive definition of the manner of the presence being made, men of different sentiments may agree in the same acts of worship, without being obliged to declare their opinion, or being understood to do any thing contrary to their several persuasions." Thus hath the Church of England corrected her teachers, and reformed her first reformers.

10.—Neither the word substance nor miracles, which Calvin places in the Eucharist, are admitted by them.

Moreover, the English Reformation neither under Edward nor Elizabeth, ever employed, in the explanation of the Eucharist, the substance of the body, nor those incomprehensible operations which Calvin so much exalts. These expressions too much favored a real presence, and it was for this reason they were not made use of either in Edward's reign, when that was designedly excluded, or in Elizabeth's, when the thing was to be left undetermined; and England was very sensible that these words of Calvin, little suitable to the doctrine of the figurative sense, could not be introduced into it otherwise, than by forcing too visibly their natural sense.

11.—The Queen's Supremacy in spirituals is established in spite of all her scruples.

The article of Supremacy now remains to be considered. True, it is, Elizabeth opposed it, and this title, of Head of the Church, in her judgment too great for kings, seemed to her still more insupportable in a queen, not to say ridiculous. "A famous preacher among those of the reformation," says Mr. Burnet, "put this scruple about in her head,"[21] that is, some remains of shame were still to be met with in the English Church; nor was it without some little remorse that she gave up her authority to the secular power; but policy got the better even in this point. As much ashamed as the queen was in her heart of this title of the Church's supreme head, she accepted of it, and exercised it under another name. By an act which passed in 1559, "The supremacy was again annexed to the crown, and declared that the authority of visiting, correcting, and reforming all things in the Church is for ever annexed to the regal dignity, and whosoever should refuse to swear and acknowledge the queen to be the supreme governor in all causes, as well ecclesiastical as temporal, within her dominions, was to forfeit any office he had either in Church or State; and to be thenceforth disabled to hold any employment during life."[22] This is what the queen's scruple ended in; and all she did to moderate the laws of Henry VIII, with regard to the king's supremacy, was, that whereas, denying the supremacy in King Henry's time, cost men their lives, in Elizabeth's it cost them but a forfeiture of their goods.[23]

12.—*Resolution of the Catholic Bishops.*

The Catholic bishops on this occasion were not forgetful of their duty, and being inflexibly attached to the Catholic Church and Holy See, were deposed for having constantly refused to subscribe the queen's supremacy, no less than the other articles of the Reformation. But Parker, the Protestant Archbishop of Canterbury, was of all the most zealous in submitting to the yoke. It was to him complaints were addressed of the queen's scruples respecting her title of Supreme head; to him was rendered an account of what was done to engage the Catholics to acknowledge it, and finally the English Reformation could no longer be compatible with the liberty and authority which Jesus Christ had given to his Church. What had been resolved on in the Parliament in 1559, in favor of the queen's supremacy, was received in the synod of London by the common consent of all the clergy, of the first as well as of the second order.

13.—*Declaration of the Clergy regarding the Supremacy of Elizabeth.*

There the supremacy was inserted among the articles of faith in these terms:—"The royal majesty has sovereign power in the kingdom of England, and in her other dominions, and the sovereign government of all her subjects, lay and ecclesiastical, belongs to her in all matters, without being subjected to any foreign power."[24] By these last words they intended to exclude the Pope; but as the other words, "in all matters"[25] put in without restriction, as had been done in the act of parliament, imported a full sovereignty, even in ecclesiastical causes, without excepting those of faith, they were ashamed of proceeding to such great excess, and introduced the following modification: "Whereas we attribute to the royal majesty this sovereign government, at which we learn that many ill-disposed individuals are displeased, we do not grant to our kings the administration of the word and of the sacraments, as is clearly shown by the ordinances of our Queen Elizabeth; but we merely give to her the prerogative, which the Scripture attributes to pious princes, of being able to keep to their duty all orders, whether lay or ecclesiastical, and to check the stubborn by the sword of the civil power.

14.—*This served but as a clumsy palliation for a great evil.*

This explanation is conformable to a declaration which the queen had published, where she said at first "that she was far from wishing to administer holy things." The Protestants, ready to afford satisfaction on the subject of ecclesiastical authority, thought thereby to be sheltered from whatever evil its supremacy was attended with, but all in vain; for the question was not whether the English invested royalty with the administration of the word and of the sacraments. Who has ever accused them of wishing that their kings should ascend the pulpit, or administer communion and baptism? And what is there so uncommon in this declaration, wherein Queen Elizabeth avows that the ministry appertains not to her? The question was to know, whether in such matters the royal majesty has a mere direction and an external execution, or whether it influences fundamentally the validity of ecclesiastical acts. But whilst it was apparently reduced in this article to the mere execution, the contrary appeared but too manifest in practice. Permission to preach was granted by letters patent and under the great seal. The queen made bishops with the same authority as the king her father and the king her brother, and for a limited time if she pleased. The commission for their consecration emanated from the royal power. Excommunications were decreed by the same authority. The queen regulated by her edicts not only the exterior worship, but also faith and the dogma, or caused them to be regulated by her parliament, whose acts received their validity from her; and there is nothing more unheard of in the Christian Church, than what was done at that time.

15.—*The Parliament continues to assume the decision in points of faith.*

The parliament pronounced directly on heresy. It regulated the conditions on which a doctrine should pass for heretical, and where these conditions were not found in this doctrine, it prohibited its condemnation, "and reserved to itself the cognizance of it." The question is not to know whether the rule which parliament prescribed is good or bad; but whether the parliament, a secular body, whose acts received their validity from the prince, can decide on matters of faith, and reserve to itself the cognizance of them; that is, whether they may challenge it to themselves, and take away the exercise of it from the bishops, on whom Christ had bestowed it; for the parliament's saying they would judge with the assent of the clergy in their convocation[26] was nothing but an illusion; since, in the end, this was still reserving to the parliament the supreme authority, and hearing the pastors rather as counsellors whose lights they borrowed, than as natural judges, to whom only the decision appertained of divine right. I cannot think that a Christian heart can hear of such an invasion of the pastoral authority and the rights of the sanctuary without a sigh.

16.—*On what is grounded the Validity of the English Ordinations.*

But lest it should be imagined, that all these attempts of the secular authority on the rights of the sanctuary were nothing but usurpations of the laity, the clergy not consenting to them, and this under pretext of the above explanation given by the said clergy to the Queen's supremacy in the thirty-seventh article of the Confession of Faith, what precedes, and what follows, evince the contrary. What precedes, inasmuch as this synod being composed, as just observed, of both houses of the clergy intending to set forth the validity of the ordination of bishops, of priests, and deacons, grounds it on a form contained in the book of consecration of archbishops and bishops, and ordaining of priests and deacons, lately set forth in the time of King Edward VI, and confirmed by authority of parliament.[27] Weak bishops! wretched clergy! who choose rather to take the form of their ordination from a book made lately, but ten years ago in King Edward's time, and confirmed by the authority of parliament, than from the sacramentary of St. Gregory, the author of their conversion, wherein they might still read the form, according to which their predecessors and the holy monk St. Augustin, their first apostle, had been consecrated; although this book was warranted, not indeed by the authority of parliaments, but by the universal tradition of all Christian churches.[28]

17.—*Sequel of this Matter.*

Upon this it was that these bishops founded the validity of their consecration, and the orders of their priests and deacons; and this was done pursuant to a decree of parliament in 1559, wherein the doubt concerning the ordination, which was joined to King Edward's liturgy: so that had not the parliament made these acts, the ordination of their whole clergy had still remained dubious.[29]

18.—*Decision of Faith reserved in the Royal Authority, by the Declaration of the Bishops.*

The bishops and their clergy, who had thus enslaved the ecclesiastical authority, conclude in a manner corresponding to such a beginning: when, after having set forth their faith in all the foregoing articles to the number of thirty-nine, they conclude with this ratification, wherein they declare, "That these articles being authorized by the consent and assent of Queen Elizabeth, ought to be received and executed throughout the whole realm of England." Where we find the Queen's approbation, and not only her consent by submission, but also her assent, as I may say, by express deliberation, mentioned in the act as a condition that makes it valid; insomuch that the decrees of bishops in matters the most within the verge of their ministry, receive their last form and validity, in the same style with acts of parliament from the Queen's approbation, these weak bishops never daring all this while to remonstrate, after the example of all past ages, that their decrees, valid of themselves, and by that sacred authority, which Jesus Christ had annexed to their character, required nothing else from the regal power, but an entire submission and exterior protection. Thus, whilst they forget the primitive institutions of their church, together with the head whom Jesus Christ had given them, and set up princes for their heads whom Jesus Christ had not appointed for that end, they degraded themselves to that degree, that no ecclesiastical act, not even those which regard preaching, censures, liturgy, sacraments, nay, faith itself, have any force in England, but inasmuch as they are approved and made valid by Kings; which in the main gives to Kings more than the word, and more than the administration of the sacraments, since it renders them the sovereign arbiters of one and the other.

19.—The same Doctrine in Scotland.—1568.

It is for the same reason that we behold the first Confession of Scotland, since she became Protestant, published in the name of the parliament; and a second Confession of the same kingdom, bearing this title: "A general Confession of the true Christian Faith according to the word of God, and the acts of our Parliaments."[30]

A great multitude of different declarations was requisite to explain how these acts did not attribute the episcopal jurisdiction to the crown; but all was nothing but mere words, since after all, it still stands incontestable that no ecclesiastical act hath any force in that kingdom, no more than in England, unless ratified by the King and parliament.

20.—The English Doctrine, which makes the King head of the Church,
condemned by the Calvinists.

Our Calvinists, I own, seem far remote from this doctrine; and I find, not only in Calvin, as already observed, but also in the national synods, express condemnations of those who confound the civil government with that of the church, by making the magistrate head of the church, or by subjecting the ecclesiastical government to the people.[31] But there is nothing but will go down with these men, provided you are an enemy to the Pope and Rome; insomuch that, by stress of equivocations and explanations, the Calvinists were gained, and brought in England even to subscribe the supremacy.

21.—All that remained to the Church seized upon.

It appears by the whole tenor of the acts which I have reported, how vain it is to pretend that, in the reign of Elizabeth, this supremacy was reduced to more reasonable terms than in the precedent reigns, there being, on the contrary, no alteration to be found in the main.[32] Among other fruits of the supremacy, one was the Queen's invading the revenues of the church under the pretence of giving the full value of them,[33] even those of the bishops, such as, till then, had remained sacred and inviolate. Treading in the steps of the King her father, in order to engage the nobility in the interests of the supremacy and reformation, she made them a present of a share in these consecrated goods; and this state of the church, enslaved both in her temporals and spirituals, is called the English Reformation, the re-establishment of evangelical purity!

22.—A remarkable passage in Mr. Burnet, concerning the English Reformation.

Nevertheless, if we may form a judgment of this reformation according to the gospel-rule, by its fruits, there was never any thing more deplorable: seeing the effect which this miserable subjection of the clergy did produce, was, that from thence-forwards religion was no more than a state-engine always veering at the breath of the prince. Edward's reformation, which had entirely changed that of Henry VIII, was changed itself in an instant under Mary, and Elizabeth destroyed in two years all that Mary had done before.

The bishops, reduced to fourteen in number, stood firm, together with about fifty or sixty ecclesiastics;[34] but, excepting so small a number in so great a kingdom, all the rest paid obedience to the Queen's injunctions, yet with so little good will for the new doctrine they were made to embrace, "that probably," says Mr. Burnet,"if Queen Elizabeth had not lived long, and a prince of another religion had succeeded before the death of all that generation, they had turned about again to the old superstitions as nimbly as they had done in Queen Mary's time."[35]

23.—Inamissibility of Justice rejected by the Church of England

In the same Confession of Faith, which had been confirmed under Elizabeth in 1562, there are two important points relating to justification. In one of them, the inamissibility of justice is rejected clearly enough by this declaration. "After we have received the Holy Ghost, we may depart from grace given, and arise again, and amend our lives."[36] In the other, the certainty of predestination seems quite excluded, when, after saying that "The doctrine of predestination is full of comfort to godly persons, by confirming their faith of eternal salvation to be enjoyed through Jesus Christ," they add, "It is the downfall for carnal persons either into a desperation, or into recklessness of most unclean living." And, in conclusion, that "we must receive God's promises, as they be generally set forth to us in holy scripture; and in our doings, that will of God is to be followed, which we have expressly declared unto us in the word of God;" which seems to exclude that special certainty, whereby each of the faithful is obliged to believe in particular, as of faith, that he is in the number of the elect, and comprehended within that absolute decree, by which God wills their salvation: a doctrine not agreeable, it seems, to the Protestants of England, although they not only bear with it in the Calvinists, but also the deputies from their church have confirmed it, as we shall see in the synod of Dort.[37]

24.—The beginning of the disturbances in France fomented by Elizabeth.— Change of the Calvinistic Doctrine.

Queen Elizabeth secretly encouraged that disposition which those of France were in towards a rebellion; nearly at the same time that the English reformation was modelled under that queen, they declared themselves. Our reformed, after about thirty years, grew weary of deriving their glory from their sufferings; their patience could hold out no longer; nor did they from that time exaggerate their submission to our kings.[38] This submission lasted but whilst they were in a capacity of curbing them. Under the strong reigns of Francis I and Henry II, they were in reality very submissive, and made no show of an intention to levy war. The reign, no less weak than short, of Francis II, inspired them with boldness. The fire, so long concealed, blazed forth in the conspiracy of Amboise. Yet a sufficient strength still remained in the government to have quenched it at the beginning: but during the minority of Charles IX, and under the regency of a queen, all whose policy aspired no further than to maintain her power by dangerous and trimming measures, the revolt became entire and the conflagration universal over all France. A particular account of these intrigues and wars comes not within my sphere, nor should I even have spoken of these commotions, if, contrary to all preceding declarations and protestations, they had not produced this new doctrine in the reformation, that it is lawful to take up arms against prince and country, in the cause of religion.

25.—*The Calvinists took arms from maxims of Religion.*

It had been well foreseen, that the new reformed would not be slack in proceeding to such measures. Not to trace back the wars of the Albigenses, the seditions of the Wickliffites in England, the furies of the Taborites in Bohemia, it had been but too apparent what was the result of all the fine protestations of the Lutherans in Germany.[39] The leagues and wars so much detested at first, as soon as ever the Protestants were sensible of their strength, became lawful, and Luther added this new article to his gospel. The ministers too of the Vaudois had but just taught this doctrine, when the war was commenced in the valleys against their sovereigns the Dukes of Savoy. The new reformed of France were not backward to follow these examples, nor is there any doubt but they were spirited up to it by their doctors.

26.—*Beza owns that the conspiracy of Amboise was entered upon from a maxim of Conscience.*

As for the conspiracy of Amboise, all historians testify us much; even Beza owns it in his ecclesiastical history. It was from the influence of the doctors, that the Prince of Condé believed himself innocent, or affected to believe it, although so heinous an attempt had been undertaken by his orders.[40] It was resolved on by the party, to furnish him with men and money, to the end he might have a competent force: so that the design then on foot, after the seizure of the two Guises in the very castle of Amboise, where the King was in person, and forcibly carrying them away, was nothing less than from that very time to light up the torch of civil war throughout the whole kingdom. The whole body of the Reformation came into this design, and on this occasion the province of Xaintonge is praised by Beza, for having done their duty like the rest.[41] The same Beza testifies an extreme regret, that so just an enterprise should have failed, and attributes the bad success of it to the perfidiousness of certain people.

27.—*Four demonstrations that the riot of Amboise was the work of Protestants, and that the motive to it was Religion.—First demonstration.*

The Protestants, it is true, were desirous of giving to this enterprise, as they do to all others of this nature, a pretext of public good, in order to inveigle some Catholics into it, and to screen the reformation from the infamy of so wicked an attempt. But four reasons demonstrate that it was in reality an affair of religion, and an enterprise carried on by the reformed. In the first place, because it was set on foot on the occasion of the executions of some of the party, and especially of Anne du Bourg, that famous pretended martyr. Beza, after relating this execution, together with the other evil treatments the Lutherans underwent, (then all the reformed were so called,) introduces the history of this conspiracy, and at the head of the motives which gave birth to it, places these manifestly tyrannical ways of proceeding, and the menaces that on this occasion were levelled at the greatest men of the kingdom, such as the Prince of Condé and the Chastillons. "Then it was," says he,"that many lords awaked as from a profound sleep: so much the more," continues this historian, "as they considered, that the Kings Francis and Henry never would attempt any thing against the men of quality, contenting themselves with awing the great ones by the correction of the meaner sort, that now quite different measures were taken; whereas, in consideration of the number concerned, they should have applied less violent remedies, rather than thus open a gate to a million seditions."

28.—Second demonstration, wherein the advice of Beza
and the Divines of the Party is reported.

The confession is sincere, I must own. Whilst nothing but the dregs of the people were punished, the lords of the party did not stir, but let them go quietly to execution. When they, like the rest, were threatened, they bethought themselves of their weapons, or, as the author expresses it, "Each man was forced to look at home, and many began to range themselves together, to provide for a just defence, and to resettle the ancient and lawful government of the kingdom." This last word was necessary to disguise the rest; but what goes before shows plainly enough the design in hand, and the sequel evinces it still more clearly. For these means of a just defence imported, that the thing[42] "having been proposed to lawyers and men of renown in France and Germany, as likewise to the most learned divines; it was discovered that they might lawfully oppose the government usurped by the Guises, and take up arms, in case of need to repel their violence, provided the princes of the blood, who in such cases are born lawful magistrates, or one of them, would but undertake it, especially at the request of the estates of France, or of the most sound part thereof." Here then is a second demonstration against the new Reformation, because the divines whom they consulted, were Protestants, as it is expressly specified by De Thou,[43] with them an unexceptionable author. And Beza insinuates it plainly enough, when he says, they took the advice "of the most learned divines," who, in his judgment, could be none else but the reformed. As much may we believe in regard to the lawyers, no Catholic having ever been so much as named.

29.—Third Demonstration.

A third demonstration, arising from the same words is, that these princes of the blood, "born magistrates in this affair," were reduced to the sole Prince of

Condé, a declared Protestant, although there were five or six more at the least, and amongst others, the King of Navarre, the prince's elder brother, and first prince of the blood; but whom the party feared rather than depended on; a circumstance that leaves not the least doubt that the design of the new Reformation was to command the enterprise.

30.—*Fourth Demonstration.*

Nay, not only the prince is the sole person placed at the head of the whole party, but what makes the fourth and last conviction against the Reformation is, that this, "the most sound part of the Estates, whose concurrence was demanded, were almost all reformed."[44] The most important and the most special orders were addressed to them, and the enterprise regarded them alone; for the end they proposed to themselves therein was, as Beza owns, that "a confession of faith might be presented to the king assisted by a good and lawful council."[45] It is plain enough, this council would never have been good and lawful, unless the Prince of Condé, with his party, had governed it, and the reformed obtained all they desired. The action was to begin by a request they would have presented to the king for obtaining liberty of conscience; and he who managed the whole affair, was La Renaudie, a man condemned to rigorous penalties for forgery, by a decree in parliament, at which court he sued for a benefice; after this, sheltering himself at Geneva, turning heretic out of spite, "burning with a desire of revenge, and of defacing, by some bold action, the infamy of his condemnation,"[46] he undertook to stir up to rebellion, as many disaffected persons as he could meet with; and at last, retiring into the house of a Huguenot lawyer at Paris, had the direction of all matters in conjunction with Antony Chandieu, the Protestant minister of Paris, who afterwards gave himself the name of Sadael.

31.—*The Huguenots that discovered the conspiracy do not justify the party.*

True it is, the Huguenot lawyer with whom he lodged, and Ligueres, another Huguenot, had a horror of so atrocious a crime, and discovered the plot; but that does not excuse the Reformation, but shows only there were some particular men in the sect, whose conscience was better than that of the divines and ministers, and that of Beza himself and the whole body of the party,[47] who ran headlong into the conspiracy over all the provinces of the realm. Accordingly, we have seen the same Beza accusing of perfidiousness these two faithful subjects who alone, of all the party, had an abhorrence of, and discovered the plot; so that, in the judgment of the ministers, those that came into this black conspiracy are the honest men, and those who detected it are the traitors.

32.—*The protestation of the Conspirators does not justify them.*

It is to no purpose to say, that La Renaudie and all the conspirators protested they had no design of attempting any thing against the king or queen, or the royal family; for is a man to be deemed innocent because he had not formed the design of so execrable a parricide?[48] Was it so light a matter in a state, to call in question the king's majority, and elude the ancient laws, which had fixed it at fourteen years of age, by the joint consent of all the orders of the realm? To presume, on this pretext, to appoint him such counsel as they thought fit? To rush, armed, into his palace; to assault and force him; to ravish from this sacred asylum, and out of the king's arms, the Duke of Guise and the Cardinal of Lorrain because the king made use of them in his council; to expose the whole court and the king's own person to all the violence and all the bloodshed, that so tumultuous an attack, and the darkness of the night, might produce? In a word, to fly to arms over all the kingdom, with a resolution not to lay them down, till the king should be forced into a compliance with all that they desired. Were the particular injury done to the Guises here only to come in question, what right had the prince of Condé to dispose of these princes, to deliver them up to the hands of their enemies, who, as Beza himself owns,[49] made a great part of the conspirators, and to employ the sword against them, as De Thou says,[50] should they not consent voluntarily to relinquish all state-affairs? What! under pretext of a particular commission, given, as Beza words it,[51] "To men of a well-approved and wise conduct (such as La Renaudie) in order to inquire secretly, though thoroughly and exactly, into all the employments heaped upon the Guises," shall a prince of the blood, of his private authority, hold them as legally convicted, and put them in the power of those, whom he knows to be "spurred on with the spirit of revenge for outrages received from them, as well in their own persons, as those of their kindred and relations;" for these are Beza's words.[52] What becomes of society, if such wicked attempts be allowed? But what becomes of royalty, if men dare to execute them, sword in hand, in the king's own palace, seize on his ministers, and tear them from his side; put him under tuition; his sacred person in the power of rebels, who would have possessed themselves of his castle, and upheld such a treason, with a war set on foot over all the kingdom? This is the fruit resulting from the councils "of the most learned Protestant divines and lawyers, of the best renown." This is what Beza approves, and what Protestants defend even to this day.[53]

33.—The suppleness and connivance of Calvin.

Calvin is cited,[54] who, after the contrivance had miscarried, wrote two letters, wherein he testifies, he had never approved it. But, after having had notice of a conspiracy of this nature, is it enough to blame it, without giving himself any further concern to stop the progress of so flagitious an undertaking? Had Beza believed that Calvin did as much detest this deed as it deserved, would he have approved it himself; would he have boasted to us the approbation of the most learned divines of the party? Who does not, therefore, perceive, that Calvin acted here too remissly; and provided he could exculpate himself, in case of ill success, was nowise averse to the conspirators hazarding the event? If we believe Brantome, the Admiral[55] was much better disposed; and the

Protestant writers vapor much at what he wrote in the life of this nobleman, viz., "That none durst ever speak to him about this enterprise, because they held him for a man of probity, a man of worth, a lover of honor, who accordingly would have sent back the conspirators well rebuked, and detected the whole; nay, would himself have been aiding to quell them."[56] Still, however, the thing was done, and the historians of the party relate with complacency, what ought not to be mentioned but with horror.

34.—Reflections on the uncertainty of histories useless on this occasion.

There is no room here for eluding a certain fact, by descanting on the uncertainty of histories, and the partiality of historians.[57] These commonplace topics are only fit to raise a mist. Should our reformed arraign the credit of De Thou, whose works they printed at Geneva, and whose authority, we have been lately told by a Protestant historian, none ever disputed; they have but to read La Popliniere, one of their own, and Beza, one of their chiefs, to find their party convicted of a crime, which the Admiral, Protestant as he was, judged so unworthy a man of honor.

35.—The first wars under Charles XI, in which all the party concurred.—1562.

Yet this great man of honor, who had such an abhorrence of the conspiracy of Amboise, either because it did not succeed, or because the measures were ill concerted, or because he found open war more to his advantage, made no scruple, two years after, of putting himself at the head of the rebellious Calvinists. Then the whole party declared themselves. Calvin made no resistance for this time, and rebellion was the crime of all his disciples. Those whom their histories celebrate as the most moderate, only said they ought not to begin.[58] However, this was their joint opinion, that to suffer themselves to be butchered, like sheep, was not the profession of men of courage; but to be men of courage in this way, they must renounce the title of Reformers, and much more—that of Confessors of the Faith and Martyrs; for it is not in vain that St. Paul said, after David, "We are accounted as sheep for the slaughter;"[59] and Jesus Christ himself: "Behold! I send you forth as sheep in the midst of wolves."[60] I have by me Calvin's own letters, well attested, wherein, at the beginning of the troubles of France, he thinks he does enough, in writing to the Baron des Adrets, against pillaging and violence, against image-breaking, and against the depredation of shrines and church treasures, without public authority. To be satisfied, as he is, with telling the soldiers thus enrolled, "Do violence to no man, and be content with your pay,"[61] adding nothing more; is speaking of this militia as you do of a lawful militia: and it is thus that St. John the Baptist decided in behalf of those who bore arms under their lawful princes. The doctrine, which allowed taking them up in the cause of religion, was afterwards ratified, I do not say by the ministers in particular only, but also in common by their synods, and it was necessary to proceed to this decision in order to engage in the war those Protestants, who, from a sense of the ancient principles of Christian Faith, and the submission they had so frequently promised at the beginning of the new Reformation, did not believe that a Christian should maintain the liberty of conscience otherwise than by suffering, according to the gospel, in all patience and humility. The brave and wise La Noue, who was at first of this opinion, was drawn into a contrary sentiment and practice by the authority of the ministers and synods. The Church was for that time infallible, and they yielded blindly to her authority against their own consciences.

36.—Decisions of the Calvinistic national Synods, in approbation of taking up arms.—1563.

Now the express decisions relating to this matter were, for the most part, made in provincial synods; but, that there be no occasion to search for them there, it will be sufficient to observe, that these decisions were preceded by the national Synod of Lyons in 1563, Art. 38, by particular facts of this import,—"That a minister of Limousin, who, in other respects had behaved uprightly, terrified by the threats of his enemies, had wrote to the queen-mother, that he never had consented to the bearing of arms, although he had consented and contributed thereto. Item, that he had promised not to preach till the king should grant him leave. Since that time, having a sense of his fault, he had made a public confession of it before all the people, on a day of celebrating the Supper, in the presence of all the ministers of the country and of all the faithful. The query is, whether he may resume his pastoral charge? the opinion is, he may: nevertheless, he shall write to him by whom he had been tempted, to notify to him his repentance, and shall entreat him to let the queen know as much, and all whomsoever this scandal to his Church might have reached; and it shall be in the breast of the Synod of Limousin to remove him to some other place, as they shall think most prudent."

37.—Another decision.

It is so Christian and so heroic an act, in the new Reformation, to make war against their sovereign for religion's sake, that it is made criminal in a minister to have repented of, and asked pardon for it of his queen. Reparation must be made before all the people in the most solemn acts of religion, namely, at the Supper, for respectful excuses made to the queen; and so far must the insolence be carried, as to have it declared to her in person, that this tender of respect is recalled, to the end she may be assured that, from henceforth, they will have no manner of regard for her; nay, they are not certain, after all this reparation and retracting, whether or not the scandal which this submission had caused amongst the reformed people would be quite defaced. Therefore it cannot be denied that obedience was scandalous to them: this it is decided by a national synod. But here is, in the forty-eighth article, another decision which will not appear less wonderful: an abbot arrived to the knowledge of the Gospel, had burnt all his titles, and during six years had not suffered Mass to be sung in the abbey. What a Reformation! but here lies the stress of his encomium: Nay, hath always comported himself *faithfully, and borne arms for the maintenance of the Gospel.* A holy abbot, indeed, who far remote from popery, no less than from the discipline of St. Bernard and St. Benedict, would not endure either Mass or vespers in his abbey, whatever might have been the founder's express injunction; and moreover, dissatisfied with those spiritual weapons which St. Paul so much recommended, yet too feeble for our warrior's courage, has generously carried arms, and drawn the sword against his prince in defence of the new Gospel. Let him be admitted to the Supper, concludes the whole national Synod, and this mystery becomes the remuneration for that war he had waged against his country.

38.—The same Doctrine perpetuated in the succeeding Synods till our days.

This tradition of the party has been handed down to subsequent times successively; and the Synod of Alais, in 1620, return thanks to M. de Chastillon for his letter, wherein "He protested to them, that he would employ whatever was in his power after the example of his predecessors, for the advancement of the kingdom of Jesus Christ." This was their style. The juncture of times and the affairs of Alais, explain the intention of this lord; and what the Admiral de Chastillon and Dandelot, his predecessors, meant by the kingdom of Christ is well known.

39.—The spirit of the Huguenots in these wars.

The ministers, who taught this doctrine, thought to impose upon the world, by setting up that fine discipline in their troops so much commended by De Thou. It lasted indeed about three months: after this, the soldiers soon carried away into the most grievous excesses, thought themselves well excused, if they did but cry out Long live the Gospel; and the Baron des Adrets, who knew full well the temper of this militia, upon his being reproached, as a Huguenot historian[62] relates, that after quitting them he had done nothing worthy of his first exploits, excused himself by saying, there was nothing he durst not enterprise "with a soldiery, whose pay was revenge, passion, and honor," whom "he had bereft of all hopes of pardon" by the cruelties he had engaged them in. If we believe the ministers, our Reformed are still in the same dispositions; and the most voluminous of all their writers, the author of new systems, and the interpreter of prophesies, has but lately published in print, that "The fury, at this day, those are in who have suffered violence, and *the rage* they have conceived at being forced, strengthens the love and attachment they had to truth."[63] This, according to the ministers, is the spirit that animates these new martyrs.

40.—Whether the example of Catholics vindicates the Huguenots.

It serves not the turn of our Reformed, to excuse themselves, as to the civil wars, by the examples of Catholics under Henry III and Henry IV, since, besides the incongruity of this Jerusalem's defending herself by the authority of Tyre and Babylon, they are very sensible that the body of Catholics which detested these excesses, and remained faithful to their kings, was always great: whereas, in the Huguenot party, scarce two or three persons of note can be found that stood firm in their loyalty.

41.—*Vain pretext of Calvinists, who pretend that these wars did not properly concern Religion.*

Here again they make fresh efforts to show that these wars were merely political, and nothing appertaining to religion. These empty pretexts deserve not refutation, nothing more being necessary for discovering the drift of these wars, than to read the treaties of peace and the edicts of pacification.—of which liberty of conscience, with some other privileges for the Protestants, was always the main import: but because, at this time, men are bent more than ever upon darkening the clearest fact, duty requires of me I should speak something on this head.

42.—*Illusions of Mr. Burnet.*

Mr. Burnet,[64] who hath taken in hand the defence of the conspiracy of Amboise, enters also the lists in vindication of the civil wars; but after a manner which shows plainly he is acquainted with no more of our history and laws than what he has picked up from the most ignorant and the most passionate of all Protestant authors. I forgive his mistaking that famous Triumvirate under Charles IX, for the union of the King of Navarre with the Cardinal of Lorrain, whereas, unquestionably, it was that of the Duke of Guise, of the Constable of Montmorency, and the Marshal of St. Andrew: nor should I even have thought it worth my while to have pointed out these sorts of blunders, were it not that they convict him, who fell into them, of not having so much as seen one good author. It is a thing less supportable to have taken, as he has done, the disorder of Vassi for a premeditated enterprise of the Duke of Guise, with a design to break the edicts, although De Thou,[65] whose testimony he must not reject, and (except Beza, too prejudiced by passion to be credited on this occasion) even Protestant authors, aver the contrary. But to say that the regency had been given to Antony, King of Navarre; to descant, as he does, on the authority of a regent; to affirm that this prince, having outstripped his power in the revocation of the edicts, the people might join themselves to the first prince of the blood after him, namely, to the prince of Condé; to carry on this empty reasoning, and say that, after the death of the King of Navarre, the regency devolved to the prince his brother, and that the foundation of the civil wars was the refusal made to this prince "of the government, to whom it of right belonged,"[66] is, to speak plainly of a man so positive, mixing too much passion with too much ignorance of our affairs.

43.—*His gross blunders and great ignorance of the affairs of France.*

For, in the first place, it is certain, that in the reign of Charles IX the regency was conferred upon Catherine of Medicis by the unanimous consent of the whole kingdom, and even of the King of Navarre. Mr. Burnet's lawyers, who proved, as he pretends, "that no woman might be admitted to the regency," were ignorant of a standing custom, confirmed by many examples ever since the time of Queen Blanche and St. Louis.[67] These same lawyers, according to Mr. Burnet's relation, presumed even to say, "that two and twenty was the soonest that any King of France had been ever held to be of age to assume the government," contrary to the express tenor of the ordinance of Charles the Fifth, in 1374, which has always been a standing law in the whole kingdom without any contradiction.[68] To quote these lawyers, and make a law for France of their ignorant and iniquitous decisions, is erecting into a state law the pretext of rebels.

44.—Sequel of Mr. Burnet's Fallacies.

Neither did the Prince of Condé ever pretend to the regency, no, not even after the death of the King his brother; and so far was he from calling in question the authority of Queen Catherine, that, on the contrary, at his rising in arms, he grounded himself on nothing but the secret orders he pretended to have received. But what deceived Mr. Burnet is, perchance, his having heard it said, that those who joined themselves to the Prince of Condé for the King's defence, who, they pretended, was a prisoner in the hands of the Guises, gave to the Prince the title of lawful Protector and Defender of the King and kingdom.[69] An Englishman, dazzled with the title of Protector, imagined he saw in this title, according to the usage of his country, the authority of a regent. The Prince never so much as dreamt of it, since even his elder brother, the King of Navarre, was still living; on the contrary, this empty title of Protector and Defender of the kingdom, which in France signifies just nothing, was given him on no other account but because it was very well perceived there was no lawful title that could be given him.

45.—The French Calvinists extricate themselves no better out of this difficulty.

Let us then leave Mr. Burnet, who, though a foreigner, pronounces thus peremptorily on our laws, without knowing so much as the first rudiments of them. The French give the thing a different turn, and ground themselves on some of the Queen's letters, "who begged the Prince to preserve the mother and children, and the whole kingdom, against those who had a mind to ruin all."[70] But two convincing reasons leave no shelter for this vain pretext. In the first place, because the Queen, who in this manner addressed herself privately to the Prince, exceeded her power; it being agreed that the regency was conferred upon her on condition that she did nothing of consequence except in council, with the participation and by the advice of the King of Navarre, as the first Prince of the blood, and lieutenant-general, established by the consent of the Estates in all the provinces and armies during the minority. As, therefore, the King of Navarre felt that she was driving all to ruin through that restless ambition which tormented her, of preserving her authority, and that she wholly turned on the side of the Prince and the Huguenots, the just fear he was in of their becoming masters, and lest the Queen, through despair, should at length even cast herself into their arms together with the King, made him break all the measures of this Princess. The other Princes of the blood joined with him, no less than the chief men of the kingdom and the parliament. The Duke of Guise did nothing but by the orders of this King; and the Queen so well knew she exceeded her power in what she requested of the Prince, that she never durst use any other words, in her addresses to him, than those of invitation; so that these so boasted letters are nothing else, in reality, but the anxieties of Catharine, not the lawful injunctions of a regent; so much the more (and it is the second proof) as the Queen gave ear to the Prince but for a moment, and through the vain terror she had conceived of being stripped of her authority; insomuch that it was easily believed, says De Thou, she would come off from this design as soon as ever she should get the better of her fears.[71]

46.—*The Calvinists convicted by Beza.*[72]

Accordingly, the event discovers that she enters sincerely into the measures of the King of Navarre, and thenceforward never left negotiating with the prince in order to reclaim him to his duty. Wherefore, these letters of the Queen, and all that followed thereupon, are counted nothing by historians but a vain pretext. Nay, Beza makes it plain enough that all turned on religion, on the breach of edicts, and on the pretended murder of Vassi.[73] The Prince neither stirred, nor gave orders to the Admiral to take up arms, but "requested, and more than entreated, by those *of the new religion*, to grant them his protection, under the name and authority of the King and his edicts."

47.—*The first War resolved upon by the advice of all the Ministers,* *and the peace concluded notwithstanding their opposition.—Testimony of Beza.*

It was in an assembly, at which were present the chief men of their Church, that the question was proposed, whether they might in conscience execute justice on the Duke of Guise, and that with no great hazard, for thus the case was worded; and the answer returned was, that "it was better to suffer what might, please God, putting themselves only on the defensive, should necessity reduce the churches to that point. Yet, whatever might happen, they ought not to be the first to draw the sword."[74] Here, then, is a point resolved in the new reformation, that they may, without scruple, make war on a lawful power, at least in their own defence. Now, they took for an assault the revocation of the edicts; so that the reformation laid it down for a certain doctrine, that she might fight for the liberty of conscience, in contradiction not only to the faith and practice of the Apostles, but also to the solemn protestation Beza had but just made at his demanding justice of the King of Navarre; viz., "that it appertained to the Church of God to suffer blows, and not to give them; but that he ought to remember, this anvil had worn out many a hammer."[75] This saying, so much extolled by the party, proved a deceit, since, after a while, the anvil itself commenced to strike contrary to nature, and, wearied with bearing blows, repaid them in its turn. Beza, who glories in this conceit, in another place makes this important declaration in the face of all Christendom, "that he had warned of their *duty* as well the Prince of Condé as the Admiral, and all the other lords and men of every degree, that made profession of the Gospel, to induce them to maintain, *by all means possible to them*, the authority of the King's edicts and the innocence of the poor oppressed; and ever after hath continued in this same will, exhorting, nevertheless, every person to use his arms in the most modest manner possible, and to seek, next to God's honor, peace in all things, provided they do not suffer themselves to be deceived and imposed upon."[76] What a delusion to persuade himself, whilst he actually authorizes a civil war, that he has fulfilled his duty by recommending modesty to a people up in arms! And as for peace, did he not see that the security he required for it would always afford pretexts, either of keeping it at a distance, or of breaking it? In the meantime he was by his preaching, as he himself confesses, one of the principal inciters to the war. One of the fruits of his gospel was, to teach this new duty to subjects and officers of the crown. All the ministers concurred in his sentiments, and he owns himself,[77] that when peace was mentioned, the ministers so much opposed it, that the prince, resolved on concluding it, was forced to exclude all of them from the debate; for they were determined to hinder the party from suffering the least exception to that edict, which was most favorable to them, namely that of January. But the prince, who had consented, for peace sake, to some light restrictions," caused them to be read before the nobility, suffering none else but the gentlemen bearing arms to speak their opinions, as he declared openly in the assembly; so that the ministers, after that time, were neither heard nor admitted to give in their advice;"[78] by this means peace was made, and all clauses of the new edict make it appear that nothing but religion was contended for in this war. Nay, it is manifest, had the ministers been hearkened to, it would have been continued in hopes of gaining more advantageous conditions which they proposed at large in writing, adding many things even to the edict of January; and they made, says Beza, a declaration of them, "to the end posterity might be informed how they comported them- selves in this affair.[79] This, therefore, stands an eternal testimony, that the ministers approved the war, and were more bent than the princes and the armed soldiers themselves, on pursuing it from the sole motive of religion, which they pretend, at present, was quite out of the question; yet was the fundamental cause of the first wars, by the consent of all authors, both Catholic and Protestant.

48.—*The other wars are destitute of all pretext.*

The rest of the wars have not so much as a color of pretext, the queen then concurring with all the powers of the state; neither was there any other excuse alleged but discontents and contraventions; things which, in the end, have no kind of weight, but in presupposing this error, that subjects have a right in the cause of religion to take up arms against their king, although religion prescribes nothing but to suffer and obey.

49.—*Answers of Mr. Jurieu.*

I now leave the Calvinists to examine whether there be the least appearance of solidity in all Mr. Jurieu's discourses, where he says, that this same is a quarrel "wherein religion came in merely by chance, and to serve for a pretext only;"[80] it is manifest, religion was at the bottom of it, and the reformation of the government was nothing but a cloak to cover their shame for having begun a war of religion, after so many protestations how much they abhorred all such conspiracies.

But here is another kind of excuse which this artful minister prepares for his party as to the conspiracy of Amboise, when he answers, that, "be it as it will, it is no otherwise criminal than by the gospel rules."[81] It is then a trifle for Reformers who boast nought to us but the gospel, to form a conspiracy that is condemned by the gospel; nor will they be much concerned, provided it only militates against these sacred ordinances. But what follows in Mr. Jurieu will make it evident he understands as little of morality as Christianity, since he even dares to write these words:—"The tyranny of the princes of Guise could not be overthrown without a great effusion of blood; the spirit of Christianity suffers not that: but if this enterprise be scanned according to the rules of worldly morality, it is not at all criminal."[82] It was, nevertheless, according to the rules of worldly morality, that the Admiral condemned the conspiracy as so shameful and detestable, and, according to the dictates of a man of honor, not barely of a Christian, that he conceived such a horror of it; nor is the corruption of the world as yet advanced so far as to discover innocence in deeds equally subversive of all laws human and divine.

The minister succeeds no better in his design when, instead of vindicating his pretended Reformers in their rebellions, he sets himself to point out the corruption of the court against which they rebelled, as if reformers could have been ignorant of that apostolical command, "Obey your masters, though they be forward."[83]

His long recriminations, with which he fills a volume, are not a whit more to the purpose, since this the main question will always return, whether those who are boasted of to us as the reformers of mankind, have diminished or increased its evils, and whether they are to be considered as Reformers who correct them, or rather as scourges whom God sends to punish them.

50.—*Question concerning the spirit of the Reformation.*—*Whether it was a spirit of meekness or of violence.*—*1514.*

Here might that question be considered, whether it be true that the Reformation, as she boasts, never aimed at establishing herself by force; but the doubt is easily resolved by all the above mentioned facts. As long as the Reformation was weak, it is true she always seemed submissive; nay, gave out for a fundamental point of her religion that she believed it not only unlawful to use force, but even to repel it.[84] But it was soon discovered this was of that kind of modesty which fear inspires, a fire hidden in ashes; for no sooner could the Reformation attain to be uppermost in any kingdom, but she was for ruling uncontrolled. In the first place, no security was there for priests and bishops; secondly, the true Catholics were proscribed, banished, deprived of their goods, and in some places of life, by the law of the state, as for instance, in Sweden. The fact is certain, whatever may have been said to the contrary. This was what they came to who at first cried so loud against violence; and there needs but to consider the acrimony, the bitterness, and insolence which was diffused through the first books and the first sermons of these Reformers; their bloody invectives, the calumnies they blacked our doctrine with, the sacrilege, the impieties, the idolatries with which they incessantly reproached us; the hatred they inspired against us, the plundering which were the result of their first preaching, "the spite and violence"[85] which appeared in their seditious libels set up against the Mass; in order to form a judgment of what was to be expected from such beginnings.

51.—Sequel of the violent spirit which predominated in the Reformation.

But many wise men, say they, condemned these libels;[86] so much the worse for the Protestant party, whose transports were so extreme, that all the wise men who remained in it could not repress them. These libels were spread all over Paris, posted up and dispersed in every street; fixed even to the door of the king's chamber;[87] nor did the wise ones who disapproved this, use any efficacious measures for its prevention. When that pretended martyr, Anne du Bourg, had declared in the tone of a prophet to the president Minard, whom he challenged, that in spite of his refusing to absent himself, and decline hearing his cause, he never should sit as judge in it,[88] the Protestants knew full well how to make good his prophecy, and accordingly the president was murdered towards the evening on entering his house. It was known afterwards, that Le Maitre and St. André, both of them very averse to the new gospel, would have met with the like fate, had they come to the court; so dangerous a thing it is to offend the Reformation, though weak! And we learn from Beza himself, that Stuart, a relation of the queen's, "a man ready for any execution, and a most zealous Protestant, made frequent visits to the prisoners held in the parliament jail on the score of religion."[89] He could not be convicted of having struck the blow, yet we see at least through what channel the communication might flow; and howsoever that may be, neither did the party want men of desperate resolution; nor can any be accused of this combination, but those who interested themselves for Anne du Bourg. It is no hard matter to vent prophecies, when such angels are at hand to execute them. The assurance of Anne du Bourg in foretelling so distinctly what was to happen, discovers plainly the good intelligence he had received; and what is said in the history of De Thou, in order to show him a prophet, rather than an accomplice of such a crime, smells rank of an addition from Geneva. We must not, therefore, wonder that a party which nursed such daring spirits, should take off the mask as soon as ever a weak reign opened a prospect of success, which we have seen they never failed to do.

52.—*Vain excuses.*

A new Defender of the Reformation is persuaded, from the dissolute behaviour, and entire conduct of the Prince of Condé, that there was "more of ambition than religion in what he did;" and he owns, that religion "was of no other use to him, than to furnish him with instruments of revenge."[90] He thinks by that means to resolve all into policy, and justify his own religion: not reflecting this is the very thing we charge them with, viz. that of a religion styling itself reformed, was so prompt an instrument of revenge to an ambitious prince. It is nevertheless the crime of the whole party. But what does this author say to us of the pillaging of churches and vestries, of breaking down images and altars? Why truly he thinks to clear all by saying that "the prince, neither by prayers, nor by remonstrances, nor even by chastisements, could put a stop to these disorders."[91] This is no manner of excuse; it is a conviction of that violence, which reigned in the party, whose fury the very heads could not restrain. But I am very much afraid that they acted by the same spirit with Cranmer and the rest of the English reformers, who, upon the complaints that were made against image-breakers, "although they had a mind to check the heat of the people and keep it within compass, yet were unwilling it should be done after such a manner as to dishearten their friends too much."[92] This was the case of the chief leaders of our Calvinists, who, though they judged themselves obliged in honor to blame these enormities, yet we do not find they ever did justice on the authors of them. Beza's history will suffice to show, that our Reformed were always ready at the least signal to run to arms, to break open prisons, to seize on churches, nor was there any thing ever seen more factious. Who is ignorant of the cruelties exercised by the Queen of Navarre against priests and religious? The towers from which the Catholics were cast headlong, and the deep pits they were flung into, are shown to this day. The wells of the bishop's palace at Nismes, and the cruel instruments employed to force them to the Protestant sermons, are not less known to the whole world. We have still the information and decrees, by which it appears that these bloody executions were the deliberate resolves of Protestants in council assembled. We have the original orders of generals, and those of cities, at the request of consistories, to compel the Papists to embrace the Reformation, by taxes, by quartering soldiers upon them, by demolishing their houses, and uncovering the roofs. Those who withdrew, to escape these violences, were stripped of their goods: the records of the town-houses of Nismes, Montauban, Alais, Montpellier, and other cities of the party, are full of such decrees; nor should I mention them, were it not for the complaints with which our fugitives alarm all Europe. These are the men who boast their meekness. What a cruelty to persecute such people merely for religion, who warrant all they do from Scripture, and chant so harmoniously their psalms in rhyme! No fear, they soon found means to shelter themselves from martyrdom, after the example of their doctors, who always were in security themselves whilst they encouraged others; both Luther and Melancthon, Bucer and Zuinglius, Calvin and Œcolampadius, with all the rest of them, speedily betook themselves to secure sanctuaries; nor am I acquainted, amongst the heads of the reformers, with any, even false martyrs, unless perchance such a one as Cranmer, whom we have seen, after a repeated abjuration of his faith, unresolved to die in the profession of it, till he was convinced his renouncing it would be unavailable to save his life.

53.—*Answer to those who might say, this is foreign to our subject.*

But to what purpose, it may be objected, the reflecting on these past transactions, which a peevish minister will say is only done to exasperate them the more, and aggravate their misfortunes? Such fears ought not to hinder me from relating what appertains so manifestly to my subject; and all that equitable Protestants can, in a history, require from me is, that, not relying wholly on the credit of their adversaries, I also give ear to their own historians. I do more than this, and, not content with hearing them, I join issue with them on their evidence. Let our brethren open then their eyes; let them cast them on the ancient Church, which, during so many ages of so cruel a persecution, never flew out, not for a moment, nor in one single person; but was seen as submissive under Dioclesian, nay, under Julian the apostate, when she was spread over all the earth, as under Nero and Domitian, when but in her infancy; there indeed appeared the finger of God truly visible. But the case is quite different, when men rebel as soon as able; and when their wars last much longer than their patience. Experience sufficiently shows us in all kinds of sects, that conceited opinion and strong prejudice can mimic fortitude, at least for a while; but maxims of Christian meekness are never in the heart, when men so readily exchange them, not only for opposite practices, but also for opposite maxims, with deliberation and by express decisions, as it is plain our Protestants have done. Here is, therefore, a true variation in their doctrine, and an effect of that perpetual instability, which cannot but fix on their Reformation a character suitable to those works, which having but what is human in them, of course must "come to naught,"[93] according to Gamaliel's maxim.

54.—*The Assassination of the Duke of Guise, by Poltrot, held by the Reformation as an act of Religion.*—1562.

The assassination of Francis, Duke of Guise, ought not to pass unmentioned in this history, inasmuch as the author of this murder mingled his religion with his crime. It is Beza that represents to us Poltrot as excited by some secret impulse, at the time he resolved upon this infamous exploit; and in order to make us understand that this secret impulse was from God, he also describes the same Poltrot just ready to enter on the execution of this black design,[94] "Praying to God most ardently, that he would vouchsafe to change his will, if what he intended was displeasing to him; otherwise, that he would give him constancy, and strength sufficient to slay this tyrant, and by that means free Orleans from destruction, and the whole kingdom from so miserable a tyranny. Thereupon, and in the evening of the same day, proceeds Beza, he struck the blow; that is, during this enthusiasm, and just rising up from that ardent prayer."[95] As soon as ever our Reformed knew the thing was done, "they solemnly returned thanks to God with great rejoicings."[96] The Duke of Guise had always been the object of their hatred. No sooner were they in a condition to effect it, but we have seen them conspire his ruin, and this by the advice of their doctors. After the riot at Vassi, although it was certain he had used all his endeavors to appease it, the party rose up against him with hideous clamors;[97] and Beza, who carried their complaints to court, acknowledges, "He had desired and begged of God innumerable times, either to change the heart of the Duke of Guise, which, nevertheless, he could not hope, or that he would rid the kingdom of him; whereof he calls to witness all those who have heard his prayers and preaching."[98] It was therefore in his preaching, and in public, that he offered up innumerable times these seditious prayers; after the example of those of Luther, whereby, we have observed, he knew so well how to animate mankind, and stir up individuals to fulfil his prophecies. By the like prayers the Duke of Guise was represented as a hardened persecutor, from whom it was necessary to beseech God that he would deliver the world by some extraordinary stroke of Providence. What Beza says in his own excuse, "that he did not publicly name the Duke of Guise,"[99] is much too silly. What signifies the naming a man when you know both how to point him out by his characters, and explain yourself in particular to those who might sufficiently have understood you? These mysterious innuendoes, in sermons and divine service, are more likely to exasperate men's minds, than more explicit declarations. Beza was not the only one that inveighed most bitterly against the Duke; all the ministers railed in the same manner. No wonder then, that amongst so many "men disposed for execution," with which the party abounded, some should be found that thought they did God service in delivering the Reformation from such an enemy. The still blacker enterprise of Amboise had met with the approbation of Beza and their doctors. This, in the conjuncture of the siege of Orleans, when the bulwark of the party together with this city was just falling into the Duke's hands, was of a far different importance; and Poltrot believed he did more for his religion than La Renaudie. Accordingly, he talked openly of his design as of a thing that would be well approved of. Although he was known in the party for a man sworn to kill the Duke of Guise, cost what it would, neither the generals, nor the soldiers, nor even the pastors dissuaded him from it. Let any one that pleases believe what Beza says,[100] that those words were taken "for the vagaries of a giddy-headed person," that would never have vented his design had he resolved to execute it. But the more sincere D'Aubigné is agreed, that it was hoped in the party he would strike the blow: which, he says, "he had learnt from good authority."[101] It is also very certain, that Poltrot did not pass for one that was hair-brained.[102] Soubize, whose servant he was, and the Admiral, considered him as a useful person, and employed him in affairs of consequence; and the manner of his explaining himself spoke him rather a man resolute at all events, than one giddy-headed and crazy. "He presented himself (they are Beza's words) to Mr. Soubize, a leading man in the party, to acquaint him that he had resolved with himself in cold blood to deliver France from so many miseries, by killing the Duke of Guise; which he durst boldly undertake, *cost what it would*."[103] The answer which Soubize returned him was not calculated to make him relent in his undertaking; for he only tells him"To do his accustomed duty;" and as for the matter proposed, "God knew well how to take care of it by other means." So faint a reply, in an action which ought not to be spoken of without horror, must have discovered to Poltrot, in Soubize's mind, either the apprehension that the thing would not be executed successfully, or the design of exculpating himself, rather than an express condemnation of it. The rest of the chiefs spoke to him with no less indifference: they were satisfied with telling him "he ought to beware of extraordinary vocations."[104] This, instead of dissuasion, was working up a belief in him that his enterprise had something in it of what was heavenly and inspired; and, as D'Aubigné expresses it in his animated style, "Their remonstrances, under the appearance of dissuading, really urged him on." Accordingly, he was but the more determined on his black undertaking: he spoke of it to every body; and, continues Beza, "had his mind so bent on it, as to make it the common topic of his discourse." During the siege of Rouen, at which the King of Navarre was killed, this death being mentioned, Poltrot, "fetching a deep sign from the bottom of his breath, Ha! says he, this is not enough, a much greater victim must still be sacrificed."[105] When asked what it might be: he answered, "It is the great Guise;" and at the same time, lifting up his right arm, "This is the arm," cried he, "that will do the deed, and put an end to our misfortunes." This he repeated often, and always with the like energy. All these discourses bespeak a man determined, scorning to conceal himself, because persuaded he is doing a meritorious action: but what more discovers the disposition of the whole party, is that of the Admiral, whom they held up to the whole world as a pattern of virtue and the glory of the Reformation. I shall not speak here of Poltrot's evidence, accusing him and Beza of having induced him to this design. Let us lay aside the testimony of a witness, who has perhaps varied too much to be entirely credited on his own word: but the facts avowed by Beza[106] in his history cannot be called in question, much less those that are contained in the declaration which the Admiral and he jointly on the assassin's accusation, sent to the Queen.[107] Thence, therefore, it remains evident, that Soubize despatched Poltrot with a packet of letters to the Admiral when still near Orleans endeavoring to relieve the town; that it was with the Admiral's consent that Poltrot went to the Duke of Guise's camp, and pretended to surrender himself to him, as one who was tired of bearing arms against the king;[108] that the Admiral, who other-wise could not be ignorant of a design made public by Poltrot, learnt from his own mouth that he persisted in it still, since he owns that Poltrot, in departing on his enterprise, "went so far as to tell him, it would be an easy matter to kill the Duke of Guise;" that the Admiral spoke not a word to turn him from it; nay, on the contrary, though conscious of his design, gave him at one time twenty crowns, and a hundred at another, to mount himself well:[109] in those days a considerable supply, and absolutely necessary both to facilitate his undertaking and escape.[110] Nothing can be more frivolous than what the Admiral alleges in his own defence. He says, "that when Poltrot mentioned to him his killing the Duke of Guise, he, the Admiral, never opened his mouth to incite him to undertake it." There was no need of inciting a man whose resolution was so well taken; and in order that he might accomplish his design, the Admiral had no more to do than, as he did, to despatch him to the place where he might execute it. The Admiral, not content to send him thither, gives him money to support himself there, and for the supply of all necessaries for such a design, not forgetting even that of a good horse and furniture.[111] What the Admiral alleged farther, that he sent Poltrot into the camp only to gain intelligence, is manifestly nothing but a cloak to that design, which he would not own. As for the money, nothing is more weak than what the Admiral replies, viz. "that he gave it to Poltrot, without ever specifying to him the killing or not killing the Duke of Guise."[112] But the reason he brings in his justification for not dissuading him from so wicked an attempt, discovers the bottom of his heart. He confesses then, "before these last troubles, he knew the men who had determined to kill the Duke of Guise; that far from inducing them to this design, or approving it, he had diverted them from it, and even given notice of it to Madame de Guise; that, since the affair of Vassi, he had prosecuted the Duke as a public enemy; nevertheless it cannot be discovered that he *had approved* any attempt should be made on his person, till he had notice given him that the Duke had drawn in certain persons to kill him and the Prince of Condé." It follows, therefore, that after this notice given (as to the truth whereof we ought not to believe an enemy on his bare word) "he did approve" attempting on the Duke's life: but "since that time, he acknowledges, when he heard one say, if he could he would kill the Duke of Guise even in his camp, he did not dissuade him from it:" by which it appears at once, that this bloody design was common in the Reformation, and the chiefs of it, the most esteemed for their virtue, such was undoubtedly the Admiral, did not think themselves under any obligation of opposing it; on the contrary, they concurred in it in every way the most effectually they were able; so little did an assassination disturb their consciences, provided religion were its motive.

55.—*Sequel.*

Should it be asked, what could induce the Admiral to confess facts which bore so hard upon him? it was not from his ignorance of the difficulties he incurred; but, says Beza[113] "the Admiral, being downright and truly sincere, if any man of his quality ever was, made answer, that if afterwards, upon confronting, he should happen to make some further confession, he might give occasion to think that even then he did not discover the whole truth;" that is, if rightly understood, this sincere and downright man feared the force of truth at confronting, and prepared his subterfuges, as is usual to guilty persons, whose conscience, and fear of being convicted, makes them often confess more than could be drawn from witnesses. Nay, it seems, if the manner of the Admiral's explaining himself be well-considered, that he feared men should think him innocent, that he shunned only the formal acknowledgment and a juridical conviction, and, what is more, took pleasure in displaying his revenge. But the most politic thing he did for his acquittal was desiring that Potrot might be kept to be confronted with him, relying on his alleged excuses and the conjuncture of the times, which forbade driving to extremes the chief of so formidable a party.[114] Neither was the court ignorant of this, and accordingly the process was concluded. Poltrot, who had retracted the charge brought in by him against the Admiral and Beza, persisted in acquitting Beza, even to death;[115] but, as for the Admiral, he impeached him anew by three declarations, one after another, even amidst the tortures of his punishment, of having induced him to perpetrate this murder for God's service. As for Beza, it does not appear that he had any share in this action otherwise than by his seditious preaching, and the approbation he had given of the much more criminal conspiracy of Amboise; but very certain it is, that before the fact was committed, he did nothing to prevent it, although he could not be ignorant of the design, and, when it was over, omitted nothing that might give it all the appearance of an inspired action. The reader may judge of the rest; and here there is more than sufficient to make it evident what spirit those were animated with, who thus boast their meekness.

56.—*Catholics and Protestants agreed on the question of punishing Heretics.*

There is no need here of explaining myself on that question, whether or not Christian princes have a right to use the sword against their subjects, enemies to sound doctrine and the Church, the Protestants being agreed with us in this point. Luther and Calvin have written books expressly to make good the right and duty of the magistrate in this point.[116] Calvin reduced this to practice against Servetus and Valentine Gentili.[117] Melancthon approved of this procedure by a letter he wrote to him on this subject.[118] The discipline of our reformed likewise permits recourse to the secular arm in certain cases; and amongst the articles of discipline of the Geneva Church,[119] it appears that the ministers ought to inform the magistrate against the incorrigible, who despise spiritual penalties, and especially against those, without distinction, who teach new doctrine. And even at this day, the author[120] that most bitterly of all the Calvinist writers upbraids the Roman Church on this subject, with the cruelty of her doctrine, subscribes to it in the main, inasmuch as he permits the exercise of the power of the sword in matters of religion and conscience; a thing which in truth cannot be called in question without enervating, and, as it were, maiming the power of the legislature; so that there cannot be a more dangerous illusion, than to set down sufferance as a characteristic of the true Church; nor do I know amongst Christians any but Socinians and Anabaptists that oppose this doctrine. In a word, the right is certain, but moderation is not less necessary.

57.—*Calvin's Death.*

Calvin died at the beginning of these troubles. It is a weakness to look for something extraordinary in the death of such men; God does not always exhibit such examples. Since he permits heresies for the trial of his elect, we ought not to wonder that, to complete this trial, he suffers the spirit of seduction, with all the fine appearances wherewith it decks itself out, to predominate in them even to the end; and without further informing myself about Calvin's life and death, it is enough that he kindled aflame in his country which the effusion of so much blood could not extinguish, and is gone to appear before God's judgment-seat without the least remorse for so great a crime.

58.—*New Confession of Faith of the Helvetic Churches.*

His death made no alterations in the affairs of the party; but the instability natural to new sects was always furnishing the world with some new spectacle, and Confessions of Faith went on at their usual rate. In Switzerland, the defenders of the figurative sense, far from being satisfied with so many confession of faith made in France and elsewhere, in exposition of their doctrine, were not even satisfied with those that were made amongst themselves. We have seen that of Zuinglius in 1530, we have seen another published at Basil in 1532, and another of the same town in 1536; another in 1554, agreed to with the joint consent of the Swiss and those of Geneva: all these confessions of faith, although ratified by divers acts, were not deemed sufficient; and it was necessary to proceed to a fifth in 1566.[121]

59.—*The frivolous reasons of the Ministers for this new Confession of Faith.*

The ministers who published it were sensible that these alterations, in a thing of that importance, and which ought to be so firm and simple as a Confession of Faith, discredited their religion. For which reason, they set forth a preface, wherein they strove to account for this last change; and here is the whole of their defence: viz., "Although many nations have already published different confessions of faith, and they themselves have also done the same thing by public writings, nevertheless, they also propose this" (reader, observe) "because those writings may perchance have been forgotten, or be spread in divers places, and explain the thing so much at large that all the world have not time to read them."[122] Yet, it is visible that these two first confessions of faith, which the Swiss had published, scarce take up five leaves; and another, which might be joined to them, is much about the same length; whereas, this last mentioned, which ought to be the shortest, has more than sixty. And, allowing their confessions of faith had been forgotten, nothing was more easy than to publish them anew, were they contented with them: so that there was no necessity for publishing a fourth, but because they found themselves obliged to it for a reason they durst not utter; which was the variety of new sentiments continually rising in their minds; and as they must not own their daily loading their confessions with such novel fancies, they cloak their changes with such frivolous pretexts.

60.—*Imputed Justice begins but then to be known amongst the Swiss.*

We have seen that Zuinglius was an apostle and reformer without so much as knowing what was that grace by which we are Christians; and he who saved even philosophers by virtue of their morality, was an entire stranger to imputed justice. Accordingly, nothing appeared of it in the Confessions of Faith of 1532 and 1536.[123] Grace was acknowledged there in such a manner as Catholics might have approved, had it been less indefinite; and nothing was so much as mentioned in them against the merit of works. In the convention made with Calvin in 1554, it appears that Calvinism began to gain ground; and, accordingly, imputed justice then shows itself; they had been reformed nearly forty years without knowing this fundamental article of the reformation. The thing was not thoroughly explained till 1566, and it was by such a gradation that, from Zuinglius's excesses, they passed insensibly to those of Calvin.

61.—*The merit of Good Works, how rejected.*

In the chapter concerning good works, they speak of them in the same sense that other Protestants do, as the necessary fruits of faith, and reject their merit, whereof, we have seen, not a word was said in the precedent confessions. To condemn them, they here make use of a saying, often inculcated by St. Austin, but they quote it incorrectly; for whereas St. Austin says, and incessantly repeats it, "That God crowns his own gifts, when he crowns our merits;" they make him say, "He crowns in us, not our merits, but his own gifts."[124] The difference of these two expressions is easily perceived, one of which joins the merits with the gifts, and the other separates them. It seems, nevertheless, as if they had a mind to insinuate, at the close, that they condemned merit only as opposed to grace; their conclusion running this: "We, therefore, condemn those who so defend merit, as to deny grace." In reality, then, no error but that of the Pelagians is here condemned; for the merit, which we admit, is so little contrary to grace, that it is the very gift and fruit thereof.

62.—*Faith appropriated to the Elect.—Certainty of Salvation. —Inamissibility of Justice.*

In the tenth chapter, true faith is attributed to the predestinated alone, by these words: "Every man must hold it for unquestionable, that, if he believes, and abides in Jesus Christ, he is predestinated." And a little father on, "If we communicate with Jesus Christ, and he belongs to us, and we to him, by true faith, this is to us a sufficiently clear and sure testimony that we are written in the book of life."[125] Hence it is plain that true faith, namely, justifying faith, appertains only to the elect; that this faith and this justice can never be lost finally; and that temporary faith is not the true justifying faith. These same words seem to conclude for the absolute certainty of predestination; for, although they make it depend on faith, it is a doctrine received amongst the whole Protestant party, that a believer, in saying, "I believe," feels in himself the true faith. But herein they are insensible of the seduction of our self-love, of the mixture of our passions, so strangely complicated, that our own dispositions, and the true motives which actuate us, are often what we, of all things, know with the lest degree of certainty; so that, in saying with that disconsolate father in the gospel, "I believe"[126] how greatly soever we may think ourselves moved, though we should cry out lamentably as he did, and with a flood of tears; we ought, nevertheless, to subjoin, with him, "Lord, help thou my unbelief;" and show by that means, that saying "I believe," is rather an effort in us to produce so great an act, than an absolute certainty of our having produced it.

63.—Conversion ill-explained.

How prolix soever be the discourse, which the Zuinglians make on free-will, in the ninth chapter of their Confession,[127] this little is all that is material in it. Three states of man are well distinguished: That of his first institution, wherein he had the power of inclining to good, and declining from evil; that of his fall, when, unable to do good, he yet is free to evil, because he embraces it voluntarily, and by consequence with liberty, although God frequently prevents the effect of his choice, and hinders him from accomplishing his evil purposes; and that of his regeneration, when, reinstated by the Holy Ghost in the power of voluntarily doing good, he is free, yet not fully, on account of the infirmity of concupiscence remaining in him, acting, nevertheless, not passively; these are their terms—odd enough, I own—for what is it to act passively? And how is it possible such an idea should enter any man's head? However, this manner of speech pleased our Zuinglians. Acting (they continue to speak of man regenerated,) not passively, but actively in the choice of good, and in the operation by which he accomplishes it. How much was this short of a clear and full explanation? They ought to have joined to these three states, that of man between corruption and regeneration, when, touched with grace, he begins to bring forth the spirit of salvation amidst the pangs of repentance. This state is not that of corruption, in which he wills nought but evil, since he begins, in this state, to will good; and if the Zuinglians would not consider it as a state, it being rather a passage from one state to another, they ought to explain, at least in some other place, that, in this passage, and previously to regeneration, the effort man makes, through grace, to convert himself, is not an evil. Our Reformed are strangers to these necessary precisions; they ought also to have explained whether, in this passage, when drawn towards good by grace, we can resist it; and again, whether, in the state of corruption, we do evil so of ourselves as not to be able even to abstain from one evil rather than another; and lastly, whether in the state of regeneration, working good, through grace, we be so forcibly attracted to it, as not to have it then in our power to decline to evil. All these things were necessary to give a right understanding of the operation and even notion of free-will, which these doctors leave confused by terms too indefinite and equivocal.

64.—*Monstrous Doctrine on Free-Will.*

But what ends the chapter displays still better the perplexity of their thoughts. "We doubt not," say they, "that men regenerate, or not regenerate, have equally their free-will in common actions; because man, being not inferior to beasts, hath that in common with them, to will certain things, reject others; thus he may speak or hold his tongue, go out of doors, or remain within." Strange doctrine! To make us free like beasts! They have not a more elevated idea of man's liberty, having said a little before, "that, by his fall, he is not altogether changed into a long or stone;"[128] Which is as much as to say, he wants but little of it. However that may be, the Swiss Zuinglians aim no higher; nay, the Protestants of Germany grovel still lower, when they say, that in man's conversion, to wit, in the most noble action he is capable of—in the action by which he unites himself with his God,—he acts no more than a stone or log, though he acts differently on other occasions.[129] How dost thou debase thyself, Oh man, thus meanly accounting for thy free-will! But, in fine, since man is not a log, and, in ordinary actions, his free-will is made to consist in being able to do certain things, or not to do them, it ought to be considered, that not finding in ourselves a different manner of acting, in natural actions, from what we do in others, this same liberty accompanies us throughout; and that God knows how to preserve it, even when he elevates us by his grace to actions supernatural—it being unworthy of His Holy Spirit to make us act any more in these than in others, like to beasts, or rather, like stocks and stones.

65.—*Our Calvinists are more sparing in their explanations, and why.*

It may perhaps seem strange, that we spoke nothing of any of these matters in treating of the confession of the Calvinists. But the reason is, they themselves pass them all in silence, nor think it worth their while to speak of the manner in which man acts; as if it were a thing indifferent to man himself, or did not appertain to faith to know, in point of liberty, together with one of the most beautiful lineaments God has traced in man, to make him in his own image, that very thing which renders us worthy of blame or praise before God and man.

66.—*The Supper without Substance, and the Presence only in virtue.*

The article of the Supper still remains, in which the Swiss will show themselves more sincere than ever. Those indeterminate phrases, which we have seen them employ once only, in 1536, by Bucer's advice, and in condescension to the Lutherans, are no longer satisfactory to them. Even Calvin, their very good friend, cannot bring them over to the proper substance, nor the incomprehensible miracles, whereby the Holy Ghost, notwithstanding the distance of place, makes us partakers of it. They say, therefore, "that indeed we receive, not an imaginary nourishment, but the proper body, the true body of our Lord given for us, but interiorly, spiritually by the Holy Ghost, who gives and applies to us the things which the body and blood of our Lord have merited for us, namely, the forgiveness of sins, the deliverance of our souls, and life eternal."[130] This is, then, what is called the thing received in this sacrament. This thing received indeed, is the forgiveness of sins, and spiritual life; and if the body and blood are also received, it is by their benefit and effect; or, as is afterwards subjoined, by their figure, by their commemoration, and not by their substance. For which reason, after having said, "That the body of our Lord is no where but in heaven, where he ought to be adored, and not under the species of bread,"[131] in order to explain the manner in which he is present, "He is not," say they, "absent from the Supper. Though the sun be in heaven absent from us, he is present to us efficaciously, that is, present by his virtue. How much more is Jesus Christ present to us by his vivifying operation?" Who does not perceive that what is present to us only by its virtue, has no need of communicating its proper substance? These two ideas are incompatible, nor has any man ever said seriously, that he receives the proper substance of the sun and stars, under pretext that he receives their influences. Thus Zuinglians and Calvinists, who, of all that have separated from Rome, boast most of being united among themselves, nevertheless reform each other in their several confessions of faith, and never could agree in one common and simple explanation of their doctrine.

67.—*Nothing particular in the Supper.*

True it is, that of the Zuinglians leaves nothing peculiar to the Supper. The body of Jesus Christ is no more there than in any other actions of a Christian; and it was in vain that Jesus Christ said in the Supper only, with so much energy, "This is my body;" since with these powerful words he was able to work nothing in it that is singular. This is the inevitable weak side of the figurative sense, which the Zuinglians were well aware of, and owned sincerely: "This spiritual nourishment is taken," say they, "out of the Supper; and how often soever a person believes, this believer hath already received and enjoyeth this food of everlasting life; but for the same reason, when he receives the sacrament, that which he receiveth is nothing; *non nihil accipit.*" What is our Lord's Supper reduced to? all they can say for it is, that what you receive in it "is next to quite nothing. For," proceed our Zuinglians, "we continue there to partake of the body and blood of our Lord." So the Supper hath nothing singular in it. "Faith is stirred up, increases, is nourished with some spiritual food; for as long as we live it receives a continual increase." It receives, therefore, as much of all this out of the Supper as in the Supper, nor is Jesus Christ a whit more there than any where else. In this manner, after saying that the particular thing received in the Supper is not a mere nothing, and in fact reducing it to so small a matter, they are not yet able to tell us what is that little they have left in it. Here is a great vacuum I must own; it was in order to supply this emptiness that Calvin and the Calvinists invented their big swelling words. They thought to fill up this frightful chasm by saying in their Catechism, that out of the Supper, Jesus Christ is received in part only; whereas, in the Supper, he is received fully. But to what purpose promising such great matters when you mean nothing by them? I like far better the sincerity of Zuinglius and the Swiss, who own the scantiness of their Supper, than the false plenty of our Calvinists, sumptuous in nothing but in words.

68.—*The Swiss the most sincere of all the defenders of the Figurative Sense.*

Thus much am I then obliged to say in behalf of the Zuinglians, that their Confession of Faith is of all the most natural and simple; and this is not only with reference to the Eucharistic point, but in regard to all the others; in a word, of all the Protestant confessions of faith, that of 1566, with all its defects, speaks the most clearly what it means to speak.

69.—*Remarkable Confession of the Polonian Zuinglians, in which the Lutherans are roughly handled.—1570.*

Among the Polish separatists from the Church of Rome, there were some that maintained the figurative sense, and these had subscribed, in 1567, the confession of faith, which the Swiss had drawn up the year before. They rested content with it for three whole years; but in 1570, they thought it reasonable to frame another in a synod held at Czenger, which is to be met with in the collection of Geneva, in which they particularly signalize themselves on the Supper-article.[132]

They condemn the reality, as well in respect to the delirium of Catholics, who say the bread is changed into the body, as in respect to the folly of the Lutherans, who place the body with the bread: they declare particularly against the latter, that the reality, which they admit, cannot subsist without a change of substance, such as happened in the waters of Egypt, in the wand of Moses, and in the water at the nuptial feast of Cana; thus they clearly own that transubstantiation is necessary, even by the principles of the Lutherans. They hold them in such abhorrence, as to vouchsafe them no other appellation than that of "eaters of human flesh," ascribing every where to them a "carnal and bloody" manner of communicating, as if they ate raw flesh.[133] After condemning the Papists and the Lutherans, they speak of others under error, whom they call Sacramentarians. "We reject," say they, the phrensy of those who believe that the Supper is an empty sign of our absent Lord." By these words, they aim at the Socinians, as introducers of an empty supper, though unable to show that their own is better furnished, nothing at all being to be found in either of them with respect to the body and the blood, but signs, commemoration, and virtue.[134] To place some difference betwixt the Zuinglian and Socinian Supper, they say in the first place, that the Supper is not the sole memorial of Jesus Christ absent, and make an express chapter concerning the presence of Jesus Christ in this mystery. But endeavoring to expound it, they confound themselves with terms that are not of any language, words so uncouth and barbarous, as not to be translated. Jesus Christ, say they, is present in the supper both as God and man: as God, *entèr, præsentèr;* render these words who can: by his Jehova divinity, that is, in common speech, by his divinity properly so called, and expressed by the incommunicable name, "As the vine in its branches, and the head in its members." All this is true, but nothing to the Supper, where the question relates to the body and blood. They proceed, therefore, to say that Jesus Christ is present as man in four ways. "In the first place," say they, "by his union with the word, inasmuch as he is united to the word who is every where. Secondly, he is present in his promise by the word and by faith, communicating himself to his elect as the vine communicates itself to its branches, and the head to its members, though distant from it. Thirdly, he is present by his sacramental institution, and the infusion of his holy spirit. Fourthly, by his office of dispenser, or by his intercession for his elect." They add, "he is not present carnally, nor locally, it being requisite he should be no where corporally till the day of universal judgment, except in heaven."[135]

70.—Ubiquity taught by the Polish Zuinglians.

The three last of these four ways of presence are well enough known amongst the defenders of the figurative sense. But will they be able to make us comprehend the first, agreeably to their sentiments? have they ever taught, as the Poles of their communion do, that "Jesus Christ is present as man, in the Supper, by his union with the word, because the word is every where present?" This is the reasoning of Ubiquitarians, who attribute to Jesus Christ an omnipresence as to place, even according to his human nature; but this extravagance of the Ubiquitarians is no where maintained but amongst the Lutherans. The Zuinglians and Calvinists reject it equally with the Catholics. Yet this notion is borrowed by the Polish Zuinglians, who, not fully satisfied with the Zuinglian confession which they had subscribed, append to it this new dogma.

71.—Their agreement with the Lutherans and Vaudois.

They did more, and that very year united themselves with the Lutherans, whom they had but just condemned as gross and carnal men, as men who taught a cruel and bloody communion. They sued for their communion, and those eaters of human flesh became their brethren. The Vaudois entered into this agreement, and all, assembled together at Sendomir, subscribed what had been defined concerning the Supper-article in the confession of faith called Saxonic.

But for the better understanding of this triple union betwixt the Zuinglians, Lutherans, and Vaudois, it will be necessary to know who these Vaudois were, who then appeared in Poland. It may not be amiss to know moreover what were the Vaudois in general, they being at last turned Calvinists; and many Protestants doing them so much honor as to assert even that the Church, persecuted by the Pope, preserved her succession in this society—so gross and manifest a delusion, that I must strive once for all to cure them of it.

Notes

[1] Burn. l. iii. p. 374.
[2] Ibid, p. 376.
[3] Ibid.
[4] Ibid. pp. 397, and 376.
[5] Ibid. 398.
[6] Thuan, l. xxi. An. 1559.
[7] Burn. l. iii. p. 397.
[8] Ibid. p. 376.
[9] Ibid. p. 392.
[10] Ibid.
[11] Calv. dilucid. explic. opusc. p. 861. p. ii. l. i. p. 104.
[12] Ibid. l. iii. pp. 405, 406.
[13] Calv. dilucid. explic. opusc. l. iii. p. 397.
[14] P. 405.
[15] John i. 10, 11.
[16] P. ii. p. 392.
[17] Ibid. l. i. p. 170.
[18] Burn. l. iii. p. 406.
[19] P. 392.
[20] Life of B. Bedell, pp. 137, 138.
[21] Burnet, l. iii. p. 386.
[22] Ibid. l. iii. pp. 385, 386.
[23] Ibid. l. iii. 386.
[24] Syn. Lond. art. 7.
[25] Syn. gen. p. i. pag. 107.
[26] Syn. gen. i. pag. 107.
[27] Syn. Lon. art. 36. Syn. Gen. p. 107. Bur. 385.
[28] Ibid.
[29] Burn. Ibid. p. 392.
[30] Synt. Gen. part i. p. 109 Ibid. p. 126. 1588.
[31] Syn. of Paris, 1565. Syn. of Rochelle, 1571.
[32] Burn l. iii. p. 394, &c.
[33] Thuan. lib. xxi. 1559. Burn. lib. iii. p. 394.
[34] Burnet, l. iii. p. 401.
[35] Ibid.
[36] Synt. Gen. par 1. Conf. Aug. Art. xvi. xvii. p. 102.
[37] Book xiv.
[38] Burn. l. iii. pp. 415, 416.
[39] Thuan. lib. xxvii. 1560, t. ii. p. 17. La Poplin l. vii. pp. 246, 255.

[40] Thuan. t. i. l. xxiv. p. 752. La Poplin, livre vi. Bez. Hist. Eccl. livre iii. p. 250, 254, 270.—1560.
[41] Ibid. 313.
[42] Beza, Hist. Eccl. liv. iii. 249.
[43] Lib. xxiv. p. 372, edit. Gen.
[44] La Poplin. Ibid. p. 164, &c.
[45] Hist. Eccl. l. iii. p. 313.
[46] Thuan. Ibid. pp. 733, 738.
[47] Beza. Thuan. La Poplin. Ibid. S. n. 26. 1.
[48] Ord. de Charles V, 1373 and 74, et seq. Vid. la Poplin. l. vi. 155, et seq.
[49] Beza, p. 250.
[50] Thuan. pp. 732, 738.
[51] Beza, p. 250.
[52] Ibid.
[53] Burn. l. iii. p. 415.
[54] Crit. de Maimb. t. i. Lett. xv. N. 6. p. 263. Cal. Ep. p. 312, 313.
[55] Crit. de Maimb. Lett. ii. N. 2.
[56] Brant. vie de l'Amiral de Chastil.
[57] Crit. de Maimb. N. 1. 4. Burn. t. 1. Pref.
[58] La Poplin. l. viii. Beza, t. ii. l. vi. p. 5.
[59] Rom. viii. 36.
[60] Matt. x. 16.
[61] Luke iii. 14.
[62] D. Aub. t. i. l. iii. ch. ix. pp. 155, 156.
[63] Jur. Accompliss. des Proph. Avis à tous les Chrét. Towards the middle of his Preface or Introduction.
[64] Part ii. l. iii. p. 415, &c.
[65] Thuan. l. xxix. p. 77, et seq. La Poplin, l. vii. pp. 283, 284.
[66] Part 2. l. iii. p. 416.
[67] Vide la Poplin. l. vi. pp. 155, 156.
[68] Vide la Poplin l. vi. pp. 616.
[69] Thuan. l. xxix. 1562. La Poplin. l. viii.
[70] Critiq. du P. Maimb. let. xvii. N. 5. p. 303. Thuan l. xxix. An. 1552, pp. 79. 81. Thuan l. xxvi. p. 787, &c.
[71] Thuan. l.xxvi. p. 79.

[72] Lib. vi.

[73] Ibid. p. 4.

[75] Ibid. p. 6.

[75] Beza, l. vi. p. 3.

[76] Ibid. p. 298.

[77] Ibid. pp. 280, 282.

[78] Ibid. p. 285.

[79] Beza, 1. vi. p. 285.

[80] Apol. pour la Reform. part 1. ch. x. p. 301.

[81] Ibid. ch. xv. p. 453.

[82] Ibid.

[83] 1 Pet. ii. 18.

[84] Crit. t. i. Lett. viii, N. 1. p. 129, et seq. Lett. xvi. N. 9, p. 315, &c.

[85] Beza, l. i. p. 16.

[86] Beza, l. i. p. 16.

[87] Thuan. lib. xxiii. An. 1559, p. 169.

[88] Beza, l. i. La Poplin. l. v. p. 144.

[89] L. iii. p. 248, An. 1560.

[90] Crit. t. i. Lett. ii. N. 3. p. 45, et seq. Ibid. Lett. xviii. p. 331.

[91] Ibid. Lett. xvii. N. 8.

[92] Burn. part. ii. l. i. p. 9.

[93] Acts v. 38.

[94] L. vi. pp. 267, 268.

[95] Ibid. p. 290.

[96] Ibid.

[97] Thuan. lib. xxxix. pp. 77, 78.

[98] L. vi. 299.

[99] Ibid.

[100] L. vi. p. 268.

[101] D'Aub. p. 1. l. iii. c. xvii. p. 176.

[102] Beza, pp. 268, 295, 297.

[103] Ibid. pp. 266, 268.

[104] D'Aub. t. i. p. 176.

[105] Thuan l. xxxiii. p. 207.

[106] L. vi. pp. 291, 308.

[107] Ibid. pp. 294, 295, et seq.

[108] P. 209.

[109] P. 308.

[110] Ibid. pp. 297, 391.

[111] L. vi. pp. 297, 391.

[112] Ibid. p. 297.

[113] Beza, p. 308.

[114] Beza, p. 308.

[115] Pp. 312, 319, 327.

[116] Luth. de Magist. t. iii.

[117] Calvin opusc. p. 592. Ibid. 600, 659.

[118] Melan. Calvino inter Calv. Ep. p. 169.

[119] Jur. Syst. ii. chap. 22, 33. Lett. Past. de la 1 Année, 1, 2, 3.

[120] Hist. du Papis. 2. Recrim. ch. 2, et seq.

[121] Synt. Gen. 1st part, p. 1.

[122] Synt. Gen. init. Præfat.

[123] Conf. 1532. Art. ix. Synt. Gen. i. p. 68. 1536. Art. 2, 3. Ibid. p. 72. Consens. Art. iii. opusc. Cal. 751. Conf. fid. c. xv. Synt. Gen. part i. p. 26.

[124] Synt. Gen. part. i. p. 26.

[125] Cap. x. p. 15.

[126] Mark ix. 24.

[127] Cap. ix. p. 12.

[128] Cap. ix. pp. 12, 13.

[129] Concord. p. 662, §5. S. l. viii. n. 48.

[130] Cap. xxi. p. 48.

[131] Cap. xxi. p. 50.

[132] Synod. Czen. Synt. Conf. part i. p. 148. Cap. de Cœn. Dom. p. 153.

[133] Cap. de Sacramentariis, p. 155.

[134] Cap. de Sacramentariis, p. 153, 154. Cap. de Præs. in Cœna. p 155.

[135] P. 155.

Book XI

A SHORT HISTORY OF THE ALBIGENSES, THE VAUDOIS, THE WICKLIFFITES, AND HUSSITES.

A brief Summary.—A short history of the Albigenses and Vaudois.—That they are two different Sects.—The Albigenses are complete Manicheans. —Their origin explained.—The Paulicians are a branch of the Manicheans in Armenia, whence they pass into Bulgaria, thence into Italy and Germany, where they are called Cathari; and into France, where they took the name of Albigenses.—Their prodigious errors, and their hypocrisy, are discovered by all contemporary authors.—The illusions of Protestants endeavoring to excuse them.—The testimony of St. Bernard, who is wrongfully accused of credulity.—The origin of the Vaudois.—The ministers in vain make them the disciples of Berengarius.—They believed Transubstantiation.—The seven Sacraments acknowledged by them. —Confession and sacramental Absolution.—Their error, a kind of Donatism.—They make the Sacraments depend on the holiness of their Ministers, and allow the administration of them to pious laymen.—Origin of the Sect called the Brethren of Bohemia.—That they are not Vaudois, which origin they contemn; nor the disciples of John Huss, though they boast of it.—Their deputies sent over all the world to seek for Christians of their belief, without being able to find any.—Wickliff's impious doctrine.—John Huss, who glories in being his disciple, abandons him in regard of the Eucharist.—The disciples of John Huss divided into Taborites and Calixtins.—The confusion of all these Sects.—The Protestants can draw from thence no advantage for the establishment of their Mission, and succession of their Doctrine.—The agreement of the Lutherans, of the Bohemians, and the Zuinglians in Poland—The divisions and reconciliations of sectaries make equally against them.

1.—What is the succession of Protestants.

IT is incredible what pains our reformed have been at, in order to find themselves predecessors in all foregoing ages. Whilst in the fourth age, of all the most illustrious, none could be found but Vigilantius alone, that opposed the honor paid to saints and the veneration of their relics, he is looked on by Protestant as the person who preserved the Depositum, namely, the succession of apostolic doctrine, and is preferred to St. Jerome, who has the whole Church on his side. For the same reason, too, Arius ought to be considered

361

as the only one whom God enlightened in the same century, for he alone rejected the sacrifice which every where else, in the East as well as the West, was offered for the relief of the dead. But, unluckily, he was an Arian; and they were ashamed to count amongst the witnesses of the truth, a man that denied the Divinity of the Son of God. But I am amazed they stuck at that. Claude of Turin was an Arian, and the disciple of Felix of Urgel, that is, a Nestorian besides.[1] But because he broke Images, he finds place amongst the forefathers of the Protestants. It matters not how far soever the rest of the Iconoclasts, as well as he, have outstretched this point, even to say, that God forbade the arts of painting and sculpture; it is sufficient that they taxed the rest of Christians with idolatry, to be enrolled amongst the first rate witnesses of the truth. Berengarius impugned nothing but the Real Presence, leaving all the rest as he found it; but the rejecting of one only tenet was sufficient to make him a Calvinist, and a doctor of the true Church. Wickliff will be of that number, notwithstanding all the impieties we shall see taught; though even by asserting that kings, lords, magistrates, priests, pastors, are no longer such from their falling into mortal sin, he has equally subverted all order in the Church and state, and filled both with tumult and sedition. John Huss followed this doctrine, and, what is more, said Mass to the end of his life, and adored the Eucharist; yet for standing up against the Church of Rome in other points, he must be placed by our reformed in the calendar of their martyrs. In a word, provided they have muttered against any one point of our tenets, especially inveighed against the pope, in other respects, be they what they will, and of what opinion soever, they stand on the list of Protestant ancestry, and are deemed worthy to keep up the succession of that Church.

2.—*The Vaudois and Albigenses a weak support to Calvinists.*

But of all the predecessors the Protestants have made choice of, the most welcome to them, at least to the Calvinists, are the Vaudois and Albigenses. What can be their aim in this? It were but a weak support. To make their antiquity rise some ages higher, (for the Vaudois, allowing them all they desire, and Peter de Bruis, with his disciple Henry, reach no further than the eleventh age,) and there to stop short unable to show one before them, is being forced to stand much beneath the time of the Apostles; it is calling for help from men as weak and as much put to it as themselves; who, alike with them, are challenged to show their predecessors; who, no more than they, are able to produce them; who, by consequence, are guilty of the same crime of innovation they are accused of; so that naming them in this cause, is naming accomplices of the same crime, not witnesses that may lawfully depose in their defense.

3.—*Why the Calvinists lay a stress on them.*

Nevertheless, this support, such as it is, is eagerly embraced by our Calvinists, and the reason is this. The Vaudois and Albigenses, it seems, formed churches separated from Rome, which Berengarius and Wickliff never did. Making them therefore their ancestors, is giving themselves, in some manner, a series of church succession. As the origin of these churches, no less than the faith they made profession of, was as yet somewhat obscure at the time of the pretended Reformation, the people were made to believe that they were of a very ancient date, and sprung from the first ages of Christianity.

4.—*Ridiculous pretensions of the Vaudois and of Beza.*

I wonder not that Leger, one of the Vaudois Barbes (for so they called their pastors) and their most celebrated historian, has given into this error, for he was unquestionably the most bold and ignorant of all mankind. But there is reason to wonder that it was embraced by Beza, and that he has written in his Ecclesiastical History, not only that the Vaudois, time immemorial, had opposed the abuses of the Church of Rome,[2] but also, in the year 1541, entered on record, by a public and authentic act, the doctrine taught from them as from father to son down from the year 120, after Christ's nativity, as their ancient predecessors always had informed them.[3]

5.—*False origin boasted of by the Vaudois.*

Here is certainly a fine tradition, had it but the least proof to countenance it. But, unfortunately, Waldo's first disciples did not trace it up so high; and the remotest antiquity they challenged was of withdrawing from the Church of Rome at the time when, under Pope Sylvester I, she accepted the temporal domains that Constantine, the first Christian Emperor, endowed her with. This is so frivolous a cause of rupture, and the pretension withal so ridiculous, as not to deserve refuting. A man must have lost his wits to persuade himself that, ever since St. Sylvester's time, that is about the year 320, there was a sect amongst Christians which the Fathers knew nothing of. We have in the councils held in the communion of the Roman Church, anathemas pronounced against an infinity of different sects; we have the catalogues of heresies drawn by St. Epiphanius, by St. Austin, and several other church authors. The most obscure and the least followed sects, those which appeared in a corner of the world, as that of certain women called Collyridians, who were to be met with only in some part of Arabia, that of the Tertullianists or Abelians, who were only in Carthage, or in some villages near Hippo, and many others equally obscure, did not escape their knowledge.[4] The zeal of pastors that labored to bring back he strayed sheep, discovered all to save all; none but these separatists on account of ecclesiastical revenues were unknown to every body. These men, more temperate than an Athanasius, a Basil, an Ambrose, and all the other doctors, more wise than all the councils, who, without rejecting goods given to the Church, were contented with making rules for their just administration; so well, I say, did these men play their part, as never to have been heard of by them. The assurance to assert this, was certainly the height of impudence in the first Vaudois; but, with Beza, to trace back this sect, unknown to all ages, up to the year of our Lord 120, is giving himself ancestors and church succession by too glaring an imposition.

6.—The design of this Eleventh Book, and what is to be shown therein.

The Reformed, disgusted at their novelty, which they were continually upbraided with, stood in need of this weak support. But, in order to derive some advantage from it, it was also requisite to set other artifices on foot; it was requisite to conceal carefully the true state of these Albigenses and Vaudois. Of two quite different sects they made but one; and this, lest the Reformed should discover amongst their ancestors a too manifest contrariety. But, above all, their abominable doctrine was kept a secret; no notice taken that these Albigenses were complete Manicheans, no less than Peter de Bruis and Henry his disciple; not a word that these Vaudois had separated from the Church upon grounds equally detested by the new Reformation, and by the Church of Rome. The same dissimulation was used in regard of the Polish Vaudois, who were but nominally such; and the people kept ignorant that their doctrine was neither that of the ancient Vaudois, nor that of the Calvinists, nor that of the Lutherans. The history I am going to furnish of these three sects, although epitomized, will be nevertheless supported with such pregnant proofs, as to make the Calvinists ashamed of the ancestors whom they have selected for themselves.

THE HISTORY OF THE NEW MANICHEANS, CALLED THE HERETICS OF TOULOUSE AND ALBY.

7.—Errors of the Manicheans, progenitors of the Albigenses.

In order to understand what follows, you must not be wholly ignorant what these Manicheans were. Their whole theology turned on the question of the origin of evil; they beheld it in the world, and were for discovering its principle. It could not be God, because he is infinitely good. It was therefore necessary, said they, to acknowledge another principle, which, being evil by its nature, might be the cause and origin of evil. Here then is the foundation of the error; two first principles, one of good, the other of evil; enemies by consequence, and of a contrary nature; which having fought and mixed in the strife, one diffused good on the world, the other evil; one light, the other darkness; and so on—for it is needless to relate here all the impious extravagances of this abominable sect. It sprung from Paganism, and its principles may be seen even in Plato. It reigned amongst the Persians. Plutarch has acquainted us with the names they gave to the good and evil cause. Manes, a Persian, strove to introduce this prodigy into the Christian religion in Aurelian's reign, viz. towards the end of the third century. Marcion had begun some years before; and his sect, divided into many branches, had prepared the way for the impieties and reveries Manes grafted on it.

8.—Consequences of the false Principle of the Manicheans.

Now the consequences which these heretics drew from this doctrine were no less absurd than impious. The Old Testament, with all its severity, was but a fable, or at best, but the product of the evil principle; the mystery of the incarnation an illusion; and the flesh of Jesus Christ a phantom; for flesh being the work of the evil principle, Jesus Christ, the son of the good God, could not, in truth, have vested himself with it. As our bodies came from the bad principle, and our souls from the good, or rather were the very substance of it, it was not lawful to beget children, nor unite the substance of the good principle with that of the bad; so that marriage, or rather the generation of children, was prohibited. The flesh of animals, and every thing proceeding from it, as white meats, was the work of the evil cause; the same of wine: all these were impure by nature, and the use of them criminal. Here then are manifestly those men seduced by devils, of whom St. Paul speaks, that were "In latter times . . . to forbid to marry," and command "to abstain from meats," as unclean, "which God hath created."[5]

9.—*The Manicheans endeavored to justify themselves by the usages of the Church.*

These wretches, who sought only to deceive the world by appearances, endeavored to justify themselves by the example of the Catholic Church, wherein the number of those that forbore marriage, from the profession of continence, was very great, and abstinence from certain meats was either practised always, as by many Anchorets after Daniel's example, or at particular times, as in Lent. But the holy fathers replied, that there was a great difference between those that condemned the procreation of children, as the Manicheans did expressly, and those that preferred continence to it with St. Paul and Jesus Christ himself, and judged it unlawful for them to look back, after making profession of so perfect a state of life.[6] Besides, it was a different thing to abstain from certain meats, either to signify some mystery, as in the Old Testament, or to mortify the senses, as was still continued in the new; a different thing to condemn them with the Manicheans, as impure, as evil, as the work, not of God, but of the bad principle. And the fathers observed, that the apostle expressly impugned this latter sense, which was that of the Manicheans, by these words: every creature of God is good. And, again, by these: nothing is to be refused of all God has created; from thence concluding, that there was no wonder the Holy Ghost had warned the faithful so long before, by the mouth of St. Paul, against so great an abomination.

10.—*Three other Characteristics of the Manicheans.—First, the Spirit of Seduction.*

Such were the principal points of the Manichean doctrine. But this sect had, besides, two remarkable characteristics; one, that in the midst of these impious absurdities, which the devil had inspired them with, they yet mixed something in their discourses of so specious a nature, so prodigiously seducing, that St. Austin himself, so great a genius, was ensnared thereby, and remained amongst them nine whole years, a great zealot of this sect.[7] It was observed, likewise, that this was one of those heresies which it is most difficult to be reclaimed from; for, to impose upon the vulgar, it had juggling and unaccountable delusions, so far even as to be taxed with sorcery; in a word, none of the implements of seduction were wanting to it.

11.—*Second Characteristic, Hypocrisy.*

The second characteristic of the Manicheans is, their knowing how to conceal what was most detestable in their sect, with so profound an artifice, that not only strangers, but even those of the profession, passed a long time amongst them in ignorance thereof. For beneath the colorable pretext of chastity they hid impurities not to be named, and which made part of their very mysteries. Amongst them were several degrees. Those whom they called auditors, knew not the bottom of their sect; and their elect, namely, those that were let into the whole mystery, carefully kept close from their probationers the abominable secret, till they had been prepared for it by several gradations. They made a show of abstinence and the exterior of a life not only good, but mortified; and one part of the seduction was, the arriving as it were by stages to that which was believed the more perfect, because hidden.

12.—*Third Characteristic: Mixing with the Catholics in the Churches, and concealing themselves.*

For the third characteristic of these heretics, we may further observe in them a surprising dexterity in mixing with the faithful, and concealing themselves under the appearance of the same profession; for this dissimulation was one of the artifices they employed to inveigle men into their sentiments.[8] They were seen promiscuously with others in the churches; there they received the communion; and although they never received the blood of our Lord, as well because they detested wine used in consecration, as also because they did not believe Jesus Christ had true blood, the liberty allowed in the Church of partaking of one or both kinds, was the cause that, for a long time, the perpetual affectation of their rejecting that of wine, passed unperceived. At length, St. Leo discovered them by this mark: but their cunning to elude the notice of the Catholics, however vigilant, was so great, that they still concealed themselves, and scarce were discovered under the pontificate of St. Gelasius. At that time, therefore, in order to render them wholly distinguishable to the people, it was necessary to proceed to an express prohibition of communicating otherwise than under both kinds; and to show that this prohibition was not founded on the necessity of always taking them conjointly, St. Gelasius[9] grounds it in formal terms on this ground, because those who refused the sacred wine did it through a certain superstition; an evident proof, that, were it not for this superstition, which rejected one of the parts of this mystery as evil, the usage in its nature had been free and indifferent, even in solemn assemblies. Protestants that believed this word, superstition, was not strong enough to express the abominable practices of the Manicheans, did not reflect that this word, in the Latin tongue, signifies all false religion; but that it is particularly appropriated to the Manichean sect, on account of their abstinence and superstitious observances: the books of St. Austin proves this sufficiently.[10]

13.—*The Paulicians or Manicheans of Armenia.*

This so hidden a sect, so abominable, so full of seduction, of superstition, and hypocrisy, notwithstanding imperial laws which condemned its followers to death, yet maintained and diffused itself. The Emperor Anastasius, and the Empress Theodora, wife to Justinian, had given it countenance. The followers thereof are to be seen under the children of Heraclius, that is, in the seventh age, in Armenia, a province bordering on Persia, the birthplace of this detestable superstition, and formerly subject to the empire. They were then settled,[11] or confirmed by one named Paul, from whom the name of Paulicians was given them in the East, by one named Constantine, and, finally, by one named Sergius. They arrived to such great power in that country, either by the weakness of the government, or the protection of the Saracens, or even by the favor of the Emperor Nicephoras, much wedded to this sect, that at length, being persecuted by the Empress Theodora, the wife of Basil, they were able to build cities, and take up arms against their sovereigns.[12]

14.—*History of the Paulicians, by Peter of Sicily, addressed to the Archbishop of Bulgaria.*

These wars were long and bloody under the reign of Basil the Macedonian, to wit, at the close of the ninth century. Peter of Sicily[13] was sent by this Emperor to Tibrica in Armenia, which Cedrenus calls Tephrica, a stronghold of these heretics, to treat about the exchange of prisoners. During this time, he became thoroughly acquainted with the Paulicians, and dedicated a book concerning their errors to the Archbishop of Bulgaria, for reasons hereafter specified. Vossius acknowledges we are much obliged to Raderus for giving us, in Greek and Latin, so particular and so excellent a history.[14] There, Peter of Sicily[15] paints out to us these heretics in their proper characters, their principles, the contempt they had for the Old Testament, their prodigious address in concealing themselves when they pleased, and the other marks already mentioned. But he notices two or three which must not be forgotten, viz., their particular aversion to the Images of Christ crucified,[16] a natural consequence of their error, forasmuch as they rejected the passion and death of the Son of God; their contempt of the Holy Virgin, whom they did not account the mother of Jesus Christ, since they denied his human flesh; and above all, their abhorrence of the Eucharist.[17]

15.—*The conformity of the Paulicians with the Manicheans, whom St. Austin refuted.*

Cedrenus,[18] who has taken the greatest part of what he writes of the Paulicians from this historian, instances, after him, these three characteristics, namely, their aversion to the Cross, to the blessed Virgin, and the holy Eucharist. The same sentiments had the Manicheans of old. We learn from St. Austin,[19] that their Eucharist was different from ours, and something so execrable as not to be thought on, much less written. But the new Manicheans had also received, from the ancient, another doctrine, we are to observe. So long as St. Austin's time, Faustus, the Manichean, upbraided the Catholics with their idolatry in the honor they paid the holy martyrs, and in the sacrifices they offered on their relics.[20] St. Austin pointed out to them that this worship had nothing common with that of the heathens, because it was not the worship of Latria, or of subjection and perfect servitude; and if they offered to God the holy oblation of the body and blood of Jesus Christ, at the tombs and on the relics of the martyrs, they were far from offering to them this sacrifice, but hoped only "To excite themselves thereby to the imitation of their virtues, to be brought into partnership with their merits; and, lastly, to be assisted by their prayers." So clear an answer did not prevent the new Manicheans from continuing the calumnies of their forefathers. Peter of Sicily[21] acquaints us, that a Manichean woman seduced an ignorant layman called Sergius, by telling him, Catholics honored the saints as divinities, and for that reason laymen were hindered from reading the Holy Scripture, lest they should discover a number of like errors.

16.—*The design of the Paulicians on the Bulgarians; and Peter of Sicily's instruction to hinder the effect.*

It was by such calumnies as these the Manicheans seduced the ignorant. A great desire of enlarging their sect was always remarked amongst them. Peter of Sicily[22] discovered, whilst ambassador at Tibrica, that it was resolved in the council of the Paulicians, to send preachers of their sect into Bulgaria, in order to seduce those new converts. Thrace, bordering on this province, had been infected with this heresy long before. So there was but too much reason to fear the worst for the Bulgarians, should the Paulicians, the most cunning of the Manichean sect, attempt to seduce them; and it was this which induced Peter of Sicily to inscribe the above-mentioned book to their archbishop, to secure them against such dangerous heretics. In spite of all his pains, it is certain the Manichean heresy took deep root in Bulgaria, and thence soon after spread itself over the other parts of Europe; whence came, as we shall see, the name of Bulgarians, given as the followers of this heresy.

17.—*The Manicheans begin to appear in the West after the year of our Lord one thousand.*

A thousand years had elapsed since the birth of Jesus Christ, and the prodigious relaxation of discipline threatened the Western Church with some extraordinary disaster. Besides, it was not unlikely the dreadful time when Satan was to be let loose, foretold in the Revelations,[23] after a thousand years, which may denote a thousand years after the strong-armed, to wit, the victorious Satan, was bound by Jesus Christ at his coming into the world.[24] Howsoever that may be, in this time and in 1017, during King Robert's reign, heretics were discovered at Orleans, of such a doctrine, as long before had been unheard of amongst the Latins.[25]

18.—Manicheans that came from Italy, discovered at Orleans in the time of King Robert.

An Italian woman brought into France this abominable heresy. Two Canons of Orleans,[26] one called Stephen or Heribert; the other Lisoius, both men of reputation, were the first inveigled. There was great difficulty in discovering their secret. But at length a person, named Arifaste, suspecting what it might be, having insinuated himself into their familiarity, these heretics and their followers confessed, after a great deal of pains, that they denied the human flesh of Jesus Christ; that they did not believe remission of sins was given in baptism; nor that the bread and wine could be changed into the body and blood of Jesus Christ. It was discovered, they had a particular Eucharist, by them called the celestial food. It was cruel and abominable, and wholly suitable to the Manichean genius, although not found amongst those of old. But besides what was seen at Orleans, Guy of Nogent[27] also takes notice of it in other countries; nor is it to be wondered at that new prodigies are to be met with in so close a sect, whether invented by them, or but newly brought to light.

19.—Sequel.

Here are the general characteristics of Manicheism. We have seen these heretics reject the incarnation. As for baptism, St. Austin[28] says expressly, the Manicheans did not give it, and believed it useless. Peter of Sicily,[29] and after him Cedrenus,[30] tell us the same of the Paulicians; altogether they show us that the Manicheans had a different Eucharist from ours. What was said by the heretics of Orleans, that we ought not to beg the saints' assistance, was also of the same stamp, and sprung, as is seen above, from the ancient source of this sect.

20.—Sequel.

They said nothing openly of the two principles, but spoke with contempt of the creation, and the books which record it, meaning the Old Testament; and confessed, at the very time of their execution, that they had entertained evil sentiments concerning the Lord of the universe.[31] The reader will remember, that he was judged the evil principle by the Manicheans. They went to the stake with joy, in hopes of a miraculous delivery, so strangely were they possessed with the spirit of seduction. Now this was the first instance of the like punishment. It is known, the Roman laws condemned the Manicheans to death; the holy King Robert judged them worthy of the flames.[32]

21.—The same Heresy in Gascony and at Toulouse.

At the same time, the same heresy is discovered in Aquitaine and Toulouse, as appears by the history of Ademarus,[33] of Chabanes, monk of the Abbey of St. Cibard, in Angouleme, contemporary with these heretics. An ancient writer of the history of Aquitaine, published by the celebrated Peter Pithou,[34] informs us that they were discovered in this province, whereof Perigord made part, "Manicheans, that rejected baptism, the sign of the holy cross, the church, and the Redeemer himself; denying his incarnation and passion, and the honor due to saints, lawful marriage, and the use of meat." And the same author shows us they were of the same sect with the heretics of Orleans, whose error came from Italy.

22.—*The Manicheans of Italy called Cathari, and why.*

In effect, we see the Manicheans had settled in that country. They were called Cathari, as much as to say, pure. Formerly other heretics had assumed that name, the Novatians, in the persuasion that their life was more pure than that of others, on account of the severity of their discipline. But the Manicheans, elated with their continency and abstinence from flesh, which they believed unclean, accounted themselves not only Cathari, or pure, but also, as St. Austin[35] relates, Catharists, namely, purifiers, by reason of that part of the divine substance, which was mixed with the herbs and pulse together with the contrary substance, from which, in eating them, they separated and purified this divine substance. These, I own, are monstrous opinions; and it were hardly to be believed, that men could have been so strangely infatuated, had not experience taught us that God sets, to man's proud mind, examples of the blindness he may fall into, when abandoned to himself. This, then, is the true original of the heretics of France, sprung from the Cathari of Italy.

23.—*Origin of the Manicheans of Toulouse and Italy.—Proof that they came from Bulgaria.*

Vignier, whom our reformed have accounted the restorer of history in the last age, speaks of this heresy, and the discovery thereof made in the Council of Orleans whose date he places, by mistake, in 1022, and observes, that "In this year many people were taken and burnt, for the crime of heresy, in that presence of king Robert; for it is written," continues he, "that they spoke ill of God and the Sacraments, to wit, of baptism and the body and blood of Jesus Christ, as likewise of marriage;" nor would eat meats that had blood and fat, reputing them unclean.[36] He reports, also, that the chief of these heretics was called Stephen, whereof he cites Glaber as a witness, with the chronicle of St. Cibard; "according to whose testimony," proceeds he, "many other followers of the same heresy, called Manicheans, were executed elsewhere, as at Toulouse and in Italy." No matter though this author was mistaken in the date, and some other circumstances of his history; he had not seen the acts, which have been recovered since that time. It is enough that his heresy of Orleans, which had Stephen for one of its authors, on the enormities of which king Robert took vengeance, and whose history Glaber hath reported, be acknowledged for Manichean by Vignier; that he held it for the source of that heresy which afterwards was punished at Toulouse, and that all this impiety, as we are going to see, was derived from Bulgaria.

24.—*The same Origin proved by an ancient Author quoted by Vignier—*
(addition to the Second Part.)

An ancient author, cited in the additions of the same Vignier, leaves no room to doubt of it. The passage of this author, which Vignier transcribes entire in Latin, imports, "that as soon as the heresy of the Bulgarians began to spread itself in Lombardy, they had for Bishop a certain man called Mark, who had received his ordination from Bulgaria, and under whom were the Lombards, the Tuscans, and those of Mark Ancona; but that another Pope, named Nicetas, came from Constantinople into Lombardy, who impeached the ordination of Bulgaria; and that Mark had received his from Drungaria."[37]

25.—*Sequel of the same Passage.*

What country he meant by Drungaria I have no need to examine. Renier, thoroughly acquainted, as we shall see, with all these heresies, tells us of the Manichean churches of Dugranicia and Bulgaria, whence come all the rest of the sect both in Italy and France;[38] which perfectly well agrees, as is plain, with Vignier's author.[39] In this same ancient author of Vignier, we see that this heresy, brought from beyond sea, to wit, from Bulgaria, thence spread itself through other provinces, where afterwards it was in great vogue, into Languedoc, Toulouse, and especially into Gascony; whence the name of Albigenses, as, for the like reason, that of Bulgares, was conferred on the sect, on account of its origin. I shall not repeat what Vignier[40] observes, how the name Bulgare was turned to its present signification in our language. The word is too infamous, but its derivation is certain; nor is it less certain that the Albigenses were called by this name in token of the place they came from, namely from Bulgaria.

26.—*Council of Tours and Toulouse against the Manicheans of this last city.*

There needs no more to convict these heretics of Manicheism. But, in process of time, the evil grew more apparent, principally in Languedoc and Toulouse, for this city was like the metropolis of the sect, "whence the heresy, extending itself," as speaks the Canon of Alexander III, in the Council of Tours, "like a cancer, into the neighboring countries, infected Gascony and the other provinces."[41] As the source of the evil, as I may say, there took its rise, there also the remedy was first applied. The Pope, Callixtus II, held a Council at Toulouse,[42] where were condemned the heretics that "rejected the sacrament of our Lord's body and blood, infant baptism, the priesthood, and all, ecclesiastical orders, with lawful marriage." The same canon was repeated in the general Council of Lateran[43] under Innocent II. The character of Manicheism is here seen in the condemnation of marriage. And again, in rejecting the sacrament of the Eucharist; for it ought to be particularly observed, that the canon imports, not that these heretics had some error respecting the sacrament, but that they rejected it, as we have seen the Manicheans did likewise.

27.—Their conformity with the Manicheans known by St. Austin.
—The same Heresy in Germany.

As for the priesthood and all ecclesiastical orders, the total subversion of the hierarchy introduced by the Manicheans, and the contempt they had of all church subordination, may be seen in St. Augustin and other authors.[44] In respect of infant baptism, we shall observe hereafter, that the new Manicheans impugned it with particular industry; and although they rejected baptism in general, what struck men with surprise was chiefly the refusal they made of this sacrament to children, whilst the Church in general showed so much eagerness to confer it on them. Therefore, the sensible characteristics, whereby this Toulousian, afterwards called Albigensian heresy, made itself known, were specified in this canon of Toulouse and Lateran. The bottom of the error lay more deeply concealed. But the more this cursed offspring from Bulgaria diffused itself in the West, their Manichean tenets became the more palpable. They penetrated into the heart of Germany, and the Emperor Henry IV there discovered them at Goslar, a city of Suabia, towards the middle of the eleventh century, surprised whence could proceed this Manichean progeny.[45] These here were known by their abstaining "from the flesh of animals of what kind whatsoever, and believing their use prohibited." The error soon spread in Germany on all sides; and in the twelfth century, many of these heretics were met with near about Cologne. The name of Cathari made the sect known, and Ecbert, a contemporary author and able divine, shows us, in these Cathari near Cologne, all the Manichean characters;[46] the same detestation of flesh and marriage; the same contempt of baptism; the same abhorrence of communion; the same repugnance to believe the truth of the Son of God's incarnation and passion: in short, other similar marks which it is needless to repeat.

28.—Sequel of Ecbert's Sentiments concerning the Manicheans of Germany.

But as heresies change, or in time show themselves plainer, so, many new tenets and usages are perceptible in this. For instance, in explaining to us, amongst the rest, the contempt the Manicheans had of baptism, Ecbert informs us, that although they rejected the baptism of water, they gave, with lighted torches, a certain baptism of fire, the ceremony of which he sets forth.[47] They were firmly opposed to infant baptism, which I notice once more, it being one of the distinguishing marks of these new Manicheans.[48] They had likewise another not less remarkable; their maintaining that the sacraments lost their virtue by the bad life of those that administered them. Wherefore, they exaggerated the corruption of the clergy, in order to make it appear that we had no longer any sacraments amongst us; and this is one of the reasons for which we have seen they were accused of rejecting all ecclesiastical orders, together with the priesthood.

29.—It is discovered that they held two first Principles.

The belief of these new heretics, as to the two principles, was not as yet fully brought to light. For although men were very sensible this was the foundation of their rejecting the union of both sexes, and whatever proceeded from it in all animals, as flesh, eggs, and white meats, yet, as far as I can find, Ecbert is the first that objects this error to them in express terms. Nay, he says, "he had most certainly discovered," that their private motive for abstaining from flesh was, "because the devil was the creator of it."[49] You see how difficult it was to dive to the bottom of their doctrine; yet it appeared sufficiently by its consequences.

30.—Variations of these Heretics.

We learn from this same author,[50] that these heretics showed themselves, at times, more moderate in regard to marriage. One called Hartuvinus allowed a youth amongst them to marry a maiden, but required they should be both virgins, and not proceed beyond the first child; which I take notice of, in order to show the oddities of a sect contradictory to itself, and often forced to act counter to its own principles.

31.—Their industry to conceal themselves.

But the most certain mark by which to know these heretics, was the pains they took to coneal themselves, not only by receiving the sacraments with us, but also by answering like us when urged regarding their faith. This was the spirit of the sect from its beginning, and we have before taken notice of it, ever since the time of St. Austin and St. Leo. Peter of Sicily,[51] and after him Cedrenus, show us the same character in the Paulicians. They did not only deny in general that they were Manicheans, but also, when interrogated in particular concerning each tenet of their faith, they feigned themselves Catholics, betraying their sentiments by manifest lies, or at least disguising them by equivocations worse than lies, because more artful and more fraught with hypocrisy.[52] For example, when spoken to concerning the water of baptism, they received it, understanding by the water of baptism, the doctrine of our Lord, whereby souls are purified. All they say abounded with the like allegories; and men took them for orthodox, unless from long custom they had learned to see through their equivocations.

32.—Their equivocations when interrogated about faith.

Ecbert informs us of one which it was impossible to guess at. It was known that they rejected the Eucharist; and when, to sound them on so important an article, they were asked whether they made the body of our Lord? they answered readily, They made it, understanding that their own body, which they made in some wise by their food, was the body of Jesus Christ, by reason that, according to St. Paul, they were the members of it.[53] By these artifices they appeared, outwardly, good Catholics. But, what is yet more unaccountable, one of their tenets was, that the Gospel forbade swearing for whatsoever cause:[54] nevertheless, when examined concerning their religion, they believed it lawful not only to lie, but to forswear themselves; and had learned from the ancient Priscillianists, another branch of the Manicheans known in Spain, this verse, cited by St. Austin: "*Jura, perjura, secretum prodere noli*: Swear true or false, as long as thou betrayest not the secret of the sect."[55] For which reason Ecbert styled them obscure men, men that did not preach but whispered in the ear, who lurked in corners, and muttered rather in private than explained their doctrine.[56] This was one of the sect's allurements; there was something of a charm in this impenetrable secret observed amongst them; and as the wise man said, "Those waters you drink by stealth are the pleasantest."[57] St. Bernard, who was well acquainted with these heretics, as we shall soon see, remarks in them this particular character, that whereas other heretics, urged on by the spirit of pride, sought only to make themselves known; these on the contrary, strove only to conceal themselves—others aimed at victory; but these, more mischievous, sought only to annoy, lurking silently in the grass, that they might instil their poison the more securely as the bite was less expected.[58] The thing was, their error, once discovered, was already half vanquished by its own absurdity; wherefore they betook themselves to the ignorant, to mechanics, to silly women, to peasants, and recommended nothing so much to them as this mysterious secret.

33.—*Enervin consults St. Bernard about the Manicheans near Cologne.*

Enervin, who served God in a church near Cologne, at the time these new Manicheans, whom Ecbert speaks of, were discovered there, gives in the main the same account of them as this author; and not finding in the Church a greater doctor to whom he could address himself for their conviction than the great St. Bernard, Abbot of Clairvaux, he wrote him that fine letter which the learned Francis Mabillon has given us in his Analects.[59] Therein, besides the dogmas of these heretics, which it is needless to repeat, we see the particularities which occasioned their discovery; we see the distinction between "the Auditors and the Elect," a certain character of Manicheism specified by St. Austin; we there see that they had their Pope, a truth which afterwards became more manifest; and in fine, that they boasted, "their doctrine had a continued succession down to us, but hidden ever since the time of the martyrs, and after that in Greece, and in some other countries; which is very true, since it came from Marcion and Manes, heresiarchs of the third century; and thereby it is apparent in whose shop was first vended this method of maintaining the Church's perpetuity, by a hidden series, and doctors scattered here and there without any manifest and legitimate succession.

34.—*These Heretics interrogated before all the people.*

But, lest it should be said the doctrine of these heretics was, perchance, calumniated for want of being well understood, it appears, as well by Enervin's letter as by Ecbert's sermons,[60] that the examination of these heretics was made in public; and that it was one of their bishops, with a companion of his, who defended their doctrine to their utmost, in the presence of the archbishop, the whole clergy, and all the people.

35.—*The tenets of these Heretics refuted by St. Bernard,*
who was well acquainted with them at Toulouse.

St. Bernard, whom the pious Enervin excited to confute these heretics, then composed the two fine sermons on the Canticles, in which he so vigorously impugned the heretics of his time. They carry so manifest a relation to Enervin's letter, that it is plain this gave occasion to them; but it is no less plain by St. Bernard's firm and positive way of speaking, that he had also other informations, and knew more of the matter than Enervin himself. And, indeed, it was now above twenty years since Peter de Bruis and his disciple Henry had secretly spread their errors in Dauphiny, in Provence, and especially in the neighborhood of Toulouse. St. Bernard took a journey into that country expressly to root up this bad seed, and the miracles he there wrought in confirmation of the Catholic truth are more conspicuous than the sun. But the material point to be observed is, that he spared no pains to inform himself fully concerning a heresy he was going to oppose; and after frequent conferences with the disciples of these heretics, he could not be ignorant of their doctrine. Now he distinctly instances, together with their condemnation "of infant baptism,"[61] the invocation of saints, the oblations for the dead," that of "the use of marriage, and of all that proceeded," far or near, "from the union of both sexes, as flesh and white meats."[62] He taxes them likewise with not admitting the Old Testament, and their receiving the Gospel only. Another, also, of their errors remarked by St. Bernard was,[63] that a sinner ceased to be a bishop, and that the popes, the archbishops, the bishops, and priests, were neither capable of giving nor receiving the sacraments, by reason they were sinners. But what he most insists on, is their hypocrisy, not only in the deceitful appearance of their austere and penitential life, but also in the custom they constantly observed of receiving the sacraments with us, and professing our doctrine publicly, which they inveighed against in secret.[64] St. Bernard shows their piety was all dissimulation. In appearance they blamed commerce with women, and nevertheless were all seen to pass days and night apart with them. The profession they made of abhorring the sex, seemed to warrant their not abusing it. They believed all oaths forbidden, yet, examined concerning their faith, did not stick at perjury; such oddness and inconstancy is there in extravagant minds![65] From all these things St. Bernard concluded this was "the mystery of iniquity" foretold by St. Paul,[66] so much the more to be feared in proportion as it was more hidden; and that these were they whom the Holy Ghost made known to the same apostle, as "giving heed to seducing spirits and doctrines of devils, speaking lies in hypocrisy, having their conscience seared with a hot iron, forbidding to marry, and commanding to abstain from meats which God has created."[67] All the characters agree too clearly with them to need insisting on. Behold here the fine ancestors whom the Calvinists have selected for themselves!

36.—Peter de Bruis and Henry.

To say these heretics of Toulouse, of whom St. Bernard speaks, are not the same with those vulgarly called Albigenses, were too gross a fallacy. The ministers are agreed that Peter de Bruis and Henry are two chiefs of this sect, and that Peter, the venerable Abbot of Cluny, their contemporary, of whom we shall soon speak, attacked the "Albigenses under the name of Petrobusians."[68] If the chiefs are convicted of Manicheism, the disciples have not degenerated from this doctrine, and these bad trees may be judged of by their fruit; for although it be certain, from St. Bernard's letters, and from the authors then living, that he converted many of these Toulousian heretics, the disciples of Peter de Bruis and Henry, yet the race was not extinguished, which the more private it kept itself the more proselytes it gained.[69] They were called "the good men" from their apparent meekness and simplicity; but their doctrine became manifest in an interrogatory many of them underwent at Lombez, a little town near Alby, n a council held there in 1176.[70]

37.—The Council of Lombez.—Famous examination of these Heretics.

Gaucelin, Bishop of Lodeve, equally well acquainted with their artifices and with sound doctrine, was there commissioned to examine them concerning their faith. They shuffle in many articles; they lie in others; but own in express terms, that "They reject the Old Testament; that they believe the consecration of the body and blood of Jesus Christ, equally good whether made by laymen or clergy, if good men; that all swearing is unlawful; and that bishops and priests, devoid of the qualities prescribed by St. Paul, are neither bishops nor priests." They never could be brought, whatever was said, to approve of marriage, nor infant baptism; and the obstinate refusal to acknowledge such certain truths, was taken for a confession of their error. They were condemned also from the Scripture as men that refused to confess their faith; and, on all the points proposed, were hard pressed by Ponce, Archbishop of Narbonne, by Arnold, Bishop of Nismes, by the abbots, and especially by Gaucelin, Bishop of Lodeve, whom Gerald, Bishop of Alby, there present, and ordinary of Lombez, before the place was erected into a bishopric, had vested with his authority. I do not think there can be seen, in any council, either a more regular procedure, or Scripture better employed, or a dispute more precise and convincing. Let men come and tell us after this, that what is said of the Albigenses is all mere calumny.

38.—History of the same Council by a contemporary Author.

An historian of those times recites at length this council, and gives a faithful abridgment of more ample acts which have been since recovered.[71] He begins his account thus: "There were heretics in the province of Toulouse, who would have themselves be called good men, and were maintained by the soldiers of Lombez. Those said, they neither received the law of Moses, nor the Prophets, nor the Psalms, nor the Old Testament, nor the Doctors of the

New, except the Gospels, St. Paul's Epistles, the seven canonical Epistles, the Acts, and Revelation." Setting all the rest aside, here is enough to make our Protestants blush for the errors of their ancestors.

39.—*Why these Heretics are called Arians.*

But in order to raise a suspicion of some calumny in the proceedings against them, they observe, they were not called Manicheans but Arians; yet the Manicheans were never accused of Arianism; a mistake, say they, which Baronius himself has owned.[72] What a feint that is, to cavil about the title men give a heresy, when they see it specified, not to mention other marks, by that of rejecting the Old Testament! But we must also show these contentious spirits, what reason there was to accuse the Manicheans of Arianism. It was because, as Peter of Sicily expressly tells us, "They professed the Trinity in words, but denied it in their hearts, and turned the mystery into impertinent allegories."[73]

40.—*The sentiments of the Manicheans concerning the Trinity, from St. Austin.*

This is likewise what St. Austin fully informs us of. Faustus, bishop of the Manicheans, had written: "We confess under three names one only and the same Divinity of God the Father Almighty, of Jesus Christ his Son, and of the Holy Ghost."[74] But then he further adds, "that the Father dwelt in the principal and sovereign light called by St. Paul inaccessible. As for the Son, he resided in the second light, which is visible; and being twofold, according to the Apostle who speaks of the power and wisdom of Jesus Christ, his power resided in the sun, and his wisdom in the moon; and finally, in regard of the Holy Ghost, his habitation was in our ambient air.[75] This is what Faustus said: whereby St. Austin convicts him of separating the Son from the Father even by corporeal spaces; nay, of separating him from himself, and of separating the Holy Ghost from them both; to situate them also, as did Faustus, in places so unequal, was placing between the divine persons a too manifest inequality. Such were these allegories fraught with ignorance, by which Peter of Sicily convicted the Manicheans of denying the Trinity. Such an explanation as this was far from a confession of it; but, as St. Austin says, "was squaring the belief of the Trinity by the rule of his own conceits." An author of the twelfth century, contemporary with St. Bernard,[76] acquaints us that these heretics declined saying, "Gloria Patri;" and Renier states it expressly that the Cathari or Albigenses did not believe that the Trinity was one only God, but believed that the Father was greater than the Son and the Holy Ghost.[77] No wonder then that the Catholics have sometimes ranked the Manicheans with those that denied the blessed Trinity, and, on this consideration, given them the name of Arians.

41.—*Manicheans at Soissons.—The Testimony of Guy of Nogent.*

To return to the Manicheism of these heretics: Guy of Nogent,[78] a celebrated author of the twelfth age, and more ancient than St. Bernard, shows us heretics near Soissons that made a phantom of the incarnation; that rejected infant baptism; that held in abhorrence the mystery wrought at the Altar; yet took the sacraments with us; that rejected all manner of flesh, and whatsoever proceeds from the union of both sexes. They made, after the example of those heretics above seen at Orleans, a Eucharist and sacrifice not fit to be described; and, to show themselves completely like the other Manicheans, "they concealed themselves like them, and mixed clandestinely amongst us," confessing and swearing any thing, to save themselves from punishment.[79]

42.—Testimony of Radulphus Ardens concerning the Heretics of the Agenois.

Let us add to these witnesses Radulphus ardens, a renowned author of the eleventh age, in the description he gives us of the heretics of the Agenois, who "boast of leading the life of the Apostles; who say, they do not lie, they do not swear; who condemn the use of flesh and marriage; who reject the Old Testament, and receive a part only of the New; and, what is more terrible, admit two Creators; who say the Sacrament of the Altar is nothing but mere bread; who despise baptism and the resurrection of bodies."[80] Are not these Manicheans in their proper colors? Now we descry no other characteristics in them than in those of Toulouse and Alby, whose sect, we have seen, extended itself into Gascony and the adjacent provinces. Agen also had its particular doctors: but, be that as it will, the same spirit is discernible every where, and all is of the same stamp.

43.—The same Heretics in England.

Thirty of these heretics of Gascoy took shelter in England in the year 1160. They were called Poplicans or Publicans. But let us see what was their doctrine from Gulielmus Neobridgensis, an historian near to those times, whose testimony Spelman, a Protestant author, has inserted in the second volume of his English Councils.[81] "These heretics," says he, "were brought before the council held at Oxford. Girard, the only person of any learning, answered well as to the substance of the heavenly physician: but proceeding to the remedies he had left us, they spoke very ill, abhorring baptism, the Eucharist and marriage, and despising Catholic unity." Protestants put in the catalogue of their ancestors these Gascoign heretics, for speaking ill (in the sentiment of the English nation, then believing the Real Presence) of the Eucharistic sacrament.[82] But they ought to have considered, that these Poplicans stand accused, not of denying the Real Presence, but of abhorring the Eucharist, no less than baptism and marriage,—three visible characteristics of Manicheism: nor do I hold these heretics wholly justified as to the other points, under pretext that they did not answer amiss; for we have seen too much of the wiles of these people; and at best they would not the less be Manicheans for mitigating some few errors of this sect.

44.—That the Poplicans, or Publicans, are Manicheans.

Even the name of Publicans or Poplicans was a name of the Manicheans, as is manifestly seen from the testimony of William le Breton. This author, the the life of Philip Augustus, dedicated to his eldest son Lewis, speaking of these heretics, vulgarly called Poplicans, says, "that they rejected marriage; accounted it a crime to eat flesh; and had other superstitions specified by St. Paul in a few words: viz., in the first to Timothy."[83]

45.—The ministers make the Vaudois Manicheans, in making them Poplicans.

Our Reformed nevertheless think they do an honor to the disciples of Waldo by ranking them amongst the Poplicans. There needed no more to condemn the Vaudois. But I shall take no advantage from this mistake: I shall leave to the Vaudois their particular heresies, it being enough for me here to have shown the Poplicans convicted of Manicheism.[84]

46.—The Manicheans of Ermengard.

I own, with the Protestants, that Ermengard's treatise ought not to have been entitled, "against the Vaudois," as it was by Gretser, for he speaks in no respect concerning these heretics; but the fact is, in Gretser's time, the general name of Vaudois was given to all sects separate from Rome ever since the eleventh or twelfth century down to Luther's days: which was the reason that this author, publishing divers treatises against these sects, gave them this common title, "against the Vaudois."[85] Yet he did not omit to preserve to each book the title he had found in the manuscript. Now Ermengard or Ermengaud had entitled his book thus: "A treatise against these Heretics, who say it is the devil and not God, that created the world and all things visible."[86] He refutes in particular, chapter by chapter, all the errors of these heretics, which are all those of Manicheism so frequently noticed by us. [87] If they speak against the Eucharist, they speak no less against baptism; if they reject the worship of saints, and our other doctrinal points, they do no less reject the creation, the incarnation, the law of Moses, marriage, eating of flesh, and the resurrection; so that to value themselves on the authority of this sect, is placing their glory in infamy itself.

47.—An Examination of the Authors who treat of the Manicheans and Vaudois is proceeded to.

I pass by many other witnesses which, after so many convincing proofs, are no longer necessary; but some there are not to be omitted, for this reason, that they insensibly lead us to the knowledge of the Vaudois.

48.—Proof from Alanus that the Heretics of Montpellier are Manicheans.

In the first place, I produce Alanus, a famous monk of the Cistercian order, and one of the first authors that wrote against the Vaudois. He dedicated a treatise against the heretics of his time to the Count of Montpellier, his lord, and divided it into two books. The first regards the heretics of his country. To them he ascribes the two principles, the denial of Jesus Christ's incarnation, and attributing to him a fantastical body, and all the other points of Maniche-ism, against the law of Moses, against the Resurrection, against the use of Flesh, and Marriage;[88] to which he adds some other things we had not as yet seen in the Albigenses; amongst others, the damnation of St. John the Baptist, for having doubted of the coming of Jesus Christ, for they took it for a doubt, in his holy precursor, what he caused his disciples to say to our Saviour, "Art thou he that should come?" a most extravagant notion, but very conformable to what Faustus, the Manichean, writes, as St. Austin testifies. The other authors who wrote against these new Manicheans, unanimously lay the same error to their charge.

49.—*The same author distinguishes the Vaudois from the Manicheans.*

In the second part of his work, Alanus treats concerning the Vaudois, and there makes a list of their errors, which we shall see in due place; it suffices to observe here, that there is nothing amongst them savoring of Manicheism, and that at first sight, these two heresies are quite distinct.

50.—*Peter of Vaucernay distinguishes very clearly these two sects, and shows the Albigenses are Manicheans.*

That of Waldo was as yet a novelty. It took its rise at Lyons, in the year 1160, and Alanus wrote in 1202, at the beginning of the thirteenth century. A little after, and about the year 1209, Peter of Vaucernay compiled his history of the Albigenses, where, treating on the different sects and heresies of his time, he begins with the Manicheans, and specifies their several parties, wherein are always to be seen some characteristics of those above observed in Manicheism, although in some strained higher, and in others more tempered, according to the fancy of these heretics.[89] Be that as it will, the whole is bottomed on Manicheism, and this is the peculiar characteristic of that heresy which Vaucernay represents to us in the province of Narbonne, namely, the heresy of the Albigenses, whose history he undertakes. Nothing like this does he attribute to the other heretics of whom he treats. "There were," says he, "other heretics called Vaudois, from a certain Waldius of Lyons. These doubtless were bad, but nothing in comparison with the first." Then he observes, in a few words, four of their capital errors, and immediately after returns to his Albigenses. But these errors of the Vaudois are far remote from Manicheism, as will soon appear; here, then, we have again the Albigenses and Vaudois, two sects thoroughly distinct, and the last clear from any character of Manicheism.

51.—*Peter of Vaucernay in his plain way has well specified the characteristics of the Manicheans.*

The Protestants will have it that Peter of Vaucernay spoke of the Albigensian heresy without well knowing what he said, on account of his charging them with blasphemies which are not to be found even in the Manicheans. But who can answer for all the secrets and new inventions of this abominable sect? What Peter of Vaucernay makes them speak regarding the two Jesuses, whereof one was born in the visible and terrestrial Bethlehem, the other in the celestial and invisible, is much of a piece with the other extravagances of the Manicheans. This invisible Bethlehem does not ill suit with the supernatural Jerusalem, which Peter of Sicily's Paulicians called the mother of God, whence Jesus Christ proceeded.[90] Say what they will of the visible Jesus, that he was not the true Christ, that he was accounted evil by these heretics, I see nothing in all that more extravagant than the other blasphemies of the Manicheans. We meet in Renier with heretics holding something of the principles of the Manicheans, and acknowledging a Christ, son of Joseph and Mary, evil at first and a sinner, but afterwards turned good, and the restorer of their sect.[91] Certain it is these Manichean heretics were much addicted to change. Renier, one of their number, distinguishes the new from the ancient opinions, and observes many novelties to have arisen amongst them in his time, and since the year 1230.[92] Ignorance and extravagance seldom hold long in the same state, and know no bounds in man. However it be, if hatred conceived against the Albigenses made men charge them with Manicheism, or, if you please, something worse than hatred; whence proceeds that care they took to excuse the Vaudois, since it cannot be supposed they were better loved than those, or less declared enemies to the Church of Rome? Yet we have already two authors very zealous for the Catholic doctrine, and very averse to the Vaudois, who carefully distinguish them from the Manichean Albigenses.

52.—*Distinction of the two sects by Ebrard of Bethune.*

Here is also a third not less considerable. It is Ebrard, native of Bethune, whose book, entitled, "Anti-heresy," was composed against the heretics of Flanders.[93] These heretics were called Piples or Piphles, in the language of that country. A Protestant author does not conjecture ill, imagining this word Piphles to be a corruption from that of Poplicans; and thence it may be known that these Flemish heretics, like the Poplicans, were perfect Manicheans, nevertheless good Protestants, if we believe the Calvinists, and worthy to be their ancestors. But not to dwell on the other name, we need but give ear to Ebrard, an author of that country, in his description of these heretics. The first characteristic which he gives them is, that they rejected the Law, and the God that gave it; the rest is of the same stamp, they not only despising marriage, but the use of flesh meat, and the sacraments.[94]

53.—*The Vaudois well distinguished from the Manicheans.*

After methodically digesting all he had to say against this sect, he proceeds to speak against that of the Vaudois, which he distinguishes, like the rest, from that of the new Manicheans; and this is the third witness we have to produce.[95] But here is a fourth, of greater importance in this fact than all the rest.

54.—*Testimony of Renier, who had been of the sect of Manicheans,*
in Italy, seventeen years.

It is Renier, of the order of Dominican friars, from whom we have already cited some passages. He wrote about the year 1250 or '54, and the title he gave his book was, "De Hæreticis," "of Heretics," as he testifies in his preface. He styles himself "Brother Renier, formerly an Heresiarch, and now a priest," on account of his having been seventeen years among the Cathari, as he twice acknowledges.[96] This author is well known among Protestants, who never cease boasting the fine description he has given of the manners of the Vaudois. He is the more to be credited on the occasion, as he tells us both good and bad with so great sincerity. Now it cannot be alleged he had not a competent knowledge of the several sects of his time. He had been frequently present at the examination of heretics, and there it was that the minutest differences were most narrowly scanned of so many obscure and cunning sects, wherewith Christendom, at that time, was overrun. Many of them were converted, and disclosed all the mysteries of the sect, which had been so carefully concealed. A thorough knowledge of the distemper is half the cure. Over and above this, Renier applied his study to the reading of heretical books, as of that great volume of John of Lyons,[97] a leading man amongst the new Manicheans, and from thence extracted the articles of his doctrine which he reports. No wonder, then, this author has given us a more exact account than any other, of the differences in his contemporary sects.

55.—*He distinguishes them very clearly from the Vaudois.*—*The Characteristics*
of Manicheism in the Cathari.

The first he instances in is that of the "poor men" of Lyons, descended from Peter Waldo, all whose dogmas he sets down even to the nicest minutiæ. All therein is far remote from Manicheism, as we shall see hereafter. Thence he proceeds to the other sects of the Manichean race; and comes at length to the Cathari, whose secrets he was entirely acquainted with;[98] for besides his having been, as already observed, seventeen years amongst them, and thoroughly initiated in the sect, he had heard their greatest doctors preach, and amongst others, one called Nazarius, the most ancient of them all, who boasted of having been formed, sixty years before, under the discipline of the two chief pastors of the Bulgarian Church. However, observe this extraction always from Bulgaria. It was from thence the Cathari of Italy, amongst whom Renier dwelt, derived their authority; and as he had been conversant amongst them so many years, it is not to be wondered that he has explained more accurately, and more minutely, their errors, their sacraments, their ceremonies, the different parties formed amongst them, with the affinities as well as the diversities of one from the other. In him, every where are to be seen very clearly the principles, the impieties, and the whole spirit of Manicheism. The distinction of the Elect and Auditors, a particular characteristic of the sect, frequent in St. Austin, and other authors, is found here distinguished under another name. We learn from Renier, that these heretics, besides the Cathari or Pure, the most consummate of the sect, had also another class which they called "their Believers," made up of all sorts of people.[99] These were not admitted to all the mysteries; and the same Renier relates that the number of the perfect Cathari, in his time, when the sect was weakened, "did not exceed four thousand in all Christendom;" but "that the believers were innumerable; a computation," says he, "which several times has been made amongst them."[100]

> 56.—*A remarkable list of the Manichean Churches.—The Albigenses comprised*
> *in it.—All of them descended from Bulgaria.*

Amongst the Sacraments of these heretics, their imposition of hands, in order to remit sins, is chiefly to be observed; they called it consolation; it served both instead of baptism and penance. You see it in the above Council of Orleans, in Ecbert, in Enervin, and in Ermengard. Renier gives the best account of it, as an adept in the mysteries of the sect.[101] But the most remarkable thing in Renier's book is the exact list of the Churches of the Cathari, and his account of the state they were in at his time. They counted sixteen in all, and amongst the rest he reckons the Church of France, the Church of Toulouse, the Church of Cahors, the Church of Alby, and in fine, the Church of Bulgaria, and the Church of Drunganicia, "whence," says he, "sprung all the rest." This considered, I see not how the Manicheism of the Albigenses can be called in question, nor their descent from the Manicheans of Bulgaria. The reader has but to call to mind the two orders of Bulgaria and Drungaria, mentioned by Vignier's author, and which united themselves in Lombardy. I repeat once more that there is no necessity of searching what this Drungaria can be. These obscure heretics often took their name from unknown places. Renier tells us of Runcarians, a Manichean sect of his time, whose name was taken from a village.[102] Who knows but this word, Runcarians, was a corruption of Druncarians?

We find in the same author, and elsewhere, so many different names of these heretics, that it were labor lost to inquire into their origin. Patarians, Poplicans, Toulousians, Albigenses, Cathari, were, under different names, and often with some diversity in sect, Manicheans, all of Bulgarian descent; whence also they took the name most in use among the vulgar.

> 57.—*The same origin proved from Matthew Paris.—The Pope of the*
> *Albigenses in Bulgaria.*

So certain is this origin, that we find it acknowledged even in the thirteenth century. "At this time," says Matthew Paris, (viz. in the year 1223,) "the Albigensian heretics made themselves an Antipope, called Bartholomew, in the confines of Bulgaria, Croatia, and Dalmatia."[103] It appears afterwards, that the Albigenses went in crowds to consult him; that he had a vicar at Carcassonne and Toulouse, and despatched his Bishops far and near; which comes up manifestly to what was said by Enervin, that these heretics had their Pope; although the same author informs us that all did not own him. And that no doubt might remain as to the error of the Albigenses, mentioned by Matthew Paris; the same author assures us, "the Albigenses of Spain," that took up arms in 1234, amongst many other errors, "particularly denied the mystery of the incarnation."

58.—The great hypocrisy of these Heretics from Enervin.

Notwithstanding such great impieties, the outward appearance of these heretics was surprising. Enervin introduces them, speaking in these terms:—"You, for your part," said they to the Catholics, "join house to house, and field to field: the most perfect amongst you, as the monks and canons regular, if they possess no goods in property, have them at least in common. We, the poor of Jesus Christ, without repose, without settled habitations, wander from town to town like sheep in the midst of wolves, and suffer persecution like the martyrs and apostles."[104] They boasted next of their abstinence, their fasts, the narrow way they walked in, and called themselves the only followers of the apostolic life, for that, contented with necessaries, they had neither house, nor land, nor riches, "for this reason," said they, "because Jesus Christ neither had, nor possessed the like things, nor suffered his disciples to possess them."

59.—And from St. Bernard.—Conformity of their discourse with that of Faustus the Manichean, in St. Austin.

According to St. Bernard, there was "nothing more Christian in appearance" than their speech, nothing more blameless than their manners. Therefore they called themselves the Apostolic, and boasted of leading the lives of the apostles. Methinks, I hear over again Faustus the Manichean, who, in St. Austin, thus speaks to Catholics:—"You ask me whether I receive the gospel? you see I do, inasmuch as I observe what the gospel prescribes: of you I ought to ask whether you receive it, since I see no mark of it in your lives. For my part, I have forsaken father, mother, wife and children, gold, silver, meat, drink, delights, pleasures; content with having what is sufficient for life from day to day. I am poor, I am peaceable, I weep, I suffer hunger and thirst, I am persecuted for justice sake, and do you question whether I receive the gospel?"[105] After this, must persecutions be still taken for a mark of the true Church and true piety? it is the language of Manicheans.

60.—Their hypocrisy confounded by St. Austin and St. Bernard.

But St. Austin and St. Bernard show them that their virtue was nothing but vain ostentation. To carry the abstinence from meats so far as to say that they are unclean and evil in their nature, and continence, even to the condemnation of marriage, is, on the one hand, to attack the Creator, and on the other, loosing the reins to evil desires by leaving them absolutely without a remedy.[106] Never believe any good of those who run virtue to extremes. The depravation of their minds venting itself in such extravagance of speech, introduces into their lives disorders without end.

61.—*The infamy of the Heretics and chiefly of the Patarians.*

St. Austin informs us that these people, who debarred themselves of marriage, allowed liberty for every thing else. What, according to their principles, they had an abhorrence of, (I am ashamed to be forced to repeat it,) was properly conception; whence it appears what an inlet was opened to the abominations whereof the old and new Manicheans stand convicted. But, as among the different sects of these new Manicheans there were degrees of weakness, the most infamous of all were those called Patarians; which I the more willingly take notice of, by reason that our Reformed, who place them expressly amongst the Vaudois, glory in descending from them."[107]

62.—*Doctrine of these Heretics, that the effect of the Sacraments depends on the sanctity of the Ministers.*

Those that make the greatest ostentation of their virtue and the purity of their lives, generally speaking, are the most corrupt. It may have been observed how these impure Manicheans prided themselves, at their beginning, and through the whole progress of the sect, in a virtue more severe than that of others; and with the view of enhancing their own merit, said that the sacraments and mysteries lost their efficacy in impure hands. It is necessary to take good notice of this part of their doctrine, which we have seen in Enervin, in St. Bernard, and in the Council of Lombez. Wherefore Renier repeats twice, that this imposition of hands, by them called Consolation, and wherein they placed the remission of sins, was unprofitable to the receiver, if the giver of it were in sin, though hidden.[108] Their manner of accounting for this doctrine, according to Ermengard, was because a person having lost the Holy Ghost, is no longer empowered to give it; which was the very reason alleged by the Donatists of old.

63.—*They condemn all Oaths and Punishment of Crimes.*

It was moreover for show of Sanctity and to raise themselves above others, that they said, a Christian ought never to affirm the truth by oath for what cause soever, not even in a court of judicature, and that it was unlawful to put any one to death, however criminal. The Vaudois, as we shall see, borrowed from them all these extravagant maxims and all this vain exterior of piety.[109]

[* Here begins a new section whose number, 64, and heading, *Réponse des Ministres que l'imputation du Manichéisme est calumnieuse. Démonstration du contraire*, were omitted by the English translators. Ed.] Such were the Albigenses by the testimony of all their contemporary authors, not one excepted. The Protestants blush for them; and all they can answer is, that these excesses, these errors, and all these disorders of the Albigenses, are the calumnies of their enemies. But have they so much as one proof for what they advance, or even one author of those times, and for more than four hundred years after, to support them in it? For our parts, we produce as many witnesses as have been authors in the whole universe who have treated of this sect. Those that were educated in their principles have revealed to us their abominable secrets after their conversion. We trace up the damnable sect even to its source; we show whence it came, which way it steered its course, all its characteristics, and its whole pedigree branching from the Manichean root. They oppose against us conjectures; nay, what conjectures? We shall take a view of them, for I mean to produce here those that carry the best appearance.

65.—*Examination of Peter de Bruis's doctrine.—the Minister's objection taken from Peter of Cluny.*

The greatest effort of our adversaries is in order to justify Peter de Bruis and his disciple Henry. St. Bernard, say they, accuses them of condemning meats and marriage. But Peter the Venerable, Abbot of Cluny, who, much about that time, refuted Peter de Bruis, speaks nothing of these errors, and accuses him of five only: of denying infant baptism; of condemning hallowed churches; of breaking crosses, instead of venerating them; of rejecting the Eucharist; of ridiculing oblations and prayers for the dead.[110] St. Bernard avers that this heretic and his followers "received only the Gospel." But Peter the Venerable, speaks doubtingly of it. "Fame," says he, "has published that you do not wholly believe either in Jesus Christ, or the Prophets, or the Apostles; but reports, frequently deceitful, are not to be lightly credited, there being some even that say, you reject the whole Canon of the Scriptures."[111] Whereupon he adds: "I will not blame you for what is uncertain." Here Protestants commend the prudence of Peter the Venerable, and blame St. Bernard's credulity, as one too easily assenting to confuted reports.

66.—*Peter de Bruis's doctrine according to Peter of Cluny.*

But, in the first place, to take only what the Abbot of Cluny reproves as certain in this heretic, there is more than enough to condemn him. Calvin[112] has numbered amongst blasphemies the doctrine condemning infant baptism. The denying it, with Peter de Bruis and his disciple Henry, was refusing salvation to the most innocent age of man; it was saying, that for so many ages, during which scarce any were baptized but children, there had been no baptism in the world, no sacrament, no church, no Christians. It is what excited horror in the Abbot of Cluny. The rest of Peter de Bruis's errors, refuted by this venerable author, are not less insupportable. Let us give ear to what he is reproached with in regard of the Eucharist by this holy abbot, who hath just declared to us, that he will object nothing to him but what is certain. "He denies," says he, "that the body and blood of Jesus Christ can be made by virtue of the divine word and ministry of the priest, and avers, that all that is done at the altar is unprofitable."[113] This is not only denying the truth of the body and blood, but, like the Manicheans, rejecting absolutely the Eucharist. For which reason the holy abbot subjoins a little after, "Were your heresy contained within the bounds of that of Berengarius, who, in denying the truth of the body, did not deny the sacrament or the appearance and figure of it, I would refer you to the authors that have refuted him. But," proceeds he, a little after, "you add error to error, heresy to heresy; and not only deny the truth of the flesh and blood of Jesus Christ, but their sacrament, their figure, and their appearance, and so leave God's people without a sacrifice."

67.—St. Bernard as circumspect as Peter of Cluny.

As for the errors of which this holy abbot does not speak, and those he doubts of, it is easy to comprehend that the reason of this was, their not being as yet sufficiently proved, nor all the secrets of a sect, which had so many windings and turnings, thoroughly disclosed at the beginning. They came to light by degrees; and Peter the Venerable, assures us himself, that Henry, the disciple of Bruis, had added a great deal to the five chapters condemned in his master.[114] He had by him the writing wherein all this heresiarch's new errors were collected from his own mouth. But this holy abbot waited, before he refuted them, for still further assurance. St. Bernard, who had beheld these heretics at close view, knew more of them than Peter the Venerable, who wrote only from report; nor did he know all, and for that reason would not venture to call them complete Manicheans;[115] for he was not less circumspect than Peter the Venerable, to impute nothing to them but what was certain. Accordingly, observe how he speaks of their impurities: "Men say, they do shameful things in private."[116] "Men say," implies, he had not as yet a full assurance of them, for which reason he durst not speak positively. Those who knew them, have spoken of them; but this circumspection of St. Bernard shows us clearly the certainty of that which he objects to them.

68.—Answer to the objection regarding the credulity of St. Bernard.

But, say they, he was credulous, and Otho of Frisingen, an author of the time, has reproached him with it. We must still hear this conjecture, which Protestants lay so much stress on. It is true, Otho of Frisingen finds St. Bernard too credulous, because he caused the manifest errors of Gilbert of Poiree, Bishop of Poictiers, to be condemned, whom his disciple Otho endeavored to excuse. This reproach of Otho is then an excuse, which a fond disciple draws up for his master. Let us see, however, in what he makes the credulity of St. Bernard to consist. "This abbot," said Otho, "both by the fervor of his faith, and by his natural goodness, had a little too much credulity; so that the doctors, who trusted too much to human reason, and to the wisdom of the age, became suspected by him; and if it was mentioned to him, that their doctrine was not altogether conformable to the faith, he easily believed it."[117] Was he wrong? Unquestionably not; and experience sufficiently shows that Peter Abelard, who became suspected by him in consequence of this; and Gilbert, who explained the Trinity rather according to the topics of Aristotle than according to tradition and the rule of faith, strayed from the right path, since their errors, condemned in the councils, are equally condemned by Catholics and Protestants.

69.—*St. Bernard imputes nothing, of which he is not certain, to Peter de Bruis and Henry, the seducers of the Toulousians.*

Let us not then here arraign the credulity of St. Bernard. If he has represented to us Henry, the disciple of Peter de Bruis, and the seducer of the Toulousians, as the most wicked and the most hypocritical of all men, all writers of the time have passed the same judgment on him. The errors which he attributes to the disciples of these heretics have been acknowledged and discovered by themselves more and more every day, as the sequel of this history will show. It was not without reason that St. Bernard imputed to them those which we find in his sermons. "I wish," said he, "to recount to you their extravagances, which we have ascertained, either by the answers which they have given, without intending it, to Catholics, or by the mutual reproaches, which their divisions have caused to burst forth, or by the things which they did, after having been converted." Thus, then, those extravagances were discovered, which St. Bernard subsequently calls blasphemies. When there was nothing else in the Henricans, but their blind attachment for those women, whom they kept in their company, as St. Bernard states, and with whom they spent their lives, shut up in the same room night and day, that were sufficient for their being held in detestation. However, the matter was so public, that St. Bernard wished that they should be known by this mark. "Tell me," said he to them, "my friend, what woman is this? Is she your wife?"—"No," say they, "that suits not my profession." "Is she your daughter, your sister, your niece?"—"No; she is no way related to me."—"But do you know that it is not allowed, according to the laws of the Church, to those who have professed continence, to cohabit with women? Put her away, then, if you wish not to scandalize the Church; otherwise, this fact, which is manifest, will make us suspect the rest, which is not so much so." He was not too credulous in this suspicion, and the turpitude of these pretendedly chaste individuals has since been disclosed to the entire world.

70.—*Conclusion.*

Whence comes it then, that Protestants undertake the defence of these wicked men? The reason is obvious. It is their ambition to procure themselves predecessors. They find none others who reject the worship of the cross, the prayers of the saints, and oblations for the dead. They are annoyed at finding the commencement of their reformation only among the Manicheans. Because they grumble against the Pope and the Church of Rome, the reformation is well disposed in their favor. The Catholics of that time reproach them with their bad notions concerning the Eucharist. Our Protestants would have been glad if they had been but mere Berengarians, displeased with the Eucharist in part, not Manicheans, averse to it in the whole. But though it had been so, these reformed, whom you will have your brethren, concealed their doctrine, "frequented our churches, honored our priests, went to the oblation; confessed their sins, communicated, received with us," continues St. Bernard, "the body and blood of Jesus Christ."[118] Behold them, therefore, in our assemblies, which in their hearts they detested as the conventicles of Satan; present at mass, which, in their error, they accounted an idolatry and sacrilege; and, in short, practising the usages of the Church of Rome, which they believed was the kingdom of Antichrist. Are these the disciples of Him, who commanded his gospel to be preached on the house-tops? Are these the children of light? Are these the works which shine forth before men, or rather such as should be hid in darkness? In a word, are these fit fathers for the Reformation to choose and boast of?

A HISTORY OF THE VAUDOIS

71.—*Beginning of the Vaudois, or Poor Men of Lyons.*

The Vaudois serve them no better with regard to establishing a legitimate succession. Their name is derived from Waldo, the author of the sect. Lyons was the place of their nativity. They were called the "poor men" of Lyons, on account of the poverty affected by them; and as the city of Lyons was then called, in Latin, Leona, they had also the appellation of Leonists, or Lionists.

72.—*The names of the Sect.*

They were also called the Insabbatized, from an ancient word signifying shoes, whence have proceeded other words of a like signification, still in use in several other languages as well as ours.[119] They took, therefore, the name of the Insabbatized from a sort of shoes of a particular make, which they cut in the upper part, to show their feet naked like the Apostles, as they said; and this fashion was affected by them in token of their apostolic poverty.

73.—*Their History bipartite.—Their beginnings specious.*

Now, here is an abridgment of their history. At their first separation, they held but few tenets contrary to ours, if any at all. In the year 1160, Peter Waldo, a merchant of Lyons, at a meeting held, as was customary, with the other rich traders of the town, was so lively struck with the sudden death of one of the most eminent amongst them, that he immediately distributed all his means, which were considerable, to the poor of that city; and having, on that account, gathered a great number of them, he preached to them voluntary poverty, and the imitation of the life of Jesus Christ and his Apostles. This is what Renier says, whom the Protestants, pleased with the encomiums we shall find he bestows on the Vaudois, will have us believe in this matter preferably to all other authors.[120] But we are going to see, what misguided piety can arrive to. Peter Pylicdorf, who beheld the Vaudois in their most flourishing condition, and related, not only their dogmas, but deportment too, with much simplicity and learning, says, that Waldo, moved with those words of the gospel so highly favorable to poverty, believed the apostolic life was no longer to be found on earth. Bent on restoring it, he sold all he had. "Others, touched with compunction, did the same," and united together in this undertaking.[121] At the first rise of this obscure and timorous sect, either they had none, or did not publish any particular tenet; which was the reason that Ebrard of Bethune remarks nothing singular in them but the affectation of a proud and lazy poverty.[122] One might see these Insabbatized or Sabbatized, so he calls them, with their naked feet, or rather with "their shoes cut open" at the top, waiting for alms, and living only on what was given them.[123] Nothing was blamed in them, at first, but ostentation, and, without ranking them as yet amongst heretics, they were reproached only with imitating their pride.[124] But let us hear the sequel of their history: "After living awhile in this pretended apostolic poverty, they bethought themselves that the Apostles were not only poor, but also preached the gospel."[125] They set themselves, therefore, to preach, according to their example, that they might wholly imitate the apostolic life. But the apostles were sent; and these men, whose ignorance rendered them incapable of such mission, were excluded by the prelates, and lastly, by the Holy See, from a ministry which they had usurped without their leave. Nevertheless, they continued it in private, and murmured against the clergy, that hindered them from preaching, as they said, through jealousy, and on account that their doctrine and holy life cast a reproach on the corrupt manners of the other.[126]

74.—*Whether Waldo were a man of learning.*

Some Protestants have asserted, that Waldo was a man of learning; but Renier says only, "he had a small tincture of it;" *aliquantulum literatus.*[127] Other Protestants, on the contrary, take advantage from the great success he had in his ignorance. But it is but too well known, what a dexterity often may be met with in the minds of the most ignorant men, to attract to them those that are alike disposed, and Waldo seduced none but such.

75.—*The Vaudois condemned by Lucius III.*

This sect, in a little time, made a great progress. Bernard, abbot of Fontcauld, who saw their beginnings, remarks their increase under Pope Lucius III.[128] This Pope's pontificate commences in 1181, to wit, twenty years after Waldo had appeared at Lyons. Twenty years at least were requisite to make a body and so considerable a sect as to deserve notice. At that time, therefore, Lucius III condemned them; and as his pontificate held but four years, this first condemnation of the Vaudois must have fallen between the year 1181, when this Pope was raised to St. Peter's chair, and the year 1185, wherein he died.

76.—*They come to Rome.—They are not accused of any thing in respect to the Real Presence.*

Conrade, abbot of Ursperg, thoroughly acquainted, as we shall find, with the Vaudois, has written, that Pope Lucius placed them in the number of heretics, on account of some dogmas and superstitious observances. As yet these dogmas are not specified; but there is no question, that, if the Vaudois had denied such remarkable points as that of the Real Presence (a matter become so notorious by Berengarius's condemnation,) it had not been thought sufficient to say in general, they held "some superstitious dogmas."[129]

77.—*Another proof that their errors did not regard the Eucharist.*

Much about the same time, in the year 1194, a statute of Alphonsus or Ildephonsus, King of Arragon, reckons the Vaudois or Insabbatized, otherwise the poor men of Lyons, amongst heretics anathematized by the Church, and this is manifestly in consequence of the sentence pronounced by Lucius III. After this Pope's death, when in spite of his decree these heretics spread themselves far and near, and Bernard, Archbishop of Narbonne, who condemned them anew after a great inquest, could not stem the current of their progress, many pious persons, Ecclesiastics and others, procured a conference, in order to reclaim them in an amicable manner. "Both sides agreed to choose for umpire" in the conference, a holy priest called Raimond of Daventry, "a man illustrious for birth, but much more so for the holiness of his life." The assembly was very solemn, "and the dispute was long." Such passages of Scripture, as each party grounded itself on, were produced on both sides. The Vaudois were condemned, and declared heretics in regard to all the heads of accusation.[130]

78.—*Proof of the same truth by a famous Conference, wherein all points were discussed.*

Thence it appears that the Vaudois, though condemned, had not as yet broken all measures with the Church of Rome, inasmuch as they had agreed to the umpirage of a Catholic and a priest. The Abbot of Fontcauld, present at the conference, did commit to writing, with much judgment and perspicuity, the debated points, and the passages alleged on both sides: so that nothing can give us a clearer insight into the whole state of the question, such as it then was, and at the beginning of the sect.

79.—*Articles of the Conference.*

The dispute chiefly turned on the obedience due to pastors. It is plain, the Vaudois refused it, and, notwithstanding all their prohibitions, believed they had a right to preach, both men and women. As this disobedience could be grounded on nothing else but the pastor's unworthiness, the Catholics, in proving the obedience due to them, prove it is due even to the wicked, and that grace, be its channel what it will, never ceases to diffuse itself on the faithful.[131] For the same reason they showed, that slandering of pastors (whence was taken the pretext of disobedience) was forbidden by the laws of God.[132] Then they attack the liberty, which laymen gave themselves, of preaching without the pastors' leave, nay, in spite of their prohibitions, and show that this seditious preaching tends to the subversion of the weak and ignorant.[133] Above all, they prove from the Scripture,[134] that women, to whom silence is enjoyed, ought not to interfere in teaching.[135] Lastly, it is remonstrated to the Vaudois, how much they are in the wrong, to reject prayer for the dead, so well grounded in Scripture, and so evidently handed down by tradition; and, whereas, these heretics absented themselves from the churches, in order to pray apart in their houses, they are made sensible, that they ought not to abandon the house of prayer, whose sanctity the whole Scripture and the Son of God himself had so much recommended.

80.—*The Eucharist is not there spoken of.*

Without examining here which side was right or wrong in this debate, it is plain, what was the ground of it, and which were the points contested; and it is more clear than day, that in these beginnings, far from bringing the Real Presence, transubstantiation, or the sacraments into question, they did not as yet so much as mention praying to saints, nor relics, nor images.

81.—*Alanus, who makes a list of the errors of the Vaudois, objects nothing concerning the Eucharist.*

It was nearly about this time, that Alanus wrote the book above mentioned; wherein, after carefully distinguishing the Vaudois from the other heretics of his time, he undertakes to prove, in opposition to their doctrine, "That none ought to preach without mission; that prelates should be obeyed, and not only good, but also evil ones; that their bad lives derogate not from their power; that it is to the sacred order we ought to attribute the power of consecrating and that of binding and loosing, and not to personal merit; that we ought to confess to priests, and not to laymen; that it is lawful to swear in certain cases, and to execute malefactors."[136] This is much what he opposes to the errors of the Vaudois. Had they erred in relation to the Eucharist, Alanus would not have forgotten it, the very thing he was so mindful to reproach the Albigenses with, against whom he undertakes to prove both the Real Presence and transubstantiation; and after reproving so many things of less importance in the Vaudois, he would never have omitted so essential a point.

82.—*Nor Peter de Vaucernay.*

A little after Alanus's time, and about the year 1201, Peter de Vaucernay, a plain downright man, and of unquestionable sincerity, distinguishes the Vaudois from the Albigenses by their proper characters, when he tells us "the Vaudois were bad, but much less so than these other heretics," who admitted the two principles, and all the consequences of that damnable doctrine.[137] "Not to mention," proceeds the author, "their other infidelities; their error chiefly consisted in four heads: viz., their wearing sandals in imitation of the Apostles; their saying it was not lawful to swear for any cause whatsoever; nor to put to death, even malefactors; lastly, in that they said that each one of them, though but mere laymen, provided he wore sandals, (namely, as above seen, the mark of apostolic poverty,) might consecrate the body of Jesus

Christ." Here are the reality the specific characters that denote the true spirit of the Vaudois; the affectation of poverty in the sandals which were the badge of it; simplicity and apparent meekness in rejecting all oaths and capital punishments, and, what was more peculiar to this sect, the belief that the laity, provided they had embraced their pretended apostolic poverty and bore its badge, that is, provided they were of their sect, might administer and consecrate the Sacraments, even the body of Jesus Christ. The rest, as their doctrine concerning prayer for the dead, was comprised in the other infidelities of these heretics, which this author forbears to particularize. Yet, had they risen up against the Real Presence, since the disturbance this matter had caused in the Church, not only this religious would not have forgotten it, but had been far from saying, "they consecrated the body of Jesus Christ," thereby making them not to differ from Catholics in this point, except their attributing to laymen that power, which Catholics acknowledged only in the priesthood.

83.—*The Vaudois come to demand the approbation of Innocent III.*

It appears then manifestly, that the Vaudois in 1209, at the time of Peter de Vaucernay's writings, had not so much as thought of denying the Real Presence, but retained so much either true or apparent submission to the Church of Rome, that even in 1212, they came to Rome, in order to obtain "the approbation of their sect from the Holy See." It was then that Conrade, Abbot of Ursperg,[138] saw them there, as he himself reports, with their master Bernard. They may be discovered by the characters given them by this chronicler: they were "the poor men of Lyons, those whom Lucius III had put in the list of heretics," who made themselves remarkable by the affectation "of apostolic poverty, with their shoes cut open at top;" who in "their private preaching and clandestine assemblies reviled the Church and Priesthood." The Pope judged the affectation was very odd which they discovered "in those cut shoes, and in their capuches, like those of the religious, though, contrary to their custom, they wore a long head of hair like laymen." And truly, these strange affectations most commonly cover something bad; but especially men took offence at the liberty these new apostles gave themselves of going promiscuously together, men and women, in imitation, as they said, of the pious women that followed Jesus Christ and the apostles to minister to them; but very different were the times, the persons, and the circumstances.

84.—*The Vaudois begin to be treated like obstinate heretics.*

It was, says the Abbot of Ursperg, with the design of giving to the Church men truly poor, more divested of earthly goods than these false poor of Lyons, that the pope afterwards approved the institute of the Brother-Minors, assembled under the direction of St. Francis, the true pattern of humility, and miracle of the age; whilst these other poor, fraught with hatred against the Church and her ministers, notwithstanding their fallacious humility, were rejected by the Holy See; insomuch that, afterwards, they were treated as contumacious and incorrigible heretics. yet they made a show of submission till the year 1212, which was the fifteenth of Innocent III, and fifty years since their beginning.

85.—*The Church's patience in regard to the Vaudois.*

Thence a judgment may be formed of the Church's patience with respect to these heretics, using no rigor against them for fifty years together, but endeavoring to reclaim them by conferences. Besides that mentioned by Bernard, Abbot of Fontcauld, we also find another in Peter de Vaucernay,[139] about the year 1206, where the Vaudois were confounded; and lastly in 1212, when, on their coming again to Rome, the Church proceeded no further against them than by rejecting their imposture. Three years after Innocent III held the great Council of Lateran, where, in his condemnation of heretics, he particularly takes notice of "those, who, under pretext of piety, arrogate to themselves the authority of preaching without mission;" whereby he seems to have particularly pointed out the Vaudois, and distinguished them by the origin of their schism.

86.—*The sect of the Vaudois a species of Donatism.*

Here are seen evidently the beginnings of this sect. It was a kind of Donatism, but different from that impugned of old in Africa, in that the African Donatists, making the effect of the sacraments depend on the virtue of the ministers, reserved at least the power of conferring them to holy priests and bishops; whereas these new Donatists attributed it, as above seen, to laymen whose life was pure. Nor did they come to this excess but by degrees; for at first they allowed nothing to the laity but preaching. They not only reproved evil manners, which the Church no less condemned than they, but also many other things she approved of, as ceremonies, yet so as not to touch on the sacraments: for Pylicdorf,[140] who was very accurate in observing both the ancient spirit and the whole progress of the sect, observes that they discarded every thing employed by the Church to edify the faithful, "except," says he,[141] "the sacraments alone;" which shows, they left them untouched. The same author relates, moreover, "that it was a long while before they began, being laymen, to hear confessions, to enjoin penances, and give absolution; and it has been observed but a little time since," continues this author, "that one of these heretics, a mere layman, did consecrate, according to his notion, our Lord's body, and communicated himself, together with his accomplices, although somewhat reprimanded for it by the rest."

87.—*Their presumption increased by little and little.*

See how their presumption increased by degrees. The followers of Waldo, scandalized at the lives of several priests, "believed themselves," says the same Pylicdorf, better absolved by their own people, seemingly to them more virtuous, than by the ministers of the Church,[142] which proceeded from the opinion, wherein principally consisted the error of the Vaudois, that personal merit had greater influence in the sacraments than character and order.

88.—*The Vaudois doctrine concerning Church goods.*

But the Vaudois carried the merit necessary to Ministers of the Church so far as to have nothing in property; and this was one of their dogmas, that to consecrate the Eucharist, it was requisite to be poor like them: so "that Catholic priests were not the true and legitimate successors of Jesus Christ's apostles, because they possessed goods of their own;"[143] which they pretended Jesus Christ had forbidden his apostles.

89.—*No error relating to the Sacraments.*

Hitherto their whole error, in respect to the sacraments, regarded only the persons empowered to administer them; all the rest was left entire, as says expressly Pylicdorf. So they doubted not either of the real presence, or transubstantiation; and, on the contrary, this author has but just informed us, that the layman presuming to give communion, did only believe "he had consecrated the body of Jesus Christ." After all, by the manner we have seen this heresy begin, it seems as if Waldo had a good design at first; that the glory of poverty which he boasted of, did seduce both him and his followers; that, puffed up with the holiness of their lives, they swelled with a bitter zeal against the clergy, and whole Catholic Church;[144] that, exasperated with their being prohibited to preach, they fell into schism, and, as Gui says, "from schism into heresy."

90.—*Manifest insincerity of Protestant Historians, and of Paul Perrin, concerning the beginnings of the Vaudois.*

From this faithful account, and the incontestable proofs with which it is manifestly supported, it is easy to judge how much Protestant historians have abused the public credit by their relation of their origin of the Vaudois. Paul Perrin, author of their history printed at Geneva, says, that in the year 1160, when the penalty of death was denounced against all who should disbelieve the Real Presence, "Peter Waldo, a citizen of Lyons, was one of the most courageous in opposing such an invention."[145] But nothing is more false; the article of the Real Presence had been defined a hundred years before, against Berengarius: nothing had been done anew relating to this article; and so far was Waldo from opposing it, that we have seen both him and all his disciples in the common faith for fifty years together.

91.—*The Minister de la Roque.*

M. de la Roque,[146] more learned than Perrin, is not more sincere, when he says, "that Peter Waldo, having found whole nations divided from the communion of the Latin Church, joined himself to them with his followers, in order to make but one and the same body, and one and the same society, by the unity of one and the same doctrine." But, on the contrary, we have seen, in the first place, that all the contemporary authors (for not one have we omitted) have shown us the Vaudois and Albigenses as two distinct sects; secondly, that all these authors discover these Albigenses to be Manicheans; and I defy all the Protestants in the world to show me that there was any where in Europe, when Waldo arose, any one sect separate from Rome which was not either the very sect, or some branch and subdivision of Manicheism. Thus, nothing can make Waldo's cause more evidently defenceless, than to grant his abettors what they demand in his behalf, namely, that he joined himself in unity of doctrine with the Albigenses, or with such people as, at that time, were separated from the communion of Rome. In a word, though Waldo should have united himself to guiltless churches, his particular errors would not have allowed any advantage to be drawn from this union, these errors being detested, not by Catholics only, but also by the Protestants.

92.—*Whether the Vaudois afterwards changed their doctrine about the Eucharist.*

But let us proceed in the history of the Vaudois, and see whether our Protestants will discover in it any thing more favorable from the time these heretics broke off entirely from the Church. The first act we meet with against the Vaudois since the great council of Lateran, is a Canon of the Council of Tarragona, describing the Insabbatized, as men "that forbade to swear, and obey ecclesiastic and secular powers, and moreover to punish malefactors, and other such like things,"[147] not the least word appearing in regard to the Real Presence, which not only would have been expressed, but also set foremost, had they denied it.

93.—*Proof of the contrary from Renier.*

At the same time, and towards the year 1250, Renier, so often quoted, who so carefully distinguishes the Vaudois or Leonists and the poor men of Lyons, from the Albigenses, sets down moreover all their errors, reducing them to these three heads: against the Church, against the Sacraments and Saints, and against Church Ceremonies.[148] But so far from any thing appearing in all these articles against transubstantiation, you there find expressly, amongst their errors, that "transubstantiation ought to be made in the vulgar tongue; that a priest could not consecrate in mortal sin;" that when a man communicated from the hand of an unworthy priest, the transubstantiation was not made in his hand that consecrated unworthily, but in the mouth of him who worthily received the Eucharist; that one might consecrate at table, at common meals, and not in churches only, conformably to those words of Malachi, "In every place there is sacrificing, and there is offered to my name a clean obla-tion:"[149] which shows, they did not deny the sacrifice nor the oblation of the Eucharist: and that, if they rejected the Mass, it was on account of the ceremonies, making it only to consist in "the words of Jesus Christ pro-nounced in the vulgar tongue."[150] Thence it clearly appears, that they admitted transubstantiation, and in nothing differed from the doctrine of the Church as to the substance of this sacrament; but said only, that it could not be consecrated by bad priests, and might be by good laymen, according to these fundamental maxims of their sect, which Renier is always exact in observing, that every good layman is a priest, and the prayer of an evil priest availed nothing:"[151] whence also they concluded, the consecration by an evil priest is worth nothing. It is likewise to be seen in other authors, that according to their principles,[152] "a man, without being a priest, might consecrate and administer the sacrament of penance; and every laic, even women, ought to preach."

94.—A list of the Vaudois errors.

We find also in the catalogue of their errors, as well in Renier as other authors, "that it is not lawful for clergymen," namely, the ministers of the Church,[153] "to have goods; that neither lands, nor people, ought to be divided;" which aims at the obligation of setting all in common, and establishing, as necessary, this pretended apostolic poverty, which these heretics gloried in;[154] "that every oath is a mortal sin; that all princes and judges are damned, because they condemn malefactors contrary to these words:[155] 'Vengeance is mine, saith the Lord;' and again, 'Let both grow together until the harvest.'"[156] Thus did these hypocrites abuse the Scripture, and with their counterfeited lenity subvert the whole foundation of Church and State.

95.—Another list, and no mention of their erring in regard of the Eucharist.

We find in Pylicdorf, a hundred years after, an ample refutation of the Vaudois, article by article, without appearance of the least opposition in their doctrine to the Real Presence or transubstantiation. On the contrary, it always appears in this author, as in the rest, that the laymen of this sect made the body of Jesus Christ,[157] although with fear and reserve in the country wherein he wrote; nor, in short, does he observe any kind of error in these heretics relating to the Eucharist, except, that bad priests did not make it "any more than the other Sacraments."

96.—Another list.

Finally, in all the lists we have of their errors, whether in the Bibliotheca Patrum,[158] or in the Inquisitor Emerick, we meet with nothing against the Real Presence, although the least differences between these heretics and us, the minutest articles whereon they are to be interrogated, be there specified; on the contrary, Emerick the Inquisitor thus reports their error on the Eucharist: "They will have it that the bread is not transubstantiated into the body of Jesus Christ, if the priest be a sinner:"[159] which clearly evidences two things: first, that they believed transubstantiation; and secondly, believed the sacraments depended on the sanctity of the ministers.

You find in the same list all the errors of the Vaudois we have already mentioned. The errors of the new Manicheans, whom we have shown were the same with those of the Albigenses, are also related apart in the same book. It is plain from thence, that these two sects are utterly distinct, nor is there any

THE HISTORY OF THE VARIATIONS   BOOK XI

thing amongst the errors of the Vaudois that savors of Manicheism, which the
other list abounds with.

97.—*Demonstration that the Vaudois did not in the least err about Transubstantiation.*

But to return to Transubstantiation: whence could it proceed, that the
Catholics should have spared the Vaudois in a point of so essential a nature,
they who were so zealous in exposing even the least of their errors?[160] Was
it perchance that these matters, and especially that of the Eucharist, were not
of sufficient importance, or not sufficiently known, after Berengarius's
condemnation by so many councils? Was it the desire of keeping the people
ignorant that this mystery was attacked? But they were not afraid to report the
much greater blasphemies of the Albigenses, even against this mystery.
Nothing was concealed from the people of what the Vaudois said, the most
shocking against the Church of Rome, as that she was "the harlot mentioned
in the Revelations; her Pope, the chief of those that erred; her prelates and
religious, scribes and pharisees." Their excesses were pitied, but never kept
private; and had they rejected the Church's faith in regard to the Eucharist,
they would have been upbraided with it.

98.—*Sequel of the same demonstration.*—*Testimony of Claude Seyssel in 1517.*
—*Gross evasion of D'Aubertin.*

Further, in the last age, in 1517 Claude Seyssel,[161] famous for his learning
and offices of trust, held under Louis XII and Francis I, and raised by his merit
to the Archbishopric of Turin; in the search he made after these heretics,
hidden in the valleys of his diocese, in order to unite them to his flock, relates
in the minutest manner all their errors, like a faithful shepherd willing to know
the bottom of the distemper afflicting his sheep, that he might heal them; and
we read in his account all that other writers relate of them, neither more nor
less. With them he chiefly observes, as the source of their error, that "they
made the authority of ecclesiastical ministry to depend on personal merit;
thence concluding, that they ought not to obey the Pope, nor Bishops,
because being wicked, and not imitating the lives of the apostles, they have no
authority from God, either to consecrate, or absolve; and as to themselves,
they alone had this power, because they observed the law of Jesus Christ, that
the Church was no where but amongst them, and the See of Rome was that
harlot of the Revelations, and the fountain-head of all errors." This is what
that great Archbishop says of the Vaudois in his diocese. The minister
Aubertin[162] is astonished that in so exact an account as he gives of their
errors, it is not discovered, that they rejected either the Real Presence or
Transubstantiation; nor any other reply can he make to it, than that this
prelate, who had so strenuously confuted them in all other points, was, in this,
conscious of his too great weakness to resist them: as if so learned and
eloquent a man could not at least transcribe what so many other learned
Catholics had written on this subject. Instead, therefore, of so miserable a shift,
Aubertin ought to have acknowledged, that if so accurate, so knowing a

person, did not reproach the Vaudois with this error, it was in reality because he had discovered none such amongst them: wherein there is nothing particular as to Seyssel, since all the other authors have no more accused them of it than this Archbishop.

99.—*Aubertin's vain objection.*

Nevertheless, Aubertin triumphs at a passage of the same Seyssel, where he says,[163] "He did not think it worth his while to relate what some of that sect, to show themselves more learned than the rest, prattled, or rallied, rather than discoursed, concerning the substance and truth of the Eucharistic Sacrament, because, what they vented by way of secret, was so high, that the most expert divines could scarcely comprehend it." But so far are these words of Seyssel from showing the Real Presence was denied by the Vaudois, that I should, on the contrary, conclude from them, that amongst them pretended to subtilize in expounding it. And should it be allowed (yet gratuitously and without any kind of reason, since Seyssel speaks not a word of it) that these high notions entertained by the Vaudois, relating to the Eucharist, regarded the real absence, to wit, a thing the least sublime of any in the world, and the most suited to carnal sense; yet then, it is nevertheless manifest that Seyssel does not report here the belief of all, but the babble and idle discourse of some: so that, on all hands, nothing is more certain than what I have advanced, that the Vaudois never were reproached with rejecting transubstantiation; but, on the contrary, had always been supposed to believe it.

100.—*Another proof from Seyssel that the Vaudois believed in Transubstantiation.*

Accordingly, the same Seyssel,[164] introducing a Vaudois summing up all his reasons, put these words into his mouth against a wicked priest and bishop: "How can the bishop and priest, enemies to god, render God propitious to others? how can he, that is banished the kingdom of heaven, have the keys of it? in fines, since his prayer and other actions have no manner of effect, how shall Jesus Christ transform himself, at his word, under the species of bread and wine, and suffer himself to be handled by that person, who has utterly rejected him?" It is then still manifest, their error consists in a Donatism, and nothing but a priest's life hinders the bread and wine from being changed into the body and blood of Jesus Christ.

101.—*Interrogatory of the Vaudois in the library of the Marquis of Seignelay.—Two Volumes marked 1769, 1770.*

And what leaves no kind of doubt on this head is, what may be seen still at this day among the manuscripts of M. de Thou, collected together in the valuable library of the Marquis of Seignelay; there, I say, may be seen the inquests, in the original, juridically made against the Vaudois of Pragelas and the other valleys in 1495, collected in two great volumes; wherein you have the examination of one Thomas Quoti of Pragelas, who being asked whether the barbes (their priests) taught them to believe the sacrament of the altar, answers, "That the barbes both preach and teach that when a chaplain who is in orders, utters the words of consecration on the altar, he consecrates the body of Jesus Christ, and that a true change is wrought of the bread into the true body," and says moreover, "that prayer made at home, or on the road, is every whit as good as in the church." Conformably to this doctrine, the same Quoti answers at two several times, "That he received every year, at Easter, the body of Jesus Christ; and the barbes taught them, that, in order to receive it, they ought to have been well confessed, and rather by the barbes than by the chaplains," meaning the priests.

102.—*Sequel of the same Examination.*

The reason of this preference is derived from the so often repeated principles of the Vaudois; and it is pursuant to these principles the same person answers, "that the gentlemen of the church-ministry led a life too large, but the barbes led a holy and upright life." And in another answer, "that the barbes led the life of St. Peter, and had the power of absolving from sins, and this was his belief; and if the Pope did not lead a holy life, he had no power of absolving." For this reason, the same Quoti answers again in another place, "that he had given credit, without any doubting, rather to the discourses of the barbes than to those of the chaplains, because, in those times, no ecclesiastic, no cardinal, no bishop, nor priest, led the life of the apostles; and, therefore, it was better believing the barbes who were good, than an ecclesiastic that was not so."

103.—*Sequel.*

It were superfluous to relate the other examinations, the same language appearing throughout, as well in respect of the Real Presence as of all the rest; and especially it is repeated there continually, "that the barbes behaved in the world like the imitators of Jesus Christ, and had more power than the priests of the Church of Rome, who lived too much at large."

104.—*Necessity of Confession.*

Nothing is repeated there so much as these dogmas, "That it was necessary to confess their sins; that they confessed to the barbes, who had power of absolving them; that they confessed kneeling; that at each confession they gave a quart (a certain piece of money;) that the barbes imposed penances on them which generally did not exceed a Pater and Credo, but the Ave Maria was never enjoined; that they forbade them all oaths whatsoever, and taught them neither to sue for help from the saints, nor to pray for the dead." Here is enough whereby to discover the principle tenets and genius of the sect; further than this, to expect to meet with order and one constant form in such odd opinions, in all times and places, were to be deceived.

105.—Sequel of the Same Subject.

I do not find they were interrogated concerning sacraments administered by the generality of laymen, whether because the inquisitors were not apprized of this custom, or that the Vaudois had at length forsaken it.[165] And, indeed, we have observed, it was not without difficulty and contradiction first introduced amongst them with regard to the Eucharist. But, as for confession, nothing is more established in the sect, than the right good laymen have to it: "A good layman," said they, "has power to absolve; they all gloried in forgiving sins by imposition of hands; they heard confessions; enjoined penances; and lest such an extraordinary practice should be discovered, they very privately received confessions, and those of women even, in cellars, in caverns, and other unfrequented places; they preached clandestinely in corners of houses, and often in the night-time."

106.—The Vaudois exteriorly did the Duties of Catholics.

But what cannot be too much remarked is, that although they had such an opinion of us as we have seen, yet they frequented our assemblies: "There they offer," says Renier,[166] "there they confess, there they communicate, but with dissimulation." The reason was, in short, whatever they might say,[167] because "some distrust remained in them of the communion they practised among themselves." Wherefore, "they came to communicate in the church when the throng was greatest, for fear of discovery. Many also remained even four, nay, six years, without communicating, concealing themselves either in villages, or towns, at Easter time, lest notice should be taken of them. They also judged it advisable to communicate in the church, but at Easter only, and under this appearance, they passed for Christians." This is what the ancient authors say of them,[168] and what also frequently may be found in the interrogatories above mentioned. "Being asked whether he made his confession to the parish priest, and discovered his sect to him, his answer was, that he confessed yearly to him, but did not mention being a Vaudois, which the barbes had forbid discovering." They answer also as above, "that every year they communicated at Easter, and received the body of Jesus Christ; and that the barbes warned them of the necessity, before they received, of having made a good confession." Observe, there is no mention here made but of the body alone, and of one only species; as, since the Council of Constance, it was then given over all the Church, the barbes never thinking all this while of condemning it. An old author[169] has observed, "They very rarely received from their teachers either baptism or Christ's body, but as well teachers as simple believers went to seek them at the priest's hands." Nor, indeed, do we conceive how they could have acted otherwise, in regard to baptism, without discovering themselves, for it would soon have been taken notice of, had they not brought their children to church, for which they would have been called to an account. Thus, separated in sentiments from the Catholic Church, these hypocrites, as far as they were able, shewed themselves externally of the same faith with others, and exhibited no act of religion in public which did not belie their doctrine.

107.—*Whether the Vaudois had discarded any one of the Seven Sacraments.*
—*Confirmation.*

The Protestants may perceive by this example what kind of men those hidden faithful before the Reformation were, whom they extol so much, and who had not bent a knee to Baal. It might be doubted whether the Vaudois had discarded any of the Seven Sacraments. And it is already manifest, they were not accused of denying so much as one at the beginning; on the contrary, an author has been produced, who, upbraiding them with their changes, excepts the sacraments. Those Renier speaks of,[170] might be suspected of varying in this matter, he seeming to say, they rejected not only orders, but also confirmation and extreme unction; but it is manifest, he means such only as Catholics conferred. For, as to confirmation, Renier, who makes them reject it, adds, "They were astonished we permitted none but bishops to confer it:" for this reason, because they were for allowing to good laymen the power of administering this as well as the other sacraments. Wherefore these same heretics, mentioned as rejecting confirmation, boast, a little after, "of giving the Holy Ghost, by laying on of hands;"[171] which is, in other words, the very substance of this sacrament.

108.—*Extreme Unction.*

In regard to extreme unction, this is what Renier says of it: "They reject the sacrament of unction, as if given to the rich only, and because many priests are necessary thereto;"[172] words, which sufficiently evince that its nullity, which they pretended was amongst us, proceeded from imaginary abuses, not from the nature of the thing. Besides, St. James[173] having enjoined to call in the priests in the plural number, these cavillers were for believing that unction, given by a single person, as commonly practised amongst us even so long ago, was not sufficient, and this bad pretext served for their neglecting it.

109.—*What was the Ablution Renier speaks of in Baptism.*

As for baptism, notwithstanding these ignorant heretics had cast off its most ancient ceremonies with contempt, there is no doubt but they received it. One might only be surprised at Renier's words,[174] as uttered by the Vaudois, "that ablution, given to children, is of no advantage to them." But, whereas this ablution is in the list of those ceremonies of baptism, which were disapproved by these heretics, it is plain, he speaks of the wine given to children after their baptism; a custom that may be still seen in many ancient rituals, about that time, and which was a remnant of the communion heretofore administered to them under the liquid species only. This wine, put into the chalice to be given to these children, was called ablution, because this action resembled the ablution taken by the priest at Mass. Again, this word ablution is not to be found in Renier as signifying baptism; and, at all events, if men will persist to have it signify this sacrament, all they could conclude from it would be for the worst, viz., that Renier's Vaudois accounted as null whatever baptism was given by unworthy ministers, such as they believed all our priests were; an error so conformable to the principles of the sect, that the Vaudois, whom we have seen approve our baptism, could not do it without running counter to their own doctrine.

110.—*Confession.*

Here, then, already are three sacraments, which the Vaudois approved in the main, Baptism, Confirmation, and Extreme Unction. We have the whole sacrament of penance in their private confession, in the penances imposed by them, in the absolution received for the remission of sins; and if they said, oral confession was not always necessary when contrition was in the heart; they said true, in the main and in certain cases, although frequently, as above instanced, they abused this maxim by too long deferring their confession.

111.—*The Eucharist.*

There was a sect called the Siscidenses, who differed little or nothing from the Vaudois, says Renier, but in that they received the Eucharist. Not that he meant the Vaudois, or poor men of Lyons, did not receive it, he having shown, on the contrary, that they received even transubstantiation; but he means only, they had an extreme repugnance to receive it from the hands of our priests, whereas these others made less difficulty in it, or perchance, none at all.

112.—*Marriage.*—*Whether Reiner hath calumniated the Vaudois.*

Protestants accuse Renier of calumniating the Vaudois, by reproaching them, "that they condemned marriage;" but these authors mutilate his words,[175] which here you have entire: "They condemn the sacrament of marriage, by saying, married people sin mortally when they use marriage for any other end than to have children;" whereby Renier would observe only the error of these proud heretics, who, to show themselves above human infirmity, would not admit the secondary end of marriage, namely, its serving as a remedy against concupiscence. It was then in this respect only that he accused these heretics of condemning marriage, to wit, of condemning this necessary part, and making that a mortal sin, which the grace of so holy a state renders pardonable.

113.—*Demonstration that the Catholics were neither ignorant of, nor dissembled, the doctrine of the Vaudois.*

It is now seen what was the doctrine of the Vaudois or poor men of Lyons. The Catholics cannot be accused, either of not knowing it, since they dwelt and conversed amongst them, and daily received their abjurations; or, of neglecting to inform themselves, since, on the contrary, they applied themselves with so much care to report its minutest points; or, in fine, of

calumniating them, since we have seen they were so exact, not only in
distinguishing the Vaudois from the Cathari and the rest of the Manicheans,
but also in acquainting us with all the correctives applied by some of them to
the extravagances of others; and, in a word, of relating to us with so much
sincerity what was commendable in their manners, that their partisans even
now-a-days take advantage from it. For we have seen, they did not dissemble
the specious appearances at Waldo's first setting out, nor the first simplicity of
his followers. Renier,[176] who so much blames them, hesitates not to say,
"that they lived justly before men; that they believed of God what was fitting
to believe, and all that was contained in the creed;" that they were regular in
their deportment, modest in their dress, just in their dealings, chaste in their
marriages, abstemious in their diet, and so of the rest, as it is well known. We
shall have a word to say on this testimony of Renier; but, in the interim, we
see he rather flatters, as I may say, than calumniates the Vaudois; and,
therefore, it cannot be doubted that what he says besides of these heretics is
true. And though we should suppose with the ministers, that Catholic authors,
urged on by the hatred they had conceived against them, charged them with
calumnies; this is a new proof of what we have but just said concerning their
doctrine, because finally, had the Vaudois stood in opposition to transubstantiation and the adoration of the Eucharist, at a time when our adversaries agree
it was so well established amongst us, the Catholics, whom they represent so
inclined to load them with false crimes, would never have failed reproaching
them with what was so true.

114.—*Division of the Vaudois doctrine into three heads.*

Now then that we know the whole doctrine of the Vaudois, we may divide
it into three sorts of articles. Some there are which we detest together with the
Protestants: some that we approve, and Protestants reject: others that they
approve, and we condemn.

115.—*Doctrine which the Protestants we well as the Catholics reject in the Vaudois.*

The articles we condemn in common are, in the first place, that doctrine so
injurious to the Sacraments, which makes their validity depend on the holiness
of their ministers; secondly, that of rendering the administration of the
Sacraments common to priests and laity without distinction; next, that of
forbidding oaths in all cases whatsoever, thereby condemning not only St. Paul
the Apostle,[177] but even God himself who has sworn; lastly, that of condemning the just punishments of malefactors, and authorizing all crimes by
impunity.

116.—*Doctrine which the Catholics approve in the Vaudois, and Protestants condemn.*

The articles which we approve, and the Protestants reject, are that of the
Seven Sacraments, except, perchance, Orders, and in the manner above spoken
to, and what is still more important, that of the Real Presence and Transub-

stantiation. So many articles which the Protestants detest either with us, or, contrary to our sentiments, in the Vaudois, pass under the cover of five or six points, wherein these same Vaudois favor them; and notwithstanding their hypocrisy and all their errors, these heretics are made to be their ancestors.

117.—*The Vaudois have changed their Doctrine since Luther's and Calvin's time.*

Such was the state of this sect till the time of the new Reformation. Although this made so much noise ever since the year 1517, the Vaudois, whom we have seen till that date abiding in all the sentiments of their ancestors, still remained unaltered. At length in 1530, after much suffering, whether solicited to it, or taking it into their heads of themselves, they thought fit to make them their protectors, whom like themselves they had heard exclaim against the Pope so many years. Those who had withdrawn for nearly two hundred years, as Seyssel[178] remarks, into the mountains of Savoy and Dauphiny, consulted Bucer and the Swiss, their neighbors. With much commendation which they received, Gilles,[179] one of their historians, acquaints us, they received also admonitions concerning three defects observed amongst them. The first related to the decision of certain points of doctrine; the second, to the establishment of the order of discipline and ecclesiastical assemblies, to the end they might be held more openly: the third invited them, no longer to permit those that desired to be accounted members of their Churches, to be present at Mass, or to adhere, in any kind, to papal superstitions, or to acknowledge the priests of the Roman Church for pastors, or to make use of their ministry.

118.—*New Articles proposed to the Vaudois by the Protestants.*

There needs no more to confirm every thing we have said, concerning the state of these wretched Churches, which concealed their faith and worship under a contrary profession. On these advertisements of Bucer and Œcolampadius, the same Gilles assures us, new articles were proposed to the Vaudois. He owns he does not report them all: but here are five or six of such as he specifies, which sufficiently discover the ancient spirit of the sect. For in order to reform the Vaudois to the Protestant mode, it was necessary to make them say, "that a Christian may swear lawfully; that auricular confession is not commanded of God; that a Christian may lawfully exercise the office of magistrate over other Christians; that there is no determined time for fasting; that the minister may possess something in particular wherewith to maintain his family, without prejudice to apostolic community; that Jesus Christ has appointed but two Sacraments, Baptism and the holy Eucharist."[180] Hereby appears a part of what was necessarily to be reformed in the Vaudois, in order to make them Zuinglians or Calvinists, and among the rest, one of the corrections was, to admit but two Sacraments. It was also necessary to hint to them a word or two concerning predestination, which assuredly they had heard but little of; and they were informed as to this new dogma, which was then like the soul of the Reformation, that whosoever owns free-will denies predestination. It appears by these same articles that, in process of time, the

Vaudois had fallen into new errors, since it was requisite to teach them[181] "they were to cease from earthly labors on the Sabbath-day, in order to attend God's service;" and again, "that it is not lawful for a Christian to revenge himself on his enemy." These two articles show the brutality and barbarity, which these Vaudois Churches (the main support, it seems, of decayed Christianity) were fallen into, at the time the Protestants reformed them: and this confirms what Seyssel says of them, that "they were a base and bestial race of men, that hardly could distinguish, by reason, whether they were men or brutes, alive or dead."[182] Such, by Gilles's account, were the articles of reformation proposed to the Vaudois towards incorporating them with the Protestants. If Gilles mentioned no more of them, it might either proceed from a fear of exposing too great an opposition between the Vaudois and Calvinists, of whom the design then was to make but one communion, or because this was all the Vaudois could be drawn to at that time. Be that as it will, he owns nevertheless,[183] they could not come to an agreement, because some of the barbes were of opinion, that by assenting to all these conclusions, they should dishonor the memory of those who had so very prosperously conducted those churches to that time. Thus, it is manifest, the design of the Protestants was not to follow the Vaudois, but to make them change, and reform to their fashion.

119.—*Conference of the Vaudois with Œcolampadius.*

During this negotiation with the ministers of Strasburg and Basil, two of the Vaudois deputies had a long conference with Œcolampadius, which Abraham Scultet, a Protestant historian, relates whole and entire in his Evangelical Annals,[184] and declares he had transcribed it word for word.

One of the deputies opens the conversation, by owning that the ministers, of which number he was one, "being prodigiously ignorant, were incapable of teaching the people: that they lived by alms and labor, poor shepherds or husbandmen, the cause of their profound ignorance and incapacity: that they were not married, nor lived always very chastely; but when they had been caught tripping, they were expelled the company of the rest: that it was not the ministers, but the priests of the Roman Church who administered the Sacraments to the Vaudois; but that their ministers made them ask pardon of God for receiving the Sacraments from those priests, because forced to it; moreover, they admonished them not to adhere to the ceremonies of Antichrist: that they practised auricular confession, and, till then, had always owned seven Sacraments, wherein, they heard it said, they were very much mistaken." They proceed to give an account of how they rejected the Mass, purgatory, and the invocation of saints, and in order to clear up their doubts, they propose the following queries:—"Whether or not it be lawful for magistrates to put criminals to death, by reason God has said, I will not the death of the sinner?" But asked at the same time, "If it were not allowable in them to kill the false brethren who informed against them to Catholics, because, they having no jurisdiction amongst them, there was no other way to keep them in awe: whether the human and civil laws, by which the world was governed, were good, the Scripture having said, that the laws of men are vain: whether churchmen might receive donations and have anything of their own: whether it were lawful to swear: whether the distinction they made of original, venial, and mortal sin, were good: whether all children, of whatsoever nation, be saved by the merits of Jesus Christ; and whether the adult, of whatsoever religion, not having faith, may also be saved; what are the judiciary and ceremonial precepts of the law of Moses: and whether they have been abolished by Jesus Christ; and which are the canonical books." After all these queries, which so clearly confirm all we have said of the belief of the Vaudois, and the brutal ignorance these heretics were at last fallen into, their deputy speaks in these terms:—"Nothing has so much disturbed us, weak and simple as we are, as what I have read in Luther concerning free-will and predestination; for we believe all men have naturally some power and strength, which, excited by God, might do something, conformably to those words, Behold, I stand at the door and knock; and whosoever would not open, should receive according to his works: but if the thing be not so, I do not see, as says Erasmus, of what use the commandments are. As for predestination, we believe that God has foreseen from all eternity those that were to be saved or damned, and that he had made all men in order to be saved, and the reprobate become such through their own fault: but should all come to pass of necessity, as Luther says, and the predestinated not have it in their power to turn reprobate, nor contrarywise, to what end so much preaching and so much writing, since, everything happening by necessity, matters never will be better or worse?" Whatever ignorance may appear throughout this discourse, it is plain, these ignorant people, with all their rusticity, spoke better than those they had chosen for reformers; and here are the men, forsooth, they present us as the remains and refuge of Christianity.

We find nothing here in particular relating to the Eucharist; which makes it likely, that the whole of the conference was not related; nor is it difficult to guess the reason. It was, in short, because the Vaudois were, as above seen, greater Papists on this head than the Zuinglians and Lutherans desired. Moreover, this deputy speaks nothing to Œcolampadius of any Confession of Faith as in use amongst them; and we have already seen that even Beza[185] reports none but that which the Vaudois made in 1541, so long after Luther and Calvin: which shows manifestly, that the Confessions of Faith produced by them, as of the ancient Vaudois, can be but very modern, as we shall soon discover.

120.—The Vaudois nowise Calvinists, as proved from Crespin.

After all these conferences with those of Strasburg and Basil in 1536, Geneva was consulted by her neighbors the Vaudois, and then it was that their society with the Calvinists commenced, by the instructions of Farel, minister of Geneva. But we need only hear the Calvinists themselves, to be convinced how far remote the Vaudois were from their Reformation. Crespin,[186] in his History of Martyrs, says, that those of Angrogne, by a long succession, and as from father to son, had retained some purity of doctrine. But to show how small, even in their estimate, was this purity of doctrine, he says in another place, speaking of the Vaudois of Merindol, "that the *very little true light they had*, they endeavored to increase from day to day, by despatching people on all sides, even to a great distance off, wheresoever they heard some ray of light did discover itself."[187] And he agrees moreover in another place, that "their ministers, who taught them in private, did not do it with that purity, which was requisite; inasmuch as ignorance having overflowed the whole universe, and God having a right to let men go astray as he did, like brute beasts, it is no wonder these poor men had not so pure a doctrine as they have since enjoyed, and at this day more than ever."[188] These last words show the pains the Calvinists were at since the year 1536, to lead the Vaudois whither they had a mind; and after all, it is but too manifest that, from that time, this sect is not to be looked on as persisting in her ancient doctrine, but as reformed by the Calvinists.

121.—*Proof from Beza.*

We learn as much from Beza,[189] though with little precaution, when he owns in his description of them, "that the purity of doctrine was somewhat adulterated by the Vaudois;" and in his history, that "in process of time, they had somewhat swerved from piety and doctrine." Afterwards he speaks more openly, confessing that "in a long series of time the purity of doctrine had been greatly adulterated by their Ministers, insomuch that they became sensible, by the ministry of Œcolampadius, of Bucer, and others, how, by little and little, the purity of doctrine had not remained amongst them, and gave orders, by sending to their brethren in Calabria, to put all things in a better state."[190]

122.—*The change of the Calabrian Vaudois, and their entire extinction.*

These brethren of Calabria were, like them, fugitives, who, according to the maxims of the sect, held their assemblies, as Gilles reports, "in the most secret manner it was possible, *and dissembled many things* against their will."[191] What this minister endeavors to hide under these words, you must understand was, that the Vaudois of Calabria, after the example of all the rest of them, performed all the external duties of good Catholics; and I leave you to judge whether they could have been exempt from it in that country, considering what we have seen of their dissimulation in the valleys of Pragelas and Angrogne. Accordingly Gilles acquaints us, how that these Calabrians, pressed at last to withdraw from church assemblies, yet not able to take the resolution, though advised to it by this minister, "of forsaking so fine a country," were soon abolished.

123.—*The present Vaudois are not the predecessors, but followers of the Calvinists.*

Thus expired the Vaudois. As they had only subsisted by concealing what they were, they fell as soon as ever they resolved to declare themselves; for those that afterwards remained under that name, it is plain, were nothing else but

Calvinists, whom Farel and the other ministers of Geneva had formed to their mode; so that these Vaudois, whom they make their ancestors and predecessors, to speak the truth, are nothing but their successors, and new disciples whom they have proselyted to their faith.

124.—*No advantage to be derived from the Vaudois in behalf of the Calvinists.*

But, after all, what help can these Vaudois, by whom they seek to justify themselves, afford our Calvinists? It is manifest by this history that Waldo and his disciples were all mere laymen, who thrust themselves in to preach without orders, without mission, and afterwards to administer the sacraments. They separated from the Church by a manifest error, detested as much by Protestants as Catholics, which was that of Donatism; nay, this Donatism of the Vaudois is beyond comparison much worse than the African Donatism of old, so strongly confuted by St. Austin. Those Donatists of Africa said, indeed, that none but a holy person could validly administer the sacraments; but they did not arrive at the extravagance of the Vaudois, to allow the administration of the sacraments as well to holy laymen as holy priests. If the African Donatists pretended that the Catholic bishops and priests had forfeited their ministry by their crimes, they at least accused them of crimes, which were actually reproved by the law of God. But our new Donatists separate themselves from the whole Catholic clergy, and would have it, they were degraded from their orders for not observing their pretended apostolic poverty, which, at most, was but a counsel. For this was the origin of the sect, and what we have seen it stood to, as long as it persisted in its first belief. Who, therefore, does not see that such a sect is nothing at bottom, but hypocrisy boasting her poverty and other virtues, and making the sacraments depend, not on the efficacy Jesus Christ has given them, but on man's merits? And, after all, these new doctors, from whom the Calvinists derive their succession, whence came they themselves, and who sent them? Puzzled at this query no less than the Protestants, like them they went in quest of predecessors, and here is the fable trumped up by them. They were told, that in the time of St. Sylvester, when Constantine endowed the churches with revenues, "One of this Pope's companions would not consent to it, and withdrew from his communion, abiding, together with them that followed him, in the way of poverty; and then it was the Church failed in Sylvester and his adherents, and remained with them."[192] Let not this be called a calumny invented by the enemies of the Vaudois, for we have seen, that the authors, who unanimously report it, had no desire of calumniating them. This fable was still in vogue in Seyssel's time.[193] The vulgar were then told, "This sect had taken its rise from a certain man called Leo, a very religious person, in the time of Constantine the Great, who detesting the avarice of Sylvester, and Constantine's excessive liberality, chose rather to follow the poverty and simplicity of faith, than, with Sylvester, to defile himself with a fat and rich benefice, to which Leo and all those joined themselves, that judged aright in faith." These ignorant people had been made to believe, it was from this counterfeit Leo, the sect of Leonists derived their name and birth. Christians are all for finding a succession in their Church and doctrine. Protestants boast of theirs in the Vaudois, the Vaudois in their pretended companion of St. Sylvester; and both are equally fictitious.

125.—*The Calvinists have no contemporary authors to favor their pretensions to the Vaudois.*

All the truth to be found in the origin of the Vaudois is, that they took their motive of separation from   the endowing of churches and church-men, contrary, as they pretended, to that poverty Jesus Christ requires of his ministers. But as this origin is absurd, and besides, nowise serves the turn of Protestants, we have seen what an account Paul Perrin has given of it in his history of the Vaudois.[194] He represents this Waldo as a person "the most courageous in opposing" the Real Presence in the year 1160. But does he produce any author in confirmation of what he says? No, not so much as one; neither Aubertin, nor La Roque, nor Chappel—in a word, no Protestant of Germany or France hath produced, or ever will produce, any one author, either of those times, or of succeeding ages, for the space of three or four hundred years, who gives the Vaudois that origin which this historian lays for the foundation of his history. Have any of the Catholics, who wrote so copiously, whatever Berengarius and the rest objected against the Real Presence, so much as named Waldo amongst those that opposed it? None ever has dreamed of it; we have seen what they said of Waldo was far different. But why must they have spared him only? What, then, did this man, whom they make so courageous in stemming the torrent, so conceal his doctrine that none ever could perceive he impugned an article of this importance? Or, was Waldo so formidable a person, that no Catholic durst impeach him of this error at the time they impeached him of so many others? An historian that sets out with a fact of this nature, and lays it for the foundation of his history, what credit does he deserve? Nevertheless, Paul Perrin is heard, like an oracle among Calvinists, so readily do they come into whatever favors the prejudices of the sect.

126.—*Vaudois books produced by Perrin.*

But, for want of known authors, Perrin produces, for his only proof, some old books[195] of the Vaudois, in manuscript, which he pretends to have recovered; amongst the rest, one volume, wherein was "A book, concerning Antichrist, bearing date 1120, and in this same volume, many sermons of the Vaudois Barbes." But it is already evidently made out, that there neither were Vaudois nor Barbes in 1120; since Waldo, by Perrin's own account, did not appear till 1160. The word barbe was not known, nor in use among the Vaudois to signify their doctors, till many ages after, and manifestly in the latter times. So, these discourses cannot all of them be made to pass as of the year eleven hundred and twenty. Nay, Perrin himself is reduced to allow this date only to the discourse concerning Antichrist, which, by this means, he hopes to father on Peter de Bruis, who lived about that time, or on some of his disciples. But the date standing in the front, should seemingly extend to all, and consequently is utterly false in regard of the first, as it evidently is in regard of the rest. And besides, this treatise about Antichrist, which he pretends to be of 1160, is not in a different language from the other pieces of the Barbes cited by Perrin; and this language is very modern, very unlike the dialect of Provence, now in use. Not only Villehardouin's language, who wrote a hundred years since Peter de Bruis, but that also of the authors subsequent to Villehardouin, is more obsolete and obscure than that which he would date in the year eleven hundred and twenty; so that there is not a more gross and palpable imposition, than to palm on us these pieces as of remote antiquity.

127.—*Sequel.*

Nevertheless, an account of this sole date of 1120, placed, you know not by whom, you know not when, in this Vaudois volume no body knows any thing of, our Calvinists have cited this book about Antichrist as undoubtedly the work of, "some one of Peter de Bruis's" disciples, or as his own.[196] The same authors quote, with great confidence, some discourses which Perrin[197] has annexed to that concerning Antichrist, as if of the same date, 1120, although, in one of those where purgatory is handled, is cited a book which St. Austin entitled, as the original has it, "Milparlemens," that is, of a thousand sayings, as if St. Austin had written a book with this title; which can be attributed to nothing but a compilation made in the thirteenth century, bearing this title, "Milleloquim Sancti Augustini," which the ignorant author of this treatise on Purgatory took for the work of this father. Besides this, we might be able to say some thing of the age of these Vaudois books, and the alterations possibly made in them, were we told of some known library where they might be seen. Till the public has received this necessary information, we cannot but wonder such books have been produced to us for authentic as have not been seen but by Perrin alone; neither Aubertin nor La Roque citing them otherwise than on his word, without so much as telling us they have ever handled them. This Perrin,[198] who alone boasts of them to us, observes none of those marks in them whereby the date of a book may be ascertained, or its antiquity proved; and all he tell us is, they are old Vaudois volumes; which, in general, may be said of the most modern Gothic books of no more than a hundred or sixscore years' antiquity. There is then every reason for believing that these books, whence they produce what they please without any solid proof of their date, have been composed or altered by those Vaudois, whom Farel and his brethren reformed in their own way.

128.—*Confession of Faith produced by Perrin.—That it is posterior to Calvinism.*

As to the Confession of Faith published by Perrin,[199] and which all Protestants quote as an authentic piece of the ancient Vaudois, "It is extracted," says he, "from a book entitled the 'Spiritual Alamanac,' and from the 'Memoirs of George Morel'." As for the Spiritual Alamanc, I know not what to say to it, unless, that neither Perrin, nor even Leger, who speaks with so great a regard for the books of the Vaudois, have mentioned any thing of the date of this. They have not even thought it worth their while to acquaint us whether it may be a manuscript or in print; and we may hold it for certain, it is very modern, since those who would make the most of it, have not specified its antiquity. But what Perrin reports is decisive, viz., that this Confession of Faith is extracted from the memoirs of George Morel. Now it is plain from Perrin himself,[200] that Goerge Morel was the man who about 1530, (so many years after the Reformation,) went to confer with Œcolampadius and Bucer, concerning the means to bring about an union; which makes it clear enought that this Confessi8on of Faith is not, any more than the rest, produced by Perrin, of the ancient Vaudois, but of the Vaudois reformed according to the mdoel of the Protestants.

129.—*Demonstration that the Vaudois had no Confession of Faith before the pretended Reformation*

Accordingly it has been already remarked by us, that no mention of a Vaudois confession of faith was made in the Conference of 1530, between Œcolampadius and the said Vaudois. We may even boldly assert, that they never made a confession of faith till a long while after, since that Beza, so diligent in his researches into, and taking advantage from, the acts of these heretics, says nothing, as has been seen, of any such confession of faith, that he knew of, except in 1541. However that may be, never before Luther's and Calvin's Reformation had a Vaudois confession of faith been so much as heard of.[201] Seyssel, whom pastoral vigilancy and the duty of his charge engaged in those latter times, namely, in 1516 and 1517, to so exact an inquiry into all that concerned this sect, says not one word of a confession of faith: and the reason was,[202] because he had never heard of any such thing, either from juridicial examinations or from those of his own converts, who, with so great tokens of sincerity, discovered him, with tears and compunction, the whole secret of the sect. They had not, therefore, at that time, any such confession; their doctrine was to be learnt, as we have seen, by their interrogatories at tribunals; but as for a confession of faith, or any Vaudois writing, we find not a word in those authors that knew them best. On the contrary, the brethren of Bohemia, a sect of whom we shall speak presently, and which the Vaudois have frequently strove to unite themselves to, both before and since Luther's time, assure us they wrote nothing. "They never had" say they, "a Church known in Bohemia, nor had our people learnt any thing of their doctrine, by reason they never had published any writings we know of."[203] And in another place—"They would not suffer that there should be any public testimony of their doctrine." But if you will say, they had nevertheless, amongst themselves, some writing and some confessions of faith; if so, doubtless they would have communicated them to the brethren with whom they wished to unite themselves. But the brethren declare, they knew nothing as to that point, except from some articles of Merindol, "which articles," say they, "possibly might have been polished since our time." This is what a learned minister of the Bohemians writes,[204] a long while after the Reformation of Luther and

Calvin. He would have spoken more accurately if, instead of saying these articles were "polished," he had said they were coined since the Reformation. But so it was that men were willing, in the party, to give some air of antiquity to the Vaudois articles, nor would this minister entirely disclose the secret of the sect. Be that as it will, he says enough of it to convince us what we ought to credit concerning the confessions of faith produced, in his time, under the name of the Vaudois; and it is easily perceived they knew nothing of the Protestant doctrine before they had been taught it by the Protestants. Nay, they scarce knew what they themselves believed, and but confusedly delivered their minds concerning it to their best friends, so far from having confessions of faith already at hand, as Perrin would fain persuade us.

130.—*The Vaudois, in drawing their Calvinistic Confession of Faith, retained something of the Dogmas that were peculiar to them.*

And nevertheless we perceive, even in these pieces of Perrin, some footsteps of the ancient genius of the Vaudois, a confirmation of what we have already said concerning them. For example, in the book about Antichrist, it is said,[205] "That the emperors and kings supposing that Antichrist resembled the true and holy mother the Church, they loved him, and endowed him contrary to God's command," which comes up to the tenet of the Vaudois, that the clergy are forbidden to have any goods; an error, as above seen, which was the first ground-work of their separation. What is advanced in the catechism, viz., that you may know the ministers "by their true sense of the faith, and by their holy doctrine and life of good example," &c., suits also with that error, which made the Vaudois believe, that ministers of an evil life were degraded from their ministry, and lost the administration of the sacraments. For which reason, in the book that treats of Antichrist, it is also said, that one of his works is, "to attribute the Reformation of the Holy Ghost to faith exteriorly dead, and to baptize children into this faith, teaching that, by this faith, these children do receive from him baptism and regeneration:" words whereby a living faith is required in the ministers of baptism, as a thing necessary for the child's regeneration, and the contrary is ranked among the works of Antichrist. Thus, when they composed these new confessions of faith agreeable to the Reformation, which they had a design of entering into, there was no hindering them from still insinuating something that savored of the old leaven; and without further loss of time in this inquiry, it is sufficient you have observed, in these works of the Vaudois, the two errors which were the ground of their separation.

131.—*Reflections on the History of the Albigenses and Vaudois.—Artifice of the ministers.*

Such is the history of the Albigenses and Vaudois as reported by the authors of those times. Our Reformed, finding nothing therein favorable to their pretensions, connived at their being imposed upon by the most gross of all artifices. Many Catholic authors who wrote in this, or towards the end of the preceding age, have not sufficiently distinguished the Vaudois from the Albigenses, but given the general name of Vaudois alike to both of them. Whatever might have been the cause of their error, our Protestants are more able critics than to require we should credit either Mariana, or Gretser, or even De Thou, and some other moderns, to the prejudice of the ancient authors, who all unanimously, as we have seen, distinguished these two sects. Nevertheless, on so gross an error, the Protestants, after taking it for granted that the Albigenses and Vaudois were but one and the same sect, have concluded, that nought but calumny branded the Albigenses with the imputation of Manicheism, since the Vaudois, according to the ancient authors, are exempt from that blemish.

132.—*Demonstration that the Heretics, who denied the Reality in the twelfth and thirteenth centuries, were Manicheans.*—*Notoriously false supposition of the Ministers.*

They ought to reflect that these ancients, who, in accusing the Vaudois of other errors, have acquitted them of Manicheism, at the same time have distinguished them from the Albigenses whom we have convicted of it. For example, the minister de la Roque, who, as he was the last who wrote on this subject, has mustered up the subtle quirks of all the other authors of the party, and especially those of Aubertin, believes he has justified the Albigenses as to their rejecting the Old Testament, like the Manicheans, by showing from Renier's testimony, that the Vaudois received it:[206] he gains nothing, since these Vaudois are, in the same Renier,[207] thoroughly distinguished from the Cathari, the stem of the Albigensian progeny. The same La Roque[208] thinks to reap advantage from certain heretics, who, according to Radulphus Ardens, said, "That the sacrament was nothing but mere bread." It is true; but the same Radulphus adds, what La Roque no less than Aubertin have dissembled, that these same heretics "admit two Creators, and reject the Old Testament, the truth of the incarnation, marriage, and the use of flesh-meat." The same minister also cites certain heretics mentioned by Peter de Vaucernay,[209] who denied the truth of Jesus Christ's body in the Eucharist. I own it; but, at the same time, this historian[210] assures us, they admitted the two principles, with all the train of Manichean errors. La Roque would make us believe, that the same Peter de Vaucernay distinguishes the Arians and Manicheans from the Vaudois and Albigenses. The half of this statement is true: it is true that he distinguishes the Manicheans from the Vaudois, but he distinguishes them not from the heretics "that were in the country of Narbonne;" and certain it is, these are the same that were called Albigenses, and who unquestionably were Manicheans. But, continues the same La Roque,[211] Renier owns heretics who say, "the body of Jesus Christ is mere bread;" they were those he calls Ordibarians that spoke thus, and, at the same time, denied the Creation, and vented a thousand other blasphemies which Manicheism had introduced: so that these enemies of the Real Presence were at the same time no less enemies of the Creator than the Deity.

133.—Sequel.—Manicheism at Metz.—The Bogomilists.

La Roque returns to the attack with Aubertin, and believes he finds good Protestants in the persons of those heretics, who, by the testimony of Cesarius of Hesterback, "blasphemed the body and blood of Jesus Christ."[212] But the same Cesarius informs us, they admitted the two principles, and all the other Manichean blasphemies; which he avers he is very well assured of, not from hearsay, but "from his frequent conversation with them in the Diocese of Metz." A famous minister of Metz, whom I was well acquainted with, made the Calvinists of that country believe these Albigenses of Cesarius were their ancestors; and then they were plainly shown, that these ancestors he had given them, were abominable Manicheans. La Roque, in his history of the Eucharist, would fain have us believe, the Bogomilists were the same with those called, in divers places, Vaudois, poor men of Lyons, Bulgarians, Insabbatized, Gazares, Poplicans, and Turlupins. I agree that the Vaudois, the Insabbatized, and the poor men of Lyons are the same sect; but that they were called Gazares or Cathari, Poplicans, Bulgarians, or Bogomilists, is what never will be proved from any author of those times. Nevertheless, M. de la Roque must needs have these Bogomilists to be their friends; surely for this reason, because "they accounted the body and blood, which we consecrate, unworthy of all esteem." But he ought to have learned from Anna Comnena, who has given us a right notion of these heretics, "that they reduced to a phantom the incarnation of Jesus; that they taught such impurities as the modesty of her sex forbade this princess to repeat; and, in a word, that they had been convicted by the Emperor Alexius, her father, of introducing a dogma mixed with two, the most infamous of all heresies, that of the Manicheans and that of the Massalians."[213]

134.—Sequel of the suppositions of the Ministers.

The same La Roque[214] numbers also among his friends Peter Moran, who, pressed to declare his faith before all the people, confessed, "He did not believe the consecrated bread was the body of our Lord;" and he forgets that this Peter Moran, by the report of the author whose testimony he cites, was of the number of those heretics convicted of Manicheism, who were called Arians for the reason above mentioned.

135.—Another falsity.

This author reckons also amongst his friends[215] those heretics, concerning whom it is said in the Council of Toulouse, under Calixtus II, "that they rejected the sacrament of Jesus Christ's body and blood;" and he mutilates the very canon he has taken these words from, in the sequel whereof is to be seen, that these heretics, together with the sacrament of the body and blood, "rejected also infant baptism and lawful wedlock."

136.—Another passage mutilated.

With a like boldness he corrupts a passage of Emerick, the inquisitor, concerning the Vaudois. "Emerick," says he, "attributes to them, as a heresy, their saying that the bread is not transubstantiated into the true body of Jesus Christ, nor the wine into blood."[216] Who would not believe the Vaudois convicted by this testimony of denying transubstantiation? but we have given the whole passage, where you will read, "The ninth error of the Vaudois is, that the bread is not transubstantiated into the body of Jesus Christ, *if the priest who consecrate it be a sinner,*" M. la Roue cuts off these last words, and, by this falsification alone, takes from the Vaudois two important points of their doctrine: one, which is the abhorrence of all Protestants, to wit, transubstantiation; the other, which is the abhorrence of all Christians, namely, their saying, that the sacraments lose their virtue in the hands of unworthy ministers. Thus do our adversaries prove what they please by manifest falsifications, nor dread giving themselves predecessors even at this rate.

137.—Recapitulation.

These are a part of Aubertin's and La Roque's illusions with regard to the Albigenses, and Vaudois, or poor men of Lyons. In a word, they perfectly vindicate these last from Manicheism, but, at the same time, bring no kind of proof to show they denied transubstantiation; on the contrary, they corrupt the passages which prove that they admitted it. And as for those who denied it in those days, they produce none but such as are convicted of Manicheism by the testimony of the same authors that accuse them of denying the change of substance in the Eucharist; so that their ancestors either, with us, defend transubstantiation as the Vaudois, or are convicted of Manicheism with the Albigenses.

138.—Two other objections of the Ministers.

But here is what these ministers have advanced with greater subtlety. Overpowered by the number of authors, who, treating of these Toulousian and Albigensian heretics, make them perfect Manicheans, they cannot deny there were such, and even in those countries; and they were those, they say,[217] who were called Cathari or Puritans. But, they add, they were very few in number, since Renier,[218] who knew them so well, assures us, they had but "sixteen churches in the whole world;" nay, that the number of these Cathari did not exceed four thousand in all parts of the earth; "whereas," says Renier, "the believers are not to be numbered."[219] These ministers would have it understood from this passage, that these sixteen churches, and four thousand men spread in all parts of the universe, could not have caused in it all that noise and all those wars the Albigenses were authors of; it must, therefore, have happened that the name of Cathari or Manicheans was extended to some other sect more numerous, and that the Vaudois and Albigenses had the name of Manicheans given them either by mistake or calumny.

139.—Sixteen Churches of the Manicheans that comprehend the whole Sect.

Whoever wishes to see what length prejudice or illusion will go, needs but to hear, after what the ministers have said, the truth I am going to relate, or rather, call to mind what has already been related. And, in the first place, as to these sixteen churches, you have seen the word Church was taken in this place by Renier,[220] not for particular churches which were in certain towns, but often, for whole provinces: thus you find amongst these churches, the church of Sclavonia, the church of Marc-Ancona in Italy, the church of France, the church of Bulgaria, the mother of all the rest. All Lombardy was contained under the title of two churches; those of Toulouse and Alby, which in France formerly were the most numerous, comprehended all Languedoc, and so forth; so that, under the denomination of sixteen churches, the whole sect was expressed as divided into sixteen cantons, all which had their relation to Bulgaria, as above seen.

140.—The Cathari, in number four thousand.—How is this to be understood?

We have also observed, with respect to those four thousand Cathari, that none were understood by that name but the perfect of the sect, called elect in St. Austin's time; but at the same time that Renier assures us, in his time, to wit, in the middle of the thirteenth century, when the sect was weakened, though there were but four thousand perfect Cathari, yet, that the multitude of the rest of the sect, namely, of simple believers, was then infinite.

141.—Whether the word Believers, in the ancient authors, signified the Vaudois.
—Aubertin's fallacy.

La Roque, after Aubertin,[221] pretends the word "Believers" signified the Vaudois, by reason that Pylicdorf, and Renier himself, call them so. But here is again too palpable a fallacy. The word "Believers" was common to all the sects: each sect had its believers or followers. The Vaudois had their believers, *Credentes ipsorum*, whom Pyliclorf has spoken of in divers places. Not that the word "Believers" was appropriated to the Vaudois; but the thing meant was, that they had theirs like the rest. The passage cited from Renier, by the ministers, says, the heretics "had their believers, *Credentes suos*, to whom they allowed all kind of crimes." It is not the Vaudois he speaks of, since he commends their good deportment. The same Renier relates the mysteries of the Cathari, or the breaking of their bread, and says, "they admitted to this table not only the Cathari, *men and women*, but also their believers,"[222] namely, those who were not as yet arrived to the perfection of the Cathari: which shows manifestly these two orders so well known among the Manicheans; and what he further remarks, that the simple believers were admitted to this kind of mystery, makes it evident that there were other mysteries which they were not deemed worthy of. These believers of the Cathari were therefore the "innumerable" above mentioned; and these, guided by the rest of an inferior number, raised all the commotions which disturbed the world.

142.—*Conclusion: that the Vaudois concur not in sentiment with the Calvinists.*

Here have you then the subtleties, not to say artifices, the ministers are reduced to, in order to find themselves predecessors. They have none of an apparent and continued succession; of such they go in search the best way they are able, amongst obscure sects whom they strive to unite, and make of them good Calvinists, though there be nothing they all agree in, but their hatred against the Pope and Church.

143.—*What is to be believed concerning the lives of the Vaudois.*

It will be asked me, perhaps, what is my opinion concerning the manners of the Vaudois so much extolled by Renier? I can easily credit all he says, nay, if they please, more than Renier said of them; for the devil matters not by what sort of bands he secures men to him. Those Toulousian heretics, confessedly Manicheans, had not less of this apparent piety than the Vaudois. It was of them St. Bernard said: "Their manners are irreproachable; they oppress none; they injure no man; their countenances are mortified and wan with fasting; they eat not their bread like sluggards, but labor to gain a livelihood."[223] What can be more plausible than these heretics mentioned by St. Bernard? But, after all, they were Manicheans, and their piety but disguise. Inspect the foundation: it was pride, it was hatred against the clergy, it was rancor against the Church; this made them drink in the whole poison of an abominable heresy. An ignorant people may be led whither you please, when, after kindling a violent passion in their breasts, especially hatred against their guides, you use it as a chain to drag them by. But what shall we say of the Vaudois, who kept themselves so clear of the Manichean errors. The devil had accomplished his work in them, when he inspired them with the same pride; the same ostentation of their pretended Apostolic poverty; the same presumption to boast their virtues; the same hatred against the clergy, carried so far as even to despise the Sacraments in their hands; the same bitterness against their brethren, even to a rupture from them and open schism. With this hatred in their breasts, even though they were externally still more just than has been reported, St. John assures me,[224] they are murderers. Were they as chaste as angels, their lot would be no better than that of the "foolish virgins,"[225] whose lamps were void of oil, and hearts void of that sweetness which alone can nourish charity.

144.—*Sourness is the character of this Sect.—Abuse of the Scripture.*

Renier[226] has therefore justly pointed out the character of these heretics, when he resolves the cause of their error into hatred, bitterness, and rancor: *Sic processit doctrina ipsorum, et rancor.* These heretics, says he, whose exterior was so specious, read much, "and prayed little. They went to sermons, but in order to lay snares for the preacher, as the Jews did for the Son of God;" as much as to say, there was amongst them much of the spirit of contention, but little of the spirit of compunction. All of them in general, Manicheans and Vaudois, never ceased inveighing against human inventions, and citing the holy Scripture, whence they always had a text at hand upon all occasions.[227] When examined concerning faith, they eluded the question by equivocating; if reproved for this, it was Jesus Christ himself, said they, that taught them this practice when he said to the Jews: "Destroy this temple, and in three days I will raise it up;" meaning of the temple of his body what the Jews understood of that of Solomon. This text, to those that knew no better, seemed expressly made for their purpose. The Vaudois had a hundred others of this sort, which they were expert in wresting to their own purposes; and to those not thoroughly versed in Scripture, it was no easy matter to escape their snares. Another author[228] remarks a very singular character in these false professors of poverty. They did not proceed like a St. Bernard, like a St. Francis, like other apostolic preachers, and attack in the midst of the world the dissolute livers, the usurers, the gamesters, the blasphemers, and the like public sinners in order to convert them: on the contrary, whomsoever they found, in towns or villages that were peaceable and retired, it was into their houses they insinuated themselves under the covert of their exterior simplicity. Scarce durst they raise their voice, their meekness was so great: yet the topic of wicked priests and wicked monks was introduced forthwith: a keen and merciless satire put on the disguise of zeal; well-meaning people, that listened to them, were ensnared; and transported with this bitter zeal, imagined even they became better men by becoming heretics: thus an universal contagion diffused itself. Some were drawn into vice by the great scandals that appeared in the world on every side; the devil took in the simple after another manner; and, by a false horror of the wicked, alienated them from the Church, wherein the number of such was daily seen to increase.

145.—Eminent sanctity in the Catholic Church.

Nothing could be more unjust; since the Church far from approving the disorders which gave a handle to the revolt of heretics, by all her decrees detested them, and nourished at the same time in her bosom men of so eminent a holiness, that in comparison to it, all the virtue of these hypocrites appeared as nothing. St. Bernard alone, whom God raised in those days with all the graces of the Prophets and Apostles to combat these new heretics, when they were making their greatest efforts to spread themselves in France, was alone sufficient to confound them. In him might they behold a spirit truly apostolical, a sanctity of such a lustre, that even those whose errors he impugned were in admiration of it, insomuch that there were some of them who, whilst they wickedly anathematized the holy doctors, excepted St. Bernard from that sentence,[229] and thought themselves obliged to publish, that at last he had come over to their party; so much did they blush to have against them so great a witness. Amongst his other virtues, was seen to shine in him, and his brethren the holy monks of Cisteaux and Clairvaux, to mention nothing of the rest, that apostolic poverty these heretics boasted so much of; but St. Bernard and his disciples, notwithstanding they carried this poverty and Christian mortification to its utmost height, did not glory that they alone had preserved the Sacraments, nor were they the less obedient to superiors however wicked, distinguishing, with Jesus Christ, abuses from the chair and from doctrine.

146.—*Bitterness and presumption of Heretics.*

At the same time, great saints might be numbered, not only among the bishops, among the priests, among the monks, but also among the common people, and even amongst princes, in the midst of this worldly pomp; but heretics cared to look on nothing but vice, that they might say more boldly with the pharisee, "We are not as other men are;"[230] we are spotless, we are the poor beloved of God; come to us if you will receive the Sacraments.

147.—*Whether their false constancy ought to surprise us.—St. Bernard's memorable answer.*

One ought not, therefore, to be surprised at the apparent regularity of their manners, this being a part of that seduction against which we have been put on our guard by so many admonitions of the gospel. To finish the external piety of these heretics, this last stroke is added; that they suffered with a surprising patience. It is true, and this it is which completes the illusion. For the heretics of those times, and even the Manicheans, whose infamies we have beheld, after shifting and dissembling as long as ever they were able to escape punishment, when convicted, and condemned by the laws, ran to death with joy. Their false constancy amazed the world: Enervin, their accuser,[231] was nevertheless astonished, and inquired of St. Bernard with concern the meaning of such a prodigy. But the saint, too well versed in the deep wiles of Satan to be ignorant of his being able to make those he held captives mimic even martyrdom itself, answered, that by a just judgment of God, the evil one might have power, "Not only over the bodies of men, but also over their hearts;"[232] and if he was able to prevail with Judas to destroy himself, he might well work on these heretics to suffer death from the hands of others. Let us not, therefore, wonder, if we see martyrs of all religions, even of those the most monstrous, but let us learn from this example, to hold none for true martyrs but those who die in unity.

148.—*Inevitable condemnation of these Heretics, in that they denied their religion.*

But what ought to put Protestants for ever out of conceit with all these impious sects, is the detestable custom they had of denying their religion, and partaking outwardly of our worship whilst they rejected it in their hearts. It is certain the Vaudois, like the Manicheans, lived in this practice ever since the beginning of the sect, till towards the middle of the last century. Seyssel[233] could not sufficiently wonder at the false piety of their Barbes, who condemning even the minutest lies, as so many grievous sins, yet dreaded not, in presence of judges, to lie in point of faith, with an obstinacy so surprising, that the confession of it could scarcely be extorted from them by the most acute tortures. They forbade swearing, though even to bear witness to truth in courts of judicature; and at the same time stuck at no oath to conceal their sect and faith; a tradition they had received from the Manicheans, as they had also inherited from them their presumption and rancor. Men inure themselves to any thing, when once their guides have gained the ascendant over their minds; but especially when engaged in a cabal under the pretext of piety.

A HISTORY OF THE BOHEMIAN BRETHREN, VULGARLY AND FALSELY CALLED VAUDOIS.

149.—*The Sect of the Bohemian Brethren.*

We are now to speak of those who were falsely called Vaudois and Picards, and who called themselves the Brethren of Bohemia, or the Orthodox Brethren, or, barely, Brethren. They constitute a particular sect distinct from the Albigenses and the poor men of Lyons. When Luther rose up, he found some churches in Bohemia, and especially in Moravia, which he long detested. He approved afterwards of their confession of faith, corrected as we shall see. Bucer and Musculus have also bestowed great praises on them. The learned Camerarius, whom we have so much spoken of, that intimate friend of Melancthon, judged their history worthy to be written by his fine pen. His son-in-law, Rudiger,[234] though called by the Protestant churches of the Palatinate, preferred to them those of Moravia, and chose to be their minister; and of all the sects separated from Rome before Luther, this is the most commended by Protestants: but its birth and doctrine will soon evince that nothing could be drawn from it to their advantage.

150.—*They disown those who call them Vaudois, and why.*

As for is birth, many, led into a mistake by the name, and some conformity of doctrine, make these Bohemians descend from the ancient Vaudois: but for their part, they renounce this origin,[235] as appears clearly in the preface they prefixed to their Confession of Faith in 1572. There they set forth their origin in an ample manner, and say, amongst other things, that the Vaudois are more ancient than they; that these had, indeed, some churches dispersed in Bohemia when their own began first to appear, but they had no acquaintance with them; that nevertheless these Vaudois, in process of time, made themselves known to them, yet refused, say they, to make any deep research into their doctrine. "Our annals," continue they, "inform us they were never united to our churches, for two reasons: first, because they gave no testimony of their faith and doctrine; secondly, because, in order to keep peace, they made no difficulty of assisting at masses celebrated by those of the Church of Rome." Whence they concluded, not only "that they never had entered into any union with the Vaudois, but also, that they had always believed they could not enter into any such with a safe conscience." So far are these people from acknowledging a Vaudois extraction, that what is eagerly sought for by the Calvinists is rejected by them with scorn.

151.—*The sentiments of Camerarius and Rudiger.*

Camerarius writes the same thing in his history of the Bohemian brethren:[236] but Rudiger,[237] one of their pastors in Moravia, says, still more clearly, that "these churches are far different from those of the Vaudois; that the Vaudois were in being ever since the year 1160, whereas the Brethren did not begin to appear till the fifteenth century; and finally, that it is written in the annals of the Brethren, how they always with constancy refused to make any union with the Vaudois, because they did not give a full Confession of their faith, and went to Mass."

152—*The Vaudois disowned by the Brethren as well as the Picards.*

Accordingly, we see the Brethren, in all their synods and all their acts, style themselves the Brethren of Bohemia, falsely called Vaudois.[238] The name of Picards is still more detested by them: "It is very likely," says Rudiger, "that those, who first gave it to our ancestors, took it from a certain Picard, who, renewing the ancient heresy of the Adamites, introduced nudities, and shameful actions; and as this heresy penetrated into Bohemia about the time our churches were established, they were discredited by so infamous a title, as if we had been nothing but the miserable remains of that impure Picard."[239] You see thereby how these two pedigrees, from the Vaudois and the Picard, are rejected by the Brethren: "they account it even an affront to be called Picard and Vaudois;"[240] and if the first origin displeases them, the second, in which our Protestants glory, seems to them but little less shameful; but not we are going to see that which they give themselves is not much more reputable.

THE HISTORY OF JOHN WICKLIFF, AN ENGLISHMAN.

153.—*Wickliff's impious doctrine in his Trialogue.*

They boast of being the disciples of John Huss; but to judge of their pretension, we must ascend higher still, since John Huss himself gloried in having Wickliff for his master. What judgment we then ought to pass on Wickliff shall be showed in few words, without producing any other records than his own works, and the testimony of all candid Protestants.

The chief of all his works is the Trialogue, that famous book which set all Bohemia in a flame, and raised such troubles in England. This was the theology contained in it,[241] "That all happens by necessity; that he, a long while, spurned at this doctrine because it was contrary to the liberty of God; but, at last, was obliged to yield, and acknowledge at the same time, that all the sins committed in the world are necessary and inevitable:[242] that God could not prevent the sin of the first man, nor forgive it without Jesus Christ's satisfaction, but then it was impossible the Son of God should not become incarnate, should not satisfy, should not die: that God indeed might have done otherwise, had he willed it, but he could not will otherwise; that he could not but forgive man; that the sins of man proceeded from seduction and ignorance, and so it was requisite of necessity, that the divine wisdom should put on flesh to repair them. That Jesus Christ could not save the devils; that their sin was a sin against the Holy Ghost:[243] that to save them, it would have been necessary the Holy Ghost should have become incarnate, which was absolutely impossible; therefore, that[244] no possible means were left of saving the devils in general. That nothing was possible to God, but what actually came to pass; that the power admitted for things, which did not happen, was an illusion. That God can produce nothing within himself, which he does not necessarily produce, nor out of himself, which he does not likewise necessarily produce in its time. That when Jesus Christ said, he could ask of his Father more than twelve legions of angels, you must understand he could if he would, but must acknowledge at the same time he could not will it.[245] That the power of God is limited in the main, and is no otherwise infinite than because there is no greater power: in a word, that the world, and all which exists,[246] is of absolute necessity, and were there any thing possible that God should refuse a being to, he would be either impotent or envious; and as he could not refuse a being to any thing capable thereof, so can he annihilate nothing.[247] That we ought not to ask why God does not hinder sin—the reason is, because he cannot; nor, in general, why he does or does not such a thing—because he does necessarily all he can do; yet is he nevertheless free,[248] but in like manner, as he is free to produce his Son, whom nevertheless he produces necessarily. That the liberty, so called, of contradiction,[249] whereby you may do a thing or not do it,[250] is an erroneous term introduced by the doctors; and the imagination we have of our being free, is a perpetual illusion like to that of a child who thinks he walks alone whilst led: yet we deliberate,[251] we consult about our affairs, we damn our souls, but all this is inevitable, no less than all that is done or omitted in the world either by the creature,[252] or by God himself. That God has determined every thing, and necessitates as well the predestinated as the reprobate to all they do,[253] as also each particular creature to is several actions; and thence it happens that there are elect and reprobate; and thus it is not in God's power to save one single reprobate.[254] That he laughs at what is said in schools, *de sensu composito et diviso*, seeing that God can save none but such as are saved actually;[255] that there is a necessary consequence for sinning if certain things fall out; that God wills these things to happen, and that this consequence be good, because otherwise it would not be necessary: so he wills you should sin, and wills sin, on account of the good he draws from it; and although it does not please God that Peter should sin, yet the sin of Peter pleases him:[256] that God approves sinning; that he necessitates to sin. That man can do no better than he does; that sinners and the damned are nevertheless beholden to God, who shows mercy to the damned in giving them existence, which is more advantageous to, and to be wished for by them than non-existence: that indeed, he dares not wholly ascertain this opinion, nor push men on to sin by teaching that it is agreeable to God they should thus sin, and that God allows it them as a recompense; he being aware[257] that the wicked might take occasion, from this doctrine, to commit grievous crimes, which, if they may, they will commit: but if no better reasons are given him than what are commonly alleged, he shall abide confirmed in his sentiment without uttering a word."

You see thereby, he feels a secret horror of the blasphemies he vents; but he is hurried into them by the spirit of pride and singularity to which he had abandoned himself, nor does he know how to restrain the transports of his pen. This is a faithful extract of his blasphemies; they are reduced to two heads, to make a God overruled by necessity, and, what is a consequence from thence, a God, author and approver of all crimes; namely, a God whom the atheists would have reason to deny: so that the religion of so great a reformer is worse than atheism.

At the same time may be seen how many of his Dogmas were followed by Luther. As for Calvin and the Calvinists, we shall see them hereafter; nor, in this sense, is it in vain that they have reckoned this impious wretch among their predecessors.

154.—He imitates the false piety of the Vaudois.

In the midst of all these blasphemies, he was for imitating the false piety of the Vaudois, by attributing the effect of the sacraments to personal merit:[258] saying, "The keys did not operate except in the hands of holy persons; and those who do not imitate Jesus Christ cannot have the power of them: that, nevertheless, this power is not lost in the Church; that it subsists in the humble and unknown: that laymen may consecrate and administer the sacraments:[259] that it is a great crime in churchmen to possess temporal goods, a great crime in princes to have bestowed such on them, and not to employ their authority to take them from the clergy." Here you have in an Englishman, if I may be allowed to say it, the first pattern of the English Reformation, and church plundering. Some will say, it is self-interest we here combat for; no, we do but discover the mischievousness of extravagant minds, which as we see, are capable of every excess.

155.—Wickliff's Doctrine not calumniated at the Council of Constance.

M. la Roque pretends, Wickliff was calumniated at the Council of Constance,[260] and that propositions, which he did not believe, were laid to his charge, this amongst the rest: "God is obliged to obey the Devil." But we find so many blasphemies in one only work that remains of Wickliff, we may easily believe there were many others in his books, so very numerous at that time; and particularly as for this, it is a manifest consequence from the above doctrine, forasmuch as God, in all things acting by necessity, is drawn by the will of the devil to do certain things when obliged of necessity to concur to them.

156.—*Wickliff's pernicious Doctrine concerning Kings.*

Neither do we find, in the Trialogue, that proposition imputed to Wickliff,[261] "that a king ceased to be king by the commission of a mortal sin." There were other books enough of Wickliff whence this might be taken. In fact we have a conference between the Catholics of Bohemia and the Calixtins, in presence of King George Pogiebrac, wherein Hilary, Dean of Prague, maintains to Roquesane,[262] chief of the Calixtins, that Wickliff had written in express terms, "that an old woman might be king and pope, were she better and more virtuous than the pope and king; and in such cases, she might say to the king, '*Rise up, I am more worthy* than thou to sit upon the throne'." Upon Roquesane's answering this was not Wickliff's meaning, the same Hilary offered to show these propositions to the whole assembly, and this besides;[263] "that whosoever is, by his virtue, the most praiseworthy, is also the most worthy in dignity, and the most holy old woman ought to be placed in the most holy employment." Roquesane stood mute, and the fact passed for incontestable.

157.—*Such of Wickliff's Articles as were conformable to our Doctrine.*

The same Wickliff[264] consented to the invocation of saints, honored their images, acknowledged their merits, and believed in purgatory.

As for the Eucharist, what he most contended against was transubstantiation, which he said was the most detestable heresy that ever had been broached. Wherefore, it is his great article that bread is in this sacrament. With respect to the Real Presence, he has some things for, and some against it. He says, "The body is hidden in each morsel and crumb of bread." In another place, after saying according to his cursed maxim, that the sanctity of the minister is necessary to a valid consecration, he adds, "you must presume for the sanctity of priests; but," says he, "on account that we have but a bare probability of it, I adore conditionally the host which I see, and adore absolutely Jesus Christ who is in heaven." He does not, therefore, doubt of the Presence, but inasmuch as he is not certain of the holiness of the minister, which he believes absolutely necessary thereto. Other such like passages may be found in him, but it is of little consequence to know more of them.

158.—*Wickliff's Confession of Faith produced by M. de la Roque, son of the Minister.*

A fact of greater importance is advanced by M. la Roque, junior.[265] He produces a confession of faith, wherein the Real Presence is clearly owned, and transubstantiation no less clearly rejected; but most material of all is what he affirms, that this confession of faith was proposed to Wickliff in the Council of London, where happened that great earthquake, called for that reason *concilium terræ motus*; some saying the earth had a horror of the bishop's decision, and others, of Wickliff's heresy.

159.—*Proved false from Wickliff himself.*

But without further examination of this confession of faith, of which we shall speak with more certainty when we shall have seen it entire, I may venture to say beforehand, that it could not have been proposed to Wickliff by the council. I prove it from Wickliff himself,[266] who repeats four times, that "in the Council of London, where the earth trembled," *in suo concilio terræ motus*; it was defined in express terms, "that the substance of bread and wine did not remain after consecration;" wherefore it is more clear than the day, that the confession of faith wherein is rejected this change of substance, can never be of this council.

160.—*Wickliff renounces his Doctrine, and dies in the external Communion of the Church.*

I take M. la Roque for a man of too great sincerity not to yield to so clear a proof. Meanwhile, we are obliged to him for sparing us the trouble of proving here the faintheartedness of Wickliff; his recantation in the presence of the council; that "of his disciples, who at first had no more resolution than he; the shame he conceived at his dastardly comportment in departing from the notions then received,"[267] which made him break off all commerce with men; so that, since his retraction, you hear no more mention of him; and, finally, his dying in his cure, and in the exercise of his function, which proves, as also does his burial in hallowed ground, that he died externally in the communion of the Church.

I have, therefore, no more to do but conclude with this author, that Protestants can reap nothing but shame from Wickliff's conduct, "who either was an hypocritical prevaricator, or a Roman Catholic; who died in the church even whilst he assisted at the sacrifice accounted the mark of distinction between both parties."[268]

161.—*Melancthon's sentiment concerning Wickliff.*

Those who have a mind to know Melancthon's opinion of Wickliff, will find it in the preface to his "Commonplaces," where he says, "You may judge of Wickliff's spirit by the errors he abounds with. He understood nothing," says he, "of the justice of faith; he makes a jumble of gospel and politics; he maintains it unlawful for priests to have anything of their own; he speaks of the civil power after a seditious manner, and full of sophistry; with the same sophistry he cavils about the universally received opinion touching our Lord's Supper."[269] This is what Melancthon said, after reading Wickliff. He would have said more, and not spared this author, as well deciding against free-will, as making God the author of sin, had he not feared, in reproving him for these excesses, he should defame his master, Luther, under Wickliff's name.

THE HISTORY OF JOHN HUSS AND HIS DISCIPLES.

162.—*John Huss imitates Wickliff in his hatred of the Pope.*

What raised Wickliff to so high a station among the predecessors of our Reformed, was his teaching that the pope was antichrist, and that ever since the year of our Lord one thousand, when Satan was to be let loose, according to St. John's prophesy, the Church of Rome was become the whore of Babylon. John Huss, the disciple of Wickliff,[270] has merited the same honors, in having so closely followed his master in this doctrine.

163.—*John Huss says Mass, and has no other sentiments in respect of the Eucharist than those of the Church of Rome.*

In other points he forsook him. Heretofore there was a dispute concerning his sentiments on the Eucharist. But the question is adjudged by our adversaries' consent; M. la Roque having shown, in his history of the Eucharist,[271] from the authors of those times, from the testimony of Huss's first disciples, from his own writings, still extant, that he believed transubstantiation, and all the other articles of the Roman faith, not one excepted, unless communion under both kinds; and that he persisted in these sentiments even unto death. The same minister demonstrates the same thing in relation to Jerome of Prague, the disciple of John Huss, and the fact admits of no doubt.

164.—*Why Huss's Doctrine came to be doubted of.*

What gave occasion to doubt of John Huss, were some words he had uttered inconsiderately, and which were misunderstood, or retracted by him. But what more than all the rest caused him to be suspected in this matter was, the excessive praises he gave Wickliff, the enemy of transubstantiation. Wickliff, in reality, was the great doctor of John Huss and all the Hussite party; but certain it is, they did not follow his doctrine, crude as it was, but strove to explain it, as did John Huss, whom Rudiger[272] praises for having explained artfully, and courageously defended the sentiments of Wickliff. It was, therefore, agreed on in the party, that Wickliff, who, to speak the truth, was the head thereof, had carried matters much too far, and stood greatly in need of explanation. But however that may be, it is very certain John Huss gloried in his priesthood to the very last, and never intermitted saying Mass when able.

165.—*John Huss a Catholic in all the controverted points, except Communion under both kinds, and the Pope's authority.*

M. La Roque, junior, upholds strenuously his father's sentiments; and is even sincere enough to own, that "they are displeasing to several of the party, and especially to the famous Mr. ———, who generally did not relish truths which had escaped his notice."[273] Everybody knows it was Mr. Claude whose name he suppressed. But this young author carries his researches much farther than any Protestant has done before. None can any longer doubt, after

the proofs which he alleges, that John Huss prayed to saints, honored their images, acknowledged the merit of works, the seven sacraments, sacramental confession, and purgatory.[274] The dispute chiefly turned on communion under both kinds; and what was of the most importance, on that damnable doctrine of Wickliff, that authority, and especially ecclesiastical authority, was lost by sin; for John Huss maintained, on this head, things as extravagant as those advanced by Wickliff, and thence it was he drew his pernicious consequences.

166.—*All goes down with Protestants, provided you inveigh against the Pope.*

If, with such a doctrine, and saying Mass besides, every day to the end of his life, a man may not only be a true believer, but also a saint and martyr, (as all Protestants proclaim John Huss, no less than Jerome of Prague, his disciple,) there is no need of more disputing about fundamental articles: the only fundamental article is, to cry out amain against the Pope and his Church of Rome; but if with Wickliff and John Huss you stretch so far as to call that church the Church of Antichrist, this doctrine is the remission of all sins whatever, and covers all kinds of errors.

167.—*The Taborites.*

Let us return to the Brethren of Bohemia, and see how they are the disciples of John Huss. Immediately after his condemnation and execution, two sects were seen to arise under his name, the sect of Calixtins and the sect of Taborites: the Calixtins under Roquesane, who by the joint consent of all, as well Catholic as Protestant authors, was, under the pretext of reformation, the most ambitious of all mankind: the Taborites under Zisca, whose sanguinary actions are not less known than his valor and success. Without inquiring into the doctrine of the Taborites, their rebellions and cruelty have made them odious to the greatest part of Protestants. Men that carried fire and sword into the bowels of their country for twenty hears together, and whose marches may be traced by the blood and ashes they left behind, are not over qualified to be held for the principal defenders of the truth, nor to give an origin to Christian Churches.[275] Rudiger, who alone of the sect, for want of better knowledge, would have the Bohemian brethren descended from the Taborites,[276] acknowledges "that Zisca, pushed on by his particular enmities, carried the hatred he had against the monks and priests so far, that he not only set fire to churches and monasteries, wherein they served God, but also, in order to leave them no dwelling-place on earth, caused all the inhabitants of those places they possessed to be put to the sword." This is what Rudiger[277] says, an unsuspected author; to which he adds, that the brethren, whom he makes to descend from these barbarous Taborites, were ashamed of this parentage. Accordingly, they renounce it in all their Confessions of Faith and Apologies, and show even it is impossible they should have sprung from the Taborites,[278] because at the time they began to appear, this sect, in a manner crushed by the death of its generals and the universal pacification of the

Catholics and Calixtins, (who united the whole powers of the state in order to demolish them), "held but in a lingering state till Pogiebrac and Roquesane entirely brought their miserable remains to destruction; insomuch," say they, "that no more Taborites, were left on earth," which is confirmed by Camerarius in his history.[279]

168.—*The Calixtins.*

The other sect, that prided itself in the name of John Huss, was that of the Calixtins, so called, because they believed the Chalice was absolutely necessary for the people. And it is undoubtedly from this sect that the Brethren proceeded in 1457, as they themselves declared in the preface to their Confession of Faith of 1558, and again, in that of 1572, so frequently cited by us, where they speak in these terms, "Those who founded our Churches, separated themselves at that time from the Calixtins by a new separation;"[280] their meaning was, as by them explained in their apology of 1532, that as the Calixtins had separated themselves from Rome, so the Brethren separated from the Calixtins; so that this was a schism and division, in another division and schism. But what were the causes for this separation? there is no comprehending them aright without knowing both the belief and condition the Calixtins were in at that time.

169.—*The Compactatum or Articles agreed to by the Council of Basil.*

Their doctrine at first consisted in four articles. The first concerned the cup; the other three regarded the correction of public and particular sins, which they carried to some excess; the free preaching of the word of God, from which, they maintained, none could be precluded; and Church-revenues. Herein was a smack of the Vaudois errors. These four articles were regulated in the council of Basil, after such a manner as the Calixtins were contented with, and the cup granted them on certain terms which they agreed to. This agreement was called Compactatum, a name famous in the history of Bohemia. But one part of the Hussites, not resting contented with these articles, began, under the name of Taborites, those bloody wars just mentioned; and the Calixtins, the other part of the Hussites, which had accepted the agreement, stood not to it; for instead of declaring, as they had agreed at Basil, that the cup was neither necessary nor commanded by Jesus Christ, they pressed the necessity thereof, even in regard to new-baptized children.[281] This point excepted, it is allowed the Calixtins agreed in all dogmas with the Church of Rome, and their disputes with the Taborites prove as much. Lydius, a minister of Dort, has collected the acts thereof, which are not called in question by Protestants.

170.—*The Calixtins disposed to own the Pope.*

In them therefore it may be seen, that the Calixtins not only allow transubstantiation, but also with relation to the Eucharist, all and every part of the doctrine and usages received in the Church of Rome, communion only under both kinds excepted; and should that be granted by the Pope, they were ready to acknowledge his authority.[282]

171.—*Wherefore then did they so much respect the memory of Wickliff?*

Here the query might be put, their sentiments being such, how they could retain so great a respect for Wickliff as to call him by excellence, as the Taborites did, the evangelical doctor? the reason in short was, because we find nothing regular in these separated sects. Although Wickliff had inveighed with all the passion imaginable against the Church of Rome, and in particular against transubstantiation, the Calixtins excused him,[283] by answering, what he had said against this dogmas was not spoken decisively but scholastically, by way of dispute; whereby we may judge how easy a matter they found it to justify, say what you would, an author with whom they were infatuated.

172.—*The ambition of Roquesane and the Calixtins hinders their reunion with the Church.*

For all that, they were not the less disposed to submit to the Pope's authority, and Roquesane's interests alone prevented their reunion. This doctor had been contriving the reconciliation, in hopes, after so great a service, that the Pope would be easily inclined to confer on him the Archbishopric of Prague, which he much ambitioned.[284] But the Pope, unwilling to trust the care of souls and depositum of faith to so factious a person, invested Budvix with this prelacy, as much Roquesane's superior in merit as in birth. This ruined all. Bohemia saw herself reinvolved in more bloody wars than ever Roquesane, in spite of the Pope, set himself up for Archbishop of Prague, or rather for Pope in Bohemia; nor could Pogiebrac, whom he had raised to the throne by his intrigues, refuse him any thing.

173.—*Origins of the Bohemian Brethren, who separate from Roquesane and the Calixtins.*

During these disturbances, the tradesmen who had begun to grumble in the precedent reign, set themselves more than ever to confer among themselves concerning the Reformation of the Church. The Mass, transubstantiation, prayer for the dead, the veneration of saints, but especially the power of the Pope, were offensive to them. In fine, they complained that the "Calixtins romanized in every thing except the cup."[285] They undertook to correct them. Roquesane, incensed against the Holy See, seemed to them a proper instrument to manage this affair.[286] Shocked with his haughty answer, which savored of nothing but love of this world, they reproached him with his ambition; that he was a mere worldling, who would sooner abandon them than his honors. At the same time they placed at their head one Kelesiski, a master-shoemaker, who drew up for them a body of Doctrine called the Forms of Kelesiski. Afterwards they chose themselves a pastor named Matthias Convalde, a lay and ignorant person; and in 1467, divided openly from the Calixtins, as the Calixtins had done from Rome. Such was the birth of the

Bohemian Brethren; and this is what Camerarius and they themselves, as well in their Annals as in their Apologies and Prefaces to their Confessions of Faith, relate of their origin, except that they date their separation from the year 1457; and it seems to me more proper to fix it ten years after, in 1467, at the time they themselves date the creation of their new pastors.

174.—*Weak beginnings of this Sect.*

I find here some little contradiction between what they relate of their history in their Apology of 1532, and what they say in the Preface of 1572.[287] For they say in this Preface that in 1457, at the time they separated from the Calixtins, they were a people collected from all manner of degrees: and in their Apology of 1532, wherein they were somewhat less assuming, they own frankly,[288] they were made up "of the meaner sort, and of some Bohemian priests in small number, all put together but a handful of men, a small remnant, and the despicable refuse," or, translate it as you please, "*Miserabilis quisquiliæ* , left in the world by John Huss." Thus did they separate from the Calixtins, that is, from the only Hussites then in being. Thus it is that they are the disciples of John Huss; a piece broken from a piece; a schism cut off from a schism; Hussites divided from Hussites, and retaining scarce any thing of them but their disobedience and rupture from the Church of Rome.

175.—*They only took the name of John Huss, and followed not his Doctrine.*

Should it be asked, how they could own John Huss, as they every where do, for an evangelical doctor, for a holy martyr, for their master, and the apostle of the Bohemians, and at the same time reject, as sacrilegious, the Mass, which their apostle constantly said to the last, Transubstantiation, and the other dogmas he had always adhered so closely to: their answer is "that John Huss had but begun the re-establishment of the gospel," and they believed, "had time been given him, he would have changed a great deal more."[289] Still he failed not to be a martyr and apostle, though he persevered, according to them, in such damnable practices, and the Brethren celebrated his martyrdom in their churches the eighth of July, as we are informed by Rudiger.[290]

176.—*Their extreme ignorance, and their presumption in pretending to rebaptize the whole world.*

Camerarius[291] acknowledges their extreme ignorance, but says what he can in excuse thereof. This we may hold for certain, that God wrought no miracles to enlighten them. So many ages after the question of rebaptizing heretics had been determined by the unanimous consent of the whole Church, they were so ignorant as to rebaptize "all those that came to them from other churches." They persisted in this error for the space of a hundred years, as they own in all their writings, and confess in the preface of 1558, that it was but a little while since they were undeceived.[292] This error ought not to be deemed of trivial importance, since it amounted to this, that Baptism was lost

in the Universal Church, and remained only amongst them. Thus presumptuous in their notions were two or three thousand men, who had more or less
equally revolted against the Calixtins, amongst whom they had lived, and
against the Church of Rome, from which both of them had divided thirty or
forty years before. So small a parcel of another parcel, dismembered so few
years from the Catholic Church, dared to rebaptize the remainder of the
universe, and reduce the inheritance of Jesus Christ to a corner of Bohemia!
They believed themselves therefore the only Christians, since they believe that
they only were baptized; and whatever they might allege in their own
vindication, their rebaptization condemned them. All they had to answer was,
if they rebaptized the Catholics, the Catholics also rebaptized them. But it is
well enough known, that the Church of Rome never rebaptized any that had
been baptized by any person whatsoever, "in the name of Father, Son, and
Holy Ghost;" and supposing there had been, in Bohemia, such very ignorant
Catholics as not to know so notorious a thing, ought not they, who called
themselves their Reformers, to know better? After all, how came it to pass that
these new rebaptizers did not cause themselves to be rebaptized? If, at their
coming into the world, Baptism had ceased throughout all Christendom, that
which they had received was no higher in value than that of their neighbors,
and by invalidating the Baptism of those by whom they were baptized, what
became of their own? They were then obliged no less to cause themselves to
be rebaptized, than to rebaptize the rest of the universe: and in this there was
but one inconveniency; namely, that, according to their principles, there was
not a man on earth that could do them this good turn, Baptism being equally
null whatever side it came from. Thus it is when a shoemaker commences as
Reformer, one, as themselves acknowledge in a Preface to their Confession of
Faith,[293] that knew not a word of Latin, and was no less presumptuous than
ignorant. These are the men whom Protestants admire. Does the question turn
on condemning the Church of Rome?—they never cease to upbraid her with
the ignorance of her priests and monks. Is the question regarding the ignorant
individuals of these latter ages, who have set up for reforming the Church by
schism?—they are fishermen turned apostles: although their ignorance stand
eternally on record, from the first step they took. No matter; if we believe the
Lutherans in the preface they placed before the Brethren's Apology, and
printed at Wittenberg in Luther's time; if, I say, we believe them, it was in
this ignorant society, in this handful of men, that "The Church of God was
preserved when she was thought entirely lost."[294]

177.—*Their fruitless search over all the universe after a Church of their Belief.*

Nevertheless, these remains of the Church, these depositaries of the ancient
Christianity, were themselves ashamed that they could not discover in the
whole universe a Church of their belief. Camerarius informs us,[295] that it
entered into their thoughts at the beginning of their separation, to make
inquiry if they could find in some place of the earth, and chiefly in Greece or
Armenia, or some other part of the east, that Christianity, of which the west

was utterly bereft according to their sentiments. At that time, many Grecian priests, who had fled to Bohemia from the sacking of Constantinople, and to whom Roquesane gave reception in his own house, had leave to celebrate the holy mysteries according to the rites of their Church. Therein the Brethren beheld their own condemnation, and beheld it still more in conversing with those priests. But notwithstanding these Grecians assured them it was in vain for them to travel into Greece in quest of Christians formed to their mode, whom they never would find; yet they appointed three deputations of able and discreet persons, whereof some traversed all the east, others went northwards into Muscovy, and others turned their course towards Palestine and Egypt; whence all meeting at Constantinople, according to the project concerted by them, they returned at last to Bohemia, and all the answer they brought to their brethren was, that they might depend upon it there were none of their profession in the whole universe.

178.—*How they sought Orders in the Catholic Church.*

Their solitude, thus destitute of all succession and lawful ordination, raised such a horror in them, that even in Luther's time they sent some of their people, who surreptitiously stole Ordination from the Church of Rome; we learn this from one of Luther's treatises, which is quoted in another place. A poor church indeed, which, void of the principle of fecundity left by Jesus Christ to the apostles and their legitimate successors, were forced to intrude themselves amongst us to beg, or rather to purloin, sacred orders.

179.—*Reproaches made them by Luther.*

Besides, they were upbraided by Luther[296] that they knew nothing, no more than John Huss, of Justification, the very principal point of the Gospel; for they "placed it," he proceeds, "in faith and works together, as many fathers had done; and John Huss was wedded to this opinion." He was in the right; for neither the Fathers, nor John Huss, nor his master Wickliff, neither orthodox, nor heretics, nor Albigenses, nor Vaudois, had ever, before him, dreamed of his "imputed justice." Wherefore he despised the Brethren of Bohemia, "as men serious, rigid, of an austere countenance, that martyred themselves with the law and works, and never enjoyed a cheerful conscience."[297] Thus did Luther treat the most regular, to all appearance, of all the schismatic Reformers, and, as was said, the sole remnant of the true Church. But he had soon reason to be satisfied with them: the Brethren carried Lutheran Justification so far, as to run blindly into the excesses of the Calvinists, and even into such as the Calvinists now-a-days strive to clear themselves from. The Lutherans would have us justified without our co-operation, and without our having part therein. The Brethren added, it was even "without our knowledge and feeling it, as an embryo is quickened in its mother's womb."[298] After our regeneration, God begins to make himself felt; and if Luther would have us know with certainty our Justification, the brethren still further would have us entirely and indubitably assured of our perseverance and salvation. They went so far with the imputation of justice as to say, that "sins, how enormous so ever, were but venial," provided you committed them "with repugnance," and that it was of these sins St. Paul said, "there is now no condemnation to them which are in Christ Jesus."[299]

180.—Their Doctrine concerning the Seven Sacraments.

The Brethren had, like us, Seven Sacraments in the Confession of 1504, which was presented to King Ladislaus. They proved them from the Scriptures, and acknowledged them "established for the accomplishment of the promises God had made to the faithful." They must have preserved this doctrine of the Seven Sacraments even in Luther's day, since he blamed them for it. The Confession of Faith was therefore reformed, and the Sacraments were reduced to two: Baptism and the Supper, as Luther had ordained. Absolution was acknowledged, but not in quality of a Sacrament. In 1504, they spoke of the confession of sins as a thing of obligation. This obligation does no longer appear so express in the Reformed Confession, where it is merely said, "You ought to demand of the priest absolution of your sins by the keys of the Church, and obtain the forgiveness of them by this ministry ordained for that end by Jesus Christ."[300]

181.—Concerning the Real Presence.

As for the Real Presence, the defenders of the literal and the figurative sense have equally striven to turn to their advantage the Bohemian Confession of Faith.[301] For my part, the thing being indifferent to me, I shall only report their words, and here is what at first they wrote to Roquesane, as they themselves set forth in their Apology: "We believe that we receive the body and blood of our Lord under the species of bread and wine." And a little further on: "We are none of those who, ill understanding the words of our Lord, say, he has given us consecrated bread as a memorial of his body, which he pointed at with his finger, saying, 'This is my body.' Others say, this bread is the body of our Lord who is in heaven, but significantly. All these expositions appear to us far remote from Jesus Christ's intention, and are very displeasing to us."

182.—Sequel.

In their Confession of Faith of the year 1504, they speak thus: "As often as a worthy priest, with a faithful people, pronounces these words, 'This is my body, this is my blood,' the bread present is the body of Jesus Christ which was offered for us to death, and the wine his blood shed for us; and this body and this blood are present under the species of bread and wine in memory of his death." And to show the firmness of their faith, they add, they would believe as much of a stone, had Jesus Christ said it was his body.[302]

183.—They make the Sacrament depend on the merit of the minister.

Hitherto we see the same language as is used by Catholics; we see the body and blood "under the species" immediately after the words, and we see them there, not in figure, but in truth. What they have peculiar to them, is their requiring these words should be pronounced by a worthy priest. This is what they add to the Catholic doctrine. To accomplish the work of God, in the Eucharistic bread, Jesus Christ's words did not suffice, but the minister's merit was also necessary; this is what they had learned from John Wickliff and John Huss.

184.—Strong expression in favor of the Reality.

They repeat the same thing in another place: "When," say they, "a worthy priest prays with his faithful people and says, 'This is my body, this is my blood,' immediately the bread present is the same body which was given up to death, and the wine present is his blood which was shed for our redemption."[303] It is therefore plain they change nothing in the Catholic doctrine as to the real presence; on the contrary, they seem to make choice of the strongest terms to confirm it, by saying, "that immediately after the words, the bread is the true body of Jesus Christ, the same that was born of the Virgin, and was to be given up to crucifixion; and the wine his true natural blood, the same which was to be shed for our sins, and all this without delay, at the very instant, with a presence most real and true, *præsentissime,* as they speak." And the figurative sense appeared to them, say they, "so odious in one of their synods, that a certain person called John Czizco, one of theirs who had dared to maintain it, was expelled out of their communion." They add that divers writings have been published by them against this presence in sign, and those that defend it hold them for their adversaries, call them Papists, Antichrists, and Idolaters.[304]

185.—The same thing confirmed.

Another proof of their sentiment is a saying of theirs, "that Jesus Christ is present in the bread and wine by his body and blood; otherwise," proceed they, "neither those that are worthy would receive any thing but bread and wine, nor those that are unworthy would be guilty of the body and blood, it being impossible they should be guilty of what is not there."[305] Whence it follows that they are there, not only for the worthy, but also for the unworthy.

186.—Their manner of refusing Adoration confirms their Belief of the Reality, even out of the Reception.

True it is, they are against our adoring Jesus Christ in the Eucharist for two reasons: first, because he has not commanded it; secondly, because there are two presences of Jesus Christ, his personal, corporeal, and sensible presence, which ought to attract our adoration; and his spiritual or sacramental presence, which ought not to attract it. But for all this, they nevertheless acknowledge the substance of the body of Jesus Christ in the Sacrament: "we are not commanded," say they, "to honor this substance of the body of Jesus Christ consecrated, but the substance of Jesus Christ which is at the right hand of the Father."[306] Here, then, have you, in the Sacrament and in heaven, the substance of Jesus Christ's body, but adorable in heaven and not so in the Sacrament. And, lest you should wonder at this, they add, "that Jesus Christ would not even oblige men to adore him on earth when he was there present, because he waited the time of his glory;"[307] which shows their intention was not to exclude the substantial presence, when they exclude adoration; on the contrary, they supposed it, since, had they not believed it, they would have had no manner of occasion to excuse themselves for not adoring in the Sacrament what, in reality, was not there.

Let us not inquire of them now, whence they learned this rare doctrine; that, to adore Jesus Christ, it is not sufficient we know him present, and that it was not his intention we should adore him on earth, but only in his glory: I am satisfied with relating what they say of the Real Presence, nay, of the Real Presence not after the manner of the Melancthonists, in the sole use, but immediately after the Consecration.

187.—*Their uncertainty and affected Ambiguities.*

With these expression apparently so distinct and so decisive for the Real Presence, in other places they confound themselves after so strange a manner, that it seems as if they feared nothing so much as leaving a clear and certain testimony of their faith: for they repeat continually that Jesus Christ is not in the Eucharist in person.[308] It is true, they call his being there in person, being there sensibly and corporally: expressions which they always link together, and oppose to a spiritual manner of being, acknowledged by them. But what casts them into a new confusion, is that they seem to say, [309] Jesus Christ is present in the Eucharist with this spiritual Presence, as he is in Baptism and in preaching the word, as he was eaten by the ancient Hebrews in the desert, as St. John the Baptist was Elias. Nor do I comprehend what they mean by this odd expression:[310] Jesus Christ is not here "with his natural body after an existing and corporeal manner, *existenter et corporaliter*," but is here[311] "spiritually, powerfully, by way of benediction, and in virtue; *spiritualiter potenter, benedicte, in virtue.*" What they add is not intelligible, that "Jesus Christ is here in the abode of benediction," to wit, according to their language, he is in the Eucharist, "as he is at the right hand of God, but not as he is in the heavens." If he be there as he is at the right hand of God, he is there in person. Thus naturally should one conclude: but how shall we distinguish the heavens from the right hand of God? there we are at a loss. The Brethren spoke distinctly when they said: "There is but one Lord, Jesus Christ, who is the same in the Sacrament with his natural body, but who is after another manner at the right hand of his Father: for it is one thing to say, there is Jesus Christ, this is my body; and another to say, he is there after such a manner."[312] But no sooner had they expressed themselves in plain terms, than they bewilder themselves in strange subtilized notions, into which they are plunged by the confusion and uncertainty of their minds and thoughts, together with a vain desire of contenting both parties of the Reformation.

188.—The Lutherans and Calvinists both strive to draw them to their side.— They incline to the first.

The more forward they advanced, the more important and mysterious they became; and as the Lutherans and Calvinists strove each to gain them, so they also, on their side, seemed inclined to content both parties. At length this is what they said in 1558, and what they appeared resolved to stand by. They complain, at first, they were accused "of not believing that the presence of the true body and true blood was present."[313] What odd expressions, presence to be present! thus they speak in the preface; but teach in the body of the Confession, that it ought to be acknowledged that the bread is the true body of Jesus Christ, and the cup his true blood, without adding any thing of your own to his words. But whilst they forbid adding any thing to the words of Jesus Christ, they themselves add to them the word *true*, which is not there; and whereas Jesus Christ said, "This is my body," they suppose he said, "This bread is my body;" a very different thing, as elsewhere you may have seen. Now if it were allowable in them to add what they judged necessary to denote a true presence, it was no less allowable in others to add also what was requisite to remove all ambiguity; and to reject these expressions after disputes had arisen, was opposing light, and leaving the questions undecided. It was for this reason Calvin[314] wrote to them, that he could not approve of their obscure and captious brevity, and required them to explain how the bread is the body of Jesus Christ; which, should they fail to do, he maintained their confession of faith could not be subscribed without peril, and would occasion great disputes. But Luther was satisfied with them, as they approximated near to his expressions, and were more inclined towards the Confession of Augsburg. For they even continued to complain of those,[315] who denied that the bread and wine were the true body and true blood of Jesus Christ, and who called them Papists, Idolaters, and Antichrists, on account of their acknowledging the true presence. Finally, to show how far they were leaning to the side of the Real Presence, they enjoin their ministers, in distributing this sacrament,[316] and in reciting the words of our Lord, "to exhort the people to believe that the presence of Jesus Christ is present;" and in this view they enjoin, likewise, although in other respects little inclined to adoration, "That the sacrament be received kneeling."

189.—Luther gives them his approbation, and how.

By thus expounding and thus palliating as already seen, they so contented Luther, that he prefixed his approbation to a confession of faith published by them,[317] declaring, however, "That for this time they not only appeared more adorned, more free, and more polished, but also more considerable and better;" which sufficiently intimates, he approved their confession only inasmuch as it had been reformed agreeably to his maxims.

190.—*Their Festivals, their Churches, their Fasts, the Celibacy of their Priests.*

It does not appear that any uneasiness was given them in regard of the stated fasts preserved amongst them, nor in regard of the festivals they celebrated, forbidding all labor, not only in honor of our Lord, but also of the Blessed Virgin and the Saints. They were not upbraided that this was observing days contrary to the precept of the Apostle, nor that these holy days in honor of the saints were so many acts of idolatry. Neither were they accused of raising churches to saints, under the pretext that they continued, as we do, to name the Church of the Virgin, *in Templo divæ Virginis*, of St. Peter, of St. Paul, churches consecrated to God in memory of them. They are likewise suffered to enjoin their priests celibacy, and degrade them from priesthood upon marrying, for this unquestionably was their practice no less than that of the Taborites.[318] All this is harmless in the Brethren; in us only every thing is rank poison.

191.—*The perpetual Virginity of Mary, Mother of God.*

I would also have them asked, where they find in Scripture what they say of the blessed Virgin: "that she was a Virgin before and after her delivery."[319] It is true, this was the belief of the holy fathers, and the contrary rejected by them for no less than an execrable blasphemy; yet does it, nevertheless, evince that many things may be accounted blasphemies, the contrary to which is nowhere in holy writ; so that, when they boast of speaking nothing but from Scripture, they really mean no more by it than that it serves their turn to talk in this strain: nor is this apparent respect for the Scripture anything in them but a blind to the ignorant and simple.

192.—*They fly for shelter into Poland.*

It is averred that these Bohemian brethren (whose words were so meek and respectful in regard of higher powers) the more they engaged in the Lutheran sentiments, so likewise the more did they enter into their intrigues and wars. Ferdinand found them mingled in the Elector of Saxony's rebellion against Charles the Fifth, and drove them from Bohemia.[320] They took sanctuary in Poland, and it appears, from a letter of Musculus to the Protestants of Poland, in 1556, that it was but a few years since these fugitives from Bohemia were received into that kingdom.

193.—*There they unite with the Lutherans and Zuinglians in the Assembly of Sendomir.*

Some time after this, the union of the three Protestant sects of Poland was brought about, namely, of the Lutherans, the Bohemians, and the Zuinglians. The act of union was passed in 1570, at the Synod of Sendomir, and bears this title: "The union and mutual agreement made between the Churches of Poland; to wit, between those of the Augsburg Confession, those of the Confession of the Bohemian Brethren, and those of the Confession of the Helvetic churches, or Zuinglians."[321] In this act the Bohemians style themselves the Brethren of Bohemia, whom the ignorant call Vaudois. It appears then manifestly that the question here was about those Vaudois who, by mistake, were named so, as we have shown, and who accordingly disclaim this origin. For, with respect to the ancient Vaudois, we learn from an old author,[322] that there were scarce any of them in the kingdom of Cracovia, namely in that of Poland, no more than in England, in the Low Countries, in Denmark, in Sweden, in Norway, and in Prussia; and since this author's time, this little number is so dwindled away to nothing, that, in all these countries, we hear no more mention of them.

194.—*Terms of the Sendomir Agreement.*

The agreement was made in these terms. In order to explain therein the point concerning the Supper, the whole article of the Saxonic Confession, where this matter is handled, was there transcribed. We have seen that Melancthon drew up this Confession in 1551 in order to have it presented at Trent. In it was said, that "Jesus Christ is truly and substantially present in the Communion, and is given truly to those who receive the body and blood of Jesus Christ."[323] To which they add, in a strange manner of expression, "That the substantial presence of Jesus Christ is not only signified, but truly rendered present, distributed, and given to those who eat; the signs not being naked, but joined to the thing itself, agreeably to the nature of the sacraments."[324]

195.—*In this agreement the Zuinglians, more than all the rest, recede from their particular tenets.*

"The substantial presence," it seems, was had very much at heart, when in order to inculcate it the more forcibly, they said, it was not only signified but truly present; but I always distrust these strong expressions of the Reformation, which the more she diminishes the truth of the body and blood in the Eucharist, the more rich is she always in words; as if she could repair by them the loss she sustains in things. Now, when you come to the point, although this declaration abounds with equivocal expressions, and leaves subterfuges to each party whereby to preserve their particular doctrine; it is, nevertheless, the Zuinglians that take the greatest step, since whereas they said in their confession that the body of our Lord being in heaven absent from us, becomes present to us only by its virtue, the terms of the agreement import, that Jesus Christ is substantially present to us; and notwithstanding all the rules of human language, a presence in virtue becomes immediately a presence in substance.

196.—*Wherein the Lutherans recede, yet may still come off.*

There are terms in the agreement which it were difficult for the Lutherans to reconcile to their doctrine, did not men inure themselves, in the new Reformation, to expound every thing to their own sense. For instance, they seem much to depart from the belief they are in, that the body of Jesus Christ is taken by the mouth even by the unworthy, when they say in this agreement, "The signs of the Supper give by Faith to the Believers, what they signify."[325] But, besides that they may say they spoke in this manner, by reason that the real presence is not known but by faith; they may also add that, in fact, there are blessings in the Supper which are given to the Believers only, as life eternal, and the nourishment of the soul, and it is those they mean when they say, "The signs given by Faith, what they signify."

197.—Disposition of the Bohemian Brethren.

I do not wonder the Bohemians signed this agreement without difficulty. Separated about forty or fifty years before from the Catholic church, and reduced to allow Christianity in no part of the world except a corner of Bohemia, which they inhabited, upon seeing the Protestants appear, all they thought of was to support themselves with their protection. They knew how to gain Luther by their submission; by equivocating, they had all that could be desired from Bucer; the Zuinglians suffered themselves to be soothed by the general expressions of the Brethren, who said, yet without practising it, that nothing ought to be added to the words our Saviour used. The most difficult to be pleased was Calvin. We have seen in the letter[326] he wrote to the Bohemian Brethren, who had taken refuge in Poland, how he blamed the ambiguity of their confession of faith, and declared there was no subscribing it without opening an inlet to dissension or error.

198.—Reflections on this Union.

Contrary to his judgment, all was subscribed, the Helvetic Confession, the Bohemian, and the Saxonic, the presence of substance together with that of virtue only; namely, the two contrary doctrines with their equivocations favoring them both. All whatever they pleased was added to our Lord's words, even at the time they ratified the Confession of Faith, wherein was laid down for a maxim, that nothing ought to be added to them: all passed, and a peace was concluded by this means. You see how all the sects, divided from Catholic unity, separate and unite among themselves; separating from the chair of St. Peter, they separate from one another, and bear the just punishment of despising the band of their unity. When they re-unite in appearance, they are never the more united in the main; and their union, cemented only by political interests, serves but to evidence, by a new proof, that they have not so much as the idea of Christian unity, since they never do unite in one accord, in one mind, as St. Paul ordains.[327]

199.—General Reflections on the history of all these sects.

May it be allowed us at present to make a few reflections on this history of the Vaudois, the Albigenses, and the Bohemians. You see whether the Protestants were right in reckoning them among their ancestors; whether this extraction be to their credit; and in particular whether they ought to have looked on Bohemia, since the time of John Huss, as the mother of the reformed churches.[328] It is clearer than the sun, on one side, that they only bring in these sects from the necessity of finding witnesses in the foregoing ages for what they believe to be the truth; and on the other, that nothing is more despicable than to allege such witnesses as are all convicted of falsehood in capital points, and who, in the main, neither agree with Protestants, nor with us, nor with themselves. This is the first reflection Protestants should make.

200.—*Another Reflection, that these Sects so contrary, all ground themselves on the evidence of Scripture.*

The second is of no less importance. They ought to consider that all these sects, so different from one another, and withal so opposite as well to us as to Protestants, agree with them in the common principle of guiding themselves by the Scriptures: not, indeed, as the Church in all times has understood and still understands them—for this is a most certain rule; but as every man of himself is capable of understanding them. This is what has produced all those errors and all those contrarieties which we have observed. Under the pretext of Scripture, every man has followed his own notions; and the Scripture, taken in this way, so far from uniting minds, has divided them, and made very one worship the delusions of his own brain, under the name of the eternal truth.

201.—*Last and most important Reflection concerning the accomplishment of St. Paul's prediction.*

But there still remains the last and by much the most important reflection to be made on all these things we have just seen in this contracted history of the Albigenses and Vaudois. There we discover the reason of the Holy Ghost's inspiring St. Paul with this prophecy: "the spirit speaketh expressly, that, in the latter times, some shall depart from the faith, giving heed to seducing spirits, and doctrines of devils; speaking lies in hypocrisy, having their conscience seared with a hot iron; forbidding to marry, and commanding to abstain from meats, which God hath created to be received with thanksgiving: for it is sanctified by the word of God and prayer."[329] All the holy fathers are agreed that this is meant of the impious sect of Marcionites and Manicheans, who taught two principles, and attributed to the *evil* one the creation of the universe; which made them detest the propagation of mankind, and the use of many kinds of food which they believed unclean and bad in their nature, as being produced by a creator who himself was bad and impure. St. Paul points, therefore, at these accursed sects by these two their so noted tenets; and without previously mentioning the principle whence they drew these two evil consequences, he expresses the two sensible characters whereby we have seen that these infamous sects were known in all times.

202.—*The Doctrine of the two Principles pointed out by St. Paul; why this Doctrine is called the Doctrine of Devils.*

But although St. Paul does not immediately express the deep cause why these deceivers forbade the use of two things so natural, he denotes it sufficiently further on, when he says, in opposition to these errors, that "every creature of

God is good,"[330] overthrowing by this principle the detestable sentiment of
those that descried impurity in the works of God, and making us withal
sensible that the root of this lay in not knowing the creation, and in
blaspheming the Creator. Accordingly, it is what St. Paul calls, in particular,
more than all other doctrines, "the doctrine of devils,"[331] there being
nothing more suitable to the jealousy against God and against men of these
seducing spirits, than to attack the creation, condemn God's works, blaspheme
against the author of the law and the law itself, and defile human nature with
all manner of impurities and illusions. For this is what Manicheism consisted
in, and what truly is the very doctrine of devils; especially if you add these
enchantments and impostures, which all authors testify were so frequently
made use of in this sect. To wrest now the so plain and so natural sense of St.
Paul, against those who, acknowledging both marriage and all sort of meats for
the work and institution of God, yet abstain voluntarily from them to mortify
the senses and purify the mind, is a too manifest delusion, and one which we
have seen long ago exploded by the Fathers. It is, then, very perceptible
whom St. Paul aimed at, nor is it possible to mistake those he has so accurately
described by their proper characters.

203.—*Query, why the Holy Ghost, of all heresies, has only in particular foretold
Manicheism.—Character of this heresy.—Hypocrisy.—Spirit of Lying.—
Conscience cauterized.*

Why the Holy Ghost, amongst so many heresies, would only mark this so
expressly, was the admiration of the fathers, and what they endeavored to
account for, in the best way they could in their age. But time, the faithful
interpreter of prophecies, has discovered to us the deep cause; nor shall we
wonder any more that the Holy Ghost was so particularly careful to forewarn
us against this sect, after having seen it was this that infected Christianity the
longest and the most dangerously; the longest, through so many ages as we
have seen the world infected by it; and the most dangerously, not making a
glaring breach from the Church like the rest, but lurking as much as was
possible, within her precincts, and insinuating herself under the appearances of
the same faith, the same worship, and even an astonishing show of piety. For
this reason St. Paul,[332] the apostle, so expressly points out its hypocrisy.
Never has the spirit of lying, remarked by this apostle, been so justly charged
on any sect, since besides its teaching, like the rest, a false doctrine, it
exceeded all others in dissembling its belief. We have observed, that these
wretches allowed every thing you pleased; they made nothing of lying in the
most material points; they stuck not at perjury to conceal their tenets; their
readiness in betraying their consciences showed in them a certain insensibility
which St. Paul admirably well expresses by the *cautery*[333] which renders the
flesh insensible by mortifying it, as the learned Theodoret[334] hath observed
on this place; nor do I think ever prophesy could have been verified by more
sensible characters than this has been.

204.—Sequel of the reasons why the Holy Ghost has pointed out this heresy more than the rest.

No longer are we to wonder why the Holy Ghost would have the prediction of this heresy to be so particular and distinct. It was more than all other heresies the error "of the latter times," as it is called by St. Paul,[335] whether we understand by the latter times, according to the Scripture style, all the times of the new law; or understand by that period of ages when Satan was to be loosed anew.[336] So long since as the second and third century, the Church beheld the rise of Cerdon, of Marcion, of Manes, those enemies to the Creator.[337] The seeds of this doctrine are every where to be met with; you find them in Tatian, who condemned wine and marriage; and in his Concordance of the Bible had erased all the texts that expressed Jesus Christ's genealogy from the blood of David. A hundred other infamous sects had attacked the God of the Jews even before Manes and Marcion; and we learn from Theodoret, that this last did but give another turn to the impieties of Simon the magician. Thus did this heresy commence from the very beginning of Christianity; it was the true "mystery of iniquity"[338] which fell to work in St. Paul's time; but the Holy Ghost who foresaw this pestilence was one day to rage in a more glaring manner, made it be foretold by this apostle with an astonishing evidence and distinctness. Marcion and Manes have set this mystery of iniquity in a more manifest light; the abominable sect has continued its pestilent succession ever since that time. This we have seen, and never did heresy disturb the Church for a longer date, nor spread its branches to a greater distance. But after that, by the eminent doctrine of St. Austin, by St. Leo's and St. Galasius's great care and diligence, it was extinguished every where in the West, and even in Rome, where it had strove to establish itself; then was seen to arrive the fatal time of Satan's being loosed "out of his prison."[339] A thousand years after this strong armed had been bound by Jesus Christ at his coming into the world, the spirit of error grew up more than ever; the remains of Manicheism, too well sheltered in the East, broke in upon the Latin Church. What hinders our looking on those miserable times as one of the periods of Satan's being loosed, without prejudice to the other more hidden meanings?[340] If Gog and Magog only be wanting to fulfil this prophecy, we shall find in Armenia, near Samosata, the province named Gogarene, where the Paulicians dwelt, and Magog amongst the Scythians, from whence the Bulgarians took their rise. Thence came those numberless enemies of "the beloved city,"[341] who first assaulted Italy. The contagion flew, in an instant, to the extremity of the north: a spark raises a great combustion; the flame almost spreads over the whole face of the universe. In all parts of it is discovered this lurking poison; Arianism, with all kinds of heresies, together with Manicheism, shoot up again under a hundred unheard of and uncouth names. Scarcely could it be compassed to quench this fire in the space of three or four hundred years, and even some of its remains might be seen in the fifteenth century.

205.—How the Vaudois came from the Albigensian Manicheans.

Nor did the evil cease, when nothing seemed left of it but its ashes. Satan had supplied the impious sect wherewith to renew the conflagration, in a manner more dangerous than ever. Church discipline was relaxed over all the earth; the disorder and abuses, carried even to the foot of the altar, made the good to sigh, humbled them, urged them on to improve still more in their virtuous courses; but wrought a far different effect on haughty minds. The Roman Church, the mother and bond of churches, became the object of hatred to all indocile tempers; envenomed satires spirit up the world against the clergy; the Manichean hypocrite trumpets them over the whole universe, and gives the name of Antichrist to the Church of Rome, for then was that notion broached in the sink of Manicheism, and amidst the precursors of Antichrist himself. These impious men imagine they appear more holy, when they say, holiness is essentially requisite to the administration of the Sacraments. The ignorant Vaudois swallow down this poison. No longer will they receive the sacraments from odious and defamed ministers; "the net is broken"[342] on all sides, and schisms multiply. Satan no longer stands in need of Manicheism; hatred against the Church is widely diffused; the viperous sect has left a brood like to itself, and a too fruitful principle of schism. No matter, though these heretics have not the same doctrine, they are swayed by hatred and bitterness, and banded against the Church; this is enough. The Vaudois believe not like the Albigenses, but like the Albigenses they hate the Church, and proclaim themselves the only saints, the only ministers of the sacraments. Wickliff believes not like the Vaudois, but Wickliff proclaims, like the Vaudois, that the Pope and his whole clergy have forfeited all authority by their loose behaviour. John Huss does not believe like Wickliff, though he admires him; what he admires in him chiefly, and almost only follows in him is, that crimes annul authority. These despicable Bohemians, as we have seen, succeeded to this spirit, which they particularly made appear, when, amounting to no more than a handful of illiterate men, they presumed to rebaptize the whole world.

206.—How Luther and Calvin sprung from the Albigenses and Vaudois.

But a still greater apostacy was hatching by means of these sects. The world teeming with animosity, brings forth Luther and Calvin, who canton Christendom. The superstructure is different, but the foundation is the same; it is still hatred against the clergy and the Church of Rome, and no man of sincerity can deny that this was the visible cause of their surprising progress. A reformation was necessary—who denies it? but it was still more necessary to refrain from schism. Were those that promoted this schism by their preaching any better than their neighbors? They acted as if they were; this was enough to delude and "spread like a canker," according to St. Paul's expression.[343] The world was desirous of condemning and rejecting their leaders; this is called Reformation. A specious name dazzles the people, and, to stir up hatred, calumny is not spared: thus is our doctrine blackened; men hate it before they know it.

207.—The Protestant Churches seek in vain a succession of Persons in the preceding Sects.

With new doctrines, new bodies of churches are erected. The Lutherans and Calvinists make the two greatest; but they cannot find in the whole earth so much as one church that believes like them, nor whence they can derive an ordinary and lawful mission. The Vaudois and Albigenses alleged by some, are not to their purpose. We have but just shewn them to be mere laymen, as much at a loss to make out their own mission and title, as those that seek their aid. We know the Toulousian heretics were never able to delude so much as one priest. The preachers of the Vaudois were trading men or mechanics, nay women. The Bohemians had no better origin, as is already proved; and when Protestants name us all these sects, they name not their fathers, but their accomplices.

208.—Much less do they find in them a succession of Doctrine.

But, perchance, though they do not find in these sects a succession of persons, they will find in them a succession of doctrines. Much less: in certain respects like to the Hussites; in others, like the Vaudois; in some like the Albigenses and the other sectaries; in other articles they are quite contrary to them; in this manner, without lighting upon any thing that is uniform, and laying hold here and there of what seems to suit them; without succession, without unity, without true predecessors, they climb to what height they can. They are not the first to reject the honor due to Saints, nor the oblations for the dead: they find, before their days, bodies of churches of this same belief in these two points. The Bohemians embraced them, but we have seen these Bohemians seek in vain for associates through the whole earth. However, here is a church at least before Luther; this is something to such as have nothing. But, after all, this church before Luther is but fifty hears before him; they must strive to advance higher; they will find the Vaudois, and, a little more distant, the Manicheans of Africa opposed to the worship of Saints. One only, Vigilantius, follows them in this particular point, but higher than this no certain author can be found; yet thereon depends the stress of the question. They may go a little further as to oblations for the dead. The priest Aerius will appear, but alone, and without followers; an Arian besides. This is all can be found that is positive; whatever is built besides this, will be built manifestly in the air. But let us see what they will discover as to the Real Presence, and remember the question is concerning positive and certain facts. Carlostadius is not the first who maintained that the bread was not made the body; Berengarius had said as much four hundred years before him in the eleventh century. Yet neither was Berengarius the first; these Manicheans of Orleans had just said the same, and the world was still full of the rumor of their evil doctrine, when this scantling of it was picked up by Berengarius. Beyond this, I find many pretensions and actions lodged against us concerning this subject, but no averred and positive facts.

209.—*What is the succession of Heretics.*

Now the Socinians have a more manifest succession; catching up a word here and another there, they will name to you declared enemies of the divinity of Jesus Christ in all ages, and at the head of them will find Cerinthus, next to the Apostles. Notwithstanding their discovering something concordant among so many in other respects, discording witnesses, they will be never the better founded, since, when all is said, Succession and Uniformity are wanting to them. To take the thing thus, namely, should each of them, in patching up their several churches, collect here and there without bond of union, all that could be found conformable to their sentiments; there is no difficulty, as might have been observed, to trace the extraction of every sect seen at this day, or ever to be seen, even up to Simon the Magician, and to that "mystery of iniquity," (2 Thess. ii. 7) which began in the time of St. Paul.

Notes

[1] Jon. Aur. præf. cont. Claud. Taur.
[2] L. i. p. 35.
[3] Ibid. 39.
[4] Epiph. hær. 79. Aug. hær. 86, 87. Tertull.
[5] 1 Tim. iv. 1, 3.
[6] Aug. 1. xxx. cont. Faust. Man. c. 3, 4, 5, 6. Dan. 1, 8, 12. 1 Cor. ii. 26, 32, 34, 38. Matt. xix. 12. Luke ix. 62. 1 Tim. iv. 4
[7] L. ii. cont. Faus. Man. c. 19; et L. iv. Conf. c. i. Theod. l. i. hær. Fab. c. ult. de Manich. Ibid.
[8] Leo i. Serm 45. Qui est iv. de Quadr. c. 5.
[9] Gelas. in Dec. Grat. de conf. distinct. 2. c. Comperimus. Yvo. Microl. &c.
[10] De Morib. Ecc. Cath. c. 34. De morib. Manich. c. 18. Cent. Ep. fundam. c. 15.
[11] Cedr. t. i. p. 432.
[12] Ibid. t. ii. p. 480. Ibid. p. 541.
[13] Pet. Sic. Hist. de Manich. Cedr. Ib. 541.
[14] Voss. de Hist. Græc.
[15] Pet. Sic. Ib. Præf. &c.
[16] Ibid.
[17] Pet. Sic. Ib. Præf. &c.
[18] Cedr. t. ii. p. 434.
[19] Aug. hær 46, &c. Lib. xx. Cont. Faus. c. 4.
[20] Ibid. c. 21, et seq. Ibid. c. 18.
[21] Peter Sic. ibid.
[22] Peter Sic. initio lib.
[23] Rev. xx. 2, 3, 7.
[24] Matt. xii. 29. Luke xi. 21, 22.
[25] Acta Conc. Aurel. spicil. t. ii. Conc. Lab. t. ix. Glab. lib. iii. c. 8.
[26] Glab. ibid. Acta. Conc. Aurel.
[27] De Vita sua, lib. iii. c. 16.
[28] De hær. in hær. Man.
[29] Peter Sic. ib.
[30] Cedr. t. i. p. 434.
[31] Cedr. t. i. p. 434.
[32] Cond. de hær. l. 52.
[33] Bib. nov. l'Abb. t. ii. pp. 176, 180.
[34] Frag. Hist. Aquit. edita à Petro Pith. Bar. t. xi. An. 1017.
[35] De hær in hær. Man.
[36] Bib. Hist. 2 p. in the year 1022, p. 672.
[37] Bib. Hist. p. 133.
[38] Ren. cont. Wald. c. 6. t. iv.
[39] Bibl. PP. part ii. p. 759.
[40] Vignier, ib.

[41] Conc. Tur. ii. c. 3.
[42] Conc. Tol. An. 1119. Can. 3.
[43] Conc. Later. ii. An. 1139. Can. 23.
[44] Aug. de hær in hær. Man. Ecb.
Serm. i. Bib. PP. t. iv. part ii. p. 81.
Ren. cont. Wald c. 6.
[45] Herm. cont. ad an. 1052. Par. To. xi.
ad eund. An. Centuriat. in Cent.
xi. c. 5. sub fin.
[46] Ecb. Serm. xii. adv. Cath. t. iv. Bib.
PP. part ii.
[47] Serm. i. viii. xi.
[48] Serm. vii. Serm. iv. &c.
[49] Ecb. Serm. vi. p. 99.
[50] Serm. v. p. 94.
[51] Petr. Sic. init. lib. de Hist. Man.
[52] Ibid. Cedr. t. i. p. 434.
[53] Ecb. Serm. i. ii.
[54] Bern. in. Cant. Serm. lxv.
[55] De hær. in hær. Priscil. Ecb. Serm. ii.
Bern. Ib. init. lib. id. Serm. i. ii. vii,
&c.
[56] Ibid.
[57] Prov. ix. 17. Serm.lxv.in Cantic.
[58] Ibid. Ecb. init. lib. &c. Bern. Serm.
lxv. lxvi.
[59] Enervin, Ep. ad. S. Bern. Anal. iii. p.
452; Ibid. pp. 455, 456, 457.
[60] Enervin, Ep. ad S. Bern. Anal. iii. p.
453; Ecb. Serm. i.
[61] Serm. lxvi.
[62] Serm. lxv.
[63] Serm. lxvi.
[64] Serm. lxv.
[65] Ibid.
[66] 2 Thess. ii. 7.
[67] Serm. lxvi. 1 Tim. iv. 1, 2, 3.
[68] La Roq. Hist. de l'Euch., pp. 452,
453.
[69] Ep. 241, ad Tol. Vit. S. Bern. lib. iii.
c. 5.
[70] Act. Conc. Lumb. t. x. Conc. Lab.
An. 1176.
[71] Roger. Hoved. in Annal. Angl.
[72] La Roq. ib. Bar. t. xii. An. 1176, p.
674.
[73] Pet. Sic. ibid.
[74] Faust ap. Aug. lib. xx. cont.
[75] Ibid. c. 7.
[76] Herib. Mon. Ep. Annal. iii.

[77] Ren. cont. Wald. c. 6, t. iv. Bib. PP.
p.759.
[78] De vita sua, lib. iii. c. 16.
[79] De vita sua, lib. iiii. c. 16.
[80] Rodul. Ard. Serm. in Dom. viii. post
Trin.t.ii.
[81] Gul. Nes. Rer. Ang. lib. ii. c. 13.
Conc. Oxon. t. ii. Conc. Ang.
Conc. lab. t. x. An. 1160.
[82] La Roq. Hist. de l'Euch. c. xviii.
p. 460.
[83] Phil. lib. i. Duch. t. v. Hist. France,
p. 102.
[84] La Roque, p. 455.
[85] Aubert. La Roque.
[86] Tom. x. Bib. PP. part. i. p. 123.
[87] Ibid. cap. xi. Ibid. xii. Ibid. xiii. Ibid.
c. i. ii. iii. vii. Ibid. v. xv. xvi.
[88] Alan. p. 31. Mat. xi. 3. Lib. v. cont.
Faust. c. i. Ebrard. Antihær. c, xiii.
t. vi. Bib. PP. 1332. Ermeng. c. vi.
ibid. 1339, &c.
[89] Hist. Albi. Pet. Mon. Val-Cern. cap.
ii. t. v. Hist. Franc. Duchesn.
[90] Petr. Sic.
[91] Ren. cont. Wald. c. vi. t. iv. part ii.
Bib. PP. p. 753.
[92] Ibid. 759.
[93] Bib. PP. p. 1075. Pet. de Valcern.
Ibid. c. ii. La Roq. p. 454.
[94] Ibid. c. i. ii. iii. et seq.
[95] Cap. 25.
[96] Ren. cont. Wal. t. iv. Bib. PP. part
ii. p. 746. Pref. Ibid. pp. 746, 756,
757. Ibid. c. vii. p. 765. Ibid. c. iii.
p. 748.
[97] Ren. Ibid. c. vi. pp. 762, 763.
[98] Ibid. c. v. p. 749, et seq. Ibid. c. vi.
pp. 753, 754, 755, 756.
[99] Ibid. p. 756.
[100] Ibid. p. 759.
[101] T. ix. Conc. Ecb. Ren. c. xiv. t. vi.
Bib. PP. part i. p. 1254. Ibid. 759.
[102] Ren. c. xiv. pp. 753, 756.
[103] Mat. Paris. in Henr. III, An. 1223,
p. 317. Ep. Enerv. ad S. Bernard.
Anal. Mabill. iii. Ibid. 124. An. p.
395.
[104] Enervin, Anal. iii. p. 454.
[105] Serm. 65. Serm. 66. L. v. cont.
Faust. c. i.

[106] Bern. Serm. 66, in Cant.

[107] Aug. Ren. c. xvi. Ebrard. c. 26. T. iv. Bib. PP.part i. p. 1178. Ren. c. vi. T. iv. Bib. PP. part ii. p. 753. La Roq. Hist. de l'Euc. part ii. c. 18. p. 445.

[108] Ren. c. vi. Ibid. pp. 756, 759. Erm. c. xiv. de imp. Man. Bib. PP. p. 1254.

[109] Bern. Serm. 66, in Cant. Ebrard. c. xiv. xv. Erm. c. xviii. xix. Bib. PP. pp. 1134, 1136, 1260, 1261.

[110] Petr. Ven. con. Petrobr.

[111] Petr. Ven. T. xxii. Bib. Max. p. 1034. Sermon 65, in Cant. Peter Ven. Ibid. p. 1037.

[112] Opusc. cont. servet.

[113] Bib. Max. p. 107.

[114] Ep. ad episcop. Arelat &c. Ante Epist. contra Petrob. Bib. Max. p. 1034.

[115] Sermon 66.

[116] Ibid. 65.

[117] Albert La Roq. Otho. Fris. in Frid. c. 46, 47.

[118] Serm. 65, in Cant. Ecbert. Ren.

[119] Ebrard. Ibid. c. 25. Conrad. Ursper. Chron. ad An. 1212.

[120] Ren. c. v. p. 749.

[121] Lib. cont. Wal. c. i. T. iv. Bib. PP. part ii. p. 779

[122] Antih. c. 25. Bib. Max., 1168.

[123] Ibid.

[124] Bib. p. 1170.

[125] Pylicd. ib.

[126] Pylicd. ib. Ren. ib.

[127] Ren. c. vi.

[128] Bern. Abb. Fontiscal. adv. Wald. Sect. T. iv. Bib. PP. Præf. p. 1195.

[129] Chron. ad. An. 1212.

[130] Apud. Em. p. ii. direct. inq. q. xiv. p. 287, et apud Marian. Præf. in. Luc. Trid. t. iv. Bib. PP. ii. p. ii. p. 582 Bern. de Font. Cal. adversus Wal. Sect. in Præf. t. iv. Bib. PP. p. iii. p. 1195.

[131] c. 1, 2.

[132] Ib. c. 3.

[133] Ib. c. 4, et seq.

[134] Ib. c. 7.

[135] Ib. c. 8. c. 9.

[136] Alan. lib. ii. p. 175, et seq. Lib. i. p. 118, et seq.

[137] Pet. de Val. Cern. Hist. Albig. c. 2. Duch. Hist. Fran. t. v. p. 575.

[138] Conr. Ursperg. ad An. 1212.

[139] Pet. de Val. c. t. p. 561. Conc. Lat. iv. Can. 3, de Hærot.

[140] Pet. Pylicid. cont. Wald. c. i. T. iv. Bib. PP. part ii. p. 780.

[141] Ibid.

[142] Ibid.

[143] V. sup. Pet. de Valle-Cern. Refut. Error. Ibid. p. 819.

[144] Guid. Car. de Hær. in Hæresi Wald. init.

[145] Hist. des Vaudois, chap. i.

[146] Hist. de l'Euch. part ii. Ch. xviii. p. 454.

[147] Conc. Tarrac. t. xi. Conc. part. i. An 1242. p. 593.

[148] Ren. c. v. T. iv, Bib. PP. part. ii. p. 749. Ibid. 750.

[149] Malach. i. 11.

[150] Ren. Ibid.

[151] Ren. p. 751.

[152] Fragm. Pylicd. Ibid. 817. Ren. Ibid. p. 751.

[153] Ren. p. 750. Ibid. err. 820.

[154] Ibid. p. 752.

[155] Ind. err. Ibid. 831. 923.

[156] Rom. xii. 19. Matt. xiii. 30.

[157] Pylicd. cont. Wald. T. iv. Bib. PP. part ii. 778, et seq. An. 1395. Ibid. c. xxx. p. 803. Ibid. c. i. Ibid. c. xvi. xviii.

[158] Bib. PP. t. iv. part ii. p. 820, 832, 836.

[159] Director. part ii. q. 14. p. 279. Ibid. p. xiii. p. 273.

[160] Ren. c. iv. Ibid. 750. Emeric. Ibid.

[161] Adv. error. Wald. part. An. 1520. f. i. et seq. Ibid. f. 10. 11.

[162] Lib. iii. de Sacr. Euch. p. 986. Col. 2. Ibid. 987.

[163] Fol. 55, 56.

[164] F. 13.

[165] Pylicd. c. i. T. iv. Bib. PP. part ii. p. 780. Ind. Err. Ibid. p. 832. N. 12. Ren. Ibid. 750. Pylicd. Ibid. c. i. p. 780. Ibid. c. viii. p. 782. 820.

[166] Ren. Ibid. c. v. p. 752. Ibid. vii. p. 765.
[167] Ind. Err. N. 12, 13. Ibid. p. 832.
[168] Pylicd. c. xxv. Ibid. p. 796. Interrogat. of Quoti and others. Ibid.
[169] Pylicd. Ibid. c. xxiv. p. 796.
[170] C. v. pp. 750, 751.
[171] Ibid. 751.
[172] P. 751.
[173] Ch. v. 14.
[174] P. 751.
[175] C. iv. p. 751.
[176] C. iv. p. 749. Ibid. vii. p. 765.
[177] Heb. vi. pp. 13, 16, 17; and vii. 21.
[178] F. 2.
[179] Hist. Eccl. des. Egl. Ref. de Pier Gilles, c. v.
[180] Hist. Eccl. des Egl. Ref. de Pier Gilles, c. v.
[181] Gilles, c. v.
[182] F. 38.
[183] Gill. Ibid. c. v.
[184] Ann. Eccl. decad. 2. An. 1530, a. p. 294, ad 300. Heidelb.
[185] Sleid. l. ii. n. 4.
[186] Hist. des Mart. in 1536.f.111.
[187] In 1543. f. 133.
[188] In 1561. f. 532.
[189] Liv. i. p. 23. 1536.
[190] Ibid. pp. 35, 36. 1544.
[191] Gilles, ch. iii. et xxix.
[192] Ren. c. iv. v. p. 749. Pylicd. c. iv. p. 779. Frag. Pylicd. pp. 815, 816, &c.
[193] Seyss. f. 5.
[194] Hist. des Vaudois, ch. i.
[195] Hist. des Vaudois, lib. i. ch. vii. p. 57 Hist. des Vaud. et Albig. part. iii. lib. iii. ch. i. p. 253.
[196] Aub. p. 962. La Roque His. de L'Euchar. pp. 451, 459.
[197] Hist. des Vaud. part. iii. liv. iii. ch. ii. p. 305.
[198] Hist des Vaud. part iii. liv. i. ch. vii. p. 56.
[199] Hist. des Vaud. liv. i. ch. 12, p. 76. Ibid.
[200] Lett. of Œcolampad. Perr. Ibid. ch. vi. p. 46; vii. p. 59.
[201] S. n. 4.
[202] Seyss. f. 3, et seq.

[203] Esrom. Rudig. de frat. Orth. narrat. Heid. cum. Hist. Cam. 1605, pp. 147, 148. Præf. Conf. fid. frat. Bohem. An. 1572. Ibid. 173.
[204] Rud. Ibid. pp. 147, 148.
[205] Hist. des Vaud. et Albig. part. iii. l. iii. ch. i. p. 252. Ibid. part iii. l. iii. p. 157. Ibid. I. iii. p. 267.
[206] La Roq. 459, Aub. p. 967, ex. Ren. c. iii. p. 5.
[207] Ren. c. vi.
[208] La Roq. 456, Aub. p. 964. B. Rad. Ard. Serm. 8, Post Pentec.
[209] La Roq. Aub. Ibid. 965, ex. Pet. de Valle-Cern. Hist. Albig. lib. ii. cap. 6.
[210] Hist. Albig. cap. 2.
[211] La Roque, p. 457. Aub. p. 965. Ren. cap. vi.
[212] Cæsar. Hesterb. lib. v. cap. 2, in Bibl. Cisterc. La Roque p. 457. Aub. p. 964. Ferri Cat. Gen. pp. 85, 455.
[213] An. Comn. Alex. lib. xv. p. 486. et seq.
[214] La Roq. p. 458. Rog. de Hoved. An. Angl. Baron ad. 1178.
[215] La Roq. p. 451. Conc. Tolos. An. 1119. Can. iii. v. 8
[216] P. 457. Direct. part ii. p. 14.
[217] Aub. p. 968. a. La Roq. p. 460, ex.
[218] C. vi.
[219] Ibid.
[220] Ren. c. vi.
[221] Aub. 968. a. La Roq. 460. c. i.14, 18. p. 780, &c. c. i. p. 747.
[222] C. vi. p. 756.
[223] Serm. 65, in Cant.
[224] John iii. 15.
[225] Matt. xxv. 3.
[226] Ch. v. p. 749.
[227] Ren. Ibid.
[228] John ii. 19.
[229] Pylicd. c. x. p. 283.
[230] Apud. Ren. ch. vi. p. 755.
[231] Luke xviii. 11.
[232] Analect. lib. iii. p. 454.
[233] Serm. 66.in Cant. sub. fin.
[234] F. 47.
[235] De Eccl. Frat. in. Boh. et Mor. nar. Hist. Heid. 1605.

236 De Orig. Eccl. Boh. et confess. ab iis editis. Heid. An. 1605, cum Hist. Joach. Camer. p. 173.
237 Hist. p. 105. etc.
238 Rudig. de Eccl. Frat. in Bohem. et Mor. nar. p. 147.
239 In Syn. Sendom. Synt. Gen. part. ii. p. 219.
240 Rudig. Eccl. Frat. in Bohem. et Mor. nar. p. 148.
241 Apo. 1532. ap. Lyd. l. ii. p. 137.
242 Lib. iii. c. vii. viii. xxiii. p. 56, 82. Edit. 1525.
243 Ibid. c. xxiv. xxv. p. 85, etc.
244 Lib. c. xxvii. lib. i. c. x. p. 15.
245 Ibid. c. xi. p. 18.
246 Ibid. c. ii.
247 Ibid. c. iv. Ibid. c. x. p. 16.
248 Ibid. c. iv. Ib. c. x. Lib. iii. c. ix.
249 Lib. i. c. x.
250 Ib. c. xi.
251 Ib. c. x.
252 Ibid.
253 Ib. lib. iii. c. ix.
254 Ib. i. c. xiv. Lib. iii. c. iv.
255 Ibid. c. viii.
256 Ibid. c. iv.
257 Ibid. c. vi. viii. Ib. c. iv.
258 Ibid. c. viii.
259 Lib. iv. c. x. xiv. xxiii. xxv. xxxii.
260 Ibid. c. xvii. xviii. xix. xxiv.
261 Hist. de Euch. Conc. Const. Sess. viii. prop. 6.
262 Ibid. prop. xv.
263 Disput. cum. Rokys. apud. Canis. ant. lect. t. iii. p. ii. 474.
264 Disput. cum. Rokys. apud. Canis. ant. lect. t. iii. p. ii. p. 500.
265 Lib. iii. c. 30. Lib. xi. 14. Lib. iii. 5. iv. 6, 7, 40, 41. Lib. iv. 1, 6. Lib. iv. c. 1.
266 Nouv. acc. Cont. M. Varril. p. 73.
267 Lib. v. c. 36, 37, 38.
268 La Roque, Ib. 70. Ib. pp. 81, 85, 88, 89, 90.
269 La Roque, Ib.
270 Præf. ad Mycon. Hosp. p. ii. ad An. 1350, f. 115.
271 Wick. lib. iv. c. 1. &c.
272 Part ii. ch. xix. p. 484.
273 Rudig. Narr. p. 153.
274 Nouv. acc. cont. Varr. pp. 148, 150.
275 Ib. p. 158, et seq. Conc. Const. Sess. xv. prop. 11, 12, 13, &c.
276 De Frat. Narrat. p. 158.
277 Ib. 155.
278 De Frat. Narrat. p. 155.
279 Præf. Confess. 1572. seu. de orig. Eccl. boh. &c. post.
280 Hist. Camer. init. Præf. p. 176.
281 Ib. p. 267. Præf. Boh. Conf. 1558. Synt. Gen.p.164. Apol.Frat.1.part, ap. Lyd. t. ii. p. 129.
282 Lyd. Wald. t. 1. Rotcro. 1616.
283 Syn. Prague. An. 1431, ap Lyd. p. 304, et An. 1434. Ibid. pp. 332, 354.
284 Ibid. p. 472.
285 Cam. Hist. Narr. Apol. Frat. p. 115, &c.
286 Apol. 1532, part 1.
287 Camer. de Eccl. Frat. pp. 64, 84, &c. Apol. Frat. 1532, part 1.
288 De orig. Eccl. Boh. post. Hist. Camer. p. 267, part i.
289 Apol.Lyd. t. ii. 221, 222, 232, &c.
290 Apol. 1532, part i. ap. Lyd. t. ii. pp. 116, 117, 118,&c.
291 Rud. Narr. post. Camer. Hist. p. 151.
292 Cam. Hist. Narr. p. 102. Præf. Apol. 1538, apud. Lyd. t. ii. p. 105.
293 Cam. Hist. Apol. part iv. p. 274. Conf. fid. 1558. Art. xii. Synt. Gen. p. 195. Ibid. p. 170.
294 Conf. fid. 1558, Synt. Gen. part ii. p. 164.
295 Joan. Euseb. in ora. prafixa Apo. frat. sub hoc titulo: Œconomia, &c. ap. Lyd. t. ii. p. 95.
296 De Eccl. Frat. p. 91.
297 Luth. Coll. p. 286. Edit. of Franc. an. 1676.
298 Ibid.
299 Apol. part iv. ap. Lyd. t. ii. p. 244, 248. Ibid. part ii. 172, 173. part iv. p. 282. Ibid. part ii. p. 168.
300 Rom. viii. 1.
301 Conf. fid. apud Lyd. t. iii. p. 8. et seq. citat. in Apol. 1531. ap. eund. Lyd. 296 t. ii. Ihen. Germ. liv. de l'ador. p. 229, 230. Ibid. Art. xi.

xii. xiii. Ib. Art. v. xiv. Pref. fid. ad
Lad. c. de pœnitent. laps. ap. Lyd.
t. ii. p. 15.
302 Apol. 1532, part iv. ap. Lyd. p. 295.
303 Prof. fid. ad Lad. c. de Euch. ap. Lyd.
t. ii. p. 10. citat. Apol. part iv. Ib.
296. Ibid. p. xii.
304 Apol. ad Lad. Ibid. 42. Prof. fid. ad.
Lad. Ibid. p. 27. Apol. p. 66. etc.
305 Apol. 1532, part iv. p. 290. Ib. p.
298. Ibid. p. 291, 299.
306 Ibid. 309.
307 Apud Lad. p. 67, et alibi passim. Ibid.
p. 301, 306, 307, 309, 311, &c.
308 Ibid. p. 67. Prof. fid. ad Lad. p. 29.
Apol. ad eund. p. 68.
309 Apol. ad Ladis. Ib. p. 68, 69, &c. 71,
73. Ibid. p. 301, 306, 307, 309,
311, &c.
310 Ibid. p. 302, 304, 307, 308.
311 Ibid. 74.
312 Ibid.
313 Ibid. p. 71.
314 Apol. ad Ladis. p. 162.
315 Calv. Ep. ad Wald. p. 312, et seq.
316 Ibid. 195.
317 Ibid. 396.
318 P. 211.
319 Art. xv. xvii. Act. Syn. Torin. 1595.
Syn. part ii. p. 240, 242. Art. ix.
An. Silv. Hist. Boh. ap. Lyd. p.
395, 405.

320 Orat. Enc. ap. Lyd. p. 30. Art. xvii.
p. 201.
321 Syntag. Gen. part ii. p. 212.
322 Syntag. Gen. art. ii. pp. 218, 219.
323 Pylic. cont. Wald. c. 15. t. iv. Bib.
PP. part ii. p. 785.
324 V. sup. lib. viii. n. 18. Syn. Conf.
part i. p. 166, part ii. p. 72.
325 Conf. p. 146.
326 Conf. p. 164.
327 Ep. ad Wal. p. 317.
328 Phillip. ii. 2.
329 Jur. Avis aux Protes. de l'Europe at
the beginning of his Prejug. legit.
p. 9.
330 1 Tim. iv. 1, 2, 3, 4, 5.
331 Ibid. 4.
332 Ibid. 1.
333 Ante, 1 Tim.
334 Ante.
335 Comm. in hunc. locum.
336 1 Tim. iv.
337 Rev. xx. 3, 7.
338 Epip. hær. xlvi. Theod. i. hær. fab.
20. Ibid. v. c. 24.
339 Thess. ii. 7.
340 Rev. xx. 2, 3, 7. Matt. xii. 29. Luke
xi. 21, 22
341 Rev. xx, 7, 8. Boch. Phal. lib. iii. 13.
342 Rev. xx. 7, 8.
343 Luke v. 6.
344 2 Tim. ii. 17.

Book XII

A brief Summary.—The Reformed Churches disturbed about the word Substance even in France.—It is maintained as grounded on the word of God in one Synod, and in another brought to nothing in favor of the Swiss, who were angry with the decision.—One Faith for France, and another for Switzerland.—Assembly of Frankfort, and a project of a new Confession of Faith for the whole second party of Protestants.—What was to be suppressed there in favor of the Lutherans.—Detestation of the Real Presence established and suppressed at the same time.—Piscator's affair, and the doctrinal decision of four National Synods reduced to nothing.—Principles of the Calvinists, and demonstrations drawn from them in our behalf.—Du Moulin's propositions received at the Synod of Ay.—Nothing solid or serious in the Reformation.

1.—*Many pretended Reformed Churches of France are for changing the article of the Supper, in their Confession of Faith.—1581.*

THE union of Sendomir had not its effect, except in Poland. In Switzerland, the Zuinglians continued steadfast to reject equivocations. The French began already to join in their sentiments. Many maintained openly, that it was requisite to discard the word Substance, and change the thirty-sixth article of the Confession of Faith presented to Charles IX, wherein the Supper was explained. It was not particular men that made this dangerous proposal, but whole churches, even the chief churches, those of the Isle of France and Brie, that of Paris, that of Meaux, where the exercise of Calvinism commenced, and others neighboring to them. These churches were for changing so considerable an article of their Confession of Faith, which they had published but ten years before as containing nothing but the pure word of God; this must have too much discredited the new party. The Synod of Rochelle, wherein Beza presided, resolved to condemn these reformers of the Reformation in 1571.

2.—*The National Synod condemns them.—This Synod's decision full of perplexities.*

The case required a clear and distinct sentence. The contest being on foot, and the parties present, there needed no more than to decide in few words; but brevity is the fruit of clear conceptions only. Behold, therefore, word for word what was concluded, and I ask only to be allowed to divide the decree into three parts, and to recite them severally.

They begin by rejecting what is evil, and their condemnations fall justly enough. To fix upon any thing will be the grand difficulty; but let us read. "Concerning the thirty-sixth article of the Confession of Faith, the deputies of the Isle of France represented, that it would be requisite to explain this article, insomuch as it speaks of the participation of the substance of Jesus Christ. After a conference of some length, the Synod, approving the thirty-sixth article, rejects the opinion of those who refuse to receive the word Substance, by which word is not understood any confusion, commixion, or conjunction whatever after a carnal manner, or otherwise natural, but a true conjunction, very intimate, and in a spiritual way, whereby Jesus Christ himself is so made ours, and we his, that there is no conjunction of body, whether natural or artificial, so close; the which nevertheless does not tend to this end, that of his substance and person joined to our substances and persons, there should be compounded some third person and substance, but only this, that his virtue and all in him requisite to our salvation, be by this means the more strictly given and communicated to us, dissenting from those who say, we join ourselves to all his merits and gifts, and with his holy Spirit only, without he himself being ours." Here is abundance of words, and nothing said. It is no commixion, either carnal or natural; who knows not that? It has nothing in common with the vulgar mixtures; its end is divine; the manner of it is entirely celestial, and in this sense, spiritual; who questions it? But has any man ever dreamed, that of the substance of Jesus Christ united to ours, a third person was made a third substance? So much time ought not to be lost in rejecting such chimeras as never entered into any man's head.

3.—*Vain efforts of the Synod to find the substance of the Body and Blood in the Doctrine of the pretended reformed Churches.*

It is something to reject those who pretend we partake in nothing but the merits of Jesus Christ, in his gifts, and in his spirit, without his giving himself to us; it was only requisite they should add, that he gives himself to us in the proper and natural substance of his flesh and blood, for this was the point in hand, and the thing to be explained. Catholics do this very clearly, for they say, Jesus Christ in pronouncing "This is my blood, the same was shed for you,"[1] designs, not the figure of it, but the substance, which in saying "Take," he renders wholly ours, there being nothing more ours than that which is given us in this manner. This speaks; this is intelligible. Instead of delivering themselves thus clearly and distinctly, we shall see our ministers lose themselves in rambling from the point, heap texts on texts without concluding anything. Let us return to where we left off; here is what presents itself: "Not consenting," proceed they, "with those who say, we join ourselves to his merits and his gifts and his spirit only, yea, rather marvelling with the Apostle (Ephes. v.) at this secret, supernatural and incomprehensible to our reason, we believe that we are made partakers of the body given for us and the blood shed for us; that we be flesh of his flesh and bone of his bones, and receive him together with all his gifts with him by faith engendered in us by the incomprehensible influence and power of this holy spirit; thus understanding that which is said, 'whoso eateth the flesh and drinketh the blood hath life everlasting.' Item, Christ is the vine and we the branches, and that he maketh us abide in him to the end we may bring forth fruit, and that we be members of his body, of his flesh, and of his bones." They are certainly afraid of being understood, or rather do not understand themselves: thus clogging their meaning with so many useless words, so many intricate phrases, such a confused jumble of crowded texts. For after all, what they have to show is, how much those are in the wrong who, refusing to acknowledge, in the Eucharist, any other communication than that of the merits and spirit of Jesus Christ, discard from this mystery "The proper substance of his body and blood." Now this is what in no way appears in any of these numerous texts. These texts conclude, only that we receive something flowing from Jesus Christ in order to enliven us, as members receive from the Head the spirit which animates them; but do not at all conclude for our receiving the proper substance of his body and blood. None of these texts, except one only, namely, that of St. John vi., relate at all to the Eucharist; neither does that of St. John vi, if we believe the Calvinists, relate to it. And if this text, well understood, shows indeed in the Eucharist the proper substance of Jesus Christ's flesh and blood, yet it does not show it in the manner it is here employed by the ministers, since the upshot of their discourse concludes at length in this, that "We receive Jesus Christ together with all his gifts with him by faith engendered in us." Now "Jesus Christ by faith engendered in us," is nothing less than Jesus Christ united to us in the proper and true substance of his flesh and blood; the first of these being no more than a moral union wrought by pious affections of the mind; and the second, being physical, is real and immediate of body to body, and of substance to substance: thus does this great synod expound nothing less than what it proposes to expound.

4.—*Error of the Synod which seeks the Mystery of the Eucharist without producing the Institution.*

I observe in this decree, that the Calvinists having undertaken to explain the mystery of the Eucharist, and in this mystery the proper substance of Jesus Christ's body and blood, which it is grounded on, allege to us far different things from the words of the institution, "This is my body, This is my blood;" for they are very sensible, should they say, these words import the proper substance of the body and blood, that this would be making it clearly appear, that our Lord's design was to express the body and blood, not in figure, nor even in virtue, but in effect, in truth, and in substance. Thus this substance must have been not only by faith, in the minds and thoughts of the faithful, but in effect, and in truth, under the sacramental species, where Jesus Christ denotes it, and thereby, even in our bodies, into which we are ordered to receive it, to the end that we might, in every way, enjoy our Saviour and participate of our victim.

5.—The Synod's reason for establishing the Substance.—They conclude
the other Opinion to be contrary to God's word.

Now, whereas the decree had not cited any one text that concluded for the proper substance, the thing in question, but rather excluded it by showing Jesus Christ united by faith only; they come back at length to the substance by the following words: "And in fact, as we derive our death from the first Adam, inasmuch as we partake of his substance; so it is requisite we should partake truly of the second Adam, Christ Jesus, that we may derive our life from him. Wherefore all pastors, and in general, all the faithful shall be exhorted to give no way, in any kind, to opinions contrary to the above doctrine, which is grounded *expressly on the word of God.*"

6.—The Synod says more than it designed.

The holy Fathers made use of this comparison of Adam to show that Jesus Christ ought to be in us otherwise than by faith and affection, or morally; for it is not by affection and thought only, that Adam and parents are in their children; it is by the communication of the same blood, and the same substance; and therefore the union we have with our parents, and by their means with Adam, from whom we are all descended, is not only moral, but physical and substantial. The Fathers have thence concluded, that the new Adam ought to be in us after a manner equally physical and substantial, to the end that we might derive immortality from him, as from our first parent we derive mortality. Accordingly, it is what they have found, and much more abundantly, in the Eucharist than in ordinary generation, for that it is not a portion of the blood and substance, but the whole substance and the whole blood of our Lord Jesus Christ, which is therein communicated to us. To say now with the ministers, that this communication is wrought barely by faith, is not only to weaken the comparison, but also to annihilate the mystery, and deprive it of its substance; and whereas it is more abundantly in Jesus Christ than in Adam, it is making it to be much less in him, or rather not at all.

7.—A point of Doctrine was in Question among them.

Thus do our doctors confound themselves, and the more pains they take to speak their minds, the more do they obscure the subject. Nevertheless, through all these mists, you discern plainly, that among the defenders of the figurative sense there was in reality an opinion which admitted nothing in the Eucharist but the gifts and merits of Jesus Christ, or at most, nothing but his spirit, not the proper substance of his flesh and blood; but that this opinion was expressly contrary to the word of God, and not to have any admittance amongst the faithful.

8.—The Swiss believe themselves condemned by this decision.

It is no hard matter to guess who were the defenders of this opinion; it was the Swiss, the disciples of Zuinglius; and such of the French as approving their sentiment would fain reform this article. And this was the reason that the Swiss were presently heard to complain, thinking they beheld their own condemnation in the Synod of Rochelle, and the fraternity broken; since, notwithstanding the soft turn given to the decree, their doctrine was condemned in the main as contrary to the word of God, with express exhortation to allow it no shelter among the pastors or the faithful.

9.—The Synod answers them by Beza, that this Doctrine only regards France.
—The Lutherans as well as Catholics detested as Defenders of a monstrous Opinion.

Under this persuasion they wrote to Beza, and the answer returned them was surprising. Beza was ordered to acquaint them, that the decree of the synod of Rochelle did not regard them, but only certain Frenchmen; so that there was a Confession of Faith for France, and another for Switzerland, as if faith varied according to climate, and it were not equally true, that in Christ Jesus there is neither Swiss nor Frenchman, as it is true, according to St. Paul, that there is neither Scythian nor Greek. To this Beza added, in order to calm the Swiss, that the churches of France detested the substantial and carnal presence, together with the monsters of transubstantiation and consubstantiation.[2] Here then, by and by, we have the Lutherans as badly treated as the Catholics, and their doctrine accounted no less monstrous; but this only in writing to the Swiss; we have seen how far they are able to soften matters when they write to the Lutherans, and how tender they are then of consubstantiation.

10.—The Swiss, not satisfied with Beza's answer, still hold themselves for condemned.

The Swiss would not be gulled with these subtleties of the synod of Rochelle, but were very sensible that they themselves were attacked under the name of these Frenchmen. Bullinger, minister of Zurich, who was ordered to answer Beza, made no difficulty of telling him they were in fact the people condemned:[3] "You condemn," answered he, "those who reject the word 'proper substance;' and who is ignorant that we are of this number?" What Beza had added, against the carnal and substantial presence, did not remove the difficulty; Bullinger knew full well, that the Catholics no less than the Lutherans complained that a carnal presence was laid to their charge, which they did not dream of; and besides, he could not comprehend the meaning of receiving in substance what was not substantially present. Thus unable to conceive the refinements of Beza, or a substance united without being present, he answered him, "that they ought to speak plainly in matters of faith, lest they should reduce the simple to such straits as no longer to know what to believe;" whence he concluded that it was necessary to mitigate the decree, and this was the only means he proposed for a reconcilement.

11.—*They were at last forced to change the Decree, and reduce the Substance to nothing at all.*—*1572.*

They were forced to stoop to these terms, and the year following, in the synod of Nismes, substance was brought to so small a matter, that they might as well have quite suppressed it. Whereas at the synod of Rochelle, the debate was about putting a stop to an opinion contrary to that which was grounded expressly on the word of God, they endeavor now to insinuate that the question was only about a word. They raze out of the decree of Rochelle these words which contained its main force and purpose: viz. "The synod rejects the opinion of those who refuse to receive the word substance." They declare they will do no prejudice to strangers; and such is their complaisance for them, that these great words, "the proper substance of Jesus Christ's body and blood," so much affected by Calvin, so strenuously maintained by his disciples, so carefully retained at the synod of Rochelle, and at last brought to nothing by our reformed, no longer appear in their confession of faith, but as a monument of the impression of the reality and substance, which the words of Jesus Christ had naturally made in the minds of their forefathers, and even of Calvin himself.

12.—*Reflection on this weakening of the first Doctrine.*

And yet if they will but reflect on these relaxations of their first doctrine, they may observe therein in what manner the spirit of seduction has deluded them. Their fathers would not easily have deprived themselves of the substance of Jesus Christ's body and blood. Accustomed in the Church to this sweet presence of the body and blood of their Saviour, the pledge of an immense love, they would not willingly have been brought down to shadows and figures, nor to a simple virtue flowing from his body and blood. Calvin had promised them something more. They had suffered themselves to be attracted by a notion of reality and substance continually inculcated in his books, in his sermons, in his commentaries, in his confessions of faith, in his catechisms: a false notion, I confess, they being there in words only, and not in fact; but yet they were charmed with the fine idea, and believing they lost nothing of what was possessed by them in the Church, they did not fear to leave it. Now that Zuinglius has gained the ascendant by the consent of their synods, and Calvin's big words stand evidently void of force and destitute of all sense, why do not they return from their error, and seek, in the Church, that real possession with which they had been flattered?

13.—*The different Confessions of Faith a mark of the disunion of the Party.*

The Swiss Zuinglians were appeased by the explanation of the synod of Nismes: but the ground of division still subsisted. So many confessions of faith were a too convincing token of it to be dissembled. Meanwhile the French, the Swiss, the English, and the Poles, had their separate ones, which all of them kept to, without borrowing from their neighbors, and their union seemed nearer allied to policy than true concord.

14.—*The Assembly of Frankfort, there endeavors are used to bring the defenders of the figurative sense to agree in one common Confession.—1577.*

They had often sought remedies for this inconvenience, but in vain. In 1577, an assembly was held at Frankfort, where the ambassadors of Queen Elizabeth assembled with the deputies of France, of Poland, of Hungary, and of the low countries.[4] The Count Palatine, John Casimir, who, the year before, had brought into France such great succor to our reformed, procured this assembly. The whole party that defended the figurative sense, whereof this prince was one, was there assembled, except the Swiss and Bohemians. But these last had sent their declaration, submitting themselves thereby to what should be resolved: and as for the Swiss, the Palatine caused it to be declared by his ambassador that he held himself assured of them.[5] The intent of this convention, as appears by the palatine-deputy's harangue at his opening of it, was to draw up, by the unanimous consent of all the other deputies, one common confession of faith for these churches; and the reason that induced the Palatine to make this proposal was, because the Lutherans of Germany, after making the famous Book of Concord so often mentioned, were to hold an assembly at Magdeburg, there to pronounce with one accord the approbation of this book, and at the same time the condemnation of all those who should refuse to subscribe it; so as, being declared Heretics, they might be excluded from toleration granted by the empire in matters of religion. By this means, all the defenders of the figurative sense were to be banished, and the monster of ubiquity, maintained in this book to be established. It was the interest of these churches, which were to be condemned, to appear at that time numerous, powerful, and united. They were cried down as having each one their particular confession of faith, and the Lutherans, united under the common name of the Confession of Augsburg, easily resolved on the proscription of a party, which its disunion made contemptible.

15.—*A design of comprehending the Lutherans in this common Confession of Faith.*

This great grievance was colored over nevertheless, in the best way possible, with specious words; and the Palatine-deputy declared that all these Confessions of Faith, conformable in doctrine, differed in method only, and the way of speaking. But he well knew the contrary, nor were the differences but too real for these churches. Be that as it will, it was their interest, in order to put a stop to the proceedings of the Lutherans, to show them their union by a confession of faith as well received among them all, as was that of Augsburg among the Lutherans. But they had yet a more general design: for in making this new confession of faith common to the defenders of the figurative sense, their intent was to pitch on such expressions as the Lutherans, defenders of the literal sense, might agree to, and so by this means make one body of the whole party called Reformed. The deputies had no better means than this of preventing the condemnation threatened them from the Lutheran party. Wherefore, the decree they made concerning this common Confession of Faith had this turn given it. "That it ought to be made, and made clear, full, and solid, with a clear and brief refutation of all the heresies of these times; yet, with such a temper of style, as rather to attract than alienate those that adhere purely to the Confession of Augsburg, as much as truth could allow."[6]

16.—*Qualities of this new Confession of Faith.—Deputies named to draw it up.*

To make this Confession of Faith clear, to make it full, to make it solid, with a clear and brief confutation of all the heresies of those times, was a grand undertaking; fine words but the thing exceedingly difficult, not to say impossible, amongst people of such different persuasions: above all, not to exasperate any further the Lutherans, those zealous defenders of the literal sense, it was necessary to pass lightly over the Real Presence, and the other articles so often mentioned. Divines were named, who had a thorough knowledge of the grievances of the Church, to wit, of the divisions in the Reformation, and of her Confessions of Faith which kept them asunder. Rodulph Gultier, and Theodore Beza, ministers, one of Zurich and the other of Geneva, were to put the finishing stroke to the work which was afterwards to be despatched to all the churches in order to be read, examined, corrected, and augmented as judged proper.

17.—*Letter written to the Lutherans by the Assembly of Frankfort.*

To prepare a work of such great nicety, and hinder the condemnation which the Lutherans were hatching, it was concluded to write, in the name of the whole assembly, a letter capable of mollifying them. Wherefore they were acquainted,[7] that this assembly was called together from sundry parts of the Christian world, to oppose the Pope's attempts, after informations received that he was uniting the most potent princes of Christendom against them, namely, the Emperor, the King of France, and the King of Spain; but what had most afflicted them was, that certain princes of Germany, who say they invoke the same God with us, as if the Catholics had another, and detest with us the tyranny of the Roman Antichrist, were preparing to condemn the doctrine of their Churches; and so, amidst the misfortunes that distressed them, they saw themselves attacked by those, in whose virtue and wisdom they had reposed their chief trust.

18.—*The Assembly minces the difficulty of the Eucharist.*

Then they represented to those of the Confession of Augsburg, that the Pope, whilst he ruined the rest of the Churches, would not spare them. For how, proceed they, should he hate those less who first gave him the mortal stab, namely, the Lutherans, whom, by this means, they place at the head of the whole party? They propose a free council in order to unite amongst themselves, and oppose the common enemy. Lastly, after complaining they were going to be condemned without a hearing, they say, the controversy that divides them most from those of the Confession of Augsburg, viz., that of the Supper and Real Presence, has not so much difficulty as is imagined, and it is an injury done them to accuse them of rejecting the Confession of Augsburg. But they add, it stood in need of explanation in some places, and even that Luther and Melancthon had made some corrections in it; by which they evidently mean those different editions, wherein were made the above-seen changes in the lifetime of Luther and Melancthon.

19.—*The consent of the Synod of Sainte-Foy to the new Confession of Faith.*—*1578.*

The year following, the Calvinists of France held their national Synod at Sainte-Foy, where they gave power to change the Confession of Faith, which they had so solemnly presented to our Kings, and which they boasted they would maintain to the last drop of their blood. The decree of this Synod is worth our notice: it imports, "that after seeing the instructions of the assembly held at Frankfort by the means of Duke John Casimir, they enter into the design of uniting in one holy band of pure doctrine all the *reformed* Churches of *Christendom*, whereof certain Protestant Divines were for condemning the soundest and the greatest part: and approve the project of making and drawing up a formulary of a Confession of Faith common to all the Churches, as also the invitation expressly made to the Churches of this kingdom, to send to the place appointed men well approved and authorized with ample procuration, in order to treat, agree, and decide on all the points of doctrine and other things relating to the union, repose, and preservation of the Church, and God's pure service." For the execution of this project, they name four deputies to draw up this common Confession of Faith, but with much more ample powers than had been demanded for them in the assembly of Frankfort.[8] For, whereas this assembly, unable to believe the Churches could agree in one Confession of Faith, without seeing it, had ordered, that after its being seen by certain ministers and polished by others, it should be sent to all the churches for their examination and correction: this Synod, condescending beyond all that could be imagined, not only expressly charges these four deputies to be present at the place and time appointed, with ample procurations as well from the ministers, as in particular from the Viscount of Turenne; but also adds thereto, "that in case even there were no means of examining this Confession of Faith throughout all the provinces, it was left to their prudence and sound judgment to agree and conclude all the points that shall come under deliberation, whether in regard of doctrine, or any other thing concerning the welfare, union, and repose of all the Churches."

20.—*Faith trusted in the hands of four Ministers, and of the Viscount of Turenne.*

Here have you then manifestly, by the authority of a whole national Synod, the faith of our pretended churches of France left to the disposal of four ministers and of the Viscount of Turenne, with power to determine therein as they pleased, and those who will not allow, that we may refer to the judgment of the whole Church the least points of faith, refer the whole of theirs to that of their deputies.

21.—*Why M. de Turenne was put in this deputation concerning Doctrine.*

One may wonder perchance to see M. de Turenne named amongst these doctors: but you must understand that this "welfare, union, and repose of all the churches," for the sake of which this deputation was made, meant much more than appeared at first sight. Forasmuch as the Duke John Casimir, and Henry de la Tour, Viscount of Turenne, joint deputies with these ministers, had thoughts of settling this repose by other means than by arguments and Confessions of Faith; which, however, necessarily made part of the negotiation, experience having shown that these new reformed Churches could not be united in a league as they ought, without first agreeing in point of doctrine. All France was flaming with civil wars; and the Viscount de Turenne, then but young, yet full of wit and valor, whom the disaster of the times had drawn into the party but two or three years before, had immediately raised himself in it to so great an authority (not so much by his illustrious blood, which allied him to the greatest families of the kingdom, as his great capacity and courage) that he was already lord-lieutenant to the king of Navarre, afterwards Henry IV. A man of such genius entered easily into the design of reuniting all the Protestants: but God did not suffer him to accomplish it. The Lutherans were found intractable, and the Confessions of Faith, notwithstanding the resolution unanimously taken of changing them all, subsisted as containing the pure word of God, which it is neither lawful to add to, nor take from.

22.—*Letter, wherein the Calvinists own Luther and Melancthon for their Fathers.*

We see that, in the year following, namely, 1579, a union was still hoped for, since the Calvinists of the Low Countries wrote conjointly to the Lutherans, authors of the Book of Concord, to Kemnitius, Chythræus, James Andrew, and the rest of the violent defenders of Ubiquity, whom they failed not to call, not only their brethren, but their own flesh, (so intimate was their union, notwithstanding their great divisions,) inviting them "to take moderate counsels, to enter into methods of union, in order whereto the Synod of France (that of Sainte-Foy) had named deputies, and this," say they, "after the example of our holy fathers, Luther, Zuinglius, Capito, Bucer, Melancthon, Bullinger, Calvin," whose unanimity was such as you have seen. These, then, are the common fathers of the Sacramentarians and Lutherans; these are the men in whose harmony and moderate counsels the Calvinists glory!

23.—*The project of a Common Confession continued to our days, and always to no purpose.*

All these endeavors towards a union proved abortive, and the defenders of the figurative sense were so far from being able to agree with the Lutherans, defenders of the literal sense, in one common Confession of Faith, that they could not even agree among themselves.[9] The proposal was frequently renewed, and even near to our days in 1614, at the Synod of Tonins, which, in 1615, was backed by the expedients proposed by the famous Peter du Moulin. But though for this he received the thanks of the Synod of the Isle of France, held the same year at the borough of Ay, in Champagne; and notwithstanding the known credit he had, not only in France, among his own brethren, but also in England and over the whole party, all proved to no purpose. The churches, which defend the figurative sense, confessed the mighty evil of their disunion, but withal confessed it was beyond remedy; and this common Confession of Faith, so earnestly desired and endeavored at, is become a Platonic idea.

24.—Vain shifts of the Ministers.

This history would require that I should relate the answers returned by the ministers, with regard to this decree of Sainte-Foy, after it became public, and was urged against them by the Catholics. But all of them, by the above account of the fact, fall of themselves. Some said, a mutual toleration was the only thing in question; but it is plain enough a common Confession of Faith was not necessary for that end, since the effect of this toleration is, not to make one common faith, but to bear mutually with one another's faith. Others, in excuse for the great power of deciding on doctrine lodged in the hands of four deputies, answered, this was because it was known "near the matter"[10] what they could agree in; this "near the matter" is admirable. Doubtless men are not over nice in questions of faith when satisfied with knowing "near the matter" what they are to say; and little also do they know what to stick to, when, for want of such knowledge, they give their deputies so unlimited a power of concluding whatsoever they shall think fitting. The Minister Claude[11] answered, that they knew precisely what they were to say; and should the deputies have gone beyond it, they would have justly been disowned as men that had gone beyond their commission. But this answer, allowing it so, does not satisfy the chief difficulty, consisting in this, that to please the Lutherans, they must have given up to them all that tended to exclude, as well the Real Presence as the other points contested with them; that is to say, they must evidently have changed, in such important articles, a Confession of Faith expressly affirmed by them to be contained in the word of God.

25.—Difference between what was designed to be done in favor of the Lutherans at Frankfort and Sainte-Foy, and what was done at Charenton.

Care ought to be taken not to confound what was to be done then with what was done since, when the Lutherans were received into communion at the Synod of Charenton, in 1631. This last action shows only, that the Calvinists can bear with the Lutheran doctrine, as a doctrine not at all prejudicial to the *fundamentals* of faith. But it is certainly quite a different thing to tolerate, in the

Lutheran's Confession of Faith, what you believe erroneous in it, and to suppress in your own what you believe to be a truth revealed of God, and expressly declared by his word. This is what they had resolved to do in the assembly of Frankfort and at the Synod of Sainte-Foy; this is what they would have executed, had it pleased the Lutherans; insomuch that it was only the fault of the defenders of the Real Presence that all which clashed with it was not erased out of the Sacramentarian Confessions of Faith. But the reason of this was, once change, and no end of changing; a Confession of Faith which changes the doctrine of ages past, shews thereby that itself may be changed likewise; nor must we wonder the Synod of Sainte-Foy thought they had power to correct in 1578 what the Synod of Paris had established in 1559.

26.—Spirit of instability in Calvinism.

All these means of agreement now mentioned, so far from diminishing the disunion of our Reformed, did but increase it. Here were men ignorant as yet what to stick to, whose first step, at setting out, was by a breach upon the whole Christian world. Here was a religion built on the sand, which had no stability even in her Confessions of Faith, although made with such nice care, and published with such pomp. Even the professors of it could not persuade themselves that they had not a right to innovate in so changeable a religion, and it was this that produced the novelties of John Fischer, known under the name of Piscator, and those of Arminius.

27.—Piscator's dispute.

Piscator's affair will teach us many important matters, and I am the more desirous to relate it at full length, the less it is known by the generality of our reformed.

Piscator taught divinity in the academy of Herborne, a town in the earldom of Nassau, towards the end of the sixteenth century. Examining the doctrine of Imputed Justice, he says that the justice of Jesus Christ, which is imputed to us, is not that which he practised during the course of his life, but that which he underwent in bearing voluntarily the punishment of our sin on the cross; as much as to say, the death of our Lord being a sacrifice of an infinite value, whereby he paid and satisfied for us, it was also by this act alone that the Son of God was properly Saviour, without any necessity of joining to it any other acts, this being itself sufficient; so that, if we are to be justified by imputation, it is by that of this act, in virtue whereof precisely we are acquitted in the sight of God, and whereby "the hand-writing of the sentence passed against us was defaced," as St. Paul speaks, "by the blood which pacifieth both heaven and earth."[12]

28.—This doctrine detested by the National Synod of Gap.—First decision.

This doctrine was detested by our Calvinists in the Synod of Gap, anno 1603,[13] as contrary to the eighteenth, twentieth, and twenty-second articles of the Confession of Faith, and it was resolved by them, "that a letter should be addressed to Mr. Piscator, and likewise to the university in which he taught."

It is certain these three articles decided nothing as to what concerned Piscator, and for this reason we find no more mention made of the twentieth and twenty-second articles. And as to the eighteenth, in which it was pretended the decision might be found, it said no more than that "we are justified by the obedience of Jesus Christ, which is allowed us," without specifying what obedience; so that Piscator found it no hard matter to defend himself in regard to the Confession of Faith. But since they will have it that he innovated in respect to the Confession of the pretended reformed of this kingdom, which had been subscribed by those of the Low Countries, I agree to it.

29.—*Second Condemnation of Piscator's Doctrine at the Synod of Rochelle.*

Piscator was written to by order of the synod, as resolved, and his answer, modest, but firm in his sentiment, was read at the Synod of Rochelle, in 1607. After reading it, this decree was made: "As to the letter of Dr. John Piscator, Professor in the Academy of Herborne, in answer to that of the Synod of Gap, rendering account of his doctrine which teaches justification to be by the sole obedience of Christ in his death and passion, imputed as justice to the faithful, and not by the obedience of his life; the assembly *not approving* the division of causes so conjoint, hath declared, that the whole obedience of Christ in his life and death is imputed to us for the entire remission of our sins, *as being no other than one and the same obedience.*"

30.—*Important observation, that the Doctrine of the Calvinists against Piscator resolves the difficulties they urge against us in regard of the sacrifice of the Eucharist.*

In consideration of these last words, I would willingly ask our Reformed, why, in order to merit for us the forgiveness of our sins, they require, not only the obedience of the death, but also that of the whole life of our Redeemer? Is it that the merit of Jesus Christ dying is not infinite, and not more than sufficient, for our salvation? This they will not say; they must, therefore, say, that what is required as necessary after an infinite merit, does neither destroy its infiniteness nor sufficiency; but at the same time it follows, that to consider Jesus Christ, as continuing his intercession by his presence not in heaven only, but also on our Altars in the sacrifice of the Eucharist, is destroying nothing of the infiniteness of the propitiation made on the cross; it is only, as speaks the Synod of Rochelle, not dividing things conjoined, and accounting all Jesus Christ did in his life, all he did in his death, and all he now does whether in heaven, where he presents himself for us to the Father, or on our Altars, where he is present in another way, as the continuation of one and the same intercession, and of one and the same obedience which he began in his life, consummated in his death, and never ceases to renew both in heaven and in the mysteries, thereby to apply them to us effectually and perpetually.

*31.—Third decision.—Formulary and Subscription ordained against Piscator
in the Synod of Privas.—1612.*

The doctrine of Piscator had its partizans. Nothing was found against him in the eighteenth, twentieth, and twenty-second articles of the Confession of Faith. And, indeed, they abandoned the two last to fix on the eighteenth, which was no more to the purpose, as we have seen, than the others; and to drive the matter home against Piscator and his doctrine, they went so far, in the national Synod of Privas, as to oblige all the pastors to subscribe expressly against Piscator in these terms: "I underwritten N. in regard to the contents in the eighteenth article of the Confession of Faith of the Reformed Churches, regarding our justification, do declare and protest, that *I understand it according to the sense received in our church, approved by the national synods, and conformable to God's word*; which is, that our Lord Jesus Christ was subject to the moral and ceremonial law, not only for our good, but in our stead; and that all the obedience he rendered to the law is imputed to us, and that our justification does consist, not only in the remission of sins, but in the imputation of active justice; and *subjecting myself to the word of God*, I believe 'that the Son of man came not to be ministered unto, but to minister,' and that he did minister to the purpose he came for: *promising never to depart from the doctrine received in our churches, and to subject myself to the ordinances of the national on this head.*"

32.—The Scripture ill-quoted, and its whole Doctrine ill-understood.

What it avails imputed justice, that "Jesus Christ came to minister, and not to be ministered unto;" and to what purpose this text is brought abruptly and without connexion into the midst of this decree, let him guess that can. Neither do I see what use the imputation of the ceremonial law is to us, which never was made for us; nor for what reason "Jesus Christ must have been subject to it, not only for our good, but in our stead." I well comprehend how Jesus Christ, having dispersed the shadows and figures of the law, has left us free from the servitude of the ceremonial laws, which were but shadows and figures; but that it was necessary for such intent that he himself should have been subject to them in our stead, the consequence would be pernicious, since it might be equally concluded he had also set us free from the moral law, by his fulfilling it. All this shows the little exactness of our Reformed, who were more intent on showing erudition in a profusion of big empty words, than on speaking with accuracy in their decrees.

33.—Fourth decision against Piscator in the Synod of Tonins.—1614.

I am at a loss to know what could be the reason that Piscator's affair was taken so very much to heart by our French Reformed, or why the Synod of Privas descended to the utmost precautions, by enjoining the above subscription. This, however, ought to have been decisive: a formulary of faith, ordered to be subscribed by all the pastors, should have explained the matter fully and distinctly. Nevertheless, after this subscription and all the precedent decrees, it was still necessary to make a new declaration at the Synod of Tonins in 1614. Four great decrees one after another, and in such different terms, concerning a particular article, and on so limited a subject, is very extraordinary; but in the new Reformation something is always found to be added or curtailed, and never is their faith explained so sincerely, nor with so full a sufficiency, as to make them adhere precisely to the first decisions.

34.—The impiety of Imputed Justice as it is proposed by these Synods.

To conclude this affair, I shall make a short reflection on the nature of the doctrine, and some reflections on the procedure.

As to the doctrine, I very well understand how the death of Jesus Christ, and the payment he made to the divine justice of the punishment we owed it, is imputed to us, as you impute to a debtor the payment made by the security for his acquittance. But that the perfect justice fulfilled by our Lord in his life and death, and the absolute obedience he rendered to the law, should be imputed to us, or as they speak, allowed, in the same sense, that the payment of the surety is imputed to the debtor; is the same as to say, that he discharges us by his justice from the obligation of being good and virtuous, as by his punishment he discharges us from the obligation of undergoing that which our sins had merited.

35.—Plainness and simplicity of the Catholic Doctrine opposed to the obscurities of the contrary.

I understand, then, and very clearly, in another kind of manner, what it avails us to have a Saviour whose sanctity is infinite. For thereby I behold him alone worthy to obtain for us all the graces requisite to make us just. But that we should formally be made just, because Jesus Christ was just; and that his justice should be allowed us, as if he had fulfilled the law to our discharge, neither does the Scripture say it, nor can any man of good sense comprehend it.

By this means accounting as nothing our interior justice, and that which we practise through grace, they make us all in the main equally just, by reason that the justice of Jesus Christ, supposed by them the only one that renders us just, is infinite.

They likewise wrest from the elect of God that crown of justice, which the just Judge reserves for each one in particular, since they suppose all have the same justice which is infinite; or if at length they confess, this infinite justice is allowed us in different degrees, accordingly as we approach to it more or less by that particular justice we are vested with by grace, it is by extraordinary expressions, saying the same thing with the Catholics.

36.—Reflections on the procedure.—Scripture quoted therein only for form-sake.

This is, in a few words, what I had to say on the doctrine itself. I shall be still more brief as to the procedure: it has nothing but what is weak in it, nothing grave nor serious. The act of most importance is the formulary of subscription enjoined at the Synod of Privas, but, from the very beginning, they do not so much as think of convicting Piscator from the Scriptures. The point to be proved was, "That the obedience of Jesus Christ, whereby he fulfilled the whole law in his life and death, is allowed us in order to make us just," which is called in the formulary of Privas, as before in that of Gap, the imputation of the active justice.

Now, all that could be found in four synods to prove this doctrine and the imputation of the active justice, by the Scripture, is, that "the Son of Man did not come to be ministered unto, but to minister," a text so little adapted to imputed justice, that there is no discovering even to what purpose it was cited.

But so it is with these new reformers, provided they name but the word of God with emphasis, and then fling out a text or two, however wide from the purpose, they think to have answered the profession they make of believing nought but Scripture in express terms. The people are dazzled with these big promises, and are not even sensible what a sway the authority of their ministers has over them, though when all is done it is by that their assent is determined.

37.—How the Confession of Faith is quoted.

As from the word of God nothing was proved against Piscator, so likewise their Confession of Faith was opposed in vain against him.

For we have seen them at Privas immediately forego the twentieth and twenty-second articles, which were produced at Gap. The eighteenth is only insisted on, and as it spoke nothing but what was general and indeterminate, they bethought themselves of thus remedying it in the Formulary: "I declare and protest that I understand the eighteenth article of our Confession of Faith according to the sense received in our churches, approved in our synods, and conformable to the word of God."

The word of God would have sufficed alone; but as that was in dispute, to finish it there was a necessity of coming back to the authority of things judged, and abiding by the article of the Confession of Faith, understanding it, not according to its precise terms, but according to the sense received in churches, and approved in the National Synods, which finally regulates the dispute by tradition, and shows us that the most assured means of understanding what is written, is to see in what manner it always had been understood.

This is what passed, as to the affair of Piscator, in four national synods. The last of them was that of Tonins, held in 1614, where, after the subscription commanded by the Synod of Privas, all seemed determined in the most serious manner imaginable; yet after all there was nothing in it, for the year following, to go no further, that is, in 1615, Du Moulin, the most renowned of all their ministers, openly made a jest of it, with the approbation of a whole synod. The history of the thing is this:—

38.—*They laugh at all these Decrees.*—*Nothing serious in the Reformation.*—
Du Moulins remonstrance approved in the Synod of Ay.—*1615.*

The party of the Reformation opposed to Lutheranism had always been disturbed because they could never contrive among themselves a common Confession, to unite all their members, as the Confession of Augsburg united all the Lutherans. So many different Confessions of Faith showed a principal of division which weakened the party. They came back, therefore, once more to the project of a reunion. Du Moulin proposed the means in a writing sent to the Synod of the Isle of France. The whole drift of it was to dissemble the dogmas, which they could not agree in; and Du Moulin writes in express terms, that among the things it was requisite to dissemble in this new Confession of Faith, they ought to place Piscator's question regarding Justification:[14] a doctrine so much detested by four national synods, becomes indifferent all of a sudden in the opinion of this minister, and the synod of the Isle of France, with the same hand with which it had but just subscribed Piscator's condemnation, nay, the pen, as I may say, still wet with the ink it had made this subscription with, thanks M. du Moulin by express letters for this proposal:[15] such instability is there in the new Reformation, and so easily does she sacrifice the greatest matters to this common Confession which she never could attain.

39.—*Du Moulin's words.*—*Dissimulation, character of Heresy, owned in the Reformation.*

The words of Du Moulin are too remarkable not to be related. "There," says he,[16] viz., in this assembly to be held for this new Confession of Faith, "I am for no disputes about religion, for minds once heated will never be brought to yield, and each one in his return cries out in victory; but I would have laid on the table the Confession of the churches of France, of England, of Scotland, of the Low Countries, of the Palatinate, of the Swiss, &c. That out of these Confessions we might strive to form *one common* one, wherein we should *dissemble* many things, without the knowledge of which one might be saved, *as is Piscator's question* regarding Justification, and many subtle opinions proposed *by Arminius* about Free-will, Predestination and Perseverance of the Saints."

He adds, "as Satan had corrupted the Church of Rome by her having too much, namely, by avarice and ambition, so he strives to corrupt the churches of the new reformation by knowing too much, to wit, by curiosity," which in reality, is the temptation all heretics sink under, and the snare they are taken in; and concludes that, in the way of agreement, "they shall have gone the greatest part of the journey, if they can but prevail on themselves to be ignorant of many things, be contented with necessaries to salvation, and be easy in regard of others."

40.—*Reflection on these words of Du Moulin approved in the Synod of Ay.*

How to agree in this matter was the question, for if by such things, the knowledge of which is necessary to salvation, he understands those which every private man is obliged to know, under penalty of damnation, this common Confession of Faith is already made in the creed of the Apostles, and in that of Nice. The union made on this foundation would reach much beyond the newly reformed churches, nor could they hinder our being comprehended in it; but, if by "the knowledge of things necessary to salvation" he understands the full explanation of all the expressly revealed truths of God, who has revealed none the knowledge of which does not tend to secure the salvation of his faithful, there "to dissemble" what the synods have declared "expressly revealed of God," with "detestation" of the contrary errors, is laughing at the Church, is holding her decrees for imposture even after signing them, is betraying both religion and conscience.

41.—*Du Moulin's inconstancy.*

Now, when you shall perceive that this same Du Moulin, who makes so slight a matter, not of Piscator's propositions only, but also of the much more important ones of Arminius, was afterwards one of the most unmerciful censors of them, you will acknowledge, in his procedure, the perpetual inconstancy of the new Reformation, always suiting her dogmas to the occasion.

42.—*Great points to be suppressed; amongst others, that which is contrary to the Real Presence.*

To conclude the account of this project of reunion then concerted, when this common Confession of the party opposed to the Lutherans should be finished, another was to be made also, but more wide and general, in which the Lutherans might be comprehended.[17] Du Moulin here sets forth all the ways of expressing themselves, so as "not to condemn the Real Presence, nor Ubiquity, nor the necessity of Baptism," nor the rest of the Lutheran tenets; and what he cannot save by equivocations or indeterminate expressions, he wraps up in silence, in the best way he can; he hopes to abolish by this means the appellation of Lutherans, of Calvinists, of Sacramentarians, and, by force of equivocating, to make no other name remain for Protestants than the common one of the Christian Church Reformed. The whole synod of the Isle of France applauded this fine plan; and this union, thus completed, it would be time, proceeds this minister, to solicit the reconciliation of the Church of Rome—but he doubts as to their succeeding. And with good reason, for we have not one instance of her ever approving equivocations in matters of religion, or consenting to the suppression of articles she once believe revealed by God.

43.—Importance of the disputes among the defenders of the figurative sense.

But I do not allow to Du Moulin and the rest of the same party, that the differences in their Confessions of Faith are only in the method and expressions, or else in polity and ceremonies; or, if in matters of faith, in such only as had not yet passed into law or public ordinance: for we have seen, and shall see the contrary through the whole sequel of this history. And can they say, for example, that the doctrine of Episcopacy wherein the Church of England is so firm, and carries it to such a pitch as to receive no Calvinistic ministers without reordaining them, is a matter only of expression, or, at most, of mere polity and ceremony? Is it nothing to look on a Church as utterly destitute of pastors lawfully ordained? It is true the Calvinists are even with them, as we are assured by one of their famous ministers in these words: "If any of ours should teach the distinction of bishops and priests, and that there is no true ministry without bishops, we could not suffer him in our Communion, that is to say, at least in our ministry."[18] The English Protestants therefore are excluded from it. Is this a difference of small importance? This same minister does not speak so of it, he being agreed that, on account of these differences, which he will have but small, of government and discipline, they treat one another as persons excommunicated.[19] If we descend to particulars in these Confessions of Faith, how many points shall we find in some which are not in others? And in reality, were the difference in words only, their obstinacy would be too great not to agree after so frequently attempting it: if in ceremonies only, their weakness would be too great in insisting on them; but the truth is, they are all sensible how little they agree in the main; and if they boast of being well united, this only serves to confirm, that the union of the new Reformation is rather political than ecclesiastic.

Nothing now remains but to entreat our brethren to consider the great steps they have seen taken, not by private men, but by their whole churches, touching matters decided by them with all the authority, said they, of the word of God: yet all these decrees came to nothing. It is a way of speaking in the Reformation always to name the word of God: they believe a thing never the more for that, nor fear the least to suppress what they had advanced under the sanction of so great an authority; but we must not wonder at it. There is nothing in religion more authentic than Confessions of Faith; nothing ought to have been better warranted by the word of God than what the Calvinists had inserted in them against the Real Presence and the other dogmas of the Lutherans. It was not only Calvin that accounted, as detestable, the invention of the Corporeal Presence; *De corporali præsentia detestabile commentum:*[20] the whole Reformation of France had just said, in body, by the mouth of Beza, that she detested this monster, as well the Lutheran Consubstantiation as the Papistical Transubstantiation. But there is nothing sincere, nor serious in these detestations of the Real Presence, since they were ready to retrench all that had been said against it, and this, not only by decree of a national synod, but by a joint determination of the whole party solemnly assembled at Frankfort. The doctrine of the figurative sense, not to speak here of other points, after so many battles and such a number of pretended martyrs, would have been buried in eternal silence, had it but pleased the Lutherans. England, France, Germany, Switzerland, the Low Countries, in a word, all the Calvinists any where to be found, consented to this suppression. How therefore can men remain so wedded to a tenet, which they see so little revelation for, that it is already cast forth from the profession of Christianity by the concurrent wishes of the whole party.

Notes

[1] Matt. xxvi. 26, 28. Luke xxii. 19, 20. 1 Cor. xi. 24.

[2] Colos. iii. 11. Hosp. 1571. f. 344.

[3] Hosp. Ibid.

[4] Act. auth. Blon. p. 59.

[5] Ibid. p. 60.

[6] Act. auth. Bln. p. 62.

[7] Ibid. p. 63.

[8] Hist. de Pas. de Franc. Act. auth. Blon. p .63. Syn. de Sainte-Foy. Ibid. pp. 5, 6.

[9] Act. Auth. Blon. p. 72.

[10] Anon. ii. Rep. p. 365.

[11] Mr. Claude, dans la Nog. Conf. rep. à l'Expos. p. 149.

[12] Col. ii. 14.

[13] Syn. de Gap. ch. de la Conf. de Foy.

[14] Act. Aut. Blond. Piece. vi. p. 72.

[15] Ibid.

[16] Ibid. n. 4.

[17] Act. Auth. Blond. pp. 12, 13.

[18] Jur. Syst. p. 214.

[19] Id. avis. aux Prot. n. 3, at the beginning of his Prej. Legit.

[20] 2 Def. cont. Westp. Opusc. 83. S. n. 9.

Book XIII

THE DOCTRINE CONCERNING ANTICHRIST, AND VARIATIONS ON THIS SUBJECT FROM LUTHER'S TIME DOWN TO THIS.

A brief Summary.—Variations of the Protestants in regard to Antichrist.—Luther's vain predictions.—Calvin's evasion.—What Luther lays down, as to this Doctrine, is contradicted by Melancthon.—A new article of Faith added to the Confession in the Synod of Gap.—The foundation of this decree manifestly false.—This Doctrine despicable in the Reformation.—The absurdities, contrarieties, and impieties of the new interpretation of prophesies proposed by Joseph Mede, and maintained by the minister Jurieu.—The most holy Doctors of the Church enrolled amongst Blasphemers and Idolaters.

1.—*Article added to the Confession of Faith on purpose to declare the Pope Antichrist.*

THE disputes of Arminius raised great combustions in the United Provinces, and it were now time to treat of them; but as the questions and decisions resulting from them are of a more particular discussion, before I engage therein, a famous decree should be mentioned of the Synod of Gap, the account of which was deferred, not to interrupt the affair of Piscator.

It was therefore in this Synod and in 1603, that a new decree was made to declare the pope Antichrist. This decree was counted of so great importance that it passed into a new article of faith, the thirty-first in order, and took place after the thirtieth, it being there said that all true pastors are equal; so that what gives the Pope the character of Antichrist, is his styling himself superior to other bishops. If it be so, it is a great while since Antichrist has reigned; nor do I conceive why the Reformation has so long deferred enrolling in the catalogue of this great number of Antichrists she has introduced, St. Innocent, St. Leo, St. Gregory and the rest of the Popes whose epistles show us the exercise of this superiority in every page.

2.—*Luther's empty prophecies, and Calvin's as empty shift.*

Now when Luther so greatly exaggerated this new doctrine of the Antichristian papacy, he did it with that prophetic air above remarked in him.[1] We have seen in what a strain he foretold the downfall of the Papal power; and how his preaching was that breath of Jesus Christ which was to overthrow the man of sin; without arms, without violence, by himself alone, without any intervening power; so dazzled, so intoxicated was he with the unexpected effect of his eloquence! The whole Reformation was in expectation of the speedy accomplishment of this new prophesy. But when they saw the pope still keep his ground, (for many more than Luther will split against this rock,) and that the Pontifical power, so far from tumbling at the blast of this false prophet, maintained itself against the conspiracy of so many revolted powers, insomuch that the attachment of God's people to this sacred authority, which makes the band of their unity, redoubled rather than was weakened by so numerous a defection, they laughed at the illusion of Luther's prophesies, and at the weak credulity of those who took them for celestial oracles. Yet Calvin had his evasion ready when he said to one that ridiculed them, that "though the body of the Papacy subsisted still, the spirit and life had forsaken it so as to leave nothing but a dead carcass."[2] Thus men will run the hazard of a prophesy, and if the event does not answer, a flash of wit brings them off.

3.—*Daniel and St. Paul brought in to no purpose.*

But they tell us with a serious air it is a prophesy, not of Luther, but of the Scripture, and evidently to be seen (so it should since it is an article of faith) in St. Paul, and in Daniel. As for the Revelations, Luther did not think fit to employ this book, nor receive it into his canon. But for St. Paul,[3] what could be more evident, seeing that the Pope sitteth in the temple of God? In the Church, says Luther,[4] that is questionless in the true Church, the true temple of God; it being unexampled in Scripture, that a temple of idols was ever called by this name: so that the first step they must make towards a right understanding how the Pope is Antichrist, is to acknowledge that Church, wherein he presides, for the true Church. What follows is not less manifest. Who does not see how "the Pope showeth himself that he is God, exalting himself above all that is worshipped?" Chiefly in that sacrifice so much condemned by our Reformers, in which, for proof that he is God, the Pope confesses his sins with all the people; raises himself above every thing by entreating all the saints and all his brethren to beg forgiveness for him; also by declaring afterwards, and in the most holy part of this sacrifice, that he hopes this forgiveness, "not through his own merits, but through the bounty and grace, and in the name of Jesus Christ our Lord?" A new kind of Antichrist, that obliges all his adherents to place their hope in Jesus Christ, and for always having been the most firm assertor of his divinity, is placed by the Socinians at the head of all Antichrists, as the chief of them all, and as the most incompatible with their doctrine.

4.—*Protestants discredit themselves by this Doctrine.*

But again, if such a dream can deserve our serious attention, which of all these Popes is "that man of sin and the son of perdition specified by St. Paul?" We never meet in Scripture with the like expressions, unless to characterize some particular person. No matter for that: all the Popes since St. Gregory, as they said heretofore, and as they say at present, all the Popes since St. Leo, are "this man of sin, this son of perdition, and this Antichrist," though they converted to Christianity England, Germany, Sweden, Denmark, and Holland; so that all these countries, by embracing the Reformation, did publicly acknowledge that they had received Christianity from Antichrist himself.

5.—*Illusions with regard to the Revelations.*

Who can relate here the mysteries our Reformed have found in the Revelations, and the deceitful prodigies of the beast, which are the miracles Rome attributes to saints and their relics; to the end that St. Austin, and St. Chrysostom, and St. Ambrose, and the rest of the Fathers, who, they allow, published the like miracles with unanimous consent, may be the precursors of Antichrist? What shall I say of the character which the beast stamps on the forehead, which in their language means the sign even of the Cross of Jesus Christ, and the holy chrism which is employed to imprint it: to the end that St. Cyprian, and all the other bishops before and after, who most undoubtedly, as is confessed, did apply this character, may be Antichrists; and the faithful, who bore it ever since the origin of Christianity, be stigmatized with the badge of the beast; and the sign of the Son of Man, become the seal of his adversary. It is irksome to relate all their impieties, and for my part, I am verily persuaded, it was these impertinences and profanations of the holy book of the Revelations, which were seen increasing without end in the new Reformation, that brought the ministers themselves, weary of hearing them, to a resolution in the national synod of Saumur, "that no pastor should undertake the exposition of the Revelations, without the advice of a provincial synod."[5]

6.—*This Doctrine concerning Antichrist was not till then in any one act of the Reformation: Luther places it among the Smalcaldic articles, but Melancthon opposes it.*

Now although the ministers had never ceased to animate the people by these odious notions of Antichristianism, they had never ventured hitherto to let them appear in the confessions of faith, though never so outrageous against the Pope. Luther alone had placed, among his articles of Smalcald, a long article concerning the papacy, more resembling a satirical declamation than a dogmatical article, and in it inserted this doctrine;[6] but this example was followed by none else. More than this, when Luther proposed this article, Melancthon refused to subscribe it, and we have heard him say, with the general consent of the whole party, that the Pope's superiority was so great a benefit to the Church, that were it not established, it ought to be so;[7] nevertheless, it was precisely in this superiority that our Reformed acknowledged the character of Antichrist at the synod of Gap in 1603.

7.—*Decision of the Synod of Gap.—Its false Foundation.*

There they said, "that the Bishop of Rome pretended to a dominion over all the churches and pastors, and styled himself God." In what place? in what council? in what profession of faith? it is what they should have specified, this being the foundation of the decree. But they durst not do it, for then it would

have appeared they had nothing to produce but the words of some impertinent interpreter, viz., that in a certain manner, and in the sense God speaks to
Judges, "Ye are gods," the Pope might be called God. Grotius laughed at this
objection of his party, asking them since what time the hyperboles of some
flatterer were taken for received dogmas? Nor, indeed, we may safely say it,
has this reproach of the Pope's *naming himself God* any other foundation than
this. On this foundation they decide that "he is properly the Antichrist, and
the son of perdition pointed at in the word of God, and the beast clothed with
scarlet whom the Lord will discomfit, as he promised, and as he has already
begun to do:" and this is what was to constitute the thirty-first article of faith
for our pretended Reformed of France, according to the decree of Gap,
chapter concerning the Confession of Faith. This new article had for title,
"Article Omitted." The Synod of Rochelle gave orders, in 1607, that this
article of Gap, "as most true and conformable to what was foretold in
Scripture, and which we see in our days *manifestly fulfilled*, should be inserted
in the copies of the Confession of Faith which were to be printed anew." But
it was judged of dangerous consequence to suffer a religion, tolerated under
certain conditions, and under a determinate confession of faith, to multiply its
articles as its ministers should think fit, and a stop was put to the effect of the
synod's decree.

8.—*Occasion of this Decree.*

It may be asked, perhaps, what spirit moved them to this novelty. The secret
is discovered by the synod itself. We there read these words in the chapter
concerning Discipline: "Forasmuch as many are uneasy for having the Pope
called Antichrist, the company protests this is the common belief and
confession of *us all*, by ill luck omitted, nevertheless in all precedent editions,
and the foundation of our separating from the Church of Rome, a foundation
drawn from the Scripture, and sealed with the blood of so many martyrs."
Wretched martyrs, who spill their blood for a tenet absolutely forgotten in all
the Confessions of Faith! But it is true that of late it is become the most
important of all, and the most essential subject of the breach.

9.—*This Doctrine relating to Antichrist, how despised in the Reformation.*

Let us now hearken to an author, who alone makes more noise in his whole
party than all the rest, and whom they seem to have intrusted with the whole
defence of the cause, none but he any longer entering the lists. Here is what
he says in that famous book entitled, "The Accomplishment of the Prophecies."[8] He complains above every thing else, "that this controversy concerning
Antichrist had languished a whole century, and was abandoned through policy,
and in obedience to popish princes. Had this great and important truth, that
popery is Antichristianism, been placed before the eyes of the Reformed, they
would not have fallen into that remissness we see them in at this day. But it
was so long ago since they had heard the thing mentioned, that they had quite
forgotten it." Here, then, is one of the fundamentals of the Reformation; "and

nevertheless," continues this author, "it so happened, through a manifest blindness, that we were solely bent on controversies which were but *accessaries*, and neglected this, that popery is the Antichristian empire."[9] The more he enters into the subject, the warmer his imagination grows. "In my judgment," proceeds he, "this is so capital a truth, that without it, we cannot be true Christians."[10] And in another place; "Verily," says he, "I so greatly account this an article of a true Christian's faith, that I cannot hold those for good Christians who deny this truth, after the event and labors of so many great men have set it in so evident a light." Here is a new *fundamental* article which they had not as yet though on, nay, on the contrary, which the Reformation had unfortunately abandoned: "for," add he, "this controversy was so thoroughly extinguished, that our adversaries believed it dead, and imagined we had renounced this pretension, *and this foundation* of our whole reform."[11]

10.—*Confuted by the most learned Protestants, Grotius, Hammond, Jurieu himself.*

For my own part thus much is true, that I never in my life have met with any man of good sense among our Protestants, that laid stress on this article: in sincerity, they were ashamed of so great an excess, and more in pain how to excuse the transports of their own people that introduced this prodigy into the world, than we were to impugn it. Their ablest men freed us from this labor. It is well known what the learned Grotius wrote on this subject, and how clearly he has demonstrated that the Pope could not be Antichrist.[12] If the authority of Grotius seem not weighty enough to our Reformed, because truly this learned man, by studying carefully the Scriptures, and reading the ancient ecclesiastical authors, disabused himself by little and little of the errors he was born in, Doctor Hammond, that learned Englishman, was not suspected in the party. Nevertheless, he took no less pains than Grotius to destroy the frenzies of Protestants touching the Antichristianism charged on the Pope.

These authors, with some others, whom our minister is pleased to call "the shame and reproach, not only of the Reformation, but also for the Christian name,"[13] were in every body's hands, and received the praises not only of the Catholics, but likewise of all the able and moderate men amongst Protestants. M. Jurieu himself is moved with their authority. For which reason, in his book of "Lawful Prepossessions,"[14] he delivers all he says of Antichrist as a thing not unanimously received, as a thing undecided, as a picture "whose lineaments are applicable to different subjects, some whereof have already happened, and others perchance are yet to come." Accordingly, the use he makes of it is as of a prepossession against popery, not as a demonstration. But now the case is quite altered; what was undecided before, is now become the groundwork of the whole Reformation; for certainly, says our author, "I do not believe this Reformation otherwise well grounded than for this reason, that the Church we have abandoned is true Antichristianism."[15] Let them no longer perplex themselves as hitherto, in search of their fundamental articles; here is the foundation of foundations, without which the Reformation would have been unjustifiable. What will then become of it if this doctrine, "popery is true Antichristianism," falls of itself, merely by exposing it? This will be perceived clearly by a little attention to what follows.

11.—*Exposition of the Minister Jurieu's Doctrine.*

There needs only to consider that the whole mystery consists in clearly showing what it is that constitutes this pretended Antichristianism. The next point to be determined is the beginning of it, its duration and its period, the most speedy that it is possible, in order to comfort those who are wearied with so tedious an expectation. He thinks he has found, in the Revelations, an infallible light for the unfolding of this secret, and supposes, by taking the days for years, that the twelve hundred and sixty days assigned in the Revelations[16] for Antichrist's persecution, make twelve hundred and sixty years: let us take all this for truth, for our business here is not to dispute, but relate historically the doctrine given us for the groundwork of the Reformation.

12.—*M. Jurieu labors hard to abridge the time of his pretended prophecies.*

At first, he is very much puzzled about these twelve hundred and sixty years of persecution. Persecution is very wearisome, and gladly would he find a speedy end put to it: it is what our author openly manifests; for since what happened last in France, "my soul being cast," says he, "into the deepest abyss of grief that I ever felt in my life, I was wiling for my comfort to find grounds to hope a speedy deliverance for the Church."[17] Bent on this design, he goes to search "even in the fountain head of the Sacred oracles, to see," says he, "whether the Holy Ghost would not teach me, in regard to *the approaching downfall* of the Antichristian empire, something more sure and more precise than what other interpreters had discovered in them."[18]

13.—*This Author owns his prevention.*

Men generally find, right or wrong, whatever they have a mind in prophecies, that is, in obscure places and enigmatic sayings, when violent prejudices accompany them. This author acknowledges his own: "I will own it," says he, "with sincerity, that I approached theses divine oracles full of my prejudices, and entirely disposed to believe that we were near to the end of the reign and empire of Antichrist."[19] As he confesses himself prepossessed, he desires also to be read with favorable preventions:[20] if so, he is persuaded you cannot but enter into his notions; all will go on smoothly with this allowance.

14.—*He forsakes his guides, and why.*

Here is he then well convicted, by his own confession, that he commenced reading the word of God, not with a mind disengaged from his prejudices, and thereby in a fit temper to receive the impressions of divine light; but, on the contrary, with a mind "full of prejudices," disheartened with persecutions, absolutely determined to find the end of them, and the approaching overthrow of this so irksome an empire. He finds all the interpreters put it off to a distant date. Joseph Mede, whom he had chosen for his guide, and who had indeed set out so much to his liking, lost his way at last; for whereas he hoped, by the means of so good a guide, "to see the persecution ended in five and twenty or thirty years' time," to accomplish what Mede proposes, he must stay many ages. "Thus are we," says he, very much retarded and greatly remote from our reckoning: we must still wait these many ages."[21] This was too much for a man in such haste to see an end, and to publish better tidings to his brethren.

15.—*The impossibility of settling the beginning of these twelve hundred and sixty years which the Reformation allows to the persecution of Antichrist.*

But after all, do what he will, he is obliged to find full twelve hundred and sixty years of persecution. To give a speedy end to them, it is necessary to date the beginning early. The greatest number of the Calvinists had begun this reckoning from the time we began, as they pretended, to say Mass, and to adore the Eucharist; for that was the god Mauzzim, whom Antichrist was to worship, according to Daniel.[22] Among other fine allegories, there was somewhat of a resemblance in sound between Mauzzim and the Mass. Crespin makes a mighty stir with this in his "History of the Martyrs,"[23] and the whole party is ravished with the invention. But how! place the adoration of the Eucharist in the first ages? it is too soon: in the tenth or eleventh, in Berengarius's time? that may be done; those are ages the Reformation is little concerned about: but after all, supposing these twelve hundred and sixty whole years to commence in the tenth or eleventh century, there would remain still six hundred and sixty years of troublesome times to rub through. Our author is disheartened at this, and his ingenuity would be of little service, could it not furnish him with some more favorable expedient.

16.—*New date given to the birth of Antichrist by this Minister in his prepossessions.*

Until now the party had shown a regard for St. Gregory. It is true, Masses were discovered in him abundantly, even for the dead, invocations of saints in plenty, a number of relics; and what is very disagreeable to the Reformation, a strong persuasion of the authority of his see. Yet, for all this, his holy doctrine and holy life made him be revered. Luther and Calvin had called him the last bishop of Rome; his successors were nothing but Popes and Anti-christs; but as for him, it was not feasible to make him of that number. Our author was bolder, and in his "Lawful Prepossessions" (for he began there to be inspired to interpret the Revelations) after frequently deciding with all his interpreters, that Antichrist must begin with the ruin of the Roman empire, he declared, "This empire ceased when Rome ceased to be the capital city of the provinces, when this empire was dismembered into ten parts, which happened at the end of the fifth century, and at the beginning of the sixth."[24] This he repeats four or five times, that you may not doubt of it, and at last concludes thus: "It is, then, certain, that at the beginning of the sixth age, the corruptions of the Church were great enough, and the pride of the bishop of Rome already risen high enough, to make us determine *on this era* for the first birth of the Antichristian empire."²⁵ And again: "One may well reckon for the birth of the Antichristian empire a time, wherein were already seen all the sprouts of future corruption and tyranny."²⁶ And finally, "this dismembering of the Roman empire into ten pieces, happened about the year 500, a little before the end of the fifth century, and at the beginning of the sixth." It is, then, manifest we must begin from thence to count the twelve hundred and sixty years assigned for the duration of the Popish empire.

17.—*The times do not tally right with it, by reason of the sanctity of the then Popes.*

Unfortunately, the Church of Rome is not found sufficiently corrupted in those days to make an Antichristian church of her, for the Popes of those times were the most zealous defenders of the mysteries of the incarnation and redemption of mankind, and withal as illustrious for sanctity as ever the Church had. We need but hear the encomium which Dionysius Parvus,²⁷ so learned and pious a man, gives St. Gelasius, the Pope, who was seated in St. Peter's chair from the year 492 to the year 496. We shall there see, that the whole life of this holy Pope was either reading or prayer: his fasting, his poverty and, in the poverty of his life, his immense charity to the poor, his doctrine, in short, and his great watchfulness, that made him account the least remissness in a pastor of dangerous consequence to souls, formed in him such a bishop as St. Paul describes. This is the Pope whom this learned man beheld in the chair of St. Peter towards the end of the fifth century, when, it seems, Antichrist was born. Even a hundred years after him, St. Gregory the Great was seated in this chair, and the whole Church, in the East no less than in the West, was replenished with the odor of his virtues, amongst which his humility and zeal shone conspicuous. Nevertheless, he was seated in the chair which "began to be the seat of pride, and that of the beast."²⁸ These are fine beginnings for Antichrist. Had these Popes been pleased to be something more wicked, and defended with less zeal the mystery of Jesus Christ and the cause of piety, the system would fit better; but every thing is settled: Antichrist, then, was only in his minority,²⁹ and in this nonage nothing hindered his being a Saint, and a most zealous defender of Jesus Christ and his kingdom. These were our author's discoveries at the beginning of the year 1685, and when he composed his "Lawful Prepossessions."

18.—*The Author changes his mind, and is for advancing the overthrow of Antichrist.*

But upon his observing, towards the end of the same year, the revocation of the Edict of Nantes, with all the consequences of it, this great event made him change his prophecies, and advance the time of the downfall of Antichrist's kingdom. The author would have it in his power to say, he hoped to live to be an eyewitness of it. In 1686, he published his great work of the "Accomplishment of the Prophecies,"³⁰ wherein he determines the period of the Antichristian persecution at the year 1710, or at least in 1714 or 1715. But he informs his reader that, after all, he thinks it a difficult matter to mark precisely the year. "God," says he, "in his prophecies, *looks not into matters so minutely.*"

Stupendous maxim! Nevertheless, "one may say," proceeds he, "this must happen between the year 1710 and the year 1715." This we may depend upon, and what he calls persecution will be at an end for certain, at the beginning of the eighteenth century; so we draw near the point: scarce five-and-twenty years remain. Which of the zealous Calvinists would not have patience, and wait so short a term?

19.—He is obliged to make him be born in the person of St. Leo the Great.

The truth is, there is some difficulty in the thing; for the more he advances the end of the twelve hundred and sixty years, the higher must he carry the beginning of them, and settle this epoch of the Antichristian empire in still purer times. Thus to finish in 1710, or thereabouts, he must have begun the Antichristian persecution in the year 450 or 454, under the Pontificate of St. Leo; and accordingly it is what the author chooses after Joseph Mede, who, in our days, has made himself famous in England by his learned extravagancies on the Revelations, and the other prophecies employed against us.

20.—Absurdity of this System.

It seems as if God had a design to confound these impostors by filling the chair of St. Peter with the greatest men and greatest Saints it ever had, at the time which was selected to make it the seat of Antichrist. Can one but consider the letters and sermons wherein St. Leo inspires, even at this day, so forcibly into his readers the faith of Jesus Christ, and believe that an Antichrist was the author of them? But what other Pope has impugned more vigorously the enemies of Jesus Christ, has maintained with more zeal both Christian grace and ecclesiastical discipline, and, in fine, given to the world a more holy doctrine, with more holy examples? He, whose sanctity made him be revered by the barbarous Attila, and saved Rome from massacre, is the first Antichrist, and father of all the rest. It was Antichrist that held the Fourth General Council, so respected by all good Christians; it was Antichrist that dictated the divine letter to Flavian, which was the admiration of the whole church, wherein the mystery of Jesus Christ is so sublimely and so distinctly explained, that the Fathers of this great Council cried out at each word, "Peter has spoken by the mouth of Leo;" whereas they should have said, by his mouth Antichrist has spoken, or rather, Peter and Jesus Christ himself have spoken by the mouth of Antichrist. Must not a man have drunk deep, even to the dregs of that infatuating cup, the potion of the lying prophets of old, and turned his head quite giddy with its fumes, to vent to the world such delirious exorbitances?

21.—Idle shift of the Minister.

At this part of the prophecy, the new prophet foresaw the indignation of mankind, and that of Protestants no less than Catholics; for he is forced to own that, from Leo the First to Gregory the Great, inclusively, Rome had a great many good bishops,[31] of whom he must make as many Antichrists, and hopes to satisfy the world by saying they were "Antichrists commenced." But after all, if the twelve hundred and sixty years of Antichristian persecution begin then, he must either abandon the sense he gives to the prophecy, or say, that then "the holy city was trod under foot by the Gentiles;[32] the two witnesses," namely, "the small number of the faithful," were put to death, "the woman with child," to wit, the church, "was driven into the wilderness," and deprived at least of the public exercise of religion; that from that time, in short, began the execrable "blasphemies of the beast against the name of God, and against all those that dwell in heaven, and the war she waged against the Saints."[33] For it is set down expressly in St. John, that all this was to continue a thousand two hundred and threescore days, which he will have to be years. To make these blasphemies, this war, this Antichristian persecution, and this triumph of error, to begin in the Church of Rome, even from the time of St. Leo, St. Gelasius, and St. Gregory, and make it hold on for the space of all these ages, when unquestionably that church was the model of all other churches, not in faith alone, but also in piety and discipline, is the height of all extravagance.

22.—Three bad characters imputed to St. Leo.

But gain, what has St. Leo done to deserve to be the first Antichrist? He could not be Antichrist for nothing. Here are the three characters he gives to Antichristianism, which must be made to agree with the time of St. Leo, and with him in person; "Idolatry, tyranny, and corruption of manners."[34] How deplorable, to be reduced to defend St. Leo against Christians, from all these reproaches! but charity constrains us to it. Let us begin by the corruption of manners. But then nothing is objected against him on this head; nothing can be found in the life of this great Pope but examples of sanctity. In his time ecclesiastical discipline was still in its full vigor, and St. leo was the support of it. Thus you see how manners were corrupted. Let us run over the other characters, that of tyranny next, in as few words. Ever since the time of St. Leo, objects our author,[35] "who was sitting in the year 450, to that of St. Gregory the Great, the Bishops of Rome have labored to arrogate to themselves a superiority over the universal church:" but was it St. Leo that began? He dares not say it; all he says is, labored at it," for he knows full well that St. Celestin his predecessor, and St. Boniface, and St. Zozimus, and St. Innocent, to go no further back at present, acted no otherwise than St. Leo; nor were they less zealous in maintaining the authority of St. Peter's chair. Why should they not, then, be of the number, at least, of these "Antichrists commenced." The reason is, because, had he begun from their time, the twelve hundred and threescore years would have elapsed already, and the event would have belied the sense he is resolved to give the Revelations. Thus do men impose on the world, and turn the divine oracles to their own fancy.

23.—St. Leo's idolatry.—The Mauzzims of Daniel applied to the Saints.

But it is time we should come to the third character of the beast, which our adversaries are determined to find in St. Leo, and in the whole church of his time. There is a new Paganism, an idolatry worse than that of the Gentiles, in the honor paid to saints and their relics. It is on this third character the chief stress is laid: Joseph Mede[36] has the honor of the invention, who interpreting these words of Daniel, "he shall honor the God Mauzzim," to wit, as he translates it, "the God of forces;" and again, "he shall do it to fence Mauzzim with a strange God;" understands this of Antichrist, who shall call the saints his fortresses.

24.—St. Basil and the rest of the Saints of these times accused of the same Idolatry.

But how can he find that Antichrist will give the saints this name? "In this," says he, "that St. Basil has preached to all his people, or rather to the whole universe, who have read and approved his divine sermons, that the forty martyrs, whose relics they possessed, 'were towers whereby the city was defended.'[37] St. Chrysostom has also said, "that the relics of St. Peter and Paul were more secure towers for Rome than ten thousand ramparts."[38] "Is not this," concludes Mede, "raising up the gods Mauzzims?" St. Basil and St. Chrysostom are the Antichrists who erect these fortresses against the true God.

25.—Other Saints likewise Idolaters.

Yet not they alone: the poet Fortunatus hath sung after St. Chrysostom, "that Rome had two ramparts and two towers in St. Peter and St. Paul." St. Gregory has said as much of them. St. Chrysostom, "that the holy martyrs of Egypt protect us like impregnable ramparts, like unshaken rocks, against our invisible enemies." And Mede still replies, "are not these Mauzzims?" he adds, "that St. Hilary discovers likewise our bulwarks in the angels."[39] He cites St. Gregory, of Nyssa, brother to St. Basil, Gennadius, Evagrius, St. Eucherius, Theodoret, and the prayers of the Greeks, in proof of the same. He does not forget that the Cross is called our defence, and that our common expression is, "we fortify ourselves with the sign of the Cross;" *Munire se signo Crucis:*[40] the Cross comes in amongst the rest, and this sacred symbol of our salvation must also be ranked amongst the Mauzzims of Antichrist.

26.—St. Ambrose added to the rest by M. Jurieu.

M. Jurieu sets off all these fine passages of Joseph Mede to the best advantage;[41] and not to be a mere transcriber, adds to them St. Ambrose, who says, "the saints Gervase and Protase were the tutelary angels of the city of Milan." He might also have named St. Gregory Nazianzen, St. Austin, and, in short, all the Fathers who abound in as strong expressions. All this is making as many gods of the saints, because it is making of them *ramparts* and *rocks* where is found a secure sanctuary, names which the Scripture appropriates to God.

27.—The Ministers cannot believe what they say themselves.

These men know well in their own consciences, that the Fathers, whom they quote, never understood it so: but meant only to say, that God gives us in the saints, as heretofore he did in Moses, in David, and in Jeremiah, invincible protectors, whose acceptable prayers are a more secure defence to us than a thousand ramparts: for he is able to make his saints, when he pleases, and in the manner that he pleases, "impregnable fortresses, iron pillars, and brazen walls."[42] Our doctors, I say again, are convinced in their hearts that is the sense of St. Chrysostom and St. Basil, when they call the saints towers and fortresses. From these examples they ought to learn, not to take in a criminal sense other as strong expressions, and withal as innocent as these; at least not to carry impiety so far as to make these holy doctors the founders of Antichristian idolatry, this being a charge equally atrocious on the whole Church of their times, whose doctrine and worship they did but propound. Nor, indeed, ought we to imagine our ministers believed seriously what they said, and judged so many saints no better than blasphemers and idolaters. All that we can conclude from thence is, that they suffer themselves to be transported beyond all bounds, and without enlightening the understanding, seek only to kindle hatred in the heart.

28.—Why they do not make St. Basil the beginning of Antichristianism as well as St. Leo.

But after all, if we must hold for Antichrists all these pretended worshippers of Mauzzims, why do they defer to St. Leo's time the beginning of the Antichristian empire?[43] Let them show me that in this Pope's days more was done for the saints than acknowledging them for towers and impregnable fortresses? Let them show me that more trust was put in their prayers, more honor paid to their relics? You say that in 360, and 390, the worship of creatures, that is, in your notion, that of the saints, was not as yet established in the public service: show me that it was more or less so in St. Leo's time? You say, in the same year of 360, and 390, great precautions were taken not to confound the service of God with the service of creatures then commencing: show me that less was taken afterwards, and especially in St. Leo's pontificate? But who ever could have confounded things so well distinguished? We demand things of God; we demand prayers of the saints: who ever dreamed of asking either prayers of God, or the things themselves of the saints as those that gave them? Show, then, that in St. Leo's time these characters so distinct were confounded, the service of God, with the honor given to his servants for love of him? you never will undertake it. Why, therefore, stop in so fair a way? dare to utter what you think. Begin by St. Basil, and St. Gregory of Nazianzen, in the reign of Antichristian idolatry, and the blasphemies of the beast against the Eternal, and against all that dwells in heaven: turn into blasphemies against God and against the saints, what has been said ever since that time of the glory God imparted to his servants in the Church: St. Basil is no better than St. Leo; nor the Church more privileged at the end of the fourth age, than fifty years after the middle of the fifth. But I see the answer you make me in your heart, viz, that should you begin by St. Basil, all would have been completed long ago; and thus belied by the event, you could no longer amuse the people with vain hopes.

29.—*Ridiculous Calculations.*

Accordingly, our author owns[44] you might begin his whole calculation from four different epochs: viz., 360, 393, 430, and in fine, 450, 455, which is the calculation he himself follows. All these four accounts, according to him, agree admirably with the system of the new idolatry:[45] but unluckily in the two first reckonings, where all things else, as he pretends, agree so well, the chief point is wanting; to wit, that according to these computations the Popish empire should have fallen in 1620, or in 1653. Now it still exists and enjoys a small respite. As to the third calculation, it terminates in 1690, four or five years hence, says our author: it would be too much exposing himself to take so short a term. Yet every concurrence tallied with it to admiration. See what these concurrences are which they build so much on, mere dreams, visions, manifest illusions, proved notoriously such by the event.

30.—*Why St. Basil's Idolatry and that of the other Fathers is not accounted Antichristian.*

"But," says our author, "the chief reason why God will not compute the birth of Antichristianism from these years, 360, 393, and 430, notwithstanding that the new idolatry," which he will have to be the character of Antichristianism, "was then established, is, that there was a fourth characteristic of the birth of this Antichristian empire which had not as yet appeared; namely, that the Roman empire was to be destroyed; that there were to be seven Kings, to wit, according to all the Protestants, seven forms of Government in the city on seven mountains, meaning Rome."[46] The Papal empire was to make the seventh government, and it was requisite the six others should be destroyed to make room for the seventh, which was that of the Pope and Antichrist. When Rome ceased to be mistress, and the Antichristian empire was to commence, it was necessary there should be ten kings, which were to receive the sovereign power at the same time with the beast;[47] and ten kingdoms, "into which the Roman empire was to be subdivided," according to the oracle of the Revelations. All this was fulfilled in the nick of time under St. Leo: this, therefore, is the precise time of the birth of Antichrist, and there is no resisting the concurrence of such circumstances.

31.—*Infinite absurdity.*

Admirable doctrine! neither these ten kings, nor the dismembering of the empire, entered into the constitution of Antichrist, nor at farthest could this be any thing else than an exterior token of his birth; what truly constitutes him, is the corruption of manners, is the pretention to superiority, is principally the new idolatry. All this is no more to be found under St. Leo, than fourscore or a hundred years before; but God would not, as yet, impute it for Antichristianism, nor did it please him that the new idolatry, though already entirely formed, should be Antichristian. It is impossible, in fine, that such extravagances, where impiety and absurdity strive together which shall exceed, should not open the eyes of our brethren, and, at length, put them out of conceit with those who delude them with such dreams.

> 32.—*The system of the Ministers concerning the seven Kings of the Revelations evidently confounded by the very words of this prophesy.*

But let us enter into the particulars of these fine concurrences so dazzling to our Reformed, and begin with the seven Kings, who, according to St. John, are the seven heads of the beast, and with these ten horns, which, according to the same St. John, are ten other kings. The sense, say they, is manifest. "The seven heads," says St. John, "are the seven mountains on which the woman sitteth, and these are seven kings: five are fallen; one is, and the other is not yet come; and when he cometh he must continue a short space; and the beast that was and is not, even he is the eighth king, and one of the seven, and goeth into destruction."[48] The seven kings are, says our author,[49] the seven forms of government Rome had been subject to; the kings, the consuls, the dictators, the decemvirs, the military tribunes, who had consular power, the emperors, and finally the Pope. Five are fallen, says St. John: five of these governments had expired when he wrote this prophesy: one is still; the empire of the Cæsars under which he wrote: and the other must come soon; who does not espy the Papal empire? It is one of the seven kings: one of the seven forms of government, and it is also the eighth king, namely, the eighth form of government: the seventh, because the pope much resembles emperors by the dominion which he exercises; and the eighth, because he has something peculiar, his spiritual empire, his dominion over consciences; all might just, but for one little word that mars the whole. In the first place, I would fain ask, why the seven kings are seven forms of government, and not seven real kings. Let them show me in Scripture, that the forms of government are named kings; on the contrary, three verses after, I see that the ten kings are ten real kings, and not ten sorts of government. Why should these seven kings of verse the ninth, be so different from the ten kings of verse the twelfth? Does he pretend to make us believe that the consuls, annual magistrates, are kings? that the entire extirpation of the regal power of Rome is one of the seven kings of Rome? that ten men, the decemviri, are one king; and the whole series of four or six military tribunes, more or less, another king? But in good truth, is that another form of government? who is ignorant that the military tribunes differed not from consuls, except in the number? for which reason they were called *Tribuni militum Consulari potestate*; and if St. John had a mind to denote all the names of the supreme power among the Romans, why did he forget the Triumviri? had they not, at least, as much power as the Decemviri? And should it be said, it was too short to deserve notice, why should that of the

Decemviri, which held but two years, deserve it more? This is true, they may reply: let us put them in lieu of the Dictators, for there is little likelihood the Dictatorship could ever be called a form of government under which Rome continued for a certain time. It was an extraordinary magistracy, set up according to the exigency of present circumstances in all times of the republic, not a particular form of government. Let us remove them then, and put the Triumviri in their stead. I consent to it, and even willingly give to the interpretation of Protestants the best appearance it is capable of: for when all is said, there is nothing in it but illusion; one little word, as I said, will subvert the whole fabric; for in short, we read of the seventh king (who shall be, since they will have it, the seventh government) that "when he cometh, he must continue a short space.[50] St. John has but just shown him; and he immediately, says he, "he goeth into destruction." If this be the Papal empire, it must needs be short. Now it is pretended from St. John, that it must continue at least one thousand two hundred and threescore years, as long a time, as is owned by our new interpreter, "as all the other governments together."[51] Wherefore it is impossible the Papal empire should be meant by this prophesy.

33.—*Trifling reply.*

But replies our author, "one day," as says St. Peter,[52] "is with the Lord as a thousand years." A fine discovery! all equally as short to the eyes of God, and not only the reign of the seventh king, but also the reign of all the rest. Now St. John would distinguish this seventh king by comparing him with the other kings, and his reign was to be remarkable by the shortness of its continuance. To show this characteristic in the Papal government, who does not see that its being short in the sight of God, with whom nothing is durable, is not sufficient? It ought to be short in comparison with the other governments; more short by consequence than that of the military Tribunes, which scarcely subsisted thirty or forty years; more short than that of the Decemviri, which continued but two; more short at least than that of the kings, or consuls, or emperors, who filled up the greatest space of time in duration. But on the contrary, that which St. John has distinguished by the brevity of its duration, does not only hold out longer than any of the rest, but also longer than all the rest together: what more manifestly absurd! and is it not an attempt to make the prophecies ridiculous, thus to interpret them?

34.—*The Ten Kings of the Revelations manifestly as ill interpreted.*

But let us say one word of the ten kings whom our interpreter, after Joseph Mede, believes he triumphs in. There it is he ranges before us[53]—first, the Britons; second, the Saxons; third, the French; fourth, the Burgundians; fifth, the Visigoths; sixth, the Suevi and Alani; seventh, the Vandals; eighth, the Germans; ninth, the Ostrogoths in Italy, where the Lombards succeed them; tenth, the Grecians. Here are fully ten kingdoms which the Roman empire was divided into at its fall. Without disputing on the qualities, without disputing on the number, without disputing on the dates, this at least is very certain —viz., that as soon as ever these ten kings appear, St. John makes them "give their power and strength unto the Beast."[54] We own as much, say our interpreters;[55] and it is likewise the very thing that gains our cause; for these are "the ten vassal and subject kings which the Antichristian empire, namely, the Pontifical, hath always had in subjection to worship it, and maintain its power." Here is a wonderful tallying of incidents; but what, I pray, have the Arian kings contributed to the establishment of the Papal empire, such as the Visigoths and the Ostrogoths, the Burgundians and the Vandals; or the heathen kings, such as at that time were the French and Saxons? Are these the ten vassal kings of the Papacy, who had nothing else to do but worship it? But when was it that these Vandals and Ostrogoths worshipped the Popes? Was it under Theodoric and his successors, when the Pope groaned under their tyranny? or under Genseric, when with the Vandals, he pillaged Rome and carried the spoils of it into Africa? And since even the Lombards are introduced, were they also of the number that aggrandized the Church of Rome, they that did all in their power to oppress her as long as ever they subsisted, namely, for two hundred years? For what else were, during this whole space of time, the Alboini, the Astolphi, and the Didiers, but enemies to Rome, and the Church of Rome? And the Emperors of the East, who were in reality the Emperors of Rome, though ranged here the last under the name of Greeks, must they also be reckoned amongst the vassals and subjects of the Pope, they whom St. Leo and his successors, down to the time of Charlemagne, acknowledged for their sovereigns? But, you will say, these Heathen and heretical kings embraced the true faith. Right; they embraced it a long while after this division into ten kingdoms. The French had four Heathen kings: the Saxons were not converted till the time of St. Gregory, a hundred and fifty years after this division; the Goths, who reigned in Spain, were converted from Arianism at the same time. What has this to do with these kings, who, according to the pretension of our interpreters, were to begin to reign at the same time with the Beast, and give up their power to him? Besides, can no other era be found for the entrance of these kings into the Antichristian empire, but that of their turning Christians or Catholics? What a happy destiny for this pretended Antichristian empire, to be compounded of people converted to Jesus Christ! But what is it, after all, that these kings, so happily converted, have contributed to the establishment of the Pope's authority? If, at their admittance into the Church they acknowledged the First See, which was that of Rome, neither did they give him that supremacy which he had undoubtedly before their conversion, nor did they acknowledge, in the Pope, any thing more than Christians had acknowledged in him before them, to wit, the successor of St. Peter. Nor did the Popes, on their side, exercise their authority over these people otherwise than by teaching them the true faith and upholding regularity and discipline among them: nor can any man show, during this time, or four hundred years after, that they concerned themselves with any thing else, or enterprised any thing on temporals. Thus you see what were these ten kings, with whom the Papal empire was to commence.

35.—Vain reply.

But then, we are told,[56] came other ten in their place, and these are they with their kingdoms: first, Germany; second, Hungary; third, Poland; fourth, Sweden; fifth, France; sixth, England; seventh, Spain; eighth, Portugal; ninth, Italy; tenth, Scotland. Expound who can why Scotland stands here rather than Bohemia; why Sweden rather than Denmark or Norway; why, in fine, Portugal, as separated from Spain, rather than Castile, Arragon, Leon, Navarre, and the other kingdoms? But why do we lose our time in examining these fancies? Let them resolve me at least this question, whether or no these were the ten kingdoms that were to be formed out of the remnants of the Roman empire at the same time that Antichrist was to appear, and which were to resign their authority and power to him? What has Poland to do here, and the other kingdoms of the North, which Rome was not acquainted with, and which, beyond question, were not formed of her ruins when the Antichrist, St. Leo, came into the world? Is it in banter than men write, with so serious an air, such ridiculous conceits? In good truth, it ill becomes those who have nothing in their mouths but the pure word of God, thus rashly to sport with its oracles: and if they have nothing more pertinent whereby to explain the prophecies, it were much better to adore their sacred obscurity, and respect the future, which God has reserved in his own hands.

36.—Contrarieties of the new Interpreters.

We must not wonder to see these daring interpreters at variance among themselves, and destroying one another. Joseph Mede, on that verse of St. John, importing that in a great earthquake "the tenth part of the city fell,"[57] thought he had hit exactly, when he interpreted this tenth part with respect to the new Antichristian Rome, which is ten times less than ancient Rome. To come at the proof of his interpretation, he seriously compares the areas of old Rome with that of the new, and with a fine figure demonstrates that the first is ten times greater than the last: but his disciple, M. Jurieu, deprives him of so mathematical an interpretation. "He is mistaken with all the rest," cries out haughtily the new prophet,[58] "when by the city St. John speaks of, he understands only the city of Rome." "We ought to hold for certain," proceeds he in a masterly strain, "that the great city is Rome with its empire."[59] And the tenth part of the city, what shall it be? He has found it out: "France," says he, "is the tenth part."[60] But how? shall France fall? and does this prophet forebode so ill of his own country? No, no, she may be reduced indeed to a tottering condition; let her look to it, the prophet threatens her: yet shall not perish. What the Holy Ghost here means by saying she shall fall, is, "that she shall fall with respect to Popery;"[61] but then she shall rise more illustrious than ever, because she shall embrace the Reformation, and that speedily; and our kings (a thing I am loth to repeat) are on the point of being Calvinistically reformed. What patience is able to support these interpretations? But after all, he is more in the right than he imagined, by calling this a "fall:" dreadful indeed would be the "fall" into a "reformation," wherein the spirit of illusion so forcibly predominates.

> 37,—*The Englishman finds England, and the Frenchman France, in the Revelations.*

If the French interpreter finds France in the Revelations, the Englishman finds England in them: the phial poured out upon the rivers and fountains of waters, "are the Pope's emissaries, and the Spaniards vanquished in Queen Elizabeth's reign of glorious memory." But good Mr. Mede,[62] it seems, was in a gross mistake: his more enlightened disciple assures us,[63] the second and third phial "were the crusades, when God returned blood upon Catholics for the blood of the Vaudois and Albigenses spilt by them." These Vaudois and Albigenses, John Wickliff and John Huss, with all the rest of that gang, even to the bloody Taborites, appear throughout these new interpretations as faithful witnesses of the truth persecuted by the Beast; but they are now well known, and even this were enough to prove the falsity of these pretended prophesies.

> 38.—*The King of Sweden foretold, and the prediction falsified immediately after.*

Joseph Mede had outdone himself in his exposition of the fourth phial. He saw it "poured out upon the sun, upon the chief part of the heaven possessed by the Beast,"[64]—namely, the Papal empire: the meaning whereof was, that the Pope was going to lose the empire of Germany, which is his sun: nothing more clear. Whilst Mede, if you will believe him, was printing these things, "which he had meditated on long before,"[65] he heard of the wonderful achievements "of that pious, happy, and victorious king, whom God had sent from the North to defend his cause:" in a word, it was the great Gustavus. Mede can no longer doubt but his conjecture was an inspiration; and applies to this great king the same canticle that David applied to the Messiah: "Gird thy sword upon thy thigh, O most mighty King! combat for the truth, and for justice, proceed prosperously and reign."[66] But the event belied the prediction; so Mede published at once his prophecy and shame.

> 39.—*Ridiculous conceit about the Turks.*

No less remarkable is that fine passage, where, whilst Mede is contemplating the overthrow of the Turkish empire, his disciple, on the contrary, spies in it the victories gained by that empire. The Euphrates in the Revelations,[67] is to Mede[68] the empire of the Turks; and the waters of the Euphrates dried up at the effusion of the sixth phial, is the Turkish empire destroyed. He is quite in the dark: M. Jurieu[69] demonstrates to us that the Euphrates is the Archipelago and the Bosphorus, which the Turks passed in 1390, in order to possess themselves of Greece and Constantinople. More than this:[70] "there is great likelihood that the conquests of the Turks are carried on thus far in order to give them the means of contributing, together with Protestants, to the great work of God,—namely, to the destruction of the Papal empire: for though the

Turks have never been so low as at present" (this is the very thing that makes our author believe they will soon rise again,) "I look upon," says he, "this year 1685, as critical in this affair. God hath humbled the Reformed and the Turks at the same time, *to raise them up again at the same time,* and in order to make them the instruments of his revenge against the Popish empire." Who would not admire this sympathy of Turkism with the Reformation, and this common destiny of them both? Should the Turks prove successful, then will the Reformed (whilst the rest of Christians grieve at their victories) raise up their heads, and believe that the time of their deliverance is at hand. We were strangers as yet to this new excellency of the Reformation—of its being to increase and decrease as it were by sympathy with the Turks. Our author himself was puzzled at this place when he composed his allowable "Prepossessions," and knew nothing of the plagues of the two last phials wherein this mystery was locked up: but at last, "after knocking two, four, five," and "six times, with a religious attention, the door flew open,"[71] and he beheld this mighty secret.

> 40.—*Why these absurdities are tolerated in the party.*

Men of sense, you will tell me, among the Protestants, laugh at these fooleries as well as we. Yet they let them take their run, knowing them necessary to amuse the credulous multitude. It was principally by these visions that hatred was excited against the Church of Rome, and hopes fomented of her speedy overthrow. The same artifice is employed again for the same purpose, and the people, a hundred times deceived, give ear to them, as the Jews, abandoned to the spirit of error, did heretofore to false prophets. Examples are quite useless to disabuse a people possessed with prejudice. They believed they saw, in the prophecies of Luther, the expiration of the Papacy so near at hand, that there was not a Protestant who did not hope to be present at its formal funeral. It was necessary, indeed, to prolong the time, but the same spirit was kept up still, and the Reformation never ceased to be the bubble of these lying prophets, who prophesy the delusions of their frantic brain.

> 41.—*The part's Prophets are impostors.—Confession of the Minister Jurieu.*

God forbid I should lose my time in speaking here of a Cotterus, a Drabicius, a Christiana, a Comenius, and all those other visionaries, of whose predictions our minister boasts, and whose errors he acknowledges. None of them, as he pretends, no, not even the learned Usher, but must turn prophet. But the same minister frankly owns he was no less mistaken than the rest. Experience proved them all deluded, "and we discover in them," says the minister, "so many things in which they blundered, that there is no relying on them."[72] Yet he nevertheless accounts them prophets, and great prophets, Ezekiels and Jeremiahs. He finds "in their visions such majesty and loftiness, that those of the ancient prophets have not more, and a train of miracles as great as ever happened since the apostles."[73] Thus does the chief of our Protestants suffer himself to be imposed on by these false prophets, even after the event had confounded them: so prevalent is the spirit of illusion in the party; but the true prophets of the Lord deliver themselves in another strain against such impostors as abuse the name of God: "Hear thou, O Hananiah," saith Jeremiah,[74] "this word that I speak in thine ears, and in the ears of all the people. The prophets that have been before me, and before thee of old, and have prophesied good or evil to nations and to kingdoms; when their words came to pass, it was known that they were prophets whom the Lord had truly sent; and the word of the Lord came unto Jeremiah, saying, Go and tell Hananiah, saying, thus saith the Lord; thou hast broken the yokes of wood,"—in token of the people's future deliverance,—"and thou shalt make for them yokes of iron: I will aggravate the yoke of these nations" to whom thou denouncest peace. "Then said the prophet Jeremiah unto Hananiah the prophet, Hear now, Hananiah, the Lord hath not sent thee, but thou makest this people to trust in a lie; therefore, thus saith the Lord, Behold, I will cast thee from off the face of the earth: this year thou shalt die, because thou hast spoken against the Lord; and Hananiah the prophet died the same year in the seventh month." Thus did he deserve to be confounded who deceived the people in the Lord's name, and the people needed but to open their eyes and take warning.

42.—*Their interpreters no better.*

Our Reformed interpreters are not worth more than our Reformed prophets. The Revelations and the rest of the Prophecies have ever been the subject which the wits of the Reformation have thought themselves at liberty to sport with. Each one has discovered in them his concurrences, whereby the credulous Protestants were always caught. M. Jurieu reproves often, as we have seen, Joseph Mede, whom he had chosen for his guide.[75] Nay, he has pointed out the errors of Du Moulin, his grandfather,[76] whose interpretations on the prophecies were admired by the whole Reformation; and has even showed "that the foundation he built upon was destitute of fidelity." Nevertheless, there was abundance of wit, and a very extensive erudition in these visions of Du Moulin; but so it is, the more wit a man has, the more he deceives himself on these occasions; because, the more wit he has, the more he invents, and ventures the more. Du Moulin's fine wit, which must needs exercise itself on futurity, set him on a task for which he was laughed at, even in his own family; and M. Jurieu, his grandson, who, perhaps, shows more wit than the rest on this subject, will be but the more certainly the laughter of mankind.

43.—*What the Ministers have discovered in the Revelations touching their Reformers.*

I am ashamed of dwelling so long on vision more chimerical than sick men's dreams. But I ought not to forget what is of greatest importance in this vain mystery of the Protestants. According to the idea they give of the Revelations, nothing should be more distinctly marked in them than the Reformation itself, with its authors, who came to destroy the empire of the Beast; and especially it ought to be marked in the effusion of the "seven phials," in which are foretold, as they pretend, the seven plagues of their Antichristian empire. But what our interpreters descry here, is so ill contrived, that one destroys what the other builds. Joseph Mede[77] thinks he has found both Luther and Calvin when the phial is poured on the sea, that is on the Antichristian world, and when immediately this sea, "is changed into blood like to that of a dead man."[78] "Here," says he, "is the Reformation; it is a poison that kills every thing: for then every living soul died in the sea." Mede takes care to explain this blood like to that of a carcass, and says, it is as the blood of a member lopped off, on account "of the provinces and kingdoms which were then rent from the body of the papacy."[79] This is an ill-boding spectacle for Protestants, to see the reformed nations exhibited to them in no other view than that of "lopped members," which have lost, according to Mede, "all connexion with the fountain of life, all vital spirit, and all warmth," without telling us any more of the matter.

44.—The idea of the Minister Jurieu.

This is Mede's idea of the Reformation. But if he sees it in the effusion of the second phial, the other interpreter sees it only in the effusion of the seventh, "when there came," says St. John,[80] "a great voice out of the temple of heaven, from the throne, saying, it is done. And there were voices, and thunders, and lightnings; and there was a great earthquake, such as was not since men were upon the earth;" there, says he, is the Reformation.[81]

This great commotion, I must own, suits well enough with the disturbances it raised over the whole universe, such as never had been seen before on the score of religion. But here it is he shines most: "the great city was divided into three parts,[82] namely," says our author, "into the Church of Rome, the Lutheran, and the Calvinian; these are the three parties that divide the 'great city,' to wit, the Western Church." I accept the omen; the Reformation breaks unity; in breaking it, she divides herself into two, and leaves unity to the Church of Rome in St. Peter's chair, which is the centre of it. But St. John should not have forgotten that one of the divided parties, the Calvinian, broke again into two pieces, since England, reckoned to appertain to it by our minister, yet makes, in the main, a sect apart. Nor must he say, this division is but light, for, by his own confession, they mutually treat each other as "excommunicated persons."[83] Accordingly, the Church of England reckons the Calvinists, or Puritans, in the number of Nonconformists; that is, in the number of those whose service she does not allow, nor receives their ministers but by ordaining them anew as pastors, destitute of sanction or character. I might also speak of the other sects which divided the Christian world at the same time with Luther and Calvin, and which, taken together or separately, make a party sufficiently great not to have been omitted in this passage of St. John. And all considered, these men should have given their reformation a more specious character than that of overthrowing every thing, and a more creditable mark than that of pulling to pieces the Western Church, the most flourishing of the whole universe; which has been the greatest of all plagues.

Notes

[1] Sup. l. i. n. 31.
[2] Gratul. ad Ven. Presb. op. p. 331.
[3] 2 Thess. ii. 4.
[4] Sup. l. iii. n. 50.
[5] Syn. of Saumur. 1596.
[6] S. l. iv. n. 38.
[7] S. l. iii. n. 39. L. v. n. 24. 1603.
[8] Avis. t. i. p. 48.
[9] Ibid. p. 49.
[10] Ibid. Acc. des Proph. part. i. ch. xvi. p. 292.
[11] Avis. t. i. p. 49, 50.
[12] Avis. p. 4, Acc. part i. ch. xvi. p. 291.
[13] Ibid. p. 4.
[14] Prej. leg. part i. ch. iv. pp. 72. 73.
[15] Ibid. p. 50.
[16] Rev. xi. xii. xiii.
[17] Avis. p. 4.
[18] Ibid. pp. 7, 8.
[19] Ibid. p. 8.
[20] Ibid. p. 53.
[21] Accomp. part ii. ch. iv. p. 60.
[22] Dan. xi. 38.
[23] Hist. des Mart. by Cresp. l. i.
[24] Prej. leg. part. i. p. 82.
[25] Ibid. pp. 83, 85.
[26] Prej. leg. part i. p. 128.
[27] Pref. Coll. decret. cod. Hist. t. i. p. 183.
[28] Prej. leg. part i. p. 147.
[29] Ibid. 128.
[30] Acc. part ii. ch. ii. p. 18, 28.
[31] Acc. part ii. ch. ii. pp. 39, 40, 41.
[32] Rev. xi. 2.
[33] Acc. part ii. ch. x. p. 159, Rev. xii. 6, 14. xiii. 5, 6.
[34] Ibid. ch. ii. pp. 18, 28.
[35] Acc. des Proph. part ii. ch. ii. p. 41.
[36] Expos. of Dan. ch. xi. n. 36, &c. Book iii. ch. xvi, xvii. p. 666, et seq. Dan. xi. 38, 39.
[37] Ibid. ch. xvii. p. 673. Bas. Orat. in 40. Mart. Id. in Maur. Mart.
[38] Chrys. Hom. 32. ad Rom.
[39] Chrys. Hom. 32 ad Rom. p. 673. Hom. 70. ad Pop. Ant. Orat. in 40. Mart.
[40] Ibid. p. 678.
[41] Acc. des Proph. part i. ch. xiv. pp.

248, 249, et seq. Ib. p. 235. Mede ubi sub. ch. xiv.
[42] Jer. i. 18.
[43] Acc. part ii. p. 23.
[44] Acc. part ii.p. 20, &c.
[45] Ibid. p. 22.
[46] Acc. part ii. p. 23. Rev. xvii. 9.
[47] Rev. xvii. 12.
[48] Rev. xvii. 3, 9, 12.
[49] Acc. part. i. p. 11.
[50] Rev. xvii. 10.
[51] Acc. part i. p. 11.
[52] 2 Pet. iii. 8.
[53] Prej. legit. part i. ch. vii. p. 126. Acc. des Proph. part ii. pp. 27, 28.
[54] Rev. xvii. 13.
[55] Acc. part i. ch. xv. p. 266.
[56] Prej. part i. ch. vi. p. 105.
[57] Rev. xi. 13. Med. comm. in apoc. part ii. p. 489.
[58] Acc. p. ii. ch. xi. p. 194.
[59] Ibid. pp. 200, 203.
[60] Ib. 201.
[61] Ibid.
[62] Med. comm. Apo. p. 528. ad Phial. Ap. iii. p. 16.
[63] Acc. des Proph. part ii. ch. iv. p. 72. Prej. legit. part i. ch. v. pp. 98, 99.
[64] Com. Ap. p. 528. Rev. xvi. 8.
[65] Ibid. p. 529.
[66] Psalm xliv.
[67] Rev. xvi. 12.
[68] Jos. Mede, ad Ph. vi. p. 529.
[69] Acc. part ii. ch. vii. p. 99.
[70] Ibid. p. 101.
[71] Acc. part ii. ch. vii. p. 94.
[72] Avis à tous les ch., at the beginning, pp. 5, 67. Ib.
[73] Acc. des Proph. part ii. p.174. Ibid.
[74] Jer. xxviii. 7, et seq.
[75] Jur. Acc. des Proph. part i. p. 71.
[76] Part ii. p. 183.
[77] Jos. Mede, ad Ph. ii. Apo. xvi. 3.
[78] Rev. Ibid.
[79] Med. Ibid.
[80] Rev. xvi. 17.
[81] Acc. part ii. ch. viii. p. 122.
[82] Rev. Ibid.
[83] S. l. xii. n. 44.

Book XIV

[From the year 1601, to that part of the Seventeenth Century, wherein the Author wrote and concluded his History.]

A brief Summary.—The excesses of the Reformation, with respect to Predestination and Free Will, discovered in Holland.—Aminius, who owns them, falls into other excesses.—Parties of Remonstrants and Anti-Remonstrants.—The Synod of Dort, where the excesses of Calvinian Justification are clearly approved.—Monstrous Doctrine on the certainty of Salvation, and the justice of the most wicked persons.—Consequences equally absurd, concerning Infant Sanctification, decided in the Synod.—The Synod's procedure justifies the Church of Rome against Protestants.—Arminianism, in the main, left entire, notwithstanding the decisions of Dort.—Pelagianism tolerated, and the suspicion of Socinianism the sole cause of rejecting the Arminians.—The uselessness of Synodical decisions amongst Protestants.—The Synod of Dort's connivance at an infinity of capital errors, whilst bent on maintaining the particular Dogmas of Calvinism.—These Dogmas confessed at the beginning for essential, at last reduced almost to nothing.—Decree of Charenton for receiving the Lutherans to Communion.—Consequence of this decree, which changes the state of Controversies.—The distinction of articles, Fundamental and not Fundamental, obliges Protestants to own, at last, the Church of Rome for a true Church, affording salvation to her members.—Conference of Cassel between the Lutherans and Calvinists.—Their agreement, wherein decisive grounds are established for Communion under one kind.—Present state of Controversies in Germany.—The opinion concerning Universal Grace prevails in France.—Is condemned at Geneva and among the Swiss.—The question of this Formulary with respect to the Hebrew text.—Another decree concerning Faith, made at Geneva.—That Church impeached by M. Claude of making a schism from the rest of the Churches by her new decisions.—Reflections on the Test, in which the Reality remains entire.—Acknowledgment of the Protestant Church of England, that the Mass and Invocation of Saints may have good sense.

1.—Intolerable excesses of Calvinism.—Free will destroyed and God made the author of sin.—Beza's words.

THE subject of Grace and Free-will was carried to such lengths in the Reformation, that it was impossible even Protestants themselves should not be at last sensible of these exorbitances. In order to destroy Pelagianism, which they were determined to fix on the Church of Rome, they had cast themselves into the opposite extremes, insomuch that the very name of Free-will excited a horror in them. There never had been such a thing in men or angels; nay, impossible it should have been: nor had the Stoics themselves ever made Fate more rigid and inflexible. Predestination reached even to sin itself, and God was not less the cause of evil actions than of good; such were Luther's sentiments: Calvin had followed them, and Beza, the most renowned of his disciples, had published, "A Brief Exposition of the Chief Points of the Christian Religion," where he laid down this principle "that God does all things according to his determined counsel, even those that are wicked and execrable."[1]

2.—Adam's Sin ordained by God.

He had extended this principle as far as the sin of the first Man, which, according to him, was not committed but by God's will and appointment, on account, that "he having ordained the end,"[2] which was to glorify his justice in the punishment of the Reprobate, "must likewise have ordained the proportionable causes leading to that end," to wit, sins which lead to eternal damnation, and in particular that of Adam, the origin of all the rest; so "that the corruption of the principal work of God," namely, the first Man, "did not happen by chance, nor without the decree and just will of God."[3]

3.—Inevitable necessity in Adam.

It is true, this author maintains at the same time, "that the will of man, which was created good, made itself evil;[4] but then he understands and repeats several times, that what is voluntary, is withal necessary;[5] so that nothing hinders the will of sinning from being always the fatal consequence of a hard and unavoidable necessity; and if men will reply, "that they had not the power of resisting the will of God," Beza does not answer them as he ought to do, that God does not move them to sin, but says only, "they must be left to plead against him, who will be well able to defend his own cause."

4.—This Doctrine of Beza taken from Calvin.

This doctrine of Beza was taken from Calvin, who maintains, in express terms,[6] "that Adam could not avoid falling, yet was nevertheless guilty, because he fell voluntarily;" which he undertakes to prove in his Institution, and reduces the whole of his doctrine to two principles: the first, that the will of God causes in all things, even in our wills, without excepting that of Adam, an inevitable necessity; the second that this necessity is no excuse for sinners. Hereby it is plain, he preserves free-will in name only, even in the state of innocence; and after this there is no room for disputing whether he makes God the author of sin, since besides his frequently drawing this consequence, it is but too evident, by the principles he lays down, that the will of God is the sole cause of that necessity imposed on all that sin.[7]

Nor indeed are Calvin's sentiments, and those of the first reformers, any longer disputed now, as to that point; and after owning what they have said upon it, "even that God pushes on the wicked to enormous crimes, and that he is in some sort the cause of sin,"[8] his disciples think they have sufficiently justified the Reformation from these so impious expressions, by reason that "they have not been employed for more than a hundred years;"[9] as if it were not a sufficient conviction of the evil spirit she was conceived in, to confess in her very authors such horrid blasphemies.

5.—The tenets which Calvin and Beza superadded to those of Luther.

Such, therefore, was the fatality which Calvin and Beza taught after Luther; and thereto the aforesaid dogmas were added by them regarding the certainty of Salvation and the inamissibility of Justice.[10] As much as to say, true justifying faith could never be lost: those that have it are surely assured of having it, and thereby are not only assured of their present justice, as spoke the Lutherans, but also of their eternal salvation, and this with an absolute and infallible certainty; assured, by consequence, of dying just, whatever crimes they might commit; and not only of dying just, but also of continuing so in sin itself, because without that, they could not maintain the sense given by them to this test of St. Paul, "the gifts and calling of God are without repentance."[11]

6.—Every Believer certified of his Perseverance and Salvation;
and this, in Calvinism, is the chief foundation of Religion.

This is what Beza likewise decided in the same exposition of faith, where he said, "that to the elect alone was granted the gift of faith:" that this faith, which is proper and peculiar to the elect, consists in depending with certainty, each "one for himself, on their election:" whence it follows, "that whosoever hath this gift of true faith, ought to rest assured of his perseverance." For as he says, "What does it avail me to believe, if I be not assured (perseverance in faith being requisite) that perseverance will be given me?"[12] Then he reckons among the fruits of this doctrine, that it alone teaches us to be assured of our faith for the time to come: which he takes to be of such importance, "that those," says he, "who oppose this, do certainly overthrow the foundation of the Christian religion."

7.—This certainty of One's own particular Salvation, as great as if God himself
had given it to us by His own Mouth.

Thus, this certainty, which every man hath of his own faith and perseverance, is not only a certainty of faith, but also the principal foundation of the Christian religion; and to show that he speaks not here of a moral and conjectural certainty, Beza adds,[13] "that we have it in our power to know whether we be predestined to salvation, and to be assured of the glorification which we expect, on account of which all Satan's war is waged against us; yea, say I, assured," continues he, "not by our fancy, but by conclusions as certain as if we had ascended into heaven to hear that sentence from the mouth of God." He will not have the faithful aspire to less certainty than this: and after proposing the means of attaining to it, which he places in the certain knowledge we have of the faith that is in us, he concludes, "we thereby learn that we are given to the Son according to God's purpose and predestination: by consequence," proceeds he, "since that God is unalterable, since that perseverance in the faith is requisite to salvation, and being made certain of our predestination, glorification is annexed to it by an indissoluble band: how can we doubt of perseverance, and finally of our salvation?"

8.—Calvinists begin to be sensible of these Excesses.

As the Lutherans, no less than the Catholics, abominated these dogmas, and the writings of the first were read with a more favorable prevention by the Calvinists, the horror of these sentiments, unheard of till Calvin's days, spread itself by little and little among the Calvinian churches. Men began to awake, and perceive how horrible it was, that a true believer could not fear for his salvation in contradiction to this precept of the apostle: "work out your own salvation with fear and trembling."[14] If it be a temptation and weakness to fear for one's salvation, as in Calvinism men are forced to say, why does St. Paul command this fear; and can a temptation fall within the precept?

9.—They opposed this Fear commanded by St. Paul.

The answer returned by them was not satisfactory. "The believer trembles," said they, "when he regards himself, because, however just he may be, he hath nothing in himself but death and damnation; and would indeed be damned, were he judged with rigor. But resting assured that he shall not be judged, what has he to fear? the future" say they; "because should he forsake God, he would perish;" weak reasoning! since, besides their holding the condition itself impossible, they hold, moreover, that the true faithful ought to believe assuredly that they shall persevere. Thus, in all manner of ways, the fear inspired by St. Paul is banished, and salvation rendered certain.

10.—Frivolous Evasion.

When they answer,—without fearing for salvation, there are other chastise-ments enough to afford just occasion of trembling; the Catholics and Lutherans reply, that this fear mentioned by St. Paul does manifestly regard salvation; "Work out," says he, "your own salvation with fear and trembling." The apostle inspired a terror reaching so far as to fear making shipwreck in the faith, as well as in a good conscience;[15] and Jesus Christ himself hath said, "fear him who is able to destroy both soul and body in hell;"[16] a precept which concerned the faithful as well as the rest, and made them fear no less a thing than the loss of their own souls. To these proofs they added those from experience: the idolatrous and disastrous fall of a Solomon, adorned undoubt-edly at first with all the gifts of grace; the abominable crimes of a David; besides what every person is conscious of in his own regard. What, then, is it fitting that, without security against crimes, you should be secure against their penalties; and that he, who once believed himself truly faithful, should be obliged to believe that he is sure of forgiveness, let him fall into whatsoever abominations he may. But must he lose this certainty in the midst of crimes?—he must then necessarily lose the remembrance of his faith and of the grace he has received. Does he not lose it?—he must then remain as secure in crimes, as in innocence; and, provided he argue aright according to the principles of his sect, he shall find therein wherewith to condemn all doubts whatever which might arise of his conversion; so that, whilst he continues to live amidst disorders, he will be sure not to die in them: or else, will be sure he never had been a true believer when he most believed himself such; and there you see him in despair, never able to hope for more certainty of his salvation than he had enjoyed then, nor able, to do what he will ever to secure himself in this life, that he shall not relapse into the deplorable state he now is in. What remedy for all this, unless to conclude, that the infallible certainty, boasted of in Calvinism, suits not with this life, and that nothing is more rash nor pernicious than such certainty.

11.—*Justifying Faith not forfeited by sin.*

But how much is it more so, to hold one's self assured, I do not say to recover lost grace, with true justifying faith, but not to lose them in sin itself; to remain therein still just and regenerated; to preserve therein the Holy Ghost and the seed of life, as the Calvinists undoubtedly believe,[17] if they follow Calvin and Beza and the other chief doctors of their sect? For, according to them, justifying faith is peculiar to the sole elect, who are never deprived of it; and Beza said, in the exposition so often quoted, "that faith, although it be as it were buried sometimes in the elect of God, in order to make them sensible of their infirmity, yet it never is without the fear of God, and charity for our neighbor."[18] And a little further on,[19] he says two things concerning the spirit of adoption: first, "that those who are planted in the Church only for a time, do never receive it;" second, "that those who are admitted among the people of God by this spirit of adoption, do never go forth from them."

12.—*What Scripture-texts Calvinists ground themselves on.*

This doctrine was grounded on these texts: "God is not like to man, so as to be a liar; nor like to the son of man, so as to repent."[20] Which also was the reason why St. Paul said, "That the gifts and calling of God are without repentance."[21] What then, does not man lose any of the gifts of God in adulteries, in homicides, in the blackest of crimes, not even in idolatry? And if some of them at least may be lost for a time and during this state, why should not justifying faith, and the presence of the Holy Ghost, be of this number, nothing being more incompatible with the state of sin, than such Graces?

13.—*Question proposed to the Calvinists:*
whether a Believer were damned that died in his crime.

In regard to this last difficulty, a very material query was also proposed, which I beg may be attentively considered, because it will be the subject of an important dispute presently to be treated of. The Calvinist is therefore asked, whether this true believer, David for instance, fallen into adultery and murder, would be saved or damned dying in this state before he had done penance? None durst answer, he would be saved; and indeed, how can a Christian maintain that any may be saved with such crimes? This true believer would be therefore damned, dying in this state; this true believer, in this state, has therefore ceased to be just, since none will ever say of a just man, that he would be damned dying in his justice.

14.—*The Calvinists' inextricable confusion under this question.*

To answer, he shall now die in his sin, but will do penance if he be of the number of the predestinated, is saying nothing; for it is not predestination, nor the penance we shall do one day, which justifies and makes us saints; otherwise, a predestinated infidel would actually be sanctified and justified even before he had faith and repentance; since, before he had either of them he was already certainly predestinated; God had already decreed he should have them.

If it be answered, this infidel is not actually justified and sanctified, because he has not as yet had faith, and repentance, although he be to have them hereafter; whereas, the true believer has them already: here arises a new perplexity; for it would follow from thence, that faith and repentance, but once exercised by the faithful, justify and sanctify them actually and for ever, although ceasing to exercise them, and even abandoning them by abominable crimes: a thing more horrible to conceive than all hitherto said on this subject.

15.—*This no indifferent question.*

Again, this is no chimerical question; it is a question that every believer, when he sins, should make to himself: or rather, it is a judgment he ought to pronounce; were I to die in the state I am in, I should be damned. To add after this, but I am predestinated, and shall amend one day; and by reason of this future amendment, am, at this instant, just and holy and a living member of Christ Jesus, is utter blindness.

16.—*These difficulties were the occasion of many forsaking Calvinism.*

Whilst Catholics, and Lutherans more readily listened to in the new Reformation than they, urged home these arguments, many Calvinists were convinced; and seeing on the other hand amongst the Lutherans a more engaging doctrine, they were attracted by it.[22] A general will in God to save all mankind; in Jesus Christ, a sincere intention to redeem them, and means sufficient offered unto us all, was what the Lutherans taught in the book of Concord. We have seen as much; we have seen even their excesses regarding these offered means and the co-operation of free-will: they gave daily more and more into these sentiments, and the Calvinists began to listen to them, principally in Holland.

17.—Arminius's dispute and excesses.—1601,1602.

James Arminius, a famous minister of Amsterdam, and since Professor of Divinity in the University of Leyden, was the first that declared himself in the university against the maxims received in the Churches of his country: but a man of so vehement a temper was not likely to keep within just bounds. He openly blamed Beza, Calvin, Zanchius, and the rest, whom Calvinism accounted her main pillars and support.[23] But he impugned excesses with other excesses; and besides his apparently drawing near to the Pelagians, was suspected, nor without reason, of something worse; certain words falling from him made him be believed favorable to Socinianism, and a great number of his disciples turning afterwards to that side, confirmed the suspicion.

18.—Gomar's opposition to him in defence of Calvinism.—Party of
Remonstrants and Anti-Remonstrants.

He met with a terrible adversary in the person of Francis Gomar, Professor of Divinity in the University of Leyden, a rigorous Calvinist, if ever there was one. The academies divided themselves between these two Professors: the division increased; the ministers espoused the quarrel; Arminius beheld whole churches in his party. His death did not end the dispute. And the minds of men on both sides were so inflamed under the names of Remonstrants and Anti-Remonstrants, namely, of Arminians and Gomarists, that the United Provinces saw themselves on the very brink of a civil war.

19.—The Prince of Orange upholds the second, Barneveld the first Party.

Maurice, Prince of Orange, had his reasons for supporting the Gomarists. Barneveld, his enemy, was judged favorable to the Arminians; and the reason of it was his proposing mutual toleration and imposing silence on both parties.[24]

This indeed answered the wishes of the Remonstrants. A party just shooting up, and as yet but weak, asks no more than time to gather strength: but the ministers, among whom Gomar prevailed, were determined on victory, and the Prince of Orange had more skill than to let a party strike root, which he judged as opposite to his grandeur as to the primitive maxims of the Reformation.

20.—The Remonstrants or Arminians condemned in the Provincial Synods.—
Convocation of the Synod of Dort.

The provincial Synods had done nothing but aggravate the evil by condemning the Remonstrants; it was necessary to proceed at length to a greater remedy; wherefore the States-general assembled a national Synod, and invited to it all those of their religion in every country. Upon this invitation, England, Scotland, the Palatinate, Hesse, the Swiss, the republics of Geneva, of Bremen, and Embden, in a word, the whole body of the Reformation not united to the Lutherans, sent deputies, with the exception of the French, whom reasons of state prevented; and of all these deputies, in conjunction with those of the whole United Provinces, was composed that famous Synod of Dort, whose doctrine and procedure we are now to relate.

21.—*Opening of the Synod, 1618.*

This assembly opened the 14th of November, 1618, with a sermon preached by Balthasar Lydius, minister of Dort. The first sessions were taken up in regulating divers matters of discipline, or of procedure; nor was it till the 13th of December, in the thirty-first sitting, that, properly speaking, they began to treat of doctrine.

22.—*The dispute reduced to five heads.—Declaration of the Remonstrants in general touching these five heads.*

In order to understand in what manner they proceeded there, it is necessary to know that, after many books and conferences, the dispute was at length reduced to five heads. The first regarded predestination; the second, the universality of redemption; the third and the fourth, which were always treated together, regarded the corruption of man and his conversion; the fifth regarded perseverance.

On these five heads, the Remonstrants had declared in general, in full Synod, by the mouth of Simon Episcopius, Professor of Divinity at Leyden, who always appears at their head, that men of great renown and repute in the Reformation had laid down such things as agreed neither with God's wisdom, nor with his goodness and justice, nor with the love which Jesus Christ bore to all men, nor with his satisfaction and merits, nor with the sanctity of preaching and the ministry, nor with the use of the sacraments nor, in fine, with the duties of a Christian. These great men, whom they impeached, were the authors of the Reformation,—Calvin, Beza, Zanchius, and the others, whom they were not allowed to name, but whom they had not spared in their writings. After this general declaration of their sentiments, they explained themselves in particular as to the five articles;[25] and their declaration attacked principally the certainty of salvation, and the inamissibility of justice—tenets by which, they pretended, piety was ruined in the Reformation, and so fine a name discredited. I shall relate the substance of this declaration of the Remonstrants, in order that it may be better understood what chiefly was the subject matter of the deliberation and the result thereof, in the decisions of the Synod.

23.—*The import of the declaration of the Remonstrants as to each particular.—As to Predestination.*

Concerning Predestination, they said "They ought not to own in God any absolute decree, whereby he had determined to give Jesus Christ to the elect alone, no more than to give to them alone by an efficacious vocation, faith, justification, perseverance, and glory; but that he had appointed Jesus Christ the common redeemer of the whole world, and resolved, by this decree, to justify and save all those who should believe in him, and at the same time to give to all of them sufficient means in order to be saved; that none perished through want of these means, but through the abuse thereof; that the absolute and especial election of particular persons was made in view of their faith and future perseverance, nor was there any election but conditional; and that reprobation likewise was made in view of men's infidelity and perseverance in so great an evil."[26]

24.—Doctrine of the Remonstrants concerning Infant Baptism, and what they would conclude from it.

They added two points worthy of particular consideration; the first, that all children of the faithful were sanctified, and that none of them dying before the use of reason, are damned; the second, that with much more reason none of these children dying after baptism, before the use of reason, are damned.[27]

In saying that all the children of the faithful are sanctified, they did but repeat what we have clearly seen in the Calvinian Confessions of Faith; and if they be sanctified, it is evident they cannot be damned in this state. But after this first article, the second seemed unnecessary; for if these children were secure of their salvation before baptism, after its reception there could be no question of it. It was therefore with particular design that this second article was inserted, and the Remonstrants would thereby denote the inconstancy of the Calvinists, who on one hand, to salve the baptism given to all these children, said, they were all saints, and born in the covenant, the sign whereof, by consequence, could not be refused them; and to salve, on the other hand, the doctrine of the inamissibility of justice, they said that baptism given to children had not its effect, but in the predestinated alone; so that the baptized that lived ill afterwards never had been saints, not even with the baptism they had received in their infancy.

Remark, I beseech you, judicious reader, this important difficulty; it strikes home to the question of inamissibility, and it will be curious to behold how the Synod will behave in this regard.

25.—Declaration of the Remonstrants concerning the universality of Redemption.

As to the second head, regarding the universality of redemption, the Remonstrants said that "the price paid by the Son of God was not only sufficient to all, but actually offered for all and every individual person; that none were excluded from the fruit of redemption by an absolute decree, or otherwise than by their own fault; that God, prevailed with by his Son, had made a new treaty with all mankind, although sinners and damned."[28] They said, by this treaty he had bound himself in respect of all, to afford them those sufficient means as above mentioned: "but that the remission of sins, merited for all, was not given actually, except through actual faith, whereby man believed actually in Jesus Christ;" by which words they gave to understand, that whosoever lost, by his crimes, actual faith which justifies us, lost also, together with it, justifying grace and sanctity; finally, they said also "none ought to believe Jesus Christ died for him, save only those for whom he died in effect; insomuch that the reprobate, for whom Jesus Christ did not die, whatsoever some might think of them, ought not to believe that he died for them."[29] This article reached much further than it seemed. For the design of it was to show (according to the doctrine of Calvin and the Calvinists, who laid down for an undoubted dogma, that Jesus Christ did not die in any sort but for the predestinated, and in no sort for the reprobate) that it followed from thence, that to be enabled to say, Jesus Christ died for me, one ought to be assured, with an absolute certainty, of his predestination and eternal happiness, without ever being able to say, "he died for me, but I have rendered his death and redemption unserviceable to me,"—a doctrine which defeats all preaching of the word to Christians, who, if bad livers, are continually told they have made themselves unworthy of being redeemed by Jesus Christ. Accordingly, this was one of those articles by which the Remonstrants maintained, that, in the Reformation, all the sincerity and holiness of preaching was subverted, as well as this text of St. Peter—"They have denied the Lord that bought them, and brought upon themselves swift perdition."[30]

26.—*Their doctrine as to the third and fourth head.*

Regarding the third and fourth head, after saying that grace is necessary to all good, not only to finish, but also to begin it, they added, "that efficacious grace was not irresistible."[31] This was their expression, and that of the Lutherans, whose doctrine they boasted of following. Their meaning was, that one might resist all kind of grace; and thereby, as every one sees, they pretended, "That although grace were bestowed unequally, yet God gave or offered a sufficient grace to all those to whom the gospel was announced, even to those that were not converted; and offered it with a sincere and serious desire of saving them all without acting two different parts, seeming inclined to save, and at bottom unwilling to do it, and moving men interiorly to sins which he forbade exteriorly."[32] In all these places they aimed directly at the authors of the Reformation, and that insincere vocation which they attributed to God, whilst he openly called those to grace whom in reality he excluded from it, predestinating them to evil.

In order to show how far grace was resistible,[33] (these words warranted by use, must be allowed, in order to avoid circumlocution,) they had inserted an article, which said "that man could do more good by the grace of the Holy Ghost than he did, and keep at a further distance from evil than he did;" he therefore frequently resisted grace, and made it useless.

27.—*Declaration of the Remonstrants concerning the Amissibility of Justice.*

Concerning perseverance, they decided that "God gave to the true faithful, regenerated by his grace, means for preserving themselves in that state; that they might lose the true justifying faith and fall into sins incompatible with justification, even into atrocious crimes; persevere in them, die in them, recover from them likewise by repentance, nevertheless without being necessitated to it by grace."[34] Here is what they urged with the greatest efforts, "detesting," said they, "from the bottom of their hearts those impious dogmas, and contrary to good morals, which were disseminated daily among the people, viz., that the true faithful could not fall into the sins of malice, but only into the sins of ignorance and weakness; that they could not lose grace; that all the crimes of the world put together could not frustrate their election, nor deprive them of the certainty thereof; a thing," added they, "which opened a gap to carnal and pernicious security; that no crimes, how horrible soever, were imputed to them; that all manner of sins present and to come were forgiven them beforehand; that in the midst of heresies, of adulteries, of murders, for which they might be excommunicated, they could not totally and finally lose the faith."[35]

28.—Two material words which the whole dispute turned on; that one could lose grace totally and finally.

These two words, *totally* and *finally*, were what the dispute chiefly turned upon. To lose faith and the grace of justification totally, was to lose it wholly for a certain time; to lose it finally, was to lose it for ever and beyond recovery. Both the one and the other were held impossible in Calvinism, and both of these excesses were detested by the Remonstrants.

29.—Against the certainty of Salvation.

They concluded the declaration of their doctrine by saying that, as the true believer might, in the time present, be assured of his faith and good conscience, he might also be assured for that time, should he then die, of his eternal salvation;[36] that he might also be assured of being able to persevere in the faith, forasmuch as grace would never fail him for that end; but to be assured of always doing his duty, they did not see how he "could be so, nor how this assurance could be necessary for him."

30.—Foundations of the Remonstrants, viz., that there is no gratuitous preference for the Elect.

If you desire now to comprehend in few words the whole of their doctrine, the foundation of it was, that there is no absolute election, no gratuitous preference, whereby God prepares for certain chosen persons, and for them only, certain means to lead them to glory; but that God offers to all men, and especially all those to whom the gospel is published, sufficient means of conversion, which some make use of, and others not, without employing any other for his elect more than for the reprobate; so that election always is conditional, which the condition failing, may be forfeited. Whence they concluded in the first place, that we may lose justifying grace, and totally, that is entirely; and finally, that is, beyond recovery: secondly, that man could not in any wise be sure of his salvation.

31.—Wherein Catholics agreed with the Remonstrants.

Although Catholics did not agree with them in principle, they agreed with them in the last two consequences, which nevertheless they grounded on other principles, which it is not necessary to the present subject to set forth in this place; and likewise they agreed that the Calvinistic doctrine, opposite to these consequences, was impious, and an inlet to all sort of wickedness.

32.—Wherein consisted the difference between Catholics, Lutherans, and Remonstrants.

The Lutherans also agreed on this point with the Catholics and Remonstrants. But the difference between Catholics and Lutherans is, that these latter, denying the certainty of perseverance, acknowledged a certainty of present justice, in which they were followed by the Remonstrants; whereas Catholics differed from both of them, by maintaining that none could be assured either of his future good dispositions, nor even of his present ones, which by reason of the blindness of self-love, we have always grounds to distrust; so that the confidence we have on God's side, takes not away wholly the doubt we have on our own.

33.—Calvinists contrary to the Doctrine of them both.

Calvin and the Calvinists opposed the doctrine of both these, and maintained against the Lutherans and Remonstrants, that the true believer was sure, not of the present only, but also of the future, and sure, by consequence, of never losing totally, that is, entirely; nor finally, that is, beyond recovery, justifying grace or the true faith once received.

34.—The Remonstrants demand a distinct Decision.

The state of the question and the different sentiments are well understood;[37] and ever so little perspicuity in the decision of the Synod of Dort, would have made us easily comprehend what was their doctrine, which they were so much the more obliged to, as the Remonstrants, after their declaration, had summoned those that should complain of their doctrines being ill-represented by them, to reject distinctly every particular wherein they judged themselves wrongfully accused; and entreated also the Synod to deliver themselves precisely in respect of the articles that cast such a blemish on the whole Reformation.

35.—The Synod's decision.

If ever there was a necessity of speaking plainly, it was after such a declaration and in such a conjuncture. Let us now give ear to the decision of the Synod.

It pronounces on the five heads proposed in four chapters, for, as above said, the third and fourth head always went together. Each chapter has two parts: in the first, they assert: in the second, reject and condemn. This is the substance of their canons, for so did they call the decrees of this Synod.

36.—The Synod's decision on the first head.—Faith in the sole Elect: certainty of Salvation.

Concerning predestination and election they decided, "that the decree thereof is absolute and unchangeable; that God gives true and lively faith to all those he resolves to withdraw from common damnation, *and to them only*: that this faith is a gift of God: that all the elect, in their time, are assured of their election, albeit not in the same degree nor in equal measure: that this assurance is derived to them, not from the fathoming of God's secrets, but from observing in themselves, with a holy pleasure and spiritual joy, the infallible fruits of election, such as be true faith, sorrow for their sins, and the like; that the sense and certainty of their salvation always make them better; that those, who have not as yet this sense and this certain confidence, ought to desire it; and, lastly, that this doctrine should not affright any but those who, wedded to the world, are not seriously converted."[38] Here have we already for the sole elect, together with true faith, the certainty of salvation; but the thing will unfold itself hereafter much more clearly.

37.—Decision on Infant Baptism.

The seventeenth article decides, "that the word of God declaring holy the children of the faithful, not by nature, but by the covenant wherein they are comprised together with their parents, the believing parents ought not to doubt of the election and salvation of their children that die in this infant age."[39]

In this article the Synod approves the doctrine of the Remonstrants, whom we have heard say precisely the same thing:[40] nothing, therefore, is more unquestionable amongst our adversaries, than an article which we see equally taught by both parties; the sequel will manifest to us what are its consequences.

38.—Condemnation of those that denied the certainty of Salvation.

Amongst the rejected articles, we find that which asserts that "the certainty of salvation depends on an uncertain condition;"[41] that is to say, they condemn those who teach that one is sure of being saved by persevering to live well, but one is not sure of living well; which precisely is the doctrine we have heard the Remonstrants teach. The Synod declares this, "uncertain certainty" absurd; and, by consequence, establishes an absolute certainty, which it endeavors even to prove from Scripture: but proofs are not our present purpose; it is to see this doctrine well asserted, viz., that the true believer, according to the decrees of Dort, not only ought to be sure of his salvation, supposing he does his duty well, but also ought to be sure of doing it well, at least, at the end of his life. But this is nothing as yet, and we shall see this doctrine decided much more clearly.

39.—Justifying Faith gain confessed in the sole Elect.

Concerning Redemption and the Promise of Grace, they define, "that it is announced indifferently to all people; that it is through their own fault that those who believe it not do reject it, and through grace, that the true faithful do embrace it; but they are the elect only to whom God is resolved to give justifying faith, whereby they infallibly are saved." Here then, a second time, have we justifying faith in the elect alone; we must see afterwards what those shall have who do not continue to believe unto the end.

40.—Co-operation, how admitted.

The summary of the Fourth Chapter is, that although God calls seriously all those to whom the Gospel is proclaimed, so that if they perish it is not God's fault; something nevertheless particular is wrought in those that are converted, God calling them efficaciously, and giving to them faith and repentance. The sufficient grace of the Arminians, whereby "Free-will determines itself," is rejected as a Pelagian tenet.[42] Regeneration is represented as transacted "without us," not by "the exterior word, or by moral persuasion," but by an operation leaving it not "in the power of man to be *regenerated or not*," to be converted, or not converted; and nevertheless, say they in this article, "when the will is renewed, it is not only pushed on and moved by God, but acts, being moved by him, and it is man that believes and repents."

41.—The Believer's certainty.

The will therefore does not act but when converted and renewed. What then, does it not act when one begins to desire his conversion, and to pray for the grace of regeneration? Or had you it already, when you began to pray for it? This they ought to have explained, and say in general, Conversion and Regeneration is wrought "without us." Many other things might be said in this place, but our business is not disputing, it is sufficient we make the doctrine of the Synod historically well understood.

It says, in the thirteenth article, that the manner whereby this operation of regenerating grace is wrought in us is inconceivable: it is sufficient to conceive that by this grace the believer "know and feels that he believes and loves his Saviour." He "knows and feels;" here have you what is most certain within the compass of perception, to know and feel.

42.—Sequel of the same subject.

We read in the sixteenth article,[43] that as sin hath not robbed man of his nature, nor of his understanding, nor of his will; so regenerating grace acts not in him "as in a stump or log of wood;" it preserves to the will "its properties, and does not force it in spite of itself;" that is, it does not make it "will without willing." What strange theology! Are not men resolved to puzzle every thing, who thus weakly express themselves on free-will?

43.—*Habits infused.*

Amongst the rejected errors, I find that which teaches,[44] "that in the true conversion of man, God cannot communicate qualities, habits, and gifts of infusion, and that faith by which we are first converted, and from which are called faithful, is not a gift and quality by God infused, but only an act of man." I am glad to hear the infusion of these new qualities and habits; it will be of great service to us in order to explain the true idea of justification, and to show by what means it may be obtained of God. For I do not believe it can be doubted but that, in those who are come to the age of understanding, it is an act of faith inspired by God which obtains for us the grace to receive the habit of it, with that of other virtues. Yet the infusion of this habit will be nevertheless gratuitous, as will be seen in due time. But let us proceed, and come now to the last chapter, which is the most material, because the reproaches of the Remonstrants concerning the certainty of salvation and the inamissibility of justice were there to be answered fully and distinctly.

44.—*Justice not to be lost.—Monstrous doctrine of the Synod.*

Concerning inamissibility, this is what they say, viz, "That in certain particular actions the true faithful may sometimes withdraw themselves, and do so in effect, by their vices, from the guidance of grace, to follow concupiscence, even so far as to fall into atrocious crimes; and do, by these enormous sins, offend God, render themselves guilty of death, interrupt the exercise of faith, greatly wound their consciences, and *sometimes* lose, for a while, *the sense of grace*."[45] O God, is it possible, in this detestable state, they should only "lose *the sense of grace*," and not grace itself, and this, too, but "*sometimes!*"[46] But it is not yet time to exclaim; here is much worse: "God, in those dismal falls, does not *entirely* deprive them of his holy Spirit, nor suffers them to fall so as to *forfeit the grace of adoption and the state of justification,* nor so as to commit the sin unto death, nor against the Holy Ghost, and be damned." Whosoever therefore is once truly faithful and regenerated by grace, not only shall not perish in his crimes, but at the very time he abandons himself to them, "*does not fall from the grace of adoption, and the state of justification.*" Could Jesus Christ be associated with Belial, grace with sin, in a more flagrant manner?

45.—*What is the sin a true Believer cannot fall into?*

The Synod, indeed, seems willing to preserve the faithful from some crimes, when it says, "they are not so far abandoned as to fall into the sin unto death, or against the Holy Ghost," which the Scripture says is not to be forgiven; but if they understand any other sin by this than that of final impenitence, I am at a loss to know what it can be, there being no such sinner, what disorders soever he may have been guilty of, that should not be made to hope the forgiveness of them. Let us, however, leave to the Synod to determine what other explanation of this sin it my please to fancy; it is sufficient we see plainly, according to its doctrine, that all crimes possible to be named, for example, an adultery as long continued, and a murder as much premeditated as that of David's heresy, idolatry, even with all its abominations which the Synod evidently allows the true believer may fall into, are compatible "with the grace of adoption and the state of justification."

46.—*The Synod speaks plainly.*

Nor can it be said by this state the Synod understands only the right of salvation still remaining in the true believer, namely, according to the Synod, in the predestinated, in virtue of predestination; for on the contrary, the matter here in deliberation concerns the immediate right one has to salvation by actual regeneration and conversion, and concerns the state whereby one is, I do not say destined to, but really in possession as well of the true faith as of justification. In a word, the matter in debate is not whether you shall one day have this grace, but whether, after having had it, you can forfeit it one single moment; the Synod decides you cannot. Remonstrants, complain not, you have your answer, at least, in plain terms, as you desired it, and all the pernicious doctrine you say is believed in the party which you accuse, all that you reject therein with abhorrence is decided by them in express terms.

47.—*The great words "totally" and "finally."*

But to remove all equivocation, we must see in the Synod[47] these essential words, "totally" and "finally," whereon, I have shown, the whole dispute depended. We must see, I say, whether it allows the Remonstrants to assert, that a true believer "may fall totally and finally from the state of justification." The Synod, to leave no doubt of its sentiment as opposite to the total loss, says, "that the immortal seed, whereby the true faithful are regenerated, abides always in them in spite of their fall." As opposite to the final loss, the same Synod says,[48] that the reconciled one day, "*shall feel* grace anew;" they shall not recover it; no, the Synod is sure not to say that, "they shall feel it" anew. In this manner, proceeds the Synod, it happens that "neither do they lose *totally* the faith and grace nor do they remain *finally* in their sin, so as to perish in it."

Here, methinks, is enough said for inamissibility. Let us see as to certainty.

48.—*Certainty of salvation, of what kind.*

"The true faithful," says the Synod, "may be certain, and are so, of their salvation and perseverance, according to the measure of faith wherewith they *believe with certainty* that they are, and abide, living members of the Church; that they have forgiveness of their sins; and life eternal: a certainty which does not accrue to them from a particular revelation, but from faith in the promises which God hath revealed in his word, and by the testimony of the Holy Ghost, and lastly, by a good conscience, and a holy and serious application to good works."[49]

49.—*All uncertainty a temptation.*

To leave nothing unsaid, it adds "that in the temptations and doubts of the flesh, which we are to contend with, we do not always feel this fullness of faith and this certainty of perseverance:"[50] to the end that, as often as ever you feel some doubt, and dare not promise yourself with an entire certainty to persevere always in your duty, you may look on yourself obliged to reckon this doubt among the motions of the flesh, and the temptations you are to fight against.

50.—*Totally and finally.*

Among the rejected errors this afterwards is reckoned, viz. "that the true faithful may fall and do often fall, *totally and finally* from justifying faith, from grace and salvation, and that, during this life, you cannot have any security of future perseverance without special revelation."[51] They declare this doctrine brings back the doubts of Papists, because this certainty, without special revelation, was condemned in the Council of Trent.

51.—*How man justified remains guilty of death.*

It may be asked, how they reconcile with the doctrine of Inamissibility, that which is said in the Synod,[52] viz. that by great crimes, the faithful committing them, "render themselves guilty of death." This is what easily is brought to bear with the principles of the new Reformation, where it is maintained that the true believer, how much soever regenerated, remains always, by concupiscence, "guilty of death," not only in his great and less sins, but also in his good works; so that this state, rendering us guilty of death, is no hindrance, according to the terms of the Synod, to our abiding in the "state of justification and grace."

52.—*The self-contradiction of the Calvinian Doctrine.*

But then, have we not said that our Reformed could not deny, nor in effect did deny, but that, should one die in these crimes without doing penance, he would be damned? True it is, the greatest part confess it; and although the Synod decided nothing in body concerning this difficulty, it was proposed there, as we shall see, by some of the Opiners. In good truth, it is wondrous strange men can remain in an error containing so inevitable and manifest a contradiction as that is which acknowledges a state of grace, in which, nevertheless, one would be damned should he die therein. But many other contradictions are there in this doctrine; here is one unquestionably not less palpable than the other. In the new Reformation, true faith is inseparable from the love of God and good works, the necessary fruits thereof; it is the most steady dogma of this religion and here you see, nevertheless, in opposition to this dogma, true faith, not only without good works, but also in the greatest crimes. Have patience, this is not all: I see another contradiction not less manifest in the new Reformation, even by the Synod's own decree:[53] All children of the faithful are holy, and their salvation certain. Therefore, in this state, they are truly justified: therefore they cannot fall from grace, and every individual of the Reformation will be predestinated: nor can one believer, which is still more strange, have a child that is not holy and predestinated like himself: thus, all their posterity are evidently predestinated, and never can a reprobate spring from one elect. Who of them all will dare to say it? And yet, who of them can deny, that so visible and so strange an absurdity is clearly contained in the principles of the Synod and the doctrine of inadmissibility? It is therefore all over teeming with manifest absurdities, all over jarring with horrid contradictions; nor can it indeed be otherwise than the necessary result of error thus always to contradict itself.

53.—*All error contradicts itself.*

There is no error but must fall into self-contradiction some way or other; but see what befalls man possessed with strong prejudice. He first strives, what he can, to avoid seeing this inevitable and glaring contradiction: if this cannot be done, he looks on it with a prepossession, that does not allow him to form a right judgment of it; he thinks to fence against it by soothing himself with frothy reasoning and fine words: dazzled with some specious principle to which he is strongly wedded, he is resolved never to forsake it. Eutyches and his followers durst not say, Jesus Christ was not at the same time true God and true man: but fond of that unity ill-understood, which they imagined in Jesus Christ, they would have both natures confounded in this union, and were pleased and gloried in removing by this means to a greater distance than all others (though it were even to excess) from Nestorius's heresy which divided the Son of God. Thus do men entangle, thus do they prepossess themselves, thus do the prepossessed, with blind determination, lead the van and draw after them the giddy vulgar, without being willing, or able to understand, as says the Apostle, "either what they say themselves, or whereof they affirm"[54] with such assurance. This is what constitutes all opinionists; this is the pit all heretics fall into.

54.—*Certainty of salvation, a false allurement.*

Our adversaries frame to themselves and object of infinite comfort in the certainty they will needs be in of their eternal salvation. Do not expect they ever will regard, with candid equity or attention, what may deprive them of this certainty. If to maintain it they must be obliged to say, one is sure not to die in sin though he fall into it with malice aforethought, nay, though he contract a detestable habit thereof; this they will say. If they must exaggerate, beyond measure, this text of St. Paul, "The gifts and calling of God are without repentance,"[55] and say, God never takes away entirely, nor in substance, what he has given; this they will say, happen what will, whatever contradictions you may show them, whatever inconsistency, what dismal consequence soever may result from their doctrine: otherwise, besides losing the pleasure of their certainty and the charms discovered by them in the novelty of this tenet, they must also be forced to own that they were in the wrong as to the point they looked upon the most essential of their Reformation, and the Church of Rome, so much censured and hated by them, was in the right.

55.—Whether the Synod were il-understood in respect to Inadmissibility, and whether the Certainty it proposes be no more than confidence.

But, perchance, this certainty, which they teach, is nothing else at bottom than that trust which we admit. Would to God it were! Nobody denies this trust: the Lutherans maintained it, yet the Calvinists told them a hundred times, that something more was requisite. But without going forth from the Synod, the Arminians admitted this trust; for unquestionably they never said that a believer fallen into sin, which he repents of, should despair of salvation. The Synod nevertheless condemns them, because that, satisfied with this hope, they reject certainty. The Catholics in fine admitted this trust, and the holy perseverance, which the Council of Trent[56] will have us acknowledge as God's special gift, it will have us expect with confidence from his infinite bounty: and yet, because it rejects absolute certainty,[57] the Synod condemns it, and accuses the Remonstrants, who likewise condemned this certainty, of falling by this means into the doubts of Popery. Had the dogma of absolute certainty and inamissibility raised as much horror in the Synod as so hideous a doctrine should excite naturally in all minds, the ministers that composed this assembly would not have had mouths enough to proclaim throughout all the universe, that the Remonstrants, the Lutherans, and all the Catholics, laying such a blasphemy to their charge, did calumniate them; and all Europe would have rung with their clamor: but on the contrary, so far were they from defending themselves against this certainty and inamissibility objected to them by the Remonstrants, that they define it expressly, and condemn the Remonstrants for denying it. When they think themselves calumniated, they are not at all sparing of their complaints. They complain, for instance, at the close of their Synod, that their enemies, and amongst the rest, the Remonstrants, accuse them of "making God the author of sin; and of the reprobation of men without any regard to sin: of making him precipitate the children of the faithful into damnation, so as that all the prayers of the Church, and even baptism itself, are not able to withdraw them from it."[58] Why do they not complain, in like manner, they are wrongfully accused of admitting this same certainty and inamissibility. "It is true," they say in this very place,[59] they are accused "of inspiring men with carnal security, by affirming that no crime prejudices the salvation of the elect, and that they may, with full security, commit the most execrable." But is this a sufficient explanation from men that were asked for a plain and direct answer? What, does it not suffice them then for an evasion, that they acknowledged crimes, for instance, "the sin even unto death and against the Holy Ghost," whatever it may be, which the elect and true faithful never fall into? And if it was their sentiment that other crimes were equally incompatible with true faith and the state of grace, could they not have said as much in express terms, whereas, in express terms, they assert the contrary?

56.—Calvin's Doctrine expressly defined by the Synod.

Conclude we, therefore, that of the three articles wherein we have made the Calvinian justification to consist, the two first which already were insinuated in the Confessions of Faith, namely, absolute certainty of predestination, and the impossibility of forfeiting finally faith and grace once received, are expressly defined in the Synod of Dort; and that the third article, where the question is, whether a true believer may at least lose for a while, and during his continuance in sin, justifying grace and true faith, although not expressed in any confession of faith, is likewise decided conformably to Calvin's doctrine and the spirit of the new reformation.[60]

57.—Peter de Moulin's Sentiments approved by the Synod.

One may also know the sentiment of the whole Synod by that of the renowned Peter Du Moulin, minister of Paris; allowed by all the world to be unquestionably the most rigorous Calvinist of his time, and the most wedded to the doctrine which Gomar defended against Arminius. He sent to Dort his judgment on this matter, which was read and approved by the whole Synod, and inserted in the acts. He declares, that he had not leisure to handle all the questions;[61] but lays down the whole substance of the Synod's doctrine when he decides, that none is justified but he that is glorified: whereby he condemns the Arminians, in that they teach,[62] "there are men justified that lose the faith, and are damned." And still more clearly in these words: "Although the doubt of salvation enter sometimes into the minds of the true faithful, God nevertheless commands us in his word to have a certainty thereof, and we must tend with all our might to this certainty, at which we should not doubt many do arrive; and whoever is assured of his salvation, is so, at the same time, that God will never abandon him, and that he shall thus persevere even to the end."[63] One cannot more clearly regard doubting as a temptation and weakness, nor certainty, as enjoined by God's commandment. Thus the faithful are not assured that they shall not fall into the worst of crimes, and continue in them a long while, like David: but are nevertheless assured, "God never will abandon them, and that they shall persevere even to the end." This is an abridgment of the Synod: accordingly, it was resolved by the assembly to return Du Moulin thanks for the very accurate judgment passed by him on this subject, and for his assent to the doctrine of the Synod.

58.—Question whether the certainty of Salvation be a certainty of Faith.

Some would doubt whether this certainty required by the Synod in every believer for his salvation, be a certainty of faith: but their doubt will cease, if they do but observe, that the certainty in question, is always expressed by the word "Believe," which in the Synod is taken no otherwise than for true faith; to which add, that this certainty, according to the same Synod, is nothing else than the belief of the promises applied by each individual to himself and to his eternal salvation, with a certain feeling in the heart of the sincerity of his faith;

so that, to the end no kind of certainty may be wanting, you have that of faith joined to that of experience and feeling.

59.—*The Sentiment of the Divines of Great Britain.*

Of all the Opiners, those that best explain the sense of the Synod, are the Divines of Great Britain: for after confessing with all the rest, a kind of doubt in the believer concerning his salvation, but a doubt that always proceeds from temptation, they explain very clearly, "how after the temptation, the act whereby one believes that God looks upon him with the eyes of mercy, and that he shall infallibly possess eternal life, is not an act of dubious opinion, or of conjectural hope, wherein one might be deceived, *cui falsum subesse potest*; but an act of a true and lively faith excited and sealed in our hearts by the spirit of adoption":[64] wherein these Divines seem to advance further than the English Confession of Faith, which, as we have already seen, looks as if it designed to avoid speaking so clearly "on the certainty of salvation."[65]

60.—*These Divines believed that Justice could not be forfeited.—Contradiction of their Doctrine.*

Some have thought that these English Divines were not of the common opinion in respect to justice attributed to the faithful fallen into grievous crimes whilst they continue in them like to David; and what may occasion this doubt is, that these doctors decide formally, "that these faithful are in the state of damnation, and would be damned, should they die therein:"[66] whence it follows, that they are fallen from the grace of justification, at least for that time. But this is one of those places which involve all such as err in necessary contradictions: for these Divines see themselves obliged, by their erroneous principles, to acknowledge, on one side, that the faithful, thus plunged into crimes, would be damned should they then die; and on the other, "that they do not fall from the state of justification."[67]

61.—*That Faith and Charity subsist amidst the greatest Crimes.*

Nor must one persuade himself, they here confound justification with predestination: for, on the contrary, it is what they distinguish most expressly; and say,[68] that these faithful, plunged into crimes, not only are not fallen from their predestination, which is true of all the elect, but "they are not fallen from the faith, nor from that celestial seed of regeneration and those fundamental gifts, without which spiritual life can in no wise subsist;[69] insomuch, that it is impossible the gifts of charity and faith should entirely be extinguished in their hearts. They do not entirely lose the faith, sanctity, adoption:[70] they abide in this universal justification, which is justification in its most proper sense, which no particular crime can exclude them from: they abide in this justification, from which interior renovation and sanctification are insepara-ble;"[71] in a word, they are saints, who, if they died, would be damned.

62.—What it was that remained in the Faithful guilty of grievous crimes.–
The Doctrine of those of Embden.

They were extremely puzzled to explain, according to these principles, what it was that remained in the faithful who had run themselves into criminal disorders. Those of Embden were agreed, "actual faith could not remain in them, and that it was inconsistent with the consent to grievous sins."[72] What they did not lose, "was habitual faith, that," said they, "which subsists in man whilst he sleeps, or doth not act;" but then, "this habitual faith infused into man by preaching and the use of the sacraments, is the true living and justifying faith;" whence they concluded that the faithful did not, for all these enormous crimes, lose "either justice or the Holy Ghost:" and when they were asked whether it might not as well be said, they lost "faith and the Holy Ghost" afterwards to recover them, as to say, they only lost "the feeling and energy" thereof;[73] they answered, the faithful ought not to be deprived of the comfort accruing to them from the impossibility of their ever losing "either faith or the Holy Ghost, what crime soever they fell into against their conscience." "For this," said they, "would be but a cold comfort, to tell them, you have entirely lost faith and the Holy Ghost, yet perchance, God will adopt and regenerate you again, that you may be reconciled to him." Thus, what sins soever the believer may give himself up to, contrary to conscience, they are so favorable to him, that to comfort him, they are not satisfied with leaving him the hopes of a future return to the state of grace;[74] but he must also have the comfort of actually being in it, his crimes notwithstanding.

63.—What it was the Holy Ghost did in the Faithful guilty of grievous sins—
Strange idea of Christian justice.

The question still remains, what did faith and the Holy Ghost in these believers thus abandoned to sin, and whether or no they were altogether without action in them? It was answered, they were not without action; and the effect produced by them, for example in David, was that he did not sin "whole and entire: *Pecavit David, at non totus;*"[75] there being a certain sin which he did not commit. But if you urged so far as to ask, what could be "this sin the whole man falls into," and the faithful are never guilty of? they answered, "it was not a particular fall of the Christian man into such or such a crime against the first or second table, but a total and universal defection and apostasy from the gospel truth, whereby man offends not God in part and by halves, but, by an obstinate contempt, despises his whole majesty, and absolutely excludes himself from grace."[76] Thus, till you are arrived to this obstinate contempt of God, and to this universal apostasy, you still have the "comfort of being holy, of being justified and regenerated," and of having the Holy Ghost dwelling in you.

64.—The Opinion of those of Bremen.

Corresponding to this is the sentiment of Bremen, when they say, "that those who are once truly regenerated, never wander to that degree as to stray entirely from God by a universal apostacy, so as to hate him as their enemy, to sin like the Devil with a studied malice, and to deprive themselves of heavenly gifts: wherefore they never lose absolutely God's grace and favor;"[77] so that they remain in this grace and favor, well regenerated, well justified, provided only they be not the declared enemies of God, and quite as wicked as the Devil.

65.—Whether the Synod can be excused from these excesses.—The unanimous consent of all the Opiners.

So great are these excesses, that the Protestants are confounded at them; nay there have been some Catholics that could not persuade themselves the Synod was guilty of them. Nevertheless, here have you historically, with the decrees of the Synod, the votes of the principal Opiners.[78] And that there might be no doubt, in respect to those of all the rest, besides what is inserted in the Acts of the Synod, that every thing was there decided by the unanimous consent of all the voices, not one excepted, I have expressly related the opinions, wherein those that are willing to excuse the Synod of Dort find the greatest moderation.

66.—The Sanctification of all baptized Children confessed in the Synod, and the consequence of this doctrine.

Besides these important points, we see a fourth expressly decided in the Synod; and it is that of the sanctity of all children descending from the faithful. There have been different explanations of this article in the Acts of the new Reformation. We have seen this sanctity of children formally established in the Catechism of the Calvinists of France, and there it is said expressly, that all children of the faithful are sanctified, and born in the Covenant; yet we have seen the contrary in the agreement of those of Geneva with the Swiss, and the sanctification of infants, even baptized, is there restrained to the predestinated alone. Beza seems to have followed this restriction in the above-cited exposition: but the Synod of Dort pronounces in favor of the sanctity of all children born of faithful parents, and permits not the parents to doubt of their salvation; an article from which we have seen it follow demonstratively, according to the principles of the Synod, that all the children of the faithful, and all the posterity of these children to the end of time, should their race continue so long, are of the number of the predestinated.[79]

67.—Procedure of the Synod.—Petition of the Remonstrants complaining that they are judged by their Adversaries.

Whether all these decisions, which seem so authentic, be so certainly fundamental in the new Reformation, as to deprive of salvation and cut off from the Church all those that reject them, is what we are to examine by setting forth the procedure of the Council.

The first thing I observe therein, is a petition preferred by the Remonstrants, representing to the Synod[80] that they have been condemned, treated as Heretics, and excommunicated by the Anti-Remonstrants, their colleagues and parties; that they are pastors like the rest, and so naturally ought to have a seat in the Synod together with them: if they are to be excluded from it as parties in the cause, their plaintiffs ought to be excluded from it no less than they—otherwise, they would be both judges and parties at the same time, which of all procedures is the most unjust.

68.—*They employ the same arguments which the whole Protestant party insisted on against the Church.*

These were manifestly the same reasons for which the Protestants had excepted against the Council of the Catholics; for which the Zuinglians in particular had opposed the Synod of the Ubiquitarians, by whom they were condemned at Jena, as before seen. The Remonstrants did not fail to quote these examples. They instanced chiefly the complaints made against the Council of Trent, when all Protestants exclaimed, "We will have a free Council; a Council we may be present at together with the rest; a Council that comes unbiased; a Council that does not hold us for Heretics—otherwise we should be judged by our adversaries."[81] We have seen that Calvin and the Calvinists alleged the same reasons against the Synod of Jena. The Remonstrants found themselves in this very state when they beheld Francis Gomar and his adherents seated in the Council amongst their Judges, yet themselves excluded, and treated as guilty persons:[82] this was prejudging against them before examining the cause; and these reason seemed to them much the more convincing, as they were visibly the very same their fathers had urged against the Council of Trent, as they set forth in their petition.

69.—*Their mouths are stopped by the authority of the States.*

After their petition was read, it was declared to them, "the Synod thought it very strange that the accused should set laws to their judges, and prescribe them rules; which was not only injuring the Synod, but also the States-General, by whom it was assembled and authorized to judge; wherefore they had no more do but to obey."[83]

This was stopping their mouths with the authority of the secular power, but not answering their arguments, nor the example of their forefathers when they declined the judgment of the Council of Trent. And truly, little did they dwell on these considerations: the delegates of the States who were present at the Synod[84] with the whole authority of their superiors, judged the Remonstrants were not to be admitted plaintiffs, and ordered them to obey the regulations of the Synod—which, on its side, declared their propositions insolent, and their challenging the whole Synod as a party in the cause, injurious, not only to the Synod itself, but also to the supreme authority of the States-General.

70.—*The protest against the Synod.—The arguments used against them by the Synod condemn the whole Protestant party.*

The Remonstrants condemned, change their petitions into protests against the Synod. These were debated on; and as the reasons alleged by them were the same with those the Protestants had used to elude the authority of the Catholic bishops, the answers returned them were the same that the Catholics had employed against the Protestants.[85] They were told that it had never been the custom of the Church to deprive pastors of their right of suffrage against errors, because that they had opposed them: that this would be divesting them of the prerogatives of their function for having faithfully discharged their duty, and subverting the whole economy of Church judgments: that by the same reasons, the Arians, the Nestorians, and the Eutychians might have excepted against the whole Church, and left themselves no judge among Christians: that this would be the way to silence pastors and give a free scope to all kind of heresies. After all, what judges would they have? Where could they find, in the whole body of the pastors, these neutral and indifferent persons that had interested themselves no way in questions of faith and affairs of the Church? These arguments were unanswerable; but then, unluckily for our reformed, they were the same that had been objected to them when they declined the judgment of the bishops in possession of authority, at the time of their separation.

71.—*They decide that the weaker and younger party ought to yield to the greater and more ancient.*

What carried the greatest weight in the objections against the Remonstrants was, "that they were innovators, and the least party, as well as the newest, which by consequence ought to be judged by the greatest, and the most ancient; by that which was in possession, and which maintained the doctrine till then received."[86] But thereby the Catholics did most evidently gain their cause, for, after all, what antiquity did the Dutch Reformed Church allege against the Remonstrants? We will not suffer, said she,[87] any alteration to be made in the doctrine we have constantly taught "these fifty years past," for this was the utmost antiquity they could boast. If fifty years gave to this Church, that called herself reformed, so great a power against the Arminians newly crept out of her bosom, what ought to be the authority of the whole Catholic Church, of so many ages standing?

72.—*Perplexity of the Synod at the Protest of the Remonstrants.*

Among all the answers made to the Remonstrants, in relation to their Protest, what was the least taken notice of was the comparison made by them between their exceptions against the Synod of Dort, and those of the Reformed against the councils of the Catholics and those of the Lutherans.[88] Some of them said, "there was a great difference between this, and the councils of Papists and Lutherans. There you hear men, the Pope and Luther; here you hear God. There men are prepossessed; here not a man to be found that is not ready to yield to the word of God. There you have enemies to contend with; and here, none but brethren. There every things is forced; here all is free." This was solving the question by that which caused the difficulty. The question was, whether the Gomarists did not come to the Synod prepossessed; the question was, whether they were enemies or brethren; the question was, which of them had the most docile hearts in regard to truth and the word of God; whether the Protestants in general, or the Catholics, the disciples of Zuinglius or those of Luther; the Gomarists or the Arminians. And as to liberty, the authority of the States which every where interposed, and moreover was always in the mouth of the Synod,[89] that of the Prince of Orange, the declared enemy of the Arminians, the imprisonment of Grotius and the other heads of that party, and lastly, the capital punishment of Barneveld, sufficiently prove what liberty was allowed in Holland as to that matter.

73.—Strange answer of those of Geneva.

The deputies of Geneva made fewer words of the difficulty, and without stopping at the Lutherans, to whom but four years of seniority above the Zuinglians could give but little authority to be their judges, they answer in respect of the Catholics: "Our father might, as they pleased, protest against the Councils of Constance and Trent, because we are determined to have no kind of union with them; on the contrary, we despise and hate them: in all times those who declined the authority of Councils separated from their communion."[90] This is the whole of their answer; and these great doctors would have had nothing to oppose against the exceptions of the Arminians, had they but broken off from the Churches of Holland, and openly "despised" and "hated" them.

74.—According to the Synod of Dort, the Protestants were obliged to own
the council of the Catholic Church.

According to this way of answering, the Lutherans needed not have taken so much pains to heap up grievances against the Council of Trent, nor to have discussed which was party, and which was not, in this cause. To reject the authority of the Council the Catholics cited them to, they had no more to do but say downright, We are determined to break with you, we despise you, we hate you, we trouble not ourselves about your Council. But public edification, and the very name of Christian, would not suffer such an answer. Neither did the Lutherans answer in this manner;[91] on the contrary, they declared, and even at Augsburg in their own Confession,[92] that they appealed to the Council, even that Council which the Pope was to assemble. There is a like declaration in the Confession of Strasburg; so that both Protestant parties were agreed in this point. They were not for breaking with us; they did not hate us; they did not despise us to that degree as did those of Geneva. If it be therefore true, according to them, that the Remonstrants ought to have submitted themselves to the Council of the Reformation, as they were averse to schism; so the Protestants, who alike declared they would not separate from the Catholic Church, ought to have submitted to her Council.

75.—In order to silence the Remonstrants, a Synod of Calvinists is forced to have recourse to the assistance of the Holy Ghost promised to Councils.

We must not forget the answer made by a whole Synod of the Province of Holland to the exceptions of the Remonstrants: it was the Synod held at Delft, little before that of Dort. The Remonstrants objected that the Synod, which was to be convened against them, would not be infallible like that of the Apostles, and, consequently, would not bind their consciences. This they must certainly have owned, or denied all the principles of the Reformation; yet after owning it, those of Delft had these words; "Jesus Christ, who promised the Apostles the spirit of truth, whose lights were to lead them into all truth, had likewise promised to his Church to be with her even to the end of the world, and to be in the midst of two or three that should meet together in his name;"[93] whence they concluded a little after, "that when pastors should meet together from sundry countries, in order to decide, according to God's word, what ought to be taught in the churches, one ought to persuade himself with a firm confidence that Jesus Christ would be with them according to his promise."

76.—This is returning to the Catholic Doctrine.

Here, then, you see them obliged to confess two promises of Jesus Christ, that he will be present at and direct the judgments of his Church. Now the Catholics never had any other foundation than this to believe the Church infallible. They make use of the first text, in order to show he always is with her considered in her whole. They make use of the second to show we ought to hold for certain he would be in the midst of two or three, were we assured that they were truly assembled in the name of Jesus Christ. Now what is doubtful in respect to two or three assembled in private, is certain in regard to the whole Church assembled in body: we ought, therefore, to hold for certain, in such case, that Jesus Christ is there by his spirit, and by that means her judgments are infallible; or let them tell us what other use can be made of these texts in the case to which the Synod of Delft applies them.

77.—The Remonstrants are made to hope for an Œcumenical Council.

It is true, the certain accomplishment of these promises is to be found in the body of the Universal Church and in her œcumenical council. Accordingly, it was to such a council the Remonstrants had appealed. They were answered, "It was doubtful whether and when this œcumenical council could be assembled; meanwhile, the national one, called together by the states, would be like to one Œcumenical and general, forasmuch as it would be composed of the deputies of all the reformed churches;"[94] and in case they should find "themselves aggrieved by the national Synod, they would be free to appeal to an œcumenical council, provided, in the interim, they obey the national council."

78.—*The illusion of this promise.*

The reflection we ought to make here is, that to speak of an œcumenical council was, amongst these new reformed, a remnant of the language of the Church. For what could this word mean in these upstart churches? They durst not say, the deputies of all the Reformed Churches were an œcumenical council representing the Universal Church. It was, said they, not an œcumenical council, but like to an œcumenial council. What, then, should a true œcumenical council be composed of? Ought the Lutherans to be a part of it, who had excommunicated them? or the Catholics? or, in fine, some other churches? That is what the Calvinists could not tell, and in the condition they had put themselves by dividing from all the rest of Christendom, the great name of an œcumenical council, so venerable among Christians, was nothing to them but an insignificant word, which had no idea in their mind corresponding to it.

79.—*Resolution of the Synod, that the Confession of Faith might be revised, and at the same time an obligation imposed of subscribing them.*

The last observation I have to make, as to the procedure, regards the Confessions of Faith and the Catechisms received in the United Provinces. The provincial Synods obliged the Remonstrants to subscribe them.[95] These refused it absolutely, because they believed there were principles in them from which the condemnation of their doctrine might be clearly enough deduced. Upon this refusal they were treated as heretics and schismatics; and this, notwithstanding it was agreed in the provincial Synods, and expressly declared in the Synod of Dort,[96] that these Confessions of Faith, so far from passing for a certain rule, might be examined anew; so that they obliged the Remonstrants to subscribe a doctrine of faith, even without believing it themselves.

80.—*Decree of the pretended Reformed of France, at the Synod of Charenton, in order to approve that of Dort.—The certainty of Salvation acknowledged as the principal point.*

We have observed already, what is specified in the acts, that the canons of the Synod against the Remonstrants were established with the unanimous consent of all the voices, "not one excepted." The pretended reformed of France were not allowed to go to Dort though invited, but received its decisions in their national Synods, and amongst the rest in that of Charenton, in 1620, where all the canons were translated into French, and a subscription of them enjoined in this form: "I receive, approve, and embrace all the doctrine taught in the Synod of Dort, as entirely conformable to God's word and to the Confession of Faith of our churches: the doctrine of the Arminians makes God's election to depend on the will of men, brings back Paganism, disguises popery, and overthrows the whole certainty of salvation."[97] These last words show us what they judged of most importance in the decisions of Dort, and the certainty of salvation stands foremost as one of the most essential characteristics of Calvinism.

81.—*A new Subscription of the Synod of Dort, by the French Refugees.*

Even very lately, the first thing required of our ministers, who had taken refuge in Holland in these last contests about religion, was to subscribe the acts of the Synod of Dort; and so great a concourse, so many oaths, such a number of repeated acts, seem to make it plain, that nothing is more authentic in the whole party.

82.—*By the Decree of the Synod of Dort the Remonstrants stand deposed and excommunicated.*

Even the decree of the Synod shows the importance of this decision, the Remonstrants being deprived by it, "of the ministry, of their chairs of professorship in divinity, of all other functions as well ecclesiastic as academical, until, having satisfied the Church, they be fully reconciled and received to her communion:"[98] which shows they were treated as excommunicated, and that the sentence of excommunication passed against them in particular churches and synods was ratified; after which the Synod supplicates the states not to suffer "any other doctrine to be taught but that which was just defined, and to obstruct heresies and errors that were creeping in;" Which manifestly regards the Arminian articles, by them qualified "as erroneous, and as the source of hidden errors."

83.—*The Decisions of Dort not essential.—The sentiment of the Minister Jurieu.*

All these things might make one think these articles were accounted very essential to religion. M. Jurieu, nevertheless, assures us of the contrary: for after supposing "the Church of Rome was in the sentiment of the Arminians, at least during the time of the Council of Trent," he thus proceeds: "If she had no other errors, we should have done exceedingly ill to separate from her: we ought to have borne with those for peace sake, by reason that she was a church whereof we made part, and which had not banded herself to maintain grace according to St. Austin's system of divinity," etc. And accordingly, it is this which makes him conclude, "that the reason which made them cut the Remonstrants off from their communion was, that they would not submit to a doctrine which, in the first place, we believed conformable to the word of God, which, in the second, we bound ourselves, by a confederate confession, to maintain and defend against the Pelagianism of the Church of Rome."[99]

84.—*Semi-Pelagianism, according to this Author, damns none.*

Without assenting to his principles, or what he says of the Church of Rome, it suffices to relate his sentiments, which make him say in another place, "that the churches of the Swiss and Geneva Confession would exclude from their communion a Semi-Pelagian, and one that should maintain the errors of the Remonstrants; yet it would not be their design thereby to declare this man damned, as if Semi-Pelagianism did damn."[100] It, therefore, stands well grounded by the sentiments of this minister, that the doctrine of the Remonstrants may well exclude one from the particular confederation of the pretended reformed churches, but not, in general, from the fellowship of God's children: which shows that these articles are not of the number of those they call fundamental.

Lastly, the same doctor, in his "judgment concerning methods," where he labors at the reunion of the Lutherans to those of his communion, acknowledges, "that in order to stem a torrent of Pelagianism which was going to overflow the Low Countries, the Synod of Dort ought to oppose the most rigid and strict method to this Pelagian relaxation."[101] He adds, "that with this view she might have imposed on her party the necessity of maintaining St. Austin's method, and obliged, I do not say all the members of her society, but, at least, all her doctors, preachers, and the rest concerned in teaching, yet without laying other churches and other communions under the same obligation." Whence it comes the Synod, so far from binding all Christians to her tenets, does not even pretend to bind all her members, but only her preachers and doctors; which shows what these grave decisions of the new Reformation are in the main; when, after so much boasting the express word of God, all terminates at last in obliging doctors to teach, by common agreement, a doctrine which private men are neither obliged to believe nor profess.

85.—*The tenets in debate at Dort were the most popular and the most essential.*

Nor can it be answered that these are dogmas which appertain not to the knowledge of the people: for besides that all dogmas revealed by God are made for the people as well as for the rest, and there are certain cases wherein they are not allowed to be ignorant of them; that which was defined at Dort ought, above all others, to be a most popular dogma, since it principally concerned that certainty every body ought to have of his own salvation; a dogma, wherein the Calvinists laid the main foundation of the Christian religion.

86.—*The minister Jurieu makes the Synod of Dort act more by policy than truth.*

All the rest of the decisions of Dort, as you have seen, tending to this dogma of certainty, it was no question of idle speculation, but of practice, which they judged the most necessary and of the utmost consequence to religion: and, nevertheless, M. Jurieu has represented this doctrine not so much as a capital dogma, but as a method they were obliged to follow; and not as the most certain neither, but as being "the most rigid. "In order to stem," says he, "this torrent of Pelagianism, it was necessary to expose against it the most rigid and strict method, and to decide," he adds, "many things to the prejudice of that liberty of disputing *pro* and *con*, which always had subsisted among the

Reformed:"[102] as if this were a political affair, or that other things were to be considered in Church decisions than the pure truth revealed by God clearly and expressly in his word; or, after a full knowledge thereof, it were allowable to shift and decline from it.

87.—*They were ready to bear with Pelagianism in the Arminians.*

But what this minister teaches in another place, is still more surprising, since he declares to the Arminians, that it is not properly Arminianism, but Socinianism, which they reject in them.[103] "These Remonstrants," says he, "ought not to wonder we offer peace to sects that seem to be of the same mind with them in respect to the Synod of Dort, and do not offer it to them. Their Semi-Socinianism will ever be a wall of separation between them and us." Here then is what makes the separation. "It is because, at this day," proceeds he, "Socinianism is in the most elevated stations amongst them." It is plainly seen, were it not for this obstacle, that they might unite with the Arminians, without concerning themselves for "that torrent of Pelagianism with which they overflowed the Low Countries," nor for the decisions of Dort, nor even for the confederacy of all Calvinism in favor of the pretended sentiments of St. Austin.

88.—*The rest of the Ministers are of the same opinion with M. Jurieu.*

M. Jurieu is not the only one that has revealed to us this secret of the party. The minister Matthew Bochart had assured us before him that, "if the Remonstrants had only differed from the rest of the Calvinists in the five points decided at the Synod of Dort, the difference might have been adjusted,"[104] which he confirms by the opinions of other doctors of the sect, even with that of the Synod itself.

89.—*The Reformation allows private men to arrogate to themselves more capacity for understanding sound Doctrine, than all the rest of the Church.*

It is true, he says at the same time,[105] that although they were disposed to tolerate, in peaceable and modest individuals, sentiments opposite to those of the Synod, they could not have suffered them in the ministers, who ought to be better instructed than the rest: but this, however, is enough to evince, that these decisions, "which were opposed against Pelagianism," although made by the Synod with so great solemnity and with such frequent declarations of their following nothing therein but the pure and express word of God, are not very material to Christianity; and what is more surprising, is, that they hold for modest men such private persons as, after knowing the decisions of all the doctors, nay, as speaks Mr. Bochart, "of all the Churches of the party as many as there are in Europe," yet believe they are better able to understand which is sound doctrine, not only than any one of these in particular, but even than all of them together.

*90.—The Doctors themselves are very much relaxed in the observance of the
decrees of Dort.*

It is also very certain, that the doctors, in whom sentiments opposed to those
of the Synod were not to be tolerated, are greatly relaxed in that respect.[106]
The ministers who have written in latter times, and among others M.
Beaulieu, whom we have seen at Sedan one of the most learned and pacific
of them all, soften as much as they are able the dogma of inamissibiity of
justice, and even that of the certainty of salvation; and two reasons move them
to it: the first is, the dislike of Lutherans to it, whom they are willing to be
united to at any rate; the second is, the absurdity and impiety discoverable in
these tenets by ever so little an inspection. The doctors may, by degrees, inure
themselves to them in consequence of the false principles they are imbued
with; but plain and sincere people will not easily be persuaded, that every one
of them, to have true faith, must assure himself he has no damnation to fear,
let him commit what crimes he pleases; much less, that he is sure of preserving
sanctity and grace in such crimes.

    As often as our Reformed disclaim these impious tenets, let us praise God
for it, and without more disputing, entreat them only to consider that the
Holy Ghost could not have been in those that taught them, and who made a
great part of the Reformation to consist in notions so derogatory to Christian
justice.

*91.—The Synod of Dort hath done no good, and in spite
of all its decrees M. Jurieu is a Pelagian.*

This, however, we may conclude from thence: that, after all, this great Synod
has proved quite useless, and neither cured the people, nor even the pastors,
for whom it was principally intended, inasmuch as what is called Pelagianism
in the Reformation (the thing the Synod resolved to destroy) still stands its
ground; for I ask, who has been cured of this evil? Not those surely who do
not believe the Synod; nor even those who do believe it; for M. Jurieu, for
instance, who is of this number, and seems to continue so firm in the
confederation, as he calls it, of the Calvinian Churches against Pelagianism, in
reality does not disapprove it, since he maintains, as we have seen, that it is
not contrary to piety.[107] He is like those Socinians, who when asked if they
believe the eternal divinity of the Son of God, make no difficulty of
answering, they believe it: but urged a little further, will tell you, that the
contrary belief, in the main, is neither opposite to piety nor true faith. Such
are true enemies to the Son of God's divinity, since they hold the tenet for
indifferent: M. Jurieu is a Pelagian, and the enemy of grace, in the same sense.

92.—Another Pelagian saying of the same Minister, and his wretched contradictions.

In effect, what is the tendency of these words of his, "in exhortation, you
must of necessity speak like a Pelagian?" This is not the speech of a divine; for
if Pelagianism be a heresy, and a heresy that renders useless the cross of Jesus
Christ, as has been so much preached even by the Reformation, you cannot

keep at too great a distance from it in exhortation, so far from retaining the least tincture of it.[108]

This minister is no less inconsistent when he excuses the Pelagians or Semi-Pelagians of the Augsburg Confession, together with the Arminians, following the same sentiments, under pretext that, "whilst they are Semi-Pelagians in word and spirit, they are the disciples of St. Austin in the heart;" for can he be ignorant that a perverted spirit soon corrupts the heart? Men must be very closely attached to error when even truth presented does not awaken them, nay, presented by a synod made up of their whole communion.

When therefore M. Jurieu says, on one hand, that Pelagianism does not damn; and on the other, that you will "never make truly pious men of Pelagians and Semi-Pelagians,"[109] though he be ever so subtle a divine, he could not show more clearly that he does not reflect on what he says, and that, by endeavoring to save all, he loses all.

93.—*This Minister falls back into the excesses of the Reformers relating to the cause of Sin.*

He also thinks he has kept clear from that blasphemy which makes God the author of sin, into which, he pretends, none of his party has fallen "for this hundred years;" and he himself relapses into it in that very book where he pretends to show they are no longer guilty of it.[110] For after all, whilst you continue to deprive mankind of the liberty of their choice, and believe that free-will subsists together with an entire and inevitable necessity, it always will be true that neither men, nor prevaricating angels, could avoid sinning; and so the sins they fell into are the necessary consequences resulting from those dispositions their Creator placed them in. Now M. Jurieu is one of those who leave this inevitable necessity whole and entire, when he says, we know nothing of our soul, "only that she thinks," nor can we define what is requisite "to constitute her free."[111] He owns, therefore, he does not know but it is this inevitable necessity which drags us into evil as well as good, and by that means sinks into all the excesses of the first Reformers, from which he boasts that his party has been free for a whole age.

To avoid these terrible inconveniences, you must at least believe, if not arrived to the comprehension of it, that there is no admitting, without blasphemy and making God the author of sin, this invincible necessity which the Remonstrants reproached the pretended Reformers with, and from which the Synod of Dort has not justified them.

94.—*Connivance of the Synod of Dort, not only at the excesses of the pretended Reformers, but also at those of the Remonstrants.*

And in reality, I observe that nothing is said in any part of the Synod against these damnable excesses. It was willing to spare the Reformers and save the beginnings of the Reformation from eternal infamy.

Yet at least it ought not to have extended the like condescension to the Remonstrants, who opposed to the excesses of the Reformers other no less criminal excesses.

They printed in Holland in 1618, a little before the Synod, a book under this title—"The State of Controversies in the Low Countries,"[112] where it is shown it was the doctrine of the Remonstrants that certain accidents might befall God; that he was liable to change; that his prescience of certain events was not certain; that he proceeded by discoursing and conjecture in drawing, as we do, one thing from another; and other the like numberless errors, wherein the Author sides with those philosophers who destroy God's foreknowledge, for fear of lessening the liberty of man. There it is made to appear they went so far astray as to make God corporeal, to attribute to him three essences, and the rest that may be learned from that Book, which is very perspicuous and concise. It was composed in order to prepare, for the approaching Synod, the subject matter of their deliberations: but none of all these things were mentioned at it, no more than many others as materially started by the Remonstrants. The whole care of the Synod was taken up in preserving those Articles which are peculiar to Calvinism; and more zeal was exhibited by them for these opinions, than for the fundamental principles of Christianity.

95.—The Decree of Charenton receiving the Lutherans to Communion.—1631.

The great deference which we have seen was paid to the Lutherans, prevailed nothing with them in regard to an union, they still persisting to hold the whole party of the Sacramentarians for excommunicated. At last the Reformed of France, in their Synod of Charenton, made this memorable decree, wherein they declare, "that the Germans and others following the Confession of Augsburg, for so much as the Churches of the Augsburg Confession agree with the others that are reformed in the fundamental principles and tenets of the true religion, and that in their worship there is neither idolatry nor superstition, may, without making abjuration, be received to the holy table, to contract marriage with the faithful of our Confession, and to present, as god-fathers, children to baptism, in promising the Consistory they will never solicit them to act counter, directly or indirectly, to the doctrine received and professed in our Churches, but will be contented with instructing them in the principles wherein we all agree."

96.—The Consequences of this Decree.

In consequence of this decree, they were obliged to say, "that the doctrine of the Real Presence, taken in itself, has no venom in it: that it is neither contrary to piety nor God's honor, nor the good of mankind: that although the opinion of the Lutherans relating to the Eucharist infers, no less than that of Rome, the destruction of Jesus Christ's humanity, this consequence nevertheless cannot be imputed to them without calumny, inasmuch as it is formally rejected by them,"[113]—so that it is an allowed maxim that, in matters of religion, none ought to charge on others the consequences they draw from their doctrine, but only such things as they allow in express terms.

97.—The Calvinists had never advanced so far.

Never had the Sacramentarians, before this time, made so great an advance towards the Lutherans. The novelty of this decree does not consist in saying, that the Real Presence, and the other disputed points between both parties, do not regard the fundamentals of salvation; for it must be owned ingenuously, that ever since the time of the Conference of Marpurg, that is, so long ago as the year 1529,[114] the Zuinglians offered the Lutherans to hold them for brethren notwithstanding their doctrine of the Real Presence; and never, from that time, did they believe it fundamental, but required that the fraternity should be mutual, and owned equally on both sides; which being refused them by Luther, they likewise continued to disown those for brethren who were so averse to pass the same judgment in their favor: whereas, in the Synod of Charenton, it is the Sacramentarians alone that receive the Lutherans into that fellowship, notwithstanding that they are held by them for excommunicated.

98.—Memorable date of the Decree of Charenton.

The date of this decree is remarkable: it was made in 1631, when the great Gustavus was thundering in Germany, and when it was currently believed throughout the whole Reformation, that Rome itself would be soon in the power of the Lutherans. God had otherwise ordained: the year following, this victorious King was killed at the battle of Lutzen, and all the rare discoveries made concerning him in the prophecies were now to be retracted.

99.—Great change in controversies by means of this Decree.—It convicts
the Calvinists of calumny.

Meanwhile the decree passed, and the Catholics observed the greatest change imaginable in the doctrine of the Protestants.

In the first place, all that horror they had infused into the people against the doctrine of the Real Presence appeared manifestly unjust and calumnious. The doctors may say what they please of the matter: but it was the Real Presence on which the aversion of the people was chiefly bent. This doctrine had been represented to them, not only as gross and carnal, but also as brutal and full of barbarity, whereby men became Cyclopses, eaters of human flesh and human blood, parricides that eat their Father and their God. But now, since the decree of this Synod, it stands confessed, that all these exaggerations, with which the silly vulgar were fascinated for so long a time, are calumnies; and the doctrine that was made to pass for so impious and inhuman, has no longer any thing in it that is contrary to piety.

100.—The literal sense and the Real Presence necessary.

Thereby even it becomes the most credible and the most necessary; for the chief reason inducing to wrest the sense of these words—"Except ye eat the flesh of the Son of Man, and drink his blood,"[115]—and also of these—"Eat, this is my body; drink, this is my blood,"[116]—to spiritual and metaphorical meanings was, because they seemed to lead to sin by commanding to eat human flesh, and to drink human blood: so that St. Austin's rule, of interpreting spiritually what appears to incline to evil, was here to take place. But at present this reason carries no longer any the least probability; all this imaginary crime is vanished, and nothing prevents taking the words of our Saviour in their true literal sense.

The people were made to abhor the Catholic doctrine, as a doctrine that destroyed Jesus Christ's human nature, and ruined the mystery of his ascension. But they must no longer be affrighted at these consequences, since the denial of them sufficiently acquits whosoever denies them.

101.—The chief argument in behalf of the rupture rendered frivolous.

These horrors thus raised in the minds of the people were, to speak the truth, the real cause of their departure from the Church. Read in all the acts of the pretended martyrs the cause for which they suffered, and you will find everywhere, that it was for the doctrine opposite to the Real Presence. Consult a Melancthon, a Sturmius, a Peucer, all the rest that were against condemning the doctrine of the Zuinglians—you will find their chief reason to be, because it was for this doctrine that such a number of the faithful laid down their lives in France and England. These wretched martyrs persuaded themselves, in dying for this doctrine, they died for a fundamental point of faith and piety; at present this doctrine is innocent, and excludes none from the sacred table, nor from the kingdom of heaven.

102.—The hatred of the People turned against Transubstantiation, a thing
of much less importance.

To preserve in the hearts of the people their aversion to the Catholic doctrine, it was requisite to turn it on another object than the Real Presence. Transubstantiation is now the great crime: there is now no manner of difficulty in admitting Jesus Christ really present; in admitting one and the same body in different places at once; in admitting the entire body in every crumb of bread; the grand error consists in taking the bread away: what regards Jesus Christ is of small importance; what regards the bread is alone essential.

103.—Jesus Christ no longer adorable in the Eucharist, as formerly believed
by Protestants.

All the maxims, till then held for unquestionable, regarding the adoration of Jesus Christ, are now changed. Calvin and the rest of them had demonstrated, that wherever Jesus Christ, so adorable an object, was held present by so special a Presence as that acknowledged in the Eucharist, it was not lawful to withhold that adoration which is due unto him. But now, Jesus Christ's Presence in any place is not enough to make him be adored in it; he must command it, he must "declare his will, in order to be adored in such and such a state;"[117] otherwise, as much God as he is, he will meet with no worship from us. More than this, he must show himself: "if the body of Jesus Christ be in a place insensibly, and in a manner imperceptible to all the senses, he does not oblige us to worship him in such a place." His word does not suffice, it is necessary he should be seen: you may hear the voice of the king ever so much; if you see him not with your own eyes, you owe him no respect, or, at least, he must declare expressly it is his intention to be honored; otherwise you should behave as in his absence. Were it the case of an earthly king, none would question paying him what is his due the moment it is known where he is; but thus to honor the King of heaven would be idolatry, and it would be to be feared lest he should take the worship to be given to another than himself.

104.—*Interior Acts of Adoration are tolerated in the Lutherans, and the exterior, which are but the tokens of them, rejected.*

But here is a device that is new and surprising. The Lutheran, who believes Jesus Christ present, shall receive him as his God; shall put his trust in him, shall invoke him; and the Synod of Charenton decides, "there is neither idolatry, nor superstition in his worship:" but if he make any perceptible act of adoration, he idolizes; that is to say, it is allowable to have the substance of adoration, which is the interior sentiment, but not allowable to testify it; and you become an idolater in making appear, by some posture of respect, the sense of that truly sacred veneration you have in your heart.

105.—*Frivolous Answer.*

"But the reason of this is," say they, "because, should the Lutheran adore Jesus Christ in the Eucharist, who is there together with the bread, there would be danger lest the adoration should be referred to the bread alike as to Jesus Christ; or, however, lest some should think the intention was to refer it so:"[118] no question, when the wise men adored Jesus Christ, either in his crib, or in a cradle, it was to be feared lest they should worship, together with Jesus Christ, either the crib or the cradle; or in fine, lest the Blessed Virgin and St. Joseph should take them for worshippers of the cradle rather than of the divine infant lying in it. These were the subtleties introduced by the decree of Charenton.

106.—*Ubiquity tolerated.*

Moreover, the doctrine of Ubiquity, which had been accounted, and with reason, alike by the Sacramentarians and by Catholics, a most monstrous doctrine, confounding both natures of Jesus Christ, becomes the doctrine of the Saints.

For you are not to imagine the defenders of this doctrine were expected out of the union: the Synod speaks in general of the churches of the Augsburg Confession, whereof it is well known the greatest part are Ubiquitarians, and the ministers assure us,[119] Ubiquity hath nothing mortal in it, though it destroys, more expressly than ever Eutychianism did, the human nature of our Lord.

107.—*Nothing but the external Worship is looked upon as important.*

In a word, little account is made of every thing that causes no alteration in the worship, even in the external worship: for the belief, which you may have interiorly, is no obstacle to communion; nothing but the respect you show externally makes the sin; and this is what we are brought to by those who are always preaching to us adoration in spirit and truth.

108.—*The fountain of Piety formerly acknowledged by them, is changed.*

It plainly appears, without needing my intimation, that after the Synod of Charenton, neither the inamissibility of justice, nor the certainty of salvation, are any longer a necessary foundation of piety, since the Lutherans are admitted to communion with the contrary doctrine.

109.—*The disputes about Predestination concern not the Substance of Religion.*

No more must they speak to us of absolute predestination and absolute decrees as of a fundamental article, since they cannot deny, according to M. Jurieu, "but there is a piety in those great communions of Protestants, wherein both absolute decrees and grace of itself efficacious, are so roughly handled." The same minister is agreed, "that the Protestants of Germany make the foreknowledge of our faith enter into that gratuitous love whereby God has loved us in Jesus Christ." Thus the decree of predestination will not be an absolute decree, and independent of all foreknowledge, but a conditional decree, including the condition of our future faith; and this is what M. Jurieu does not condemn.[120]

110.—*Two other remarkable Novelties ensuing from the Decree of Charenton.*

But here are the two most remarkable novelties which the decree of Charenton has introduced into the pretended Reformation: first, the dispute on fundamental points; and secondly, the dispute on the nature of the Church.

111.—*Distinction of fundamental Points, and the inevitable perplexity of our Reformed.*

As to fundamental points, the Catholics thus argued with them: "If the Real Presence, if Ubiquity, if so many other important points, contested for more than a century between the Lutherans and Calvinists, be not fundamental, why should those be more so on which you dispute with the Church of Rome? Does not she believe the Trinity, the Incarnation, the whole Creed? Has she laid any other foundation than Jesus Christ? All you object against her, on this head, in order to show that she has another, are so many consequences which she denies, and which, according to your own principles, ought not to be imputed to her. Wherein, then, do you place precisely what is fundamental in religion?" To relate here all they have said concerning fundamental points, some one way, some another, and the greatest part confessing that it is all a mystery to them, and a thing rather to be felt than explained, were an endless task, and involving one's self with them in a labyrinth from whence there is no exit.

> 112.—*They are forced to own that the Church of Rome is a true Church,*
> *wherein one may be saved.*

The other dispute was not less important: for this principle being once established by them, that those who retain the principal foundations of faith, however separated in communion, are, in the main, the same Church and the same society of God's children, worthy of his holy table and his kingdom, the Catholics demand how they can be excluded from this Church and from eternal salvation? For now it will no longer serve their turn to say, the Church of Rome is a Church excluding the whole world, and which the whole world ought to exclude: for you see the Lutherans, who exclude the Calvinists, are not excluded. It is this which has produced this new system of the Church which makes so great a noise, and wherein, after all, they cannot but comprehend the Church of Rome.

> 113.—*The Conference of Cassel, where the Lutherans of Rintel come to an*
> *Agreement with the Calvinists of Marpurg.*

The Protestants of Germany have not been in all places alike inexorable in regard of the Calvinists. In 1661, a conference was held at Cassel between the Calvinists of Marpurg and the Lutherans of Rintel, where both parties entered into a brotherly fellowship. I own this union was without consequence in the other parts of Germany, and I have not been able to discover what even was the consequence of it between the contracting parties: but in the agreement there was one important article not to be forgotten.

> 113.—*Important article of this Agreement relating to the breaking of*
> *the Eucharistic Bread.*

The Calvinists reproached the Lutherans that, in the celebration of the Eucharist, they omitted the breaking of the bread, which had a divine institution.[121] It is the current doctrine of Calvinism, that the breaking makes part of the Sacrament as being a symbol of that body broken which Jesus would give to his disciples; that for this reason it was practised by Jesus Christ, that is of precept, and comprehended by our Saviour in this ordinance, "Do ye this." This is what was maintained by the Calvinists of Marpurg, and denied by the Lutherans of Rintel. They nevertheless united, each side persisting in their sentiments; and it was said by those of Marpurg, "That the breaking did not appertain to the essence, but only to the integrity of the Sacrament, as being necessary thereto by the example and commandment of Jesus Christ, so that the Lutherans, without breaking the bread, had nevertheless the substance of the Supper, and both parties might mutually tolerate each other."

115.—*Demonstration in favor of Communion under one kind.*

A minister, who answered a treatise concerning Communion under both kinds, has examined this conference which was objected against them: the fact passed for unquestionable, and the minister agreed that the breaking of the bread, although commanded by Jesus Christ, did not appertain to the essence, but only to the integrity of the Sacrament.[122] Here, then, have we the essence of the Sacrament manifestly separated from the divine precept, and reasons have been found to dispense with that which they said was commanded by Jesus Christ: after which I do not see how they can urge the precept of receiving under both kinds; forasmuch that as though we were agreed Jesus Christ had commanded the receiving of them, we should still be admitted to examine whether this divine commandment regarded the essence, or only the integrity.

116.—*Present state of Controversies in Germany.*

The present state of controversies in Germany between the Lutherans and Calvinists may be likewise seen in the same conference; where it will be perceived, that the constant doctrine of the divines of the Augsburg Confession is, that grace is universal; that it is resistible; that it is amissible; that predestination is conditional, and presupposes the foreknowledge of our faith; lastly, that the grace of conversion is annexed to an action purely natural, and depending on our own strength, namely, on our carefulness to hear sermons:[123] which the learned Beaulieu confirms by many testimonies, to which we could add many others, were not the thing past dispute, as might have been seen by the testimony of M. Jurieu,[124] and had we not spoken of this matter already.

117.—*The relaxation of the principles of the Lutherans give occasion to those of Cameron and of his disciples, touching Universal Grace.*

Accordingly, one may have seen in this history, how Melancthon had softened, among the Lutherans, that extreme rigor wherewith Luther maintained absolute and particular decrees, and how unanimously it is taught amongst them, that God wills seriously and sincerely the salvation of all men; that he offers them Jesus Christ as their redeemer; that he calls them to him by preaching and the promises of his gospel; and that his Spirit is ever ready to be efficacious in them, if they do but hearken to his word; that, finally, it is attributing to God two contrary wills, to say on one side, he proposes his gospel to all mankind; and on the other, that he will save but a very small number of them.[125] In consequence of that complaisance, still continued in behalf of the Lutherans, John Cameron of Scotland, a famous minister, and Professor of Divinity in the Academy of Saumur, there taught an universal vocation and grace, declared in behalf of all mankind by the wonders of God's works, by his word, and the Sacraments. This doctrine of Cameron was strenuously and ingeniously defended by his disciples Amiraud and Testard, professors of divinity in the same town. This entire Academy embraced it: Du Moulin put himself at the head of the contrary party, and engaged in this sentiment the Academy of Sedan, where he ruled uncontrolled; and in our days we have seen the whole Reformation divided in France, with much warmth, between Saumur and Sedan. In spite of the censures of the Synods, which suppressed the doctrine of universal grace, yet without qualifying it as heretical or erroneous, the most learned ministers undertook to defend it. Daille made its apology, to which Blondel put a preface very much to the advantage of the abettor of this sentiment; and universal grace triumphed even in Sedan, where the minister Beaulieu taught in our days.

118.—*Whether Universal Grace be contrary to the Synod of Dort.*

It had not equal success out of this kingdom, particularly in Holland, where it was judged opposite to the Synod of Dort. But on the contrary, Blondel and Daille showed,[126] that the divines of Great Britain and Bremen had maintained in the Synod "an universal will and intention" of saving all mankind, a sufficient grace given to all; a grace without which one could not renew in himself God's image. This is what these divines had publicly declared in the Synod, nor did they merit the less for it the praises and congratulations of this whole assembly.

119.—*Decree passed at Geneva against Universal Grace, and the question resolved by the Magistrate.—Helvetic Formulary.—1669-1671.*

Geneva, ever attached to Calvin's rigorous propositions, was very averse to this Universality, which nevertheless was carried into its very bowels by the French ministers. Every family was now in contention for or against it, when the Magistrate interposed. From the court of Twenty-five it was carried to that of the Two Hundred. These Magistrates did not blush to make their pastors and professors enter into a dispute before them, and set themselves up as judges in a question of the most refined theology. Powerful recommendations came from the Swiss in behalf of particular grace against universal grace; a rigorous decree was issued in condemnation of the latter. They published the formulary of a divine which the Swiss approved, wherein the system of universal grace was declared "not a little remote from the sound doctrine revealed in Scripture;" and that nothing might be wanting to it, the sovereign magistrate commanded that all doctors, ministers and professors, should subscribe the formulary in these words: "Thus do I believe; thus do I profess; thus will I teach." This is no submission of polity and order, it is a pure act of faith enjoined by the secular authority; this is what the Reformation ends in, subjecting the Church to the world, learning to ignorance, and faith to the magistrate.

120.—*Another decision of the Helvetic Formulary, concerning the Hebrew text, which the learned of the party laugh at.—Variation in regard to the Vulgate.*

This Helvetic formulary had also another clause, wherein, not concerning themselves with the Septuagint, nor the Targums, nor the original Samaritan, nor with any of the old interpreters, nor any of the ancient readings, they canonized even the points of the Hebrew text, such as we now have it, declaring it untainted with any even the least faults of the transcriber, and clear from all injuries of time. The authors of this decree were not sensible how egregiously they exposed themselves to the laughter of all learned men, even of their own communion; but they adhered to the old maxims of the Reformation, then but ignorant. They were vexed that the readings of the Vulgate, formerly taken by them for so many falsifications, were daily more and more approved by the learned of the party; and by fixing the original text, such as it is at this time, they thought to rid themselves of the necessity of tradition, never reflecting that, under the name of the Hebrew text, instead of ecclesiastic traditions, and that of the ancient Synagogue, they consecrated those even of the Rabbis.

121.—*Other decisions of Geneva and the Swiss how much condemned by M. Claude.*

Another decree passed also at Geneva concerning Faith in 1675, wherein was confirmed that of 1649, whereby they added two new Articles to the Confession of Faith; the first, importing, "that the imputation of Adam's sin was anterior to corruption;" the second, "that, in the economy of the divine decrees, the sending of Jesus Christ is after the decree of election." They ordered that all those who should refuse to subscribe these two new articles of Faith, should be excluded and deposed from the ministry and all ecclesiastical functions.

This decision was judged very odd even in the party, and Turretin, minister and professor at Geneva, was greatly upbraided for it by M. Claude,[127] as appears by a letter of this minister dated the twentieth of June, 1675, which Lewis du Moulin, son to the minister Peter du Moulin, and uncle to the minister Jurieu, caused to be printed.

M. Claude complains in this letter, "that the Swiss were solicited to draw up a Formulary conformable to that of Geneva, containing the same points and the same restrictions, in order to be added to their Confession of Faith:"[128] and it is plain from a remark of Du Moulin, inserted in the same letter,[129] that the Swiss had in fact struck this stroke which M. Claude judged so terrible.

Nevertheless, the same minister maintains that it is not lawful to add thus[130] "new articles of Faith to those of his Confession; and that it is dangerous to remove the ancient landmarks which have been set by our fathers."[131] I would to God our Reformed had always had before their eyes this maxim of the wise man, which they so frequently are obliged to return to, in order to terminate the divisions they see daily breeding in the midst of them! M. Claude proposes it to those of Geneva,[132] and is astonished that this Church "should thus make new articles of Faith and new laws of preaching;" he makes bold to say,[133] that acting in this manner is setting up gods of their own, and breaking unity with all the Churches which are not of their own opinion: to wit "with those of France, with those of England, with those of Poland, of Prussia, and Germany;" that the matter in hand is not of mere discipline, in which Churches may be allowed to vary, but that it is separating themselves in[134] "points of doctrine unalterable in their nature, which they cannot, with a good conscience, teach differently;" so that this is not only "setting up for themselves a particular ministry," but also sowing "the seeds of a fatal division" in faith itself, and, in short, "shutting their hearts" against other Churches.

If now one should be desirous to know to what length Geneva carried her rigor, he will be informed from the same letter[135]: for it specifies, "that the signing of the articles was exacted with an inconceivable severity, and exacted even from those who came to Geneva to be ordained with the design of serving elsewhere; that the same necessity of subscription was laid on them as on those of Geneva itself; that it was exacted with the same rigor from pastors already received, notwithstanding they had already grown old in the labors of the ministry:" and this, says M. Claude, "is as much as in them lies, wresting every where the cure from those that are of different opinions, namely, *from all the rest of the Churches*, and condemning themselves, as having hitherto maintained as unjust peace with people against whom they ought to have declared war."[136]

All these remonstrances were of no effect; the church of Geneva stood firm, no less than that of the Swiss, both of them in the notion that their determinations were grounded on the word of God: which still continues to make it manifest that, under the covert of this word, it is his own conceits every man pays worship to; and if they have no other principle whereby to agree in the sense of this word, there never will be amongst their Churches any other than a political and exterior union, such as subsists with those of Geneva, who in the main have broken off from all the rest; and in order to find something fixed, it is necessary, after M. Claude's example, that they should be brought back to this maxim of the wise man, "not to remove the landmarks set them by their forefathers;"[137] that is, they must hold to the decisions already made by those in matters of faith.

122.—*The Test Act in England: therein the English approach to our sentiments, and only, through manifest error, condemn the Church of Rome.*

The famous Test well deserves a place in this history, forasmuch as it was one of the principal acts of Religion in England. The parliament held at London in 1678, passed an Act enjoining the following declaration: "I, A. B. do solemnly and sincerely, in the presence of God, profess, testify, and declare, that I do believe that in the Sacrament of the Lord's Supper there is not any transubstantiation of the elements of bread and wine into the body and blood of Christ, at or after the consecration, by any person whatsoever; and that the invocation or adoration of the Virgin Mary, or any other saint, and the sacrifice of the Mass, as they are now used in the Church of Rome, are superstitious and idolatrous, &c." The particulars to be observed in this Profession of Faith, are first, that it only attacks Transubstantiation and not the Real Presence, wherein it follows the amendment which Elizabeth had made in the Reformation of Edward the Sixth. There are only added to it these words, "at or after the Consecration," which manifestly allow the belief of the Real Presence before the manducation, since they exclude nothing, as is plain, but the sole change of substance.

Thus, a good English Protestant, without blemish to his religion or conscience, may believe that the body and blood of Jesus Christ are really and substantially present in the bread and wine immediately after consecration. If the Lutherans believed as much, it is certain they would adore him. Neither do the English place any obstacle to it in their Test: and as they receive the Eucharist kneeling, nothing hinders their acknowledging and worshipping Jesus Christ there present, in the same spirit that we do: after this, to cavil with us about Transubstantiation, is a proceeding little worthy of them.

In the following words of the Test, the Invocation, or as they call it, the Adoration of the Blessed Virgin and the saints, with the sacrifice of the Mass, are condemned as acts of "superstition and idolatry:" not absolutely, but "as they are now used in the church of Rome." But the reason of this was, that the English are too well versed in antiquity to be ignorant, that the Fathers of the fourth century (to ascend no higher at present) did invoke the Blessed Virgin and the saints. They know that St. Gregory of Nazianzum approves expressly, in the mouth of a martyr, that piety which moved her to beg of the Blessed Virgin, "that she would assist a Virgin engaged in danger."[138] They know that all the Fathers have made, and solemnly approved in their Homilies, the like invocations addressed to saints: nay, in respect of them, have even used the word Invocation.[139] As for that of adoration, they know likewise, it is equivocal no less among the holy Fathers than in Scripture; and does not always signify, rendering to a person divine honors; and for this reason also St. Gregory of Nazianzum made no difficulty, in many places, of saying that the relics of the martyrs were adored, and that God did not disdain to confirm such an adoration by miracles. The English are too well read in antiquity to be ignorant of this doctrine and these practices of the ancient Church, and bear her too great a veneration to accuse her of superstition and idolatry: it is this which makes them use this restriction, which we observe in their Test, and suppose, in the church of Rome, a kind of invocation and adoration different from that of the Fathers, because they were very sensible, without this precaution, the Test would be no more subscribed with a good conscience by the learned Protestants than by Catholics.

Nevertheless it is certain, as to the fact, that we demand nothing of the saints but the partnership of their prayers, no more than the ancients did: and that we honor nothing in their relics, but what they honored in them. If we sometimes entreat the Saints, not to pray, but to give and act, the learned among the English will agree that the ancients have done it like us,[140] and like us have understood it in that sense which attributes favors received, not only to the Sovereign that distributes them, but also, to the intercessors who obtain them: so that there never will be found any real difference between the ancients, whom the English will not condemn, and us, whom they do condemn, but through mistake, and by laying to our charge what we do not believe.

I say the same of the sacrifice of Mass. The English are better skilled in antiquity than to be ignorant that in all times the same gifts were offered to God, in the sacred mysteries and the celebration of the Eucharist, as were afterwards distributed to the people, and that these were offered to him no less for the dead than for the living. The ancient Liturgies containing the form of this oblation, as well in the east as west, are in the hands of every one, and the English are far from accusing them either of superstition or idolatry. There is then a way of offering to God the Eucharistic sacrifice for the living and the dead, which the Protestant Church of England judges neither superstitious nor idolatrous: and if they reject the Roman Mass, it is by supposing that it is different from that of the ancients.

But this difference is none at all; one drop of water is not more like another, than the Roman Mass is like, as to its essence and substance, to the Mass which the Greeks and the rest of Christians received from their forefathers. For which reason the church of Rome, when she admits them to her communion, does not prescribe another Mass to them. Thus the Roman Church has not, in the main, another sacrifice than that which, by the confession of the English Protestants themselves, was offered in the east and west ever since the beginning of Christianity.

Hence it clearly follows that the Roman doctrine, as well concerning Invocation and Adoration, as the sacrifice of the Mass, is no otherwise condemned in the Test, than by presupposing that Rome receives these things in another sense, and practises them in another spirit, than that of the Fathers; which visibly is not so: so that readily, and without alleging further reasons, we may say, that abrogating the Test would be nothing else but abrogating a notorious calumny fixed on the Church of Rome.

Notes

[1] Ex. de la Foi. chez. Riv. 1560, ch. ii. Conc. 1.
[2] Ib. ch. p. iii. t. iv. art. v. p. 35.
[3] Ib. Conc. part vi. p. 38.
[4] Ex. de la Foi. chez. Riv. 1560, ch. ii. Conc. part iv. p. 39.
[5] Ib. 29, 90, 91. ch. iii. Con. part vi. p. 40.
[6] Lib. de Dei prædes. opusc. 704, 705.
[7] Lib. iii. c. xxiii. n. 7, 8. 9.
[7] De prædes de occult. provid. &c.
[8] Jr. jugem. sur les mech. Sect. xvii. pp. 142, 143.
[9] Jur. Ibid.
[10] S. l. ix. n. 3, et seq.
[11] Rom. xi. 29.
[12] Ch. viii. conc. part i. p. 66.
[13] Ib. conc. part ii. p. 121.

[14] Phil. ii. 12.
[15] Tim. i. 19.
[16] Matt. x. 28.
[17] S. l. ix. n. 15.
[18] Ch. iv. Conc. part 13. p. 74.
[19] S. l. ix. Ch. v. Conc. 6. p. 90.
[20] Conc. p. 74.
[21] Rom. xi. 29.
[22] S. l. viii. n. 52. Epit. c. xi.
    Concord p. 621. solid. rept. 669,
    805, et seq.
[23] Act. Syn. Dordr. Edit. Dordr. 1620.
    Præf. ad Eccl. ante Synod. Dordr.
[24] Ibid.
[25] Sess. xxxi. p. 112.
[26] Ibid.
[27] Art. ix. 10. Ibid.
[28] Sess. xxxiv. p. 115, et seq.
[29] Art. iv. Ibid.
[30] 2 Pet. ii. 1.
[31] Ead. Sess. xxxiv. p. 116, et seq.
[32] Ibid. p. 117.
[33] Art. vii. Ibid. p. 117.
[34] Ibid. pp. 117, 118, et seq.
[35] Ead. Sess. xxxiv. Art. iv. Ibid. p. 118.
[36] Art. vii. and viii. Ibid. p. 119.
[37] Sess. xxxiv. Ibid. pp. 121. 322.
[38] Sess. xxxvi. p. 249, et seq. Ib. Art. xii.
    et seq. p. 251.
[39] Ibid. Art. xvii. p. 252.
[40] Sup. n. 23.
[41] Ibid. Art. viii. p. 254.
[42] Art. xii. p. 265.
[43] Ibid.
[44] Ibid. vi. p. 267.
[45] Art. iv. v. p. 271.
[46] Ibid. vi. et seq.
[47] S. n. 27.
[48] Art. vii. viii. p. 272.
[49] Ib. Art. ix. pp. 272, 273.
[50] S. n. 27. Art. ii.
[51] Art. iii. p. 274. Conc. Trid. Sess. vi.
    c. xii. Can. xvi.
[52] S. n. 42.
[53] S. n. 36.
[54] 1 Tim. i. 7.
[55] Rom. xi. 29.
[56] Conc. Trid. Sess. vi.
[57] Can. xv. xvi. xxii.
[58] Syn. Dord. Concl. Sess. 136. p. 275.
[59] Ibid.

[60] S. l. ix. n. 2, 3, et seq. Conf. de Foi
    de Fr. Art. xviii. xix. xx. xxi. xxii.
    Dim. 18, 19, 36. S. l. ix. Conf.
    Bilg. Art. xxiv. Synt. Gen. part i. p.
    139.
[61] Sess. iii. civ. pp. 289, 300.
[62] Ibid. p. 291.
[63] Ibid. 300.
[64] Theolog. Mag. Brit. c. de persev. cert.
    quoad nos. Th. iii. p. 218. Ibid. Th.
    iv. p. 219.
[65] Conf. Ang. Art. xvii. Synt. Gen. i. p.
    102. S. l. x. n. 23.
[66] Theol. Mag. Brit. Th. iii. iv.
[67] Ib. Th. ii. p. 212.
[68] Ib. Th. v. p. 213. vi. 214.
[69] Ib. 215.
[70] Ibid. Th. vii. Ibid. Th. vi.
[71] Ibid. pp. 214, 218.
[72] Jud. Theo. Embd. de V. Art. Th. i. n.
    44, 52, pp. 266, 267. Ibid. n. 45.
    Ibid. 270.
[73] Ibid. n. 50, 51.
[74] Ibid. n. 30. p. 265.
[75] Ibid. n. 54, p. 267.
[76] Ibid. n. 60. p. 268.
[77] Jud. Brem. de V. Art. n. 32, 33. pp.
    254, 255.
[78] Sess. cxxv. cxxx. et præf. ad Ecc.
[79] S. l. ix. pp. 11, 12, 19. Ibid. 21. Ex
    pos. de la Foi, ch. iv. Conc. xiii. p.
    80. Sessione xxxvi. Ca. de prædest.
    Art. xvii. Sup. n. 36.
[80] Sess. xxv. p. 65. et seq.
[81] S. l. viii. n. 41. Ibid. 70, 81.
[82] Syn. Dord. Ibid. pp. 70, 71, 72, &c.
    81, &c.
[83] Syn. Dord. p. 80. Sess. xxvi. pp. 82,
    83.
[84] Sess. xxvi. p. 81.
[85] Sess. xxvii. p. 93. Ibid. n. 83, 87, 97,
    98, 100, 104, 106.
[86] Sess. xxvv. pp. 97, 103, &c.
[87] Præf. ad Ecc. Ant. Syn. Dord.
[88] P. 99.
[89] Sess. xxv. 80. xxvi. 81, 82, 83, &c.
[90] Sess. xxvi. 103.
[91] S. l. iii. n. 62.
[92] Conf. Argent. Peror. Synt. Gen. part
    i. p. 199.

[93] Oct. 24, 1618. Syn. Delph. Int. Act. Dord. Sess. xxvi. p. 86. Matt. xviii. 20.

[94] Præf. ad Ecc. Ant. Syn. Dord.

[95] Syn. Delph. Int. Act.

[96] Dord. Sess. xxv. p. 91. Sess. xxxii. 123.

[97] Sess. cxxv. cxxx. Præf. ad Ecc. Sin. de Cha. xxiii.

[98] Sent. Syn. de Remon. Sess. cxxxviii. p. 280.

[99] Syst. de l'Egl. liv. ii. ch. iii. p. 255. Ibid. ch. x. p. 305.

[100] Syst. de l'Egl. liv. ii. ch. iii. 249.

[101] Jug. sur les meth. Sect. xviii. pp. 159, 160.

[102] Jug. sur les meth. Sect. xviii. p. 59.

[103] Ib. Sect. xvi. p. 137.

[104] Diallact. c. viii. p. 126, &c. Ib. 130. Ib. 127.

[105] Ib. 126, et seq. Ib. 127.

[106] The. de Art. Just. part ii. Th. 42, 4. Item. Th. An Homo solis nat. virib, &c. Corol. 2, 3, 4, 5, 6, &c.

[107] S. n. pp. 83, 84, 87.

[108] Meth. Sect. xv. p. 131. Ibid. Sec. xiv. pp. 113, 114.

[109] S. n. 83, 84, 87. Meth. Sect. xv. pp. 113, 121.

[110] S. n. 6.

[111] Meth. Sect. pp. 129, 132.

[112] Specim. Controv. Belg. ex Offic. Elzev. pp. 2, 4, 7, &c.

[113] Daillè Apol. ch. vii. p. 43. Id. Lettre à Mongl.

[114] S. l. ii. n. 45.

[115] John vi. 53.

[116] Matt. xxvi. 26, 27, 28.

[117] Cont. Westp. Cont. Heshu. Dial. Du Minist. Boch. sur le syn. de Cha. i. p. 24. Ejusd. Dial. part ii. cap. vii. Sedani, p. 21.

[118] Dial. du Min. Boch. sur le Syn. de Cha. i. p. 24.

[119] Boch. Ibid. Dial. xv. part ii. c. vii. Jugement sur les Meth. Sect. xiv. p. 113.

[120] Ibid. sect. xviii. p. 158.

[121] Coll. Cass. q. de fract. pan.

[122] Traité de Communion sous les deux Especes. part ii. ch. xii. La Roq. Rep. part ii. ch. xvii. p. 307.

[123] Thes. de q. An. hom. in. stat. pecc. solis. nat. viribus, &c. Th. xxxi. et seq.

[124] S. n. 109. S. l. vii. n. 48, et seq.

[125] S. l. vii. n. 22, et seq. Epit. Tit. de præd. Conc. p. 617. Solida repetit. Cod. Tit. p .804.

[126] Dall. Apol. Tract. part ii. Blond. Act. auth. viii. et seq. p. 77. Jud. The. Mag. Brit. de Art. ii. inter. Act. Syn. Dord. part ii. p. 287. Jud. B rem. Ibid. p. 113, et seq.

[127] Fascic. Ep. 1676, pp. 83, 94.

[128] Ibid. p. 95.

[129] P. 101.

[130] Ibid. p. 15.

[131] Prov. xxii. 28.

[132] Fascic. Ep. p. 89.

[133] Pp. 90, 91, 98, 103.

[134] Ibid. pp. 93, 100.

[135] Fascic. Ep. pp. 94, 95.

[136] Pp. 97, 100.

[137] Prov. xxii. 28.

[138] Orat. in. Cyp. Basil. Orat. in Mam.

[139] Greg. Nyss. Orat.in Theo. Amb. Serm. de S. Vit. Greg. Naz. Orat. in Jul. i. in Machab. &c

[140] Greg. Naz. Orat. funeb. Ath. et Basil, &c. &c.

Book XV

[Variations in the Article of the Creed: I believe the Holy Catholic Church—. The unshaken steadiness of the Church of Rome]

A brief Summary.—An account of the Variations relating to the subject of the Church.—She is naturally owned to be Visible.—The difficulty of showing where the Church was, forced men upon the device of an invisible one.—The perpetual Visibility of it necessarily confessed.—Divers means of saving the Reformation under this supposition.—The state of the question, as, by the Disputes of the Ministers Claude and Jurieu, it stands at present.—They are at length forced to own that Salvation may be still had in the Church of Rome, as well as before the pretended Reformation.—Strange Variations, and the Confessions of Faith despised.—Advantages yielded to Catholics on the necessary foundation of Jesus Christ's promises in favor of perpetual Visibility.—The Church owned to be infallible.—Her sentiments acknowledged to be an infallible rule of Faith.—Vain exceptions.—All the proofs against the infallible authority of the Church brought to nothing by the Ministers.—Evidence and simplicity of the Catholic doctrine with regard to the Church.—The Reformation forsakes her first groundwork, by owning that Faith is not formed on the Scriptures.—Consent of the Ministers Claude and Jurieu on this tenet.—Unheard of absurdities of the new system concerning the Church, but necessary to defend themselves against the objections of the Catholics.—The uniformity and constancy of the Catholic Church opposed to the Variations of the Protestant Churches.—Abridgment of this fifteenth Book.—Conclusion of the whole Work.

1.—*The cause of Variations, in Protestant Churches, is their want of a true notion of what the Church is.*

AS, after observing the pernicious effects of a distemper on man's body, the cause of it is diligently inquired into, in order to apply specific remedies: in like manner, after seeing that perpetual instability of Protestant Churches, (the disastrous distemper of Christendom,) the prime source thereof ought to be traced out, to the end that a suitable relief, if possible, may be afforded. The cause of these variations, which we have observed in separate societies, is their not having known the authority of the Church, the promises she has received from heaven, nor, in short, so much as what the Church is. For that was the fixed point, in which all the steps they were to take ought to centre; and by deviating from this, heretics, either curious or ignorant, have been bewildered in the mazes of human reasoning, abandoned to their resentments, to their particular passions; the very reason they did but walk groping even in their confessions of faith, and could not shun falling under the two inconveniences specified by St. Paul concerning false teachers; one of which is "to be condemned by their own judgment;"[1] and the other, "to be ever learning, and never able to come to the knowledge of the truth."[2]

2.—*The Catholic Church ever knew herself, and never varied in her Decisions.*

This original cause of the instability of the pretended Reformation has appeared through the whole series of this work; but it is time to observe it with particular attention, by showing, in the confused sentiments of our separated brethren, relating to the article of the Church, the variations which have caused all the rest: after that we shall finish this discourse, by showing a quite contrary procedure in the Catholic Church, which, from well knowing what she was through the grace of Christ Jesus, has always so well delivered herself at the very first in all questions that arose, in order to ascertain the faith of Christians, that there never happened a necessity, I do not say of varying, but of deliberating anew, or of departing in the least tittle from the first plan.

3.—*Doctrine of the Catholic Church concerning the Article of the Church.—*
Four points essential and inseparable one from the other.

The doctrine of the Catholic Church consists in four points, whose connexion is inviolable:[3] the first, that the Church is visible; the second, that she is perpetual; the third, that the truth of the Gospel is always professed therein by the whole society; the fourth, that it is unlawful to depart from her doctrine: which is as much as to say, in other terms, that she is infallible.

The first point is grounded on a certain fact: which is, that the word Church always signifies in Scripture, and therefore, in the common language of the faithful, a visible society: Catholics take this for granted, and it was necessary for Protestants to assent to it, as will appear hereafter.

The second point, that the Church is perpetual, is not less certain, it being grounded on Jesus Christ's promises agreed on by all parties.

Hence the third point is inferred most clearly, that the truth is professed always by the society of the Church; for the Church being no otherwise visible than by the profession of the truth, it follows, that if she be always, and always be visible, she cannot but always teach and profess the truth of the Gospel: from whence the fourth point is as clearly deduced, that it is not allowable to say the Church is in error, nor to forsake her doctrine; and all this is founded on the promise allowed by all parties, since, in fine, the same promise, which makes the Church be always, makes her always be in that state which the word Church implies; is consequently always visible, and always teaching the truth. Nothing is more simple, more clear, nor more coherent than this doctrine.

4.—*Sentiments of the Protestants touching the perpetual visibility of the Church.—The Confession of Augsburg.*

So clear is this doctrine, that Protestants could not deny it; so clearly does it condemn them, that they durst not own it: wherefore, their whole thoughts were bent on perplexing it, nor were they able to avoid falling into the contradictions I am about to relate.

Let us, in the first place look into their confessions of faith; and to begin with that of Augsburg,[4] which is the first, and as it were the foundation of all the rest,—the article concerning the Church was thus delivered by it: "We teach that there is a holy Church which must eternally subsist." What now is that Church whose duration is eternal? The following words explain it: "The Church is the assembly of saints, wherein the Gospel is rightly taught, and the sacraments rightly administered."

Here may be seen three fundamental rules. First, "that the Church subsists always:" there is then an inviolate succession. Second, that she is essentially compounded of pastors and people, the administration of the sacraments and preaching of the word entering into her very definition. Third, that the word and sacraments are not only therein administered, but rightly administered, *recte*, "as they ought to be:" which also enters into the essence of a Church, since it is placed, as we see, in her definition.

5.—*This doctrine owned by Protestants is the subversion of their Reformation, and the source of their perplexities.*

Now, this being admitted, the question is, how they can possibly accuse the Church of error, either in doctrine or in administration of the sacraments; for, could that happen, the definition of the Church wherein is placed not only preaching, but true preaching of the Gospel, and not only administration, but the right administration of the sacraments, would be false; and if that cannot happen, the Reformation, which accused the Church of error, carried in her very title her own condemnation.

Observe well the difficulty; for this was the first source, in the Protestant Churches, of those contradictions we shall discover in them; but contradictions, which the remedies they thought to find for the defect of their original, made them but plunge the deeper into. In the meanwhile, till the series of facts lead us to these fruitless remedies, let us endeavor thoroughly to make known the evil.

6.—*What it was precisely that the Protestants did oblige themselves to by this Doctrine.*

On this foundation of the seventh article of the Confession of Augsburg, the Lutherans were asked, what it was they came to reform? "The Church of Rome," said they. But have you any other Church wherein the doctrine you would establish is professed? It was a fact incontestable that they could show none. Where was then that Church, in which, by your seventh article, the true preaching of God's word, and the right administration of the sacraments, were always to subsist? To name some doctors here and there, and from time to time, who, as you pretend, have taught your doctrine, allowing the fact proved, yet would be nothing to the purpose: for it was a body of a Church you were to show, a body wherein truth was preached, and wherein the sacraments were administered; by consequence, a body compounded of pastors and of people; a body, in this respect, always visible. This is what must be shown, and, consequently, there must be shown in this body a manifest succession both of doctrine and of ministry.

7.—*Perpetual Visibility of the Church Confirmed by the Apology of the Augsburg Confession.*

At the recital of the seventh article of the Confession of Augsburg, the Catholics found fault with their defining the Church "the assembly of saints;" and said, that sinners and hypocrites, who are united to the Church by the external bands, ought not to be excluded from their unity. Melancthon accounted for this doctrine in the Apology,[5] and it is not impossible that might be a dispute as much about words as things; but without stopping at this, let us observe, they persisted to say[6] that the Church was *always to last*, and to last always *visible*, preaching and the sacraments being essential to her; for let us hear how they speak: "The Catholic Church is not an exterior society of certain nations, but it is men dispersed all over the universe, who have the same sentiments with regard to the Gospel, who have the same Christ, the same Holy Ghost, and the same Sacraments."[7] And still more expressly a little after, "We never have dreamed that the Church was a Platonic city not to be found on earth; we say that the Church exists, that in it there are true believers, and men truly just spread over all the universe; we add to this, its marks, the pure Gospel, and the Sacraments, and it is such a Church that is properly the pillar of truth."[8] Here, then, at least, unquestionably is a Church very really existing; very really visible, wherein sound doctrine is very really preached, and the Sacraments very really administered as they ought to be; for, as they subjoin, the kingdom of Jesus Christ cannot subsist but with *the word and sacraments*, so that where they are not, *there can be no Church.*[9]

8.—*How they endeavored to make this Doctrine consist with the necessity of a Reformation.*

Notwithstanding, many human traditions, said they, had crept into the Church, whereby sound doctrine and the right administration of the sacraments was changed; and this was what they would reform. But if these human traditions were turned in the Church into articles of faith, where could be that purity of the word and doctrine, without which she could not subsist? Here the thing was to be palliated, and accordingly they said,[10] as has been seen, that their design was not to combat against "the Catholic Church, nor even the Church of Rome, nor to maintain opinions which the Church had condemned;" that the matter in debate was no more than some few abuses brought into the Church without any certain authority; nor was that to be taken for the doctrine of the Church of Rome, which was approved of only by the Pope, some cardinals, some bishops, and some monks.

To hear the Lutherans speak thus, one might think they did not impugn the received dogmas, but some particular opinions only, and some few abuses lately crept in without authority. This but little suited with those outrageous invectives of sacrilege and idolatry, with which they filled the whole universe, much less with an open rupture. But the fact is certain, and by these smooth words they endeavored to salve the inconsistency of owning corruption in the tenets of the Church, after having made a pure preaching of the truth essential to her.

9.—The perpetual Visibility confirmed in the Articles of Smalcald by the promises of Jesus Christ.

This immutability and perpetual duration of sound doctrine was confirmed in the articles of Smalcald,[11] subscribed by the whole Lutheran party, explaining those words of our Saviour: "On this rock will I build my Church," namely, said they, "on this ministry of the profession made by Peter." Thereunto preaching, and true preaching, was therefore necessary, without which they owned the Church could not subsist.

10.—The Saxonic Confession, in which they begin to spy out the difficulty without departing from the precedent doctrine.

Now we are upon the subject of the doctrine of the Lutheran Churches, the Saxonic Confession, known to be Melancthon's, opportunely presents itself. In it is acknowledged that "there is always some true Church; that the promises of God, who hath promised her duration, are immutable; that they speak not of the Church as of a Platonic idea, but point out a Church which is seen and heard; and that she is visible in this life, and is the assembly which embraces the Gospel of Christ Jesus, and which has the true use of the Sacraments, in which God operates efficaciously by the ministry of the Gospel, and wherein many are regenerated."[12]

They add, "she may be reduced to a small number; yet, however, there is always a remnant of the faithful, whose voice makes itself be heard on earth, and of which God, from time to time, renews the ministry." They must mean that he continues it; for the definition of the Church which, as just said, cannot subsist without the ministry, does not allow its interruption even for a moment; and immediately after it is subjoined, "that God will have the ministry of the Gospel be public; he will not have preaching shut up in darkness, but heard by all mankind; and that there are assemblies where it may resound, and where his name may be praised and invoked."[13]

Here then you see the Church always visible. True it is, they begin to see the difficulty when saying, "she may be reduced to a small number;" but after all, the Lutherans have not less difficulty in showing, at Luther's first appearance, a small society of their sentiments than a great one, and yet without that there is neither ministry nor Church.

11.—*Doctrine of the Confession of Wirtemburg, and the perpetual Visibility*
always maintained.

The Confession of Wirtemburg, which was penned by Brentius, does not degenerate from this doctrine, it being there acknowledged "that there is a Church so well governed by the Holy Ghost, that, although weak, she lasts for ever; that she judges of doctrine; and is where the Gospel is sincerely preached, and where the sacraments are administered, according to Christ's institution."[14] The difficulty still remained of showing us a Church and a society of pastors and people wherein sound doctrine had always been preserved to Luther's days.

The next chapter relates how councils may err; by reason that, although Jesus Christ has promised his Church the perpetual presence of his Holy Spirit, nevertheless, "every assembly is not the Church;" and it may happen in the Church, as in bodies politic, that the greater number of bad men may prevail over the good. This is what I shall not dispute at present; but I still insists on their showing me a Church, little or great, which, before Luther's coming, was of his sentiments.

12.—*The Confession of Bohemia.*

The Confession of Bohemia is approved by Luther. Therein is confessed "a Holy and Catholic Church, which comprehends all Christians dispersed throughout the earth, which are assembled by preaching the gospel in the faith of the Trinity and of Jesus Christ: wheresoever Jesus Christ is preached and received, and wheresoever are the words and sacraments according to the rule by him prescribed, there is the Church."[15] These men at least were fully satisfied that when they were born there was no Church in the whole universe of their belief;[16] for the deputies despatched by them every where on that errand, had well assured them of it. And yet they durst not say their assembly, such as it was, little or great, was the holy, universal Church; but only that "she was a member and a part thereof."[17] But what then was become of all the other parts? They had surveyed all corners of the world, and no tidings of them: sad extremes indeed! not to dare to say they were the Universal Church, and dare still less to say that they had met with brethren and partners of their faith in any part whatsoever of the whole universe.

Be that as it will, these are the first that seem to insinuate in a Confession of Faith, that true Christian Churches might be separated from one another, since they dare not exclude from Catholic unity, those Churches with whom they knew they had no communion; which I beg may be remarked, by reason that this doctrine will at length be the last resource of Protestants, as shall appear hereafter.

13.—*The Confession of Strasburg.*

We have seen the Confession of the Lutherans regarding the Church; we shall now hear the other party. The Confession of Strasburg, presented as before observed, to Charles V, at the same time with that of Augsburg, defines the Church,[18]"the society of those who have enlisted themselves soldiers of Jesus

Christ, amongst whom are mixed many hypocrites." There is no doubt that such a society is visible—that she must always abide in this state of visibility,—it being added, "that Jesus Christ does never abandon her; that those who do not hear her, ought to be held for heathens and publicans; that, indeed, there is no seeing what constitutes her a Church, namely, her faith; yet she makes herself be seen by her fruits, amongst which confession of the truth is one."

The following chapter sets forth[19] how that "the Church being on earth in the flesh, God also will instruct her by the exterior word, and make her faithful members preserve an exterior society by means of the sacraments." There are then necessarily both pastors and people, nor can the Church subsist without this ministry.

14.—*Two Confessions of Basil.*

The Confession of Basil in 1536 says,[20] "that the Catholic Church is the holy congregation of all the saints; and although unknown to any but God, nevertheless is she seen, is she known, is she constituted by external rites of God's appointment: to wit, by the sacraments, and by the public and lawful preaching of his word;" wherein is seen manifestly, that ministers lawfully called are comprehended, by whom it is also added, "God makes himself known to his faithful, and administers to them the remission of their sins."

In another Confession of Faith, made at Basil in 1532 "The Christian Church is likewise defined the society of the Saints, whereof all those who confess Jesus Christ are the citizens;" thus the profession of Christianity is essential to her.

15.—*The Helvetic Confession of 1566, and the perpetual Visibility thoroughly established.*

Whilst we are upon the Helvetic Confessions, that of 1566, which is the great and solemn one, defines also the Church, "which has been always, which is, and which shall ever be, the assembly of the faithful, and of the saints who know God, and serve him by the Word and the Holy Ghost."[21] Here, then, is not only the interior band, namely, the Holy Ghost, but the exterior also, which is the word and preaching; and therefore they say afterwards, "that lawful and true preaching is her chief mark, to which must be added the sacraments as God has constituted them."[22] Whence they conclude "that the Churches, which are deprived of these marks, although they boast the succession of their bishops, their unity, and their antiquity, do not belong to the true Church of Jesus Christ; nor can salvation any more be had out of the Church than out of the ark; if you will have life, you must not separate yourself from the true Church of Jesus Christ."

I desire these words may be observed, which will be of great consequence when we shall come to the last answers of the ministers; in the mean time, let us but remark, that it is impossible to teach more clearly that the Church is always visible, and that she is necessarily compounded of pastors and people, than is here done by this Helvetic Confession.

16.—They begin to vary.—The invisible Church begins to appear.

But as they were obliged, according to these ideas, always to find a ministry and a Church wherein the truth of Christianity was preserved: the difficulty was no small one, because, say what they would, they were very sensible that there was no Church, little or great, composed of pastors and people, wherein they could show that faith, which they would make pass for the only true Christian faith. They are then forced to subjoin, "that God has had his friends out of the people of Israel; that during the captivity of Babylon, the people were deprived sixty years of the sacrifice; that, through a just judgment of God, the truth of his word and worship, and the Catholic faith, are sometimes so obscured, that it seems almost as if they were extinct, and no Church at all subsisting, as happened in the time of Eli and at other times; so that the Church may be called invisible; not that the men she is composed of are so, but because she is often hidden to our eyes, and being known to God alone, escapes from the sight of men." Here is the dogma of an invisible Church, as clearly established as the dogma of the visible Church had been before; that is to say, the Reformation, struck at first with the true notion of the Church, defined it so as that her visibility came into her very essence; but afterwards fell into other notions through the impossibility of finding a Church always visible of her belief.

17.—Church invisible.—Why invented.—Confession of Minister Jurieu.

That it was this inevitable perplexity which drove the Calvinian Churches upon this chimera of a Church invisible none can doubt, after hearing M. Jurieu. "That which moved," says he "some reformed doctors (he should have said whole Churches of the reformation) in their own Confessions of Faith, to cast themselves into the *perplexity* they were entangled in upon their denying the perpetual visibility of the Church, was because they believed, by owning the Church always visible, they should find it difficult to answer the question which the Church of Rome so often asks us:—Where was our Church a hundred and fifty years ago? If the Church be always visible, your Calvinist and Lutheran Church is not the true Church, for that was not visible."[23] This is fairly owning the cause of that perplexity which disturbed his Churches; he that pretends to have refined beyond them, will not extricate himself better, as we shall see; but let us continue to observe the confusion of the Churches themselves.

18.—Belgic Confession, and sequel of the perplexity.

The Belgic Confession manifestly copies also the Helvetic, since it says, "that the Catholic or Universal Church is the assembly of all the faithful; that she has been, is, and always will be eternally, by reason that Jesus Christ, her eternal King, cannot be without subjects; although for some time she seem little, *and as it were extinct* to the eyes of men; as in the time of Achab and of those seven thousand who had not bent their knees to Baal."[24]

Nevertheless, they afterwards subjoin,[25] "that the Church is the assembly of the elect, out of which none can be saved; that it is not lawful to withdraw from her, or abide apart; but all must unite themselves to the Church, and submit to her discipline;[26] that one may see and know her, by pure preaching, right administration of the sacraments, and a good discipline; and it is thereby, say they, that we may rightly distinguish this true Church, from which it is not allowable to depart."

It seems then, on one side, as if they would say, one may easily and always know her, since she has such manifest tokens, and that it is never lawful to depart from her. And on the other side, if we press them to show us a Church of their belief, though ever so minute, always visible, they provide a subterfuge for themselves by flying to this Church which does not appear, although they dare not speak out boldly, nor say absolutely that she is extinct, but only that she seems as it were extinct.

19.—Church of England.

The Church of England speaks ambiguously. "The visible Church," says she, "is a congregation of faithful men, in which the pure word of God is preached, and the sacraments are duly ministered, according to Christ's ordinance;"[27] that is, such is she when visible, but this is not saying that she is always visible. What follows is not more clear: "As the Churches of Jerusalem, Alexandria, and Antioch, have erred, so also the Church of Rome hath erred in matters of faith:" the question is, (they thus attainting these great, and as it were, mother churches of all the rest,) whether the infection might have spread so universally, as that the profession of truth was extinguished over all the earth: but they chose rather to speak nothing of it, than to incur this terrible dilemma, which would oblige them, on one side, either to own there was no Church left on earth in which truth was confessed: or, allowing the impossibility of this, would oblige them, on the other side, to seek what they knew could not be found, to wit, a Church always subsisting and believing as they did.

20.—Confession of Scotland, and manifest contradiction.

In the Confession of Scotland, the Catholic Church is defined the Society of all the Elect: they say,[28] "She is invisible, and known to God only, who alone knows his elect;" and add, "that the true Church hath for its mark, preaching and the sacraments:" and wherever these marks be, though there should be but two or three men, there is the Church of Jesus Christ, in the mist of which he is, according to his promise: "Which is understood," say they, "not of the universal Church just spoken of, but of the particular Church of Ephesus, of Corinth, and so forth, wherein the ministry had been planted by St. Paul." Prodigious! to make Jesus Christ say the ministry may be where two or three men can be found. But they were forced into these straits; for to find one only Church of their belief, wherein was a regulated ministry, as at Ephesus or Corinth, always subsisting, was what they despaired of.

21.—Catechism of the pretended Reformed of France.

I have reserved the Confession of the pretended Reformed of France for the last, not only on account of the particular concern I ought to have for my own country, but also because in France especially the Protestants have for this long time sought most diligently for the solution of this difficulty.

Let us begin by the Catechism, wherein on the fifteenth Sunday, upon this Article of the Creed, "I believe the Holy Catholic Church," they teach that this name is given her, "to signify that as there is but one head of the faithful, so all are to be united in one body; so that there are not many Churches, but one only, which is diffused all the world over."[29] How the Lutheran or Calvinian Church was diffused all over the world, when scarcely known in some corner of it; and, how Churches of this belief are to be found, in all times and in all the world, is what constitutes the difficulty. They saw, and they obviate it in the following Sunday, where, after having asked, whether this Church may be otherwise known than by believing her, they answer thus: "There is indeed a visible Church of God conformable to the signs he hath given us to know her by; but in this place, (the Creed,) properly speaking, is meant the society of those whom God hath elected for salvation, which cannot be discovered fully by the eye."[30]

22.—Sequel in which the difficulty appears.—The Church in the Creed at length acknowledged visible.

They seem to say two things: the first, that no mention is made of the Church in the symbol of the Apostles; the second, that for want of such a Church which they might show visibly of their belief, it is sufficient to have recourse to that invisible Church which cannot be seen fully by the eye. But what follows put an obstacle to the two points of this doctrine, it being there taught, "that no man obtains pardon of his sins, unless he be first incorporated with God's people, and persevere in unity and communion with the body of Christ, and so be a member of the Church:" whence they conclude, that "out of the Church there is nothing but death and damnation; and that all those who separate themselves from the company of the faithful to make a sect apart, ought not, whilst divided, to hope for salvation." To make a sect apart, is, unquestionably, to break the exterior bonds of the unity of the Church. They suppose, therefore, that the Church, wherewith it is necessary to be in communion in order to obtain pardon of our sins, has a twofold union, the internal and external; and that both of them are necessary, first to salvation, and secondly, to the understanding the Article of the Creed touching the Catholic Church; so that this Church, confessed in the Creed, is visible and distinguishable in her exterior; for which reason also they durst not venture to say that we could not see her, but, could not see her fully, to wit, as to that which is internal; a thing no man disputes.

23.—Calvin's Sentiment.

All these notions in the Catechism came from Calvin who composed it: for, explaining the Article, "I believe the Catholic Church,"[31] he distinguishes the Church visible from the invisible known to God alone, which is the society of all the elect, and it seems as if he would say it is this the Creed speaks of: although, says he, "this Article regards, in some measure, the external Church,"[32] as if there were two Churches, and it were not, on the contrary, most evident, that the same Church, which is invisible in her internal gifts, doth manifest herself by the sacraments and profession of her faith. But so it is, that the Reformation is always in a panic when the visibility of the Church is to be acknowledged.

24.—Confession of Faith of the French Calvinists.

They act more naturally in their Confession of Faith, and elsewhere it hath been proved unanswerably, that they there own no other Church but that which is visible.[33] The fact stands incontestable, as will be seen hereafter. Nor was there, indeed, any thing that could less bear a dispute; for, from the twenty-fifth Article, where this matter begins, to the thirty-second Article, where it ends, they all along evidently suppose the Church visible; and in the twenty-fifth Article, they lay it down as a fundamental point, that "the Church cannot subsist, unless there be pastors in her that have the charge of teaching." It is, therefore, a thing absolutely necessary; and those who oppose this doctrine are detested, as fantastical. Whence they concluded, in the twenty-sixth Article, "that no man ought to withdraw apart, nor rest on self-sufficiency;" so that it is necessary to be united externally with some Church: a truth inculcated in every place, without the appearance of so much as one word of a Church invisible.

It ought however, to be observed, that in the twenty-sixth Article, where it is said, "No man ought to withdraw apart nor rest on self-sufficiency, but should join himself to some Church," they add, "and this in whatever place God shall have established a true form of a Church;" whereby it is left undecided whether or no they mean that such a form always does subsist.

25.—Sequel wherein the perpetual Visibility is always manifestly supposed.

In the twenty-seventh Article caution is given to distinguish carefully which is the true Church; words that plainly show they suppose her visible: and after having decided that she is "the congregation of truly faithful men," they add, "amongst the faithful there be hypocrites and reprobate, whose wickedness cannot deface the title of a Church," wherein the Church's visibility is again clearly supposed.

26.—The Church of Rome excluded from the title of a true Church by the twenty-eighth Article of the French Confession.

By the principles laid down in the twenty-eighth Article, the Church of Rome stands excluded from the title of a true Church, forasmuch as, after laying this foundation, "that where the word of God is not preached, and no profession is made of bringing one's self under subjection to it, and where there is no use of sacraments, properly speaking, we cannot judge that there is any Church:" they declare they "condemn the assemblies of the Papacy, considering that the pure truth of God is banished thence, and the sacraments are there corrupted, adulterated, falsified, or wholly annihilated; and all superstitions and idolatries are in vogue amongst them:" whence they draw this consequence,—"We hold that all those who join in such deeds, and communicate in them, do separate and cut themselves off from the body of Christ Jesus."

It is impossible to decide more clearly that there is no salvation in the Church of Rome. And what is subjoined by them, that there are still some "footsteps of a Church amongst us," so far from mitigating the preceding expressions, even strengthens them; inasmuch as this term implies rather some remains and traces of a Church that had formerly passed that way, than a token of her being there. Thus it was understood by Calvin, when he asserted "that the essential doctrine of Christianity was entirely forgotten by us."[34] But the difficulty of discovering a society in which God could be served, before the Reformation, has made them elude this article, as we shall see hereafter.

27.—*The thirty-first Article, in which the interruption of the Ministry, and the the cessation of the visible Church, is acknowledged.*

The same reason obliged them also to elude the thirty-first, which regards the vocation of Ministers. However trite may have been this subject, it must nevertheless, of necessity, be resumed, and so much the more, as it has given occasion to notorious variations even in our days. It begins by these words:—"We believe, (it is an article of faith, consequently revealed by God, and revealed clearly in his Scripture according to the principles of the Reformation,) we believe, then, that no man may intrude himself, of his own proper authority, into the government of the Church;" allowed, the thing is certain: "but that this ought to be done by election;" this part of the Article is not less certain than the other. You must be chosen, deputed, authorized, by somebody; otherwise you are an intruder, "and by your own particular authority;" the thing just now prohibited. But here is what annoys the Reformation; they knew not who had chosen, deputed, authorized the Reformers, and it was necessary to find out here some cloak for so visible a defect. Wherefore, after having said you ought to be elected and deputed after some form or other, without specifying any, they add, "so far forth as is possible, and God permits it:" whereby an exception is manifestly prepared in behalf of the Reformers. And, accordingly, they immediately subjoin, "which exception we add expressly, because it hath been necessary sometimes, nay, in our days, when the state of the Church was interrupted, that God should raise men in an extraordinary manner to set up the Church anew which was fallen into ruin and desolation." They could not denote in more clear and more general terms the interruption of the ordinary ministry established by God, nor carry it further than to be obliged to have recourse to an extraordinary mission which God himself despatches, and accordingly furnishes with the particular proofs of his immediate will. For they acknowledge frankly in the present case, that they can neither produce pastors that did consecrate, nor people that could elect; which implied necessarily the entire extinction of the Church in her visibility; and remarkable it was that, from the interruption of the visibility and ministry, they came to own in plain terms that the Church was fallen into ruin, without distinguishing between the visible and the invisible, because they had got into a train of simple notions by which the Scripture naturally leads us to own no Church but such as is visible.

28.—*Perplexity in the Synods of Gap and Rochelle, on account of the invisible Church having been forgotten in the Confession.*

This difficulty was at length perceived by the Reformation; and in 1603, five and forty years after the Confession of Faith had been published, was proposed to the national Synod of Gap in these terms: "The provinces are exhorted to examine thoroughly, in the provincial synods, in what terms the twenty-fifth Article of the Confession of Faith ought to be couched, so much the more as our belief, regarding the Church, whereof mention is made in the creed, being to be expressed, there is nothing in the said confession that can be understood of any other than the Church militant and visible."[35] A general command is subjoined, "that all come prepared on questions concerning the Church."

This is, therefore, a fact well avowed, that when they were to expound the doctrine of the Church, an article so essential to Christianity as to have been expressed in the creed, the idea of a Church invisible did not so much as enter into the minds of the Reformers, so distant was it from good sense, and so unnatural. However, they bethink themselves afterwards that it is necessary for their turn, it being impossible for them to find out a Church which had always visibly persisted in the faith they profess, and a remedy is therefore sought for this omission. What shall they say? That the Church might be wholly invisible? This were introducing into a Confession of Faith so crude a fancy, so repugnant to good sense, that it never entered into the heads of those that drew it up. It was therefore resolved, at last, to leave it as they found it; and four years after, in 1607, at the national Synod of Rochelle,[36] when all the provinces had thoroughly examined what was wanting to the Confession of Faith, "they concluded not to add to or diminish anything from the twenty-fifth and twenty-ninth Articles," the very same in which the visibility of the Church was expressed the most fully, "nor to meddle anew with the subject of the Church."

29.—*Vain subtlety of the Minister Claude towards eluding these Synods.*

M. Claude, of all men, was the most subtle to elude the decisions of his Church when they incommoded him;[37] but, on this occasion, he jests but too openly, for he would make us believe that all the difficulty the Synod of Gap met with in the Confession of Faith, was, that she could have wished that, instead of specifying only "the militant and visible part of the universal Church, her invisible parts, which are the Church triumphant and that which is still to come, had also been specified." Was not that, indeed, a very important, a very difficult question, to order the discussion of in all the synods and over all the provinces, towards bringing it to a decision in the next national synod? Did they so much as dream of ever raising so frivolous a question? And to believe they troubled their heads about it, must not he have forgotten the whole state of controversies ever since the beginning of the pretended Reformation? But M. Claude was not for acknowledging that the synod's perplexity proceeded from her not finding, in their Confession of Faith, the invisible Church, whilst his brother, M. Jurieu, more sincere in that particular, agrees that they thought it was necessary in the party, in order to answer the query, Where was the Church?

30.—*Remarkable decision, which they stick not to, of the Synod of Gap concerning extraordinary Vocation.*

The same Synod of Gap passed an important decision on the thirty-first article of the Confession of Faith, which spoke of the extraordinary vocation of pastors: for the question being proposed, "Whether or not it were expedient, when they should treat on the vocation of pastors who reformed the Church, to ground the authority they had to reform and teach, on the vocation they had received from the Church of Rome;" the Synod judged "they ought to refer it, according to the article, to the extraordinary vocation only whereby God interiorly stirred them up to this ministry, and not to the small remains amongst them of that corrupted ordinary vocation." Such was the decision of the Synod of Gap: but, as before frequently observed, the Reformation never hits right at first. Whereas, she enjoins here to have recourse *to an extraordinary vocation only*, the Synod of Rochelle says they must *principally* have recourse to it. But they will no more abide by the exposition of the Synod of Rochelle, than by the determination of the Synod of Gap and the whole sense of the article, so carefully explained by two Synods, shall be changed by two ministers.

31.—*The Ministers elude the decree concerning extraordinary Vocation.*

The ministers Claude and Jurieu are no longer for an extraordinary vocation by which ministers are sent immediately from God; neither does a confession of faith, nor Synods, terrify them: for as the Reformed in the main neither care for confessions of faith nor synods, and answer objections from them only for form-sake, even the slightest evasions will serve their turn. For such, M. Claude was never at a loss; "the right to teach," says he, "and to perform the pastoral functions, is one thing: the right to labor towards a reformation, is another."[38] As for the last, the vocation was extraordinary, on account of the extraordinary talents the Reformers were endowed with: but as for the vocation to the pastoral ministry, there was nothing extraordinary in it; since these first pastors were appointed by the people, in whom the source of authority and vocation naturally resides.[39]

32.—Extraordinary Vocation, established in the Confession and two national Synods, is abandoned.

They could not shift off the thirty-first Article in a more gross manner. For, it is manifest the question there regarded in no manner of way either the extraordinary labor towards a reformation, or the rare talents wherewith the Reformers were endowed; but merely the vocation for governing the Church, into which it was not lawful "for any one to intrude himself of his own proper authority." Now it was in this regard that they had recourse to an extraordinary vocation; consequently, it was in regard of the pastoral functions.

The Synod explains itself no less clearly; for without the least thought of distinguishing between the power of reforming and that of teaching, which in reality are so linked together, that the same power which authorizes to teach, authorizes likewise to reform abuses,—the question was, whether the power, as well of reforming as of teaching, ought to be founded on vocation derived from the Church of Rome, or on an extraordinary commission issuing immediately from God; and the Synod concludes for the latter.

But no longer were there any means left of maintaining it, they not having any one mark thereof: nay, two Synods could find no other warrant to authorize these extraordinary commissioned pastors, except what they said for themselves, that they had an "interior impulse to their ministry." The chiefs of the Anabaptists and Unitarians say the same, nor is there a more sure method of introducing into the pastoral charge all manner of fanatics.

33.—How important is the present state of the controversy about the Church.

Here was a fine field opened to Catholics. Nor have they failed so to press the arguments regarding the Church and ministry, that intestine divisions began to disorder the camp of the enemy; and the minister Claude, after subtilizing to a higher itch than any one had ever done before him, was not able to content the minister Jurieu. What they both have said on this subject, the steps they have taken towards the truth, the absurdities they fell into for not having sufficiently pursued their principle, have placed the question concerning the Church in such a state as not to be dissembled without omitting one of the most material occurrences of this history.

34.—They no longer contest with us the visibility of the Church.

These two ministers suppose the Church visible, and always visible, nor is it in this point they are divided. In order to put it beyond all doubt that M. Claude persisted in this sentiment to the very last, I will produce his last work on this subject. He there declares,[40] that the question between Catholics and Protestants is not whether the Church be visible; that it is not denied in his religion that the true Church of Jesus Christ, the Church which his promises relate to, is so; he very clearly decides that the text of St. Paul, in which the Church is represented as without spot or wrinkle, "regards not only the Church in heaven, but also the visible Church that is on earth: insomuch, that the visible Church is the body of Christ Jesus, or, what comes to the same thing, the body of Christ Jesus, which alone is the true Church, is visible: that this is the sentiment of Calvin and Mestresat, and that the Church of God is not to be sought out of the visible state of the ministry and world."

35.—*The promises of Jesus Christ in behalf of the Visibility are allowed.*

This is most clearly owning that she cannot subsist without her visibility and the perpetuity of her ministry: accordingly this author has acknowledged it in many places, and particularly in expounding these words: the "gates of hell shall not prevail against her;" where he speaks thus: "if in these words he understood a perpetual subsistence of the ministry in a state sufficient for the salvation of God's elect, in spite of all the efforts of hell, and in spite of all the disorders and confusions of the ministers themselves; it is no more than what I own has been promised by Jesus Christ, and therein it is that we have a sensible and palpable token of his promise."[41]

The perpetuity, therefore, of the ministry is not a thing which happens accidentally to the Church, or is only suitable to her for a time: it is a thing which is promised her by Jesus Christ himself; and it is equally certain, that the Church will never be without a visible ministry, as it is certain that Jesus Christ is the eternal truth.

36.—*Another promise equally confessed.*

This Minister proceeds still further,[42] and expounding this promise of Jesus Christ, "Go ye, baptize, teach, and lo, I am with you always even unto the end of the world," he approves this comment thereon: "with you teaching, with you baptizing," and concludes it with these words: "I acknowledge that Jesus Christ promises the Church to be with her, and to teach with her, *without interruption*, to the end of the world:" an acknowledgment from whence I shall, in due time, conclude the infallibility of the Church's doctrine, with whom Jesus Christ is always teaching: but I only employ it here to establish by his scriptures and his promises, with the consent of this Minister, his visible perpetuity of the Church ministry.

37.—*The Visibility enters into the definition which the Minister Claude has given of the Church.*

Accordingly, also, he proceeds thus to define the Church: "the Church is," says he, "the true faithful who make profession of the truth, of Christian piety, of a true sanctity under a ministry which furnishes her with the food necessary for a spiritual life, without subtracting from her any part thereof."[43] Where the profession of the truth and the perpetuity of the visible ministry are seen manifestly to enter the definition of the Church: whence it clearly follows, that as much as he is assured that she will always exists, so much is he assured that she always will be visible, since visibility appertains to her essence, and comes into her very definition.

38.—*In what manner the Society of the faithful is visible, in this Minister's opinion.*

If it be asked this minister, how he understands the Church to be visible, since he will have her be the assembly of the true faithful known to God alone, and that the profession of the truth, which might make her known, is common to her with wicked men and hypocrites, as well as the visible and exterior ministry; he answers,[44] that it is sufficient to render the assembly of the faithful visible, that we may point at the place where she abides, to wit, the body wherein she is nourished, and the visible ministry under which she is necessarily contained: by which means we may even say, "there she is," as viewing the field in which grow good corn and tares, we say, "there is the good corn;" and as, beholding the nets wherein are good and bad fish, "there are the good fish."

39.—*Before the Reformation, the Elect of God saved in the Communion, and under the Ministry of Rome.*

But what was that public and visible ministry under which were contained, before the Reformation, the true faithful whom he will have alone be the true Church? this was the grand question. No ministry was to be found throughout the whole universe that had perpetually continued, except that of the Church of Rome, or of others, whose doctrine was equally disadvantageous to Protestants. Wherefore he was obliged at last to own that "this body in which the true faithful were nourished, and this ministry whereby they received sufficient food without subtraction of any part, was the body of the Church of Rome, and the ministry of her prelates."[45]

40.—*This Minister has not recourse to the Albigenses, &c.*

This Minister is here to be praised for his penetration, exceeding that of many others, and for not having confined the Church to societies separate from Rome, as were the Vaudois and Albigenses, the Wickliffites and the Hussites: for though he considers them as the most "illustrious part of the Church because they were the most pure, the most knowing, and the most gener-ous;"[46] he well saw it was ridiculous there to place the whole defence of his cause; and, in his last work, without minding these obscure sects, whose insufficiency is now made visible, he no where places the true Church and true faithful but in the Latin ministry.

41.—*Inevitable perplexity and contradiction.*

But here lies the dilemma, which it is impossible to evade; for the Catholics return to their old query: if the true Church be always visible; if the marks to know her by, according to all your catechisms and all your confessions of faith, be the pure preaching of the Gospel, and the right administration of the

Sacraments, either the Church of Rome had these two marks, and you came in vain to reform her, or she had them not; and you can no longer say, according to your principles, that she is the body in which is contained the true Church. For, in contradiction to this, Calvin has said, "that the doctrine essential to Christianity was there buried, and she was nothing but a school of idolatry and impiety."[47] His sentiments passed into the Confession of Faith, wherein we have seen, "that the pure truth of God was banished from this Church; that the sacraments were there corrupted, falsified, and adulterated; that all superstition and idolatry were there in vogue." Whence he concluded, "that the Church was fallen into desolation and ruin, the state of the ministry interrupted, and her succession so annihilated, that there was no means of reviving it but by an extraordinary mission."[48] And in reality, if imputed justice was the foundation of Christianity; if the merit of works, and so many other received doctrines, were mortally ruinous to piety: if both kinds were essential to the Eucharist, where was the truth and sacraments? Calvin and the confession were in the right to say, according to these principles, that no Church at all was left amongst us.

42.—*The answers whereby they fall into a greater perplexity.*[49]

On the other side, neither can it be said that the Church has ceased, nor ceased to be visible; the promises of Jesus Christ are too perspicuous, and reconciled they must be, some way or other with the doctrine of the Reformation. Hence commenced the distinctions of additions and subtractions: if by subtraction you take away some fundamental truths, no longer stands the ministry: if you lay evil dogmas on these foundations; nay, though they should destroy this foundation by consequence, the ministry subsists, impure indeed, yet sufficient: and by the discernment which the faithful make of the foundation, which is Jesus Christ, from that which is superadded, they shall find all necessary nourishment in the ministry. Here then ends that purity of doctrine, and of sacraments rightly administered, which had been set as marks of the true Church. Without having so much as preaching which you can approve of, or worship which you can join in, or an entire Eucharist, still you have all necessary food without subtraction of any part thereof, still you have the purity of the word, and the sacraments well administered; what is it to contradict one's self, if this be not?

43.—*According to the Minister's principles all is entire in the Church of Rome that can be required for external Salvation.*

But here occurs another difficulty. If together with all these points of doctrine, all these practices, and all this worship of the Church of Rome, with the adoration and oblation of our Saviour's body, with the subtraction of one kind, and all the other dogmas, you have still "all necessary food without subtraction of any part," because one God is by her confessed, Father, Son, and Holy Ghost, and one only Jesus Christ as God and Saviour; it is, therefore, to be had there still: still you have in her the marks of a true Church, namely purity of doctrine, and the right administration of the sacraments to a sufficient degree: still then the true Church is there, and still therein may you save your soul.

44.—No difference between us and our fathers.

To this M. Claude would not agree; the consequences of so considerable a concession made him tremble for the Reformation. But M. Jurieu did not mince the matter, sensible as he was that the differences which M. Claude alleged between us and our fathers were too frivolous to contend for. And indeed, no more than these two were mentioned: the first is, that at present there is a body whose communion we may embrace, viz. the body of the pretended Reformed: the second is, that the Church of Rome has made many dogmas articles of faith, which in our father's time, were undecided.[50] But nothing can be more frivolous; and to convince the Minister Claude, he needs only to remember what the Minister Claude has but just told us: viz. that the Berengarians, the Vaudois, the Albigenses, the Wickliffites, the Hussites, &c., had already appeared in the world as "the most illustrious part of the Church, because they were the most pure, the most knowing, the most generous."[51] Again, he has but to remember that, even in his judgment, the Church of Rome "had already given cause sufficient of withdrawing from her communion by her anathemas against Berengarius, against the Vaudois and Albigenses, against John Wickliffe and John Huss, and by the persecutions she had exercised against them."[52] Yet he owns, nevertheless, in all these places, that, in order to salvation, it was not necessary to join with these sects, and that Rome did still contain the elect of God.

To say that the Lutherans and Calvins outshone them in brightness and lustsre, were only disputing about more or less, the substance of the thing still continuing the same. The decisions, passed against these sects, comprehended the principal part of what afterwards was defined against Luther and Calvin; and without speaking of decisions, the constant and universal practice of offering the sacrifice of the Mass, and making the most essential part of the divine worship to consist in this oblation, was no new thing, nor was it possible to remain in the Church without consenting to this worship. We had, therefore, with this worship, and with all its dependencies, all necessary food, without subtraction of any part thereof: therefore we may still have it; M. Claude could not have denied this without too gross an imposition, nor was the concession of it, lately made by M. Jurieu, otherwise than forced.

Add to this that M. Claude, who would make us believe so great a difference between the times preceding and those subsequent to the Reformation, under pretext that doctrines before undecided, are since made articles of faith, has himself destroyed this answer, by saying, "that it was not a more difficult thing to the people to abstain from believing and practising what had been made a dogma, than to abstain from believing and practising what was taught by the ministry, what was commanded by it, and what was become common;"[53] so that this mighty matter of making new Dogmas, which he sets up for such a scarecrow to his party, after all, is just nothing even in his own judgment.

> 45.—*Falsehood asserted by the Minister Claude, that one might be in the Romish Communion without Communicating in her Dogmas and Practice.*

To these inconsistencies of M. Claude's doctrine, I add also a palpable falsehood which he was bound to maintain by this system, viz. that the true faithful, whom he owns in the Church of Rome before the Reformation, "therein subsisted without communicating in her doctrines or her corrupted practices;"[54] that is to say, without coming to Mass, without confessing themselves, without communicating all their lives, or at death; in a word, without ever performing any one action of a Roman Catholic.

He has been made to see, a hundred times, what a new prodigy this would be; for without speaking of the great care that was taken through the entire Church to make inquiries after the Vaudois and Albigenses, the Wickliffites and Hussites, it is certain, in the first place, that even those whose doctrine was unsuspected, were obliged, on a hundred occasions, to show tokens of their belief, and particularly when the holy Viaticum was given them. We need but look into all the rituals antecedent to Luther's times, to be convinced of the care then taken to make those to whom they administered it, first to confess their sins, and in giving it to them, to make them own therein the truth of the body of our Lord, and adore it with a profound respect. A second incontestable fact results from thence: which is, that the concealed Vaudois and others, who wished to shelter themselves from the censures of the Church, had no other means of compassing it, than by practising the same worship with the Catholics, even by receiving communion with them:[55] this has been most clearly shown by all kinds of proofs that can be had in such a matter. But there is a third and still more certain fact, inasmuch as it is acknowledged even by the ministers, viz. that of all those who embraced either Lutheranism or Calvinism, not so much as one has been found to say, that in embracing such doctrines he did not change his belief, but only declared what he always had believed in his heart.

> 46.—*A certain fact, that before the Reformation, the Doctrine she taught was unknown.—Reflection on a book of M. Claude, after the conference of this Minister.*

To this fact distinctly stated, M. Claude is satisfied with answering insultingly, "Does M. de Meaux imagine that the disciples of Luther and Zuinglius ought to have made formal declarations of all they had thought before the Reformation; or that these declarations ought to appear publicly in print?"[56]

This is shuffling in too weak and palpable a manner, for I did not pretend that all ought to be declared, or all printed; but that they never would have omitted to write that which decided one of the most material points of the whole cause, namely, the question, whether or not, before Luther and Zuinglius, there was any one person of their faith, or whether their faith then was absolutely unknown. This question was decisive, since none being able to conceive that the truth had been wholly extinguished, it followed manifestly that what doctrine soever was undiscoverable then on earth, could not be the truth. Examples would have cleared all kind of doubt on this matter, and if any had been, it is evident they would have made them public, but they produced none; it is therefore because there were none, and the fact must stand as incontestable.

47.—Whether Luther's great success be a proof, that before his disputes men thought as he did.

All that could be answered to this was, that had men been satisfied with the doctrines and worship of Rome, the Reformation would not have met with so speedy a success.[57] But, not to repeat here what may be found elsewhere, with regard to this success, and even throughout this whole history, it is sufficient to reflect on that saying of St. Paul, "That the word of heretics will spread like to a gangrene:"[58] now the gangrene does not suppose a gangrene in the body it corrupts, nor by consequence do Heresiarchs find their error already settled in those minds which it depraves. It is true, matters were disposed,[59] as M. Claude says, by ignorance and other before-mentioned causes, for the most part little to the credit of the Reformation: but to conclude from thence with this minister, that the disciples, whom novelty gained to Luther, were already of his sentiments, is, instead of a positive fact whereof proof is demanded, substituting a consequence that is not only doubtful, but even evidently false.

48.—Absurdity of M. Claude's supposition, with respect to those who, in his judgment, lived in the communion of Rome.

Again, though it were granted M. Claude, that before the Reformation all men were asleep in the Church of Rome, even so far as to let every man act as he pleased; those that were neither present at Mass nor Communion, that never confessed their sins, never partook of the sacraments, either living or dying, lived and died quite undisturbed: none ever dreamed of requiring from such people a confession of their faith, and reparation of the scandal they had given to their brethren; after all, what does he gain by advancing such prodigies? His drift therein was to prove that men might have saved their souls whilst remaining with sincerity in communion with the Church of Rome. In proof of this, the first thing he does, is to take from those he saves all the exterior bands of communion. The most essential part of the service was the Mass; they were to take no part in it. The most manifest token of communion, was communicating at Easter: they were to abstain from it; otherwise they must have adored Jesus Christ as present, and partook but of one kind. All pulpits resounded with this worship, with this communion, and, in fine, with these doctrines deemed so corrupt. Great heed was to be taken not to give the least sign of approving them; by this means, says M. Claude, salvation might be had in communion with the Church. He ought rather to have concluded, that by this means salvation would be had out of communion with the Church, since by this means such would have violated all the ties of communion; for, in short, let them define to me what it is to be in communion with the Church. Is it to dwell in the country where this Church is owned, as Protestants did amongst us, and Catholics do now in England and Holland? Surely it cannot be that; but, perhaps, it is to appear in the churches, to hear the sermons, and be present at the assemblies without any token of approbation, and much in the same disposition with a curious traveller, without saying "amen" to their prayers, and especially without ever communicating? This is bantering, you will reply. Why, then, to communicate with a church, is at least to frequent her meetings with the marks of consent and approbation given thereto by others. To give these marks to a Church whose profession of faith is criminal, is giving consent to a crime; and refusing them, is no longer being in that exterior communion, wherein, nevertheless, you would have them be.

But if you say, the marks of approbation to be given must only fall on the truths which this Church preaches, and on the good she practises, by the same way of reasoning, one might be in communion with the Socinians, with the Deists, could they make one society, with the Mahometans, with the Jews, by receiving the several truths professed in each party, silent as to all the rest, and living withal in every respect a complete Socinian, a complete Deist: what extravagance can compare with this?

49.—*This Minister varies in what he had said of the Visibility of the Church.*

This is the state wherein M. Claude has left the controversy regarding the Church; a weak state, as is plain, and manifestly indefensible. And, indeed, he does not trust to it, nor will he deprive his party of the subterfuge, though ever so pitiful, of an invisible Church, since he supposes God may make his Church entirely vanish out of the sight of men:[60] and when he says he may, he does not mean that he can do this absolutely speaking, and it implies no contradiction, for that is not the question; nor are the metaphysical abstractions here so much as thought of; but he may do it in the hypothesis, and allowing the present plan of Christianity. It is in this sense that M. Claude decides, "That God may, when he pleases, reduce the faithful to an entire external dispersion, and preserve them in this miserable state, and that there is great difference between saying, the Church ceases to be visible, and saying, the Church ceases to be." After a hundred times repeating, that he disputes not with us the visibility of the Church;[61] after making the visibility of her ministry enter into her very definition; after grounding her perpetuity on these promises of Jesus Christ, "Lo, I am with you always, and the gates of hell shall not prevail,"—to say what we have just heard, is to forget his own doctrine, and make void the promises which are more durable than heaven and earth. But his case was this: after his utmost straining to reconcile them with his Reformation, and to maintain the Scripture doctrine of the visibility, he found it still requisite to leave himself a last refuge in the invisible Church, to fly to in case of need.

50.—*The Minister Jurieu comes in to the assistance of the Minister Claude,*
who had involved himself in an inextricable labyrinth.

In this posture was the question, when M. Jurieu published his new system of the Church.[62] No means were there of defending the difference which his brother would have placed between us and our forefathers, nor of saving one in damning the others. No less ridiculous was it, in owning that some elect are born to God, in the communion of the Church of Rome, to say, that these elect of her communion were such as took no part in her doctrine, nor in her worship, nor in her sacraments. M. Jurieu was very sensible that these pretended elect could be nothing but hypocrites or impious men; and at length, though with much ado, he opened Heaven's gate to those who lived in the communion of the Church of Rome. But lest she might glory in this advantage, he communicated it, at the same time, to all other Churches wheresoever Christianity is spread, how much soever divided amongst themselves, though never so unmercifully excommunicating one another.

51.—*He establishes Salvation in all Communions.*

He carried this notion to such a height, that he did not hesitate to call the contrary opinion inhuman, cruel, barbarous,[63] in a word an executioner's opinion, that is pleased with damning mankind, with the most tyrannical that ever was. He will not allow a truly charitable Christian can have any other sentiment than that which places the elect in all communions where Jesus Christ is known; and informs us that, "if amongst his own people this doctrine has not been hitherto much insisted on, it was from the effect of a policy which he does not approve." Nay, he has found means to render his system so far plausible in his party, that they no longer oppose any thing else to our instructions, and believe they have therein so strong a hold as not to be forced from it; so that the last resource of the Protestant party is to give to Jesus Christ a kingdom like unto that of Satan; a kingdom "divided against itself,[64] ready," by consequence, "to be brought to desolation, and whose houses are falling one upon the other."

52.—*The history of this opinion, beginning from the Socinians.—Division*
in the Reformation between M. Claude and M. Pajon.

If now one should desire to know the history and progress of this opinion, the glory of the invention belongs to the Socinians. These men, indeed, agree not with the rest of Christians in fundamental articles, for they admit but two; the unity of God and the mission of Jesus Christ. But, they say, all those who profess them with manners suitable to this profession, are true members of the Church universal, and that the dogma superadded to this foundation hinder not salvation; nor is the world ignorant of the notions and indifference of *De Dominis* on this head. After the Synod of Charenton, where the Calvinists received the Lutherans to communion, notwithstanding the separation of both societies, there resulted a necessity of acknowledging one and the same Church in different communions. The Lutherans were far from this sentiment; but Calixtus,[65] one of the most renowned and learned of them, has, in our days, brought it into vogue in Germany, and admits into the communion of the universal Church all sects preserving the foundation, without even excepting the Church of Rome. It is nearly thirty years since Huisseau, minister of Saumur, pushed on the consequence of this doctrine to a great extent. This minister, already famous in his party for his publication of Ecclesiastical Discipline compared with the decrees of national Synods, made himself much spoken of by the plan of reuniting all Christians of all sects, which he proposed in 1670; and M. Jurieu acquaints us,[66] that he had many sticklers, notwithstanding the solemn condemnation which was passed on his books and person. A little while since, M. Pajon, the famous minister of Orleans, in his answer to the Pastoral Letter of the French clergy, did not think himself able to maintain the Church system defended by M. Claude. The catholicity or universality of the Church appeared to him much more extensive than his brother had made it; and M. Jurieu gives notice to M. Nicole, "that answering M. Claude's book will be doing nothing, unless he also answer that of M. Pajon, by reason that these two gentlemen having taken different paths, one and the same answer cannot satisfy both."[67]

53.—*Sentiments of the Minister Jurieu.*

In this division of the Reformation, driven to the utmost straits on the question regarding he Church, M. Jurieu[68] sided with M. Pajon; and not affrighted with the separation of Churches, decides, "that all Christian societies which agree in some tenets, inasmuch as they agree, are united to the body of the Christian Church, though they be in schism one against another, *even to daggers drawing.*"

Notwithstanding these so general expressions, he varies in regard of the Socinians; for at first in his "allowable Prepossessions," where he spoke naturally what he thought, he begins, by enrolling them "amongst the members of the Christian Church."[69] He seems a little puzzled at the question, whether or not one may save his soul amongst them: for on one hand, he seems to allow none capable of salvation but those who live in sects wherein the divinity of Jesus Christs, with the other fundamental articles, are acknowledged; and on the other,[70] after compounding "the body of the Church of all that great heap of sects which make profession of Christianity in all provinces of the world put together," wherein the Socinians are visibly comprehended, he concludes in express terms, "that the saints and elect are spread in all parts of this vast body."

The Socinians gained their cause, and M. Jurieu was blamed, even in his own party, for having been too favorable to them; which is the reason that he restrains in some measure his ideas in his systems: for whereas, in his "Prepossessions," he place naturally in the body of the universal Church all sects whatsoever without exception: in the system, he commonly adds to it this corrective, "at least those who preserve the fundamental articles;"[71]

which he explains in behalf of the Trinity, and other points of like conse-quence. Thereby he seemed to limit his general propositions: but at last, led on by the force of his principle, he broke through all restraints laid on him by the policy of the party, and loudly owned that the true faithful may be found in the communion of a Socinian Church.

This is the history of that opinion which makes up the Catholic Church out of separate communions. In all probability, its authority among Protestants would be great, did not policy obstruct it. The disciples of Calixtus multiply in the Lutheran party. As for the Calvinists, it is plain that the new system of the Church prevails among them; and as M. Jurieu signalizes himself in that party, by defending it, and none has better laid down the principles, nor better foreseen the consequences of it, its irregularity cannot be shown better, than by relating the disorder into which that minister has cast himself by this doctrine, and the advantage he at the same time affords the Catholics.

54.—*Salvation may be had in the Church of Rome, according to this Minister.*

To dive to the bottom of his notion, his distinction of the Church considered as to its body, and of the Church considered as to its soul, must be presup-posed.[72] The profession of Christianity is sufficient to make part of the body of the Church, which he advances against M. Claude, who compounds the body of the Church, of the true faithful only; but to have part in the soul of the Church, it is necessary to be in the grace of God.

This distinction supposed, the question is, what sects are simply in the body of the Church; and what are those in which one may attain to partake of her soul, namely, of charity and the grace of God? which he explains sufficiently by an abridgment he makes of Church history. This he begins, by saying "that she was corrupted after the third century:"[73] this date must be observed. He passes over the fourth century without either approving or blaming it: "but," continues he, "in the fifth, the sixth, the seventh, and the eighth, the Church adopted divinities of a second rate, adored relics, made herself images, and prostrated herself before them even in the Churches; and then grown sickly, deformed, ulcerous, she was alive nevertheless:"[74] so that her soul was in her still, and what is worthy of observation, it was in her in the mist of idolatry.

He goes on saying, "that the universal Church divides itself into two great parties, the Greek Church, and the Latin Church. The Greek Church, before this great schism, was already subdivided into Nestorians, Eutycheans, Melchites, and divers other sects: the Latin Church into *Papists*, Vaudois, Hussites, Taborites, Lutherans, Calvinists, and Anabaptists;" and he pronounces that "it is an error to imagine all these different parties had absolutely broken off from Jesus Christ, by breaking one from the other."[75]

55.—The Church of Rome comprehended amongst the living Societies, wherein the fundamentals of Salvation are retained.

Who breaks not with Jesus Christ, breaks not from salvation and life; accordingly, he counts these societies amongst the living societies. The societies that are dead, according to this minister, are "those which ruin the foundation; to wit, the Trinity, the Incarnation, the satisfaction of Jesus Christ, and other the like articles; but this is not the case of the Greeks, the Armenians, the Cophts, the Abyssinians, the Russians, the *Papists*, and Protestants; all these societies," says he, "have composed the Church, and therein does God preserve his fundamental truths."[76]

It signifies nothing, to object that they subvert these truths by consequences drawn in good form from their principles; because, as they disown these consequences, they ought not, says this minister,[77] to be imputed to them; for which reason, he acknowledges God's elect even amongst the Eutychians, who confounded the two natures of Jesus Christ, and amongst the Nestorians, who divided his person. "There is no room to doubt," says he, "but God preserves a remnant in them according to the election of grace;"[78] and lest it should be imagined there is more difficulty with respect to the Church of Rome than for others, by reason that she is, according to him, the kingdom of Antichrist, he clears this doubt in express terms, asserting "that God's elect were preserved even in the kingdom of Antichrist, and in Babylon itself."[79]

56.—The Antichristianism of the Church of Rome no hindrance to Men's saving their souls in it.

The minister proves it by these words:—"Come out of Babylon, my people."[80] Whence he concludes that the people of God, that is, his elect, must necessarily have been in it; but, continues he, "they were not in it, as his elect are in some manner amongst the heathens, from whom they are withdrawn; for God does not call those his people who are in a state of damnation; consequently, the elect who are found in Babylon are absolutely out of this state, and in a state of grace. It is," says he, "clearer than day, that God, in these words, 'come out of Babylon, my people,' alludes to the Jews of the Babylonian captivity," who certainly, "in this state, did not cease to be jews and the people of God."

After this manner the spiritual Jews and the true Israel of God,[81] that is, his true children, are to be found in the communion of Rome, and will be found there to the end, it being evident that this sentence, "come out of Babylon, my people,"[82] is pronounced even in the fall and desolation of that mystical Babylon, which he will have to be the Church of Rome.

57.—Men may be saved amongst us whilst retaining our Faith and Worship.

In order to explain how men are saved in her, the minister distinguishes two ways: the first, which he has taken from M. Claude, is the way of separation and discernment, when one is in the communion of a Church without partaking of her errors, and of whatever may be evil in her practices: the second, added by him to that of M. Claude, is the way of toleration on God's side, when, in consideration of fundamental truths retained in a communion, God pardons errors superadded to them.

That he comprehends us in this last way he clearly gives to understand in his system, where he declares the conditions on which one may hope from God some toleration "in the sects which sap the foundation by their additions, yet without taking it away."[83] By what has been now said, it is plain he means us and those like us; and the condition under which he allows men may be saved in such a kind of sect is, "that they communicate with it in sincerity, believing that it has preserved the essence of the sacraments, and obliges to nothing against conscience," which shows (so far from obliging those who abide in these sects to reject their doctrine in order to be saved) that they who remain therein with the greatest sincerity, and are the most persuaded as well of the doctrine as of the practices in use amongst them, may be the soonest saved.

58.—One may be saved who is sincere in his conversion from Calvinism to the Church of Rome.

It is true he seems to add two other conditions also: one, of having been engaged in these sects from one's birth; and the other, of not having it in one's power to communicate with a more pure society, either because one knows none such, or "is not in a condition of breaking" with the society he happens to be in.[84] But afterwards he passes beyond these bounds: for after having proposed the question, whether it be lawful, "to be one while a Greek, another while a Latin; now a reformed, then a *Papist*; sometimes a Calvinist, sometimes a Lutheran," he answers, "no, when you make profession of believing what you do not believe in fact. But if you pass from one sect to another by way of seduction, and because you cease to be persuaded of certain opinions which you had formerly looked upon as true,"[85] he declares that "one may proceed to different communions without hazard of salvation, as well as remain in them: because those who pass into sects, which neither ruin nor subvert the foundations, are not in a different state from those who are born in them;" so that one may not only remain a Latin and Papist when born in this communion, but also come into it from Calvinism, without forsaking the way of salvation; nor are they who save their souls amongst us, such only, as said M. Claude, who abide amongst us without approving our doctrine, but such even as are sincere in the profession of it.

59.—This Doctrine of the Minister destroys all he says against us and our Idolatries.

Our brethren, the pretended Reformed, may thence be convinced, that all they are told of our idolatries is wretchedly extravagant. Never was it believed that an idolater might be saved under pretence of his sincerity; so gross an error, so manifest an impiety, is incompatible with an upright conscience. Wherefore the idolatry imputed to us is of a particular species; it is an idolatry invented to excite against us the hatred of the weak and ignorant. But it is high time they should undeceive themselves; for, to be converted is no such great misfortune, since he who cries out the loudest against our idolatries, and loads with most reproaches the converters and converted, is agreed that all of them may be true Christians.

60.—*The Ethiopians saved adding Circumcision to the Sacraments of the Church.*

Neither is the presumption imputed to us of having, on one side, augmented the number of the Sacraments, and on the other, mutilated the Supper by cutting off, as they say, a part from it, any longer to be exaggerated by them: for this minister declares it would be "a cruelty to turn out of the Church"[86] such as admit other sacraments than those two, which he pretends are only instituted by Jesus Christ, namely, Baptism and the Supper; and so far from excluding us thence for having added to them Confirmation, Extreme Unction, and the rest, he does not even exclude from it the Ethiopic Christians, who, says he, "receive circumcision, not by the politic custom, but in quality of a sacrament, although St. Paul has declared, 'If ye be circumcised, Christ shall profit you nothing.'"[87]

61.—*Communion under one kind contains, according to the Ministers, the whole substance of the Eucharistic Sacrament.*

As for what concerns communion under one kind, nothing is more common in the writings of the ministers, even of this author himself, than to say, that by so giving the Eucharistic sacrament we corrupt the foundation and essence thereof; which, in matter of sacraments, is saying "the same thing as if we no longer had them."[88] But such propositions are not to be taken literally as they stand; since M. Claude has already told us that, before the Reformation, "our Fathers receiving but in one kind, had nevertheless all necessary food without subtraction of any part thereof;"[89] and M. Jurieu says still more clearly the same thing, forasmuch as after having defined the Church "the aggregate of all the communions which preach the same Jesus Christ, which declare the same salvation, which give the same sacraments in substance, and which teach the same doctrine,"[90] he counts us expressly in this collection of communions, and in the Church; which necessarily supposes that we give the substance of the Eucharist, and by consequence, that both kinds are not essential to it. Let our brethren, therefore, no longer defer coming over to us in sincerity and truth, since their ministers have removed for them the greatest obstacle, if not the only one, which they allege against it.

62.—*The excesses of the Confession of Faith softened in our favor.*

The truth is, there appears a manifest opposition between this system and the Confessions of Faith of the Protestant Churches: for the confessions of faith, all of them, unanimously give two only marks of a true Church, "The pure preaching of God's word, and the administration of the Sacraments conformably to the institution of Jesus Christ;"[91] for which reason, the confession of faith of our pretended Reformed has concluded, "That in the Roman Church, whence the pure truth of God was banished, and where the sacraments were corrupted, or wholly annihilated, properly speaking, there was no Church at all."[92] But our minister assures us,[93] these expressions are not to be understood in their strict sense; as much as to say, there is a great deal of exaggeration and excess in what the Reformation lays to our charge.

> 63.—*The two marks of a true Church given by Protestants are sufficiently to be seen amongst us.*

However, it is something curious to behold how the minister will acquit himself as to these two marks of the true Church, so solemn in the whole Protestant party. It is true, says he, "We lay them down: we, that is to say, we Protestants: but for my part, I would give the thing," proceeds he, "another turn, and would say, that to know the body of the Christian and universal Church in general, there is but one mark requisite, viz. the confession of the name of Jesus Christ, the true Messias and Redeemer of mankind."[94]

This is not all: for after having found the marks of the body of the universal Church, "It is necessary to find those of the soul, to the end you may know in what part of this Church God preserves his elect." Here it is, answers the minister, "that we must return to our two marks, pure preaching, and pure administration of the sacraments."[95] But beware you be not deceived; "this is not to be taken in a strict sense."[96] To save the essence of a Church, the preaching is sufficiently pure when the fundamental truths are preserved, what error soever be superadded; the sacraments are sufficiently pure, notwithstanding the additions: let us add, following the aforesaid principle, notwithstanding the subtractions which spoil them: forasmuch as, in the midst of all this, the foundation subsists, and "God applies to his elect what good there is, hindering whatsoever of human institution from turning to their prejudice and destruction." We conclude, therefore, with this minister, that nothing of what has been said on this subject in the confession of Faith must be taken in a strict sense; and moreover, that the Church of Rome (Lutherans and Calvinists, calm your hatred!) the Church of Rome, I say, so much hated and so much condemned, in spite of all your confessions of faith and all your reproaches, may glory in having, in a very true sense, as far as is necessary to form the children of God, "the pure preaching of the Word, and the right administration of the Sacraments."

> 64.—*The Confession of Faith hath no longer any authority amongst the Ministers.*

If it be said, these favorable interpretations of the Confessions of Faith are quite opposite to, and destroy the text; that, for instance, what is there said of the Church of Rome, that truth is "banished from her, the sacraments either falsified or wholly annihilated, and properly speaking, that we have no such thing as a Church among us;"[97] are far different things from what we have just heard from our ministers, I own as much; but the reason in short is, they have found by experience that there is no longer any possibility of maintaining their confessions of faith, to wit, the foundations of the Reformation. Nor indeed is it less truth that, in the main, little are the ministers concerned about them; and it is only from a point of honor that they give themselves any pains to answer in their behalf; which was the cause of the minister Jurieu's inventing the aforesaid answers, more polite and better suited to his turn, than sincere and solid.

65.—*This system changes the language of Christians, and confounds their ideas, even of those of the Reformation.*

Now, to maintain this new system, a courage is requisite capable of withstanding any difficulty, and not to be startled at any novelty. Although men be animated against one another even to "daggers drawing," it must be said, they are but one body in Jesus Christ.[98] If any one rebel against the Church, and scandalize her, either by his crimes or his errors, one would think, by excommunicating him, he is cut off from the body of the Church in general, and thus have Protestants spoken as well as we: it is a mistake: this scandalous and this heretical person is cut off but from one particular flock, and do what you will, remains a member of the Catholic Church by the sole profession of the Christian name: notwithstanding that Jesus Christ has pronounced, "If any one neglect to hear the Church, look upon him,"[99] not as a man that is cut off from a particular flock and who remains in the great one of the Church in general, but look upon him as a "a heathen and publican," as an alien from Christianity, as a man that has no longer any part with God's people.

66.—*Manifest contrariety between the notions of the Minister in regard of Excommunication and those of his own Church.*

Further, what M. Jurieu here advances is a particular opinion wherein he evidently contradicts his own Church. A national Synod has defined excommunication in these terms: "to excommunicate," say they, "is to cut a man off from the body of the Church like a rotten member, and to deprive him of her communion and all her benefits."[100] And in the proper form of excommunication, the people are thus addressed: "We remove this rotten member from the society of the faithful, that he may be to you as a heathen and a publican." M. Jurieu[101] spares no pains to embroil this matter with his distinctions of sentence declaratory and sentence juridical; sentence which cuts off from the body of the Church, and sentence which cuts off only from a particular confederation. He invents these distinctions only that the reader may lose himself in the maze of these subtleties, and not perceive he is fed with empty sound. For, after all, he never will be able to show, in the pretended Reformed Churches, any other excommunication, separation, lopping off, than the abovementioned; nor can one depart more expressly from it, than does M. Jurieu. He pronounces and repeats in a hundred places and a hundred different ways, that "it is impossible to banish a man from the universal Church;"[102] and his Church says on the contrary, that the excommunicated person must be looked upon as a heathen, who no longer appertains to God's people. M. Jurieu proceeds: "All excommunication whatsoever is made by a particular

Church, and is nothing else but an expulsion from a particular Church;"[103] and we see, according to the rules of his religion, that a particular Church severs a man from the body of the Church as "one does a rotten member," which doubtless no longer cleaves to any part of the body after it is once divided from it.

67.—*Confessions of Faith but arbitrary conventions.*

Let us, nevertheless, consider again what are these particular Churches and these particular flocks, from which he supposes one is separated by excommunication. The Minister explains himself by this principle: "All whatever different flocks have no other external link than that which is made by way of voluntary and arbitrary confederation, such as was that of the Christian Churches in the third century, on account that they found themselves united under the same temporal prince."[104] So that ever since the third age, when the Church was still found in her purity, the Churches, according to the Minister, were no otherwise united than by an arbitrary confederacy, or, as he elsewhere styles it, "by accident."[105] What? Those Christians then who were not subject to the Roman Empire, those who were spread from the time of St. Irenæus, and even from the time of St Justin, amidst the Barbarians and Scythians, were they under no external band with the other Churches, and had they not a right to communicate with them? This is not the notion they have formerly given us of Christian fraternity. All that are orthodox have a right to communicate with an orthodox Church; all that are Catholic, to wit, all members of the Church universal, with the whole Church. All those who bear the mark of the children of God have a right to be admitted wherever they find the table of their common Father, provided their manners be approved: but here comes one to disturb this fine order; you are no longer in society, "but by accident;" Christian fraternity is changed into arbitrary confederacies, which you may extend at will, more or less, according to the different confessions of faith agreed upon.[106] These confessions of faith are treaties in which you insert whatever you please. Some have put in them, "that they are to teach the verities of grace as expounded by St. Austin,"[107] and these, we are told, are the pretended Reformed churches: far from truth; nobody is less, in their doctrine, than St. Austin; yet they are pleased to say so. These men are not allowed to be "Semipelagians, and the Swiss, no less than those of Geneva, would exclude them from their communions."[108] As for those who have not made the like convention, they shall be Semipelagians, if they please. What is still more, those who have entered into the confederacy of Geneva and that of the pretended Reformed, where one thinks he is obliged to maintain the grace of St. Austin, "may depart from the agreement;"[109] but then they must be contented to be separated from a confederation whose laws they have violated, and "what one would tolerate everywhere else," can be no longer tolerated in those flocks in which other conventions have been made.

68.—Independentism established contrary to the Decree of Charenton.

But what will become of those men who break the agreement of the Calvinian Reformation, or of some such other like confederacy? Shall they be then obliged to enter into league with some other Church? No such thing: "It is nowise necessary, when you separate yourself from one Church, to find out another to adhere to."[110] I am aware he is forced to say so, because otherwise he could not excuse the Protestant Churches, which, on their separation from the Church of Rome, were not able to find on earth a Church they could embrace. But we must hear the reason which authorizes such a separation. "It is," continues M. Jurieu, "because all Churches are naturally free and independent of one another;"[111] or, as he explains it in another place, "naturally and originally, all Churches are independent."

Here is exactly our doctrine, will say the Independents; we are the true Christians that defend this primitive and natural liberty of Churches. Yet Charenton has nevertheless condemned them in 1644. Therefore by anticipation has also condemned M. Jurieu, who maintains them; but let us hear the Decree. "Whereas it has been represented, that many who call themselves independents, because they teach that every church ought to govern herself by her own laws *without any dependance* on any body in Church matters, and free from any obligation of acknowledging the authority of Conferences and Synods for their conduct and government;"[112] that is, without any confederation with any other Church whatsoever; and this is exactly the case of M. Jurieu. But the Synod's answer is very different from his: for the Synod pronounces, "that it ought to be dreaded, lest this poison insensibly diffusing itself, should create," say they, "disorder and confusion amongst us, should open a gate to all kind of irregularities and extravagances, and make void all means of applying a remedy; which would be equally prejudicial to Church and State, and give room to form as many religions as there are parishes and particular assemblies." And M. Jurieu concludes, on the contrary, that by separating from one Church without adhering to another, you do nothing but retain "the liberty and independence, which naturally and originally belongs to Churches," namely, that liberty which Jesus Christ, at their formation, bestowed upon them.

69.—All authority and subordination of Churches depends on Princes.

Accordingly, there is no way of maintaining, conformably to the principles of this minister, these Conferences and Synods. For he supposes, in case a Catholic kingdom should divide itself from Rome, and then subdivide itself into many sovereignties, that each Prince might make a Patriarch, and establish, in his state, a government absolutely independent of that of its neighboring states "without appeal," without union, without correspondence;[113] for all that, in his notion, depends on the Prince; and it is for this reason that he makes the first confederation of Churches depend on the unity of the Roman Empire. But, if this be so, his uncle, Lewis du Moulin, gains his cause: for he pretends,[114] that all this subordination of Conferences and

Synods (if you consider it as ecclesiastical and spiritual) is nothing else but Popery in disguise, and the ushering in of Antichrist; consequently, that there is no power in this distribution of Churches but from the Sovereign's authority; and that excommunications and degradations made by Synods, whether provincial or national, have no authority but from thence. But by a little further extension of this argument, the excommunications of consistories will appear no more effectual than those of Synods: so that, either there will be no ecclesiastical jurisdiction, and the Independents are in the right; or, it will be lodged in the Prince's hand; and, in fine, Lewis du Moulin must have converted his nephew, who so long opposed his errors.

70.—The true Christian Unity.

See what this system comes to, wherein the whole solution of this difficulty about the Church is placed; it is matter of astonishment to hear these novelties. What an error to imagine there is no external Union between Christian Churches, but dependently on Princes, or by some other "arbitrary and voluntary confederation;" and not be sensible that Jesus Christ hath obliged his faithful to live in a Church, to wit, as is owned, in an exterior society, and to communicate with one another, not only in the same faith and the same sentiments, but also, when they meet, in the same sacraments and the same service; insomuch that, however distant churches be, yet are they but the same Church distributed into divers places, the diversity of places not hindering the unity of the holy table, at which all communicate one with another, as they do with Jesus Christ their common head.

71.—Rashness of the Minister, who owns that his System is contrary to
the Faith of all ages.

Let us now consider the origin of this new system which we have just now taken a view of. Its author boasts,[115] perhaps, as he does in other tenets, of having on his side the three first ages; and, it is likely, the opinion which includes the whole Church in one and the same communion (it being pretended so tyrannical) will be born under the empire of Antichrist: no; it was born in Asia, even in the third age: Firmilian, so great a man, and his colleagues, such great bishops, are the authors of it: it passed over into Africa, where St. Cyprian, a martyr so illustrious, and the light of the Church, embraced it with the whole council of Africa; and it was this cruel opinion which made them rebaptize all heretics, no other reason for it being alleged by them, but that heretics were not of the Catholic Church.

It must be owned St. Cyprian made use of the following bad argument: Heretics and Schismatics are not of the body of the Catholic Church; therefore they ought to be rebaptized at their coming into it. But M. Jurieu would not have the assurance to say, that the principle of the unity of the Church, abused by St. Cyprian, was as new as the consequence he drew from it, since this minister acknowledges,[116] "that the false idea of the unity of the Church was formed in the history of the two first centuries down to the middle, or end of the third. We must not wonder," continues he, "that the Church accounted all the sects which existed during those times, as entirely separated from the body of the Church, for that was true;" and he adds, "it was at that time, namely in the two first ages down to the middle of the third,[117] that they got a habit of believing that heretics did not in any manner appertain to the Church:" so that the doctrine of St. Cyprian, which he accuses of novelty, nay, of tyranny, was a habit contracted ever since the first two ages of the Church; that is, from the beginning of Christianity.

It must no less be owned that this doctrine of St. Cyprian, concerning the unity of the Church, was not invented on the occasion of rebaptizing heretics, by reason that the book, "Concerning the Unity of the Church," wherein the doctrine excluding heretics and schismatics is so clearly laid down, did precede the dispute of rebaptization; so that St. Cyprian entered naturally into this doctrine consequently to the tradition of the two foregoing ages.

Nor is it less certain that the whole Church had embraced this doctrine equally with him, long before the dispute of rebaptizing. For this dispute began under St. Stephen, Pope. Now, before this, and not only in the time of St. Lucius, his predecessor, but also from the beginning of the pontificate of St. Cornelius, predecessor to St. Lucius, Novatian and his followers[118] had been looked upon as separated from the communion of all the Bishops and Churches of the world, although they had not renounced the profession of Christianity, nor overthrown any fundamental article. From that time, therefore, even those that preserved the fundamentals, if under other pretexts they broke unity, were accounted separated from the universal Church.

Thus it is an unquestionable fact, that the doctrine impugned by M. Jurieu was received by the whole Church, not only before the quarrel about rebaptization, but even from the first origin of Christianity; and was made use of by St. Cyprian, not as a new foundation which he gave to his error, but as a common principle in which the whole world concurred.

72.—The Minister contradicts himself by asserting the Council of Nice to be of his sentiments.

The Minister had the presumption to say,[119] that his ideas of the Church are the same with those of the Nicene Council, and concludes, "that this holy council did not reject all heretics from the communion of the Church, because it did not command all of them to be rebaptized, neither requiring this in regard of the Novatians or Cathari, nor of the Donatists, nor of the rest that retained the foundation of faith, but only of the Paulianists, namely, the followers of Paul of Samosata, who denied the Trinity and Incarnation." But, waiving other arguments, the Minister needs but hear himself, in order to be convicted. He speaks of the Council of Nice "as the most universal ever held;"[120] but which, nevertheless, was not altogether so, since "the great assemblies of the Novatians and Donatists were not called to it." I desire no more than this confession to conclude, that consequently they were not accounted, at that time, as part of the universal Church, since there was not so much as the least thought of calling them to the Council expressly convened to represent her.

And, in fact, let us hear how this Council speaks of the Novations or Cathari: those, says the council, "when they shall come to the Catholic Church."[121] Enough said; the dispute is ended: in the Church, therefore, they could not be. Nor does it speak in other terms of the Paulianists whose baptism it condemns:[122] as for the Paulianists, when they ask to be received into the Catholic Church, see again; in it, therefore, they were not, according to the notions of these Fathers, and the minister agrees therein. But that he may no longer presume to say, that those whose baptism is received are in the Catholic Church, and not those whose baptism is rejected; the council puts out of the Church no less those whose baptism it approves, as the Novations, than those whom it makes be rebaptized, as the Paulianists; consequently, this difference did not at all depend on those being deputed members of the Catholic Church, and not these.

As much must be said of the Donatists, the Council of Nice neither admitting of their communion nor their bishops; on the contrary, receiving to its sessions Cecilian, bishop of Carthage, from whom the Donatists had separated. The council, therefore, looked upon the Donatists as separated from the universal Church.

Let the minister now come and tell us that the Fathers of the Nicene council are of his opinion, or that their doctrine was new, or that when they pronounced against the Arians this sentence—"The holy Catholic and Apostolic Church anathemizes them,"—they left them fellow-members of this same Catholic Church, and did but banish them from a voluntary and arbitrary confederation, which they might extend, more or less, according to their fancy: such discourses ought to appear nothing less than prodigies.

73.—The Minister is condemned by the Creeds which he receives.

The Minister counts amongst the symbols received by the whole world, that of the Apostles, that of Nice, and that of Constantinople. We are agreed, indeed, that these three creeds make but one, and that the Apostles' creed is but explained by that of the two first Œcumenical councils.[123] We have seen the sentiments of the Council of Nice. The Council of Constantinople proceeds on the same principles, in that it banishes all sects from its unity: whence it concludes, in its letter to all the bishops, that the body of the Church is not divided; and it was conformably to this same spirit that it said in its creed—"I believe *one* Holy, Catholic, and Apostolic Church,"—adding this word *one*, to those *Holy* and *Catholic,* which were in the Symbol of the Apostles, and strengthening it by that of *Apostolic,* in order to show that the Church thus defined and perfectly one by the exclusion of all sects, was that which was founded by the Apostles.

74.—*The Minister endeavors to weaken the authority of the Apostles' Creed.*

The judicious reader expects here to know what this hardy minister will say in regard of the Apostles' Creed, and touching that article, "I believe the Catholic Church." Until now it had been believed, and even in the Reformation, that this creed, so unanimously received by all Christians, was an abridgment, and as a summary of the doctrine of the Apostles and the Scripture. But the minister tells us quite the contrary,[124] for, after deciding that the Apostles were not the authors of it, he will not even grant, what none else denied till now, that, at least, it was made wholly according to their spirit. He says, therefore, "that we must look for the sense of the articles of the creed, not in the Scripture, but in the intention of those who composed it." But, proceeds he, "the creed was not made all at once: the article—'I believe the Catholic Church·'—was added in the fourth age." What does this reasoning tend to else, but to prepare himself a refuge against the creed, and give it only the authority of the fourth age? Whereas all Christians to this time have held it for a common Confession of Faith, of all ages, and of all Christian Churches, from the days of the Apostles.

75.—*A new gloss of the Minister on the Apostles' Creed.*

But let us see, nevertheless, in what manner he will define the Catholic Church conformably to the creed. He at once rejects the definition which he imputes to Catholics;[125] nor does he approve more of that which he attributes to Protestants. For his part, he, who no less raises himself above his brethren, the Protestants, than above his adversaries, the Catholics, being to define the Church of all times, he does it thus: "it is the body of those who make profession of believing Jesus Christ the true Messias; a body divided into a great number of sects;" he must add besides, which excommunicate one another, to the end that all anathematized Heresies, nay, all Schismatics, though divided from their brethren, "even to daggers drawing," (to use the minister's expression,) may have the happiness of being in the Church expressed by the creed, and in the Christian unity which it teaches us. This is what men are bold enough to say in the Reformation, and the kingdom of Jesus Christ carries among them, in its proper definition, the character of the division "whereby every kingdom (as the Gospel says) is brought to desolation."[126]

76.—*The Minister destroys the notion of a Catholic Church taught by himself when he explained the Catechism.*

The minister should at least have called to mind the Catechism, which he himself taught at Sedan so many years; wherein, after reciting "I believe the Catholic Church," it concludes, "that out of the Church there is nothing but damnation and death, and that all those who separate themselves from the community of the faithful to make a sect apart, ought not to hope salvation."[127] It is very certain, that the Church here spoken of is the universal Church; therefore, in respect to her, one may make a sect part, one may separate himself from her unity. I ask whether in this place to make "a sect apart," be a word that implies apostacy? Is it necessary for him that makes a sect part, to put on a turban, and publicly renounce his baptism: Do men speak thus? Should they speak thus, in a catechism, to an innocent child, on purpose to confound all his ideas, and that he may no longer know what to stick to?

77.—*The Schism of Jeroboam and the Twelve Tribes is justified.*

Methinks I labor for the salvation of souls, by continuing the recital of this minister's errors, the most exorbitant and palpable that the defence of a bad cause has perhaps ever cast man into. What he was forced to invent in support of the new system, is still more strange, if possible, and more unheard of than the system itself. It was necessary for him to perplex all the ideas with which the Scripture furnishes us. It speaks to us of the schism of Jeroboam[128] as of a detestable action, which began by a revolt, which maintained itself by a downright idolatry in adoring calves of gold, so far even as to forsake the ark of the covenant;[129] in fine, to renounce the law of Moses, to cast off the priesthood of Aaron, and the hole Levitical ministry, to consecrate false priests of strange gods and of devils. Yet must it be said, nevertheless, that these Schismatics, these Heretics, these Apostates from the law, these Idolaters, made part of God's people;[130] that the seven thousand whom God had reserved to himself, and the remainder of the elect in Israel, adhered to the schism; that the prophets of the Lord communicated with these Schismatics and Idolaters, and broke off from Judah, which was the place that God had chosen; and a schism aggravated with such circumstances ought not, it seems, to be counted "among those sins which destroy grace."[131] If this be true, the whole Scripture must be nothing but delusion and the most excessive exaggeration that can be found in all human language. But then, what must be said to the texts alleged by M. Jurieu? Any thing, rather than to own so enormous a doctrine, and to place manifest idolaters in the communion of God's children, for this is no proper place for a deeper research into this subject.

78.—*The Church in the Apostle's time is accused of Schism and Heresy.*

No more does the Christian than the Jewish Church escape the hands of this minister.[132] He attacks her in her prime and vigor, even in those happy days when she was governed by the Apostles. For, if we believe him, the converted Jews, namely the greatest part of the Church, there being "so many thousands of them,"[133] according to St. James's testimony, and undoubtedly its most noble part, since it comprehended those on whom the rest "were grafted;" the stock "and holy root whence the fatness of the good olive"[134] was derived to the wild branches, were Heretics and Schismatics,[135] nay, guilty of a heresy of which St. Paul has said, "it destroyed grace, and rendered Christ of no effect to them."[136] The rest of the Church, to wit, those who came from heathenism, partook of the schism and heresy by consenting to it, and by acknowledging those as holy and brethren in Jesus Christ, who entertained in their minds so strange a heresy, and in their hearts so criminal a jealousy; and the Apostles themselves were the most heretical and schismatical of all, for conniving at such crimes and errors. Such is the idea he gives us of the Christian Church under the Apostles, when the blood of Jesus Christ was, as I may say, still reeking, his doctrine fresh in their minds—the spirit of Christianity in its full strength. What an opinion will the impious have of the Church in her progress, if these so much extolled beginnings be grounded on heresy and schism; nay, if corruption even reach to those who had the first-fruits of the Spirit?

79.—*According to the Minister, one may save himself even in the Communion of Socinians.*

It seemed as if our minister was for excluding the Socinians, at least, from the communion of God's people, he having so frequently said, that they impugn directly the fundamental truths, and that these being subverted, such societies are dead and can raise no children to Almighty God. But all this was nothing but a false appearance; and the minister would heartily despise whosoever should be deluded by it.

And, indeed, the principal foundation of his doctrine is, "That the word of God is never preached in any country but God makes it effectual with regard to some people."[137] As then, very certainly, the word of God is preached amongst the Socinians, the minister concludes aright, according to his principles, "That if Socianism had been as much diffused as is, for example, Popery, God would also have found means of feeding in it his elect, and of hindering their taking part in the mortal heresies of that sect, as he found means heretofore of preserving, in Arianism, a number of elect and virtuous souls untainted with the Arian heresy."[138]

And if the Socinians, in the state they are in at present, cannot contain in their body the elect of God, it is not on account of their perverse doctrine, but, "for that they being in small numbers, and dispersed up and down without making a figure in the world, and in most places having not so much as an assembly, it is not necessary to suppose that God saves any of them."[139] Nevertheless, since it is certain the Socinians have had churches in Poland, and have at this day in Transylvania, one might ask of the minister, what is the number requisite to make a figure? But be that as it will, according to him it depends only on princes to give children of God to all societies whatsoever, by giving them assemblies; and if the devil complete his work, if taking men on that side to which their senses lean, and, by that means, multiply Socinians in the world, he also finds means of procuring them a more free and extensive exercise of their religion, he will compel Jesus Christ to form his elect among them.

80.—*By the Minister's principles, one might be saved in the exterior Communion of the Mahometans and Jews.*

The minister will answer doubtless, that if he says, you may be saved in the communion of Socinians, it is not by the way of toleration, but by that of discernment and separation; that is to say, it is not by presupposing God tolerates Socinianism as he does other sects which have preserved the foundation, but on the contrary, by presupposing that these Socinian associates, discerning the good from the evil in the doctrine of this sect, will reject in their hearts what is blasphemous therein, although they remain united therewith exteriorly.

But take his answer which way you will, it is equally full of impiety. For in the first place, this makes him inconsistent with himself in respect to the toleration of those who deny the divinity of the Son of God, since he extends this toleration even to the Arians: "To damn," says he, "all those numberless Christians who lived in the external communion of Arianism, some whereof detested its tenets, others were ignorant of them, some *tolerated them in the spirit of peace*, others held their tongues through fear and authority: to damn, I say, all those people, is the opinion of an executioner, and becoming the cruelty of Popery."[140] In this manner M. Jurieu extends his mercy, not to those only who remained in the communion of Arians, being ignorant of their sentiments, but to those also who knew them; and not only to those who, knowing and detesting them in their hearts, did not blame them through fear, but also to those who "tolerated them in the spirit of peace," namely, to those who judged that denying the divinity of Jesus Christ was a tolerable doctrine. What, then, hinders his tolerating, in the spirit of peace, even the Socinians, as he tolerates the rest, and extending his charity so far even as to save them?

But although the minister should repent himself of having carried his toleration to this excess, and would save but those only in the Socinian communion that should heartily detest their sentiments, his doctrine would be nothing the better for that; since, in short, he must always save those who, conscious of the Socinian tenets, should, nevertheless, remain in their external communion, that is, frequent their assemblies, join their prayers and worship, be present at their sermons with an exterior like to that of others who pass for men of that communion. If this dissimulation be lawful, no longer do we know what is hypocrisy, nor what this sentence means, "Depart from the tents of the wicked."[141]

Should now the minister reply, that those who frequent the Socinian assemblies in this manner, ought so to direct their intention as to partake only of that which is good amongst them, namely, of the unity of God and the mission of Jesus Christ; this is a still greater absurdity, since, in this sense, there would be likewise no difficulty of living in the communion of Jews and Turks: for you need but persuade yourself, you partake only with them in the belief of God's unity, detesting in your heart without uttering word, all they speak impiously against Jesus Christ, and should it be said, that it is enough to incur damnation to make your usual worship in an assembly where Jesus Christ is blasphemed, the Socinians, blasphemers of his divinity and so many others of his sacred truths, are no better than they.

81.—*The succession which the Minister gives his Religion, is common to him with all Heresies.*

Such are the absurdities of this new system: it was not the product of free choice, for no man takes pleasure in making himself ridiculous by advancing such paradoxes. But one false step draws on another; nor would he have plunged into this excess, but for others he had fallen into before. The Reformation had fallen into the excess of separating herself not only from the Church in which she had received her baptism, but also from all other Christian Churches. In this state, urged to answer where the Church was before the time of these Reformers, she could not keep to one constant language, and iniquity gave herself the lie. At last, quite nonplused, and little satisfied with all the answers hitherto made in our days, she thought to extricate herself by saying,[142] it is not of particular societies, of Lutherans, of Calvinists, you should ask for the visible succession of their doctrine and pastors; it being true, "they were not as yet formed two hundred years ago;" granting this, yet the universal Church, whereof these sects make a part, was visible in the communions of which Christianity was composed, viz. that of the Grecians, of the Abyssinians, of the Armenians, and Latins, which is all the succession there is occasion for. Here is the last refuge; this their whole solution. But all kinds of sects, they must allow, may say the same. There is not any, nor ever was, to take in each of them no more than the common profession of Christianity, which does not find its particular succession as our minister has found his; so that, to give a descent and an always visible perpetuity to his Church, he was forced to lavish the same favor on the most novel and impious societies.

82.—*The Minister at the same time speak* pro *and* con *with relation to the perpetual Visibility of the Church.*

The greatest offence that can be done to truth is, to know it, and, at the same time, to abandon or undermine it. M. Jurieu has owned great truths: in the first place, "that the Church is taken in Scripture for a society always visible; nay, I go," says he, "further on this head than M. de Maux."[143] With all my heart, what I had said was sufficient; but since he will allow us more, I receive it from him.

Secondly, he agrees that it cannot be denied "that the Church, which the Creed obliges us to believe is a visible Church."[144]

This was enough to demonstrate the perpetual visibility of the Church, because that, which is believed in the Creed, is eternally and unalterably true. But in order that there may be no doubt that this article of our faith is grounded on the express promises of Jesus Christ, the minister grants us moreover, that the Church to which Jesus Christ had promised that hell should not prevail against her, was a confessing Church, a Church which published the faith with St. Peter, a Church, by consequence, always exterior and visible;"[145] which he carries so far as to declare, without hesitation, "that he, who should have the faith without the profession of the faith, would not be of the Church."[146]

It is this also that makes him say, "it is essential to the Christian Church to have a ministry."[147] Equally with M. Claude, he approves[148] of our inferring from these words of our Saviour, "teach, baptize, and lo I am with you always, even unto the end of the world;"[149] "that there will be teachers with whom Jesus Christ shall teach, and that true preaching never shall cease in the Church." He says as much of the sacraments, and is agreed, "that the band of Christians, by means of the sacraments, is essential to the Church; that there is no true Church without the sacraments;"[150] whence he concludes that it is necessary "to have the essence" and foundation, to be members of the body of the Church.

From all these express passages, the minister concludes with us, that the Church is always visible, necessarily visible, and, what is more remarkable, visible not only as to its body, but also as to its soul, as he terms it, because, says he, "when I see Christian societies, wherein doctrine conformable to the word of God is preserved as much as is necessary for the essence of a Church, I know and see for certain, that there are elect in it, since, wherever are the fundamental truths, they are salutary to some people."[151]

After this chain of doctrine, which the minister confirms by so many express passages, one might think nothing could be better settled in his mind, from Scripture, from the promises of Jesus Christ, from the Creed of the Apostles, than the perpetual visibility of the Church; and yet he says the contrary, not by consequence, but in formal terms; for he says, at the same time,[152] "that this perpetual visibility of the Church is not to be found by those proofs which are called of right," that is, by Scripture, as he explain it, "otherwise than by supposing that God always preserves to himself a hidden number of the faithful, a Church, as one may say, subterraneous and unknown to the whole earth, which would be as well the body of Jesus Christ, his spouse and his kingdom, as a known Church; and, in fine, that the promises of Jesus Christ would remain inviolate, though the Church should have fallen into so great an obscurity as that it were impossible to point out and say, there is the true Church, and there does God preserve the elect."

What, then, becomes of that express acknowledgment, that the Church in the Scripture is always visible; that the promises she has received from Jesus Christ, for her perpetual duration, are addressed to a visible Church, to a Church that publishes her faith, to a Church which has the keys and a ministry, to whom the ministry is essential, and which no longer is a Church, if the profession of faith be wanting to her? This we are at a loss to know; the minister thinks he salves all by telling us, that, for his part,[153] he truly believes the Church always visible, and that she hath been ever so, may be proved from history. Who does not see what he aims at? Namely, in a word, that in case it happens a Protestant should be forced to own, according to his belief, that the Church had ceased to be visible, at most he would only have denied a fact, yet not overthrown the promises of Jesus Christ. But this is putting us on the wrong scent in too gross a manner. The question in hand is not whether the Church, by good luck, has always remained to this day in her visibility, but whether she has promises of continuing for ever in it; nor, whether M. Jurieu believes it, but whether M. Jurieu has written that all Christians are obliged to believe it as a truth from God, and as a fundamental article couched in the creed. Most certainly he has written it, as we have seen; and he goes on demonstrating, that the question touching the Church involves the ministers in such a disorder, that they know not which way to turn themselves; and if they can but meet with an evasion, it is all they aim at.

83.—Vain distinction between errors.

But no one is left them, provided they follow but ever so little the principles which they have granted; for, if the Church be visible and always visible by the confession of the truth; if Jesus Christ has promised she would be eternally so, it is clearer than day that it is not allowable to depart one moment from her doctrine, which is saying, in other words, that she is infallible. The consequence is very plain; since, departing from the doctrine of her who always teaches truth, would be too manifestly declaring enmity to truth itself; again, nothing can be more clear and distinct than this.

Let us consider, nevertheless, what method the ministers have used to ward off this stroke. Jesus Christ has promised, say they, a perpetual ministry, yet not a ministry always pure; the essence of the ministry shall subsist in the Church, because the foundations will be retained; but what shall be added to these, will corrupt it, which makes M. Claude to say,[154] that the ministry will never come to a subtraction of a fundamental truth, such as is seen, for example, in Socinianism, which rejects the divinity of Jesus Christ; but there is not a like inconvenience in corrupting, by addition, wholesome truths, as the Church of Rome has done, because the fundamentals of salvation still subsist.

Pursuant to the same principles, M. Jurieu agrees,[155] "that Jesus Christ has promised there always shall be teachers with whom he will teach, so far that true preaching shall never cease in his Church;" but he distinguishes: there always shall be teachers with whom Jesus Christ will teach the fundamental truths, he grants it; but that there never shall be errors in this ministry, he denies it:[156] so, "true preaching shall never cease in the Church; we own it," answers he, "if by true preaching he understood a preaching which announces the essential and fundamental verities; but we deny it, if by true preaching a doctrine be understood that contains no kind of errors."

84.—A single word destroys these subtleties.

To dispel all these mists, nothing more is necessary than to ask these men, where it is they have learned to put a restriction on the promises of Jesus Christ? He that is able to prevent subtractions, why must he not be able to prevent dangerous additions? What certainty, therefore, have they, that preaching shall be more pure, the ministry more privileged with regard to subtraction, than to addition? This word, "I am with you,"[157] implies an universal protection to those with whom Jesus Christ does teach. If the duration of the external and visible ministry be the work of man, it may fail equally on all sides; if, on account of the intervention of Jesus Christ, pursuant to his promises, we are assured that subtraction has never taken place therein, no longer do we comprehend how addition can find admittance.

85.—*Strange way of securing the promises of Jesus Christ.*

And assuredly it is impossible, agreeing as they do, that Jesus Christ has promised his Church that the truth should always be taught in her, and that he would eternally abide with the Ministers of this same Church, in order to teach them; it is, I say, impossible he should not have meant to say, that the truth he promised to preserve in her should be pure, and such as revealed by him; there being nothing more ridiculous than to make him promise he would always teach the truth with such as, retaining a foundation of it, were to overwhelm this foundation, nay destroy it, as is supposed, with their errors, by the inevitable consequence of their doctrine.

And, in reality, I leave the Protestants to judge whether the magnificent promises of rendering the Church immovable in the visible profession of the truth be fulfilled in the state, which the Minister has represented to us by these words:—"We say that the Church is perpetually visible; but the greatest part of the time, and *almost always*, she is more visible by the corruption of her manners, by the addition of many *false tenets*, by the decay of her ministry, *by her errors and her superstitions*, than by the truth she has preserved."[158] If such be the visibility which Christ has promised to his Church, if it be thus he promises,[159] that the truth shall always be taught in her, there is no sect, though ever so impious, which may not glory that the promise of Jesus Christ is fulfilled in her: and if Jesus Christ only promises to teach with all those that shall teach some truth, whatever error may be interwoven with it, he promises nothing more to his Church than to the Socinians, to the Deists, to Atheists themselves, since none of them are gone so far astray as not to retain some remnant of the truth.

86.—*The Minister says that the Universal Church teaches, and at the same time does not teach.*

It is now easy to understand what we have inculcated so frequently, that the article of the creed, "I believe the Catholic and Universal Church," imports necessarily the belief of her infallibility, and that there is no difference between believing *the* Catholic Church, to wit, by approving and assenting to her doctrine. The Minister rises up with contempt against this reasoning of M. de Meaux, and opposes it by two answers[160] the first is, that the Universal Church teaches nothing; the second, that, supposing she taught the truth, it would not follow that she taught it entirely pure. But he contradicts himself in these two answers: in the first, in express terms, as I am going to show; in the second, by the evident consequence of his principles, as will be shown hereafter. Let us then, observe how he speaks in his first answer. "The Universal Church," says he,[161] mentioned in the Creed cannot, properly speaking, either teach or preach the truth:" and I prove to him the contrary by his own words, he having said, but two pages before, that the Church to which Jesus Christ promises an eternal subsistence, by saying "the gates of hell shall not prevail against her, is a confessing Church, a Church that publishes her faith:"[162] now this Church is, undoubtedly, the Universal Church, and the same that the Creed speaks of; therefore the Universal Church, of which mention is made in the Creed, confesses and publishes the truth; nor can it any longer be denied by this Minister, without giving himself the lie, but that Church does confess, does preach the truth, unless publishing and confessing be different from preaching to the whole universe.

87.—Sequel of the contradictions of the Minister on this subject, that the Universal Church teaches and judges.

But let us dive farther into this Minister's sentiments in this important subject. What he most repeats, what he most insists upon in his system is, "that the Universal Church teaches nothing, decides nothing, has never passed, nor will ever pass, nor will be able ever to pass, any judgment; and that to teach, to decide, to judge, is the property of particular Churches." But this doctrine is so false, that, to see it convicted of error, no more is requisite than to continue on the reading of those places where it is asserted; for there you will find,[163] that "the subsisting communions, and those which make a figure, are the Greeks, the Latins, the Protestants, the Abyssinians, the Armenians, the Nestorians, the Russians. I say that the consent of all these communions in *teaching* certain verities, is a kind *of judgment,* nay, *of infallible judgment.*" These communions, therefore, teach; and seeing these communions, according to him, are the Universal Church, he cannot deny that the Universal Church does teach; no more can he deny that she judges in a certain sense, since he attributes to her a kind of judgment, which can be nothing less than a sentiment declared. Here is, then, by the confession of the Minister, a declared sentiment, and, moreover, an infallible sentiment of the Church he calls universal.

88.—By the Confession of the Minister, the sentiment of the Church is a certain rule of Faith in the most essential matters.

He proceeds:—"When the consent of the Universal Church is general in all ages as well as in all communions, then I maintain that this unanimous consent makes a demonstration." This is not enough; this demonstration is grounded on the perpetual assistance which, according to him, God owes his Church; "God," says he,[164] *cannot permit* great Christian societies to be engaged in mortal errors, nor to persevere in them for a long while." And a little after, "is it likely that God should so far have abandoned the Universal Church, that all communions, in all ages, should have unanimously renounced the most important truths?"

Thence it clearly follows that the sentiment of the Universal Church is a certain rule of faith, and the Minister makes the application of it to the two most important disputes, which, in his own judgment, possibly can arise among Christians. The first is that of the Socinians, which comprehends so many essential points; and thereupon "the presumption of the Socinians," says he,[165] "cannot be considered otherwise than as a prodigious temerity and a certain token of reprobation; for that, in the articles of Jesus Christ's divinity, the trinity of persons, the redemption, satisfaction, original sin, the creation, grace, immortality of the soul, and eternity of torments, they have departed from the sentiment of the whole Universal Church."[166] Again, therefore, this Universal Church has a sentiment: her sentiment carries along with it an infallible condemnation of the errors opposite thereunto, and serves as a rule for the decision of all the aforesaid articles.

89.—*This rule, according to the Minister, is sure, clear, sufficient, and the Faith it produces is not blind nor unreasonable.*

Besides this, there is another subject wherein this sentiment stands for a rule: "I believe that it is here also *the most sure rule* of judging which points are fundamental, and of distinguishing them from such as are not; so knotty, so difficult a question to resolve! Thus, all that Christians have unanimously believed, and do still everywhere believe, is fundamental and necessary to salvation."

This rule is not only certain and clear, but also fully sufficient; since the Minister, after having said that the discussion of texts, of versions, of interpretations of Scripture, and even the reading of this divine book, is not necessary to the believer in order to form his faith, concludes at last, that "a simple woman, who has learnt the Apostle's Creed, and understood it in the sense of the Universal Church (withal keeping God's commandments,) shall be, perhaps, in a more sure way than the learned, who, with so much ability, contend about the difference of versions.[167]

There must be, therefore, an easy method of discovering what is believed by the Universal Church, since this discovery is within the reach of a simple woman. There is a security in this knowledge so discovered, since this simple woman relies upon and trusts to it; lastly, there is an entire sufficiency, since this woman has nothing to seek further, and, fully instructed in her faith, needs no otherwise to be concerned than how to live well. This belief is neither blind nor unreasonable, since it is founded on clear and sure principles; and in reality, when one is weak, as we all are, it is the most excellent pitch of reason to know well whom you may rely upon.

90.—*It can be no longer objected to us, that by following the authority of the Church we follow men.*

But let us push on this argument still further. That which makes an absolute certainty in matter of faith, a certainty of demonstration, and the best rule to decide truths by, must be clearly grounded on the word of God. Now, this kind of infallibility, which the Minister attributes to the Universal Church, imports a certainty absolute, and a certainty of demonstration, and it is the most sure rule whereby to decide the most essential, and withal the most knotty truths: therefore, it is clearly grounded on the word of God.

For the future, therefore, when we shall urge the Protestants with the authority of the Universal Church, should they object to us, that we follow the authority and traditions of men; their Minister will confound them by saying, with us, that following the Universal Church is not following men, but God himself, who assists her by his spirit.

91.—*The idea which the Minister forms to himself of the Universal Church as he conceives it, is not agreeable with the sentiments of the Universal Church.*

If the Minister should answer, that we get nothing by this acknowledgment, because the Church, wherein he owns this infallibility, is not ours, and that all Christian communions enter into the notion which he gives of the Church; he will be no less confounded by his own principles, since he has but just placed among the conditions of the true faith, that the Creed be understood "in the sense of the Universal Church." We must therefore understand, in this sense, that article of the Creed, which speaks of the Universal Church itself. Now the Universal Church never has believed, that the Universal Church was the aggregate of all Christian sects: nor does the Minister find this notion in all places, or all times;[168] on the contrary, he is agreed that the notion which reduces the Church to a perfect unity, by excluding all sects from her communion, is of all ages, even of the three first: he has seen it in the two councils whose creeds he receives, namely, in that of Nice, and in that of Constantinople. It is not, therefore, in his sense, but in ours, that the simple woman, whom he makes to walk so surely in the way of salvation, ought to understand these words in the Creed, "the Catholic or Universal Church;" and when this good woman says, she believes therein, she is obliged to fix upon one certain communion, which God shall have distinguished from all the rest, and which contains in her unity none but the orthodox: a communion which must be the true kingdom of Christ Jesus perfectly united in itself, and opposite to the kingdom of Satan,[169] whose character, as before observed, is disunion.

92.—*The Minister condemns his Church by the characteristics ascribed by him to the Universal Church.*

Should the Minister think to escape by answering that, supposing we had proved a communion of this nature, we had done nothing as yet, since it still remained to be proved that this is our communion; I own, before we come to that, there are still some steps to be taken; but, in the meanwhile, and before we do this, and force the Minister, according to his principles, to take these steps with us; we find already in his principles, whereby to reject his Church. For when he gave us for a rule that which the Universal Church unanimously believes everywhere: lest he should comprehend the Socinians in this universal Church, whose authority he opposed against them, he reduced this Church to "communions which are ancient and extensive,"[170] exclusively of sects which have neither of these advantages, and which, "for this reason, could neither be called communions, nor Christian communions." Here are then two great characteristics, which, according to him, a communion ought to have to merit the denomination of Christian, antiquity and extent: now it is very certain, that the Churches of the Reformation were not, at the beginning, either ancient or extensive, no more than those of the Socinians and others which the Minister rejects; therefore, they were neither "Churches nor communions:" but if they were not so then, they could not become so afterwards: therefore, they are not so now, nor can one, consistently with the Minister's rules, too speedily forsake them.

93.—*All the Minister's means for defending his Churches are common to them with those of the Socinians and of other Sectaries rejected by the Reformation.*

It serves no purpose to answer, that these Churches had their predecessors in those great societies which were antecedent to them, and which preserved the fundamental verities; for it suits only with the Socinians to say as much. The minister urges them in vain with these words, "Let these men name us a communion which has taught their dogma. To find out the succession of their doctrine, they begin by a Cerinthus; they continue by an Artemon, by a Paul of Samosata, by a Photinus, and other such like men, who never had an assembly of four thousand people, who never had a communion, and who were the abomination of the whole Church."[171] When the Minister urges them thus, he is right in the main, but he is not right according to his principles, because the Socinians will always tell him, that the only fundamental point of salvation is to believe one only God, and one only mediator, Christ; that it is the unity of these tenets, which all the world agrees in, that makes the Church's unity; that the superadded tenets may, indeed, make particular confederations, but not another body of the Church universal; that their faith had subsisted, and does still subsist in all Christian societies; that they can live amongst the Calvinists, as the pretended elect of the Calvinists lived, before Calvin, in the Church of Rome; that they are no more obliged to show, nor to reckon their predecessors, than the Lutherans or Calvinists; that it is not true, they were "the abomination of the whole Church;" since, besides their being a part thereof, the whole Church never had the power of assembling herself against them; the whole Church "teaches nothing, decides nothing," detests nothing; that all these functions appertain only to particular Churches; that he is in the wrong to find fault with them for clandestinity, or rather for the nullity of their assemblies; that those of the Lutherans or Calvinists at the beginning were in no respect different; that, after their example, they meet together when able, and where they have the liberty: which if others have extorted by bloody wars, their cause is never the better for that; and to annex salvation to such favor or toleration, howsoever obtained from prince or magistrate, whether by negotiation or force, is making Christianity to depend on policy.

94.—*Abridgment of the foregoing arguments.*

The Minister having taken these great steps, by ever so little reflection upon his own principles, would soon join issue with us. The sentiment of the universal Church is a rule; it is a certain rule against the Socinians; therefore, an universal Church must be shown in which the Socinians are not comprehended. What excludes them from it is the want of "extent or succession:" a succession, therefore, must be pointed out to them, which they cannot meet with amongst themselves: now they meet evidently with the same succession that Calvinists boast of; namely, a succession in the principles which are common to them with other sects; it is necessary, therefore, they should find out another; it is necessary, I say, that you should find a succession in the tenets peculiar to that sect whose antiquity you would establish. Now this succession agrees not with Calvinists, who, in their peculiar tenets, have no more succession, nor antiquity, than the Socinians: you must, therefore, go forth from theirs as well as from the Socinian Church: you must, therefore, be able to find out a better antiquity and succession than either of theirs. Finding this antiquity and this succession, you will have found the certainty of faith; all, therefore, you will have to do is, to rely on the sentiments of the Church, and on her authority; and what is all this else, I pray, but owning the Church infallible? This Minister leads us then by a sure way to the infallibility of the Church.

95.—*There is no restriction with respect to Dogmas in the Church's Infallibility.*

I am sensible he lays a restriction. "The universal Church," says he, "is infallible to a certain degree, as far as those bounds which divide fundamental truths from those which are not so."[172] But we have already made it plain that this restriction is arbitrary. God hath not declared to us that he ever confined within these bounds the assistance which he promised to His Church, nor that he designed to limit his promises at the will of ministers. He gives his Holy Ghost, not to teach some truth, but to teach "all truth,"[173] because he has revealed none but such as is useful and necessary in certain cases. Never, therefore, will he permit any one of these truths to be extinguished in the body of the universal Church.

96.—*What is once believed in the whole Church, was always believed in it.*

Wherefore, whatsoever doctrine I shall show to have been once universally received, the minister must receive it according to his principles; and should he think to escape by answering that this doctrine, for instance, transubstantiation, the sacrifice, invocation of saints, veneration of images, and such like points, are indeed to be found in all the Oriental communions no less than in the Western Church, but yet were not always there, and that it is in this perpetuity that he has placed the stress of his proof and the infallibility of the universal Church: he must have misunderstood himself, because he could not have believed in the Church universal, a perpetual assistance of the Holy Ghost, without comprehending, in this acknowledgment, not only all times together, but also each time in particular: this perpetuity including them all; from whence it follows that, throughout the whole duration of the Church, he will never be able to point out a time, when the error prevails which the Holy Ghost has bound himself to preserve her from. Now it has been seen, the Holy Ghost has equally bound himself to preserve her from all error, nor from one more than another; therefore there never can be any.

97.—*The Catholic alone believes in the promises.*

What makes our adversaries stop at this, is their having nothing but a human and a wavering faith. But the Catholic, whose faith is divine and firm, will say without hesitating: if the Holy Ghost has promised his universal Church to assist her indefinitely against errors, therefore against *all*: and if against *all* therefore *always*: and as often as one shall find, in any certain time, a doctrine established in the whole Catholic Church, such can never be impeached of novelty, but by error.

98.—*The Minister can no longer deny the Infallibility which he has confessed.*

We press him too much, will he say, and at last shall force him to forsake his principles of the infallibility of the universal Church. God forbid he should forsake so true a principle, or that he should fall back into all the absurdities he sought to avoid by establishing it; for then his case would be that mentioned by St. Paul, "If I build again the things which I destroyed, I make myself a prevaricator."[174] But since he has begun to take so wholesome a medicine, he must be made to follow it to the last drop, however bitter it may seem at present; that is, he must be shown all the necessary consequences of that truth which he has once acknowledged.

99.—*The infallibility of general Councils a consequence from the infallibility of the Church.*

He puzzles himself about the infallibility of universal councils: but in the first place, supposing there were no councils, the minister is agreed that the consent of the Church, even without being assembled, would serve for a certain rule. Her consent might be known, since he supposes it is so sufficiently at present, to condemn the Socinians, and to serve for an unalterable rule in the most knotty questions. Now, by the same means that the Socinians are condemned, the other sects may also be condemned. Nor, indeed, can it be denied that the whole Church, without assembling herself, has sufficiently condemned Novation, Paul of Samosata, the Manicheans, the Pelagians, and an endless number of other sects. In like manner, what sect soever may arise, it may always be condemned like those, and the Church will be infallible in this condemnation, since her consent will be a rule. Secondly, by owning that the universal Church is infallible, how can the Councils not be so that represent her, which she receives, which she approves, wherein nothing else is proposed but to declare her sentiments in a lawful assembly?

100.—*Cavils against Councils.*

But this assembly is impossible, because there is no assembling all the pastors of the universe, and much less, so many opposite communions. What a chicanery! Did ever man take it into his head to require, in order to form an Œcumenical Council, that all pastors should be present at it? Is it not sufficient that so many come to it, and from so many places, and the rest so evidently consent to their assembly, as to become manifest that the judgment passed in it is the judgment of the whole earth? Who, therefore, can refuse his consent to such a Council, unless he that will say, Jesus Christ, contrary to his promise, has abandoned the whole Church? And if the sentiment of the Church was of much force whilst diffused, of how much more will it be, when reunited?

101.—*Excessive and monstrous power given by the Minister to those who are rebels to the Church.*

Concerning what the Minister says about opposite communions, I have but one word to tell him. If the Universal Church be infallible in opposite communions, she would be much more so, remaining in her primitive unity. Let us, then, take her in this state; let us convene her pastors in the third century, before the Church was corrupted: before, if he pleases, that Novation had separated from it: at such a time, he must allow the convention of such a council would have been a divine relief in order to prevent the progress of an error. Let us now suppose what came to pass: a proud Novation makes himself bishop in a See already filled, and makes a sect that will reform the Church. He is expelled; is excommunicated: what then; because he continues to call himself a Christian, must he be of the Church in despite of her? Because he carries his insolence to the utmost extremes, and will listen to no kind of reason, must the Church have lost her first unity, nor be able any longer to assemble, nor to form an universal Council unless his proud heart consent? Must temerity have such a power? And will there need no more than to lop off a branch, nay, a rotten branch, to say that the tree has lost its unity and root?

102.—*The Council of Nice formed contrary to the principles of the Minister.*

It is therefore a thing not to be questioned, that in spite of Novatian, in spite of Donatus, in spite of all other no less contentious than unreasonable men, the Church will have power to convene an Œcumenical Council. Will have it, do I say? Already has she exercised that power, and in despite of Novatian and Donatus held the Nicene Council. That it was necessary to call, and what is worse, to make the followers of these heresiarchs actually come to it, in order that the assembly might be lawfully held, is what was never so much as thought of. To invent such an evasion, and thirteen hundred years after the whole world (the impious part excepted) has looked on this holy council as universal; to maintain it was not so, nay, that it was impossible for the Catholic Church to hold such a council, because she could not assemble in it those rebels who had unjustly broken unity, is obliging her to depend on her enemies, and punish their rebellion on herself.

103.—*Remarkable words of a learned Englishman concerning the infallibility of the Nicene Council.*

Here is, then, a Council justly called universal, by consequence infallible, if the minister do not forget all he has just granted; and pleased am I with the opportunity of quoting to him what a learned Englishman, a staunch Protestant, has said to this purpose. "The matter under question in this Council was a main article of the Christian religion. If, in a question of this importance, it be imagined, that all the pastors of the Church could have fallen into error, and deceived all the faithful, how shall we be able to defend the word of Jesus Christ who has promised his Apostles, and in their persons, his successors, to be always with them? A promise that would not be true, the Apostles not being to live so long a time, were it not that their successors are here comprehended in the persons of the Apostles themselves;"[175] which he confirms by a passage out of Socrates, who says, "That the Fathers of this Council, although simple and not over-learned, could not fall into error, for that they were illuminated with the light of the Holy Ghost;"[176] whereby he shows us all at once the infallibility of universal Councils by the Scripture and by the tradition of the ancient Church. May the blessing of God light on the learned Doctor Bull! and in recompense of this sincere acknowledgment, and withal of that zeal he has shown in defence of Jesus Christ's divinity, may he be delivered from the prejudices which prevent him from opening his eyes to the lights of the Catholic Church, and to the necessary consequences of that truth he has confessed.

104.—*One may judge of other Councils by the Council of Nice.*

I do neither undertake the history nor the defence of all general councils; it suffices me to have remarked in one only, from avowed principles, what the attentive reader will easily extend to all the rest; and the least that can be concluded from this example is, that God having prepared in these assemblies so immediate an assistance to his troubled Church, it is renouncing faith in his providence to believe, that Schismatics may so alter the constitution of his Church, as that this remedy should become absolutely impossible to her.

105.—*The Minister forced to take from Pastors the title of Judges in matters of Faith.*

In order to enervate the authority of ecclesiastical judgments in matters of faith, M. Jurieu has ventured to say that they are not even judgments; that the pastors assembled in these cases are not judges, "but wise and experienced men, and that they act not with authority;" that the want of being let into this secret was the cause, that his brethren "have written with so little perspicuity on this subject;" and the reason he alleges for taking from councils the title of judges is, because "not being infallible, it is impossible they should be judges in decisions of faith, because the word 'judge' imports a person you must necessarily submit to."[177]

106.—This Doctrine is contrary to the sentiments of his Churches.

That the pastors are not judges in questions relative to faith, is what never has been heard of among Christians, nay, not so much as in the Reformation, where ecclesiastical authority is brought to so low an ebb. On the contrary, M. Jurieu himself produces us the words of the Synod of Dort,[178] wherein that Synod declares herself judge, and even "lawful judge, in the cause of Arminius," which certainly regarded faith.

We read also in the book of Discipline,[179] "that all the differences of a province shall be definitively judged, and without appeal, in its respective provincial Synod, except what regards suspensions and degradations....And likewise what concerns doctrine, the sacraments, and discipline in general; all which cases may, step by step, be brought up to the national Synod to receive the definitive and last judgment," which, in another place, is called "the entire and final resolution."[180]

To say with M. Jurieu,[181] that the word "judgment" is here taken "in an extensive sense," for a report of experienced men, and not for a sentence "of judges having authority to bind men's consciences," is an insult on human language; for what must be called acting with authority, and binding consciences, if it be not to push things so far as to oblige the particular condemned persons "to acquiesce from point to point, and with express disclaiming of their errors entered in a register, under penalty of being cut off from the Church?"[182]

Is this a judgment in an improper "and more extensive sense," and not rather a judgment in full rigor? And that the Synods have exerted this power, we have seen in the affair of Piscator,[183] they obliging him to subscribe a formulary which condemned his doctrine: we have seen in the affair of Arminius, and in the subscription required to the canons of the Synod of Dort; and all the registers of our reformed are full of the like subscriptions.

107.—Subscriptions disapproved by the Minister notwithstanding the practice of his Churches.

No other remedy has M. Jurieu found out for this but to say, "that when a Synod decides controversies which are not important, it ought never to oblige the condemned parties to subscribe, and to believe her decisions;"[184] but this is contrary to the express terms of their Discipline, "which obliges to acquiesce from point to point, and with an express disclaiming of their errors entered in a register, under penalty of being severed from the Church;" which M. Jurieu himself understands "of less important controversies, which neither destroy nor hurt the foundation."[185]

108.—*The Minister's evasion.*

It only reminded to say, that "cutting off from the Church," in this place, was no more than cutting off from an arbitrary confederation,[186] contrary to the express words of their Discipline, which, explaining this cutting off in the same chapter, is acquainted with no other than that which severs a rotten member from the body, and ranks it among heathens, as already seen.

109.—*Infallibility proved by the principles of the Minister.*

Wherefore it is but too manifest that this minister has changed the maxims of the sect. Let us now restore them, and joining them to the minister's own principles, we shall clearly find infallibility confessed. By the minister's principles, if councils were judges in matters of faith, they would be infallible:[187] now, by the principles of his Church, they are judges; therefore, the minister either must condemn himself, or his Church, if he allow not the infallibility of councils, of those at least, wherein is the last and final resolution: but though he should have bereft the pastors assembled of the title of judges, so as to leave them nothing but that of experienced men, yet the councils would be but the better authorized by his doctrine, there being not a man of sound sense that would not hold himself for at least as rash, in resisting the sentiment of all experienced men, as in resisting the sentence of all judges.

110.—*Strange expression of the Minister, who will have us sacrifice Truth to Peace.*

He is not less perplexed about the letters of submission, which the deputies of all provincial Synods are to carry to the national one in good form, and in these terms: "We promise before God to submit ourselves to all that shall be concluded and resolved in your holy assembly, persuaded, as we are, that God will there preside, and will lead you into all truth and equity by the rule of his word."[188] The last words demonstrate that the matter in hand was religion; nor any longer can we learn what it is to be judges, nay, and sovereign judges, if men to whom such an oath is taken be not so. I have elsewhere shown[189] that they exacted it in full rigor; that many provinces were censured for having made a difficulty of submitting "to the clause of approbation, of submission and obedience;" and that they were obliged "to make it in specific terms to all that should be concluded and decreed, without condition or modification." These words are so pressing, that after so long torturing himself to expound them, M. Jurieu at length comes to say, "that they promise this submission on regulations of discipline relating to things indifferent, or, at furthest, less important controversies, which do not destroy nor hurt the foundation of faith;"[190] so that, concludes he, "it is not strange that in such sort of things we pay the Synod an entire submission, because, in controversies which are not of the utmost importance, we ought to sacrifice truths to the good of peace."

Sacrifice truths, and the revealed truths of God! Either he knows not what he says, or he blasphemes. To sacrifice heavenly truths, if this be to renounce them, and subscribe the condemnation of them, it is a blasphemy. There is no truth revealed of God that does not deserve, so far from sacrificing it, that we should sacrifice ourselves for it. But perchance to sacrifice them, is to hold one's tongue. The expression is much too violent. Let it pass, however, provided this will satisfy; but the Synod will come upon you "after her last and final resolution," and press you in virtue of their Discipline and your own solemn oath, "to acquiesce from point to point, and with an express disclaiming of your opinion authentically entered in a register," in order to prevent all equivocation, under penalty of being cut off from God's people, and accounted as a heathen. What will you do, if unable to make your judgment bend to that of the Church? Certainly, either you will subscribe and betray your conscience, or speedily you alone will be your whole Church.

111.—*The Confession of Faith always put to the question in all Synods.*

Besides, when the minister tells us,[191] that the points of controversy which are submitted to the Synod, are not those which are contained in the "Confession of Faith," he does not reflect how many times they would have changed them in important articles out of complaisance to the Lutherans. Nay, more, he has forgotten the custom of all their Synods, wherein the first point put to debate always is, upon reading the Confession of Faith, to examine whether there be anything to be corrected in it. The fact was put to M. Claude,[192] nor was it denied by him, and besides this, it is manifest by the acts of all the Synods. Who will now wonder that nothing has escaped change in the new Reformation, since, notwithstanding so many books written, and so many Synods held, they are every day still to seek and deliberate anew about their faith?

112.—*The weak constitution of the Reformation forces at length the Ministers to change their Capital Dogma, viz. the necessity of the Scripture.*

But nothing will set in plainer light the feeble constitution of their Church, than the change I am about to relate. Nothing amongst them is more essential, nor more fundamental, than to oblige each one to form his faith on the reading of the Scripture. But one sole question proposed to them has, at length, withdrawn them from this principle. Now, they were asked, what could be the faith of those people, who as yet had neither read the Scripture nor heard it read, but were just entering on the reading of it? There needed no more than this to put them manifestly to a stand.

To say, that in this state, one has no faith, with what disposition, then, and in what spirit, will such a man read the holy Scripture? But if you say, he has, whence has he received it? All they had to answer was,[193] "that the Christian doctrine, taken in the whole, makes itself be felt; that to form an act of faith on the divinity of Scripture, it is not necessary to have read it; that it suffices to have read a summary of Christian doctrine without descending to particulars; that those who wanted the Scripture, had it nevertheless in their power to become good Christians; that the Gospel doctrine makes its divinity be felt by the simple, independently of the book in which it is contained; that supposing this doctrine were mixed with things not divine but useless, the pure and celestial doctrine blended with it would nevertheless make itself be felt; that conscience relishes truth, after which the faithful man believes such a book to be canonical, because he has found truths that sensibly affect him; in a word, that one feels truth as he feels the light in seeing it; heat, sitting near the fire; sweet and bitter, in eating."[194]

113.—*Their Faith no longer formed on Scripture.*

Heretofore it was an inextricable difficulty for the ministers to resolve this question; whether or not it is requisite, if faith be to be formed on Scripture, to have read all the books thereof? and, if sufficient to have read some of them, which are those privileged ones we must read preferably to the rest, in order to form our faith? But they have rid themselves of this perplexity by saying, there is not even a necessity of reading any one of them; nay, they have carried it so far as to make a believer form his faith without so much as knowing which are the books inspired by God.

114.—*The people have no further necessity of discerning Apocryphal from Canonical Books.*

Their thoughts were too much busied about the Confession of Faith, when they said, speaking of the divine books, "that they were known for canonical, not so much from the consent of the Church, as from the testimony and interior persuasion of the Holy Ghost."[195] The ministers, it seems, are sensible at present that this was all illusion, and how little likelihood there is that the faithful should be capable, by their interior relish, and without the assistance of tradition, to discern from a profane book, the Canticle of Canticles, or to feel the divinity of the first chapters of Genesis, and so forth; accordingly, it is decided at present, "that the examination of the question touching Apocryphal books, is not necessary for the people." M. Jurieu[196] has written a chapter expressly to prove it; and so far is it from being a requisite to torment one's self about books Canonical or Apocryphal, about text or version, or to be at the pains of discussing Scripture, or even reading it, that the Christian truths, provided you only put them together, will of themselves make you feel them as you feel cold and heat.

115.—*The importance of this change.*

M. Jurieu says all this; and what is more remarkable, says it but after M. Claude. And since these two ministers have concurred together in this point, which is as much as to say, that the party has but this sole refuge; let us stop a while to consider whence they set out, and whither they are arrived. The ministers heretofore built faith on Scripture;[197] now they form it without the Scripture. It was said in the Confession of Faith, speaking of Scripture, that "all things ought to be examined, regulated, and reformed according to it;"[198] now, not the sentiment, which men have of things, ought to be proved by Scripture, but Scripture itself is not known, nor perceived to be Scripture, otherwise than by the sentiment you have of things before you know the divine books; and religion is formed without them.

116.—*Manifest Fanaticism.*

This testimony, imagined by men to proceed from the Holy Ghost, whereby to discern divine Scripture from Scripture not divine, was held deservedly for fanaticism and a means of deceit; because this testimony, not being annexed to any positive proof, there was not a man that could not either boast of it without reason, or fancy it to himself without grounds. But the case is now much worse; whereas they said formerly, "let us see what is written, and then we will believe;" which was beginning at least by something positive and a certain fact: now, they begin by feeling things in themselves as you feel cold and heat, sweet and bitter; and when afterwards they come to read the Scripture in this disposition, God knows with what facility they turn it to what they already hold for as certain as what they have seen with their eyes and touched with their hands.

117.—*Neither Miracles, nor Prophecies, nor Scripture, nor Tradition necessary to authorize and declare Revelation.*

According to this presupposition, viz., truths necessary to salvation make themselves be felt by themselves, Jesus Christ needed not miracles, nor prophecies: Moses would have been believed, though the Red Sea had not divided itself, though the rock had not poured out torrents of water at the first touch of the wand; they had nothing to do but to propose the Gospel or the law. No more had the fathers of Nice and Ephesus, than to propose the Trinity and Incarnation, provided they proposed it with all the other mysteries; the researches into Scripture and tradition, which they made with so much care, were needless to them: on the bare exposition of truth, grace would have commanded the assent of all the faithful; God inspires all he pleases into whom he pleases, and inspiration of itself alone can do all things.

118.—*The Grace necessary to produce Faith, why annexed to certain exterior means and matters of fact.*

This was not the thing doubted of, and the power of God was well known to Catholics, no less than the necessity men stood in, of his inspiration and grace. The business was to find out the external means it makes use of, and whereto God has been pleased to annex it: one may feign or imagine that he is inspired of God without being really so; but he cannot feign, nor imagine that the sea divides itself, that the earth opens, the dead arise, those born blind receive sight, that he reads such a thing in a book, and that such and such our predecessors in the faith have so understood it; that the whole church believes, and always has believed it so. The question, therefore, at issue is, not whether those external means be sufficient without grace and divine inspiration, for none pretends that: but, in order to hinder men from feigning or imagining an inspiration, whether it has not been God's economy, and his usual conduct, to make his inspiration walk hand in hand with certain means of fact, which men can neither feign in the air without being convicted of falsehood, nor imagine without illusion. This is not the place to determine which are these facts, which these external means, which the motives of belief, since it is already certain there are some such, for the ministers hath agreed to it; it is, I say, agreed, not only that there are such certain facts, but moreover that those certain facts may serve for an infallible rule. For instance, according to him, it is a certain fact that the Christian Church has always believed the divinity of Jesus Christ, the soul's immortality, and the eternity of pains, with such and such other articles: but this certain fact, according to him, is an infallible rule, and the best of all rules, not only to decide all these articles, but also to resolve the obscure and knotty question concerning fundamentals. We have seen the passages where the Minister teaches us and proves this;[199] but when he teaches thus, and allows the universal consent to be "the most sure rule" of judging these important and knotty questions; yet, in proposing this external motive, which, according to him, implies demonstration, he did not aim at excluding grace and inward inspiration: the question, therefore, is, whether the authority of the Church, which joined to the grace of God is a sufficient motive and "most sure of all rules" in certain points, may not be so in all; and whether, setting up an inspiration exclusive of all these exterior means, and whereof you give yourself and your own sentiment for surety to yourself and others, be not the best plea that can possibly be put into the mouths of false teachers, the surest illusion to drive headstrong men to the utmost extremes.

119.—*The language of the Ministers loosens the reins to the people's licentiousness.*

After having put it into the heads of the people that they are particularly inspired by God; to complete the thing you need but also tell them that they may make themselves guides as they think fit, may depose all those that are established, may set up others to act by such power as they judge meet to communicate. This is what has been done in the Reformation. M Claude and M. Jurieu also agree together in this doctrine.

120.—*The language of the Catholic Church concerning the settlement of Pastors.*

The Catholic Church thus speaks to the Christian people. Ye are a people, a state, and a society: but Jesus Christ, who is your king, holds nothing of you, and his authority is derived from a higher source: naturally, you have no more right to give him ministers than you have to appoint him your prince; thus his ministers, who are your pastors, derive their descent still higher as he himself does, and it is necessary they should come by an order of his appointment. The kingdom of Jesus Christ is not of this world, nor can a comparison be made between his kingdom and those of the earth, which is not defective; in a word, nature affords us nothing that bears a conformity with Jesus Christ and his kingdom, nor have you any other right than that which you shall find in the laws or customs immemorial of your society. Now, these customs immemorial, to begin from the Apostolic times, are, that the pastors already constituted should constitute others: "Choose ye," say the Apostles, "and we shall appoint;"[200] it was Titus's business to appoint the pastors of Crete; and it was from Paul, appointed by Jesus Christ, that he received this power. "For this cause," says he, "left I thee in Crete, that thou shouldest reform the things that are wanting, and ordain priests in every city, as I had appointed thee."[201] Besides, those who flatter you with the notion that your consent is absolutely necessary to constitute your pastors, do not believe what they tell you, since they acknowledge those of England for true pastors, though the people has no share in their election. The example of St. Mathias, extraordinarily chosen by a divine lot, ought not to be made a precedent, nay, even then, all was not left to the people, for Peter, already established pastor by Jesus Christ, held the assembly: neither was it election that constituted Mathias; it was heaven which declared itself. Everywhere else, the authority of constituting is given to pastors already constituted: the power, which they have from above, is rendered sensible by the imposition of hands, a ceremony reserved to their order. It is thus that pastors follow successively one another: Jesus Christ, who appointed the first, has said that he would always be with those to whom they should transmit their power; ye cannot have pastors anywhere but in this succession, nor any more ought ye to apprehend its failing, than that the Church herself, preaching, and the sacraments, should fail.

121.—*Language of the Reformation.*

Thus speaks the Church, nor do the people presume beyond what is given them: but the Reformation speaks to them quite the contrary. In you, says she, is the source of celestial power; ye may not only present, but constitute your pastors. Should proofs of this power, in the people, be required from the Scriptures, she would be at a stand. To exempt herself from this task, she tells the people that it is a natural right of all societies; so that, to enjoy it, there is no need of Scripture, it being sufficient that Scripture has not recalled this right allowed by nature. The turn is cunning, I must own; but beware of it, ye people, who are fed with this delusion! To make yourselves a lord on earth, it suffices to acknowledge him for such, and every man carries this power in his own will. But the case is not the same in making yourselves a Christ, a Saviour, a celestial King, and appointing him his ministers. And will ye then, indeed, ye people, impose your hands on them on being told it appertains to you to appoint them? They dare not: but are again encouraged when assured this ceremony of imposition of hands is not necessary. What! is it not sufficient to judge it necessary, that you so often find it in Scripture, and do not find, either in Scripture or in all tradition, that ever pastor was made any other way, no, not one but was made by other pastors? No matter, do it nevertheless, O people! believe ye that the power of loosing and binding, of appointing and rejecting, is in you, and that your pastors have no power but as your representatives; that the authority of their Synod flows from you, that they are no more than your delegates; believe, I say, all these things, although you find not a word thereof in Scripture; and believe, beyond every thing else, that, when you shall think yourselves inspired by God to reform the Church, whensoever you shall be assembled in whatsoever way, you have the power to do with your pastors just what you please, none having a right to deprive you of this liberty, it being derived from nature. Thus is the Reformation preached; thus is Christianity destroyed root and branch, and the way paved for Antichrist.

122.—*The Sects issuing from the Reformation, proofs of her evil constitution.—Comparison of the Ancient Church ill alleged.*

With such maxims and such a spirit, (for although it shoots out more manifest in our days, the root was always the same in the Reformation), it is no longer to be wondered that we have seen it, from its first origin, run from change to change, productive of so many sects of so many kinds. M. Jurieu has had the face to answer, that herein, as in all other things, it resembles the primitive Church.[202] In good truth, this is too notoriously abusing the people's credulity and the venerable name of the primitive Church. The sects which divided from her were not the consequence or natural effect of her constitution. Two kinds of sects did arise in primitive Christianity; some purely heathen in their foundation, as that of the Valentinians, the Simonians, the Manicheans, and others of that stamp which entered themselves, in appearance, on the list of Christians, only to set themselves off with the great name of Jesus Christ; nor have these sects anything in common with those of the latter ages. The other sectaries, for the most part, were Christians, which, unable to bear the loftiness, and, as I may say, the whole weight of faith, sought to ease reason now of one article, then of another: thus, some deprived Christ of his divinity; others, unable to unite the divinity and humanity, mutilated, as it were, in diverse ways, both one and the other. Against the like rocks split the proud spirit of Martin Luther. He sunk in reconciling grace and free-will, which, in truth, is a grand mystery; he kept no compass in matter of predestination, and no longer saw anything for men but a fatal and inevitable necessity, wherein good and evil are equally comprehended. We have seen how these extravagant maxims produced those of the Calvinists, still more extravagant. When laying aside all temper, by carrying to extremes predestination and grace, men fell into such visible excesses as were no longer to be supported: the horror they conceived thereof cast them into the opposite extreme; and from Luther's excess, who went beyond bounds with grace, (however incredible it may seem), they passed to the excess of the Demipelagians, who destroy it. Whence have we the Arminians, who, in our days, have produced the Pajonists, complete Pelagians, whose author was M. Pajon, the late minister of Orleans. On the other side, the same Luther, cast down by the force of these words,—"This is my body, this is my blood," could not find in his heart to reject the Real Presence; but at the same time was resolved, in compliance with human sense, to rid it of the change of substance. Things stopped not there; and the Real Presence was soon assaulted. Human sense took a pleasure in its own inventions, and its exceptions being satisfied with regard to one mystery, stood up for the same concession in all the rest. As Zuinglius and his followers pretended that the Real Presence was a remnant of Popery still to be reformed in Lutheranism, the Socinians now a days say the same of the Trinity and Incarnation; and these great mysteries, which had stood free from all insult of heresy for twelve hundred years, are entered on the footing of disputable points in an age when all kinds of novelties think they have a right to show their heads.

123.—Socinians united with the Anabaptists, and both of them deriving their origin from Luther and Calvin.

We have seen the illusions of the Anabaptists, and are sensible it was by following the principles of Luther and the rest of the Reformers that they rejected baptism without immersion and infant baptism; for this reason, that they did not find them in the Scripture, where they were made to believe all was contained. The Unitarians or Socinians united with them, yet not so as to keep within the limits of their maxims, because the principles they had borrowed from the Reformers led them much further.

M. Jurieu remarks that they came forth a long while since the Reformation, from the midst of the Church of Rome. Where is the wonder! Luther and Calvin came forth from her as well as they. The question is, whether the constitution of the Church of Rome was the cause of these innovations, and not rather the new Church-frame set up by the Reformers. Now this question is easily decided by the history of Socinianism.[203] In 1545, and in the years subsequent to this date, twenty years after Luther had removed the bounds set by our forefathers, when all minds were in a ferment, and the world, teeming with novelty from his disputes, was always ready to bring forth some strange offspring. Lelio Socinus and his companions held their clandestine conventicles in Italy against the divinity of the Son of God. George Blandratus and Faustus Socinus, Lelio's nephew, maintained this doctrine in 1558 and in 1573, and formed the party. By the same method employed by Zuinglius to elude these words, "This is my body," the Socinians and their followers eluded those by which Christ is called God. Zuinglius believed himself forced to the figurative interpretation by the impossibility of comprehending a human body whole and entire everywhere that the Eucharist was distributed, the Unitarians believed they had the same right over all the other mysteries equally incomprehensible; and after it had been set them for a rule to understand figuratively those passages of Scripture which bore hard on human reasoning, they did but extend this rule to whatsoever the mind of man had to suffer the like violence from. To these evil dispositions introduced by the Reformation, let us join the general foundations it had laid, the authority of the Church despised, the succession of pastors held for nothing, precedent ages impeached of error, the Fathers themselves basely handled, all fences laid open, and human curiosity abandoned entirely to itself; what else could be the issue but what has been seen, namely an unbridled licentiousness in all matters of religion? But experience has proved that these hardy innovators saw not the least possibility of settling amongst us; it was to the Churches of the Reformation they betook themselves; those upstart Churches, which, set in motion, and still giddy with their own changes, were susceptible of all others. It was in the bosom of these Churches, at Geneva, amongst the Swiss and the Polish protestants, that the Unitarians sought a sanctuary. Repulsed by some of these Churches, they raised themselves a sufficient number of disciples amongst the rest of them to make a separate body. This, beyond question, was their origin. You need but look into the Testament of George Schoman, one of the Unitarian chiefs, and the account given by Andrew Wissonats, "in what manner the Unitarians separated themselves from the Reformed,"[204] to be convinced that this sect was nothing but a progress of, and a sequel from the dogmas of Luther, of Calvin, of Zuinglius, of Menon, the last of whom was one of the heads of the Anabaptists. There you will find all those sects were but "the first draught, and, as it were, the dawn of the Reformation, and that Anabaptism, joined to Socinianism, is the mid-day."[205]

124.—*Constitution of the Reformation how unlike to that of the Primitive Church.*

No longer, therefore, let them object to us the sects of the ancient Church, and no longer boast of resembling her. Never did the ancient Church vary in her doctrine; never, in her confessions of faith, did she suppress the truths which she believed were revealed by God; she never retouched her decisions, never deliberated new on matters once determined; never, not once, proposed new expositions of faith, save when some new questions arose. But the Reformation, quite on the contrary, never could content herself; her creeds have nothing that is certain; the decrees of her synods nothing fixed; her confessions of faith are confederacies and arbitrary contracts; what is an article of faith amongst them, is not so for all, nor always—they go apart by caprice, and meet again by policy. When, therefore, sects arose in the ancient Church, it was from the commn and inveterate depravation of mankind; and when they now arise in the Reformation, it is from the novel and particular constitution of the Churches she has modelled.

125.—*A memorable instance of Variation in the Protestant Church of Strasburg.*

To make this truth the more apparent, I shall choose for an example the Protestant Church of Strasburg, as one of the most learned of the Reformation, and by her proposed, ever since the beginning, as a pattern of discipline to all the rest. This great city was one of the first that fell by Luther's preaching, and did not think, at that time, of disputing the Real Presence. All the complaints made against her senate were, that "it took away images, and made communion be given in both kinds."[206] It was in 1523 that, by the means of Bucer and Capito, she turned Zuinglian. After she had for some years heard their invectives against the Mass, without wholly abolishing it, and

THE HISTORY OF THE VARIATIONS   BOOK XV

without a full assurance of its being evil, the senate decreed "it should be suspended until it were proved a worship acceptable to God."[207] Here is a new provision in matter of faith; and though I had not mentioned that this decree came from the senate, it would easily have been understood, that the assembly where it was made had nothing in it that was ecclesiastical. The decree passed in 1529. The same year, those of Strasburg,[208] having never been able to agree with the Lutherans, joined in a league with the Swiss, who were Zuinglians like themselves. So far did they carry Zuinglius's notion and their hatred of the Real Presence, as to refuse to subscribe the Confession of Augsburg in 1530,[209] and to make themselves a particular Confession, which we have seen under the name of the Confession of Strasburg, or of the four towns.[210] The very next year,[211] they shuffled so much, and with so much art on this subject, as to get themselves comprehended in the league of Smalcald, from which the rest of the Sacramentarians were excluded. But they went still further in 1536, inasmuch as they subscribed the Wittemberg agreement, wherein, as we have seen, was confessed the substantial presence and the communion of the true body and true blood in the unworthy, although void of faith.[212] Thereby they passed over insensibly to Luther's sentiment, and from that time were counted among the defenders of the Confession of Augsburg which they subscribed. They declared, nevertheless, in 1548,[213] that this was without departing from their first Confession, which, although formerly it had made them reject that of Augsburg, was found conformable to it now. In the mean time, Strasburg was so wedded to the agreement of Wittemberg and the Confession of Augsburg,[214] that Peter Martyr and Zanchius, the two greatest men at that time of the Sacramentarians, were forced at length to withdraw from that city; one for refusing to subscribe the agreement, and the other for having subscribed the Confession with a restriction; so zealous were they become at Strasburg for the Real Presence. In 1598, this city subscribed the book of Concord; and after having been for so long a time the chief, as it were, of those cities that opposed the Real Presence, she stretched her Confession, in spite of Sturmius, to the prodigious tenet of Ubiquity.[215] The cities of Linden and Memmingen, formerly her associates in the hatred of the Real Presence, followed this example.[216] At this time the ancient Agenda was changed, and Marbachius's book was printed at Strasburg, in which he maintained that "Jesus Christ, before his ascension, was in heaven, as to his humanity; that this visible ascension was nothing, in reality, but an appearance; that the Heaven wherein Jesus Christ's humanity was received, contained not only God and all the saints, but moreover all the devils and all the damned; and that Jesus Christ was, according to his human nature, not only in the bread and wine of the Supper, but also in all the pots and all the glasses." To these extremities were men driven, when, forsaking the sure guidance of Church authority, they gave themselves up to human opinions like to a changeable and impetuous wind.

126.—Constancy of the Catholic Church.

If now, to the variations and giddiness of these new Churches, you oppose the constancy and gravity of the Catholic Church, it will easily be judged where it is the Holy Ghost presides; and because I neither can, nor ought to relate, in this work, all the judgments she has passed in matters of faith, that uniformity and steadiness I commend her for, shall be made appear in those very articles wherein we have seen the inconstancy of our Reformed.

127.—Example in the Question moved by Berengarius concerning the Real Presence.

The first who made a sect in the Church, and dared to condemn her, in regard to the Real Presence, was unquestionably Berengarius. What our adversaries say of Ratramnus[217] is nothing less than a certain fact, as above seen; and though it were granted that Ratramnus favored them (which is false), an ambiguous author, by all of them made to speak in behalf of their several opinions, would be in nowise proper to make a sect. I say the same of John Scot, whose error was personal, and had no continued succession.

128.—The Church's behaviour in regard of Innovators.

The Church does not always anathematize rising errors; nor does she censure them as long as there are hopes they will vanish of themselves; nay, often fears rendering them famous by her anathemas. Thus Artemon, and some others who had denied Jesus Christ's divinity before Paul of Samosata, drew not such signal condemnations on themselves as he did, they not being judged capable of raising a sect. As for Berengarius, certain it is he attacked openly the faith of the Church, and had disciples of his own name like other heresiarchs, although his heresy was soon extinguished.

129.—Beginning of Berengarius's Sect, and his Condemnation.

It appeared about the year 1030; not but that we have already remarked, some years before, even from the year 1017, the Real Presence manifestly impugned by the heretics of Orleans, who were Manicheans.[218] Such were the first authors of that doctrine, one article of which was maintained by Berengarius. But as that sect kept concealed, the Church was surprised at this novelty, yet not much disturbed with it at that time. It was against Berengarius that the first decision was made on this subject in 1052, in a council of a hundred and thirteen bishops called together at Rome from all sides by Nicholas II.[219] Berengarius submitted himself, and the first who made a sect of the Sacramentarian heresy, was the first also that condemned it.

130.—First Confession of Faith required of Berengarius.

No one is ignorant of that famous Confession of Faith, which begins, "Ego Berengarius," where this Heresiarch acknowledges, "that the bread and the wine which are placed on the altar after consecration are not only the sacrament, but also the true body and the true blood of our Lord Jesus Christ, and are sensibly touched by the hands of the priest, broken and bruised between the teeth of the faithful, not only in sacrament, but in truth."

There were none but understood, that the body and blood of Jesus Christ was broken in the Eucharist, in the same sense that we say a man is torn, he is wet, when the clothes he actually wears are torn or wet. When his clothes are not on him, we use not the same way of speaking: so that the meaning was that Jesus Christ was as truly under the species, which are broken and eaten, as we are truly in the clothes we wear. It was said, moreover, that Jesus Christ is sensibly received and touched, because he is in person and in substance under the sensible species which are touched and received; and all this imported that Jesus Christ is received and eaten, not in his proper species and under the exterior of man, but under a foreign species, and under the exterior of bread and wine. And if the Church said also, in a certain sense, that the body of Jesus Christ is broken, it was not from her being ignorant that, in another sense, it was not so: just as when saying, in a certain sense, we are torn and wet when our clothes are so; we are still sensible, at the same time, that, in another sense, we are neither one nor the other, as to our persons. Thus the Fathers justly said to Berengarius what we still say,[220] "that the body of Jesus Christ is all entire in the whole Sacrament, and all entire in every particle thereof; everywhere the same Jesus Christ always entire, inviolable and indivisible, communicating himself without dividing himself, as the word to a whole audience, and as our soul to all our members." But what obliged the Church to say, after many Fathers, and after St. Chrysostom, that the body of Jesus Christ is broken, was, that Berengarius, under pretext of doing honor to the Saviour of the world, was accustomed to say, "God forbid that man may break with the tooth or divide Jesus Christ, in the same manner as we put under the tooth, and divide these things,"[221] namely, the bread and wine. The Church, which always took care to combat in heretics the most precise and strongest words they made use of to explain their error, opposed against Berengarius the contradictory of that proposition he had advanced, and placed in some manner the Real Presence under the eyes of Christians, by saying to them what they received in the sacrament, after consecration, was as really the body and the blood, as before consecration it was really bread and wine.

131.—*Berengarius's second Confession of Faith, where the change of Substance is more clearly explained, and why.*

Besides, when the faithful were told that the bread and wine of the Eucharist were in truth the body and the blood, they were accustomed to understand, not that they were so by their nature, but became such by the consecration, so that the change of substance was contained in that expression, although what principally was aimed at by it, was to render the presence sensible, which likewise was principally impugned. Some while after it was perceptible that Berengarius and his disciples varied. For we learn from authors of those times[222] that, in the course of the dispute, they acknowledged in the Eucharist the substance of the body and blood, but with that of bread and wine, employing even the term of impanation and that of invination, and asserting that Jesus Christ was, as I may say, impanate in the Eucharist, as he became incarnate in the Virgin's womb. This, says Guitmondus,[223] was as a last entrenchment to Berengarius; nor was it without difficulty that this subtlety of the sect was discovered. But the Church, which always follows heretics step by step to condemn their errors as they disclose them, after having so well established the Real Presence in Berengarius's first Confession of Faith, proposed also another to him, in which the change of substance was expressed more distinctly. He confessed, therefore, under Gregory VII, in a Council held at Rome,[224] which was the sixth held under that Pope in 1079, "that the bread and wine which are placed on the altar, by the mystery of holy prayer and the words of Jesus Christ, are substantially changed into the true, life-giving, and proper flesh of Jesus Christ, &c." And the same is said of the blood. It is specified that the body here received "is the same that was born of the Virgin, that was nailed to the cross, that is seated at the right hand of the Father, and the blood is the same that flowed from his side;" and in order that no room might be left for equivocation, whereby heretics delude mankind, it is added, this is done "not in sign and in virtue by a simple sacrament, but in the propriety of nature and the truth of substance."

132.—*The change of Substance was opposed to Berengarius from the beginning.*

Berengarius again subscribed, and this second time condemned himself; but he was now so hampered, that no room for equivocation was left him, no subterfuge for his error. And if the change of substance was here insisted on more precisely, it was not that the Church had before in the least doubted of it, since, from the beginning of the dispute against Berengarius, Hugo of Langres had said, "that the bread and wine did not remain in their first nature, but pass into another; that they were changed into the body and blood of Jesus Christ by the omnipotence of God, against which Berengarius opposed himself in vain."[225] And as soon as ever this heretic had declared himself, Adelman, Bishop of Bresse, his schoolfellow, and the first discoverer of his error, warned him, "that he stood in opposition to the sense of the whole Catholic Church, and that it was as easy for Jesus Christ to change the bread into his body, as to change water into wine, and create light by his word alone."[226] It was, therefore, a constant doctrine of the universal church, not that the bread and wine contained the body and blood of Jesus Christ, but that they became his body and blood by a change of substance.

133.—*A certain fact, that the Faith opposed to Berengarius was that of the whole Church and of all Christians.*

Nor was it Adelman only that reproached Berengarius with the novelty and singularity of his doctrine; all authors unanimously upbraid him as with a certain fact, that the faith he impugned was that of the whole universe; that he scandalized the whole Church by the novelty of his doctrine; that to come over to his faith, it was necessary to believe there was no such thing as a

Church on earth; that there was not so much as one town, no, not one village of his opinion; that the Greeks, the Armenians, in a word, all Christians had, in this regard, the same faith with those of the west; so that nothing could be more ridiculous than to censure, as incredible, what was believed by the whole world. Nor did Berengarius deny this fact, but, like all heretics, answered disdainfully, that wise men ought not to follow "the sentiments, or rather the follies, of the vulgar." But Lanfranc and the rest of them remonstrated, and what he called the vulgar, was the whole clergy and all the people of the universe; and upon the certainty of this fact, wherein he feared no contradiction, he concluded, that if Berengarius's doctrine were true, "the inheritance promised to Jesus Christ was made void, and his promises annihilated:" lastly, that "the Catholic Church was no more, and, if she was no more, she never had been."[227]

134.—All Innovators always find the Church
in a full and constant possession of that Doctrine they attack.

A remarkable fact likewise may be here observed; namely, that Berengarius, like all other heretics, found the Church firm and universally united in the dogma which he impugned; this is what has always happened in like cases. Of all the dogmas which we believe, not so much as one can be named, which was not found invincibly and universally established when the contrary dogma began to make a sect; and wherein the Church has not remained, if possible, still more fixed from that very time, a thing alone sufficient to make palpable the perpetual succession and immutability of her faith.

135.—There was no need of an universal Council against Berengarius.

There was not more necessity for convening an universal council against Berengarius than against Pelagius; the decisions of the holy See, and of the Councils then held, were unanimously received by the whole Church, and the heresy of Berengarius, quickly crushed, found no longer any sanctuary but with the Manicheans.

136.—Decision of the great Council of Lateran.—The word Transubstantiation
pitched upon, and why.

It has been seen in what manner these Manicheans began to spread themselves all over the west, filling it with their blasphemies against the Real Presence, and at the same time, with their equivocating language, on purpose to conceal themselves from the Church, whose assemblies they were determined to frequent.[228] In order, therefore, that she might defeat these equivocations, the Church thought herself obliged to employ some precise terms, as she had done formerly with so much advantage against the Arians and Nestorians, which she did in this manner under Innocent III, in the great council of Lateran in the year of our Lord 1215. "There is one only universal Church of the faithful out of which there is no salvation, in which Jesus Christ is himself the sacrificer and the victim, whose body and blood are truly contained under the species of bread and wine in the Sacrament of the altar, the bread and wine being transubstantiated, one into the body, and the other into the blood of our Lord by the divine power, to the end that, for accomplishing the mystery of unity, we should take of his what he himself took of ours."[229] There is no one who does not see, that this new word transubstantiation here employed, without adding any thing to the idea of a change of substance which we have seen already owned against Berengarius, did but declare it by an expression, the bare signification of which served for a mark to the faithful against the subtleties and equivocations of heretics, as did heretofore the Homoousion of Nice, and the Theotocos of Ephesus. Such was the decision of the council of Lateran, the greatest and the most numerous that ever had been held, its authority being so great, that posterity has called it, by excellence, the *General* Council.

137.—*The plainness of the Decisions of the Church.*

By these decisions may be seen, with what brevity, with what precision, with what uniformity, the Church explains herself. Heretics, always in search after their faith, walk groping in the dark, and vary. The Church, which always carries her faith entirely formed in her heart, seeks only to explain it without intricacy and ambiguity; for which reason her decisions are never clogged with a multiplicity of words. Besides, as she beholds without surprise the most sublime difficulties, she proposes them without reserve, convinced that she shall always find in her children a mind ready to captivate itself, and a docility capable of the whole weight of the divine mystery. Heretics, who seek to indulge human sense and the animal part unsusceptible of the divine secret, take great pains to bend the Scripture to their taste and fancy. On the contrary, the Church only thinks of taking it in its plain sense. She hears our Saviour say, "This is my body," and cannot apprehend that what he calls "body" so absolutely, should be anything else than the body itself; wherefore she believes without difficulty, that it is the body in substance, because the body in substance is nothing else but the true and proper body: thus the word substance enters naturally into her expressions. But then Berengarius never thought of using that word; and Calvin, who used it, though agreeing in the main with Berengarius, has thereby made it but manifest, that the figure which Berengarius admitted, did not answer the whole expectation, nor the whole idea of a Christian.

The same simplicity, which made the Church believe the body present in the Sacrament, has made her believe that it was the whole substance of it, Jesus Christ not having said, "My body is here," but "This is it;" and as it is not so by its nature, it becomes, and is made so by the divine power. This is what imports a conversion, a transformation, a change; a word so natural to this mystery, that it could not fail taking place in Berengarius's case, and the more so, as it was everywhere already found in the Liturgies and Fathers.

138.—*Decision of the Council of Trent.*

These reasons, so plain and natural, were opposed to Berengarius. We have no other, even at this day, to oppose against Calvin and Zuinglius: we have received them from Catholics that wrote against Berengarius, as they had received them from those who preceded them; nor has the Council of Trent added anything to the decisions of our forefathers, unless what was necessary for a further elucidation of what Protestants studied to perplex and darken, as will easily be perceived by those who have the least knowledge of the history of our controversies.[230]

But it was necessary, for instance, to explain more distinctly, that Jesus Christ rendered himself present, not only in the actual use of the Sacrament, as is the opinion of the Lutherans,[231] but immediately after the Consecration, because it is not there said, "This shall be," but "This is;" which, nevertheless, was, in the main, what had been formerly said against Berengarius when the presence was annexed, not to the manducation, or to the faith of him who received the Sacrament, but to the "sacred prayer and the word of our Saviour;" whereby also did appear, not the adoration only, but likewise the truth of the oblation and sacrifice, as we have seen confessed by the Protestants:[232] so that, in the end, there remains no difficulty but in the Real Presence, wherein we have the advantage to discover, that those even who in fact depart from our doctrine, do always endeavor (so sacred is it!) to draw as near to it as they are able.

139.—*Reason for the Decision of the Council of Constance, touching Communion under one kind.*

The decision of Constance, in approbation of and for retaining communion under one kind, is one of those, wherein our adversaries think they have they most advantage. But in order to be convinced of the gravity and constancy of the Church in this decree, we need but remember that the Council of Constance,[233] when they passed it, had found the custom of communicating under one kind established, beyond contradiction, many ages before. The case was much the same with that of Baptism by immersion, as clearly grounded on Scripture as communion under both kinds could be, and which, nevertheless, had been changed into infusion, with as much ease and as little contradiction, as communion under one kind was established; so that the same reason stood for retaining one as the other.

140.—*Reasons determining the maintenance of the ancient custom.*

It is a fact most certainly avowed in the Reformation, although at present some will cavil at it, that Baptism was instituted by immersing the whole body into water; that Jesus Christ received it so, and caused it to be so given by his Apostles; that the Scripture knows no other Baptism than this; that antiquity so understood and practised it; that the word itself implies it, to baptize being the same as to dip: this fact, I say, is unanimously acknowledged by all the

Divines of the Reformation, nay, by the Reformers themselves, and those even who best understood the Greek language and the ancient customs as well of the Jews as Christians; by Luther, by Melancthon, by Calvin, by Casaubon, by Grotius, by all the rest, and lately even by Jurieu, the most contradicting of all ministers.[234] Nay, Luther has observed, that the German word signifying Baptism was derived from thence, and this Sacrament named Tauf, from profundity or depth, because the baptized were deeply plunged into water. If then, any fact in the world can be deemed certain, it is this same: but it is not less certain even by all these authors, that Baptism without immersion is valid, and that the Church is in the right to retain the custom. It is therefore plain, in a parallel fact, what ought to be our judgment as to the decree of communion under one kind, and that all which is opposed against it, is nothing but chicane.

And, indeed, if there was reason to maintain Baptism without immersion, because, in rejecting it, it would follow, there had been no such thing as Baptism for many ages, consequently, no such thing as a Church, it being impossible for the Church to subsist without the substance of the Sacraments; no less impossible was it, without the substance of the Supper. The same reason, then, subsisted for maintaining communion under one kind, as for maintaining Baptism by infusion; and the Church, in maintaining these two practices which tradition showed equally indifferent, did nothing else but, according to custom, maintain against contentious spirits that authority, whereon the faith of the people reposed.

Whoever desires to see more on this subject, may turn back to those places of this history where it is handled, and among others, to those where may be seen, that communion under one kind was settled with so little contradiction, that it was not impugned by the greatest enemies of the Church, not even by Luther, at the beginning.[235]

141.—*Question about Justification.*

Next to the question of the Eucharist, the principal one of our controversies is that of justification, in relation to which the gravity of the decisions of the Church may be easily understood, in that she did but repeat in the Council of Trent, what the Fathers and St. Austin had decided formerly, when this question was debated with the Pelagians.

142.—*Inherent justice acknowledged on both sides.—Consequence of this Doctrine.*

And, in the first place, it must be supposed that there is no question between us, whether or not a sanctity and justice infused into the soul by the Holy Ghost should be acknowledged in man justified; for the qualities and infused habits are, as above seen, confessed by the Synod of Dort.[236] The Lutherans are no less steady in defending them; and, in a word, all Protestants are agreed, that by the regeneration and sanctification of the new man, a sanctity and justice is formed in him like a permanent habit: the question is, whether this sanctity and this justice be what justifies us in the sight of God. But where is

37889

67845678099

the difficulty of this? A sanctity which does not make us saints, a justice which does not make us just, were a subtlety quite unintelligible. But a sanctity and justice formed in us by Almighty God, and yet not pleasing to him; or, if agreeable to him, not making that person in whom it is found agreeable to him, would be another nicety still more unworthy the sincerity of a Christian.

143.—*The Church in the Council of Trent does but repeat her ancient Decisions touching the notion of justifying Grace.*

But, after all, when the Church defined in the Council of Trent, that remission of sins was given to us, not by a simple imputation of the justice of Jesus Christ outwardly, but by a regeneration which changes and renews us inwardly; she did but repeat what formerly she had defined against the Pelagians in the Council of Carthage, "that children are truly baptized in the remission of sins, to the end that regeneration should purify in them the sin which they contracted by generation."[237] Conformably to these principles, the same Council of Carthage[238] understands by "justifying grace, not only that which remits to us sins committed, but that also which assists us to commit them no more" not only by enlightening our minds, but also by inspiring charity into our hearts, to the end, that "we might fulfil God's commandments." Now, the grace which works these things is not a simple imputation, but is also an emanation of the justice of Jesus Christ: wherefore justifying grace is a different thing from such an imputation; and what was said in the Council of Trent is nothing but a repetition of the Council of Carthage, whose decrees appeared by so much the more inviolable to the Fathers at Trent, as the Fathers of Carthage were sensible, in proposing them, they proposed nothing else on this subject, but what "had always been approved of in the Catholic Church spread over the entire earth."[239]

144.—*Touching gratuity.*

Our forefathers, therefore, did not believe, in order to destroy human glory and attribute all to Jesus Christ, that it was necessary, either to take from man that justice which was in him, or to diminish the value, or deny the effect thereof: but believed they ought to acknowledge it as proceeding from God only by a gratuitous bounty, and this also was what the Fathers of Trent acknowledged after them, as above seen in many places of this work.[240]

It is in this sense that the Catholic Church had always confessed after St. Paul, that "Jesus Christ is made unto us wisdom,"[241] not by simply imputing to us that wisdom which is in him, but by infusing into our souls that wisdom which flows from his; that he is "unto us justice and sanctity," in the same sense that he is redemption, not by covering our crimes only, but by defacing them entirely by his Holy Spirit poured into our hearts: moreover, that we are "made the justice of God in Jesus Christ,"[242] in a manner more intimate than Jesus Christ "had been made to be sin for us, since God had made him sin," to wit, the victim for sin, by treating him as a sinner though he were just; whereas, he "had made us the justice of God in him," not by leaving us our sins, and merely by treating us as just men, but by taking from us our sins, and by rendering us just.

145.—*Touching the preparations to Grace, that they all proceed from Grace.*

In order to make this grace inherent in us absolutely gratuitous, our forefathers did not believe that it was necessary to say, one cannot dispose himself for them by good desires, nor obtain them by prayers; but they believed these good desires and prayers were themselves inspired of God; and this is what the Council of Trent[243] has done after their example, when it said, that all our good dispositions came "from a prevenient grace;" that we could not "dispose and prepare ourselves" for grace, but as we are "excited and assisted by grace itself;" that God is the source of all justice, and in this quality ought to be beloved; and that there was "no believing, hoping, loving, nor repenting as we ought, so that the grace of justification might be conferred upon us, without a prevenient inspiration of the Holy Ghost."[244] Wherein this Holy Council has done no more than repeat what we read in the Council of Orange, viz. "that we can neither will, nor believe, nor think, nor love as we ought to do, and advantageously, but by the inspiration of prevenient grace;"[245] that is to say, they would not dispute either against heretics, or against infidels, or even against heathens, or, in a word, against any others who imagine they love God, and who feel in effect inclinations so like those to the faithful: but without entering with them into an impossible discussion of the precise differences of their sentiments from those of the just, they were satisfied with defining, that what is performed without grace, is not "as it ought to be," nor agreeable to God, since "without faith it is impossible to please him."[246]

146.—*Touching the necessity of preserving Free-will together with Grace.*

If the Council of Trent, in defending the grace of God, hath, at the same time, maintained Free-will, this also was a faithful repetition of the sentiments of our forefathers, when they defined, against the Pelagians, "that grace destroyed not free-will, but set it at liberty, to the end that, from being darkened it might become full of light; from sick, healthy; from depraved, upright; from imprudent, provident and wise;"[247] for which reason the grace of God was called "an aid and a succor of the free-will;" consequently, something which, far from destroying, conserved and perfected it.

147.—*Touching the merit of good-works.*

According to so pure a notion, far from fearing the word merit, which indeed naturally expressed the dignity of good-works, our Fathers maintained it against the remnant of Pelagians in the same Council of Orange,[248] by these words repeated in that of Trent, "the goodness of God is so great to all mankind, that what he gives us, he will even have to be our merit;"[249] from whence it follows, as likewise the same Fathers of the Council of Orange have decided, "that all the works and merits of the saints ought to be referred to

God's glory, because none can please him except by the things which he has given."[250]

Lastly, if at Trent they did not fear to acknowledge, with a holy confidence, that eternal recompense is due to good-works, it is still in conformity with, and on the same principles that our Fathers had said in the Council of Orange, "that merits do not precede grace, and that recompense is only due to good-works on account that grace, which was not due, did not precede them."[251]

148.—*Touching the fulfilling of God's commandments.*

By this means we find in the Christian a true justice, but which is given him by God together with his love, and which accordingly makes him accomplish his commandments, wherein the Council of Trent likewise does not but follow that rule of the Fathers of Orange: viz., "after having received the grace by baptism, all the baptized, with the grace and co-operation of Jesus Christ, can and ought to fulfil what appertains to salvation, if they will labor faithfully;"[252] where these Fathers have united Jesus Christ's co-operating grace with man's labor and faithful correspondence, agreeably to that saying of St. Paul, "Yet, not I, but the grace of God with me."[253]

149.—*Touching the Truth, and withal, the imperfection of our Justice.*

Notwithstanding this opinion which we have of Christian justice, yet we do not believe that it is perfect and wholly irreprehensible, since we place the principal part thereof in continually demanding the forgiveness of sins: and if we believe these sins, whereof the most just are obliged daily to implore forgiveness, do not hinder them from being truly just, the Council of Trent has moreover taken this so necessary a decision from the Council of Carthage, which declares "that the saints are they who say humbly and truly at the same time, 'forgive us our trespasses;' that the apostle St. James, although holy and just, said, nevertheless, 'we all offend in many things:' that Daniel also, though holy and just, yet did say, 'we have sinned.'"[254] Whence it follows that such sins hinder not holiness and justice, because they hinder not the love of God from reigning in our hearts.

150.—*God accepts our good works for the love of Jesus Christ.*

Now, if the Council of Carthage, on account of these sins, will have us continually say to God, "Enter not into judgment with thy servant, for no man living shall be justified in thy sight;"[255] we understand this, as does that Council, of perfect justice, without excluding from the just man a true justice; acknowledging, nevertheless, that it is also by an effect of a gratuitous bounty, and for the love of Jesus Christ, that God, who could have set at as high a price as he pleased, to condemned persons as we were, so great a good as life eternal, did not exact of us a righteousness without blemish, and, on the contrary, has consented to judge us, not with extremity of rigor, but with a rigor tempered and suited to our weakness, which obliged the Council of

Trent to acknowledge "that man hath not wherewith to glorify himself, but all his glory is in Christ Jesus, in whom we live, in whom we merit, in whom we satisfy, doing worthy fruits of penance which derive from him their virtue; by him are offered to his Father, and for the love of him are accepted by his Father."[256]

151.—*That the Holy Fathers have detested no less than we, as a blasphemy, the doctrine which makes God equally predestinate to good and evil.*

The rock to be feared in celebrating the mystery of Predestination, was the admitting it equally in respect of good and evil; and if the Church abhorred the crime of the pretended Reformers guilty of this excess, she did but walk in the steps of the Council of Orange, which pronounces an eternal "anathema, with utter detestation, against those who should dare to say that man is predestinated to evil by the divine power;"[257] and of the Council of Valentia, deciding, in like manner, "that God, by his fore-knowledge, doth impose on no man the necessity of sinning, but foresees only what man would be by his own will; so that the wicked do not perish on account that they had not the power of being good, but because they would not become good, or because they would not remain in the grace they had received."[258]

152.—*The Church always found in the same situation.*

Thus, when a question has been once judged in the Church, as she never fails to decide it according to the tradition of all past ages, so, should it happen to be moved again in succeeding times, you find the Church, after a thousand or twelve hundred years, always in the same situation, always ready to oppose against the enemies of truth the same decrees which the Holy Apostolic See and Catholic Unanimity had pronounced, without ever adding anything thereto, save what is necessary against new errors.

153.—*Our Fathers have rejected, as well as we, the certainty of Salvation and Righteousness.*

To conclude what remains on the subject of justifying grace, I find no decision touching the certainty of salvation, because as yet nothing had obliged the Church to pronounce on this point: yet none has contradicted St. Austin, who teaches "that this certainty is not beneficial in this state of temptation, in which assurance might produce pride;"[259] which also extends itself, as is plain, to the certainty one might have of present righteousness, so that the Catholic Church, whilst she inspires into her children so great a confidence as to exclude perturbation and trouble, yet leaves in them, after the example of the Apostles, the counterpoise of fear, and no less teaches man to distrust himself than to trust absolutely in God.

154.—*Malancthon agrees that the article of Justification is easy to be reconciled.*

In fine, if all that has been seen granted in this work by our adversaries, touching justification and the merits of the saints, be reviewed, it will entirely convince a man that there is not the least occasion to complain of the doctrine of the Church.[260] Melancthon, so zealous for this article, owns nevertheless that "it is easy to come to an agreement on both sides:" what he seems most to insist upon is the certainty of justice; but every humble Christian will easily rest contented with the same certainty with respect to justice as to eternal salvation: all the comfort man ought to have in this life is that of excluding by hope, not only despair, but also trouble and anguish; nor is there anything to reproach a Christian with, who, assured on God's side, has no longer anything to fear or doubt but from himself.

155.—*The clearness of the decisions of the Church.*—*She cuts away the root of abuses in regard of Prayer to the Saints.*

The decisions of the Catholic Church are not less clear and precise than they are firm and lasting, always obviating whatever might give occasion to the mind of man going astray.[261] Honoring the Saints in her assemblies, was honoring God, the author of their sanctity and bliss; and demanding of them the partnership of their prayers, was joining ourselves to the choirs of angels, to the spirits of the perfectly just, and to the Church of the first-born which are in heaven. So holy a practice may be discovered ever since the first ages, nor is the beginning of it to be discovered there, since none can then be found who were noted for innovation in that regard. The thing most to be feared with respect to the ignorant was, lest they should make the invocation of saints too like to that of God, and their intercession too like that of Jesus Christ: but the Council of Trent[262] instructs us fully as to these two points, by warning us that the saints pray,—which places them at an infinite distance from him who gives; and that they pray through Jesus Christ,—which places them infinitely beneath him who is heard through himself.

156.—*Regarding Images.*

Setting up images is rendering sensible the mysteries and examples which sanctify us. The thing to be feared in respect of the ignorant is, lest they should believe that the divine nature might be represented, or rendered present in images, or, at all events, lest they should look upon them as filled with some virtue for which they are honored; these are the three characters of idolatry. But the Council has rejected them in plain terms,[263] so that it is not lawful to attribute to one image more virtue than to another, nor, by consequence, to frequent one more than another, unless in memory of some miracles, or some pious history which might excite devotion.[264] The use of images being thus purified, Luther himself and the Lutherans will demonstrate that images of this kind are not what the Decalogue speaks of, and the honor rendered to them will be manifestly nothing else than a sensible and exterior testimony of the pious remembrance they excite, and the simple and natural effect of that mute language which accompanies these pious representations, and whose usefulness is so much the greater, as it is capable of being understood by all mankind.

157.—*Regarding Worship in general.*

In general, worship is referred to the interior and exterior exercise of faith, of hope, and of charity, and principally to that of this last virtue, whose property is to unite us with God; so that a worship in spirit and in truth exists everywhere, wherever there is to be found the exercise of charity towards God or towards our neighbor, conformably to that saying of St. James, "Pure religion, and undefiled before God is this, to visit the fatherless and widows, and to keep himself unspotted from the world;"[265] and every act of piety not animated with this spirit is imperfect, carnal, or superstitious.

158.—*Against those who accuse the Council of Trent of having spoken ambiguously.*

Under pretext that the Council of Trent declined entering into many difficulties, our adversaries, after Fra Paolo, are continually blaming it as having explained the dogmas in general, obscure, and equivocal terms, with the design of pleasing in appearance the greatest number: but they would entertain more equitable sentiments, did they but consider, that God, who knows how far he designs to guide our understanding in revealing to us some truth, or some mystery, does not always reveal to us either the ways of explaining it, or the circumstances which accompany it, or even wherein it consists as to its utmost precision or, as we speak in schools, as to its specific difference; so that, in Church decisions, it is often necessary to keep to general expressions, in order to retain that measure of faith so much commended by St. Paul,[266] and not to transgress his precept forbidding us to be more wise than we ought to be.

159.—*The Principles of Protestants prove the necessity of Purgatory.*

For example, in the controversy concerning Purgatory, the Council of Trent has firmly believed as a truth revealed by God, that just souls may depart this life without being wholly purified. Grotius proves evidently,[267] that this truth is confessed by Protestants, by Mestresat, by Spanheim, by Calvin himself, on this common ground-work of the Reformation, viz. that in the whole course of this life the soul is never entirely pure, whence it follows that she is still defiled at her departure from the body. But the Holy Ghost hath pronounced that "not anything that is polluted shall enter into the holy city;"[268] and the minister Spanheim[269] proves unanswerably, that the soul cannot be presented to God till she be "without spot or wrinkle, all holy, pure, and irreproachable," conformably to the doctrine of St. Paul,[270] which he allows she cannot be, during this mortal life.

160.—*Protestants do not reject the purification of souls after this life.*

After this still remains the question, whether or not this purification of the soul be wrought in this life at the last moment, or after death; and Spanheim leaves the thing undecided: "The main point," says he, "is uncertain, but the manner and circumstances are not so."[271] But without further pressing this author with the principles of the sect, the Catholic Church advances beyond this: for the tradition of all ages having taught her to pray in behalf of the dead, for the comfort of their souls, for the forgiveness of their sins, and their relief, she has held it for a certain truth, that the perfect purification of souls was performed after death, and this by secret pains not alike explained by the holy doctors, but of which they said only, that they might be mitigated and wholly remitted by prayers and oblations, answerably to the Liturgies of all Churches.

161.—*Moderation of the Church in not determining anything but what is certain.*

Without examining in this place whether this sentiment be good or bad, it were no longer equitable, or candid, to refuse granting us, that in this presupposition at least, the Council ought to have formed its decree in a general expression, and defined as it has done:[272] first, that there is a Purgatory after this life; secondly, that the prayers of the living may afford relief to faithful souls departed, without descending to particulars, either of their pains or the manner in which they are purified, because tradition did not explain it; but showing only that they are purified by Jesus Christ alone, they being purified only by prayers and oblations made in his name.

162.—*The difference of general terms, from indefinite, perplexed, or ambiguous terms.*

The same judgment ought to be passed on other decisions, and are taken not to confound, as our reformed here do, general with indefinite, intricate, or ambiguous terms. Indefinite terms signify nothing; ambiguous terms signify equivocally, and leave in the mind no determinate sense; intricate terms raise a mist of confused ideas; but although general terms carry not the evidence as far as the utmost precision, they are, however, to a certain degree perspicuous.

163.—*General terms are clear in their way.*

Our adversaries will not deny that the passages of Scripture, which say that the holy Ghost proceeds from the Father, denote clearly some truth, since they denote, beyond all doubt, that the third person of the Trinity derives his origin from the Father no less than the second, although they do not express specifically wherein his procession consists, nor wherein it is different from that of the Son. It is, therefore, plain, that general expressions cannot be blamed, without blaming at the same time Jesus Christ and the Gospel.

164.—*In what consists the clearness of a decision.*

It is in this that our adversaries always show themselves unjust to the Council, sometimes blaming it for descending too much to particulars, and sometimes requiring it should have decided all the disputes of the Scotists and Thomists, under penalty of being convicted of affected obscurity: as if they were ignorant that, in decisions of faith, a free scope ought to be allowed to divines for proposing different means of explaining the Christian truths, and, consequently, that a council, waiving their several and particular opinions, ought to keep itself within the compass of such essential points, as they all defend in common. This method of defining the articles of our faith is so far from speaking equivocally, that, on the contrary, it is an effect of clearness to define so plainly that which is certain, as not to involve in the decision what is doubtful; nor is there anything more becoming the authority and majesty of a Council, than to repress the impetuosity of those who would advance beyond these bounds.

>165.—*That which is certain in regard of the Pope's authority, acknowledged in the Council and by the Catholic Doctors.*

Conformably to this rule, a form for explaining the Pope's authority having been proposed at Trent in such terms as that his superiority over the general Council might in some manner be inferred, the Cardinal of Lorraine and the Bishops of France being opposed to it, Cardinal Pallavicini himself relates in his history, that the form was suppressed, and the Pope answered, that "Nothing ought to be defined but what all the Fathers should unanimously agree to;"[273] an admirable rule in order to separate what is certain from what is doubtful! Whence it also came to pass that the Cardinal du Perron, although a zealous defender of the interests of the Court of Rome, declared to the King of England, "That the dispute concerning the Pope's authority, whether in its spiritual regard to Œcumenical Councils, or in its temporal regard to secular jurisdictions, is not a dispute about things that are held for articles of faith, or are inserted and required in the Confession of Faith, or that could hinder his Majesty from entering into the Church, should he be satisfied in other points."[274] And even in our days, the renowned Andrew du Val,[275] doctor of Sorbonne, to whom those on the other side of the Alps referred the defence of their cause, decided that the doctrine denying the Pope's infallibility is not absolutely against faith; and that which places the Council above the Pope cannot be branded with any censure, either of heresy, or error, or even of temerity.

>166.—*With this moderation, Melancthon would have owned the pope's authority.*

Thereby it appears that doctrines, not supported by a certain and perpetual tradition, cannot strike root in the Church, since they make not a part of her confession of faith; and that even those who teach them, teach them as their particular doctrine and not as the doctrine of the Catholic Church.[276] To reject the supremacy and authority of the Holy See, with this wholesome moderation, is to reject the band of Christians, is to be at enmity with order and peace, and to envy the Church that good which Melancthon himself wished it might enjoy.[277]

>167.—*Abridgment of this last book, and first, touching the perpetual Visibility of the Church.*

After what has been seen, there is nothing left at present that can hinder our reformed from submitting to the Church; the shelter of a Church invisible is abandoned: no longer is it allowable to allege in its defence the obscurities of the Jewish Church; the ministers have freed us from the trouble of answering on that head, by showing clearly, that the true worship was never interrupted, not even under Achaz and Manasses:[278] the Christian society, more extensive than that of the Jews, according to the conditions of its covenant, has likewise stood more firm, and the perpetual visibility of the Catholic Church can be no longer doubted of.

168.—A remark on the Confession of Augsburg.

Those of the confession of Augsburg are yet more obliged to acknowledge it than the Calvinists:[279] the Invisible Church has neither found place in their Confession of Faith, nor in their apology, wherein, on the contrary, we have seen the Church spoken of in the Creed vested with a perpetual visibility, and, according to these principles, they should be able to show us an assembly made up of pastors and people, in which sound doctrine and the Sacraments have ever flourished.

169.—The arguments brought by them against the authority of the Church,
are resolved by the Ministers.

All the arguments that were formed against the authority of the Church are given up. Yielding to the authority of the Universal Church, is now no longer acting unadvisedly nor submitting to men, since they own that her sentiments are the rule, nay, the most sure rule, for deciding the most important truths of religion.[280] They agree, if this rule had been followed, and men had proposed to themselves the understanding holy Scripture as it was understood by the Universal Church, that there never would have been Socinians; never should we have heard the divinity of Jesus Christ called in question, the immortality of the soul, the eternity of pains, the creation, God's foreknowledge, the spirituality of his essence: things so firmly believed among Christians, that they did not so much as think they could be ever doubted of, and which at present are impugned with such captious arguments, that many weak minds are ensnared thereby. They agree that the authority of the Universal Church is an infallible remedy against this disorder; so that the authority of the Church, far from being, what was said in the Reformation, a means of introducing all manner of new-fangled doctrines amongst Christians, is, on the contrary, a certain means of putting a stop to the licentiousness of men's minds, of preventing the abuse they make of the sublimity of Scripture, after a manner so dangerous to the salvation of souls.

The Reformation has discovered these truths at last; and if the Lutherans will not receive them from the hands of a Calvinist minister, they have but to explain to us how they can resist the authority of the Church after having owned that the truth is always manifest in her.[281]

170.—Salvation to be had in the Church of Rome.

None now, of whatever separate communions, should any longer hesitate to come and seek eternal life in the bosom of the Church of Rome, since it is confessed[282] that God's true people and his true elect are still in her, as it hath always been confessed that they were before the pretended Reformation. But it is perceived at length, that the difference put between the ages that preceded, and those which followed it, was vain, and that the difficulty which was made of acknowledging this truth, proceeded from evil policy.

Should the Lutherans here start new difficulties, and not suffer themselves to be persuaded by the sentiments of Calixtus, let them show us what the Church of Rome has done since Luther's time to forfeit the title of a true Church, and so to lose her fecundity, that the elect can be no longer born in her womb.

171.—*The Ministers are not to be believed when they make Salvation so difficult in the Church of Rome.*

True it is, when the ministers acknowledge you may be saved in the Church of Rome, they would make you believe you must do it as in an infected air, and by a kind of miracle, by reason of her impieties and idolatries. But men should learn to distinguish, in the ministers, what hatred has made them add, from what truth has forced them to confess. If the Church of Rome made profession of impiety and idolatry, no salvation could have been had in her, either before or after the Reformation; and if, both before and after, salvation may be had in her body, the accusation of impiety and idolatry is unworthy and calumnious.

172.—*Excesses of the Ministers who prefer the Arian Sect to the Church of Rome.*

And, indeed, the hatred they show to her is but too visible, since they are so far transported as to say, that without doubt a man may save his soul in that communion, but with greater difficulty than "amongst the Arians,"[283] who deny the divinity of the Son of God and of the Holy Ghost; who, by consequence, believe themselves devoted to creatures by baptism; who, in the Eucharist, look on the flesh of a man, who is not God, as the source of life; who believe that, without being God, a man has saved them, and was able to pay the price of their redemption; who invoke him as the person to whom all power is given in heaven and on earth; who are consecrated to the Holy Ghost, namely, to a creature, to become his temples; who believe that a creature, to wit, the same Holy Ghost, distributes grace to them as he pleases, regenerates them, and sanctifies them by his presence. This is the sect they prefer to the Church of Rome; and is not this saying to all that are capable of understanding, Believe not one word we say; when we speak of that Church, hatred possesses and sets us beside ourselves.

173.—*The Protestants can no longer excuse themselves from Schism.*

Lastly, there is no longer any possibility for our reformed to avoid being reckoned amongst the number of those "who separate themselves, and who make a sect apart," contrary to the precept of the Apostles, particularly St.

Jude,[284] and contrary to the import of their own Catechism.[285] Here are
its very words in the exposition of the Creed: "The article of forgiveness of
sins is placed after that of the Catholic Church, because no one obtains pardon
for his sins except beforehand he be incorporated with God's people, and
persevere in unity and communion with the body of Christ, and so be a
member of the Church; insomuch that, out of the Church, there is nothing
but death and damnation; for all those who separate from the society of the
faithful, *to make a sect apart*, ought not to hope for salvation whilst they are in
division."

The article speaks clearly of the Universal Church, visible and always
visible, and in this we have seen that they are agreed:[286] they are agreed
likewise, as to a fact certain and notorious, that the Churches, which call
themselves reformed, at their renouncing the communion of the Church of
Rome, did not find on earth one Church which they united with: they
therefore made a sect apart from the whole body of Christians and the
Universal Church; and, according to their own doctrine, renounce the grace
of forgiveness of sins, which is the fruit of the blood of Jesus Christ; and death
and damnation is their lot.

174.—Short repetition of the absurdities of the new System.

The absurdities, necessarily attending the answer to this argument, plainly
discover how invincible it is; for after a thousand fruitless shifts, they were, in
fine, driven into such straits as even to say,[287] that you remain in the
Catholic and Universal Church, in renouncing the communion of all
Churches in the world, and in making a Church apart; that you remain in the
same Universal Church although driven from it by a just censure; that you
cannot go forth from it by any other crime than that of apostacy, by
renouncing Christianity and your baptism; that all the Christian sects, how
divided soever they be, are one and the same body, and one and the same
Church in Jesus Christ; that Christian Churches have no exterior band of
union by the appointment of Jesus Christ; that their band is arbitrary; that the
Confessions of Faith whereby they unite themselves, are arbitrary likewise, and
contracts susceptible of what terms you please, which yet may not be broken
without incurring the guilt of Schism: that the union of Churches depends on
empires and the will of princes; that all Christian Churches are naturally, and
by their origin, independent one of another, whence it follows that the
Independents, so grievously censured at Charenton, do nothing else but stand
up for the natural liberty of Churches; that, provided you find means of
assembling together either with consent or by violence so as "to make a figure
in the world," you are a true member of the body of the Catholic Church;
that no heresy ever has, or can be, condemned by a judgment of the Universal
Church; nay, that there is not, nor can be, any ecclesiastical judgment in
matters of faith; that men have no right to exact subscriptions to the decrees
of Synods respecting faith; that one may save his soul in the most perverse
sects, even in that of the Socinians.

175.—The height of the absurdities, viz. the kingdom of Jesus Christ confounded with the kingdom of Satan.

There would be no end were I to repeat all the absurdities it was necessary to vent in order to save the Reformation from the sentence pronounced against those "who make a sect apart." But, besides that it is needless to enter into a detail of them, they are all comprised in this one which has been always more or less maintained in the Reformation, and wherein the whole defence of the cause is placed now more than ever; viz. "that the Catholic Church," whereof the Creed speaks, is one heap of sects divided amongst one another, and which anathematize one another;[288] insomuch that the character of the kingdom of Jesus Christ is the same with that given by Jesus Christ to the kingdom of Satan, as above explained.

But nothing is more opposite to the doctrine of Christ himself. According to his doctrine, the kingdom of Satan is divided against itself,[289] and must fall, house upon house, to utter desolation. On the contrary, according to the promise of Jesus Christ, his Church, which is his kingdom built on the rock,[290] on the same Confession of Faith, and the same ecclesiastical government, is perfectly united: whence it follows that she is immovable, and the gates of hell shall not prevail against her; that is to say, division, the cause of weakness and the character of hell, shall not get the better of unity, the cause of strength, and the character of the Church. But all this order is changed in the Reformation; and the kingdom of Jesus Christ being divided like to that of Satan, no wonder men have said, conformably to such a principle, that it was fallen to ruin and desolation.

176.—The immovable steadfastness of the Church.—Conclusion of this Work.

These maxims of division were the ground-work of the Reformation, inasmuch as it was established by an universal rupture, and a Church-unity has never been known therein: and therefore its Variations, whose history we have at length concluded, have shown us what it was, to wit, a kingdom disunited, divided against itself, and which must fall sooner or later; whilst the Catholic Church, so unalterably attached to decrees once pronounced, that not the least variation since the origin of Christianity can be discovered in her, shows herself a Church built on the rock, always in full security from the promises she has received, firm in her principles, and guided by a Spirit which never contradicts himself.

May He who holds in his hand the hearts of men, and who alone knows the bounds he has set to rebellious sects, and to the afflictions of his Church, cause all his stray children quickly to return to her unity; and may we have the joy to behold with our eyes Israel, so unfortunately divided, unite under one and the same head with Judah.[291]

Notes

¹ Tit. iii. 11.

² 2 Tim. iii. 7.

³ Conf. avec M. Cl. p. 13, et seq.

⁴ Conf. Aug. Art. vii.

⁵ Apol. Tit. de Ecc. p. 144.

⁶ Ibid. pp. 145, 146.

⁷ Ibid.

⁸ Ibid. p. 48.

⁹ Ibid. p. 156.

¹⁰ S. lib. iii. n. 59.

¹¹ Art. Smal. Concord. p. 345.

¹² Cap. de Ecc. Syn. Gen. part ii. p. 72.

¹³ Cap. de Cœn. p. 72.

¹⁴ Cap. de Ecc. Ibid. p. 132. Ibid. c. de Conc. p. 134.

¹⁵ Syn. Gen. Art. viii. p. 186.

¹⁶ S. l. xi. n. 176.

¹⁷ Syn. Gen. p. 187.

¹⁸ Conf. Argent. c. xv. de Eccl. Synt. Gen. part i. p. 191.

¹⁹ Ibid. cap. xvi.

²⁰ Ibid. Art. 14, 15.

²¹ Syn. Gen. cap. xvii. p. 31.

²² Ibid. pp. 33, 34.

²³ Syst. p. 226.

²⁴ Syn. Gen. Art. 27. p. 140.

²⁵ Ib. Art. 28.

²⁶ Ib. Art. 29.

²⁷ Syn. Gen. Art. 19, p. 103.

²⁸ Ibid. Art. 16, de Eccl. p. 118, Art. 18, p. 119.

²⁹ Catech. Dim. xv.

³⁰ Dim. xvi.

³¹ Instit. l. iv. c. 1. n. 2.

³² N. 3.

³³ Conf. avec. M. Cl. p. 9, et seq.

³⁴ Instit. iv. c. xi. n. 2.

³⁵ Synod. de Gap. ch. de la Conf. de Foi.

³⁶ Syn. de la Roch. 1607.

³⁷ Rep. au Disc. de M. de Cond. p. 220.

³⁸ Def. de la Rep. p. i. ch. iv. et p. iv. ch. iv. Rep. à M. de Cond. pp. 313, 333.

³⁹ Ibid. pp. 307, 313.

⁴⁰ Rep. au Disc. de M. de Cond. p. 73. Ib. pp. 82, 83, et seq.

⁴¹ Rep. au Disc. de M. de Cond. p. 105. Matt. xvi. 18.

⁴² Conf. avec M. Cl. p. 36. Rep. au. Disc. de M. de Cond. pp. 106, 107.

⁴³ Rep. au Disc.

⁴⁴ Rep. au Disc. de M. de Cond. pp. 79, 95, 115, 121, 146, 243.

⁴⁵ Ibid. pp. 130, &c. 145, &c. 360, 369, &c. 373, 378.

⁴⁶ Def. de la Rep. p. iii. ch. v. p. 289. Rep. au Disc. de M. de Cond.

⁴⁷ Inst. l. iv. c. ii. n. 2. S. n. 26.

⁴⁸ Ibid.

⁴⁹ Rep. de M. Cl. au Disc. de M. de Meaux, pp. 128, 146, 149, 247, 561, &c.

⁵⁰ Def. de la Ref. p. 265. Rep. au Disc. de M. de Cond. p. 370, 358 &c.

⁵¹ Ibid. p. iii. ch. v. p. 289.

⁵² Rep. au Disc. de Cond. p. 368.

⁵³ Rep. au Disc. de M. de Cond. p. 357.

⁵⁴ Ibid. pp. 360, 361, &c. 369, &c.

⁵⁵ Sup. l. xi. n. 106, 107, 117, 149, &c.

⁵⁶ Rep. au Disc. de M. de Cond. p. 460.

⁵⁷ Rep. au Disc. de M. de Cond. p. 363. Rep. à la Let. Past. de M. de Meaux.

⁵⁸ 2 Tim. ii. 17.

⁵⁹ Ibid.

⁶⁰ Def. de la Rep. pp. 47, 49, 314. Rep. au Disc. de M. de Cond. pp. 89, 92, 245, 247.

⁶¹ P. 63, et seq.

⁶² Syst. de l'Egl. l. i. ch. xx. xxi., &c.

⁶³ System. Pref. towards the end.

⁶⁴ Luke xi. 17, 18.

⁶⁵ Calixt. de fid. et stud. Conc. Ecc. n. 1, 2, 3, 4, &c Ludg. Bat. 1651.

⁶⁶ Avert. aux. Prot. de l'Eur. at the beginning of the Prejug. p. 19.

⁶⁷ Ibid. p.12.

⁶⁸ Prejug. p. 4.

⁶⁹ Prej. leg. p.4.

⁷⁰ Ibid. p. 4, &c. p. 8.

⁷¹ Ibid. p. 133, &c.

⁷² Prej. leg. ch. i. Syst. l. i. ch. i.

⁷³ Prej. leg. ch. i. Syst. l. i. ch. i. p. 5.

⁷⁴ Ibid.

⁷⁵ Ibid. p. 6.

⁷⁶ Syst. pp. 147, 149.

⁷⁷ Ibid. p. 155.

[78] Prej. ch. i. p. 16.
[79] Ibid.
[80] Syst. p. 145.
[81] Gal. vi. 16.
[82] Rev. xviii. 4.
[83] Syst. pp. 173, 174.
[84] Syst. pp. 158, 164, 259.
[85] Ibid. pp. 174, 175, 195.
[86] Syst. pp. 539, 548.
[87] Gal. v. 2.
[88] Syst. p. 548.
[89] S. n. 37, 41.
[90] Ibid. p. 216.
[91] Prej. legit. p. 24.
[92] Art. xxviii. S. n. 26.
[93] Ibid.
[94] Prej. legit. p. 25. Syst. p. 214.
[95] Ibid. p. 25.
[96] Ibid.
[97] Art. xxviii.
[98] Ibid. S. n. 15.
[99] Matt. xviii. 17.
[100] 2 Syn. of Par. 1565. Disci. ch. 5. Art. 17. p. 102.
[101] Syst. l. ii. ch. iii.
[102] Syst. p. 24, &c.
[103] Ibid.
[104] Prej. p. 6. Syst. pp. 246, &c. 254, 262, 269, 305, 557.
[105] Ibid. p. 265.
[106] Syst. p. 254.
[107] Ibid.
[108] Ibid. p. 249.
[109] Ibid. p. 254.
[110] Lib. iii. ch. xv. p. 547.
[111] Ibid.
[112] Disc. ch. vi. of the union of Churches. Notes on the 2d Art. p. 118.
[113] Syst. p. 546.
[114] Fasci. Ep. Lud. Moli.
[115] Syst. l. i. ch. vii. viii.
[116] Ibid. p. 55.
[117] Syst. l. i. ch. vii. viii. p. 56.
[118] Epist. Cyp. ad Antonian, &c.
[119] Syst. p. 61.
[120] Syst. p. 234.
[121] Conc. Nic. Can. viii.
[122] Ibid. Can. xix.
[123] Conc. c. p. Epist. ad Omn. Episc.
[124] Prej. leg. ch. ii. pp. 27, 28. Syst. p. 217.

[125] Prej. p. 29.
[126] Luke xi. 17.
[127] Catechism of the Prot. Ref. Dim. 17.
[128] Kings iii. 12, 2 Par. ix. 13.
[129] 2 Paralip. xi. 15.
[130] Syst. l. i. ch. xiii.
[131] Syst. l. i. ch. xx. p. 153.
[132] Ibid. ch. xiv, xxi. p. 167.
[133] Acts xxi.
[134] Rom. xi. 17, &c.
[135] Syst. Ibid. ch. xx. p. 167.
[136] Gal. v. 2, 4.
[137] Prej. leg. pp. 4, 5, &c.
[138] Syst. pp. 147, 149, &c. Prej. leg. p. 16. Syst. 1. i. ch. xii. pp. 98, 102; ch. xix. p. 149, &c.; ch. xx. p. 15 &c.
[139] Ibid.
[140] Prej. p. 22.
[141] Num. xvi. 26.
[142] Syst. 1. i. ch. xxix. p. 226.; l. iii. ch. xvii.
[143] Syst. p. 215.
[144] Ibid. p. 217.
[145] Ibid. p. 215.
[146] Syst. p. 2
[147] L. iii. ch. xv. p. 549, &c.
[148] Ibid. pp. 228, 229.
[149] Matt. xxviii. 19, 20.
[150] Syst. pp. 539, 548.
[151] Prej. leg. ch. ii. pp. 21, 22, &c. Syst. p. 221.
[152] Prej. leg. pp. 21, 22, &c. Syst. p. 221.
[153] Syst. p. 125. Prej. p. 22.
[154] Rep. an disc. de M. de Cond. p. 383, et seq.
[155] Syst. pp. 228, 229.
[156] Ibid.
[157] Matt. xxviii. 20.
[158] Prej. leg. p. 21.
[159] Matt. xvi. 18.
[160] Syst. i. ch. xxvi. pp. 217, 218.
[161] Ibid. p. 218.
[162] Ibid. p. 215.
[163] Syst. pp. 6, 218, 233, 234, 235, 236.
[164] Syst. p. 27.
[165] Ibid.
[166] Syst. p. 237.
[167] Syst. l. iii. ch. iv. p. 463.
[168] See Sect. 71, of this Book, et seq.
[169] Luke xi. 17.

[170] Syst. l. ii. ch. i. p. 238.
[171] Ibid.
[172] P. 236.
[173] John xvi. 13.
[174] Gal. ii. 18.
[175] Dr. Bull, def. fid. Nic. prœm, n. 2. p. 2. Ibid. n. 3.
[176] Socra. l. i. c. 9.
[177] Syst. l. iii. ch. ii. p. 243. ch. iii. p. 251 .ch. iv. p. 258. Ibid. 243. p. 255.
[178] Syst. l. iii. ch. ii. p. 243. ch. iii. p. 251. ch. iv. p. 258. Ibid. 243. p. 257.
[179] Disc. ch. viii. Art. x
[180] Ibid. v. Art. xxxii. p. 114.
[181] Syst. p. 257.
[182] Disc. Ibid.
[183] S. l. xii.
[184] Syst. p. 306.
[185] Ibid. p. 270.
[186] Syst. p. 269. Ibid. Art. xvii.
[187] Sup. n. 105. S. 106, et seq.
[188] Disc. p. 144.
[189] Expos. ch. xix. Conference with M. Claude, pp. 52, 337.
[190] Syst. pp. 270, 271.
[191] Syst. p. 270.
[192] Conference with M. Claude, p. 378.
[193] Syst. p. 428.
[194] Ibid. p. 453, et seq.
[195] Confess. Art. iv.
[196] Syst. l. iii. Ib. ch. ii. p.3.
[197] Def. of the Ref. part ii. ch. ix. p. 296.
[198] Confession of Faith, Art. v.
[199] S. n. 38, et seq.
[200] Acts vi. 3, 6, 7.
[201] Tit. i. 5.
[202] History of Calvin, part i. ch. iv.
[203] Vid. Bibl. Anti-Trinit.
[204] Test. Georg. Sch. et relat. Wisson. in Biblioth. Anti-Trin. Sand. pp. 191, 209.
[205] Ib.
[206] Sleid. lib. iv. fol. 60.
[207] Ibid. lib. vi. fol. 93.
[208] Ibid. fol. 100.
[209] Ibid. lib. viii. fol. 104.
[210] S. lib. iii. n. 3.
[211] Sleid. lib. viii. fol. 125.

[212] S. lib. iv. n. 23. Hosp. part ii. n. 23.
[213] Hosp. An. 1548. fol. 203.
[214] Ibid. An. 1556 et 1563.
[215] Ibid. Conc. discors. c. lvi. p. 278.
[216] Ibid. Conc. discors. c. lvi. fol. 99.
[217] S. lib. iv. n. 32.
[218] S. lib. xi. n. 17, et seq.
[219] Concil. Rom. sub. Nic. II. An. 1059. t. ix. Con. Lab. Guit. lib. iii. t. xv iii. Bib. PP. Max. p. 462, &c.
[220] Guit. lib. i. adv. Beren. Bib. PP. t. xviii. p. 443, 449.
[221] Ber. apud Guit. Ibid. p. 441.
[222] Guit. ante pp. 441, 442, 462, 463, 464. Alg. de Sac. Corp. et Sang. Præf. t. xxi. p. 251.
[223] Ibid.
[224] Conc. Rom. vi. sub Greg. VII. t. x. Conc. Lab. An. 1079.
[225] Bib. PP. Max. t. xviii. p. 417.
[226] Bib. PP. Max. t. xviii. pp. 438, 439.
[227] Ascel. Ep. ad Ber. Guit. Ibid. lib. iii. pp. 462, 463. Lanfranc de Corp. et Sang. Dom. Ibid. c. ii. iv. v. xxii. pp. 765, 766, 776. Ibid. c. iv. p. 765. Ibid. c. xxii. p. 776.
[228] S. l. xi. n. 31, 2, &c.
[229] Conc. Lat. iv. t. xi. Conc. Lab. p. 143.
[230] Dur. Troarn. t. xviii. Bib. PP. p. 422. Guit. Ibid. 462, &c.
[231] S. n. 131. S. l. iii. n. 51, et seq. as far as 56; l. vi. n. 26, 31, et seq.
[232] S. l. ix. n. 26, 27, 28, et seq. as far as n. 75.
[233] Conc. Const. Sess. viii.
[234] Luth. de Sacr. Bapt. t. i. Mel. loc. com. c. de Baptist. Cal. Inst. iv. 15, 19, &c. Casau. not. in Matt. iii. 6. Grot. Ep. 36. Jur. Syst. l. iii. ch. xx. p. 583.
[235] S. l. ii. 10. iii. 60, 61, et seq. vii. 67. xi. 106. xiv, 114, 115. S. n. 43. 61.
[236] S. l. xiv. n. 43.
[237] Conc.Carth.cap.i.
[238] Ibid. cap. iii. iv. v.
[239] Ibid. c. iv.
[240] S. l. iii. n. 20, et seq.
[241] 1 Cor. i. 29, 30, 31.
[242] 2 Cor. v. 21.
[243] Sess. vi. c. v. vi.

[244] Can. i.

[245] Con. Ara. ii. c. 6, 7, 25.

[246] Heb. xi. 6.

[247] Auct. sed. Apost. de grat. inter. dec. Cœlest. P. P.

[248] Conc. Ara.

[249] Conc. Trid. Sess. vi. 16.

[250] Conc. Ara. v.

[251] Ibid. c. xviii.

[252] Conc. Trid. Sess. vi. can. 11. can. 18. cap. xxv.

[253] 1 Cor. xv. 10.

[254] Cap. vii. viii.

[255] Cap. vii. viii.

[256] Sess. xiv. c. viii.

[257] Conc. Arau. c. xxv.

[258] Conc. Valent. iii. c. ii. v.

[259] De correct. et. grat. c. xiii. de Civ. Dei. xi. 12.

[260] S. l. iii. n. 25, et seq., viii. 22, et seq. Sent. Phil. Mel. de pace Ec. p. 10. Bern. Ser. i. de Sept.

[261] S. l. xiii. xiv.

[262] Sess. xxv. decr. de invoc. S. S.

[263] Ibid.

[264] S. l. ii. n. 28.

[265] Jas. i. 27,

[266] Rom. xii. 3.

[267] Grot. Ep. extraor. pp. 575, 578, 579.

[268] Rev. xxi. 27.

[269] Span. dub. Ev. Tem. iii. dub. 141. n. vi. vii.

[270] Ephes. v. 27.

[271] N. vii.

[272] Sess. xxv. dec. de Purg.

[273] Hist. Conc. Trid. interp. Giattin. lib. xix. c. xi. xiii. xiv. xv.

[274] Reply, l. vi. Præf. p. 858.

[275] Du Val. Elench. p. 9. it. tract. de Sup. Rom. Pont. potes. part ii. q. l. p. 4. q. 7 ,8.

[276] Vid. l. iv. 39. v. 24, 25.

[277] Mel. de pace, c. de pot. Pontif. P. 6.

[278] 4 Reg. xvi. 4, 15. xxi. Jur. Syst. pp. 222, 223.

[279] S. n. 4. et seq. to n. 10.

[280] S. n. 86, 87, et seq.

[281] S. n. 4. et seq.

[282] S. n. 50, 51 et seq. as far as n. 59.

[283] Prej. leg. part i. ch. i. Syst. p. 225.

[284] Jud. xvii. 18.

[285] Dim. xvi.

[286] S. n. 21, 22, 34, 35, et seq. 68, 81, 82, 83.

[287] S. n. 65, &c.

[288] S. n. 51, &c.

[289] Luke xi.

[290] Matt. xvi.

[291] Hosea i. 11.

A MATERIAL APPENDIX

TO THE FOURTEENTH BOOK

1.—*A new Book written by the Minister Jurieu concerning the union of the Calvinists with the Lutherans.*

AFTER this work was finished, a Latin book fell into my hands, which the indefatigable Jurieu has just brought to light, and whereof it is requisite I should give the public some account. The title is, "An Amicable Consultation concerning Peace between the Protestants." Therein he treats of this subject with the Doctor Daniel Severin Scultet, who, on his side, proposes to himself to smooth the difficulties of this peace, so frequently and so unsuccessfully attempted. The question chiefly in debate is that of predestination and grace. The Lutheran cannot digest what was defined at the Synod of Dort touching absolute decrees and irresistible grace: he judges still more insupportable what the Synod teaches of the inamissibility of justice, and the certainty of salvation, there being nothing, in his notion, more impious than to give to man once justified, a certain assurance in the midst of the most heinous crimes, that they shall neither make him forfeit his salvation in eternity, nor in time even the Holy Ghost and the grace of adoption. I repeat not the explanation of these questions, which the reader must have understood from the account given of them in this history;[1] but shall only say, that this is what is called, among the Lutherans, the *particularism* of the Calvinists: so abominable a heresy that they charge it with nothing less than of making God the author of sin, and of subverting all Christian morality, by inspiring with a pernicious security those who are abandoned to the most abominable enormities. M. Jurieu does not deny that the Synod of Dort taught these dogmas laid to its charge: he endeavors only to clear them from those evil consequences which are thence drawn; and he himself carries so far the certainty of salvation, the very dogma we have seen all centre in, as to say, that taking it from the faithful is making a Christian's life an insufferable torment.[2] He grants then, in the main, the sentiments imputed to the Calvinists: but in order to bring about a peace, notwithstanding so great an opposition in such important articles, after proposing some mitigations consisting in words only, he concludes for a mutual toleration. The reasons he grounds himself on are reduced to two, one whereof is recrimination, and the other a compensation of dogmas.

629

2.—The recriminations of the Minister Jurieu against the Lutherans, concerning Luther's blasphemies.

As for recrimination, M. Jurieu's reasoning is as follows: You accuse us, says he to Doctor Scultet, of making God the author of sin;[3] it is Luther you must accuse of this, not us: and thereupon cites to him those passages we have above related, where Luther decides "that God's prescience renders free-will impossible; that Judas, for this reason, could not help betraying his master; that all that passes in man, whether good or evil, happens by pure and inevitable necessity; that it is God who operates in man all the good and evil that is done by him, and makes man guilty of damnation by necessity; that David's adultery is no less the work of God than the vocation of St. Paul; lastly, that it is no more unworthy of God to damn the innocent, than to forgive, as he does, the guilty."

The Calvinist then shows, that Luther does not speak here in a doubting manner, but with that terrible decision above specified, and which suffers no reply on this head: "You," says he, "that hear me, never forget that I am the man who thus teaches, and without any inquiry submit to this word."[4]

The Lutheran thought to escape, by saying that Luther had recanted; but the Calvinist nonplusses him when he demands, "where is this recantation of Luther? It is true," proceeds he, "he has begged we would excuse, in his first books, some remnants of Popery in regard to indulgences: but as to what regards Free-will, he never changed a tittle of his doctrine."[5] And, indeed, it is very certain that the above-said monsters of impiety were far from being derived from Popery, which, as Luther acknowledges in all these places, held them in execration.

M. Jurieu, in that respect, is of the same opinion with us, and declares, "he holds in abhorrence these Dogmas of Luther, as impious, horrible, frightful, deserving every anathema, introductive to Manicheism, and subversive of all religion."[6] He is sorry to see himself obliged to speak thus of the head of the Reformation. "I speak it," says he, "with grief, and favor, as much as I am able, the memory of this great man." This is, therefore, one of those confessions, which the evidence of truth extorts from men, how much soever against their will; and, in fine, the author of the Reformation, by the very confession of the Reformed, is convicted of being an impious blasphemer againt God: *a great man*, after this, as much as they please; for to have sounded the alarm against Rome, is merit enough in the Reformation for any titles whatever. Melancthon is guilty of this wicked doctrine, which destroys all religon. M. Jurieu has convicted him of uttering the same blasphemies as his master;[7] and instead of detesting them, as they deserved, of never having retracted them but too faintly and with diffidence. You see on what corner-stones the Reformation was built.

3.—Whether Calvin has less blasphemed than Luther.

But because M. Jurieu here seems willing to excuse Calvin, he need but cast his eyes on the passages of this author already quoted by me in this history:

there will he find "that Adam could not avoid his fall, and was nevertheless guilty, because he fell voluntarily; that it was ordained by God, and comprised in his secret decrees."[8] There will he find, "that a hidden counsel of God is the cause of hardness of heart; that we must not deny that God willed and decreed the defection of Adam, since he does all he wills; that this decree, he must confess, raises horror; yet, after all, it cannot be denied that God foresaw the fall of man, because he had ordained it by his own decree; that we ought not to use the word permission, since it is an express order; that the will of God makes the necessity of things; and all he hath willed happens necessarily; that it was for this reason Adam fell by an order of God's providence, and because God had so judged it fitting, although he fell through his own fault; that the reprobate are inexcusable, although they cannot shun the necessity of sinning; and that this necessity befalls them by God's appointment; that God speaks to them, but on purpose to make them the more deaf; that he places light before their eyes, but on purpose to blind them; that he applies sound doctrine to them, but on purpose to render them the more insensible; that he sends them remedies, but to the end they may not be cured."[9]

Whast is here wanting to make Calvin as complete a Manichean as Luther?[10]

What, therefore, does it avail M. Jurieu to have quoted us some passages of Calvin, where he seems to say that man was free in Adam, and fell in Adam by his own will; since it is otherwise certain from Calvin himself that this will of Adam was the necessary effect of a special decree of God? And, indeed, the truth is, this minsiter has not pretended absolutely to excuse Calvin, but contents himself with saying only, "he was sober in comparison to Luther;"[11] but we have just heard him speak not less extravangly and impiously than Luther.

I have also produced Beza's words,[12] which manifestly refer all sins to the will of God as their first cause. Thus, beyond all dispute, the heads of both parties of the Reformation, Luther and Melancthon on one side, Calvin and Beza on the other, the master and disciples, equally are convicted of Manicheism and impiety; and M. Jurieu has had rason to confess candidly of the Reformers in general, that they taught that "God drove on wicked men to enormous crimes."[13]

4.—*Another recrimination of the Minister Jurieu.—The Lutherans convicted of Pelagianism.*

The Calvinist returns to the charge, and here is another recrimination not less remarkable. You upbraid us, says he to the Lutherans, with our irresistible grace: but in order to make it resistible you run to the opposite extreme; and, unlike to your master Luther, who in matter of grace, so far outwent all bounds "as to make himself suspected of Manicheism," you do the like in Free-will, so as to turn Demi-Pelagians, since you attribute to it the beginning of salvation.[14] Which he makes evident by the same proofs we have made use of in this history, by showing the Lutherans that, according to them, the grace of conversion depends on the care they themselves take to hear the word preached. I have clearly demonstrated this Demi-Pelagianism of the Lutherans from the book of Concord, and from other testimonies; but the minister strengthens my proofs with the testimony of his adversary, Scultet, who confesses in as many words, "that God converts men, when men themselves receive the word preached with respect and attention."[15] Accordingly, it is in this manner the Lutherans explain the universal will of saving all mankind, and say with Scultet, "that God will infuse contrition and a lively faith into the hearts of all the adult, provided, nevertheless, they do *beforehand* the ncessary duty for man's conversion." Thus, what they attribute to the divine power, is that grace which goes hand in hand with preaching; and what they attribute to Free-will, is rendering itself beforehand, by its own strenght, attentive to the word announced; which is saying, as clearly as ever the Demi-Pelagians have done, that the beginning of salvation comes purely from Free-will; and, that there may be no doubt that this is the error of the Lutherans, M. Jurieu produces moreover a passage from Calixtus, where he transcribes word for word the propositions condemned in the Demi-Pelagians; for he says, in express terms, "that there remains in all men some strength of the understanding, of the will, and of natural knowledge, which, if they make right use of, in laboring what they are able for their salvation, God will afford them the necessary means to arrive at the perfection which revelation leads us to;"[16] which once more makes grace depend on what man precedently does by his own strength.

I was right, then, in affirming that the Lutherans are become true Demi-Pelagians, namely, Pelagians in the most dangerous part of this heresy, it being that by which human pride is the most flattered. For the greatest mischief of Pelagianism is placing man's salvation finally in his own hands, independently of grace. Now this is done by those, who, like the Lutherans, make the conversion and justificastion of a sinner dependent on a beginning introductive of all the rest, and which, nevertheless, the sinner gives to himself merely by his Free-will without grace, as I have proved evidently, and as M. Jurieu has also but just made apparent from the Confession of the Lutherans.

They ought not, therefore, to flatter themselves, as if they had escaped the Anathema merited by the Pelagians, under pretext that they are only such by halves; since we see that this part swallowed by them of so mortal a poison, as that of Pelagianism, contains its own malignity: from whence one may perceive the deplorable condition of the whole Protestant party; since, on one side, the Calvinists know no way of maintaining Christian grace against the Pelagians, but by making it inamissible with all the other aforesaid inconveniences; and on the other, that Lutherans believe there is no avoiding this detestable *particularism* of Dort and of the Calvinists, but by turning Pelagians, and abandoning man's salvation to his own Free-will.

5.—*Sequel of Recriminations.*—*The Lutherans convicted of denying the necessity of good works.*

The Calvinist pursues his point: and, says he to the Lutherans, "it is impossible to dissemble" your doctrine against the necessity of good works. "I will not," proceeds he, "go in quest of the harsh propositions of your Doctors, ancient and modern, on this subject."[17] As I take it, he glances at the Decree of Worms, where we have observed that it was decided that good works are not necessary to salvation. But without insisting on this assembly, and other like decrees of the Lutherans, I shall observe only (says he to Scultet) what you yourself have taught: "That it is not lawful for us to give any alms to the poor, no, not a farthing, with the design of obtaining forgiveness of our sins."[18] And, again, "That the habit and exercise of virtue is not absolutely necessary for the justified in order to be saved: that the exercise of the love of God, neither in the course of life, nor even at the hour of death, is a necessary condition without which we cannot be saved." Lastly, "That neither the habit nor exercise of virtue is necessary to a dying person, in order to obtain forgiveness of his sins;" that is to say, "a man is saved," as this minister concludes, "without having done so much as one good work, either in his life or at death."

6.—*Another recrimination on the certainty of Salvation.*—*The Lutherans convicted of contradiction and blindness.*

These are just and terrible recriminations, of which Dr. Scultet will never clear himself: again, here is another no less remarkable. You object to us as a crime (says M. Jurieu[19] to him), the certainty of salvation defined in the Synod of Dort; but you, who object it to us, hold the same yourselves. Thereupon he produces the Theses, wherein Doctor John Gerard (the third man after Luther and Chemnicius of the Reformation, if we believe their testimony who approved his works) advances this proposition. "We maintain against the Papists the certainty of salvation as a certainty of faith."[20] And again, "The predestinate has in himself God's testimony, and says interiorly to himself, 'he that predestinated me from all eternity, calls me, and justifies me in time by his word'." It is certain he wrote these things, and others every whit as strong, alleged by M. Jurieu:[21] they are usual with the Lutherans. But this Minister reproaches them, with reason, that they are not consistent with their doctrine of the amissibility of justice, which they account as a capital point; accordingly, it is what I have remarked in this history, nor have I forgotten the solution proposed by the Lutherans, and even by Dr. Gerard: but I do not vouch for the contradictions the Minister Jurieu upbraids them with in these words:—"It is a thing incredible that wise men, having eyes in their heads, should have fallen into so stupendous a blindness, as to believe one is assured of his salvation with a certainty of faith, and, at the same time, that the true believer may lose the faith and eternal salvation."[22] From thence he takes occasion to reproach them, that their doctrne is self-contradictory, that their universalism, introduced contrary to Luther's principles, has brought such a confusion into their theology "that there is none but is sensible that it has no longer any manner of coherence; that it cannot be self-consistent; that they have no excuse left them."[23] Thus you see how these men treat one another when in peace; what do not they do when at mortal war?

7.—Another recrimination.—The monster of Ubiquity.

Besides what regards grace, the Minister also charges the Lutherans very home with their monstrous doctrine of Ubiquity, "worthy," says he, "of all the eulogiums you bestow on the decisions of Dort, a frightful, huge, and horrid monster, of a prodigious deformity in itself, and still more prodigious in its consequences; since it brings back the confusion of natures in Jesus Christ, and not only that of the soul with the body, but also that of the divinity with the humanity, and, in a word, Eutychianism, so unanimously detested by the whole Church."[24]

He shows them they have added to the Confession of Augsburg this monster of Ubiquity, and to Luther's doctrine their excessive universalism, which has made them fall back into the error of the Pelagians. All these reproaches are very true, as we have made appear;[25] and here you behold the Lutherans, the first of those that took up the title of Reformers, convicted by the Calvinists of being all at once Pelagians in formal terms, and Eutychians by consequences indeed,[26] but such as the whole world is sensible of, and which are as clear as the noon-day.

8.—The compensation of Dogmas proposed to the Lutherans by the Minister Jurieu.

After all these vigorous recriminations, one would think that the Minister Jurieu[27] must conclude to detest, in the Lutherans, so many abominable excesses, so many visible contradictions, so manifest a blindness: no such thing. He accuses the Lutherans of so many enormous errors, only to conclude a peace by a mutual toleration on both sides, notwithstanidng the gross errors both stand convicted of by the testimonies of each other.

Here, then, he proposes that marvellous compensation, that bartering of doctrine, where all terminates in concluding "if our particularism be an error, we offer you a toleration for errors much more strange." Let us make up peace on this foundation, and mutually declare one another God's faithful servants, without any obligation on either side of correcting anything in our tenets. We allow you all the prodigies of your doctrine:[28] we allow you that monstrous Ubiquity: we allow you your Demi-Pelagianism, which places the beginning of man's salvation purely in his own hands: we allow you that horrid dogma,[29] which denies that good works and the habit of charity, any more than the exercise thereof, are necessary to salvation, either in life or at death: we tolerate you, we receive you to the holy table, we own you for God's children, notwithstanding all these errors: overlook, then, in our behalf, and in behalf of the Synod of Dort, these absolute decrees with irresistible grace, the certainty of salvation with the inamissibility of justice, together with all the rest of our particular dogmas, how much soever you abhor them.

This is the bargain he proposes; this, what he negotiates in the face of teh whole Christian world: a peace between Churches calling themselves not only Christian, but also Reformed: not by agreeing in the doctrine which they believe expressly revealed by God, but by forgiving mutually each other the most unpardonable errors.

What shall be the issue of this treaty? I am loth to foresee it: but will be bold to say the Calvinists shal gain nothing else by it but an addition to their own errors of those of the Lutherans, which they make themselves accomplices in by admitting to the holy table those as the true children of God who professedly maintain them. As for the Lutherans, if it be true, as it is insinuated by M. Jurieu,[30] that they begin for the most part to become more tractable in regard to the Real Presence, and offer peace to the Calvinists, provided only they receive their Demi-Pelagian Universalism, the whole universe will be witnesss that they have made a peace by sacrificing to the Sacramentarians what Luther most defended against them, even to his death, to wit, the reality; and by making them profess what the same Luther most detested, namely, Pelagianism, to which he preferred the opposite extreme, even the horror of making God the author of sin.

9.—*The means proposed by M. Jurieu for advancing this agreement.*—Princes sovereign Judges of Religion.

But let us also see the means which M. Jurieu proposes for attaining this wonderful agreement.[31] "In the first place," says he, "this pious work cannot be brought about without the concurrence of the princes of both parties, by reason that," proceeds he, "the whole Reformation was made by their authority." Wherefore, in order to promote it, we must assemble—"not Ecclesiastics, always too much wedded to their own sentiments—but politicians,"[32] who, in all appearance, will part with their religion at an easier rate. These, therefore, shall examine "the importance of each tenet, and weigh with equity, whether such and such a proposition, supposing it an error, be capable of being agreed to, or incapable of being tolerated;"[33] that is to say, what is most essential to religion must be debated in this assembly, it being to decide what is fundamental, and what not; what may be, and what may not be tolerated. Here lies the grand difficulty: but in this difficulty, so essential to religion, "the divines are to speak as lawyers, the politicians are to hearken and judge under the authority of their princes."[34] Here, then, manifestly are princes become supreme arbiters of religion, and the substance of faith trusted absolutely in their hands. Whether this be religion, or a mere political agreement, I refer to the reader.

Nevertheless, it must be owned, the reason alleged by M. Jurieu for submitting the whole to princes, is convincing, since in reality, as he has just told us, "the whole Reformation was made by their authority."[35] It is what we have shown through the whole series of this history: but now, at least, this fact, so ignominious to Protestants, can no longer be disputed. M. Jurieu confesses it in plain terms; nor must we wonder that princes have vested in themselves the supreme authority of judgment, in regard to a Reformation which they themselves have made.

For which reason, the Minister has laid it down for the groundwork of the agreement, "that previously to all conferenes and disputes, the divines on both sides shall make oath to obey the judgment of the delegates of their princes, and to do nothing contrary to the agreement."[36] The princes and their delegates are now turned infallible: obedience is sworn to them beforehand, enjoin what they will: that must be believed essential or indifferent, tolerable or intolerable, in religion, which shall please them. And the fundamental points of Christianity must be decided by policy.

10.—The Calvinists ready to subscribe the Confession of Augsburg.

One no longer knows what country he is in, nor whether they are Christians he hears speak, when he sees the foundation of religion given up to temporal authority, and the sovereign disposal of it resigned to princes. But this is not all; after this a Confession of Faith must be agreed to, and hence should arise their main perplexity: but the expedient is easy.[37] They are to make one in indefinite and general terms, which the whole world shall be satisfied with; each must dissemble what may be displeasing to his companion: silence is a remedy for all evils: every man shall believe in his hesart just what he likes,—Pelagian, Eutychian, or Manichean; provided he hold his tongue, all will go well, and Jesus Christ will not fail to look on both one and the other for Christians well united. What shall we say? Let us deplore the blindness of our brethren, and beseech God that the enormity of their error may at length open their eyes, so as to become sensible thereof.

But here is the finishing stroke. We have seen what Zuinglius and the Zuinglians, Calvin and the Calvinists, judged of the Confession of Augsburg:[38] how from its first beginning they refused to subscribe it, and separated themselves from its defenders; how those of France in all succeeding times, in receiving all the rest, have ever excepted the tenth article relating to the Supper. We have seen, among other things, what was said at the conference of Poissy;[39] nor forgotten what Calvin then wrote, "no less of the suppleness than of the obscure and defective brevity" of this Confession, which was the cause, said he, "that it displeased people of good sense, and even that Melancthon, its author, repented he ever made it;" but during the present great prevalency of that fond desire of uniting with the Lutherans! they are ready to subscribe this Confession; for they are very sensible the Lutherans will never depart from it. Well then, says our minister, "is no more required of us than to subscribe it? The business is done: we are ready for this subscription, provided you will receive us."[40] Thus you see this Confession, which had been so stoutly rejected these hundred and fifty years, all of a sudden, without any alteration in it, will become the common rule of Calvinists as it is of Lutherans, upon condition each one shall have the liberty of interpreting and adapting it to his own notions. I leave the reader to decide which of the two ought most to be lamented, the Calvinists, who turn with every wind, or the

Lutherans, whose Confession is subscribed only with a view of discovering in it a doctrine suitable to their notions, by the means of those equivocal expressions, of which it is accused. No man but sees now vain, to say no worse, would be this projected union; what would ensue from it of some real consequence is, however, as says M. Jurieu, "that one might make thereof a good confederacy, and that the Protestant party would make the Papists tremble."[41] These were the hopes of M. Jurieu, who would be well enough satisfied with the success of his negotiation, if, failing as to a sincere agreement of minds, it could at least unite them so as to set all Europe in a flame; but, luckily for Christendom, leagues are not made as doctors wish.

11.—*Wondrous motives for an union proposed to the Lutherans.*

In this marvellous negotiation nothing is more surprising than the artfulness M. Jurieu uses to mollify the hard-hearted Lutherans. What, says he,[42] will you always be insensible of the complaisance we have shown, in allowing you your corporal presence? "Besides all these philosophical absurdities which we were forced to digest, how perilous are the consequences of this dogma?" Those experience it, proceeds he, who are obliged to endure, in France, this continual reproach: "Why do you reject the Catholics after having received the Lutherans? Our people make answer, The Lutherans take not away the substance of the bread: they do not adore the Eucharist: they offer it not in sacrifice: they deprive not the people of one kind: so much the worse for them, we are told, it is in this they argue ill, nor follow their own principles. For, if the body of Jesus Christ be really and carnally prsent, we ought to adore him: if he be present, we ought to offer him up to his Father: if he be present, Jesus Christ is whole and entire under each species. Do not say you deny these consequences; for, after all, they flow better and more nasturally from your dogma than those you impute to us. It is certain your doctrine regarding the Supper was the beginning of error: the change of substance was grounded thereupon: thereupon was adoration commanded; nor is it easy to withstand it: human reason directs us to adore Jesus Christ wheresoever he is. Not that this reason is alway good, for God is in a piece of wood and in a stone, yet we may not adore a stone or wood; but, after all, the mind is carried to it by its own propensity," and as natural as the elements tend to their centre: a great struggle is required "to hinder our falling into this precipice"—(this precipice is worshipping Jesus Christ where he is present); "and I nowise doubt," proceeds our Author, "but that the simple amongst you would fall into it, were they not prevented by the continual contests with the Papists." Open your eyes, ye Lutherans, and suffer the Cathoilics to speak thus to you in their turn. We do not propose that you should worship wood or stone because God is in them; we propose to you to worship Jesus Christ where you acknowledge he is, by so special a presence, attested by so particular and divine a testimony: "reason directs you to it of course; the mind is carried to it by its own propensity." Simple minds, void of contention, would follow so natural a bent, if continual disputes did not restrain them; nor is it anything but the spirit of contention that can hinder the adoration of Jesus Christ where he is believed so present.

12.—Both parties irreconcilable in the main, according to the Minister Jurieu.

Such are the conditions of the agreement at this day in treaty between the Lutherans and Calvinists; such are the means they are to use for attaining it; and such the reasons employed to persuade and move the Lutherans. And let not these people go away with the notion, that our speaking of it in this manner proceeds from some fear we may be in of their re-union, which, after all, will never be anything better than grimace and cabal; for in short, for them to convince one another is a thing judged impossible even by M. Jurieu. "Never," says he, "will either of the parties suffer itself to be led in triumph; and to propose an agreement between the Lutherans and Calvinists, on condition that one party shall renounce its doctrine, is the same as if you should propose to the Spaniards as a means of agreement, to give up all their provinces and fortresses into the hands of the French. That," says he, "is neither just nor possible."[43] Who does not see, on this foundation, that the Lutherans and Calvinists are in the main two nations as irreconcilable and incompatible as any? They may join in confederacies, but that they ever will be able to arrive at a Christian agreement by the conformity of sentiments, were manifest folly to believe. Nevertheless, they will still continue to say, and one as much as the other, that the Scripture is clear, although conscious in their hearts that this alone can never terminate the least dispute; and all they can do is to patch up agreements, and dissemble what they believe to be the truth clearly revealed by God, or at all events to disguise it, as they have endeavored a thousand times to do, under equivocal expressions.

Let them, therefore, do what they think fit, and whatsoever God shall suffer them to do in respect to these vain projects of agreements; they will be eternally the mutual punishment and grievance of each other: they will bear eternal testimony one against another, how unhappily they usurped the title of Reformers, and that the method they took for the correction of abuses, could tend to nothing but the subversion of Christianity.

13.—Query put to the Lutherans and Calvinists.

But here is something still worse for them. Supposing they were arrived at this mutual toleration, we should then ask them in what rank they would place Luther and Calvin, who make God, in express terms, the author of sin, and thereby stand convicted of a dogma which their disciples now abhor? Who does not see that of two things one will happen, either that they must place this blasphemy, this Manicheism, this "impiety which subverts all religion," amongst the tenets that may be tolerated; or in fine, to the eternal ignominy of the Reformation, Luther must become the horror of the Lutherans, and Calvin of the Calvinists?

Notes

1 L. ix. xiv.
2 P. i. c. viii. p. 2, c. vi. p. 191, &c. xi. 253, 254.
3 S. l. ii. n. 17. Jur. part ii. c. viii. p. 210, et seq.
4 S. l. ii. n. 17.
5 Jur. Ibid. pp. 217, 218.
6 Jur. part ii. c. viii. pp. 211, 214, et seq.
7 Jur. part. ii. c. viii. p. 24.
8 S. l. xiv. n. 4. Opusc. de præd. pp. 704, 705, Inst. iii. xxiii. i. pp. 1, 7, 8, 9.
9 S. l. xxiv. n. 13.
10 Jur. part ii. c. xiii. ibid. p. 214.
11 Jur. part ii. c. xiii. ibid. p. 214.
12 S. l. xiv. n. 2, 3.
13 Ibid. n. 4.
14 Jur. part ii. c. viii. p. 117. S. l. viii. n. 83. et seq. xiv. 116.
15 Jur. p. 117.
16 Jur. p. 118. Calix. Ep.
17 Ib. part ii. c. ii. p. 243.
18 S. l. iii. n. 12. viii. n. 32. pp. 243, 244.
19 Jur. part i. c. viii. pp. 128, 129.
20 Gerard. de elect. et rep. c. xiii. Thes. pp. 210, 211.

21 Jur. part i. c. viii. p. 129. Sup. l. iii. n. 39. viii. n. 60, 61.
22 Ibid.
23 Ibid. pp. 213, 129, 131, 135.
24 Jur. part i. c. viii. 242.
25 S. l. viii. n. 46.
26 Jur. ibid.
27 Jur. part ii. c. iii. et seq. x. xi. p. 240.
28 Part i. c. viii. p. 123.
29 Jur. part i. c. viii. 243.
30 Jur. part ii. c. xii. p. 261.
31 Ibid. p. 260, n. 1.
32 Ibid. n. 4.
33 Ibid. p. 263, n. 8.
34 Jur. part ii. c. xii. p. 263, n. 8.
35 Ibid.
36 Ibid.
37 Ibid.c. xi. p. 245, et seq. c. xii. 268.
38 S. l. iii. n. 3. ix. n. 88, 89, 100, et seq.
39 Ibid. n. 107.
40 Ibid. c. xiii. p. 171.
41 p. 262.
42 p. 240.
43 Jur. ii. p. cap. i. pp. 138, 141.

In the Index of the English translation references are to the pages. Here the numbers indicate the Book and the Section respectively. Thus 11:19 refers to Book XI, Section 19. This method enables the reader to consult readily not only the original English translation, but also the French text of the various editions. In most of them the Sections within each Book are usually indicated with a number on the margin together with the French text of the caption which the English translation carries in front of each Section.

INDEX

*Ablution. What the ablution was which the Vaudois condemned in Baptism, 11:109

*Absolution, Sacramental, owned by the Lutherans, 3:46—and by the English, under Henry VIII, 7:37.

*Abstinence from flesh retained in England, 7:92—the Church of Rome justified by the English in her abstinence from flesh, ib.

*Adam. The sin of Adam ordained by God, according to the Calvinists, 14:2

*Adoration, the Protestants cannot endure the adoration rendered to Jesus Christ in the Eucharist, 6:21—Luther's doctrine implies adoration, 6:35—the adoration of Jesus Christ in the Eucharist suppressed in England under Edward VI, 7:94—of Jesus Christ in the Eucharist, rejected by the Brethren of Bohemia, 11:186—alterations made by the Calvinists in respect to the Adoration of Jesus Christ in the Eucharist, 14:103—they tolerate in the Lutherans the internal acts of this Adoration, and reject the external, which are but tokens thereof, 14:104

*Aerius. The Lutherans' contradictory sentiments on the doctrine of Aerius against prayer for the dead, 3:55

*Ailly, (Cardinal Peter D',) his opinions concerning the Reformation of the Church, 1:1-4

*Albert, of Brandebourg, Great Master of the Teutonic Order, turns Lutheran, and why, 8:10

*Albigenses. (The) well treated by the Calvinists, and why, 11:3—those of Toulouse bore the name of Petrobusians, 11:36—Council of Lombez against them. Famous examination of these Heretics, 11:37—why they are called Arians, 11:39—the Albigenses are Manicheans, and, by consequence, different from the Vaudois, 11:48, et seq.—The Albigenses comprised by Renier in the list of the Manichean Churches, 11:56

—they came from the Manicheans of Bulgaria,—their profound hypocrisy, 11:58 the agreeableness of their propositions with those of Faustus the Manichean, 11:59—their hypocrisy confounded by St. Bernard, 11:60—their infamy, 11:61—they teach that the effect of the Sacraments depends on the holiness of the Ministers, 11:62—they damn all oaths and punishment of crimes, 11:63—proof of their being Manicheans, 11:63 et seq.—Protestants reap nothing but shame by challenging the Albigenses for their ancestors, 11:70—reflections on the history of the Albigenses and Vaudois; artifice of the Ministers, 11:131—the Albigenses unquestionably Manicheans, 11:132 —the Albigenses of Metz were Manicheans, 11:133—sixteen Churches of the Manicheans comprehended the whole Sect, 11:139—inevitable condemnation of these Heretics from their denying their religion, 11:148—how the Vaudois sprung from the Manichean Albigenses, 11:205

*Amboise. Conspiracy of Amboise, 10:26—entered upon from a maxim of conscience, according to Beza, ib.— the riot of Amboise was the work of Protestants, and had religion for its motive, 10:27—the Huguenots' discovering the conspiracy, does not justify the party, 10:31—the protestation of the conspirators does not justify them, 10:32—what is said by M. Jurieu concerning the conspiracy of Amboise, 10:49

*Amissibility of justice owned in the Confession of Augsburg, 3:37—received in 1557, by the Calvinists of France, 9:89—of justice received by the English under Elizabeth, 10:23—doctrine of the Arminians concerning the amissibility of justice, 14:27

*Amsdorf, (Nicholas,) ordained Bishop of Naumburg by Luther, 1:27

641

of the Calvinian wars in France, 10: 46—how he authorizes the civil wars, 10:47—what he says touching the assassination of the Duke of Guise by Poltrot, 10:54—Beza's ridiculous pretensions in favor of the antiquity of the Vaudois, 11:4—what he says of their Doctrine shows they were not Calvinists, 11:121—in 1571 Beza presides in the national Synod of Rochelle, where those that were for changing the Supper article in the Confession of Faith are condemned, 12:1—by the Synod's orders, he answers the Swiss offended at its decision, that it only regarded France, 12:9—he is of the number of those that were deputed by the Frankfort assembly to draw up one common Confession of Faith, 12:16—he makes God the author of sin, 14:1-3—this doctrine of Beza taken from Calvin, 14:4—the Dogmas he adds to those of Luther, 15:5—what he says of the certainty of particular men's salvation, 14:6-7—he teaches, after Calvin, that justifying Faith is not lost in a criminal state, 14:11

*Bishops, authority of Bishops despised by Protestants, 5:7—Melancthon is for owning Bishops, 5:24—all the Bishops in England subscribe the decisions of Henry VIII, 7:30—the Bishops of England take out new commissions from Edward VI, 7:76—the Bishops of England have no share in matters of religion and faith, 7:78 —Constancy of the English Catholic Bishops, who are deposed for refusing to own Queen Elizabeth's supremacy, 10:12, 22—decisions in matters of Faith reserved to the royal authority by the declaration of the English Protestant Bishops, 10:18

*Blandratus. George Blandratus, one of the heads of the Socinians, 15:123

*Bohemia. The sect of the Bohemian Brethren falsely called Vaudois, 11: 149—why they disown those who call them Vaudois, 11:150-151,—and Picards, 11:152—they boast their descent from John Huss, 11:153—they divide from the Calixtins, 11:168,173-174—the bloody wars of the Calixtins trouble all Bohemia, 11:172 —they make to themselves an ignorant lay Pastor, 11: 173—weak beginning of this Sect, 11: 174—they only took the name of John Huss but did not follow his doctrine;

their extreme ignorance and assurance to re-baptize the whole world, 11:175-176—fruitless search throughout the universe after a Church of their belief, 11:177—how they sought Ordination in the Catholic Church; reproaches made them by Luther, 11:178,179—their Doctrine in respect to the seven Sacraments, 11:180—they change it in their Reformed Confessions of Faith, ib.— what they thought of the Eucharist, 11:181 et seq.—the manner in which they refuse to adore Jesus Christ, a proof that they believed the Reality even out of the actual use of the Sacrament, 11:186—their uncertainty and affected ambiguities, 11:187—the Calvinists and Lutherans each strive to bring them to their side; they incline to the latter, 11:188—Luther gives them his approbation; their Festivals, their Temples, their Fasts, and the Celibacy of their Priests, 11:189-190—they take shelter in Poland, 11:192—there they unite with the Lutherans and Zuinglians, 11:193—what disposition they were in for this agreement, 11:197—reflections on this union, 11:198

*Bohemians, their separation condemned by Luther, 1:21—The buffooneries of Luther, 1:33, 6:39

*Brags of Calvin, 10:80

*Breaking. Important article of the Conference of Cassel, concerning the breaking of the Eucharistic Bread, 14:114

*Brentius, a famous Protestant, favors Osiander, 8:31, 33

*Bucer gives a figurative sense to the words of the institution, 2:25—he was present at the Conference of Marpurg, 2:45—he draws up the Strasburg Confession of Faith, 3:3—his character, ib.—his fruitfulness in equivocations,— ib. 3:12—his doctrine on the merit of good works, 3:42—he undertakes the defence of the prayers of the Church, and shows in what sense the merits of Saints are useful to us, 3:43—he is despatched by the Landgrave of Hesse to have an interview with Luther and Zuinglius, 4:1—his transactions with Luther, 4:3—his equivocating shifts in order to reconcile the parties, 4:4—the agreement by him proposed, no more than verbal, 4:5—his equivocations on the words Sacrament and Mystery, 4:10—he plays with words, 4:13—he

owns that the unworthy receive the body of Jesus Christ really, 6:18, 8:7—he grants six Articles to Luther concerning the Supper, 4:23—he deceives Luther, and evades the terms of agreement, 4:24—his equivocations owned by Calvin, 4:25—those even of Zurich make a jest of them, 4:28—explication of the doctrine, and the return of the towns from his belief to that of the Real Presence, 4:30—he satisfies the Lutherans in the assembly of Smalkald, 4:34—Bucer's testimony concerning the hypocrisy of the Protestants, 5:14—he is sent to Luther by the Landgrave to obtain leave for this Prince to marry a second wife, his first still living, 6:3—he makes a new Confession of Faith, 6:18—his perplexities with relation to the communion of the impious, 6:19—his doctrine about the Eucharist not hearkened to in England, 6:19—he is present at the Conference of Ratisbon, 8:4—he makes a new Confession of Faith, 8:7—he dies in England without having been able to change any thing in the articles of Peter Martyr, 8:9
Bull, a learned English protestant, maintains the Infallibility of the Council of Nice and that of the other general Councils, 15:103
Burnet, (Mr.) a new piece published by Mr. Burnet about Luther's sentiment touching on a reconciliation with the Zuinglians, 6:42—he owns that the Reformation began in England by a man equally rejected by both parties, 7:3—Mr. Burnet's magnificent words concerning the English Reformation, 7:2—the heroes of Mr. Burnet's history even by his own testimony are not always very virtuous men, 7:7—what he relates of Montluc, Bishop of Valence, *ib.*—what he says of Cranmer, Archbishop of Canterbury, 7:8—what he says of the oath Cranmer took at his Consecration, 7:11—what he says of the cruelties and excesses of Henry VIII, 7:16—the praises he gives to Queen Catharine, the lawful wife of Henry VIII, 7:20—what he says of the disorderly behaviour of Anne Boleyn, *ib.*—he comes off lamely in his excuse of Cranmer's cowardice, 7:22—how he excuses the Protestants of England for subscribing the decisions of Henry VIII, who approved the principal points of

the Catholic doctrine, 7:30—his vain artifices to excuse the hypocrisy of Thomas Cromwell, 7:35—he is ashamed of that sentence which annulled the marriage of Henry VIII with Anne of Cleves, 7:36—he owns that scarce any thing was changed in the offices and Rituals of the Church under Henry VIII, 7:39—what he says of Cranmer's resisting the Six Articles of Henry VIII, 7:40-41—he is confounded at Cranmer's doctrine about the power of ministers of the Church, 7:44—he laments his seeing in England the ecclesiastical power in the hands of seculars, *ib.*—he sets down two points of Reformation under Henry VIII, 7:63 *et seq.*—a proof, from Mr. Burnet, of the snares laid for the weak and simple by the pretended perspicuity of Scripture, 7:67—Mr. Burnet's confession of the belief of the Greek Church, 7:83—he vindicates us in the observance of Saints-days and abstinence from flesh, 7:90 *et seq.*—his vain efforts to justify Cranmer in little things, without saying a word of great ones, 7:98—he ill compares Cranmer's twice abjuring his faith to the denial of St. Peter, 7:104—he badly excuses the Reformers, 7:106—the fallacy in the examples alleged by him, 7:107—his facts far from being certain, 7:108—his imposition with regard to Fra Paolo, 7:109—his error concerning the pallium, 7:110—his gross error concerning Celibacy and the Roman Pontifical, 7:112—His imposition in asserting that the Doctrine established under Edward VI was not changed, 10:8—what Mr. Burnet says of the indifference of the English as to the Real Presence, 10:9— A memorable passage of Mr. Burnet concerning the English Reformation, 10:22—his illusion in regard to the wars of the Huguenots, 10:42—his gross mistakes and prodigious ignorance relating to the affairs of France, 10:43–sequel of his fallacies, 10:44

Calixtins. The Sect of the Calixtins rises up in Bohemia, 11:167—why called Calixtins, 11:168—the Compactatum, or the four articles allowed to the Calixtins by the Council of Basil, 11:169—the Calixtins disposed to acknowledge the pope, 11:170—the reason of their so great respect for Wickliff's memory; their ambition hinders them from re-uniting with the Church, 11:171-172—the Bohemian Brethren separate from them, 11:173

Calixtus, a famous Lutheran, establishes in Germany the union of Sects, and is followed in France by the Minister d'Husseau, 15:52

Calumny. The decree of the Synod of Charenton in 1631 convicts the Calvinists of calumny, 14:99

Calumnies of Protestants against the Church on the point of Justification, 3:21—other calumnies on the merit of good works, 3:25—three other calumnies against the invocation of Saints, and concerning Images, 3:58

Calvin, his esteem for Luther, Preface, 10, 1:6—what Calvin writes to Melancthon upon the strange division of Protestants, 2:43—his sentiments on equivocations in matters of Faith, 4:25——what he writes to Bullinger and Melancthon about the tyranny of Luther, 5:15—what he says of the adoration of the blessed Sacrament retained by Luther, 6:34—he favors Henry VIII in his divorce, 7:56—he rejects the ceremonies of the Church, 9:75—what he says of Osiander's profane temper, 8:12—the incompatibility of his sentiments with those of Melancthon, 8:38—he draws up a Confession of Faith, 8:63—his genius; his refinements surpass those of Luther, 9:1—he adds to imputed justice the certainty of salvation, 9:3—he teaches that justice cannot be lost, 9:5—he teaches that Baptism is not necessary to salvation, 9:6—he maintains that the children of the faithful are born in grace, 9:10—Calvin's principles but supposed, he argued better than Luther, but swerved wider from truth, 9:13—two tenets of Calvin's concerning children, not suiting with his principles, 9:19—his agreement with those of Geneva and Zurich, 9:20—the contradictions of his doctrine upon Infant Baptism, 9:21-22—his refinements upon the Eucharist, 9:23—he shows that, after fifteen years' disputing, the Lutherans and Zuinglians had not understood one another on this point, 9:24-—Calvin, already known on account of his Institutions, makes himself more so by his treatise on the Supper, 9:25—his doctrine on the Eucharist almost forgot-

ten by his followers, 9:26—he is not satisfied with receiving a sign only in the Supper, 9:27—not even an efficacious sign, nor the virtue and merit of Jesus Christ, 9:28-29—his doctrine partakes somewhat of that of Bucer's and of the Articles of Wittenberg, 9:30—he endeavors to reconcile Luther and Zuinglius, 9:36—with what force he speaks of the Reality, 9:37—a new effect of Faith, according to Calvin, 9:39—he will have the proper substance, and that we receive the body and blood of Jesus Christ otherwise than did the ancient Hebrews, 9:41—according to his expressions it must be believed that the reception of the body of Jesus Christ is independent of Faith, 9:42—and that the true body is in the Sacrament, 9:43—he maintains that the body is under the sign of bread, as the Holy Ghost is under the dove, 9:44—he makes Jesus Christ present in the bread as God was in the ark, 9:45—he says he disputes but of the manner, and admits the things as much as we, 9:46—he admits a presence of the body which is miraculous and ineffable, 9:47—he admits a presence that is proper and peculiar to the Supper, 9:49—the communion of the unworthy, how real, according to Calvin, 9:51—a comparison by him made use of to enforce the truth of the body's being received by the unworthy, 9:53—he speaks inconsequently, 9:54—he explains as we do that saying, "that flesh profiteth nothing," 9:55—he weakens his own expressions, and eludes the miracle which he owns in the Supper, 9:57—he is sensible of the insufficiency of his doctrine to explain the miracle of the Eucharist, 9:59—his perplexities and contradictions in the defence of the figurative sense, 9:61—the cause of his perplexity, 9:62—he saw further into the difficulty than the rest of the Sacramentarians: how he endeavors to salve it, 9:63—the examples which he drew from Scripture; that of Circumcision convicts instead of helping him, 9:64—another example nothing to the purpose, viz. that the Church is called the body of Jesus Christ, 9:65—he makes new efforts to salve the notion of reality impressed by the Institution of Jesus Christ, 9:66—how his doctrine is ex-

plained in the book entitled, "Du Pré-servatif," &c. 9:68—he would make one understand more than he really meant to say, 9:71—a passage of Calvin's for a Real Presence independent of Faith, 9:74—he rejects ceremonies, 9:75—his pride and boastings, 9:77-78—the difference between Calvin and Luther, 9:79—how he bragged of his eloquence, 9:80—he has as much violence and more acrimony than Luther, 9:82—the contempt he passes on the Fathers, 9:83—whether he has varied in his doctrine, 9:85—why he was not in person at the Conference of Poissy, 9:91—the instruction he sends to the Ministers during the Conference, 9:101—what he says of the Confession of Augsburg, 9:102—his special caution with regard to the tenth Article of the Augsburg Confession, 9:104—his connivance at the conspiracy of Amboise, 10:33—his death, 10:57—in what manner issued from the Vaudois and Albigenses, 11:206—his evasions in regard to the vain predictions of Luther concerning the Papacy, 13:2—he made God the author of Adam's sin, 14:4—the Dogmas by him added to those of Luther, 14:5—his Doctrine of the Certainty of Salvation defined by the Synod of Dort, 14:56
*Calvinists (The) give in to the Semi-pelagianism of the Lutherans, 8:59—they have two tenets concerning children not conformable with their principles, 9:19—the present Calvinists have abandoned the doctrine of Calvin about the Supper, 9:68—they were more sensible that a miracle ought to be admitted in the Eucharist than they did indeed admit one, 9:60—what opinion other Protestants had of the Calvinists, 9:76—Variations in the Acts of Calvinists, 9:86—they send a Confession of Faith into Germany, which is not consistent with the figurative sense, 9:87—they send thither another Confession of Faith, in which they deliver themselves more strongly in favor of the Real Presence than the Lutherans themselves, 9:88—they own all the Articles of the Augsburg Confession except the tenth, 9:89—they depute the ablest men among them to the Conference of Poissy, 9:91—there they present their Confession of Faith to Charles IX, 9:93—their explanation of the Supper Arti-

cle, full of intricate words, 9:94—they refuse to sign the tenth Article of the Augsburg Confession, 9:100—which they receive throughout in all other points, but only out of policy, 9:101—how many different parts they at that time played with respect to the Confession of Augsburg, 9:102—Calvinists of France receive the English Doctrine, making the King head of the Church, 10:20—change of their doctrine, 10:24—their conspiracy at Amboise, ib.—they take up arms by a maxim of Religion, 10:25—the first civil wars which the whole Calvinists Party concurs to, 10:35—decisions of their national Synods in approbation of their arming, 10:36—what spirit actuated them in these wars, 10:39—their false pretence that these wars did not concern Religion, 10:41—perplexity of the French Calvinists to justify these wars, 10:45—they are convicted by Beza, 10:46—their other wars destitute of all pretext, 10:48—whether the spirit of their Reformation were a spirit of meekness or violence, 10:50—fatal consequences of their violent spirit, 10:51—their vain excuses, 10:52—their cruelties, ib.—why our Calvinists examine less into the question of Free-will than the Zuinglians, 10:65—the reason of their keeping such a stir about the Albigenses and Vaudois, 11:3—the present Vaudois are their Disciples, 11:123—they have not one contemporary Author that favors their pretensions touching the Vaudois, 11:125—all are welcome to the Calvinists, if they but exclaim against the pope, 11:166—in what manner they descended from the Albigenses and Vaudois, 11:206—they seek in vain the succession of Persons in the precedent Sects, 11:207—still less do they find amongst them the succession of Doctrine, 11:208—many Calvinists of France are for changing the article of the Supper in the Confession of Faith, but are condemned by a national Synod, 12:1-2—they assemble at St. Foy, and give the power to four Ministers of changing their Confession of Faith, 12:19—a letter wherein the Calvinists own Luther and Melancthon for their fathers, 12:22—they have continued to our days the project of a common Confession, but always to no purpose, 12:

23—they receive the Lutherans to their Communion, 14:95—the unsettled spirit of Calvinism, 12:26—the Calvinists detest Piscator's Doctrine, 12:28—the Doctrine of the Calvinists against Piscator solves all the difficulties they object to us on the sacrifice of the Mass, 12:30 —the impiety of their Doctrine touching imputed justice, as it is proposed by the Synods which condemn Piscator, 12:34—reflection on their procedure against Piscator, 12:36—they add an article to their Confession of Faith in order to declare the Pope Antichrist, 13:1—intolerable excesses of Calvinism concerning Free-will, 14:1 —they make God the author of sin, ib.—they believe as a fundamental point that every one of the faithful is sure of his perseverance and salvation, 14:6—they are sensible of these excesses, so contrary to the fear and trembling prescribed by St. Paul, 14:8—they maintain that justifying Faith is not lost in a criminal state, 14:11— what texts of Scripture they ground themselves on, 14:12—the perplexity they are under to answer this question, "What would become of a Believer should he die in his sin?" 14:13 et seq.—these difficulties have reclaimed many Calvinists, 14: 16—they are contrary to both the Lutherans and Remonstrants in the point of Grace, 14:33—contradiction of their Doctrine, 14:52—they promise the Arminians an Œcumenical Council, 14:77—the illusion of this promise, 14:78—the Calvinists of France receive the Synod of Dort, 14: 80—their union with the Lutherans in 1631, 14:95—they never before had advanced so far towards it, 14:97—this conduct of theirs convicts them of calumny, 14:99—they tolerate in the Lutherans the interior acts of Adoration, and reject the exterior, which are but tokens of the former, 14:104—their perplexity concerning the distinction of fundamental points, 14: 111—they are forced to own that the Church of Rome is a true Church, wherein salvation may be had, 14:112 —the Calvinists of Marpurg agree with the Lutherans of Rintel in the Conference of Cassel, 14:113—what is said by the Calvinists of France concerning the visibility of the Church, 15:21 they own that the Church of the Creed is

visible, 15:22—they always suppose the Church's perpetual visibility, 15:25— they exclude the Church of Rome from the title of a true Church, 15:26—they own the interruption of the Ministry, and the cessation of the visible Church, 15: 27—their perplexity in that the invisible Church had been forgotten in their Confession, 15:28
*Camerarius, Melancthon's friend, does not approve the preparations for war made by the Princes of Germany, 4:2 —writes the history of the Bohemian Brethren, 11:149—he says, they disown those who called them Vaudois, 11:150
*Cameron's and his Disciples', concerning universal grace, 14:117.
*Capito, Minister of Strasburg, his confession of the insolence of his Reformed brethren, and the injury done to the Church by their rejecting the pope, 5:7
*Carlostadius attacks the reality, 2:7—his character, ib.—the sense he gave to the words of the Institution, ib.—the origin of his contests with Luther, 2:8—he pulls down images, and sets up communion under both kinds, ib.—he is driven from Wittenberg, 2:11—he unites himself with the Anabaptists, ib.—he tumultuates the people of Orlemond, ib.—he drinks with Luther, and promises him to write against the Real Presence, ib.— he marries, 2:13—he is reconciled to Luther, 2:25
*Catharine, Queen of England, divorced by Henry VIII against all laws, 7:13— death of this Princess; a comparison between her and Anne Boleyn, 7:20— she maintains to death the truth of her marriage and the dignity of a Queen, 7:21
*Catharine Howard, mistress to Henry VIII, 7:34—this Prince first parries, then puts her to death, 7:36
*Catharine Medici causes the Conference of Poissy to be held, 9:91
*Catholics (The) by the Confession of Sacramentarians themselves, understand the words of the Eucharistic Institution better than the Lutherans, 2:31-33— even by the Confession of a whole Synod, 2:33—their sense in this point is the most natural, 2:37—they alone have a consistent doctrine, 6:38—they are justified by the divisions of the Protestants, 11:200—the sentiments of Catholics on these words, "This is my body,"

decision on extraordinary vocation, 15:30

Gardiner, Bishop of Winchester, imprisoned by the orders of Cranmer, Archbishop of Canterbury, 7:102

Geneva. Calvin makes an agreement with those of Geneva, 9:20—compared with the Catechism and Confession of France, 9:86—Calvin rules Geneva, 9:91. Strange answer of those of Geneva to the Arminians' request at the Synod of Dort, 14:73—decree passed at Geneva against universal Grace, and the question resolved by the Magistrate, 14:119—the Church of Geneva adds two articles to her Confession of Faith, 14:121

George, Duke of Saxony, shamefully treated by Luther, 2:44—he is an enemy to the Lutherans, *ib.*

Gerard, a Lutheran doctor; in what manner he explains the certainty of salvation taught by his party, 8:61

Germany, set all in a flame by Luther's writings, 2:11-12—the Lutherans by a great armament make all Germany tremble, 2:44—all Germany in arms at a writing of Luther's, 4:1-2. Present state of controversies in Germany, 14:116

Gerson, Chancellor of the University of Paris, his opinion about the Reformation of the Church, 1:1,4—he is praised by Luther, 3:10—he is cited to a wrong sense by Mr. Burnet, 7:111

God the author of all crimes, according to Luther's Doctrine, 2:17—Wickliff's Theology concerning the liberty, the goodness, and the power of God, 11:153—God author of sin, according to the Calvinists, 14:1-4. Strange doctrine of the Lutherans concerning the love of God, 3:44

Gog, and *Magog*, 11:204

Gomar maintains Calvinism against Arminius; his disciples take the name of Counter-Remonstrants, and the Prince of Orange upholds them, 14:18-19

Gomarists, or Counter-Remonstrants, 14:18

Goods, of Monasteries, pillaged in England, 7:19—the goods of the Church sold at a low price in England, 7:31—the goods of the Church exposed to the plunder of the laity under Edward VI, 7:96

Grace. Grace once received can never be lost, according to Calvin, 9:5—difficulties of this Doctrine, 9:21-22—The inamissibility of, grace defined at Dort, 14:44—Doctrine of the Arminians on Grace, 14:25 *et seq.*—Cameron's and his disciples' sentiments on universal Grace admitted by the Doctors of the Dort Synod, 14:117-118—Sufficient Grace admitted by them, 14:118—decree passed at Geneva against universal Grace, 14: 119.

Gregory (St.) Pope, under whom the English were converted, had no other sentiments than we have of the authority of the Holy See, 7:73

Gropper. By the advice of the learned Gropper, Herman, Archbishop of Cologne, holds very holy councils, 8:2—he is present at the Conference of Ratisbon, 8:4

Grotius demonstrates that the pope cannot be Antichrist, 13:10—he proves from the Protestants, that, by their own confession, souls may depart out of the body without being wholly purified, 15:159

Hebrew. Decision of the Swiss, touching the Hebrew text, ridiculed by the learned of the sect, 14:120

Helding, titular Bishop of Sidon, president at the Conference of Ratisbon, and there revises the book of the Interim, 8:6

Henry, disciple of Peter de Bruis, in the eleventh century, 11:2—secretly diffuses his master's errors in Dauphiny, Provence, and about Toulouse, 11:35—his doctrine, 11:65 *et seq.*

Henry II, King of France, did his utmost to depress the Calvinists, 9:87

Henry VIII, King of England, is basely handled by Luther, 2:5, 2:18—he reproaches Luther with his scandalous marriage and errors,—he is for marrying a second wife, the first still living, ceremonies, 7:1, 24 *et seq*, 51, etc.—what was the Faith of this Prince, 7:4—he assumes the title of supreme head of the Church of England, *ib.*—what were the instruments he made use of in his Reformation, 7:5—he marries Anne Boleyn, 7:13—he becomes enraged against the Holy See, 7:14—he puts to death Thomas More, and Fisher, Bishop of Rochester, 7:15—and the remarkable date of his cruelties, 7:16—all England takes the oath of Supremacy, 7:17—he appropriates to himself the goods of Monasteries, 7:19—he puts Anne Boleyn to death in favor of Jane Seymour, 7:23—he confirms the Doctrine of the Church with regard to penance, 7:24—the Eucharist and Images, 7:25-26—and invocation of Saints and Ceremonies, 7:26-27—and Purgatory and Masses for the dead, 7:28—by his own authority he pronounces on matters of Faith, 7:29—he confirms anew the Faith of the Church, 7:33—he marries Anne of Cleves; falls in love with Catharine Howard, and executes Cromwell, 7:34—he repudiates Anne of Cleves, 7:36—he marries Catharine Howard and puts her to death, ib.—he confirms again the Faith of the Church, 7:37—he makes all Ecclesiastical power proceed from the Crown, 7:42—his vices the beginning of the English Reformation, 7:49—examen of his first marriage, and the frivolous pretexts with which he covered his passion, 7:51—he bribes some Catholic Doctors, 7:59—what judgment ought to be passed on the pretended consultation of the faculty of Paris concerning Henry's divorce, 7:60—testimony of the Civilian Charles du Moulin, 7:61—in what manner he allows the people to read the Scriptures, 7:64—he will have the Church of every country regulate her Faith independently of all other Churches, 7:68—his death, 7:74—a total change in England after his death, 7:75

Heretics. Why Heretics are forced to mimic the language of the Church, 9:72—Catholic and Protestants agreed in the punishing of Heretics, 10:56—memorable answer of St. Bernard on the false constancy of Heretics, 11:147—what is the succession of Heretics, 12:209—character of Heresy owned in the Reformation, 12:39

Herman, Archbishop of Cologne, calls the Protestants into his Diocese; his extreme ignorance, 8:2

Heshusius, a Lutheran Minister, sadly abused by Calvin on the subject of the Eucharist

Humility, apparent, of Luther, 1:20

Huss, (John) inspires the people with a hatred of the Clergy, 1:5—his Doctrine is approved by Luther, 1:25—Huss a disciple of Wickliff, 11:162,164—he imitates Wickliff in his hatred of the Pope, 11:162—says Mass, 11:1,164—and judges no otherwise concerning the Eucharist than those of the Church of Rome, 11:163—why John Huss's doctrine was doubted of, 11:164—he was a Catholic in all the now controverted points, except Communion under both kinds, and the pope, 11:165—the Bohemian Brethren account him a great martyr, although they follow not his doctrine, 11:175—Luther accuses John Huss of his ignorance in the point of Justification, 11:179

Hussites (The) divided among themselves, 11:173-174.

Illyricus, (Flaccius) his jealousy, and his hidden designs against Melancthon's Doctrine about Free-will, 8:26,34.

Images, pulled down by Carlostadius, 2:10—Luther's opinion concerning Images, 2:28—Calumnies of the Protestants with respect to the honor we show Images, ib., 3:60—Luther praises God for that the Church of Rome preserves the Images of the Crucifix, 3:60—the Doctrine of the Church concerning Images confirmed by Henry VIII, King of England, 7:26, 37—artifices employed to excite young Edward VI against the Church's Doctrine with relation to Images, 7:95—Queen Elizabeth, at first, is for retaining images, 10:3—she is persuaded by false reasons to condemn them, nevertheless retains the crucifix in her chapel, ib.—images broken by Claude of Turn, an Arian, 11:1—they are honored by Wickliff, 11:157—and John Huss, 11:165

Impanation, set up by some Lutherans, and rejected by Luther, 2:3

Imputation, imputed justice—*Vide* Justification

Inamissibility of justice rejected by the English under Elizabeth, 10:23—taught by the Swiss, 10:62—the Dort Synod's prodigious doctrine on inamissibility of justice, 14:44—whether it was right understood, 14:55

Incarnation. This mystery an imposition, according to the Manicheans, 11:8—and according to the Albigenses, 11:133

Indulgences, attacked by Luther, 1:6—the indulgence that Luther preached, 1:8

owned by John Huss, 11:165—the Trent Council's Doctrine concerning the merit of good works, 15:147

*Ministers (The) decide that the Calvinists may take up arms, 10:28, 36—the first Huguenot war resolved on by the advice of all the Ministers, and peace made notwithstanding their opposition, 10:47—proof against the Ministers that the Albigenses were Manicheans 11:63, et seq.—artifices of the Ministers in respect to the history of the Vaudois and Albigenses, 11:131—notoriously false supposition of the Ministers, in order to confound the Vaudois with the Albigenses, 11:132—two objections of the Ministers to the same purpose refuted, 11:138—the Faith of the French Calvinists trusted in the hands of four Ministers, 11:20—the Ministers cannot believe what they say, 13:27—vain shifts of the Ministers relating to the business of Sainte-Foy, 12:24—the System of the Ministers touching the seven kings of the Revelations evidently confounded by the very terms of this prophecy, 13:32—their fallacious answer, 13:33—they account as ill for the ten kings of the Revelations, 13:34—what it is the Ministers have discovered in the Revelations concerning their Reformers, 14:43—the Ministers declare that Semi-Pelagianism doth not damn, 14:84—and that they were ready to bear with it in the Arminians, 14:87—the Ministers themselves very much relaxed in the observance of the Dort decrees, 14:90—the Ministers elude the decree of the Gap Synod, and the thirty-first article of their Confession touching extraordinary vocation, 15:29-31

*Ministry. Interruption of the Church's Ministry owned by the Calvinists of France, 15:27—before the Reformation, the Elect saved in the Roman Ministry by M. Claude's confession, 15:39

*Miracle. Luther requires of the Anabaptists that they should warrant their pretended mission by Miracles, 1:28—the miracles Luther boasts of, 1:29—the Zuinglians will not bear the mention of any miracle in the Eucharist, 4:29—Calvin confesses a miraculous presence of the Body of Jesus Christ in the Eucharist, 9:47—he shifts off the miracle which he admits in the Supper, 9:58—what is the miracle of the Eucha-

rist according to the Fathers, ib.—The Calvinists were more sensible of the necessity of admitting a miracle in the Eucharist than they did in fact admit one, 9:60. Under Edward VI and under Elizabeth, none of the Miracles admitted by Calvin in the Eucharist are employed, 10:10

*Mission. Luther pretends his mission was extraordinary, 1:27—he confesses the necessity of mission, 1:28—he receives his mission from the Prince, in order to make his Ecclesiastical visitations, 5:9

*Monastery. Pillaging of monasteries under Henry VIII, 7:19

*Monks. Monks reckoned among the Saints in the Apology of the Augsburg Confession, 3:36

*Montpellier, the Heretics of, were Manicheans, 11:48

*Montluc, Bishop of Valence; what Mr. Burnet says of him, 7:7—he is present at the Conference of Poissy, 9:92—he endeavors to find out some ambiguous formulary for the Supper, 9:94—his empty discourses on the Reformation of manners, 9:99—his private marriage, ib.

*More, Thomas, Lord Chancellor of England, is condemned to death for not owning the King supreme head of the Church, 7:15

*Muncer, Father of the Anabaptists, preaches without mission, 1:28—Luther condemned him on this head only, ib.

*Mystery. Equivocations of the Sacramentarians on this word, 4:10—all the mysteries of Jesus Christ are signs in some respect, 4:12—What is that Mystery of Iniquity specified by St. Paul? 11:204

*Naumburg, assembly of the Lutherans at, and what passed there, 8:43

*Nismes. The national Synod of Nismes in 1572; changes the decree of that of Rochelle concerning the Substance of Jesus Christ's body in the Eucharist, 12:11

*Oblation of the Eucharist cut off from the Lutheran Mass, 3:52—what was invented in order to render this Oblation odious, 3:53—how oblation of Eucharist is profitable to the whole world, 3:56—it is a necessary consequence from the Real Presence; the

Lutherans themselves own as much, 6:23-25, 34-35—it is suppressed in England under Edward VI, upon a false pretence, 7:86, 94—*Vide* Mass
Œcolampadius takes up the defence of Carlostadius, 2:19—his character, 2:24—what Erasmus says of his marriage, and the rest of his behaviour *ib.*—he writes against the Real Presence, 2:25—his death, 4:3—he had admonished Bucer, that there was nothing but trick in his equivocations, 4:14
Operation, ex opere operato, ill-understood by Protestants, 3:32, 56—it is admitted by them, 3:23
Ordibarians, who they were, 11:32
Ordination of Pastors still preserved in the Church of Rome by Luther's own Confession, 3:60—ordination of Bishops and priests regulated by the Parliament in England, 7:76—Validity of Ordinations, whereon grounded in England, 10:16—how the Bohemian Brethren seek their Ordinations in the Catholic Church, 11:178
Origin of the contests between Luther and Carlostadius, 2:8
Orlemonde, a town in Thuringia, where Carlostadius takes shelter, 2:11—he there raises great disturbances, and drinking with Luther declares war against him, *ib.*
Ornaments preserved in the Lutheran Mass, 3:51—and in England, 7:90
Osiander, renews the doctrine of impanation, 2:3—he is present at the Conference of Marpurg, 2:45—his sister marries Thomas Cranmer, 7:9—Osiander's character and his Doctrine about Justification, 8:11—the profane spirit of Osiander observed by Calvin, 8:12—the notions that Protestants had of Osiander, 8:13—he keeps within no bounds, 8:14—his Doctrine on Justification is spared at the Conference of Worms, 8:33—his triumph in Prussia, 8:35

Parker, Protestant Archbishop of Canterbury, is the first that subscribes Elizabeth's supremacy, 10:12
Paris. The pretended consultation of the Paris faculty of Divinity concerning the divorce of Henry VIII, 7:59-61
Paschasius Radbertus, 4:32
Patarians, who they were, 11:56—their infamy, 11:61

Paulicians, or Manicheans of Armenia, their history, 11:13-14—their conformity with the Manicheans refuted by St. Austin, 11:15—their design on the Bulgarians, 11:16
Peasants rebel in Germany, instigated by Luther's Doctrine, 1:12, 4:1
Pelagianism. Spite of the Dort decrees, M. Jurieu maintains that Pelagianism is not contrary to piety, 14:84, 92
Penance. The Lutherans acknowledge the Sacrament of Penance and Sacramental Absolution, 3:46—Henry VIII confirms the Church's Faith of the Sacrament of Penance, 7:37
Perrin (Paul) quotes not so much as one contemporary Historian in his History of the Vaudois, 11:125—the books of the Vaudois produced by him, 11:126—their Confession of Faith which he produces is posterior to Calvinism, 11:128
Peter D'Ailly. The sentiments of Cardinal Peter D'Ailly, Bishop of Cambray, on the Reformation of the Church, 1:1,3
Peter de Bruis appears in the eleventh Century, 11:2—he clandestinely disseminates his errors in Dauphiny, Provence, and in the neighborhood of Toulouse, 11:35—he is chief of the Albigenses, 11:36—examination of his Doctrine, 11:65—St. Bernard charges him with nothing but what is true, 11:69
Peter Martyr is called into England to begin the Reformation there. His Doctrine on the Eucharist, 7:81—his opinion of the equivocations of the rest of the Ministers, 9:96
Peter du Moulin—Vide Du Moulin
Peter of Sicily writes the History of the Paulicians and Manicheans of Armenia, 11:14—endeavors to prevent the spreading of their Sect in Bulgaria, 11:16
Petrobusians, who they were, 11:36.
Picards (The) disowned by the Bohemian Brethren, 11:152
Piercy, Lord, Anne Boleyn falsely declares that she was married to him before she was wedded to Henry VIII, 7:21—what the engagement which Lord Piercy had with Anne Boleyn, *ib.*
Piscator, who he was, and his Doctrine on imputed Justice, 12:27—his Doctrine is detested by the national Synod of Gap, 12:28—by that of Rochelle in

proceeding from their ignorance of what the Church is, 15:1—their sentiments relating to the perpetual Visibility of the Church, 15:4—this Doctrine the ruin of their Reformation, and the source of their perplexities, 15:5—what precisely the Protestants are obliged to by this Doctrine, 15:6.—they vary on this head, 15:16—and why, 15:17

*Prussia set all in commotion by Osiander, 8:10—this country turns Lutheran, ib.

*Pflugius, Bishop of Naumburg, present at the Conference of Ratisbon, 8:4—he puts the finishing stroke to the book of the Interim, 8:6—he presides in the Conference of Worms, 8:31

*Purgatory. The Church's doctrine on Purgatory confirmed by Henry VIII, 7:28, 37—retained for a while, then abolished under Edward VI, 7:88 Purgatory believed by Wickliff, 11:157—and John Huss, 11:165—what precisely is to be believed concerning Purgatory agreeably to the Council of Trent, 15:159—Protestants' principles prove the necessity of Purgatory, ib.— the Purification of souls after this life owned by them, 15:160—they agree as to the main point, but leave the manner undecided, ib.

*Puritans. What James I, King of England, said of the Puritans, 9:76

*Ratisbon. Conference at Ratisbon in 1541, and what passed at it, 8:4—another Conference at Ratisbon in 1546, and what passed at it, 8:6

*Ratramnus. Ratramnus's Book puzzles Melancthon, 4:32—what the dispute in Ratramnus's time, ib.

*Reality. Luther had at the beginning a great mind to subvert the reality, from a very strange motive, 2:1—the reality attacked by Carlostadius, 2:7, 11—impugned by Zuinglius, 2:23—strongly defended by Luther, 2:30—Melancthon labors to place the reality during the time of the sole use of the Sacrament, 6:20—Calvin makes vain efforts to keep up the idea of reality, 9:66—he cannot satisfy the notion of reality impressed by our Lord's institution, 9:67—the reality well expressed by the Prelates assembled at Poissy, 9:97— Queen Elizabeth will not suffer her Divines to censure the Reality, 10:5—indifference of the Eng-

lish, in respect of the Reality, 10:8-9—the Reality condemned by the Zuinglians of Poland, 10:69—the Reality denied by the Albigenses, 11:65—believed by the Vaudois, 11:77-92—manifest proof that the Heretics, who denied the Reality in the twelfth and thirteenth centuries, were Manicheans, 11:132—Reality believed by John Huss, 11:163—strong expressions of the Bohemian Brethren for the Reality, 11:181—the Reality free from venom, 14:96, Vide Eucharist, Real Presence

*Rebaptization of the Bohemian Brethren, 11:176

*Redemption. The Doctrine of the Arminians concerning the universality of Redemption, 14:25

*Reformation of the Church desired more than an age ago, 1:1—the Reformation that was desired touched only discipline, and not faith, 1:2—two ways of desiring the Reformation of the Church, 1:5—the Reformation of Protestants established by seditions and wars, 1:34—the Reform makes two separate bodies in Germany by different Confessions of Faith, 2:43—it is resolved in the new Reformation to take arms, 4:1—no Reformation of manners in the Protestant Church, 5:13,33; 6:11—the causes of its progress, 5:5—no authority in the Reformation to terminate their disputes, 5:22, 23, 26, 31—Reformation in England, vide England: whether the progress of the Reformation be due to the reading of Scripture, and how, 7:65—foundation of the Reform laid on the ruins of ecclesiastical authority, 7:76—the Reformation under Edward began in England by Peter Martyr, and Bernardin Ochin, 7:81—all order subverted in the English Reformation, 7:93—whether any advantage can be drawn from the sudden progress of pretended Reformation, 7:96—the Reformation goes from one excess to another, 8:27, 58—vain discourses of the Bishop of Valence on the Reformation of manners, 9:99—Queen Elizabeth approves not the Reformation of Edward VI in all its points, 10:1—whether the spirit of the Reformation was a spirit of meekness or violence, 10:50—effects of that violent spirit which predominated in the Reformation, 10:51—the Reformation allows private men

to arrogate to themselves greater abili-
ties for understanding sound Doctrine
than all the rest of the Church, 14:89—
Sects born in the Reformation, 15:122
*Reformers, or the heads of the Refor-
mation, careful to secure themselves:
Cranmer the only one among them that
dies for this cause, 8:10
*Relics. Vigilantius, in the fourth centu-
ry, opposes honoring of Relics, 11:1—
St. Leo, St. Basil, and the rest of the
Saints of that time, accused of Idolatry
by the Ministers, on account of the
veneration they showed to Saints and
Relics, 13:23-26
*Remission of sins—Vide Sin
*Rome. The Church of Rome praised
and respected by Luther, 1:21
*Remonstrants—Vide Arminians
*Renaudie (La) chief of the Amboise
conspiracy; his character, 10:30
*Revelations. Illusions of the Protestant
relating to the Revelations, 13:5—exposition of the Minister Jurieu's Doctrine
on the eleventh, twelfth, and thirteenth
chapters of the Revelations, 13:11—the
system of the Minister concerning the
seven Kings of the Revelations evidently confuted by the very terms of the
prophecy, 13:32—the ten Kings of the
Revelations as evidently ill accounted
for, 13:34—contrarieties of the new
Interpreters of the Revelations, 13:36
—the Englishman finds England, and
the Frenchman France, in the Revelations, 13:37—what it is that the Ministers have discovered in the Revelations
touching their Reformers, 13:43
*Revenues of the Church plundered by
Elizabeth, Queen of England, 10:21
*Revolt. Beginnning of the Calvinists'
revolt in France, 10:24—open revolt of
the whole party, 10:35
*Rochelle. The national synod of Ro-
chelle in 1571 condemns those of the
party that were for changing the Supper-article in the Confession of Faith,
12:2—decision of this Synod full of
perplexity, ib.—vain efforts of this
Synod to find the substance of the body
in the Calvinian Doctrine, 12:3—error
of this Synod endeavoring to explain
the mystery of the Eucharist without
producing the institution, 12:4—reason
of the Synod for establishing the substance; there it is concluded that the
other opinion is contrary to the word of

God, 12:5—it says more than it designed, 12:6—the Swiss believe themselves condemned by this decision, but
the Synod takes care they should be
answered that this doctrine only concerns France, 12:8-9—the decree of this
Synod is changed in that of Nismes,
12:11—the Synod of Rochelle in 1607
condemns Piscator's Doctrine, 12:29—it
gives orders that the decree of the Synod of Gap, declaring the Pope Antichrist, be printed in all the copies of
the Confession of Faith, 13:7—this
Synod declares that nothing ought to be
added or taken from the twenty-fifth
and twenty-ninth articles of the Confession of Faith, where the Church is
treated of, 15:28
*Roque (M. de la). His want of sincerity
touching the Vaudois, 11:91—this Minister artfully confounds the Vaudois
with the Albigenses, 11:132—his false
pretence that Wickliff's Doctrine was
slandered at the Council of Constance,
11:155—he proves that John Huss and
Jerome of Prague died in the belief of
the Church of Rome, especially in what
regards the Eucharist, 11:163
*Roque (M. de la) son of the Minister,
produces a Confession of Faith of Wickliff's, where the Reality is clearly
established, 11:158
*Roquesane, chief of the sect of the
Calixtins, 11:167—he utterly destroys
the Taborites, ib.—his ambition prevents the Calixtins re-uniting with the
Church, 11:172—he makes himself
Pope in Bohemia, ib.—he permits several Greek Priests to celebrate the holy
mysteries according to their Church
rites, 11:177
*Runcarians, who they were, 11:56

*Sacrament. In the Lutheran doctrine the
Sacraments operate ex opere operato,
3:23—What the Lutherans think of the
seven Sacraments, 3:48—equivocation
of the Sacramentarians on the word
Sacrament, 4:10—the seven Sacrament
retained by the English under Henry
VIII, 7:37—The Albigenses taught that
the effect of the Sacraments depends on
the holiness of the Ministers, 11:62
—the Vaudois taught that the merit of
persons acted in the Sacraments more
than order and character, 6:86—the
Vaudois were in no error as to the

674 INDEX

signs in certain respects, 4:12—Calvin is not content with receiving a sign in the Supper, 9:27

*Sin. Errors of the Zuinglians on original sin, 2:21—the forgiveness of sins purely gratuitous, according to the Council of Trent, 3:24—enumeration of sins retained in confession by the Lutherans, 3:47—forgiveness of sins conserved in the Church of Rome by Luther's Confession, 3:60—a considerable article in the Confession of Saxony on mortal and venial sins, 8:29. God the Author of Sin according to the Calvinists, 14:1 et seq.—M. Jurieu relapses into the excesses of the Reformers with respect to the cause of Sin, 14:93

*Siscidenses (The), a sect of the Vaudois that refused not to receive the Eucharist from the hands of a Priest, 11:111

*Smalkald. The Lutherans labor to form the Smalkaldic Confederacy, 4:1—The Assembly of Smalkald occasioned by the Council called by Paul III, 4:34—Luther flies out against the pope in the Articles of Smalkald, 5:38—in the Assembly of Smalkald, Melancthon is of opinion that they should own the Council summoned by the Pope, 5:25

*Socini. Fausto Socini and Lelio heads of the Socinians, 15:123

*Socinians. The Socinians and the Anabaptists sprung from Luther and Calvin, 15:123—united together, ibid.

*Soissons. Manicheans at Soissons, 11:41—their history, 11:42

*Somerset (Duke of) begins the Reformation in England, 7:80—whether this Duke had any thing to show of a Reformer, 7:97

*Song. Latin Song retained in the Lutheran Mass, 3:51

*Strasburg. The Strasburg Confession of Faith, or of the four cities, 3:3—equivocal terms of this Confession on the Article of the Supper, 3:12—the Confession of Strasburg explains Justification in the same manner as the Church of Rome, 3:41—they at the same time receive at Strasburg two contrary Confessions of Faith, 8:8. Variation of the Church of Strasburg, 15:125—The senate of Strasburg destroys images, and enjoins the communion under both kinds, ib.—suspends the celebration of Mass, ib.—those of Strasburg turn Zuinglians, afterwards return to the Confes-

sion of Augsburg, ib.—they fall into ubiquity, ib.

*Substance. Why this word is employed in the Eucharist, 3:16—Neither under Edward VI, nor under Elizabeth, is the word Substance employed, which Calvin admits in the Eucharist, 10:10—the Zuinglian Supper void of Substance, 10:66—vain endeavors of the national Synod of Rochelle in 1571 to prove the Substance of the body and blood of Jesus Christ in the Doctrine of the pretended Reformed of France, 12:3—the Substance reduced to nothing in the national Synod of Nismes, 12:11

*Succession. Protestants seek in vain for the Succession of Persons and Doctrine in the Vaudois and Albigenses, 12:207—what is the Succession of heretics, 12:209

*Supper. The Supper of the Swiss or Zuinglians without substance, and a presence in virtue only, 10:66—difference which the Zuinglians of Poland place between their Supper and that of the Socinians, 10:69—several pretended reformed Churches of France are for changing the Supper-article in the Confession of Faith, 12:1

*Supremacy of the Kings of England is there established, notwithstanding Queen Elizabeth's qualms of conscience, 10:11—the Catholic Bishops refuse to sign it, 10:12—declaration of the Protestant Clergy in England in favor of this Supremacy, 10:13—this doctrine condemned by the Calvinists, 10:20

*Swiss, (The) are incensed against Luther, 4:18—New Confession of Faith of the Helvetic Churches or Swiss, 10:58—frivolous reasoning of the Ministers concerning this Confession, 10:59—the Swiss begin but then to know any thing of imputed justice, 10:60—they reject the merit of good works, 10:61—they attribute true Faith to the Elect alone, 10:62—they teach the Certainty of Salvation, and the Inamissibility of Grace, and ill explain conversion, 10:62-63—their monstrous Doctrine on Free-will, 10:64—according to them, the Supper is void of substance, and no presence but in virtue, 10:66—they leave nothing peculiar to the Supper, 10:67—they are the most sincere defenders of the figurative sense, 10:68—

the Swiss believe themselves condemned by the decision of the national Synod of Rochelle in 1571, 12:88—they are not satisfied with Beza's answer, but still hold themselves condemned, 12:10—they are specified by the explication of the Synod of Nismes, 12:11—Swiss formulary against Universal Grace, 14:119—another Swiss decision on the Hebrew Text laughed at by the learned of the party, 14:120—another decision of the Swiss and Geneva reproved by M. Claude, 14:121

*Taborites. The sect of Taborites arises in Bohemia, 11:167—their rebellion and cruelties ib.—their total destruction, ib.
*Temples erected in honor of the Saints by the Bohemian Brethren, 11:190
*Test. Test Act in England, wherein the English draw near to our sentiments, and condemn us only by manifest mistakes, 14:122
*Testament. The Old Testament rejected by the Manicheans as fabulous, 11:8—rejected by the Albigenses, 11:37—received by the Vaudois, 11:132
*Theses (The) of Luther, to excite the Lutherans to take up arms, 8:1
*Thomas Aquinas. Luther's odd doubt of the salvation of this Saint, 3:10
Thomas (St.) of Canterbury, razed out of the list of Saints by the English, 7:114—the behaviour of this Saint quite different from that of Thomas Cranmer, ib.
*Thomas Cranmer—vide Cranmer
*Thomas Cromwell—Vide Cromwell
*Thomas More—Vide More
*Thomas Muncer—Vide Muncer
*Tonins. The national Synod of Tonins in 1614 condemns Piscator, 12:33
*Tournon, (Cardinal of,) Archbishop of Lyons, presides in the Conference of Poissy, 11:92
*Toulouse. The Manicheans of Toulouse, 11:35—are the same with the Albigenses, 11:36
*Transubstantiation attacked by Luther, 2:2—Variation of Luther on Transubstantiation, 2:4, 42—it follows from his expressions, 2:2: 4:37—and from that of Melancthon in the Apology, 6:26—Transubstantiation destroys not the Sacrament, 2:38—why the name of bread retained, 2:39—why the Church makes use of the word transubstantia-

tion, 3:16—Transubstantiation, according to the Zuinglians, is established by Luther's doctrine, 2:31—and according to the Divines of Leipsic and Wittenberg, 6:35—the doctrine of Transubstantiation confirmed by Henry VIII, 7:37—and abolished under Edward VI, 7:94—Manifest proof that the Vaudois did no wise err as to that point, 11:97—this Doctrine impugned by Wickliff, 11:157—retained by John Huss and Jerome of Prague, 11:163—and by the Calixtins, 11:170—rejected by the Bohemian Brethren, 11:173—the hatred of the Calvinist people turned against Transubstantiation ever since the Synod of Charenton in 1631, 14:102—the word Transubstantiation chosen at the Council of Lateran, 15:136—and why
*Trent. The Council of Trent hath added nothing to the decisions of the Ancients, 15:138—it does but repeat the ancient decisions in respect to justifying Grace, 14:143—in respect to its gratuity, 15:144—in respect to the preparations to Grace, 15:145—to the inseparable union of liberty and Grace, 15:146—to the merit of good works, 15:147—in respect to the fulfilling of God's commandments, 15:148—it has cut away the root of all abuses relating to the honor paid to Images, 15:156—its moderation in determining nothing but what is certain, 15:161—it speaks not with ambiguity, 15:162-164—it has determined all that regards the true authority of the pope, 15:165—in it, those are opposed who were for making a formulary whence the pope's superiority over a general council might be inferred, ib.—this formulary suppressed with the Pope's consent, ib.
*Trinity. The ancient Manicheans' sentiment as to the Trinity, 11:40—is the same with that of the Toulouse Albigenses, 11:42
*Turenne (M.) Synod of Sainte-Foy trusts its Faith in the hands of four ministers and of M. Turenne, 12:20—why M. Turenne was employed in this deputation concerning doctrine, 12:21
*Turk. Luther's strange doctrine about war against the Turk, 1:19—Jurieu's ridiculous conceit relating to the Turk, 13:39

6:37—the Divines of Wittenberg come back to Luther's sentiments, and why, 6:38
*Works. Satisfactory works owned in the Apology of the Augsburg Confession, 3:36—the merit of good works, vide Merit.—The necessity of good works, in order to salvation, condemned by the Lutherans, 8:32
*Worms. The Conference of Worms, in order to reconcile both religions, 8:31—Assembly at Worms in 1557, whither the Reformed Churches of France and Geneva send Beza and Farel, 9:87

*Zisca, chief of the Taborites, his bloody feats, 11:167
*Zuinglius, his character and doctrine on the salvation of Heathens, 2:19—his errors on original sin, 2:21—his errors on baptism, 2:22—he forces the Scripture in every thing, 2:23—his contempt of antiquity, ib.—he writes against the Real Presence, 2:25—he takes from the Eucharist all that raises it above the senses, 2:26—a Spirit appears to him, and suggests that text to him where the sign of the Institution received immediately the name of the thing, 2:27—why Zuinglius is worse handled by Luther than the rest of the Sacramentarians, 2:28—Zuinglius preaches the Reformation in Switzerland, ib.—he is present at the Conference of Marpurg, where he confers with Luther, 2:45—he sends his Confession of Faith to the emperor, 3:1,3—his Confession of Faith free from equivocations, 3:14—what presence of the body of Jesus Christ he acknowledges in the Supper, ib.—Zuinglius's death in battle, 4:3

*Zuinglians prove to Luther that the Catholics understand the literal sense better than he, 2:31—a whole synod of Zuinglians in Poland assert the same truth, 2:33—they prove to Luther that he admits a kind of figurative sense, 2:35—they will not hear a miracle or omnipotence spoken of in the Eucharist, 4:29—they reprove Luther for always having the Devil in his mouth, and call him madman, 6:16—Luther's last sentiments concerning the Zuinglians, 6:40—Zuinglianism gains ground in England, 7:80—the Zuinglians are condemned by the Lutherans, 8:42—their scoffs at the Confession of Augsburg, 8:44—The Zuinglians make a new Confession of Faith, 10:58—they go over to Calvin's notions concerning Grace, 10:60—man's conversion ill explained by them, 10:63—their monstrous doctrine concerning Free-will, 10:64—according to them, the Supper is void of Substance, and the Presence but in virtue, 10:66—they leave nothing peculiar to the Supper, 10:67—they are the most sincere defenders of the figurative sense, 10:68—remarkable Confession of Faith of the Polish Zuinglians, 10:69—they teach Ubiquity, 10:70—their union with the Bohemians and Lutherans at Sendomir, 11:193—the Zuinglians, most of them, recede from their particular principles in this union, 11:195—reflection on this union, 11:198
*Zurich. The Mass abolished at Zurich, 2:27—those of Zurich laugh at Bucer's equivocations, 4:28—Calvin makes an agreement with those of Zurich, 9:20